D1414230

MICROPROCESSORS AND MICROCOMPUTER-BASED SYSTEM DESIGN

Mohamed Rafiquzzaman, Ph.D.

Professor
California State Polytechnic University
Pomona, California
and
Adjunct Professor
University of Southern California
Los Angeles, California

CRC Press
Boca Raton   Ann Arbor   Boston

Library of Congress Cataloging-in-Publication Data

Rafiquzzaman, Mohamed.
    Microprocessors and microcomputer-based system design / Mohamed
Rafiquzzaman.
        p.   cm.
    Includes bibliographical references.
    ISBN 0-8493-4275-9
    1. System design.   2. Microprocessors.   3. Microcomputers.
I. Title.
QA76.9.S88R32   1990
004.2'1--dc20   89-23875
                                                                              CIP

Acquiring Editor: Russ Hall
Production Director: Sandy Pearlman
Coordinating Editors: Jocelyn Makepeace/Janice Morey
Cover Design: Chris Pearl
In-Text Graphics: Cynthia Tarpley, Advanced Graphics Xpress
Copy Editor: Naomi Lynch
Keyboarding: Betty Grunza
Indexing: Sharon Smith, Professional Indexing
Composition: CRC Press, Inc.
Printer and Binder: R.R. Donnelley & Sons Company

PREFACE

The concept behind *Microprocessors and Microcomputer-Based System Design* is to present the capabilities, interfaces, and trade-offs in the practical design of microcomputer-based systems. The book accomplishes this by exploring the architectures and system design concepts associated with several popular microprocessors.

Coverage includes an 8-bit microprocessor (Intel's 8085), several 16-bit microprocessors (Intel's 8086, 80186, 80286, and Motorola's 68000), 32-bit microprocessors (Intel's 80386 and Motorola's 68020 and 68030), and a RISC microprocessor (Motorola's MC88100).

The audience of this book can be college students or practicing microprocessor system designers in industry. As a text it is for a junior, senior, or graduate course in electrical engineering, computer engineering, or computer science. Practitioners of microprocessor system design in industry will find greater detail and comparison considerations than are found in manufacturers' manuals. The book assumes a familiarity with digital logic and topics such as Boolean algebra and K-maps.

Microprocessors and Microcomputer-Based System Design has evolved from notes I have developed for courses I teach at the California State Polytechnic University, Pomona, at the University of Southern California, and in short courses for Motorola, Inc. in the Southern California area. I have made the extensive information related to the microprocessors easily understandable by the use of numerous examples, illustrations, tables, data sheets, questions, problems, and a systematic presentation.

This may well be the most voluminous book currently available on this subject. But the reader need not try to digest all of the material covered in a single course. Because of the systematic coverage, courses can be taught from this book using either the Motorola or Intel materials, or both in a combined and comparative context. Students and practitioners will wish to keep the book as a one-place reference as they consider the trade-offs of design.

Chapter 1 introduces the reader to the evolution of microprocessors, microcomputer hardware, systems software, and programming concepts, addressing modes and instructions, basic features of microcomputer development systems, a system development flowchart, and typical practical applications, such as personal computers, robotics, real-time controllers, and fault-tolerant systems.

Chapter 2 provides a detailed coverage of 8085 hardware, software, I/O, timing, and system design.

Chapters 3 through 8 provide detailed descriptions of the architectures, addressing modes, instruction sets, I/O, and system design concepts of Intel's 8086, 80186, 80286, and 80386 and Motorola's 68000, 68020, 68030, and 88100 microprocessors.

Chapter 9 covers the basics of peripheral interfacing. Topics include keyboard/display interfacing, DMA controllers, printer interfaces, CRT and graphics controllers, floppy disk interface, and coprocessors.

Chapter 10 offers two detailed design problems. The purpose of these is to offer an opportunity to apply some of the design principles covered in the preceding chapters.

The appendices include materials on the HP 64000 microcomputer development system, data sheets on the Motorola 68000 and support chips, data sheets on the Intel 8085, 8086 microprocessors and support chips, and a glossary.

Mohamed Rafiquzzaman
Pomona, California

ACKNOWLEDGMENTS

The author wishes to express his sincere appreciation to his students Marc Langer, Clyde Soo, Laurie Polumbo, James Moses, Larry Keller, Mark Walker, Francis Thomson, and others; to his colleague Professor Rajan Chandra of California State Polytechnic University, Pomona; to Rata Truong of Hughes Aircraft; to Mehdi Mirfattah of Rafi Systems, Inc., Ontario, California; and to others for making constructive suggestions.

The author is also grateful to Dr. W. C. Miller of the University of Windsor, Canada, to his brother and his wife Captain and Mrs. Zaman, and to his friend Rick Hefler for their support and inspiration throughout the writing effort.

The reviewers of the manuscript are to be commended for their comments and constructive criticisms. They are Dr. Kenneth J. Breeding, Department of Electrical Engineering and Computer and Information Science, Ohio State University; Dr. Darrow F. Dawson, Department of Electrical Engineering, University of Missouri-Rolla; Dr. David G. Green, Department of Electrical Engineering, University of Alabama at Birmingham; Dr. Martin E. Kaliski, Department of Electronic and Electrical Engineering, California State Polytechnic University, San Luis Obispo; Dr. David W. Knapp, Department of Computer Science, University of Illinois, Urbana Champaign; Dr. Michel Lynch, Department of Electrical Engineering, University of Florida; Dr. Alan B. Marcovitz, Department of Computer Engineering, Florida Atlantic University; Dr. Kay M. Purcell, Department of Electrical Engineering, Southern Illinois University at Carbondale; and Dr. Joseph G. Tront, Department of Electrical Engineering, Virginia Polytechnic Institute and State University.

The author is especially indebted to Janice Morey, Sandy Pearlman, and Russ Hall of CRC Press, Inc. for their personal commitment, dedication, and outstanding job in bringing this book to publication. To all the others on the staff of CRC Press who literally worked round the clock in order to complete the final stages of preparation, the author expresses his sincere appreciation.

Finally, the author is grateful to Nancy, Mary, Karen, Francis, and Melanie for typing all of the manuscript.

THE AUTHOR

Dr. Rafiquzzaman obtained his Ph.D. in Electrical Engineering in Canada in 1974. He worked for Esso/Exxon and Bell Northern Research for approximately 5 years. Dr. Rafiquzzaman is presently a professor of electrical and computer engineering at California State Polytechnic University, Pomona. He was Chair of the department there in 1984–1985. Dr. Rafiquzzaman is also an adjunct professor of electrical engineering systems at the University of Southern California, Los Angeles. He consulted for ARCO, Rockwell, Los Angeles County, and Parsons Corporation in the areas of computer applications. He has published four books on computers which have been translated into Russian, Chinese and Spanish, and has published numerous papers on computers.

Dr. Rafiquzzaman is the founder of Rafi Systems, Inc., a manufacturer of biomedical devices and computer systems consulting firm in Ontario, California. In 1984, he managed the Olympic Swimming, Diving and Synchronized Swimming teams. He has also managed Swiss timing, scorekeeping, and computer systems.

Dr. Rafiquzzaman is presently an advisor to the President of Bangladesh on computers.

To my Parents,
my wife Reba, son Tito
and brother Elan

To Dr. Richard J. Hermsen,
for his friendship
and constant encouragement

CONTENTS

Chapter 1

INTRODUCTION TO MICROPROCESSORS AND MICROCOMPUTER-BASED DESIGN

This chapter provides a brief summary of the features of microprocessors and microcomputer development systems.

The basic elements of a computer are the Central Processing Unit (CPU), the Memory, and Input/Output (I/O) units. The CPU translates instructions, performs arithmetic or logic operations, and temporarily stores instructions and data in its internal high-speed registers. The memory stores programs and data. The I/O unit interfaces the computer with external devices such as keyboard and display.

With the advent of semiconductor technology, it is possible to integrate the CPU in a single chip. The result is the microprocessor. Metal Oxide Semiconductor (MOS) technology is typically used to fabricate the standard off-the-shelf microprocessors such as those manufactured by Intel and Motorola. Appropriate memory and I/O chips are interfaced to the microprocessor to design a microcomputer. Single-chip microcomputers are available these days in which the microprocessor, memory, and I/O are all fabricated in the same chip. These single-chip microcomputers offer limited capabilities. However, they are ideal for certain applications such as peripheral controllers.

The efficient development of microprocessor-based systems necessitates the use of a microcomputer development system. The microcomputer development system is used for the design, debugging, and sometimes the documentation of a microprocessor-based system.

This chapter first covers the evolution of 8-, 16-, and 32-bit microprocessors along with an overview of programming languages, microcomputer hardware, and software. The attributes of typical microcomputer development systems features as well as methods used to design and debug some specific microprocessor applications are then included.

1

1.1 EVOLUTION OF THE MICROPROCESSOR

Intel Corporation introduced the first microprocessor, the 4004, in 1971. The 4004 evolved from a development effort while designing a calculator chip set.

Soon after the 4004 appeared in the commercial market, three other microprocessors were introduced. These were the Rockwell International PPS-4, the Intel 8-bit 8008, and the National Semiconductor 16-bit IMP-16.

The microprocessors introduced between 1971 and 1973 were the first-generation systems. They were designed using the PMOS (P-type MOS) technology. This technology provided low cost, slow speed, and low output currents and was not compatible with TTL (Transistor Transistor Logic).

After 1973, second-generation microprocessors such as Motorola 6800 and 6809, Intel 8085, and Zilog Z80 evolved. These processors were fabricated using the NMOS (N-type MOS) technology. The NMOS process offers faster speed and higher density than PMOS and is TTL-compatible.

After 1978, the third-generation microprocessors were introduced. These processors are 16 bits wide and include typical processors such as Intel 8086/80186/80286 and Motorola 68000/68010. These microprocessors are designed using the HMOS (high-density MOS) technology. HMOS provides the following advantages over NMOS:

- Speed-Power-Product (SPP) of HMOS is four times better than NMOS:

  NMOS ≈4 Picojoules (PJ)
  HMOS ≈1 Picojoule (PJ)

Note that Speed-Power-Product

  = speed × power
  = nanosecond × milliwatt
  = picojoules

- Circuit densities provided by HMOS are approximately twice those of NMOS:

  NMOS = 4128 gates/μm^2
  HMOS = 1852.5 gates/μm^2

where 1 μm (micrometer) = 10^{-6} meter.

Recently, Intel utilized the HMOS technology to fabricate the 8085A. Thus, Intel offers a high-speed version of the 8085A called 8085AH. The price of the 8085AH is higher than the 8085A.

In 1980, fourth-generation microprocessors evolved. Intel introduced the first commercial 32-bit microprocessor, the problematic Intel 432. This processor was eventually discontinued by Intel. Since 1985, more 32-bit microprocessors have been introduced. These include Motorola's MC 68020 and 68030 and Intel 80386. These processors are fabricated using the low-power version of the HMOS technology called the HCMOS.

The performance offered by the 32-bit microprocessor is more comparable to that of superminicomputers such as Digital Equipment Corporation's VAX11/750 and VAX11/780. Recently, Motorola has introduced a 32-bit RISC (Reduced Instruction Set Computer) microprocessor with a simplified instruction set called the MC88100.

The trend in microprocessors is not toward introduction of 64-bit microprocessors. Extensive research is being carried out for implementation of more on-chip functions and for improvement of the speeds of memory and I/O devices.

1.2 MICROCOMPUTER HARDWARE

In this section, some unique features associated with various microcomputer components will be provided.

The microcomputer contains a microprocessor, a memory unit, and an input/output unit. These elements are explained in the following in detail. Figure 1.1 shows a simplified block diagram of a microcomputer.

1.2.1 THE SYSTEM BUS
The system bus contains three buses. These are the address bus, the data bus, and the control bus. These buses connect the microprocessor to

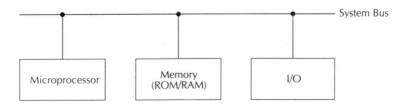

FIGURE 1.1 Simplified block diagram of a microprocessor.

each of the memory and I/O elements so that information transfer between the microprocessor and any of the other elements can take place.

On the address bus, information transfer takes place only in one direction, from the microprocessor to the memory or I/O elements. Therefore, this is called a unidirectional bus. This bus is usually 8 to 32 bits wide. The number of unique addresses that the microprocessor can generate on this bus depends on the width of this bus. For example, for a 16-bit address bus, the microprocessor can generate $2^{16} = 65,536$ different possible addresses. A different memory location or an I/O element can be represented by each one of these addresses.

The data bus is a bidirectional bus, that is, information can flow in both directions, to or from the microprocessor.

The control bus is used to transmit signals that are used to synchronize the operation of the individual microcomputer elements. Typical control signals include READ, WRITE, and RESET. Some signals on the control bus such as READ and WRITE are unidirectional, while some others such as RESET may be bidirectional.

1.2.2 THE MICROPROCESSOR

The commercial microprocessor, fabricated using the MOS technology, is normally contained in a single chip. The microprocessor is comprised of a register section, one or more ALUs (Arithmetic Logic Units), and a control unit. Depending on the register section, the microprocessor can be classified either as an accumulator-based or a general-purpose register-based machine.

In an accumulator-based microprocessor such as the Intel 8085 and Motorola 6809, one of the operands is assumed to be held in a special register called the "accumulator". All arithmetic and logic operations are performed using this register as one of the data sources. The result after the operation is stored in the accumulator. One-address instructions are very predominant in this organization. Eight-bit microprocessors are usually accumulator-based.

The general-purpose register-based microprocessor is usually popular with 16- and 32-bit microprocessors, such as Intel 8086/80386 and Motorola 68000/68020, and is called general-purpose, since its registers can be used to hold data, memory addresses, or the results of arithmetic or logic operations. The number, size, and types of registers vary from one microprocessor to another. Some registers are general-purpose registers, while others are provided with dedicated functions. The general-purpose registers are used to store addresses or data for an indefinite period of time and then retrieve data when needed.

A general-purpose register is also capable of manipulating the stored data by shift left or right operations. These registers are normally 8, 16, and 32 bits wide. For example, all general-purpose registers in 68000 are 32 bits and can be used as either 8, 16, or 32 bits. Typical dedicated registers include the Program Counter (PC), the Instruction Register (IR), Status Register (SR), the Stack Pointer (SP), the Index Register, and the Barrel Shifter.

The PC normally contains the address of the next instruction to be executed. Upon activating the microprocessor chip's RESET input, the PC is normally initialized with the address of the first instruction, such as 0000H for 8085. The first instruction of a program must be stored at this address. In order to execute the instruction, the microprocessor normally places the PC contents on the address bus and reads (fetches) the first instruction from external memory. The program counter contents are then automatically incremented by the ALU. The microcomputer thus executes a program sequentially unless it encounters a jump or branch instruction. The size of the PC varies from one microprocessor to another depending on the address size. For example, the 8085 has a 16-bit PC, while the 68020 contains a 32-bit PC.

The instruction register (IR) contains the instruction to be executed. After fetching an instruction from memory, the microprocessor places it in the IR for translation.

The status register contains individual bits with each bit having a special meaning. The bits in the status register are called flags. Each flag is usually set or reset by an ALU operation. The flags are used by the Conditional Branch instructions. Typical flags include carry, sign, zero, and overflow.

The carry (C) flag is used to reflect whether or not an arithmetic operation such as ADD generates a carry. The carry is generated out of the 8th bit (bit 7) for byte operation, 16th bit (bit 15) for 16-bit, or 32nd bit (bit 31) for 32-bit operations. The carry is used as the borrow flag for subtraction. In multiple word arithmetic operations, any carry from a low-order word must be reflected in the high-order word for correct result.

The zero (Z) flag is used to indicate whether the result of an arithmetic or logic operation is zero. $Z = 1$ for a zero result and $Z = 0$ for a non-zero result. The sign flag (sometimes also called the negative flag) indicates whether a number is positive or negative. $S = 1$ indicates a negative number if the most significant bit of the number is one; $S = 0$ indicates a positive number if the most significant bit of the number is zero.

The overflow (V) flag is set to one if the result of an arithmetic operation on signed (two's complement) numbers is too large for the microprocessor's maximum word size; the C flag is overflow for unsigned numbers. The overflow flag for signed numbers can be shown as $V = C7 \oplus C6$, where C7 is the final carry and C6 is the previous carry. This can be illustrated by the numerical examples shown below:

$$
\begin{array}{r}
0000\ 0100 \\
+\ 0000\ 0010 \\
\hline
C7=0 \leftarrow 0000\ 0110 \\
\end{array}
\qquad
\begin{array}{r}
04_{10} \\
+\ 02_{10} \\
\hline
06_{10} \\
\end{array}
$$

$$C6 = 0 \leftarrow 0 \qquad 6_{16}$$

From the above, the result is correct when C6 and C7 have the same values (0 in this case). When C6 and C7 are different, an overflow occurs. For example, consider the following:

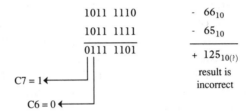

$$
\begin{array}{r}
1011\ 1110 \\
1011\ 1111 \\
\hline
0111\ 1101 \\
\end{array}
\qquad
\begin{array}{r}
-\ 66_{10} \\
-\ 65_{10} \\
\hline
+\ 125_{10(?)} \\
\text{result is} \\
\text{incorrect}
\end{array}
$$

$$C7 = 1 \leftarrow$$
$$C6 = 0 \leftarrow$$

The result is incorrect. Since $V = C6 \oplus C7 = 0 \oplus 1 = 1$, the overflow flag is set. Note that this applies to signed numbers only.

     The stack pointer (SP) register addresses the stack. A stack is Last-In First-Out (LIFO) read/write memory in the sense that items that go in last will come out first. This is because stacks perform all read (POP) and write (PUSH) operations from one end. The stack can be implemented by using hardware or software.

     The hardware stack is designed by using a set of high-speed registers to provide a fast response. The disadvantage of a hardware stack is that the stack size is limited. Earlier microprocessors such as the Intel 4040 4-bit microprocessor used hardware stacks. The software stack, on the other hand, is implemented by using a number of RAM locations. The software stack provides an unlimited stack size but is slower than the hardware stack. It is very popular with 8-, 16-, and 32-bit microprocessors. The stack is addressed by a register called the stack pointer (SP). The size of the SP is dependent on the microprocessor's logical address size. The stack is normally used by subroutines or interrupts for saving certain registers such as the program counter.

Two instructions, PUSH (stack write) and POP (stack read), can usually be performed by the programmer to manipulate the stack. If the stack is accessed from the top, the stack pointer is decremented after a PUSH and incremented before a POP. On the other hand, if the stack is accessed from the bottom, the SP is incremented after a PUSH and decremented after a POP. Typical microprocessors access stack from the top. Depending on the microprocessor, an 8-, 16-, or 32-bit register can be pushed onto or popped from the stack. The value by which the SP is incremented or decremented after POP or PUSH operations depends on the register size. For example, values of "one" for an 8-bit register, "two" for 16-bit registers, and "four" for 32-bit registers are used. Figure 1.2 shows the stack data when accessed from the top before and after PUSHing a 16-bit register onto the stack or POPping 16 bits from the stack into the 16-bit register. Note that stack items PUSHed must be POPped in reverse order. The item pushed last must be popped first.

Consider the PUSH operation in Figure 1.2a when the stack is accessed from the top. The SP is decremented by 2 after the PUSH. The SP is decremented since it is accessed from the top. A decrement value of 2 is used since the register to be pushed is 16 bits wide.

The POP operation shown in Figure 1.2b is the reverse of the PUSH. The SP is incremented after POP. The contents of locations 5008_{16} and 5009_{16} are assumed to be empty.

An index register is typically used as a counter for an instruction or for general storage functions. The index register is useful with instructions where tables or arrays of data are accessed. In this operation, the index register is used to modify the address portion of the instruction. Thus appropriate data in a table can be accessed. This is called indexed addressing. The effective address for an instruction using the indexed addressing mode is determined by adding the address portion of the instruction to the contents of the index register. Some microprocessors such as the 8085 do not offer indexing. However, the indexed mode in 8085 can be achieved by using proper instructions. The general-purpose register-based microprocessor can use any general-purpose register as the index register.

Typical 32-bit microprocessors such as the Intel 80386 and Motorola 68020/68030 include a special type of shifter called barrel shifter for performing fast shift operations.

The barrel shifter is an on-chip component for 32-bit microprocessors and provides fast shift operations. For example, the 80386 barrel shifter can shift a number from 0 through 64 positions in one clock period (clock rate is 16.67 MHz).

The ALU in the microprocessors performs all arithmetic and logic

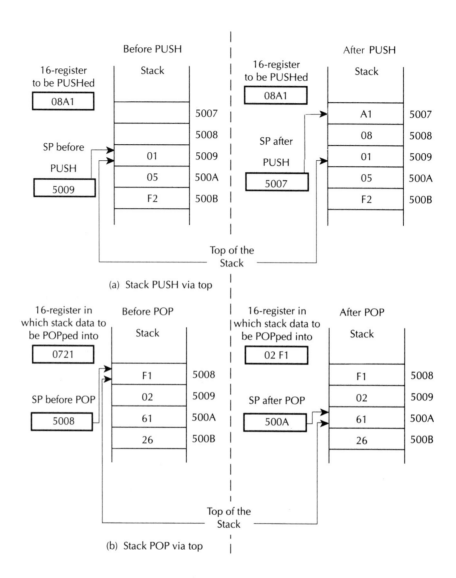

FIGURE 1.2 PUSH and POP operations via top.

operations on data. The size of the ALU defines the size of the microprocessor. For example, Intel 8086 is a 16-bit microprocessor since its ALU
is 16 bits wide. The Intel 8088 is also a 16-bit microprocessor since its ALU
is 16 bits wide, even though its data bus is 8 bits wide. Motorola 68030
is a 32-bit microprocessor since its ALU is 32 bits wide. The ALU usually
performs operations such as binary addition and subtraction. The 32-bit
microprocessors include multiple ALUs for parallel operations and thus
achieve fast speed.

The control unit of the microprocessor performs instruction interpreting and sequencing. In the interpretation phase, the control unit reads instructions from memory using PC as a pointer. It then recognizes the instruction type, gets the necessary operands, and routes them to the appropriate functional units of the execution unit. Necessary signals are issued to the execution unit to perform the desired operations, and the results are routed to the specified destination.

In the sequencing phase, the control unit determines the address of the next instruction to be executed and loads it into the PC. The control unit is typically designed using one of three techniques:

- Hardwired control
- Microprogramming
- Nanoprogramming

The hardwired control unit is designed by physically connecting typical components such as gates and flip-flops. Zilog's 16-bit microprocessor Z8000 is designed using hardwired control. The microprogrammed control unit includes a control ROM for translating the instructions. Intel 8086 is a microprogrammed microprocessor. Nanoprogramming includes two ROMs inside the control unit. The first ROM (microROM) stores all the addresses of the second ROM (nanoROM). If the microinstructions (which is the case with the 68000/68020/68030) repeat many times in a microprogram, use of two-level ROMs provides tremendous memory savings. This is the reason that the control units of the 68000, 68020, and 68030 are nanoprogrammed. The control unit generates certain control signals for other microcomputer elements or reads in control inputs and activates functions such as RESET and interrupts. The RESET input of a typical microprocessor is activated to initialize PC so that the microprocessor knows where to find the first instruction. For example, the 8085 loads PC with 0000_{16} after activation of the RESET pin via an external circuit. This means that the 8085 executes the first instruction at 0000_{16}. Therefore, the user's memory map must include this address.

1.2.3 MEMORY ORGANIZATION
1.2.3.a Introduction
A memory unit is an integral part of any microcomputer system and its primary purpose is to hold programs and data. The major design goal of a memory unit is to allow it to operate at a speed close to that of the processor. However, the cost of a memory unit is so prohibitive that it is practically not feasible to design a large memory unit with one technology that guarantees a high speed. Therefore, in order to seek a trade-off

between the cost and operating speed, a memory system is usually designed with different technologies such as solid state, magnetic, and optical.

In a broad sense, a microcomputer memory system can be logically divided into three groups:

- Processor memory
- Primary or main memory
- Secondary memory

Processor memory refers to a set of CPU registers. These registers are used to hold temporary results when a computation is in progress. Also, there is no speed disparity between these registers and the microprocessor because they are fabricated using the same technology. However, the cost involved in this approach forces a microcomputer architect to include only a few registers (usually 8 or 16) in the microprocessor.

Primary memory is the storage area in which all programs are executed. The microprocessor can directly access only those items that are stored in primary memory. Therefore, all programs and data must be within the primary memory prior to execution. MOS technology is normally used these days in primary memory design. Usually the size of the primary memory is much larger than processor memory and its operating speed is slower than the processor registers by a factor of 25.

Secondary memory refers to the storage medium comprising slow devices such as magnetic tapes and disks. These devices are used to hold large data files and huge programs such as compilers and data base management systems which are not needed by the processor frequently. Sometimes secondary memories are also referred to as auxiliary or backup store.

Primary memory normally includes ROM (Read-only Memory) and RAM (Random Access Memory). As the name implies, a ROM permits only a read access. Some ROMs are custom made, that is, their contents are programmed by the manufacturer. Such ROMs are called mask programmable ROMs. A typical example for a mask programmable ROM is the character generator ROM 2513. Since these ROMs are mass produced, they are inexpensive. Sometimes a user may have to program a ROM in the field. For instance, in a fusible-link ROM, programmable read-only memory (PROM) is available. The main disadvantage of a PROM is that it cannot be reprogrammed.

In practice, when programs are in the development stage, it is necessary that they be altered before they become a marketable product. ROMs that allow reprogramming are called Erasable Programmable Read-Only Memories (EPROMs).

In an EPROM, programs are entered using electrical impulses and the stored information is erased by using ultraviolet rays. Usually an EPROM is programmed by inserting the EPROM chip into the socket of a PROM programmer and providing program addresses and voltage pulses at the appropriate pins of the chip. Typical erase times vary between 10 and 30 minutes.

With advances in IC technology, it is possible to achieve an electrical means of erasure. These new ROMs are called Electrically Alterable ROMs (EAROMs) or Electrically Erasable PROMs (EEPROMs) and these ROM chips can be programmed even when they are in the circuit board. These memories are also called Read Mostly Memories (RMMs), since they have much slower write times than read times. EAROMs are well suited for these applications in which the read operations are more frequent than write operations.

Information stored in semiconductor random access memories will be lost if the power is turned off. This property is known as volatility and, hence, RAMs are usually called volatile memories. RAMs can be backed up by batteries for a certain period of time and are sometimes called nonvolatile RAMs. Stored information in a magnetic tape or magnetic disk is not lost when the power is turned off. Therefore, these storage devices are called nonvolatile memories. Note that a ROM is a nonvolatile memory.

In a semiconductor memory constructed using bipolar transistors, the information is stored in the form of voltage levels in flip-flops. These voltage levels do not usually get drifted away. Such memories are called static RAMs because the stored information remains constant for some period of time.

On the other hand, in semiconductor memories that are designed using MOS transistors, the information is held in the form of electrical charge in capacitors. Here, the stored charge has the tendency to get leaked away. Therefore, a stored 1 would become a 0 if no precautions are taken. These memories are referred to as dynamic RAMs. In order to prevent any information loss, dynamic RAMs have to be refreshed at regular intervals. Refreshing means boosting the signal level and writing it back. This activity is performed by a hardware unit called "refresh logic" which is usually a part of the processor.

Since the static RAM maintains information in active circuits, power is required even when the chip is inactive or in standby mode. Therefore, static RAMs require large power supplies. Also, each static RAM cell is about four times larger in area than an equivalent dynamic cell; a dynamic RAM chip contains about four times as many bits as a static RAM chip using the same or comparable semiconductor technology. Figure 1.3

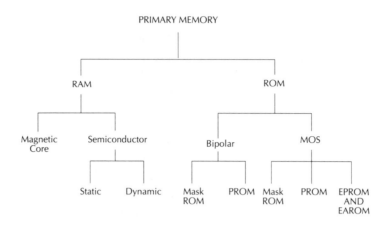

FIGURE 1.3 Subcategories of RAMs and ROMs.

shows the subcategories of ROMs, RAMs, and their associated technologies.

One of the best known read/write memories is the ferrite core memory. In this case, the reading process destroys the stored information. This property is called destructive readout (DRO) and it is unique with respect to ferrite cores. Note that a semiconductor memory does not exhibit this property and for this reason solid-state memories are referred to as nondestructive readout (NDRO) memories. Whenever data are read from the ferrite core memory, they are first transferred to a buffer, and from this buffer, data are rewritten into the location from where they are originally read. It is interesting to note that the inclusion of the memory buffer register (MBR) as a part of a RAM unit is the direct consequence of the phenomenon of DRO.

1.2.3.b Main Memory Array Design

In many applications, a memory of large capacity is often realized by interconnecting several small-size memory blocks. In this section, design of a large main memory using small-size memories as building blocks is presented.

There are two types of techniques used for designing the main memory. These are linear decoding and fully decoding. We will illustrate the concepts associated with these techniques in the following.

First, consider the block diagram of a typical static RAM chip shown in Figure 1.4.

The capacity of this chip is 8192 bits and these bits are organized as 1024 words with 8 bits/word. Each word has a unique address and this is

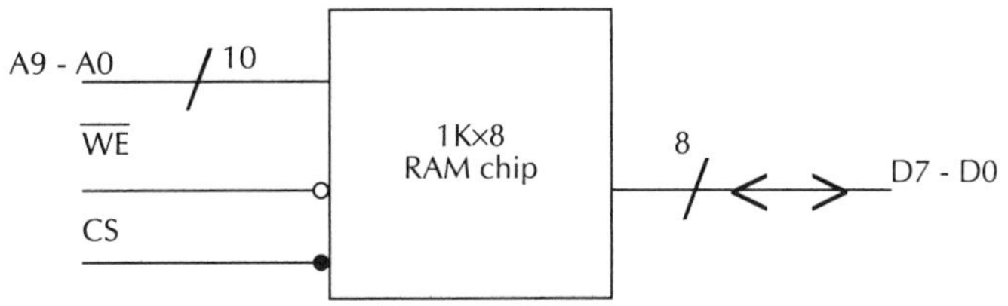

FIGURE 1.4 Block diagram of a typical 1KX8 static RAM chip.

specified on 10-bit address lines A9—A0 (note that 2^{10} = 1024). The inputs and outputs are routed through the 8-bit bidirectional data lines D7 through D0. The operation of this chip is governed by the two control inputs: $\overline{WE}$ (write Enable) and CS (chip select). The truth table that describes the operation of this chip is shown in Table 1.1.

TABLE 1.1
Truth Table for 1K × 8 Static RAM

CS	$\overline{WE}$	MODE	Status of the bidirectional data lines D7—D0	Power
L	X	Not selected	High impedance	Standby
H	L	Write	Acts as an input bus	Active
H	H	Read	Acts as an output bus	Active

Note: H — high, L — low, X — don't care.

From this table, it is easy to see that when CS input is low, the chip is not selected and thus the lines D7 through D0 are driven to the high impedance state. When CS = 1 and $\overline{WE}$ = 0, data on lines D7—D0 are written into the word addressed by A0 through A9. Similarly, when CS = 1 and $\overline{WE}$ is high, the contents of the memory word (whose address is specified on address lines A9 through A0) will appear on lines D7 through D0. Note that when the chip select input CS goes to low, the device is disabled and the chip automatically reduces its power requirements and remains in this low-power standby mode as long as CS remains low. This feature results in system power savings as high as 85% in larger systems, where the majority of devices are disabled.

1.2.3.b.i Linear Decoding

This technique uses the unused address lines of the microprocessor as chip selects for the memory chips.

A simple way to connect an 8-bit microprocessor to a 6K RAM system using linear decoding is shown in Figure 1.5. In this approach, the address lines A9 through A0 of the microprocessor are used as a common input to each $1K \times 8$ RAM chip. The remaining 6 high-order lines are used to select one of the 6 RAM chips. For example, if A15A14A13A12A11A10 = 000010, then the RAM chip 1 is selected. The address map realized by this arrangement is summarized in Figure 1.6. This method is known as the linear select decoding technique. The principal advantage of this method is that it does not require any decoding hardware. However, this approach has some disadvantages:

- Although with a 16-bit address bus we connect 64K bytes of RAM, we are able to interface only 6K bytes of RAM. This means that this idea wastes address space.
- The address map is not contiguous; rather, it is sparsely distributed.
- If both A11 and A10 are high at the same time, both RAM chips 0 and 1 are selected and thus a bus conflict occurs. This can be avoided by proper memory map to select the desired memory chip and deselect the others.
- Also, if all unused address lines are not utilized as chip selects for memory, then these unused pins become don't cares (can be 0 or 1). This results in foldback, meaning that a memory location will have its image in the memory map. For example, if A15 is don't care in design and if A14 to A0 address lines are used, then address 0000_{16} and address 8000_{16} are the same locations. This is called foldback and it wastes memory space.

1.2.3.b.ii Fully Decoding

The difficulties such as the bus conflict and sparse address distribution are eliminated by the use of the fully decoded addressing technique. To see this, consider the organization shown in Figure 1.7. In this setup, we use a 2-to-4 decoder and interface the 8-bit microprocessor with 4K bytes of RAM. In particular, the four combinations of the lines A11 and A10 select the RAM chips as follows:

A11	A10	Device selected
0	0	RAM chip 0
0	1	RAM chip 1
1	0	RAM chip 2
1	1	RAM chip 3

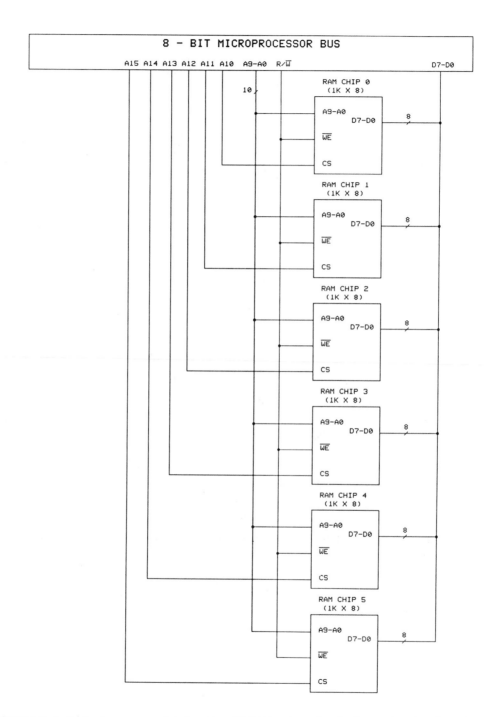

FIGURE 1.5 An 8-bit microprocessor interfaced to a 6K RAM system using the linear select decoding technique.

Binary Address Pattern	Device Selected	Address Assignment in Hex
A15 A14 A13 A12 A11 A10 A9 A8 A7 A6 A5 A4 A3 A2 A1 A0		
0 0 0 0 0 1 0 0 0 0 0 0 0 0 0 0 . . . . 0 0 0 0 0 1 1 1 1 1 1 1 1 1 1 1	RAM CHIP 0	0400 to 07FF
0 0 0 0 1 0 0 0 0 0 0 0 0 0 0 0 . . . . 0 0 0 0 1 0 1 1 1 1 1 1 1 1 1 1	RAM CHIP 1	0800 to 0BFF
0 0 0 1 0 0 0 0 0 0 0 0 0 0 0 0 . . . . 0 0 0 1 0 0 1 1 1 1 1 1 1 1 1 1	RAM CHIP 2	1000 to 13FF
0 0 1 0 0 0 0 0 0 0 0 0 0 0 0 0 . . . . 0 0 1 0 0 0 1 1 1 1 1 1 1 1 1 1	RAM CHIP 3	2000 to 23FF
0 1 0 0 0 0 0 0 0 0 0 0 0 0 0 0 . . . . 0 1 0 0 0 0 1 1 1 1 1 1 1 1 1 1	RAM CHIP 4	4000 to 43FF
1 0 0 0 0 0 0 0 0 0 0 0 0 0 0 0 . . . . 1 0 0 0 0 0 1 1 1 1 1 1 1 1 1 1	RAM CHIP 5	8000 to 83FF

FIGURE 1.6 Address map realized by the system shown in Figure 1.5.

Also observe that this hardware makes sure that the memory system is enabled only when the lines A15 through A12 are zero. The complete address map corresponding to this organization is summarized in Figure 1.8.

1.2.3.c Memory Management Concepts

Due to the massive amount of information that must be saved in most systems, the mass storage is often a disk. If each access is to a disk (even a hard disk), then system throughput will be reduced to unacceptable levels.

An obvious solution is to use a large and fast locally accessed semiconductor memory. Unfortunately the storage cost per bit for this solution is very high. A combination of both off-board disk (secondary memory) and on-board semiconductor main memory must be designed into a system. This requires a mechanism to manage the two-way flow of information between the primary (semiconductor) and secondary (disk) media. This mechanism must be able to transfer blocks of data efficiently, keep track of block usage, and replace them in a nonarbitrary way. The primary memory system must therefore be able to dynamically allocate memory space.

An operating system must have resource protection from corruption or abuse by users. Users must be able to protect areas of code from each other,

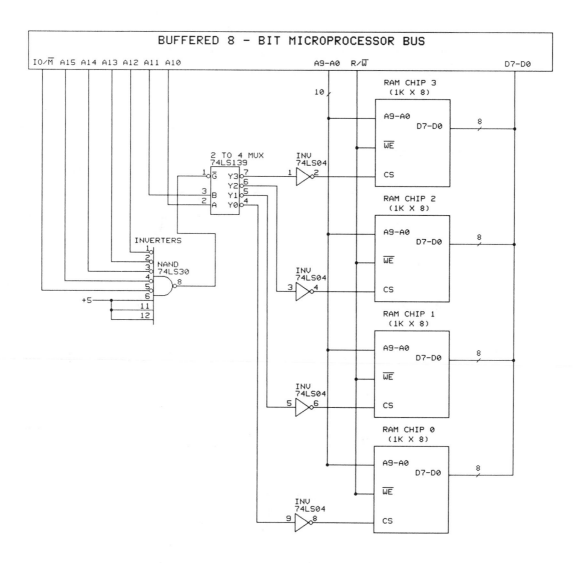

FIGURE 1.7 An 8-bit microprocessor interfaced to a 4K RAM system using a fully decoded addressing technique.

while maintaining the ability to communicate and share other areas of code. All these requirements indicate the need for a device, located between the microprocessor and memory, to control accesses, perform address mappings, and act as an interface between the logical and microprocessor and physical (memory) address spaces. Since this device must manage the memory use configuration, it is appropriately called the memory management unit (MMU). Typical 32-bit microprocessors such as Motorola 68030 and Intel 80386 include on-chip MMU.

Binary Address Pattern																Device Selected	Address Assignment to Hex
A15	A14	A13	A12	A11	A10	A9	A8	A7	A6	A5	A4	A3	A2	A1	A0		
0	0	0	0	0	0	0	0	0	0	0	0	0	0	0	0	RAM CHIP 0	0000 to 03FF
0	0	0	0	0	0	1	1	1	1	1	1	1	1	1	1		
0	0	0	0	0	1	0	0	0	0	0	0	0	0	0	0	RAM CHIP 1	0400 to 07FF
0	0	0	0	0	1	1	1	1	1	1	1	1	1	1	1		
0	0	0	0	1	0	0	0	0	0	0	0	0	0	0	0	RAM CHIP 2	0800 to 0BFF
0	0	0	0	1	0	1	1	1	1	1	1	1	1	1	1		
0	0	0	0	1	1	0	0	0	0	0	0	0	0	0	0	RAM CHIP 3	0C00 to 0FFF
0	0	0	0	1	1	1	1	1	1	1	1	1	1	1	1		

FIGURE 1.8 Address map corresponding to the organization shown in Figure 1.7.

The MMU reduces the burden of memory management function on the operating system.

The basic functions provided by the MMU are address translation and protection. The MMU translates logical program addresses to physical memory addresses. Note that in assembly language programming, addresses are referred to by symbolic names. These addresses in a program are called logical addresses since they indicate the logical positions of instructions and data. The MMU translates these logical addresses to physical addresses provided by the memory chips. The MMU can perform address translation in one of two ways:

1.   By using the substitution technique as shown in Figure 1.9a
2.   By adding an offset to each logical address to obtain the corresponding physical address as shown in Figure 1.9b

Address translation using substitution is faster than the offset method. However, the offset method has the advantage of mapping a logical address to any physical address as determined by the offset value.

Memory is usually divided into small manageable units. The terms "page" and "segment" are frequently used to describe these units. Paging divides the memory into equal-sized pages, while segmentation divides the memory into variable-sized segments.

It is relatively easier to implement the address translation table if the logical and main memory spaces are divided into pages. The term "page" is associated with logical address space, while the term "block" usually refers to a page in main memory space.

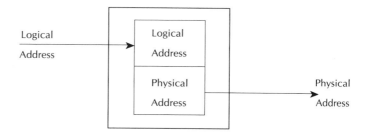

FIGURE 1.9a Address translation using substitution technique.

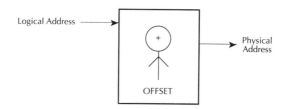

FIGURE 1.9b Address translation by offset technique.

There are three ways to map logical addresses to physical addresses. These are paging, segmentation, and combined paging/segmentation.

In a paged system, a user has access to a larger address space than physical memory provides. The virtual memory system is managed by both hardware and software. The hardware included in the memory management unit handles address translation. The memory management software in the operating system performs all functions including page replacement policies in order to provide efficient memory utilization. The memory management software performs functions such as removal of the desired page from main memory to accommodate a new page, transferring a new page from secondary to main memory at the right instant of time, and placing the page at the right location in memory.

If the main memory is full during transfer from secondary to main memory, it is necessary to remove a page from main memory to accommodate the new page. Two popular page replacement policies are first-in first-out (FIFO) and least recently used (LRU). The FIFO policy removes the page from main memory that has been resident in memory for the longest amount of time. The FIFO replacement policy is easy to implement. One of the main disadvantages of the FIFO policy is that it is likely to replace heavily used pages. Note that heavily used pages are resident in main memory for the longest amount of time. Sometimes this replacement policy might be a poor choice. For example, in a time-shared system, several users normally share a copy of the text editor in order to type and correct programs. The FIFO policy on such a system might replace a heavily used editor page to make room for a new page. This editor page might be recalled to main memory immediately. The FIFO, in this case, would be a poor choice.

The LRU policy, on the other hand, replaces that page which has not been used for the longest amount of time.

In the segmentation method, the MMU utilizes the segment selector to obtain a descriptor from a table in memory containing several descriptors. A descriptor contains the physical base address for a segment, the segment's privilege level, and some control bits. When the MMU obtains a logical address from the microprocessor, it first determines whether the segment is already in the physical memory. If it is, the MMU adds an offset component to the segment base component of the address obtained from the segment descriptor table to provide the physical address. The MMU then generates the physical address on the address bus for selecting the memory. On the other hand, if the MMU does not find the logical address in physical memory, it interrupts the microprocessor. The microprocessor executes a service routine to bring the desired program from a secondary memory such as disk to the physical memory. The MMU determines the physical address using the segment offset and descriptor as above and then generates the physical address on the address bus for memory. A segment will usually consist of an integral number of pages, say, each 256 bytes long. With different-sized segments being swapped in and out, areas of valuable primary memory can become unusable. Memory is unusable for segmentation when it is sandwiched between already allocated segments and if it is not large enough to hold the latest segment that needs to be loaded. This is called external fragmentation and is handled by MMUs using special techniques. An example of external fragmentation is given in Figure 1.10.

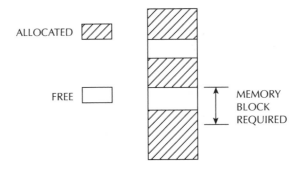

FIGURE 1.10 Memory fragmentation (external).

The advantages of segmented memory management are that few descriptors are required for large programs or data spaces, and internal fragmentation (to be discussed later) is minimized. The disadvantages include external fragmentation, involved algorithms for placing data are required, possible restrictions on starting address, and longer data swap times are required to support virtual memory.

Address translation using descriptor tables offers a protection feature. A segment or a page can be protected from access by a program section of a lower privilege level. For example, the selector component of each logical address includes one or two bits indicating the privilege level of the program requesting access to a segment. Each segment descriptor also includes one or two bits providing the privilege level of that segment. When an executing program tries to access a segment, the MMU can compare the selector privilege level with the descriptor privilege level. If the segment selector has the same or higher privilege level, then the MMU permits the access. If the privilege level of the selector is lower than the descriptor, the MMU can interrupt the microprocessor informing of a privilege level violation. Therefore, the indirect technique of generating physical address provides a mechanism of protecting critical program sections in the operating system. Since paging divides the memory into equal-sized pages, it avoids the major problem of segmentation-external fragmentation. Since the pages are of the same size, when a new page is requested and an old one swapped out, the new one will always fit into the vacated space. However, a problem common to both techniques remains — internal fragmentation. Internal fragmentation is a condition where memory is unused but allocated due to memory block size implementation restrictions. This occurs when a module needs, say, 300 bytes and page is 1K bytes, as shown in Figure 1.11.

In the paged-segmentation method, each segment contains a number

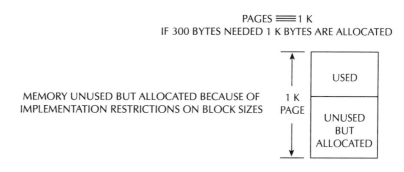

FIGURE 1.11 Memory fragmentation (internal).

of pages. The logical address is divided into three components: segment, page, and word. The segment component defines a segment number, the page component defines the page within the segment, and the word component provides the particular word within the page. A page component of n bits can provide up to 2^n pages. A segment can be assigned with one or more pages up to a maximum of 2^n pages; therefore, a segment size depends on the number of pages assigned to it.

Protection mechanism can be assigned either on physical address or logical address. Physical memory protection can be accomplished by using one or more protection bits with each block to define the access type permitted on the block. This means that each time a page is transferred from one block to another, the block protection bits must be updated. A more efficient approach is to provide a protection feature in logical address space by including protection bits in the descriptors of the segment table in the MMU.

1.2.3.d Cache Memory Organization

The performance of a microcomputer system can be significantly improved by introducing a small, expensive, but fast memory between the microprocessor and main memory. This memory is called cache memory and this idea was first introduced in the IBM 360/85 computer. Later on, this concept was also implemented in minicomputers such as PDP-11/70. With the advent of VLSI technology, the cache memory technique is gaining acceptance in the microprocessor world. For example, a small on-chip cache memory is implemented in Intel's 32-bit microprocessor, the 80386, and Motorola's 32-bit microprocessor, the MC 68020/68030.

The block diagram representation of a microprocessor system that employs a cache memory is shown in Figure 1.12. Usually, a cache memory is very small is size and its access time is less than that of the main memory by a factor of 5. Typically, the access times of the cache and main memories are 100 and 500 ns, respectively.

If a reference is found in the cache, we call it a cache hit and the data pertaining to the microprocessor reference is transferred to the microprocessor from the cache. However, if the reference is not found in the cache, we call it a cache miss. When there is a cache miss, the main memory is accessed by the microprocessor and the data are then transferred to the microprocessor from the main memory. At the same time, a block of data containing the desired data needed by the microprocessor is transferred from the main memory to the cache. The block normally contains 4 to 16 words, and this block is placed in the cache using the standard replacement policies such as FIFO (First-In First-Out) or LRU (Least Recently Used).

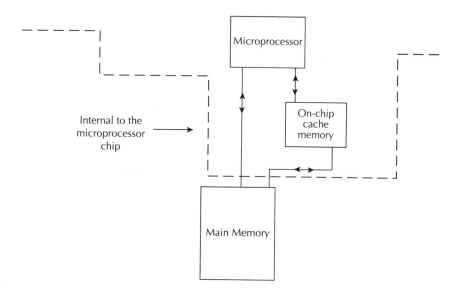

FIGURE 1.12 Memory organization of a computer system that employs a cache memory.

This block transfer is done with a hope that all future references made by the microprocessor will be confined to the fast cache.

The relationship between the cache and main memory blocks is established using mapping techniques. Three widely used mapping techniques are

- Direct mapping
- Fully-associative mapping
- Set-associative mapping

In direct mapping, the main memory address is divided into two fields: an index field and a tag field. The number of bits in the index field is equal to the number of address bits required to access the cache memory.

Assume that the main memory address is m bit wide and the cache memory address is n bit wide. Then the index field requires n bits and the tag field is (m – n) bit wide. The n-bit address accesses the code. Each word in the cache includes the data word and its associated tag. When the microprocessor generates an address for main memory, the index field is used as the address to access the cache. The tag field of the main memory is compared with the tag field in the word read from cache. A hit occurs if the tags match. This means that the desired data word is in cache. A miss occurs if there is no match and the required word is read from main memory. It is written in the cache along with the new tag. A random access memory is used as the cache memory.

One of the main drawbacks of direct mapping is that numerous misses may occur if two or more words with addresses having the same index but different tags are accessed several times. This can be minimized by having such words far apart in the address range.

The fastest cache memory utilizes an associative memory. The method is known as fully associative mapping. Each associative memory content contains main memory address and its content (data). When the microprocessor generates a main memory address, it is compared associatively (simultaneously) with all addresses in the associative memory. If there is a match, the corresponding data word is read from the associative cache memory and sent to the microprocessor. If a miss occurs, the main memory is accessed, and the address and its corresponding data are written to the associative cache memory. If the cache is full, certain policies such as FIFO (first-in first-out) are used as replacement algorithm for the cache. The associative cache is expensive but provides fast operation.

The set-associative mapping is a combination of direct and associative mapping. Each cache word stores two or more main memory words using the same index address. Each main memory word consists of a tag and its data word. An index with two or more tags and data words forms a set. When the microprocessor generates a memory request, the index of the main memory address is used as the cache address. The tag field of the main memory address is then compared associatively (simultaneously) with all tags stored under the index. If a match occurs, the desired data word is read. If a miss occurs, the data word, along with its tag, is read from main memory and also written into the cache. The hit ratio improves as the set size increases. This is because more words with the same index but different tags can be stored in cache.

There are two ways of writing into cache: the write-back and write-through methods. In the write-back method, whenever the microprocessor writes something into a cache word, a dirty bit is assigned to the cache word. When a dirty word is to be replaced with a new word, the dirty word is first copied into the main memory before it is overwritten by the incoming new word. The advantage of this method is that it avoids unnecessary writing into main memory.

In the write-through method, whenever the microprocessor alters a cache address, the same alteration is made in the main memory copy of the altered cache address. This policy can be easily implemented and also it insures that the contents of the main memory are always valid. This feature is desirable in a multiprocessor system where the main memory is shared by several processors. However, this approach may lead to several unnecessary writes to main memory.

One of the important aspects of cache memory organization is to devise a method that insures proper utilization of the cache. Usually, the tag directory contains an extra bit for each entry. This additional bit is called a valid bit. When the power is turned on, the valid bit corresponding to each cache block entry of the tag directory is reset to zero. This is done in order to indicate that the cache block holds invalid data. When a block of data is first transferred from the main memory to a cache block, the valid bit corresponding to this cache block is set to 1. In this arrangement, whenever the valid is a zero, it implies that a new incoming block can overwrite the existing cache block. Thus, there is no need to copy the contents of the cache block being replaced into the main memory.

1.2.4 INPUT/OUTPUT (I/O)

This section describes the basic input and output techniques used by microcomputers to transfer data between the microcomputer and an external device. The general characteristics of I/O are described. One communicates with a microcomputer system via the I/O devices interfaced to it. The user can enter programs and data using the keyboard on a terminal and execute the programs to obtain results. Therefore, the I/O devices connected to a microcomputer system provide an efficient means of communication between the computer and the outside world. These I/O devices are commonly called peripherals and include keyboards, CRT displays, printers, and disks.

The characteristics of the I/O devices are normally different from those of the microcomputer. For example, the speed of operation of the peripherals is usually slower compared to the microcomputer, and the word length of the microcomputer may be different from the data format of the peripheral device. To make the characteristics of the I/O devices compatible with those of the microcomputer, interface hardware circuitry between the microcomputer and I/O devices is necessary. Interfaces provide all input and output transfers between the microcomputer and peripherals by using an I/O bus. An I/O bus carriers three types of signals: device address, data, and command status.

For 16- and 32-bit microcomputers, a separate intelligent I/O processor (IOP) or data channel is provided to route all I/O transfers. To make 8-bit microcomputer systems inexpensive, a separate interface rather than a smart I/O processor is provided with each I/O device. I/O processors control all major I/O functions and relieve the microcomputer of these tasks.

The microprocessor uses the I/O bus when it executes an I/O instruction. A typical I/O instruction has three fields. When the microcomputer executes an I/O instruction, the control unit decodes the op-code field and identifies it as an I/O instruction. The microprocessor then places the device address and command from the respective fields of the I/O instruction onto the I/O bus. The interfaces for various devices connected to the I/O bus decode this address, and appropriate interface is selected. The identified interface decodes the command lines and determines the function to be performed. Typical functions include receiving data from an input device into the microprocessor or sending data to an output device from the microprocessor.

In a typical microcomputer system, the user gets involved with two types of I/O devices: physical I/O and virtual I/O. When the microcomputer has no operating system, the user must work directly with physical I/O devices and perform detailed I/O design.

There are three ways of transferring data between the microcomputer and a physical I/O device:

- Programmed I/O
- Interrupt driven I/O
- Direct memory access (DMA)

The microcomputer executes a program to communicate with an external device via a register called the I/O port for programmed I/O.

An external device requests the microcomputer to transfer data by activating a signal on the microcomputer's interrupt line during interrupt I/O. In response, the microcomputer executes a program called the interrupt-service routine to carry out the function desired by the external device.

Data transfer between the microcomputer's memory and an external device occurs without microprocessor involvement with direct memory access.

For a microcomputer with an operating system, the user works with virtual I/O devices. The user does not have to be familiar with the characteristics of the physical I/O devices. Instead, the user performs data transfers between the microcomputer and the physical I/O devices indirectly by calling the I/O routines provided by the operating system using virtual I/O instructions.

1.2.4.a Programmed I/O

As described earlier, the microcomputer communicates with an external device via one or more registers called I/O ports using programmed I/

O. These I/O ports are occasionally fabricated by the manufacturer in the same chip as the memory chip to achieve minimum chip count for small system applications. For example, the Intel 8355/8755 contains 2K bytes of ROM/EPROM with two I/O ports. The Motorola 6846 has 2K bytes of ROM and an 8-bit I/O port.

I/O ports are usually of two types. For one type, each bit in the port can be individually configured as either input or output. For the other type, all bits in the port can be set up as either all parallel input or output bits. Each port can be configured as an input or output port by another register called the command, or data-direction register. The port contains the actual input or output data. The data-direction register is an output register and can be used to configure the bits in the port as inputs or outputs.

Each bit in the port can usually be set up as an input or output by respectively writing a 0 or a 1 in the corresponding bit of the data-direction register. As an example, if an 8-bit data-direction register contains 34_{16}, then the corresponding port is defined as follows:

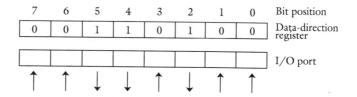

In the preceding example, since 34_{16} ($0011\ 0100_2$) is sent as an output into the data-direction register, bits 0, 1, 3, 6, and 7 of the port are set up as inputs, and bits 2, 4, and 5 of the port are defined as outputs. The microcomputer can then send outputs to external devices, such as LEDs, connected to bits 2, 4, and 5 through a proper interface. Similarly, the microcomputer can input the status of external devices, such as switches, through bits 0, 1, 3, 6, and 7. To input data from the input switches, the 8-bit microcomputer assumed here inputs the complete byte, including the bits to which LEDs are connected. While receiving input data from an I/O port, however, the microcomputer places a value, probably 0, at the bits configured as outputs and the program must interpret them as "don't cares". At the same time, the microcomputer's outputs to bits configured as inputs are disabled.

For parallel I/O, there is only one data-direction register, known as the command register for all ports. A particular bit in the command register configures all bits in the port as either inputs or outputs.

Consider two I/O ports in an I/O chip along with one command register. Assume that a 0 or a 1 in a particular bit position defines all bits of ports A or B as inputs or outputs.

For example,

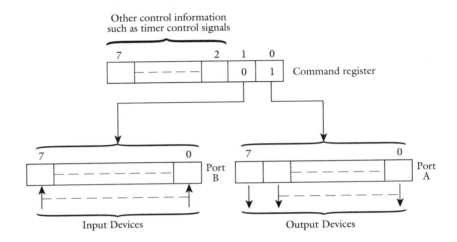

Some I/O ports are called handshake ports. Data transfer occurs via these ports through exchanging of control signals between the I/O controller and an external device.

1.2.4.b Standard I/O Versus Memory-Mapped I/O

I/O ports are addressed using either standard I/O or memory-mapped I/O techniques. The standard I/O, also called isolated I/O, uses the IO/$\overline{\text{M}}$ control pin on the microprocessor chip. The processor outputs a HIGH on this pin to indicate to memory and the I/O chips that an I/O operation is taking place. A LOW output from the processor to this pin indicates a memory operation. Execution of IN or OUT instructions makes the IO/$\overline{\text{M}}$ HIGH, whereas memory-oriented instructions, such as LDA and STA, drive the IO/$\overline{\text{M}}$ to LOW. In standard I/O, the processor uses the IO/$\overline{\text{M}}$ pin to distinguish between I/O and memory. For 8-bit processors, an 8-bit address is typically used for each I/O port. This is because 8 bits are the basic data unit for these processors. Eight-bit processors are usually capable of directly addressing 64K bytes of memory using 16 address lines. With an 8-bit I/O port address, these processors are capable of addressing 256 ports. However, in a typical application, there are usually four or five I/O ports required. Some of the address bits of the microprocessor are normally decoded to obtain the I/O port addresses. With memory-mapped I/O, the processor does not differentiate between I/O and memory and, therefore, does not use the IO/$\overline{\text{M}}$ control pin. The processor uses a portion of the memory addresses to represent I/O ports. The I/O ports are mapped into the processor's main memory and, hence, are called *memory-mapped I/O*. Each method has its advantages and disadvantages. For example, when standard I/O is used, an 8085 processor normally uses the 2-byte IN or OUT instruction as follows:

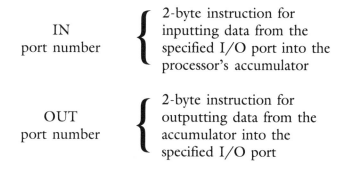

With memory-mapped I/O, an 8-bit processor normally uses 3-byte instructions, namely, LDA and STA, as follows:

LDA
   xx }   Port address   { 3-byte instruction
   xx }   mapped into memory   for inputting a byte
                                                     into accumulator

STA
   xx }   Port address   { 3-byte instruction
   xx }   mapped into memory   for outputting data
                                                     into the specified port

In memory-mapped I/O, the most significant bit (MSB) of the address is typically used to distinguish between I/O and memory. If the MSB of address is 1, an I/O port is selected. If the MSB of address is 0, a memory location is accessed. Sixteen and thirty-two bit microprocessors provide special control signals for performing memory-mapped I/O. Thus, these processors do not use MSB of the address lines. The processor can perform operations on port data without moving it into a microprocessor register through memory-mapped I/O. The port data must be moved into the accumulator for further processing while using standard I/O.

1.2.4.c Unconditional and Conditional Programmed I/O

The processor can send data to an external device at any time during unconditional I/O. The external device must always be ready for data transfer. A typical example is when the processor outputs a 7-bit code through an I/O port to drive a seven-segment display connected to this port.

In conditional I/O, the processor outputs data to an external device via handshaking. Data transfer occurs by the exchanging of control signals between the processor and an external device. The processor inputs the status of the external device to determine whether the device is ready for data transfer. Data transfer takes place when the device is ready.

The concept of conditional I/O will now be demonstrated by means of data transfer between a processor and an analog-to-digital (A/D) converter. Consider, for example, the A/D converter shown in the accompanying figure.

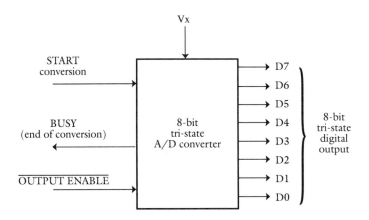

The A/D converter just shown transforms an analog voltage Vx into an 8-bit binary output at pins D7—D0. A pulse at the START conversion pin initiates the conversion. This drives the BUSY signal LOW. The signal stays LOW during the conversion process. The BUSY signal goes HIGH as soon as the conversion ends. Since the A/D converter's output is tristated, a LOW on the OUTPUT ENABLE transfers the converter's output. A HIGH on the OUTPUT ENABLE drives the converter's output to a high impedance state.

The concept of conditional I/O can be demonstrated by interfacing the A/D converter to an 8-bit processor. Figure 1.13 shows such an interfacing example.

The user writes a program to carry out the conversion process. When this program is executed, the processor sends a pulse to the START pin of

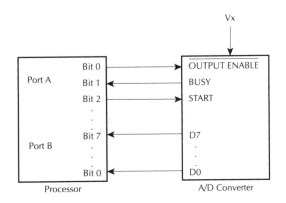

FIGURE 1.13 Interfacing an A/D converter to an 8-bit processor.

the converter via bit 2 of port A. The processor then checks the BUSY signal by bit 1 of port A to determine if the conversion is completed. If the BUSY signal is HIGH (indicating the end of conversion), the processor sends a LOW to the $\overline{\text{OUTPUT ENABLE}}$ pin of the A/1 converter. The processor then inputs the converter's D0—D7 outputs via port B. If the conversion is not completed, the processor waits in a loop checking for the BUSY signal to go HIGH.

1.2.4.d Typical Microcomputer I/O Circuits

The tristate output circuit shown in Figure 1.14 utilizes totem pole-type output called a PUSH-PULL circuit providing low-output currents. Therefore, current amplifier (buffer) is required to drive devices such as LEDf.

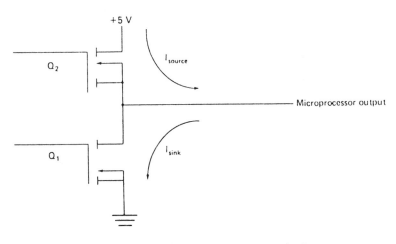

FIGURE 1.14 Typical microprocessor output circuit.

In the preceding figure, when Q_1 is ON, Q_2 is OFF and I_{sink} will flow from the external device into Q_1. Also, when Q_2 is ON, Q_1 is OFF and I_{source} will flow from Q_2 into the output device. Figure 1.15 shows a hardware interface circuit using the push-pull circuit for driving an external device such as LED.

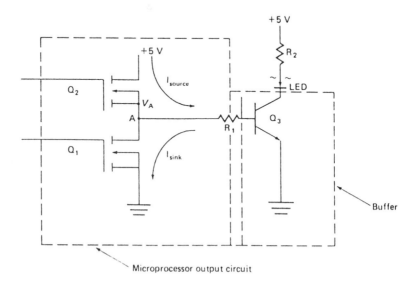

FIGURE 1.15 Microprocessor I/O interfaces for driving on LED.

Assume I_{source} to be 400 μA (usually represented by a negative sign such as I_{OH} = −400 μA; the negative sign indicates that the chip is losing current) with a minimum voltage V_A of 2.4 at point A, and that the LED requires 10 mA at 1.7 V. Therefore, a buffer such as a transistor is required at the output circuit to increase the current drive capability to drive the LED. In order to design the interface, the values of R_1, R_2 and minimum β of the transistor will be determined in the following:

$$R_1 = \frac{V_A - V_{BE}(Q_3)}{400 \ \mu A} = \frac{2.4 - 0.7}{400 \ \mu A} = 4.25 \ k\Omega$$

Since I_{LED} = 10 mA at 1.7 V and assuming that V_{CE} (saturation) ≈ 0 V,

$$R_2 = \frac{5 - 1.7 - V_{CE}(Q_3)}{10 \ mA} = \frac{3.3}{10 \ mA} = 330 \ \Omega$$

Since $I_{source} = 400\ \mu A = I_B(Q_3)$, β for transistor Q_3 is

$$\beta = \frac{I_C(Q_3)}{I_B(Q_3)} = \frac{10\ mA}{400\ \mu A} = \frac{10 \times 10^{-3}}{400 \times 10^{-6}} = 25$$

Therefore, the interface design is complete, and a transistor with a mimimum of saturation β of 25 and $R_1 = 4.25\ k\Omega$ and $R_2 = 330\ \Omega$ is required.

In the input mode of the tristate I/O pin configured by the data direction register, an input switch shown in Figure 1.16 can be interfaced.

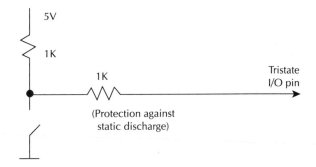

FIGURE 1.16 Switch interface to a tristate pin.

1.2.4.e Interrupt Driven I/O

A disadvantage of conditional programmed I/O is that the microcomputer needs to check the status bit (BUSY signal for the A/D converter) by waiting in a loop. This type of I/O transfer is dependent on the speed of the external device. For a slow device, this waiting may slow down the capability of the microprocessor to process other data. The interrupt I/O technique is efficient in this type of situation.

Interrupt I/O is a device-initiated I/O transfer. The external device is connected to a pin called the *interrupt* (INT) pin on the processor chip. When the device needs an I/O transfer with the microcomputer, it activates the interrupt pin of the processor chip. The microcomputer usually completes the current instruction and saves at least the contents of the current program counter on the stack.

The microcomputer then automatically loads an address into the program counter to branch to a subroutine-like program called the interrupt-service routine. This program is written by the user. The external device wants the microcomputer to execute this program to transfer data. The last instruction of the service routine is a RETURN, which is typically the same instruction used at the end of a subroutine. This instruction normally loads the address (saved in the stack before going to the service routine) in the program counter. Then, the microcomputer continues executing the main program.

1.2.4.e.i Interrupt Types

There are typically three types of interrupts: external interrupts, traps or internal interrupts, and software interrupts.

External interrupts are initiated through the microcomputer's interrupt pins by external devices such as A/D converters. A simple example of an external interrupt was given in the previous section.

External interrupts can further be divided into two types: maskable and nonmaskable. A maskable interrupt is enabled or disabled by executing instructions such as EI or DI. If the microcomputer's interrupt is disabled, the microcomputer ignores the maskable interrupt. Some processors, such as the Intel 8086, have an interrupt-flag bit in the processor status register. When the interrupt is disabled, the interrupt-flag bit is 1, so no maskable interrupts are recognized by the processor. The interrupt-flag bit resets to zero when the interrupt is enabled.

The nonmaskable interrupt has higher priority than the maskable interrupt. If both maskable and nonmaskable interrupts are activated at the same time, the processor will service the nonmaskable interrupt first. The nonmaskable interrupt is typically used as a power failure interrupt. Processors normally use +5 V DC, which is transformed from 110 V AC. If the power falls below 90 V AC, the DC voltage of +5 V cannot be maintained. However, it will take a few milliseconds before the AC power can drop this low (below 90 V AC). In these few milliseconds, the power failure-sensing circuitry can interrupt the processor. An interrupt service routine can be written to store critical data in nonvolatile memory such as battery-backed CMOS RAM. The interrupted program can continue without any loss of data when the power returns.

Some processors are provided with a maskable handshake interrupt. This interrupt is usually implemented by using two pins — INTR and $\overline{\text{INTA}}$. When the INTR pin is activated by an external device, the processor completes the current instruction, saves at least the current program counter onto stack, and generates an interrupt acknowledge ($\overline{\text{INTA}}$). In response to the $\overline{\text{INTA}}$, the external device provides an instruction, such as CALL, using external hardware on the data bus of the microcomputer. This instruction is then read and executed by the microcomputer to branch to the desired service routine.

Internal interrupts, or traps, are activated internally by exceptional conditions such as overflow, division by zero, or execution of an illegal opcode. Traps are handled the same way as external interrupts. The user writes a service routine to take corrective measures and provide an indication to inform the user that an exceptional condition has occurred.

Many processors include software interrupts, or system calls. When one of these instructions is executed, the processor is interrupted and serviced similarly to external or internal interrupts. Software interrupt instructions are normally used to call the operating system. These instructions are shorter than subroutine calls, and no calling program is needed to know the operating system's address in memory. Software interrupt instructions allow the user to switch from user to supervisor mode. For some processors, a software interrupt is the only way to call the operating system, since a subroutine call to an address in the operating system is not allowed.

1.2.4.e.ii Interrupt Address Vector

The technique used to find the starting address of the service routine (commonly known as the *interrupt address vector*) varies from one processor to another. With some processors, the manufacturers define the fixed starting address for each interrupt. Other manufacturers use an indirect approach by defining fixed locations where the interrupt address vector is stored.

1.2.4.e.iii Saving the Microprocessor Registers

When a processor is interrupted, it saves at least the program counter on the stack so the processor can return to the main program after executing the service routine. Some processors save only one or two registers, such as the program counter and status register. Other processors save all microprocessor registers before going to the service routine. The user should know the specific registers the processor saves prior to executing the service routine. This will enable the user to use the appropriate return instruction at the end of the service routine to restore the original conditions upon return to the main program.

1.2.4.e.iv Interrupt Priorities

A processor is typically provided with one or more interrupt pins on the chip. Therefore, a special mechanism is necessary to handle interrupts from several devices that share one of these interrupt lines. There are two ways of servicing multiple interrupts: polled and daisy chain techniques.

Polled interrupts are handled by software and therefore are slower when compared with daisy chaining. The processor responds to an interrupt by executing one general service routine for all devices. The priorities of devices are determined by the order in which the routine polls each device. The processor checks the status of each device in the general service routine, starting with the highest-priority device to service an interrupt. Once the processor determines the source of the interrupt, it branches to the service routine for the device.

In a daisy chain priority system, devices are connected in a daisy chain fashion to set up a priority system. Suppose one or more devices interrupt the processor. In response, the processor pushes at least the PC and generates an interrupt acknowledge ($\overline{\text{INTA}}$) signal to the highest-priority device. If this device has generated the interrupt, it will accept the $\overline{\text{INTA}}$. Otherwise it will pass the $\overline{\text{INTA}}$ onto the next device until $\overline{\text{INTA}}$ is accepted. Once accepted, the device provides a means for the processor to find an interrupt address vector by using external hardware. The daisy chain priority scheme is based on mostly hardware and is therefore faster than the polled interrupt.

1.2.4.f Direct Memory Access (DMA)

Direct Memory Access (DMA) is a technique that transfers data between a microcomputer's memory and I/O device without involving the microprocessor. DMA is widely used in transferring large blocks of data between a peripheral device and the microcomputer's memory. The DMA technique uses a DMA controller chip for the data-transfer operation. The main functions of a typical DMA controller are summarized as follows:

- The I/O devices request DMA operation via the DMA request line of the controller chip.
- The controller chip activates the microprocessor HOLD pin, requesting the CPU to release the bus.
- The processor sends HLDA (hold acknowledge) back to the DMA controller, indicating that the bus is disabled. The DMA controller places the current value of its internal registers, such as the address register and counter, on the system bus and sends a DMA acknowledge to the peripheral device. The DMA controller completes the DMA transfer.

There are three basic types of DMA: block transfer, cycle stealing, and interleaved DMA.

For block-transfer DMA, the DMA controller chip takes the bus from the microcomputer to transfer data between the memory and I/O device. The microprocessor has no access to the bus until the transfer is completed. During this time, the microprocessor can perform internal operations that do not need the bus. This method is popular with microprocessors. Using this technique, blocks of data can be transferred.

Data transfer between the microcomputer memory and an I/O device occurs on a word-by-word basis with cycle stealing. Typically, the microprocessor clock is enabled by ANDing an $\overline{\text{INHIBIT}}$ signal with the system clock. The system clock has the same frequency as the microprocessor clock.

The DMA controller controls the $\overline{\text{INHIBIT}}$ line. During normal operation, the $\overline{\text{INHIBIT}}$ line is HIGH, providing the microprocessor clock. When DMA operation is desired, the controller makes the $\overline{\text{INHIBIT}}$ line LOW for one clock cycle. The microprocessor is then stopped completely for one cycle. Data transfer between the memory and I/O takes place during this cycle. This method is called cycle stealing because the DMA controller takes away or steals a cycle without microprocessor recognition. Data transfer takes place over a period of time.

With interleaved DMA, the DMA controller chip takes over the system bus when the microprocessor is not using it. For example, the microprocessor does not use the bus while incrementing the program counter or performing an ALU operation. The DMA controller chip identifies these cycles and allows transfer of data between the memory and I/O device. Data transfer takes place over a period of time for this method.

The DMA controller chip usually has at least three registers normally selected by the controller's register select (RS) line: an address register, a terminal count register, and a status register. Both the address and terminal count registers are initialized by the microprocessor. The address register contains the starting of the data to be transferred, and the terminal count register contains the desired block to be transferred. The status register contains information such as completion of DMA transfer.

1.2.4.g Summary of Microcomputer I/O Methods

Figure 1.17 summarizes the I/O structure (explained so far) of typical microcomputers.

1.2.4.h Coprocessors

In typical 8-bit microprocessors such as the Intel 8085 and Z-80, technology places a limit on the chip area. In consequence, these microprocessors include no hardware or firmware for performing scientific computations such as floating-point arithmetic, matrix manipulation, and graphic-data processing. Therefore, users of these systems must write these programs. Unfortunately, this approach is unacceptable in high-speed applications, since program execution takes a significant amount of time. To eliminate this problem, coprocessors are used.

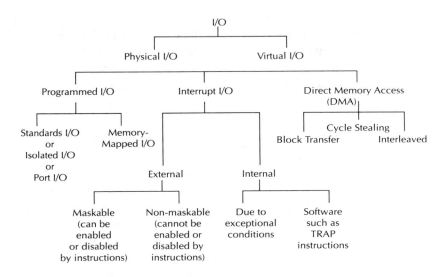

FIGURE 1.17 I/O structure of a typical microcomputer.

In this approach, a single chip is built for performing scientific computations at high speed. However, the chip is regarded as a companion to the original or host microprocessor. Typically, each special operation is encoded as an instruction that can be interpreted only by the companion processor. When the companion microprocessor encounters one of these special instructions, it assumes the processing functions independent of the host microprocessor. The companion microprocessor that operates in this manner is called the coprocessor. Therefore, this concept not only extends the capabilities of the host microprocessor, but also increases the processing rate of the system. The coprocessor concept is widely used with typical 32-bit microprocessors such as the Motorola 68020 and Intel 80386.

Functionally, the coprocessor provides a logical extension of the programmer's model in the way of instructions, registers, and operand types. This extension is transparent to the programmer.

It is important to make the distinction between standard peripheral hardware and a coprocessor. A coprocessor is a device that has the capability of communicating with the main processor through the protocol defined as the coprocessor interface. As mentioned before, the coprocessor also adds additional instructions, registers, and data types that are not directly supported by the main processor. The coprocessor provides capabilities to the user without appearing to be hardware external to the main processor.

Standard peripheral hardware, on the other hand, is generally accessed through the use of interface registers mapped into the memory space of the main processor. The programmer uses standard processor instructions to access the peripheral interface registers and thus utilize the services provided by the peripheral. It should be pointed out that even though a peripheral can provide capabilities equivalent to a coprocessor for many applications, the programmer must implement the communication protocol between the main processor and the peripheral necessary to use the peripheral hardware. Two main techniques may be used to pass commands to a coprocessor. These are intelligent monitor interface and coprocessors using special signals.

In the *intelligent monitor interface,* the coprocessor monitors the instruction stream by obtaining commands directly from the bus at the same time as the main processor. The Intel 8087 floating-point coprocessor is of this type, as it monitors the instruction stream simultaneously with a main processor such as the Intel 8086. This has the obvious advantage of requiring no additional bus cycles to pass the content of the instruction word to the coprocessor. One of the main disadvantages of this approach is that each coprocessor in the system must duplicate the bus monitoring circuitry and instruction queue, tracking all branches, wait states, operand fetches, and instruction fetches.

In the second type, the coprocessor may be explicitly addressed by certain instructions, which initiate a special sequence of microinstructions in the main processor to effect command and operand transfer.

In this approach, when the main processor executes a coprocessor instruction, it decodes the instruction and writes a command in the command register (one of the interface registers) specifying the operation required by the coprocessor. In response, the coprocessor writes data back in a register called the *response register* (one of the interface registers). The main processor can read these data, and it tells the main processor certain information such as whether additional information is required by the coprocessor to carry out the operation. If such data are required, the main processor provides this; otherwise, the coprocessor carries out the operation concurrently with the main and provides the result.

An advantage of this approach is that no special signals are required for the coprocessor interface.

One of the main disadvantages of this method is that once the main processor detects a coprocessor instruction, the main has to use bus bandwidth and timing to transmit the command to the appropriate coprocessor. The Motorola 68881 (floating-point coprocessor) is of this type.

1.3 MICROCOMPUTER SYSTEM SOFTWARE AND PROGRAMMING CONCEPTS

In the early days of computer system design, the high cost of hardware components completely overshadowed the labor costs of software design. Now, hardware costs have dropped so low that software development time has become the critical factor in achieving low-cost microcomputer-based products. The system software in a microcomputer allows one to develop application programs for microprocessor-based systems. In this section, the basic concepts associated with system software and programming will be discussed.

1.3.1 SYSTEM SOFTWARE

Typical microcomputer system software includes editors, assemblers, compilers, interpreters, debuggers, and an operating system.

The editor is used to create and change source programs. Source programs can be written in assembly language, a high-level language such as Pascal, or be data tables. The editor has commands to change, delete, or insert lines or characters. The text editor is a special type of editor that is used to enter and edit text in a general-purpose computer, whether the text is a report, a letter, or a program.

An assembler translates a source text that was created using the editor into a target language such as binary or object code.

High-level language contains English-like commands that are readily understandable by the programmer. High-level languages normally combine a number of assembly-level statements into a single high-level statement. A compiler is used to translate the high-level languages such as Pascal into machine languages. The advantages of high-level languages over assembly language are ease of readability and maintainability. Also, the code multiplicity of high-level languages increases the productivity of the programmers. This is assuming, of course, that the problem is better suited to being solved using such a language and not an assembly language.

Like a compiler, an interpreter usually processes a high-level language program. Unlike a compiler, an interpreter actually executes the high-level language program one statement at a time, rather than translating the whole program into a sequence of machine instructions to be run later. Interpreters may be microcoded firmware rather than software.

The debugger provides an interactive method of executing and debugging the user's software one or a few instructions at a time, allowing the user to see the effects of small pieces of the program and thereby isolate programming errors.

An operating system performs resource management and human-to-machine translation functions. A resource may be the microprocessor, memory, or an I/O device. Basically, an operating system is another program that tells the machine what to do under a variety of conditions. Major operating system functions include efficient sharing of memory, I/O peripherals, and the microprocessor among several users. An operating system is

1. The interface between hardware and users
2. The manager of system resources in accordance with system policy to achieve system objectives

Operating systems for microcomputers became available when microcomputers moved from process control applications to the general-purpose computer applications. It was appropriate to write a process control program in assembly language because the microcomputer was required to perform dedicated real-time control functions. But when the microcomputers evolved to the point of controlling several I/O devices (disks, printers), an organized operating system was needed.

Modern operating systems handle all memory and I/O interfacing between the user and the microcomputer. A user writing application programs using a high-level language such as FORTRAN or Pascal may never be aware of the memory or I/O requirements of the program because the user relies on the operating system to supply the routines needed to compile, link, and execute the program.

1.3.2 PROGRAMMING CONCEPTS

In general, programs are developed using machine, assembly, and high-level languages.

1.3.2.a Machine Language Programming

One way to write a program is to assign a fixed binary pattern for each instruction and represent the program by sequencing these binary patterns. Such a program is called a machine language program or an object program. A typical example of a machine language program is shown on the following page. This program will readily run on a Z-80 based microcomputer. But the program is hard to understand and difficult to debug.

```
0011    1110    ;    Load A register with
0000    0101    ;    value 5
0000    0110    ;    Load B register with
0000    1010    ;    value 10
1000    0000    ;    (A) ← (A) + (B)
0011    1010    ;    store the result
0110    0100    ;    into the memory location
0000    0000    ;    whose address is 100 (decimal)
0111    0110    ;    halt processing
```

1.3.2.b Assembly Language Programming

Program designers realized the importance of symbols in programming to improve readability and expedite the program development process. As a first step, they came up with the idea of giving a symbolic name for each instruction. These names are called mnemonics, and a program written using such mnemonics is called an assembly language program. Given below is a typical Z-80 assembly language equivalent for the previous machine language program:

```
LD  A,5      ;    load A reg with 5
LD  B,10     ;    load B reg with 10
ADD A,B      ;    (A) ← (A) + (B)
LD  (100),A  ;    save the result in the location 100
HALT         ;    halt processing
```

From this example, it is clear that the usage of mnemonics (in our example LD, ADD, HALT are the mnemonics) has improved the readability of our program significantly.

An assembly language program cannot be executed by a machine directly, as it is not in binary form. Usually, we refer to a symbolic program as a source program. An assembler is needed in order to translate an assembly language (source) program into the object code executable by the machine. This is illustrated in Figure 1.18.

Assembly language provides improved readability, but the programmer

FIGURE 1.18 Assembly process.

needs to know the internal architecture of the microprocessor. The assembly language program written for one processor will not usually run another processor. The assembly language instructions include input/ output instructions and, therefore, this programming method is normally used for writing I/O routines.

1.3.2.c High-Level Language Programming

Typical examples of high-level languages include FORTRAN, BASIC, Pascal, and C. The program shown below is written in FORTRAN, in order to obtain the sum of the first N natural numbers:

```
        READ  (5,10)  N
10      FORMAT (I4)
        NSUM = N*(N+1)/2
        WRITE (2,10)  NSUM
        STOP
        END
```

A translator called a compiler is needed to translate a program written in a high-level language into binary form. Running a source program or a program written in a high-level language using a microcomputer is a two-

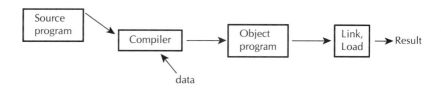

FIGURE 1.19 Compilation process.

stage process. This is explained in Figure 1.19.

In the first step, the compiler reads each line of the source program and produces an object program executable on a given target machine. In the second step, the object program is executed with the given data in order to produce results. Note that most compilers make several passes through the source code before translation is complete. In order to execute the same program many times with different data, there is no need to read the source program for the second run. In this way, a compiler improves the efficiency of the whole process. This idea works very well in a professional environment where one has to think of many production runs of the same program.

High-level language programs are portable. That is, a particular high-level language written for one processor will run on another processor provided a compiler for that language is available. Also, the programmer does not have to know the internal architecture of the processor. Finally, the high-level language C includes I/O instructions.

Another way to process symbolic language programs is by using an interpreter. This is illustrated in Figure 1.20.

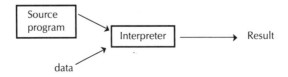

FIGURE 1.20 Interpretation process.

Executing a program using an interpreter is a single-stage process. An interpreter reads each line of the source program and translates and executes it immediately. In general, interpreters will go to the next line after executing the current line.

1.4 MICROCOMPUTER TYPICAL ADDRESSING MODES AND INSTRUCTIONS

In this chapter, some important characteristics and properties of microcomputer instruction sets are discussed. Topics include addressing modes and instruction types.

1.4.1 INTRODUCTION

An instruction manipulates the stored data, and a sequence of instructions constitutes a program. In general, an instruction has two components:

- Op-code field
- Address field(s)

The op-code field specifies how data are to be manipulated. The data items may reside within a microprocessor register or in the main memory.

The purpose of the address field is to indicate the data address. When operations require data to be read from or stored into two or more addresses, the address field may contain more than one address. For example, consider the following instruction:

```
        ADD                     R1, R0
    op-code field            address field
```

Assume that this microcomputer uses R1 as the source register and R0 as the destination register. The preceding instruction then adds the contents of registers R0 and R1 and saves the sum in register R0. The number and types of instructions supported by a microcomputer vary from one microcomputer to another and depend primarily on the architecture of a particular machine.

Depending on the number of addresses specified, one can have the following instruction formats:

- Three-address
- Two-address
- One-address
- Zero-address

1.4.2 ADDRESSING MODES

The sequence of operations that a processor has to carry out while executing an instruction is called its *instruction cycle*. One of the activities in an instruction cycle is the determination of the addresses of the operands involved in that instruction.

The way in which a processor accomplishes this task is called the *addressing mode*. Typical addressing modes supported by the instruction sets of popular processors will be examined.

An instruction is said to have an *inherent* addressing mode if its op-code indicates the address of the operand, which is usually the contents of a register. For example, consider the following instruction:

STC. Set the carry flag in the status register. Since the op-code implies the address of the operand, the processor does not have to compute the operand address. This mode is very common with 8-bit microprocessors such as the 8085, Z 80, and MC6809.

Whenever an instruction contains the operand value, it is called an *immediate mode* instruction. For example, consider the following instruction:

$$\text{ADD \#25,R1; R1} \leftarrow \text{R1 + 25}$$

In this instruction, the symbol # indicates that it is an immediate-mode instruction. This convention is adopted in the assemblers for processors such as the MC6809 and MC68000. In these systems, the machine representation of this instruction occupies two consecutive memory words. The first word holds the op-code, whereas the next word holds the data value. (For the preceding case, it is 25.)

To execute this instruction, the processor has to access memory twice.

An instruction is said to have an *absolute addressing mode* if it contains the address of the operand. For example, consider the following move instruction:

$$\text{MOVE 5000, R2; R2} \leftarrow \text{[5000]}$$

This instruction copies the contents of memory location 5000 in the register R2.

An instruction is said to have a *register mode* if it contains a register address as opposed to a memory address. For example, consider the following register mode and instruction:

$$\text{ADD R2, R3; R3} \leftarrow \text{R2 + R3}$$

Whenever an instruction specifies a register that holds the address of an operand, the resulting addressing mode is known as the *register indirect* mode. From this definition, it follows that the EA of an operand in the register-indirect mode is the contents of the register R. More formally, this result is written as follows:

$$\text{EA = [R]}$$

To illustrate this idea clearly, consider the following instruction:

$$\text{MOVE (R2), (R3);   [R3]} \leftarrow \text{[R2]}$$

Assume that the following configuration exists:

$$[R2] = 5000_{16}$$
$$[R3] = 4000_{16}$$
$$[5000] = 1256_{16}$$
$$[4000] = 4629_{16}$$

This instruction copies the contents of the memory location, whose address is specified by the register R2, into the location whose address is specified by the register R3. Thus, after the execution of this instruction, the memory location 4000 will contain the value 1256.

1.4.3 INSTRUCTION TYPES

In general, instructions available in a processor may be broadly classified into five groups:

- Data transfer instructions
- Arithmetic instructions
- Logical instructions
- Program control instructions
- I/O instructions

Data transfer instructions are primarily concerned with data transfers between the microprocessor registers or between register and memory. An example is MOVE R0, R1 which transfers the contents of register R0 to register R1.

Typical arithmetic instructions include ADD and SUBTRACT instructions. For example, ADD R0, R1 adds the contents of R0 to R1 and stores the result in R1.

Logical instructions perform Boolean AND, OR, NOT, and EXCLU-SIVE-OR operations on a bit-by-bit basis. An example is OR R0, R1 which logically ORes the contents of R0 with R1 and places the result in R1.

Typical program control instructions include unconditional and conditional branch and subroutine CALL instructions. For example, JMP 2035H unconditionally branches to the 16-bit address 2035H.

I/O instructions perform input and output operations. An example is IN PORTA which inputs the contents of an I/O port called port A into a microprocessor register such as the accumulator.

1.5 BASIC FEATURES OF MICROCOMPUTER DEVELOPMENT SYSTEMS

When the first 4- and 8-bit microprocessors appeared on the market, the hardware costs associated with a microprocessor system were so high that the labor costs (logic design, software, debugging) were of lesser impact on the total project cost. With the constantly decreasing cost of new microprocessor components, the labor costs of developing new products have taken on a more significant role. The microcomputer development system's main function is to simplify the product development stage and therefore obtain the maximum efficiency from the design team, whether it be a single engineer or a large team.

Development systems allow the parallel design of hardware and software so that the design can be tested and debugged before any actual hardware simulations occur. Some development systems allow the simulation of software without any of the final hardware being available to the software engineer.

Development systems fall into one of two categories: systems supplied by the device manufacturer and systems built by after-market manufacturers. The main difference between the two categories is the range of microprocessors that a system will accommodate. Systems supplied by the device manufacturer (Intel, Motorola, RCA) are limited to use for the particular chip set manufactured by the supplier. In this manner, an Intel development system may not be used to develop a Motorola-based system. The other category contains systems that are more universal in usage. Software and emulation hardware are available for the universal systems (Tektronix, Hewlett-Packard, AMI) to develop most of the popular microprocessors.

Within both categories of development systems, there are basically three types available: single-user systems, time-shared systems, and networked systems. A single-user system consists of one development station that can be used by one user at a time. Single-user systems are low in cost and may be sufficient for small systems development. Time-shared systems usually consist of a "dumb"-type terminal connected by data lines to a centralized microcomputer-based system that controls all operations. A networked system usually consists of a number of smart Cathode Ray Tubes (CRTs) capable of performing most of the development work and can be connected over data lines to a larger central computer. The central microcomputer in a network system usually is in charge of allocating disk storage space and will download some programs into the user's work station computer. The networked development systems are becoming more popular because they allow more throughput of data which allows the user to develop the programs faster and more easily. The cost per station of networked systems is less than that of the single-user system as the number of stations increases.

A microcomputer development system is a combination of the hardware necessary for microprocessor design and the software to control the hardware. The basic components of the hardware are the central processor, the CRT terminal, mass storage device (floppy or hard disk), and usually an In-Circuit Emulator (ICE).

The central processor is the heart of the development system. Whether a microprocessor in a single-user system or a large processor in a time-shared multiuser system, the central processor is responsible for the overall control of the development system. In a single-user system, the central processor executes the operating system software, handles the Input/Output (I/O) facilities, executes the development programs (editor, assembler, linker), and allocates storage space for the programs in execution. In a large multiuser networked system the central processor may be responsible for mass storage allocation, while a local processor may be responsible for the I/O facilities and execution of development programs.

The CRT terminal provides the interface between the user and the operating system or program under execution. The user enters commands or data via the CRT keyboard and the program under execution displays data to the user via the CRT screen. In early development systems, CRTs were not used and a mechanical teletype was used to communicate with the development system. The current CRTs communicate with the operating system at speeds in excess of ten times the speed of the old teletypes. The CRT of a single-user system may be connected directly to the central processor, while CRTs in time-shared systems may be connected to remote microcomputers via phone lines (using modems).

A disk drive of some kind is necessary for mass storage of user data. Some of the current complex operating systems and high-level development programs require large amounts of system Random Access Memory (RAM) to operate, and little memory is left available for user data such as source code for the program under development. For this reason, the operating system must allocate the available memory and store unused portions of the program on a disk. A common technique for memory management is the use of *overlay* files. An overlay is a portion of a program that is not always needed and is therefore not kept in the limited RAM space. When the overlay is needed, it is read from the disk and overlays another program in memory that is no longer needed. The use of overlays and other memory management techniques allows the use of complex programs that would otherwise not be available for use on the smaller microcomputers in popular use today. The user's files, such as source code, are also stored on the disk.

Most of the single-user systems use a flexible (floppy) disk for mass storage, while the time-shared and networked systems tend to use a hard disk for mass storage. Cost and performance are directly related in the disk systems. The cost of flexible disk systems is low, but the storage capability is also low. The access time of a flexible disk (the delay time before the data are available after they have been requested) is also slow compared with hard disks or standard memory. The access time of a hard disk is much shorter than a flexible disk and the storage capability is much greater, but the higher cost of a hard disk system may be prohibitive to a small user. If a hard disk system is purchased, the cost can usually be returned in decreased development times.

Each program (whether system software or user program) is stored in an ordered format on the disk. Each separate entry on the disk is called a *file*. The operating system software contains the routines necessary to interface between the user and the mass storage unit. When the user requests a file by a specific *file name*, the operating system finds the program stored on disk by the file name and loads it into main memory. More advanced development systems contain *memory management* software that protects a user's files from unauthorized modification by another user. This is accomplished via a unique user identification code called USER ID. A user can only access files that have the user's unique code.

The equipment listed above comprises a basic development system, but most systems have other devices such as printers and PROM programmers attached. A printer is needed to provide the user with a hard copy record of the program under development. Many simple programs may be developed completely on the CRT, but a printer is needed to provide the documentation necessary for advanced program development. After a program has been fully debugged and tested, the PROM programmer is used to load the machine code into a PROM for final prototype testing. Figure 1.21 shows a typical development system.

MODEM (MOdulator-DEModulator) interfaces allow serial communication between systems using telephone lines. The modulator on the transmitting end converts the serial data into distinct tones which are demodulated on the receiver end back into serial data. MODEMs are also used to connect a user's CRT to a master development system at a remote

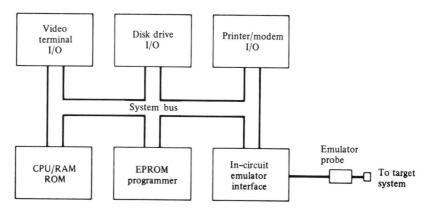

FIGURE 1.21 Block diagram of a typical development system.

installation. Communication rates for MODEMs are usualy limited to about 1200 bits per second and are therefore much slower than directly connected CRTs. Microcomputer development systems can be interfaced to a minicomputer via MODEMs to provide software development capabilities for many different microprocessors.

Program development and documentation call for the availability of printed listings of the programs. These listings are referred to as *hard copy* and are printed on the system line printer.

After the target system software has been completely developed and debugged, it needs to be permanently stored for execution in the target hardware. The PROM programmer takes the machine code and programs it into a PROM or EPROM. Erasable/Programmable Read Only Memories (EPROMs) are more generally used in system development as they may be erased and reprogrammed if the program changes. PROM programmers usually interface to circuits particularly designed to program a specific PROM. These interface boards are called personality cards and are available for all the popular PROM configurations.

Most development systems support one or more in-circuit emulators. The ICE is one of the most advanced tools for microprocessor hardware development. To use an ICE, the microprocessor chip is removed from the system under development (called the target processor) and the emulator plugged into the socket that the processor was removed from. The ICE will functionally and electrically act identically to the target processor with the exception that the ICE is under the control of development system software. In this manner the development system may exercise the hardware that is being designed and monitor all status information available about the operation of the target processor. Using an ICE, processor register contents may be displayed on the CRT and operation of the hardware observed in a single-stepping mode. In-circuit emulators can find hardware and software bugs quickly that might take many hours using conventional hardware testing methods.

Architectures for development systems can be generally divided into two categories: the master/slave configuration and the single-processor configuration. In a master/slave configuration, the master (host) processor controls all development functions such as editing, assembling, and so on. The master processor controls the mass storage device and processes all I/O (CRT, printer).

The software for the development systems is written for the master processor which is usually not the same as the slave (target) processor. The slave microprocessor is typically connected to the user prototype via a 40-pin connector (the number varies with the processor) which links the slave processor to the master processor.

Some development systems such as the HP 64000 completely separate the system bus from the emulation bus and therefore use a separate block of memory for emulation. This separation allows passive monitoring of the software executing on the target processor without stopping the emulation process. A benefit of the separate emulation facilities allows the master processor to be used for editing, assembling, and so on, while the slave processor continues the emulation. A designer may therefore start an emulation running, exit the emulator program, and at some future time return to the emulation program.

Another advantage of the separate bus architecture is that an operating system needs to be written only once for the master processor and will be used no matter what type of slave processor is being emulated. When a new slave processor is to be emulated, only the emulator probe needs to be changed.

A disadvantage of the master/slave architecture is that the memory is not continuous because it is in isolated blocks. This separation makes it a little harder to work with in some systems. Under some situations, the higher cost associated with the master/slave architecture is a disadvantage, but in a system capable of simultaneously running two emulators (such as the HP 64000 system), the increased throughput may make the master/slave system cheaper than two individual development systems. In single-processor architecture, only one processor is used for system operation and target emulation.

The single processor does both jobs of executing system software as well as acting as the target processor. Since there is only one processor involved, the system software must be rewritten for each type of processor that is to be emulated. Since the system software must reside in the same memory used by the emulator, not all memory will be available to the emulation process, which may be a disadvantage when large prototypes are being developed.

System cost is lower because less hardware is required, but, as mentioned in the section on master/slave systems, the cost is a viable factor only if a single development facility is needed.

The hardware for a development system is necessary, but would be useless without the proper development software. As the developments become more and more advanced, the operating systems remove many of the routine tasks from the user, making the user's time more productive. Many development systems are self-promoting, freeing the user from the responsibility of looking up commands and procedures in operating manuals.

The main programs necessary to microprocessor development are the operating system, editor, assembler, linker, compiler, and debugger.

The operating system is responsible for executing the user's commands. The operating system (such as CP/M, MP/M, UNIX) handles I/O functions, memory management, and loading of programs from mass storage into RAM for execution. The larger the development system, the larger and more capable the operating system.

The editor is usually the first program used in developing the software for the systems being developed. The editor allows the user to enter the source code (either assembly language or some high-level language) into the development system. The editor includes commands that facilitate changing (additions or deletions) the source code whenever necessary.

The editor functions start by loading a segment of the input file into the development system RAM. The program segment is displayed to the user in some manner and the user edits the segment to make any needed changes. When the changes for a segment are complete, the segment is stored back on disk and the next segment loaded into RAM.

There are two types of editors currently in use: the line-oriented editor and the character-oriented editor.

The first editors developed were line-oriented editors. Line editors have fewer features than character editors and are therefore less expensive. Line editors are limited mostly to home computer systems and are rarely found on modern development systems. The main difference between line editors and character editors is that line editors do not display any changes in the file until the user prints the file, whereas character editors will display the change when the user makes the change.

Modern line-oriented editors allow the user to enter lines without line numbers. The user enters lines by positioning a *pointer* to the location in the program where the new line is desired and the new line is typed into

RAM. The user may also position the pointer to locations within a line, thus allowing characters to be added or deleted without retyping the entire line. This type of line editor supports more advanced features than the line number-based line editor, but is still inferior to the character-oriented editor.

Almost all current microprocessor development systems use the character-oriented editor, more commonly referred to as the screen editor. The editor is called a screen editor because the text is dynamically displayed on the screen and the display automatically updates any edits made by the user.

The screen editor uses the pointer concept to point to the character(s) that need editing. The pointer in a screen editor is called the cursor and special commands allow the user to position the cursor to any location displayed on the screen. Other commands allow the user to scroll the display forward or backward to allow display of any segment of the file. When the cursor is positioned, the user may insert characters, delete characters, or simply type over the existing characters.

Complete lines may be added or deleted using special editor commands. By placing the editor in the *insert* mode, any text typed will be inserted at the cursor position when the cursor is positioned between two existing lines. If the cursor is positioned on a line to be deleted, a single command will remove the entire line from the file.

Search commands allow the user to search the file for occurrences of specific characters of text called *strings*. The user can specify a string of text and the editor will compare the file text for any matches with the string and then display the segment of text that holds the matched string. A similar function of *find and replace* is also available where the user can specify one string that is to be found and another string that is to replace the first string. This feature is extremely valuable for correcting misspelled words or phases.

Other useful commands allow portions of other files to be merged into the current file, move segments to other positions in the file, delete old files, copy files, and perform many other functions that speed up the process of writing and debugging source code.

Screen editors implement the editor commands in different fashions. Some editors use dedicated keys to provide some cursor movements. The cursor keys are usually marked with arrows to show the direction of cursor movement. Other special editor functions are accomplished with the use of *control keys*. A control key is activated by pressing a special key (usually labeled control or CTRL) simultaneously with a normal key. This combination of key strokes creates a new character that is sent to the editor program.

More advanced editors (such as the HP 64000) use *soft keys*. A soft key is an unmarked key located on the keyboard directly below the bottom of the CRT screen. The mode of the editor decides what functions the keys are to perform. The function of each key is displayed on the screen directly above the appropriate key. The soft key approach is valuable because it frees the user from the problem of memorizing many different special control keys. The soft key approach also allows the editor to reassign a key to a new function when necessary.

The source code generated on the editor is stored as ASCII characters and cannot be executed by a microprocessor. Before the code can be executed, it must be converted to a form acceptable by the microprocessor. An assembler is the program used to translate the assembly language source code generated with an editor into object code or machine code which may be executed by a microprocessor.

Assemblers recognize four *fields* on each line of source code. The fields consist of a variable number of characters and are identified by their position in the line. The fields, from left to right on a line, are the label field, the mnemonic or op-code field, the operand field, and the comment field. Fields are separated by characters called *delimiters* which serve as a flag to the assembler that one field is done and the next one is to start. Typical delimiters and their uses are

space	used to separate fields
TAB	used to separate fields
,	used between addresses or data in the operand field
;	used before a comment statement
:	used after a label

A few typical lines of 8085 source code are

```
LABEL  | OP CODE | OPERAND | COMMENT FIELD
FIELD  | FIELD   | FIELD   |
       |         |         |
       | MVI     | A,5     | ; LOAD A 5 INTO A
LOOP   | DCR     | A       | ; DECREMENT THE COUNT
       | JNZ     | LOOP    | ; REPEAT LOOP IF COUNT NOT ZERO
       | RET     |         | ; RETURN TO CALLER WHEN LOOP DONE
```

As can be seen in the above example, tab keys are used instead of spaces to separate the fields to give a more *spread out* line which is easier to read during debugging.

In order for the assembler to differentiate between numbers and labels, specific rules are set up which apply to all assemblers. A label must start with a letter. After the letter, a combination of letters and numbers (called alphanumerics) may be used. For example, when grouping lines of code by function, a common alphabetic string may be used followed by a unique number for the label: LOOP01, LOOP02, LOOP10, and so on.

A numeric quantity must start with a number, even though the number may be in hex (which may start with a letter). Most assemblers assume that a number is expressed in the decimal system and if another base is desired, a special code letter is used immediately following the number. The usual letter codes used are

B	binary
C	octal
H	hex (Motorola uses $ before the number)

To avoid confusion when hex quantities are used, a leading zero is inserted to tell the assembler that the quantity is a number and not a label (for example, the quantity FA in hex would be represented by 0FAH in the source code).

PSEUDOINSTRUCTIONS (ASSEMBLER DIRECTIVES)

Pseudoinstructions are instructions entered into the source code along with the assembly language. Pseudoinstructions do not get translated into object code but are used as special instructions to the assembler to perform some special functions. The assembler will recognize pseudoinstructions that assign memory space, assign addresses to labels, format the pages of the source code, and so on.

The pseudoinstruction is usually placed in the op-code field. If any labels or data are required by the pseudoinstruction, they are placed in the label or operand field as necessary.

Some common pseudoinstructions will now be discussed in detail.

a. ORIGIN (ORG). The ORG statement is used by the programmer when it is necessary to place the program in a particular location in memory. As the assembler is translating the source code, it keeps an internal counter (similar to the microprocessor program counter) that keeps track of the address for the machine code. The counter is incremented automatically and sequentially by the assembler. If the programmer wishes to alter the locations where the machine code is going to be located, the ORG statement is used.

For example, if it is desired to have a subroutine at a particular location in memory, such as 2000H, the ORG statement would be placed immediately before the subroutine to direct the assembler to alter the internal program counter:

```
        ORG 2000H  ; SET PROGRAM COUNTER TO 2000H
   SUB  MVI A,5    ; SUBROUTINE PUTS A 5 IN 'A'
        RET        ; RETURN TO CALLER
```

Most assemblers will assume a starting address of zero if no ORG statement is given in the source code.

b. EQUATE (EQU). The EQU instruction is used to assign the data value or address in the operand field to the label in the label field. The EQU instruction is valuable because it allows the programmer to write the source code in symbolic form and not be concerned with the numeric value needed. In some cases, the programmer is developing a program without knowing what addresses or data may be required by the hardware. The program may be written and debugged in symbolic form and the actual data added at a later time. Using the EQU instruction is also helpful when a data value is used several times in a program. If, for example, a counter value was loaded at ten different locations in the program, a symbolic label (such as COUNT) could be used and the label count defined at the end of the program. By using this technique, if it is found during debugging that the value in COUNT must be changed, it need only be changed at the EQU instruction and not at each of the ten locations where it is used in the program.

As an example of EQU, consider the following 8085 code:

```
PORTA   EQU  00         ;  ASSIGN A DUMMY VALUE
PORTB   EQU  00         ;  ANOTHER DUMMY VALUE
        MVI  A, OFFH    ;  DATA TO BE SENT TO OUTPUTS
        OUT  PORTA      ;  INITIALIZE PORT A
        OUT  PORTB      ;  AND PORT B TOO
```

In the example, the programmer does not know the hardware addresses of output ports A and B, but may still write the source code. When the I/O addresses are known, they may be used to replace the 00 in the EQU statement.

c. DEFINE BYTE (DEFB or DB). The DB instruction is used to set a memory location to a specific data value. The DB instruction is usually used to create data tables or to preset a flag value used in a program. As the name implies, the DB instruction is used for creating an 8-bit value.

For example, if a table of four values, 45H, 34H, 25H, and 0D3H, had to be created at address 2000H, the following code could be written:

```
        ORG  2000H              ; SET  TABLE  ADDRESS
  TABLE  DB   44H,34H,25H,0D3H  ; PRESET  TABLE  VALUES
```

The commas are necessary for the assembler to be able to differentiate between data values. When the code is assembled, the machine code would appear as follows:

```
        . . .
        2000  45
        2001  34
        2002  25
        2003  D3
        . . .
```

d. DEFINE WORD (DEFW or DW). Similarly to DB, DW defines memory locations to specific values. As the name implies, the memory allotted is in word lengths which are usually 16 bits wide. When assigning a 16-bit value to memory locations, two 8-bit memory locations must be used. By convention, most assemblers store the least significant byte of the 16-bit value in the first memory location and the most significant byte of the 16-bit value in the next memory location. This technique is sometimes referred to as *Intel style,* because the first microprocessors were developed by Intel, and this storage method is how the Intel processors store 16-bit words.

Data tables may be created with the DW instruction, but care must be taken to remember the order in which the 16-bit words are stored. For example, consider the following table:

```
        ORG        2500H
  DATA  DW  4000H,2300H,  4BCAH
```

The machine code generated for this table would appear as follows:

```
        . . .
        2500  00
        2501  40
        2502  00
        2503  23
        2504  CA
        2505  4B
        . . .
```

e. TITLE. TITLE is a formatting instruction that allows the user to name the program and have the name appear on the source code listing. Consider the following line:

TITLE   'MULTIPLICATION ROUTINE'

When the assembler generates the program listing, each time it starts a new page the title MULTIPLICATION ROUTINE appears at the top of each page.

f. PAGE (also called EJECT). PAGE is another formatting instruction that causes the assembler to skip to the next page. The PAGE instruction is used to keep subroutines or modules of source code on separate pages which makes the source code easier to read and debug.

g. SPACE. The SPACE instruction simply instructs the assembler to skip a line.

h. END. The END pseudoinstruction signals to the assembler that the source code is complete. Any lines after the END statement will be ignored by the assembler. Some assemblers require an END statement while some assemblers merely assume an END after the last line of the source code has been processed.

i. LIST. The LIST instruction is a direct command to the assembler and will cause the assembler to print the entire source code program.

Several types of assemblers are available, the most common of which are the one-pass assembler, the two-pass assembler, the macroassembler, cross assemblers, resident assemblers, and the metaassembler.

a. One-Pass Assembler. The one-pass assembler was the first type to be developed and is therefore the most primitive. Very few systems use a one-pass assembler because of the inherent problem that only *backward references* may be used.

In a one-pass assembler the source code is processed only once. As the source code is processed, any labels encountered are given an address and stored in a table. Therefore, when the label is encountered again, the assembler may look backward to find the address of the label. If the label has not been defined yet (for example, a jump instruction that skips forward), the assembler issues an error message.

Since only one pass is used to translate the source code, a one-pass assembler is very fast, but because of the forward reference problem the one-pass assembler is seldom used.

b. Two-Pass Assembler. The two-pass assembler is similar in operation to the one-pass assembler with one important difference. The first pass made through the source code is specifically for the purpose of assigning an address to all labels. When all labels have been stored in a table with the appropriate addresses, a second pass is made to actually translate the source code into machine code.

The two-pass style assembler is the most popular type of assembler currently in use.

c. Macroassembler. A macroassembler is a type of two-pass assembler that allows the programmer to write the source code in *macros*. A macro is a sequence of instructions that the programmer gives a name. Whenever the programmer wishes to duplicate the sequence of instructions, the macro name is inserted into the source code.

A macroutine is *not* the same as a subroutine call in assembly language. An assembly language call is a function of the microprocessor. When the CALL (8085) instruction is encountered in the machine code, the 8085 will save the address of the next sequential instruction to be executed and alter the program counter to the address given in the CALL instruction. When a macro is used, it is a function of the assembler and not the microprocessor. Every time the macro name is encountered in the source file, the macroassembler substitutes the macro sequence in place of the macro name.

Conditional assembly is included with most macroassemblers (as well as with most two-pass assemblers) and is very useful under certain conditions. In some cases a program is being written which will execute on two or more hardware systems which are similar, but have minor differences. Instead of writing a customized program for each system, the same program may be used with conditional assembly. A flag is defined in the source code as either true or false depending on which system is going to execute the program. A conditional statement is then inserted at the locations in the program where different actions must be taken, depending on the hardware.

d. Cross Assemblers. A cross assembler may be of any of the types already mentioned. The distinguishing feature of a cross assembler is that it is not written in the same language used by the microprocessor that will execute the machine code generated by the assembler.

Cross assemblers are usually written in a high-level language such as

FORTRAN which will make them machine independent. For example, an 8085 assembler may be written in FORTRAN and then the assembler may be executed on another machine such as the Motorola 6800. Microprocessors will provide cross assemblers to develop machine code for one of their microprocessors using their own development system that uses another microprocessor.

e. Resident Assembler. A resident assembler is almost the complete opposite of the cross assembler because it is written to run on the same machine that will execute the source code. For example, an 8085 assembler that is written in 8085 assembly language is a resident assembler.

f. Metaassembler. The most powerful assembler is the metaassembler because it will support many different microprocessors. The programmer merely specifies at the start of the source code which microprocessor assembly language will be used and the metaassembler will translate the source code to the correct machine code.

The output file from most development system assemblers is an object file. The object file is usually relocatable code that may be configured to execute at any address. The function of the linker is to convert the object file to an *absolute* file which consists of the actual machine code at the correct address for execution. The absolute files thus created are used for debugging and finally for programming PROMs.

A compiler will take the source code written in a high-level language (such as FORTRAN, COBOL, PL/M, Pascal) and translate it into machine language.

Interpreters are another form of high-level language but they do not convert to assembly language. The interpreter (such as BASIC) is a program that is written for the system and the interpreter directly executes the high-level statements one at a time.

Debugging a microprocessor-based system may be divided into two categories: software debugging and hardware debugging. Both debug processes are usually carried out separately from each other because software debugging can be carried out on an emulator without having the final system hardware.

The usual software development tools provided with the development system are

- Single-step facility
- Breakpoint facility
- Simulator program

A single-stepper simply allows the user to execute the program being debugged one instruction at a time. A single-stepper allows the user to follow program logic one step at a time, examining all processor information before allowing the next instruction to be executed. During debugging it is usually helpful to examine the state of the data bus, the address bus, the status flags, and the control lines. By examining the state of the processor during each step, the debugger can detect such program faults as incorrect jumps, incorrect addressing, erroneous op codes, and so on.

A breakpoint allows the user to execute an entire section of a program being debugged.

There are two types of breakpoint systems: hardware and software. The hardware breakpoint uses hardware to monitor the system address bus and detect when the program is executing the desired breakpoint location. When the breakpoint is detected, the hardware uses the processor control lines to either halt the processor for inspection or cause the processor to execute an interrupt to a breakpoint routine. Hardware breakpoints can be used to debug both ROM- and RAM-based programs. Software breakpoint routines may only operate on a system with the program in RAM because the breakpoint instruction must be inserted into the program that is to be executed.

Breakpoint routines are extremely useful for debugging programs because they allow the user to execute a large portion of the program before stopping execution. An entire subroutine may be executed and then halted to examine the processor registers to see if the subroutine executed properly. When the breakpoint is no longer needed, it may be removed and the program will execute normally.

Most debuggers combine single-steppers and breakpoint routine to provide a complete package. The user may insert a breakpoint (either manually or automatically, depending on the system) at the desired point and let the program execute up until that point. When the program stops at the breakpoint the user may use a single-stepper to then examine the program one instruction at a time.

A simulator is a program that allows the execution of a program to be simulated while keeping track of all parameters (address, data, flags) of the target processor. The processor that executes the simulator does not need to be of the same type as the target processor because the program to be debugged is not actually executed by the development system processor. The simulator operates by taking one instruction at a time and then simulating all actions that the target processor would perform for that instruction.

Simulators are usually very large programs which will include all the software debugging tools (single-stepper, breakpoints) necessary in a complete software development program.

There are two main hardware debugging tools: the logic analyzer and the in-circuit emulator.

Logic analyzers are usually used to debug hardware faults in a system. The logic analyzer is the digital version of an oscilloscope because it allows the user to view logic levels in the hardware.

In-circuit emulators can be used to debug and integrate software and hardware.

Two other features associated with a typical microcomputer development system are disassembly and command files.

Disassembly is the reverse process of assembly and is generally used during debugging to verify that the hex machine code being executed actually matches the assembly language that the user thinks is being executed. Most emulators and debuggers have a disassembler built into the program. A typical disassembly of a section of machine code may appear as follows:

```
0100    21   00   05    LXI  H,0500
0103    06   05         MVI, B05
0105    AF              XRA  A
```

By using the disassembly feature of a debugger, some bugs may be found without actually referring to the source code listing because the code may be displayed in assembly language form on the CRT.

A command file is a file created by the user that contains a sequence of commands that are to be executed. Instead of the programmer entering an identical sequence of commands over and over while debugging a program, the programmer uses a command file to perform the operations. A typical command file may hold the commands necessary to load a program into an emulator, set the emulator parameters, and execute the program. A command file saves the programmer time while at the same time providing repeatability by removing the possibility of operator error from command entry.

1.6 SYSTEM DEVELOPMENT FLOWCHART

The total development of a microprocessor-based system typically involves three phases: software design, hardware design, and program diagnostic design. A systems programmer will be assigned the task of writing the application software, a logic designer will be assigned the task of designing the hardware, and typically both designers will be assigned the task of developing diagnostics to test the system. For small systems, one engineer may do all three phases, while on large systems several engineers may be assigned to each phase. Figure 1.22 shows a flowchart for the total development of a system. Notice that software and hardware development may occur in parallel to save time.

1.6.1 SOFTWARE DEVELOPMENT

The first step in developing the software is to take the system specifications and write a flowchart to accomplish the desired tasks that will implement the specifications. The flowchart should be properly structured to ensure efficient program flow.

The assembly language or high-level source code may now be written from the system flowchart. Individual software designers may be given portions of the flowchart to develop individual modules that will be linked together after they are debugged. As much hardware information as possible should be made available at this point so that hardware-dependent portions of the program may be entered with the proper data.

After the source code has been written, it may be entered into the editor. Labels should be used whenever possible and symbols should be used in place of direct data.

Once the complete source code has been entered, it may be assembled. The assembler will check for syntax errors and print error messages to help in the correction of errors. Many advanced assemblers will assemble source code for many different microprocessors. In order to identify which microprocessor is to be used, a special command is entered in the source code to tell the assembler what microprocessor is in use.

The normal output of an assembler is the object code and a program listing. The object code will be used later by the linker. The program listing may be sent to a disk file for use later or it may be directed to the printer I/O if a printer is available.

The linker can now take the object code generated by the assembler and create the final absolute code that will be executed on the target system. The emulation phase will take the absolute code and load it into the development system RAM. From here, the program may be tested using breakpoints or single-stepping. Single-stepping allows the designer to watch the program execute one instruction at a time and monitor program status. During single-stepping, registers may be displayed to detect any program problems that may occur.

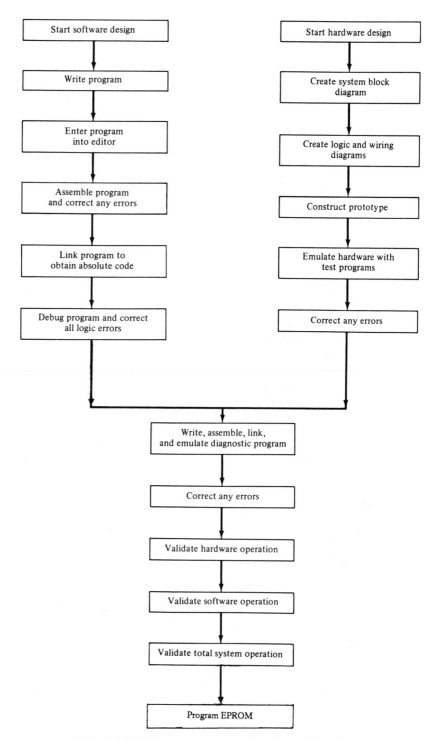

FIGURE 1.22 Microprocessor system development flowchart.

1.6.2 HARDWARE DEVELOPMENT

Working from the system specifications, a block diagram of the hardware must be developed. The block diagram will include all major hardware sections and show how they interconnect.

The logic diagram may now be drawn using the block diagram as a guide. Great care should be taken to design a system that uses the most efficient logic available. Minimum parts count may be important if space is limited. In a system where cost is a limiting factor, parts count may be increased if less expensive parts are available which will perform the same function.

A wiring list and parts layout diagram is then made from the logic diagram. Care should be taken to ensure that all pin connections are correct, for in most cases the design engineer will not be constructing the prototype and will therefore not be able to detect any errors during construction. A prototype may now be constructed and tested for wiring errors.

When the prototype has been constructed it may be debugged for correct operation using standard electronic testing equipment such as oscilloscopes, meters, logic probes, and logic analyzers.

After the prototype has been debugged electrically, the development system in-circuit emulator may be used to check it functionally. The ICE will verify addressing, correct I/O operation, and so on.

The next step in the system development is to validate the complete system by running operational checks on the prototype with the finalized application software installed. The EPROM is then programmed with the error-free programs.

1.7 TYPICAL PRACTICAL APPLICATIONS

Microprocessors are being extensively used in a wide variety of applications. Typical applications include dedicated controllers, personal workstations, and real-time robotics control. Some of these applications will be described in the following.

1.7.1 TWO-POSITION CONTROLLER

The control law of the two-position controller can be stated as:

$$\text{Valve output} \quad = \quad 100\% \text{ for } E > 0$$
$$= \quad 0\% \text{ for } E < 0$$

where the error E = PV-SP, PV is the process variable measurement, and SP is the set point.

The above relationship means that when the measured value is greater than the set point, the two-position controller must completely open the valve. When it is smaller than the set point, the controller must close the valve. An example is a home furnace which is either turned ON or OFF depending on the "opened" or "closed" status of a switch controlled by a thermostat, the temperature sensor. When the temperature drops below the set point, the switch is closed, the furnace is turned on, and the temperature rises. When the temperature is higher than the set point, the controller opens the switch and thus the furnace is turned OFF. The up and down cycling continues indefinitely. To avoid cycles from changing too fast and thus becoming destructive to the equipment, a gap called the neutral zone is built into the controller so that nothing happens until the temperature passes the set point and goes beyond the neutral zone boundaries. A microcomputer can be used as the two-position controller.

The following example illustrates this concept. Consider Figure 1.23.

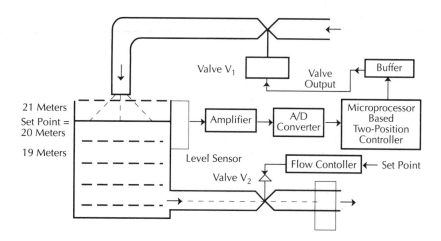

FIGURE 1.23 Microprocessor-based two-position controller.

The cylindrical tank in the figure is emptied by a constant flow. This outflow is maintained by controlling the valve, V_2.

The microprocessor-based two-position controller opens the valve V_1 if the level measured by the level sensor drops below 19 meters and closes the valve if the level exceeds 21 meters. The neutral zone is 2 meters.

The level sensor measures the level and converts it to electrical analog voltage. The amplifier is used to amplify this voltage to make it compatible for analog-to-digital conversion. The program in the microcomputer inputs this digital (binary) data and compares it with the lower and upper bounds of the neutral zone. The microcomputer then outputs HIGH or LOW to the buffer. The buffer is used to amplify the current for making the microcomputer output compatible for turning the valve V_1 solenoid (relay) ON or OFF.

1.7.2 PERSONAL WORKSTATIONS

Personal workstations are designed using the high-performance 16- and 32-bit microprocessors. A dedicated single user (rather than multiple users sharing resources of a single microcomputer) can obtain significant computing power from these workstations.

The workstations currently under production are using 32-bit microprocessors to provide certain sophisticated functions such as IC layout, 3D graphics, and stress analysis. Typical workstations designed using an 8- and 16-bit microprocessor cost about $10,000 per machine. With 32-bit microprocessors, the cost of the workstations can be lowered since the functions performed by discrete components and special-purpose hardware will be performed by the high-performance 32-bit microprocessor.

1.7.3 FAULT-TOLERANT SYSTEMS

In many applications such as control of life-critical systems, control of nuclear waste, and unattended remote system operation, the reliability of the hardware is of utmost importance. The need for such a reliable system resulted in fault-tolerant systems. These systems use redundant computing units to provide reliable operation. However, the cost of fault-tolerant systems can be very high if the performance requirements of the application need high-performance VAX-type computers. Since the performance levels of 32-bit microprocessors are comparable to the VAX-type computer, use of multiple 32-bit microprocessors in a redundant configuration will outperform the VAXs. Thus, the 32-bit microprocessors will provide efficient fault-tolerant systems.

1.7.4 REAL-TIME CONTROLLERS

Real-time controllers such as flight-control systems for aircraft, flight simulators, and automobile engine control require high-performance computers. Some of these applications were handled in the past by using mainframe computers which resulted in high cost and the controllers occupied large spaces.

Next-generation flight simulators currently under production use multiple 32-bit microprocessors to perform graphic manipulation, data gathering, and high-speed communications. Obviously, an application such as real-time automobile engine control using mainframe computers is not practical since these systems are not small enough to fit under a car hood. These controllers are currently being designed using the small-sized 32-bit microprocessors to perform high-speed data manipulation and calculation.

1.7.5 ROBOTICS

The processing requirements of complex robots attempting to emulate human activities exceed the capabilities of 8- and 16-bit microprocessors. With 32-bit microprocessors, it is now feasible to design these controllers at low cost. In many cases, the microprocessor is used as the brain of the robot. In a typical application, the microprocessor will input the actual arm angle measurement from a sensor, compare it with the desired arm angle, and will then send outputs to a motor to position the arm.

Mitsubishi recently announced the first 68020-based system robot control system.

1.7.6 SUMMARY

Microcomputers, therefore, are being used in diversified applications. With improvements in speed of memory and I/O devices in the future, high-speed real-time applications will be more feasible with 16- and 32-bit microprocessors.

QUESTIONS AND PROBLEMS

1.1 What is the basic difference between the microprocessor and the microcomputer?

1.2 What is meant by an 8-bit microprocessor and a 16-bit microprocessor?

1.3 What is the main advantage of a barrel shifter?

1.4 Determine the carry, sign, overflow, and zero flags for the following operation:

$$231F_{16} \text{ ADD } 82A1_{16}$$

1.5 What is the difference between EPROM and EAROM?

1.6 What is the difference between static and dynamic RAMS?

1.7 Assume the following ROM chip and the microprocessor:

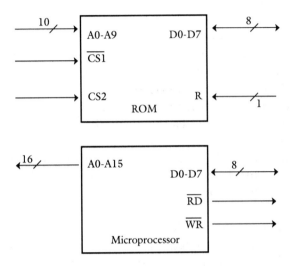

Connect the microprocessor to the ROM to obtain the following memory map: 0000_{16} through $03FF_{16}$. Use only the signals shown. Draw a neat schematic and analyze the memory map.

1.8 Assume the following microprocessor and the RAM chip:

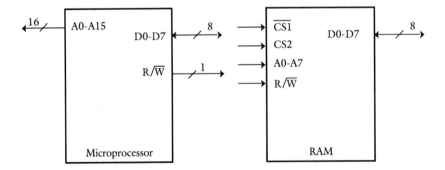

Draw a neat schematic showing connections between the above microprocessor and the RAM chip using only the signals shown to include the memory map 0200_{16} through $02FF_{16}$. Use linear decoding.

1.9 Use the following chips to design a microcomputer memory to include the map 3000_{16} through $33FF_{16}$.

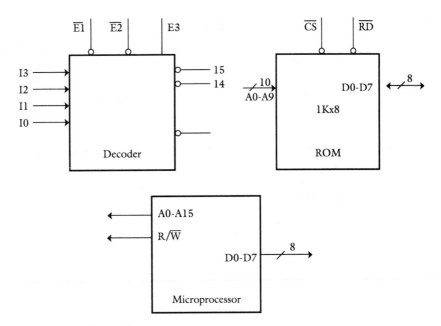

Draw a neat schematic.

1.10 What is meant by foldback in linear decoding?

1.11 Define the three basic types of I/O.

1.12 What is the difference between:

    i)   Standard and memory-mapped programmed I/O
    ii)   Maskable and nonmaskable interrupts
    iii) Internal and external interrupts
    iv) Block transfer and interleaved DMA
    v)   Polled and daisy chain
    vi) One-pass and two-pass assemblers

1.13 Discuss the main features of IOP.

1.14 Comment on the importance of the following architectural features in an operating system implementation:

a)   Address translation
b)   Protection
c)   Program relocation

1.15 Explain clearly the differences between segmentation and paging. Can you think of a situation where it would be advantageous to define a virtual memory that is smaller than available physical memory?

1.16 What is the purpose of cache memory? Discuss briefly the various types of cache.

1.17 Discuss the main features of typical coprocessors.

1.18 What is the difference between software breakpoint and hardware breakpoint?

1.19 Discuss the basic features of microcomputer development systems.

Chapter 2

INTEL 8085

This chapter describes hardware, software, and interfacing aspects of the Intel 8085. Topics include 8085 register architecture, addressing modes, instruction set, and system design.

2.1 INTRODUCTION

The Intel 8085 is an 8-bit microprocessor. Intel redesigned the 8080 in order to enhance its performance and came up with the 8085. For example, Intel 8080 requires +5-, −5-, and 12V power supplies while the 8085 only requires a +5-V supply. The 8080 requires external chips to generate the clock signal and to support system control and interrupts. The 8085, on the other hand, has integrated the clock generation, system control, and interrupt circuitry in the microprocessor chip. The 8085 has a 320-ns clock and is more than 50% faster than the 8080, which requires a 500-ns clock. As far as the instructions are concerned, the 8085 includes all 8080 instructions plus two new ones related to interrupts called RIM and SIM. Both 8080 and 8085 are designed using NMOS in 40-pin DIP (Dual In-line Package). The 8085 can be operated from either 3.03 MHz maximum (8085A) or 5 MHz maximum (8085A-2) internal clock frequency.

The 8085 has three enhanced versions, namely, the 8085AH, 8085AH-2, and 8085AH-1. These enhanced processors are designed using the HMOS (High-density MOS) technology. Each is packaged in a 40-pin DIP like the 8085. These enhanced microprocessors consume 20% lower power than the 8085A. The internal clock frequencies of the 8085AH, 8085AH-2, and 8085AH-1 are 3, 5, 6 MHz, respectively. These HMOS 8-bit microprocessors are expensive compared to the NMOS 8-bit 8085A.

Figure 2.1 shows a simplified block diagram of the 8085 microprocessor. The accumulator connects to the data bus and the Arithmetic and Logic Unit (ALU). The ALU performs all data manipulation, such as incrementing a number or adding two numbers.

The temporary register feeds the ALU's other input. This register is invisible to the programmer and is controlled automatically by the microprocessor's control circuitry.

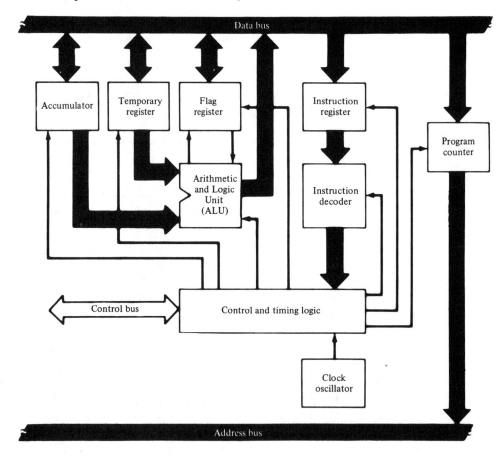

FIGURE 2.1 Simplified 8085 block diagram.

The flags are a collection of flip-flops that indicate certain characteristics of the result of the most recent operation performed by the ALU. For example, the zero flag is set if the result of an operation is zero. The zero flag is tested by the JZ instruction.

The instruction register, instruction decoder, program counter, and control and timing logic are used for fetching instructions from memory and directing their execution.

2.2 REGISTER ARCHITECTURE

The 8080 and 8085 have the same registers and flags. The registers and status flags are shown in Figure 2.2.

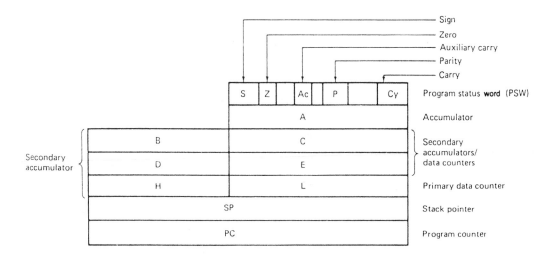

FIGURE 2.2 8085 microprocessor registers and status flags.

The accumulator (A) is an 8-bit register and has its usual meaning. Most arithmetic and logic operations are performed using the accumulator. All I/O data transfers between the 8085 and the I/O devices are performed via the accumulator. Also, there are a number of instructions that move data between the accumulator and memory.

The B, C, D, E, H, and L are each 8 bits long. Registers H and L are the memory address register or data counter. This means that these two registers are used to store the 16-bit address of 8-bit data being accessed from memory. This is the implied or register indirect addressing mode. There are a number of instructions, such as MOV reg, M, and MOV M, reg, which move data between any register and memory location addressed by H and L. However, using any other memory reference instruction, data transfer takes place between a memory location and the only 8085 register, the accumulator. The instruction LDAX B is a typical example.

Registers B, C, D, and E are secondary accumulators or data counters. There are a number of instructions to move data between any two registers. There are also a few instructions that combine registers B and C or D and E, as a 16-bit data counter with high byte of a pair contained in the first register and low byte in the second. These instructions typically include LDAX B, LDAX D, STAX B, and STAX D, which transfer data between memory and the accumulator.

Each of these 8-bit registers can be incremented and decremented by a single byte instruction. There are a number of instructions which combine two of these 8-bit registers to form 16-bit register pairs as follows:

A	and	PSW
B	and	C
D	and	E
H	and	L

high-order byte   low-order byte

The 16-bit register pair obtained by combining the accumulator and the program status word (PSW) is used only for stack operations. Arithmetic operations use B and C, D and E, or H and L as 16-bit data registers.

The **program status word** consists of five status flags. These are described below.

The **carry flag (Cy)** reflects the final carry out of the most significant bit of any arithmetic operation. Any logic instruction resets or clears the carry flag. This flag is also used by the shift and rotate instructions. The 8085 does not have any CLEAR CARRY instruction. One way of clearing the carry will be by ORing or ANDing the accumulator with itself.

The **parity status flag (P)** is set to 1 if an arithmetic or logic instruction generates an answer with even parity, that is, containing an even number of 1 bits. This flag is 0 if the arithmetic or logic instruction generates an answer with odd parity, that is, containing an odd number of 1s.

The **auxiliary carry flag (Ac)** reflects any carry from bit 3 to bit 4 (assuming 8-bit data with bit 0 as the least significant bit and bit 7 as the most significant bit) due to an arithmetic operation. This flag is useful for BCD operations.

The **zero flag (Z)** is set to 1 whenever an arithmetic or logic operation produces a result of 0. The zero flag is cleared to zero for a nonzero result due to arithmetic or logic operation.

The **sign status flag (S)** is set to the value of the most significant bit of the result in the accumulator after an arithmetic or logic operation. This provides a range of -128_{10} to $+127_{10}$ (with 0 being considered positive) as the 8085's data-handling capacity.

The 8085 does not have any overflow flag. Note that execution of arithmetic or logic instructions in the 8085 affects the flags. All conditional instructions in the 8085 instruction set use one of the status flags as the required condition.

The **stack pointer (SP)** is 16 bits long. All stack operations with the 8085 use 16-bit register pairs. The stack pointer contains the address of the last data byte written into the stack. It is decremented by 2 each time 2 bytes of data are written or pushed onto the stack and is incremented by 2 each time 2 bytes of data are read from or pulled (popped) off the stack, that is, the top of the stack has the lowest address in the stack that grows downward.

The **program counter (PC)** is 16 bits long to address up to 64K of memory. It usually addresses the next instruction to be executed.

2.3 MEMORY ADDRESSING

When addressing a memory location, the 8085 uses either register indirect or direct memory addressing. With register indirect addressing, the H and L registers perform the function of the memory address register or data counter; that is, the H, L pair holds the address of the data. With this mode, data transfer may occur between the addressed memory location and any one of the registers A, B, C, D, E, H, or L.

Also, some instructions, such as LDAX B, LDAX D, STAX B, and STAX D, use registers B and C or D and E to hold the address of data. These instructions transfer data between the accumulator and the memory location addressed by registers B and C or D and E using the register indirect mode.

There are also a few instructions, such as the STA ppqq, which use the direct-memory addressing mode to move data between the accumulator and the memory. These instructions use 3 bytes, with the first byte as the OP code followed by 2 bytes of address.

As mentioned before, the stack is basically a part of the RAM. Therefore, PUSH and POP instructions are memory reference instructions.

All 8085 JUMP instructions use direct or absolute addressing and are 3 bytes long. The first byte of this instruction is the OP code followed by a 2-byte address. This address specifies the memory location to which the program would branch.

2.4 8085 ADDRESSING MODES

The 8085 has five addressing modes:

1. **Direct** — Instructions using this mode specify the effective address as a part of the instruction. These instructions contain 3 bytes, with the first byte as the OP code followed by 2 bytes of address of data (the low-order byte of the address in byte 2, the high-order byte of the address in byte 3). Consider LDA 2035H. This instruction loads accumulator with the contents of memory location 2035_{16}. This mode is also called the absolute mode.

2. **Register** — This mode specifies the register or register pair that contains data. For example, MOV B, C moves the contents of register C to register B.

3. **Register Indirect** — This mode contains a register pair which stores the address of data (the high-order byte of the address in the first register of the pair, and the low-order byte in the second). As an example, LDAX B loads the accumulator with the contents of a memory location addressed by B, C register pair.

4. **Implied or Inherent** — The instructions using this mode have no operands. Examples include STC (Set the Carry Flag).

5. **Immediate** — For an 8-bit datum, this mode uses 2 bytes, with the first byte as the OP code, followed by 1 byte of data. On the other hand, for 16-bit data, this instruction contains 3 bytes, with the first byte as the OP code followed by 2 bytes of data. For example, MVI B, 05 loads register B with the value 5, and LXIH, 2050H loads H with 20H and L with 50H.

A JUMP instruction interprets the address that it would branch to in the following ways:

1. **Direct** — The JUMP instructions, such as JZ ppqq, use direct addressing and contain 3 bytes. The first byte is the OP code, followed by 2 bytes of the 16-bit address where it would branch to unconditionally or based on a condition if satisfied. For example, JMP 2020 unconditionally branches to location 2020H.

2. **Implied or Inherent Addressing** — This JUMP instruction using

this mode is 1 byte long. A 16-bit register pair contains the address of the next instruction to be executed. The instruction PCHL unconditionally branches to a location addressed by the H, L pair.

2.5 8085 INSTRUCTION SET

As mentioned before, the 8085 uses the 16-bit address. Since the 8085 is a byte-addressable machine, it follows that it can directly address 65,536 (2^{16}) distinct memory locations. The addressing structure of the 8085 processor is shown in Figure 2.3.

From this figure, we notice that two consecutive memory locations may be used to represent a 16-bit data item. However, according to the Intel convention, the high-order byte of a 16-bit quantity is always assigned to the high memory address.

The 8085 instructions are 1 to 3 bytes long and these formats are shown in Figure 2.4. The 8085 instruction set contains 74 basic instructions and they support conventional addressing modes such as immediate, register, absolute, and register indirect addressing modes.

Table 2.1 lists the 8085 instructions in alphabetical order; the object codes and instruction cycles are also included. When two instruction cycles are shown, the first is for "condition not met", while the second is for "condition met". Table 2.2 provides the 8085 instructions affecting the status flags. Note that not all 8085 instructions affect the status flags. The 8085 arithmetic and logic instructions normally affect the status flags.

In describing the 8085 instruction set, we will use the symbols in Table 2.3.

The 8085 move instruction transfers 8-bit data from one register to another, register to memory, and vice versa. A complete summary of these instructions is presented in Table 2.4.

The 8085 instruction set also accomplishes the 8- and 16-bit data transfers using the load and store instructions. These instructions are summarized in Table 2.5.

From Table 2.5 we notice that we adopt the following convention when we specify a register pair in the instruction.

Symbol	Register pair used
B	B,C
D	D,E
H	H,L

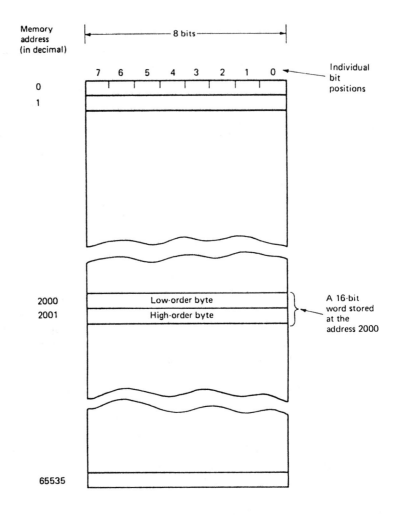

FIGURE 2.3 8085 addressing structures.

Also, observe that in Table 2.5 the 8085 processor does not provide LDAX H instruction. This is because the same result can be obtained by using the MOV A,M instruction. The 8085 includes a one-byte exchange instruction, namely, XCHG. The XCHG exchanges the contents of DE with HL. That is, it performs the following operation:

$$[D] \leftrightarrow [H]$$

$$[E] \leftrightarrow [L]$$

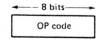

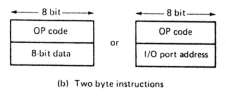

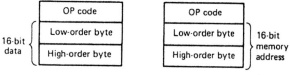

FIGURE 2.4 8085 instruction formats.

TABLE 2.1
Summary of 8085 Instruction Set

Instruction	OP Code	Bytes	Cycles	Operations performed
ACI DATA	CE	2	7	[A] ← [A] + second instruction byte + [Cy]
ADC A	8F	1	4	[A] ← [A] + [A] + [Cy]
ADC B	88	1	4	[A] ← [A] + [B] + [Cy]
ADC C	89	1	4	[A] ← [A] + [C] + [Cy]
ADC D	8A	1	4	[A] ← [A] + [D] + [Cy]
ADC E	8B	1	4	[A] ← [A] + [E] + [Cy]
ADC H	8C	1	4	[A] ← [A] + [H] + [Cy]
ADC L	8D	1	4	[A] ← [A] + [L] + [Cy]
ADC M	8E	1	7	[A] ← [A] + [[H L]] + [Cy]
ADD A	87	1	4	[A] ← [A] + [A]
ADD B	80	1	4	[A] ← [A] + [B]
ADD C	81	1	4	[A] ← [A] + [C]
ADD D	82	1	4	[A] ← [A] + [D]
ADD E	83	1	4	[A] ← [A] + [E]

TABLE 2.1 (continued)
Summary of 8085 Instruction Set

Instruction	OP Code	Bytes	Cycles	Operations performed
ADD H	84	1	4	[A] ← [A] + [H]
ADD L	85	1	4	[A] ← [A] + [L]
ADD M	86	1	7	[A] ← [A] + [[H L]]
ADI DATA	C6	2	7	[A] ← [A] + second instruction byte
ANA A	A7	1	4	[A] ← [A] ∧ [A]
ANA B	A0	1	4	[A] ← [A] ∧ [B]
ANA C	A1	1	4	[A] ← [A] ∧ [C]
ANA D	A2	1	4	[A] ← [A] ∧ [D]
ANA E	A3	1	4	[A] ← [A] ∧ [E]
ANA H	A4	1	4	[A] ← [A] ∧ [H]
ANA L	A5	1	4	[A] ← [A] ∧ [L]
ANA M	A6	1	4	[A] ← [A] ∧ [[H L]]
ANI DATA	E6	2	7	[A] ← [A] ∧ second instruction byte
CALL ppqq	CD	3	18	Call A subroutine addressed by ppqq
CC ppqq	DC	3	9/18	Call a subroutine addressed by ppqq if Cy = 1
CM ppqq	FC	3	9/18	Call a subroutine addressed by ppqq if S = 1
CMA	2F	1	4	[A] ← 1's complement of [A]
CMC	3F	1	4	[Cy] ← 1's complement of [Cy]
CMP A	BF	1	4	[A] – [A] and affects flags
CMP B	B8	1	4	[A] – [B] and affects flags
CMP C	B9	1	4	[A] – [C] and affects flags
CMP D	BA	1	4	[A] – [D] and affects flags
CMP E	BB	1	4	[A] – [E] and affects flags
CMP H	BC	1	4	[A] – [H] and affects flags
CMP L	BD	1	4	[A] – [L] and affects flags
CMP M	BE	1	7	[A] – [[H L]] and affects flags
CNC ppqq	D4	3	9/18	Call a subroutine addressed by ppqq if Cy = 0
CNZ ppqq	C4	3	9/18	Call a subroutine addressed by ppqq if Z = 0

TABLE 2.1 (continued)
Summary of 8085 Instruction Set

Instruction	OP Code	Bytes	Cycles	Operations performed
CP ppqq	F4	3	9/18	Call a subroutine addressed by ppqq if S = 0
CPE ppqq	EC	3	9/18	Call a subroutine addressed by ppqq if P = 1
CPI DATA	FE	2	7	[A] – second instruction byte and affects flags
CPO ppqq	E4	3	9/18	Call a subroutine addressed by ppqq if P = 0
CZ ppqq	CC	3	9/18	Call a subroutine addressed by ppqq if Z = 1
DAA	27	1	4	Decimal adjust accumulator
DAD B	09	1	10	[HL] ← [HL] + [BC]
DAD D	19	1	10	[HL] ← [HL] + [DE]
DAD H	29	1	10	[HL] ← [HL] + [HL]
DAD SP	39	1	10	[HL] ← [HL] + [SP]
DCR A	3D	1	4	[A] ← [A] – 1
DCR B	05	1	4	[B] ← [B] – 1
DCR C	0D	1	4	[C] ← [C] – 1
DCR D	15	1	4	[D] ← [D] – 1
DCR E	1D	1	4	[E] ← [E] – 1
DCR H	25	1	4	[H] ← [H] – 1
DCR L	2D	1	4	[L] ← [L] – 1
DCR M	35	1	4	[[HL]] ← [[HL]] – 1
DCX B	0B	1	6	[BC] ← [BC] – 1
DCX D	1B	1	6	[DE] ← [DE] – 1
DCX H	2B	1	6	[HL] ← [HL} – 1
DCX SP	3B	1	6	[SP] ← [SP] – 1
DI	F3	1	4	Disable interrupts
EI	FB	1	4	Enable interrupts
HLT	76	1	5	Halt
IN PORT	DB	2	10	[A] ← [specified port]
INR A	3C	1	4	[A] ← [A] + 1
INR B	04	1	4	[B] ← [B] + 1
INR C	0C	1	4	[C] ← [C] + 1
INR D	14	1	4	[D] ← [D] + 1

TABLE 2.1 (continued)
Summary of 8085 Instruction Set

Instruction	OP Code	Bytes	Cycles	Operations performed
INR E	1C	1	4	[E] ← [E] + 1
INR H	24	1	4	[H] ← [H] + 1
INR L	2C	1	4	[L] ← [L] + 1
INR M	34	1	4	[[HL]] ← [[HL]] +1
INX B	03	1	6	[BC] ← [BC] +1
INX D	13	1	6	[DE] ← [DE] + 1
INX H	23	1	6	[HL] ← [HL] + 1
INX SP	33	1	6	[SP] ← [SP] + 1
JC ppqq	DA	3	7/10	Jump to ppqq if Cy = 1
JM ppqq	FA	3	7/10	Jump to ppqq if S = 1
JMP ppqq	C3	3	10	Jump to ppqq
JNC ppqq	D2	3	7/10	Jump to ppqq if Cy = 0
JNZ ppqq	C2	3	7/10	Jump to ppqq if Z = 0
JP ppqq	F2	3	7/10	Jump to ppqq if S = 0
JPE ppqq	EA	3	7/10	Jump to ppqq if P = 1
JPO ppqq	E2	3	7/10	Jump to ppqq if P = 0
JZ ppqq	CA	3	7/10	Jump to ppqq if Z = 1
LDA ppqq	3A	3	13	[A] ← [ppqq]
LDAX B	0A	1	7	[A] ← [[BC]]
LDAX D	1A	1	7	[A] ← [[DE]]
LHLD ppqq	2A	3	16	[L] ← [ppqq],[H] ← [ppqq + 1]
LXI B	01	3	10	[BC] ← second and third instruction bytes
LXI D	11	3	10	[DE] ← second and third instruction bytes
LXI H	21	3	10	[HL] ← second and third instruction bytes
LXI SP	31	3	10	[SP] ← second and third instruction bytes
MOV A,A	7F	1	4	[A] ← [A]
MOV A,B	78	1	4	[A] ← [B]
MOV A,C	79	1	4	[A] ← [C]
MOV A,D	7A	1	4	[A] ← [D]
MOV A,E	7B	1	4	[A] ← [E]
MOV A,H	7C	1	4	[A] ← [H]
MOV A,L	7D	1	4	[A] ← [L]

TABLE 2.1 (continued)
Summary of 8085 Instruction Set

Instruction	OP Code	Bytes	Cycles	Operations performed
MOV A,M	7E	1	7	[A] ← [[HL]]
MOV B,A	47	1	4	[B] ← [A]
MOV B,B	40	1	4	[B] ← [B]
MOV B,C	41	1	4	[B] ← [C]
MOV B,D	42	1	4	[B] ← [D]
MOV B,E	43	1	4	[B] ← [E]
MOV B,H	44	1	4	[B] ← [H]
MOV B,L	45	1	4	[B] ← [L]
MOV B,M	46	1	7	[B] ← [[HL]]
MOV C,A	4F	1	4	[C] ← [A]
MOV C,B	48	1	4	[C] ← [B]
MOV C,C	49	1	4	[C] ← [C]
MOV C,D	4A	1	4	[C] ← [D]
MOV C,E	4B	1	4	[C] ← [E]
MOV C,H	4C	1	4	[C] ← [H]
MOV C,L	4D	1	4	[C] ← [L]
MOV C,M	4E	1	7	[C] ← [[HL]]
MOV D,A	57	1	4	[D] ← [A]
MOV D,B	50	1	4	[D] ← [B]
MOV D,C	51	1	4	[D] ← [C]
MOV D,D	52	1	4	[D] ← [D]
MOV D,E	53	1	4	[D] ← [E]
MOV D,H	54	1	4	[D] ← [H]
MOV D,L	55	1	4	[D] ← [L]
MOV D,M	56	1	7	[D] ← [[HL]]
MOV E,A	5F	1	4	[E] ← [A]
MOV E,B	58	1	5	[E] ← [B]
MOV E,C	59	1	4	[E] ← [C]
MOV E,D	5A	1	4	[E] ← [D]
MOV E,E	5B	1	4	[E] ← [E]
MOV E,H	5C	1	4	[E] ← [H]
MOV E,L	5D	1	4	[E] ← [L]
MOV E,M	5E	1	7	[E] ← [[HL]]
MOV H,A	67	1	4	[H] ← [B]
MOV H,B	60	1	4	[H] ← [A]
MOV H,C	61	1	4	[H] ← [C]

TABLE 2.1 (continued)
Summary of 8085 Instruction Set

Instruction	OP Code	Bytes	Cycles	Operations performed
MOV H,D	62	1	4	[H] ← [D]
MOV H,E	63	1	4	[H] ← [E]
MOV H,H	64	1	4	[H] ← [H]
MOV H,L	65	1	4	[H] ← [L]
MOV H,M	66	1	7	[H] ← [[HL]]
MOV L,A	6F	1	4	[L] ← [A]
MOV L,B	68	1	4	[L] ← [B]
MOV L,C	69	1	4	[L] ← [C]
MOV L,D	6A	1	4	[L] ← [D]
MOV L,E	6B	1	4	[L] ← [E]
MOV L,H	6C	1	4	[L] ← [H]
MOV L,L	6D	1	4	[L] ← [L]
MOV L,M	6E	1	7	[L] ← [[HL]]
MOV M,A	77	1	7	[[HL]] ← [A]
MOV M,B	70	1	7	[[HL]] ← [B]
MOV M,C	71	1	7	[[HL]] ← [C]
MOV M,D	72	1	7	[[HL]] ← [D]
MOV M,E	73	1	7	[[HL]] ← [E]
MOV M,H	74	1	7	[[HL]] ← [H]
MOV M,L	75	1	7	[[HL]] ← [L]
MVI A, DATA	3E	2	7	[A] ← second instruction byte
MVI B, DATA	06	2	7	[B] ← second instruction byte
MVI C, DATA	0E	2	7	[C] ← second instruction byte
MVI D, DATA	16	2	7	[D] ← second instruction byte
MVI E, DATA	1E	2	7	[E] ← second instruction byte
MVI H, DATA	26	2	7	[H] ← second instruction byte
MVI L, DATA	2E	2	7	[L] ← second instruction byte
MVI M, DATA	36	2	10	[[HL]] ← second instruction byte
NOP	00	1	4	No operation
ORA A	B7	1	4	[A] ← [A]∨ [A]
ORA B	B0	1	4	[A] ← [A]∨ [B]
ORA C	B1	1	4	[A] ← [A]∨ [C]
ORA D	B2	1	4	[A] ← [A]∨ [D]
ORA E	B3	1	4	[A] ← [A]∨ [E]
ORA H	B4	1	4	[A] ← [A]∨ [H]

TABLE 2.1 (continued)
Summary of 8085 Instruction Set

Instruction	OP Code	Bytes	Cycles	Operations performed
ORA L	B5	1	4	$[A] \leftarrow [A] \vee [L]$
ORA M	B6	1	7	$[A] \leftarrow [A] \vee [[HL]]$
ORI DATA	F6	2	7	$[A] \leftarrow [A] \vee$ second instruction byte
OUT PORT	D3	2	10	[specified port] $\leftarrow [A]$
PCHL	E9	1	6	$[PCH]^a \leftarrow [H], [PCL]^a \leftarrow [L]$
POP B	C1	1	10	$[C] \leftarrow [[SP]], [SP] \leftarrow [SP] + 2$ $[B] \leftarrow [[SP] + 1]$
POP D	D1	1	10	$[E] \leftarrow [[SP]], [SP] \leftarrow [SP] + 2$ $[D] \leftarrow [[SP] + 1]$
POP H	E1	1	10	$[L] \leftarrow [[SP]], [SP] \leftarrow [SP] + 2$ $[H] \leftarrow [[SP] + 1]$
POP PSW	F1	1	10	$[A] \leftarrow [[SP] + 1],$ $[PSW] \leftarrow [[SP]], [SP] \leftarrow [SP] + 2$ $[[SP] - 1] \leftarrow [B],$ $[SP] \leftarrow [SP] - 2$
PUSH B	C5	1	12	$[[SP] - 2] \leftarrow [C]$
PUSH D	D5	1	12	$[[SP] - 1] \leftarrow [D], [[SP] - 2] \leftarrow [E]$ $[SP] \leftarrow [SP] - 2$
PUSH H	E5	1	12	$[[SP] - 1] \leftarrow [H],$ $[SP] \leftarrow [SP] - 2$ $[[SP] - 2] \leftarrow [L]$
PUSH PSW	F5	1	12	$[[SP] - 1] \leftarrow [A],$ $[SP] \leftarrow [SP] - 2$ $[[SP] - 2] \leftarrow [PSW]$
RAL	17	1	4	
RAR	1F	1	4	
RC	D8	1	6/12	Return if carry; $[PC] \leftarrow [SP]]$
RET	C9	1	10	$[PCL]^a \leftarrow [[SP]],$ $[SP] \leftarrow [SP] + 2$ $[PCH]^a \leftarrow [[SP] + 1]$

TABLE 2.1 (continued)
Summary of 8085 Instruction Set

Instruction	OP Code	Bytes	Cycles	Operations performed
RIM	20	1	4	Read interrupt mask
RLC	07	1	4	
RM	F8	1	6/12	Return if minus; [PC] ← [[SP]]
RNC	D0	1	6/12	Return if no carry; [PC] ← [[SP]]
RNZ	C0	1	6/12	Return if result not zero; [PC] ← [[SP]]
RP	F0	1	6/12	Return if positive; [PC] ← [[SP]], [SP] ← [SP] + 2
RPE	E8	1	6/12	Return if parity even; [PC] ← [[SP]], [SP] ← [SP] + 2
RPO	E0	1	6/12	Return if parity odd; [PC] ← [[SP]], [SP] ← [SP] + 2
RRC	0F	1	4	
RST0	C7	1	12	Restart
RST1	CF	1	12	Restart
RST2	D7	1	12	Restart
RST3	DF	1	12	Restart
RST4	E7	1	12	Restart
RST5	EF	1	12	Restart
RST6	F7	1	12	Restart
RST7	FF	1	12	Restart
RZ	C8	1	6/12	Return if zero; [PC] ← [[SP]]
SBB A	9F	1	4	[A] ← [A] – [A] – [Cy]
SBB B	98	1	4	[A] ← [A] – [B] – [Cy]
SBB C	99	1	4	[A] ← [A] – [C] – [Cy]
SBB D	9A	1	4	[A] ← [A] – [D] – [Cy]
SBB E	9B	1	4	[A] ← [A] – [E] – [Cy]
SBB H	9C	1	4	[A] ← [A] – [H] – [Cy]
SBB L	9D	1	4	[A] ← [A] – [L] – [Cy]
SBB M	9E	1	7	[A] ← [A] – [[HL]] – [Cy]
SBI DATA	DE	2	7	[A] ← [A] – second instruction byte – [Cy]

TABLE 2.1 (continued)
Summary of 8085 Instruction Set

Instruction	OP Code	Bytes	Cycles	Operations performed
SHLD ppqq	22	3	16	[ppqq] ← [L], [ppqq + 1] ← [H]
SIM	30	1	4	Set interrupt mask
SPHL	F9	1	6	[SP] ← [HL]
STA ppqq	32	3	13	[ppqq] ← [A]
STAX B	02	1	7	[[BC]] ← [A]
STAX D	12	1	7	[[DE]] ← [A]
STC	37	1	4	[Cy] ← 1
SUB A	97	1	4	[A] ← [A] − [A]
SUB B	90	1	4	[A] ← [A] − [B]
SUB C	91	1	4	[A] ← [A] − [C]
SUB D	92	1	4	[A] ← [A] − [D]
SUB E	93	1	4	[A] ← [A] − [E]
SUB H	94	1	4	[A] ← [A] − [H]
SUB L	95	1	4	[A] ← [A] − [L]
SUB M	96	1	7	[A] ← [A] − [[HL]]
SUI DATA	D6	2	7	[A] ← [A] − second instruction byte
XCHG	EB	1	4	[D] ↔ [H], [E] ↔ [L]
XRA A	AF	1	4	[A] ← [A] ⊕ [A]
XRA B	A8	1	4	[A] ← [A] ⊕ [B]
XRA C	A9	1	4	[A] ← [A] ⊕ [C]
XRA D	AA	1	4	[A] ← [A] ⊕ [D]
XRA E	AB	1	4	[A] ← [A] ⊕ [E]
XRA H	AC	1	4	[A] ← [A] ⊕ [H]
XRA L	AD	1	4	[A] ← [A] ⊕ [L]
XRA M	AE	1	7	[A] ← [A] ⊕ [[HL]]
XRI DATA	ee	2	7	[A] ← [A] ⊕ second instruction byte
XTHL	E3	1	16	[[SP]] ↔ [L], [[SP] + 1]] ↔ [H]

[a] PCL — program counter low byte; PCH — program counter high byte.

All mnemonics copyright Intel Corporation 1976.

TABLE 2.2
8085 Instructions Affecting the Status Flags

Instructions[a]	Status flags[b]				
	Cy	**Ac**	**Z**	**S**	**P**
ACI DATA	+	+	+	+	+
ADC reg	+	+	+	+	+
ADC M	+	+	+	+	+
ADD reg	+	+	+	+	+
ADD M	+	+	+	+	+
ADI DATA	+	+	+	+	+
ANA reg	0	1	+	+	+
ANA M	0	1	+	+	+
ANI DATA	0	1	+	+	+
CMC	+				
CMP reg	+	+	+	+	+
CMP M	+	+	+	+	+
CPI DATA	+	+	+	+	+
DAA	+	+	+	+	+
DAD rp	+				
DCR reg		+	+	+	+
DCR M		+	+	+	+
INR reg		+	+	+	+
INR M		+	+	+	+
ORA reg	0	0	+	+	+
ORA M	0	0	+	+	+
ORI DATA	0	0	+	+	+
RAL	+				
RAR	+				
RLC	+				
RRC	+				
SBB reg	+	+	+	+	+
SBB M	+	+	+	+	+
SBI DATA	+	+	+	+	+
STC	+				
SUB reg	+	+	+	+	+
SUB M	+	+	+	+	+
SUI DATA	+	+	+	+	+

TABLE 2.2 (continued)
8085 Instructions Affecting the Status Flags

Instructions[a]	Status flags[b]				
	Cy	Ac	Z	S	P
XRA reg	0	0	+	+	+
XRA M	0	0	+	+	+
XRI DATA	0	0	+	+	+

[a] reg — 8-bit register; M — memory; rp — 16-bit register pair.

[b] Note that instructions which are not shown in the table do not affect the flags. + indicates that the particular flag is affected; 0 or 1 indicates that these flags are always 0 or 1 after the corresponding instructions are executed.

All mnemonics copyright Intel Corporation 1976.

TABLE 2.3
Symbols to be Used in 8085 Instruction Set

Symbol	Interpretation
r1, r2	8-bit register
rp	Register pair
data8	8-bit data
data16	16-bit data
M	Memory location indirectly addressed through the register pair H,L
addr16	16-bit memory address

TABLE 2.4
8085 MOVE Instructions

| Instruction | Symbolic description | Addressing mode | | Illustration | |
		Source	Destination	Example	Comments
MOV r1, r2	(r1) ← (r2)	Register	Register	MOV A, B	Copy the contents of the register B into the register A
MOV r, M	(r) ← M((HL))	Register indirect	Register	MOV A, M	Copy the contents of the memory location whose address is specified in the register pair H,L into the A register
MVI r, data8	(r) ← data8	Immediate	Register	MVI A, 08	Initialize the A register with the value 08
MOV M, r	M((HL)) ← (r)	Register	Register indirect	MOV M, B	Copy the contents of the B register into the memory location addressed by H,L pair
MVI M, data8	M((HL)) ← data8	Immediate	Register indirect	MVI M, 07	Initialize the memory location whose address is specified in the register pair H,L with the value 07

TABLE 2.5
8085 Load and Store Instructions

Instruction	Symbolic description	Restriction	Addressing mode	Example	Comments
					Illustration
LDA addr16	(A) ← M(addr16)	The destination is always the accumulator register	Absolute	LDA 2000H	Load the accumulator with the contents of the memory location whose address is 2000H
LHLD addr16	(L) ← M(addr16) (H) ← M(addr16+1)	The destination is always the register pair H,L	Absolute	LHLD 2000H	Load the H and L registers with contents of the memory locations 2001H and 2000H, respectively
LXI rp, data16	(rp) ← data16	rp may be HL, DE, BC, or SP	Immediate	LXI H, 2024H	$H \leftarrow 20_{16}, L \leftarrow 24_{16}$
LDAX rp	(A) ← M((rp))	Destination is always the accumulator; also rp may be either B,C or D,E	Register indirect	LDAX B	Load the accumulator with the contents of the memory location whose address is specified with the register pair B,C
STA addr16	M(addr16) ← (A)	Source is always the accumulator register	Absolute	STA 2001H	Save the contents of the accumulator into the memory location whose address is 2001H
SHLD addr16	M(addr16) ← (L) M(addr16+1)←(H)	The source is always the register pair H,L	Absolute	SHLD 2000	M(2000) ← (L) M(2001) ← (H)

TABLE 2.5 (continued)
8085 Load and Store Instructions

Instruction	Symbolic description	Restriction	Addressing mode	Example	Illustration Comments
STAX rp	M((rp)) ← (A)	The source is always the accumulator register and the register pair may be B,C or D,E	Register indirect	STAX D	Save the contents of the accumulator register into the memory location whose address is specified with the register pair D,E
XCHG	[D] ↔ [H], [E] ↔ [L]		Inherent	XCHG	Exchanges [DE] with [HL]

The arithmetic instructions provided by the 8085 processor allow one to add (or subtract) two 8-bit data with or without carry (or borrow). The subtraction operation is realized by adding the two's complement of the subtrahend to the minuend. During the subtraction operation, the carry flag will be treated as the borrow flag. Table 2.6 lists these instructions. For some instructions such as ADD M, examples and comments are not included. This is due to limited space in the table.

As far as logical operations are concerned, the 8085 includes some instructions to perform traditional Boolean operations such as AND, OR, EXCLUSIVE-OR. In addition, instructions are available to complement the accumulator and to set the carry flag. The 8085 COMPARE instructions subtract the specified destination from the contents of the accumulator and affect the status flags according to the result. However, in this case the result of the subtraction is not provided in the accumulator. All 8085 logical instructions are specified in Table 2.7. For some instructions in this figure, examples and comments are not provided. This is due to limited space in the table.

The AND instruction can be used to perform a masking operation. If the bit value in a particular bit position is desired in a word, the word can be logically ANDed with appropriate masking data to accomplish this. For example, the bit value at bit 3 of the word $1011\ X011_2$ can be determined as follows:

	1011	X011	Word
and	0000	1000	Masking Data
	0000	X000	Result

If the bit value X at bit 3 is 1, then the result is nonzero ($Z = 0$); otherwise the result is zero ($Z = 1$). The Z-flag can be tested using JZ (jump if $Z = 1$) or JNZ (jump if $Z = 0$) to determine whether $X = 0$ or 1. The AND instruction can also be used to determine whether a binary number is odd or even by checking the least significant bit (LSB) of the number (LSB = 0 for even and LSB = 1 for odd). XRA instruction can be used to find ones compliment of a binary number by exclusive-ORing the number with all ones as follows:

	1010	1001	Original number
XOR	1111	1111	
	0101	0110	Ones complement of the original number

TABLE 2.6
8085 Arithmetic Instructions

Operation	Instruction	Interpretation	Addressing mode	Example	Illustration Comments
8-bit addition	ADD r	$(A) \leftarrow (A) + (r)$	Register	ADD B	$(A) \leftarrow (A) + (B)$
	ADI data8	$(A) \leftarrow (A) + data8$	Immediate	ADI 05	$(A) \leftarrow (A) + 05$
	ADD M	$(A) \leftarrow (A) + M((HL))$	Register indirect	—	—
8-bit addition with a carry	ADC r	$(A) \leftarrow (A) + (r) + Cy$	Register	ADC C	$(A) \leftarrow (A) + (C) + Cy$
	AC data8	$(A) \leftarrow (A) + data8 + Cy$	Immediate	ACI 07	$(A) \leftarrow (A) + 07 + Cy$
	ADC M	$(A) \leftarrow (A) + M((HL)) + Cy$	Register indirect	—	—
8-bit subtraction	SUB r	$(A) \leftarrow (A) - (r)$	Register	SUB C	$(A) \leftarrow (A) - (C)$
	SUI data8	$(A) \leftarrow (A) - data8$	Immediate	SUI 03	$(A) \leftarrow (A) - 03$
	SUB M	$(A) \leftarrow (A) - M((HL))$	Register indirect	—	—
8-bit subtraction with a borrow	SBB r	$(A) \leftarrow (A) - (r) - Cy$	Register	SBB D	$(A) \leftarrow (A) - (D) - Cy$
	SBI data8	$(A) \leftarrow (A) - data8 - Cy$	Immediate	SBI 04	$(A) \leftarrow (A) - 04 - Cy$
	SBB M	$(A) \leftarrow (A) - M((HL)) - Cy$	Register indirect	—	—
16-bit addition	DAD rp	$(HL) \leftarrow (HL) + (rp)$	Register	DAD B	$(HL) \leftarrow (HL) + (BC)$
Decimal adjust	DAA	Convert the 8-bit number stored in the accumulator into BCD	Inherent	—	—
8-bit increment	INR r	$(r) \leftarrow (r) + 1$	Register	INR B	$(B) \leftarrow (B) + 1$
	INR M	$M((HL)) \leftarrow M((HL)) + 1$	Register indirect	—	—

16-bit increment[a]	INX rp	$(rp) \leftarrow (rp) + 1$	Register	INX D	$(DE) \leftarrow (DE) + 1$
8-bit decrement	DCR r	$(r) \leftarrow (r) - 1$	Register	DCR B	$(B) \leftarrow (B) - 1$
	DCR M	$M((HL)) \leftarrow M((HL)) - 1$	Register indirect	—	—
16-bit decrement[a]	DCX rp	$(rp) \leftarrow (rp) - 1$	Register	—	—

[a] rp = BC, DE, HL, or SP.

TABLE 2.7
8085 Logical Instructions

Operation	Instruction	Interpretation	Illustration Addressing mode	Illustration Example	Illustration Comments
Boolean AND	ANA r	$(A) \leftarrow (A) \wedge (r)$	Register	ANA B	$(A) \leftarrow (A) \wedge (B)$
	ANI data8	$(A) \leftarrow (A) \wedge$ data8	Immediate	ANI 0FH	$(A) \leftarrow (A) \wedge 00001111_2$
	ANA M	$(A) \leftarrow (A) \wedge M((HL))$	Register indirect	—	—
Boolean OR	ORA r	$(A) \leftarrow (A) \vee (r)$	Register	ORA C	$(A) \leftarrow (A) \vee (C)$
	ORI data8	$(A) \leftarrow (A) \vee$ data8	Immediate	ORI 08H	$(A) \leftarrow (A) \vee 00001000_2$
	ORA M	$(A) \leftarrow (A) \vee M((HL))$	Register indirect	—	—
Boolean EXCLUSIVE-OR	XRA r	$(A) \leftarrow (A) \oplus (r)$	Register	XRA A	$(A) \leftarrow (A) \oplus (A)$
	XRI data8	$(A) \leftarrow (A) \oplus$ data8	Immediate	XRI 03H	$(A) \leftarrow (A) \oplus 00000011_2$
	XRA M	$(A) \leftarrow (A) \oplus M((HL))$	Register indirect	—	—
Compare	CMP r	$(A) - (r)$ and affect flags	Register	CMP D	Compare (A) register with (D) register
	CPI data8	$(A) -$ data8 and affect flags	Immediate	CPI 05	Compare (A) with 05
	CMP M	$(A) - M((HL))$ and affect flags	Register indirect	—	—
Complement	CMA	$(A) \leftarrow (A)'$	Inherent	—	—

Bit manipulation	STC	$Cy \leftarrow 1$ (set carry to 1)	Inherent	—	—
	CMC	$Cy \leftarrow Cy'$ (complement carry flag)	Inherent	—	—

One of the applications of the compare instruction is to find a match in an array. The number to be matched can be loaded in the accumulator and compared with each element in the array. The JZ (jump if Z = 1) can then be executed to find the match. If the subtraction instruction is used in place of the COMPARE, the number to be matched in the accumulator will be lost after each subtraction, and therefore the number needs to be loaded for the next subtraction.

The 8085 instruction set includes rotating the contents of the A register to the left or right without or through the carry flag. These instructions are listed in Table 2.8.

TABLE 2.8
8085 Rotate Instructions

Instruction	Interpretation	Illustration
RLC	Rotate left accumulator by one position without the carry flag Cy	
RRC	Rotate right accumulator by one position without the carry flag Cy	
RAR	Rotate right accumulator by one position through the carry flag	
RAL	Rotate left accumulator by one position through the carry flag	

In the 8085, absolute mode branch instruction is of the form JMP addr16. There is also a one-byte implied unconditional jump instruction, namely, PCHL. The PCHL loads [H] into PC high byte and [L] into PC low byte. That is, PCHL performs an unconditional JUMP to a location addressed by the contents of H and L. The general format of an 8085 conditional branch instruction is J (condition code) addr16 where the condition code may represent one of the following conditions:

Conditional jumps	Condition	Comment
JZ	$Z = 1$	Z flag is set (result equal to zero)
JNZ	$Z = 0$	Z flag is reset (result not equal to zero)
JC	$Cy = 1$	Cy flag is set
JNC	$Cy = 0$	Cy flag is reset
JPO	$P = 0$	The parity is odd
JPE	$P = 1$	The parity is even
JP	$S = 0$	S flag is reset (or the number is positive)
JM	$S = 1$	S flag is set (or the number is negative)

For example, the following instruction sequence causes a branch to the memory address 2000_{16} only if the contents of the A and B registers are equal:

CMP B
JZ 2000H

In the 8085, the subroutine call instruction is of the form

CALL addr16

The instruction RET transfers the control to the caller, and it should be the last instruction of the subroutine. Both instructions use the PC and SP for subroutine linkage.

For example, consider the following:

Main program		**Subroutine**	
	—	**SUB**	—
	—		—
	—		—
CALL SUB			—
START	—		—
	—		—
	—		**RET**
	—		

The call SUB instruction pushes or saves the current PC contents (START which is the address of the next instruction) onto the stack and loads PC with the starting address of the Subroutine (SUB) specified with the CALL instruction. The RET instruction at the end of the subroutine pops or reads the address START (saved onto the stack by the CALL instruction) into PC and transfers control to the right place in the main program.

There are a number of conditional call instructions. These include:

```
CC      addr    (call if Cy = 1)
CNC     addr    (call if Cy = 0)
CZ      addr    (call if Z = 1)
CNZ     addr    (call if Z = 0)
CM      addr    (call if S = 1)
CP      addr    (call if S = 0)
CPE     addr    (call if P = 1)
CPO     addr    (call if P = 0)
```

Also, there are a number of conditional return instructions. These include:

```
RC      (Return if Cy = 1)
RNC     (Return if Cy = 0)
RZ      (Return if Z = 1)
RNZ     (Return if Z = 0)
RPE     (Return if P = 1)
RPO     (Return if P = 0)
RM      (Return if S = 1)
RP      (Return if S = 0)
```

There are eight one-byte call instructions (RST 0 to 7) which have predefined addresses. The format for these instructions is

```
11   XXX   111
            XXX = 000 for RST0
                = 001 for RST1
                = 010 for RST2
                = 011 for RST3
                = 100 for RST4
                = 101 for RST5
                = 110 for RST6
                = 111 for RST7
```

RSTs are one-byte call instructions used mainly with interrupts. Each RST has a predefined address. However, RST0 and hardware reset vector have the same address 0000_{16}. Therefore, use of RST0 is not usually recommended. The RSTs cause the 8085 to push PC onto the stack. The 8085 then loads the PC with a predefined address based on the particular RST being used.

A 3-bit code in the OP code for a particular RST determines the address to which the program would branch. This is shown in Figure 2.5.

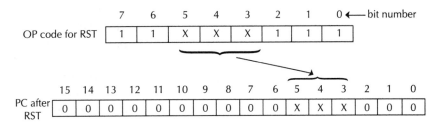

FIGURE 2.5 Execution of the RST instruction.

The vector addresses for the RSTs are listed in Table 2.9. Note that a limited number of locations are available for each RST instruction. This may not provide enough locations for writing a complete subroutine. Therefore, one may place an unconditional JUMP at the vector address to JUMP to an address in RAM where the actual subroutine is written.

TABLE 2.9
RST0-RST7 Vector Addresses

Instruction	OP code (hexadecimal)	Vector address (hexadecimal)
RST0	C7	0000
RST1	CF	0008
RST2	D7	0010
RST3	DF	0018
RST4	E7	0020
RST5	EF	0028
RST6	F7	0030
RST7	FF	0038

The 8085 stack manipulation instructions allow one to save and retrieve the contents of the register pairs into and from the stack, respectively. For example, the following instruction saves the register pair B,C into the stack:

```
PUSH B ; (SP) ← (SP) - 1
       ; M((SP)) ← (B)
       ; (SP) ← (SP) - 1
       ; M((SP)) ← (C)
```

Similarly, the instruction POP D retrieves the top two words of the stack and places them into the registers E and D in that order as follows:

```
POP D  ; (E) ← M((SP))
       ; (SP) ← (SP) + 1
       ; (D) ← M((SP))
       ; (SP) ← (SP) + 1
```

This means that all 8085 registers can be saved onto the stack using the following instruction sequence:

```
PUSH PSW ; save the A and flags register
PUSH B   ; save the D,E pair
PUSH D   ; save the D,E pair
PUSH H   ; save the H,L pair
```

Similarly, the saved status can be restored by using the following sequence of POP instructions:

```
POP H    ; restore H,L pair
POP D    ; restore D,E pair
POP B    ; restore B,C pair
POP PSW  ; restore A and flags register
```

There are two other stack instructions: SPHL and XTHL. SPHL is a one-byte instruction. It moves the [L] to SP high byte and [H] to SP low byte. XTHL is also a one-byte instruction. It exchanges the [L] with the top of the stack addressed by SP and [H] with the next stack addressed by SP + 1. That is, XTHL performs the following:

$$[[SP]] \longleftrightarrow [L]$$
$$[[SP + 1]] \longleftrightarrow [H]$$

The 8085 can use either standard or memory-mapped I/O. Using standard I/O, the input and output instructions have the following format:

```
IN    (8-bit port address)    ; input instruction
OUT   (8-bit port address)    ; output instruction
```

For example, the instruction IN 02H transfers the contents of the input port with address 02_{16} into the accumulator. Similarly, the instruction OUT 00H transfers the contents of the accumulator to the output port with address 00_{16}. Using memory-mapped I/O, LDA addr and STA addr can be used as input and output instructions, respectively.

The 8085 HLT instruction forces the 8085 to enter into the halt state. Similarly, the dummy instruction NOP neither achieves any result nor affects any CPU registers. This is a useful instruction for producing software delay routines and to insert diagnostic messages.

The 8085 8-bit increment (INR) and decrement (DCR) instructions affect the status flags. However, the 16-bit increment (INX) and decrement (DCX) instructions do not affect the flags. Therefore, while using these instructions in a loop counter value greater than 256_{10}, some other instructions must be used with DCX or INX to affect the flags after their execution. For example, the following instruction sequence will affect the flags for DCX:

```
       LXI B,16-BIT DATA        ; Load
        —                       ; initial
        —                       ; 16-bit loop
        —                       ; count to BC
        —
        —
        —                       ; Decrement
Loop   DCX B                    ; counter
       MOV A,B                  ; Move B to A to
                                  test for zero
       ORA C                    ; Logically or with
                                  A
       JNZ Loop                 ; Jump if not zero
        —
        —
        —
```

There are four one-byte 8085 interrupt instructions. These are DI, EI, RIM, and SIM.

DI disables the 8085's maskable interrupt capability. EI, on the other hand, enables the 8085 maskable interrupt capability.

RIM is a one-byte instruction. It loads the accumulator with 8 bits of data as shown in Figure 2.6.

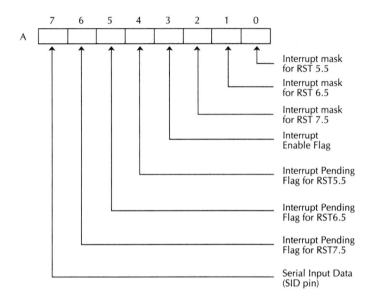

FIGURE 2.6 Accumulator data format after execution of the RIM.

Bits 0, 1, and 2 provide the values of the RST 5.5, RST 6.5, and RST 7.5 mask bits, respectively. If the mask bit corresponding to a particular RST is one, the RST is disabled; a zero in a specific RST (bits 0, 1, and 2) means that RST is enabled.

If the interrupt enable bit (bit 3) is 0, the 8085's maskable interrupt capability is disabled; the interrupt is enabled if this bit is one.

A "one" in a particular interrupt pending bit indicates that an interrupt is being requested on the identified RST line; if this bit is zero, no interrupt is waiting to be serviced. The serial input data (bit 7) indicate the value of the SID pin.

The SIM instruction outputs the contents of the accumulator to define interrupt mask bits and the serial output data line. The bits in the accumulator before execution of the SIM are defined as shown in Figure 2.7.

If the mask set enable bit is set to one, interrupt mask bits for RST 7.5, RST 6.5, and RST 5.5 are sent out; a zero value at the mask set enable does not affect the interrupt mask bits. A one at a particular interrupt mask disables that interrupt and a zero enables it.

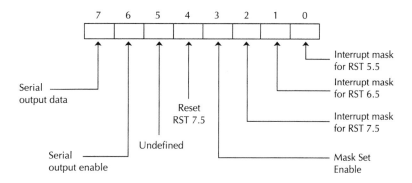

FIGURE 2.7 Accumulator data format before execution of the SIM.

The RESET RST 7.5, if set to one, resets as internal flip-flop to zero in order to disable the 7.5 interrupt.

If the serial output enable is one, the serial output data are sent to the SOD pin.

The interrupt instructions will be covered in detail during discussion of the 8085 interrupts.

Example 2.1

Write an 8085 assembly language program to add a 16-bit number in locations 5000H (high byte) and 5001H (low byte) with another 16-bit number stored in 5002H (high byte) and 5003H (low byte). Store result in BC.

Solution

```
        ORG     2000H
        LDA     MEM2        ; Load low byte of
        LXI     H,5003H     ; number 1
        ADD     M           ; Add with low
                            ; byte of number 2
        MOV     C, A        ; Store result in C
        LDA     MEM1        ; Load high byte
        DCX     H           ; of number 1
        ADC     M           ; Add with
                            ; high byte and Cy
        MOV     B, A        ; Store result
                            ; in B
        HLT                 ; stop
        ORG     5000H
MEM1    DB                  DATA1
MEM2    DB                  DATA2
MEM3    DB                  DATA3
MEM4    DB                  DATA4
```

Example 2.2

Write an 8085 assembly language program to perform a parity check on an 8-bit word in location 5000_{16}. If the parity is odd, store DD16 in location 5000_{16}. However, if the parity is even, store EE16 in location 5000_{16}.

Solution

```
            ORG  3000H
            LDA  PARITY         ; Load 8-bit
                                ; data into A
            ADI  00H            ; Add with
                                ; 00H to affect
                                ; flags
            JPO  ODD            ; Check for
                                ; odd parity
            MVI  A,0EEH         ; If parity
                                ; even, store
                                ; EEH
            STA  PARITY         ; in 5000H
            HLT                 ; Stop
    ODD     MVI  A,0DDH         ; If parity
                                ; odd store
            STA  PARITY         ; DDH in 5000H
            HLT                 ; stop
            ORG  5000 H
PARITY      DB DATA
```

Note that address 3000H at ORG 3000H is arbitrarily chosen.

Example 2.3

Write a program in 8085 assembly language to perform an unsigned 8-bit by 8-bit multiplication via repeated addition. Assume that the multiplicand is in "B" register and the multiplier is in "C" register. Store the product in HL.

Solution

```
        ORG  5000H
        LXI  H,0000H        ; Initialize the
                            ; 16-bit product to zero
```

```
          MVI  C, MULT         ;  Move multiplier to C
          MOV  E,B             ;  Move multiplicand
                               ;  to register E
          MVI  D,OOH           ;  Convert multiplicand
                               ;  to unsigned 16-bit
START     DAD  D               ;  Perform 16-bit
                               ;  addition
          DCR  C               ;  Decrement
                               ;  multiplier
          JNZ  START           ;  Jump if multiplier
                               ;  not zero
          HLT                  ;  Stop. Product
                               ;  is in HL
```

Example 2.4

Write a subroutine in 8085 assembly language to check whether an 8-bit number in location 3000_{16} is odd or even. If the number is odd, store DD16 in location 3000_{16}; if the number is even, store EE16 in location 3000_{16}.

Also, write the main program to initialize stack pointer 5020_{16}, load the 8-bit number to be checked for odd or even into A, store DD16 or EE16 depending on the result, and stop.

Solution

```
Main Program
          ORG  4000H
          LXI  SP, 5020H       ;  Initialize SP
          LDA  START           ;  Load number
          CALL CHECK           ;  Call subroutine
          STA  START           ;  Store DD16 or EE16
          HLT                  ;  stop
          ORG  3000H
START     DB DATA


Subroutine
          ORG  7000H
CHECK     RAR                  ;  Rotate 'A' for checking
          JNC  EVEN            ;  Jump if even
          MVI  A,ODDH          ;  Store DD16 if
          JMP  RETURN          ;  odd and return
EVEN      MVI  A,OEEH          ;  Store EE16
RETURN    RET                  ;  if even and return
```

Example 2.5

Write an 8085 assembly language program to clear 100_{10} consecutive bytes starting at 2050_{16}.

Solution

```
        ORG  2000H
        MVI  A, 64H    ;     Load 'A' with number of
                       ;     bytes to be cleared
        LXI  H,2050H   ;     Load HL with 2050H
LOOP    MVI  M, 00H    ;     Clear memory location
        INX  H         ;     Increment address
        DCR  A         ;     Decrement loop counter
        JNZ  LOOP      ;     Jump to loop if
                       ;     loop counter zero
        HLT            ;     Stop
```

Example 2.6

Write an 8085 assembly language program to find the square root of a number using the successive approximation algorithm as follows: let B be the value for which the square root is desired and A be the guess value of B. The value of A is squared and compared with the value of B. If A^2 is greater than B, A is decreased, but if A^2 is less than B, then A is increased by an arbitrary number (user choice). This procedure is repeated until A^2 is approximately equal to B. The user decides how close A^2 needs to be with respect to B before the loop is terminated. When the loop is terminated, A is the value of the square root of B.

Solution

```
137                        *SQUARE ROOT ROUTINE
138                        *
139                        *
140  0347  26 80    SQRT   MVI   H,80H  ;SET  MSB  OF  SHIFT COUNTER
141  0349  2E 00           MVI   L,0    ;CLEAR  THE  BINARY  VALUE
142  0348  70       SQRT1  MOV   A,L    ;GET  BINARY  VALUE
143  034C  B4              ORA   H      ;SET  A BIT  IN  L
144  034D  6F              MOV   L,A
145  034E  47              MOV   B,A    ;SQUARE  BINARY  VALUE
146  034F  CD 037A         CALL  SQRB
147  0352  7A              MOV   A,D    ;IS  B>D?  YES,  RESET  BIT
148  0353  B8              CMP   B      ;NO,  LEAVE  BIT
149  0354  DA 035F         JC    RSTBIT
```

```
150  0357  C2 0362           JNZ   SHFTCTR;IS  B = D?  NO,  LEAVE  BIT
                                            SET
151  035A  7B                MOV   A,E     ;YES,  COMPARE  LO BYTE
152  035B  B9                CMP   C       ;IS  C>E?  YES,   RESET  BIT
153  035C  D2 0362           JNC   SHFTCTR;NO,  LEAVE  BIT  SET
154  035F  7D        RSTBIT  MOV   A,L     ;GET THE BIT SET LAST
155  0360  AC                XRA   H       ;RESET THAT BIT IN BINARY
                                            VALUE
156  0361  6F                MOV   L,A
157  0362  7C        SHFTCTRMOV   A,H     ;GET   THE   COUNTER
158  0363  1F                RAR           ;SHIFT RIGHT
159  0364  67                MOV   H,A     ;HAS IT BEEN SHIFTED 8
                                            TIMES?
160  0365  D2  034B          JNC   SQRT1   ;YES, FALL THRU
161  0368  45                MOV   B,L     ;SQUARE L
162  0369  CD  037A          CALL  SQRB
163  036C  7B                MOV   A,E     ;GET LO BYTE OF HL
164  036D  91                SUB   C       ;SUBTRACT LO BYTE L**2
165  036E  BD                CMP   L       ;IS DIFFERENCE < L OR = L
166  036F  DA  0376          JC    DONE    ;YES, L**2 IS CLOSER
167  0372  CA  0376          JZ    DONE
168  0375  2C                INR   L       ;NO,  (L + 1)**2 IS CLOSER
169  0376  4D        DONE    MOV   C,L     ;SQUARE ROOT TO REG C
170  0377  C3  0397          HLT   CDA     ;HALT
171                  *
172                  *
173                  *
174                  *SUBROUTINE FOR SQUARING REGISTER B
175                  *RESULT IN RP B_C
176                  *
177  037A  D5        SQRB    PUSH  D
178  037B  1E  08            MVI   E,08H   ;MULTIPLY COUNT
179  037D  0E  00            MVI   C,00H
180  037F  50                MOV   D,B
181  0380  B7        SHIFT1  ORA   A       ;CLEAR CARRY
182  0381  79                MOV   A,C     ;SHIFT 16 BITS LEFT
183  0382  17                RAL
184  0383  4F                MOV   C,A
185  0384  78                MOV   A,B
186  0385  17                RAL
187  0386  47                MOV   B,A
188  0387  D2  0391          JNC   SQRB1
189  038A  7A                MOV   A,D     ;GET DATA
190  038B  81                ADD   C
191  038C  4F                MOV   C,A
192  038D  78                MOV   A,B
193  038E  CE  00            ACI   00H
194  0390  47                MOV   B,A
```

```
195  0391  1D        SQRB1 DCR   E       ;CHECK  IF  DONE
196  0392  C2  0380        JNZ   SHIFT1
197  0395  D1              POP   D
198  0396  C9              RET           ;DONE
199                  *
```

2.6 TIMING METHODS

Timing concepts are very important in microprocessor applications. Typically, in sequential process control the microprocessor is required to provide time delays for on-off devices such as pumps or motor-operated valves. DELAY routines are used to provide such time delays. Time delay programs reside in microcomputer memory and are not capable of handling complicated timing requirements. To keep things simple, however, we only consider delay routines in this section.

A delay program typically has an input register that contains the initial count. The register pair D,E is used for this purpose. A typical delay subroutine is given below:

```
DELAY   DCX D       ;  Decrement the D,E contents
        MOV A,D     ;
        ORA E       ;  Are the contents zero?
        JNZ DELAY   ;  Jump if not zero
        RET
```

We now calculate the total time required by the DELAY routine using the following data:

Instruction	Number of cycles
CALL	18
DCX D	6
MOV A,D	4
ORA E	4
JNZ	7/10
RET	10

Note that in the above, if the JNZ condition is met (Z = 0), ten cycles are required and the program branches back to the DCX D instruction. However, if the JNZ condition is not met (Z = 1), the seven cycles are required, and the program executes the next instruction, that is, the RET instruction. Also, note that the CALL instruction is used in the main program written by the user, and the 3-byte instruction CALL DELAY is used.

For each iteration in which the JNZ condition is met (Z = 0), the number of cycles is equal to cycles for DCX D + cycles for MOV A,D + cycles for ORA E + cycles for JNZ = 6 + 4 + 4 + 10 = 24 cycles.

These 24 cycles will be performed (y − 1) times, where y is the initial contents of D,E. For the final iteration in which no jump is performed and the JNZ condition is not satisfied (Z ≠ 0), the number of cycles is equal to cycles for DCX D + cycles for MOV A,D + cycles for ORA E + cycles for JNZ + cycles for RET = 6 + 4 + 4 + 7 + 10 = 31 cycles. Therefore, the time used, including a CALL instruction, is

$$18 + 31 + 24(y − 1) = 49 + 24(y − 1) \text{ clock cycles}$$

Suppose that in a program a delay time of 1/3 ms is desired. The DELAY routine can be used to accomplish this in the following way. Each cycle of the 8085 clock is 1/3 μs (3 MHz). The number of cycles required in the DELAY routine is

$$\frac{1/3 \text{ ms}}{1/3 \text{ μs}} = \frac{10^{-3}}{10^{-6}} = 1000 \text{ cycles}$$

Therefore, the initial counter value y of the D,E register pair can be calculated:

$$49 + 24 (y\text{-}1) = 1000$$
$$24 (y\text{-}1) = 951$$
$$y = \frac{951}{24} + 1 \cong 40_{10} = 28_{16}$$

Therefore, in the program the D,E register pair can be loaded with 0028_{16} and the DELAY routine can be called to obtain 1/3 ms of time delay. Table 2.10 shows initial counts for various time delays.

TABLE 2.10
Time Intervals along with Initial Counts

3-MHz clock milliseconds	Initial count (hexadecimal)
1/3	0028
1	007C
2	00F9
10	04E1
100	30D3

The following program produces a delay of 10 ms:

```
LXI SP, 5000H     ;  Set stack pointer
LXI D, 04E1H      ;  Load D,E with initial count
                     value of 04E1 to provide 10 ms
                     of delay
CALL DELAY        ;  Call DELAY routine
HLT               ;  STOP
```

The delay times can be increased by using a counter. Suppose that a delay of 5 s is desired in a program. From Table 2.10 an initial count of $30D3_{16}$ produces a 100-ms delay. We can use a counter along with the 100-ms delay to obtain the 5-s delay as follows

$$(100 \text{ ms}) \times X = 5 \text{ s}$$

where X is the value of the counter. Then

$$X = \frac{5}{100 \times 10^{-3}} = \frac{5}{10^{-1}} = 50$$

Therefore, a counter of 50_{10} or 32_{16} is required. Now the program for the 5-s delay can be written as follows:

```
         LXI  SP,  5000H        ;  Set stack pointer
         MVI  C,  32H           ;  Do DELAY loop 50   times
                                   by loading C with count
                                   32
START    LXI  D,  30D3H         ;  Load initial count
         CALL DELAY             ;  Call DELAY loop
         DCR  C                 ;  Decrement C and check if
                                   zero: if not, do another
                                   delay
         JNZ  START             ;  Loop back
         HLT                    ;  STOP
```

In the above, since execution times of DCR C and JNZ START are very small compared to 5 s, they are not considered in computing the delay.

2.7 8085 PINS AND SIGNALS

The 8085 is housed in a 40-pin dual in-line package (DIP). Figure 2.8 shows the 8085 pins and signals.

The low-order address byte and data lines AD0 to AD7 are multiplexed. These lines are bidirectional. The beginning of an instruction is indicated by the rising edge of the ALE signal. At the falling edge of ALE, the low byte of the address is automatically latched by some of the 8085 support chips such as 8155 and 8355: AD0 to AD7 lines can then be used as data lines. Note that ALE is an input to these support chips. However, if the support chips do not latch AD0 to AD7, then external latches are required to generate eight separate address lines A7 to A0 at the falling edge of ALE.

Pins A8 to A15 are unidirectional and contain the high byte of the address.

Table 2.11 lists the 8085 pins along with a brief description of each.

The $\overline{\text{RD}}$ pin signal is output LOW by the 8085 during a memory or I/O READ operation. Similarly, the $\overline{\text{WR}}$ pin signal is output LOW during a memory or I/O WRITE.

Next, we explain the purpose of IO/$\overline{\text{M}}$, S0, and S1 signals. The IO/$\overline{\text{M}}$ signal is output HIGH by the 8085 to indicate execution of an I/O instruction such as IN or OUT. This pin is output LOW during execution of a memory instruction such as LDA 2050H.

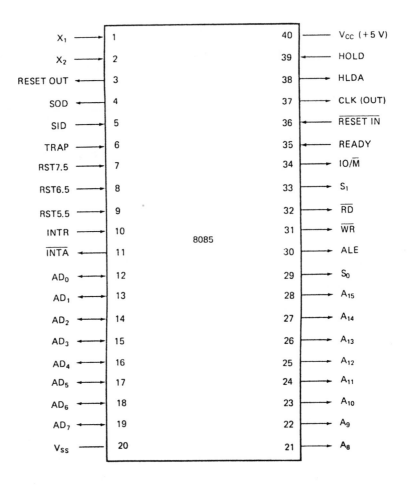

FIGURE 2.8 8085 microprocessor signals and pin assignments.

The IO/$\overline{\text{M}}$, S0, and S1 are output by the 8085 during its internal operations, which can be interpreted as follows:

IO/$\overline{\text{M}}$	S1	S0	Operation performed by the 8085
0	0	1	Memory WRITE
0	1	0	Memory READ
1	0	1	I/O WRITE
1	1	0	I/O READ
0	1	1	OP code fetch
1	1	1	Interrupt acknowledge

TABLE 2.11
8085 Signal Description Summary

Pin name	Description	Type
AD0-AD7	Address/data bus	Bidirectional, tristate
A8-A15	Address bus	Output, tristate
ALE	Address latch enable	Output, tristate
$\overline{\text{RD}}$	Read control	Output, tristate
$\overline{\text{WR}}$	Write control	Output, tristate
IO/$\overline{\text{M}}$	I/O or memory indicator	Output, tristate
S0, S1	Bus state indicators	Output
READY	Wait state request	Input
SID	Serial data input	Input
SOD	Serial data output	Output
HOLD	Hold request	Input
HLDA	Hold acknowledge	Output
INTR	Interrupt request	Input
TRAP	Nonmaskable interrupt request	Input
RST5.5	Hardware vectored	Input
RST6.5	Hardware vectored interrupt request	Input
RST7.5	Hardware vectored	Input
$\overline{\text{INTA}}$	Interrupt acknowledge	Output
$\overline{\text{RESET IN}}$	System reset	Input
RESET OUT	Peripherals reset	Output
X1, X2	Crystal or RC connection	Input
CLK (OUT)	Clock signal	Output
Vcc, Vss	Power, ground	

Figure 2.9 illustrates the utilization of ALE and AD0 to AD7 signals for interfacing an EPROM and a RAM.

The 2716 is a 2K × 8 EPROM with separate address and data lines without any built-in latches. This means that a separate latch such as the 74LS 373 must be used to isolate the 8085 low byte address and D0-D7 data lines at the falling edge of ALE (Figure 2.9a).

The 8155 contains 256-byte static RAM, three user ports, and a 14-bit timer. The 8155 is designed for 8085 in the sense that it has built-in latches with ALE as input along with multiplexed address (low byte) and data lines, AD0 to AD7. Therefore, as shown in Figure 2.9b, external latches are not required.

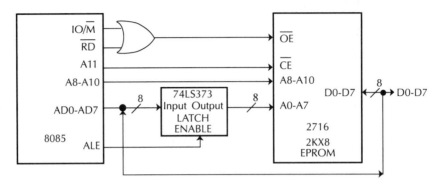

(a) 8155 - 2716 interface using internal latches.

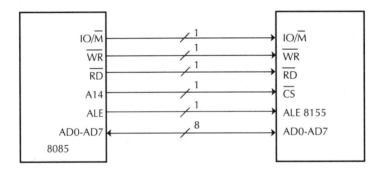

(b) 8085 - 8155 interface using ALE and AD0-AD7

FIGURE 2.9 8085's interface to external device using ALE and the multiplexed AD0 to AD7 pins.

The READY input can be used by the slower external devices for obtaining extra time in order to communicate with the 8085. The READY signal (when LOW) can be utilized to provide wait-state clock periods in the 8085 machine. If READY is HIGH during a read or write cycle, it indicates that the memory or peripheral is ready to send or receive data.

The Serial Input Data (SID) and Serial Output Data (SOD) lines are associated with the 8085 serial I/O transfer. The SOD line can be used to output the most significant bit of the accumulator. The SID signal can be input into the most significant bit of the accumulator.

The HOLD and HLDA signals are used for the Direct Memory Access (DMA) type of data transfer. The external devices place a HIGH on HOLD line in order to take control of the system bus. The HOLD function is acknowledged by the 8085 by placing a HIGH output on the HLDA pin.

The signals on the TRAP, RST7.5, RST6.5, RST5.5, INTR, and $\overline{\text{INTA}}$ are related to the 8085 interrupt signal. TRAP is a nonmaskable interrupt; that is, it cannot be enabled or disabled by an instruction. The TRAP has the highest priority. RST7.5, RST6.5, and RST5.5 are maskable interrupts used by the external devices whose vector addresses are generated automatically. $\overline{\text{INTA}}$ is an interrupt acknowledge signal which is pulsed LOW by the 8085 in response to the interrupt INTR request. In order to service INTR, one of the eight OP codes (RST0 to RST7) has to be provided on the 8085 AD0-AD7 bus by external logic. The 8085 then executes this instruction and vectors to the appropriate address to service the interrupt.

The 8085 has the clock generation circuit on the chip and, therefore, no external oscillators need to be designed. The 8085A can operate with a maximum clock frequency of 3.03 MHz and the 8085A-2 can be driven with a maximum of 5 MHz clock. The 8085 clock frequency can be generated by a crystal, an LC tuned circuit, or an external clock circuit. The frequency at X1X2 is divided by 2 internally. This means that in order to obtain 3.03 MHz, a clock source of 6.06 MHz must be connected to X1X2. For crystals with less than 4 MHz, a capacitor of 20 pF should be connected between X2 and a ground to ensure the starting up of the crystal at the right frequency (Figure 2.10).

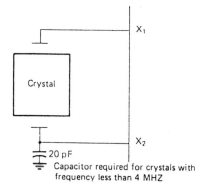

FIGURE 2.10 Crystal connection to X1 and X2 pins.

A **parallel-resonant LC circuit**, shown in Figure 2.11, can also be used as the frequency source for the 8085. The values of L_{ext} and C_{ext} can be chosen using the formula:

$$f = 1/2\pi L_{ext}(C_{ext} + C_{int})$$

To minimize variations in frequency it is recommended that a value for C_{ext} should be chosen which is twice that C_{int}, or 30 pF. The use of LC circuit is not recommended for external frequencies higher than approximately 5 MHz.

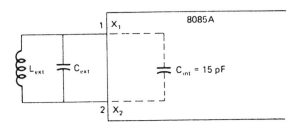

FIGURE 2.11 LC tuned circuit clock driver.

An RC circuit may also be used as the clock source for the 8085A if an accurate clock frequency is of no concern. Its advantage is the low component cost. Figure 2.12 shows a clock circuit for generating an approximate external frequency of 3 MHz. Note that frequencies greatly higher or lower than 3 MHz should not be attempted on this circuit.

There is a TTL signal which is output on pin 37, called the CLK (OUT) signal. This signal can be used by other external microprocessors or by the host microprocessor's internal circuitry.

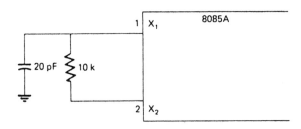

FIGURE 2.12 RC circuit clock source.

The $\overline{\text{RESET IN}}$ signal, when pulsed LOW, causes the 8085 to execute the first instruction at the 0000_{16} location. In addition, the 8085 resets instruction register, interrupt mask (RST5.5, RST6.5, and RST7.5) bits, and other registers. The $\overline{\text{RESET IN}}$ must be held LOW for at least three clock periods. A typical 8085 reset circuit is shown in Figure 2.13. In this circuit, when the switch is activated, $\overline{\text{RESET IN}}$ is driven to LOW with a large time constant providing adequate time to reset the system.

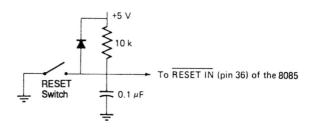

FIGURE 2.13   8085 reset circuit.

The 8085 requires a minimum operating voltage of 4.75 V. Upon applying power, the 8085A attains this voltage after 500 µs. The reset circuit of Figure 2.13 resets the 8085 upon activation of the switch. The voltage across the 0.1-µF capacitor is zero on power-up. The capacitor then charges Vcc after a definite time determined by the time constant RC. The chosen values of RC in the figure will drive the $\overline{\text{RESET IN}}$ pin to low for at least three clock periods. In this case, after activating the switch, $\overline{\text{RESET}}$ $\overline{\text{IN}}$ will be low (assuming capacitance charge time is equal to the discharge time) for 10K*0.1 µF = 1 ms, which is greater than three clock periods (3*1/3 µs = 1 µs) of the 3-MHz 8085A. During normal operation of the 8085, activation of the switch will short the capacitor to ground and will discharge it. When the switch is opened, the capacitor charges and the $\overline{\text{RESET IN}}$ pin becomes HIGH. Upon hardware reset, the 8085 clears PC, IR, HALT flip-flop, and some other registers; the 8085 registers PSW, A, B, C, D, E, H, and L are unaffected. Upon activation of the $\overline{\text{RESET IN}}$ to low, the 8085 outputs HIGH at the RESET OUT pin which can be used to reset the memory and I/O chips connected to the 8085. Note that since hardware reset initializes PC to 0, the 8085 fetches the first instruction for address 0000_{16} after reset.

2.8 8085 INSTRUCTION TIMING AND EXECUTION

An 8085 instruction's execution consists of a number of machine cycles. These cycles vary from one to five (M1 to M5) depending on the instruction. Each machine cycle contains a number of 320-ns clock periods. The first machine cycle will be executed by either four or six clock periods, and the machine cycles that follow will have three clock periods. This is shown in Figure 2.14.

The shaded MCs indicate that these machine cycles are required by certain instructions. Similarly, the shaded clock periods (T5 and T6) mean that they are needed in M1 by some instructions.

The clock periods within a machine cycle can be illustrated as shown in Figure 2.15. Note that the beginning of a new machine cycle is indicated on the 8085 by outputting the Address Latch Enable (ALE) signal HIGH. During this time, lines AD0 to AD7 are used for placing the low byte of the address.

When the ALE signal goes LOW, the low byte of the address is latched so that the AD0 to AD7 lines can be used for transferring data.

We now discuss the timing diagrams for instruction fetch, READ, and WRITE.

FIGURE 2.14 8085 machine cycles.

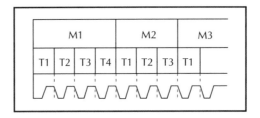

FIGURE 2.15 Clock periods within a machine cycle.

2.8.1 BASIC SYSTEM TIMING

Figure 2.16 shows the 8085 basic system timing. An instruction execution includes two operations: OP code fetch and execution.

The OP code fetch cycle requires either four (for one-byte instructions such as MOV A,B) or six cycles (for 3 byte instructions such as LDA 2030H). The machine cycles that follow will need three clock periods.

The purpose of an instruction fetch is to read the contents of a memory location containing an instruction addressed by the program counter and to place it in the instruction register. The 8085 instruction fetch timing diagram shown in Figure 2.16 can be explained in the following way:

1. The 8085 puts a LOW on the IO/$\overline{M}$ line of the system bus, indicating a memory operation.
2. The 8085 sets S0 = 1 and S1 = 1 on the system bus, indicating the memory fetch operation.
3. The 8085 places the program counter high byte on the A8 to A15 lines and the program counter low byte on the AD0 to AD7 lines of the system bus. The 8085 also sets the ALE signal to HIGH. As soon as the ALE signal goes to LOW, the program counter low byte on the AD0 to AD7 is latched automatically by some 8085 support chips such as 8155 (if 8085 support chips are not used, these lines must be latched using external latches), since these lines will be used as data lines for reading the OP code.
4. At the beginning of T2 in M1, the 8085 puts the $\overline{RD}$ line to LOW indicating a READ operation. After some time, the 8085 loads the OP code (the contents of the memory location addressed by the program counter) into the instruction register.
5. During the T4 clock period in M1, the 8085 decodes the instruction.

The Machine Cycle M2 of Figure 2.16 shows a memory (or I/O) READ operation as seen by the external logic, and the status of the S0 and S1 signals indicates whether the operation is instruction fetch or memory READ; for example, S1 = 1, S0 = 1 during instruction fetch and S1 = 1, S0 = 0 during memory READ provided IO/$\overline{M}$ = 0.

The purpose of the memory READ is to read the contents of a memory location addressed by a register pair, such as the H,L pair, or a memory location specified with the instruction and the data placed in a microprocessor register such as the accumulator. In contrast, the purpose of the memory fetch is to read the contents of a memory location addressed by PC into IR. The machine cycle M3 of Figure 2.16 indicates a memory (or

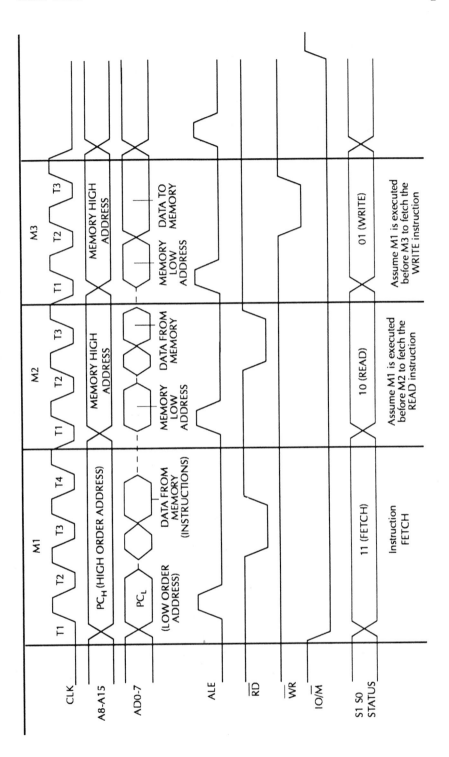

FIGURE 2.16 Basic system timing.

I/O) write operation. In this case, S1 = 0 and S0 = 1 indicate a memory write operation when IO/$\overline{\text{M}}$ = 0 and an I/O write operation when IO/$\overline{\text{M}}$ = 1.

2.8.2 8085 MEMORY READ (IO/$\overline{\text{M}}$ = 0, $\overline{\text{RD}}$ = 0) AND I/O READ (IO/$\overline{\text{M}}$ = 1, $\overline{\text{RD}}$ = 0)

Figure 2.17a shows an 8085A clock timing diagram. The machine cycle of M1 of Figure 2.16 shows a memory READ timing diagram.

The purpose of the memory READ is to read the contents of a memory location addressed by a register pair, such as the accumulator. Let us explain the 8085 memory READ timing diagram of Figure 2.17b along with the READ timing signals of Figure 2.16:

1. The 8085 uses machine cycle M1 to fetch and decode the instruction. It then performs the memory READ operation in M2.
2. The 8085 continues to maintain IO/$\overline{\text{M}}$ at LOW in M2 indicating a memory READ operation (or IO/$\overline{\text{M}}$ = 1 for I/O READ).
3. The 8085 puts S0 = 0, S1 = 1, indicating a READ operation.
4. The 8085 places the contents of the high byte of the memory address register, such as the contents of the H register, on lines A8 to A15.
5. The 8085 places the contents of the low byte of the memory address register, such as the contents of the L register, in lines AD0 to AD7.
6. The 8085 sets ALE to high, indicating the beginning of M1. As soon as ALE goes to low, the memory chip must latch the low byte of the address lines, since the same lines are going to be used as data lines.
7. The 8085 puts the $\overline{\text{RD}}$ signal to LOW, indicating a READ operation.
8. The 8085 gets the data from the memory location addressed by the memory address register, such as the H,L pair, and places the data into a register such as the accumulator. In case of I/O, the 8085 inputs data from the I/O port into the accumulator.

2.8.3 8085 MEMORY WRITE (IO/$\overline{\text{M}}$ = 0, $\overline{\text{WR}}$ = 0) AND I/O WRITE (IO/$\overline{\text{M}}$ = 1, $\overline{\text{WR}}$ = 0)

The machine cycle M3 of Figure 2.16 shows a memory WRITE timing diagram. As seen by the external logic, the signals S0 = 1, S1 = 0, and $\overline{\text{WR}}$ = 0 indicate a memory WRITE operation.

The purpose of a memory WRITE is to store the contents of the 8085 register, such as the accumulator, into a memory location addressed by a pair, such as H,L.

The WRITE timing diagram of Figure 2.16 can be explained as follows:

1. The 8085 uses machine cycle M1 to fetch and decode the instruction. It then executes the memory WRITE instruction in M3.
2. The 8085 continues to maintain IO/$\overline{\text{M}}$ at LOW, indicating a memory operation (or IO/$\overline{\text{M}}$ = 1 for I/O WRITE).
3. The 8085 puts S1 = 0, S1 = 1, indicating a WRITE operation.
4. The 8085 places the Memory Address Register high byte, such as the contents of the H register, on lines A8 to A15
5. The 8085 places the Memory Address Register low byte, such as the contents of L register, on lines AD0 to AD7.
6. The 8085 sets ALE to HIGH, indicating the beginning of M3. As soon as ALE goes to LOW, the memory chip must latch the low byte of the address lines, since the same lines are going to be used as data lines.
7. The 8085 puts the $\overline{\text{WR}}$ signal to LOW, indicating a WRITE operation.
8. It also places the contents of the register, say, accumulator, on data lines AD0 to AD7.
9. The external logic gets data from the lines AD0 to AD7 and stores the data in the memory location addressed by the Memory Address Register, such as the H,L pair. In case of I/O, the 8085 outputs [A] to an I/O port.

Figures 2.17a through c show the 8085A clock and read and write timing diagrams. Table 2.12 lists the various timing parameters.

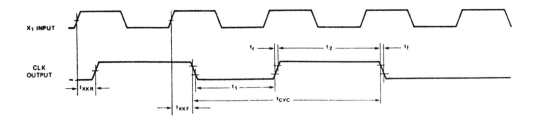

FIGURE 2.17a 8085A clock timing waveform.

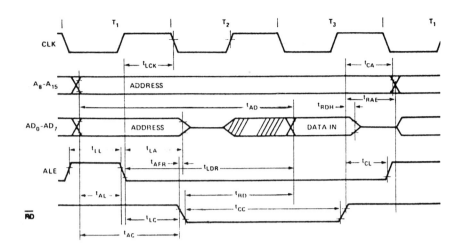

FIGURE 2.17b 8085A read operation.

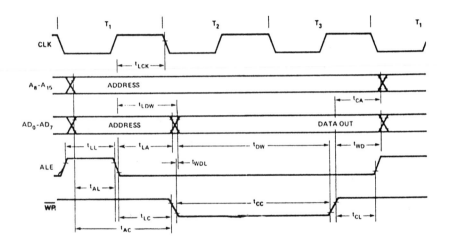

FIGURE 2.17c 8085A write operation.

TABLE 2.12
8085A Timing Parameters in Nanoseconds

	8085A $\left(\dfrac{\text{MAX}}{3.03\ \text{MHz}}\right)$			8085A-2 $\left(\dfrac{\text{MAX}}{5\ \text{MHz}}\right)$	
t_{AL}	—	$(1/2)\,T - 45$	MIN	$(1/2)\,T - 50$	MIN
t_{LA}	—	$(1/2)\,T - 60$	MIN	$(1/2)\,T - 50$	MIN
t_{LL}	—	$(1/2)\,T - 20$	MIN	$(1/2)\,T - 20$	MIN
t_{LCK}	—	$(1/2)\,T - 60$	MIN	$(1/2)\,T - 50$	MIN
t_{LC}	—	$(1/2)\,T - 30$	MIN	$(1/2)\,T - 40$	MIN
t_{AD}	—	$(5/2 + N)\,T - 225$	MAX	$(5/2 + N)\,T - 150$	MAX
t_{RD}	—	$(3/2 + N)\,T - 180$	MAX	$(3/2 + N)\,T - 150$	MAX
t_{RAE}	—	$(1/2)\,T - 10$	MIN	$(1/2)\,T - 10$	MIN
t_{CA}	—	$(1/2)\,T - 40$	MIN	$(1/2)\,T - 40$	MIN
t_{DW}	—	$(3/2 + N)\,T - 60$	MIN	$(3/2 + N)\,T - 70$	MIN
t_{WD}	—	$(1/2)\,T - 60$	MIN	$(1/2)\,T - 40$	MIN
t_{CC}	—	$(3/2 + N)\,T - 80$	MIN	$(3/2 + N)\,T - 70$	MIN
t_{CL}	—	$(1/2)\,T - 110$	MIN	$(1/2)\,T - 75$	MIN
t_{ARY}	—	$(3/2)\,T - 260$	MAX	$(3/2)\,T - 200$	MAX
t_{HACK}	—	$(1/2)\,T - 50$	MIN	$(1/2)\,T - 60$	MIN
t_{HABF}	—	$(1/2)\,T + 50$	MAX	$(1/2)\,T + 50$	MAX
t_{HABE}	—	$(1/2)\,T + 50$	MAX	$(1/2)\,T + 50$	MAX
t_{AC}	—	$(2/2)\,T - 50$	MIN	$(2/2)\,T - 85$	MIN
t_1	—	$(1/2)\,T - 80$	MIN	$(1/2)\,T - 60$	MIN
t_2	—	$(1/2)\,T - 40$	MIN	$(1/2)\,T - 30$	MIN

t_{RV} —   (3/2) T – 80   MIN
t_{LDR} —   (4/2) T – 130   MAX

Note: N is equal to the total WAIT states.
T = t_{CYC}.

t_{RV} —   (3/2) T – 80   MIN
t_{LDR} —   (4/2) T – 180   MAX

Note: N is equal to the total WAIT states.
T = t_{CYC}.

2.9 8085 INPUT/OUTPUT (I/O)

The 8085 I/O transfer techniques are discussed. The 8355/8755 and 8155/8156 I/O ports and 8085 SID and SOD lines are also included.

2.9.1 8085 PROGRAMMED I/O

There are two I/O instructions in the 8085, namely, IN and OUT. These instructions are 2 bytes long. The first byte defines the OP code of the instruction and the second byte specifies the I/O port number. Execution of the IN PORT instruction causes the 8085 to receive one byte of data into the accumulator from a specified I/O port. On the other hand, the OUT PORT instruction, when executed, causes the 8085 to send one byte of data from the accumulator into a specified I/O port.

The 8085 can access I/O ports using either standard I/O or memory-mapped I/O.

In standard I/O, the 8085 inputs or outputs data using IN or OUT instructions.

In memory-mapped I/O, the 8085 maps I/O ports as memory addresses. Hence, LDA addr or STA addr instructions are used to input or output data to or from the 8085. The 8085's programmed I/O capabilities are obtained via the support chips, namely, 8355/8755 and 8155/8156. The 8355/8755 contains a 2K-byte ROM/EPROM and two 8-bit I/O ports (ports A and B).

The 8155/8156 contains 256-byte RAM, two 8-bit and one 6-bit I/O ports, and a 16-bit programmable timer. The only difference between the 8155 and 8156 is that chip enable is LOW on the 8155 and HIGH on the 8156.

2.9.1.a 8355/8755 I/O Ports

Two 8-bit ports are included in the 8355/8755. These are ports A and B. Another 8-bit port, called the data direction register, is associated with each one of these ports. These registers (DDRA and DDRB) can be used to configure each bit in ports A or B as either input or output. For example, a "0" written into a bit position of the data direction register sets up the corresponding bit in the I/O port as input. On the other hand, a "1" written in a particular bit position in the data direction register sets up the corresponding bit in the I/O port as output. For example, consider the following instruction sequence:

```
MVI A, 05H
OUT DDRA
```

The above instruction sequence assumes DDRA as the data direction register for port A. The bits of port A are configured as follows:

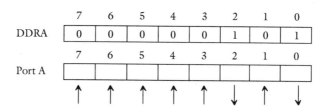

The 8355/8755 uses the IO/$\overline{\text{M}}$ pin on the chip in order to distinguish between standard and memory-mapped I/O. This pin is controlled by the 8085 as shown in Figure 2.18.

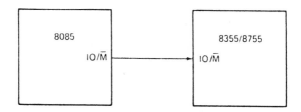

FIGURE 2.18 Interfacing the 8085 with 8355/8755 via the IO/$\overline{\text{M}}$ pin.

The 8085 outputs a HIGH on the IO/$\overline{\text{M}}$ pin when it executes either an IN or OUT instruction. This means that IO/$\overline{\text{M}}$ in the 8355/8755 becomes HIGH after execution of IN or OUT. This, in turn, tells the 8355/8755 to decode the AD1 and AD0 lines in order to obtain the 8-bit address of various ports in the chip as follows:

AD1	AD0	
0	0	Port A
0	1	Port B
1	0	Data Direction Register A
1	1	Data Direction Register B

The other 6 bits of each 8-bit port address are don't care conditions. This means that these bits can be either one or zero. The 8085/8355/8755 standard I/O is illustrated in Figure 2.19.

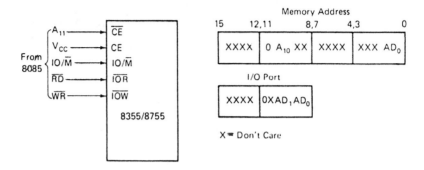

FIGURE 2.19 8355/8755 standard I/O.

Since the 8355/8755 is provided with 2K bytes of memory, 11 address lines A0 to A10 are required for memory addressing. Since the 8085 has 16 address pins A0 to A15, A11 to A15 will not be used for memory addressing. Note that the 8355/8755 includes two chip enables CE and $\overline{CE}$. In Figure 2.19 these two chip enables are connected to Vcc and A11, respectively. It should be pointed out that the 8085 duplicates low and high bytes of the 16-bit address lines with the port address when it executes an IN or OUT instruction. This means that if the 8085 executes IN 01 instruction, it takes 0101_{16} on the 16 address lines. Note that in Figure 2.19, A11 = 0 for both memory and port addressing. This is because A11 = 0 enables this chip. When the 8085 executes an LDA addr or STA addr instruction, IO/$\overline{M}$ becomes LOW. This tells the 8355/8755 to interpret A0 to A10 as memory addresses. On the other hand, when the 8085 executes an IN PORT or OUT PORT instruction, the 8085 drives IO/$\overline{M}$ to HIGH. This tells the 8355/8755 to decode AD1 and AD0 for I/O port addresses. The port addresses are as follows:

| | A15 | A14 | A13 | A12 | A11 | A10 | A9 | A8 | Address |
	AD7	AD6	AD5	AD4	AD3	AD2	AD1	AD0	
Port A =	X	X	X	X	0	X	0	0	$= 00_{16}$
Port B =	X	X	X	X	0	X	0	1	$= 01_{16}$
DDRA =	X	X	X	X	0	X	1	0	$= 02_{16}$
DDRB =	X	X	X	X	0	X	1	1	$= 03_{16}$

X is don't care. Assume X is zero in the above.

Let us now discuss 8355/8755 memory-mapped I/O. Figure 2.20 provides such an example. In Figure 2.20, A11 must be zero for selecting the 8355/8755 and A15 is connected to IO/$\overline{\text{M}}$ of the 8355/8755. When A15 = 1, IO/$\overline{\text{M}}$ becomes HIGH. This tells the 8355/8755 chip to decode AD1 and AD0 for obtaining I/O port addresses. For example, if we assume all don't cares in the I/O port address are 1, then the I/O port addresses will be mapped into memory locations as follows:

Port name	16-bit memory address
I/O port A	$F7FC_{16}$
I/O port B	$F7FD_{16}$
DDRA	$F7FE_{16}$
DDRB	$F7FF_{16}$

Note that in Figure 2.20 memory addresses are mapped as 7000_{16} through $77FF_{16}$ assuming all don't cares to be ones.

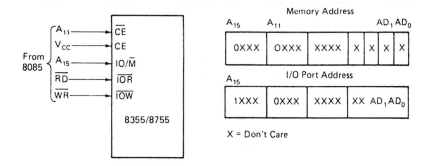

FIGURE 2.20 8355/8755 memory-mapped I/O.

Note that the above port addresses may not physically exist in memory. However, input or output operations with these ports can be accomplished by generating the necessary signals by executing LDA or STA instructions with the above address. For example, outputting to DDRA or DDRB can be accomplished via storing to locations $F7FE_{16}$ or $F7FF_{16}$, respectively. The instructions STA F7FEH or STA F7FFH will generate all of the required signals for OUT DDRA or OUT DDRB, respectively. For example, upon execution of the STA F7FEH, the 8085 sends a LOW to the

$\overline{WR}$ pin and places F7FE16 on the address bus. This will make A15 = 1, A11 = 0, AD1 = 1, AD0 = 0, and thus will make the IO/$\overline{M}$ = 1, $\overline{CE}$ = 0, $\overline{IOW}$ = 0 on the 8355/8755 in Figure 2.20. When ALE goes to LOW, the 8085 places the contents of the accumulator on the AD7 to AD0 pins. The 8355/8755 then takes this data and writes into DDRA. Therefore, STA F7FEH is equivalent to OUT DDRA instruction, although the location F7FEH is nonexistent in 8085-based microcomputer memory map.

2.9.1.b 8155/8156 I/O Ports

The 8155 or 8156 includes 256 bytes of static RAM and three parallel I/O ports. These ports are port A (8-bit), port B (8-bit), and port C (6-bit). By parallel it is meant that all bits of the port are configured as either all input or all output. Bit-by-bit configuration like the 8355/8755 is not permitted. The only difference between the 8155 and 8156 is that the 8155 has LOW chip enable (CE), while the 8156 includes a HIGH chip enable (CE). The 8155/8156 ports are configured by another port called the command status register (CSR). When data are output to CSR via the accumulator, each bit is interpreted as a command bit to set up ports and control timer as shown in Figure 2.21. Port C can be used as a 6-bit parallel port or as a control port to support data transfer between the 8085 and an external device via ports A and B using handshake. Note that handshake means data transfer via exchange of control signals. Two bits (bits 2 and 3) are required in CSR to configure port C. Note that port A interrupt and port B interrupt are associated with handshaking and are different from the 8085 interrupts. For example, port A interrupt is HIGH when data are ready to be transferred using handshaking signals such as port A buffer full and port A strobe. The port A interrupt (PC0 in ALT3) can be connected to an 8085 interrupt pin and data can be transferred to or from the 8085 via port A by executing appropriate instructions in the interrupt service routine.

When the 8085 reads CSR, it accesses the status register and information such as status of handshaking signals and timer interrupt is obtained.

Three bits are used to decode the 8155 six ports (CSR, port A, port B, port C, timer high port, timer low port) as follows:

AD2	AD1	AD0	Port selected
0	0	0	CSR
0	0	1	Port A
0	1	0	Port B
0	1	1	Port C
1	0	0	Timer-low port
1	0	1	Timer-high port

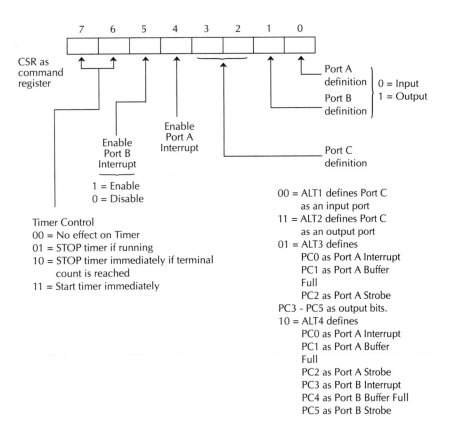

FIGURE 2.21 CSR format as command register.

A typical interface between the 8085 and 8155 is shown in Figure 2.22. Consider Figure 2.22a. Since the 8085 duplicates low byte address bus with the high byte address (i.e., AD7 to AD0 same as A15 to A8 for 8085 standard I/O), the address pins AD2 to AD0 will be the same as A10 to A8. This means that the pins A10 to A8 must not be used as chip enables since they will be used for decoding of port addresses. Therefore, A14 is used as chip enable in the figure. The unused address lines A11 to A13 and A15 are don't cares and are assumed to be zero in the following. Therefore, the port addresses are

A15 AD7	A14 AD6	A13 AD5	A12 AD4	A11 AD3	A10 AD2	A9 AD1	A8 AD0	Address
0	0	0	0	0	0	0	0	= 00H = CSR
0	0	0	0	0	0	0	1	= 01H = Port A

A15	A14	A13	A12	A11	A10	A9	A8	
AD7	AD6	AD5	AD4	AD3	AD2	AD1	AD0	Address
0	0	0	0	0	0	1	0	= 02H
								= Port B
0	0	0	0	0	0	1	1	= 03H
								= Port C

For memory-mapped I/O, consider Figure 2.22b. In this case, the 8085 low byte and high byte address bus are not duplicated. The ports will have 16-bit addresses as follows. Assume the unused address pins A8 to AD3 to be zeros.

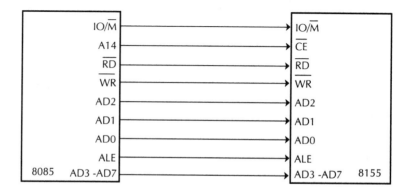

(a) 8085 - 8155 Interface using standard I/O

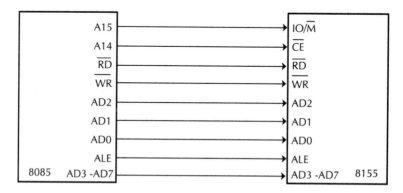

(b) 8085 - 8155 Interface using memory-mapped I/O

FIGURE 2.22 8085-8155 interface for I/O ports.

Port address	AD0	AD1	AD2	AD3	AD4	AD5	AD6	AD7	A8	A9	A10	A11	A12	A13	A14	A15
$= 8000_{16}$ CSR	0	0	0	0	0	0	0	0	0	0	0	0	0	0	0	1
$= 8001_{16}$ (Port A)	1	0	0	0	0	0	0	0	0	0	0	0	0	0	0	1
$= 8002_{16}$ (Port B)	0	1	0	0	0	0	0	0	0	0	0	0	0	0	0	1
$= 8003_{16}$ (Port C)	1	1	0	0	0	0	0	0	0	0	0	0	0	0	0	1

Like the 8355/8755 memory-mapped I/O, the above port addresses may not physically exist in the microcomputer's main memory map. However, read or write operations with them will generate the necessary signals for input or output transfer with the ports. Assuming all don't cares to be zeros, the memory map of either configuration of Figure 2.22a or b includes addresses 0000H through 00FFH.

Example 2.7

An 8085-8355-based microcomputer is required to drive an LED connected to bit 0 of port A based on the input conditions set by a switch on bit 1 of port A. The input/output conditions are as follows: if the input to bit 1 of port A is HIGH then the LED will be turned ON; otherwise the LED will be turned OFF. Assume that a HIGH will turn the LED ON and a LOW will turn it OFF. Write an 8085 assembly language program.

Solution

```
            ORG  5000H
PORT A      EQU  00H
DDRA        EQU  02H
            MVI  A, 01H ; Configure Port A
            OUT  DDRA
START       IN PORT A  ; Input Port A
            RAR         ; Rotate switch to LED position
            OUT  PORT A ; Output to LED
            JMP  START   ; Stop
```

Example 2.8

An 8085-8155-based microcomputer is required to drive an LED connected to bit 0 of port A based on two switch inputs connected to bits 6 and 7 of port A. If both switches are either HIGH or LOW, turn the LED on; otherwise turn it OFF. Assume that a HIGH will turn the LED ON and a LOW will turn it OFF. Use port addresses of CSR and port A as 20_{16} and 21_{16}, respectively.

Write an 8085 assembly language program to accomplish this.

Solution

```
          ORG    3000H
CSR       EQU    20H
PORT A    EQU    21H
START     MVI    A, 00H    ;    Configure Port A
          OUT    CSR       ;    as input
          IN     PORT A    ;    Input Port A
          ANI    COH       ;    Retain bits 6 and 7
          JPE    LEDON     ;    If both switches HIGH,
                           ;    turn LED ON
          MVI    A, 01H    ;    Otherwise, configure
          OUT    CSR       ;    Port A as output
          MVI    A, 00H    ;    and turn LED OFF.
          OUT    PORT A    ;
          JMP    START     ;    Jump to START
LEDON     MVI    A, 01H    ;    Configure Port A as
          OUT    CSR       ;    output
          OUT    PORT A    ;    Turn LED ON
          JMP    START     ;    Jump to START
```

Example 2.9

Write an 8085 assembly language program to turn on an LED connected to bit 4 of the 8155 I/O port B. Use address of port B as 22_{16}.

Solution

```
               ORG    5000H
Port B    EQU    22H
          MVI    A, 02H    ;  Configure
          OUT    CSR       ;  Port B as output
          MVI    A, 10H    ;  Output HIGH
          OUT    PORT B    ;  to LED
          HLT
```

Example 2.10

An 8085-8355-based microcomputer is required to drive a common anode seven-segment display connected to port A as follows:

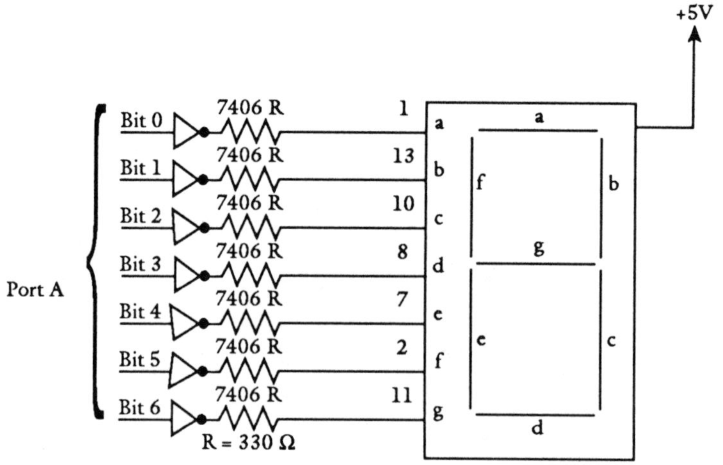

Write an 8085 assembly language program to display a single hexidecimal digit (0 to F) from location 4000_{16}. Use a look-up table. Note that the 7406 shown in the figure contains six inverting buffers on one 7406. Therefore, two 7406 or one 7406 and one transistor are required for the seven segments. Use port addresses of DDRA and port A as 42H and 40H, respectively.

Solution

The decode table can be obtained as follows:

	Bits								
Hex digit	**7**	**6**	**5**	**4**	**3**	**2**	**1**	**0**	**Decode byte**
		g	f	e	d	c	b	a	
0	0	0	1	1	1	1	1	1	3F
1	0	0	0	0	0	1	1	0	06
2	0	1	0	1	1	0	1	1	5B
3	0	1	0	0	1	1	1	1	4F
4	0	1	1	0	0	1	1	0	66
5	0	1	1	0	1	1	0	1	6D
6	0	1	1	1	1	1	0	1	7D
7	0	0	0	0	0	1	1	1	07
8	0	1	1	1	1	1	1	1	7F

Hex digit	Bits								Decode byte
	7	6	5	4	3	2	1	0	
9	0	1	1	0	0	1	1	1	67
A	0	1	1	1	0	1	1	1	77
B	0	1	1	1	1	1	0	0	7C
C	0	0	1	1	1	0	0	1	39
D	0	1	0	1	1	1	1	0	5E
E	0	1	1	1	1	0	0	1	79
F	0	1	1	1	0	0	0	1	71

```
              ORG     5000H
       DDRA   EQU     42H
       Port A         EQU 40H
       MVI    A,7FH
       OUT    DDRA    ;    Port A
       LXI    H,4015H ;    Load HL with
                      ;    starting address of table
       LXI    D,0000H ;    Load 0000H to DE
       LDA    DIGIT   ;    Load digit to be
                      ;    On into A
       MOV    E,A     ;    Move digit to E
       DAD    D       ;    Determine digit address
       MOV    A,M     ;    Load decode byte to A
       OUT    Port A  ;    Outport decode byte
       HLT            ;    to display
              ORG     4015H
TABLE  DB     3FH, 06H, 5BH, 4FH
       DB     66H, 6DH, 7DH, 07H
       DB     7FH, 67H, 77H, 7CH
       DB     39H, 5EH, 79H, 71H
              ORG     4000H
DIGIT  DB     DATA
```

2.9.2 8085 INTERRUPT SYSTEM

The 8085 chip has five interrupt pins, namely, TRAP, RST7.5, RST6.5, RST5.5, and INTR. If the signals on these interrupt pins go to HIGH simultaneously, then TRAP will be serviced first (i.e., highest priority) followed by RST7.5, RST6.5, RST5.5, and INTR. Note that once an interrupt is serviced, all the interrupts except TRAP are disabled. They can be enabled by executing the Enable Interrupts (EI) instruction.

1. TRAP — TRAP is a nonmaskable interrupt. That is, it cannot be disabled by an instruction. In order for the 8085 to service this interrupt, the signal on the TRAP pin must have a sustained HIGH level with a leading edge. If this condition occurs, then the 8085 completes execution of the current instruction, pushes the program counter onto the stack, and branches to location 0024_{16} (interrupt address vector for the TRAP). Note that the TRAP interrupt is disabled by the falling edge of the signal on the pin.

2. RST7.5 — RST7.5 is a maskable interrupt. This means that it can be enabled or disabled using the SIM instruction. The 8085 responds to the RST7.5 interrupt when the signal on the RST7.5 pin has a leading edge. In order to service RST7.5, the 8085 completes execution of the current instruction, pushes the program counter onto the stack, and branches to 003C16. The 8085 remembers the RST7.5 interrupt by setting an internal D flip-flop by the leading edge.

3. RST6.5 — RST6.5 is a maskable interrupt. It can be enabled or disabled using the SIM instruction. RST6.5 is HIGH level sensitive. In order to service this interrupt, the 8085 completes execution of the current instruction, saves the program counter onto the stack, and branches to location 0034_{16}.

4. RST5.5 — RST5.5 is a maskable interrupt. It can be enabled or disabled by the SIM instruction. RST5.5 is HIGH level sensitive. In order to service this interrupt, the 8085 completes execution of the current instruction, saves the program counter onto the stack, and branches to 0020_{16}.

5. INTR — INTR is a maskable interrupt. This is also called the handshake interrupt. INTR is HIGH level sensitive. When no other interrupts are active and the signal on the INTR pin is HIGH, the 8085 completes execution of the current instruction, and generates an interrupt acknowledge, INTA, LOW pulse on the control bus. The 8085 then expects either a 1-byte CALL (RST0 through RST7) or a 3-byte CALL. This instruction must be provided by external hardware. In other words, the INTA can be used to enable a tristate buffer. The output of this buffer can be connected to the 8085 data lines. The buffer can be designed to provide the appropriate op code on the data lines. Note that the occurrence of INTA turns off the 8085 interrupt system in order to avoid multiple interrupts from a single device. Also note that there are eight RST instructions (RST0 through RST7). Each of these RST instructions has a vector address. These were shown in Table 2.9.

Let us now identify the characteristics of an interrupt acknowledge (INTA) machine cycle. The INTA machine cycle is the same as the instruction fetch cycle with the following differences:

1. The 8085 generates an INTA pulse rather than MEMR pulse. An RST instruction is then fetched and executed.
2. The 8085 does not increment the program counter contents in order to return to the proper location after servicing the interrupt.
3. The generation of INTA disables the 8085 interrupt capability in order to avoid multiple interrupts.

The interrupt acknowledge timing diagram is shown in Figure 2.23a and 2.23b. In response to a HIGH on the INTR, the 8085 proceeds with the sequence of events shown in Figure 2.23a and 2.23b, if the 8085 system interrupt is enabled by the EI instruction. Before the MC1.T1 cycle, the 8085 checks all the interrupts. If INTR is the only interrupt and if the 8085 system interrupt is enabled, the 8085 will turn off the system interrupt and then make the INTA LOW for about two T-states (T2 and T3 cycles of MC1 in Figure 2.23a). This INTA signal can be used to enable an external hardware to provide an op code on the data bus. The 8085 can then read this op code. Typically, the 1-byte RST or 3-byte CALL instruction can be used as the op code. If the 3-byte CALL is used, then the 8085 will generate two additional INTA cycles in order to fetch all 3 bytes of the instruction. However, on the other hand, if RST is used, then no additional INTA is required. Figures 2.23a and 2.23b show that in response to INTA, a CALL op code is generated on the data bus during MC1. The call op code could have been placed there by a device like the 8259 programmable interrupt controller. At this point, only the op code for the CALL (CD16) is fetched by the 8085. The 8085 executes this instruction and determines that it needs two more bytes (the address portion of the 3-byte instruction). The 8085 then generates a second INTA cycle in MC2 followed by a third INTA cycle in MC3 in order to fetch the address portion of the CALL instruction from the 8259. The 8085 executes the CALL instruction and branches to the interrupt service routine located at an address specified in the CALL instruction. Note that the 8085 does not increment the program counter contents during the three INTA cycles so that the appropriate program counter value is pushed in the stack during MC4 and MC5. Also note that the recognition of any maskable interrupt (RST7.5,

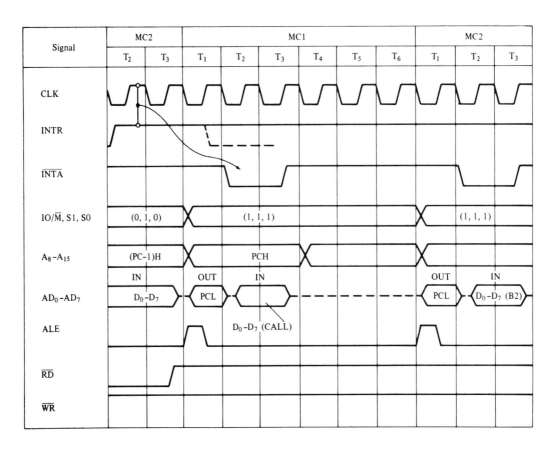

FIGURE 2.23a Interrupt acknowledge machine cycles (with CALL instruction in response to INTR).

RST6.5, RST5.5, and INTR) disables all maskable interrupts.

Therefore, in order that the 8085 can accept another interrupt, the last two instructions of the interrupt service routine will be EI followed by RET.

One can produce a single RST instruction, say RST7 (op code FF in HEX), using 74LS244. The inputs I0 to I7 of the 74LS244 (Figure 2.24) are connected to HIGH and its enable line ($\overline{OE}$) is tied to a $\overline{INTA}$. In response to $\overline{INTA}$ LOW, the 74LS244 places FF in hex (RST7) on the data bus. Figure 2.24 shows a typical circuit.

An 8-to-3 encoder such as the 74LS148 (Figure 2.25) can be used along with the 74LS244 in order to generate all eight RST instructions. This is shown in Figure 2.25. The encoder generates active LOW outputs. This means that if the input R4 is connected to the 74LS148, the encoder converts the 3-bit binary code $100_2(4)$ into $011_2(3)$.

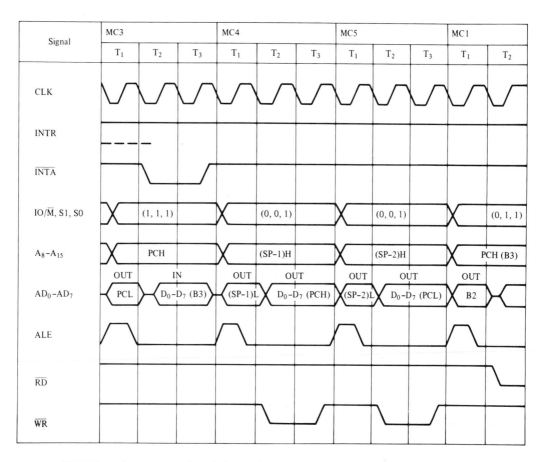

FIGURE 2.23b Interrupt acknowledge machine cycles (with CALL instruction in response to INTR).

As mentioned before, the op code for RST instruction is

```
11 CCC   111
         where CCC is   000 for RST0
                        001 for RST1
                        010 for RST2
                        011 for RST3
                        100 for RST4
                        101 for RST5
                        110 for RST6
                        111 for RST7
```

In the above circuit, the output of the encoder Q2, Q1, Q0 provides CCC for the RST instruction.

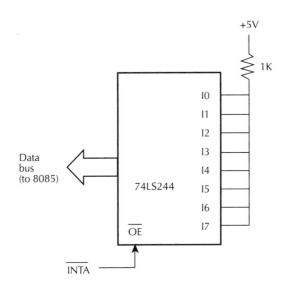

FIGURE 2.24 Using an octal buffer to provide RST7 instruction.

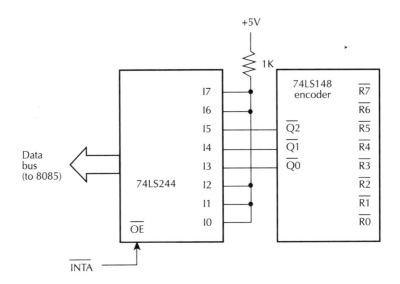

FIGURE 2.25 Forming eight RST instructions with a priority encoder.

Table 2.13 provides a summary of the 8085 interrupts and the regular RST instructions. Figure 2.26 shows the 8085 interrupt structure. Now in Figure 2.25 the encoder provides three active-low output bits to a 74LS244. The purpose is to place one of the eight RST instructions on the data bus of the 8085 in response to the $\overline{INTA}$ signal. Note that in Figure 2.25 the inputs to the encoder should be synchronized to $\overline{INTA}$ in order to avoid any erratic results. Now, we know that the inputs and outputs of a 74LS148 encoder are active LOW. As a result, a LOW level on input R0 produces the RST7 instruction (op code FF16) and input R7 produces the RST0 instruction (op code $C7_{16}$) which has the same address as RESET. The encoder only differentiates between simultaneous active inputs and produces an output which corresponds to the highest priority input.

Let us elaborate on Figure 2.26. Execution of the EI instruction sets the RS flip-flop of Figure 2.26 and makes one of the inputs to the AND gates #1 through #4 HIGH. Hence, in order for all the interrupts (except

TABLE 2.13
Summary of 8085 Interrupts and Regular RST Instructions

Instruction or input	op code (hex)	Vector address (hex)
RST0	C7	0000
RST1	CF	0008
RST2	D7	0010
RST3	DF	0018
RST4	E7	0020
TRAP	Hardware interrupt	0024
RST5	EF	0028
RST5.5	Hardware interrupt	002C
RST6	F7	0030
RST6.5	Hardware interrupt	0034
RST7	FF	0038
RST7.5	Hardware interrupt	003C

TRAP) to work, the interrupt system must be enabled. Execution of Disable Interrupts (DI) clears the RS flip-flop and disables all interrupts except TRAP. The SIM instruction outputs the contents of the accumulator which can be interpreted as shown in Figure 2.27. The interrupt mask function is only executed if the mask set enable bit is 1. Suppose that if 06_{16} is stored in the accumulator and the SIM instruction is executed, 1 will be sent to the interrupt mask for RST7.5 and RST6.5, and 0 will be sent to RST5.5. That is, in Figure 2.26, 1 will be sent to the inputs of the AND gates #1 and #2, and 0 will be sent to the AND gate #3, then inverted at the AND gate inputs (shown by circles), giving two LOW outputs dis-

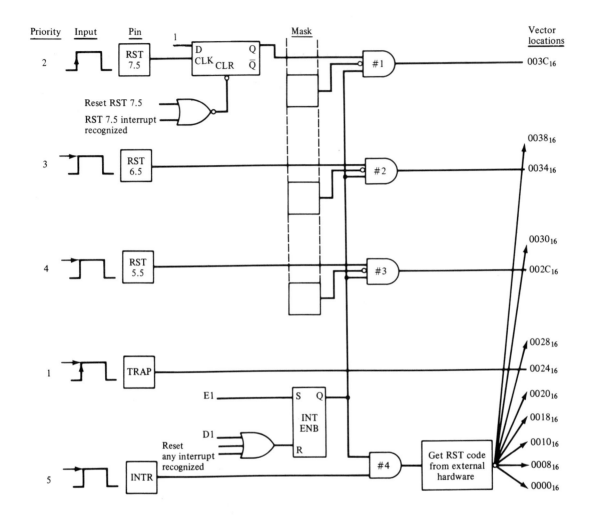

FIGURE 2.26 8085 interrupt structure.

abling RST7.5, RST6.5, and a HIGH input to AND gate #3. Therefore, in order to enable RST7.5, RST6.5, or RST5.5, the interrupt system must be enabled, the appropriate interrupt mask bit must be LOW, and the appropriate interrupt signal (leading edge or high level) at the respective pins must be available. For example, consider the RST7.5 interrupt. When the EI and SIM instructions are executed, the interrupt system can be enabled and also the interrupt mask bit for RST7.5 can be set to LOW, making the two inputs to AND gate #1 HIGH. The third input to this AND gate can be set to a HIGH by a leading edge at the RST7.5 pin. This sets the D flip-flop, thus making the output of the AND gate #1 HIGH, enabling the RST7.5. The 8085 branches to location $003C_{16}$ where a 3-byte JMP instruction takes the program to the service routine. The RST5.5 and RST6.5 can similarly be explained from Figure 2.26.

From Figure 2.26 it can also be seen that a leading edge and a HIGH level at the TRAP interrupt pin take the 8085 to location 0024_{16} where a 3-byte CALL can be executed to go to the service routine. Note that TRAP cannot be disabled by any instruction and is nonmaskable.

Finally, if the INTR is HIGH and the interrupt system is enabled, the output of the AND gate #4 is HIGH, interrupting the 8085. After executing the current instruction, the 8085 puts the $\overline{INTA}$ signal to a LOW. As mentioned before, this LOW at the $\overline{INTA}$ can be used to enable an external device such as the 74LS244 to provide an RST code on the 8085 data lines.

The RIM instruction can be used to check whether one or more of the RST7.5, RST6.5, and RST5.5 interrupts are waiting to be serviced. The RIM instruction also provides the mask bits for RST7.5, RST6.5, and RST5.5 and the status of the SID pin (HIGH or LOW). After execution of the RIM instruction, the 8085 loads the accumulator with 8 bits of data which can be interpreted as shown in Figure 2.28.

The bits are interpreted as follows:

Mask bits — Bits 0, 1, and 2 are the status of the mask bits for RST5.5, RST6.5, and RST7.5.

Interrupt Enable bit — This bit indicates whether one maskable interrupt capability is enabled (if this bit = 1) or disabled (if this bit = 0).

Interrupt Pending bits — A one in a particular bit position indicates that the particular RST is waiting to be serviced, while a 0 indicates that no interrupt is pending.

Serial Input data — These data indicate the status of the SID pin.

The 8085 disables the maskable interrupt handling capability by internally executing a DI instruction automatically when it services a maskable interrupt. This is done in order to avoid multiple interrupts from the same device when executing a service routine. The RIM instruction can be used to read the interrupt pending bits in the accumulator. These bits can then be checked by software to determine whether any higher priority interrupts are pending. For example, suppose that RST6.5 and RST5.5 interrupts are used in a system. If RST5.5 interrupt first occurs, assuming no other higher level interrupts, the 8085 will execute the RST5.5 service routine. Note that while in this service routine, the RST6.5 interrupt (higher priority than

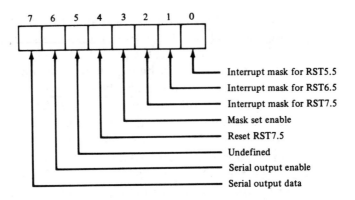

FIGURE 2.27 Interpretation of data output by the SIM instruction.

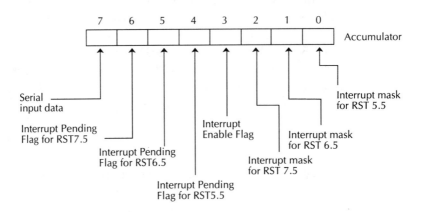

FIGURE 2.28 Execution of RIM instruction.

RST5.5 interrupt) may occur. Since the 8085's maskable interrupt capability is disabled, the user can check whether the RST6.5 is pending while executing the RST5.5 service routine in one of two ways:

- By executing EI at the beginning of the RST5.5 service routine provided that the level at RST5.5 pin is LOW (RST5.5 disabled). This will service the RST6.5 immediately if pending and will then complete RST5.5 service routine.
- By executing RIM and using rotate instruction to check whether

RST6.5 is pending. The RIM instruction can be executed at several places in the RST5.5 service routine. If the RST6.5 is found to be pending, the interrupt can be enabled by executing EI in the RST5.5 service routine.

Example 2.11

Design the interface hardware using a simplified block diagram between the 8085-based microcomputer and A/D converter. Use RST6.5 interrupt first and then repeat the example using INTR (say RST6) interrupt.

Solution

The A/D converter used is the Teledyne 8703 8-bit with tristate outputs. The timing diagrams of the Teledyne 8703 A/D Converter can be drawn from the manufacturer's specification as shown in Figure 2.29a. The 8085 can be programmed to send an INITIATE CONVERSION pulse to the 8703 for at least 500 ns. This can be accomplished by sending a HIGH and then a LOW to the INITIATE CONVERSION pin of the 8703. Either the DATA VALID or the BUSY signal can be connected to the interrupt pin (RST6.5 or INTR in this example) of the 8085 to interrupt the processor after the conversion is complete.

Figure 2.29b shows the interfacing of the 8703 A/D to the 8085-based microcomputer using RST6.5 and data valid signals. In the interface circuit, the 8085 can be programmed to send a HIGH output through bit 0 of port B and a LOW output through bit 0 of port B to provide the INITIATE CONVERSION pulse for at least 500 ns. The 8085 then waits for the DATA VALID signal to go to a LOW, indicating the conversion is complete. This waiting can be accomplished using the HLT instruction in the program. When the DATA VALID signal goes to a LOW, and the RST6.5 is unmasked and enabled, the 8085 will be interrupted. The 8085 will complete the current instruction and branch to location 0034_{16} where a 3-byte JMP instruction can be placed to branch to the interrupt service routine. The first few instructions of the service routine will be to send a LOW output through bit 1 of port B to enable the output of the A/D converter. Then the 8085 can be programmed to input the A/D converter output through port A.

Note that the 8703 latches the data when the DATA VALID signal goes to a HIGH after 5 μs. Therefore, the data must be input into the 8085 5 μs after the occurrence of the interrupt. In the above, the duration between the occurrence of the interrupt and the outputting of the A/D output into the 8085 is much more than 5 μs.

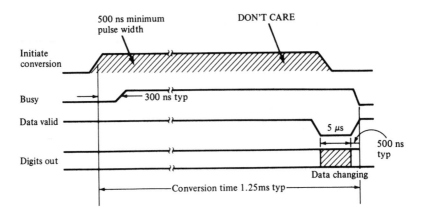

FIGURE 2.29a   8703 timing diagram.

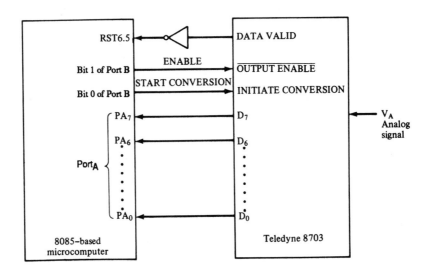

FIGURE 2.29b   Interfacing 8703 to 8085 using DATA VALID signal.

Next we consider using the INTR and the DATA VALID signals.
**Using the 8085 INTR (RST 6) interrupt and the DATA VALID
signal** — The hardware interface can be designed as shown in Figure 2.30.
In Figure 2.30 as before, the 8085 can be programmed to send a HIGH
output through bit 0 of port B and a LOW output through bit 0 of port
B to provide the INITIATE CONVERSION pulse. The HLT instruction
can then be used in the program for the 8085 to wait until the conversion

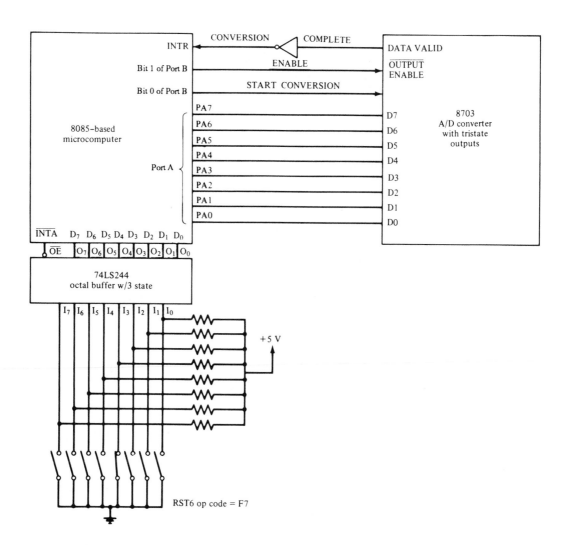

FIGURE 2.30 8085-8703 schematic.

is complete. As soon as the DATA VALID signal goes to a LOW, indicating the conversion is complete, the INTR is set to a HIGH. Now, if the interrupt is enabled, the 8085 will be interrupted. The processor will complete the current instruction and will output the interrupt acknowledge ($\overline{\text{INTA}}$) LOW, which will enable the 74LS244 tristate buffer where the op code for RST6 (F7_{16}) can be placed by means of DIP switches. Thus, upon enabling the 74LS244 by the $\overline{\text{INTA}}$ signal, the RST6 instruction will be strobed onto the data lines. This will cause the processor to jump to location 8085 where a 3-byte CALL instruction can be executed to branch to the interrupt service routine. The interrupt service routine can be written to send a LOW output through bit 1 of port B to enable the $\overline{\text{OUTPUT}}$ $\overline{\text{ENABLE}}$ and then input the 8-bit A/D output through the I/O port A. Note that as in the RST6.5, the duration between the occurrence of the INTR and inputting of the A/D output into the 8085 is much more than 5 μs. This means that the A/D output is input into the 8085 after the 8703 latches the data.

2.9.3 8085 DMA

The Intel 8257 DMA controller chip is a 40-pin DIP and is programmable. It is compatible with the 8080/8085 microprocessor. The 8257 is a four-channel DMA controller with priority logic built into the chip. This means that the 8257 provides for DMA transfers for a maximum of up to four devices via the DMA request lines DRQ0 to DRQ3 (DRQ0 has the highest priority and DRQ3 the lowest). Associated with each DRQ is a DMA acknowledge ($\overline{\text{DACK0}}$ to $\overline{\text{DACK3}}$ for four DMA requests DRQ0 to DRQ3). Note that the $\overline{\text{DACK}}$ signals are active LOW. The 8257 uses the 8080/8085 HOLD pin in order to take over the system bus. After initializing the 8257 by the 8080/8085, the 8257 performs the DMA operation in order to transfer a block of data of up to 16,384 bytes between the memory and a peripheral without involving the microprocessor. A typical 8085-8257 interface is shown in Figure 2.31. An I/O device, when enabled by the 8085, can request a DMA transfer by raising the DMA request (DRQ) line of one of the channels of the 8257. In response, the 8257 will send a HOLD request (HRQ) to the 8085. The 8257 waits for the HOLD acknowledge (HLDA) from the 8085. On receipt of HLDA from the 8085, the 8257 generates a LOW on the DACK lines for the I/O device. Note that DACK is used as a chip select bit for the I/O device. The 8257 sends the READ or WRITE control signals, and data are transferred between the I/O and memory. On completion of the data transfer, the DACK0 is set to HIGH, and the HRQ line is reset to LOW in order to transfer control of the bus to the 8085. The 8257 utilizes four clock cycles in order to transfer 8 bits of data.

The 8257 has three main registers. These are a 16-bit DMA address register, a terminal count register, and a status register. Both address and terminal count registers must be initialized before a DMA operation. The DMA address register is initialized with the starting address of the memory to be written into or read from. The low-order 14 bits of the terminal

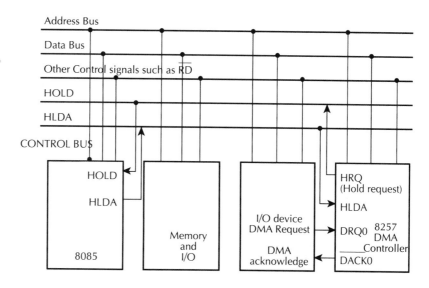

FIGURE 2.31 An 8085-8257 interface.

count register are initialized with the value $(n - 1)$, where n is the desired number of DMA cycles. A Terminal Count (TC) pin on the 8257 is set to HIGH in order to indicate to the peripheral device that the present DMA cycle is the last cycle. An 8-bit status register in the 8257 is used to indicate which channels have attained a terminal count.

2.9.4 8085 SID AND SOD LINES

Serial I/O is extensively used for data transfer between a peripheral device and the microprocessor. Since microprocessors perform internal operations in parallel, conversion of data from parallel to serial and vice versa is required to provide communication between the microprocessor and the serial I/O. The 8085 provides serial I/O capabilities via SID (Serial Input Data) and SOD (Serial Output Data) lines.

One can transfer data to or from the SID or SOD lines using the instruction RIM and SIM. After executing the RIM instruction, the bits in the accumulator are interpreted as follows:

1. Serial input bit is bit 7 of the accumulator.
2. Bits 0 to 6 are interrupt masks, the interrupt enable bit, and pending interrupts.

The SIM instruction sends the contents of the accumulator to the interrupt mask register and serial input line. Therefore, before executing the SIM, the accumulator must be loaded with proper data. The contents of the accumulator are interpreted as follows:

1. Bit 7 of the accumulator is the serial output bit.
2. The SOD enable bit is bit 6 of the accumulator. This bit must be 1 in order to output bit 7 of the accumulator to the SOD line.
3. Bits 0 to 5 are interrupt masks, enables, and resets.

Example 2.12

An 8085/8155-based microcomputer is required to input a switch via the SID line and output the switch status to an LED connected to the SOD line. Write an 8085 assembly language program to accomplish this.

Solution

```
        ORG    5000H
START   RIM           ; Bit 7 of 'A' is SID
        ORI    40H    ; Set SOD Enable to one
        SIM           ; output to LED
        JMP    START  ; REPEAT
```

2.10 8085-BASED SYSTEM DESIGN

In order to illustrate the concepts associated with 8085-based system design, a microcomputer with 2K EPROM (2716), 256 byte RAM, and 3 ports (8155) is designed. A hardware schematic is included. Also, an 8085 assembly language program is provided to multiply 4-bit numbers entered via DIP switches connected to port A. The 8-bit product is displayed on two seven-segment displays interfaced via port B. Repeated addition will be used for multiplication. Figure 2.32 shows a schematic of the hardware design. Full decoding using the 74LS138 decoder is utilized. Texas Instruments TIL 311's displays with on-chip decoder are used. The memory and I/O maps are given in the following:

1.   Memory map

2716

A15 A14 A13 A12 A11 A10 A9   A8   AD7 AD6 AD5 AD4 AD3 AD2 AD1 AD0
0   0   0   0   0   {--------------------------all ones or zeros------------------------}

Result 0000H-07FFH

8155

A15 A14 A13 A12 A11 A10 A9   A8   AD7 AD6 AD5 AD4 AD3 AD2 AD1 AD0
0   0   0   0   1   0   0   0   {---------------all ones or zeros--------------}

Result 0800H-08FFH

2.   I/O map using standard I/O

Ports

A15	A14	A13	A12	A11	A10	A9	A8		
AD7	AD6	AD5	AD4	AD3	AD2	AD1	AD0		
0	0	0	0	1	0	0	0	CSR	08H
0	0	0	0	1	0	0	1	Port A	09H
0	0	0	0	1	0	1	0	Port B	0AH
0	0	0	0	1	0	1	1	Port C	0BH

A listing of the 8085 assembly language program for performing 4 bit × 4 bit multiplication is provided below:

```
CSR     EQU  08H
PORT A  EQU  09H
PORT B  EQU  0AH
REPEAT  MVI  A,02H   ; Configure Port A as input
        OUT  CSR     ; and Port B as output
        MVI  L,00H   ; Initialize product to zero
        IN   Port A  ; Input multiplier and
                       multiplicand
```

```
            MOV    B,A      ; Save multiplicand and
                              multiplier in B
            ANI    0FH      ; Mask multiplicand and retain
                                  multiplier
            MOV    C,A      ; Save 4-bit multiplier in C
            MOV    A,B      ; Move multiplicand and
                              multiplier to A
            RAR             ; Move 4-bit multiplicand
            RAR             ; (upper nibble of A)
            RAR             ; into LOW nibble
            RAR             ; of
                            ; accumulator
            ANI    0FH      ; Mask high nibble and retain
                              multiplicand
    START   ADD    L        ; Perform repeated addition
            DCR    C        ; Decrement multiplier value
            JNZ    START    ; if Z=0, repeat addition
                            ; else product in L
            MOV    A,L      ; Move product to A
            ANI    0FH      ; Retain product LOW nibble and
            MOV    H,A      ; Save in H
            MOV    A,L      ; Move product to A
            RAR             ; Move
            RAR             ; high nibble
            RAR             ; of product
            RAR             ; to LOW nibble
                            ; of A
            ANI    2FH      ; Retain high nibble of product
                              and enable latch
            OUT    PORT B   ; of high hex display and
                              disable low latch
                            ; Display high nibble of
                              product
            MOV    A,H      ; Move LOW product nibble to A
            ANI    1FH      ; Enable LOW latch and disable
                              high latch
            OUT    PORT B   ; Display LOW nibble of product
            JMP    REPEAT   ; On low display and continue
```

The above program can be assembled. The 2716 can then be programmed by using an EPROM programmer with the machine code of the

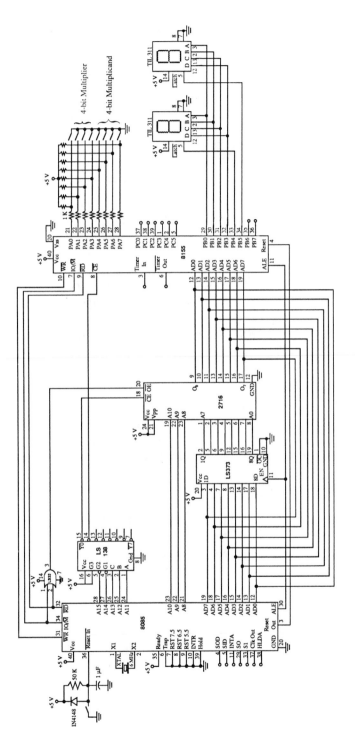

FIGURE 2.32 8085-based system design.

preceding program starting at location 0000H. Then upon activation of the switch at the 8085 reset input, the dip switch low and high nibbles will be multiplied and the result of the multiplication will be displayed on the two TIL311s. By changing DIP switch inputs at port A, new results can be displayed.

QUESTIONS AND PROBLEMS

2.1   i)   Summarize the basic differences between 8080 and 8085.

         ii)   Compare the main differences of 8085AH, 8085AH-2, and 8085AH-1 with the 8085.

2.2   What is the primary purpose of the 8085 H-L pair with respect to external memory? List two of its main functions.

2.3   Identify the addressing modes of the following instructions:

         i)   MOV A, M

         ii)   RAR

         iii) STAX D

         iv) LDA START

2.4   Assume register pair BC contains $7F02_{16}$. For the following 8085 assembly language program, determine the carry, zero, parity, and sign flags after execution of the M V I A, 05H instruction:

```
ORG    4000H
LXI    SP, 2050H
PUSH   B
MVI    A,02H
ADI    03H
POP    PSW
MVI    A,  05H
HLT
```

2.5   What function is performed by each of the following 8085 instructions:

         i)   **XOR A**

         ii)   **MOV D,D**

         iii) **DAD H**

2.6 i) What is the function of the 8085 ALE pin?

ii) If a crystal of 4 MHz is connected to the 8085 X1X2 pins, what is the 8085 internal clock period?

2.7 Write an 8085 assembly language program to divide an 8-bit unsigned number in accumulator by 4. Neglect remainder. Use minimum number of instructions. Store result in A.

2.8 Using the simplest possible algorithm, write an 8085 assembly language program with minimum number of instructions to divide a 16-bit unsigned number in DE by 16. Neglect remainder. Store result in DE.

2.9 Assume the contents of DE are 2050H. Write an 8085 assembly language program to unconditionally branch to 2050H. Do not use any conditional or unconditional Jump or CALL or return instructions. Use three instructions maximum.

2.10 Write an 8085 assembly language program using minimum number of instructions to add the 16-bit numbers in BC, DE, and HL. Store the 16-bit result in DE.

2.11 Write an 8085 assembly language program to add two 24-bit numbers located in memory address 2000_{16} through 2005_{16} with the most significant byte of the first number in 2000_{16} and the most significant byte of the second number in 2003_{16}. Store the 24-bit result in three consecutive bytes starting at address 2000_{16}.

2.12 Write a subroutine in 8085 assembly language to divide a 16-bit unsigned number in BC by 32_{10}. Neglect the remainder. Use the simplest possible algorithm. Also, write the main program in 8085 assembly language to perform all the initializations. The main program will then call the subroutine, store the 16-bit quotient in DE, and stop.

2.13 Write an 8085 assembly language program to shift the contents of the 8085 DE register twice to left without using any ROTATE instructions. After shifting, if the contents of DE are nonzero, store $FFFF_{16}$ in HL pair. On the other hand, if the contents of DE pair are zero, then store 0000_{16} in HL pair.

2.14 Write an 8085 assembly language program to check the parity of an 8-bit number in "A" without using any instructions involving the parity flag. Store EE16 in location 3000_{16} if the parity is even; otherwise, store DD16 in location 3000_{16}.

2.15 Write an 8085 assembly language program to move a block of data of length 100_{10} from the source block starting at 2000_{16} to the destination block starting at 3000_{16}.

2.16 Write a subroutine in 8085 assembly language to divide an 8-bit unsigned number Xi by 2. Also, write the main program in 8085 assembly language which will call the subroutine to compute

$$\sum_{i=1}^{3} Xi / 2$$

Store the result in location 5000_{16}. Use minimum number of instructions.

2.17 Assume an 8085/8355-based microcomputer. Suppose that four switches are connected to bits 0 through 3 of port A, an LED to bit 4 of port A, and another LED to bit 2 of port B. If the number of low switches is even, turn the port A LED ON and port B LED OFF. If the number of low switches is odd, turn port A LED OFF and port B LED ON. Write an 8085 assembly language program to accomplish the above.

2.18 Draw a simplified diagram using an 8085, one 8156, and one 8355 to include the following memory map and I/O ports:
  i)   *8355*   *8156*
        2000_{16} thru $27FF_{16}$ 4000_{16} thru $40FF_{16}$
  ii)   Using memory-mapped I/O, configure ports A and B of 8355 as addresses 8000_{16} and 8001_{16}. Show only connections for the lines which are pertinent.

2.19 It is desired to interface a pump to a 8085/8355/8156-based microcomputer. The pump will be started by the microcomputer at the trailing edge of a start pulse via the SOD pin. When the pump runs, a HIGH status signal from the pump called "Pump Running" will be used to interrupt the microcomputer via its INTR interrupt. In response, the microcomputer will turn an LED on connected to bit 7 of the 8355 port A. Assume DDRA as the data direction register for this port.
  i)   Draw a simplified schematic for accomplishing the above.
  ii) Write the main and interrupt service routines using the 8085 assembly language programs.

2.20

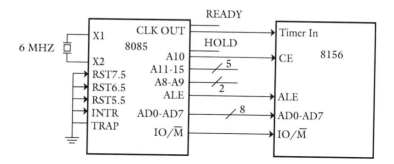

Will the above circuit work? If so, determine the memory and I/O. Maps in Hex? If not, justify briefly and then modify the above circuit and then determine the memory and I/O maps. Use only the pins and signals as shown. Also, assume all don't cares to be zeros.

2.21

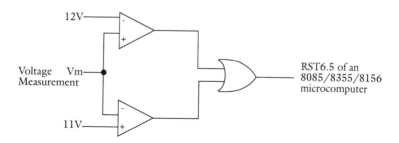

In the above, if Vm > 12 V, turn an LED ON connected at bit 3 of port A. On the other hand, if Vm < 11 V, turn the LED OFF. Use ports, registers, and memory locations as needed.

    i)   Draw a hardware block diagram showing the microcomputer and the connections of the above diagram to its ports.

    ii)   Write service routines in 8085 assembly language.

2.22 Interface the following 8156 RAM chip to obtain the following memory map: 0400H thru 04FFH.

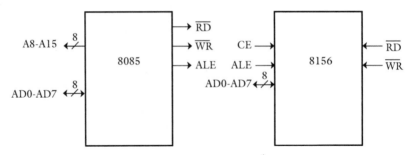

Show only the connections for the pins which are shown. Assume all unused address lines to be zero.

2.23

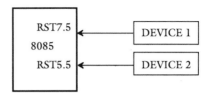

If device 2 is presently being serviced by the 8085 and the device 1 interrupt occurs, explain briefly what the user needs to do in the service routine of device 2 in order that device 1 will be serviced before device 2.

2.24 Assume an 8085/8355 microcomputer. Suppose that two switches are connected to bit 1 of Port A and the SID line. Also, an LED is connected to the SOD line. It is desired to turn the LED ON if both switches are HIGH; otherwise the LED is to be turned off. Write an 8085 assembly language program to input both switches and turn the LED ON or OFF based on the above conditions.

2.25 It is desired to interface a pump and an A/D converter to an 8085/8355/8156-based microcomputer as follows:

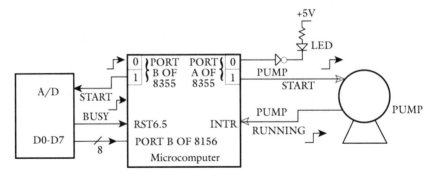

The pump can be started by a HIGH at the pump start signal. If the pump starts, the pump-running signal goes to HIGH; otherwise the pump running stays LOW. The A/D converter can be started by a HIGH and the conversion is completed when the Busy signal is HIGH. Start the pump and A/D converter nearly at the same time. If the pump runs, the LED is to be turned on. On the other hand, if the Busy signal goes to HIGH, the A/D converter's output is to be read.

     i)   Draw a simplified hardware schematic to accomplish the above.

     ii)   Write main program and service routines in 8085 assembly language. Include the interrupt priority concept in the programs.

2.26   Assume an 8085/8355-based microcomputer. Write an 8085 assembly language program to turn an LED (LED 1) ON connected to bit 3 of port A if a 16-bit number in DE register pair is negative after shifting once to the left; if the number is positive after shifting, turn the LED (LED 1) OFF. Also, after shifting, if there is a sign change of the 16-bit number, turn another LED (LED 2) ON connected to bit 1 of port A; otherwise, turn the LED (LED 2) OFF.

2.27   Design an 8085/2716/8155-based microcomputer to obtain the following:

     i)   4K EPROM, 512 bytes static RAM, four 8-bit and two 6-bit ports. Use standard I/O and linear decoding.

     ii)   Repeat i) except use fully decoding using a 3×8 decoder.

     iii) Repeat i) except use memory-mapped I/O.

     iv) Repeat i) except use memory-mapped I/O and fully decoding.

Draw a neat schematic of your design and also determine memory and I/O maps in each case.

Chapter 3

INTEL 8086

This chapter describes the internal architecture, addressing modes, instruction set, and I/O techniques associated with the 8086 microprocessor. Interfacing capabilities to typical memory and I/O chips such as the 2716, 2142, and 8255 are included.

A design technique is presented showing interconnection of the 8086 to 2716 EPROM, 2142 RAM, and 8255 I/O chips. The memory and I/O maps are then determined.

3.1 INTRODUCTION

The 8086 is Intel's first 16-bit microprocessor. Its design is based on the 8080 but it is not directly compatible with the 8080.

The 8086 is designed using the HMOS technology and contains approximately 29,000 transistors. The 8086 is packaged in a 40-pin DIP (Dual In-line Package) and requires a single 5V power supply. The 8086 can be operated at three different clock speeds. The standard 8086 runs at 5 MHz internal clock frequency, whereas the 8086-2 and 8086-4 run at internal clock frequencies of 8 and 4 MHz, respectively. An external clock generator/driver chip such as the Intel 8284 is needed to generate the 8086 clock input signal. The 8086 divides the external clock connected at the CLK pin internally by three. This means that for a 5-MHz internal clock, the 8284 must generate a 15-MHz clock output which should be connected at the 8086 CLK pin.

The 8086 has a 20-bit address and, hence, it can directly address up to one megabyte (2^{20}) of memory. The 8086 uses a segmented memory. An interesting feature of the 8086 is that it prefetches up to six instruction bytes from memory and queues them in order to speed up instruction execution.

The memory of an 8086-based microcomputer is organized as bytes. Each byte can be uniquely addressed with 20-bit addresses of 00000_{16}, 00001_{16}, 00002_{16}, ...$FFFFF_{16}$. An 8086 16-bit word consists of any two consecutive bytes; the low-addressed byte is the low byte of the word and the high-addressed byte contains the high byte as follows:

Low byte of the word	High byte of the word
07_{16}	26_{16}
Address 00520_{16}	Address 00521_{16}

The 16-bit word stored at the even address 00520_{16} is 2607_{16}.

Next consider a word stored at an odd address as follows:

Low byte of the word	High byte of the word
05_{16}	$3F_{16}$
Address 01257_{16}	Address 01258_{16}

The 16-bit word stored at the odd address 01257_{16} is $3F05_{16}$. Note that for word addresses, the programmer uses the low-order address (odd or even) to specify the whole 16-bit word.

The 8086 always accesses a 16-bit word to or from memory. The 8086 can read a 16-bit word in one operation if the first byte of the word is at an even address. On the other hand, the 8086 must perform two memory accesses to two consecutive memory even addresses, if the first byte of the word is at an odd address. In this case, the 8086 discards the unwanted bytes of each. For example, consider MOV BX, ADDR. Note that the X or H (or L) following the 8086 register name in an instruction indicates whether the transfer is 16-bit or 8-bit. For example, MOV ADDR, BX moves the contents of the 20-bit physical memory location addressed by ADDR into the 8086 16-bit register BX. Now, if ADDR is a 20-bit even address such as 30024_{16}, then this MOV instruction loads the low (BL) and high (BH) bytes of the 8086 16-bit register BX with the contents of memory locations 30024_{16} and 30025_{16}, respectively, in a single access. Now, if ADDR is an odd address such as 40005_{16}, then the MOV BX, ADDR instruction loads BL and BH with the contents of memory locations 40005_{16} and 40006_{16}, respectively, in two accesses. Note that the

8086 accesses locations 40004_{16} and 40005_{16} in the first operation but discards the contents of 40004_{16}, and in the second operation accesses 40006_{16} and 40007_{16} but ignores the contents of 40007_{16}.

Next, consider a byte move such as MOV BH, ADDR. If ADDR is an even address such as 50002_{16}, then this MOV instruction accesses both 50002_{16} and 50003_{16}, but loads BH with the contents of 50002_{16} and ignores the contents of 50003_{16}. However, if ADDR is an odd address such as 50003_{16}, then this MOV loads BH with the contents of 50003_{16} and discards the contents of 50002_{16}.

The 8086 family consists of two types of 16-bit microprocessors — the 8086 and 8088. The main difference is how the processors communicate with the outside world. The 8088 has an 8-bit external data path to memory and I/O, while the 8086 has a 16-bit external data path. This means that the 8088 will have to do two read operations to read a 16-bit word into memory. In most other respects, the processors are identical. Note that the 8088 accesses memory in bytes. No alterations are needed to run software written for one microprocessor on the other. Because of similarities, only the 8086 will be considered here. The 8088 is used in designing the IBM Personal computer.

An 8086 can be configured as a small uniprocessor system (minimum mode if the MN/$\overline{\text{MX}}$ pin is tied to HIGH) or as a multiprocessor system (maximum mode when MN/$\overline{\text{MX}}$ pin is tied to LOW). In a given system, the MN/$\overline{\text{MX}}$ pin is permanently tied to either HIGH or LOW. Some of the 8086 pins have dual functions depending on the selection of the MN/$\overline{\text{MX}}$ pin level. In the minimum mode (MN/$\overline{\text{MX}}$ pin high), these pins transfer control signals directly to memory and input/output devices. In the maximum mode (MN/$\overline{\text{MX}}$ pin low), these same pins have different functions which facilitate multiprocessor systems. In the maximum mode, the control functions normally present in minimum mode are assumed by a support chip, the 8288 bus controller.

Due to technological advances, Intel introduced the high performance 80186 and 80188 which are enhanced versions of the 8086 and 8088, respectively. The 8-MHz 80186/80188 provides two times greater throughput than the standard 5-MHz 8086/8088. Both have integrated several new peripheral functional units such as a DMA controller, a 16-bit timer unit, and an interrupt controller unit into a single chip. Just like the 8086 and 8088, the 80186 has a 16-bit data bus and the 80188 has an 8-bit data bus; otherwise, the architecture and instruction set of the 80186 and 80188 are identical. The 80186/80188 has an on-chip clock generator so that only an external crystal is required to generate the clock. The 80186/80188 can operate at either 6 or 8 MHz internal clock. Like the 8085, the crystal frequency is divided by 2 internally. In other words, external crystals of 12 or 16 MHz must be connected to generate the 6- or 8-MHz internal clock frequency. The 80186/80188 is fabricated in a 68-pin package. Both processors have on-chip priority interrupt controller circuits to provide five interrupt pins. Like the 8086/8088, the 80186/80188 can directly address one megabyte of memory. The 80186/80188 is provided with 10 new instructions beyond the 8086/8088 instruction set. Examples of these instructions include INs and OUTs for inputting and outputting string byte or string word. The 80286, on the other hand, has added memory protection and management capabilities to the basic 8086 architecture. An 8-MHz 80286 provides up to six times greater throughput than the 5-MHz 8086. The 80286 is fabricated in a 68-pin package. The 80286 can be operated at 4, 6, or 8 MHz clock frequency. An external 82284 clock generator chip is required to generate the clock. The 80286 divides the external clock by two to generate the internal clock. The 80286 is typically used in a multiuser or multitasking system. The 80286 can be operated in two modes, real address and protected virtual address. The real address mode emulates a very high performance 8086. In this mode, the 80286 can directly address one megabyte of memory. The 80286, in the virtual address mode, can directly address 16 megabytes of memory. The virtual address mode provides (in addition to the real address mode capabilities) virtual memory management, task management, and protection. The programmer can select one of these modes by loading appropriate data in the 16-bit machine status word (MSW) register by using load and store instructions. Two examples of these instructions are LMSW (Load MSW register) and SMSW (Store MSW register). The 80286 is used as the CPU of the IBM PC/AT Personal computer. An enhanced version of the 80286 is at the 32-bit 80386 microprocessor which will be covered later. The 80386 is used as the CPU in the IBM's newest PC.

3.2 8086 ARCHITECTURE

Figure 3.1 shows a block diagram of the 8086 internal architecture. As shown in the figure, the 8086 microprocessor is internally divided into two separate functional units. These are the Bus Interface Unit (BIU) and the Execution Unit (EU). The BIU fetches instructions, reads data from memory and ports, and writes data to memory and I/O ports. The EU executes instructions that have already been fetched by the BIU. The BIU and EU function independently. The BIU interfaces the 8086 to the

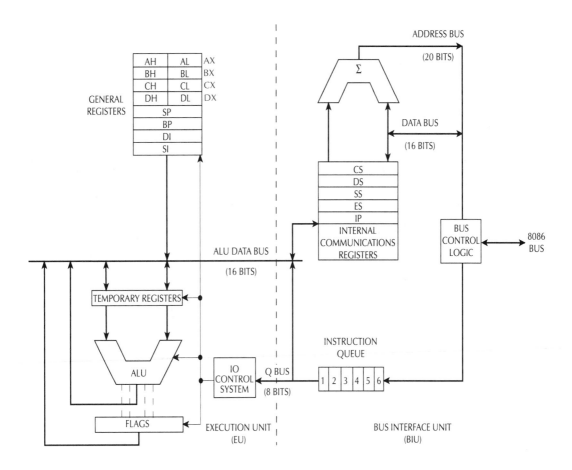

FIGURE 3.1 Internal architecture of the 8086.

outside world. The BIU provides all external bus operations. The BIU contains segment registers, instruction pointer, instruction queue, and address generation/bus control circuitry to provide functions such as fetching and queuing of instructions, and bus control.

The BIU's instruction queue is a First-In-First-Out (FIFO) group of registers in which up to six bytes of instruction code are prefetched from memory ahead of time. This is done in order to speed up program execution by overlapping instruction fetch with execution. This mechanism is known as pipelining. If the queue is full and the EU does not request BIU to access memory, the BIU does not perform any bus cycle. On the other hand, if the BIU is not full and if it can store at least two bytes and the EU does not request it to access memory, the BIU may prefetch instructions. However, if BIU is interrupted by EU for memory access while the BIU is in the process of fetching an instruction, the BIU first completes fetching and then services the EU: the queue allows the BIU to keep the EU supplied with prefetched instructions without tying up the system bus. If an instruction such as Jump or subroutine call is encountered, the BIU will reset the queue and begin refilling after passing the new instruction to the EU.

The BIU contains a dedicated adder which is used to produce the 20-bit address. The bus control logic of the BIU generates all the bus control signals such as read and write signals for memory and I/O.

The BIU has four 16-bit segment registers. These are the Code Segment (CS) register, the Data Segment (DS) register, the Stack Segment (SS) register, and the Extra Segment (ES) register. The 8086's one megabyte memory is divided into segments of up to 64K bytes each. The 8086 can directly address four segments (256K byte within the 1 Mbyte memory) at a particular time. Programs obtain access to code and data in the segments by changing the segment register contents to point to the desired segments. All program instructions must be located in main memory pointed to by the 16-bit CS register with a 16-bit offset in the segment contained in the 16-bit instruction pointer (IP). The BIU computes the 20-bit physical address internally using the programmer-provided logical address (16-bit contents of CS and IP) by logically shifting the contents of CS four bits to left and then adding the 16-bit contents of IP. In other words, the CS is multiplied by 16_{10} by the BIU for computing the 20-bit physical address. This means that all instructions of a program are relative to the contents of the CS register multiplied by 16 and then offset is added provided by the 16-bit contents of IP. For example, if $[CS] = 456A_{16}$ and $[IP] = 1620_{16}$, then the 20-bit physical address is generated by the BIU as follows:

$$\text{Four times logically shifted } [CS] \text{ to left} = 456A0_{16}$$

$$+ [IP] \text{ as offset} \qquad\qquad = \ 1620_{16}$$

$$\text{20-bit physical address} \qquad\qquad = 46CC0_{16}$$

The BIU always inserts four zeros for the lowest 4-bits of the 20-bit starting address (physical) of a segment. In other words, the CS contains the base or start of the current code segment, and IP contains the distance or offset from this address to the next instruction byte to be fetched. Note that immediate data are considered as part of the code segment.

The SS register points to the current stack. The 20-bit physical stack address is calculated from SS and SP for stack instructions such as PUSH and POP. The programmer can use the BP register instead of SP for accessing the stack using the based addressing mode. In this case, the 20-bit physical stack address is calculated from BP and SS.

The DS register points to the current data segment; operands for most instructions are fetched from this segment. The 16-bit contents of Source Index (SI) or Destination Index (DI) are used as offset for computing the 20-bit physical address.

The ES register points to the extra segment in which data (in excess of 64K pointed to by DS) is stored. String instructions always use ES and DI to determine the 20-bit physical address for the destination.

The segments can be contiguous, partially overlapped, fully over-lapped, or disjoint. An example of how five segments (segment 0 through segment 4) may be stored in physical memory are shown below:

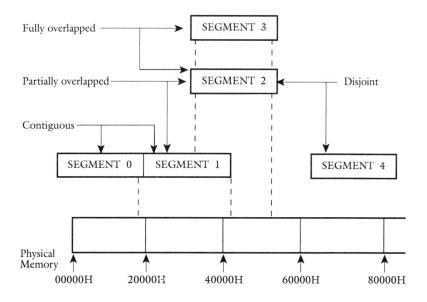

In the above SEGMENTs 0 and 1 are contiguous (adjacent), SEGMENTs 1 and 2 are partially overlapped, SEGMENTs 2 and 3 are fully overlapped, and SEGMENTs 2 and 4 are disjoint. Every segment must start on 16-byte memory boundaries.

Typical examples of values of segments should then be selected based on physical addresses starting at 00000_{16}, 00010_{16}, 00020_{16}, 00030_{16}, ... $FFFF0_{16}$. A physical memory location may be mapped into (contained in) one or more logical segments. Many applications can be written to simply initialize the segment registers and then forget them.

A segment can be pointed to by more than one segment register. For example, DS and ES may point to the same segment in memory if a string located in that segment is used as a source segment in one string instruction and as a destination segment in another string instruction. Note that for string instructions, a destination segment must be pointed to by ES.

It should be pointed out that codes should not be written within 6 bytes of the end of physical memory. Failure to comply with this guideline may result in an attempted op code fetch from nonexistent memory, hanging the CPU if READY is not returned. One example of four currently addressable segments is shown below:

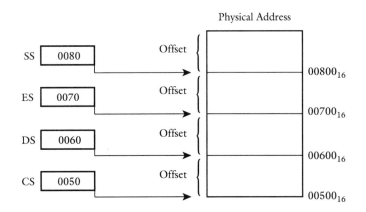

The EU decodes and executes instructions. A decoder in the EU control system translates instructions. The EU has a 16-bit ALU for performing arithmetic and logic operations.

The EU has eight 16-bit general registers. These are AX, BX, CX, DX, SP, BP, SI, and DI. The 16-bit registers AX, BX, CX, and DX can be used as two 8-bit registers (AH, AL, BH, BL, CH, CL, DH, DL). For example, the 16-bit register DX can be considered as two 8-bit registers DH (high byte of DX) and DL (low byte of DX). The general-purpose registers AX, BX, CX, and DX are named after special functions carried out by each one of them. For example, the AX is called the 16-bit accumulator while the AL is the 8-bit accumulator. The use of accumulator registers is assumed by some instructions. The Input/Output (IN or OUT) instructions always use AX or AL for inputting/outputting 16- or 8-bit data to or from an I/O port.

Multiplication and division instructions also use AX or AL. The AL register is the same as the 8085 A register.

BX register is called the base register. This is the only general-purpose register, the contents of which can be used for addressing 8086 memory.

All memory references utilizing these register contents for addressing use DS as the default segment register. The BX register is similar to 8085 HL register. In other words, 8086 BH and BL are equivalent to 8085 H and L registers, respectively.

The CX register is known as the counter register. This is because some instructions such as shift, rotate, and loop instructions use the contents of CX as a counter. For example, the instruction LOOP START will automatically decrement CX by 1 without affecting flags and will check if [CX] = 0. If it is zero, the 8086 executes the next instruction; otherwise the 8086 branches to the label START.

The data register DX is used to hold high 16-bit result (data) in 16 × 16 multiplication or high 16-bit dividend (data) before a 32 ÷ 16 division and the 16-bit remainder after the division.

The two pointer registers, SP (stack pointer) and BP (base pointer), are used to access data in stack segment. The SP is used as an offset from the current SS during execution of instructions that involve stack segment in external memory. The SP contents are automatically updated (incremented or decremented) due to execution of POP or PUSH instruction.

The base pointer contains an offset address in the current SS. This offset is used by the instructions utilizing the based addressing mode.

The FLAG register in the EU holds the status flags typically after an ALU operation. Figure 3.2 shows the 8086 registers.

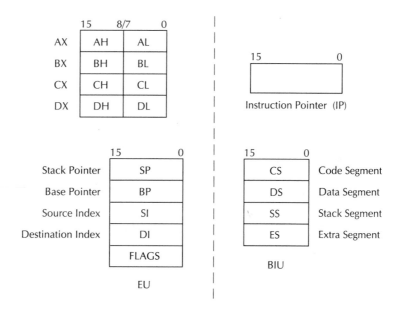

FIGURE 3.2 8086 registers.

15		12	11	10	9	8	7	6	5	4	3	2	1	0
	. . .		OF	DF	IF	TF	SF	ZF		AF		PF		CF

FIGURE 3.3 8086 flag register.

The 8086 has six one-bit flags. Figure 3.3 shows the flag register. Let us explain the 8086 flags. AF (Auxiliary carry Flag) is used by BCD arithmetic instructions. AF = 1 if there is a carry from the low nibble (4-bit) into the high nibble or a borrow from the high nibble into the low nibble of the low-order 8-bit of a 16-bit number. CF (Carry Flag) is set if there is a carry from addition or borrow from subtraction. OF (Overflow Flag) is set if there is an arithmetic overflow, that is, if the size of the result exceeds the capacity of the destination location. An interrupt on overflow instruction is available which will generate an interrupt in this situation. SF (Sign Flag) is set if the most significant bit of the result is one (negative) and is cleared to zero for non-negative result. PF (Parity Flag) is set if the result has even parity; PF is zero for odd parity of the result. ZF (Zero Flag) is set if result is zero; ZF is zero for nonzero result.

The 8086 has three control bits in the flag register which can be set or reset by the programmer: setting DF (Direction Flag) to one causes string instructions to autodecrement and clearing DF to zero causes string instructions to autoincrement. Setting IF (Interrupt Flag) to one causes the 8086 to recognize external maskable interrupts; clearing IF to zero disables these interrupts. Setting TF (Trace Flag) to one places the 8086 in the single-step mode. In this mode, the 8086 generates an internal interrupt after execution of each instruction. The user can write a service routine at the interrupt address vector to display the desired registers and memory locations. The user can thus debug a program.

3.3 8086 ADDRESSING MODES

The 8086 has 12 basic addressing modes. The various 8086 addressing modes can be classified into five groups:

1.   Addressing modes for accessing immediate and register data (register and immediate modes)

2.   Addressing modes for accessing data in memory (memory modes)
3.   Addressing modes for accessing I/O ports (I/O modes)
4.   Relative addressing mode
5.   Implied addressing mode

3.3.1 ADDRESSING MODES FOR ACCESSING IMMEDIATE AND REGISTER DATA (REGISTER AND IMMEDIATE MODES)

3.3.1.a Register Addressing Mode

This mode specifies the source operand, destination operand, or both to be contained in an 8086 register. An example is MOV DX, CX which moves the 16-bit contents of CX into DX. Note that in the above both source and destination operands are in register mode. Another example is MOV CL, DL which moves 8-bit contents of DL into CL. MOV BX, CH is an illegal instruction; the register sizes must be the same.

3.3.1.b Immediate Addressing Mode

In immediate mode, 8- or 16-bit data can be specified as part of the instruction. For example, MOV CL, 03H moves the 8-bit data 03H into CL. On the other hand, MOV DX, 0502H moves the 16-bit data 0502H into DX. Note that in both of the above MOV instructions, the source operand is in immediate mode and the destination operand is in register mode.

A constant such as "VALUE" can be defined by the assembler EQUATE directive such as VALUE EQU 35H. An 8086 instruction with immediate mode such as MOV BH, VALUE can then be used to load 35H into BH. Note that even though the immediate mode specifies data with the instruction, these immediate data must be located in the memory addressed by the 8086 CS and IP registers. This is because these data are considered as part of the instruction.

3.3.2 ADDRESSING MODES FOR ACCESSING DATA IN MEMORY (MEMORY MODES)

As mentioned before, the Execution Unit (EU) has direct access to all registers and data for register and immediate operands. However, the EU cannot directly access the memory operands. It must use the BIU in order to access memory operands. For example, when the EU needs to access a memory location, it sends an offset value to the BIU. This offset is also called the Effective Address (EA). Note that EA is displacement of the desired location from the segment base. As mentioned before, the BIU generates a 20-bit physical address after shifting the contents of the desired segment register four bits to the left and then adding the 16-bit EA to it. The 8086 must use a segment register whenever it accesses the memory. Also, every memory addressing instruction uses an Intel-defined standard default segment register. However, a segment override prefix can be placed before most of the memory addressing instructions whose default segment register is to be overridden. For example, INC BYTE PTR [START] will increment the 8-bit content of memory location in DS with offset START by one. However, segment DS can be overridden by ES as follows: INC ES: BYTE PTR [START]; segments cannot be overridden for stack reference instructions (such as PUSH and POP). Destination segment of a string segment which must be ES (if a prefix is used with string instruction, only the source segment DS can be overridden) cannot be overridden. The Code Segment (CS) register used in program memory addressing cannot be overridden. There are six modes in this category. These are

a.   Direct addressing mode
b.   Register indirect addressing mode
c.   Based addressing mode
d.   Indexed addressing mode
e.   Based indexed addressing mode
f.   String addressing mode

3.3.2.a Direct Addressing Mode

In this mode, the 16-bit effective address (EA) is taken directly from the displacement field of the instruction. The displacement (unsigned 16-bit or sign-extended 8-bit number) is stored in the location following the Instruction op code. This EA or displacement is the distance of the memory location from the current value in the data segment (DS) register in which the data are stored. The BIU shifts the [DS] four times to left and adds the EA to generate the 20-bit physical address. The register can be overridden by the programmer by using a segment override instruction to tell the BIU to add EU to some other segment base for producing the 20-bit physical address. As an example of 16-bit read from memory, consider MOV CX, START. This instruction moves the contents of memory location which is offset by START from the current DS value into register CX.

Note that in the above instruction, the source is in direct addressing mode. If the 16-bit value assigned to the offset START by the programmer using an assembler pseudoinstruction such as DW is 0040_{16} and [DS] = 3050_{16}, then the BIU generates the 20-bit physical address 30540_{16} on the

8086 address pins and then initiates a memory read cycle to read the 16-bit data from memory location starting at 30540_{16} location. The memory logic places the 16-bit contents of locations 30540_{16} and 30541_{16} on the 8086 data pins. The BIU transfers these data to the EU; the EU then moves these data to CX; $[30540_{16}]$ to CL and $[30541_{16}]$ to CH. Now, for 8-bit read from memory consider MOV CH, START. If $[DS] = 3050_{16}$, the value of START is 0040_{16}, then the 8-bit content of memory location 30540_{16} is moved to register CH. An example of 16-bit write to memory is MOV START, BX with $[DS] = 3050_{16}$. If the value of START is 0040_{16}, then this MOV instruction moves $[BL]$ and $[BH]$ to locations 30540_{16} and 30541_{16}, respectively. Similarly, an example of 8-bit data write is MOV START, BL. The 8086 does not have a MOVE instruction for moving 8-bit or 16-bit data from one memory location to another in which both source and destination operands are in direct addressing mode. String addressing mode (to be discussed later) allows string memory operation such as block move from source memory array to a destination memory array. Note that START in the above can be defined as an address by using the assembler DB (Define Byte) or DW (Define Word) pseudoinstructions.

3.3.2.b Register Indirect Addressing Mode

In this mode, the EA is specified in either a pointer register or an index register. The pointer register can be either base register BX or base pointer register BP and index register can be either Source Index (SI) register or Destination Index (DI) register. The 20-bit physical address is computed using DS and EA. For example, consider MOV [DI], BX. The destination operand of the above instruction is in register indirect mode, while the source operand is in register mode. The instruction moves the 16-bit content of BX into a memory location offset by the value of EA specified in DI from the current contents in DS. Now, if $[DS] = 5004_{16}$, $[DI] = 0020_{16}$, and $[BX] = 2456_{16}$, then after MOV [DI], BX, content of BX (2456_{16}) is moved to memory locations 50060_{16} and 50061_{16}.

Using this mode, one instruction can operate on many different memory locations if the value in the base or index register is updated. The LEA (Load Effective Address) might be used to change the register value.

3.3.2.c Based Addressing Mode

In this mode, EA is obtained by adding a displacement (signed 8-bit or unsigned 16-bit) value to the contents of BX or BP. The segment registers used are DS and SS. When memory is accessed, the 20-bit physical address is computed from BX and DS. On the other hand, when the stack is accessed, the 20-bit physical address is computed from BP and SS. This allows the programmer to access the stack without changing the SP contents. As an example of this mode, consider MOV AL, START [BX]. Note that some assemblers use MOV AL, [BX + START] rather than MOV AL, START [BX]. The source operand in the above instruction is in based mode. EA is obtained by adding the value of START and [BX]. The 20-bit physical address is produced from DS and EA. The 8-bit content of this memory location is moved to AL. The displacement START can be either unsigned 16-bit or signed 8-bit. However, a byte is saved for the machine code representation of the instruction if 8-bit displacement is used. The 8086 sign-extends the 8-bit displacement and then adds it to [BX] in the above MOV instruction for determining EA. On the other hand, the 8086 adds an unsigned 16-bit displacement directly with [BX] for determining EA.

Based addressing provides a convenient way to address structure which may be stored at different places in memory:

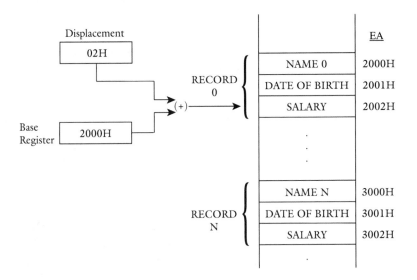

For example, the element salary in record 0 of the employee NAME 0 can be loaded into an 8086 internal register such as AL using the instruction MOV AL, ALPHA [BX], where ALPHA is the 8-bit displacement 02H and BX contains the starting address of the record 0. Now, in order to access the salary of RECORD N, the programmer simply changes the contents of the base register to 3000H.

If BP is specified as a base register in an instruction, the 8086 automatically obtains the operand from the current SS (unless a segment override prefix is present). This makes based addressing with BP a very convenient way to access stack data. BP can be used as a stack pointer in SS to access local variables. Consider the following instruction sequence:

```
PUSH BP                 ; Save BP
MOV BP, SP              ; Establish BP
PUSH DX                 ; Save
PUSH AX                 ; registers
SUB SP, 4               ; Allocate 2 words of
                        ; stack for accessing stack
MOV [BP - 6], AX        ; Arbitrary instructions for
MOV [BP - 8], BX        ; accessing stack data using BP
ADD SP, 4               ; Deallocate storage
POP AX                  ; Restore
POP DX                  ; all registers
POP BP                  ; that were pushed before
```

This instruction sequence is arbitrarily chosen to illustrate the use of BP for accessing the stack.

Figure 3.4 shows the 8086 stack during various stages. Figure 3.4A shows the stack before execution of the instruction sequence.

The instruction sequence from PUSH BP to SUB SP, 4 pushes BP, DX, and AX and then subtracts 4 from SP, and this allocates 2 words of the stack. The stack at this point is shown in Figure 3.4B. Note that in 8086, SP is decremented by 2 for PUSH and incremented by 2 for POP. The [BP] is not affected by PUSH or POP. The instruction sequence MOV [BP – 6], AX saves AX in the stack location addressed by [BP – 6] in SS. The instruction MOV [BP – 8], BX writes the [BX] into the stack location [BP – 8] in SS. These instructions are arbitrarily chosen to illustrate how BP can be used to access the stack. These two local variables can be accessed by the subroutine using BP. The instruction ADD SP, 4 releases two words of the allocated stack. The stack at this point is shown in Figure 3.4C. The last three POP instructions restore the contents of AX, DX, and BP to their original values and return the stack as it was before the instruction sequence was executed. This shown in Figure 3.4D.

3.3.2.d Indexed Addressing Mode

In this mode, the effective address is calculated by adding the unsigned 16-bit or sign-extended 8-bit displacement and the contents of SI or DI.

As an example, MOV BH, START [SI] moves the contents of the 20-bit address computed from the displacement START, SI and DS into BH.

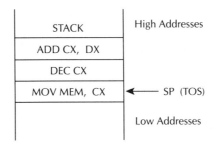

A) Stack before executing the instruction sequence.

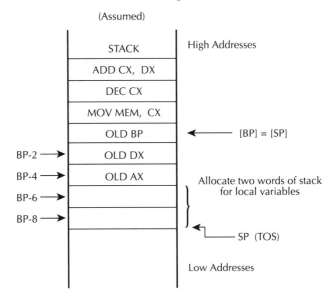

B) Stack after execution of the instruction sequence
from PUSH BP to SUB SP, 4

FIGURE 3.4 Accessing stack using BP.

The 8-bit displacement is provided by the programmer using the assembler pseudoinstruction such as EQU. For 16-bit displacement, the EU adds this to SI to determine EA. On the other hand, for 8-bit displacement the EU sign-extends it to 16 bits and then adds to SI for determining EA.

Note that for both based and indexed modes, the 8086 obtains the Effective Address (EA) by using the equation EA = RA + M, where RA is the Reference Address and M is the Modifier. In case of based addressing mode, RA is held in a register such as BX or BP and the modifier M is unsigned 16-bit or signed 8-bit displacement and is included as part of the instruction. The based mode is useful in accessing segmented memory in

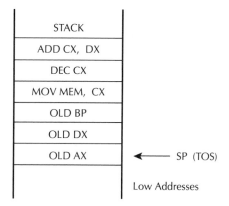

C) Stack after execution of ADD SP, 4

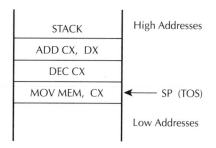

D) Stack before execution of POP BP.

FIGURE 3.4 (continued)

which BX or BP holds the base address of a segment. In indexed addressing mode, on the other hand, RA is included as part of the instruction and the 8086 register SI or DI contains the value of M. RA can be unsigned 16-bit or sign-extended 8-bit.

Indexed addressing mode can be used to access a single table. The displacement can be the starting address of the table. The content of SI or DI can then be used as an index from the starting address to access a particular element in the table.

3.3.2.e Based Indexed Addressing Mode

In this mode, the EA is computed by adding a base register (BX or BP), an index register (SI or DI), and a displacement (unsigned 16-bit or sign-extended 8-bit). As an example, consider MOV ALPHA [SI] [BX], CL if [BX] = 0200H, value of ALPHA = 08H, [SI] = 1000H, and [DS] = 3000 H, then 8-bit content of CL is moved to 20-bit physical address 31208_{16}.

Based indexed addressing mode provides a convenient way for a subroutine to address an array allocated on a stack. Register BP can be loaded with the offset in segment SS (top of the stack after the subroutine has saved registers and allocated local storage). The displacement can be the value which is the difference between the top of the stack and the beginning of the array. An index register can then be used to access individual array elements as follows:

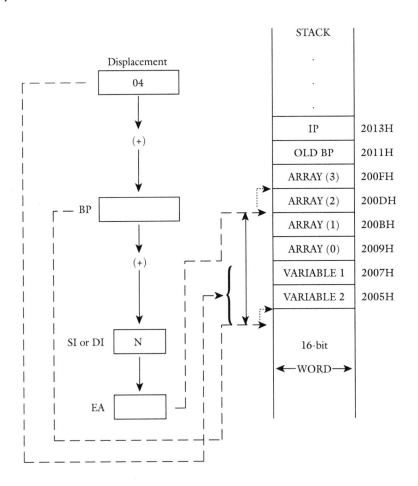

In the above, [BP] = top of the stack = 2005H; displacement = difference between the top of the stack and start of the array = 04H; [SI or DI] = N = 16-bit number (0, 2, 4, 6 in the example). As an example, the instruction MOV DX, 4 [SI] [BP] with [SI] = 6 will read the array (3) which is the content of 200FH in SS into DX. Since in the based indexed mode, the contents of two registers such as BX and SI can be varied, two-dimensional arrays such as matrices can also be accessed.

3.3.2.f String Addressing Mode

This mode uses index registers. The string instructions automatically assume SI to point to the first byte or word of the source operand and DI to point to the first byte or word of the destination operand. The contents of SI and DI are automatically incremented (by clearing DF to 0 by CLD instruction) or decremented (by setting DF to 1 by STD instruction) to point to the next byte or word. The segment register for the source is DS and may be overridden.

The segment register for the destination must be ES and cannot be overridden. As an example, consider MOVS BYTE. If $[DF] = 0$, $[DS] = 2000_{16}$, $[SI] = 0500_{16}$, $[ES] = 4000_{16}$, $[DI] = 0300_{16}$, $[20500]_{16} = 38_{16}$, and $[40300_{16}] = 45_{16}$, then after execution of the MOVS BYTE, $[40300_{16}] = 38_{16}$, $[SI] = 0501_{16}$, and $[DI] = 0301_{16}$. The contents of other registers and memory locations are unchanged. Note that SI and DI can be used in either the source or destination operand of a two-operand instruction, except for string instructions in which SI points to the source (may be overridden) and DI must point to the destination.

3.3.3 ADDRESSING MODES FOR ACCESSING I/O PORTS (I/O MODES)

Standard I/O uses port addressing modes. For memory-mapped I/O, memory addressing modes are used. There are two types of port addressing modes: direct and indirect.

In direct port mode, the port number is an 8-bit immediate operand. This allows fixed access to ports numbered 0 to 255. For example, OUT 05H, AL outputs [AL] to 8-bit port 05H. In indirect port mode, the port number is taken from DX allowing 64K 8-bit ports or 32K 16-bit ports. For example, if $[DX] = 5040_{16}$, then IN AL, DX inputs the 8-bit content of port 5040_{16} into AL. On the other hand, IN AX, DX inputs the 8-bit contents of ports 5040_{16} and 5041_{16} into AL and AH, respectively. Note that 8-bit and 16-bit I/O transfers must take place via AL and AX, respectively.

3.3.4 RELATIVE ADDRESSING MODE

Instructions using this mode specify the operand as a signed 8-bit displacement relative to PC. An example is JNC START. This instruction means that if carry = 0, then PC is loaded with current PC contents plus the 8-bit signed value of START; otherwise the next instruction is executed.

3.3.5 IMPLIED ADDRESSING MODE

Instructions using this mode have no operands. An example is CLC which clears the carry flag to zero.

3.4 8086 INSTRUCTION SET

The 8086 instruction set includes equivalents of the 8085 instructions plus many new ones. The new instructions contain operations such as signed and unsigned multiplication and division, bit manipulation instructions, string instructions, and interrupt instructions.

The 8086 has approximately 117 different instructions with about 300 op codes. The 8086 instruction set contains no operand, single operand, and two operand instructions. Except for string instructions which involve array operations, the 8086 instructions do not permit memory-to-memory operations. Table 3.1 lists a summary of 8086 instructions in alphabetical order. Tables 3.A-1 through 3.A-12 (supplied at the end of the chapter) provide a detailed description of the 8086 instructions.

TABLE 3.1
Summary of 8086 Instructions

Instructions	Interpretation	Comments
AAA	ASCII adjust [AL] after addition	This instruction has implied addressing mode; this instruction is used to adjust the content of AL after addition of two ASCII characters
AAD	ASCII adjust for division	This instruction has implied addressing mode; converts two unpacked BCD digits in AX into equivalent binary numbers in AL; AAD must be used before dividing two unpacked BCD digits by an unpacked BCD byte
AAM	ASCII adjust after multiplication	This instruction has implied addressing mode; after multiplying two unpacked BCD numbers, adjust the product in AX to become an unpacked BCD result; ZF, SF, and PF are affected
AAS	ASCII adjust [AL] after subtraction	This instruction has implied addressing mode used to adjust [AL] after subtraction of two ASCII characters
ADC mem/reg 1, mem/reg 2	[mem/reg 1] ← [mem/reg 1] + [mem/reg 2] + CY	Memory or register can be 8- or 16-bit; all flags are affected; no segment registers are allowed; no memory-to-memory ADC is permitted
ADC mem, data	[mem] ← [mem] + data + CY	Data can be 8- or 16-bit; mem uses DS as the segment register; all flags are affected

TABLE 3.1 (continued)

Instructions	Interpretation	Comments
ADC reg, data	[reg] ← [reg] + data + CY	Data can be 8- or 16-bit; register cannot be segment register; all flags are affected; reg is not usually used as AX or AL
ADC A, data	[A] ← [A] + data + CY	'A' can be AL or AX register; all flags are affected
ADD mem/reg 2, mem/reg 1	[mem/reg 1] ← [mem/reg 2] + [mem/reg 1]	Add two 8- or 16-bit data; no memory-to-memory ADD is permitted; all flags are affected; mem uses DS as the segment register; reg 1 or reg 2 cannot be segment register
ADD mem, data	[mem] ← [mem] + data	Mem uses DS as the segment register; data can be 8- or 16-bit; all flags are affected
ADD reg, data	[reg] ← [reg] + data	Data can be 8- or 16-bit; no segment registers are allowed; all flags are affected; this instruction should not be used to add AL or AX with 8- or 16- bit immediate data
ADD A, data	[A] ← [A] + data	Data can be 8- or 16-bit; 'A' can be AL or AX; all flags are affected
AND mem/reg 1, mem/reg 2	[mem/reg 1] ← [mem/reg 1] ∧ [mem/reg 2]	This instruction logically ANDS 8- or 16-bit data in [mem/reg 1] with 8- or 16-bit data in [mem/reg 2]; all flags are affected; OF and CF are cleared to zero; no segment registers are allowed; no memory-to-memory operation is allowed; mem uses DS as the segment register
AND mem, data	[mem] ← [mem] ∧ data	Data can be 8- or 16-bit; mem uses DS as the segment register; all flags are affected with OF and CF always cleared to zero
AND reg, data	[reg] ← [reg] ∧ data	Data can be 8- or 16-bit; reg cannot be segment register; this instruction should not be used to AND AL or AX with 8- or 16-bit immediate data; all flags are affected with OF and CF cleared to zero
AND A, data	[A] ← [A] ∧ data	Data can be 8- bit or 16-bit; 'A' must be AL or AX; all flags are affected with OF and CF cleared to zero
CALL PROC (NEAR)	Call a subroutine in the same segment with signed 16-bit displacement (to CALL a subroutine in ±32K)	NEAR in the statement BEGIN PROC NEAR indicates that the subroutine 'BEGIN' is in the same segment and BEGIN is 16-bit signed; CALL BEGIN instruction decrements SP by 2 and then pushes IP onto the stack and then adds the signed 16-bit value of BEGIN to IP and CS is unchanged; thus, a subroutine is called in the same segment (intrasegment direct)

TABLE 3.1 (continued)

Instructions	Interpretation	Comments
CALL Reg 16	CALL a subroutine in the same segment addressed by the contents of a 16-bit general register	The 8086 decrements SP by 2 and then pushes IP onto the stack, then specified 16-bit register contents (such as BX, SI, and DI) provide the new value for IP; CS is unchanged (intrasegment indirect)
CALL Mem 16	CALL a subroutine addressed by the content of a memory location pointed to by 8086 16-bit register such as BX, SI, and DI	The 8086 decrements SP by 2 and pushes IP onto the stack; the 8086 then loads the contents of a memory location addressed by the content of a 16-bit register such as BX, SI, and DI into IP; [CS] is unchanged (intrasegment indirect)
CALL PROC (FAR)	CALL a subroutine in another segment	FAR in the statement BEGIN PROC FAR indicates that the subroutine 'BEGIN' is in another segment and the value of BEGIN is 32 bit wide
		The 8086 decrements SP by 2 and pushes CS onto the stack and moves the low 16-bit value of the specified 32-bit number such as 'BEGIN' in CALL BEGIN into CS; SP is again decremented by 2; IP is pushed onto the stack; IP is then loaded with high 16-bit value of BEGIN; thus, this instruction CALLS a subroutine in another code segment (intersegment direct)
CALLDWORD PTR [reg 16]	CALL a subroutine in another segment	This instruction decrements SP by 2, and pushes CS onto the stack; CS is then loaded with the contents of memory locations addressed by [reg 16 + 2] and [reg 16 + 3] in DS; the SP is again decremented by 2; IP is pushed onto the stack; IP is then loaded with the contents of memory locations addressed by [reg 16] and [reg 16 + 1] in DS; typical 8086 registers used for reg 16 are BX, SI, and DI (intersegment indirect)
CBW	Convert a byte to a word	Extend the sign bit (bit 7) of AL register into AH
CLC	$CF \leftarrow 0$	Clear carry to zero
CLD	$DF \leftarrow 0$	Clear direction flag to zero
CLI	$IF \leftarrow 0$	Clear interrupt enable flag to zero to disable maskable interrupts
CMC	$CF \leftarrow CF'$	One's complement carry
CMP mem/reg 1, mem/reg 2	[mem/reg 1] – [mem/reg 2], flags are affected	Mem/reg can be 8- or 16-bit; no memory-to-memory comparison allowed; result of subtraction is not provided; all flags are affected

TABLE 3.1 (continued)

Instructions	Interpretation	Comments
CMP mem/reg, data	[mem/reg] – data, flags are affected	Subtracts 8- or 16-bit data from [mem or reg] and affects flags; no result is provided
CMP A, data	[A] – data, flags are affected	Subtract 8- or 16-bit data from AL or AX, respectively, and affects flags; no result is provided
CMPS BYTE or CMPSB	FOR BYTE [[SI]] – [[DI]], flags are affected [SI] ← [SI] ± 1 [DI] ← [DI] ± 1	8- or 16-bit data addressed by [DI] in ES is subtracted from 8- or 16-bit data addressed by SI in DS and flags are affected without providing any result; if DF = 0, then SI and DI are incremented by one for byte and two for word; if DF = 1, then SI and DI are decremented by one for byte and two for word; the segment register ES in destination cannot be overridden
CMPS WORD or CPSW	FOR WORD [[SI]] – [[DI]], flags are affected [SI] ← [SI] + 2 [DI] ← [DI] + 2	
CWD	Convert a word to 32 bits	Extend the sign bit of AX (bit 15) into DX
DAA	Decimal adjust [AL] after addition	This instruction uses implied addressing mode; this instruction converts [AL] into BCD; DAA should be used after BCD addition
DAS	Decimal adjust [AL] after subtraction	This instruction uses implied addressing mode; converts [AL] into BCD; DAS should be used after BCD subtraction
DEC reg 16	[reg 16] ← [reg 16] – 1	This is a one-byte instruction; used to decrement a 16-bit register except segment register; does not affect the carry flag
DEC mem/reg 8	[mem] ← [mem] – 1 or [reg 8] ← [reg 8] – 1	Used to decrement a byte or a word in memory or an 8-bit register content; segment register cannot be decremented by this instruction; does not affect carry flag
DIV mem/reg	16/8 bit divide: $\dfrac{[AX]}{[mem\ 8/reg\ 8]}$ [AH] ← Remainder [AL] ← Quotient 32/16 bit divide: $\dfrac{[DX]\ [AX]}{[mem\ 16/reg\ 16]}$ [DX] ← Remainder [AX] ← Quotient	Mem/reg is 8-bit for 16-bit by 8-bit divide and 16-bit for 32-bit by 16-bit divide; this is an unsigned division; no flags are affected; division by zero automatically generates an internal interrupt
ESC external OP code, source	ESCAPE to external processes	This instruction is used to pass instructions to a coprocessor such as the 8087 floating point coprocessor which simultaneously monitors the system bus with the 8086; the coprocessor OP codes are 6-bit wide; the

TABLE 3.1 (continued)

Instructions	Interpretation	Comments
ESC external OP code, source (continued)		coprocessor treats normal 8086 instructions as NOP's; the 8086 fetches all instructions from memory; when the 8086 encounters an ESC instruction, it usually treats it as NOP; the coprocessor decodes this instruction and carries out the operation using the 6-bit OP code independent of the 8086; for ESC OP code, memory, the 8086 accesses data in memory for the co-processor; for ESC data, register, the coprocessor operates on 8086 registers; the 8086 treats this as an NOP
HLT	HALT	Halt
IDIV mem/reg	Same as DIV mem/reg	Same as DIV mem/reg
IMUL mem/reg	For 8 × 8 [AX] ← [AL] * [mem 8/reg 8] FOR 16 × 16 [DX] [AX] ← [AX]* [mem 16/reg 16]	Mem/reg can be 8- or 16-bit; only CF and OF are affected; signed multiplication
IN AL, DX	[AL] ← [PORT DX]	Input AL with the 8-bit content of a port addressed by DX; this is a one-byte instruction
IN AX, DX	[AX] ← [PORT DX]	Input AX with the 16-bit content of a port addressed by DX and DX + 1; this is a one-byte instruction
IN AL, PORT	[AL] ← [PORT]	Input AL with the 8-bit content of a port addressed by the second byte of the instruction
IN AX, PORT	[AX] ← [PORT]	Input AX with the 16-bit content of a port addressed by the 8-bit address in the second byte of the instruction
INC reg 16	[reg 16] ← [reg 16] + 1	This is a one-byte instruction; used to increment a 16-bit register except the segment register; does not affect the carry flag
INC mem/reg 8	[mem] ← [mem] + 1 or [reg 8] ← [reg 8] + 1	This is a two-byte instruction; can be used to increment a byte or word in memory or an 8-bit register content; segment registers cannot be incremented by this instruction; does not affect the carry flag
INT n (n can be zero thru 255)	[SP] ← [SP] − 2 [[SP]] ← Flags IF ← 0 TF← 0	Software interrupts can be used as supervisor calls; that is, request for service from an operating system; a different interrupt type can be used for each type of service that

TABLE 3.1 (continued)

Instructions	Interpretation	Comments
INT n (continued)	$[SP] \leftarrow [SP] - 2$ $[[SP]] \leftarrow [CS]$ $[CS] \leftarrow 4n + 2$ $[SP] \leftarrow [SP] - 2$ $[[SP]] \leftarrow [IP]$ $[IP] \leftarrow 4n$	the operating system could supply for an application or program; software interrupt instructions can also be used for checking interrupt service routines written for hardware-initiated interrupts
INTO	Interrupt on Overflow	Generates an internal interrupt if OF = 1; executes INT 4; can be used after an arithmetic operation to activate a service routine if OF = 1; when INTO is executed and if OF = 1, operations similar to INT n take place
IRET	Interrupt Return	POPS IP, CS and Flags from stack; IRET is used as return instruction at the end of a service routine for both hardware and software interrupts
JA/JNBE disp 8	Jump if above/jump if not below original	Jump if above/jump if not below nor equal with 8-bit signed displacement; that is, the displacement can be from -128_{10} to $+127_{10}$, zero being positive; JA and JNBE are the mnemonic which represent the same instruction; Jump if both CF and ZF are zero; used for unsigned comparison
JAE/JNB/JNC disp 8	Jump if above or equal/jump if not below/jump if no carry	Same as JA/JNBE except that the 8086 Jumps if CF = 0; used for unsigned comparison
JB/JC/JNAE disp 8	Jump if below/jump if carry/ jump if not above or equal	Same as JA/JNBE except that the jump is taken CF = 1, used for unsigned comparison
JBE/JNA disp 8	Jump if below or equal/jump if not above	Same as JA/JNBE except that the jump is taken if CF = 1 or ZF = 0; used for unsigned comparison
JCXZ disp 8	Jump if CX = 0	Jump if CX = 0; this instruction is useful at the beginning of a loop to bypass the loop if CX = 0
JE/JZ disp 8	Jump if equal/jump if zero	Same as JA/JNBE except that the jump is taken if ZF = 1; used for both signed and unsigned comparison
JG/JNLE disp 8	Jump if greater/jump if not less or equal	Same as JA/JNBE except that the jump is taken if ((SF + OF) or ZF) = 0; used for signed comparison
JGE/JNL disp 8	Jump if greater or equal/ jump if not less	Same as JA/JNBE except that the jump is taken if (SF + OF) = 0; used for signed comparison

TABLE 3.1 (continued)

Instructions	Interpretation	Comments
JL/JNGE disp 8	Jump if less/Jump if not greater nor equal	Same as JA/JNBE except that the jump is taken if (SF + OF) = 1; used for signed comparison
JLE/JNG disp 8	Jump if less or equal/ jump if not greater	Same as JA/JNBE except that the jump is taken if ((SF + OF) or ZF) = 1; used for signed comparison
JMP Label	Unconditional Jump with a signed 8-bit (SHORT) or signed 16-bit (NEAR) displacement in the same segment	The label START can be signed 8-bit (called SHORT jump) or signed 16-bit (called NEAR jump) displacement; the assembler usually determines the displacement value; if the assembler finds the displacement value to be signed 8-bit (–128 to +127, 0 being positive), then the assembler uses two bytes for the instruction: one byte for the OP code followed by a byte for the displacement; the assembler sign extends the 8-bit displacement and then adds it to IP; [CS] is unchanged; on the other hand, if the assembler finds the displacement to be signed 16-bit (±32 K), then the assembler uses three bytes for the instruction: one byte for the OP code followed by 2 bytes for the displacement; the assembler adds the signed 16-bit displacement to IP; [CS] is unchanged; therefore, this JMP provides a jump in the same segment (intrasegment direct jump)
JMP Reg 16	[IP] ← [reg 16] [CS] is unchanged	Jump to an address specified by the contents of a 16-bit register such as BX, SI, and DI in the same code segment; in the example JMP BX, [BX] is loaded into IP and [CS] is unchanged (intrasegment memory indirect jump)
JMP mem 16	[IP] ← [mem] [CS] is unchanged	Jump to an address specified by the contents of a 16-bit memory location addressed by 16-bit register such as BX, SI, and DI; in the example, JMP [BX] copies the content of a memory location addressed by BX in DS into IP; CS is unchanged (intrasegment memory indirect jump)
JMP Label (FAR)	Unconditionally jump to another segment	This is a 5-byte instruction: the first byte is the OP code followed by four bytes of 32-bit immediate data; bytes 2 and 3 are loaded into IP; bytes 4 and 5 are loaded into CS to JUMP unconditionally to another segment (intersegment direct)

TABLE 3.1 (continued)

Instructions	Interpretation	Comments
JMP DWORD PTR [reg 16]	Unconditionally jump to another segment	This instruction loads the contents of memory locations addressed by [reg 16] and [reg 16 + 1] in DS into IP; it then loads the contents of memory locations addressed by [reg 16 + 2] and [reg 16 + 3] in DS into CS; typical 8086 registers used for reg 16 are BX, SI, and DI (intersegment indirect)
JNE/JNZ disp 8	Jump if not equal/jump if not zero	Same as JA/JNBE except that the jump is taken if ZF = 0; used for both signed and unsigned comparison
JNO disp 8	Jump if not overflow	Same as JA/JNBE except that the jump is taken if OF = 0
JNP/JPO disp 8	Jump if no parity/jump if parity odd	Same as JA/JNBE except that the jump is taken if PF = 0
JNS disp 8	Jump if not sign	Same as JA/JNBE except that the jump is taken if SF = 0
JO disp 8	Jump if overflow	Same as JA/JNBE except that the jump is taken if OF = 1
JP/JPE disp 8	Jump if parity/jump if parity even	Same as JA/JNBE except that the jump is taken if PF = 1
JS disp 8	Jump if sign	Same as JA/JNBE except that the jump is taken if SF = 1
LAHF	[AH] ← Flag low-byte	This instruction has implied addressing mode; it loads AH with the low byte of the flag register; no flags are affected
LDS reg, mem	[reg] ← [mem] [DS] ← [mem + 2]	Load a 16-bit register (AX, BX, CX, DX, SP, BP, SI, DI) with the content of specified memory and load DS with the content of the location that follows; no flags are affected; DS is used as the segment register for mem
LEA reg, mem	[reg] ← [offset portion of address]	LEA (load effective address) loads the value of the source operand rather than its content to register (such as SI, DI, BX) which are allowed to contain offset for accessing memory; no flags are affected
LES reg, mem	[reg] ← [mem] [ES] ← [mem + 2]	DS is used as the segment register for mem; in the example LES DX, [BX], DX is loaded with 16-bit value from a memory location addressed by 20-bit physical address computed from DS and BX; the 16-bit content of the next memory is loaded into ES; no flags are affected
LOCK	LOCK bus during next instruction	Lock is a one-byte prefix that causes the 8086 (configured in maximum mode) to assert its bus LOCK signal while following

TABLE 3.1 (continued)

Instructions	Interpretation	Comments
LOCK (continued)		instruction is executed; this signal is used in multiprocessing; the LOCK pin of the 8086 can be used to LOCK other processors off the system bus during execution of an instruction; in this way, the 8086 can be assured of uninterrupted access to common system resources such as shared RAM
LODS BYTE or LODSB	FOR BYTE [AL] ← [[SI]] [SI] ← [SI] + 1	Load 8-bit data into AL or 16-bit data into AX from a memory location addressed by SI in segment DS; if DF = 0, then SI is incremented by 1 for byte or incremented
LODS WORD or LODSW	FOR WORD [AX] ← [[SI]] [SI] ← [SI] + 2	by 2 for word after the load; if DF = 1, then SI is decremented by 1 for byte or decremented by 2 for word; LODS affects no flags
LOOP disp 8	Loop if CX not equal to zero	Decrement CX by one, without affecting flags and loop with signed 8-bit displacement (from –128 to +127, zero being positive) if CX is not equal to zero
LOOPE/LOOPZ disp 8	Loop while equal/loop while zero	Decrement CX by one without affecting flags and loop with signed 8-bit displacement if CX is equal to zero, and if ZF = 1 which results from execution of the previous instructions
LOOPNE/LOOPNZ disp 8	Loop while not equal/loop while not zero	Decrement CX by one without affecting flags and loop with signed 8-bit displacement if CX is not equal to zero and ZF = 0 which results from execution of previous instruction
MOV mem/reg 2, mem/reg 1	[mem/reg 2] [mem/reg 1]	mem uses DS as the segment register; no memory-to-memory operation allowed; that is, MOV mem, mem is not permitted; segment register cannot be specified as reg or reg; no flags are affected; not usually used to load or store 'A' from or to memory
MOV mem, data	[mem] ← data	mem uses DS as the segment register; 8- or 16-bit data specifies whether memory location is 8- or 16-bit; no flags are affected
MOV reg, data	[reg] ← data	Segment register cannot be specified as reg; data can be 8- or 16-bit; no flags are affected
MOV A, mem	[A] ← [mem]	Takes fewer bytes than reg, mem; mem uses DS as segment register; 'A' can be AL or AX; no flags are affected

TABLE 3.1 (continued)

Instructions	Interpretation	Comments
MOV mem, A	[mem] ← [A]	mem uses DS as segment register; 'A' can be AL or AX; no flags are affected; needs fewer bytes than MOV mem, reg
MOV segreg, mem/reg	[segreg] ← [mem/reg]	mem uses DS as segment register; used for initializing CS, DS, ES, and SS; no flags are affected
MOV mem/reg, segreg	[mem/reg] ← [segreg]	mem uses DS as segment register; no flags are affected
MOVS BYTE or MOVSB	FOR BYTE [[DI]] ← [[SI]] [SI] ← [SI] + 1	Move 8-bit or 16-bit data from the memory location addressed by SI in segment DS location addressed by DI in ES; segment DS can be overridden by a prefix but destination segment must be ES and cannot be overridden; if DF = 0, then SI is incremented by one for byte or incremented by two for word; if DF = 1, then SI is decremented by one for byte or by two for word
MOVS WORD or MOVSW	FOR WORD [[DI]] ← [[SI]] [SI] ← [SI] + 2	
MUL mem/reg	FOR 8 × 8 [AX] ← [AL]* [mem/reg] FOR 16 × 16 [DX] [AX] ← [AX]* [mem/reg]	mem/reg can be 8- or 16-bit; only CF and OF are affected; unsigned multiplication
NEG mem/reg	[mem/reg] ← [mem/reg]' + 1	mem/reg can be 8- or 16-bit; performs two's complement subtraction of the specified operand from zero, that is, two's complement of a number is formed; all flags are affected except CF = 0 if [mem/reg] is zero; otherwise CF = 1
NOP	NO Operation	8086 does nothing
NOT reg	[reg] ← [reg]'	mem and reg can be 8- or 16-bit; segment registers are not allowed; no flags are affected; ones complement reg
NOT mem	[mem] ← [mem]'	mem uses DS as the segment register; no flags are affected; ones complement mem
OR Mem/reg 1, Mem/reg 2	[mem/reg 1] ← [mem/reg 1] ∨ [mem/reg 2]	No memory-to-memory operation is allowed; [mem] or [reg 1] or [reg 2] can be 8- or 16-bit; all flags are affected with OF and CF cleared to zero; no segment registers are allowed; mem uses DS as segment register
OR mem, data	[mem] ←[mem] ∨ data	mem and data can be 8- or 16-bit; mem uses DS as segment register; all flags are affected with CF and OF cleared to zero

TABLE 3.1 (continued)

Instructions	Interpretation	Comments
OR reg, data	[reg] ← [reg] ∨ data	reg and data can be 8- or 16-bit; no segment registers are allowed; all flags are affected with CF and OF cleared to zero; should not be used to OR AL or AX with immediate data
OR A, data	[A] ← [A] ∨ data	Data can be 8- or 16-bit; A must be AL or AX; all flags are affected with OF and CF cleared to zero
OUT DX, AL	[PORT] ← [AL] DX	Output the 8-bit contents of AL into an I/O Port addressed by the 16-bit content of DX; this is a one-byte instruction
OUT DX, AX	[PORT] ← [AX] DX	Output the 16-bit contents of AX into an I/O Port addressed by the 16-bit content of DX; this is a one-byte instruction
OUT PORT, AL	[PORT] ← [AL]	Output the 8-bit contents of AL into the Port specified in the second byte of the instruction
OUT PORT, AX	[PORT] ← [AX]	Output the 16-bit contents of AX into the Port specified in the second byte of the instruction
POP mem	[mem] ← [[SP]] [SP] ← [SP] + 2	mem uses DS as the segment register; no flags are affected
POP reg	[reg] ← [[SP]] [SP] ← [SP] + 2	Cannot be used to POP segment registers or flag register
POP segreg	[segreg] ← [[SP]] [SP] ← [SP] + 2	POP CS is illegal
POPF	[Flags] ← [[SP]] [SP] ← [SP] + 2	This instruction pops the top two stack bytes in the 16-bit flag register
PUSH mem	[SP] ← [SP] − 2 [[SP]] ← [mem]	mem uses DS as segment register; no flags are affected; pushes 16-bit memory contents
PUSH reg	[SP] ← [SP] − 2 [[SP]] ← [reg]	reg must be a 16-bit register; cannot be used to PUSH segment register or Flag register
PUSH segreg	[SP] ← [SP] − 2 [[SP]] ← [segreg]	PUSH CS is illegal
PUSHF	[SP] ← [SP] − 2 [[SP]] ← [Flags]	This instruction pushes the 16-bit Flag register onto the stack
RCL mem/reg, 1	ROTATE through carry left once byte or word in mem/reg	FOR BYTE FOR WORD

TABLE 3.1 (continued)

Instructions	Interpretation	Comments
RCL mem/reg, CL	ROTATE through carry left byte or word in mem/reg by [CL]	Operation same as RCL mem/reg, 1 except the number of rotates is specified in CL for rotates up to 255; zero or negative rotates are illegal
RCR mem/reg, 1	ROTATE through carry right once byte or word in mem/reg	FOR BYTE FOR WORD
RCR mem/reg, CL	ROTATE through carry right byte or word in mem/reg by [CL]	Operation same as RCR mem/reg, 1 except the number of rotates is specified in CL for rotates up to 255; zero or negative rotates are illegal
RET	.POPS IP for intrasegment CALLS .POPS IP and CS for intersegment CALLS	The assembler generates an intrasegment return if the programmer has defined the subroutine as NEAR; for intrasegment return, the following operations take place: [IP] ← [[SP]], [SP] ← [SP] + 2; on the other hand, the assembler generates an inter-segment return if the subroutine has been defined as FAR; in this case, the following operations take place: [IP] ← [[SP]], [SP] ← [SP] + 2, [CS] ← [[SP]], [SP] ← [SP] + 2; an optional 16-bit displacement 'START' can be specified with the intersegment return such as RET START; in this case, the 16-bit displacement is added to the SP value; this feature may be used to discard parameter pushed onto the stack before the execution of the CALL instruction
ROL mem/reg, 1	ROTATE left once byte or word in mem/reg	FOR BYTE FOR WORD

TABLE 3.1 (continued)

Instructions	Interpretation	Comments
ROL mem/reg, CL	ROTATE left byte or word by the content of CL	[CL] contains rotate count up to 255; zero and negative shifts are illegal; CL is used to rotate count when the rotate is greater than once; mem uses DS as the segment register
ROR mem/reg, 1	ROTATE right once byte or word in mem/reg	FOR BYTE FOR WORD
ROR mem/reg, CL	ROTATE right byte or word in mem/reg by [CL]	Operation same as ROR mem/reg, 1; [CL] specifies the number of rotates for up to 255; zero and negative rotates are illegal; mem uses DS as the segment register
SAHF	[Flags, low-byte] ← [AH]	This instruction has the implied addressing mode; the content of the AH register is stored into the low-byte of the flag register; no flags are affected
SAL mem/reg, 1	Shift arithmetic left once byte or word in mem or reg	FOR BYTE FOR WORD Mem uses DS as the segment register; reg cannot be segment registers; OF and CF are affected; if sign bit is changed during or after shifting, the OF is set to one
SAL mem/reg, CL	Shift arithmetic left byte or word by shift count on CL	Operation same as SAL mem/reg, 1; CL contains shift count for up to 255; zero and negative shifts are illegal; [CL] is used as shift count when shift is greater than one; OF and SF are affected; if sign bit of [mem] is changed during or after shifting, the OF is set to one; mem uses DS as segment register

TABLE 3.1 (continued)

Instructions	Interpretation	Comments
SAR mem/reg, 1	SHIFT arithmetic right once byte or word in mem/reg	FOR BYTE FOR WORD
SAR mem/reg, CL	SHIFT arithmetic right byte or word in mem/reg by [CL]	Operation same as SAR mem/reg, 1; however, shift count is specified in CL for shifts up to 255; zero and negative shifts are illegal
SBB mem/reg 1, mem/reg 2	[mem/reg 1] ← [mem/reg 1] – [mem/reg 2] – CY	Same as SUB mem/reg 1, mem/reg 2 except this is a subtraction with borrow
SBB mem, data	[mem] ← [mem] – data – CY	Same as SUB mem, data except this is a subtraction with borrow
SBB reg, data	[reg] ← [reg] – data – CY	Same as SUB reg, data except this is a subtraction with borrow
SBB A, data	[A] ← [A] – data – CY	Same as SUB A, data except this is a subtraction with borrow
SCAS BYTE or SCASB	FOR BYTE [AL] – [[DI]], flags are affected, [DI] [DI] ± 1	8- or 16-bit data addressed by [DI] in ES is subtracted from 8- or 16-bit data in AL or AX and flags are affected without affecting [AL] or [AX] or string data; ES cannot be overridden; if DF = 0, then DI is incre-
SCAS WORD or SCASW	FOR WORD [AX] – [[DI]], flags are affected, [DI] ← [DI] ± 2	mented by one for byte and two for word; if DF = 1, then DI is decremented by one for byte or decremented by two for word
SHL mem/reg, 1	SHIFT logical left once byte or word in mem/reg	Same as SAL mem/reg, 1
SHL mem/reg, CL	SHIFT logical left byte or word in mem/reg by the shift count in CL	Same as SAL mem/reg, CL except overflow is cleared to zero
SHR mem/reg, 1	SHIFT right logical once byte or word in mem/reg	FOR BYTE FOR WORD

TABLE 3.1 (continued)

Instructions	Interpretation	Comments

SHR
  mem/reg, CL
	SHIFT right logical byte or
	  word in mem/reg by [CL]
		Operation same as SHR mem/reg, 1;
		  however, shift count is specified in CL for
		  shifts up to 255; zero and negative shifts
		  are illegal

STC	CF ← 1	Set carry to one
STD	DF ← 1	Set direction flag to one
STI	IF ← 1	Set interrupt enable flag to one to enable maskable interrupts

STOS BYTE
  or STOSB
	FOR BYTE
	  [[DI]] ← [AL]
	  [DI] ← [DI] ± 1
		Store 8-bit data from AL or 16-bit data from
		  AX into a memory location addressed by DI
		  in segment ES; segment register ES cannot

STOS WORD
  or STOSW
	FOR WORD
	  [[DI]] ← [AX]
	  [DI] ← [DI] ± 2
		be overridden; if DF = 0, then DI is
		  incremented by one for byte or incremented
		  by two for word after the store

SUB mem/reg 1,
  mem/reg 2
	[mem/reg 1] ←
	  [mem/reg 1] – [mem/reg 2]
		No memory-to-memory SUB permitted; all
		  flags are affected; mem uses DS as the
		  segment register

SUB mem, data	[mem] ← [mem] – data	Data can be 8- or 16-bit; mem uses DS as the segment register; all flags are affected

SUB reg, data	[reg] ← [reg] – data	Data can be 8- or 16-bit; this instruction is
		  not usually used for subtracting data from
		  AX or AL; SUB A, data is used for this; all
		  flags are affected

SUB A, data	[A] ← [A] – data	'A' can be AL or AX; data can be 8- or 16- bit; all flags are affected

TEST mem/reg 1,
  mem/reg 2
	[mem/reg 1] – [mem/reg 2],
	  no result; flags are affected
		No memory-to-memory TEST is allowed; no
		  result is provided; all flags are affected with
		  CF and OF cleared to zero; [mem], [reg 1]
		  or [reg 2] can be 8- or 16-bit; no segment
		  registers are allowed; mem uses DS as the
		  segment register

TEST
  mem/data
	[mem] – data,
	  no result; flags are affected
		Mem and data can be 8- or 16-bit; no result
		  is provided; all flags are affected with CF
		  and OD cleared to zero; mem uses DS as
		  the segment register

TEST
  reg, data
	[reg] – data,
	  no result; flags are affected
		Reg and data can be 8- or 16-bit; no result
		  is provided; all flags are affected with CF
		  and OF cleared to zero; reg cannot be
		  segment register; should not be used to test
		  AL or AX with immediate data

TEST
  A, data
	[A] – data,
	  no results; flags are affected
		'A' must be AX or AL; data can be 8- or 16-
		  bit; no result is provided; all flags are
		  affected with CF and OF cleared to zero

TABLE 3.1 (continued)

Instructions	Interpretation	Comments
WAIT	8086 enters wait state	Causes CPU to enter wait state if the 8086 TEST pin is high; while in wait state, the 8086 continues to check TEST pin for low; if TEST pin goes back to zero, the 8086 executes the next instruction; this feature can be used to synchronize the operation of 8086 to an event in external hardware
XCHG AX, reg	[AX] ↔ [reg]	Reg must be 16-bit; no flags are affected; reg cannot be segment register
XCHG mem, reg	[mem] ↔ [reg]	Reg and mem can be both 8- or 16-bit; mem uses DS as the sement register; reg cannot be segment register; no flags are affected
XCHG reg, reg	[reg] ↔ [reg]	Reg not used to exchange reg with AX; reg can be 8- or 16-bit; reg cannot be segment register; no flags are affected
XLAT	[AL] ← [AL] + [BX]	This instruction is useful for translating characters from one code such as ASCII to another such as EBCDIC; this is a no-operand instruction and is called an instruction with implied addressing mode; the instruction loads AL with the contents of a 20-bit physical address computed from DS, BX, and AL; this instruction can be used to read the elements in a table where BX can be loaded with a 16-bit value to point to the starting address (offset from DS) and AL can be loaded with the element number (0 being the first element number); no flags are affected; the XLAT instruction is equivalent to MOV AL, [AL] [BX]
XOR mem/reg 1, mem/reg 2	[mem/reg 1] ← [mem/reg 1] ⊕ [mem/reg 2]	No memory-to-memory operation is allowed; [mem] or [reg 1] or [reg 2] can be 8- or 16-bit; all flags are affected with CF and OF cleared to zero; mem uses DS as the segment register
XOR mem, data	[reg] ← [mem] ⊕ data	Data and mem can be 8- or 16-bit; mem uses DS as the segment register; mem cannot be segment register; all flags are affected with CF and OF cleared to zero
XOR Reg, data	[reg] ← [reg] ⊕ data	Same as XOR mem, data; should not be used for XORing AL or AX with immediate data
XOR A, data	[A] ← [A] ⊕ data	'A' must be AL or AX; data can be 8- or 16-bit; all flags are affected with CF and OF cleared to zero

Explanation of Table 3.A-1 Instructions

- MOV CX, DX copies the 16-bit content of DX into CX. MOV AX, 0205H moves immediate data 0205H into 16-bit register AX. MOV CH, [BX] moves the 8-bit content of memory location addressed by BX in segment register DS into CH. If [BX] = 0050H, [DS] = 2000H, [20050H] = 08H, then after MOV CH, [BX], the content of CH will be 08H.

  MOV START [BP], CX moves the 16-bit (CL to first location and then CH) content of CX into two memory locations addressed by the sum of the displacement START and BP in segment register SS. For example, if [CX] = 5009H, [BP] = 0030H, [SS] = 3000H, START = 06H, then after MOV START [BP], CX physical memory location [30036H] = 09H and [30037H] = 50H. Note that the segment register SS can be overridden by CS using MOV CS: START [BP], CX.

- PUSH START [BX] pushes the 16-bit contents of two memory locations starting at the 20-bit physical address computed from START, BX, and DS after decrementing SP by 2.

- POP ES pops the top stack word into ES and then increments SP by 2.

- XCHG START [BX], AX exchanges the 16-bit word in AX with the contents of two consecutive memory locations starting at 20-bit physical address computed from START, BX, and DS. [AL] is exchanged with the content of the first location and [AH] is exchanged with the content of the next location.

- XLAT can be used to convert a code such as ASCII into another code such as EBCDIC.

Suppose that an 8086-based microcomputer is interfaced to an ASCII keyboard and an IBM printer (EBCDIC code). In such a system, any number entered into the microcomputer will be in ASCII code which must be converted to EBCDIC code before outputting to the printer. If the number entered is 4, then the ASCII code for 4 (34H) must be translated to the EBCDIC code for 4 (F4H). A look-up table containing EBCDIC code for all the decimal numbers (0 to 9) can be stored in memory at the 16-bit starting address (offset) in DS, 3030H with the code for 0 stored at 3030H, code for 1 at 3031H, and so on. Now, if AL is loaded with the ASCII code 34H and BX is loaded with 3000H, then by using the XLAT instruction, content of memory location 3034H in DS containing the EBCDIC code for 4 (F4H) from the look-up table is read into AL, thus replacing the ASCII code for 4 with the EBCDIC code for 4.

- Note that MOV A, mem can also be obtained from MOV mem/reg 2, mem/reg 1. This means that MOV A, mem has two different OP codes; one obtained from MOV mem/reg 2, mem/reg 1 and the other from the dedicated MOV A, mem instruction. The assembler usually provides the OP code for the MOV A, M since it takes fewer bytes. The same concept applies to other instructions involving "A" which have more than one OP code.
- Symbolic names such as START can be defined as an address containing a byte or word by using the DB or DW assembler directive. To define the symbolic name as a constant for immediate data, one can use the EQU directive.

Explanation of Table 3.A-2 Instructions

- Consider fixed port addressing in which the 8-bit port address is directly specified as part of the instruction. IN AL, 38H inputs 8-bit data from port 38H into AL. IN AX, 38H inputs 16-bit data from ports 38H and 39H into AX. OUT 38H, AL outputs the contents of AL to port 38H. OUT 38H, AX, on the other hand, outputs the 16-bit contents of AX to ports 38H and 39H.
- For the variable port addressing, the port address is 16-bit and is specified in the DX register. Consider ports addressed by 16-bit address contained in DX. Assume $[DX] = 3124_{16}$ in all the following examples:

> IN AL, DX inputs 8-bit data from 8-bit port 3124_{16} into AL.
> IN AX, DX inputs 16-bit data from ports 3124_{16} and 3125_{16} into AX.
> OUT DX, AL outputs 8-bit data from AL into port 3124_{16} data.
> OUT DX, AX outputs 16-bit data from AX into ports 3124_{16} and 3125_{16}.

Variable port addressing allows up to 65,536 ports with addresses from 0000H to FFFFH. The port addresses in the variable port addressing can be calculated dynamically in a program. For example, assume that an 8086-based microcomputer is connected to three printers via three separate ports. Now, in order to output to each one of the printers, separate programs are required if fixed port addressing is used. However, with variable port addressing one can write a general subroutine to output to the printers and then supply the address of the port for a particular printer in which data output is desired to register DX in the subroutine.

Explanation of Table 3.A-3 Instructions

- LEA reg, mem loads an offset (mem) in DS directly into the specified register. The XLAT and string instructions assume that certain registers point to operands. LEA can be used to load these addresses. For example, LEA can be used to load the address of the table used by the XLAT instructions. Consider converting an ASCII code into EBCDIC code. Suppose that EBCDIC codes for the first seven symbols NUL (NULL), SOH (Start of Heading), STX (Start Text), and ETX (End Text); EOT (End of Transmission), ENQ (Enquiry), and ACK (Acknowledge) are stored in memory.

Starting at location TABLE 1 as follows:

```
TABLE 1:    00H; EBCDIC Code for NUL
            01H; Code for SOH
            02H; Code for STX
            03H; Code for ETX
            37H; Code for EOT
            2DH; Code for ENQ
            2EH; Code for ACK
```

Suppose that the ASCII codes for these characters are stored in memory starting at address TABLE 2 as follows:

```
TABLE 2:    00H; ASCII Code for NUL
            01H; Code for SOH
            02H; Code for STX
            03H; Code for ETX
            04H; Code for EOT
            05H; Code for ENQ
            06H; Code for ACK
```

Now, in order to translate an ASCII Code for a symbol such as EOT into its EBCDIC Code, ASCII Code for EOT (04H) can be loaded into AL, BX can be initialized with the value of TABLE 1 using LEA, and XLAT can then be used to load the ABCDIC Code for EOT (37H) into AL as follows:

```
LEA BX, TABLE 1 ; Load the value TABLE 1 into BX
MOV AL, 04H     ; Load ASCII Code for EOT into AL
XLAT            ; Load the content of memory loca-
                  tion addressed by [TABLE 1 + 04H]
                  into AL.
```

- LDS reg, mem can be used to initialize SI and DS to point to the start of the source string before using one of the string instructions. For example, LDS SI, [BX] loads the 16-bit contents of memory offset by [BX] in DS into SI and the 16-bit contents of memory offset by [BX + 2] in DS into DS.

- LES reg, mem can be used to point to the start of the destination string before using one of the string instructions. For example, LES DI, [BX] loads the 16-bit contents of memory offset by [BX] in DS to DI and then initializes ES with the 16-bit contents of memory offset by [BX + 2] in DS.

Table 3.A-4 is self-explanatory.

Explanation of Table 3.A-5 Instructions

- Numerical data received by an 8086-based microcomputer from a terminal is usually in ASCII code. The ASCII codes for numbers 0 to 9 are 30H through 39H. Two 8-bit data can be entered into an 8086-based microcomputer via a terminal. The ASCII codes for these data (with 3 as the upper middle for each type) can be added. AAA instruction can then be used to provide the correct unpacked BCD. Suppose that ASCII codes for 2 (32_{16}) and 5 (35_{16}) are entered into an 8086-based microcomputer via a terminal. These ASCII codes can be added and then the result can be adjusted to provide the correct unpacked BCD using AAA instructions as follows:

```
ADD CL, DL    ; [CL] = 32₁₆ = ACSII for 2
              ; [DL] = 35₁₆ = ASCII for 5
              ; Result [CL] = 67₁₆
MOV AL, CL    ; Move ASCII result
              ; into AL since AAA
              ; adjust only [AL]
AAA           ; [AL] = 07, unpacked
              ; BCD for 7
```

Note that in order to send the unpacked BCD result 07_{16} back to the terminal, [AL] = 07 can be ORed with 30H to provide 37H, the ASCII code for 7.

- DAA is used to adjust the result of adding two packed BCD numbers in AL to provide a valid BCD number. If after the addition, the low 4-bit of the result in AL is greater than 9 (or if AF = 1), then the DAA adds 6 to the low 4 bits of AL. On the other hand, if the high 4 bits of the result in AL is greater than 9 (or if CF = 1), then DAA adds 60H to AL. As an example, consider adding two packed BCD digits 55 with 18 as follows:

```
ADD AL, DL   ; [AL] = 55 BCD
             ; [DL] = 18 BCD
             ; Result = [AL] = 6DH

DAA          ; Since low nibble
```

$; D = 1101_2 > 9, \text{add i.e. } 1101_2 + 0110_2 \rightarrow$

$$\underbrace{10011}_{}{}_2$$

3BCD

carry

- The ASCII codes for two-bit numbers in an 8086-based microcomputer can be subtracted. Assume

```
[AL] = 35H = ASCII for 5
[DL] = 37H = ASCII for 7
```

The following instruction sequence provides the correct subtraction result:

```
SUB AL, DL   ; [AL] = 1111 1110₂ = subtraction
             ;   result
             ; in 2's complement
             ; CF = 1
AAS          ; [AL] = BCD02
             ; CF = 1 means
             ; borrow to be
             ; used in multi BCD subtraction
```

AAS adjusts [AL] and leaves zeros in the upper nibble. To output to the terminal from the microcomputer, BCD data can be ORed with 30H to produce the correct ASCII code.

- DAS can be used to adjust the result of subtraction in AL of two packed BCD numbers to provide the correct packed BCD. If low 4-bit in AL is greater than 9 (or if AF = 1), then DAS subtracts 6 from the low 4-bit of AL. On the other hand, if the upper 4-bit of the result in AL is greater than 9 (or if CF = 1), DAS subtracts 60 from AL.

While performing these subtractions, any borrows from LOW and HIGH nibbles are ignored. For example, consider subtracting BCD 55 in DL from BCD 94 in AL.

```
SUB AL, DL  ; [AL] = 3FH → Low nibble = 1111
DAS         ; CF = 0                  -6 = 1010
                                           1001
            ; [AL] = 39 BCD            1
                                        ignore
```

- IMUL mem/reg provides signed 8×8 or signed 16×16 multiplication. As an example, if $[CL] = FDH = -3_{10}$, $[AL] = FEH = -2_{10}$, then after IMUL CL, register AX contains 0006H.
- Consider 16×16 unsigned multiplication, MUL WORDPTR [BX]. If $[BX] = 0050H$, $[DS] = 3000H$, $[30050H] = 0002H$, $[AX] = 0006H$, then after MUL WORDPTR [BX], $[DX] = 0000H$, $[AX] = 000CH$.
- Consider DIV BL. If $[AX] = 0009H$, $[BL] = 02H$, then after DIV BL,

$$[AH] = Remainder = 01H$$
$$[AL] = Quotient = 04H$$

- Consider IDIV.WORDPTR [BX]. If $[BX] = 0020H$, $[DS] = 2000H$, $[20020H] = 0004H$, $[DX] [AX] = 00000011H$, then after IDIV. WORDPTR [BX],

$$[DX] = Remainder = 0001H$$
$$[AX] = Quotient = 0004H$$

- AAD converts two unpacked BCD digits in AH and AL to an equivalent binary number in AL. AAD must be used before dividing two unpacked BCD digits in AX by an unpacked BCD byte. For example, consider dividing $[AX] =$ unpacked BCD 0508 (58 decimal) by $[DH] = 07H$. $[AX]$ must first be converted to binary by using AAD. The register AX will then contain 003AH = 58 decimal. After DIV DH, $[AL] =$ quotient = 08 unpacked BCD, $[AH] =$ remainder = 02 unpacked BCD.
- Consider CBW. This instruction extends the sign from the AL register to AH register. For example, if $[AL] = E2H$, then after CBW, AH will contain FFH since the most significant bit of E2H is one. Note that sign extension is useful when one wants to perform an arithmetic

operation on two signed numbers of different sizes. For example, the 8-bit signed number 02H can be subtracted from 16-bit signed number 2005H as follows:

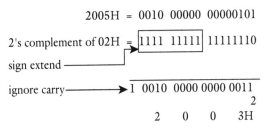

$$2005H = 0010\ 00000\ 00000101$$

2's complement of 02H = $\boxed{1111\ 11111}\ 11111110$

sign extend

ignore carry → 1 0010 0000 0000 0011
$$2$$
$$2 \quad 0 \quad 0 \quad 3H$$

Another example of sign extension is that in order to multiply a signed 8-bit number by a signed 16-bit number, one must first sign-extend the signed 8-bit into a signed 16-bit number and then the instruction IMUL can be used for 16×16 signed multiplication.

- AAM adjusts the product of two unpacked BCD digits in AX. If [AL] = BCD3 = 00000011_2 and [CH] = BCD8 = $0000\ 1000_2$, then after MUL CH, [AX] = 0000000000011000_2 = 0018H, and after using AAM, [AX] = $00000010\ 00000100_2$ = unpacked 24. The following instruction sequence accomplishes this:

MUL CH
AAM

Note that the 8086 does not allow multiplication of two ASCII codes. Therefore, before multiplying two ASCII bytes received from a terminal, one must mask the upper 4-bits of each one of these bytes and then multiply them as two unpacked BCD digits and then use AAM for adjustment. In order to convert the unpacked BCD product back to ASCII, for sending back to the terminal, one must OR the product with 3030H.

Table 3.A-6 is self-explanatory.

Explanation of Table 3.A-7 Instructions

- LODS can be represented in four forms:

For Byte   **LODS BYTE**
                                 or
                             LODSB

For Word   **LODS WORD**
                                 or
                             LODSW

If [SI] = 0020H, [DS] = 3000H, [30020H] = 05H, DF = 0, then after LODS BYTE or LODSB, [AL] = 05H, [SI] = 0021H.

- [DS] = 2000H, [ES] = 3000H, [SI] = 0020H, [DI] = 0050H, DF = 0, [20020H] = 0205H, [30050H] 4071H, then after execution of MOVSW or MOVS WORD, memory location 30050H will contain 0205H. Since DF = 0, register SI will contain 0022H and register DI will contain 0052H.

- REP, a one-byte prefix, can be used with MOVS to cause the instruction MOVS to continue executing until CX = 0. Each time the instructions such as REP MOVSB or REP MOVSW are executed, CX is automatically decremented by 1, and if [CX] ≠ 0, MOVS is reexecuted and then CX is decremented by 1 until CX = 0; the next instruction is then executed. REP MOVSB or REP MOVSW can be used to move string bytes until the string length (loaded into CX before the instructions REP MOVSB or REP MOVSW) is decremented for zero.

    REPE/REPZ or REPNE/REPNZ prefix can be used with CMPS or SCAS to cause one of these instructions to continue executing until ZF = 0 (for REPNE/REPNZ prefix) and CX = 0. Note that REPE and REPZ are two mnemonics for the same prefix byte. Similarly, REPNE and REPNZ also provide the same purpose. If CMPS is prefixed with REPE or REPZ, the operation is interpreted as "compare while not end-of-string (CX not zero) and strings are equal (ZF = 1)". If CMPS is preceded by REPNE or REPNZ, the operation is interpreted as "compare while not end-of-string (CX not zero) and strings not equal (ZF = 0)". Thus, repeated CMPS can be used to find matching or differing string elements. If SCAS is prefixed with REPE or REPZ, the operation is interpreted as "scan while not end-of-string (CX not 0) and string-element = scan-value (ZF = 1)". This form may be used to scan for departure from a given value. If SCAS is prefixed with REPNE or REPNZ, the operation is interpreted as "scan while not end-of-string (CX not 0) and string-element is not equal to scan-value (ZF = 0)". This form may be used to locate a value in a string. Repeated string instructions are interruptible; the processor recognizes the interrupt before processing the next string element. Upon return from the interrupt, the repeated operation is resumed from the point of interruption. When multiple prefixes (such as LOCK and segment override) are specified in addition to any of the repeat prefixes, program execution does not resume properly upon return from interrupt.

    The processor remembers only one prefix in effect at the time of the interrupt, the prefix that immediately precedes the string instructions. Upon return from interrupt, program execution resumes at this point but any additional prefixes specified are not recognized. The multiple prefix must be used with a string instruction; maskable interrupts should be disabled for the duration of the repeated execution. However, this will not prevent a nonmaskable interrupt from being recognized.

- Note that the segment register for destination for all string instructions is always ES and cannot be overridden. However, DS can be overridden for the source using a prefix. For example, ES: MOVSB instruction uses the segment register as ES for both source and destination.

Table 3.A-8 is self-explanatory.

Explanation of Table 3.A-9 Instructions

All 8086 conditional branch instructions use 8-bit signed displacement. That is, the displacement covers a branch range of -128_{10} to $+127_{10}$ with 0 being positive. In order to branch out of this range, the 8086 unconditional jump instructions (having direct mode) must be used.

Conditional jumps are typically used with compare instructions to find the relationship (equal to, greater than, or less than) between two numbers. The use of conditional instructions depends whether the numbers to be compared are signed or unsigned. The 8-bit number $1111\ 1110_2$, when considered as signed, has a value of -2_{10}; the same number has a value of $+254_{10}$ when considered as unsigned. This number, when considered signed, will be smaller than zero, and when unsigned will be greater than zero. Some new terms are used to differentiate between signed and unsigned conditional transfers. For the unsigned numbers, the terms used are "below and above", while for signed numbers, the terms "less than and greater than" are used. In the above, the number $1111\ 1110_2$ when considered signed is greater than $0000\ 0000_2$, while the same number $1111\ 1110_2$ when considered unsigned is above $0000\ 0000_2$. The conditional transfer instructions for equality of two numbers are the same for both signed and unsigned numbers. This is because when two numbers are compared for equality irrespective of whether they are signed or unsigned, they will provide a zero result (ZF = 1) if equal or a nonzero result (ZF = 0) if not equal. Therefore, the same instructions apply for both signed and unsigned numbers for "equal to" or "not equal to" conditions, and the various signed and unsigned conditional branch instructions for determining the relationship between two numbers are as follows:

Signed		Unsigned	
Name	**Alternate name**	**Name**	**Alternate name**
JE disp8 (JUMP if equal)	JZ disp8 (JUMP if result zero)	JE disp8 (JUMP if equal)	JZ disp8 (JUMP if zero)
JNE disp8 (JUMP if not equal)	JNZ disp8 (JUMP if not zero)	JNE disp8 (JUMP if not equal)	JNZ disp8 (JUMP if not zero)
JG disp8 (JUMP if greater)	JNLE disp8 (JUMP if not less or equal)	JA disp8 (JUMP if above)	JNBE disp8 (JUMP if not below or equal)
JGE disp8 (JUMP if greater or equal)	JNL disp8 (JUMP if not less)	JAE disp8 (JUMP if above or equal)	JNB disp8 (JUMP if not below)
JL disp8 (JUMP if less than)	JNGE disp8 (JUMP if not greater or equal)	JB disp8 (JUMP if below)	JNAE disp8 (JUMP if not above or equal)
JLE disp8 (JUMP if less or equal)	JNG disp8 (JUMP if not greater)	JBE disp8 (JUMP if below or equal)	JNA disp8 (JUMP if not above)

3.4.1 SIGNED AND UNSIGNED CONDITIONAL BRANCH INSTRUCTIONS

There are also conditional transfer instructions that are concerned with the setting of status flags rather than relationship between two numbers. The table below lists these instructions:

JC disp8	JUMP if carry, i.e., CF = 1
JNC disp8	JUMP if no carry, i.e., CF = 0
JP disp8	JUMP if parity, i.e., PF = 1
JNP disp8	JUMP if no parity, i.e., PF = 0
JO disp8	JUMP if overflow, i.e., OF = 1
JNO disp8	JUMP if no overflow, i.e., OF = 0
JS disp8	JUMP if sign, i.e., SF = 1
JNS disp8	JUMP if no sign, i.e., SF = 0
JZ disp8	JUMP if result zero, i.e., Z = 1
JNZ disp8	JUMP if result not zero, i.e., Z = 0

3.4.2 CONDITIONAL JUMPS AFFECTING INDIVIDUAL FLAGS

The JP and JNP instructions use alternate names. They are JPE (Jump if Parity Even) and JPO (Jump if Parity Odd), respectively.

Now, let us look at the flag settings for the conditional transfer instructions concerned with the relationship between two numbers. These are listed in the table below:

Flag Settings for Instructions Concerned with Relationships between Two Numbers

Instruction	Flag setting
JE/JZ	ZF = 1
JNE/JNZ	ZF = 0
JL/JNGE	SF + OF = 1
JNL/JGE	SF + OF = 0
JG/JNLE	((SF + OF) OR ZF) = 0
JNG/JLE	((SF × + OR OF) OR ZF) = 1
JB/JNAE	CF = 1
JNB/JAE	CF = 0
JA/JNBE	(CF OR ZF) = 0
JNA/JBE	(CF OR ZF) = 1

The meanings of JE/JZ (ZF = 1) and JNE/JNZ (ZF = 0) are obvious.

If two signed numbers are compared and if the "less than" condition is satisfied (SF = 1) with no overflow (OF = 0), the processor after execution of the JL/JNGE instruction branches to a label with the specified displacement; otherwise the next instruction is executed. In this case, SF + OF = 1. Similarly, the meaning of JNL/JGE can be explained.

The processor when executing the JG/JNLE instruction (after comparing two signed numbers) branches to the label with the specified displacement if OF = 0 and SF = 0 (i.e., result is greater than zero). In this case, ((SF + OF) OR ZF) = 0. Similarly, the meaning of JNG/JLE can be explained.

The overflow flag OF is not involved while considering unsigned numbers. After comparing two unsigned numbers, the processor when executing the JB/JNAE instruction branches to a label with the specified displacement if result is below zero (i.e., CF = 1 indicating a borrow). Similarly, the meaning of JNB/JAE can be explained.

After comparing two unsigned numbers, the processor when executing the JA/JNBE instruction branches to a label with the specified displacement if result is above zero (CF = 0) or not equal to zero (ZF = 0). Similarly, the meaning of JNA/JBE can be explained.

Tables 3.A-10, 3.A-11, and 3.A-12 are self-explanatory.

3.5 8086 INSTRUCTION FORMAT

The 8086 instruction sizes vary from one to six bytes. The general 8086 instruction format is shown in Figure 3.5. The op code, register direction bit (D) and data size bit (W) in byte 1 are defined by Intel as follows:

- Op code occupies six bits and it defines the operation to be carried out by the instruction.
- Register Direction bit (D) occupies one bit. It defines whether the register operand in byte 2 is the source or destination operand. D = 1 specifies that the register operand is the destination operand; on the other hand, D = 0 indicates that the register is a source operand.
- Data size bit (W) defines whether the operation to be performed is on 8- or 16-bit data. W = 0 indicates 8-bit operation while W = 1 specifies 16-bit operation.
- The second byte of the instruction usually identifies whether one of

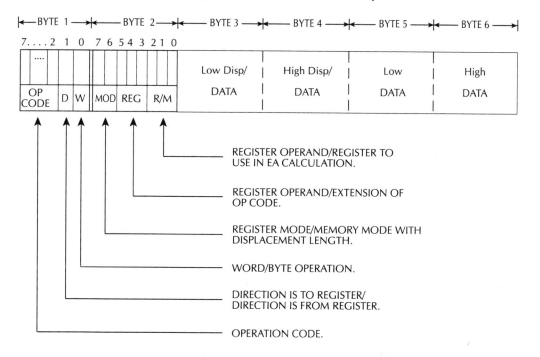

FIGURE 3.5 8086 Instruction format.

the operands is in memory or whether both are registers: this byte contains three fields. These are the Mode (MOD) field, the Register (REG) field, and the Register/Memory (R/M) field and are defined as follows.

The 2-bit MOD field specifies whether the operand is in register or memory as follows:

MOD	Interpretation
00	Memory mode with no displacement follows except for 16-bit displacement when R/M = 110
01	Memory mode with 8-bit displacement
10	Memory mode with 16-bit displacement
11	Register mode (no displacement)

REG field occupies 3 bits. It defines the register for the first operand which is specified as the source or destination by the D-bit (byte 1). The definition of REG and W fields are given below:

REG	W = 0	W = 1
000	AL	AX
001	CL	CX
010	DL	DX
011	BL	BX
100	AH	SP
101	CH	BP
110	DH	SI
111	BH	DI

The R/M field occupies 3 bits. The R/M field along with the MOD field defines the second operand as shown below:

MOD 11			Effective address calculation			
R/M	W = 0	W = 1	R/M	MOD = 00	MOD 01	MOD 10
000	AL	AX	000	(BX) + (SI)	(BX) + (SI) + D8	(BX) + (SI) + D16
001	CL	CX	001	(BX) + (DI)	(BX) + (DI) + D8	(BX) + (DI) + D16
010	DL	DX	010	(BP) + (SI)	(BP) + (SI) + D8	(BP) + (SI) + D16
011	BL	BX	011	(BP) + (DI)	(BP) + (DI) + D8	(BP) + (DI) + D16
100	AH	SP	100	(SI)	(SI) + D8	(SI) + D16
101	CH	BP	101	(DI)	(DI + D8	(DI) + D16

MOD 11			Effective address calculation			
R/M	W = 0	W = 1	R/M	MOD = 00	MOD 01	MOD 10
110	DH	SI	110	DIRECT ADDRESS	(BP) + D8	(BP) + D16
111	BH	DI	111	(BX)	(BX) + D8	(BX) + D16

In the above, encoding of the R/M field depends on how the mode field is set. If MOD = 11 (register-to-register mode), then R/M identifies the second register operand. If MOD selects memory mode, then R/M indicates how the effective address of the memory operand is to be calculated.

• Bytes 3 through 6 of an instruction are optional fields that normally contain the displacement value of a memory operand and/or the actual value of an immediate constant operand. As an example, consider the instruction MOV CH, BL. This instruction transfers the 8-bit content of BL into CH. We will determine the machine code of this instruction. The 6-bit op code for this instruction is 100010_2. The D-bit indicates whether the register specified by the REG field of byte 2 is a source or destination operand. Let us define the BL in the REG field of byte 2. D = 0 indicates that the REG field of the next byte is the source operand. The W-bit of byte 1 is 0 since this is a byte operation.

In byte 2, since the second operand is a register, MOD field is 11_2. The R/M field = 101_2 specifies that the destination register is CH and, therefore, R/M = 101_2. Hence the machine code for MOV CH, BL is $\underbrace{10001001}_{\text{BYTE 1}} \quad \underbrace{11011101}_{\text{BYTE 2}}$

= $89DD_{16}$.

As another example, consider SUB BX, [DI]. This instruction subtracts the 16-bit content of memory location addressed by DI and DS from BX. The 6-bit op code for SUB is 001010_2.

D = 1 so that the REG field of byte 2 is the destination operand and W = 1 indicates 16-bit operation. Therefore, byte 1 = $\underbrace{0010}_{2} \quad \underbrace{1011}_{B}$

= $2B_{16}$. Hence the machine code = $2\ B1D_{16}$.

3.6 8086 ASSEMBLER-DEPENDENT INSTRUCTIONS

Some 8086 instructions do not define whether an 8-bit or 16-bit operation is to be executed. Instructions with one of the 8086 registers as an operand typically define the operation as 8-bit or 16-bit based on the register size. An example is MOV CL, [BX] which moves an 8-bit number with the offset defined by [BX] in DS into register CL; MOV CX, [BX], on the other hand, moves the number from offsets [BX] and [BX + 1] in DS into CX.

Instructions with single-memory operand may define 8-bit or 16-bit operation by adding B for byte or W for word with the mnemonic. Typical examples are MULB [BX] and CMPB [ADDR]. The string instructions may define this in two ways. Typical examples are MOVSB or MOVS BYTE for 8-bit and MOVSW or MOVS WORD for 16-bit. Memory offsets can also be specified by including .BYTE PTR for 8-bit and .WORD PTR for 16-bit with the instruction. Typical examples are INC .BYTE PTR [BX] and INC.WORD PTR [BX].

3.7 ASM-86 ASSEMBLER PSEUDOINSTRUCTIONS

The ASM-86 is the assembler written by Intel for the 8086 microprocessor. The ASM-86 allows the programmer to assign the values of CS, DS, SS, and ES. One of the requirements of the ASM-86 assembler is that a variable's type must be declared as byte (8-bit), word (16-bit), or double word (4 bytes or 2 words) before using in a program. Some examples are included below:

```
START DB 0  ;    START is declared
            ;    as a byte offset
            ;    and initialized to zero.

BEGIN DW 0  ;    BEGIN is declared
            ;    as a word offset
            ;    and initialized to zero.
```

```
NAME DD 0      ;    NAME is declared
               ;    as a double word
               ;    (4 bytes) offset
               ;    and initialized to zero.
```

The EQU directive can be used to assign a name to constants. For example, the statement JOHN EQU 21H directs the assembler to assign the value 21H every time it finds JOHN in the program. This means that the assembler reads the statement MOV BH, JOHN as MOV BH, 21H. As mentioned before, DB, DW, and DD are the ASM-86 directives used to assign names and specify data types for variables in a program. For example, after execution of the statement BOB DW 2050H, the ASM-86 assembler assigns 50H to the offset name BOB and 20H to the offset name BOB + 1. This means that the program can use the instruction MOV BX, BOB to load the 16-bit content of memory starting at the offset BOB in DS into BX. The DW sets aside storage for a word in memory and gives the starting of this word the name BOB. Next, typical 8086 addressing mode examples for the ASM-86 assembler are given below:

```
MOV AH, BL         ;    Both source and
                   ;    destination are in
                   ;    register mode.

MOV CH, 8          ;    Source is in
                   ;    immediate mode
                   ;    and destination is in
                   ;    register mode.

MOV AX, START      ;    Source is in memory
                   ;    direct mode and
                   ;    destination is in
                   ;    register mode.

MOV CH, [BX]       ;    Source is in register
                   ;    indirect mode and
                   ;    destination is in register
                   ;    mode.

MOV [SI], AL       ;    Source is in register
                   ;    mode and destination
                   ;    is in register indirect
                   ;    mode.
```

```
      MOV [DI], BH           ;   Source is in register
                             ;   mode and destination
                             ;   is in register
                             ;   indirect mode.


      MOV BH, VALUE          ;   Source is in register
          [DI]               ;   indirect with
                             ;   displacement mode
                             ;   and destination is
                             ;   in register mode
                             ;   VALUE is typically
                             ;   defined by the
                             ;   EQU directive prior
                             ;   to this instruction.


      MOV AX, [DI + 4]       ;   Source is in
                             ;   indexed with
                             ;   displacement mode and
                             ;   destination is in
                             ;   register mode.


      MOV SI, [BP + 2]       ;   Source is in
              [DI]           ;   bused indexed
                             ;   with displacement
                             ;   mode and
                             ;   destination is in
                             ;   register mode.


      OUT 30H, AL            ;   Source is in
                             ;   register mode and
                             ;   destination is
                             ;   in direct port
                             ;   mode.


      IN AX, DX              ;   Source is in
                             ;   indirect port mode and
                             ;   destination is
                             ;   in register mode.
```

Note that in the above, START must be previously defined by a data allocation statement such DB and DW.

In the following, typical ASM-86 assembler directives such as SEG-MENT, ENDS, ASSUME, and DUP will be discussed.

3.7.1 SEGMENT AND ENDS

A section of a program or a data array can be defined by the SEG-MENT and ENDS directives as follows:

```
JOHN        SEGMENT

X1            DB          0
X2            DB          0
X3            DB          0
JOHN        ENDS
```

The segment name is JOHN. The assembler will assign a numeric value to JOHN corresponding to the base value of the data segment. The programmer must use the 8086 instructions to load JOHN into DS as follows:

```
MOV BX,  JOHN
MOV DS,  BX
```

Note that the segment registers must be loaded via a 16-bit register such as AX or by content of a memory location.

3.7.2 ASSUME DIRECTIVE

As mentioned before, the 8086, at any time, can directly address four physical segments which include a code segment, a data segment, a stack segment, and an extra segment. The 8086 may contain a number of logical segments containing codes, data, and stack. The ASSUME pseudoinstruction assigns a logical segment to a physical segment at any given time. That is, the ASSUME directive tells the ASM-86 assembler what addresses will be in the segment registers at execution time.

For example, the statement ASSUME CS: PROGRAM 1, DS: DATA 1, SS: STACK 1 directs the assembler to use the logical code segment PROGRAM 1 as CS containing the instructions, the logical data segment DATA 1 as DS containing data, and the logical STACK segment STACK 1 as SS containing the stack.

3.7.3 DUP DIRECTIVE

The DUP directive can be used to initialize several locations to zero. For example, the statement START DW 4 DUP (0) reserves four words starting at the offset START in DS and initializes them to zero. The DUP directive can also be used to reserve several locations which need not be initialized. A question mark must be used with DUP in this case. For example, the statement BEGIN DB 100 DUP (?) reserves 100 bytes of uninitialized data space to an offset BEGIN in DS. Note that BEGIN should be typed in the label field, DB in the op field, and 100 DUP (?) in the operand field.

A typical example illustrating the use of these directives is given below:

```
DATA 1        SEGMENT
ADDR 1        DW 3005H
ADDR 2        DW 2003H
DATA 1        ENDS
STACK 1       SEGMENT
              DW 60 DUP (0)     ;  Assign 60₁₀ words
                                ;  of stack with zeros.
STACK-TOP     LABEL WORD        ;  Initialize Stack-Top
                                ;  to the next
STACK 1       ENDS              ;  location after the
                                ;  top of the stack.
CODE 1        SEGMENT
              ASSUME CS: CODE 1, DS: DATA 1, SS:
              STACK 1
              MOV AX,  STACK 1
              MOV SS,  AX
              LEA SP,  STACK-TOP
              MOV AX,  DTATA 1
              MOV DS,  AX
              LEA SI,  ADDR 1
              LEA DI,  ADDR 2
              -
              -           }    Main Program
              -           }        Body
              -
CODE 1        ENDS
```

Note that LABEL is a directive used to initialize STACK-TOP to the next location after the top of the stack. The statement STACK-TOP LABEL WORD gives the name STACK-TOP to the next address after the 60 words are set aside for the stack. The WORD in this statement indicates that PUSH into and POP from the stack are done as words.

In the above program, the ASSUME directive tells the assembler the names of the logical segments to use as code segment, data segment, and stack segment. The extra segment can be assigned a name in a similar manner. When the instructions are executed, the displacements in the instructions along with the segment register contents are used by the assembler to generate the 20-bit physical addresses. The segment register, other than the code segment, must be initialized by instructions before they are used to access data.

When the ASM-86 assembler translates an assembly language program, it computes the displacement, or offset, of each instruction code byte from the start of a logical segment that contains it. For example, in the above program the CS: CODE 1 in the ASSUME statement directs the assembler to compute the offsets or displacements by the following instructions from the start of the logical segment CODE 1. This means that when the program is run, the CS will contain the 16-bit value where the logical segment CODE 1 is located in memory. The assembler keeps track of the instruction byte displacements which are loaded into IP. The 20-bit physical address generated from CS and IP are used to fetch each instruction.

Another example to store data bytes in a data segment and to allocate stack is given in the following:

```
DSEG        SEGMENT
ARRAY       DB 02H, F1H, A2H      ; Store 3 bytes
                                  ; of data in an
DSEG        ENDS                  ; address  defined
            -                     ; by DSEG as DS
            -                     ; and ARRAY as
            -                     ; offset
SSEG        SEGMENT
            DW 10 DUP (0)         ; Allocate
                                  ; 10 word stack
STACK-TOP   LABEL  WORD           ; Label initial
                                  ; TOS
SSEG        ENDS
            -
            -
            -
            -
            MOV AX, DSEG          ; Initialize
            MOV DS, AX            ; DS
            MOV AX, SSEG          ; Initialize
            MOV SS, AX            ; SS
```

```
MOV SP, STACK-TOP    ;  Initialize SP
-
-
-
```

A logical segment is not normally given a physical starting address when it is declared. After the program is assembled, the programmer uses the linker to assign physical address.

Example 3.1
Determine the effect of each one of the following 8086 instructions:

i) **PUSH [BX]**
ii) **DIV DH**
iii) **CWD**
iv) **MOVSB**
v) **MOV START [BX], AL**

Assume the following data prior to execution of each one of the above instructions independently. Assume all numbers in hexadecimal.

[DS]	= 3000H	[SI]	= 0400H
[ES]	= 5000H	[DI]	= 0500H
[DX]	= 0400H	DF	= 0
[SP]	= 5000H	[BX]	= 6000H
[SS]	= 6000H	Value of START	= 05H
[AX]	= 00A9H		

[36000H] = 02H, [36001H] = 03H
[50500H] = 05H
[30400H] = 02H, [30401H] = 03H

Solution

i) 20-bit physical memory addressed by DS and BX = 36000H. 20-bit physical location pointed to by SP and SS = 65000H. PUSH [BX] pushes [36001H] and [36000H] into stack locations 64FFFH and 64FFEH, respectively. The SP is then decremented by 2 to contain the 20-bit physical address 64FFEH (SS = 6000H, SP = 4FFEH). Therefore, [64FFFH] = 03H and [64FFEH] = 02H.

ii) Before unsigned division, [DX] = 0400H, DH contains 04H, and [AX] = 00A9H = 169_{10}. After DIV DH, [AH] = remainder = 01H and [AL] = quotient = 2AH = 42_{10}.

iii) CWD sign extends AX register into the DX register. Since the sign bit of [AX] = 0, after CWD [DX AX] = 000000A9H.

iv) MOVSB moves the content of memory addressed by the source [DS] and [SI] to the destination addressed by [ES] and [DI] and then it increments SI and DI by 1 for byte move. Since DF = 0, [DS] = 3000H, [SI] = 0400H, [ES] = 5000H, [DI] = 0500H, and the content of physical memory location 30400H is moved to physical memory 50500H. Since [30400H] = 02H, the location 50500H will also contain 02H. Since DF = 0 after MOVSB, [SI] = 0401H, [DI] = 0501H.

v) Since [BX] = 6000H, [DS] = 3000H, START = 05H, and the physical memory for destination = 36005 H. After MOV START [BX], AL, memory location 36005H will contain A9H.

Example 3.2

Write 8086 assembly program to clear 100_{10} consecutive bytes. Assume CS and DS are already initialized.

Solution

```
        LEA BX, ADDR    ;   Initialize BX
        MOV CX, 100     ;   Initialize loop count
START   MOV [BX], 00H   ;   Clear memory byte
        INC BX          ;   Update pointer
        LOOP START      ;   Decrement CX and loop
        HLT
```

Example 3.3

Write 8086 assembly program to compute $\sum_{i=1}^{N} XiYi$ where Xi and Yi are signed 8-bit numbers. N = 100. Assume CS and DS are already initialized. Assume no overflow.

Solution

```
        MOV CX, 100     ;   Initialize Loop count
        LEA BX, ADDR 1  ;   Load ADDR 1 into BX
        LEA SI, ADDR 2  ;   Load ADDR 2 into SI
        MOV DX, 0000H   ;   Initialize sum to zero
START   MOV AL, [BX]    ;   Load data into AL
        IMUL [SI]       ;   Signed multiplication
        ADD DX, AX      ;   Sum XiYi
```

```
            INC BX              ;   Update
            INC SI              ;   Pointers
            LOOP START          ;   Decrement CX and Loop
            HLT
```

Example 3.4

Write 8086 assembly language program to add two words; each word contains four packed BCD digits. The first word is stored in two consecutive locations with the low byte at the offset pointed by SI at 0500H, while the second word is stored in two consecutive locations with the low byte pointed by BX at the offset 1000H. Store the result in memory pointed to by BX. Assume CS and DS are already initialized.

Solution

```
            MOV CX, 2           ;   Initialize loop count
            MOV SI, 0500H       ;   Initialize SI
            MOV BX, 1000H       ;   Initialize BX
            CLC                 ;   Clear carry
    START   MOV AL, [SI]        ;   Move data
            ADC AL, [BX]        ;   Perform addition
            DAA                 ;   BCD adjust
            MOV [BX], AL        ;   Store result
            INC SI              ;   Update
            INC BX              ;   Pointers
            LOOP START          ;   Decrement CX and loop
            HLT
```

Example 3.5

Write an 8086 assembly language program to add two words; each contains two ASCII digits. The first word is stored in two consecutive locations with the low byte pointed to by SI at offset 0300H, while the second byte is stored in two consecutive locations with the low byte pointed to by DI at offset 0700H. Store the result in DI. Assume CS and DS are already initialized.

Solution

```
            MOV CX, 2           ;   Initialize loop count
            MOV SI, 0300H       ;   Initialize SI
```

```
            MOV DI, 0700H    ;  Initialize DI
            CLC              ;  Clear carry
START       MOV AL, [SI]     ;  Move data
            ADC AL, [DI]     ;  Perform addition
            AAA              ;  ASCII adjust
            MOV [DI], AL     ;  Store result
            INC SI           ;  Update
            INC DI           ;  Pointers
            LOOP START       ;  Decrement CX and Loop
            HLT
```

Example 3.6

Write an 8086 assembly language program to compare a source string of 50_{10} words pointed to by an offset of 2000H in DS with a destination string pointed to by an offset 3000H in ES. The program should be halted as soon as a match is found or the end of string is reached. Assume CS and DS are initialized.

Solution

```
            MOV SI, 2000H   ;  Initialize SI
            MOV DI, 3000H   ;  Initialize DI
            MOV CX, 50      ;  Initialize CX
            CLD             ;  DF is cleared
                            ;  so that SI and DI
                            ;  will autoincrement
                            ;  after compare
            REPNE CMPSW     ;  Repeat CMPSW
                            ;  unit CX = 0 or
                            ;  until compared
                            ;  words are equal.
            HLT             ;  STOP
```

Example 3.7

Write a subroutine in 8086 assembly language which can be called by a main program in a different code segment. The subroutine will multiply a signed 16-bit number in CX by a signed 8-bit number in AL. The main program will call this subroutine, store the result in two consecutive memory words, and stop. Assume SI and DI contain the signed 8-bit and 16-bit data, respectively.

Solution

Main Program

```
MAIN PROG SEGMENT                    ;  Give assembler
          ASSUME CS: MAIN PROG ;  CS name
          MOV AX, 5000H            ;  Initialize
          MOV DS, AX               ;  DS to 5000H
          MOV AX, 6000H            ;  Initialize
          MOV SS, AX               ;  SS to 6000H
          MOV SP, 0020H            ;  Initialize SP
          MOV BX, 2000H            ;  Initialize BX
          MOV AL, [SI]             ;  Move 8-bit data
          MOV CX, [DI]             ;  Move 16-bit data
          CALL MUL                 ;  Call multiplica-
                                   ;  tion
                                   ;  subroutine
          MOV [BX], DX             ;  Store high
                                   ;  word of result
          MOV [BX + 2], AX         ;  Store low
                                   ;  word of result
          HLT
MAIN PROG ENDS
```

Subroutine

```
SUBR      SEGMENT
          ASSUME  CS:  SUBR
MUL       PROC    FAR          ;  Must be called
                               ;  from another code
                               ;  segment
CBW                            ;  Sign extend AL
IMUL CX                        ;  [DX] [AX] ← [AX]
                               ;  * [CX]
RET                            ;  Return
MUL       ENDP                 ;  End of Procedure
                               ;  MUL
SUBR      ENDS
```

Note that in the above programs SEGMENT, ASSUME, ENDP, and ENDS are used as assembler directives.

3.8 SYSTEM DESIGN USING 8086

This section covers the basic concepts associated with interfacing the 8086 to its support chips such as memory and I/O. Topics such as timing diagrams and 8086 pins and signals will also be included.

3.8.1 PINS AND SIGNALS

The 8086 pins and signals are shown in Figure 3.6. Unless otherwise indicated, all 8086 pins are TTL compatible. As mentioned before, the 8086 can operate in two modes. These are minimum mode (uniprocessor system — single 8086) and maximum mode (multiprocessor system — more than one 8086). MN/$\overline{\text{MX}}$ is an input pin used to select one of these modes. When MN/$\overline{\text{MX}}$ is HIGH, the 8086 operates in the minimum mode. In this mode, the 8086 is configured (that is, pins are defined) to support small, single processor systems using a few devices that use the system bus.

When MN/$\overline{\text{MX}}$ is LOW, the 8086 is configured (that is, pins are defined in the maximum mode) to support multiprocessor systems. In this case, the Intel 8288 bus controller is added to the 8086 to provide bus controls and compatibility with the multibus architecture. Note that in a particular application, the MN/$\overline{\text{MX}}$ must be tied to either HIGH or LOW. AD0-AD15 lines are a 16-bit multiplexed address/data bus. During the first clock cycle AD0-AD15 are the low order 16 bits of address. The 8086 has a total of 20 address lines. The upper four lines are multiplexed with the status signals for the 8086. These are the A16/S3, A17/S4, A18/S5, and A19/S6. During the first clock period of a bus cycle (read or write cycle), the entire 20-bit address is available on these lines. During all other clock cycles for memory and I/O operations, AD15-AD0 contain the 16-bit data, and S3, S4, S5, and S6 become status lines. S3 and S4 lines are decoded as follows:

A17/S4	A16/S3	Function
0	0	Extra segment
0	1	Stack segment
1	0	Code or no segment
1	1	Data segment

Common Signals		
Name	Function	Type
AD15-AD0	Address/Data Bus	Bidirectional, 3-State
A19/S6-A16/S3	Address/Status	Output, 3-State
$\overline{BHE}$/S7	Bus High Enable/ Status	Output, 3-State
MN/$\overline{MX}$	Minimum/Maximum Mode Control	Input
$\overline{RD}$	Read Control	Output, 3-State
$\overline{TEST}$	Wait On Test Control	Input
READY	Wait State Control	Input
RESET	System Reset	Input
NMI	Non-Maskable Interrupt Request	Input
INTR	Interrupt Request	Input
CLK	System Clock	Input
Vcc	+5V	Input
GND	Ground	

Minimum Mode Signals (MN/MX = Vcc)		
Name	Function	Type
HOLD	Hold Request	Input
HLDA	Hold Acknowledge	Output
$\overline{WR}$	Write Control	Output, 3-State
M/$\overline{IO}$	Memory/IO Control	Output, 3-State
DT/$\overline{R}$	Data Transmit/ Receive	Output, 3-State
$\overline{DEN}$	Data Enable	Output, 3-State
ALE	Address Latch Enable	Output
$\overline{INTA}$	Interrupt Acknowledge	Output

Maximum Mode Signals (MN/MX = GND)		
Name	Function	Type
$\overline{RQ}$/$\overline{GT}$1, 0	Request/Grant Bus Access Control	Bidirectional
$\overline{LOCK}$	Bus Priority Lock Control	Output, 3-State
$\overline{S2}$-$\overline{S0}$	Bus Cycle Status	Output, 3-State
QS1, QS0	Instruction Queue Status	Output

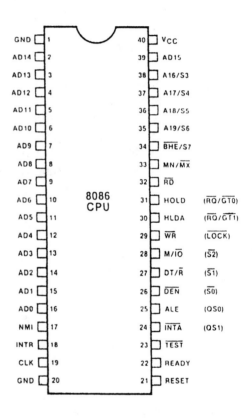

MAXIMUM MODE PIN FUNCTIONS (e.g., $\overline{LOCK}$)
ARE SHOWN IN PARENTHESES

FIGURE 3.6 Pin definitions.

Therefore, after the first clock cycle of an instruction execution, the A17/S4 and A16/S3 pins specify which segment register generates the segment portion of the 8086 address. Thus, by decoding these lines and then using the decoder outputs as chip selects for memory chips, up to 4 megabytes (one megabyte per segment) can be provided. This provides a degree of protection by preventing erroneous write operations to one segment from overlapping into another segment and destroying information in that segment. A18/S5 and A19/S6 are used as A18 and A19, respectively, during the first clock period of an instruction execution. If an I/O instruction is executed, they stay low during the first clock period. During all other cycles, A18/S5 indicates the status of the 8086 interrupt enable flag and A19/S6 becomes S6, and a low A19/S6 pin indicates that the 8086 is on the bus. During a "Hold Acknowledge" clock period, the 8086 tristates the A19/S6 pin and thus allows another bus master to take control of the system bus.

The 8086 tristates AD0-AD15 during Interrupt Acknowledge or Hold Acknowledge cycles.

$\overline{BHE}$/S7 is used as $\overline{BHE}$ (Bus High Enable) during the first clock cycle of an instruction execution. The 8086 outputs a low on this pin during read, write, and interrupt acknowledge cycles in which data are to be transferred in a high-order byte (AD15-AD8) of the data bus. $\overline{BHE}$ can be used in conjunction with AD0 to select memory banks. A thorough discussion is provided later. During all other cycles $\overline{BHE}$/S7 is used as S7 and the 8086 maintains the output level ($\overline{BHE}$) of the first clock cycle on this pin.

$\overline{RD}$ is LOW whenever the 8086 is reading data from memory or an I/O location.

$\overline{TEST}$ is an input pin and is only used by the WAIT instruction. The 8086 enters a wait state after execution of the WAIT instruction until a LOW is seen on the $\overline{TEST}$ pin. This input is synchronized internally during each clock cycle on the leading edge of the CLK pin.

INTR is the maskable interrupt input. This line is not latched and, therefore, INTR must be held at a HIGH level until recognized to generate an interrupt.

NMI is the nonmaskable interrupt input activated by a leading edge.

RESET is the system reset input signal. This signal must be high for at least four clock cycles to be recognized, except after power-on which requires a 50-μs reset pulse. It causes the 8086 to initialize registers DS, SS, ES, IP and flags to all zeros. It also initializes CS to FFFFH. Upon removal of the RESET signal from the RESET pin, the 8086 will fetch its next instruction from 20-bit physical address FFFF0H (CS = FFFFH, IP = 0000H).

When the 8086 detects the positive going edge of a pulse on RESET, it stops all activities until the signal goes LOW. When the reset is low, the 8086 initializes the system as follows:

8086 component	Content
Flags	Clear
IP	0000H
CS	FFFFH
DS	0000H
SS	0000H
ES	0000H
Queue	Empty

The reset signal to the 8086 can be generated by the 8284. The 8284 has a Schmitt Trigger input ($\overline{RES}$) for generating reset from a low active external reset.

To guarantee reset from power-up, the reset input must remain below 1.05 volts for 50 microseconds after Vcc has reached the minimum supply voltage of 4.5V. The $\overline{RES}$ input of the 8284 can be driven by a simple RC circuit as shown in Figure 3.7.

The values of R and C can be selected as follows:

$$Vc \ (t) = V \ (1 - \exp - (t/RC))$$

where t = 50 microseconds, V = 4.5 V, Vc = 1.05V, and RC = 188 microseconds. For example, if C is chosen arbitrarily to be 0.1 μF, then R = 1.88 KΩ.

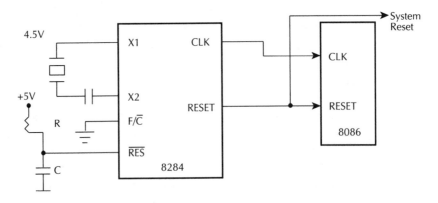

FIGURE 3.7 8086 reset and system reset.

As mentioned before, the 8086 can be configured in either minimum or maximum mode using the MN/$\overline{\text{MX}}$ input pin. In minimum mode, the 8086 itself generates all bus control signals. These signals are

- DT/$\overline{\text{R}}$ (Data Transmit/Receive). DT/$\overline{\text{R}}$ is an output signal required in minimum system that uses an 8286/8287 data bus transceiver. It is used to control direction of data flow through the transceiver.
- $\overline{\text{DEN}}$ (Data Enable) is provided as an output enable for the 8286/8287 in a minimum system which uses the transceiver.
- $\overline{\text{DEN}}$ is active LOW during each memory and I/O access and for $\overline{\text{INTA}}$ cycles.
- ALE (Address Latch Enable) is an output signal provided by the 8086 and can be used to demultiplex the AD0-AD15 into A0-A15 and D0-D15 at the falling edge of ALE. The 8086 ALE signal is same as the 8085 ALE.
- M/$\overline{\text{IO}}$. This 8086 output signal is similar to the 8085 IO/$\overline{\text{M}}$. It is used to distinguish a memory access (M/$\overline{\text{IO}}$ = HIGH) from an I/O access (M/$\overline{\text{IO}}$ = LOW). When the 8086 executes an I/O instruction such as IN or OUT, it outputs a LOW on this pin. On the other hand, the 8086 outputs HIGH on this pin when it executes a memory reference instruction such as MOVE AX, [SI].
- $\overline{\text{WR}}$. The 8086 outputs LOW on this pin to indicate that the processor is performing a write memory or write I/O operation, depending on the M/$\overline{\text{IO}}$ signal.
- $\overline{\text{INTA}}$. The 8086 $\overline{\text{INTA}}$ is similar to the 8085 $\overline{\text{INTA}}$. For Interrupt Acknowledge cycles (for INTR pin), the 8086 outputs LOW on this pin.
- HOLD (input), HLDA (output). These pins have the same purpose as the 8085 HOLD/HLDA pins and are used for DMA. A HIGH on the HOLD pin indicates that another master is requesting to take over the system bus. The processor receiving the HOLD request will output HLDA high as an acknowledgment. At the same time, the processor tristates the system bus. Upon receipt of LOW on the HOLD pin, the processor places LOW on the HLDA pin. HOLD is not an asynchronous input. External synchronization should be provided if the system cannot otherwise guarantee the setup time.
- CLK (input) provides the basic timing for the 8086 and bus controller.

The maximum clock frequencies of the 8086-4, 8086, and 8086-

2 are 4 MHz, 5 MHz, and 8 MHz, respectively. Since the design of these processors incorporates dynamic cells, a minimum frequency of 2 MHz is required to retain the state of the machine. The 8086-4, 8086, and 8086-2 will be referred to as 8086 in the following. Minimum frequency requirement, single stepping, or cycling of the 8086 may not be accomplished by disabling the clock. Since the 8086 does not have on-chip clock generation circuitry, an 8284 clock generator chip must be connected to the 8086 CLK pin as shown in Figure 3.8.

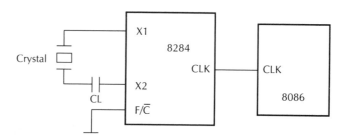

FIGURE 3.8 8284 clock generator connections to the 8086.

The crystal must have a frequency three times the 8086 internal frequency. That is, the 8284 divides the crystal clock frequency by 3. In other words, to generate 5 MHz 8086 internal clock, the crystal clock must be 15 MHz. To select the crystal inputs of the 8284 as the frequency source for clock generation, the $F/\overline{C}$ input must be strapped to ground. This strapping option allows either the crystal or the external frequency input as the source for clock generation. When selecting a crystal for use with the 8284, the crystal series resistance should be as low as possible. The oscillator delays in the 8284 appear as inductive elements to the crystal and cause the 8284 to run at a frequency below that of the pure series resonance; a capacitor CL should be placed in series with the crystal and the X2 pin of the 8284. This capacitor cancels the inductive element. The impedance of the capacitor XC = $1/2\pi FCL$, where F is the crystal frequency. It is recommended that the crystal series resistance plus XC be kept less than 1 kohm. As the crystal frequency increases, CL should be decreased. For example, a 12-MHz crystal may require CL ≈ 24 PF, while 22 MHz may require CL ≈ 8 PF. If very close correlation with the pure series resonance is not necessary, a nominal CL value of 12 to 15 PF may be used with a 15-MHz crystal. Two crystal manufacturers recommended by Intel are Crystle Corp. model CY 15A (15 MHz) and CTS Knight Inc. model CY 24 A (24 MHz).

Note that the 8284 can be used to generate the 8086 READY input signal based on inputs from slow memory and I/O devices which are not capable of transferring information at the 8086 rate.

In the maximum mode, some of the 8086 pins in the minimum mode are redefined. For example, pins HOLD, HLDA, $\overline{WR}$, M/$\overline{IO}$, DT/$\overline{R}$, $\overline{DEN}$, ALE, and $\overline{INTA}$ in the minimum mode are redefined as $\overline{RQ}/\overline{GT0}$, $\overline{RQ}/\overline{GT1}$, $\overline{LOCK}$, $\overline{S2}$, $\overline{S1}$, $\overline{S0}$, QS0, and QS1, respectively. In maximum mode, the 8288 bus controller decodes the status information from $\overline{S0}$, $\overline{S1}$, $\overline{S2}$ to generate bus timing and control signals required for a bus cycle. $\overline{S2}$, $\overline{S1}$, $\overline{S0}$ are 8086 outputs and are decoded as follows:

$\overline{S2}$	$\overline{S1}$	$\overline{S0}$	
0	0	0	Interrupt Acknowledge
0	0	1	Read I/O port
0	1	0	Write I/O port
0	1	1	Halt
1	0	0	Code access
1	0	1	Read memory
1	1	0	Write memory
1	1	1	Inactive

- $\overline{RQ}/\overline{GT0}$, $\overline{RQ}/\overline{GT1}$. These request/grant pins are used by other local bus masters to force the processor to release the local bus at the end of the processor's current bus cycle. Each pin is bidirectional, with $\overline{RQ}/\overline{GT0}$ having higher priority than $\overline{RQ}/\overline{GT1}$. These pins have internal pull-up resistors so that they may be left unconnected. The request/grant function of the 8086 works as follows:

  1. A pulse (one clock wide) from another local bus master ($\overline{RQ}/\overline{GT0}$ or $\overline{RQ}/\overline{GT1}$ pins) indicates a local bus request to the 8086.
  2. At the end of 8086 current bus cycle, a pulse (one clock wide) from the 8086 to the requesting master indicates that the 8086 has relinquished the system bus and tristated the outputs. Then the new bus master subsequently relinquishes control of the system bus by sending a LOW on $\overline{RQ}/\overline{GT0}$ or $\overline{RQ}/\overline{GT1}$ pins. The 8086 then regains bus control.

- $\overline{LOCK}$. The 8086 outputs LOW on the $\overline{LOCK}$ pin to prevent other bus masters from gaining control of the system bus. The $\overline{LOCK}$ signal is activated by the 'LOCK' prefix instruction and remains active until the completion of the instruction that follows.

- QS1, QS0. The 8086 outputs to QS1 and QS0 pins to provide status to allow external tracking of the internal 8086 instruction queue as follows:

QS1	QS0	
0	0	No operation
0	1	First byte of op code from queue
1	0	Empty the queue
1	1	Subsequent byte from queue

QS0 and QS1 are valid during the clock period following any queue operation. The 8086 can be operated from a +5V to +10V power supply. There are two ground pins on the chip to distribute power for noise reduction.

3.8.2 8086 BASIC SYSTEM CONCEPTS

This section describes basic concepts associated with 8086 bus cycles, address and data bus, system data bus, and multiprocessor environment.

3.8.2.a 8086 Bus Cycle

In order to communicate with external devices via the system bus for transferring data or fetching instructions, the 8086 executes a bus cycle. The 8086 basic bus cycle timing diagram is shown in Figure 3.9. The minimum bus cycle contains four CPU clock periods called T States. The bus cycle timing diagram depicted in Figure 3.9 can be described as follows:

1. During the first T State (T1), the 8086 outputs the 20-bit address computed from a segment register and an offset on the multiplexed address/data/status bus.
2. For the second T State (T2), the 8086 removes the address from the bus and either tristates or activates the AD15-AD0 lines in preparation for reading data via AD15-AD0 lines during the T3 cycle. In case of a write bus cycle, the 8086 outputs data on AD15-AD0 lines. Also, during T2, the upper four multiplexed bus lines switch from address (A19-A16) to bus cycle status (S6, S5, S4, S3). The 8086 outputs LOW on $\overline{\text{RD}}$ (for read cycle) or $\overline{\text{WR}}$ (for write cycle) during portions of T2, T3, and T4.

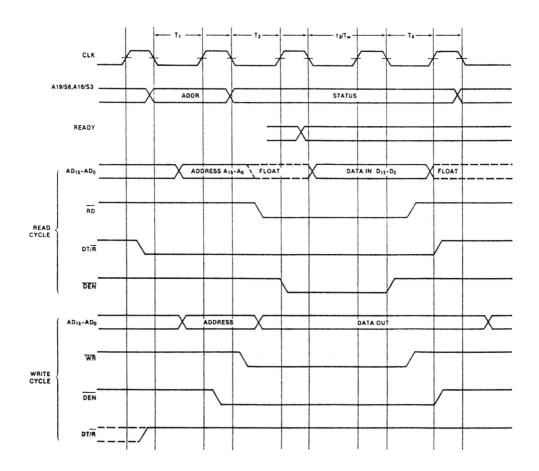

FIGURE 3.9 Basic 8086 bus cycle.

3. During T3, the 8086 continues to output status information on the four A19-A16/S6-S3 lines and will either continue to output write data or input read data to or from AD15-AD0 lines. If the selected memory or I/O device is not fast enough to transfer data at the 8086, the memory or I/O device activates the 8086's READY input line low by the start of T3. This will force the 8086 to insert additional clock cycles (wait states TW) after T3. Bus activity during TW is the same as T3. When the selected device has had sufficient time to complete the transfer, it must activate the 8086 READY PIN HIGH. As soon as the TW clock periods end, the 8086 executes the last bus cycle, T4. The 8086 will latch data on AD15-AD0 lines during the last wait state or during T3 if no wait states are requested.

4. During T4, the 8086 disables the command lines and the selected memory and I/O devices from the bus. Thus, the bus cycle is terminated in T4. The bus cycle appears to devices in the system as an asynchronous event consisting of an address to select the device, a register or memory location within the device, a read strobe, or a write strobe along with data.

5. $\overline{\text{DEN}}$ and DT/$\overline{\text{R}}$ pins are used by the 8286/8287 transceiver in a minimum system. During the read cycle, the 8086 outputs $\overline{\text{DEN}}$ LOW during part of T2 and all of T3 cycles. This signal can be used to enable the 8286/8287 transceiver. The 8086 outputs LOW on the DT/$\overline{\text{R}}$ pin from the start of T1 and part of T4 cycles. The 8086 uses this signal to receive (read) data from the receiver during T3-T4. During a write cycle, the 8086 outputs $\overline{\text{DEN}}$ LOW during part of T1, all of T2 and T3, and part of T4 cycles. The signal can be used to enable the transceiver. The 8086 outputs HIGH on DT/$\overline{\text{R}}$ throughout the four bus cycles to transmit (write) data to the transceiver during T3-T4.

3.8.2.b 8086 Address and Data Bus Concepts

The majority of memory and I/O chips capable of interfacing to the 8086 require a stable address for the duration of the bus cycle. Therefore, the address on the 8086 multiplexed address/data bus during T1 should be latched. The latched address is then used to select the desired I/O or memory location. Note that the 8086 has a 16-bit multiplexed address and data bus, while the 8085's 8-bit data lines and LOW address byte are multiplexed. Hence, the multiplexed bus components of the 8085 family are not applicable to the 8086. To demultiplex the bus, the 8086 provides an ALE (Address Latch Enable) signal to capture the address in either the 8282 (noninverting) or 8283 (inverting) 8-bit bistable latches. These latches propagate the address through to the outputs while ALE is HIGH and latch the address in the following edge of ALE. This only delays address access and chip select decoding by the propagation delay of the latch. Figure 3.10 shows how the 8086 demultiplexes the address and data buses.

The programmer views the 8086 memory address space as a sequence of one million bytes in which any byte may contain an eight-bit data element and any two consecutive bytes may contain a 16-bit data element. There is no constraint on byte or word addresses (boundaries). The address space is physically implemented on a 16-bit data bus by dividing the address space into two banks of up to 512K bytes as shown in Figure 3.11. These banks can be selected by $\overline{\text{BHE}}$ and A0 as follows:

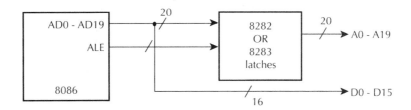

FIGURE 3.10 Separate address and data buses.

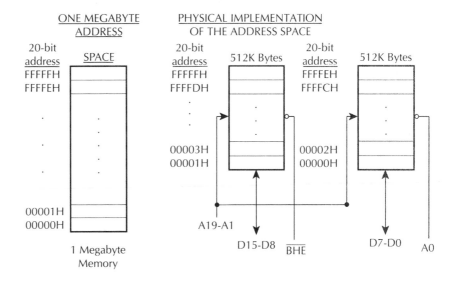

FIGURE 3.11 8086 memory.

BHE	A0	Byte transferred
0	0	Both bytes
0	1	Upper byte to/from odd address
1	0	Lower byte to/from even address
1	1	None

One bank is connected to D7-D0 and contains all even addressed bytes (A0 = 0). The other bank is connected to D15-D8 and contains odd-addressed bytes (A0 = 1). A particular byte in each bank is addressed by A19-A1. The even-addressed bank is enabled by LOW A0 and data bytes transferred over D7-D0 lines. The 8086 outputs HIGH on $\overline{BHE}$ (Bus High Enable) and thus disables the odd-addressed bank. The 8086 outputs

LOW on $\overline{\text{BHE}}$ to select the odd-addressed bank and HIGH on A0 to disable the even-addressed bank. This directs the data transfer to the appropriate half of the data bus. Activation of A0 and $\overline{\text{BHE}}$ is performed by the 8086 depending on odd or even addresses and is transparent to the programmer. As an example, consider execution of the instruction MOV DH, [BX]. Suppose the 20-bit address computed by BX and DS is even. The 8086 outputs LOW on A0 and HIGH on $\overline{\text{BHE}}$. This will select the even-addressed bank. The content of the selected memory is placed on the D7-D0 lines by the memory chip. The 8086 reads this data via D7-D0 and automatically places it in DH. Next, consider accessing a 16-bit word by the 8086 with low byte at an even address as shown in Figure 3.12.

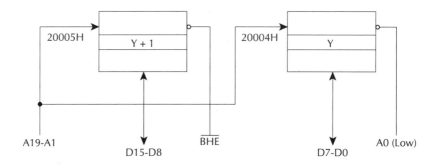

FIGURE 3.12 Even-addressed word transfer.

For example, suppose that the 8086 executes the instruction MOV [BX], CX. Assume [BX] = 0004H, [DS] = 2000H. The 20-bit physical address for the word is 20004H. The 8086 outputs LOW on both A0 and $\overline{\text{BHE}}$, enabling both banks simultaneously. The 8086 outputs [CL] to D7-D0 lines and [CH] to D15-D8 lines with $\overline{\text{WR}}$ LOW and M/$\overline{\text{IO}}$ HIGH. The enabled memory banks obtain the 16-bit data and write [CL] to location 20004H and [CH] to location 20005H. Next, consider accessing an odd-addressed 16-bit word by the 8086. For example, suppose the 20-bit physical address computed by the 8086 is 20005H. The 8086 accomplishes this transfer in two bus cycles. In the first bus cycle, the 8086 outputs HIGH on A0, LOW on $\overline{\text{BHE}}$, and thus enables the odd-addressed bank and disables the even-addressed bank. The 8086 also outputs LOW on $\overline{\text{RD}}$ and HIGH on M/$\overline{\text{IO}}$ pins. In this bus cycle, the odd memory bank places [20005H] on D15-D8 lines. The 8086 reads this data into CL. In the second bus cycle, the 8086 outputs LOW on A0, HIGH on $\overline{\text{BHE}}$, and thus enables the even-addressed bank and disables the odd-addressed bank.

The 8086 also outputs LOW on $\overline{RD}$ and HIGH on $M/\overline{IO}$ pins. The selected even-addressed memory bank places [20006H] on D7-D0 lines. The 8086 reads this data into CH. This is shown in Figure 3.13.

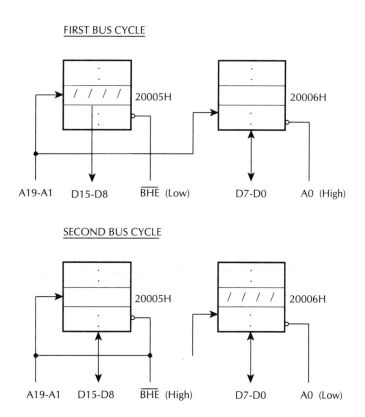

FIGURE 3.13. Odd-addressed word transfer.

During a byte read, the 8086 floats the entire D15-D0 lines during portions of T2 cycle even though data are expected on the upper or lower half of the data bus. As will be shown later, this action simplifies the chip select decoding requirements for ROMs and EPROMs. During a byte write, the 8086 will drive the entire 16-bit data bus. The information on the half of the data bus not transferring data is indeterminate. These concepts also apply to I/O transfers.

If memory of I/O devices are directly connected to the multiplexed bus, the designer must guarantee that the devices do not corrupt the address on the bus during T1. To avoid this, the memory or I/O devices should have an output enable controlled by the 8086 read signal. This is shown in Figure 3.14.

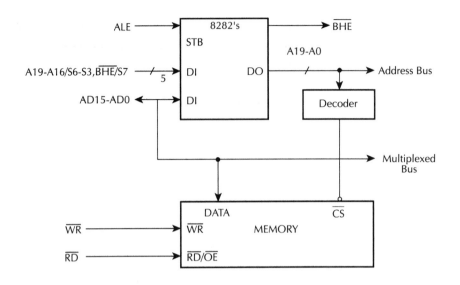

FIGURE 3.14 Devices with output enabling the multiplexed bus.

The 8086 timing guarantees that the read is not valid until after the address is latched by ALE as shown in Figure 3.15.

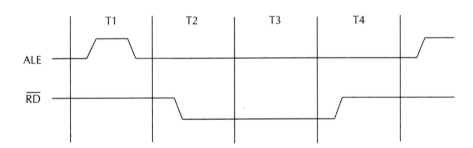

FIGURE 3.15 Relationship of ALE and Read.

All Intel peripherals, EPROMs, and RAMs for microprocessors provide output enable for read inputs to allow connection to the multiplexed bus. Several techniques are available for interfacing the devices without output enables to the 8086 multiplexed bus. However, these techniques will not be discussed here.

3.8.3 INTERFACING WITH MEMORIES

Figure 3.16 shows a general block diagram of an 8086 memory array. In Figure 3.16, the 16-bit word memory is partitioned into high and low

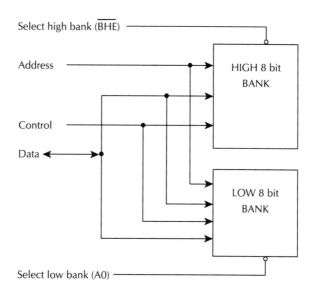

FIGURE 3.16 8086 memory array.

8-bit banks on the upper and lower halves of the data bus selected by $\overline{\text{BHE}}$ and A0.

3.8.3.a ROM and EPROM

ROMs and EPROMs are the simplest memory chips to interface to the 8086. Since ROMs and EPROMs are read-only devices, A0 and $\overline{\text{BHE}}$ are not required to be part of the chip enable/select decoding (chip enable is similar to chip select except chip enable also provides whether the chip is in active or standby power mode). The 8086 address lines must be connected to the ROM/EPROM chips starting with A1 and higher to all the address lines of the ROM/EPROM chips. The 8086 unused address lines can be used as chip enable/select decoding. To interface the ROMs/ RAMs directly to the 8086 multiplexed bus, they must have output enable signals. Figure 3.17 shows the 8086 interfaced to two 2716s.

Byte accesses are obtained by reading the full 16-bit word onto the bus with the 8086 discarding the unwanted byte and accepting the desired byte. If $\overline{\text{RD}}$, $\overline{\text{WR}}$, and M/$\overline{\text{IO}}$ are not decoded to generate separate memory and I/O commands for memory and I/O chips and the I/O space overlaps with the memory space of ROM/EPROM, then M/$\overline{\text{IO}}$ must be a condition of chip select decode.

3.8.3.b Static RAMs

Since static RAMs are read/write memories, both A0 and $\overline{\text{BHE}}$ must

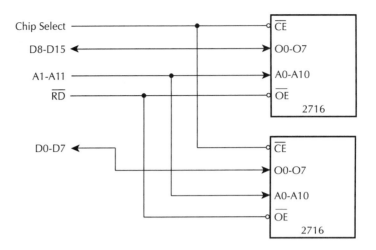

FIGURE 3.17 ROM/EPROM interface to the 8086.

be included in the chip select/chip enable decoding of the devices and write timing must be considered in the compatibility analysis.

For each static RAM, the memory data lines must be connected to either the upper half AD15-AD0 or lower half AD7-AD0 of the 8086 data lines.

For static RAMs without output enable pins, read and write lines must be used as enables for chip select generation to avoid bus contention. If read and write lines are not used to activate the chip selects, static RAMs with common input/output data pins such as 2114 will face extreme bus contentions between chip selects and write active. The 8086 A0 and $\overline{BHE}$ pins must be used to enable the chip selects. A possible way of generating chip selects for high and low static RAM banks is given in Figure 3.18. Note that Intel 8205 has three enables $\overline{E1}$, $\overline{E2}$, and E3, three inputs A0-A2, and eight outputs O0-O7.

For devices with output enables such as 2142, one way to generate chip selects for the static RAMs is by gating the 8086 $\overline{WR}$ signal with $\overline{BHE}$ and A0 to provide upper and lower bank write strobes. A possible configuration is shown in Figure 3.19. Since the Intel 2142 is a 1024×4 bit static RAM, two chips for each bank with a total of 4 chips for $2K \times 8$ static RAM is required. Note that DATA is read from the 2142 when the output disable OD is low, $\overline{WE}$ is HIGH, and DATA is written into 2142. When the output disable OD is HIGH, $\overline{WE}$ is LOW, CS2 is HIGH, and $\overline{CS1}$ is LOW. If multiple chip selects are available with the static RAM, BHE and A0 may be used directly as the chip selects. A possible configuration for $2K \times 8$ array is shown in Figure 3.20.

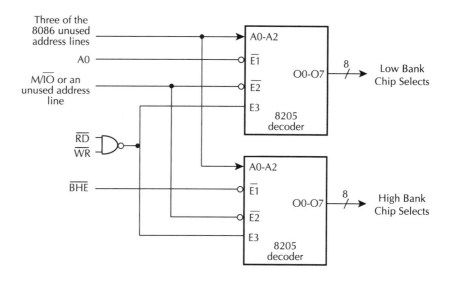

FIGURE 3.18 Generating chip selects for static RAMs without output enables.

3.8.3.c Dynamic RAM

Dynamic RAMs store information as charges in capacitors. Since capacitors can hold charges for a few milliseconds, refresh circuitry is necessary in dynamic RAMs for retaining these charges. Therefore, dynamic RAMs are complex devices to design a system. To relieve the designer of most of these complicated interfacing tasks, Intel provides the 8202 dynamic RAM controller as part of the 8086 family of peripheral devices. The 8202 can be interfaced with the 8086 to build a dynamic memory system. A thorough discussion on this topic can be found in Intel manuals.

3.8.4 8086 PROGRAMMED I/O

The 8086 can be interfaced to 8- and 16-bit I/O devices using either standard or memory-mapped I/O. The standard I/O uses the instructions IN and OUT and is capable of providing 64K bytes of I/O ports. Using standard I/O, the 8086 can transfer 8- or 16-bit data to or from a peripheral device. The 64K byte I/O locations can then be configured as 64K 8-bit ports or 32K 16-bit ports. All I/O transfer between the 8086 and the peripheral devices take place via AL for 8-bit ports (AH is not involved) and AX for 16-bit ports. The I/O port addressing can be done either directly or indirectly as follows:

DIRECT   •   IN AL, PORTA or IN AX, PORTB inputs 8-bit
               contents of port A into AL or 16-bit contents of port

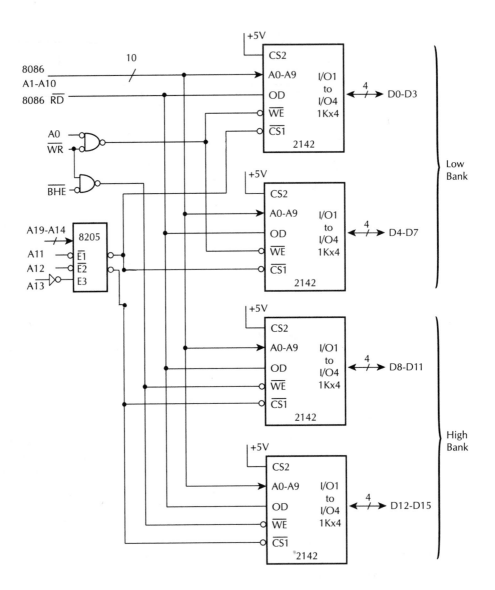

FIGURE 3.19 2K × 8 static RAM array for the 8086.

B into AX, respectively. Port A and port B are assumed as 8- and 16-bit ports, respectively.

- OUT PORTA, AL or OUT PORT B, AX outputs 8-bit contents of AL into port A or 16-bit contents of AX into port B, respectively.

INDIRECT   •   IN AX, DX or IN AL, DX inputs 16-bit data addressed

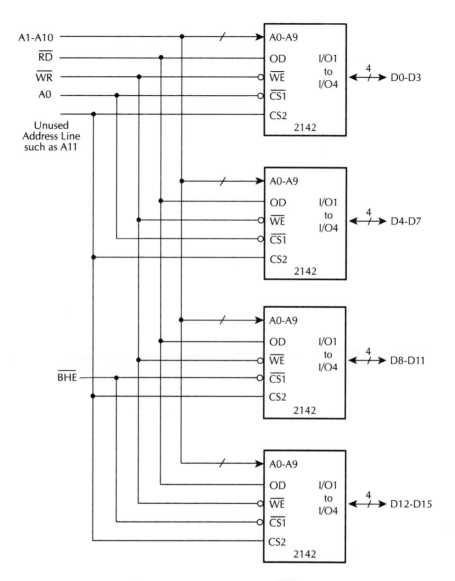

FIGURE 3.20 2K × 8 static RAM array with A0 and $\overline{BHE}$ as direct chip select inputs.

by DX into AX or 8-bit data addressed by DX into AL, respectively.

- OUT DX, AX or OUT DX, AL outputs 16-bit contents of AX into the port addressed by DX or 8-bit contents of AL into the port addressed by DX, respectively. In indirect addressing, register DX is used to hold the port address.

Data transfer using the memory-mapped I/O is accomplished by using memory-oriented instructions such as MOV reg 8 or reg 16, [BX] and MOV [BX], reg 8 or reg 16 for inputting and outputting 8- or 16-bit data from or to an 8-bit register or a 16-bit register addressed by the 20-bit memory-mapped port location computed from DS and BX.

Note that the indirect I/O transfer method is desirable for service routines that handle more than one device such as multiple printers by allowing the desired device (a specific printer) to be passed to the procedure as a parameter.

3.8.4.a Eight-Bit I/O Ports

Devices with 8-bit I/O ports can be connected to either the upper or lower half of the data bus. Bus loading is distributed by connecting an equal number of devices to the upper and lower halves of the data bus. If the I/O port chip is connected to the 8086 lower half of the data lines (AD0-AD7), the port addresses will be even (A0 = 0). On the other hand, the port addresses will be odd (A0 = 1) if the I/O port chip is connected to the upper half of the 8086 data lines (AD8-AD15). A0 will always be one or zero for a partitioned I/O chip. Therefore, A0 cannot be used as an address input to select registers within a particular I/O chip. If two chips are connected to the lower and upper halves of the 8086 address bus that differ only in A0 (consecutive odd and even addresses), A0 and $\overline{\text{BHE}}$ must be used as conditions of chip select decode to avoid a write to one I/O chip from erroneously performing a write to the other. Figure 3.21 shows two ways of generating chip selects for I/O port chip.

The first method shown in Figure 3.21A uses separate 8205s to generate chip selects for odd- and even-addressed byte peripherals. If a 16-bit word transfer is performed to an even-addressed I/O chip, the adjacent odd-addressed I/O chip is also selected. Figure 3.21B generates chip selects for byte transfers only.

3.8.4.b Sixteen-Bit I/O Ports

For efficient bus utilization and simplicity of I/O chip selection sixteen-bit I/O ports should be assigned even addresses. Both A0 and $\overline{\text{BHE}}$ should be the chip select conditions to ensure that the I/O chip is selected only for word operations. Figure 3.22 shows a method for generating chip for 16-bit ports. Note that in Figure 3.22, the 8086 will output low on both A0 and $\overline{\text{BHE}}$ when it executes a 16-bit I/O instruction with an even port address such as IN AX, 0006H. This instruction inputs the 16-bit contents of ports 0006H and 0007H in AX.

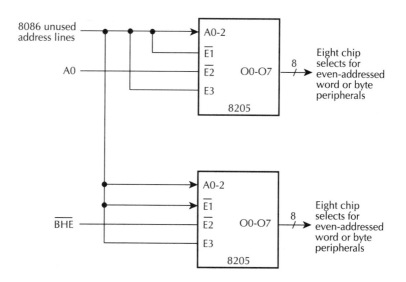

FIGURE 3.21A Techniques for generating I/O device chip selects.

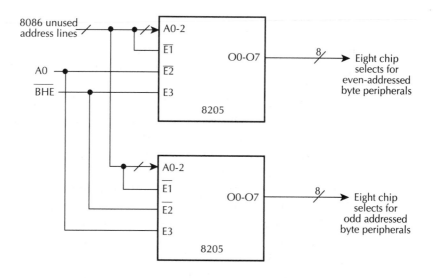

FIGURE 3.21B Techniques for generating I/O device chip selects.

3.8.5 8086-BASED MICROCOMPUTER

In this section, an 8086 will be interfaced in the minimum mode to provide 2K × 16 EPROM, 1K × 16 static RAM, and six 8-bit I/O ports. 2716 EPROM, 2142 static RAM, and 8255 I/O chips will be used for this purpose. Memory and I/O maps will also be determined. Figure 3.23 shows a hardware schematic for accomplishing this.

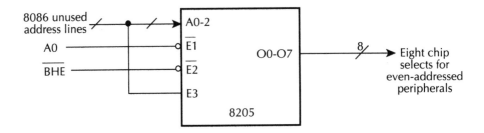

FIGURE 3.22 Chip selects for 16-bit ports.

Three 8282 octal latches are used. These are numbered as 8282-1, 8282-2, and 8282-3. The STB input of the 8282 strobes the eight inputs at the DI0-7 pins into the internal data latches. When $\overline{OE}$ is low, 8-bit data at the data latches are transferred to the output pins DO0-7. The 8086 ALE pin is used as the STB input for all the three latches and $\overline{OE}$ is tied to ground. The 8282-1 latches A16-A9 and $\overline{BHE}$. Pins DI5-7 and DO5-7 pins are not used for the 8282-1 chip. The 8282-2 and 8282-3 chips provide the A15-A8 and A7-A0, respectively. The 2716 is a 2K × 8 ultraviolet EPROM with eleven address pins A0-A10 and eight data pins O0-7. Two 2716s numbered as 2716-1 and 2716-2 are used. The 2716-1 provides all the even-addressed data and the 2716-2 contains all the odd-addressed data. The 8086 A1-A11 pins are connected to the A0-A10 pins of these chips. The 2716-1 even EPROM's O0-7 pins are connected to the 8086 D0-D7 pins. This is because the 8086 reads data via the D0-D7 pins for even addresses. On the other hand, the O0-7 pins of the 2716-2 are connected to the 8086 D8-D15 pins. The 8086 reads data via D8-D15 pins for odd addresses.

The 8205 is a 3 to 8 decoder with three enable pins $\overline{E1}$, $\overline{E2}$, and E3. E3 is tied to high. $\overline{E1}$ and $\overline{E2}$ are enabled by the 8086 A15 and A16 pins. The 8205 input pins A0-A2 are connected to the 8086 A12-A14. The 8205 is used to provide the fully decoding technique for addressing 2716s, 2142s, and 8255s. The 8205 3 × 8 decoder is used for future expansion.

The memory map for the 2716s can be determined as follows. A19-A17 pins are don't cares and are assumed to be high.

For 2716-1   (EVEN # EPROM)

A19	A18	A17	A16	A15	A14	A13	A12	A11	A10	A9	....	A1	A0
1	1	1	1	1	1	1	1	0	0	0	....	0	0
											to		
	F				F			1	1	1	....	1	0

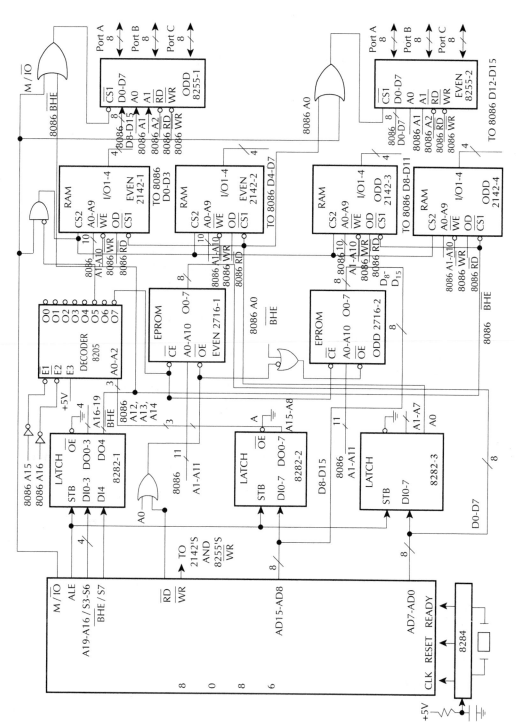

FIGURE 3.23 8086 interface to memory and I/O.

Note that A17-A19 pins are don't cares. A16 and A15 are used via inverters to enable $\overline{E1}$ and $\overline{E2}$ of the 8205. The 8086 address pins A12-A14 are used to provide the A2-A0 inputs of the 8205. Therefore, the memory map of the 2716-1 contains all even addresses, FF000H, FF002H, ... FFFFEH.

Note that the reset vector FFFF0H (CS = FFFFH, IP = 0000H) is included in this map. For any 8086-based design, the memory map must include the reset vector FFFF0H. Similarly, the 2716-2 contains the odd addresses FF001H, FF003H, ..., FFFFFH.

Next, the memory map for the 2142 RAMs will be determined. The 2142 is a 1K × 4 bit static RAM. Therefore, four 2142 RAM chips (2142-1, 2142-2, 2142-3, 2142-4) are required. Four-bit data are read from the 2142 when $\overline{CS1}$ = 0, CS2 = 1, $\overline{WE}$ = 1, and $\overline{OD}$ = 0. On the other hand, four-bit data are written into the 2142 when $\overline{CS1}$ = 0, CS2 = 1, $\overline{WE}$ = 0, and OD = 0. The 2142-1 and 2142-2 RAM chips provide the even addresses since the 8086 A0 pin is used to enable them. The 8086 A1-A10 pins are connected to the A0-A9 pins of these chips. The 8086 D0-D3 and D4-D7 pins are respectively connected to I/O 1-4 pins of the 2142-1 and 2142-2. Both chips are enabled simultaneously by enabling CS2 by ANDing the 8205 decoder output $\overline{O5}$ and $M/\overline{IO}$. The 2142-3 and 2142-4 contain the odd addresses since the 8086 $\overline{BHE}$ pin is used to enable them. Also, these chips are simultaneously enabled by CS2 via ANDing $\overline{O3}$ and $M/\overline{IO}$. The 8086 A11 pin is not required for the 2142s and is assumed to be one. The 2142-1 and the 2142-2 contain all even addresses FD800H, FD802H...FDFFEH. The memory map for the 2142-3 and the 2142-4 include all odd addresses FD801H, FD803H, ... FDFFFH assuming A11 = 1.

The memory map can therefore be summarized as follows:

Chip	Physical address (20-bit)	Logical address Segment register (16-bit)	Offset (16-bit)
2716-1 (even)	FF000H, FF002H, ..., FFFFEH	FF00H	0000H, 0FFEH, ..., 0FFEH
2716-2 (odd)	FF001H, FF003, ..., FFFFFH	FF00H	0001H, 0003H, ..., 0FFFH
2142-1, 2142-2 (even)	FD800H, FD802H, ..., FDFFEH	FD00H	0800H, 0802H, ..., 0FFEH
2142-3, 2142-4 (odd)	FD801H, FD803H, ..., FDFFFH	FD00H	0801H, 0803H, ..., 0FFFH

In the preceding table, the physical address FFFF0H can also be translated into the logical address with segment register value FFFFH and offset 0000H (reset vector).

For I/O ports, chips 8255-1 and 8255-2 are used. The 8255 is a general-purpose programmable I/O chip. The 8255 has three 8-bit I/O ports: ports A, B, and C. Ports A and B are latched 8-bit ports for both input and output. Port C is also an 8-bit port with latched output but the inputs are not latched. Port C can be used in two ways. It can either be used as a simple I/O port or as a control port for data transfer using handshaking via ports A and B.

The 8086 can configure the three ports by outputting appropriate data to the 8-bit control register. The ports can be decoded by two 8255 input pins A0 and A1 as follows:

A1	**A0**	
0	0	Port A
0	1	Port B
1	0	Port C
1	1	Control register

The structure of the control register is given below:

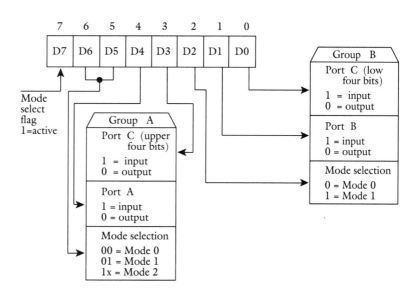

The bit 7 (D7) of the control register must be one to send the above definitions for bits 0 through 6 (D0-D6).

In this format bits D0-D6 are divided into two groups: groups A and B. Group A configures all 8 bits of port A and upper 4 bits of port C, while

Group B defines all 8 bits of port B and lower 4 bits of Port C. All bits in a port can be configured as a parallel input port by writing a 1 at the appropriate bit in the control register by the 8086 OUT instructions, and a 0 in a particular bit position will configure the appropriate port as a parallel output port. Group A has three modes of operation. These are modes 0, 1, and 2. Group B has two modes: modes 0 and 1. Mode 0 for both groups A and B provides simple I/O operation for each of the three ports. No handshaking is required. Mode 1 for both groups A and B is the strobed I/O mode used for transferring I/O data to or from a specified port in conjuction with strobes or handshaking signals. Ports A and B use the lines on port C to generate or accept these handshaking signals.

The mode 2 of group A is the strobed bidirectional bus I/O and may be used for communicating with a peripheral device on a single 8-bit data bus for both transmitting and receiving data (bidirectional bus I/O). Handshaking signals are required. Interrupt generation and enable/disable functions are also available.

When D7 = 0, the bit set/reset control word format is used for the control register as follows:

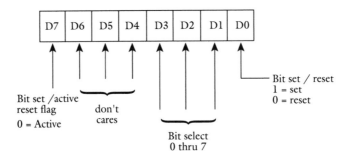

This format is used to set or reset the output on a pin of port C or when enabling of the interrupt output signals for handshake data transfer is desired. For example, the 8-bits 0   X X X   1 1 0   0
                                                    ↑   don't   bit 6   ↑
                                          bit set/   cares   clear
                                          reset mode

will clear bit 6 of port C to zero. Note that the control word format can be output to the 8255 control register by using the 8086 OUT instruction.

Next, the mode 0 of the 8255 will only be considered in the following discussion to illustrate 8086's programmed I/O capability.

Now, let us define the control word format for mode 0 more precisely by means of numerical example. Consider that the control word format is $1\,000\,0\,010_2$. With this data in the control register, all 8 bits of port A are configured as outputs, 8 bits of port C are also configured as outputs, but all 8 bits of port B are defined as inputs. On the other hand, outputting $1\,0\,011\,011_2$ into the control register will configure all 3 8-bit ports (ports A, B, and C) as inputs.

Let us decode the I/O port addresses. The 8255-1 will contain the odd-addressed ports since it is enabled by $\overline{BHE}$, while the 8255-2 will include the even-addressed ports since it is enabled by A0.

Since the 8086 A1 and A2 pins are utilized in addressing the ports, bits A3-A7 are don't cares and are assumed to be ones here. Note that A0 = 1 for odd-addressed ports, while A0 = 0 for even-addressed ports.

For 8255-1 (Odd-Addressed Ports)

	Address								
Port name	A7	A6	A5	A4	A3	A2	A1	A0	
Port A	1	1	1	1	1	0	0	1	= F9H
Port B	1	1	1	1	1	0	1	1	= FBH
Port C	1	1	1	1	1	1	0	1	= FDH
Control Register	1	1	1	1	1	1	1	1	= FFH

For 8255-2 (Even-Addressed Ports)

	Address								
Port name	A7	A6	A5	A4	A3	A2	A1	A0	
Port A	1	1	1	1	1	0	0	0	= F8H
Port B	1	1	1	1	1	0	1	0	= FAH
Port C	1	1	1	1	1	1	0	0	= FCH
Control Register	1	1	1	1	1	1	1	0	= FEH

In the above, standard I/O technique is used. The 8255s can also be interfaced to the 8086 using memory-mapped I/O. In this case the 8086 $M/\overline{IO}$ pin will not be used. The 20-bit physical addresses for the ports can be determined in a similar way by considering any unused 8086 address bits (A3-A19) as don't cares.

Example 3.8

Assume an 8086/8255 configuration with the following port addresses:

Port A	=	F9H
Port B	=	FBH
Control Register	=	FFH

Port A has three switches connected to bits 0, 1, and 2 and port B has an LED connected to bit 2 as follows:

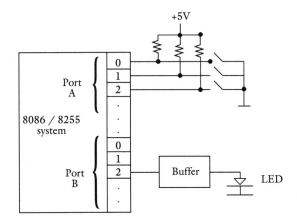

Write an 8086 assembly language program to turn the LED ON if port A has an odd number of HIGH switch inputs; otherwise turn the LED OFF. Do not use any instructions involving the parity flag.

Solution

```
PORT A    EQU  0F9H
PORT B    EQU  0FBH
CNTRL     EQU  0FFH
          MOV AL, 90H   ; Configure Port A as input
          OUT CNTRL, AL ; Port B as output
BEGIN     IN AL, PORTA  ; Input switches
          AND AL, 07H   ; Mask high five bits
          CMP AL, 07H   ; Are all three inputs HIGH?
          JZ ODD        ; If so, turn LED ON
          CMP AL, 01H   ; Is input 0 HIGH?
          JZ ODD        ; If so, turn LED ON
```

```
          CMP  AL,  02H    ;  Is  input  1  HIGH?
          JZ   ODD         ;  If  so,  turn  LED  ON
          CMP  AL,  04H    ;  Is  input  2  HIGH?
          JZ   ODD         ;  If  so,  turn  LED  ON.
          MOV  AL,  00H    ;  Else  turn  LED
          OUT  PORTB,  AL  ;  OFF
          JMP  BEGIN       ;  REPEAT
   ODD    MOV  AL,  04H    ;  Turn  LED
          OUT  PORTB,  AL  ;  ON
          JMP  BEGIN       ;  REPEAT
```

3.9 8086 INTERRUPT SYSTEM

The 8086 interrupts can be classified into three types. These are

1.   Predefined interrupts
2.   User-defined software interrupts
3.   User-defined hardware interrupts

The interrupt vector addresses for all the 8086 interrupts are determined from a table stored in locations 00000H through 003FFH. The starting addresses for the service routines for the interrupts are obtained by the 8086 using this table. Four bytes of the table are assigned to each interrupt: two bytes for IP and two bytes for CS. The table may contain up to 256 8-bit vectors. If fewer than 256 interrupts are defined in the system, the user need only provide enough memory for the interrupt pointer table for obtaining the defined interrupts.

The interrupt address vector (contents of IP and CS) for all the interrupts of the 8086 assigns every interrupt a type code for identifying the interrupt. There are 256 type codes associated with the 256 table entries. Each entry consists of two addresses, one for storing the IP contents and the other for storing the CS contents. Each 8086 interrupt physical address vector is 20 bits wide and is computed from the 16-bit contents of IP and CS.

For obtaining an interrupt address vector, the 8086 calculates two addresses in the pointer table where IP and CS are stored for a particular interrupt type.

For example, for the interrupt type nn (instruction INT nn), the table address for IP = 4 * nn and the table address for CS = 4 * nn + 2. For servicing the 8086's nonmaskable interrupt (NMI pin), the 8086 assigns the type code 2 to this interrupt. The 8086 automatically executes the INT2 instruction internally to obtain the interrupt address vector as follows:

```
Address for IP = 4 * 2 = 00008H
Address for CS = 4 * 2 + 2 = 0000AH
```

The 8086 loads the values of IP and CS from the 20-bit physical address 00008H and 0000AH in the pointer table. The user must store the desired 16-bit values of IP and CS in these locations. Similarly, the IP and CS values for other interrupts are calculated. The 8086 interrupt pointer table layout is shown in Table 3.2.

TABLE 3.2
8086 Interrupt Pointer Table

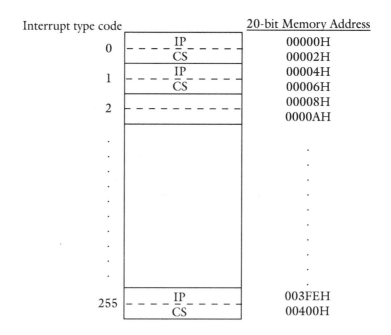

In response to an interrupt, the 8086 pushes flags, CS, and IP onto the stack, clears TF and IF flags, and then loads IP and CS from the pointer table using the type code.

Interrupt service routine should be terminated with the IRET (Interrupt Return) instruction which pops the top three stack words into IP, CS, and flags, thus returning to the right place in the main program. The 256 interrupt type codes are assigned as follows:

- Types 0 to 4 are for the predefined interrupts.
- Types 5 to 31 are reserved by Intel for future use.
- Types 32 to 255 are available for maskable interrupts.

3.9.1 PREDEFINED INTERRUPTS (0 TO 4)

The predefined interrupts include DIVISION BY ZERO (type 0), SINGLE STEP (type 1) NONMASKABLE INTERRUPT pin (type 2), BREAKPOINT-INTERRUPT (type 3), and INTERRUPT ON OVER-FLOW (type 4). The user must provide the desired IP and CS values in the interrupt pointer table. The user may also imitate these interrupts through hardware or software. If a predefined interrupt is not used in a system, the user may assign some other function to the associated type.

The 8086 is automatically interrupted whenever a division by zero is attempted. This interrupt is nonmaskable and is implemented by Intel as part of the execution of the divide instruction. When the TF (TRAP flag) is set by an instruction, the 8086 goes into the single step mode. The TF can be cleared to zero as follows:

```
PUSHF                         ;  Save flags
MOV BP, SP                    ;  Move [SP] → [BP]
AND [BP + 0],    0FEFFH       ;  Clear TF
POPF                          ;  Pop flags
```

Note that in the above [BP + 0] rather than [BP] is used since BP cannot be used without displacement. Now, to set TF, the AND instruction in the above should be replaced by OR [BP + 0], 0100H.

Once TF is set to one, the 8086 automatically generates a TYPE 1 interrupt after execution of each instruction. The user can write a service routine at the interrupt address vector to display memory locations and/ or register to debug a program. Single step is nonmaskable and cannot be enabled by STI (enable interrupt) or CLI (disable interrupt) instruction. The nonmaskable interrupt is initiated via the 8086 NMI pin.

It is edge triggered (LOW to HIGH) and must be active for two clock cycles to guarantee recognition. It is normally used for catastrophic failures such as power failure. The 8086 obtains the interrupt vector address by automatically executing the INT2 (type 2) instruction internally.

Type 3 interrupt is used for breakpoint and is nonmaskable. The user inserts the one-byte instruction INT3 into a program by replacing an instruction. Breakpoints are useful for program debugging.

The INTERRUPT ON OVERFLOW is a type 4 interrupt. This interrupt occurs if the overflow flag (OF) is set and the INTO instruction is executed. The overflow flag is affected, for example, after execution of signed arithmetic such as MULS (signed multiplication) instruction. The user can execute the INTO instruction after the MULS. If there is an overflow, an error service routine written by the user at the type 4 interrupt address vector is executed.

3.9.2 USER-DEFINED SOFTWARE INTERRUPTS

The user can generate an interrupt by executing a two-byte interrupt instruction INT nn. The INT nn instruction is not maskable by the interrupt enable flag (IF). The INT nn instruction can be used to test an interrupt service routine for external interrupts. Type codes 0 to 255 can be used. If predefined interrupt is not used in a system, the associated-type code can be utilized with the INT nn instruction to generate software (internal) interrupts.

3.9.3 USER-DEFINED HARDWARE (MASKABLE INTERRUPTS)

The 8086 maskable interrupts are initiated via the INTR pin. These interrupts can be enabled or disabled by STI (IF = 1) or CLI (IF = 0), respectively. If IF = 1 and INTR is active (HIGH) without occurrence of any other interrupts, the 8086, after completing the current instruction, generates $\overline{\text{INTA}}$ LOW twice, each time for about 2 cycles.

The state of the INTR pin is sampled during the last clock cycle of each instruction. In some instances, the 8086 samples the INTR pin at a later time. An example is execution of POP to a segment register. In this case, the interrupts are sampled until completion of the following instruction. This allows a 32-bit pointer to be loaded to SS and SP without the danger of an interrupt occurring between the two loads.

$\overline{\text{INTA}}$ is only generated by the 8086 in response to INTR, as shown in Figure 3.24. The interrupt acknowledge sequence includes two $\overline{\text{INTA}}$ cycles separated by two idle clock cycles. ALE is also generated by the 8086 and will load the address latches with indeterminate information. The ALE is useful in maximum systems with multiple 8259A priority interrupt controllers. During the $\overline{\text{INTA}}$ bus cycles, DT/$\overline{\text{R}}$ and $\overline{\text{DEN}}$ are LOW (see 8086 minimum mode bus cycle). The first $\overline{\text{INTA}}$ bus cycle indicates that an interrupt acknowledge cycle is in progress and allows the system to be ready

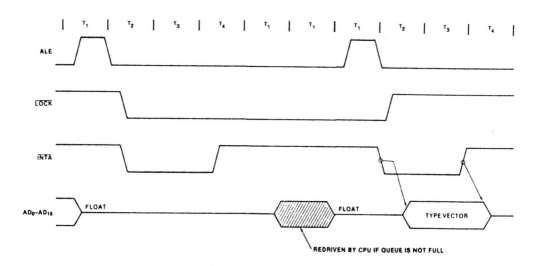

FIGURE 3.24 Interrupt acknowledge sequence.

to place the interrupt type code on the next $\overline{\text{INTA}}$ bus cycle. The 8086 does not obtain the information from the bus during the first cycle. The external hardware must place the type code on the lower half of the 16-bit data bus during the second cycle.

In the minimum mode, the $M/\overline{IO}$ is low indicating I/O operation during the $\overline{\text{INTA}}$ bus cycles. The 8086 internal $\overline{\text{LOCK}}$ signal is also low from T2 of the first bus cycle until T2 of the second bus cycle to avoid the BIU from accepting a hold request between the two $\overline{\text{INTA}}$ cycles. Figure 3.25 shows a simplified interconnection between the 8086 and 74LS244 for servicing the INTR. $\overline{\text{INTA}}$ enables 74LS244 to place the type code nn on the 8086 data bus.

In the maximum mode, the status lines S0 to S2 will enable the $\overline{\text{INTA}}$

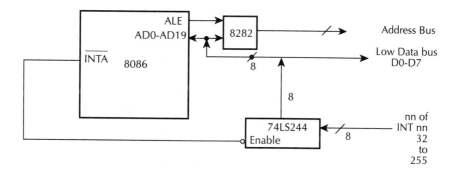

FIGURE 3.25 Servicing the INTR in the minimum mode.

output for each cycle via the 8288. The 8086 $\overline{\text{LOCK}}$ output will be active from T2 of the first cycle until T2 of the second to prevent the 8086 from accepting a hold request on either $\overline{\text{RQ}/\text{GT}}$ input and to prevent bus arbitration logic from releasing the bus between $\overline{\text{INTAs}}$ in multimaster systems. The $\overline{\text{LOCK}}$ output can be used in external logic to lock other devices off the system bus, thus ensuring the $\overline{\text{INTA}}$ sequence to be completed without intervention.

Once the 8086 has the interrupt-type code (via the bus for hardware interrupts, from software interrupt instructions INT nn or from the predefined interrupts), the type code is multiplied by four to obtain the corresponding interrupt vector in the interrupt vector table. The four bytes of the interrupt vector are least significant byte of the instruction pointer, most significant byte of the pointer, least significant byte of the code segment register, and most significant byte of the code segment register. During the transfer of control, the 8086 pushes the flags and current code segment register and instruction pointer into the stack. The new CS and IP values are loaded. Flags TF and IF are then cleared to zero. The CS and IP values are read by the 8086 from the interrupt vector table. No segment registers are used when accessing the interrupt pointer table. S4S3 has the value 10_2 to indicate no segment register selection.

As far as the 8086 interrupt priorities are concerned, single-step interrupt has the highest priority, followed by NMI, followed by the software interrupts (all interrupts except single step, NMI, and INTR interrupts). This means that a simultaneous NMI and single step will cause the NMI service routine to follow single step; a simultaneous software interrupt and single step will cause the software interrupt service routine to follow single step and a simultaneous NMI and software interrupt will cause the NMI service routine to be executed prior to the software interrupt service routine. An exception to this priority scheme occurs if all three nonmaskable interrupts (single step, software, and NMI) are pending. For this case, software interrupt service routine will be executed first followed by the NMI service routine, and single stepping will not be serviced. However, if software interrupt and single stepping are pending, single stepping resumes upon execution of the instruction causing the software interrupt (the next instruction in the routine being single stepped).

The INTR is maskable and has the lowest priority. If the user does not wish to single step before INTR is serviced, the single-step routine must disable interrupts during execution of the program being single stepped, and reenable interrupts on entry to the single-step routine. To avoid single stepping before the NMI service routine, the single-step routine must check the return address on the stack for the NMI service routine address and return control to that routine without single step enabled. Figure

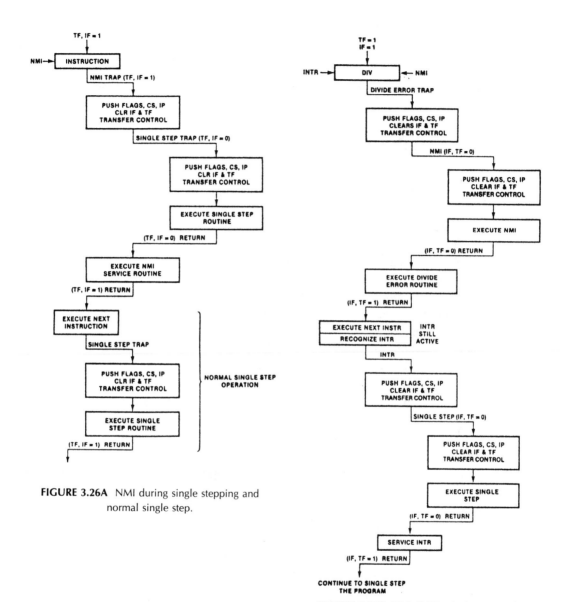

FIGURE 3.26A NMI during single stepping and normal single step.

FIGURE 3.26B NMI, INTR, single-step, and divide error simultaneous interrupts.

3.26A and B illustrate this. In Figure 3.26A single step and NMI occur at the same time, whereas in Figure 3.26B NMI, INTR, and a divide error occur during a divide instruction being single stepped.

A priority interrupt controller such as the 8259A can be used with the 8086 INTR to provide eight levels of interrupts. The 8259A has built-in features for expansion of up to 64 levels with additional 8259As. The

8259A is programmable and can be readily used with the 8086 to obtain multiple interrupts from the single 8086 INTR pin.

3.10 8086 DMA

When configured in the minimum mode (MN/$\overline{\text{MX}}$ pin HIGH), the 8086 provides HOLD (DMA request) and HLDA (DMA acknowledge) signals to take over the system bus for DMA applications. The Intel DMA controller chips 8257 and 8237 can be used with the 8086. The 8257 or 8237 can request DMA transfer between the 8086 memory and I/O device by activating the 8086 HOLD pin. The 8086 will complete the current bus cycle (if there is one presently in progress) and then output HLDA, relinquishing the system bus to the DMA controller. The 8086 will not try to use the HOLD pin until it is negated.

As mentioned before, the 8086 memory addresses are organized in two separate banks — one containing even-addressed bytes and the other containing odd-addressed bytes. An 8-bit DMA controller must alternately select these two banks to access logically adjacent bytes in memory. The 8089 I/O processor can interface a high-speed 8-bit device to an 8086-based microcomputer via DMA. The 8089 I/O processor will be discussed in the next section.

3.11 8089 I/O PROCESSOR

An input-output processor (IOP) is a microprocessor system with DMA capabilities that can directly communicate with I/O devices. A microcomputer with IOP configuration typically consists of a memory unit and one or more IOPs. Each IOP performs all I/O functions and, there-fore, off-loads the microprocessor of these functions. The Intel 8089 is an IOP and performs the functions of an intelligent DMA controller. The 8089 is primarily designed for the Intel 8086.

The 8089 contains two I/O channels. Each channel in the 8089 provides the basic features of a microprocessor along with those of a DMA controller.

The 8089 can be used in managing files and buffers for peripheral devices such as hard disk and floppy disk controllers. Other typical applications with the 8089 include CRT control functions, such as cursor control and autoscrolling keyboard control, and general I/O functions.

The 8086 initiates an I/O operation by forming a message in the main memory that specifies the function to be performed by the 8089. The 8089 reads this message from memory, performs the operation, and informs the 8086 upon completion of the task. All I/O device controller overheads such as DMA data block transfer functions are accomplished by the 8089 without any 8086 intervention.

The 8086 communicates with the 8089 in two distinct modes: initialization and command. The initialization sequence is usually performed when the system is powered up or reset. The 8086 initializes the 8089 by forming a series of message blocks in memory. On receipt of a command from the 8086, the 8089 reads these blocks and determines how the data buses are configured and how access to the buses is to be controlled.

Upon initialization, the 8086 directs all communications to either of the 8089's two channels. Each channel has the ability to execute programs and has its own set of ten registers and associated control logic that monitors its operation during data transfer. All 8086 to 8089 communication is based on the channel control block (CCB). The CCB is located in the 8086's memory space and its address is padded to the 8089 during initialization. The CCB contains information such as the busy flag and the Channel Command Word (CCW). The busy flag indicates whether the channel is in the midst of an operation or is available for a new 8086 command. Each channel maintains this flag. The 8086 sets the CCW to indicate the type of operation the 8089 is to perform. Six different commands allow the 8086 to start and stop programs, remove interrupt requests, etc.

If the 8086 is commanding a channel to run a program, it directs the channel to a parameter block (PB) and a task block (TB). The PB contains variable data that the channel program uses in carrying out its assignment. The PB may also contain space for the result that the channel is to return to the 8086. A TB is a channel program sequence of 8089 instructions that will perform the desired operation. A typical channel program might use the PB data to set up the 8089, and an I/O device controller for a transfer, to carry out the transfer, return the results, and then halt.

After initializing the CCW and linking the TB to a PB and the PB to the CCB, the 8086 normally activates the CA (channel attention) and SEL (channel select) pins of the 8089. The SEL pin at the falling edge of CA line selects channel 1 or channel 2.

An 8089 channel attention line (CA) is similar in concept to an 8086 interrupt. When the channel identifies the CA, it stops the current program and checks the command in the CCW. If the 8086 commands the 8089 to start a program, the 8089 reads the PB and TB into its internal registers, sets its busy flag, and starts executing the channel program. After sending the CA, the 8086 may perform other functions and the 8089 may carry on with the desired function in parallel.

Upon completion of the function, the 8089 informs the 8086 by clearing the busy flag in the CCB. Optionally, the 8089 may interrupt to inform the 8086 of its completion of the desired function.

The 8086/8089 communication structure is shown in Figure 3.27.

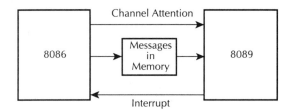

FIGURE 3.27 8086/8089 communication.

Almost all communications occur via messages in shared memory. The only direct hardware communications between the 8086 and the 8089 are channel attentions and interrupt requests.

The two 8089 channels can operate independent of each other. Each channel contains its own registers, channel attention, interrupt request, and DMA control signals.

A channel may be idle, may execute a program, carry out a DMA transfer, or respond to the 8086 channel attention at any particular time. The two channels cannot perform data transfer simultaneously. Only one of the two channels can be active at a time. However, in some cases, the two channels can be active concurrently operating in sequence. For example, during the successive DMA cycles of channel 1, instructions may be executed by channel 2. The 8089 assembly language programming (ASM-89) is used to write channel programs. The 8089 includes 50 instructions. These include data transfer, simple arithmetic, logical and address manipulation operations, unconditional and conditional jumps, calls, bit manipulations, and DMA transfer instructions.

The 8089 DMA transfer instruction makes the channel ready for a DMA transfer. The 8089 completes execution of one additional instruction, then stops program execution and goes into DMA transfer mode. Before execution of the DMA transfer instruction, the user must initialize the channel register which monitors the DMA transfer.

Data are transferred from one memory area to another in the 8086 memory space, from one I/O area to another within the 8089, or from memory in 8086 to I/O spaces in 8089 and vice versa.

QUESTIONS AND PROBLEMS

3.1 What is the basic difference between the 8086 and 8088 microprocessors? Name one reason why these two microprocessors are included in the i APX 86 family by Intel.

3.2 List the 8086 minimum and maximum mode signals. How are these modes selected?

3.3 What are the functions provided by 8288 bus controller and 8289 bus arbiter in a maximum mode 8086 system?

3.4 Which bit of the 8086 FLAG register is used by the string instructions? How? Illustrate this by using the 8086 MOVSB instruction.

3.5 What is the relationship between the 8086 external and internal clocks? Does the 8086 have an on-chip clock circuitry? Comment.

3.6 Write an 8086 instruction sequence to set the TF bit in the FLAG register for single stepping.

3.7 If $[BL] = 36_{16}$ (ASCII code for 6) and $[CL] = 33_{16}$ (ASCII code for 3), write an 8086 assembly program which will add the contents of BL and CL, and then provide the result in decimal. Store result in CL.

3.8 What happens to the contents of the AX register after execution of the following 8086 instruction sequence:

```
MOV  AX,  0F180H
CBW
CWD
```

3.9 Write an 8086 assembly program to implement the following Pascal segment:

```
SUM:= 0; for i: = 0 to 15 do
SUM:= SUM + A(i)
```

Assume CS and DS are already initialized. A(i)s are 16-bit numbers.

3.10 Write an 8086 assembly program to add two 128-bit numbers stored in memory in consecutive locations.

3.11 Write an 8086 subroutine in assembly language to compute

$$Y = \sum_{i=1}^{N} \frac{Xi^2}{N}$$

where Xis are signed 8-bit integers and N = 100. The numbers are stored in consecutive locations. Assume SI to point to Xis and SP, DS, SS are already initialized.

3.12 Write an 8086 assembly program to move a block of data bytes of length 100_{10} from the source block starting at location 2000H in DS to the destination block starting at location 3000H in ES. Assume DS and ES are already initialized.

3.13 Write an 8086 assembly program to logically shift a 128-bit number stored in location starting at 4000H in DS twice to the right. Store the result in memory location starting at 5000H in DS. Assume DS is initialized.

3.14 Determine the number of 2732 4K × 8 EPROMs and 2142 1K × 4 static RAMs to provide 4K word EPROM and 1K word RAM. Draw a neat schematic and determine the map.

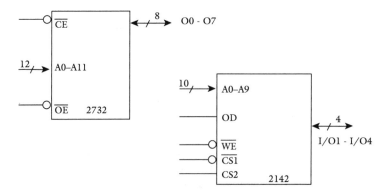

3.15 Assume the memory and I/O maps of Figure 3.23. Interface the following A/D to the 8086/2716/2142/8255 of the figure:

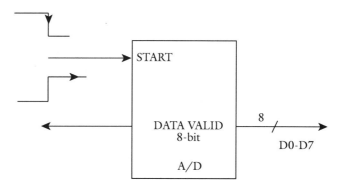

Write an 8086 assembly program to input the A/D converter and turn an LED ON connected to bit 5 of port A of 8255-2 if the number read from A/D is odd; otherwise turn the LED OFF. Assume that the LED is turned ON by a HIGH and turned OFF by a LOW.

3.16 Repeat problem 3.15 using 8086 INTR interrupt.

3.17 Identify the 8086 and 8089 signals required to interface these two chips and discuss them.

3.18 Write 8086 assembly language program to add a 16-bit number stored in DX (bits 0 to 7 containing the high-order byte of the number and bits 8 to 15 containing the low-order byte) with another 16-bit number stored in BX (bits 0 to 7 containing the low-order 8 bits of the number and bits 8 through 15 containing the high-order 8 bits). Store the result in CX.

TABLE 3.A-1
8086 Data Transfer Instructions

Operation	Instructions	Interpretation	Source	Destination	Example	Comments
			Addressing mode			**Illustration**
MOVE	MOV mem/reg 2, mem/reg 1	[mem/reg 2] ← [mem/reg 1]	Memory or register	Memory or register	MOV BX, CX	mem uses DS as the segment register; no memory-to-memory operation allowed; that is, MOV mem, mem is not permitted Segment register cannot be specified as reg1 or reg2; no flags are affected; not usually used to load or store 'A' from or to memory
	MOV mem, data	[mem] ← data	Immediate	Memory	MOV [DI], 3476H	mem uses DS as the segment register; 8- or 16-bit data specify whether memory location is 8- or 16-bit; no flags are affected
	MOV reg, data	[reg] ← data	Immediate	Register	MOV SI, 0F125H	Segment register cannot be specified as reg; data can be 8- or 16-bit; no flags are affected
	MOV A, mem	[A] ← [mem]	Memory	Register	MOV AL, START	Takes fewer bytes than reg, mem; mem uses DS as segment register; 'A' can be AL or AX; no flags are affected
	MOV mem, A	[mem] ← [A]	Register	Memory	MOV BEGIN, AX	mem uses DS as segment register; 'A' can be AL or AX; no flags are affected; needs fewer bytes than MOV mem, reg
	MOV segreg, mem/reg	[segreg] ← [mem/reg]	Memory or register	Register	MOV DS, CX	mem uses DS as segment register; used for initializing CS, DS, ES, and SS; no flags are affected
	MOV mem/reg, segreg	[mem/reg] ← [segreg]	Register	Memory or register	MOV CX, DS	mem uses DS as segment register; no flags affected

TABLE 3.A-1 (continued)
8086 Data Transfer Instructions

Operation	Instructions	Interpretation	Source	Destination	Example	Comments
			Addressing mode			**Illustration**
PUSH	PUSH mem	$[SP] \leftarrow [SP] - 2$ $[[SP]] \leftarrow [mem]$	Memory	—	PUSH [BX]	mem uses DS as segment register; no flags are affected; PUSH as 16-bit memory contents
	PUSH reg	$[SP] \leftarrow [SP] - 2$ $[[SP]] \leftarrow [reg]$	Register	—	PUSH DX	reg must be a 16-bit register; cannot be used to PUSH segment register or flag register
	PUSH segreg	$[SP] \leftarrow [SP] - 2$ $[[SP]] \leftarrow [segreg]$	Register	—	PUSH ES	PUSH CS is illegal
POP	POP mem	$[mem] \leftarrow [[SP]]$ $[SP] \leftarrow [SP] + 2$	Memory	—	POP [DI]	mem uses DS as the segment register; no flags are affected
	POP reg	$[reg] \leftarrow [[SP]]$ $[SP] \leftarrow [SP] + 2$	Register	—	POP CX	Cannot be used to POP segment registers or flag register
	POP segreg	$[segreg] \leftarrow [[SP]]$ $[SP] \leftarrow [SP] + 2$	Register	—	POP DS	POP CS is illegal
Exchange	XCHG AX, reg16	$[AX] \leftrightarrow [reg16]$	Register	Accumulator	XCHG AX, CX	reg must be 16-bit; no flags are affected; reg cannot be segment register
	XCHG mem, reg	$[mem] \leftrightarrow [reg]$	Register	Memory	XCHG [BX], DX	reg and memory can be both 8- or 16-bit; mem uses DS as the segment register; reg cannot be segment register; no flags are affected
	XCHG reg, reg	$[reg] \leftrightarrow [reg]$	Register	Register	XCHG CL, DL	Not used to exchange reg with AX; reg can be 8- or 16-bit; reg cannot be segment register; no flags are affected

TABLE 3.A-1(continued)
8086 Data Transfer Instructions

Operation	Instructions	Interpretation	Addressing mode		Example	Comments
			Source	Destination		Illustration
Translate table	XLAT	[AL] ← [[AL] + BX]	—	—	XLAT	This instruction is useful for translating characters from one code such as ASCII to another such as EBCDIC; this is a no-operand instruction and is called an instruction with implied addressing mode; the instruction loads AL with the contents of a 20-bit physical address computed from DS, BX, and AL; this instruction can be used to read the elements in a table where BX can be loaded with a 16-bit value to point to the starting address (offset from DS) and AL can be loaded with the element number (0 being the first element number); no flags are affected; the XLAT instruction is equivalent to MOV AL, [AL] [BX]

TABLE 3.A-2
8086 I/O Instructions

Operation	Instructions	Interpretation	Addressing mode Source	Addressing mode Destination	Example	Illustration Comments
I/O	IN AL, DX	[AL] ← [PORT DX]	Register indirect (port)	Register (AL only)	IN AL, DX	Input AL with the 8-bit contents of a port addressed by DX; this is a one-byte instruction
	IN AX, DX	[AX] ← [PORT DX]	Register indirect (port)	Register (AX only)	IN AX, DX	Input AX with the 16-bit contents of a port addressed by DX and DX + 1; this is a one-byte instruction
	IN AL, PORT	[AL] ← [PORT]	Register (port)	Register (AL only)	IN AL, PORT A	Input AL with the 8-bit contents of a port addressed by the second byte of the instruction
	IN AX, PORT	[AX] ← [PORT]	Register (port)	Register (AX only)	IN AX, PORT	Input AX with the 16-bit contents of a port addressed by the 8-bit address in the second byte of the instruction
	OUT DX, AL	[PORT] ← [AL] DX	Register (AL only)	Register indirect (port)	OUT DX, AL	Output the 8-bit contents of AL into an I/O port addressed by the contents of DX
	OUT DX, AX	[PORT DX] ← [AX]	Register (AX only)	Register indirect (port)	OUT DX, AX	Output the 16-bit contents of AX into an I/O port addressed by DX
	OUT PORT, AL	[PORT] ← [AL]	Register (AL only)	Register indirect (port)	OUT PORT, AL	Output the 8-bit contents of AL into the port specified in the second byte of the instruction
	OUT PORT, AX	[PORT] ← [AX]	Register (AX only)	Register (port)	OUT PORT, AX	Output the 16-bit content of AX into the port specified in the second byte of the instruction

TABLE 3.A-3
Address Object Transfers[a]

| Operation | Instructions | Interpretation | Addressing mode | | Illustration | |
			Source	Destination	Example	Comments
Load EA	LEA reg, offset	[reg] ← offset portion of address in DS	Memory	Register	LEA SI, ADDR (the value ADDR is loaded into SI which can then be used as offset for memory in DS LEA DI, ADDR + 5 loads the value ADDR + 5 into DI	LEA (load effective address) loads the value in the source operand rather than its content to register (such as SI, DI, BX), which are allowed to contain offset for accessing memory; no flags are affected LEA is useful if address computation is required during program execution
Load pointer using DS	LDS reg, mem	[reg] ← [mem] [DS] ← [mem + 2]	Memory	Register	LDS BX, BEGIN	Load a 16-bit register (such as BX, BP, SI, DI) with the content of specified memory and load DS with the content of the location that follows; no flags are affected; DS is used as the segment register for mem
Load pointer using ES	LES reg, mem	[reg] ← [mem] [ES] ← [mem + 2]	Memory	Register	LES SI, [BX]	DS is used as the segment register for mem; in the example, SI is loaded with 16-bit value from memory location addressed by 20-bit physical address computed from DS and BX. The 16-bit content of the next memory is loaded into ES; no flags are affected

[a] Address object transfers — provides programmer with some control over the addressing mechanism.

TABLE 3.A-4
8086 Flag Register Instructions

Operation	Instructions	Interpretation	Addressing mode		Illustration	
			Source	Destination	Example	Comments
Load AH from flags	LAHF	[AH] ← [Flags low-byte]	—	—	LAHF	This instruction has implied addressing mode; it loads AH with low byte of the flag with register; no flags are affected
Store AH in flags	SAHF	[Flags low-byte] ← [AH]	—	—	SAHF	This instruction has the implied addressing mode; the content of the AH register is stored into low-byte of the flag register; all flags are affected (low byte of SR)
Push flags into stack	PUSHF	[SP] ← [SP] – 2 [[SP]] ← [Flags]	—	—	PUSHF	This instruction pushes the 16-bit flag register onto the stack; no flags are affected
Pop flags off stack	POPF	[Flags] ← [[SP]] [SP] ← [SP] + 2	—	—	POPF	This instruction pops the top two stack bytes in the 16-bit flag register; all flags are affected (low byte of SR)

TABLE 3.A-5
Arithmetic Instructions

Operation	Instructions	Interpretation	Addressing mode		Example	Comments
			Source	Destination		**Illustration**
ADD	ADD mem/reg 2, mem/reg 1	[mem/reg 2] ← [mem/reg 2] + [mem/reg 1]	Memory or register	Memory or register	ADD BL, [SI]	Add two 8- or 16-bit data; no memory-to-memory ADD is permitted; all flags are affected; mem uses DS as the segment register; reg 1 or reg 2 cannot be segment register
	ADD mem, data	[mem] ← [mem] + data	Immediate	Memory	ADD START, 02H	mem uses DS as the segment register; data can be 8- or 16-bit; all flags areaffected
	ADD reg, data	[reg] ← [reg] + data	Immediate	Register	ADD BX, 0354H	Data can be 8- or 16-bit; no segment registers are allowed; all flags are affected; this instruction should not be used to add AL or AX with 8- or 16-bit immediate data
	ADD A, data	[A] ← [A] + data	Immediate	Register	ADD AL, 05H	Data can be 8- or 16-bit; 'A' can be AL or AX; all flags are affected
ADD with carry	ADC mem/reg 2, mem/reg 1	[mem/reg 2] ← [mem/reg 2] + [mem/reg 1] + CY	Memory or register	Memory or register	ADC [SI], BL	Memory or register can be 8- or 16-bit; all flags are affected; no segment registers are allowed; no memory-to-memory ADC is permitted

TABLE 3.A-5 (continued)
Arithmetic Instructions

Operation	Instructions	Interpretation	Addressing mode Source	Addressing mode Destination	Example	Illustration Comments
ADD with carry (continued)	ADC mem, data	[mem] ← [mem] + data + CY	Immediate	Memory	ADC [BX], 05H	Data can be 8- or 16-bit; mem uses DS as the segment register; all flags are affected
	ADC reg, data	[reg] ← [reg] + data + CY	Immediate	Register	ADC SI, 05FIH	Data can be 8- or 16-bit; register cannot be segment register; all flags are affected; reg is not usually used as AX or AL
	ADC A, data	[A] ← [A] + data + CY	Immediate	Register	ADC AH, 05H	'A' can be AL or AX register; all flags are affected
Increment	INC reg16	[reg16] ← [reg16] + 1	—	Register	INC BX	This is a one-byte instruction; used to increment a 16-bit register except the segment register; does not affect the carry flag
	INC mem/reg 8	[mem] ← [mem] + 1 or [reg8] ← [reg8] + 1	Memory or register	— —	INC BYTE PTR ADDR BYTE PTR is an assembler directive to indicate that ADDR is a byte address	This is a two-byte instruction; can be used to increment a byte or word in memory or an 8-bit register content; segment register cannot be incremented by this instruction; does not affect the carry flag

TABLE 3.A-5 (continued)
Arithmetic Instructions

Operation	Instructions	Interpretation	Addressing mode		Example	Illustration
			Source	Destination		Comments
ASCII adjust after addition	AAA	ASCII adjust [AL] after addition	—	—	AAA	This instruction has implied addressing mode; this instruction is used to adjust the content of AL after addition of two ASCII characters; adjust means convert results to correct binary number
Decimal adjust [AL] after addition	DAA	Decimal adjust [AL] after addition	—	—	DAA	This instruction uses implied addressing mode; this instruction converts [AL] into BCD; DAA should be used after BCD addition
Subtraction	SUB mem/reg 1, mem/reg 2	[mem/reg 1] ← [mem/reg 1] − [mem/reg 2]	Memory or register	Memory or register	SUB CX, DX or SUB BH, BH	No memory-to-memory SUB permitted; all flags are affected; mem uses DS as the segment register
	SUB mem, data	[mem] ← [mem] − data	Immediate	Memory	SUB ADDR, 02H	Data can be 8- or 16-bit; mem used DS as the segment register; all flags are affected
	SUB reg, data	[reg] ← [reg] − data	Immediate	Memory	SUB CL, 03H	Data can be 8- or 16-bit; this instruction is not usually used for subtracting data from AX or AL − SUB A, data is used for this; all flags are affected

TABLE 3.A-5 (continued)
Arithmetic Instructions

| Operation | Instructions | Interpretation | Addressing mode | | Example | Illustration |
			Source	Destination		Comments
Subtraction (continued)	SUB A, data	[A] ← [A] − data	Immediate	Register	SUB AL, 02H	'A' can be AL or AX; data can be 8- or 16-bit; all flags are affected
Subtraction with borrow	SBB mem/reg 1, mem/reg 2	[mem/reg 1] ← [mem/reg 1] − [mem/reg 2] − CY	Memory or register	Memory or register	SBB, BX, CX	Same as SUB mem/reg 1, mem/reg 2 except this is a subtraction with borrow
	SBB mem, data	[mem] ← [mem] − data − CY	Immediate	Memory	SBB ADDR, 05H	Same as SUB mem, data except this is a subtraction with borrow
	SBB reg, data	[reg] ← [reg] − data − CY	Immediate	Register	SBB BX, 0302H	Same as SUB reg, data except this is a subtraction with borrow
	SBB A, data	[A] ← [A] − data − CY	Immediate	Register	SBB AL, 05H	Same as SUB A, data except this is a subtraction with borrow
Decrement	DEC reg16	[reg16] ← [reg16] − 1	—	Register	DEC CX	This is a one-byte instruction used to decrement a 16-bit register except segment register; does not affect the carry flag
	DEC mem/reg8	[mem] ← [mem] − 1 or [reg8] ← [reg8] − 1	—	Memory or register	DEC BYTE PTR ADDR or DEC BL	Used to decrement a byte or a word in memory or an 8-bit register content; segment register cannot be decremented by this instruction; does not affect carry flag

TABLE 3.A-5 (continued)
Arithmetic Instructions

| Operation | Instructions | Interpretation | Addressing mode | | Example | Illustration Comments |
			Source	Destination		
ASCII adjust after subtraction	AAS	ASCII adjust [AL] after subtraction	—	—	AAS	This instruction has implied addressing mode; used to adjust [AL] after subtraction of two ASCII characters
Decimal adjust [AL] after subtraction	DAS	Decimal adjust [AL] after subtraction	—	—	DAS	This instruction uses implied addressing mode; converts [AL] into BCD; DAS should be used after BCD subtraction
Negation	NEG mem/reg	[mem/reg] ← [mem/reg]' + 1	—	Memory or register	NEG BL or NEG BYTE PTR ADDR	mem/reg can be 8- or 16-bit; performs two's complement subtraction of the specified operand from zero; that is, two's complement of a number is formed; all flags are affected except CF = 0 if [mem/reg] is zero; otherwise CF = 1
Compare	CMP mem/reg 1, mem/reg 2	[mem/reg 1] − [mem/reg 2] → flags are affected; no result	Memory or register	Memory or register	CMP BH, CL	mem/reg can be 8- or 16-bit; no memory comparison allowed; result of subtraction is not provided; all flags are affected

TABLE 3.A-5 (continued)
Arithmetic Instructions

Operation	Instructions	Interpretation	Addressing mode		Example	Comments
			Source	Destination		Illustration
Compare (continued)	CMP mem/reg, data	[mem/reg] – data → flags are affected; no result	Immediate	Memory or register	CMP ADDR, 0561H or CMP BL, 02H	Subtracts 8- or 16-bit data from [mem/reg] and affects flags; no result is provided
	CMP A, data	[A] – data → flags are affected; no result	Immediate	Register	CMP AL, 05H	Subtract 8- or 16-bit data from AL or AX, respectively, and affect flags; no result is provided
Multiplication (unsigned)	MUL mem/reg	For 8 × 8 [AX] ← [AL]* [mem8/reg8] For 16 × 16 [DX] [AX] ← [AX]* [mem16/reg16]	Memory or register	—	MUL BH MUL WORD PTR [BX]	mem/reg can be 8- or 16-bit; only CF and OF are affected; unsigned multiplication
Multiplication (signed)	IMUL mem/reg	For 8 × 8 [AX] ← [AL]* [mem8/reg8] For 16 × 16 [DX] [AX] ← [AX]* [mem16/reg16]	Memory or register	—	IMUL CL or IMUL BYTE PTR	mem/reg can be 8- or 16-bit; only CF and OF are affected; signed multiplication
ASCII adjust after multiplication	AAM	ASCII adjust after multiplication	—	—	AAM	This instruction has implied addressing mode; after multiplying two unpacked BCD numbers, adjust the product in AX to become an unpacked BCD result; ZF, SF, and PF are affected

TABLE 3.A-5 (continued)
Arithmetic Instructions

Operation	Instructions	Interpretation	Addressing mode Source	Addressing mode Destination	Illustration Example	Illustration Comments
Division (unsigned)	DIV mem/reg	16 ÷ 8 [AX] [mem8/reg8] → [AH] ← Remainder [AL] ← Quotient 32 ÷ 16 [DX] [AX] [mem16/reg16] → [DX] ← Remainder [AX] ← Quotient	Memory or register	—	DIV BL or DIV WORD PTR ADDR	mem/reg is 8-bit for 16-bit by 8-bit divide and 16-bit for 32-bit by divide; this is an unsigned division; no flags are affected; division by zero automatically generates an internal interrupt
Division (signed)	IDIV mem/reg	Same as DIV mem/reg	Memory or register	—	IDIV BL or IDIV WORD PTR ADDR	Same as DIV mem/reg except signed division
ASCII adjust for division	AAD	ASCII adjust for division	—	—	AAD	This instruction has implied addressing mode; converts two unpacked BCD digits in AX into equivalent binary number in AL; AAD must be used before dividing two unpacked BCD digits by an unpacked BCD byte
Sign extension	CBW	Convert a byte to a word	—	—	CBW	Extend the sign bit (bit 7) of AL register into AH
	CWD	Convert a word to a doubleword (32-bit)	—	—	CWD	Extend the sign bit of AX (bit 15) into DX

TABLE 3.A-6
Logical Instructions

Operation	Instructions	Interpretation	Addressing mode		Illustration	
			Source	Destination	Example	Comments
AND	AND mem/reg 1, mem/reg 2	[mem/reg 1] ← [mem/reg 1] ∧ [mem/reg 2]	Memory or register	Memory or register	AND BL, CH	This instruction logically ANDS 8- or 16-bit data in [mem/reg 1] with 8- or 16-bit in [mem/reg 2]; all flags are affected; OF and CF are cleared to zero; no segment registers are allowed; no memory to memory operation is allowed; mem uses DS as the segment register
	AND mem, data	[mem] ← [mem] ∧ data	Immediate	Memory	AND START, 02H	Data can be 8- or 16-bit; mem uses DS as the segment register; all flags are affected with OF and CF always cleared to zero
	AND reg, data	[reg] ← [reg] ∧ data	Immediate	Register	AND CX, 027IH	Data can be 8- or 16-bit; reg cannot be segment register; this instruction should not be used to AND AL or AX with 8- or 16-bit immediate data; all flags are affected with OF and CF cleared to zero
	AND A, data	[A] ← [A] ∧ data	Immediate	Register	AND AL, 02H	Data can be 8- or 16-bit; A must be AL or AX; all flags are affected with OF and CF cleared to zero

TABLE 3.A-6 (continued)
Logical Instructions

| Operation | Instructions | Interpretation | Addressing mode | | Example | Illustration Comments |
			Source	Destination		
NOT (ones complement)	NOT reg	[reg] ← [reg]'	—	Register	NOT BX	Finds ones complemented of a register; mem and reg can be 8- or 16-bit; segment registers are not allowed; no flags are affected
	NOT mem	[mem] ← [mem]'	—	Memory	NOT [SI]	mem uses DS as the segment register; no flags are affected
OR	OR mem/reg 1, mem/reg 2	[mem/reg 1] ← [mem/reg 1] ∨ [mem/reg 2]	Memory or register	Memory or register	OR BX, CX	No memory-to-memory operation is allowed; [mem] or [reg1] or [reg2] can be 8- or 16-bit; all flags are affected with OF and CF cleared to zero; no segment registers are allowed; mem uses DS as segment register
	OR mem, data	[mem] ← [mem] ∨ data	Immediate	Memory	OR [DI], 02H	mem and data can be 8- or 16-bit; mem uses DS as segment register; all flags are affected with CF and OF cleared to zero
	OR reg, data	[reg] ← [reg] ∨ data	Immediate	Register	OR BL, 03H	reg and data can be 8- or 16-bit; no segment registers are allowed; all flags are affected with CF and OF cleared to zero; should not be used to OR AL or AX with immediate data
	OR A, data	[A] ← [A] ∨ data	Immediate	Register	OR AX, 2050H	Data can be 8- or 16-bit; A must be AL or AX; all flags are affected with OF and CF cleared to zero

TABLE 3.A-6 (continued)
Logical Instructions

| Operation | Instructions | Interpretation | Addressing mode | | Example | Illustration |
			Source	Destination		Comments
TEST	TEST mem/reg 1, mem/reg 2	[mem/reg 1] ∧ [mem/reg 2] → no result; flags are affected	Memory or register	Memory or register	TEST CL, BL	No memory-to-memory TEST is allowed; no result is provided; all flags are affected with CF and OF cleared to zero; [mem], [reg 1] or [reg2] can be 8- or 16-bit; no segment registers are allowed; mem uses DS as the segment register
	TEST mem, data	[mem] ∧ data → no result; flags are affected	Immediate	Memory	TEST START, 02H	mem and data can be 8- or 16-bit; no result is provided; all flags are affected, with CF and OF cleared to zero; mem uses DS as the segment register
	TEST reg, data	[reg] ∧ data → no result, flags are affected	Immediate	Register	TEST CL, 02H	reg and data can be 8- or 16-bit; no result is provided; all flags are affected with CF and OF cleared to zero; reg cannot be segment register; should not be used to test AL or AX with immediate data
	TEST A, data	[A] ∧ data → no result; flags are affected	Immediate	Register	TEST AL, 02H	A must be AX or AL; data can be 8- or 16-bit; no result is provided; all flags are affected with CF and OF cleared to zero

TABLE 3.A-6 (continued)
Logical Instructions

Operation	Instructions	Interpretation	Addressing mode Source	Addressing mode Destination	Example	Illustration Comments
XOR	XOR mem/reg 1, mem/reg 2	[mem/reg 1] ← [mem/reg 1] ⊕ [mem/reg 2]	Memory or register	Memory or register	XOR BL, CL	No memory-to-memory operation is allowed; [mem] or [reg1] or [reg2] can be 8- or 16-bit; all flags are affected, with CF and OF cleared to zero; mem uses DS as the segment register
	XOR mem/data	[mem] ← [mem] ⊕ data	Immediate	Memory	XOR START	Data and mem can be 8- or 16-bit; mem uses DS as the segment register; mem cannot be segment registers; all flags are affected with CF and OF cleared to zero
	XOR reg, data	[reg] ← [reg] ⊕ data	Immediate	Register	XOR BL, 03H	reg or mem can be 8- or 16-bit; mem uses DS as the segment register; all flags are affected with CF and OF cleared to zero; should not be used for XORing AL or AX with immediate data
	XOR A, data	[A] ← [A] ⊕ data	Immediate	Register	XOR AL, 05H	A must be AL or AX; data can be 8- or 16-bit; all flags are affected with CF or OF cleared to zero
SHIFTS and ROTATES	SAL Mem/reg, 1	Shift arithmetic left once byte or word in mem or reg	Immediate	Memory or register	SAL BYTE PTR START, 1 SAL BL, 1	FOR BYTE

TABLE 3.A-6 (continued)
Logical Instructions

FOR WORD

Operation	Instructions	Interpretation	Addressing mode		Example	Illustration
			Source	Destination		Comments
SHIFTS and ROTATES (continued)	SAL mem/reg, CL	Shift arithmetic left byte or word by shift count on CL	Register	Memory or register	SAL BYTE PTR [SI], CL or SAL BX, CL	mem uses DS as segment register; mem cannot be segment registers; OF and CF are affected; if sign bit is changed during or after shifting, the OF is set to one. Operation same as SAL mem/reg 1; CL contains shift count for up to 255; zero and negative shifts are illegal; [CL] is used as shift count when shift is greater than one; OF and SF are affected; if sign bit of [mem] is changed during or after shifting, the OF is set to one; mem uses DS as segment register
	SHL mem/reg, 1	SHIFT logical left once byte or word in mem/reg	Immediate	Memory or register	SHL BL, 1	Same as SAL mem/reg, 1
	SHL mem/reg, CL	SHIFT logical left byte or word in mem/reg by the shift count in CL	Register	Memory or register	SHL BYTE PTR [SI], CL	Same as SHL mem/reg, CL

TABLE 3.A-6 (continued)
Logical Instructions

Operation	Instructions	Interpretation	Source	Destination	Example	Illustration	Comments
			Addressing mode				
SHIFTS and ROTATES (continued)	SAR mem/reg, 1	SHIFT arithmetic right once byte or word in mem/reg	Immediate	Memory or register	SAR AX, 1	FOR BYTE / FOR WORD	
	SAR mem/reg, CL	SHIFT arithmetic right byte or word in mem/reg by [CL]	Register	Memory or register	SAR DX, CL		Operation same as SAR mem/reg, 1; however, shift count is specified in CL for shifts up to 255_{10}; zero and negative shifts are illegal
	SHR mem/reg, 1	SHIFT right logical once byte or word in mem/reg	Immediate	Memory or register	SHR BX, 1	FOR BYTE / FOR WORD	
	SHR mem/reg, CL	SHIFT right logical byte or word in mem/reg by [CL]	Register	Memory or register	SHR BX, CL		Operation same as SHR mem/reg, 1; however, shift count is specified in CL for shifts up to 255_{10}; zero and negative shifts are illegal

TABLE 3.A-6 (continued)
Logical Instructions

| Operation | Instructions | Interpretation | Addressing mode | | Example | Illustration |
			Source	Destination		
SHIFTS and ROTATES (continued)	ROL mem/reg, 1	ROTATE left once byte or word in mem/reg	Immediate	Memory or register	ROL BX, 1	FOR BYTE FOR WORD
	ROL mem/reg, CL	ROTATE left byte or word by the content of CL	Register	Memory or register	ROL DX, CL	[CL] contains rotate count up to 255$_{10}$; zero and negative shifts are illegal; CL is used as rotate count when the rotate is greater than once; mem uses DS as the segment register
	ROR mem/reg, 1	ROTATE right once byte or word in mem/reg	Immediate	Memory or register	ROR AX, 1	FOR BYTE FOR WORD

TABLE 3.A-6 (continued)
Logical Instructions

Operation	Instructions	Interpretation	Addressing mode		Example	Illustration	Comments
			Source	Destination			
SHIFTS and ROTATES (continued)	ROR mem/reg, CL	ROTATE right byte or word in mem/reg by [CL]	Register	Memory or register	ROR AX, CL		Operation same as ROR mem/reg, 1; [CL] specifies the number of rotates for up to 255_{10}; zero and negative rotates are illegal; mem uses DS as the segment register
	RCL mem/reg, 1	ROTATE through carry left once byte or word in mem/reg	Immediate	Register	RCL BX, 1	FOR BYTE FOR WORD	
	RCL mem/reg, CL	ROTATE through carry left byte or word in mem/reg by [CL]	Register	Memory or register	RCL DX, CL		Operation same as RCL mem/reg, 1 except the number of rotates is specified in CL for rotates up to 255_{10}; zero or negative rotates are illegal
	RCR mem/reg, 1	ROTATE through carry right once	Immediate	Memory or register	RCR AX, 1	FOR BYTE	

TABLE 3.A-6 (continued)
Logical Instructions

| Operation | Instructions | Interpretation | Addressing mode | | Example | Illustration |
			Source	Destination		Comments
SHIFTS and ROTATES (continued)						FOR WORD
	RCR mem/reg, CL	ROTATE through carry right byte or word in mem/reg by [CL]	Register	Memory or register	RCR DX, CL	Operation same as RCR mem/reg, 1 except the number of rotates is specified in CL for rotates up to 255_{10}; zero or negative rotates are illegal

TABLE 3.A-7
String Instructions

Operation	Instructions	Interpretation	Addressing Mode — Source	Addressing Mode — Destination	Example	Illustration — Comments
Load string	LODS BYTE or LODSB	For byte [AL] ← [[SI]] [SI] ← [SI] ± 1 For Word [AX] ← [[SI]] [SI] ← [SI] ± 2	Byte or word	—	LODS BYTE or LODSB	Load 8-bit data into AL or 16-bit data into AX from a memory location addressed by SI in segment DS; if DF = 0, then SI is incremented by 1 for byte or incremented by 2 for word after the load; if DF = 1, then SI is decremented by 1 for byte or decremented by 2 for word; LODS affects no flags
					LODS WORD or LODSW	
MOVE string	MOVS BYTE or MOVSB	For byte [[DI]] ← [[SI]] [SI] ← [SI] ± 1 [DI] ← [DI] ± 1 For Word [[DI]] ← [[SI]] [SI] ← [SI] ± 2 [DI] ← [DI] ± 2	Byte or word	—	MOVS BYTE or MOVSB	Move 8-bit or 16-bit data from the memory location addressed by SI in segment DS location addressed by DI in ES; segment DS can be overridden by a prefix but destination segment must be ES and cannot be overridden; if DF = 0, then SI and DI are incremented by 1 for byte or 2 for word; if DF = 1, then SI and DI are decremented by 1 for byte or by 2 for word
	MOVS WORD or MOVSW				MOVS WORD or MOVSW	
STORE string	STOS BYTE or STOSB	For byte [[DI]] ← [AL] [DI] ← [DI] ± 1 For word [[DI]] ← [AX] [DI] ← [DI] ± 2	Byte or word	—	STOS BYTE or STOSB	Store 8-bit data from AL or 16-bit data from AX into a memory location addressed by DI in segment ES; segment register ES cannot be overridden; if DF = 0, then DI is incremented by one for byte or incremented by two for word after the store; if DF = 1, then DI is decremented by 1 for byte or by 2 for word; no flags are affected
	STOS WORD or STOSW				STOS WORD or STOSW	

TABLE 3.A-7 (continued)
String Instructions

Operation	Instructions	Interpretation	Addressing Mode Source	Addressing Mode Destination	Illustration Example	Illustration Comments
Compare string	CMPS BYTE or CMPSB	For Byte [[SI]] – [[DI]] → Flags [SI] ← [SI] ± 1 [DI] ← [DI] ± 1	Byte or word	—	CMPS BYTE or CMPSB	8- or 16-bit data addressed by [DI]; ES is subtracted from 8- or 16-bit data addressed by SI in DS and flags are affected without providing any result; if DF = 0, then SI and DI are incremented by one for byte and two for word after the compare; if DF = 1, then SI and DI and decremented by one for byte and two for word; the segment register ES in destination cannot be overridden
	CMPS WORD or CPMSW	For Word [[SI]] – [[DI]] → flags affected [SI] ← [SI] ± 2 [DI] ← [DI] ± 2			CMPS WORD or CPMSW	
Compare memory with AL or AX	SCAS BYTE or SCASB	For Byte [AL] – [[DI]] ⇒ flags are affected [DI] ← [DI] ± 1	Byte or word	—	SCAS BYTE or SCASB	8- or 16-bit data addresses by [DI] in ES is subtracted from 8- or 16-bit data in AL or AX and flags are affected without affecting [AL] or [AX] or string data; ES cannot be overridden; if DF = 0, then DI is incremented by one for byte and two for word; if DF = 1, then DI is decremented by one for byte or decremented by two for word
	SCAS WORD or SCASW	For Word [AX] – [[DI]] ⇒ flags are affected [DI] ← [DI] ± 2			SCAS WOED or SCASW	

TABLE 3.A-8
Unconditional Transfers

Operation	Instructions	Interpretation	Addressing mode		Example	Illustration
			Source	Destination		Comments
CALL subroutine (intrasegment direct)	CALL PROC (NEAR)	Call a subroutine in the same segment with signed 16-bit displacement (to CALL a subroutine in ±32K)	Relative	—	A subroutine can be declared as NEAR by using an assembler directive; the subroutine can then be called in the same segment by using the CALL instruction	NEAR in the statement BEGIN PROC NEAR indicates that the subroutine "BEGIN" is in the same segment and BEGIN is 16-bit signed; CALL BEGIN instruction decrements SP by 2 and then pushes IP onto the stack and then adds the signed 16-bit value of BEGIN to IP and CS is unchanged; thus, a subroutine is called in the same segment (intrasegment direct)
CALL subroutine (intrasegment indirect)	CALL reg16	CALL a subroutine in the same segment addressed by the contents of a 16-bit general register	Register	—	CALL BX	The 8086 decrements SP by 2 and then pushes IP onto the stack, then specified 16-bit register contents (such as BX, SI, and DI) provide the new value for IP; CS is unchanged (intrasegment indirect)
	CALL mem16	CALL a subroutine addressed by the content of a memory location pointed to by an 8086 16-bit	Memory indirect		CALL [BX]	The 8086 decrements SP by 2 and pushes IP onto the stack; the 8086 then loads the contents of a memory location addressed by the content of a 16-bit register

TABLE 3.A-8 (continued)
Unconditional Transfers

Operation	Instructions	Interpretation	Addressing mode — Source	Addressing mode — Destination	Example	Illustration — Comments
CALL subroutine (intrasegment indirect) (continued)		register such as BX, SI, and DI				such as BX, SI, and DI into IP; [CS] is unchanged (intrasegment indirect)
CALL subroutine (intersegment direct)	CALL PROC (FAR)	CALL a subroutine in another segment	Memory		A subroutine can be declared as FAR by using the statement BEGIN PROC FAR; the subroutine BEGIN can be called from another segment by using CALL BEGIN	FAR in the statement BEGIN PROC FAR indicates that the subroutine "BEGIN" is in another segment and the value of BEGIN is 32 bit wide. The 8086 decrements SP by 2 and pushes CS onto the stack and moves the low 16-bit value of the specified 32-bit number such as "BEGIN" in CALL BEGIN into CS; SP is again decremented by 2; IP is pushed onto the stack; IP is then loaded with high 16-bit value of BEGIN; thus, this instruction CALLS a subroutine in another code segment (intersegment direct)
CALL a subroutine in another segment (intersegment indirect)	CALL DWORD PTR [reg16]	CALL a subroutine in another segment	Memory indirect	—	Call DWORD PTR [BX] loads into IP the contents of memory	This instruction decrements SP by 2, and pushes CS onto the stack; CS is then loaded with the contents of memory locations addressed

TABLE 3.A-8 (continued)
Unconditional Transfers

Operation	Instructions	Interpretation	Addressing mode		Illustration	
			Source	Destination	Example	Comments
CALL a subroutine in another segment (intersegment indirect) (continued)					location addressed by [BX] and [BX + 1] in DS; it then loads into CS the contents of memory location addressed by [BX + 2] and [BX + 3] in DS	by [reg16 + 2] and [reg16 + 3] in DS. The SP is again decremented by 2; IP is pushed onto the stack; IP is then loaded with the contents of memory locations addressed by [reg16] and [reg16 + 1] in DS. Typical 8086 registers used for reg16 are BX, SI, and DI (intrasegment indirect)
Return	RET	• POPS IP for intrasegment CALLS • POPS IP and CS for intersegment CALLS	—	—	RET	The assembler generates an intrasegment return if the programmer has defined the subroutine as NEAR; for intrasegment return, the following operations take place: [SP] ← [SP] + 2; on the other hand, the assembler generates on intersegment return if the subroutine has been defined as FAR; in this case, the following operations take place: [IP] ← [[SP]], [SP] ← [SP] + 2, [CS] ← [[SP]], [SP] ← [SP] + 2; an

TABLE 3.A-8 (continued)
Unconditional Transfers

Operation	Instructions	Interpretation	Addressing mode		Example	Comments
			Source	Destination		
Return (continued)						optional 16-bit displacement 'START' can be specified with the intersegment return such as RET START; in this case, the 16-bit displacement is added to the SP value; this feature may be used to discard parameter pushed onto the stack before the execution of the CALL instruction
Unconditional jump (intrasegment direct)	JMP label	Unconditional jump with a signed 8-bit (short) or signed 16-bit (NEAR) displacement in the same segment	Relative	—	JMP START	The label START can be signed 8-bit (called SHORT jump) or signed 16-bit (called NEAR jump) displacement; the assembler usually determines the displacement value; if the assembler finds the displacement value to be signed 8-bit (−128 to +127, 0 being positive), then the assembler uses two bytes for the instruction; one byte for the OP code followed by a byte for the displacement; the assembler sign extends the 8-bit displace-

TABLE 3.A-8 (continued)
Unconditional Transfers

Operation	Instructions	Interpretation	Addressing mode Source	Addressing mode Destination	Example	Illustration Comments
Unconditional jump (intrasegment direct) (continued)						ment and then adds it to IP; [CS] is unchanged; on the other hand, if the assembler finds the displacement to be signed 16-bit (±32K), then the assembler uses three bytes for the instruction: one byte for the OP code followed by 2 bytes for the displacement; the assembler adds the signed 16-bit displacement to OP; [CS] is unchanged; therefore, this JMP provides a jump in the same segment (intrasegment direct jump)
Unconditional jump (intrasegment indirect)	JMP reg16	[IP] ← [reg 16] [CS] is unchanged	Register indirect		JMP BX	Jump to an address specified by the contents of a 16-bit register such as BX, SI, and DI in the same code segment; in the example JMP BX, [BX] is loaded into IP and [CS] is unchanged (intrasegment register indirect jump)
Unconditional jump (intrasegment	JMP mem16	[IP] ← [mem] [CS] is unchanged	Memory indirect		JMP [BX]	Jump to an address specified by the contents of a 16-bit memory location

TABLE 3.A-8 (continued)
Unconditional Transfers

Operation	Instructions	Interpretation	Addressing mode — Source	Addressing mode — Destination	Example	Illustration — Comments
Memory (indirect jump)						addressed by 16-bit register such as BX, SI, and DI; in the example, JMP [BX] copies the content of a memory location addressed by BX in DS into IP; CS is unchanged (intrasegment memory indirect jump)
Unconditional jump (intrasegment direct)	JMP label (FAR)	Unconditionally jump to another segment	Memory	—	A jump can be declared as FAR by using the statement START PROC FAR; the instruction JMP START can be used after this to jump to the label START in another segment	This is a 5-byte instruction; the first byte is the OP code followed by four bytes of 32-bit immediate data; bytes 2 and 3 are loaded into IP; bytes 4 and 5 are loaded into CS to jump unconditionally to another segment (intersegment direct)
Jump unconditionally to another segment (intersegment indirect)	JMP DWORD PTR [reg16]	Unconditionally jump to another segment	Memory	—	JMP DWORD PTR [BX] loads into IP the contents of memory locations	This instruction loads the contents of memory locations addressed by [reg16] and [reg16 + 1] in DS into IP; it then loads the contents of memory

TABLE 3.A-8 (continued)
Unconditional Transfers

| Operation | Instructions | Interpretation | Addressing mode | | Illustration | |
			Source	Destination	Example	Comments
Jump unconditionally to another segment (intersegment indirect) (continued)					addressed by [BX] and [BX + 1] in DS; it then loads into CS the contents of memory locations addressed by [BX + 2] and [BX + 3] in DS	locations addressed by [reg 16 + 2] and [reg16 +3] in DS into CS; typical 8086 register used for reg16 are BX, SI, and DI (intersegment indirect)

TABLE 3.A-9
Conditional Branch Instructions

Operation	Instructions	Interpretation	Addressing mode — Source	Addressing mode — Destination	Example	Illustration — Comments
Conditional branch instruction	JA/JNBE disp 8	Jump if above/ jump if not below original	Relative	—	JA/JNBE START	Jump if above/jump if not below nor equal with 8-bit signed displacement; that is, the displacement can be from -128_{10} to $+127_{10}$, zero being positive JA and JNBE are the mnemonic which represent the same instruction; jump if both CF and ZF are zero; used for unsigned comparison
	JAE/JNB/JNC disp 8	Jump if above or equal/jump if not below/jump if no carry	Relative	—	JAE/JNB/ JNC START	Same as JA/JNBE except that the 8086 jumps if CF = 0; used for unsigned comparison
	JB/JC/JNAE disp 8	Jump if below/ jump if carry/ jump if not above or equal	Relative	—	JB/JC/JNAE START	Same as JA/JNBE except that the jump is taken if CF = 1; used for unsigned comparison
	JBE/JNA disp 8	Jump if below or equal/jump if not above	Relative		JBE/JNA START	Same as JA/JNBE except that the jump is taken if CF = 1 or Z = 1; used for unsigned comparison
	JE/JZ disp 8	Jump if equal/ jump if zero	Relative		JE/JZ START	Same as JA/JNBE except that the jump is taken if ZF = 1; used for both signed and unsigned comparison
	JG/JNLE disp 8	Jump if greater/ jump if not less or equal	Relative		JG/JNLE START	Same as HA/JNBE except that the jump is taken if ((SF + OF) or ZF) = 0; used for signed comparison
	JGE/JNL disp 8	Jump if greater or equal/jump if not less	Relative		JGE/JNL START	Same as JA/JNBE except that the jump is taken if (SF + OF) = 0; used for signed comparison

TABLE 3.A-9 (continued)
Conditional Branch Instructions

| Operation | Instructions | Interpretation | Addressing mode | | Example | Illustration |
			Source	Destination		Comments
Conditional branch instruction (continued)	JL/JNGE disp 8	Jump if less/ jump if not greater nor equal	Relative		JL/JNGE START	Same as JA/JNBE except that the jump is taken if (SF + OF) = 1; used for signed comparison
	JLE/JNG disp 8	Jump if less or equal/jump if not greater	Relative		JLE/JNG START	Same as JA/JNBE except the jump is taken if ((SF + OF) or ZF) = 1; used for signed comparison

TABLE 3.A-10
Loop Instructions

Operation	Instructions	Interpretation	Addressing Mode		Illustration	
			Source	Destination	Example	Comments
Loop instructions	LOOP disp 8	Loop if CX $\neq$ 0	Relative		LOOP START	Decrement CX by 1, without affecting flags and loop with signed 8-bit displacement (from -128_{10} to $+127_{10}$, zero being positive) if CX $\neq$ 0
	LOOPE/LOOPZ disp 8	Loop while equal/loop while zero	Relative		LOOP E/LOOPZ START	Decrement CX by one without affecting flags and loop with signed 8-bit displacement if CX $\neq$ 0, and ZF = 1 while results from execution of the previous instructions
	LOOPNE/LOOPNZ disp 8	Loop while not equal/loop while not zero	Relative		LOOPNE/LOOPNZ START	Decrement CX by one without affecting flags and loop with signed 8-bit displacement if CX $\neq$ 0 and ZF = 0, which results from execution of the previous instructions
	JCXZ disp 8	Jump if CX = 0	Relative		JCXZ START	Jump if CX $\neq$ 0; this instruction is useful at the beginning of a loop to bypass the loop if CX = 0

TABLE 3.A-11
Interrupt Instructions

Operation	Instructions	Interpretation	Source	Destination	Example	Comments
			Addressing Mode			**Illustration**
Interrupt instructions	INT n (n can be 0 thru 255_{10})	$[SP] \leftarrow [SP] -2$ $[[SP]] \leftarrow$ Flags $IF \leftarrow 0$ $TF \leftarrow 0$ $[SP] \leftarrow [SP] - 2$ $[[SP]] \leftarrow [CS]$ $[CS] \leftarrow 4n + 2$ $[SP] \leftarrow [SP] - 2$ $[[SP]] \leftarrow [IP]$ $[IP] \leftarrow 4n$	Immediate		INT 50	Software interrupts can be used as supervisor calls, that is, request for service from an operating system; a different interrupt type can be used for each type of service that the operating system could supply for an application program; software interrupt instructions can also be used for checking interrupt service routines written for hardware-initiated interrupts
	INTO	Interrupt on overflow			INTO	Generates an internal interrupt if OF = 1; executes INT4; can be used after an arithmetic or logic operation to activate a service routine if OF = 1; when INTO is executed and if OF = 1, operations similar to INTn take place
	IRET	Interrupt return			IRET	POPS IP, CS and Flags from stack; IRET is used as return instruction at the end of a service routine for both hardware and sofware interrupts

TABLE 3.A-12
Processor Control Instructions

| Operation | Instructions | Interpretation | Addressing Mode | | Example | Illustration |
			Source	Destination		Comments
Flag operations, external synchronization, and no operation	STC	CF ← 1	—	—	STC	Set carry to one
	CLC	CF ← 0	—	—	CLC	Clear carry to zero
	CMC	CF ← CF′	—	—	CMC	Ones complement carry
	STD	DF ← 1	—	—	STD	Set direction flag to 1
	CLD	DF ← 0	—	—	CLD	Clear direction flag to zero
	STI	IF ← 1	—	—	STI	Set interrupt enable flag to one to enable maskable interrupts
	CLI	IF ← 0	—	—	CLI	Clear interrupt enable flag to zero to disable maskable interrupts
	NOP	NO operation	—	—	NOP	8086 does nothing
	HLT	HALT	—	—	HLT	Halt
	WAIT	8086 enters wait state	—	—	WAIT	Causes CPU to enter wait state if the 8086 TEST pin is high; while in wait state, the 8086 continues to check TEST pin for low; if TEST pin goes back to zero, the 8086 executes the next instruction; this feature can be used to synchronize the operation of the 8086 to an event in external hardware
	ESC external OP code, source	ESCAPE external processes	Immediate	Register or memory	ESC data, register or memory	This instruction is used to pass instructions to a coprocessor such as the 8087 floating point coprocessor which simultaneously monitors the system bus with the 8086; the coprocessor OP codes are 6 bit wide; the coprocessor treats normal 8086 instructions as NOP's; the 8086 fetches all instructions from memory; when

TABLE 3.A-12 (continued)
Processor Control Instructions

| Operation | | Addressing Mode | | Illustration | |
Instructions	Interpretation	Source	Destination	Example	Comments
					the 8086 encounters an ESC instruction, it usually treats this as a NOP; the coprocessor decodes this instruction and carries out the operation using the 6-bit OP code independent of the 8086; for ESC OP code, memory, the 8086 accesses data in memory for the coprocessor; for ESC data, register the coprocessor operates on 8086 register, the 8086 treats this as a NOP
LOCK	LOCK bus during next instruction	—	—	LOCK	Lock is a one-byte prefix that causes the 8086 (configured in maximum mode) to assert its bus LOCK signal while the following instruction is executed; this signal is used in multiprocessing; the LOCK pin of the 8086 can be used to lock other processors off the system bus during execution of an instruction; in this way, the 8086 can be assured of uninterrupted access to common system resources such as shared RAM

Chapter 4

INTEL 80186/80286/80386

This chapter describes the internal architecture, addressing modes, instruction set, and I/O techniques associated with the 80186, 80286, and 80386 microprocessors. Interfacing capabilities to typical memory and I/O chips are also included. Finally, virtual memory concepts associated with the 80286 and 80386 are covered.

4.1 INTEL 80186 AND 80286

This section will cover the two enhanced versions of the 8086 microprocessor: Intel 80186 and 80286. The state-of-the-art technology has allowed fabrication of thousands of transistors on a single chip. This, in turn, has led to the Intel 80186 and 80286 microprocessors. The Intel 80186 includes the Intel 8086 and six separate functional units in a single chip, while the 80286 has integrated memory protection and management into the basic 8086 architecture.

4.1.1 INTEL 80186

The Intel 80186 family contains two microprocessors: Intel 80186 and 80188. The only difference between them is that the 80186 has a 16-bit data bus, while the 80188 includes an 8-bit data bus. The 80186 is packaged in a 68-pin leadless package. The 80186 can be operated at two different clock speeds: 8 MHz (80186) and 6 MHz (80186-6). It can directly address one megabyte of memory. The 80186 contains the 8086-2 microprocessor and several additional functional units. The major on-chip circuits include a clock generator, two independent DMA channels, a a programmable interrupt controller, three programmable 16-bit timers, and a chip select unit.

The 80186 provides double the performance of the standard 8086. The 80186 includes 10 new instructions beyond the 8086. The 80186 is completely object code compatible with the 8086. It contains all the 8086 registers and generates the 20-bit physical address from a 16-bit segment register and a 16-bit offset in the same way as the 8086. The 80186 does not have the MN/$\overline{\text{MX}}$ pin. The 80186 has enough pins to generate the minimum mode-type pins. S0-S3 status signals can be connected to external bus controller chips such as 8288 for generating the maximum mode type signals.

Figure 4.1 shows the 80186 functional block diagram. The DMA unit provides two DMA channels. Each DMA channel contains 20-bit source and destination pointers used to address the source and destination of the data transferred. Each of these pointers may independently address either memory or I/O. After each DMA cycle, these pointers are incremented,

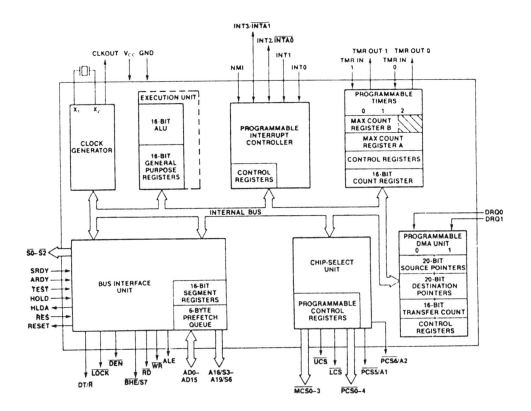

FIGURE 4.1 80186 functional block diagram.

decremented, or kept constant. A 16-bit transfer count register is included in each channel which contains a number of DMA transfers to be performed. Data can be transferred either by the byte or by 16-bit words. Each data transfer takes 2 bus cycles (a minimum of 8 clocks): one cycle to read data and the other to store data. Each channel contains a 16-bit control register. This register specifies information such as: (1) whether 8- or 16-bit data are to be transferred; (2) whether DMA operation will be terminated when count register is zero; (3) whether source and destination pointers will be incremented, decremented, or maintained constant; (4) whether interrupts will be generated after the last transfer; and (5) whether source or destination pointers will address memory or I/O. No separate DMA acknowledge pulse is provided since both source and destination pointers are maintained. A read from a requesting source or a write to a requesting destination should be used as the DMA acknowledge signal. A chip select line can be used as the DMA acknowledge signal, since the chip select lines can be programmed to be active for a given block of memory or I/O space. The DMA channel may be programmed such that one channel has priority over the other. DMA cycles will take place whenever the ST/STOP bit in the control register is set to one.

The 80186 contains three independent 16-bit timers/counters. Two of these timers can be programmed to count external events. The third timer is not connected to any external pins. This timer only counts the 80186 clock cycles and can be used to interrupt the 80186 after a programmed amount of time to provide a count pulse to the DMA unit after a specific amount of time. The mode/control register allows the 80186 to operate in two modes. These are non-iRMX-86 and iRMX-86 modes. The non-iRMX-86 is also called the master mode. In the master mode, the interrupt controller acts as the master interrupt controller for the system, while in iRMX-86 mode, the interrupt controller operates as a slave to an external interrupt controller, such as the 8259, for the system. The 8086 interrupt controller can be placed in the iRMX-86 mode by setting the iRMX mode bit in the peripheral control block relocation register. Some of the interrupt controller registers and interrupt controller pins change definition between these modes, but their functions are basically identical. Upon reset, the 80186 operates in the non-iRMX-86 (master) mode.

The 80186 interrupt controller allows the 80186 to receive interrupts from internal or external sources. Internal interrupt sources (timers and DMA channels) can be disabled by their own control registers or by mask bits within the interrupt controller. The interrupt controller has a special iRMX-86 compatibility that allows the use of the 80186 within the iRMX-86 operating system interrupt structure. The 80186 will accept external interrupts only in the master mode. The 80186 is provided with five dedicated pins for external interrupts. These pins are NMI, INT0, INT1, INT2/$\overline{\text{INTA0}}$, and INT3/$\overline{\text{INTA}}$. NMI is the only nonmaskable interrupt.

In the master mode, the interrupt controller provides three modes of operation. These are fully nested mode, cascade mode, and special fully nested mode. In the fully nested mode, all four maskable interrupt pins are used as direct interrupt requests. The interrupt vectors are obtained by the 80186 internally. In the cascade mode, INT0 is used as the interrupt pin and can be connected to the 8259 INT pin (output) and the INT2/$\overline{\text{INTA0}}$ is used as the interrupt acknowledge pin for the INT0. The INT2/$\overline{\text{INTA0}}$ can be connected to the 8259 $\overline{\text{INTA}}$ input pin. Similarly, the INT3/$\overline{\text{INTA1}}$ can be used as the interrupt acknowledge pin for the INT1 via the 8259. The use of dedicated acknowledge signal eliminates the need for external hardware to generate $\overline{\text{INTA}}$ and device select signals.

When the 8259 receives an interrupt from an external device, it activates the 80186 INT0 or INT1. The interrupt acknowledge pins INT2/$\overline{\text{INTA0}}$ or INT3/$\overline{\text{INTA1}}$ can then be used to enable an octal buffer to place the interrupt-type number on the 80186 low data byte. The 80186 thus determines the address vector. The special fully nested mode is entered by setting the proper bits in INT0 or INT1 control register. It enables complete nestability with external 8259 masters. This allows multiple interrupts via a single pin. Upon acceptance of an interrupt (hardware, INT instructions, or instruction exceptions such as divide by 0), the 80186 pushes CS, IP, and status word onto the slack just like the 8086. Also, similar to the 8086, an interrupt pointer table with 256 entries provides interrupt address vectors (IP and CS) for each interrupt. This vector identifies the appropriate table entry. Nonmaskable interrupts use an internally supplied vector, while the vectors for maskable interrupts are provided by the user via external hardware. The vectors for INT instructions and instruction exceptions are generated internally by the 80186. The 80186 includes an on-chip clock generator/crystal oscillator circuit. Like the 8085, a crystal connected at the 80186 X1 X2 pins is divided by 2 internally. The built-in chip select unit is an address decoder. This unit can be programmed to generate six memory chip selects ($\overline{\text{LCS}}$, $\overline{\text{UCS}}$, and $\overline{\text{MCS0}}$ — 3 pins) and seven I/O or peripheral chip selects ($\overline{\text{PCS0-4}}$, $\overline{\text{PCS5}}$/A1, and $\overline{\text{PCS6}}$/A2 pins). This unit can be programmed to generate an active low chip select when a memory or port address in a particular range is sent out. For example, the 80186 outputs low on the $\overline{\text{LCS}}$ (lower chip select) pin when it accesses an address between 00000H and a higher address (in the range of 1K to 256K) programmable by the user via a control word. On the other hand, the 80186 outputs low on the $\overline{\text{UCS}}$

(upper chip select) pin when it accesses an address between a user programmable lower address (by placing some bits in a control word via an instruction) and upper fixed address FFFFFH. The four middle chip select pins ($\overline{\text{MCS0-3}}$) are activated low by the 80186 when it accesses an address in the mid range. For peripheral chip selects, a base address can be programmed via a control word. The 80186 sends low on the $\overline{\text{PCS0}}$ when it accesses a port address located in a block from this base address to up to 128 bytes. The 80186 sends low on the other chip selects $\overline{\text{PCS1-6}}$ when one of six contiguous 128-byte blocks above the block for $\overline{\text{PCS0}}$. Like the 8086, memory for the 80186 is set up as odd ($\overline{\text{BHE}}$ = 0) and even A0 = 0) memory banks.

The 80186 provides eight addressing modes. These include register, immediate, direct, register indirect (SI, DI, BX, or BP), based (BX or BP), indexed (SI or DI), based indexed, and based indexed with displacement modes.

Typical data types provided by the 80186 include signed integer, ordinal (unsigned binary number), pointer, string, ASCII, BCD, unpacked/ packed BCD, and floating point. The 80186 instruction set is divided into seven types. These are data transfer, arithmetic, shift/rotate, string, control transfer, high level instructions (for example, the BOUND instruction detects values outside prescribed range), and processor control. As mentioned before, the 80186 includes 10 new instructions beyond the 8086. These 10 additional instructions are listed below:

Data Transfer
PUSHA	— Push all registers onto stack
POPA	— Pop all registers from stack
PUSH immediate	— Push immediate numbers onto stack

Arithmetic
IMUL destination register, source, immediate data means immediate
data* source → destination

Logical
SHIFT/ROTATE destination, immediate data shifts/rotates register or
memory contents by the number of times
specified in immediate data

String Instructions
INS	— Input string byte or string word
OUTS	— Output string byte or string word

High Level Instructions

ENTER — Format stack for procedure entry
LEAVE — Restore stack for procedure exit
BOUND — Detect values outside predefined range

Let us explain some of these instructions.

- IMUL destination, source, immediate data. This is a signed multiplication. This instruction multiplies signed 8- or 16-bit immediate data with 8- or 16-bit data in a specified register or memory location and places the result in a general-purpose register. As an example, IMUL DX, CX, 03H multiplies the contents of CX by 3 and places the lower 16-bit result in DX. Note that the immediate 8-bit data of 03H are sign extended to 16-bit prior to multiplication. A 32-bit result is obtained but only the lower 16-bit is saved by this instruction.
- ROL/ROR/SAL/SAR destination, immediate data. Like the 8086, data can be specified in CL up to a maximum of 32_{10}. Unlike the 8086, the immediate data of up to 32_{10} can be specified as immediate data in the 80186 instruction. Note that the 8086 allows an immediate data of one only.
- INS/INSB/INSW inputs a byte of a word from a port addressed by DX to a memory location in ES pointed to by DI. If DF = 0, DI will automatically be incremented (by 1 for byte and 2 for word) after execution of this instruction. On the other hand, if DF = 1, DI is automatically decremented (by 1 for byte and 2 for word) after execution of this instruction. The instructions INSB (or INS BYTE PTR) for byte and INSW (or INS WORD PTR) for word are used.
- OUTS/OUTSB/OUTSW string similarly provides outputting to a port addressed by DX from a source string in DS with offset in SI. A typical example of inputting 50 bytes of I/O data via a port into a memory location is given below (assume ES is already initialized):

```
        STD                 ; Set DF to 1.
        MOV DI, ADDR        ; Initialize DI.
        MOV DX, 0E124H      ; Load port address.
        MOV CX, 50          ; Initialize count.
        REP INSB            ; Input port until CX = 0.
STOP    JMP STOP            ; Halt.
```

The instructions OUTSB (or OUTS BYTE PTR) for byte and OUTSW (or OUTS WORD PTR) for word are used.

- The ENTER instruction is used at the beginning of an assembly language subroutine which is to be called by a high level language program such as Pascal. The main purpose of ENTER is to reserve space on the stack for variables used in the subroutine.

The ENTER instruction has two immediate operands:

$$\text{ENTER imm16, imm8}$$

The first operand imm16 specifies the total memory area allocated to the local variables, which is 16 bits wide (0 to 64K bytes). The second operand imm8, on the other hand, is 8 bits wide and specifies the number of nested subroutines.

For the main subroutine, imm8 = 0. Note that nested subroutines mean a subroutine calling another subroutine. For example, if there are three subroutines SUB1, SUB2, and SUB3 such that the main program M calls SUB1, SUB1 calls SUB2 and SUB2 calls SUB3, then imm8 = 2. ENTER can be used to allocate temporary stack space for local variables for the subroutines.

In the second operand, imm8 = 0, the ENTER instruction pushes the frame printer BP onto the stack. ENTER then subtracts the first operand imm16 from the stack pointer and sets the frame pointer, BP, to the current stack pointer value.

The LEAVE instruction is used at the end of an assembly language subroutine (usually before the RET instruction) which is to be called by a high level language program. The LEAVE does not have any operand. The LEAVE instruction should be used with the ENTER instruction. The ENTER allocates space in stack for variables used in the subroutine, while the LEAVE instruction deallocates this space and ensures that SP and BP have the original values that they had prior to execution of the ENTER. The RET instruction then returns to the appropriate address in the main program.

As an example of application of ENTER and LEAVE instructions, suppose that a subroutine requires 16 bytes of stack for local variables. The instructions ENTER 16, 0 at the subroutine's entry point and a LEAVE before the RET instruction will accomplish this. The 16 local bytes may be accessed. When the 80186 accesses an array, the BOUND instruction can be used to ensure that data outside the array are not accessed. When the BOUND is executed, the 80186 compares the content of a general-purpose register (initialized by the user with the offset of the array element currently being accessed) with the lower and upper bounds of the array (loaded by the user prior to BOUND). The format for BOUND is BOUND reg16, memory32. The first operand is the register containing the array index and the second operand is a memory location containing the array bounds. If the index value violates the array bounds, an exception (maskable interrupt 5) takes place. A service routine can be executed by the user to indicate that the array element being accessed is out of bounds. As an example, consider BOUND SI, ADDR. The lower bound of the array is contained in address ADDR and the upper bound is in address ADDR + 2. Both bounds are 16 bits wide. For a valid access [SI] must be greater than or equal to [ADDR] and less than or equal to [ADDR + 2]; otherwise interrupt 5 occurs. The BOUND instruction is normally placed just before the array itself, making the array addressable via a constant from the start of the array.

4.1.2 INTEL 80286

The Intel 80286 is a high-performance 16-bit microprocessor with on-chip memory protection capabilities primarily designed for multiuser/multitasking systems. The IBM PC/AT and its clones capable of multi-tasking operations use the 80286 as their CPU. The 80286 can address 16 megabytes (2^{24}) of physical memory and 1 gigabyte (2^{30}) of virtual memory per task. The 80286 can be operated at three different clock speeds. These are 4 MHz (80286-4), 6 MHz (80286-6), and 8 MHz (80286).

The 80286 has two modes of operations. These are real address mode and protected virtual address mode (PVAM). In the real address mode, the 80286 is object code compatible with the Intel iAPX 86/88 family. In protected virtual address mode, the 80286 is source code compatible with the iAPX 86/88 family and may require some software modification to use virtual address features of the 80286.

The 80286 includes special instructions to support operating systems. For example, one instruction can end a current task execution, save its state, switch to a new task, load its state, and begin executing the new task.

The 80286's performance is up to six times faster than the standard 5-MHz 8086. The 80286 is housed in a 68-pin leadless flat package. Figure 4.2 shows a functional diagram of the 80286. It contains four separate processing units. These are the Bus Unit (BU), the Instruction Unit (IU), the Address Unit (AU), and the Execution Unit (EU). The BU provides all memory and I/O read and write operations. The BU also performs data transfer between the 80286 and coprocessors such as the 80286. The prefetcher in the BU prefetches instructions of up to 6 bytes and places them in a queue.

The Instruction Unit (IU) translates or decodes up to 3 prefetched instructions and places them in a queue for execution by the execution unit.

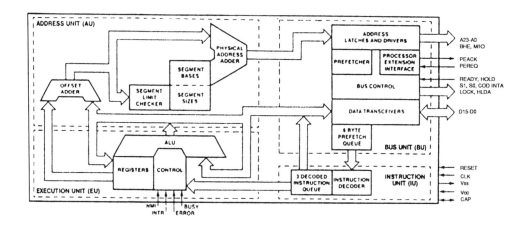

FIGURE 4.2 80286 internal block diagram.

The Execution Unit (EU) executes instructions from the IU sequentially. The EU contains an 8086 flag register, general-purpose registers, pointer registers, index registers, and one 16-bit additional register called the machine status word (MSW) register. The lower four bits of the MSW are used. One bit places the 80286 into PVAM mode while the other three bits control the processor extension (coprocessor) interface. The LMSW and SMSW can load and store MSW in real address mode.

The Address Unit (AU) calculates a 20-bit physical address based on the 16-bit contents of a segment register and a 16-bit offset just like the 8086. In this mode, the 80286 addresses one megabyte of physical memory. The 80286 has 24 address pins. However, in the real address mode, pins A23-A20 are ignored and A19-A0 pins are used. In the protected virtual address mode (PVAM), the AU operates as a memory management unit (MMU) and utilizes all 24 address lines to provide 16 megabytes of physical memory. The BU outputs memory or I/O addresses to devices connected to the 80286 after receiving them from the AU.

The 80286 does not have on-chip clock generator circuitry. Therefore, an external 82284 chip is required. The 80286 has a single CLK pin for a single-phase clock input. The external clock is divided by 2 internally. The 82284 also provides the 80286 RESET and $\overline{\text{READY}}$ signals.

The 80286 external memory is configured as odd ($\overline{\text{BHE}}$ = 0) and even (A0 = 0) memory banks just like the 8086. The 80286 operates in a mode similar to the 8086 maximum mode. Some of the 80286 pins such as M/$\overline{\text{IO}}$, $\overline{\text{S0}}$, $\overline{\text{S1}}$, HOLD, HLDA, $\overline{\text{READY}}$, and $\overline{\text{LOCK}}$ have identical functions as the 8086. Two external interrupt pins (NMI and INTR) are provided. The nonmaskable interrupt NMI is serviced in the same way as the 8086. The INTR and COD/$\overline{\text{INTA}}$ are used together to provide an interrupt-type code on the data bus via external hardware. Note that the 80186 $\overline{INTA}$ is multiplexed with another function called the COD (code). This pin distinguishes instruction fetch cycles from memory data read cycles. Also, it distinguishes interrupt acknowledge cycles from I/O cycles. $M/\overline{IO}$ = HIGH and COD/INTA = HIGH define instruction fetch cycle. On the other hand, $M/\overline{IO}$ = LOW and COD/$\overline{INTA}$ = LOW specify interrupt acknowledge cycle.

A new pin called the CAP is provided on the chip. The 80286 MOS substrate must be applied with a negative voltage for maximum speed. The negative voltage is obtained from the +5V. An external capacitor can be connected to the CAP pin for filtering this bias voltage.

Four pins are provided to interface the 80286 with a coprocessor. These are PEREQ, $\overline{PEACK}$, $\overline{BUSY}$, and $\overline{ERROR}$. The PEREQ (Processor Extension Request) input pin can be activated by the coprocessor to tell the 80286 to perform data transfer to or from memory for it. When the 80286 is ready, it activates the PEACK (Processor Extension Acknowledge) signal to inform the coprocessor of the start of the transfer. The 80286 $\overline{BUSY}$ signal input, when activated LOW by the coprocessor, stops 80286 program execution on WAIT and some ESC instructions until $\overline{BUSY}$ is HIGH. If a coprocessor finds some error during processing, it will activate the 80286 $\overline{ERROR}$ input pin. This will generate an interrupt. A service routine for this interrupt can be written to provide an indication to inform the user of the error.

Upon hardware reset, the 80286 operates in real (physical) address mode. In this mode, 20-bit physical addresses are generated by adding a 16-bit offset to the shifted (4 times to the left) segment register just like the 8086.

The 80286 on-chip MMU is disabled in the real address mode. In this mode, the 80286 acts functionally as a high-performance 8086. This mode averages $2 \frac{1}{2}$ times the performance of an 8086 running at the same clock frequency. All instructions of the 8086, 80186, plus a few more such as LMSW (Load Machine Status Word) and SMSW (Store Machine Status Word) are available with the 80286 in the real address mode. In this mode, the 80286 supports only the 8086 data types. When interfaced with an 80287 floating point coprocessor, the 80286 supports 8087 floating point data types also. Upon hardware reset, the 80286 operates in real address mode unless the user sets a bit in the MSW by using the LMSW instruction to change the 80286 mode to Protected Virtual Address Mode (PVAM). The 80286, in real address mode, can run 8086 or 8088 software. Now, to change the 80286 mode from real address to PVAM, the user should read the contents of MSW, set just the Protection Enable (PE) bit to 1 without changing the other bits, and then load the new data into the MSW.

The following instruction sequence will accomplish this:

```
SMSW CX  ; Store MSW into a general register such as CX
OR CX, 1 ; Set only the PE bit (bit 0 in MSW)
LMSW CX  ; Load the new value back to MSW.
```

After the above instruction sequence is executed, the 80286 operates in PVAM with memory management capabilities. In the PVAM, the 80286 is compatible with the 8086/8088 at the source code level but not at the machine code level. This means that most 8086/8088 programs must be recompiled or reassembled.

When the 80286 is in the protected mode, the on-chip MMU is enabled which expects several address-mapping tables to exist in memory. The 80286, in this mode, will automatically access these tables for translating the virtual addresses used by the user to physical addresses. The 80286 supports the following data types:

- 8-bit or 16-bit signed binary numbers (integers)
- Unsigned 8- or 16-bit numbers (ordinal)
- A 32-bit pointer comprised of a 16-bit segment selector and 16-bit offset
- A contiguous sequence of bytes or words (strings)
- ASCII
- Packed and unpacked BCD
- Floating point

The 80286 provides 8 addressing modes. These include register, immediate, direct, register indirect, based, indexed, based index, and based indexed with displacement modes. The 80286 includes all 80186 instructions plus more. The new instructions are for supporting the PVAM of the 80286 via an operating system.

These instructions are listed in the following and are used by the operating system:

CTST	Clear task switched flag to zero located in the MSW register
LGDT	Load global descriptor table register from memory
SGDT	Store global descriptor table register into memory
LIDT	Load interrupt descriptor table register from memory
LLDT	Load selector and associated descriptor into LDTR (local descriptor table register)
SLDT	Store selector from LDTR in specified register or memory
LTR	Load task register and descriptor for TSS (task state segment)

STR	Store selector from task register in register or memory
LMSW	Load MSW register from register or memory
SMSW	Store MSW register in register or memory
LAR	Load access rights byte of descriptor into register or memory
LSL	Load segment limit from descriptor into register or memory
ARPL	Adjust register privilege Level of selector
VERR	Determine if segment addressed by a selector is readable
VERW	Determine if segment pointed to the selector is writeable

Next, the 80286 will be considered from an operating systems point of view. In this context, the memory management capabilities protection and task switching features of the 80286 will be covered. Using these features a multitasking operating system can be implemented in the 80286-based microcomputer system.

The 80286 memory management features provide the operating system with the following capabilities:

- An operating system can separate tasks from each other. This avoids an 80286 system failure due to task errors.
- As tasks begin and end, the operating system can optimize memory usage by moving them around, a process referred to as dynamic relocation. This is because a program can be executed in different parts of memory without being reassembled or recompiled.
- Use of virtual memory becomes easy. Note that virtual memory is a method for executing programs larger than the main memory by automatically transferring parts of the programs between main memory and disk.
- Controlled sharing of information between tasks.

The 80286 protection features allow:

- An operating system to protect itself from malicious users in a multi-user environment
- Critical subsystems such as disk I/O from being destroyed by program bugs under development

The 80286 task switching provides:

- Fast task switching due to 80286's hardware implementation for accomplishing this feature. This permits the 80286 to spend more time on task execution than switching. Real-time systems can thus be supported by the 80286 since they may require fast task switching. Note that an exception in a running task or an interrupt from a peripheral device requires task switching.

The above 80286 features are not available in the 8086. Upon reset, the 80286 operates in real mode and provides all features of the 8086. An 80286 initialization program in the real mode can be executed to operate the 80286 in virtual mode in which the functions of memory management, protection, and task switching are available.

4.1.2.a 80286 Memory Management

The 80286 memory management is based on address translation. That is, the 80286 translates logical addresses (addresses used in programs) to physical addresses (addressing required by memory hardware). The 80286 memory pointer includes two 16-bit words: one word for a segment selector and the other as an offset into the selected segment. The real and virtual modes compute physical addresses from these selector and offset values in different ways.

In the real address mode, the 80286 computes the physical address from a 16-bit (selector) content and a 16-bit offset just like the 8086/80186. It shifts the 16-bit selector four times to the left and then adds the 16-bit offset to determine the 20-bit physical address. As mentioned before, even though the 80286 has 24 address pins (A0-A23), in the real address mode pins A0-A19 are used and A20-23 pins are ignored.

In the Protected Virtual Address Mode (PVAM or virtual mode for short), the 32-bit address is called a virtual address. Just like the logical address, the virtual address includes a 16-bit selector and a 16-bit offset. The 80286 determines the 24-bit physical address by first obtaining a 24-bit value from a table in memory using the segment value (selector) as an index (rather than shifting the segment value 4 times to left as in the real mode) and then adding the 16-bit offset. Figure 4.3 shows the 80286 virtual address translation scheme.

The 16-bit selector is divided into a 13-bit index, one-bit Table Indicator (TI), and two-bit Requested Privilege Level (RPL). The 13-bit index is used as a displacement to access the selected table. Each entry in the table is termed a descriptor. An index can start from a value of 0 to a higher value. The index value refers to a descriptor in the table. For example, index value K refers to the descriptor K. Each descriptor is 8 bytes wide and contains the 24-bit base address required for physical address calculation. This address only occupies three bytes of the 8-byte descriptor. The meaning of the other bytes will be explained later. The single-bit TI

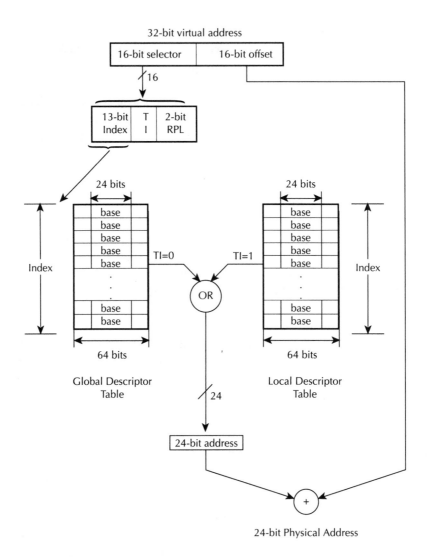

FIGURE 4.3 80286 virtual address translation.

tells the 80286 to select one of two tables: Global Descriptor Table (GDT) and Local Descriptor Table (LDT). All tasks in the 80286 share a common single table called the GDT, while each task has its own LDT. Therefore, the 24-bit base addresses required in physical address calculation for segments to be shared by all tasks are stored in the GDT and the base addresses for segments dedicated to a particular task are stored in its LDT. When TI = 0, the GDT is used as the look-up table, and when TI = 1, the LDT is used as the look-up table. The 2-bit RPL is used by the operating system for implementing the 80286's protection features. RPL is not used in physical address calculation.

The 24-bit physical address is then generated by the 80286 by adding the 24-bit base address of the selected descriptor and the 16-bit offset.

Note that in the above, when TI = 0 (GDT selector) and Index = 0, a null selector is selected. The selector does not correspond to the 0th GDT descriptor. Null selectors can be loaded into a segment register, but use of null selectors in virtual address translation would generate an 80286 exception.

Figure 4.4 shows the 80286 address translation registers. The segment registers CS, DS, SS, and ES have already been discussed before. The GDT and LDT registers are only used in the 80286 virtual mode address translation. The GDT register stores the 24-bit base address and the length of the GDT (in bytes) minus one. During system initialization, the GDT is loaded and is usually kept unchanged after this. The 80286 generates an exception when indexing beyond the GDT limit is attempted.

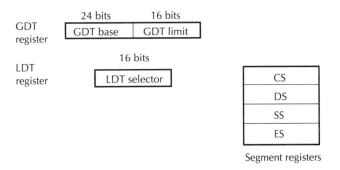

FIGURE 4.4 80286 address translation registers.

The LDT register stores a 16-bit selector for a selector in the present LDT. A GDT descriptor is indexed by this selector. The LDT register makes task switching very fast. For example, the 80286 local address space can be modified during task switching by updating the LDT register.

Figure 4.5 shows a flowchart showing steps for accessing a memory byte. In the flowchart, it can be seen that when accessing memory the 80286 address translation scheme requires two 8-bit descriptors in memory (for LDT) and two 24-bit additions.

The 80286 has improved the speed of these memory accesses via additional hardware. This is accomplished by providing an internal register called the shadow register with the LDT register and four shadow registers with the four segment registers (one for CS, one for DS, one for SS, and

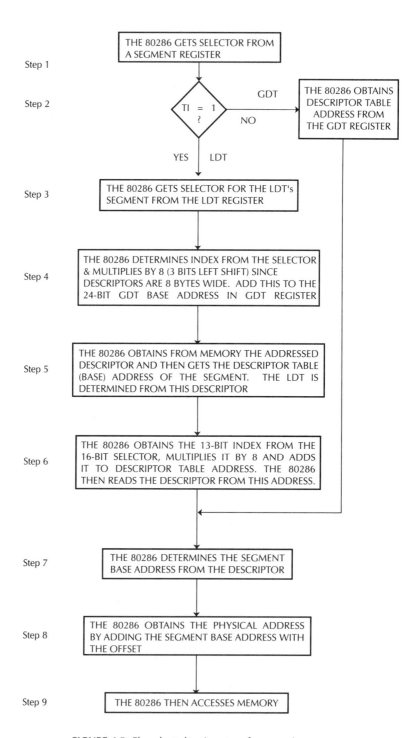

FIGURE 4.5 Flowchart showing steps for accessing memory.

one for ES). The shadow registers are internal to the 80286 and are not accessible via software. They are implemented in the 80286 hardware. The shadow registers store respective descriptors associated with the LDT registers and the segment register. Whenever the LDT register or a segment register is loaded with a selector, the associated descriptor is automatically moved into the corresponding shadow register. The 80286 internally performs steps 1 to 6 of the flowchart via hardware to load a shadow register with the associated descriptor. In order to compute the physical address, the 80286 obtains the segment base address from the descriptor, adds it to the offset, and then accesses memory with this physical address.

In summarizing the topic of shadow registers, these registers are provided to speed up memory references. The shadow registers are internal and cannot be accessed by instructions. Whenever a selector is moved into a segment register, the associated shadow register is updated with its descriptor automatically. Therefore, any memory accessed with respect to the segment register does not require referral to a look-up table, since the descriptor loaded into the shadow register contains the base address of the selected segment.

Note that in the virtual mode, the 80286 descriptor table can store a maximum of 2^{13} (13-bit index) descriptors and each segment can specify a segment of up to 2^{16} bytes. Therefore, a task can have its own address space of up to $2^{13} \times 2^{16} = 2^{29}$ bytes and can share 2^{29} bytes with all other tasks. Therefore, an address space of 1 gigabyte (2^{30} bytes) can be assigned to a task.

The following 80286 memory management instructions include loading and storing the address translation register and checking the contents of descriptors:

LGDT	Load GDT register
SGDT	Store GDT register
LLDT	Load LDT register
SLDT	Store LDT register
LAR	Load Access Rights
LSL	Load Segment Limit

4.1.2.b Protection

In this section, two topics will be covered. These are (1) protecting one 80286 task from another and (2) activating an operating system to protect itself.

The 80286 provides protection mechanism for supporting multitasking and virtual memory features. The 80286 includes certain basic protection features such as segment limit and segment usage checking. These basic protections are useful even though multitasking and virtual memory may not be available in a system. The basic protection mechanism also allows assignment of privilege levels to virtual memory space in a hierarchical manner.

The 80286 privilege level mechanism uses certain rules to define the hierarchical order. This allows protection of the operating system independent of the user. The 80286 includes special descriptor table entries named call gates to permit CALLS to higher privilege code segments at specific valid entry points. In order to protect the operating system, the 80286 does not allow accessing a higher privilege entry point without its accessible gate.

The 80286 provides some instructions controlled by its IOPL (Input/Output Privilege Level) feature to protect shared system resources. The I/O instructions are permitted at the lowest privilege level.

The 80286 on-chip protection features handle basic violations such as trying to access code segment instead of stack segment by trapping into the operating systems's appropriate routine. Thus, the operating system recovers a faulty task by taking whatever actions are necessary. The 80286 protection hardware provides information such as stack status to inform the operating system of the fault type.

The 80286 on-chip protection hardware provides up to four privilege levels in a hierarchical manner which can be used to protect the operating system from unauthorized access. The 80286 can read specific bits in its segment descriptor to obtain privilege levels of each code and data segment. Figure 4.6 shows the format for a segment descriptor for code or data segment.

The descriptors include four words. Bit 3 of the 3-bit-type field of the access rights byte is called the Executable (E) bit. E = 1 identifies a code segment descriptor, while E = 0 identifies the segment as a data segment descriptor. The two-bit DPL (Descriptor Privilege Level) provides the privilege level of the descriptor. The DPL field specifies a hierarchical privilege system of four levels 0 thru 3.

Level 0 is the highest level while level 3 is the lowest. Privilege level provides protection within a task. Operating system routines, interrupt handlers, and other system software can be included and protected within the virtual address space of each task using the four levels of privileges. Each task in the system has a separate stack for each of its privilege levels. Typical examples of privilege levels are summarized as follows:

Code or Data Segment Descriptor

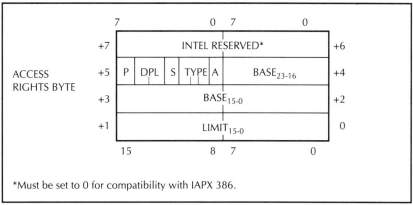

*Must be set to 0 for compatibility with IAPX 386.

Access Rights Byte Definition

Bit Position	Name	Function		
7	Present (P)	P = 1	Segment is mapped into physical Memory.	
		P = 0	No mapping to physical memory eexists, base and limit are not used.	
6-5	Decriptor Privilege Level (DPL)		Segment privilege attribute used in privilege test.	
4	Segment Descriptor (S)	S = 1	Code or data (includes stacks) segment descriptor	
		S = 0	System Segment Descriptor or Gate Descriptor	
3	Executable (E)	E = 0	Data segment descriptor type is:	If Data Segment (S =1, E = 0)
2	Expansion Direction (ED)	ED = 0	Expand up segment, offsets must be ≤ limit.	
		ED = 1	Expand down segment, offsets must be > limit.	
1	Writeable (W)	W = 0	Data segment may not be written into.	
		W = 1	Data segment may be written into.	
3	Executable (E)	E = 1	Code Segment Descriptor type is:	If Code Segment (S =1, E = 0)
2	Conforming (C)	C = 1	Code segment may only be executed when CPL ≥ DPL and CPL remains unchanged.	
1	Readable (R)	R = 0	Code segment may not be read.	
		R = 1	Code segment may be read.	
0	Accessed (A)	A = 0	Segment has not been accessed.	
		A = 1	Segment selector has been loaded into segment register or used by selector test instructions.	

FIGURE 4.6 Code and data segment descriptor formats.

- A single privilege level can be assigned to the codes of a dedicated 80286. In this case, all load/store and I/O instructions are available. The 80286 can be initialized by setting the PE bit in MSW to one and then loading the GDTR with appropriate values to address a valid global descriptor table.

- Privilege levels can be assigned to user and supervisor mode types of applications. In this case, all system software can be defined as level 0 (higher level) and all other programs at some lower privilege level.

- For large applications, the system software can be divided into critical and noncritical. All critical software can be defined as a kernel with the highest privilege level (level 0), the noncritical portion of the system software is defined with levels 1 and 2, while all user application programs are defined with the lowest level (level 3).

Upon enabling the protected mode bit, the 80286 basic protection features are available irrespective of a single 80286-type application or user/supervisor configuration or for a large application. The descriptors limit field (the maximum offset from the base) and the access rights byte provides the 80286's basic protection features.

Segment limit checking ensures that all memory accesses are physically available in the segment. For all read and write operations with memory, the 80286 in the protected mode automatically checks the offset of an effective address with the descriptor limit (predefined). This limit checking feature ensures that a software fault in a segment does not interfere with any other segments in the system.

The descriptor access rights byte complements the limit checking. It differentiates code segments from data segments. The access right byte along with limit checking ensures proper usage of the segments. At least three types of segments can be defined using the access byte. Data segments can be defined as read/write or read-only. Code segments can be designated as execute-only and can be defined as conforming segments. A code segment in a particular privilege level can be accessed by using 80286 CALL or JMP instruction without a privilege level transition. A segment of equal or lower privilege level than another segment (defined as conforming via the access byte) can access that segment.

The operating system can be protected from unauthorized accesses by malicious users by using the 80286's hierarchical privilege levels. The higher privilege level segments can be protected from the lower ones by using the 80286 protection features.

The hierarchical protection levels have four logical rules. These are summarized below:

- The Current Privilege Level (CPL) at any instant of time represents the level of the code segment presently being executed. This is provided by the privilege level in the access rights byte of the descriptor. The 80286 gives the value of CPL in its code register.

- Since every privilege level has its own stack, a stack segment rule is implemented in the 80286 to ensure using the proper stack. According to this rule, the stack segment (stack addressed by the stack segment register) and the current code segment must have the identical privilege level.

- As far as the data segments are concerned, the DPL (Descriptor Privilege Level) of an accessed data segment must be less than or equal to the CPL. This rule allows protection of privileged data segments from unprivileged codes.

- The 80286 is provided with a rule which pertains to accessing data segments. The 80286 can access data segments of equal or less privilege with respect to the CPL. For example, if CPL is 1, the 80286 codes in current code segment can access data segments with privilege levels of 1, 2, or 3, but not 0.

- The 80286 allows CALLing a subroutine in a code segment with higher privilege level using call gates technique and returns to code with lower privilege code segments. This is called the flow control rule and it protects higher privilege code segments. For example, if the CPL is 2, all code segments with level 3 can be accessed by the 80286; code segments of levels 0 or 1 cannot be accessed directly. However, higher privilege level accesses can be done directly. Also, higher privilege level accesses can be controlled by special descriptor table entries known as call gates. A call gate is 8 bytes wide and is stored like a descriptor in a descriptor table.

The main difference between a descriptor and a call gate is that a descriptor's contents refer to a segment in memory. On the other hand, a gate refers to a descriptor.

A descriptor includes a 24-bit physical base address, while a gate contains a 32-bit virtual address. When the effective address of an intersegment CALL references a call gate, the 80286 redirects control to the destination address defined within the gate. The 32-bit virtual address (selector and offset) of the gate can be used by the 80286 to access a higher privilege code segment.

The 80286 controls the use of I/O instructions. The user may choose the level at which these I/O instructions can be used. This level is called the IOPL (Input Output Privilege Level).

IOPL is a two-bit flag whose value varies from 0 to 3. In a user/ supervisor configuration in which all supervisor code is at level 0 (highest) and all user code is at lower levels, the IOPL should be 0. This zero value of IOPL allows the supervisor code to carry out I/O operations but ensures that the user code cannot execute these I/O instructions. Protection of a task from unauthorized access by another is provided by the 80286 both in virtual and physical memory spaces. The 80286 provides a multitasking feature via its virtual memory capabilities. As mentioned before, the virtual memory space consists of two spaces: global and local. The local space is unique to the present task being executed. This uniqueness of the local spaces provides intertask protection in the virtual memory space. The 80286's limit checking feature in the physical memory space avoids illegal accesses of segments beyond the defined segment limits and thus provides protection.

The 80286 is especially designed to execute several different tasks simultaneously (appears to be simultaneous). This is called multitasking. If the present task needs to wait for some external data, the 80286 can be programmed to switch to another task until such data are available. This mechanism of switching from one task to another is called task switching. The 80286 automatically performs all the necessary steps in order to properly switch from one task to another. When a task switching takes place, the 80286 stores the state of the present task (typically most of the 80286 registers), loads the state of the new task, and starts executing the new task. If execution of the outgoing task is desired after completion of the incoming one, the 80286 can automatically go back to the right place where the task switch took place.

Task switching may occur due to hardware or software reasons. For example, task switching may take place due to 80286 external interrupt requests (hardware reason) or due to the operating system's desire to time-share the 80286 among multiple user tasks (software reason). The task to be executed due to interrupts is termed interrupt-scheduled, while the task to be executed due to time-sharing by the operating system is called software-scheduled.

As soon as an interrupt-scheduled or a software-scheduled task is ready to be run by the 80286, it becomes the currently active (incoming) task. All inactive tasks (outgoing) have code and data segments saved in memory or disk by the 80286. Each outgoing task has a Task State Segment (TSS) associated with it. The TSS holds the task register state of an inactive task.

The TSS includes a special access right byte in its descriptor in the GDT in order that the 80286 can identify it as code or data segments. TSSs are referenced by 16-bit selectors (each task has a unique selector) that identify a TSS descriptor in the GDT. The 80286 stores the TSS selector of the presently active task in its Task State Segment register (TR). The first 44 bytes of a TSS store the complete state of a task. Information such as selectors and 80286 registers is saved.

In summary, the 80286 provides the capability of automatically performing all steps required for task switching and task state loading/storing. The 80286 saves the state of a task in a Task State Segment (TSS). Each task has a unique TSS and an associated descriptor. The 80286 maintains a Task Register (TR) to store the TSS selector of the presently active task.

The 80286 switches from one task to another when it executes an intersegment CALL or JMP with the destination operand addressing a TSS or task gate. The 80286 stores registers in the present TSS and then reads in the new TSS selector into the task register. The 80286 also loads register and flags from the new TSS and identifies the new task's TSS descriptor-type code as busy. The processor automatically traps if the segments required in the new task's TSS are not resident in the main memory. A trap service routine can be executed to load these segments by the operating system. The 80286 sets the Nested Task (NT) bit in the flag word of the incoming task to one if the task switching is due to CALL or interrupt. The back link field in the new TSS references the previous TSS. On the other hand, if the task switching occurs due to JMP or IRET, the 80286 identifies the outgoing task's TSS descriptor-type code as not busy, indicating that the outgoing task is not busy anymore. The new task returns to the program at the right place as defined by the CS and IP values in the TSS.

Example 4.1

Discuss the 80286's performance impact on memory management while executing the following program:

```
        MOV DS,  Segment selector   ; Load data selector
        MOV BX,  Displ               ; Load offset
        MOV CX,  Count               ; Load loop count
BEGIN   MOV DX,  data                ; Move 16-bit data to
                                       DX
        CMP DX,  .WORD PTR[BX]       ; Find match
        JZ DONE                      ; If match
        JMP BEGIN                    ; found, stop
                                     ; else compare
DONE    HLT
```

Solution

The 80286 memory management capabilities are only utilized when loading the selector value (first instruction in the above program). By loading the selector value into DS, the 80286 chooses a descriptor from a descriptor table and then automatically determines the physical address of that segment using the descriptor. Thus, by executing the first instruction MOV DS, segment selector, the 80286 automatically determines the segment's physical address (transparent to the user).

After determining the segment's physical address, the 80286 executes all other instructions that follow. The 80286 reads data from the data segment every time it goes through the BEGIN loop. The 80286 does not refer to the descriptor table because of its on-chip cache.

Like any other memory management system, the 80286 will have some overhead for performing the virtual address to the physical address translation. This is transparent to the user's application programs and is automatically carried out by the 80286. The memory management overhead (virtual to physical address translation) is minimized due to on-chip cache. This overhead takes place once only. One of the main characteristics of on-chip MMU is that after the descriptor is read into the on-chip cache memory, no overhead occurs. Therefore, the overhead is kept at a minimum, thus providing good performance.

4.2 INTEL 80386

The 80386 is a 32-bit microprocessor and is a logical extension of the Intel 80286.

The 80386 provides multitasking support, memory management, pipelined architecture, address translation caches, and a high-speed bus interface in a single chip.

The 80386 is software compatible at the object code level with the Intel 8086, 80186, and 80286. The 80386 includes separate 32-bit internal and external data paths along with eight general-purpose 32-bit registers. The processor can handle 8-, 16-, and 32-bit data types. It has separate 32-bit data and address pins and generates a 32-bit physical address. The 80386 can directly address up to four gigabytes of physical memory and 64 tetrabytes (2^{46}) of virtual memory. The 80386 can be operated from a 12.5-, 16-, 20-, 25-, or 33-MHz clock. The chip has 132 pins and is housed in a Pin Grid Array (PGA) package. The 80386 is designed using high-speed CHMOS III technology.

The 80386 is highly pipelined and can perform instruction fetching, decoding, execution, and memory management functions in parallel. The on-chip memory management and protection hardware translates logical addresses to physical addresses and provides the protection rules required in a multitasking environment. The 80386 includes special hardware for task switching. A single instruction or an interrupt is required for the 80386 to perform complete task switching. A 16-MHz 80386 can save the state of one task (all registers), load the state of another task (all registers, segment, and paging registers if needed), and resume execution in less than 16 microseconds.

The 80386 contains a total of 129 instructions. The 80386 protection mechanism, paging, and the instructions to support them are not present in the 8086. Also, the semantics of all instructions that affect segment registers (PUSH, POP, MOV, LES LDS) and those affecting program flow (CALL, INTO, INT, IRET, JMP, RET) are quite different than the 8086 on the 80386 in protected mode.

The main differences between the 80286 and the 80386 are the 32-bit addresses and data types and paging and memory management. To provide these features and other applications, several new instructions are added in the 80386 instruction set beyond those of the 80286.

The internal architecture of the 80386 includes six functional units (Figure 4.7) that operate in parallel. The parallel operation is known as pipelined processing. Fetching, decoding, execution, memory management, and bus access for several instructions are performed simultaneously. The six functional units of the 80386 are

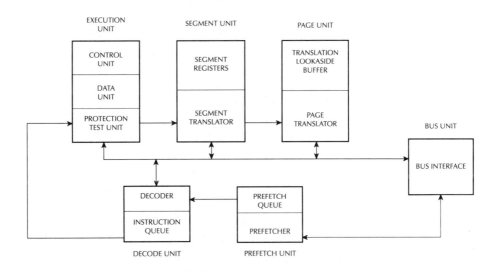

FIGURE 4.7 80386 functional units.

- Bus interface unit
- Code prefetch unit
- Execution unit
- Segmentation unit
- Paging unit
- Decode unit

The bus interface unit interfaces between the 80386 with memory and I/O. Based on internal requests for fetching instructions and transferring data from the code prefetch unit, the 80386 generates the address, data, and control signals for the current bus cycles.

The code prefetch unit prefetches instructions when the bus interface unit is not executing bus cycles. It then stores them in a 16-byte instruction queue for execution by the instruction decode unit.

The instruction decode unit translates instructions from the prefetch queue into microcodes. The decoded instructions are then stored in an instruction queue (FIFO) for processing by the execution unit.

The execution unit processes the instructions from the instruction queue. It contains a control unit, a data unit, and a protection test unit.

The control unit contains microcode and parallel hardware for fast multiply, divide, and effective address calculation.

The data unit includes an ALU, 8 general-purpose registers, and a 64-bit barrel shifter for performing multiple bit shifts in one clock. The data unit carries out data operations requested by the control unit. The protection test unit checks for segmentation violations under the control of the microcode.

The segmentation unit translates logical addresses into linear addresses at the request of the execution unit.

The translated linear address is sent to the paging unit. Upon enabling of the paging mechanism, the 80386 translates these linear addresses into physical addresses. If paging is not enabled, the physical address is identical to the linear addresses and no translation is necessary.

Figure 4.8 shows a typical 80386 system block diagram.

The 80287 or 80387 numeric coprocessor extends the instruction set of the 80386 to include instructions such as floating point operations. These instructions are executed in parallel by the 80287 or 80387 with the 80386 and thus off-load the 80386 of these functions.

The 82384 clock generator provides system clock and reset signals. The 82384 generates both the 80386 clock (CLK2) and a half-frequency clock (CLK) to drive the 80286-compatible devices that may be included in the system. It also generates the 80386 RESET signal.

The 8259A interrupt controller provides interrupt control and man-

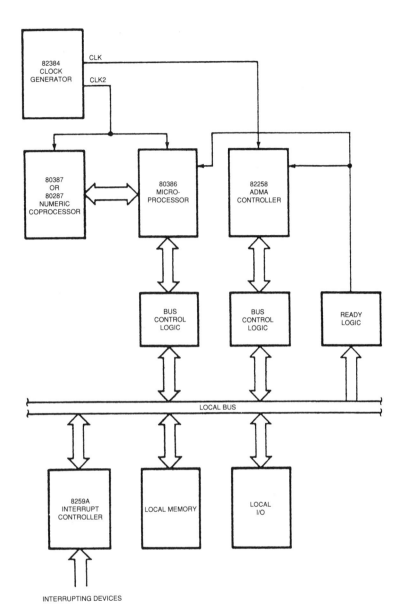

Component	Description
80386 Microprocessor	32-bit high-performance microprocessor with on-chip memory management and protection
80287 or 80387 Numeric Coprocessor	Performs numeric instruction in parallel with 80386; expands instruction set
82384 Clock Generator	Generates system clock and RESET signal
8259A Programmable Interrupt Controller	Provides interrupt control and management
82258 Advanced DMA	Performs direct memory controller access (DMA)

FIGURE 4.8 80386 system block diagram.

agement functions. Interrupts from as many as eight external sources are accepted by one 8259A and up to 64 interrupt requests can be handled by connecting several 8259A chips. The 8259A manages priorities between several interrupts, then interrupts the 80386 and sends a code to the 80386 to identify the source of the interrupt.

The 82258 DMA controller performs DMA transfers between the main memory and the I/O device such as a hard disk or floppy disk. The 82258 Advanced DMA (ADMA) controller provides four channels and all signals necessary to perform DMA transfers.

The 80386 has three processing modes: protected mode, real-address mode, and virtual 8086 mode.

Protected mode is the normal 32-bit application of the 80386. All instructions and features of the 80386 are available in this mode.

Real-address mode (also known as the "real mode") is the mode of operation of the processor upon hardware RESET. This mode appears to programmers as a fast 8086 with a few new instructions. This mode is utilized by most applications for initialization purposes only.

Virtual 8086 mode (also called V86 mode) is a mode in which the 80386 can go back and forth repeatedly between V86 mode and protected mode at a fast speed. The 80386, when entering into the V86 mode, can execute an 8086 program. The processor can then leave V86 mode and enter protected mode to execute an 80386 program.

As mentioned before, the 80386 enters real address upon hardware reset. In this mode, the Protection Enable (PE) bit in a control register called the Control Register 0 (CR0) is cleared to zero. Setting the PE bit in CR0 places the 80386 in protected mode. When in protected mode, setting the VM (Virtual Machine) bit in the flag register (called the EFLAGS register) will place the 80386 in V86 mode. Details of these modes will be discussed later.

4.2.1 BASIC 80386 PROGRAMMING MODEL
The 80386 basic programming model includes the following aspects:

a)   Memory organization and segmentation
b)   Data types
c)   Registers
d)   Instruction format
e)   Addressing modes
f)   Features of interrupts and exceptions of interest to application programmers

I/O is not included as part of the basic programming model. This is because systems designers may select to use I/O instructions for application programs or may select to reserve them for the operating system. Therefore, 80386 I/O capabilities will be covered during the discussion of systems programming.

4.2.1a Memory Organization and Segmentation

The 4-gigabyte physical memory of the 80386 is structured as 8-bit bytes. Each byte can be uniquely accessed by a 32-bit address.

The programmer can write assembly language programs without knowledge of physical address space.

The memory organization model available to applications programmers is determined by the system software designers. The memory organization model available to the programmer for each task can vary between the following possibilities:

- A "flat" address space includes a single array of up to 4 gigabytes. Even though the physical address space can be up to 4 gigabytes, in reality it is much smaller. The 80386 maps the 4-gigabyte flat space into the physical address space automatically by using an address translation scheme transparent to the applications programmers.
- A segmented address space includes up to 16,383 linear address spaces of up to 4 gigabytes each. In a segmented model, the address space is called the logical address space and can be up to 2^{46} bytes (64 tetrabytes). The processor maps this address space onto the physical address space (up to 4 gigabytes by an address translation technique).

To applications programmers, the logical address space appears as up to 16,383 one-dimensional subspaces, each with a specified length. Each of these linear subspaces is called a segment. A segment is a unit of contiguous address space with sizes varying from one byte up to a maximum of 4 gigabytes.

A pointer in the logical address space consists of a 16-bit segment selector identifying a segment and a 32-bit offset addressing a byte within a segment.

4.2.1.b Data Types

Data types can be byte (8-bit), word (16-bit with low byte addressed n and high byte by address n + 1), and double word (32-bit with byte 0 addressed by address n and byte 3 by address n + 3). All three data types can start at any byte address. Therefore, the words are not required to be aligned at even-numbered addresses and double words need not be aligned at addresses evenly divisible by 4. However, for maximum performance, data structures (including stacks) should be designed in such a way that, whenever possible, word operands are aligned at even addresses and double-word operands are aligned at addresses evenly divisible by 4.

Depending on the instruction referring to the operand, the following additional data types are available: integer (signed 8-, 16-, or 32-bit), ordinal (unsigned 8-, 16-, or 32-bit), near pointer (a 32-bit logical address which is an offset within a segment), far pointer (a 48-bit logical address consisting of a 16-bit selector and a 32-bit offset), string (8-, 16, or 32-bit from 0 bytes to 2^{32} −1 bytes), bit field (a contiguous sequence of bits starting at any bit position of any byte and may contain up to 32 bits), bit string (a contiguous sequence of bits starting at any position of any byte and may contain up to 2^{32} − 1 bits), and packed/unpacked BCD. When the 80386 is interfaced to a coprocessor such as the 80287 or 80387, then floating point numbers (signed 32-, 64-, or 80-bit real numbers) are supported.

4.2.1.c 80386 Registers

Figure 4.9 shows 80386 registers. The 80386 has 16 registers classified as general, segment, status, and instruction.

The eight general registers are the 32-bit registers EAX, EBX, ECX, EDX, EBP, ESP, ESI, and EDI. The low-order word of each of these eight registers has the 8086/80186/80286 register names AX (AH or AL), BX (BH or BL), CX (CH or CL), DX (DH or DL), BP, SP, SI, and DI. They are useful for making the 80386 compatible with the 8086, 80186, and 80286 processors.

The six 16-bit segment registers (CS, SS, DS, ES, FS, and GS) allow systems software designers to select either a flat or segmented model of memory organization. The purpose of CS, SS, DS, and ES is obvious. Two additional data segment registers FS and GS are included in the 80386. The four data segment registers (DS, ES, FS, GS) can access four separate data areas and allow programs to access different types of data structures. For example, one data segment register can point to the data structures of the current module, another to the exported data of a higher level module, another to dynamically created data structure, and another to data shared with another task.

The flag register is a 32-bit register named EFLAGS. Figure 4.10 shows the meaning of each bit in this register. The low-order 16 bits of EFLAGS is named FLAGS and can be treated as a unit. This is useful when executing 8086/80186/80286 code, because this part of EFLAGS is the same as the FLAGS register of the 80286/80186/80286. The 80386 flags

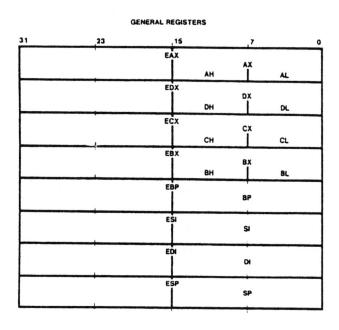

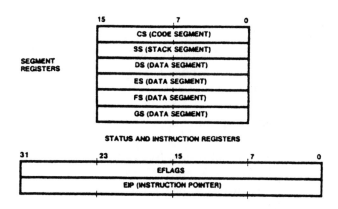

FIGURE 4.9 80386 applications register set.

are grouped into three types: the status flags, the control flags, and the system flags.

The status flags include CF, PF, AF, ZF, SF, and OF like the 8086/80186/80286. The control flag DF is used by strings like the 8086/80186/80286. The system flags control I/O, maskable interrupts, debugging, task switching, and enabling of virtual 8086 execution in a protected,

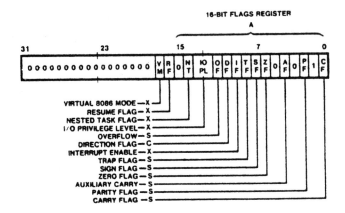

FIGURE 4.10 EFLAGS register.

multitasking environment. The purpose of IF and TF is identical to the 8086/80186/80286. Let us explain the other flags:

- IOPL (I/O Privilege Level) — This is a 2-bit field and supports the 80386 protection feature. The IOPL field defines the privilege level needed to execute I/O instructions. If the present privilege level is less than or equal to IOPL (privilege level is specified by numbers), the 80386 can execute I/O instructions; otherwise it takes a protection exception.

- NT (Nested Task) — The NT bit controls the IRET operation. If NT = 0, a usual return from interrupt is taken by the 80386 by popping EFLAGS, CS, and EIP from the stack. If NT = 1, the 80386 returns from an interrupt via task switching.

- RF (Resume Flag) — If RF = 1, the 80386 ignores debug faults and does not take another exception so that an instruction can be restarted after a normal debug exception. If RF = 0, the 80386 takes another debug exception to service debug faults.

- VM (Virtual 8086 Mode) — When VM bit is set to one, the 80386 executes 8086 programs. When VM bit is zero, the 80386 operates in the protected mode.

The RF, NT, DF, and TF can be set or reset by an 80386 program executing at any privilege level. The VM and IOPL bits can be modified by a program running at only privilege level 0 (the highest privilege level).

An 80386 with I/O privilege level can only modify the IF bit. The IRET instruction or a task switch can set or reset the RF and VM bits. The other control bits can also be modified by the POPF instruction.

The instruction pointer register (EIP) contains the offset address relative to the start of the current code segment of the next sequential instruction to be executed. The EIP is not directly accessible by the programmer; it is controlled implicitly by control-transfer instructions, interrupts, and exceptions. The low-order 16 bits of EIP is called IP and is useful when the 80386 executes 8086/80186/80286 instructions.

4.2.1.d Instruction Format

The 80386 instruction is formatted to include information such as operation to be performed, operand types to be manipulated, and the location of these operands. In general, all 80386 instructions are subsets of a general instruction format which includes one or two primary op code bytes followed by two bytes (an address specified for mod r/m byte and a scaled index byte), a displacement (1, 2, or 4 bytes or none) if required, and an immediate data field (1, 2, or 4 bytes or none) if required.

The op code byte field varies depending on the class of operation. This field defines information such as direction of the operation, displacement sizes, register encoding, or sign extension.

Almost all instructions referring to an operand in memory have an addressing mode byte following the primary op code byte(s). This byte (the mod r/m byte) specifies the addressing mode to be used. Certain encodings of the mod r/m byte indicate a second addressing byte. For example, the scale-index-base byte that follows the mod r/m byte fully specifies the addressing mode. The scale-index-base byte specifies the scale factor for scale index addressing mode with a general register as index register and a general register as base register.

The displacement field can be 8, 16, or 32 bits if the addressing mode includes a displacement. The last field of the instruction is the immediate data which can be 8, 16, or 32 bits if the addressing mode is immediate.

4.2.1.e 80386 Addressing Modes

The 80386 has 11 addressing modes which are classified into register/immediate and memory addressing modes. Register/immediate type includes two addressing modes, while the memory addressing type contains the nine modes.

1. Register/Immediate Modes — Instructions using these register or immediate modes operate on either register or immediate operands.
    i) Register Mode — The operand is contained in one of the 8, 16,

or 32-bit general registers. An example is DEC ECX which decrements the 32-bit register ECX by one.

ii)   Immediate Mode — The operand is included as part of the instruction. An example is MOV EDX, 5167812FH which moves the 32-bit data $5167812F_{16}$ to EDX register. Note that the source operand in this case is in immediate mode.

2.   Memory Addressing Modes — The other 9 addressing modes specify the effective memory address of an operand. These modes are used when accessing memory. An 80386 address consists of two parts: a segment base address and an effective address. The effective address is computed by adding any combination of the following four components:

*   Displacement: 8- or 32-bit immediate data following the instruction; 16-bit displacements can be used by inserting an address prefix before instruction.
*   Base: The contents of any general-purpose register can be used as base. Compilers normally use these base registers to point to the beginning of the local variable area.
*   Index: The contents of any general-purpose register except ESP can be used as an index register. The elements of an array or a string of characters can be accessed via the index register.
*   Scale: The index register's contents can be multiplied (scaled) by a factor of 1, 2, 4, or 8. Scaled index mode is efficient for accessing arrays or structures.

The nine memory addressing modes are a combination of the above four elements. Of these nine modes, eight of them are executed with the same number of clock cycles, since the Effective Address calculation is pipelined with the execution of other instructions; the mode containing base, index, and displacement components requires one additional clock.

As shown in Figure 4.11, the Effective Address (EA) of an operand is computed according to the following formula:

$$EA = \text{Base reg} + (\text{Index Reg} * \text{Scaling}) + \text{Displacement}$$

1.   Direct Mode — The operand's effective address is included as part of the instruction as an 8-, 16-, or 32-bit displacement. An example is DEC WORD PTR [4000H].
2.   Register Indirect Mode — A base or index register contains the operand's effective address. An example is MOV EBX, [ECX].
3.   Based Mode — The contents of a base register are added to a

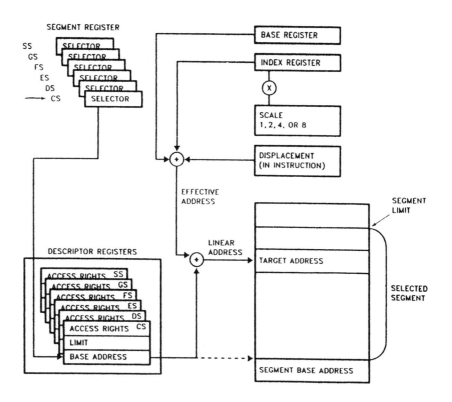

FIGURE 4.11 Addressing mode calculations.

displacement to obtain the operand's effective address. An example is MOV [EDX + 16], EBX.

4. Index Mode — The contents of an index register are added to a displacement to obtain the operand's effective address. An example is ADD START [EDI], EBX.

5. Scaled Index Mode — The contents of an index register are multiplied by a scaling factor (1, 2, 4, or 8) which is added to a displacement to obtain the operand's effective address. An example is MOV START [EBX * 8], ECX.

6. Based Index Mode — The contents of a base register are added to the contents of an index register to obtain the operand's effective address. An example is MOV ECX, [ESI] [EAX].

7. Based Sealed Index Mode — The contents of an index register are multiplied by a scaling factor (1, 2, 4, or 8) and the result is added to the contents of a base register to determine the operand's effective address. An example is MOV [ECX * 4] [EDX], EAX.

8. Based Index Mode with Displacement — The operand's effective

address is obtained by adding the contents of a base register and an index register with a displacement. An example is MOV [EBX] [EBP + 0F24782AH], ECX.

9. Based Scaled Index Mode with Displacement — The contents of an index register are multiplied by a scaling factor, and the result is added to the contents of a base register and a displacement to obtain the operand's effective address. An example is MOV [ESI*8] [EBP + 60H], ECX.

The 80386 can execute 8086/80186/80286 16-bit instructions in real and protected modes. This is provided in order to make the 80386 software compatible with the 80286, 80186, and the 8086. The 80386 uses the D bit in the segment descriptor register (8 bytes wide) to determine whether the instruction size is 16 or 32 bits wide. If D = 0, the 80386 uses all operand lengths and effective addresses as 16 bits long. On the other hand, if D = 1, then the default length for operands and addresses is 32 bits. Note that in the protected mode, the operating system can set or reset the D bit using proper instructions. In real mode, the default size for operands and addresses is 16 bits. Note that real address mode does not use descriptors.

Irrespective of the D-bit definition, the 80386 can execute either 16- or 32-bit instructions via the use of two override prefixes such as operand size prefix and address length prefix. These prefixes override the D bit on an individual instruction basis. These prefixes are automatically included by Intel assemblers. For example, if D = 1 and the 80386 wants to execute INC.WORD PTR [BX] to increment a 16-bit memory location, the assembler automatically adds the operand length prefix to specify only a 16-bit value.

The 80386 uses either 8- or 32-bit displacements and any register as base or index register while executing a 32-bit code. However, the 80386 uses either 8- or 16-bit displacements with the base and index registers conforming to the 80286 while executing 16-bit code. The base and index registers utilized by the 80386 for 16- and 32-bit addresses are given in the following:

	16-bit addressing	**32-bit addressing**
Base Register	BX, BP	Any 32-bit general-purpose register
Index Register	SI, DI	Any 32-bit general-purpose register except ESP
Scale Factor	None	1, 2, 4, 8
Displacement	0, 8, 16 bits	0, 8, 32 bits

4.2.2 80386 INSTRUCTION SET

The 80386 extends the 8086/80186/80286 instruction set in two ways: 32-bit forms of all 16-bit instructions are included to support the 32-bit data types and 32-bit addressing modes are provided for all memory reference instructions. The 32-bit extension of the 8086/80186/80286 instruction set is accomplished by the 80386 via the default bit (D) in the code segment descriptor and by having 2 prefixes to the instruction set.

The 80386 instruction set is divided into nine types:

Data transfer
Arithmetic
Shift/rotate
String manipulation
Bit manipulation
Control transfer
High-level language support
Operating system support
Processor control

These instructions are listed in Table 4.1.

TABLE 4.1
80386 Instructions

Data Transfer

General purpose
MOV	Move operand
PUSH	Push operand onto stack
POP	Pop operand off stack
PUSHA	Push all registers on stack
POPA	Pop all registers off stack
XCHG	Exchange operand, register
XLAT	Translate

Conversion
MOVZX	Move Byte or Word, Dword, with zero extension
MOVSX	Move Byte or Word, Dword, sign extended
CBW	Convert Byte to Word, or Word to Dword
CDW	Convert Word to Dword
CDWE	Convert Word to Dword extended
CDQ	Convert Dword to Qword

TABLE 4.1 (continued)
80386 Instructions

Input/output
    IN   Input operand from I/O space
    OUT   Output operand to I/O space
Address object
    LEA   Load effective address
    LDS   Load pointer into D segment register
    LES   Load pointer into E segment register
    LFS   Load pointer into F segment register
    LGS   Load pointer into G segment register
    LSS   Load pointer into S (stack) segment register
Flag manipulation
    LAHF   Load A register from flags
    SAHF   Store A register in flags
    PUSHF   Push flags onto stack
    POPF   Pop flags off stack
    PUSHFD   Push Eflags onto stack
    POPFD   Pop Eflags off stack
    CLC   Clear carry flag
    CLD   Clear direction flag
    CMC   Complement carry flag
    STC   Set carry flag
    STD   Set direction flag

Arithmetic Instructions

Addition
    ADD   Add operand
    ADC   Add with carry
    INC   Increment operand by 1
    AAA   ASCII adjust for addition
    DAA   Decimal adjust for addition
Subtraction
    SUB   Subtract operand
    SBB   Subtract with borrow
    DEC   Decrement operand by 1
    NEG   Negate operand
    CMP   Compare operands
    AAS   ASCII adjust for subtraction

TABLE 4.1 (continued)
80386 Instructions

Multiplication
   MUL   Multiply double/single precision
   IMUL   Integer multiply
   AAM   ASCII adjust after multiply
Division
   DIV   Divide unsigned
   IDIV   Integer divide
   AAD   ASCII adjust after division

String Instructions

MOVS   Move Byte or Word, Dword string
INS   Input string from I/O space
OUTS   Output string to I/O space
CMPS   Compare Byte or Word, Dword string
SCAS   Scan Byte or Word, Dword string
LODS   Load Byte or Word, Dword string
STOS   Store Byte or Word, Dword string
REP   Repeat
REPE/REPZ   Repeat while equal/zero
RENE/REPNZ   Repeat while not equal/not zero

Logical Instructions

Logicals
   NOT   "NOT" operand
   AND   "AND" operand
   OR   "Inclusive OR" operand
   XOR   "Exclusive OR" operand
   TEST   "Test" operand
Shifts
   SHL/SHR   Shift logical left or right
   SAL/SAR   Shift arithmetic left or right
   SHLD/   Double shift left or right
    SHRD
Rotates
   ROL/ROR   Rotate left/right
   RCL/RCR   Rotate through carry left/right

TABLE 4.1 (continued)
80386 Instructions

Bit Manipulation Instructions

Single bit instructions
BT	Bit test
BTS	Bit test and set
BTR	Bit test and reset
BTC	Bit test and complement
BSF	Bit scan forward
BSR	Bit scan reverse

Bit string instructions
IBTS	Insert bit string
XBTS	Exact bit string

Program Control Instructions

Conditional transfers
SETCC	Set byte equal to condition code
JA/JNBE	Jump if above/not below nor equal
JAE/JNB	Jump if above or equal/not below
JB/JNAE	Jump if below/not above nor equal
JBE/JNA	Jump if below or equal/not above
JC	Jump if carry
JE/JZ	Jump if equal/zero
JG/JNLE	Jump if greater/not less nor equal
JGE/JNL	Jump if greater or equal/not less
JL/JNGE	Jump if less/not greater nor equal
JLE/JNG	Jump if less or equal/not greater
JNC	Jump if not carry
JNE/JNZ	Jump if not equal/not zero
JNO	Jump if not overflow
JNP/JPO	Jump if not parity/parity odd
JNS	Jump if not sign
JO	Jump if overflow
JP/JPE	Jump if parity/parity even
JS	Jump if sign

Unconditional transfers
CALL	Call procedure/task
RET	Return from procedure/task
JMP	Jump

TABLE 4.1 (continued)
80386 Instructions

Iteration controls
    LOOP   Loop
    LOOPE/LOOPZ   Loop if equal/zero
    LOOPNE/   Loop if not equal/not zero
     LLOPNZ
    JCXZ   JUMP if register CX = 0
Interrupts
    INT   Interrupt
    INTO   Interrupt if overflow
    IRET   Return from interrupt
    CLI   Clear interrupt enable
    SLI   Set interrupt enable

High Level Language Instructions

BOUND   Check array bounds
ENTER   Setup parameter block for entering procedure
LEAVE   Leave procedure

Protection Model

SGDT   Store global descriptor table
SIDT   Store interrupt descriptor table
STR   Store task register
SLDT   Store local descriptor table
LGDT   Load global dedcriptor table
LIDT   Load interrupt descriptor table
LTR   Load task register
LLDT   Load local descriptor table
ARPL   Adjust requested privilege level
LAR   Load access rights
LSL   Load segment limit
VERR/VERW   Verify segment for reading or writing
LMSW   Load machine status word (lower 16 bits of CR0)
SMSW   Store machine status word

Processor Control Instructions

HLT   Halt
WAIT   Wait until BUSY # negated
ESC   Escape
LOCK   Lock bus

The 80386 instructions include zero-operand, single-operand, two-operand, and three-operand instructions. Most zero-operand instructions such as STC occupy only one byte. Single operand instructions are usually two bytes wide. The two-operand instructions usually allow the following types of operations:

Register-to-register
Memory-to-register
Immediate-to-register
Memory-to-memory
Register-to-memory
Immediate-to-memory

The operands can be either 8, 16, or 32 bits wide. In general, operands are 8 or 32 bits long when the 80386 executes the 32-bit code. On the other hand, operands are 8 or 16 bits wide when the 80386 executes the existing 80286 or 8086 code (16-bit code). Prefixes can be added to all instructions which override the default length of the operands. That is, 32-bit operands for 16-bit code or 16-bit operands for 32-bit code can be used.

The 80386 various instructions affecting the status flags are summarized in Table 4.2.

TABLE 4.2
Status Flag Summary

Status Flags' Functions

Bit	Name	Function
0	CF	Carry flag — Set on high-order bit carry or borrow; cleared otherwise
2	PF	Parity flag — Set if low-order eight bits of result contain an even number of 1 bits; cleared otherwise
4	AF	Adjust flag — Set on carry from or borrow to the low-order four bits of AL; cleared otherwise; used for decimal arithmetic
6	ZF	Zero flag — Set if result is zero; cleared otherwise
7	SF	Sign flag — Set equal to high-order bit of result (0 is positive, 1 if negative)
11	OF	Overflow flag — Set if result is too large a positive number or too small a negative number (excluding sign-bit) to fit in destination operand; cleared otherwise

TABLE 4.2 (continued)
Key to Codes

T	Instruction tests flag
M	Instruction modifies flag (either sets or resets depending on operands)
0	Instruction resets flag
—	Instruction's effect on flag is undefined
Blank	Instruction does not affect flag

Instruction	OF	SF	ZF	AF	PF	CF
AAA	—	—	—	TM	—	M
AAS	—	—	—	TM	—	M
AAD	—	M	M	—	M	—
AAM	—	M	M	—	M	—
DAA	—	M	M	TM	M	TM
DAS	—	M	M	TM	M	TM
ADC	M	M	M	M	M	TM
ADD	M	M	M	M	M	M
SBB	M	M	M	M	M	TM
SUB	M	M	M	M	M	M
CMP	M	M	M	M	M	M
CMPS	M	M	M	M	M	M
SCAS	M	M	M	M	M	M
NEG	M	M	M	M	M	M
DEC	M	M	M	M	M	
INC	M	M	M	M	M	
IMUL	M	—	—	—	—	M
MUL	M	—	—	—	—	M
RCL/RCR 1	M					TM
RCL/RCR count	—					TM
ROL/ROR 1	M					M
ROL/ROR count	—					M
SAL/SAR/SHL/SHR 1	M	M	M	—	M	M
SAL/SAR/SHL/SHR count	—	M	M	—	M	M
SHLD/SHRD	—	M	M	—	M	M
BSF/BSR	—	—	M	—	—	—
BT/BTS/BTR/BTC	—	—	—	—	—	M
AND	0	M	M	—	M	0
OR	0	M	M	—	M	0
TEST	0	M	M	—	M	0
XOR	0	M	M	—	M	0

Table 4.3 lists the various conditions referring to the relation between two numbers (signed and unsigned) for Jcond and SETcond instructions.

TABLE 4.3
Condition Codes
(For Conditional Instructions Jcond, and SETcond)

Mnemonic	Meaning	Instruction subcode	Condition tested
O	Overflow	0000	OF = 1
NO	No overflow	0001	OF = 0
B	Below		
NAE	Neither above nor equal	0010	CF = 1
NB	Not below	0011	CF = 0
AE	Above or equal		
E	Equal	0100	ZF = 1
Z	Zero		
NE	Not equal	0101	ZF = 0
NZ	Not zero		
BE	Below or equal	0110	(CF or ZF) = 1
NA	Not above		
NBE	Neither below nor equal	0111	(CF or ZF) = 0
A	Above		
S	Sign	1000	SF = 1
NS	No sign	1001	SF = 0
P	Parity	1010	PF = 1
PE	Parity even		
NP	No parity	1011	PF = 0
PO	Parity odd		
L	Less	1100	$(SF \oplus OF) = 1$
NGE	Neither greater nor equal		
NL	Not less	1101	$(SF \oplus OF) = 0$
GE	Greater or equal		
LE	Less or equal	1110	$((SF \oplus OF)$ or ZF$) = 1$
NG	Not greater		

TABLE 4.3 (continued)
Condition Codes
(For Conditional Instructions Jcond, and SETcond)

Mnemonic	Meaning	Instruction subcode	Condition tested
NLE	Neither less nor equal	1111	((SF $\oplus$ OF) or ZF) = 0
G	Greater		

Note: The terms "above" and "below" refer to the relation between two unsigned values (neither SF nor OF is tested). The terms "greater" and "less" refer to the relation between two signed values (SF and OF are tested.

All new 80386 instructions along with those which have minor variations from the 80286 are listed in alphabetical order below in Table 4.4.

TABLE 4.4
80386 Instructions (New Instructions beyond Those of 8086/80186/80286)

Instruction	Comment
ADC EAX, imm32 ADC reg32/mem32, imm32 ADC reg32/mem32, imm8	Add CF with sign-extended immediate byte and 32-bit data in reg32 or mem 32
ADC reg32/mem32, reg32 ADC reg32, reg32/mem32 ADD EAX, imm32	

ADD reg32/mem32, imm32
ADD reg32/mem32, imm8
ADD reg32/mem32, reg32
ADD reg32, reg32/mem32
	Immediate data byte is sign-extended before addition

TABLE 4.4 (continued)
80386 Instructions (New Instructions beyond Those of 8086/80186/
80286)

Instruction	Comment
AND EAX, imm32	
AND reg32/mem32, imm32	
AND reg32/mem32, imm8	
AND reg32/mem32, reg32	
AND reg32, reg32/mem32	
BOUND reg32, mem64	Check if reg32 is within bounds specified in mem64; the first 32 bits of mem64 contain the lower bound and the second 32 bits contain the upper bound
BSF	Bit scan forward
BSR	Bit scan reverse
BT	Bit test
BTC	Bit test and complement
BTR	Bit test and reset
BTS	Bit test and set
CALL label	There are several variations of the label such as disp16, disp32, reg16, reg32, mem16, mem32, ptr16:16, ptr16:32, mem16:16, and mem16:32; NEAR CALLS use reg16/ mem16, reg32/mem32, and disp16/ disp32 and the CALL is the same segment with CS unchanged; CALL disp16 or disp32 adds a signed 16- or 32-bit offset to the address of the next instruction (current EIP) and the result is stored in EIP; when disp16 is used, the upper 16 bits of EIP are cleared to zero; CALL reg16/mem16 or reg32/mem32 specifies a register or memory location from which the offset is obtained; near-return instruction should be used for these

TABLE 4.4 (continued)
80386 Instructions (New Instructions beyond Those of 8086/80186/80286)

Instruction	Comment
	CALL instructions; the far calls CALL ptr16:16 or ptr16:32 uses a four-byte or six-byte operand as a long pointer to the procedure called; the CALL mem16:16 or mem16:32 reads the long pointer from the memory location specified (indirection); in real-address mode or virtual 86 mode, the long pointer provides 16 bits for CS and 16 or 32 bits for EIP depending on operand size; the far-call instruction pushes CS and IP (or EIP) and return addresses; in protected mode, both long pointers have different meaning; consult Intel manuals for details
CDQ	Convert doubleword to quadword EDX:EAX ← sign extend EAX
CMP reg32/mem32, imm32	$\left[\begin{array}{c} \text{reg32} \\ \text{or} \\ \text{mem32} \end{array}\right]$ – imm32 ⇒ affects flags
CMP EAX, imm32	
CMP reg32/mem32, imm8	Compare sign extended 8-bit data with reg32 or mem32
CMP reg32mem32, reg32	
CMP reg32, reg32/mem32	
CMPSD	
CMPS mem32, mem31	
CWDE	EAX ← sign extend AX
DEC reg32/mem32	
DIV EAX, reg32/mem32	Unsigned divide EDX:EAX by reg32 or mem32 (EAX = quotient, EDX = remainder)
ENTER imm16, imm8	Create a stack frame before entering a procedure

TABLE 4.4 (continued)
80386 Instructions (New Instructions beyond Those of 8086/80186/
80286)

Instruction	Comment
IDIV EAX, reg32/mem32	Signed divide; everything else is same as DIV
IMUL reg32/mem32	Signed multiply EDX: EAX ← EAX * reg32 or mem32
IMUL reg32, reg32/mem32	reg32 ← reg32 *reg32 or mem32; upper 32 bits of the product are discarded
IMUL reg16, reg16/mem16	reg16 ← reg16* reg16/mem16; result is low 16 bits of the product
IMUL reg16, reg16/mem16, imm8	reg16 ← reg16/mem16 * (sign extended imm8); result is low 16 bits of the product
IMUL reg32, reg32/mem32, imm8	reg32 ← reg32/mem32* (sign extended imm8); result is low 32 bits of the product
IMUL reg16, imm8	In all IMUL instructions, size of the result is defined by the size of the destination (first) operand; the other bits of the result are discarded if the result size is greater than the size of destination
IMUL reg32, imm8	
IMUL reg16, reg16/mem16, imm16	
IMUL reg32, reg32/mem32, imm32	
IMUL reg16, imm16	
IMUL reg32, imm32	
IN EAX, imm8	Input 32 bits from immediate port into EAX
IN EAX, DX	Input 32 bits from port DX into EAX
INC reg32/mem32	
INS reg32/mem32, DX or INSD	
IRET/IRETD	In real-address mode, IRET pops IP, CS, and FLAGS, and IRETD POPS EIP, CS, and EFLAGS; for protection mode, consult Intel manuals
Jcc label	cc can be any of the 31 conditions, including the flag settings and less, greater, above, equal, etc.; label can

TABLE 4.4 (continued)
80386 Instructions (New Instructions beyond Those of 8086/80186/
80286)

Instruction	Comment
	be disp8 as with the 80286; in 80386, however, one can have disp16 and disp32 as label; all these are signed displacements; the 80386 includes the 80286 JCXZ disp8 instruction; furthermore, the 80386 includes a new instruction called JECXZ disp8; (Jump if ECX = 0)
JMP label	The label can be specified in the same way as the CALL label instruction; see CALL label explanation for near-jump and far-jump explanations
LAR reg32, reg32/mem32	Load access right byte; reg32 ← reg32 or mem32 masked by 00FXFF00H
LEA reg32, m	Calculate the effective address (offset part) m and store it in reg32
LEAVE	LEAVE releases the stack space used by a procedure for its local variables; LEAVE reverses the action of ENTER instruction; LEAVE sets ESP to EBP and then POPS EBP
LGS/LSS/LDS/LES/LFS	Load full pointer; explained later
LODS mem32 or LODSD	To be explained later
LOOP disp8	To be explained later
LOOPcond disp8	To be explained later
MOV reg32/mem32, reg32	
MOV reg32, reg32/mem32	
MOV EAX, mem32	Move 32 bits from mem32 to EAX
MOV MEM32, EAX	
MOV reg32, imm32	
MOV reg32/mem32, imm32	
MOV reg32, CR0/CR2/CR3	CRs are control registers
MOV CR0/CR2/CR3, reg32	

TABLE 4.4 (continued)
80386 Instructions (New Instructions beyond Those of 8086/80186/
80286)

Instruction	Comment
MOV reg32, DR0/DR1/DR2/D3	DRs are debug registers
MOV reg32, DR6/DR7	
MOV DR0/DR1/DR2/DR3, reg32	
MOV DR6/DR7, reg32	
MOV reg32, TR6/TR7	TRs are test registers
MOV TR6/TR7, reg32	
MOVS mem32, mem32 or MOVSD	To be explained later
MOVSX	Move with sign extend; to be discussed later
MOVZX	Move with zero extend; to be discussed later
MUL EAX, reg32/mem32	Unsigned multiply; EDX: EAX ← EAX * (reg32 or mem32)
NEG reg32/mem32	Two's complement negate 32 bits in reg32 or mem32
NOT reg32/mem32	Ones complement
OR d,s	The definitions for d and s are same as AND
OUT imm8, EAX	Output 32-bit EAX to immediate port number
OUT DX, reg32/mem32 or OUTSD	To be explained later
POP reg32	To be explained later
POP mem32	To be explained later
POP FS	To be explained later
POP GS	To be explained later
POPAD	To be explained later
POPFD	To be explained later
PUSH reg32	To be explained later
PUSH mem32	To be explained later
PUSH FS	To be explained later
PUSH GS	To be explained later
PUSHAD	To be explained later
PUSHFD	To be explained later
RCL reg32/mem32, 1	Rotate reg32 or mem32 thru CF once to left

TABLE 4.4 (continued)
**80386 Instructions (New Instructions beyond Those of 8086/80186/
80286)**

Instruction	Comment
RCL reg32/mem32, CL	Rotate reg32 or mem32 thru CF to left CL times
RCL reg32/mem32, imm8	
RCR reg32/mem32, 1	
RCR reg32/mem32, CL	
RCR reg32/mem32, imm8	
ROL reg32/mem32, 1	
ROL reg32/mem32, CL	
ROL reg32/mem32, imm8	
ROR reg32/mem32, 1	
ROR reg32/mem32, CL	
ROR reg32/mem32, imm8	
SAL/SAR/SHL/SHR d, n	d and n have same definitions as RCL/RCR/ROL/ROR
SBB d,s	d and s have same definitions as ADD d,s
SCAS mem32 or SCASD	To be explained later
SET cc	To be explained later
SHLD	To be explained later
SHRD	To be explained later
STOS mem32 or STOSD	To be explained later
SUB d,s	d and s have same definitions as ADD
TEST EAX, imm32	
TEST reg32/mem32, imm32	
TEST reg32/mem32, reg32	
XCHG reg32, EAX	Exchange 32-bit register contents with EAX
XCHG EAX, reg32	
XCHG reg32/mem32, reg32	
XCHG reg32, reg32/mem32	
XLATB	Set AL to memory byte DS: [EBX + unsigned AL]
XOR d,s	d and s have same definitions as AND

A detailed description of most of the new 80386 instructions is given in the following.

4.2.2.a Arithmetic Instructions

There are two new instructions beyond those of 80286. These are CWDE and CDQ. CWDE sign extends the 16-bit contents of AX to a 32-bit doubleword in EAX. CDQ instruction sign extends a doubleword (32 bits) in EAX to a quadword (64 bits) in EDX: EAX.

4.2.2.b Bit Instructions

The following lists the 80386 six-bit instructions:

```
BSF    Bit scan forward
BSR    Bit scan reverse
BT     Bit test
BTC    Bit test and complement
BTR    Bit test and reset
BTS    Bit test and set
```

The above instructions are discussed in the following:

* BSF (Bit Scan Forward)

```
BSF    d , s
       reg16, reg16
       reg16, mem16
       reg32, reg32
       reg32, mem32
```

The 16-bit (word) or 32-bit (doubleword) number defined by s is scanned (checked) from right to left (bit 0 to bit 15 or bit 31). The bit number of the first one found is stored in d. If the whole 16-bit or 32-bit number is zero, the zero flag is set to one; if a one is found, the zero flag is reset to zero. For example, consider BSF EBX, EDX. If $[EDX] = 01241240_{16}$, then $[EBX] = 00000006_{16}$ and ZF = 0. This is because the bit number 6 in EDX (contained in second nibble of EDX) is the first one when EDX is scanned from the right.

- BSR (Bit Scan Reverse)

```
BSR      d , s
         reg16,  reg16
         reg16,  mem16
         reg32,  reg32
         reg32,  mem32
```

BSR scans or checks a 16-bit or 32-bit number specified by s from the most significant bit (bit 15 or bit 31) to the least significant bit (bit 0). The destination operand d is loaded with the bit index (bit number) of the first set bit. If the bits in the number are all zero, the ZF is set to one and operand d is undefined; ZF is reset to zero if a one is found.

- BT (Bit Test)

```
BT       d , s
         reg16,  reg16
         mem16,  reg16
         reg16,  imm8
         mem16,  imm8
         reg32,  reg32
         mem32,  reg32
         reg32,  imm8
         mem32,  imm8
```

BT assigns the bit value of operand d (base) specified by operand s (the bit offset) to the carry flag. Only the CF is affected. If operand s is an immediate data, only eight bits are allowed in the instruction. This operand is taken modulo 32, so the range of immediate bit offset is from 0 to 31. This permits any bit within a register to be selected. If d is a register, the bit value assigned to CF is defined by the value of the bit number defined by s taken modulo the register size (16 or 32). If d is a memory bit string, the desired 16-bit or 32-bit can be determined by adding s (bit index) divided by operand size (16 or 32) to the memory address of d. The bit within this 16- or 32-bit word is defined by d modulo the operand size (16 or 32). If d is a memory operand, the 80386 may access four bytes in memory starting at

Effective address + (4* [bit offset divided by 32]). As an example, consider BT CX, DX. If [CX] = 081F$_{16}$, [DX] = 0021$_{16}$, then since the content of DX is 33$_{10}$, the bit number one (remainder of 33/16 = 1) of CX (value 1) is reflected in the CF and therefore CF = 1.

- BTC (Bit Test and Complement)

BTC d , s

d and s have the same definitions as the BT instruction. The bit of d defined by s is reflected in the CF. After CF is assigned, the same bit of d defined by s is ones complemented. The 80386 determines the bit number from s (whether s is immediate data or register) and d (whether d is register or memory bit string) in the same way as the BT instruction.

- BTR (Bit Test and Reset)

BTR d , s

d and s have the same definitions as for the BT instruction. The bit of d defined by s is reflected in CF. After CF is assigned, the same bit of d defined by s is reset to zero. Everything else that is applicable to the BT instruction also applies to BTR.

- BTS (Bit Test and Set)

BTS d , s

Same as BTR except the specified bit in d is set to one after the bit value of d defined by s is reflected into CF. Everything else applicable to the BT instruction also applies to BTS.

4.2.2.c Byte-Set-On Condition Instructions

These instructions set a byte to one or reset a byte to zero depending on any of the 16 conditions defined by the status flags. The byte may be located in memory or in a one-byte general register. These instructions are very useful in implementing Boolean expressions in high level languages such as Pascal. The general structure of this instruction is SETcc (set byte on condition cc) which sets a byte to one if condition cc is true; or else, reset the byte to zero. The following is a list of these instructions:

Instruction	Condition codes	Description
SETA/SETNBE reg18/mem8	CF = 0 and ZF = 0	Set byte if above or not below/equal
SETAE/SETNB/SETNC reg8/mem8	CF = 0	Set if above/equal, set if not below, or set if not carry
SETB/SETNAE/SETC reg8/mem8	CF = 1	Set if below, set if not above/equal, or set if carry
SETBE/SETNA reg8/mem8	CF = 1 or ZF = 1	Set if below/equal or set if not above
SETE/SETZ reg8/mem8	ZF = 1	Set if equal or set if zero
SETG/SETNLE reg8/mem8	ZF = 0 or SF = OF	Set if greater or set if not less/equal
SETGE/SETNL reg8/mem8	SF = OF	Set if greater/equal or set if not less
SETL/SETNGE reg8/mem8	SF ≠ OF	Set if less or set if not greater/equal
SETLE/SETNG reg8/mem8	ZF = 1 and SF ≠ OF	Set if less/equal or set if not greater
SETNE/SETNZ reg8/mem8	ZF = 0	Set if not equal or set if not zero
SETNO reg8/mem8	OF = 0	Set if no overflow
SETNP/SETPO reg8/mem8	PF = 0	Set if no parity or set if parity odd
SETNS reg8/mem8	SF = 0	Set if not sign
SETO reg8/mem8	OF = 1	Set if overflow
SETP/SETPE reg8/mem8	PF = 1	Set if parity or set if parity even
SETS reg8/mem8	SF = 1	Set if sign

As an example, consider SETB BL. If $[BL] = 52_{16}$ and CF = 1, then after this instruction is executed $[BL] = 01_{16}$ and CF remains at 1; all other flags (OF, SF, ZF, AF, PF) are undefined. On the other hand, if CF = 0, then after execution of SETB BL, BL contains 00_{16}, CF = 0 and ZF = 1; all other flags are undefined. Similarly, the other SETcc instructions can be explained.

4.2.2.d Conditional Jumps and Loops

JECXZ disp18 jumps if ECX is zero. disp8 means a relative address range from 128 bytes before the end of the instruction. JECXZ tests the contents of ECX register for zero and not the flags. If [ECX] = 0, then after execution of JECXZ instruction, the program branches with signed 8-bit relative offset ($+127_{10}$ to -128_{10} with 0 being positive) defined by disp8.

JECXZ instruction is useful at the beginning of a conditional loop that terminates with a conditional loop instruction such as LOOPNE label. The JECXZ prevents entering the loop with ECX = 0, which would cause the loop to execute up to 2^{32} times instead of zero times.

LOOP Instructions

Instruction	Description
LOOP disp8	Decrement CX/ECX by one and jump if CX/ECX ≠ 0
LOOPE/LOOPZ disp8	Decrement CX/ECX by one and jump if CX/ECX ≠ 0 and ZF = 1
LOOPNE/LOOPNZ disp8	Decrement CX/ECX by one and jump if CX/ECX ≠ 0 and ZF = 0

The 80386 LOOP instructions are similar to those of 8086/80186/80286, except that if the counter is more than 16 bits, ECX register is used as the counter.

4.2.2.e Data Transfer

- Move instructions description

```
MOVSX  d,s     Move and sign extend
MOVZX  d,s     Move and zero extend
```

The d and s operands are defined as follows:

```
MOVSX    d,s
or
MOVZX    reg16,  reg8
         reg16,  mem8
         reg32,  reg8
         reg32,  mem8
         reg32,  reg16
         reg32,  mem16
```

MOVSX reads the contents of the effective address or register as a byte or a word from the source and sign-extends the value to the operand size of the destination (16 or 32 bits) and stores the result in the destination. No flags are affected. MOVZX, on the other hand, reads the contents of the effective address or register as a byte or a word and zero-extends the value to the operand size of the destination (16 or 32 bits) and stores the result in the destination. No flags are affected. For example, consider MOVSX BX, CL. If CL = 81_{16} and [BX] = $21AF_{16}$, then after execution of MOVSX BX, CL, register BX will contain $FF81_{16}$ and CL contents do not change. Also, consider MOVZX CX, DH. If CX = $F237_{16}$ and [DH] = 85_{16}, then after execution of this MOVZX, CX register will contain 0085 and DH contents do not change.

- PUSHAD and POPAD Instructions — There are two new PUSH and POP instructions in the 80386 beyond those of 80286. These are PUSHAD and POPAD. PUSHAD saves all 32-bit general registers (the order is EAX, ECX, EDX, EBX, original ESP, EBP, ESI, and EDI) onto the 80386 stack. PUSHAD decrements the stack pointer (ESP) by 32_{10} to hold the eight 16-bit values. No flags are affected. POPAD reverses a previous PUSHAD. It pops the eight 32-bit registers (the order is EDI, ESI, EBP, ESP, [BX,EDX], ECS, and EAX). The ESP value is discarded instead of loading onto ESP. No flags are affected. Note that ESP is actually popped but thrown away, so that [ESP], after popping all the registers, will be incremented by 32_{10}.

- Load Pointer Instruction — There are five instructions in this category. These are LDS, LES, LFS, LGS, and LSS. The first two instructions LDS and LES are available in the 80286. However, the 80286 loads 32 bits from a specified location (16-bit offset and DS) into a specified 16-bit register such as BX and the other into DS for LDS or ES for LES. The 80386, on the other hand, can have four versions of these instructions as follows:

```
LDS     reg16,  mem16:  mem16
LDS     reg32,  mem16:  mem32
LES     reg16,  mem16:  mem16
LES     reg32,  mem16:  mem32
```

Note that mem16: mem16 or mem16: mem32 defines a memory operand containing four pointers composed of two numbers. The number to the left of the colon corresponds to the pointer's segment selector. The number to the right corresponds to the offset. These instructions read a full pointer from memory and store it in the selected segment register: specified register. The instruction loads 16 bits into DS (for LDS) or into ES (for LES). The other register loaded is 32 bits for 32-bit operand size and 16 bits for 16-bit operand size. The 16- and 32-bit registers to be loaded are determined by reg16 or reg32 register specified.

The three new instructions LFS, LGS, and LSS associated with segment registers FS, GS, and SS can similarly be explained.

4.2.2.f Flag Control

There are two new 80386 instructions beyond those of the 80286. These are PUSHFD and POPFD. PUSHFD decrements the stack pointer by 4 and saves the 80386 EFLAGS register to the new top of the stack. No flags are affected. POPFD, on the other hand, pops the 32-bit (double-word) from the stack-top and stores the value in EFLAGS. All flags except VM and RF are affected.

4.2.2.g Logical

There are two new 80386 logical instructions beyond those of 80286. These are SHLD and SHRD.

Instruction	Description
SHLD d,s, count	Shift left double
SHRD d,s, count	Shift right double

The operands are defined as follows:

d	s	count
reg16	reg16	imm8
mem16	reg16	imm8
reg16	reg16	CL
mem16	reg16	CL
reg32	reg32	CL
mem32	reg32	imm8
reg32	reg32	CL
mem32	reg32	CL

For both SHLD and SHRD, the shift count is defined by the low five bits and, therefore, shifts up to 0 to 31 can be obtained.

SHLD shifts by the specified shift count the contents of d:s with the result stored back into d; d is shifted to the left by the shift count with the low-order bits of d being filled from the high-order bits of s. The bits in s are not altered after shifting. The carry flag becomes the value of the bit shifted out of the most significant bit of d.

If the shift count is zero, the instruction works as a NOP. For a specified shift count, the SF, ZF, and PF flags are set according to the result in d. CF is set to the value of the last bit shifted out. OF and AF are undefined.

SHRD, on the other hand, shifts the contents of d:s by the specified shift count to the right with the result being stored back into d. The bits in d are shifted right by the shift count with the high-order bits being filled from the low-order bits of s. The bits in s are not altered after shifting.

If the shift count is zero, this instruction operates as a NOP. For the specified shift count, the SF, ZF, and PF flags are set according to the value of the result. CF is set to the value of the past bit shifted out. OF and AF are undefined.

As an example, consider SHLD BX, DX, 2. If $[BX] = 183F_{16}$, $[DX] = 01F1_{16}$, then after this SHLD, $[BX] = 60FC_{16}$, $[DX] = 01F1_{16}$, CF = 0, SF = 0, ZF = 0, and PF = 1.

Similarly, the SHRD instruction can be illustrated.

4.2.2.h String

*   **Compare String** — There is a new instruction CMPS mem32, mem32 (or CMPSD) beyond the compare string instruction available with the 80286. This instruction compares 32-bit words ES:EDI (second operand) with DS:ESI and affects the flags. The direction of subtraction of CMPS is [[ESI]] – [[EDI]]. The left operand ESI is the source and the right operand EDI is the destination. This is a reverse of the normal Intel convention in which the left operand is the destination and the right operand is the source. This is true for byte (CMPSB) or word (CMPSW) compare instructions. The result of subtraction is not stored; only the flags are affected. For the first operand (ESI), the DS is used as segment unless a segment override byte is present, while the second operand (EDI) must use ES as the segment register and cannot be overridden. ESI and EDI are incremented by 4 if DF = 0, while they are decremented by 4 if DF = 1. CMPSD can be preceded by the REPE or REPNE prefix for block comparison. All flags are affected.

- **Load and Move Strings** — There are two new 80386 instructions beyond those of 80286. These are LODS mem32 (or LODSD) and MOVS mem32, mem32 (or MOVSD). LODSD loads the doubleword (32-bit) from a memory location specified by DS:ESI into EAX. After the load, ESI is automatically incremented by 4 if DF = 0, while ESI is automatically decremented by 4 if DF = 1. No flags are affected. LODS can be preceded by REP prefix. LODS is typically used within a loop structure because further processing of the data moved into EAX is normally required. MOVSD copies the doubleword (32-bit) at memory location addressed by DS:ESI to the memory location at ES:EDI. DS is used as the segment register for the source and may be overridden. ES must be used as the segment register and cannot be overridden. After the move, ESI and EDI are incremented by four if DF = 0, while they are decremented by 4 if DF = 1. MOVS can be preceded by the REP prefix for block movement of ECX doublewords. No flags are affected.

- **String I/O Instructions** — There are two new 80386 string I/O instructions beyond those of the 80286. These are INS mem32, DX (or INSD) and OUTS DX, mem32 (or OUTSD). INSD inputs 32-bit data from a port addressed by the content of DX into a memory location specified by ES:EDI. ES cannot be overridden. After data transfer, EDI is automatically incremented by 4 if DF = 0, while it is decremented by 4 if DF = 1. INSD can be preceded by the REP prefix for block input of ECX doublewords. No flags are affected. OUTSD instruction outputs 32-bit data from a memory location addressed by DS:ESI to a port addressed by the content of DX. DS can be overridden. After data transfer, ESI is incremented by 4 if DF = 0 and decremented by 4 if DF = 1. OUTSD can be preceded by the REP prefix for block output of ECX doublewords.

- **Store and Scan Strings** — There is a new 80386 STOS mem32 (or STOSD) instruction. STOS stores the contents of the EAX register to a doubleword addressed by ES and EDI. ES cannot be overridden. After storing, EDI is automatically incremented by 4 if DF = 0 and decremented by 4 if DF = 1. No flags are affected. STOS can be preceded by the REP prefix for a block fill of ECX doublewords. There is a new scan instruction called the SCAS mem32 (or SCASD) in the 80386. SCASD performs the 32-bit subtraction [EAX] –

[memory addressed by ES and EDI]. The result of subtraction is not stored, and the flags are affected.

4.2.2.i Table Look-Up Translation Instruction

There is a modified version of the 80286 XLAT instruction available in the 80386.

XLAT mem8 (or XLATB) replaces the AL register from the table index to the table entry. AL should be the unsigned index into a table addressed by DS:BX for 16-bit address (available in 80286 and 80386) and DS:EBX for 32-bit address (available only in 80386). DS can be overridden. No flags are affected. ES cannot be overridden. If DF = 0, EDI is incremented by 4 and if DF = 1, EDI is decremented by 4.

SCASD can be preceded by the REPE or REPNE prefix for block search of ECX doublewords. All flags are affected.

4.2.2.j High-Level Language Instructions

The three instructions ENTER, LEAVE, and BOUND (also available with 80186/80286) in this category have been enhanced in 80386.

The ENTER imm16, imm8 instruction creates a stack frame. The data imm8 defines the nesting depth of the subroutine and can be from 0 to 31. The value 0 specifies the first subroutine only. The data imm8 defines the number of stack frame pointers copied into the new stack frame from the preceding frame.

After the instruction is executed, the 80386 uses EBP as the current frame pointer and ESP as the current stack pointer. The data imm16 specifies the number of bytes of local variables for which the stack space is to be allocated.

If imm8 is zero, ENTER pushes the frame pointer EBP onto the stack; ENTER then subtracts the first operand imm16 from the ESP and sets EBP to the current ESP.

For example, a procedure with 28 bytes of local variables would have an ENTER 28, 0 instruction at its entry point and a LEAVE instruction before every RET. The 28 local bytes would be addressed as offset from EBP. Note that the LEAVE instruction sets ESP to EBP and then pops EBP. For 80186 and 80286, ENTER and LEAVE instructions use BP and SP instead of EBP and ESP. The 80386 uses BP (low 16 bits of EBP) and SP (low 16 bits of ESP) for 16-bit operands, and EBP and ESP for 32-bit operands.

The formal definition of the ENTER instruction is given in the following:

```
LEVEL denotes the value of the second operand,
imm8:
Push EBP
Set a temporary value FRAME-PTR: = ESP
If LEVEL > 0 then
      Repeat (LEVEL-1) times:
             EBP: = EBP-4
             Push the doubleword pointed to by EBP
      End repeat
      Push FRAME-PTR
End if
EBP: = FRAME-PTR
ESP: = ESP - first operand, imm16
```

BOUND ensures that a signed array index is within the limits specified by a block of memory containing an upper and a lower bound. The 80386 provides two forms of the BOUND instruction:

$$\text{BOUND reg16, mem32}$$
$$\text{BOUND reg32, mem64}$$

The first form is for 16-bit operands and is also available with the 80186 and 80286. The second form is for 32-bit operands and is included in the 80386 instruction set. For example, consider BOUND EDI, ADDR. Suppose [ADDR] = 32-bit lower bound, d_L and [ADDR + 4] = 32-bit upper bound du. If, after execution of this instruction, [EDI] $<d_L$ and $>$ du, the 80386 traps to interrupt 5; otherwise the array is accessed.

Example 4.2

Determine the effect of each one of the following 80386 instructions:
  i) **CDQ**
 ii) **BTC CX, BX**
iii) **MOVSX ECX, E7H**

Assume [EAX] = FFFFFFFFH, [ECX] = F1257124H, [EDX] = EEEE EEEEH, [BX] = 0004H, [CX] = 0FA1H, prior to execution of each of the above instructions.

  i) After CDQ,
     [EAX] = FFFF FFFFH
     [EDX] = FFFF FFFFH

ii) After BTC CX, BX, bit 4 of register CX is reflected in the ZF and then ones complemented in CX.
Before

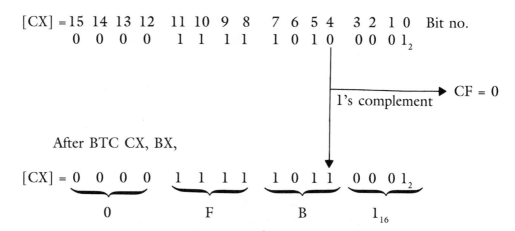

$[CX] = $ 15 14 13 12 11 10 9 8 7 6 5 4 3 2 1 0 Bit no.
        0 0 0 0   1 1 1 1 1 0 1 0 0 0 0 1$_2$

1's complement → CF = 0

After BTC CX, BX,

$[CX] = $ 0 0 0 0 1 1 1 1 1 0 1 1 0 0 0 1$_2$

          0   F   B   1$_{16}$

Hence, $[CX] = 0FB1H$ and $[BX] = 0004H$

ii)   MOVSX ECX, E7H copies the 8-bit data E7H into low byte of ECX and then sign-extends to 32 bits. Therefore, after MOVSX ECX, E7H, $[ECX] = FFFFFFE7H$.

Example 4.3

Write an 80386 assembly language program to multiply a signed 8-bit number by a signed 32-bit number in ECX. Store result in EAX. Assume that the segment registers are already initialized and also that the result fits within 32 bits.

Solution

```
IMUL ECX, data8    ;  Perform signed
                   ;  multiplication
MOV EAX, ECX       ;  Store result
HLT                ;  in EAX and stop
```

Example 4.4

Write an 80386 assembly program to move two columns of 10,000 32-bit numbers from A (i) to B (i). In other words, move A (1) to B (1), A (2) to B (2), and so on.

Solution

```
MOV ECX, 10,000        ; Initialize counter
MOV BX, SOURCE SEG     ; Initialize DS
MOV DS, BX             ; register
MOV BX, DEST SEG       ; Initialize ES
MOV ES, BX             ; register
MOV ESI, SRC INDX      ; Initialize ESI
MOV EDI, DEST INDX     ; Initialize EDI
SED                    ; Set DF to Autoincrement
REP MOVSD              ; MOV A (i) to
                       ; B (i) until ECX = 0
HLT
```

4.2.3 Memory Organization

Memory on the 80386 is structured as 8-bit (byte), 16-bit (word), or 32-bit (doubleword) quantities. Words are stored in two consecutive bytes with low byte at the lower address and high byte at the higher address. The byte address of the low byte addresses the word. Doublewords are stored in four consecutive bytes in memory with byte 0 at the lowest address and byte 3 at the highest address. The byte address of byte 0 addresses the doubleword.

Memory on the 80386 can also be organized as pages or segments. The entire memory can be divided into one or more variable length segments which can be shared between programs or swapped to disks. Memory can also be divided into one or more 4K-byte pages. Segmentation and paging can also be combined in a system. The 80386 includes three types of address spaces. These are logical or virtual, linear, and physical. A logical or virtual address contains a selector (contents of a segment register) and offset (effective address) obtained by adding the base, index, and displacement components discussed earlier. Since each task on the 80386 can have a maximum of 16K selectors and offsets can be 4 gigabytes (2^{32} bits), the programmer views a virtual address space of 2^{46} or 64 tetrabytes of logical address space per task.

The 80386 on-chip segment unit translates the logical address space to 32-bit linear address space. If the paging unit is disabled, then the 32-bit linear address corresponds to the physical address. On the other hand, if the paging unit is enabled, the paging unit translates the linear address space to the physical address space. Note that the physical addresses are generated by the 80386 on its address pins.

The main difference between real and protected modes is how the 80386 segment unit translates logical addresses to linear addresses. In real mode, the segment unit shifts the selector to the left four times and adds the result to the offset to obtain the linear address. In protected mode, every selector has a linear base address. The linear base address is stored in one of two operating system tables (local descriptor table or global descriptor table). The selector's linear base address is summed with the offset to obtain the linear address. Figure 4.12 shows the 80386 address translation mechanism.

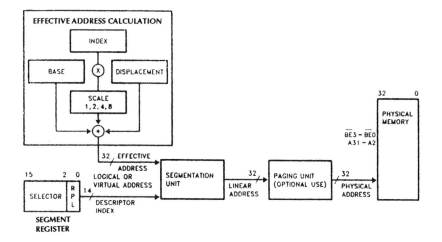

FIGURE 4.12 Address translation mechanism.

There are three main types of 80386 segments. These are code, data, and stack segments. These segments are of variable size and can be from 1 byte to 4 gigabytes (2^{32} bits) in length.

Instructions do not explicitly define the segment type. This is done in order to obtain compact instruction encoding. A default segment register is automatically selected by the 80386 according to Table 4.5.

In general, DS, SS, and CS use the selectors for data, stack, and code. Segment override prefixes can be used to override a given segment register as per Table 4.5.

TABLE 4.5
Segment Register Selection Rules

Type of memory reference	Implied (default) segment use	Segment override prefixes possible
Code Fetch	CS	None
Destination of PUSH, PUSHA instructions	SS	None
Source of POP, POPA instructions	SS	None
Other data references, with effective address using base register of:		
[EAX]	DS	CS,SS,ES,FS,GS
[EBX]	DS	CS,SS,ES,FS,GS
[ECX]	DS	CS,SS,ES,FS,GS
[EDX]	DS	CS,SS,ES,FS,GS
[EBX]	DS	CS,SS,ES,FS,GS
[ESI]	DS	CS,SS,ES,FS,GS
[EDI]	DS	CS,SS,ES,FS,GS
[EBP]	SS	CS,DS,ES,FS,GS
[ESP]	SS	CS,DS,ES,FS,GS

4.2.4 I/O SPACE

The 80386 supports both standard and memory-mapped I/O. The I/O space contains 64K 8-bit ports, 32K 16-bit ports, 16K 32-bit ports, or any combination of ports up to 64K bytes. I/O instructions do not go through the segment or paging units. Therefore, the I/O space refers to physical memory. The M/$\overline{\text{IO}}$ pin distinguishes between the memory and I/O.

The 80386 includes IN and OUT instructions to access I/O ports with port address provided by DL, DX, or EDX registers. All 8- and 16-bit port addresses are zero-extended on the upper address lines. The IN and OUT instructions drive the 80386 M/$\overline{\text{IO}}$ pin to low.

I/O port addresses 00F8H through 00FFH are reserved by Intel. The coprocessors in the I/O space are at locations 800000F8H through 800000FFH.

4.2.5 80386 INTERRUPTS

Earlier, features and exceptions of interrupts and exceptions which are of interest to application programmers were discussed. In this section, details of these interrupts and exceptions are covered. The difference between interrupts and exceptions is that interrupts are used to handle asynchronous external events and exceptions handle instruction faults. The 80386 also treats software interrupts such as INT n as exceptions.

The 80386 interrupts and exceptions are similar to those of the 8086.

There are three types of interrupts/exceptions. These are hardware interrupts, exceptions, and software interrupts.

Hardware interrupts can be of two types. The 80386 provides the NMI pin for the nonmaskable interrupt. When the NMI pin encounters a LOW to HIGH transition by an external device such as an A/D converter, the 80386 services the interrupt via the internally supplied instruction INT2. The INT2 instruction does not need to be provided via external hardware.

The 80386 services a maskable interrupt when its INTR pin is activated HIGH and the IF bit is set to one. An 8-bit vector can be supplied by the user via external hardware which identifies the interrupt source.

The IF bit in the EFLAG registers is reset when an interrupt is being serviced. This, in turn, disables servicing additional interrupts during an interrupt service routine.

When an interrupt occurs, the 80386 completes execution of the current instruction. The 80386 then pushes the EIP, CS and flags onto the stack. Next, the 80386 obtains an 8-bit vector via either external hardware (maskable) or internally (nonmaskable) which identifies the appropriate entry in the interrupt table. The table contains the starting address of the interrupt service routine. At the end of the interrupt service routine, IRET can be placed to resume the program at the appropriate place in the main program.

The software interrupt due to execution of INT n has the same effect as the hardware interrupt. A special case of the software interrupt INT n is the INT3 or breakpoint interrupt. Like the 8086, the single-step interrupt is enabled by setting the TF bit. The TF bit is set by altering the stack image and executing a POPF or IRET instruction. The single step uses INT1. Exceptions are classified as faults, traps, or aborts depending on the way they are reported and whether or not the instruction causing the exception is restarted. Faults are exceptions that are detected and serviced before the execution of the faulting instruction. A fault can occur in a virtual memory system when the 80386 references a page or a segment not present in the main memory. The operating system can execute a service routine at the fault's interrupt address vector to fetch the page or segment from disk. Then the 80386 restarts the instruction traps and immediately reports the cause of the problem via the execution of the instruction.

Typical examples of traps are user-defined interrupts. Aborts are exceptions which do not allow the exact location of the instruction causing the exception to be determined. Aborts are used to report severe errors such as a hardware error or illegal values in system tables.

Therefore, upon completion of the interrupt service routine, the 80386 resumes program execution at the instruction following the interrupted instruction. On the other hand, the return address from an exception fault routine will always point to the instruction causing the exception. Table 4.6 lists the 80386 interrupts along with to where the return address points.

TABLE 4.6
Interrupt Vector Assignments

Function	Interrupt number	Instruction which can cause exception	Return address points to faulting instruction	Type
Divide error	0	DIV, IDIV	Yes	Fault
Debug exception	1	Any instruction	Yes	Trap[a]
NMI interrupt	2	INT 2 or NMI	No	NMI
One-byte interrupt	3	INT	No	Trap
Interrupt on overflow	4	INTO	No	Trap
Array bounds check	5	BOUND	Yes	Fault
Invalid OP-code	6	Any illegal instruction	Yes	Fault
Device not available	7	ESC, WAIT	Yes	Fault
Double fault	8	Any instruction that can generate an exception		Abort
Coprocessor segment	9	Coprocessor tries to access data past the end of a segment	No	Trap[b]
Invalid TSS	10	JMP, CALL, IRET, INT	Yes	Fault
Segment not present	11	Segment register instructions	Yes	Fault
Stack fault	12	Stack references	Yes	Fault
General protection fault	13	Any memory reference	Yes	Fault

TABLE 4.6 (continued)
Interrupt Vector Assignments

Function	Interrupt number	Instruction which can cause exception	Return address points to faulting instruction	Type
Page fault	14	Any memory access or code fetch	Yes	Fault
Coprocessor error	16	ESC, WAIT	Yes	Fault
Intel reserved	17—32			
Two-byte interrupt	0—255	INT n	No	Trap

[a] Some debug exceptions may report both traps on the previous instruction and faults on the next instruction.

[b] Exception 9 no longer occurs on the 80386 due to the improved interface between the 80386 and its coprocessors.

The 80386 can handle up to 256 different interrupts/exceptions. For servicing the interrupts, a table containing up to 256 interrupt vectors must be defined by the user. These interrupt vectors are pointers to the interrupt service routine. In real mode, the vectors contain two 16-bit words: the code segment and a 16-bit offset. In protected mode, the interrupt vectors are 8-byte quantities, which are stored in an interrupt descriptor table. Of the 256 possible interrupts, 32 are reserved by Intel and the remaining 224 are available to be used by the system designer.

If there are several interrupts/exceptions occurring at the same time, the 80386 handles them according to the following priorities:

Priority	Interrupt/exception
1. (Highest)	Exception faults
2.	TRAP instructions
3.	Debug traps for this instruction
4.	Debug faults for next instruction
5.	NMI
6. (Lowest)	INTR

As an example, suppose an instruction causes both a debug exception (interrupt no. 1) and page fault (interrupt vector 14). According to the built-in priority mechanism, the 80386 will first service the page fault by executing the exception 14 handler. The exception 14 handler will be interrupted by the debug exception handler (1). An address in the page fault handler will be pushed onto the stack and the service routine for the debug handler (1) will be completed. After this, the exception 14 handler will be executed. This permits the system designer to debug the exception handler.

4.2.6 80386 RESET AND INITIALIZATION

Upon hardware reset, the 80386 registers contain the values as shown in Table 4.7.

TABLE 4.7
Register Values after Reset

Flag word	UUUU0002H
Machine status word (CR0)	UUUUUUU0H
Instruction pointer	0000FF0H
Code segment	F000H
Data segment	0000H
Stack segment	0000H
Extra segment (ES)	0000H
Extra segment (FS)	0000H
Extra segment (GS)	0000H
All other registers	Undefined

Note: U means undefined.

The 80386 executes instructions near the top of the physical memory at address FFFFFFF0H. When the 80386 executes the first intersegment jump or call, address lines A20-A31 will go low and the 80386 executes instruction in the lower megabyte of physical memory. This allows the system designer to use a ROM at the top of physical memory to initialize the system and take care of resets. The 80386 is reset by activating its RESET pin high for at least 78 CLK2 periods.

4.2.7 TESTABILITY

The 80386 provides capability to perform self-test. The self-test checks all of the control ROM and the associate nonrandom logic inside the

80386. Self-test feature is performed when the 80386 RESET pin goes from HIGH to LOW and the BUSY # pin is LOW. The self-test takes above 30 milliseconds with a 16-MHz clock. After self-test, the 80386 performs reset and begins program execution. If the self-test is successful, the contents of both EAX and EDX are zero; otherwise the contents of EAX and EDX are not zero, indicating a faulty chip.

4.2.8 DEBUGGING

In addition to the software breakpoint and single-stepping features, the 80386 also includes six program-accessible 32-bit registers for specifying up to four district breakpoints. Unlike the INT3 which only allows instruction breakpointing, the 80386 debug registers permit breakpoints to be set for data accesses. Therefore, a breakpoint can be set up if a variable is accidentally being overwritten. Thus, the 80386 can stop executing the program whenever the variable's contents are being changed.

4.2.9 80386 PINS AND SIGNALS

As mentioned before, the 80386 is a 132-pin ceramic Pin Grid Array (PGA). Pins are arranged 0.1 inch (2.54 mm) center-to-center, in a 14 × 14 matrix, three rows around.

A number of sockets are available for low insertion force or zero insertion force mountings. Three types of terminals include soldertail, surface mount, or wire wrap. These application sockets are manufactured by Amp, Inc. of Harrisburg, PA, Advanced Interconnections of Warwick, RI, and Textool Products of Irving, TX.

Figure 4.13 shows the 80386 pinout as viewed from the pin side of the chip. Table 4.8 provides the 80386 pinout functional grouping description.

Figure 4.14 shows functional grouping of the 80386 pins. A brief description of the 80386 pins and signals is provided in the following. The # symbol at the end of the signal name indicates the active or asserted state when it is low. When the symbol # is absent after the signal name, the signal is asserted when high.

The 80386 has 20 Vcc and 21 GND pins for power distribution. These multiple power and ground pins reduce noise. Preferably, the circuit board should contain Vcc and GND planes.

CLK2 pin provides the basic timing for the 80386. This clock is divided by 2 internally to provide the internal clock used for instruction execution.

There are two phases (phase one and phase two) of the internal clock. Each CLK2 period defines a phase of the internal clock. Figure 4.15 shows the relationship. The 80386 is reset by activating the RESET pin for at least

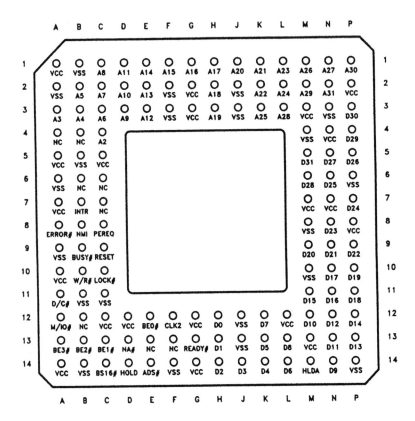

FIGURE 4.13 80386 PGA pinout view from pin side.

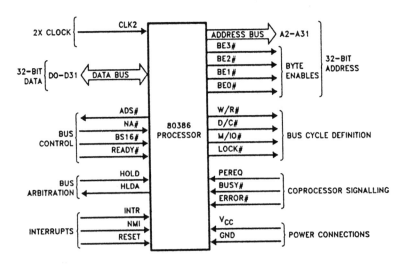

FIGURE 4.14 Functional signal groups.

TABLE 4.8
80386 PGA Pinout Functional Grouping

Pin/signal		Pin/signal		Pin/signal		Pin/signal	
NS	A31	M5	D31	A1	Vcc	A2	Vss
P1	A30	P3	D30	A5	Vcc	A6	Vss
M2	A29	P4	D29	A7	Vcc	A9	Vss
L3	A28	M6	D28	A10	Vcc	B1	Vss
N1	A27	N5	D27	A14	Vcc	B5	Vss
M1	A26	P5	D26	C5	Vcc	B11	Vss
K3	A25	N6	D25	C12	Vcc	B14	Vss
L2	A24	P7	D24	D12	Vcc	C11	Vss
L1	A23	N8	D23	G2	Vcc	FS	Vss
K2	A22	P9	D22	G3	Vcc	F3	Vss
K1	A21	N9	D21	G12	Vcc	F14	Vss
J1	A20	M9	D20	G14	Vcc	J2	Vss
H3	A19	P10	D19	L12	Vcc	J3	Vss
H2	A18	P11	D18	M3	Vcc	J12	Vss
H1	A17	N10	D17	M7	Vcc	J13	Vss
G1	A16	N11	D16	M13	Vcc	M4	Vss
F1	A15	M11	D15	N4	Vcc	M8	Vss
E1	A14	P12	D14	N7	Vcc	M10	Vss
E2	A13	P13	D13	P2	Vcc	N3	Vss
E3	A12	N12	D12	P8	Vcc	P6	Vss
D1	A11	N13	D11			P14	Vss
D2	A10	M12	D10				
D3	A9	N14	D9	F12	CLK2	A4	N.C.
C1	A8	L13	D8			D4	N.C.
C2	A7	K12	D7	E14	ADS#	B6	N.C.
C3	A6	L14	D6			B12	N.C.
B2	A5	K13	D5	B10	W/R#	C6	N.C.
B3	A4	K14	D4	A11	D/C#	C7	N.C.
A3	A3	J14	D3	A12	M/IO#	E13	N.C.
C4	A2	H14	D2	C10	LOCK#	F13	N.C.
A13	BE3#	H13	D1				
B13	BE2#	H12	D0	D13	NA#	C8	PEREQ
C13	BE1#			C14	BS16#	B9	BUSY#
E12	BE0#			G13	READY#	A8	ERROR#
		D14	HOLD				
C9	RESET	M14	HLDA	B7	INTR	B8	NMI

15 CLK2 periods. The RESET signal is level-sensitive. When the RESET pin is asserted, the 80386 ignores all input pins and drives all other pins to idle bus state. The 82384 clock generator provides system clock and reset signals.

D0-D31 provides the 32-bit data bus. The 80386 can transfer 16- or 32-bit data via the data bus.

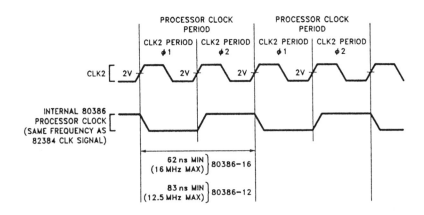

FIGURE 4.15 CLK2 signal and internal processor clock.

The address pins A2-A31 along with the byte enable signals BE0# thru BE3# generate physical memory or I/O port addresses. Using these pins, the 80386 can directly address 4 gigabytes by physical memory (00000000H thru FFFFFFFFH) and 64 kilobytes of I/O addresses (00000000H thru 0000FFFFH). The coprocessor addresses range from 800000F8H thru 800000FFH. Therefore, coprocessor select signal is generated by the 80386 when M/IO # LOW and A31 HIGH.

The byte enable outputs, BE0# thru BE3# by the 80386, define which bytes of D0-D31 are utilized in the current data transfer. These definitions are given below:

BE0# is low when data is transferred via D0-D7
BE1# is low when data is transferred via D8-D15
BE2# is low when data is transferred via D16-D23
BE3# is low when data is transferred via D24-D31

The 80386 asserts one or more byte enables depending on the physical size of the operand being transferred (1, 2, 3, or 4 bytes).

When the 80386 performs a word memory write or word I/O write cycle via D16-D31 pins, it duplicates this data on D0-D15.

W/R#, D/C#, M/IO#, and LOCK# output pins specify the type of bus cycle being performed by the 80386. W/R# pin, when HIGH, identifies write cycle and, when LOW, indicates read cycle. D/C# pin, when HIGH, identifies data cycle and, when LOW, indicates control cycle. M/IO# differentiates between memory and I/O cycles. LOCK# distinguishes between locked and unlocked bus cycles. W/R#, D/C#, and M/IO# pins define the primary bus cycle. This is because these signals are valid when ADS# (address status output) is asserted. LOCK# output is valid as soon as the bus cycle begins, but due to address pipelining LOCK# may be valid later than ADS# asserted. Table 4.9 defines the bus cycle definitions.

The 80386 bus control signals include ADS# (address status), READY# (transfer acknowledge), NA# (next address request), and BS16# (bus size 16).

The 80386 outputs LOW on the ADS# pin to indicate a valid bus cycle (W/R#, D/C#, M/IO#) and address (BE0#-BE3#, A2-A31) signals.

TABLE 4.9
Bus Cycle Definition

M/IO#	D/C#	W/R#	Bus cycle type		Locked?
Low	Low	Low	INTERRUPT ACKNOWLEDGE		Yes
Low	Low	High	Does not occur		—
Low	High	Low	I/O DATA READ		No
Low	High	High	I/O DATA WRITE		No
High	Low	Low	MEMORY CODE READ		No
High	Low	High	HALT:	SHUTDOWN:	No
			Address = 2	Address = 0	
			(BE0# High	(BE0# Low	
			BE1# High	BE1# High	
			BE2# Low	BE2# High	
			BE3# High	BE3# High	
			A2-A31 Low)	A2-A31 Low)	
High	High	Low	MEMORY DATA READ		Some cycles
High	High	High	MEMORY DATA WRITE		Some cycles

When READY# input is asserted during a read cycle or an interrupt acknowledge cycle, the 80386 latches the input data on the data pins and ends the cycle. When READY# is low during a write cycle, the 80386 ends the bus cycle.

The NA# input pin is activated low by an external hardware to request address pipelining. A low on this pin means that the system is ready to receive new values of BE0#-BE3#, A2-A31, W/R#, D/C#, and M/IO# from the 80386 even if the completion of the present cycle is not acknowledged on the READY# pin.

BS16# input pin permits the 80386 to interface to 32- and 16-bit data buses. When the BS16# input pin is asserted low by an external device, the 80386 uses the low-order half (D0-D15) of the data bus corresponding to BE0# and BE1# for data transfer. If the 80386 asserts BE2# or BE3# during a bus cycle, then assertion of BS16# by an external device in this cycle will automatically cause the 80386 to transfer the upper byte(s) via only D0-D15. For 32-bit data operands with BS16# asserted, the 80386 will automatically execute two consecutive 16-bit bus cycles to accomplish this.

HOLD (input) and HLDA (output) pins are 80386 bus arbitration signals. These signals are used for DMA transfers. PEREQ, BUSY#, and ERROR# pins are used for interfacing coprocessors such as 80287 or 80387 to the 80386. A HIGH on PEREQ (coprocessor request) input pin indicates that a coprocessor is requesting the 80386 to transfer data to or from memory. The 80386 thus transfers data between the coprocessor and memory. This signal is level-sensitive. A LOW on the BUSY# (coprocessor Busy) input pin means that the coprocessor is still executing an instruction and is not capable of accepting another instruction. The BUSY# pins avoid interference with a previous coprocessor instruction.

ERROR# (coprocessor error) input pin, when asserted LOW by the coprocessor, indicates that the previous coprocessor instruction generated a coprocessor error of a type not masked by the coprocessor's control register. This input pin is automatically sampled by the 80386 when a coprocessor instruction is encountered and, if asserted, the 80386 generates exception 7 for executing the error-handling routine.

There are two interrupt pins on the 80386. These are INTR (maskable) and NMI(nonmaskable) pins. INTR is level-sensitive. When INTR is asserted and if IF bit in the EFLAGS is 1, the 80386 (when ready) responds to the INTR by performing two interrupt acknowledge cycles and at the end of the second cycle latches an 8-bit vector on D0-D7 to identify the source of interrupt. To ensure INTR recognition, it must be asserted until the first interrupt acknowledge cycle starts.

NMI is leading-edge sensitive. It must be negated for at least 8 CLK2 periods and then be asserted for at least 8 CLK2 periods to assure recognition by the 80386. The servicing of NMI was discussed earlier.

Table 4.10 summarizes the characteristics of all 80386 signals.

TABLE 4.10
80386 Signal Summary

Signal name	Signal function	Active state	Input/ output	Input synch or asynch to CLK2	Output high impedance during HDLA?
CLK2	Clock	—	I	—	—
D0-D31	Data bus	High	I/O	S	Yes
BE0#-BE3#	Byte enables	Low	O	—	Yes
A2-A31	Address bus	High	O	—	Yes
W/R#	Write-read indications	High	O	—	Yes
D/C#	Data-control indication	High	O	—	Yes
M/IO#	Memory-I/O indication	High	O	—	Yes
LOCK#	Bus lock indication	Low	O	—	Yes
ADS#	Address status	Low	O	—	Yes
NA#	Next address request	Low	I	S	—
BS16#	Bus size 16	Low	I	S	—
READY#	Transfer acknowledge	Low	I	S	—
HOLD	Bus hold request	High	I	S	—
HLDA	Bus hold acknowledge	High	O	—	No
PEREQ	Coprocessor request	High	I	A	—
BUSY#	Coprocessor busy	Low	I	A	—
ERROR#	Coprocessor error	Low	I	A	—
INTR	Maskable interrupt request	High	I	A	—

TABLE 4.10 (continued)
80386 Signal Summary

Signal name	Signal function	Active state	Input/ output	Input synch or asynch to CLK2	Output high impedance during HDLA?
NMI	Nonmaskable interrupt request	High	I	A	—
RESET	Reset	High	I	A (note)	—

Note: If the phase of the internal processor clock must be synchronized to external circuitry, RESET falling edge must meet setup and hold times t_{25} and t_{26}.

4.2.10 80386 BUS TRANSFER TECHNIQUE

The 80386 uses one or more bus cycles to perform all data transfers. The 32-bit address is generated by the 80386 from BE0#-BE3# and A2-A32 as follows:

80386 address signals

Physical base address			80386 address pins and BE0#-BE3# signals			
A31—A2	A1	A0	A31—A2	BE3#	BE2#	BE1#	BE0#
A31—A2	0	0	A31—A2	X	X	X	Low
A31—A2	0	1	A31—A2	X	X	Low	High
A31—A2	1	0	A31—A2	X	Low	High	High
A31—A2	1	1	A31—A2	Low	High	High	High

Dynamic bus sizing feature connects the 80386 with 32-bit or 16-bit data buses for memory or I/O. A single 80386 can be connected to both 16- and 32-bit buses. During each bus cycle, the 80386 dynamically determines bus width and then transfers data to or from 32- or 16-bit devices. During each bus cycle, the 80386 BS16# pin can be asserted for 16-bit ports or negate BS16# for 32-bit ports by the external device. With BS16# asserted all transfers are performed via D0-D15 pins. Also, with

BS16# asserted, the 80386 automatically performs data transfers larger than 16 bits or misaligned 16 bits transfers in multiple cycles as needed. Note that 16-bit memory or I/O devices must be connected on D0-D15 pins.

Asserting BS16# only affects the 80386 when BE2# and/or BE3# are asserted during the cycle. Assertion of BS16# does not affect the 80386 if data transfer is only performed via D0-D15. On the other hand, the 80386 is affected by assertion of the BS16# pin, depending in which byte enable pins are asserted during the current bus cycle. For example, asserting BS16# during "upper half only" reads causes the 80386 to read data on the D0-D15 pins and ignores data on the D16-D31. Data that would have been read from D16-D31 (as indicated by BE2# and BE3#) will instead be read from D0-D15.

A 32-bit-wide memory can be interfaced to the 80386 by utilizing its BS16#, BE0#-BE3#, and A2-A31 pins. Each 32-bit memory word starts at a byte address that is a multiple of 4. BS16# is connected to HIGH (negated) for all bus cycles for 32-bit transfers. A2-A31 and BE0#-BE3# are used for addressing the memory.

For 16-bit memories, each 16-bit memory word starts at an address which is a multiple of 2. The address is decoded to assert BS16# only during bus cycles for 16-bit transfers.

A2-A31 can be used to address 16-bit memory also. A1 and two-byte enable signals are also required.

To obtain A1 and two-byte enables for 16-bit transfers, BE0#-BE3# should be decoded as in Table 4.11.

Figure 4.16 shows a block diagram interfacing 16- and 32-bit memories to 80386.

Finally, if an operand is not aligned such as a 32-bit doubleword operand beginning at an address not divisible by 4, then multiple bus cycles are required for data transfer.

4.2.11 80386 READ AND WRITE CYCLES

The 80386 performs data transfer during bus cycles (also called read or write cycles).

Two choices of address timing are dynamically selectable. These are nonpipelined and pipelined. One of these timing choices is selectable on a cycle-by-cycle basis with the Next Address (NA#) input.

After a bus idle state, the 80386 always uses nonpipelined address timing. However, the NA# may be asserted by an external device to select pipelined address timing, for the next cycle is made available before the present bus cycle is terminated by the 80386 by asserting READY#. In

TABLE 4.11
Generating A1, BHE#, and BLE# for Addressing 16-Bit Devices

80386 signals				16-bit bus signals			
BE3#	BE2#	BE1#	BE0#	A1	BHE#	BLE# (A0)	Comments
H*	H*	H*	H*	x	x	x	x — no active bytes
H	H	H	L	L	H	L	
H	H	L	H	L	L	H	
H	H	L	L	L	L	L	
H	L	H	H	H	H	L	
H*	L*	H*	L*	x	x	x	x — not contiguous bytes
H	L	L	H	L	L	H	
H	L	L	L	L	L	L	
L	H	H	H	H	L	H	
L*	H*	H*	L*	x	x	x	x — not contiguous bytes
L*	H*	L*	H*	x	x	x	x — not contiguous bytes
L*	H*	L*	L*	x	x	x	x — not contiguous bytes
L	L	H	H	H	L	L	
L*	L*	H*	L*	x	x	x	x — not contiguous bytes
L	L	L	H	L	L	H	
L	L	L	L	L	L	L	

Note: BLE# asserted when D0-D7 of 16-bit bus is active; BHE# asserted when D8-D15 of 16-bit bus is active; A1 low for all even words; A1 high for all odd words.

Key: x = don't care
      H = high voltage level
      L = low voltage level
      * = a nonoccurring pattern of Byte Enables; either none are asserted, or the pattern has Byte Enables asserted for noncontiguous bytes

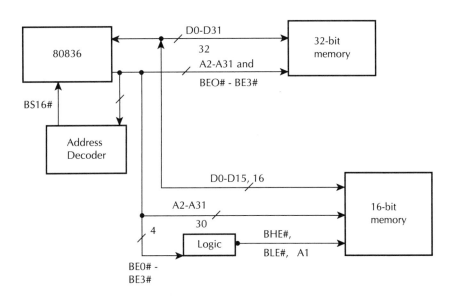

FIGURE 4.16 Interfacing 80386 16- and 32-bit memories.

general, the 80386 samples NA# input during each bus cycle to select the desired address timing for the next bus cycle.

Physical data bus width (16- or 32-bit) is selected by the 80386 by sampling the BS16# (bus size 16) input pin near the end of the bus cycle. Assertion of BS16# indicates a 16-bit data bus, while negation of BS16# means a 32-bit data bus.

A read or write cycle is terminated by the 80386 on a low READY# (assertion) from the external device. Until the READY# is asserted, the 80386 inserts wait states to permit adjustment for the speed of any external device when a read cycle is terminated, and the 80386 latches the information present at its data pins. When a write cycle is acknowledged, the 80386 write data remain valid throughout phase one of the next bus state, to provide write data hold time.

To illustrate the concept of 80386 bus cycle timing, a mixture of read and write cycles with nonpipelined address timing is shown in Figure 4.17.

This diagram shows the fastest possible cycles with nonpipelined address timing having two bus states (T1 and T2) per bus cycle. In phase one T1, the address signals and bus control signals are valid and the 80386 activates ADS# low to indicate their availability.

During read cycle, the 80386 tristates its data signals to permit driving by the external device being addressed. During write cycle, the 80386

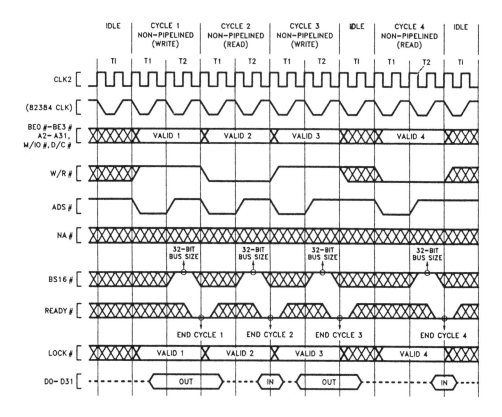

FIGURE 4.17 Bus cycles with nonpipelined address (zero wait states).

places data on the data bus starting in phase two of T1 until phase one of the bus state following cycle acknowledgment.

4.2.12 80386 MODES

The 80386 can be operated in real, protected, or virtual 8086 mode. These modes are described below.

4.2.12.a 80386 Real Mode

Upon reset or power-up, the 80386 operates in real mode. In real mode, the 80386 can access all the 8086 registers along with the 80386 32-bit registers. The memory addressing, memory size, and interrupts of 80386 in this mode are the same as those of the 80286 in real mode.

The 80386 can execute all the instructions in real mode. The main purpose of real mode is to initialize the 80386 for protected mode operation.

In real mode, the 80386 can directly address up to one megabyte of memory. The address lines A2-A19, BE0-BE3 are used by the 80386 in this mode. Paging is not provided in real mode. Therefore, linear addresses are identical to physical addresses. The 20-bit physical address is formed by adding the shifted (four times to the left) segment registers to an offset as shown in Figure 4.18.

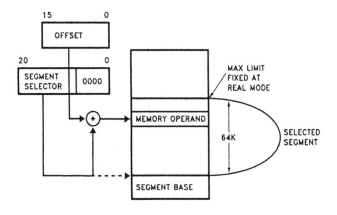

FIGURE 4.18 Real address mode addressing.

All segments in real mode are exactly 64K bytes wide. Segments can be overlapped in this mode. There are two memory areas which are reserved in real mode for system initialization and interrupt pointer table. Addresses 00000H thru 002FFH are reserved for the interrupt pointer table, while addresses FFFFFFF0H thru FFFFFFFFH are reserved for system initialization. Many of the exceptions listed in Table 4.6 are not applicable to real mode. Exceptions 10, 11, 12, and 14 will never occur in this mode. Also, other exceptions have minor variations as follows:

Function	Interrupt number	Related instructions	Return address location
Interrupt table Limit too small	8	INT vector is not within table limit	Before instruction
Segment overrun exception	13	Word memory reference with off-set = FFFFH or an attempt to execute an instruction past the end of a segment	Before instruction

4.2.12.b Protected Mode

The total 80386 capabilities are available when the 80386 operates in protected mode. This mode increases the linear space to four gigabytes (2^{32} bytes) and permits the execution of virtual memory programs of 64 tetrabytes (2^{46} bytes). Also, in protected mode, the 80386 can run all existing 8086 and 80286 programs with on-chip memory management and protection features. The protected mode includes new instructions to support multitasking operating systems. The main difference between protected mode and real mode from a programmer's viewpoint is the increased memory space and a differing addressing mechanism. Similar to real mode, protected mode also includes two elements (16-bit selector for determining a segment's base address and a 32-bit offset or effective address) to obtain a 32-bit linear address. This 32-bit linear address is either used as the 32-bit physical address or, if paging is enabled, the paging mechanism translates this 32-bit linear address to a 32-bit physical address. Figure 4.19 shows the protected mode addressing mechanism. The selector is used to specify an index into a table defined by the operating system. The table includes the 32-bit base address of a given segment. The physical address is obtained by summing the base address obtained from the table to the offset.

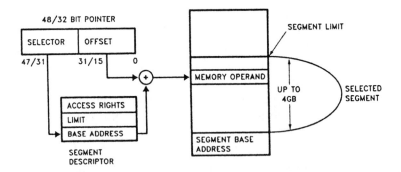

FIGURE 4.19 Protected mode addressing.

With the paging mechanism enabled, the 80386 provides additional memory management mechanism. The paging feature manages large 80386 segments.

The paging mechanism translates the protected linear addresses from the segmentation unit into physical addresses. Figure 4.20 shows this translation scheme.

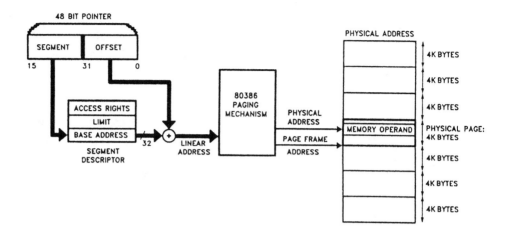

FIGURE 4.20 Paging and segmentation.

Let us now discuss 80386 segmentation, protection, and paging features.

Segmentation provides both memory management and protection. All information about the segments is stored in an 8-byte data structure called a descriptor. All the descriptors are stored in tables identified by the 80386 hardware. There are three types of tables holding 80386 descriptors: global descriptor table (GDT), local descriptor table (LDT), and interrupt descriptor table (IDT). These tables are memory arrays of variable lengths. Their sizes can vary from 8 bytes to 64K bytes. Each table can store up to 8192 8-byte descriptors. The upper 13 bits of a selector are used as an index into the descriptor table. The tables have associated registers which store a 32-bit linear base address and a 16-bit limit for each table. Each table has a set of registers, namely, GDTR (32-bit), LDTR (16-bit), and IDTR (32-bit), associated with it. The 80386 instructions LGDT, LLDT, and LIDT are used to load the base and 16-bit limit of the global, local, and interrupt descriptor tables into the appropriate registers. The SGDT, SLDT, and SIDT instructions store the base and limit values.

The GDT contains descriptors which are available to all the tasks in the system. In general, the GDT contains code and data segments used by the operating system, task state segments, and descriptors for LDTs in a system.

LDTs store descriptors for a given task. Each task has a separate LDT, while the GDT contains descriptors for segments which are common to all tasks.

The IDT contains the descriptors which point to the location of up to 256 interrupt service routines. Every interrupt used by a system must have an entry into the IDT. The IDT entries are referenced via INT instructions, external interrupt vectors, and exceptions.

The object to which the selector points to is called a descriptor. Descriptors are eight bytes wide containing attributes about a given segment. These attributes contain the 32-bit base linear address of the segment, segment length, protection level, read/write/execute privileges, the default operand size (16 or 32 bits), and segment type.

In order to provide operating system compatibility between the 80286 and 80386, the 80386 supports all of the 80286 segment descriptors. The only differences between the 80286 and 80386 formats are that the values of the type fields and the limit and base address fields have been expanded for the 80386.

The 80286 system segment descriptors contain a 24-bit base address and 16-bit limit, while the 80386 system segment descriptors have a 32-bit base address, a 20-bit limit field, and a granularity bit. Note that the segment length is page granular if the granularity bit is one; otherwise, the segment length is byte granular.

By supporting 80286 segments the 80386 is able to execute 80286 application programs on a 80386 operating system. This is possible because the 80386 automatically can differentiate between the 80286-type and 80386-type descriptors. In particular, if the upper word of a descriptor is zero, then that descriptor is a 80286-type descriptor.

The only other differences between the 80286 and 80386 descriptors are the interpretation of the word count field of call gates and the B bit. The word count field specifies the number of 16-bit quantities to copy for 80286 call gates and 32-bit quantities for 80386 call gates. The B bit controls the size of pushes when using a call gate. If B = 0, then pushes are 16 bits, while pushes are 32 bits for B = 1.

The 80386 provides four protection levels for supporting a multi-tasking operating system to isolate and protect user programs from each other and the operating system. The privilege level controls the use of privileged instructions, I/O instructions, and access to segments and segment descriptors. The 80386 includes the protection as part of its memory management unit. The 80386 also provides an additional type of protection when paging is enabled.

The four-level hierarchical privilege system is shown in Figure 4.21. It is an extension of the user/supervisor privilege mode used by minicomputers. Note that the user/supervisor mode is supported by the 80386 paging

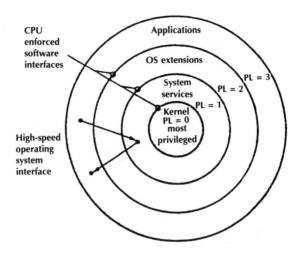

FIGURE 4.21 Four-level hierarchical protection.

mechanism. The Privilege Levels (PL) are numbered 0 thru 3. Level 0 is the most privileged level.

The 80386 provides the following rules of privilege to control access to both data and procedures between levels of a task:

- Data stored in a segment with a privilege level 0 can be accessed only by code executing at a privilege level at least as privileged as 0.
- A code segment/procedure with privilege level 0 can only be called by a task executing at the same or a lesser privilege level than 0.

The 80386 supports task gates (protected indirect calls) to provide a secure method of privilege transfers within a task.

The 80386 also supports a rapid task switch operation via hardware. It saves the entire state of the machine (all of the registers, address space, and a link to the previous task), loads a new execution state, performs protection checks, and commences execution in the new task in approximately 17 microseconds.

Paging is another type of memory management for virtual memory multitasking operating systems. The main difference between paging and segmentation is that paging divides programs/data into several equal-sized pages, while segmentation divides programs/data into several variable-sized segments.

There are three elements associated with the 80386 paging mechanism. These are page directory, page tables, and the page itself (page frame). Paging mechanism does not have memory fragmentation since all pages have the same size of 4K bytes. Figure 4.22 shows the 80386 paging mechanism.

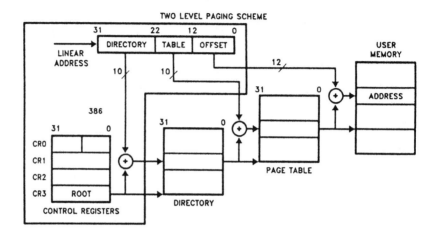

FIGURE 4.22 Paging mechanism.

There are four 32-bit control registers (CR0-CR3) associated with the paging mechanism. CR2 is the page fault linear address register and contains the 32-bit linear address which caused the last page fault detected.

CR3 is the page directory physical base address register and contains the physical starting address of the page directory. The lower 12 bits of CR3 are always zero to ensure that the page directory is always page aligned. CR1 is reserved for future Intel processors. CR0 contains 6 defined bits for control and status purposes. The low-order 16 bits of CR0 are known as the machine status word and include special control bits such as the enable bit and the protection enable bit.

The page directory is 4K bytes wide and permits up to 1024 page directory entries. Each page directory entry contains the address of the next level of tables, page tables, and information about the page table. The upper 10 bits of the linear address (A22-A31) are used as an index to select the correct page directory entry.

Each page table is 4K bytes and holds up to 1024 page table entries. Page table entries contain the starting address of the page frame and statistical information about the page such as whether the page can be read or written in supervisor or user mode. Address bits A12-A21 are used as index to select one of the 1024 page table entries. The 20 upper-bit page frame address is concatenated with the lower 12 bits of the linear address to form the physical address. Page tables can be shared between tasks and swapped to disks.

The lower 12 bits of the page table entries and page directory entries contain statistical information about pages and page tables, respectively. As an example, the P (present) bit indicates whether a page directory or page table entry can be used in address translation. If P = 1, the entry can be used in address translation, and if P = 0, the entry cannot be used for translation and all other 31 bits are available for use by the software. These 31 bits can be used to indicate where on a disk the page is located.

The 80386 provides a set of protection attributes for paging systems. The paging mechanism provides two levels of protection: user and supervisor. The user level corresponds to level 3 of the segmentation-based protection and the supervisor level combines all of the other protection levels (0, 1, 2). Programs executing at level 0, 1, or 2 bypass the page protection, although segmentation-based protection is still enforced by hardware.

The 80386 takes care of the page address translation process, relieving the burden from an operating system in a demand-paged system. The operating system is responsible for setting up the initial page tables and the handling of any page faults. The operating system initializes the tables by loading CR3 with the address of the page directory and allocates space for the page directory and the page tables. The operating system also implements a swapping policy and handles all of the page faults.

4.2.12.c Virtual 8086 Mode

The virtual 8086 mode permits the execution of 8086 applications while taking full advantage of the 80386 protection mechanism. In particular, the 80386 permits concurrent execution of 8086 operating systems and applications, an 80386 operating system, and both 80286 and 80386 application. For example, in a multiuser 80386-based microcomputer, one person can run an MD-DOS spreadsheet, another person can use MS-DOS, and a third person can run multiple UNIX utilities and applications.

One of the main differences between 80386 real and protected modes is how the segment selectors are interpreted. In virtual 8086 mode, the segment registers are used in the same way as the real mode. The contents of the segment register are shifted 4 times to the left and added to the offset to obtain the linear address.

The paging hardware permits the simultaneous execution of several virtual mode tasks and provides protection.

The paging hardware allows the 20-bit linear address produced by a virtual mode program to be divided up into 256 pages. Each one of the pages can be located anywhere within the maximum 4-gigabyte physical address space of the 80386.

The paging hardware also permits sharing of the 8086 operating system code by several 8086 applications. All virtual mode programs execute at privilege level 3. Therefore, virtual mode programs are subject to all of the protection checks defined in protected mode. This is different from real mode which executes programs in level 0.

QUESTIONS AND PROBLEMS

4.1 Write an 80186 assembly program to multiply a 16-bit signed number in BX by 00F3H. Assume that the result is 16 bits wide.

4.2 Identify the peripheral functional blocks integrated into the 80186.

4.3 What is the purpose of the relocation register in the 80186 peripheral control block?

4.4 What is the relationship between internal and external clocks of the 80186?

4.5 Identify the basic differences between 8086 and 80186.

4.6 Identify the main differences between the 80186 and 80286.

4.7 How much physical and virtual memory can the 80286 address?

4.8 What is the difference between the 80286 real address mode and PVAM? Explain how these two modes can be switched back and forth.

4.9 Explain how the 80286 determines where in memory the global descriptor table and the present local descriptor table are located.

4.10 Discuss briefly the 80286 protection mechanism.

4.11 What is meant by the 80286 task state segment for each active task? How can this be accessed?

4.12 Explain the meaning of 80286 call gates.

4.13 Discuss briefly the 80286 memory management features and task switching.

4.14 What is the purpose of 80286 CAP, COD/$\overline{\text{INTA}}$ pins?

4.15 Identify the 80286 pins used for interfacing it to a coprocessor.

4.16 Discuss the issues associated with isolating a user program from a supervisor program and then utilize the 80286's protection features for protection. Assume that no task switching is involved. Also, assume that the supervisor program will perform all I/O operations and be present in the virtual memory space.

4.17 Compare the features of the 80386 with those of the 80286 from the following point of view: registers, clock rate, number of pins, number of instructions, modes of operation, memory management, and protection mechanism.

4.18 What are the basic differences between the 80386 real, protected, and virtual 8086 modes?

4.19 Assume the following register contents:

$$[EBX] \ = \ 0000 \ 2000H$$
$$[ECX] \ = \ 0500 \ 0000H$$
$$[EDX] \ = \ 5000 \ 5000H$$

prior to execution of each of the 80386 instructions listed below. Determine the effective address after execution of each instruction and identify the addressing modes of both source and destination:

```
i)   MOV  [EBX * 2] [ECX], EDX
ii)  MOV  [EBX * 4] [ECX + 20H], EDX
```

4.20 Determine the effect of each of the following 80386 instructions:

    i)   **MOVZX ECX, BX**
          assume [ECX] = F1250024H
                  [BX] = F130H

       prior to execution of the MOVZX instruction.

    ii) **SHLD CX, BX, 0 if**
        [CX] = 0025H, [BX] = F27H

       prior to execution of the SHLD instruction.

4.21 Write an 80386 assembly language program to divide a signed 64-bit number in EBX:EAX by a 16-bit signed number in AX. Store the 32-bit quotient and remainder in memory locations.

4.22 Write an 80386 assembly program to compute Xi^2/N where $N = 100$ and Xi's are signed 32-bit numbers. Assume that Xi^2 can be stored as a 32-bit signed number without overflow.

4.23 Write an 80386 assembly program to input 100 32-bit string data via a port addressed by DX. The program will then store the data in memory locations addressed by [DS] and [ESI].

4.24 Discuss how the following situation will be handled by the 80386: The 80386 executing an instruction causes both a general protection fault (interrupt 13) and coprocessor segment overrun (interrupt 9).

4.25 How does the 80386 generate the 32-bit physical address from A2-A31 and BE0#-BE3#?

4.26 What are the purposes of NA#, D/C#, BS16#, and ERROR# pins?

4.27 For 16- and 32-bit transfers, what is the logic level of the BS16# pin?

4.28 Discuss briefly 80386 segmentation unit, paging unit, and protection.

4.29 How many bits are required for the address in real and protected modes?

4.30 Discuss the basic differences between 80286 and 80386 descriptors.

4.31 What is the four-level hierarchical protection in protected mode?

4.32 Discuss briefly 80386 virtual mode.

Chapter 5

MOTOROLA MC68000

This chapter describes the details of the Motorola 68000 microprocessor. The basic architecture, addressing modes, instruction set, and interfacing features of the Motorola 68000 are included.

5.1 INTRODUCTION

The MC68000 is Motorola's first 16-bit microprocessor. All 68000 address and data registers are 32 bits wide and its ALU is 16 bits wide. The 68000 is designed using HMOS technology. The 68000 requires a single 5V supply. The processor can be operated from a maximum internal clock frequency of 25 MHz. The 68000 is available in several frequencies. These include 6 MHz, 8 MHz, 10 MHz, 12.5 MHz, 16.67 MHz, and 25 MHz. The 68000 does not have on-chip clock circuitry and, therefore, requires a crystal oscillator or external clock generator/driver circuit to generate the clock.

The 68000 has several different versions. These include 68008, 68010, and 68012. The 68000 and 68010 are packaged in a 64-pin DIP (Dual In-line Package) with all pins assigned or in a 68-pin quad pack or Pin Grid Array (PGA) with some unused pins. The 68000 is also packaged in 68-terminal chip carrier. The 68008 is packaged in a 48-pin dual in-line package while the 68012 is packaged in 84-pin grid array. The 68008 provides the basic 68000 capabilities with inexpensive packaging. It has an 8-bit data bus which facilitates interfacing of this chip to inexpensive 8-bit peripheral chips.

The 68010 provides hardware-based virtual memory support and efficient looping instructions. Like the 68000, it has a 16-bit data bus and a 24-bit address bus.

The 68012 includes all the 68010 features with a 31-bit address bus.

The clock frequencies of the 68008, 68010, and 68012 are the same as the 68000.

The following table summarizes the basic differences among the 68000 family members:

	68000	**68008**	**68010**	**68012**
Data size (bits)	16	8	16	16
Address bus size (bits)	24	20	24	31
Virtual memory	No	No	Yes	Yes
Control registers	None	None	Three	Three
Directly addressable memory	16 Mbytes	1 Mbyte	16 Mbytes	2 gigabytes

In order to implement operating systems and protection features, the 68000 can be operated in two modes. These are supervisor and user modes. The supervisor mode is also called the operating system mode. In this mode, the 68000 can execute all instructions. However, in the user mode, the 68000 operates in one of these modes based on the S-bit of the Status register. When the S-bit is one, the 68000 operates in the supervisor mode. On the other hand, the 68000 operates in the user mode when $S = 0$.

Table 5.1 lists the basic differences between 68000 user and supervisor modes.

From Table 5.1 it can be seen that the 68000 executing a program in supervisor mode can enter the user mode by modifying the S-bit of the Status register to zero via an instruction. Instructions such as MOVE to SR, ORI to SR, EORI to SR can be used to accomplish this. On the other hand, the 68000 executing a program in user mode can enter the supervisor mode only via recognition of a trap, reset, or interrupt. Note that upon hardware reset, the 68000 operates in the supervisor mode and can execute all instructions. An attempt to execute privileged instructions (instructions that can only be executed in supervisor mode) in user mode will automatically generate an internal interrupt (trap) by the 68000.

The logical level in the 68000 Function Code pin (FC2) indicates to the external devices whether the 68000 is currently operating in user or supervisor mode. The 68000 has three function code pins (FC2, FC1, and FC0) which indicate to the external devices whether the 68000 is accessing

TABLE 5.1
68000 User and Supervisor Modes

	Supervisor mode	User mode
Enter mode by	Recognition of a trap, reset, or interrupt	Clearing status bit S
System stack pointer	Supervisor stack pointer	User stack pointer
Other stack pointers	User stack pointer and registers A0—A6	registers A0—A6
Instructions available	All including STOP RESET MOVE to/from SR ANDI to/from SR ORI to/from SR EORI to/from SR MOVE USP to (An) MOVE to USP RTE	All except those listed under supervisor mode
Function code pin FC2	1	0

supervisor program/data, user program/data, or performing an interrupt acknowledge cycle. These three pins are used for memory protection and for enabling an external chip such as the 74LS244 to provide an interrupt address vector.

The 68000 can operate on five different data types. These are bit, 4-bit BCD digit, 8-bit byte, 16-bit word, and 32-bit long word.

The 68000 provides 56 basic instructions. With 14 addressing modes, 56 instructions, and 5 data types, the 68000 includes more than 1000 op codes. The fastest instruction is MOVE reg, reg and is executed in 500 ns at 8-MHz clock. The slowest instruction is 32-bit by 16-bit divide, which is executed in 21.25 μs at 8-MHz clock.

Like the 8-bit Motorola microprocessors such as Motorola 6800 and 6809, the 68000 supports memory-mapped I/O. Thus, the 68000 instruction set does not include any IN or OUT instruction.

The 68000 is a general-purpose register-based microprocessor since any data register can be used as an accumulator or as a scratch pad register. Even though the 68000 program counter is 32 bits wide, only the low-order 24 bits are used for PC. With 24 bits as address, the 68000 can directly address 16 megabytes (2^{24}) of memory.

5.2 68000 PROGRAMMING MODEL

The register architecture of the 68000 is shown in Figure 5.1.

The 68000 chip contains eight 32-bit data registers (D0-D7) and nine 32-bit address registers (A0-A7, A7′). The 68000 uses A7 or A7′ as the user or supervisor stack pointer, depending on the mode of operation. Data items such as bytes (8 bits), words (16 bits), Long words (32 bits), and BCD numbers (4 bits) are usually stored in the data registers. On the other hand, the address of the operand is usually stored in an address register. Since the address sizes used by 68000 instructions can be either 16 or 24 bits, the address registers can only be used as 16- or 32-bit registers. While using the address registers as 32 bits, the 68000 discards the uppermost eight bits (bits 24 thru 31).

The 68000 status register consists of two bytes. These are a user byte and a system byte (Figure 5.2). The user byte includes the usual condition codes such as C, V, N, Z, and X. The meaning of C, V, N, and Z flags is obvious. However, the X-bit (extend bit) has a special meaning. The 68000 does not have any ADDC or SUBC instructions; rather, it has ADDX or

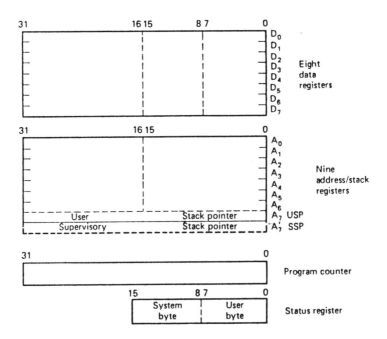

FIGURE 5.1 MC68000 programming model.

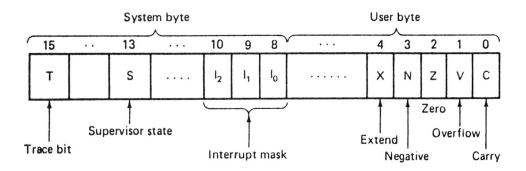

FIGURE 5.2 68000 status register.

SUBX instructions. For arithmetic operations, the carry flag C and the extend flag X are affected in an identical manner. This means that one can use ADDX or SUBX to include carries or borrows while adding or subtracting high-order long words in multiprecision additions or subtractions.

The system byte contains a 3-bit interrupt mask (I2, I1, I0), a supervisor flag (S), and a trace flag (T). The interrupt mask bits (I2, I1, I0) provide the status of the 68000 interrupt pins $\overline{IPL2}$, $\overline{IPL1}$, and $\overline{IPL0}$. I2 I1 I0 = 000 indicates no interrupt, while I2 I1 I0 = 111 means nonmaskable interrupt. The other combinations of I2, I1, and I0 provide the 68000 maskable interrupt levels. It should be pointed out that signals on $\overline{IPL2}$, $\overline{IPL1}$, and $\overline{IPL0}$ pins are inverted and then reflected on I2, I1, and I0, respectively. When the S-bit in SR is 1, the 68000 operates in the supervisor mode. When S = 0, the 68000 assumes user mode operation. When the TF (trace flag) is set to one, the 68000 generates an internal interrupt (trap) after execution of each instruction. A debugging routine can be written at the interrupt address vector to display registers and/or memory after execution of each instruction. This provides single-stepping facility. The 68000 can be placed in the single-step mode by setting the TF bit in SR to one by executing a logical privileged instruction such as ORI # $8000, SR in the supervisor mode.

5.3 68000 ADDRESSING STRUCTURE

The 68000 supports 8-bit bytes, 16-bit words, and 32-bit long words as shown in Figure 5.3. Byte addressing contains both odd and even

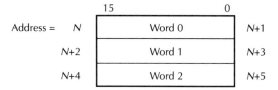

(a) 68000 Words Stored as Bytes (4 bytes).

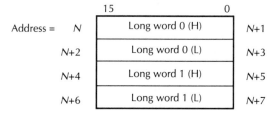

(b) 68000 Word Structure (3 Words).

15   0

Address =	N	Long word 0 (H)	N+1
	N+2	Long word 0 (L)	N+3
	N+4	Long word 1 (H)	N+5
	N+6	Long word 1 (L)	N+7

(c) 68000 Long Word Structure (2 long words).

For byte addressing (not shown in this figure), each byte can be uniquely addressed with bit 0 as the least significant bit and bit 7 as the most significant bit.

FIGURE 5.3 68000 addressing structure.

addresses (0, 1, 2, 3, 4, ...); word addressing includes only even addresses in increments of 2 (0, 2, 4, 6, ...); and long-word addressing contains only even addresses in increments of 4 (0, 4, 8, ...). As an example of the addressing structure, consider MOVE.L D0, $102050. If [D0] = $12345678, then after this MOVE, [$102050] = $12, [$102051] = $34, [$102052] = $56, and [$102053] = $78.

5.4 68000 INSTRUCTION FORMAT

The 68000 instructions are zero-operand, single-operand, or two-operand types. These instructions must always start on the word boundary and can occupy one to five words. The first word is the operation word and it specifies the type of operation, sizes of operands, and their addressing modes. The remaining words contain other information such as immediate data or extensions to the effective addressing mode specified in the operation word. Figure 5.4 shows the 68000 instruction format structure.

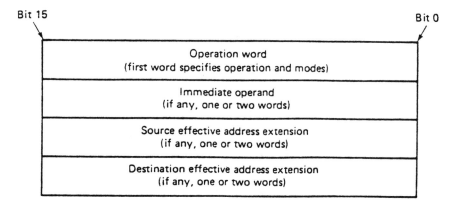

FIGURE 5.4   68000 instruction format.

The 68000 contains more than 18 different instruction formats. Table 5.2 provides a description of some of them.

As an example, consider the instruction format number 1. The two-bit operand-type field specifies the operand size (01 for byte, 11 for word, and 10 for long word). The 6-bit operand field is divided into a 3-bit addressing mode field and a 3-bit register field. In 68000, all registers cannot be used in all modes. This means that a specific mode allows only a particular set of registers. For example, with an 8-bit MOVE instruction, an address register cannot be used as destination. Because of this limitation, a register field of three bits is used to address 16 registers (D0-D7 and A0-A7).

Further, several two-address instructions require one of the operands in the register mode. For example, the ADD instruction (Format 2 of Table 5.2) provides a total of three combinations of source and destination. These are register-to-register, memory-to-register, and register-to-memory. The ADD instruction does not perform memory-to-memory addition.

A few 68000 instructions contain multiple formats. For example, the ROL (rotate left) instruction includes two different forms: one for the memory rotate and the other for the register rotate.

Format numbers 4 and 5 allow the instructions to use small constants. For example, format number 4 permits one to move an 8-bit 2's comple-

TABLE 5.2
Some 68000 Instruction Formats

Format number	Number of fields	Name of the field	Field size (in bits)	Instructions that use this format
1	4	OP code	2	MOVE
		Operand type	2	
		Operand 1	6	
		Operand 2	6	
2	4	OP code	4	ADD, AND, CMP, SUB
		Register	3	
		Mode	3	
		Operand	6	
3	5	OP code 1	4	MOVEP
		Register 1	3	
		Mode	3	
		OP code 1	3	
		Register	3	
4	4	OP code 1	4	MOVEQ
		Register	3	
		OP code 2	1	
		Data	8	
5	5	OP code 1	4	ADDQ, SUBQ
		Data (small constant)	3	
		OP code 2	1	
		Operand type	2	
		Operand	6	

ment number to a data register and convert it to a signed 32-bit number. The instruction MOVEQ $0A1,D5 will move the 8-bit immediate number $A1_{16}$ into low byte of D5 and sign-extends it so that D5 will finally contain $FFFFFFA1_{16}$.

Using format number 5, byte, word, or long word in a register or memory location can be incremented or decremented by as much as 7. The instruction ADDQ.B#5, D1 will increment the low byte of D1 by 5 without affecting the upper bytes of D1.

5.5 68000 ADDRESSING MODES

Table 5.3 lists the 14 addressing modes of the 68000. The addressing modes are divided into six basic groups. These are register direct, address register indirect, absolute, program counter relative, immediate, and implied.

As mentioned in the last section, the 68000 contains three types of instructions: zero-operand, single-operand, and two-operand. The zero-operand instructions have no operands in the operand field. A typical example is CLC (Clear carry) instruction. The single-operand instructions contain the effective address, EA, in the operand field. The EAs of these instructions are calculated by the 68000 using the addressing mode specified for this operand. For two-operand instructions, one of the operands usually contains the EA and the operand is usually a register or memory location. The EAs in these instructions are calculated by the 68000 based on the addressing modes used for the EAs. Some two-operand instructions have EA in both operands. This means that the operands in these instructions can use two different addressing modes.

As mentioned before, the 68000 address registers do not support byte-sized operands. Therefore, when an address register is used as a source operand, either the low-order word or the entire long-word operand is used depending on the operation size. On the other hand, when an address register is used as the destination operand, the entire register is affected regardless of the operation size. If the operation size is a word, and the destination operand is an address register, then the 68000 performs the 16-bit operation, places the result in the low 16 bits of the address register, and then sign-extends the address register to 32 bits. An example is MOVEA.W #$8050,A5. In this case, the source operand is 16-bit immediate datum 8050_{16} which is moved to the low 16 bits of A5, and the result is then sign-extended to 32 bits so that $[A5] = FFFF8050_{16}$. Data registers support data operands of byte, word, and long-word size.

5.5.1 REGISTER DIRECT ADDRESSING

In this mode, the eight data registers (D0-D7) or seven address registers (A0-A6) contain the data operand. For example, consider ADD $005000, D0. The destination operand of this instruction is in data register direct mode.

TABLE 5.3
68000 Addressing Modes

Mode	Generation	Assembler syntax
1. Register direct addressing		
Data register direct	EA = Dn	Dn
Address register direct	EA = An	An
2. Address register indirect addressing		
Register indirect	EA = (An)	(An)
Postincrement register indirect	EA = (An), An ← An + N	(An)+
Predecrement register indirect	An ← An – N, EA = (An)	–(An)
Register indirect with offset	EA = (An) + d16	d(An)
Indexed register indirect with offset	EA = (An) + (Ri) + d8	d(An, Ri)
3. Absolute data addressing		
Absolute short	EA = (Next word)	xxxx
Absolute long	EA = (Next two words)	xxxxxxxx
4. Program counter relative addressing		
Relative with offset	EA = (PC) + d16	d
Relative with index and offset	EA = (PC) + (Ri) + d8	d(Ri)
5. Immediate data addressing		
Immediate	DATA = Next word(s)	#xxxx
Quick immediate	Inherent data	#xx
6. Implied addressing		
Implied register	EA = SR, USP, SP, PC	

Notes:

EA = effective address
An = address register
Dn = data register,
Ri = address or data register used as index register
SR = status register
PC = program counter
USP = user stack pointer

SP = active system stack pointer (user or supervisor)
d8 = 8-bit offset (displacement)
d16 = 16-bit offset (displacement)
N = 1 for byte, 2 for words, and 4 for long words
( ) = contents of
← = replaces

Now, if $[005000] = 0002_{16}$, $[D0] = 0003_{16}$, then after execution of ADD \$005000, D0 the contents of D0 = 0002 + 0003 = 0005. Note that in the above instruction, the \$ symbol is used to represent hexadecimal numbers by Motorola. Also, note that instructions using address registers are not available for byte operations. In addition, in the 68000, the first operand of a two-operand instruction is the source and the second operand is the destination. Recall that in the 8086, the first operand is the destination while the second operand is the source.

5.5.2 ADDRESS REGISTER INDIRECT ADDRESSING

There are five different types of address register indirect mode. In the register indirect mode, an address register contains the effective address. For example, consider CLR (A1). If [A1] = \$003000, then after execution of CLR (A1), the contents of memory location \$003000 will be cleared to zero.

The postincrement address register indirect mode increments an address register by 1 for byte, 2 for word, and 4 for long word after it is used. For example, consider CLR.L (A0) + If $[A0] = 005000_{16}$, then after execution of CLR.L (A0) +, the contents of locations 005000_{16} through 005003_{16} are cleared to zero and [A0] = 005004. The postincrement mode is typically used with memory arrays stored from LOW to HIGH memory locations. For example, in order to clear 1000_{16} words starting at memory location 003000_{16}, the following instruction sequence can be used:

```
           MOV.W #$1000,D0      ; Load length of data
                                  into D0
           MOVEA.L#$3000,A0     ; Load starting address
                                  into A0
REPEAT     CLR.W (A0)+          ; Clear a location
                                  pointed to by A0 and
                                  increment A0 by 2
           SUBQ#1,D0            ; Decrement D0 by 1
           BNE REPEAT           ; Branch to REPEAT if Z
                                  = 0, else go to next
                                  instruction

           —
           —
           —
```

Note that in the above, CLR.W (A0)+ automatically points to the next location by incrementing A0 by 2 after clearing a memory location.

The predecrement address register indirect mode, on the other hand, decrements an address register by 1 for byte, 2 for word, and 4 for long word before using a register. For example, consider CLR.W – (A0). If [A0] = 002004, then after execution of CLR.W – (A0), the content of A0 is first decremented by 2; that is, [A0] = 002002_{16}, and the 16-bit contents of memory location 002002 are then cleared to zero.

The predecrement mode is used with arrays stored from HIGH to LOW memory locations. For example, in order to clear 1000_{16} words starting at memory location 4000_{16} and below, the following instruction sequence can be used:

```
          MOVE.W  #$1000,D0    ; Load length of data into
                                 D0
          MOVEA.L #$4002, A0   ; Load starting address
                                 plus 2 into A0
REPEAT    CLR.W - (A0)         ; Decrement A0 by 2 and
                                 clear the memory location
                                 addressed by A0
          SUBQ#1, D0           ; Decrement D0 by one
          BNE REPEAT           ; If Z = 0, branch to
                                 REPEAT;
          –                    ; otherwise, go to next
          –                      instruction
          –
```

In the above, CLR.W – (A0) first decrements A0 by 2 and then clears the location. Since the starting address is 004000_{16}, A0 must initially be initialized with 004002_{16}.

It should be pointed out that the predecrement and postincrement modes can be combined in a single instruction. A typical example is MOVE.W(A5) +, –(A3). The two other address register modes provide accessing of the tables by allowing offsets and indices to be included to an indirect address pointer. The address register indirect with offset mode determines the effective address by adding a 16-bit signed integer to the contents of an address register. For example, consider MOVE.W $10 (A5), D3 in which the source operand is in address register indirect with offset mode. If [A5] = 00002000_{16}, $[002010]_{16} = 0014_{16}$, then after execution of MOVE.W $10(A5), D3, register D3 will contain 0014_{16}.

The indexed register indirect with offset determines the effective address by adding an 8-bit signed integer and the contents of a register (data or address register) to the contents of an address (base) register. This mode is usually used when the offset from the base address register needs to be varied during program execution. The size of the index register can be a 16-bit integer or a 32-bit value.

As an example, consider MOVE.W $10(A4, D3.W), D4 in which the source is in the indexed register indirect with offset mode. Note that in this instruction A4 is the base register and D3.W is the 16-bit index register (sign extended to 32 bits). This register can be specified as 32 bits by using D3.L in the instruction, and 10_{16} is the 8-bit offset which is sign-extended to 32 bits. If $[A4] = 00003000_{16}$, $[D3] = 0200_{16}$, $[003210_{16}] = 0024_{16}$, then the above MOVE instruction will load 0024_{16} into low 16 bits of register D4.

The address register indirect with offset mode can be used to access a single table where the offset (maximum 16 bits) can be the starting address of the table (fixed number) and the address register can hold the index number in the table to be accessed. Note that the starting address, plus the index number, provides the address of the element to be accessed in the table. For example, consider MOVE.W $3400 (A5), D1. If A5 contains 04, then this move instruction transfers the contents of 3404 (i.e., the fifth element, 0 being the first element) into low 16 bits of D1. The indexed register indirect with offset, on the other hand, can be used to access multiple tables, where the offset (maximum 8 bits) can be the element number to be accessed. The address register pointer can be used to hold the starting address of the table containing the lowest starting address, and the index register can be used to hold the difference between the starting address of the table being accessed and the table with the lowest starting address. For example, consider three tables with Table 1 starting at 002000_{16}, Table 2 at 003000_{16}, and Table 3 at 004000_{16}. Now, in order to transfer element 7 (0 being the first element) in Table 2 to the low 16 bits of register D0, the instruction MOVE.W$06 (A2, D1.W), D0 can be used, where $[A2]$ = starting address of the table, with the lowest address = 002000_{16} in this case and $[D1]_{low\ 16\ bits}$ = difference between the starting address of the table being accessed and the starting address of the table, with the lowest address = $003000_{16} - 002000_{16} = 1000_{16}$. Therefore, the above MOVE instruction will transfer the contents of address 003006_{16} (seventh element in Table 2) to register D0.

5.5.3 ABSOLUTE ADDRESSING

In this mode, the effective address is part of the instruction. The 68000 has two absolute addressing modes: absolute short addressing in which a 16-bit address is used (the address is sign-extended to 32 bits before use) and absolute long addressing in which a 24-bit address is used. For example, consider ADD $2000, D2 as an example of absolute short mode. If $[\$2000] = 0012_{16}$, $[D2] = 0010_{16}$, then after execution of ADD $2000, D2, the address $2000 is sign-extended to 32 bits, whose low 24 bits are used as the address, and register D2 will therefore contain 0022_{16}. The absolute long addressing is used when the address size is more than 16 bits. For example, MOVE.W $240000, D5 loads the 16-bit contents of location $240000 into low 16 bits of D5. The absolute short mode includes an address ADDR in the range $0 \leq ADDR \leq \$7FFF$ or $\$FF8000 \leq ADDR \leq \$FFFFFF$. Note that a single instruction may use both short and long absolute modes, depending on whether the source or destination address is less than, equal to, or greater than the 16-bit address. A typical example is MOVE.W $500002, $1000.

5.5.4 PROGRAM COUNTER RELATIVE ADDRESSING

The 68000 has two program counter relative addressing modes: relative with offset, and relative with index and offset. In relative with offset, the effective address is obtained by adding the contents of the current PC with a sign-extended 16-bit displacement. This mode can be used when the displacement needs to be fixed during program execution. Typical branch instructions such as BEQ, BRA, and BLE use relative mode with offset. This mode can also be used by some other instructions. For example, consider ADD*+$30, D5 in which the source operand is relative to the offset mode. Note that typical assemblers use the symbol * to indicate offset. Now suppose that the current PC contents are 002000_{16}, the contents of 002030_{16} are 0005_{16}, and the low 16 bits of D5 contain 0010_{16}; after execution of this ADD instruction, D5 will contain 0015_{16}.

In relative with index and offset, the effective address is obtained by adding the contents of the current PC, a signed 8-bit displacement (sign-extended to 32 bits), and the contents of an index register (address or data register). The size of the index register can be 16 or 32 bits wide. For example, consider ADD.W $4 (PC, D0.W), D2. If $[D2] = 00000012_{16}$, $[PC] = 002000_{16}$, $[D0]_{low\ 16\ bits} = 0010_{16}$, and $[002014] = 0002_{16}$, then after this ADD, $[D2]_{low\ 16\ bits} = 0014_{16}$. This mode is used when the displacement needs to be changed during program execution.

5.5.5 IMMEDIATE DATA ADDRESSING MODE

There are two immediate modes available with the 68000. These are the immediate and quick immediate modes. In the immediate mode, the operand data are constant data, which is part of the instruction. For example, consider ADD #$0005, D0. If $[D0] = 0002_{16}$, then after this ADD instruction, $[D0] = 0002_{16} + 0005_{16} = 0007_{16}$. Note that the # symbol is used by Motorola to indicate the immediate mode.

The quick immediate mode allows one to increment or decrement a register by a number from 0 to 7. For example, ADDQ #1, D0 increments the contents of D0 by 1. Note that the data is inherent in the op code with the op code length of one word (16-bit). Data 0 to 7 are represented by three bits in the op code.

5.5.6 IMPLIED ADDRESSING

There are two types of implied addressing modes: implicit and explicit.

The instructions using the implicit mode do not require any operand, and registers such as PC, SP, or SR are implicitly referenced in these instructions. For example, RTE returns from an exception routine to the main program by using implicitly the PC and SR. The JMP add instruction, on the other hand, allows loading a value into the PC, although the PC is not explicitly defined in the instruction.

All 68000 addressing modes of Table 5.3 can further be divided into four functional categories as follows:

- Data Addressing Mode. An addressing mode is said to be a data addressing mode if it references data objects. For example, all 68000 addressing modes, except the address register direct mode, fall into this category.
- Memory Addressing Mode. An addressing mode that is capable of accessing a data item stored in the memory is classified as memory addressing mode. For example, the data and address register direct addressing modes cannot satisfy this definition.
- Control Addressing Mode. This refers to an addressing mode that has the ability to access a data item stored in the memory without the need to specify its size. For example, all 68000 addressing modes except the following are classified as control addressing modes:

  - Data register direct
  - Address register direct
  - Address register indirect with postincrement
  - Address register indirect with predecrement
  - Immediate

- Alterable Addressing Mode. If the effective address of an addressing mode is written into, then that mode is called alterable addressing mode. For example, the immediate and the program counter relative addressing modes will not satisfy this definition.

The addressing modes are classified into the four functional categories as shown in Figure 5.5.

	Addressing Categories			
Addressing Mode	Data	Memory	Control	Alterable
Data register direct	X	-	-	X
Address register direct	-	-	-	X
Address register indirect	X	X	X	X
Address register indirect with postincrement	X	X	-	X
Address register indirect with predecrement	X	X	-	X
Address register indirect with displacement	X	X	X	X
Address register indirect with index	X	X	X	X
Absolute short	X	X	X	X
Absolute long	X	X	X	X
Program counter with displacement	X	X	X	-
Program counter with index	X	X	X	-
Immediate	X	X	-	-

FIGURE 5.5 68000 addressing-functional categories.

5.6 68000 INSTRUCTION SET

The 68000 instruction set contains 56 basic instructions. Table 5.4 lists them in alphabetical order. Table 5.5 lists those affecting the condition codes. The repertoire is very versatile and offers an efficient means to handle high-level language structures (such as arrays and linked lists). Note that in order to identify the operand size of an instruction, the following is placed after a 68000 mnemonic:.B for byte, .W or none for word, .L for long word. For example:

```
ADD.B           D0, D1 ; [D1]8  ← [D8]8  + [D1]8
ADD.W or ADD    D0, D1 ; [D1]16 ← [D0]16 + [D1]16
ADD.L           D0, D1 ; [D1]32 ← [D0]32 + [D1]32
```

TABLE 5.4
68000 Instruction Set

Instruction	Size	Length (words)	Operation
ABCD – (Ay), –(Ax)	B	1	–[Ay]10 + – [Ax]10 + X → [Ax]
ABCD Dy, Dx	B	1	[Dy]10 + [Dx]10 + X → Dx
ADD (EA), (EA)	B, W, L	1	[EA] + [EA] → EA
ADDA (EA), An	W, L	1	[EA] + An → An
ADDI #data, (EA)	B, W, L	2 for B, W / 3 for L	data + [EA] → EA
ADDQ #data, (EA)	B, W, L	1	data + [EA] → EA
ADDX – (Ay), –(Ax)	B, W, L	1	–[Ay] + –[Ax] + X → [Ax]
ADDX Dy, Dx	B, W, L	1	Dy + Dx + X → Dx
AND (EA), (EA)	B, W, L	1	[EA] ∧ [EA] → EA
ANDI #data, (EA)	B, W, L	2 for B, W / 3 for L	data ∧ [EA] → EA
ANDI #data8, CCR	B	2	data8 ∧ [CCR]→ CCR
ANDI #data16, SR	W	2	data16 ∧ [SR] → SR
ASL Dx, Dy	B, W, L	1	
ASL #data, Dy	B, W, L	1	
ASL (EA)	B, W, L	1	
ASR Dx, Dy	B, W, L	1	
ASR#data, Dy	B, W, L	1	

ASL Dx, Dy operation diagram:

```
C ←─────────────── Dy ──────────────── ← 0
X ←
      number of shifts determined by [Dx]
```

ASL #data, Dy operation diagram:

```
C ←─────────────── Dy ──────────────── ← 0
X ←
      number of shifts determined
            by # data
```

ASL (EA) operation diagram:

```
C ←─────────────── [EA] ──────────────── ← 0
X ←
            shift once
```

ASR Dx, Dy operation diagram:

```
      ─────────────── Dy ───────────────  → C
                                          → X
      number of shifts determined
            by [Dx]
```

ASR#data, Dy operation diagram:

```
      ─────────────── Dy ───────────────  → C
                                          → X
      number of shifts determined
         by immediate data
```

TABLE 5.4 (continued)
68000 Instruction Set

Instruction	Size	Length (words)	Operation
ASR (EA)	B, W, L	1	

shift once

Instruction	Size	Length (words)	Operation
BCC d	B, W	1 for B 2 for W	Branch to PC + d if carry = 0; else next instruction
BCHG Dn, (EA)	B, L	1	[bit of [EA], specified by Dn]' → Z [bit of [EA] specified by Dn]' → bit of [EA]
BCHG #data, (EA)	B, L	2	Same as BCHG Dn, [EA] except bit number is specified by immediate data
BCLR Dn (EA)	B, L	1	[bit of [EA]]' → Z 0 → bit of [EA] specified by Dn
BCLR #data, (EA)	B, L	2	Same as BCLR Dn, [EA] except the bit is specified by immediate data
BCS d	B, W	1 for B 2 for W	Branch to PC + d if carry = 1; else next instruction
BEQ d	B, W	1 for B 2 for W	Branch to PC + d if Z = 1; else next instruction
BGE d	B, W	1 for B 2 for W	Branch to PC + d if greater than or equal; else next instruction
BGT d	B, W	1 for B 2 for W	Branch to PC + d if greater than; else next instruction
BHI d	B, W	1 for B 2 for W	Branch to PC + d if higher; else next instruction
BLE d	B, W	1 for B 2 for W	Branch to PC + d if less or equal; else next instruction
BLS d	B, W	1 for B 2 for W	Branch to PC + d if low or same; else next instruction
BLT d	B, W	1 for B 2 for W	Branch to PC + d if less than; else next instruction
BMI d	B, W	1 for B 2 for W	Branch to PC + d if N = 1; else next instruction
BNE d	B, W	1 for B 2 for W	Branch to PC + d if Z = 0; else next instruction
BPL d	B, W	1 for B 2 for W	Branch to PC + d if N = 0; else next instruction
BRA d	B, W	1 for B 2 for W	Branch always to PC + d

TABLE 5.4 (continued)
68000 Instruction Set

Instruction	Size	Length (words)	Operation
BSET Dn (EA)	B, L	1	[bit of [EA]]' → Z 1 → bit of [EA] specified by Dn
BSET #data, (EA)	B, L	2	Same as BSET Dn, [EA] except the bit is specified by immediate data
BSR d	B, W	1 for B 2 for W	PC → –[SP] PC + d → PC
BTST Dn, (EA)	B, L	1	[bit of [EA] specified by Dn]' → Z
BTST #data, (EA)	B, L	2 2 for W	Same as BTST Dn, [EA] except the bit is specified by data
BVC d	B, W	1 for B 2 for W	Branch to PC + d if V = 0; else next instruction
BVS d	B, W,	1 for B 2 for W	Branch to PC + d if V = 1; else next instruction
CHK (EA), Dn	W	1	If Dn < 0 or Dn > [EA], then trap
CLR (EA)	B, W, L	1	0 → EA
CMP (EA), Dn	B, W, L	1	Dn – [EA] → Affect all condition codes except X
CMP (EA), An	W, L	1	An – [EA] → Affect all condition codes except X
CMPI #data, (EA)	B, W, L	2 for B, W 3 for L	[EA] – data → Affect all flags except X-bit
CMPM (Ay) +, (Ax)+	B, W, L	1	[Ax]+ – [Ay]+ → Affect all flags except X; update Ax and Ay
DBCC Dn, d	W	2	If condition false, i.e., C = 1, then Dn – 1 → Dn; if Dn ≠ –1, then PC + d → PC; else PC + 2 → PC
DBCS Dn, d	W	2	Same as DBCC except condition is C = 1
DBEQ Dn, d	W	2	Same as DBCC except condition is Z = 1
DBF Dn, d	W	2	Same as DBCC except condition is always false
DBGE Dn, d	W	2	Same as DBCC except condition is greater or equal
DBGT Gn, d	W	2	Same as DBCC except condition is greater than
DBHI Dn, d	W	2	Same as DBCC except condition is high
DBLE Dn, d	W	2	Same as DBCC except condition is less than or equal
DBLS Dn, d	W	2	Same as DBCC except condition is low or same

TABLE 5.4 (continued)
68000 Instruction Set

Instruction	Size	Length (words)	Operation
DBLT Dn, d	W	2	Same as DBCC except condition is less than
DBMI Dn, d	W	2	Same as DBCC except condition is N = 1
DBNE Dn, d	W	2	Same as DBCC except condition Z = 0
DBPL Dn, d	W	2	Same as DBCC except condition N = 1
DBT Dn, d	W	2	Same as DBCC except is always true
DBVC Dn, d	W	2	Same as DBCC except condition is V = 0
DBVS Dn, d	W	2	Same as DBCC except condition is V = 1
DIVS (EA), Dn	W	1	Signed division $[Dn]32/[EA]16 \rightarrow$ $[Dn]0\text{-}15$ = remainder $[Dn]16\text{-}31$ = quotient
DIVU (EA), Dn	W	1	Same as DIVS except division is unsigned
EOR Dn, (EA)	B, W, L	1	$Dn \oplus [EA] \rightarrow EA$
EORI #data, (EA)	B, W, L	3 for L 2 for B, W	$data \oplus [EA] \rightarrow EA$
EORI #d8, CCR	B	2	$d8 \oplus CCR \rightarrow CCR$
EORI #d16, SR	W	2	$d16 \oplus SR \rightarrow SR$
EXG Rx, Ry	L	1	$Rx \acute{\leftrightarrow} Ry$
EXT Dn	W, L	1	Extend sign bit of Dn from 8-bit to 16-bit or from 16-bit to 32-bit depending on whether the operand size is B or W
JMP (EA)	Unsized	1	$[EA] \rightarrow PC$ Unconditional jump using address in operand
JSR (EA)	Unsized	1	$PC \rightarrow -[SP]; [EA] \rightarrow PC$ Jump to subroutine using address in operand
LEA (EA), An	L	1	$[EA] \rightarrow An$
LINK An, # –d	Unsized	2	$An \leftarrow -[SP]; SP \rightarrow An; SP - d \rightarrow SP$
LSL Dx, Dy	B, W, L	1	
LSL #data, Dy	B, W, L	1	Same as LSL Dx, Dy except immediate data specify the number of shifts from 0 to 7
LSL (EA)	B, W, L	1	Same as LSL Dx, Dy except left shift is performed only once

TABLE 5.4 (continued)
68000 Instruction Set

Instruction	Size	Length (words)	Operation
LSR Dx, Dy	B, W, L	1	
LSR #data, Dy	B, W, L	1	Same as LSR except immediate data specifies the number of shifts from 0 to 7
LSR (EA)	B, W, L	1	Same as LSR, Dx, Dy except the right shift is performed once only
MOVE (EA), (EA)	B, W, L	1	$[EA]_{source} \rightarrow [EA]_{destination}$
MOVE (EA), CCR	W	1	$[EA] \rightarrow CCR$
MOVE (EA), SR	W	1	If S = 1, then $[EA] \rightarrow SR$; else TRAP
MOVE SR, (EA)	W	1	$SR \rightarrow [EA]$
MOVE An, USP	L	1	If S = 1, then An $\rightarrow$ USP; else TRAP
MOVE USP, An	W, L	1	$[USP] \rightarrow$ An
MOVEM register list, (EA)	W, L	2	Register list $\rightarrow [EA]$
MOVEM (EA), register list	W, L	2	$[EA] \rightarrow$ register list
MOVEP Dx, d (Ay)	W, L	2	Dx $\rightarrow$ d[Ay]
MOVEP d (Ay), Dx	W, L	2	d[Ay] $\rightarrow$ Dx
MOVEQ #d8, Dn	L	1	d8 sign extended to 32-bit $\rightarrow$ Dn
MULS (EA)16, (Dn)16	W	1	Signed 16 × 16 multiplication $[EA]16$ *$[Dn]16 \rightarrow [Dn]32$
MULU (EA)16, (Dn)16	W	1	Unsigned 16 × 16 multiplication $[EA]16$ *$[Dn]16 \rightarrow [Dn]32$
NBCD (EA)	B	1	$0 - [EA]10 - X \rightarrow EA$
NEG (EA)	B, W, L	1	$0 - [EA] \rightarrow EA$
NEGX (EA)	B, W, L	1	$0 - [EA] - X \rightarrow EA$
NOP	Unsized	1	No operation
NOT (EA)	B, W, L	1	$[EA]' \rightarrow EA$
OR (EA), (EA)	B, W, L	1	$[EA] \vee [EA] \rightarrow EA$
ORI #data, (EA)	B, W, L	2 for B, W 3 for L	data $\vee [EA] \rightarrow EA$
ORI #d8, CCR	B	2	d8 $\vee$ CCR $\rightarrow$ CCR

TABLE 5.4 (continued)
68000 Instruction Set

Instruction	Size	Length (words)	Operation
ORI #d16, SR	W	2	If S = 1, then d16 ∨ SR → SR; else TRAP
PEA (EA)	L	1	[EA]16 sign extend to 32 bits → −[SP]
RESET	Unsized	1	If S = 1, then assert RESET line; else TRAP
ROL Dx, Dy	B, W, L	1	
ROL #data, Dy	B, W, L	1	Same as ROL Dx, Dy except immediate data specifies number of times to be rotated from 0 to 7
ROL (EA)	B, W, L	1	Same as ROL Dx, Dy except [EA] is rotated once
ROR Dx,Dy	B, W, L	1	
ROR #data, Dy	B, W, L	1	Same as ROR Dx, Dy except the number of rotates is specified by immediate data from 0 to 7
ROR (EA)	B, W, L	1	Same as ROR Dx, Dy except [EA] is rotated once
ROXL Dx, Dy	B, W, L	1	
ROXL #data, Dy	B, W, L	1	Same as ROXL Dx, Dy except immediate data specifies number of rotates from 0 to 7
ROXL (EA)	B, W, L	1	Same as ROXL Dx, Dy except [EA] is rotated once

TABLE 5.4 (continued)
68000 Instruction Set

Instruction	Size	Length (words)	Operation
ROXR Dx, Dy	B, W, L	1	
ROXR #data, Dy	B, W, L	1	Same as ROXR Dx, Dy except immediate data specifies number of rotates from 0 to 7
ROXR (EA)	B, W, L	1	Same as ROXR Dx, Dy except [EA] is rotated once
RTE	Unsized	1	If S = 1, then [SP]+ → SR; [SP]+ → PC, else TRAP
RTR	Unsized	1	[SP] +→ CC; [SP] +→ PC
RTS	Unsized	1	[SP] +→ PC
SBCD –(Ay), –(Ax)	B	1	–(Ax)10 — (Ay)10 – X → (Ax)
SBCD Dy, Dx	B	1	[Dx]10 – [Dy]10 – X → Dx
SCC (EA)	B	1	If C = 0, then 1s → [EA] else 0s → [EA]
SCS (EA)	B	1	Same as SCC except the condition is C = 1
SEQ (EA)	B	1	Same as SCC except if Z = 1
SF (EA)	B	1	Same as SCC except condition is always false
SGE (EA)	B	1	Same as SCC except if greater or equal
SGT (EA)	B	1	Same as SCC except if greater than
SHI (EA)	B	1	Same as SCC except if high
SLE (EA)	B	1	Same as SCC except if less or equal
SLS (EA)	B	1	Same as SCC except if low or same
SLT (EA)	B	1	Same as SCC except if less than
SMI (EA)	B	1	Same as SCC except if N = 1
SNE (EA)	B	1	Same as SCC except if Z = 0
SPL (EA)	B	1	Same as SCC except if N = 0
ST (EA)	B	1	Same as SCC except condition always true
STOP #data	Unsized	2	If S = 1, then data → SR and stop; TRAP if executed in user mode
SUB (EA), (EA)	B, W, L	1	[EA] – [EA] → EA
SUBA (EA), An	W, L	1	An – [EA] → An

TABLE 5.4 (continued)
68000 Instruction Set

Instruction	Size	Length (words)	Operation
SUBI #data, (EA)	B, W, L	2 for B,W 3 for L	[EA] – data → EA
SUBQ #data, (EA)	B, W, L	1	[EA] – data → EA
SUBX – (Ay), – (Ax)	B, W, L	1	–[Ax] – –[Ay] – X → [Ax]
SUBX Dy, Dx	B, W, L	1	Dx – Dy – X → Dx
SVC (EA)	B	1	Same as SCC except if V = 0
SVS (EA)	B	1	Same as SCC except if V = 1
SWAP Dn	W	1	Dn [31:16] ↔ Dn [15:0]
TAS (EA)	B	1	[EA] tested; N and Z are affected accordingly; 1 → bit 7 of [EA]
TRAP #vector	Unsized	1	PC → –[SSP], SR → –[SSP], (vector) → PC; 16 TRAP vectors are available
TRAPV	Unsized	1	If V = 1, then TRAP
TST (EA)	B, W, L	1	[EA] – 0 → condition codes affected; no result provided
UNLK An	Unsized	1	An → SP; [SP]+ → An

All 68000 instructions may be classified into eight groups, as follows:

i)   Data movement instructions

ii) Arithmetic instructions

iii) Logical instructions

iv) Shift and rotate instructions

v)   Bit manipulation instructions

vi) Binary-coded decimal instructions

vii) Program control instructions

viii) System control instructions

5.6.1 DATA MOVEMENT INSTRUCTIONS

These instructions allow data transfers from register to register, register to memory, memory to register, and memory to memory. In addition,

TABLE 5.5
68000 Instructions Affecting the Condition Codes

Instruction	X	N	Z	V	C
ABCD	+	U	+	U	—
ADD, ADDI, ADDQ, ADDX	+	+	+	+	+
AND, ANDI	—	+	+	0	0
ASL, ASR	+	+	+	+	+
BCHG, BCLR, BSET, BTST	—	—	+	—	—
CHK	—	+	U	U	U
CLR	—	0	1	0	0
CMP CMPA, CMPI, CMPM	—	+	+	+	+
DIVS, DIVU	—	+	+	+	0
EOR, EORI	—	+	+	0	0
EXT	—	+	+	0	0
LSL, LSR	+	+	+	0	+
MOVE (EA), (EA)	—	+	+	0	0
MOVE TO CC	+	+	+	+	+
MOVE TO SR	+	+	+	+	+
MOVEQ	—	+	+	0	0
MULS, MULU	—	+	+	0	0
NBCD	+	U	+	U	+
NEG, NEGX	+	+	+	+	+
NOT, OR, ORI	—	+	+	0	0
ROL, ROR	—	+	+	0	+
ROXL, ROXR	+	+	+	0	+
RTE, RTR	+	+	+	+	+
SBCD	+	U	+	U	+
STOP	+	+	+	+	+
SUB, SUBI, SUBQ, SUBX	+	+	+	+	+
SWAP	—	+	+	0	0
TAS	—	+	+	0	0
TST	—	+	+	0	0

Note: +, affected; — , not affected; U, undefined.

there are also special data movement instructions such as MOVEM (Move multiple registers). Typically, byte, word, or long-word data can be transferred. Table 5.6 lists the 68000 data movement instructions.

TABLE 5.6
68000 Data Movement Instructions

Instruction	Size	Comment
EXG Rx, Ry	L	Exchange the contents of two registers; Rx or Ry can be any address or data register; no flags are affected
LEA (EA), An	L	The effective address [EA] is calculated using the particular addressing mode used and then loaded into the address register; [EA] specifies the actual data to be loaded into An
LINK An, #-displacement	Unsized	The current contents of the specified address register are pushed onto the stack; after the push, the address register is loaded from the updated SP; finally, the 16-bit sign-extended displacement is added to the SP; a negative displacement is specified to allocate stack
MOVE (EA), (EA)	B, W, L	[EA]s are calculated by the 68000 using the specific addressing mode used; [EA]s can be register or memory location; therefore, data transfer can take place between registers, between a register and a memory location, and between different memory locations; flags are affected; for byte-size operation, address register direct is not allowed; An is not allowed in the destination [EA]; the source [EA] can be An for word or long-word transfers
MOVEM reg list, (EA) or (EA), reg list	W, L	Specified registers are transferred to or from consecutive memory locations starting at the location specified by the effective address
MOVEP Dn, d (Ay) or d (Ay), Dn	W, L	Two [W] or four [L] bytes of data are transferred between a data register and alternate bytes of memory,

TABLE 5.6 (continued)
68000 Data Movement Instructions

Instruction	Size	Comment
MOVEP Dn, d (Ay) or d (Ay), Dn (continued)		starting at the location specified and incrementing by 2; the high-order byte of data is transferred first, and the low-order byte is transferred last This instruction has the address register indirect with displacement-only mode
MOVEQ #data, Dn	L	This instruction moves the 8-bit inherent data into the specified data register; the data are then sign-extended to 32 bits
PEA (EA)	L	Computes an effective address and then pushes the 32-bit address onto the stack
SWAP Dn	W	Exchanges 16-bit halves of a data register
UNLK An	Unsized	An → SP; [SP] +→ An

- [EA] in LEA [EA], An can use all addressing modes except Dn, An, [An] +, –[An], and immediate.
- Destination [EA] in MOVE [EA], [EA]can use all modes except An, relative, and immediate.
- Source [EA] in MOVE [EA], [EA] can use all modes.
- Destination [EA] in MOVEM reg list, [EA] can use all modes except Dn, An, [An]+, relative, and immediate. Source [EA] in MOVEM [EA], reg list can use all modes except Dn, An, –[An], and immediate.
- [EA] in PEA [EA]) can use all modes except Dn, An, [An]+, –[An], and immediate.

5.6.1.a MOVE Instructions

The format for the basic MOVE instruction is MOVE.S (EA), (EA), where S = .L, .W, or .B. (EA) can be a register or memory location depending on the addressing mode used. Consider MOVE.B D2, D0 which uses a data register direct mode for both the source and destination.

Now if $[D2] = 03_{16}$, $[D0] = 01_{16}$, then after execution of this MOVE instruction $[D2] = 03_{16}$ and $[D0] = 03_{16}$.

There are several variations of the MOVE instruction. For example, MOVE.W CCR, (EA) moves the content of the low-order byte of the SR, i.e., CCR, to the low-order byte of the destination operand, and the upper byte of SR is considered as zero. The source operand is a word. Similarly, MOVE.W (EA), CCR moves an 8-bit immediate number or low-order 8-bit data from a memory location or register into the condition code register; the upper byte is ignored. The source operand is a word. Data can also be transferred between (EA) and SR or USP using the following instructions:

```
MOVE.W (EA),  SR
MOVE.W SR,  (EA)
MOVE.L USP,  An
MOVE.L An,  USP
```

MOVEA.W or .L (EA), An can be used to load an address into an address register. Word size source operands are sign-extended to 32 bits. Note that (EA) is obtained using an addressing mode. As an example, MOVEA.W #$8000, A0 moves the 16-bit word 8000_{16} into the low 16 bits of A0 and then sign-extends 8000_{16} to the 32-bit number $FFFF8000_{16}$.

Note that sign extension means extending bit 15 of 8000_{16} from bit 16 through bit 31. As mentioned, sign extension is required when an arithmetic operation between two signed binary numbers of different sizes is performed. (EA) in MOVEA can use all addressing modes. MOVEM instruction can be used to PUSH or POP multiple registers to or from the stack. For example, MOVEM.L D0-D7/A0-A6, – (SP) saves the contents of all of the 8 data registers and 7 address registers in the stack. This instruction stores address registers in the order A6-A0 first, followed by data registers in the order D7-D0, regardless of the order in the list. MOVEM.L (SP)+, D0-D7/A0-A6 restores the contents of the registers in the order D0-D7,A0-A6 regardless of the order in the list. MOVEM instruction can also be used to save a set of registers in memory. In addition to the above predecrement and postincrement modes for the effective address, MOVEM instruction allows all the control modes. If the effective address is in one of the control modes, such as absolute short, then the registers are transferred starting at the specified address and up through higher addresses. The order of transfer is from D0 to D7 and then from A0 to A7. For example, MOVEM.W A4/D1/D3/A0-A2, $8000 transfers the low 16-bit contents of D1, D3, A0, A1, A2, and A4 to locations $8000, $8002, $8004, $8006, $8008, and $800A, respectively.

The MOVEQ.L #d8, Dn moves the immediate 8-bit data into the low byte of Dn. The 8-bit data are then sign-extended to 32 bits. This is a one-word instruction. For example, MOVEQ.L #$FF, D0 moves $FFFFFFFF into D0. In order to transfer data between the 68000 data registers and 6800 (8-bit) peripherals, the MOVEP instruction can be used. This instruction transfers two to four bytes of data between a data register and alternate byte locations in memory, starting at the location specified in increments of 2.

Register indirect with displacement is the only addressing mode used with this instruction. If the address is even, all the transfers are made on the high-order half of the data bus. The high-order byte from the register is transferred first and the low-order byte is transferred last. For example, consider MOVEP.L $0050 (A0), D0. If $[A0] = 00003000_{16}$, $[003050] = 01_{16}$, $[003052] = 03_{16}$, $[003054] = 02_{16}$, $[003056] = 04_{16}$, then after the execution of the above MOVEP instruction, D0 will contain 01030204_{16}.

5.6.1.b EXG and SWAP Instructions

The EXG Rx, Ry instruction exchanges the 32-bit contents of Rx with that of the Ry. The exchange is between two data registers, two address registers, or between an address and a data register. The EXG instruction exchanges only 32-bit-long words. The data size (L) does not have to be specified after the EXG instruction since this instruction has only one data size. No flags are affected.

The SWAP Dn instruction, on the other hand, exchanges the low 16 bits of Dn with the high 16 bits of Dn. All condition codes are affected.

5.6.1.c LEA and PEA Instructions

The LEA.L (EA), An moves an effective address (EA) into the specified address register. The (EA) can be calculated based on the addressing mode of the source. For example, LEA $00456074, A1 moves $00456074 to A1. This instruction is equivalent to MOVEA.L #$00456074, A1. Note that $00456074 is contained in the PC.

LEA instruction is very useful when address calculation is desired during program execution. (EA) in LEA specifies the actual data to be loaded into An, whereas (EA) in MOVEA specifies the address of actual data. For example, consider LEA $06 (A2, D5.W), A0. If $[A2] = 00003000_{16}$, $[D5] = 0044_{16}$, then the LEA instruction moves 0000304A16 into A0. On the other hand, MOVEA $06(A2 D5.W), A0 moves the contents of 0000304A16 into A0. Therefore, it is obvious that if address calculation is required, the instruction LEA is very useful.

The PEA (EA) computes an effective address and then pushes it onto the stack. This instruction can be used when the 16-bit address used in absolute short mode is required to be pushed onto the stack. For example, consider PEA $8000 in the user mode. If [USP] = $00005004, then $8000 is sign-extended to 32 bits and pushed to stack. The low-order 16 bits ($8000) are pushed at 005002_{16}$ and the high-order 16 bits ($FFFF) are pushed at 005000_{16}.

5.6.1.d LINK and UNLK Instructions

Before calling a subroutine, the main program quite often transfers values of certain parameters to the subroutine. It is convenient to save these variables onto the stack before calling the subroutine. These variables can then be read from the stack and used by the subroutine for computations. The 68000 LINK and UNLK instructions are used for this purpose. In addition, the 68000 LINK instruction allows one to reserve temporary storage for the local variables of a subroutine. This storage can be accessed as needed by the subroutine and be released using UNLK before returning to the main program. The LINK instruction is usually used at the beginning of a subroutine to allocate stack space for storing local variables and parameters for nested subroutine calls. The UNLK instruction is usually used at the end of subroutine before the RETURN instruction to release the local area and restore the stack pointer contents so that it points to the return address.

The LINK An, #-displacement causes the current contents of the specified An to be pushed onto the system (user or supervisor) stack. The updated SP contents are then loaded into A$_n$. Finally, a sign-extended 2's complement displacement value is added to the SP. No flags are affected. For example, consider LINK A0, #-100. If [A0] = 00005100 [USP] = 00002104_{16} then after execution of the LINK instruction the situation shown in Figure 5.6 occurs.

This means that after the LINK instruction, [A0] = 00005100 is

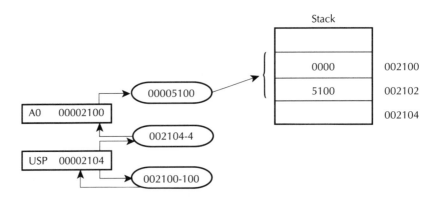

FIGURE 5.6 Execution of the link instruction.

pushed onto the stack, the [updated USP] = 002100 is loaded into A0. USP is then loaded with 002000 and, therefore, 100 locations are allocated to subroutine at the beginning of which the above LINK instruction can be used. Note that A0 cannot be used in the subroutine.

The UNLK instruction at the end of this subroutine before the RETURN instruction releases the 100 locations and restores the contents of A0 and USP to those prior to using the LINK instruction. For example, UNLK A0 will load [A0] = 00002100 into USP, the two stack words 00005100 into A0, and USP is then incremented by 4 to contain 00002104. Therefore, the contents of A0 and USP prior to using the LINK are restored. In the above example, after execution of the LINK, addresses 001999 and below can be used as the stack. One hundred locations starting at 002000 and above can be reserved for storing the local variables of the subroutine. These variables can then be accessed with an address register such as A0 as a base pointer using the address register indirect with displacement mode such as MOVE.W d(A0), D2 for read and MOVE.W D2, d(A0) for write.

5.6.2 ARITHMETIC INSTRUCTIONS

These instructions allow:

- 8-, 16-, or 32-bit additions and subtractions
- 16-bit by 16-bit multiplication (both signed and unsigned)
- Compare, clear, and negate instructions
- Extended arithmetic instructions for performing multiprecision arithmetic
- Test (TST) instruction for comparing the operand with zero
- Test and set (TAS) instruction which can be used for synchronization in multiprocessor system

The 68000 arithmetic instructions are summarized in Table 5.7.

TABLE 5.7
68000 Arithmetic Instructions

Instruction	Size	Operation
Addition and Subtraction Instructions		
ADD (EA), (EA)	B, W, L	[EA] + [EA] → EA
ADDI #data, (EA)	B, W, L	[EA] + data → EA
ADDQ #d8, (EA)	B, W, L	[EA] + d8 → EA
		d8 can be an integer from 0 to 7

TABLE 5.7 (continued)
68000 Arithmetic Instructions

Instruction	Size	Operation
ADDA (EA), An	W, L	An + [EA] → An
SUB (EA), (EA)	B, W, L	$[En]_{dest} - [EA]_{source}$ → EA_{dest}
SUBI # data, (EA)	B, W, L	[EA] – data → EA
SUBQ #d8, (EA)	B, W, L	[EA] – d8 → EA
		d8 can be an integer from 0 to 7
SUBA (EA), An	W, L	An – [EA] → An

Multiplication and Division Instructions

Instruction	Size	Operation
MULS (EA), Dn	W	[Dn]16 * [EA]16 → [Dn]32 (signed multiplication)
MULU (EA), Dn	W	[Dn]16 * [EA]16 → [Dn]32 (un-signed multiplication)
DIVS (EA), Dn	W	[Dn]32 / [EA]16 → [Dn]32 (signed division, high word of Dn contains remainder and low word of Dn contains the quotient)
DIVU (EA), Dn	W	[Dn]32 / [EA]16 → [Dn]32 (unsigned division, remainder is in high word of Dn and quotient is in low word of Dn

Compare, Clear, and Negate Instructions

Instruction	Size	Operation
CMP (EA), Dn	B, W, L	Dn – [EA] → No result; affects flags
CMPA (EA), An	W, L	An – [EA] → No result; affects flags
CMPI #data, (EA)	B, W, L	[EA] – data → No result; affects flags
CMPM (Ay) +, (Ax) +	B, W, L	[Ax]+ – [Ay]+ → No result; affects flags; Ax and Ay are incremented depending on operand size
CLR (EA)	B, W, L	0 → EA
NEG (EA)	B, W, L	0 – [EA] → EA

Extended Arithmetic Instructions

Instruction	Size	Operation
ADDX Dy, Dx	B, W, L	Dx + Dy + X → Dx
ADDX – (Ay), – (Ax)	B, W, L	–[Ax] + –[Ay] + X → [Ax]

TABLE 5.7 (continued)
68000 Arithmetic Instructions

Instruction	Size	Operation
EXT Dn	W, L	If size is W, then sign-extended low byte of Dn to 16 bits; if size is L, then sign extend low 16 bits of Dn to 32 bits
NEGX (EA)	B, W, L	$0 - [EA] - X \rightarrow EA$
SUBX Dy, Dx	B, W, L	$Dx - Dy - X \rightarrow Dx$
SUBX – (Ay), – (Ax)	B, W, L	$-[Ax] - -[Ay] - X \rightarrow [Ax]$

Test Instruction

TST (EA)	B, W, L	$[EA] - 0 \rightarrow$ flags affected

Test and Set Instruction

TAS (EA)	B	If $[EA] = 0$, then set $Z = 1$; else $Z = 0$, $N = 1$ and then always set bit 7 of $[EA]$ to 1

Note: If [EA] in the ADD or SUB instruction is an address register, the operand length is WORD or LONG WORD. [EA] in any instruction is calculated using the addressing mode used. All instructions except ADDA and SUBA affect condition codes.

- Source [EA] in the above ADDA and SUBA can use all modes.
- Destination [EA] in ADDI and SUBI can use all modes except An relative, and immediate.
- Destination [EA] in ADDQ and SUBQ can use all modes except relative and immediate.
- [EA] in all multiplication and division instructions can use all modes except An.
- Source [EA] in CMP and CMPA instructions can use all modes.
- Destination [EA] in CMPI can use all modes except An, relative, and immediate.
- [EA] in CLR and NEG can use all modes except An, relative, and immediate.
- [EA] in NEGX can use all modes except An, relative, and immediate.
- [EA] in TST can use all modes except An, relative, and immediate
- [EA] in TAS can use all modes except An relative, and immediate.

5.6.2.a Addition and Subtraction Instructions

- Consider ADD.W $245000, D0. If $[245000_{16}] = 2014_{16}$ and $[D0] = 1004_{16}$, then after execution of this ADD instruction, the low 16 bits of D0 will contain 3018_{16}.

- ADDI instruction can be used to add immediate data to register or memory location. The immediate data follows the instruction word. For example, consider ADDI.W #$0062, $500000. If $[500000_{16}] = 1000_{16}$, then after execution of this ADDI instruction, memory location 500000_{16} will contain 1062_{16}. ADDQ, on the other hand, adds a number from 0 to 7 to the register or memory location in the destination operand. This instruction occupies 16 bits and the immediate data. 0 to 7 is specified by 3 bits in the instruction word. For example, consider ADDQ.B#4, D0. If $[D0]_{\text{low byte}} = 60_{16}$, then after execution of this ADDQ, low byte of register D0 will contain 64_{16}.

- For ADD or SUB, if the destination is Dn, then the source (EA) can use all modes; if the destination is a memory location (all modes except Dn, An, relative, and immediate), then the source must be Dn.

- All subtraction instructions subtract source from destination. For example, consider SUB.W D0, $500000. If $[D0]_{\text{low word}} = 3003_{16}$ and $[500000_{16}] = 5005_{16}$, then after execution of this SUB instruction, memory location 500000_{16} will contain 2002_{16}.

- Consider SUBI.W# $0004, D0. If $[D0]_{\text{low word}} = 5004_{16}$, then after execution of this SUBI instruction, D0 will contain 5000_{16}. Note that the same result can be obtained by using a SUBQ.W# $4, D0. However, in this case the data 4 is inherent in the instruction word.

5.6.2.b Multiplication and Division Instructions

The 68000 instruction set includes both signed and unsigned multiplication of integer numbers.

- MULS (EA), Dn multiplies two 16-bit signed numbers and provides a 32-bit result. For example, consider MULS #-2, D0. If $[D0] = 0004_{16}$, then after this MULS, D0 will contain the 32-bit result $FFFFFFF8_{16}$ which is −8 in decimal. MULU (EA), Dn, on the other hand, performs unsigned multiplication. Consider MULU (A_1), D2. If $[A1] = 00002000_{16}$, $[002000] = 0400_{16}$, and $[D2] = 0300_{16}$, then after this MULU, D2 will contain 32-bit result $000C0000_{16}$.

- Consider DIVS #4, D0. If $[D0] = -9_{10} = FFFFFFF7_{16}$, then after this DIVS, register D0 will contain

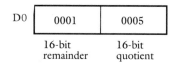

D0 | FFFF | FFFE

16-bit remainder = -1_{10} 16-bit quotient = -2_{10}

Note that in 68000, after DIVS, the sign of the remainder is always the same as the dividend unless the remainder is equal to zero. Therefore, in the example above, since the dividend is negative (-9_{10}), the remainder is negative (-1_{10}). Also, division by zero causes an internal interrupt automatically. A service routine can be written by the user to indicate an error, N = 1 if the quotient is negative, and V = 1 if there is an overflow. The DIVU instruction is the same as the DIVS instruction except that the division is unsigned. For example, consider DIVU #2, D0. If [D0] = 11_{10} = $0000000B_{16}$, then after execution of this DIVU, register D0 contains:

D0 | 0001 | 0005

16-bit remainder   16-bit quotient

As with the DIVS, division by zero using DIVU causes trap. Also, V = 1 if there is an overflow.

5.6.2.c Compare, Clear, and Negate Instructions

*   The COMPARE instructions affect condition codes, but do not provide the subtraction result. Consider CMPM.W (A1)+, (A2)+. If [A1] = 00400000_{16}, [A2] = 00500000_{16}, [400000] = 0008_{16}, [500000] = 2006_{16}, then after this CMP instruction N = 0, C = 0, X = 0, V = 0, Z = 0, [A1] = 00400002_{16}, and [A2] = 00500002_{16}.
*   CLR.L D3 clears all 32 bits of D3 to zero.
*   Consider NEG.W (A1). If [A1] = 00500000_{16}, [500000] = 0007_{16}, then after this NEG instruction, the low 16 bits of location 500000_{16} will contain $FFFF9_{16}$.

5.6.2.d Extended Arithmetic Instructions

*   ADDX and SUBX instructions can be used in performing multiple precision arithmetic since there are no ADDC (add with carry) or SUBC (subtract with borrow) instructions. For example, in order to perform a 64-bit addition, the following two instructions can be used:

```
ADD.L D2, D3     Add low 32 bits of data and
                 store in D3
ADDX.L D4, D5    Add high 32 bits of data along
                 with any carry from the low 32-
                 bit addition and store result in
                 D5
```

Note that in the above D5 D3 contains one 32-bit data and D4 D2 contains the other 32-bit data. The 32-bit result is stored in D5 D3.

- Consider EXT.W D5. If [D5] low byte = $F8_{16}$, then after the EXT, [D5] = $FFF8_{16}$.

5.6.2.e Test Instructions

- Consider TST.W (A1). If [A1] = 00700000_{16}, [700000] = $F000_{16}$, then after the TST.W (A1), the operation $F000_{16}$-0000_{16} is performed internally by the 68000, Z is cleared to zero, and N is set to 1. V and C flags are always cleared to zero.

5.6.2.f Test and Set Instruction

A multiprocessor system includes a mechanism to safely access resources such as memory shared by two or more processors. This mechanism is called mutual exclusion.

Mutual exclusion allows a processor to lock out other processors from accessing a shared resource. This shared resource is also called a Critical Program Section, since once a processor starts executing the program sequence in this section, it must complete it before another processor accesses it.

A binary flag called semaphore stored in the shared memory is used to indicate whether the shared memory is free (semaphore = 0) to be accessed or busy (semaphore = 1; the shared memory being used by another processor). Testing and setting the semaphore is a critical operation and must be executed in an indivisible cycle by a processor so that the other processors will not access the semaphore simultaneously.

The test and set instruction, along with a hardware lock mechanism, can initialize a semaphore. The test and set instruction tests and sets a semaphore. The processor, when executing this instruction, generates a signal to provide the lock mechanism during the execution time of the instruction. This prevents other processors from altering the semaphore between the processor's testing and setting the semaphore.

The 68000 provides the TAS instruction to test and set a semaphore. During execution of the TAS, the 68000 generates LOW on the $\overline{AS}$

(address strobe) pin which can be used to lock out other processors from accessing the semaphore.

Let us explain the application of the TAS instruction. TAS(EA) is usually used to synchronize two processors in multiprocessor data transfers. For example, consider two 68000-based microcomputers with shared RAM shown in Figure 5.7.

Suppose that it is desired to transfer the low byte of D0 from processor 1 to the low byte of D2 in processor 2. A memory location, namely, TRDATA, can be used to accomplish this. First, processor 1 can execute the TAS instruction to test the byte in the shared RAM with address TEST for zero value. If it is zero, the processor 1 can be programmed to move the low byte of D0 into location TRDATA in the shared RAM. The processor 2 can then execute an instruction sequence to move the contents of TRDATA from the shared RAM into the low byte of D2. The following instruction sequence will accomplish this:

Processor 1 Routine	**Processor 2 Routine**
Proc 1 TAS TEST	Proc 2 TAS TEST
BNE Proc 1	BNE Proc 2
MOVE.B D0, TRDATA	MOVE.B TRDATA, D2
CLR.B TEST	CLR.B TEST
—	—
—	—
—	—

Note that in the above, TAS TEST checks the byte addressed by TEST for zero. If [TEST] = 0, then Z is set to one; otherwise Z = 0 and N = 1. After this, bit 7 of [TEST] is set to 1. Note that a zero value of TEST indicates that the shared RAM is free for use and the Z bit indicates this after the TAS is executed. In each of the above instruction sequences, after a data transfer using the MOVE instruction, TEST is cleared to zero so that the shared RAM is free for use by the other processor. Note that bit 7 of memory location TEST is called the semaphore.

In order to avoid testing of the TEST byte simultaneously by two proc-

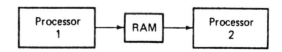

FIGURE 5.7 Two 68000s interfaced via shared RAM.

essors, the TAS is executed in a Read-Modify-Write cycle. This means that once the operand is addressed by the 68000 executing the TAS, the system bus is not available to the other 68000 until the TAS is completed.

5.6.3 LOGICAL INSTRUCTIONS

These instructions include logical OR, EOR, AND, and NOT as shown in Table 5.8.

TABLE 5.8
68000 Logical Instructions

Instruction	Size	Operation
AND (EA), (EA)	B, W, L	$[EA] \wedge [EA] \rightarrow EA$
ANDI #data, (EA)	B, W, L	$[EA] \wedge$ #data $\rightarrow EA$; [EA] cannot be address register
ANDI #data8, CCR	B	$CCR \wedge$ #data $\rightarrow CCR$
ANDI #data16, SR	W	$SR \wedge$ #data $\rightarrow SR$
EOR Dn, (EA)	B, W, L	$Dn \oplus [EA] \rightarrow EA$; [EA] cannot be address register
EORI #data, (EA)	B, W, L	$[EA] \oplus$ #data $\rightarrow EA$; [EA] cannot be address register
NOT (EA)	B, W, L	One's complement of $[EA] \rightarrow EA$
OR EA, (EA)	B, W, L	$[EA] \vee [EA] \rightarrow EA$
ORI #data, (EA)	B, W, L	$[EA] \vee$ #data $\rightarrow EA$; [EA] cannot be address register
ORI #data8, CCR	B	$CCR \vee$ #data8 $\rightarrow CCR$
ORI #data16, SR	W	$SR \vee$ #data $\rightarrow SR$

- Source [EA] in AND and OR can use all modes except An.
- Destination [EA] in AND or OR or EOR can use all modes except Dn, An, relative, and immediate.
- Destination [EA] in ANDI, ORI, and EORI can use all modes except An, relative, and immediate.
- [EA] in NOT can use all modes except An, relative, and immediate.

- Consider AND.W D2, D6. If $[D2] = 0005_{16}$, $[D6] = 0FF1_{16}$, then after execution of this AND, the low 16 bits of D6 will contain 0001_{16}.
- Consider ANDI.B #$80, CCR. If $[CCR] = 0F_{16}$, then after this ANDI, register CCR will contain 00_{16}.

- Consider EOR.W D2, D6. If $[D2] = 000F_{16}$ and $[D6] = 000F_{16}$, then after execution of this EOR, register D6 will contain 0000_{16}, and D2 will remain unchanged at $000F_{16}$.
- Consider NOT.B D0. If $[D0] = 04_{16}$, then after execution of this NOT instruction, the low byte of D0 will contain FB_{16}.
- Consider ORI #$1008, SR. If $[SR] = A011_{16}$, then after execution of this ORI, register SR will contain $B019_{16}$. Note that this is a privileged instruction since the high byte of SR containing the control bits is changed and therefore can only be executed in the supervisor mode.

5.6.4 SHIFT AND ROTATE INSTRUCTIONS
The 68000 shift and rotate instructions are listed in Table 5.9.

TABLE 5.9
68000 Shift and Rotate Instructions

Instruction	Size	Operation
ASL, Dx, Dy	B, W, L	
		Shift [Dy] by the number of times to left specified in Dx; the low 6 bits of Dx specify the number of shifts from 0 to 63
ASL #data, Dn	B, W, L	Same as ASL Dx, Dy except that the number of shifts is specified by immediate data from 0 to 7
ASL (EA)	B, W, L	[EA] is shifted one bit to left; the most significant of [EA] goes to x and c, and zero moves into the least significant bit
ASR Dx, Dy	B, W, L	
		Arithmetically shift [Dy] to the right by retaining the sign bit; the low 6 bits of Dx specify the number of shifts from 0 to 63
ASR #data, Dn	B, W, L	Same as above except the number of shifts is from 0 to 7

TABLE 5.9 (continued)
68000 Shift and Rotate Instructions

Instruction	Size	Operation
ASR (EA)	B, W, L	Same as above except [EA] is shifted once to the right
LSL Dx, Dy	B, W, L	

Low 6 bits of Dx specify the number of shifts from 0 to 63

Instruction	Size	Operation
LSL #data, Dn	B, W, L	Same as above except the number of shift is specified by immediate data from 0 to 7
LSL (EA)	B, W, L	[EA] is shifted one bit to the left
LSR Dx, Dy	B, W, L	

Same as LSL Dx, Dy except shift is to the right

Instruction	Size	Operation
LSR #data, Dn	B, W, L	Same as LSL #data, Dn, except shift is to the right by immediate data from 0 to 7
LSR (EA)	B, W, L	Same as LSL [EA] except shift is to the right
ROL Dx, Dy	B, W, L	

Low 6 bits of Dx specify the number of times [Dy] to be shifted

Instruction	Size	Operation
ROL #data, Dn	B, W, L	Same as above except that the immediate data specify that [Dn] to be shifted from 0 to 7
ROL (EA)	B, W, L	[EA] is rotated once to the left
ROR Dx, Dy	B, W, L	

Low 6 bits of Dx specify the number of shifts from 0 to 63

Instruction	Size	Operation
ROR #data, Dn	B, W, L	Same as ROL #data, Dn except the shift is to the right by immediate data from 0 to 7

TABLE 5.9 (continued)
68000 Shift and Rotate Instructions

Instruction	Size	Operation
ROR (EA)	B, W, L	[EA] is rotated once to the right
ROXL Dx, Dy	B, W, L	

Low 6 bits of Dx contain the number of rotates from 0 to 63

ROXL #data, Dy	B, W, L	Same as above except immediate data specify number of rotates from 0 to 7
ROXL (EA)	B, W, L	[EA] is rotated one bit to right
ROXR Dx, Dy	B, W, L	

Same as ROXL Dx, Dy except the rotate is to the right

ROXR #data, Dy	B, W, L	Same as ROXL #data, Dy, except rotate is to the right by immediate data from 0 to 7
ROXR (EA)	B, W, L	Same as ROXL [EA] except rotate is to the right

Note: [EA] in ASL, ASR, LSL, LSR, ROL, ROR, ROXL, and ROXR can use all modes except Dn, An, relative, and immediate.

- All the instructions in Table 5.9 affect N and Z flags according to the result. V is reset to zero except for ASL.
- Note that in the 68000 there is no true arithmetic shift left instruction. In true arithmetic shifts, the sign bit of the number being shifted is retained. In the 68000, the instruction ASL does not retain the sign bit, whereas the instruction ASR retains the sign bit after performing the arithmetic shift operation. Consider ASL.W D3, D0. If $[D3]_{\text{low 16 bits}} = 0003_{16}$, $[D0]_{\text{low 16 bits}} = 87FF_{16}$, then after this ASL instruction $[D0]_{\text{low 16 bits}} = 3FF8_{16}$, C = 0, and X = 0. Note that the sign of the contents of D0 is changed from 1 to 0, and therefore the overflow is set. ASL sets the overflow bit to indicate sign change during the shift. In the example, the sign bit of D0 is changed after

shifting [D0] three times. ASR, on the other hand, retains the sign bit. For example, consider ASR.W #2, D5. If [D5] = $8FE2_{16}$, then after this ASR, the low 16 bits of [D5] = $E3F8_{16}$, C = 1, and X = 1. Note that the sign bit is retained. ASL (EA) or ASR (EA) shifts (EA) one bit to the left or right, respectively. For example, consider ASL.W (A2). If [A2] = 00004000_{16} and [004000] = $F000_{16}$, then after execution of the ASL, [004000] = $E000_{16}$, X = 1, and C = 1. On the other hand, after ASR.W (A2), memory location 004000_{16} will contain 7800_{16}, C = 0, and X = 0. Note that only memory-alterable modes are allowed for (EA). Also, only 16-bit operands are allowed for (EA) when the destination is memory location.

- LSL and ASL instructions are the same in the 68000 except that with the ASL, V is set to 1 if there is a sign change of the number during the shift.
- Consider LSR.W# 0002, D0. If [D0] = $F000_{16}$, then after the LSR, [D0] = $3C00_{16}$, X = 0, and C = 0.
- Consider ROL.B# 02, D2. If [D2] = $B1_{16}$ and C = 1, then after execution of the ROL, the low byte of [D2] = $C7_{16}$ and C = 0. On the other hand, with [D2] = $B1_{16}$ and C = 1, consider ROR.B # 02, D2. After execution of this ROR, register D2 will contain EC_{16} and C = 0.
- Consider ROXL.W D2, D1. If [D2] = 0003_{16}, [D1] = F201, C = 0, and X = 1, then the low 16 bits after execution of this ROXL are [D1] = $900F_{16}$, C = 1, and X = 1.

5.6.5 BIT MANIPULATION INSTRUCTIONS

The 68000 has four bit manipulation instructions, and these are listed in Table 5.10.

- In all the above instructions, the 1's complement of the specified bit is reflected in the Z flag. The specified bit is then 1's complemented, cleared to zero, set to one, or unchanged by BCHG, BCLR, BSET, or BTST, respectively. In all the instructions in Table 5.10, if (EA) is Dn, then length of Dn is 32 bits; otherwise, the length of the destination is one byte.
- Consider BCHG.B #2, $003000. If [003000] = 05_{16}, then after execution of this BCHG instruction, Z = 0 and [003000] = 01_{16}.
- Consider BCLR.L # 3, D1. If [D1] = $F210E128_{16}$, then after execution of this BCLR, register D1 will contain $F210E120_{16}$ and Z = 0.
- Consider BSET.B #0, (A1). If [A1] = 00003000_{16}, [003000] = 00_{16}, then after execution of this BSET, memory location 003000 will contain 01_{16} and Z = 1.

TABLE 5.10
68000 Bit Manipulation Instructions

Instruction	Size	Operation
BCHG Dn, (EA) BCHG #data, (EA)	B, L	A bit in [EA] specified by Dn or immediate data is tested; the 1's complement of the bit is reflected in both the Z flag and the specified bit position
BCLR Dn, (EA) BCLR #data, (EA)	B, L	A bit in [EA] specified by Dn or immediate data is tested and the 1's complement of the bit is reflected in the Z flag; the specified bit is cleared to zero
BSET Dn, (EA) BSET #data, (EA)	B,L	A bit in [EA] specified by Dn or immediate data is tested and the 1's complement of the bit is reflected in the Z flag; the specified bit is then set to one
BTST Dn, (EA) BTST #data, (EA)	B,L	A bit in [EA] specified by Dn or immediate data is tested; the 1's complement of the specified bit is reflected in the Z flag

- [EA] in the above instructions can use all modes except An, relative, and immediate.
- If [EA] is memory location, then data size is byte; if [EA] is Dn then data size is long word.

- Consider BTST.B #2, $002000. If $[002000] = 02_{16}$, then after execution of this BTST, Z = 0 and $[002000] = 02_{16}$.

5.6.6 BINARY-CODED DECIMAL INSTRUCTION

The 68000 instruction set contains three BCD instructions, namely, ABCD for adding, SBCD for subtracting, and NBCD for negating. These instructions always include the extent (X) bit in the operation. The BCD instructions are listed in Table 5.11.

- Consider ABCD D1, D2. If $[D1] = 25_{16}$, $[D2] = 15_{16}$, X = 0, then after execution of the ABCD instruction, $[D2] = 40_{16}$, X = 0, and Z = 0.
- Consider SBCD − (A2), − (A3). If $[A2] = 00002004_{16}$, $[A3] =$

TABLE 5.11
68000 Binary-Coded Decimal Instructions

Instruction	Operand size	Operation
ABCD Dy, Dx	B	$[Dx]10 + [Dy]10 + X \rightarrow Dx$
ABCD – (Ay), – (Ax)	B	$-[Ax]10 + -[Ay]10 + X \rightarrow [Ax]$
SBCD Dy, Dx	B	$[Dx]10 - [Dy]10 - X \rightarrow Dx$
SBCD – (Ay), –(Ax)	B	$-[Ax]10 - -[Ay]10 - X \rightarrow [Ax]$
NBCD (EA)	B	$0 - [EA]10 - X \rightarrow EA$

Note: [EA] in NBCD can use all modes except An, relative, and immediate.

  00003003_{16}, $[002003] = 05_{16}$, $[003002] = 06_{16}$, then after execution of this SBCD, $[003002] = 00_{16}$, $X = 0$, and $Z = 1$.
- Consider NBCD (A1). If $[A1] = [00003000_{16}]$, $[003000] = 05$, $X = 1$, then after execution of the NBCD, $[003000] = FA_{16}$.

5.6.7 PROGRAM CONTROL INSTRUCTIONS
These instructions include branches, jumps, and subroutine calls as listed in Table 5.12.

TABLE 5.12
68000 Program Control Instructions

Instruction	Size	Operation
Bcc d	B,W	If condition code cc is true, then PC + d →PC; the PC value is current instruction location plus 2; d can be 8- or 16-bit signed displacement; if 8-bit displacement is used, then the instruction size is 16 bits with the 8-bit displacement as the low byte of the instruction word; if 16-bit displacement is used, then the instruction size is two words with 8-bit displacement field (low byte) in the instruction word as zero and the second word following the instruction word as the 16-bit displacement

TABLE 5.12 (continued)
68000 Program Control Instructions

Instruction	Size	Operation
Bcc d (continued)		There are 14 conditions such as BCC (Branch if Carry Clear), BEQ (Branch if result equal to zero, i.e., $Z = 1$), and BNE (Branch if not equal, i.e., $Z = 0$) Note that the PC contents will always be even since the instruction length is either one word or two words depending on the displacement widths
BRA d	B,W	Branch always to PC + d where PC value is current instruction location plus 2; as with Bcc, d can be signed 8 or 16 bits; this is an unconditional branching instruction with relative mode; note that the PC contents are even since the instruction is either one word or two words
BSR d	B,W	$PC \rightarrow -[SP]$ $PC + d \rightarrow PC$ The address of the next instruction following PC is pushed onto the stack; PC is then loaded with PC + d; as before, d can be 8 or 16 bits; this is a subroutine call instruction using relative mode
DBcc Dn, d	W	If cc is false, then $Dn - 1 \rightarrow Dn$, and if Dn $= -1$, then $PC + 2 \rightarrow PC$; If $Dn \neq -1$, then $PC + d \rightarrow PC$; if cc is true, $PC + 2 \rightarrow PC$
JMP (EA)	Unsized	$[EA] \rightarrow PC$ This is an unconditional jump instruction which uses control addressing mode
JSR (EA)	Unsized	$PC \rightarrow -[SP]$ $[EA] \rightarrow PC$ This is a subroutine call instruction which uses control addressing mode
RTR	Unsized	$[SP] + \rightarrow CCR$ $[SP]+ \rightarrow PC$ Return and restore condition codes

TABLE 5.12 (continued)
68000 Program Control Instructions

Instruction	Size	Operation
RTS	Unsized	Return from subroutine [SP] + → PC
Scc (EA)	B	If cc is true, then the byte specified by [EA] is set to all ones, otherwise the byte is cleared to zero

- [EA] in JMP and JSR can use all modes except Dn, An, (An) +, –(An), and immediate.
- [EA] in Scc can use all modes except An, relative, and immediate.

- Consider Bcc d. There are 14 branch conditions. This means that cc in Bcc can be replaced by 14 conditions providing 14 instructions. These are BCC, BCS, BEQ, BGE, BGT, BHI, BLE, BLS, BLT, BMI, BNE, BPL, BVC, and BVS. It should be mentioned that some of these instructions are applicable to both signed and unsigned numbers, some can be used with only signed numbers, and some instructions are applicable to only unsigned numbers as shown below:

For both signed and unsigned numbers	For signed numbers	For unsigned numbers
BCC d (Branch if C = 0)	BGE d (Branch if greater or equal)	BHI d (Branch if high)
BCS d (Branch if C = 1)	BGT d (Branch if greater than)	BLS d (Branch if low or same)
BEQ d (Branch if Z = 1)	BLE d (Branch if less than or equal)	
BNE d (Branch if Z = 0)	BLT d (branch if less than)	
	BMI d (Branch if N = 1)	
	BPL d (Branch if N = 0)	
	BVC d (Branch if V = 0)	
	BVS d (Branch if V = 1)	

After signed arithmetic operations such as ADD or SUB the instructions such as BEQ, BNE, BVS, BVC, BMI, and BPL can be used. On the other hand, after unsigned arithmetic operations, the instructions such as BCC, BCS, BEQ, and BNE can be used.

If V = 0, BPL and BGE have the same meaning. Likewise, if V = 0, BMI and BLT perform the same function.

The conditional branch instructions can be used after typical arithmetic instructions such as subtraction to branch to a location if cc is true. For example, consider SUB.W D1, D2. Now if [D1] and [D2] are unsigned numbers, then

$$BCC \text{ d can be used if } [D2] > [D1]$$
$$BCS \text{ d can be used if } [D2] < [D1]$$
$$BEQ \text{ d can be used if } [D2] = [D1]$$
$$BNE \text{ d can be used if } [D2] \neq [D1]$$
$$BHI \text{ d can be used if } [D2] > [D1]$$
$$BLS \text{ d can be used if } [D2] \leq [D1]$$

On the other hand, if [D1] and [D2] are signed numbers, then after SUB.W D1, D2, the following branch instructions can be used:

$$BEQ \text{ d can be used if } [D2] = [D1]$$
$$BNE \text{ d can be used if } [D2] \neq [D1]$$
$$BLT \text{ d can be used if } [D2] < [D1]$$
$$BLE \text{ d can be used if } [D2] \leq [D1]$$
$$BGT \text{ d can be used if } [D2] > [D1]$$
$$BGE \text{ d can be used if } [D2] \geq [D1]$$

Now, as an example consider BEQ* + $20. If [PC] = 000200_{16}, then after execution of the BEQ instruction, program execution starts at 000220_{16} if Z = 1; if Z = 0, program execution continues at 000200. Note that * is used by some assemblers to indicate displacement.

- The instruction BRA and JMP are unconditional JUMP instructions. The BRA instruction uses the relative addressing mode, whereas the JMP uses only control addressing modes. For example, consider BRA * + $20. If [PC] = 000200_{16}, then after execution of the BRA, program execution starts at 000220_{16}.

    Now consider JMP (A1). If [A1] = 00000220_{16}, then after execution of the JMP, program execution starts at 000220_{16}.

- The instructions BSR and JSR are subroutine CALL instructions. BSR uses relative mode, whereas JSR uses control addressing mode. Consider the following program segment:

Main program	**Subroutine**

```
Main program                          Subroutine

         —            SUB  MOVEM.L  D0-D7/A0-A6, –(SP)
         —                   —    ⎫
         —                   —    ⎬  main body of
    JSR SUB                  —    ⎬    the subroutine
START                        —    ⎭
         —
         —            MOVEM.L  (SP)+ , D0-D7/A0-A6
                      RTS
```

In the above, JSR SUB instruction calls the subroutine called SUB. In response to JSR, the 68000 pushes the current PC contents called START onto the stack and loads the starting address SUB of the subroutine into PC. The first MOVEM in the SUB pushes all registers onto the stack and after the subroutine is executed, the second MOVEM instruction pops all the registers back. Finally, RTS pops the address START from the stack into PC, and the program control is returned to the main program. Note that BSR SUB could have been used instead of JSR SUB in the main program. In that case, the 68000 assembler would have considered the SUB with BSR as a displacement rather than as an address with the JSR instruction.

The 68000 can pass data between a main program and a subroutine using the following method:

1. Using 68000 registers
2. Using 68000 stack
3. Using parameter areas in memory
4. By coding argument values after subroutine CALL

Note that the information required by a subroutine is called parameters. In high-level languages, parameters provide general information for the subroutine. The subroutine can then be called by specific values called arguments in the main program. The arguments replace the parameters with specific values and provide results. For example, in FORTRAN, a subroutine SUMSQ with two parameters (Q,R) can be defined as follows: subroutine SUMSQ (Q,R). This subroutine can be called with various arguments in the main program as long as the arguments and parameters are the same data types such as real, integer, and floating-point. The subroutine can be called by the main program by using CALL (5.0,

RESULT). The subroutine uses the value 5.0 for Q and provides the answer in a location called RESULT. The specific value can be changed to get other results. In the above, Q and R are parameters, while 5.0 and RESULT are arguments.

Now let us discuss the methods of passing the arguments between the main program and the subroutine.

5.6.7.a Using 68000 Registers

The eight data registers (D0-D7) and seven address registers (A0-A6) can be used to pass arguments. Data can be passed via D0-D7, while addresses can be passed via A0-A6. For example, the following instruction sequence in the main program loads a 32-bit value in D5 and an indirect pointer in A4; the subroutine TRIG can use the values directly from the registers D5 and A4 to accomplish the desired function:

```
MOVE.L #DATA, D5
LEA.L ADDR, A4
BSR TRIG
```

This method is simple, requires small memory, but the number of arguments to be passed is limited by the number of registers.

5.6.7.b Using 68000 Stack

A 68000 stack can be formed by using A0-A6 registers as stack pointers. This stack can then be used to pass arguments by pushing the arguments onto the stack before calling the subroutine. The main program can use postincrement or predecrement modes for pushing the arguments. The following instruction sequence initializes A5 as the stack pointer and passes four arguments:

```
MOVEA.L      # STACKPTR,   A5    ;   Define A5 as SP
MOVE .L      DATA1, (A5)+        ;   Push first data
MOVE .L      DATA2, (A5)+        ;   Push second data
Move .L      DATA3, (A5)+        ;   Push third data
MOVE .L      DATA4, (A5)+        ;   Push fourth data
BSR          START               ;   Call subroutine
                                 ;   START
```

In the above, STACKPTR defines the bottom of the stack and the stack grows from low to high addresses.

The four arguments can be retrieved by the subroutine START as follows:

```
MOVE.L    —    (A5),  DATA 4    ;   Get  DATA  4
MOVE.L    —    (A5),  DATA 3    ;   Get  DATA  3
MOVE.L    —    (A5),  DATA 2    ;   Get  DATA  2
MOVE.L    —    (A5),  DATA 1    ;   Get  DATA  1
```

The stack pointer, now A5, contains the value STACKPTR.

The system stack can also be used to pass arguments. The arguments can be pushed by the main program before calling the subroutine as follows:

```
MOVE.L    DATA 1, — (USP)   ;  Push  DATA  1
MOVE.L    DATA 2, — (USP)   ;  Push  DATA  2
PEA.W     LOC               ;  Push  LOC
BSR       START             ;  Call  Subroutine
                            ;  START
```

Since BSR START pushes PC onto the stack top, this must be popped from the stack temporarily before popping the arguments as follows:

```
MOVE.L    (USP)+, A0    ;   Save  PC  temporarily
MOVE.L    (USP)+, A1    ;   Obtain  LOC
MOVE.L    (USP)+, D0    ;   Obtain  DATA  2
MOVE.L    (USP)+, D1    ;   Obtain  DATA  1
          —
          —
          —
          —

MOVE.L    A0, — (USP)   ;   RESTORE  PC
RTS                     ;   Return  to
                        ;   Main  Program
```

This method is normally used by the user program and, hence, USP is used as the stack pointer.

5.6.7.c Using Parameter Areas in Memory

A parameter area is usually created when several parameters need to be passed. This parameter area contains the data or the addresses to be accessed by subroutine after the subroutine has been passed the beginning address of the parameter area by the main program.

The main program can create a parameter area of three parameters as follows:

```
MOVE.L     DATA 1,     BEGIN      ;   Store DATA 1
MOVE.L     DATA 2,     BEGIN+4    ;   Store DATA 2
MOVE.L     DATA 3,     BEGIN+8    ;   Store DATA 3
MOVEA.L    BEGIN, A5              ;   Initialize
                                  ;   A5 with the
                                  ;   starting address
                                  ;   of the area
BSR        START                  ;   Call subroutine
  —                               ;   START
  —
  —
```

The subroutine START now can access any parameter using indirect addressing with displacements. For example, the instruction MOVE.L 4(A5), D3 will load the second data to D3.

5.6.7.d By Coding Argument Values after Subroutine Call

This method specifies values of argument that are fixed and are unchanged after assembly. These constant values can be defined by using the DC (Define Constant) assembler pseudoinstruction after the subroutine call. For example, in order to PASS the values 5 and 8 to a subroutine, the following instruction sequence can be executed:

```
           BSR      BEGIN
START      DC.W     5
           DC.W     8
            —
            —
            —
```

BSR BEGIN in the above pushes the address START onto the system stack (USP or SSP). DC.W directive stores 5 in location START and 8 in location START+2. The subroutine must return to address START+4 in main program.

In order to obtain the arguments 5 and 8, the subroutine must execute the following instruction sequence (assume user mode):

```
MOVEA.L  (USP), A5     ;   Obtain PC into A5
MOVE.W   (A5)+, D2     ;   Obtain 5 into D2
MOVE.W   (A5)+, D3     ;   Obtain 8 into D3
MOVEA.L  A5, (USP)     ;   Save START+4 in stack
  —
  —
  —
RTS
```

The MOVEA instruction loads the PC value START in A5. The first MOVE loads the content (5) of memory location START to low word of D2 and increments A5 to START+2. The second MOVE moves the content (8) of location START+2 to low word of D3 and updates A5 to START+4. The MOVEA instruction then pushes START+4 to stack. RTS instruction at the end of the subroutine pops START+4 to PC and returns control to the right place in the main program.

The use of stack to save temporary variables during subroutine execution can be facilitated by utilizing a stack frame. The stack frame is a set of locations in stack used for saving return addresses, local variables, and I/O parameters. Local variables such as loop counters used in the subroutine are used by the subroutine and are not returned to the main program. The stack frame can be utilized by the subroutine to access a new set of parameters each time the main program calls it.

In 68000, the stack frame can be created by the main program and the subroutine using the LINK and UNLK instructions. The subroutine can access the variables on the stack by using displacements from a base register called a frame pointer. The 68000 LINK instruction can be used to create a stack frame and define the frame pointer.

As an example of LINK/UNLK, the instruction LINK A5, #-100 creates a stack frame of 100_{10} with A5 as the frame pointer. The instruction such as MOVE.W d (A5), D1 and MOVE.W D1,d(A5) can then be used to access the stack frame.

A typical instruction sequence illustrating the use of LINK and UNLK is given below:

```
        Main Program
        MOVE.L Const,-(USP)        ;  Push address of 32-bit
                                      constant to be passed
        PEA.W ADDR                 ;  Push starting address of
                                      a table to be passed
        JSR START                  ;  Jump to the subroutine
                                      START
          —
          —
          —
        Subroutine
START   LINK A3,#-12               ;  Allocate 12 bytes
          —
          —
          —
        MOVE.L DATA 1,-4 (A3),     ;  Push local variable 1
        MOVE.L DATA 2,-8 (A3),     ;  Push local variable 2
```

```
                    MOVE.L DATA 3,-12 (A3)    ;  Push local variable 3

Instructions   ⎛   MOVEA.L 8 (A3), A4        ;  Obtain ADDR
arbitrarily    ⎨   MOVE.L (A4), D1           ;  Read data from table
chosen         ⎬   SUBQ.L #5,-12 (A3)        ;  Subtract 5 from local
               ⎪                             ;  variable 3
               ⎝   MOVE.L 12 (A3), D4        ;  Read the 32-bit constant
                    —
                    —
                    —
                    UNLK  A3                  ;  Restore original values
                    RTS                       ;  RETURN
```

The following illustrates the stack contents at various points:

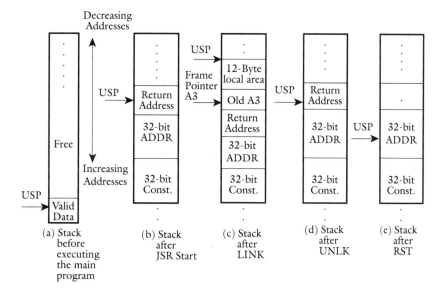

(a) Stack before executing the main program
(b) Stack after JSR Start
(c) Stack after LINK
(d) Stack after UNLK
(e) Stack after RST

In the main program, it is assumed that the 68000 is in user mode and, therefore, USP is used in the program. It is assumed that the main program passes to the subroutine a 32-bit constant, and the starting address ADDR of a table to be accessed by the subroutine. The subroutine allocates 12 bytes to save three 32-bit local variables by using the LINK instruction. Several instructions are arbitrarily chosen (to illustrate the concept) to be executed by the subroutine to read data from the table, decrement the local variable 3 by 5, and read the 32-bit constant so that they can be used in the instruction sequence that follows (not shown in the subroutine). The

UNLK instruction restores the original conditions and the RTS allows the program to return to the right place in the program.

- DBcc Dn, d tests both the condition codes and the value in a data register. DBcc first checks if cc (NE, EQ, GT, etc.) is satisfied. If satisfied, the next instruction is executed. If cc is not satisfied, the specified data register is decremented by 1. If $[Dn] = -1$, then next instruction is executed; if $Dn \neq -1$, then a branch is taken to PC + d. For example, consider DBNE D5, * -4 and $[D5] = 00003002_{16}$, $[PC]$ $= 002006_{16}$. If $Z = 1$, then $[D5] = 00003001_{16}$; since $[D5] \neq -1$, program execution starts at 002002_{16}. There is a false condition in the DBcc instruction, and this instruction is the DBF (some assemblers use DBRA for this). In this case, the condition is always false. This means that after execution of this instruction, Dn is decremented by 1 and if $[Dn] = -1$, then the next instruction is executed; if $[Dn] \neq -1$, then branch to PC + d is taken.
- Consider SPL(A5). If $[A5] = 00200020_{16}$ and $N = 0$, then after execution of the SPL, memory location 200020_{16} will contain 11111111_2.

5.6.8 SYSTEM CONTROL INSTRUCTIONS

The 68000 contains some system control instructions which include privileged instructions, trap instructions, and instructions that use or modify SR. Note that the privileged instructions can only be executed in the supervisor mode. The system control instructions are listed in Table 5.13.

- The RESET instruction, when executed in supervisor mode, outputs a signal on the RESET pin of the 68000 in order to initialize the external peripheral chips. The 68000 reset pin is bidirectional. A bidirectional buffer circuitry can be connected to the reset pin. The 68000 can be reset by asserting the reset pin using hardware, whereas the peripheral chips can be reset using the software RESET instruction.
- MOVE.L USP, (An) or MOVE.L (An), USP can be used to save, restore, or change the contents of USP in supervisor mode. The USP must be loaded in supervisor mode since MOVE USP is a privileged instruction.
- Consider TRAP # n. There are 16 TRAP instructions with n ranging from 0 to 15. The hexadecimal vector address is calculated using the following equation:

$$\text{Hexadecimal vector address} = 80 + 4*n$$

TABLE 5.13
68000 System Control Instructions

Instruction	Size	Operation
Instruction	**Size**	**Operation**

Privileged Instructions

RESET	Unsized	If supervisory state, then assert reset line; else TRAP
RTE	Unsized	If supervisory state, then restore SR and PC; else TRAP
STOP #data	Unsized	If supervisory state, then load immediate data to SR and then STOP; else TRAP
ORI to SR MOVE USP ANDI to SR EORI to SR MOVE (EA) to SR	}	These instructions were discussed earlier

Trap and Check Instructions

TRAP # vector	Unsized	PC → − [SSP] SR → − [SSP] Vector address → PC
TRAPV	Unsized	TRAP if V = 1
CHK (EA), Dn	W	If Dn < 0 or Dn > [EA], then TRAP

Status Register

ANDI to CCR EORI to CCR MOVE (EA) to CCR ORI to CCR MOVE SR to (EA)	}	Already explained earlier

Note: (EA) in CHK can use all modes except An.

The TRAP instruction first pushes the contents of PC and then the SR onto the system (user or supervisor) stack. The hexadecimal vector address is then loaded into PC. The TRAP is basically a software interrupt.

One of the 16 trap instructions can be executed in the user mode to execute a supervisor program located at the specified trap routine. Using the TRAP instruction, control can be transferred to the supervisor mode from the user mode.

There are other traps which occur due to certain arithmetic errors. For example, division by zero automatically traps to location 14_{16}. On the other hand, an overflow condition, i.e., if $V = 1$, will trap to address $1C_{16}$ if the instruction TRAPV is executed.

- The CHK (EA), Dn instruction compares [Dn] with (EA). If $[Dn]_{\text{low 16 bits}} < 0$ or if $[D]_{\text{low 16 bits}} > (EA)$, then a trap to location 0018_{16} is generated. Also, N is set to 1 if $[Dn]_{\text{low 16 bits}} < 0$ and N is reset to zero if $[Dn]_{\text{low 16 bits}} > (EA)$. (EA) is treated as a 16-bit 2's complement integer. Note that program execution continues if $[Dn]_{\text{low 16 bits}}$ lies between 0 and (EA).

Consider CHK (A5), D2. If $[D2]_{\text{low 16 bits}} = 0200_{16}$, $[A5] = 00003000_{16}$, $[003000_{16}] = 0100_{16}$, then after execution of the CHK, the 68000 will trap since $[D2] = 0200_{16}$ is greater than $[003000] = 0100_{16}$.

The purpose of the CHK instruction is to provide boundary checking by testing if the content of a data register is in the range from zero to an upper limit. The upper limit used in the instruction can be set equal to the length of the array. Then every time the array is accessed, the CHK instruction can be executed to make sure that the array bounds have not been violated.

The CHK instruction is usually placed following the computation of an index value to ensure that the limits of this index value are not violated. This allows checking whether or not the address of an array being accessed is within the array boundaries when the address register indirect with index mode is used to access an element in the array. For example, the instruction sequence shown below will allow accessing of an array with base address in A3 and array length of 125_{10} bytes:

```
        —
        —
CHK #124, D5
MOVE.B 0 (A3, D5.W), D4
        —
        —
        —
```

In the above, if low 16 bits of D5 is greater than 124, the 68000 will trap to location 0018_{16}.

In the above, it is assumed that D5 is computed prior to execution of the CHK instruction. Also, the 68000 assemble requires that a displacement value of 0 be specified as in the instruction MOVE.B0 (A3, D5.W), D4.

5.6.9 STACKS AND QUEUES

A stack is a last-in-first-out (LIFO) memory, while the queue is a first-in-first-out (FIFO) memory. When data are added to a stack or a queue, they are "pushed" onto the structure; when they are removed, they are "popped" from the structure.

The 68000 supports stacks and queues with the address register indirect postincrement and predecrement addressing modes. A queue can be implemented using a linked list. Each entry in the linked list contains the address to the next entry in the list, along with data for each element. A linked list with three elements is shown below:

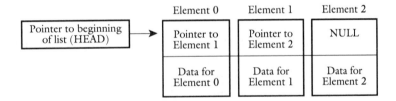

An advantage of linked list is that the items or elements in the list need not be stored in memory in a sequential order, since each element includes the pointer to the next element. This means that in order to change the order of one or more elements, the address pointers must be moved, while the data associated with each element are not required to be moved. Addition, deletion, and insertion of elements are easier with linked lists. The element 2 (last element) in the above figure includes a special symbol identified as NULL to indicate the end of the list. In 68000, a NULL value of 0000_{16} can be used, since no data will be stored at address 0000_{16}. If the address HEAD contains 0000_{16}, the list is assumed to be empty.

5.6.9.a Stacks

In addition to SP, all seven address registers A0-A6 can be used as stack pointers by using appropriate addressing modes.

Subroutine calls, traps, and interrupts automatically use the system stack pointers: USP when S = 0 and SSP when S= 1. Subroutine calls push

PC onto the stack, while RTS pops PC from the system stack. Traps and interrupt push both PC and SR onto the system, while RTE pops PC and SR from the system stack.

These stack operations fill data from high memory to low memory. This means that the system SP is decremented by 2 (word) or 4 (long word) after push and incremented by 2 (for word) or 4 (for long word) after pop. As an example, suppose that a 68000 call instruction (JSR or BSR) is executed when PC = $0031 F200; then after execution of the subroutine call the stack will push the PC as follows:

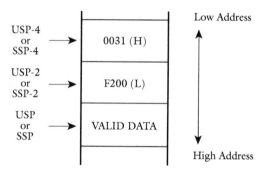

Note that the system stack pointer always points to valid data.

Stacks can be created by the user by using address register indirect with postincrement or predecrement modes. Using one of the seven (A0-A6) address registers, the user may create stacks which can be filled from either high memory to low memory or vice versa.

Stack from high to low memory is implemented with predecrement mode for push and postincrement mode for pop. On the other hand, stack from low to high memory is implemented with postincrement for push and predecrement for pop. For example, consider the following stack growing from high to low memory addresses in which A5 is used as the stack pointer:

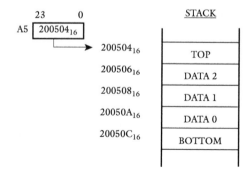

In order to push 16-bit content 0504_{16} of memory location 305016_{16}, the instruction MOVE.W \$305016, $-$(A5) can be used as follows:

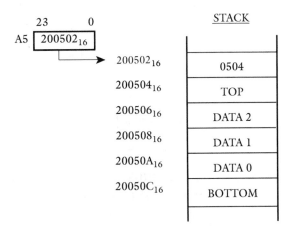

The 16-bit data 0504_{16} can be popped from the stack into low 16 bits of D0 by using MOVE.W (A5)+, D0. A5 will contain 200504_{16} after the POP. Note that in this case, the stack pointer A5 points to valid data.

Next, consider the stack growing from low to high memory addresses in which, say, A6 is used as the stack pointer:

Now, in order to PUSH 16-bit contents 2070_{16} of the low 16 bits of D5, the instruction MOVE.W D5, (A6)+ can be used as follows:

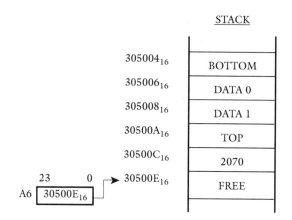

The 16-bit data 2070_{16} can be popped from the stack into 16-bit memory location 417024_{16} by using MOVE.W– (A6), \$417024.

Note that in this case, the stack pointer A6 points to the free location above the valid data.

5.6.9.b Queues

Queues are used to store data in the order in which they will be used. Operating systems store tasks in queues so that they will be executed in the right order.

User queues can be created with the address register indirect with postincrement or predecrement modes. Using two address registers of A0-A6, the user may implement queues which are filled from either high memory to low memory addresses or vice versa. Since queues are pushed from one end and popped from the other, two address registers (Put Pointer and Get Pointer) are used.

For low to high memory addresses, data are placed in the queue using one of A0-A6 such as A5 with postincrement mode as the put pointer, while data are obtained from the queue using a different A0-A6 register such as A4 with postincrement mode. After a put operation, the put address register addresses the next free space in the queue, while the unchanged get register addresses the next data to be read from the queue. After a get operation, the get address register addresses the next data to be read from the queue and the unchanged put address register addresses the next free space in the queue. This situation is shown in the following:

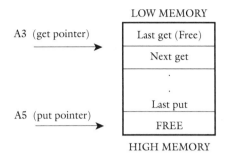

To put data from, for example, low word of D1 into the FREE space, the instruction MOVE.W D1, (A5)+ can be used. To get data into a 24-bit memory location 451724_{16}, the instruction MOVE.W (A3)+, \$451724 can be used.

For high to low memory queue, data are placed in the queue using one of A0-A6 with predecrement mode as the put pointer. Data can be obtained from the queue using a different A0-A6 with predecrement mode. After a put operation, the put address register addresses the last data placed in the queue and the unchanged get address register addresses the last data read from the queue. After a get operation, the get address register addresses the last data read from the queue and the unchanged put address register addresses the last data placed in the queue. This situation is shown below:

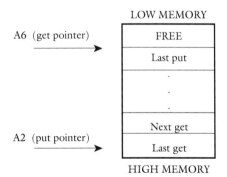

Now, to put 32-bit data from, for example, D2 into the free space, the instruction MOVE.L D2, –(A6) can be used. To get data into low 16-bit D3, the instruction MOVE.W –(A2), D3 can be used.

Example 5.1

Determine the effect of each one of the following 68000 instructions:

- CLR D0
- MOVE.L D1, D0
- CLR.L (A0)+
- MOVE − (A0), D0
- MOVE 20(A0), D0
- MOVEQ.L #$D7, D0
- MOVE 21(A1, A0.L), D0

Assume the following initial configuration before each instruction is executed. Also, assume all numbers in hex.

$$
\begin{aligned}
[D0] &= 22224444 \\
[D1] &= 55556666 \\
[A0] &= 00002224 \\
[A1] &= 00003333 \\
[002220] &= 8888 \\
[002222] &= 7777 \\
[002224] &= 6666 \\
[002226] &= 5555 \\
[002238] &= AAAA \\
[00556C] &= FFFF
\end{aligned}
$$

Solution

Instruction	Effective address	Net effect (HEX)
CLR D0	Destination EA = D0	[D0] = 22220000
MOVE.L D1, D0	Destination EA = D0	[D0] ← 55556666
	Source EA = D1	
CLR.L (A0)+	Destination EA = [A0]	[002224] = 0000
		[002226] = 0000
		[A0] ← 00002228
MOVE −(A0), D0	Source EA = [A0] − 2	[A0) ← 00002222
	Destination EA = D0	[D0] = 22227777
MOVE 20 (A0), D0	Source EA = [A0] + 20_{10} (or 14_{16}) = 002238	[D0] = 2222AAAA
	Destination EA = D0	

Solution (continued)

Instruction	Effective address	Net effect (HEX)
MOVEQ.L#$D7, D0	Source data = $D7_{16}$	$[D0] \leftarrow$ FFFFFFD7
	Destination EA = D0	
MOVE 21(A0, A1.L), D0	Source EA = [A0] + [A1] + 21_{10} = 556C	$[D0]$ = 2222FFFF
	Destination EA = D0	

. . .

Example 5.2

Write a 68000 assembly program segment that implements each one of the following Pascal segments. Assume the following information about the variables involved in this problem.

Variable	Comments
X	Address of a 16-bit signed integer of array 1 of 10 elements
Y	Address of a 16-bit signed integer of array 2 of 10 elements
SUM	Address of the sum

    (a) If X ≥ Y, then X := X + 10;
       else Y :=Y – 12.
       . . .
       . . .
    (b) Sum := 0; for i := 0 to 9, do
       sum := sum + A (i).
       . . .
       . . .

Solution

(a)

```
        LEA  X,  A0      ;   Point A0 to X
        LEA  Y,  A1      ;   Point A1 to Y
        MOVE (A0),  D0   ;   MOVE [X] into D0
        CMP  (A1),  D0   ;   COMPARE [X] WITH
                             [Y]

        BGE  THRPT
```

```
            SUBI #12, (A1)    ;     Execute else part
            BRA NEXT
THRPT       ADDI#10, (A0)     ;     Execute then part
NEXT  . . .
```

(b)
```
            LEA SUM, A1       ;       Point to SUM
            LEA Y, A0         ;   Point A0 to Y [0]
            CLR D0            ;   Clear the sum to
                                  zero
            MOVEQ.L #9,D1     ;   Initialize D1 with
                                  loop limit
     LOOP   ADD (A0) +, D0    ;   Perform the
                                  iterative
            DBF D1,LOOP       ;       Summation
            MOVE D0, (A1)     ;   Transfer the
                                  result

            . . .
```

Note that condition F in DBF is always false and thus we exit from the loop only when the content of the register D1 becomes –1. Therefore, we repeat the addition process for 10 times as desired.

. . .

Example 5.3

Write 68000 assembly program to clear 85_{16} consecutive bytes.

Solution

```
            ORG $2000
            MOVEA.L#$3000,A0  ;   LOAD A0 WITH $3000
            MOVE #$84, D0     ;   MOVE 84₁₆ INTO D0
     LOOP   CLR.B(A0)+        ;   CLEAR [3000₁₆] AND
                              ;   POINT TO NEXT
                                  ADDRESS
            DBF D0, LOOP      ;   DECREMENT AND
                                  BRANCH
FINISH      JMP FINISH        ;   HALT
```

Note that the 68000 has no HALT instruction in the user mode. The 68000 has the STOP instruction in supervisor mode. Therefore, the unconditional JUMP to same location such as FINISH JMP FINISH in the above program must be used. Since DBF is a word instruction and considers D0's low 16-bit word as that loop count, D0 must be initialized by a word MOVE rather than byte MOVE, even though 84_{16} can be accommodated in a byte. Also, one should be careful about using MOVEQ, since MOVEQ sign extends a byte to a long word.

Example 5.4

Write 68000 assembly program to compute

$$\sum_{i=1}^{N} Xi\ Yi$$

where Xi and Yi are signed 16-bit numbers, N = 100. Assume no overflow.

Solution

```
        ORG  $1000
        MOVEQ.L#99,D0  ;      MOVE  99₁₀ INTO D0
        LEA  P, A0     ;      LOAD ADDRESS P INTO A0
        LEA  Q, A1     ;      LOAD ADDRESS Q INTO A1
        CLR.L D1       ;      Initialize D1 to zero
LOOP    MOVE (A0)+, D2       ;     MOVE [X] TO D2
        MULS (A1)+, D2       ;     D2 ← [X] * [Y]
        ADDL.L D2, D1 ;  D1 ← Σ Xi Yi
        DBF  D0, LOOP  ;  DECREMENT AND BRANCH
FINISH  JMP FINISH     ;      HALT
```

Example 5.5

Write a 68000 subroutine to compute

$$Y = \sum_{i=1}^{N} Xi^2/N.$$

Assume the Xi's are 16-bit signed integers and N = 100. The numbers are stored in consecutive locations. Assume A0 points to the Xi's and SP is already initialized. Assume no overflow.

Solution

```
SQRE   MOVEM.L D2/D3/A0,-(SP)   ;   Save registers
       CLR.L D1                 ;   Clear sum
       MOVEQ.L #99,D2           ;   Initialize
                                        loop count
LOOP   MOVE.W (A0)+, D3         ;   Move Xis into D3
       MULS D3,D3               ;   Computer Xi²
       ADD.L D3, D1
       DBF D2, LOOP             ;   Store Xi² into D1
       DIVS #100, D1            ;   Compute Σ Xi²/N
       MOVEM.L (SP)+, D2/D3/A0  ;   Restore registers
       RTS
```

Example 5.6

Write a 68000 assembly language program to move block of data length 100_{10} from the source block starting at location 002000_{16} to the destination block starting at location 003000_{16}.

Solution

```
       MOVEA.L #$2000, A4       ;   Load A4 with
                                        source address
       MOVEA.L #$3000, A5       ;   Load A5 with
                                        destination
                                        address
       MOVEQ.L #99, D0          ;   Load D0 with count
                                        -1 = 99₁₀
START  MOVE.W (A4)+, (A5)+      ;   MOVE source data
                                        to destination
       DBF D0, START            ;   Branch if D0 ≠ -1
END    JMP END                  ;   HALT
                                . . .
```

Example 5.7

Assume the following linked list:

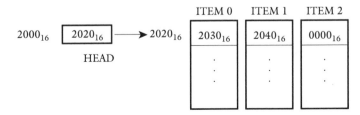

Write a 68000 assembly language program to insert a new item as item 0 containing data starting at address 2010_{16} as follows:

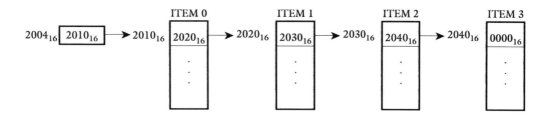

Solution

```
ADDR1   EQU   $2010
HEAD    EQU   $2000
        ORG   $5000
        MOVEA.W  HEAD, A5      ;      MOVE old head to
                                      A5
        MOVE.W   A5, ADDR1     ;      MOVE starting
                                      address of
                               ;      old Item 0 to NEW
                               ;      Item 0 first
                                      content
        MOVE.W   #$2010,HEAD   ;      Update HEAD
STOP    JMP   STOP
```

5.7 68000 PINS AND SIGNALS

The 68000 is housed in one of the following packages:

- 64-pin dual in-line package (DIP)
- 68-Terminal Chip Carrier
- 68-pin Quad Pack
- 68-pin Grid Array

Figure 5.8 shows the pin diagrams of the 68-pin grid array. Pin diagrams for the other three packages are shown in Appendix B.

The 68000 is provided with several Vcc and ground pins. Power is thus distributed in order to reduce noise problems at high frequencies.

In order to build a prototype to demonstrate that the paper design for

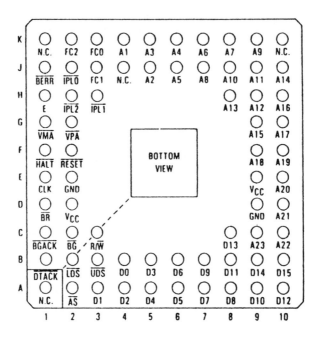

FIGURE 5.8 68-pin grid array.

the 68000-based microcomputer is correct, one must use either wire-wrap or solder for the actual construction. Prototype board must not be used. This is because at high frequencies above 4 MHz, there will be noise problems due to stray capacitances.

D0-D15 is the 16-bit data bus. All transfers to and from memory and I/O devices are conducted over the 16-bit bus. A1-A23 are the 23 address lines. A0 is obtained by encoding $\overline{\text{UDS}}$ (Upper Data Strobe) and $\overline{\text{LDS}}$ (Lower Data Strobe) lines. The 68000 operates on a single-phase TTL level clock at 4 MHz, 6 MHz, 8 MHz, 10 MHz, 12.5 MHz, 16.67 MHz, or 25 MHz. The 68000 also has a lower-power HCMOS version called the MC68HC000 which can run at 8 MHz, 10 MHz, 12.5 MHz, and 16.67 MHz.

There is no on-chip clock generator/driver circuitry and therefore the clock must be generated externally. This clock input is utilized internally by the 68000 to generate additional clock signals for synchronizing the 68000's internal operation.

Figure 5.9 shows the 68000 CLK waveform and clock timing specifications.

AC ELECTRICAL SPECIFICATIONS – CLOCK TIMING

Characteristic	Symbol	8 MHz		10 MHz		12.5 MHz		Unit
		Min	Max	Min	Max	Min	Max	
Frequency of Operation	f	4.0	8.0	4.0	10.0	4.0	12.5	MHz
Cycle Time	t_{cyc}	125	250	100	250	80	250	ns
Clock Pulse Width	t_{CL}	55	125	45	125	35	125	ns
	t_{CH}	55	125	45	125	35	125	
Rise and Fall Times	t_{Cr}	–	10	–	10	–	5	ns
	t_{Cf}	–	10	–	10	–	5	

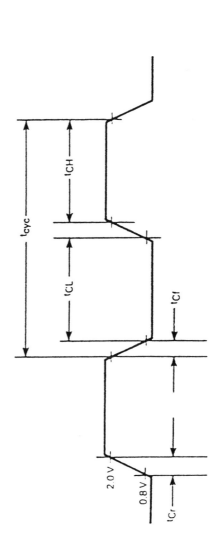

FIGURE 5.9 Clock input timing diagram.

NOTE: Timing measurements are referenced to and from a low voltage of 0.8 volts and a high voltage of 2.0 volts, unless otherwise noted. The voltage swing through this range should start outside and pass through the range such that the rise or fall will be linear between 0.8 and 2.0 volts.

The clock is at TTL compatible voltage. The clock timing specification provides data for three different clock frequencies: 8 MHz, 10 MHz, and 12.5 MHz.

The 68000 CLK input can be provided by a crystal oscillator or by designing an external circuit. Figure 5.10 shows a simple oscillator to generate the 68000 CLK input. The above circuit uses two inverters connected in series. Inverter 1 is biased in its transition region by the resistor R. Inverter 1 inputs the crystal output (sinusoidal) to produce logic pulse train at the output of inverter 1. Inverter 2 sharpens the wave and drives the crystal. For this circuit to work, HCMOS logic (74HC00, 74HC02, or 74HC04) must be used and a coupling capacitor should be connected across the supply terminals to reduce the ringing effect during high-frequency switching of the HCMOS devices. Additionally, the output of this oscillator is fed to the clock input of a D-flip-flop (74LS74) to further reduce the ringing. Hence, a clock signal of 50% duty cycle at a frequency of 1/2 the crystal frequency is generated.

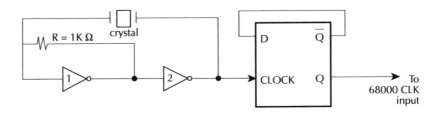

FIGURE 5.10 External clock circuitry.

The 68000 consumes about 1.5 watts of power.

The 68000 signals can be divided into five functional categories. These are

1. Synchronous and asynchronous control lines
2. System control lines
3. Interrupt control lines
4. DMA control lines
5. Status lines

5.7.1 SYNCHRONOUS AND ASYNCHRONOUS CONTROL LINES

The 68000 bus control is asynchronous. This means that once a bus cycle is initiated, the external device must send a signal back in order to complete it. The 68000 also contains three synchronous control lines that facilitate interfacing to synchronous peripheral devices such as Motorola's inexpensive MC6800 family. Note that synchronous operation means that bus control is synchronized or clocked using a common system clock signal. In 6800 family peripherals, this common clock is a phase 2 (Ø2) or an E clock signal depending on the particular chip used.

With synchronous control, all READ and WRITE operations must be synchronized with the common clock. However, this may create problems when interfacing slow peripheral devices. This problem does not arise with asynchronous bus control.

Asynchronous operation is not dependent on a common clock signal. The 68000 utilizes the asynchronous control lines to transfer data between the 68000 and peripheral devices via handshaking. Using asynchronous operation, the 68000 can be interfaced to any peripheral chip regardless of the speed. The 68000 has three control lines to transfer data over its bus in a synchronous manner. These are E (enable), $\overline{\text{VPA}}$ (valid peripheral address), and $\overline{\text{VMA}}$ (valid memory address).

The E clock corresponds to phase 2 clock of the 6800. The E clock is output at a frequency that is 1/10th of the 68000 input clock. The $\overline{\text{VPA}}$ is an input which tells the 68000 that a 6800 device is being addressed and therefore data transfer must be synchronized with the E clock. The $\overline{\text{VMA}}$ is processor's response to $\overline{\text{VPA}}$. $\overline{\text{VPA}}$ is asserted when the memory address is valid. This also tells the external device that the next data transfer over the data bus will be synchronized with the E clock. $\overline{\text{VPA}}$ can be generated by decoding the address pins and address strobe ($\overline{\text{AS}}$). Note that the 68000 asserts $\overline{\text{AS}}$ low when the address on the address bus is valid. $\overline{\text{VMA}}$ is typically used as chip select of the 6800 peripheral. This ensures that the 6800 peripherals are selected and deselected at the correct time. The 6800 peripheral interfacing sequence is provided in the following:

1. The 68000 initiates a cycle by starting a normal read or write cycle.
2. The 6800 peripheral defines the 6800 cycle by asserting the 68000 $\overline{\text{VPA}}$ input. If the $\overline{\text{VPA}}$ is asserted as soon as possible after the assertion of $\overline{\text{AS}}$, then $\overline{\text{VPA}}$ will be recognized as being asserted on the falling edge of S4. If the $\overline{\text{VPA}}$ is not asserted at the falling edge of S4, the 68000 inserts wait states until $\overline{\text{VPA}}$ is recognized by the 68000 as asserted. $\overline{\text{DTACK}}$ should not be asserted while $\overline{\text{VPA}}$ is asserted. The 6800 peripheral must remove $\overline{\text{VPA}}$ within one clock after $\overline{\text{AS}}$ is negated.
3. The 68000 monitors enable (E) until it is low. The 68000 then

synchronizes all read and write operations with the E clock. $\overline{\text{VMA}}$ output pin is asserted low by the 68000.

4. The 68000 peripheral waits until E is active (HIGH) and then transfers the data.

5. The 68000 waits until E goes low (on a read cycle the data is latched as E goes low internally). The 68000 then negates $\overline{\text{VMA}}$, $\overline{\text{AS}}$, $\overline{\text{UDS}}$, and $\overline{\text{LDS}}$. The 68000 thus terminates the cycle and starts the next cycle.

The 68000 provides five lines to control address and data transfers asynchronously. These are $\overline{\text{AS}}$ (Address Strobe), R/$\overline{\text{W}}$ (Read/Write), $\overline{\text{DTACK}}$ (Data Acknowledge), $\overline{\text{UDS}}$ (Upper Data Strobe), and $\overline{\text{LDS}}$ (Lower Data Strobe).

The 68000 outputs $\overline{\text{AS}}$ to notify the peripheral device when data are to be transferred. $\overline{\text{AS}}$ is active LOW when the 68000 provides a valid address on the address bus. The R/$\overline{\text{W}}$ is HIGH for read and LOW for write. The $\overline{\text{DTACK}}$ is used to tell the 68000 that a transfer is to be performed.

When the 68000 wants to transfer data asynchronously, it first activates the $\overline{\text{AS}}$ line and, at the same time, the 68000 generates the required address on the address lines in order to select the peripheral device.

Since the $\overline{\text{AS}}$ line tells the peripheral chip when to transfer data, the $\overline{\text{AS}}$ line should be part of the address decoding scheme. After enabling the $\overline{\text{AS}}$, the 68000 enters the wait state until it receives the $\overline{\text{DTACK}}$ from the selected peripheral device. On receipt of the $\overline{\text{DTACK}}$, the 68000 knows that the peripheral device is ready for data transfer. The 68000 then utilizes the R/$\overline{\text{W}}$ and data lines to transfer data.

$\overline{\text{UDS}}$ and $\overline{\text{LDS}}$ are defined as follows:

$\overline{\text{UDS}}$	$\overline{\text{LDS}}$	Data Transfer occurs via	Address
1	0	D0-D7 pins for byte	Odd
0	1	D8-D15 pins for byte	Even
0	0	D0-D15 pins for word or Long word	Even

$\overline{\text{UDS}}$ and $\overline{\text{LDS}}$ are used to segment the memory into bytes instead of words. When the $\overline{\text{UDS}}$ is asserted, contents of even addresses are transferred on the high-order 8 lines of the data bus, D8-D15. The 68000 internally shifts these data to the low byte of the specified register. When $\overline{\text{LDS}}$ is asserted, contents of odd addresses are transferred on the low-order 8 lines of the data bus, D0-D7. During word and long word transfers, both $\overline{\text{UDS}}$ and $\overline{\text{LDS}}$ are asserted and information is transferred on all 16 data lines, D0-D15. Note that during byte memory transfers, A0 corresponds to $\overline{\text{UDS}}$ for even addresses (A0 = 0) and to $\overline{\text{LDS}}$ for odd addresses (A0 = 1). The circuit in Figure 5.11 shows how even and odd addresses are interfaced to the 68000.

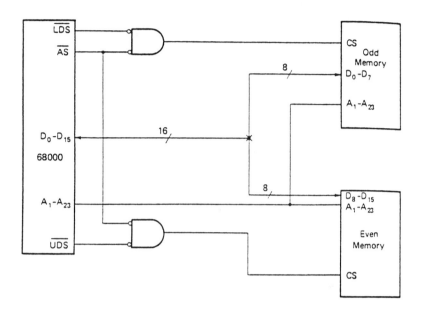

FIGURE 5.11 Interfacing of the 68000 to even and odd addresses.

5.7.2 SYSTEM CONTROL LINES

The 68000 has three control lines, namely, $\overline{\text{BERR}}$ (Bus Error), $\overline{\text{HALT}}$, and $\overline{\text{RESET}}$, that are used to control system-related functions.

The $\overline{\text{BERR}}$ is an input to the 68000 that is used to inform the processor that there is a problem with the instruction cycle currently being executed. With asynchronous operation, this problem may arise if the 68000 does not receive $\overline{\text{DTACK}}$ from a peripheral device. An external timer can be used to activate the $\overline{\text{BERR}}$ pin if the external device does not send $\overline{\text{DTACK}}$ within a certain period of time. On receipt of the $\overline{\text{BERR}}$, the 68000 does one of the following:

- Reruns the instruction cycle which caused the error
- Executes an error service routine

The troubled instruction cycle is rerun by the 68000 if it receives a

$\overline{\text{HALT}}$ signal along with the $\overline{\text{BERR}}$ signal. On receipt of LOW on both $\overline{\text{HALT}}$ and $\overline{\text{BERR}}$ pins, the 68000 completes the current instruction cycle and then goes itself into the high impedance state. On removal of both $\overline{\text{HALT}}$ and $\overline{\text{BERR}}$ (that is, when both $\overline{\text{HALT}}$ and $\overline{\text{BERR}}$ are HIGH), the 68000 reruns the troubled instruction cycle. The cycle can be rerun repeatedly if both $\overline{\text{BERR}}$ and $\overline{\text{HALT}}$ are enabled/disabled continually.

On the other hand, an error service routine is executed only if the $\overline{\text{BERR}}$ is received without $\overline{\text{HALT}}$. In this case, the 68000 will branch to a bus error vector address where the user can write a service routine. If two simultaneous bus errors are received via the $\overline{\text{BERR}}$ pin without $\overline{\text{HALT}}$, the 68000 automatically goes into the $\overline{\text{HALT}}$ state until it is reset.

The $\overline{\text{HALT}}$ line can also be used by itself to perform single-stepping or to provide DMA. When $\overline{\text{HALT}}$ input is activated, the 68000 completes the current instruction and goes into a high impedance state until $\overline{\text{HALT}}$ is returned to HIGH. By enabling/disabling the $\overline{\text{HALT}}$ line continually, the single-stepping debugging can be accomplished. However, since most 68000 instructions consist of more than one instruction cycle, single-stepping using $\overline{\text{HALT}}$ is not normally used. Rather, the trace bit in the status register is used to single-step the complete instruction.

One can also use $\overline{\text{HALT}}$ to perform microprocessor-halt DMA. Since the 68000 has separate DMA control lines, DMA using the $\overline{\text{HALT}}$ line will not normally be used.

The $\overline{\text{HALT}}$ pin can also be used as an output signal. The 68000 will assert the $\overline{\text{HALT}}$ pin LOW when it goes into a $\overline{\text{HALT}}$ state as a result of a catastrophic failure. The double bus error (activation of $\overline{\text{BERR}}$ twice) is an example of this type of error. When this occurs, the 68000 goes into a high impedance state until it is reset. The $\overline{\text{HALT}}$ line informs the peripheral devices of the catastrophic failure.

The $\overline{\text{RESET}}$ line of the 68000 is also bidirectional. In order to reset the 68000, both the $\overline{\text{RESET}}$ and $\overline{\text{HALT}}$ pins must be asserted at the same time. The 68000 executes a reset service routine automatically for loading the PC with the starting address of the program. The 68000 $\overline{\text{RESET}}$ pin can also be used as an output line. A LOW can be sent to this output line by executing the $\overline{\text{RESET}}$ instruction in the supervisor mode in order to reset external devices connected to the 68000. The execution of the $\overline{\text{RESET}}$ instruction does not affect any data, address, or status register. Therefore, the $\overline{\text{RESET}}$ instruction can be placed anywhere in the program whenever the external devices need to be reset. An external bidirectional buffer circuit is needed in order to use the $\overline{\text{RESET}}$ pin as both input and output.

The $\overline{\text{RESET}}$ line of the 68000 is bidirectional. This means that the

68000 $\overline{\text{RESET}}$ pin can be used as an input or an output line. For hardware reset, this $\overline{\text{RESET}}$ pin must be activated LOW by an external circuit. This will initialize 68000 PC, SP, and status register. The $\overline{\text{RESET}}$ pin can also be used as an output pin. The $\overline{\text{RESET}}$ instruction can be executed by the 68000 in supervisor mode to output a LOW on the $\overline{\text{RESET}}$ pin to reset the memory and I/O chips. In order to use the $\overline{\text{RESET}}$ pin as an I/O pin, bidirectional buffer will be required. However, the reset input pins of the memory and I/O chips can be connected to the 68000 $\overline{\text{RESET}}$ pin along with the reset circuit. Activation of the 68000 $\overline{\text{RESET}}$ pin via the reset circuit will reset the 68000, memory, and I/O chips. In this case, bidirectional buffers are not required.

In order to reset the 68000, both the $\overline{\text{RESET}}$ and $\overline{\text{HALT}}$ pins must be asserted simultaneously by an external circuit. Figure 5.12 shows the timing diagram for the 68000 reset operation.

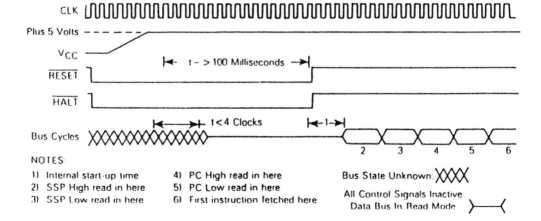

FIGURE 5.12 68000 reset operation timing diagram.

Upon hardware reset, the 68000 performs the following:

1. The 68000 reads four words from addresses $000000, $000002, $000004, and $000006. The 68000 loads the supervisor stack pointer high and low words with the contents of locations $000000 and $000002, respectively. Also, the program counter high and low words are loaded with the contents of locations $000004 and $000006, respectively.
2. The 68000 initializes the status register to an interrupt level of seven.
3. No other registers are affected by hardware reset.

When a RESET instruction is executed, the 68000 drives the $\overline{\text{RESET}}$ pin low for 124 clock periods. In this case, the processor is trying to reset the rest of the system. Therefore, there is no effect on the internal state of the 68000. All of the 68000 internal registers and the status register are unaffected by the execution of a reset instruction. All external devices connected to the $\overline{\text{RESET}}$ line will be reset at the completion of the reset instruction.

Asserting the $\overline{\text{RESET}}$ and $\overline{\text{HALT}}$ lines for 10 clock cycles will cause a processor reset, except when Vcc is initially applied to the 68000. In this case, an external reset must be applied for at least 100 milliseconds.

The reset circuit (used for 8085) depicted in Figure 5.13a satisfies the 68000 reset requirements mentioned above.

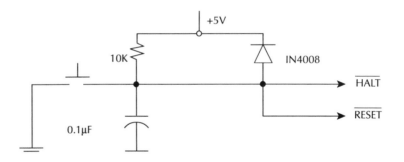

FIGURE 5.13a 68000 RESET circuit (simple).

The above circuit is similar to the 8085 reset circuit except that the output goes to both $\overline{\text{RESET}}$ and $\overline{\text{HALT}}$ lines of the 68000. A more accurate $\overline{\text{RESET}}$ circuit is shown in Figure 5.13b.

The Motorola MC1455 in Figure 5.13b is a timer chip that provides accurate time delays or oscillation. The timer is precisely controlled by external resistors and capacitors. The timer may be triggered by an external trigger input (falling waveform) and can reset by external reset input (falling waveform).

The reset circuit in Figure 5.13b will assert the 68000 $\overline{\text{RESET}}$ pin for at least 10 clock cycles. From the MC1455 data sheet, the internal block diagram of the MC1455 is shown in Figure 5.13c.

When the input voltage (Vcc) to the trigger comparator (COMPB) falls below 1/3 Vcc, the comparator output (COMPA) triggers the flip-flop so that its output becomes low. This turns the capacitor discharge transistor OFF and drives the digital output to the HIGH state. This condition permits the capacitor to charge at an exponential rate set by the

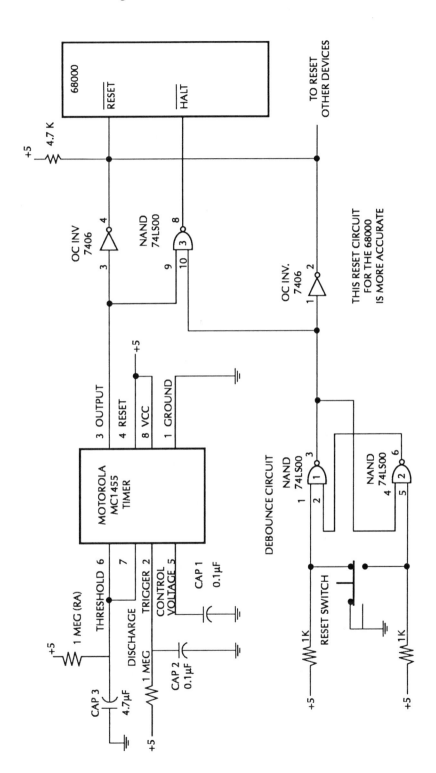

FIGURE 5.13b 68000 $\overline{\text{RESET}}$ circuit.

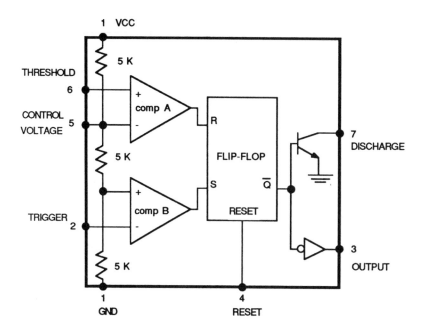

FIGURE 5.13c MC1455 internal block diagram.

RC time constant. When the capacitor voltage reaches $^2/_3$ Vcc, the threshold comparator resets the flip-flop. The action discharges the timing capacitor and returns the digital output to the LOW state. The output will be HIGH for t = 1.1 R_AC seconds, where R_A = 1M and C = 4.7 μF.

The MC1455 can be connected so that it will trigger itself and the capacitor voltage will oscillate between $^1/_3$ Vcc and $^2/_3$ Vcc. Once the flip-flop has been triggered by an input signal, it cannot be retriggered until the present timing period has been completed. A reset pin is provided to discharge the capacitor, thus interrupting the timing cycle. The reset pin should be tied to Vcc when not in use. With proper trigger input as in the figure, the MC1455 output will stay HIGH for 1.1 R_AC = 5.17 s (1.1 * 10^6 * 4.7 * 10^{-6}). The 68000 requires the $\overline{\text{RESET}}$ and $\overline{\text{HALT}}$ lines to be low for at least 10 cycles. If the 68000 clock cycle is 0.125 μs (8-MHz clock), then the 68000 $\overline{\text{RESET}}$ and $\overline{\text{HALT}}$ pins must be LOW for at least 0.125 μs * 10 = 1.25 μs. Since the MC1455 output is connected to the 68000 $\overline{\text{RESET}}$ pin through an inverter, the $\overline{\text{RESET}}$ pin will be held LOW for 5.17 s (greater than 1.25 μs). Hence, the timing requirement for the 68000 $\overline{\text{RESET}}$ pin is satisfied. The $\overline{\text{HALT}}$ pin is activated by NANDing the MC1455 true output and the debouncing circuit output. The $\overline{\text{HALT}}$ pin is LOW when both inputs to NAND gate #3 are HIGH. The MC1455 output is HIGH for 5.17 s and the output of the debounce circuit is HIGH when the push button is activated. This will generate a LOW at the $\overline{\text{HALT}}$ pin for 5.17 s (greater than 1.25 μs). The timing requirements of the 68000 $\overline{\text{RESET}}$ and $\overline{\text{HALT}}$ pins will be satisfied by the reset circuit of Figure 5.13b.

Note that when the reset circuit is not activated, the top input of AND gate #1 is HIGH and the bottom input of AND gate #2 is LOW (HIGH is grounded to LOW, see Figure 5.13b). Since a NAND gate always produces a HIGH output when one of the inputs is LOW, the output of NAND gate #2 will be HIGH. This will make the bottom input of NAND gate #1 HIGH and thus the output of NAND gate #1 will be LOW, which in turn will make the output of NAND gate #3 HIGH. Therefore, the 68000 will not be reset when the push button is not activated. Upon activation of the push button, the top input of NAND gate #1 is LOW (HIGH is grounded to LOW); this will make the output of NAND gate #1 HIGH. Hence, both inputs of NAND gate #3 will be HIGH providing a LOW at the $\overline{\text{HALT}}$ pin for 5.17 s (greater than 1.25 μs).

5.7.3 INTERRUPT CONTROL LINES

$\overline{\text{IPL0}}$, $\overline{\text{IPL1}}$, and $\overline{\text{IPL2}}$ are interrupt control lines. These lines provide for seven interrupt priority levels ($\overline{\text{IPL2}}$, $\overline{\text{IPL1}}$, $\overline{\text{IPL0}}$ = 111 means no interrupt and $\overline{\text{IPL2}}$, $\overline{\text{IPL1}}$, $\overline{\text{IPL0}}$ = 000 means nonmaskable interrupt). $\overline{\text{IPL2}}$, $\overline{\text{IPL1}}$, $\overline{\text{IPL0}}$ = 001 through 110 provides six maskable interrupts. The 68000 interrupts will be discussed later in this chapter.

5.7.4 DMA CONTROL LINES

$\overline{\text{BR}}$ (Bus Request), $\overline{\text{BG}}$ (Bus Grant), and $\overline{\text{BGACK}}$ (Bus Grant Acknowledge) lines are used for DMA purposes. The 68000 DMA will be discussed later in this chapter.

5.7.5 STATUS LINES

The 68000 has three output lines called the function code pins (FC2, FC1, and FC0). Table 5.14 shows how these lines tell external devices whether user data, user program, supervisor data, or supervisor program is being addressed. These lines can be decoded to provide user or supervisor programs and/or data, and interrupt acknowledge as shown in Table 5.14.

The FC2, FC1, and FC0 pins can be used to partition memory into four functional areas: user data memory, user program memory, supervisor data memory, and supervisor program memory. Each memory partition can directly access up to 16 megabytes, and thus the 68000 can be used to directly address up to 64 megabytes of memory. This is shown in Figure 5.14.

TABLE 5.14
Function Code Lines

FC2	FC1	FC0	Operation
0	0	0	Unassigned
0	0	1	User data
0	1	0	User program
0	1	1	Unassigned
1	0	0	Unassigned
1	0	1	Supervisor data
1	1	0	Supervisor program
1	1	1	Interrupt acknowledge

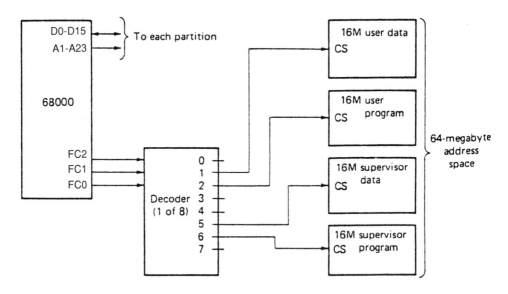

FIGURE 5.14 Partitioning 68000 address space using FC2, FC1, and FC0 pins.

5.8 68000 SYSTEM DIAGRAM

Figure 5.15 shows a simplified version of the 68000 basic system diagram.

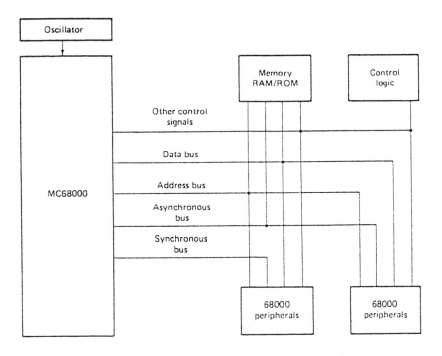

FIGURE 5.15 68000 basic system.

5.9 TIMING DIAGRAMS

The 68000 family of processors (68000, 68008, 68010, and 68012) uses a handshaking mechanism to transfer data between the processors and the peripheral devices. This means that all these processors can transfer data asynchronously to and from peripherals of varying speeds.

Figure 5.16 shows 68000 read and write cycle timing diagrams.

During the read cycle, the 68000 obtains data from a memory location or an I/O port. If the instruction specifies a word such as MOVE.W$020504, D1 or a long word such as MOVE.L $030808, D0, the 68000 reads both upper and lower bytes at the same time by asserting $\overline{UDS}$ and $\overline{LDS}$ pins. When the instruction is for a byte operation the 68000 utilizes an internal bit to find which byte to read and then outputs the data strobe required for that byte. For byte operations, when the address is even (A0 = 0), the 68000 asserts $\overline{UDS}$ and reads data via D8-D15 pins into low byte of the

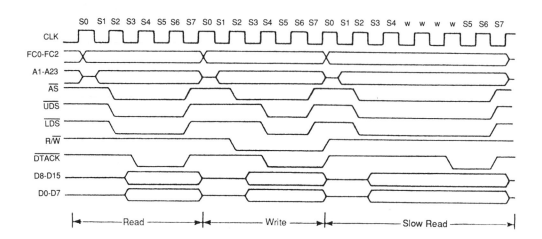

FIGURE 5.16 Read and write cycle timing diagrams.

specified data register. On the other hand, for reading data byte from an odd address (A0 = 1), the 68000 outputs LOW on $\overline{\text{LDS}}$ and reads data byte via D0-D7 pins into low byte of the specified data register. For example, consider MOVE.B $507144, D5. The 68000 outputs LOW on $\overline{\text{UDS}}$ (since A0 = 0) and high on $\overline{\text{LDS}}$. The memory chip's 8 data lines must be connected to the 68000 D8-D15 pins. The 68000 reads the data byte via D8-D15 pins into low byte of D5. Note that for reading a data byte from an odd location by executing an instruction such as MOVE.B $507145, D5, the 8 data lines of the memory chip must be connected to 68000 D0-D7 pins. The 68000, in this case, outputs low on $\overline{\text{LDS}}$ (A0 = 0) and high on $\overline{\text{UDS}}$, then reads the data byte into low byte of D5.

Now, let us discuss the read timing diagram of Figure 5.16. Consider Figure 5.16 for word read timing. During S0, address and data signals are in high impedance state. At the start of S1, the 68000 outputs the address on its address pins (A1-A23). During S0, the 68000 outputs FC2-FC0 signals. $\overline{\text{AS}}$ is asserted at the start of S2 to indicate valid address on bus. $\overline{\text{AS}}$ can be used at this point to latch the signals on the address pins. The 68000 asserts $\overline{\text{UDS}}$ and $\overline{\text{LDS}}$ pins to indicate a word transfer. The 68000 also outputs high on the R/$\overline{\text{W}}$ pin to indicate a read operation.

The 68000 now waits for the peripheral device to assert $\overline{\text{DTACK}}$. Upon placing data on the data bus, the peripheral device asserts $\overline{\text{DTACK}}$. The 68000 samples $\overline{\text{DTACK}}$ signal at the end of S4. If $\overline{\text{DTACK}}$ is not asserted by the peripheral device, the processor automatically inserts wait states (W).

However, upon assertion of $\overline{\text{DTACK}}$, the 68000 negates $\overline{\text{AS}}$, $\overline{\text{UDS}}$, and

$\overline{\text{LDS}}$ signals and then latches the data from data bus into an internal register at the end of the next cycle. Once the selected peripheral device senses that the 68000 has obtained data from the data bus (by recognizing the negation of $\overline{\text{AS}}$, $\overline{\text{UDS}}$, or $\overline{\text{LDS}}$), the peripheral device must negate $\overline{\text{DTACK}}$ immediately, so that it does not interfere with the start of the next cycle.

If $\overline{\text{DTACK}}$ is not asserted by peripherals at the end of state 4 (Figure 5.16), the 68000 inserts wait states. The 68000 outputs valid addresses on the address pins and keeps asserting $\overline{\text{AS}}$, $\overline{\text{UDS}}$, and $\overline{\text{LDS}}$ until the peripheral asserts $\overline{\text{DTACK}}$. The 68000 always inserts an even number of wait states if $\overline{\text{DTACK}}$ is not asserted by the peripheral, since all 68000 operations are performed using the clock with two states per clock cycle. Note that in Figure 5.16, the 68000 inserts 6 wait states or 3 cycles.

As an example of word read, consider that the 68000 is ready to execute the MOVE.W $602122, D0 instruction.

The 68000 performs the following:

1. The 68000, at the end of S0, places the upper 23 bits of the address 602122_{16} on A1-A23.
2. At the end of S1 state, the 68000 asserts $\overline{\text{AS}}$, $\overline{\text{UDS}}$, and $\overline{\text{LDS}}$.
3. The 68000 continues to output high on R/W pin from the beginning of the read cycle, indicating a READ operation.
4. At the end of S0, the 68000 places appropriate outputs on FC2-FC0 pins to indicate whether supervisor or user read.
5. If the peripheral asserts $\overline{\text{DTACK}}$ at the end of S4, the 68000 reads the contents of 602122_{16} and 602123_{16} via D8-D15 pins and D0-D7 pins, respectively, into high and low bytes of D0 at the end of S6. If the peripheral does not assert $\overline{\text{DTACK}}$ at the end of S4, the 68000 continues to insert wait states.

Consider Figure 5.16 for 68000 write word timing. The 68000 outputs the address of the location to be written into the address bus at the start of S1. During S0, the 68000 places the proper function code values at the FC2, FC1, and FC0 pins. If the 68000 uses the data bus in the previous cycle, then it places all data pins in the high impedance state and then outputs LOW on $\overline{\text{AS}}$ and R/W pins. At the start of S3, the 68000 places data on D0-D15 pins. The 68000 then asserts $\overline{\text{UDS}}$ and $\overline{\text{LDS}}$ pins at the beginning of S4.

For the memory or I/O device, if $\overline{\text{DTACK}}$ is not asserted by memory or I/O device by the end of S4, the 68000 automatically inserts wait states into the write cycle.

The 68000 provides a special cycle called the read-modify-write cycle during execution of only the TAS instruction. This instruction reads a data byte, sets condition codes according to the byte value, sets bit 7 of the byte, and then writes the byte back into memory. The TAS instruction can be used in providing data transfer between two 68000 processors using shared RAM. The data byte mentioned above is held in the shared RAM. The read/modify/write cycle is indivisible. That is, it cannot be interrupted by any other bus request.

5.10 68000 MEMORY INTERFACE

One of the advantages of the 68000 is that it can easily be interfaced to memory chips. This is because the 68000 goes into a wait state if $\overline{DTACK}$ is not asserted by the memory devices at the end of S4.

A simplified schematic showing an interface of a 68000 to two 2716s and two 6116s is shown in Figure 5.17. The 2716 is a 2 K×8 EPROM and the 6116 is a 2 K×8 static RAM. For a 4-MHz clock, each cycle is 250 ns. The 68000 samples $\overline{DTACK}$ at the falling edge of the S4 (third clock cycle) and latches data at the falling edge of S6 (fourth clock cycle). $\overline{AS}$ is used to assert $\overline{DTACK}$. $\overline{AS}$ goes to LOW after 500 ns (two clock cycles). The time delay between $\overline{AS}$ going LOW and the falling edge of S6 is 500 ns.

Since the access times of the 2716 and 6116 are, respectively, 450 and 120 ns, delay circuits for $\overline{DTACK}$ are not required. Note that $\overline{LDS}$ and $\overline{UDS}$ must be used as chip selects as in the figure. They must not be connected to A0 of the memory chips, since in that case half of the memory in each chip will be wasted. For example, consider Figure 5.18 in which A0 of the even 2716 is connected to 68000 $\overline{UDS}$ pin via an inverter. Assume that the 2716's $\overline{OE}$ and $\overline{CE}$ are enabled (not shown in the figure).

The 2716 has eleven address pins. These 11-bit locations accessed by the 68000 in the 2716s can be obtained as follows:

Even 2716 (when $\overline{UDS}$ = 0, A0 is 0)

A10	A9	A8	A7	A6	A5	A4	A3	A2	A1	A0	*Hex Address*
0	0	0	0	0	0	0	0	0	0	0	= $000
0	0	0	0	0	0	0	0	0	1	0	= $002
—		—					—				
—		—					—				
—		—					—				
1	1	1	1	1	1	1	1	1	1	0	= $7FE

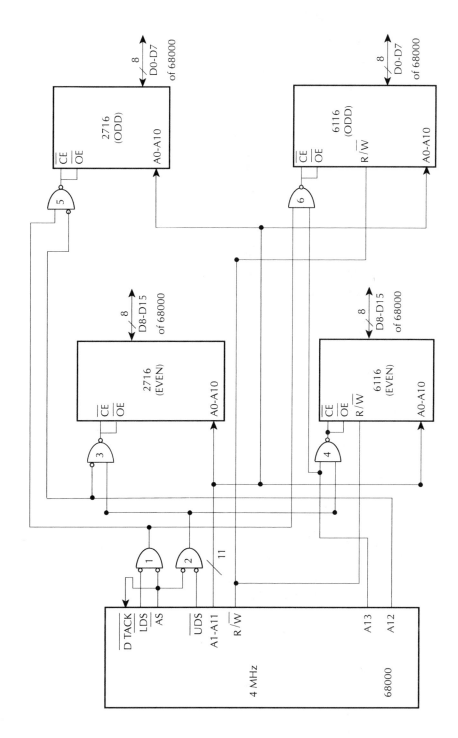

FIGURE 5.17 68000 interface to 2716/6116.

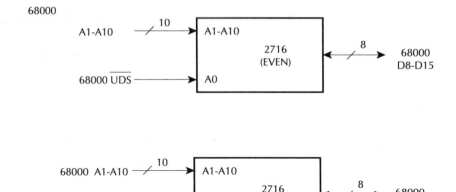

FIGURE 5.18 Connecting A0 of memory chips to 68000 $\overline{\text{LDS}}$ or $\overline{\text{UDS}}$ (not recommended).

Odd 2716 (when $\overline{\text{LDS}}$ = 0, A0 is 1)

A10	A9	A8	A7	A6	A5	A4	A3	A2	A1	A0	*Hex Address*
0	0	0	0	0	0	0	0	0	0	1	= $001
0	0	0	0	0	0	0	0	0	1	1	= $003
—	—	—				—					
—	—	—				—					
—	—	—				—					
1	1	1	1	1	1	1	1	1	1	1	= $7FF

Therefore, in the even 2716, alternate locations $000, $002, $004 ... are addressable by the 68000. Similarly, for the odd 2716, alternate locations $001, $003, $005 ... are accessible. This means that half of the memory of each memory chip will not be accessed by the 68000 if $\overline{\text{UDS}}$ and $\overline{\text{LDS}}$ are connected to A0 of even and odd memory chips, respectively. Therefore, the configuration of Figure 5.18 is not recommended. Let us determine the memory map of Figure 5.17. Assume the don't care values of A23-A14 to be zeros.

Memory map for even 2716 (A12 must be zero to select even 2716 and A13 must be zero to deselect even 6116)

A23	A22	A21	A20	A19	A18	A17	A16	A15	A14	A13	A12	A11	...	A1	A0
0	0	0	0	0	0	0	0	0	0	0	0				0

can be from all zeros to all ones

The memory map includes the addresses $000000, $000002, $00004, ... $000FFE.

Memory map for odd 2716 (A12 must be 0 to select odd 2716 and A13 must be 0 to deselect odd 6116)

A23	A22	A21	A20	A19	A18	A17	A16	A15	A14	A13	A12	A11...A1	A0
0	0	0	0	0	0	0	0	0	0	0	0		1

can be from all zeros to all ones

The memory map includes the addresses $000001, $000003, $000005, ... $000FFF.

Memory map for even 6116 (A12 must be one to deselect even 2716 and A13 must be one to select even 6116)

A23	A22	A21	A20	A19	A18	A17	A16	A15	A14	A13	A12	A11...A1	A0
0	0	0	0	0	0	0	0	0	0	1	1		0

can be from all zeros to all ones

The memory map includes the addresses $003000, $003002, . . . , $003FFE.

Memory map for odd 6116 (A12 must be one to deselect odd 2716 and A13 must be one to select to odd 6116)

A23	A22	A21	A20	A19	A18	A17	A16	A15	A14	A13	A12	A11 ... A1	A0
0	0	0	0	0	0	0	0	0	0	1	1		1

can be from all zeros to all ones

The memory map includes the addresses $003001, $003003, . . . , $003FFF.

In summary, the memory for the schematic in Figure 5.16 is shown in the following:

```
EVEN 2716 EPROM   $000000, $000002, $000004, ......
                  $000FFE
ODD 2716 EPROM    $000001, $000003, $000005, ......
                  $000FFF
EVEN 6116 RAM     $003000, $003002, $003004, ......
                  $003FFE
ODD 6116 RAM      $003001, $003003, $003005, ......
                  $003FFF
```

In the following, some examples will be considered to illustrate the use of memory map of the schematic of Figure 5.17 due to execution of 68000 MOVE instruction.

Consider MOVE.B $000004, D. Upon execution of this MOVE instruction, the 68000 reads the [$000004] from even 2716 to low byte of D1. In order to execute the instruction, the processor places the upper 23 bits of $000004 on its A23-A1 pins, and asserts $\overline{UDS}$ and $\overline{AS}$. Since A12 = 0, the output of AND gate 2 = 1, the output of AND gate 3 generates a LOW, making $\overline{CE}$ and $\overline{OE}$ of the even 2716 LOW. When the 68000 samples $\overline{DTACK}$ (asserted by $\overline{AS}$ in Figure 5.17), data placed on the 68000 D8-D15 lines by the even 2716 are read by the processor into low byte of D1. Similarly, a byte read operation from the odd 2716 can be explained.

Consider MOVE.W $000004, D1. The 68000 asserts both $\overline{UDS}$ and $\overline{LDS}$ in this case. The outputs of AND gates 3 and 5 are LOW. Both the even 2716 and the odd 2716 are selected. Data placed on D0-D7 pins and D8-D15 pins of the 68000 from locations $000004 and $000005 of the even 2716 and odd 2716 are read by the processor, respectively, into bits 8-15 and bits 0-7 of D0.

Consider MOVE.B D2, $003001. The 68000 asserts $\overline{LDS}$, $\overline{AS}$ and outputs HIGH on A12 and A13. The output of AND gate 6 is LOW and thus selects odd 6116. Since $R/\overline{W} = 0$, the odd 6116 writes the low byte of D2 from 68000 D0-D7 pins into location $003001. Similarly, other byte operations from the RAMs can be illustrated.

Consider MOVE.L D3, $003002. The 68000 asserts $\overline{AS}$, and both $\overline{UDS}$ and $\overline{LDS}$. It also outputs HIGH on A12 and A13. Both RAMs are selected. The high 16 bits of the 32-bit data placed on D0-D15 pins by the 68000 are written into locations #003002 (byte 0) and $003003 (byte 1), and the low 16 bits of the 32-bit data placed on D0-D15 pins by the 68000 are written into locations $003004 (byte 2) and $003005 (byte 3), respectively, of the even and odd 6116s. Similarly, the other long word operations can be illustrated.

5.11 68000 PROGRAMMED I/O

As mentioned before, the 68000 uses memory-mapped I/O. Programmed I/O can be achieved in the 68000 using one of the following ways:

1. By interfacing the 68000 asynchronously with its own family of peripheral devices such as the MC-68230, Parallel Interface/Timer chip

2. By interfacing the 68000 synchronously with 6800 peripherals such as the MC6821 (note that synchronization means that every READ or WRITE operation is synchronized with the clock).

5.11.1 68000-68230 INTERFACE

The MC68230 parallel interface/timer (PI/T) provides double buffered parallel interfaces and a timer for 68000 systems. Note that double buffering means that the ports have dual latches. Double buffering allows simultaneous reading of data from a port by the microprocessor and placing of data into the same port by an external device via handshaking. Double buffering is most useful in situations where a peripheral device and the processor are capable of transferring data at nearly the same speed. If there is a large difference in speed between the microprocessor and the peripheral, little or no benefit of double buffering is achieved. In these cases, however, there is no penalty for using double buffering. Double buffering permits the fetch operation of the data transmitter to be overlapped with the store operation of the data receiver.

The parallel interfaces provided by the 68230 can be 8 or 16 bits wide with unidirectional or bidirectional modes. In the unidirectional mode, a data direction register configures each port as an input or output. In the bidirectional mode, the data direction registers are ignored and the direction is determined by the state of four handshake pins.

The 68230 allows use of interrupts, and also provides a DMA request pin for connection to a DMA controller chip such as the MC68450. The timer contains a 24-bit-wide counter. This counter can be clocked by the output of a 5-bit (divide by 32) prescaler or by an external timer input pin (TIN).

Table 5.15 provides the signal summary and Figure 5.19 shows the 68230 pin diagram. The 68230 is a 48-pin device.

The purpose of D0-D7, R/$\overline{\text{W}}$, and CS pins is obvious. RS1-RS5 are five register select input pins for selecting the 23 internal registers.

During read or interrupt acknowledge cycles, $\overline{\text{DTACK}}$ is asserted after data have been provided on the data bus and during write cycles it is asserted after data have been accepted at the data bus. A pullup resistor is required to maintain $\overline{\text{DTACK}}$ high between bus cycles.

Upon activation of the $\overline{\text{RESET}}$ input, all control and data direction registers are cleared and most internal operations are disabled by the assertion of $\overline{\text{RESET}}$ LOW.

TABLE 5.15
Signal Summary of the MC68230

Signal name	Input/output	Active state	Edge/level sensitive	Output states
CLK	Input		Falling and rising edge	
CS	Input	Low	Level	
D0-D7	Input/output	High = 1, low = 0	Level	High, low, high impedance
$\overline{\text{DMAREQ}}$	Output	Low		High, Low
DTACK	Output	Low		High, low, high impedance[a]
H1(H3)[b]	Input	Low or high	Asserted edge	
H2(H4)[c]	Input or output	Low or high	Asserted edge	High, low high impedance
PA0-PA7,[c]	Input/output,	High = 1, low = 0	Level	High, low high impedance
PB0-PB7,[c] PC0-PC7	Input or output input or output			
$\overline{\text{PIACK}}$	Input	Low	Level	
$\overline{\text{PIRQ}}$	Output	Low		Low, high impedance[a]
RS1-RS5	Input	High = 1, low = 0	Level	
R/$\overline{\text{W}}$	Input	High read, low write	Level	
$\overline{\text{RESET}}$	Input	Low	Level	
$\overline{\text{TIACK}}$	Input	Low	Level	
TIN (external clock)	Input		Rising edge	
TIN (run/halt)	Input	High	Level	
TOUT (square wave)	Output	Low		High, low
TOUT ($\overline{\text{TIRQ}}$)	Output	Low		Low, high impedance[a]

[a] Pullup resistors required.
[b] H1 is level sensitive for output buffer control in modes 2 and 3.
[c] Note these pins have internal pullup resistors.

The clock pin has the same specifications as the 68000.

PA0-PA7 and PB0-PB7 pins provide two 8-bit ports that may be concatenated to form a 16-bit port in certain modes. The ports may be controlled in conjunction with handshake pins H1-H4. A simple example of a handshake operation for input of data is for the I/O device to indicate

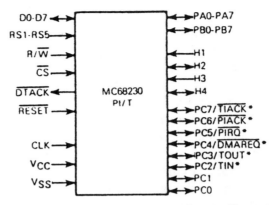

* Individually Programmable Dual-Function Pin

FIGURE 5.19 Logical pin assignment.

to the port that new data are available at the port by activating H1 to HIGH. After input of data by the 68000, the H2 output of the 68230 is set to HIGH to indicate to the I/O device that data have been read and it may now provide another data byte to the port.

Handshake pins H1-H4 are multipurpose pins that provide an interlocked handshake, a pulsed handshake, an interrupt input, or simple I/O pins. The interlocked and pulsed I/O handshake modes are selected via port A control register (PACR) and port B control register (PBCR). For pulsed or interlocked mode, H1 and H2 are used with port A, while H3 and H4 are used with port B.

In the interlocked I/O handshake protocol, the handshake pins H2 and H4 are defined as output pins. For interlocked input protocol, H2 and H4 are asserted automatically by the 68230 when the port input latches are ready to accept new data. When both double-buffered latches are full, H2 (or H4) remain negated until data are removed by a read of port A (or port B) data register. Therefore, any time the H2 (or H4) output is asserted, new data may be input by asserting H1 (or H3).

In the interlocked output protocol, H2 and H4 are also output pins. H2 (or H4) is asserted two clock cycles after data are transferred to the double-buffered output latches. The data remain stable and H2 (or H4) stays asserted until the next asserted edge of H1 (or H3). At that time, H2 (or H4) is asynchronously negated. As soon as the next data are available, they are output to the latches, and H2 (or H4) is asserted. H1 (or H3) is used by the external device to receive data.

For pulsed input handshake protocol, H2 (or H4) is asserted exactly as the interlocked input handshake and remains asserted up to four clock cycles. As soon as the asserted edge of H1 (or H3) occurs, H2 (or H4) is negated asynchronously.

For pulsed output handshake protocol, H2 (or H4) is an output pin and is asserted exactly in the same way as the interlocked output protocol up to four cycles. But if H1 (or H3) asserted edge occurs before termination of the pulse, H2 (or H4) is negated asynchronously.

Note that the 68230 automatically asserts or negates the handshake pins when they are output pins. The handshake pins, when acting as inputs, are provided by the external device.

In the interrupt mode, the handshake pins can be defined as interrupt input pins. In the I/O mode, they can be configured as general purpose I/O pins.

PC0-PC7 pins can be used as eight general purpose I/O pins or any combination of six special function pins and two general purpose I/O pins (PC0, PC1).

Port C can be configured as input or output by the port C data direction register.

The alternate function pins TIN, TOUT, and $\overline{\text{TIACK}}$ are timer I/O pins. For example, the PC2 pin can also be used as a timer input TIN. When the 68230 timer is used as an event counter, the counter value can be decremented upon application of pulses at TIN by external circuitry. This means that TIN is the timer clock input. TIN can also be configured as the timer run/halt input. In this case, a HIGH at TIN enables the 68230 internal timer clock. Therefore, the 68230 timer runs when TIN = 1. On the other hand, a low on TIN disables the 68230 internal clock and stops the timer. TOUT may provide an active low timer interrupt request output or a general purpose square output, initially high. $\overline{\text{TIACK}}$ is an active low high-impedance input used for timer interrupt acknowledge.

Ports A and B have an independent pair of active low interrupt request $(\overline{\text{PIRQ}})$ and interrupt acknowledge $(\overline{\text{PIACK}})$ pins. $\overline{\text{PIRQ}}$ is an output pin and is used by the 68230 when it implements an interrupt-driven parallel I/O configuration. Therefore, PC2-PC7 pins may or may not be available for general purpose I/O. The 68230 $\overline{\text{PIRQ}}$ pin can be connected to one of the 68000 $\overline{\text{IPL}}$ pins and the 68230 $\overline{\text{PIACK}}$ pin can be connected to the NANDed output of 68000 FC2 FC1 FC0 pins. Since FC2 FC1 FC0 = 111_2 indicates interrupt acknowledge, $\overline{\text{PIACK}}$ is asserted when the 68000 is ready to service the interrupt. The $\overline{\text{DMAREQ}}$ pin provides an active low direct memory access controller request pulse for three clock cycles, compatible with MC68450 DMA controller chip.

Tables 5.16 and 5.17 provide the 68230 register addressing assignments and the register model. Table 5.17 shows each of the 68230 twenty-three registers and the function of each of the bits. These registers configure modes of operation of I/O ports and timer, input and output data to or from I/O devices, and provide status information of the ports and the timer.

TABLE 5.16
68230 Register Addressing Assignments

Register		Register select bits 5	4	3	2	1	Accessible	Affected by reset	read cycle
Port General Control Register	(PGCR)	0	0	0	0	0	R W	Yes	No
Port Service Request Register	(PSRR)	0	0	0	0	1	R W	Yes	No
Port A Data Direction Register	(PADDR)	0	0	0	1	0	R W	Yes	No
Port B Data Direction Register	(PBDDR)	0	0	0	1	1	R W	Yes	No
Port C Data Direction Register	(PCDDR)	0	0	1	0	0	R W	Yes	No
Port Interrupt Vector Register	(PIVR)	0	0	1	0	1	R W	Yes	No
Port A Control Register	(PACR)	0	0	1	1	0	R W	Yes	No
Port B Control Register	(PBCR)	0	0	1	1	1	R W	Yes	No
Port A Data Register	(PADR)	0	1	0	0	0	R W	No	a
Port B Data Register	(PBDR)	0	1	0	0	1	R W	No	a
Port A Alternate Register	(PAAR)	0	1	0	1	0	R	No	No
Port B Alternate Register	(PBAR)	0	1	0	1	1	R	No	No
Port C Data Register	(PCDR)	0	1	1	0	0	R W	No	No
Port Status Register	(PSR)	0	1	1	0	1	R W[b]	Yes	No
Timer Control Register	(TCR)	1	0	0	0	0	R W	Yes	No
Timer Interrupt Vector Register	(TIVR)	1	0	0	0	1	R W	Yes	No
Counter Preload Register High	(CPRH)	1	0	0	1	1	R W	No	No
Counter Preload Register Middle	(CPRM)	1	0	1	0	0	R W	No	No
Counter Preload Register Low	(CPRL)	1	0	1	0	1	R W	No	No
Count Register High	(CNTRH)	1	0	1	1	1	R	No	No
Count Register Middle	(CNTRM)	1	1	0	0	0	R	No	No
Count Register Low	(CNTRL)	1	1	0	0	1	R	No	No
Timer Status Register	(TSR)	1	1	0	1	0	R W[b]	Yes	No

Note: R = read; W = write.

[a] Mode dependent.
[b] A write to this register may perform a special status resetting operation.

TABLE 5.17
68230 Register Modes

5	4	3	2	1	7	6	5	4	3	2	1	0	Register value after RESET (hex value)	
0	0	0	0	0	Port Mode Control	H34 Enable	H12 Enable	H4 Sense	H3 Sense	H2 Sense	H1 Sense		0 0	Port General Control Register
0	0	0	0	1	*	SVCRQ Select		IPF Select		Port Interrupt Priority Control			0 0	Port Service Request Register
0	0	0	1	0	Bit 7	Bit 6	Bit 5	Bit 4	Bit 3	Bit 2	Bit 1	Bit 0	0 0	Port A Data Direction Register
0	0	0	1	1	Bit 7	Bit 6	Bit 5	Bit 4	Bit 3	Bit 2	Bit 1	Bit 0	0 0	Port B Data Direction Register
0	0	1	0	0	Bit 7	Bit 6	Bit 5	Bit 4	Bit 3	Bit 2	Bit 1	Bit 0	0 0	Port C Data Direction Register
0	0	1	0	1	Interrupt Vector Number						*	*	0 F	Port Interrupt Vector Register
0	0	1	1	0	Port A Submode		H2 Control			H2 Int Enable	H1 SVCRQ Enable	H1 Stat Ctrl	0 0	Port A Control Register
0	0	1	1	1	Port B Submode		H4 Control			H4 Int Enable	H3 SVCRQ Enable	H3 Stat Ctrl	0 0	Port B Control Register
0	1	0	0	0	Bit 7	Bit 6	Bit 5	Bit 4	Bit 3	Bit 2	Bit 1	Bit 0	* *	Port A Data Register
0	1	0	0	1	Bit 7	Bit 6	Bit 5	Bit 4	Bit 3	Bit 2	Bit 1	Bit 0	* *	Port B Data Register
0	1	0	1	0	Bit 7	Bit 6	Bit 5	Bit 4	Bit 3	Bit 2	Bit 1	Bit 0	* * *	Port A Alternate Register

TABLE 5.17 (continued)
68230 Register Modes

Register select bits					7	6	5	4	3	2	1	0	Register value after $\overline{RESET}$ (hex value)	
5	4	3	2	1										
0	1	0	1	1	Bit 7	Bit 6	Bit 5	Bit 4	Bit 3	Bit 2	Bit 1	Bit 0	* * *	Port B Alternate Register
0	1	1	0	0	Bit 7	Bit 6	Bit 5	Bit 4	Bit 3	Bit 2	Bit 1	Bit 0	* * * *	Port C Data Register
0	1	1	0	1	H4 Level	H3 Level	H2 Level	H1 Level	H4S	H3S	H2S	H1S	* * * *	Port Status Register
0	1	1	1	0	*	*	*	*	*	*	*	*	0 0	(Null)
0	1	1	1	1	*	*	*	*	*	*	*	*	0 0	(Null)
1	0	0	0	0	TOUT/$\overline{TIACK}$ Control		Z D Ctrl	*	Clock Control		Timer Enable		0 0	Timer Control Register
1	0	0	0	1	Bit 7	Bit 6	Bit 5	Bit 4	Bit 3	Bit 2	Bit 1	Bit 0	0 F	Timer Interrupt Vector Register
1	0	0	1	0	*	*	*	*	*	*	*	*	0 0	(Null)
1	0	0	1	1	Bit 23	Bit 22	Bit 21	Bit 20	Bit 19	Bit 18	Bit 17	Bit 16	* *	Counter Preload Register (High)
1	0	1	0	0	Bit 15	Bit 14	Bit 13	Bit 12	Bit 11	Bit 10	Bit 9	Bit 8	* *	Counter Preload Register (Mid)
1	0	1	0	1	Bit 7	Bit 6	Bit 5	Bit 4	Bit 3	Bit 2	Bit 1	Bit 0	* *	Counter Preload Register (Low)
1	0	1	1	0	*	*	*	*	*	*	*	*	0 0	(Null)
1	0	1	1	1	Bit 23	Bit 22	Bit 21	Bit 20	Bit 19	Bit 18	Bit 17	Bit 16	* *	Count Register (High)
1	1	0	0	0	Bit 15	Bit 14	Bit 13	Bit 12	Bit 11	Bit 10	Bit 9	Bit 8	* *	Count Register (Mid)

TABLE 5.17 (continued)
68230 Register Modes

Register select bits													Register value after $\overline{\text{RESET}}$ (hex value)	
5	4	3	2	1	7	6	5	4	3	2	1	0		
1	1	0	0	1	Bit 7	Bit 6	Bit 5	Bit 4	Bit 3	Bit 2	Bit 1	Bit 0	* *	Count Register (Low)
1	1	0	1	0	*	*	*	*	*	*	*	ZDS	0 0	Timer Status Register
1	1	0	1	1	*	*	*	*	*	*	*	*	0 0	(Null)
1	1	1	0	0	*	*	*	*	*	*	*	*	0 0	(Null)
1	1	1	0	1	*	*	*	*	*	*	*	*	0 0	(Null)
1	1	1	1	0	*	*	*	*	*	*	*	*	0 0	(Null)
1	1	1	1	1	*	*	*	*	*	*	*	*	0 0	(Null)

Note: * Unused, read as zero; ** value before $\overline{\text{RESET}}$; *** current value on pins; **** undetermined value.

The 68230 ports can be configured for various modes of operation. For example, consider ports A and B. Bits 6 and 7 of the port general control register, PGCR (R0) are used for configuring ports A and B in one of four modes as follows:

```
PGCR
bits
7  6
0  0     Mode 0    (unidirectional 8-bit mode)
0  1     Mode 1    (unidirectional 16-bit mode)
1  0     Mode 2    (bidirectional 8-bit mode)
1  1     Mode 3    (bidirectional 16-bit mode)
```

The other pins of PGCR are defined as follows:

PGCR	
bit 5	H34 Enable
0	Disabled
1	Enabled
bit 4	H12 Enable
0	Disabled
1	Enabled
bit 3	
0	H4 sense at high level when negated and low level when asserted
1	H4 sense at low level when negated and high level when asserted
bit 2 (H3 sense), bit 1 (H2 sense) and bit 0 (H1 sense)	same definition as H4 sense

The modes 0 and 2 configure ports A and B as unidirectional or bidirectional 8-bit ports. Modes 1 and 3, on the other hand, combine ports A and B together to form a 16-bit unidirectional or bidirectional port. Ports configured as unidirectional must further be programmed as submodes of operation using bits 7 and 6 of PACR (R6) and PBCR (R7) as follows:

For unidirectional 8-bit mode (mode 0)

	Bit 7 of PACR or PBCR	Bit 6 of PACR or PBCR	
Submode 00	0	0	Pin-definable double-buffered input or single-buffered output
Submode 01	0	1	Pin-definable double-buffered output or non-latched input
Submode 1X	1	X	Bit I/O (pin-definable single-buffered output or nonlatched input)

Note that in the above X means don't care. Nonlatched inputs are latched internally but the bit values are not available at the port.

The submodes define the ports as parallel input ports, parallel output modes, or bit-configurable I/O ports. In addition to these, the submodes further define the ports as latched input ports, interrupt-driven ports, DMA ports, and with various I/O handshake operations. From Table 5.17 it can be seen that R0 through R13 registers of the 68230 configure and control the operation of these ports. Therefore, some of these registers are considered in detail in the following.

As mentioned earlier, PGCR is register R0. Bits 7 and 6 of R0 configure ports A and B in one of four modes of operation. The other bits of PGCR are used to enable and sense the handshake lines H1 through H4. For example, bit 5 of PGCR is the H34 enable bit. It must be set to HIGH to enable the H3 and H4 lines. Similarly, H12 is used to enable or disable the H1 and H2 lines. Bits 0 through 3 of PGCR are sense bits for H1 through H4. These bits are programmable. For example, setting one or more of these bits to one will result in using high voltage level as the active level of the corresponding handshake pins (H1-H4). On the other hand, making one or more of these bits to 0 will set the low voltage level as the active state.

Register R1 is the port service request register (PSRR). This control port is used to interface 68230 to 68000 for interrupt-driven mode of operation for I/O. The bits in this port are used

1. To define the bits of port C as interrupt request and interrupt acknowledge signals instead of I/O lines
2. To set up a priority scheme for the handshake lines H1-H4
3. To operate ports A and B in DMA mode

In Figure 5.20, the format for R1 is shown. Bits 5 and 6 of PSRR are identified as SVCRQ (service request) select. These bits define whether the PC4/$\overline{\text{DMAREQ}}$ pin of port C is used as an I/O pin PC4 or as the DMA-request pin, $\overline{\text{DMAREQ}}$. Outputting 0 to bit 6 of PSRR configures the PC4/$\overline{\text{DMAREQ}}$ pin as an I/O pin and outputting 1 makes it the $\overline{\text{DMAREQ}}$ pin. The DMA mode, bit 6 of PSRR defines whether DMA operations with the selected port are with respect to H1 or H3. For example, bits 6, 5 of PSRR as 11 will choose DMA operation with H3 and port B.

Bits 3 and 4 configure the operation of the PC5/$\overline{\text{PIRQ}}$ and PC6/$\overline{\text{PIACK}}$ pins of the 68230. For example, outputting 10 to these bits will select PC5/$\overline{\text{PIRQ}}$ as an I/O pin and PC6/$\overline{\text{PIACK}}$ as the $\overline{\text{PIACK}}$ pin.

Finally, bits 0, 1, and 2 define H2 as the highest priority, H1 next highest, H3 next, and H4 as the lowest.

Port Service Request Register (PSRR)

7	6	5	4	3	2	1	0
•	SVCRQ Select		Operation Select		Port Interrupt Priority Control		

PSRR

6 5   SVCRQ Select

0 X   The PC4 / $\overline{\text{DMAREQ}}$ pin carries the PC4 function; DMA is not used.

PSRR   SVCRQ Select

1 0   The PC4 / $\overline{\text{DMAREQ}}$ pin carries the $\overline{\text{DMAREQ}}$ function and is associated with double-buffered transfers controlled by H1. H1 is removed from the PI / T's interrupt structure, _and thus_ does not cause interrupt requests to be generated. To obtain $\overline{\text{DMAREQ}}$ pulses, port A control register bit 1 (H1 SVCRQ enable) must be a one.

1 1   The PC4 $\overline{\text{DMAREQ}}$ pin carries the $\overline{\text{DMAREQ}}$ function and is associated with double-buffered transfers controlled by H3. H3 is removed from the PI / T's interrupt structure, _and thus_ does not cause interrupt requests to be generated. To obtain $\overline{\text{DMAREQ}}$ pulses, port B control register bit 1 (H3 SVCRQ enable) must be one.

PSRR

4 3   Interrupt Pin Function Select

0 0   The PC5/$\overline{\text{PIRQ}}$ pin carries the PC5 function, no interrupt support.
             The PC6/$\overline{\text{PIACK}}$ pin carries the PC6 function, no interrupt support.

0 1   The PC5/$\overline{\text{PIRQ}}$ pin carries the $\overline{\text{PIRQ}}$ function, supports autovectored interrupts.
             The PC6/$\overline{\text{PIACK}}$ pin carries the PC6 function, supports autovectored interrupts.

1 0   The PC5/$\overline{\text{PIRQ}}$ pin carries the PC5 function.
             The PC6/$\overline{\text{PIACK}}$ pin carries the $\overline{\text{PIACK}}$ function.

1 1   The PC5/$\overline{\text{PIRQ}}$ pin carries the $\overline{\text{PIRQ}}$ function, supports vectored interrupts.
             The PC6/$\overline{\text{PIACK}}$ pin carries the $\overline{\text{PIACK}}$ function, supports vectored interrupts.

Bits 2, 1 and 0 determine port interrupt priority. The priority as shown below is in descending order left to right.

PSRR Port Interrupt Priority Control

2 1 0	Highest ....Lowest				2 1 0	Highest ....Lowest			
0 0 0	H1S	H2S	H3S	H4S	1 0 0	H3S	H4S	H1S	H2S
0 0 1	H2S	H1S	H3S	H4S	1 0 1	H3S	H4S	H2S	H1S
0 1 0	H1S	H2S	H4S	H3S	1 1 0	H4S	H3S	H1S	H2S
0 1 1	H2S	H1S	H4S	H3S	1 1 1	H4S	H3S	H2S	H1S

FIGURE 5.20 PSRR (R1) format details.

Registers R2, R3, and R4 are, respectively, the port A data direction register (PADDR), port B data direction register (PBDDR), and port C data direction register (PCDDR). The bits in these control ports configure the corresponding bits in the associated ports as input or output for unidirectional mode of operation. A '0' in a particular bit position in a DDR is used to configure the corresponding bit in the associated port as input and a '1' is used to program the bit as output. For example, to set up all bits of port A as input lines, 00_{16} must be output to PADDR.

R5 is the interrupt vector register (PIVR). It is used with the interrupt-driven mode for the ports. The upper 6 bits of an interrupt vector number are loaded into the bits 2-7 of PIVR.

Bits 0 and 1 of PIVR are provided internally by the 68230 for indicating the priority of the active handshake line. R6 and R7 are, respectively, the port A control register (PACR) and port B control register (PBCR). As mentioned earlier, bits 7 and 6 of these ports define the submodes. The formats for PACR and PBCR are shown in Figure 5.21. Figure 5.22 provides port mode layout and Table 5.18 shows port mode control summary. In the figure, for mode 0 (defined by PGCR) with submode 00, port A is defined as an 8-bit latched double-buffered input port. By latching, it is meant that at the logic level transition of H1, data at port A pins are latched internally by the 68230 flip-flops. Note that the active level of H1 can be set to 1 or 0 by the sense bit in PGCR. As mentioned before, double buffering means that there are dual latches in the 68230 ports. This allows simultaneous reading of port A data by the 68000 and placing of new data into port A by the I/O device.

The other bits of PACR and PBCR are for handshake operations.

R8 and R9 are port A and port B data registers, PADR and PBDR. Each bit in these registers refers to one of the bits in the corresponding I/O port.

In the following, an example is given to illustrate interfacing of 68230 to a 68000 in a simplified manner. The 68230 ports A and B are used along with mode 0 (bits 7,6 of PGCR = 00).

In mode 0, bit I/O is available by programming submode 1X in PACR or PBCR for port A or port B. This submode can be used in applications where several independent devices are to be controlled or monitored. Data output to the specified port is single buffered. If a bit in the data direction register is a one (output), the output buffer is enabled. If it is a zero (input), data written are still latched, but are not available at the pin. Data read from the data register are the instantaneous value of the pin or what was written to the data register, depending on the contents of the data direction register.

Port A Request Register (PACR)

7	6	5	4	3	2	1	0
Port A Submode		H2 Control			H2 Interrupt Enable	H1 SVCRQ Enable	H1 Status Control

Port B Request Register (PBCR)

7	6	5	4	3	2	1	0
Port B Submode		H4 Control			H4 Interrupt Enable	H3 SVCRQ Enable	H3 Status Control

PACR

| 7 6 | | Port A Submode |
| 0 0 | | Submode XX |

PACR

5 4 3		H2 Control
0 X 0		Input pin - edge-sensitive status input, H2S is set on an asserted edge.
1 X 0		Output pin - negated, H2S is always cleared.
1 X 0		Output pin - asserted, H2S is always cleared.

PACR

2		H2 Interrupt Enable
0		The H2 interrupt is disabled.
1		The H2 interrupt is enabled.

PACR

1		H1 SVCRQ Enable
0		The H1 interrupt is disabled.
1		The H1 interrupt is enable.

PACR

| 0 | | H1 status Control |
| X | | H1 is an edge-sensitive status input. H1S is set by an asserted edge of H1. |

PBCR

| 7 6 | | Port B Submode |
| 0 0 | | Submode X1 |

PBCR

5 4 3		H4 Control
0 X X		Input pin - edge-sensitive status input, H4S is set on an asserted edge.
1 0 0		Output pin - negated, H4S is always cleared.
1 0 1		Output pin - asserted, H4S is always cleared.
1 1 0		Output pin - interlocked input handshake protocol.
1 1 1		Output pin - pulsed input handshake protocol.

FIGURE 5.21 PACR and PBCR.

PBCR
2   H4 Interrupt Enable
0   The H4 interrupt is disabled.
1   The H4 interrupt is enabled.

PBCR
1   H3 SVCRQ Enable
0   The H3 interrupt is disabled.
1   The H3 interrupt is enable.

PBCR
0   H3 status Control
0   The H2S status bit is set when either the initial or final output latch
                ports A and B can accept new data. It is clear when both latches are
                full and cannot accept new data.
1   The H3S status bit is set when both the initial and final output latch
                ports A and B are empty
                The H2S status bit is clear when at least one set of output latches is

FIGURE 5.21 (continued)

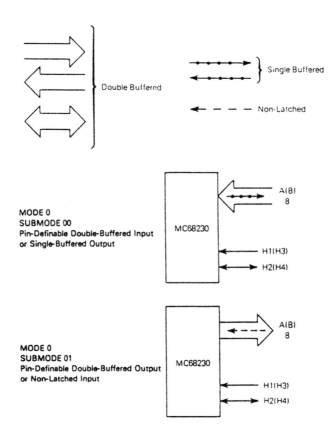

FIGURE 5.22 Port mode layout.

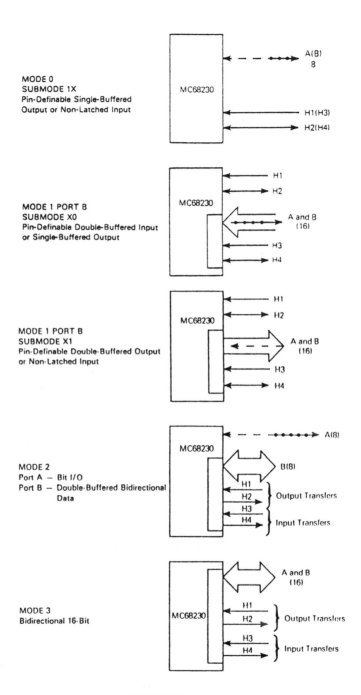

FIGURE 5.22 (continued)

TABLE 5.18
Port Mode Control Summary

Mode 0 (unidirectional 8-bit mode)
Port A
    Submode 00 — pin-definable double-buffered input or single-buffered output
      H1 — latches input data
      H2 — status/interrupt generating input, general purpose output, or operation with H1 in the interlocked or pulsed hand-shake protocols
    Submode 01 — pin-definable double-buffered output or nonlatched input
      H1 — indicates data received by peripheral
      H2 — status/interrupt generating input, general purpose output, or operation with H1 in the interlocked or pulsed hand-shake protocols
    Submode 1X — pin-definable single-buffered output or nonlatched input
      H1 — status/interrupt generating input
      H2 — status/interrupt generating input or general purpose output
Port B
    H3 and H4 — identical to port A, H1 and H2

Mode 1 (unidirectional 16-bit mode)
Port A — most significant data byte or nonlatched input or single-buffered output
    Submode XX — (not used)
      H1 — status/interrupt generating input
      H2 — status/interrupt generating input or general purpose output
Port B — least significant data byte
    Submode X0 — pin-definable double-buffered input or single-buffered output
      H3 — latches input data
      H4 — status/interrupt generating input, general purpose output, or operation with H3 in the interlocked or pulsed hand-shake protocols
    Submode X1 — pin-definable double-buffered output or nonlatched input

**TABLE 5.18 (continued)
Port Mode Control Summary**

H3 — indicates data received by peripheral

H4 — status/interrupt generating input, general purpose output, or operation with H3 in the interlocked or pulsed handshake protocols

Mode 2 (bidirectional 8-bit mode)

Port A — bit I/O

Submode XX — (not used)

Port B — double-buffered bidirectional data

Submode XX — (not used)

H1 — indicates output data received by the peripheral and controls output drivers

H2 — operation with H1 in the interlocked or pulsed output handshake protocols

H3 — latches input data

H4 — operation with H3 in the interlocked or pulsed input handshake protocols

Mode 3 (bidirectional 16-bit mode)

Port A — double-buffered bidirectional data (most significant data byte)

Submode XX — (not used)

Port B — double-buffered bidirectional data (least significant data byte)

Submode XX — (not used)

H1 — indicates output data received by peripheral and controls output drivers

H2 — operation with H1 in the interlocked or pulsed output handshake protocols

H3 — latches input data

H4 — operation with H3 in the interlocked or pulsed input handshake protocols

Figure 5.23 shows a simplified schematic for the 68000-68230 interface. A23 is chosen to be HIGH to select the 68230 chip so that the port addresses are different than the 68000 reset vector addresses 000000_{16} through 000006_{16}. The configuration in the figure will provide even port addresses, since $\overline{\text{UDS}}$ is used for enabling the 68230 $\overline{\text{CS}}$.

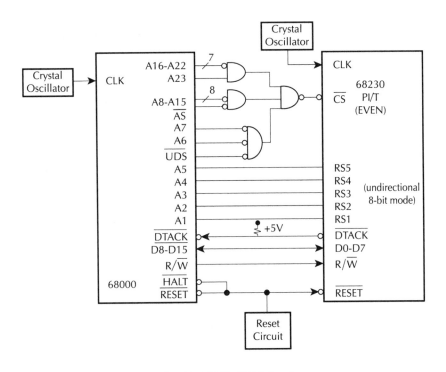

FIGURE 5.23 68000-68230 interface.

From the figure, addresses are for registers PGCR (R0), PADDR (R2), PBDDR (R3), PACR (R6), PBCR (R7), PADR (R8), and PBDR (R 9). Consider PGCR.

$$
\begin{array}{cccccccccccc}
A23 & A22 & A21 & A20 & \dots & A6 & A5 & A4 & A3 & A2 & A1 & A0 \\
1 & 0 & 0 & 0 & \dots 0 & & 0 & 0 & 0 & 0 & 0 & 0
\end{array} = \$800000
$$

$$\underbrace{\qquad\qquad}_{\text{RS5 — RS1}} \qquad \overset{\uparrow}{\overline{\text{UDS}}}$$

Similarly,

address for PADDR	= \$800004
address for PBDDR	= \$800006
address for PACR	= \$80000C
address for PBCR	= \$80000E
address for PADR	= \$800010
address for PBDR	= \$800012

As an example, the following instruction sequence will select mode 00, submode 1X and configure bits 0-3 of port A as outputs, bits 4-7 as inputs, and port B as an output port:

```
PGCR    EQU  $800000
PADDR   EQU  $800004
PBDDR   EQU  $800006
PACR    EQU  $80000C
PBCR    EQU  $80000E


        MOVE.B  #$00,  PGCR   ;   Select mode 0
        MOVE.B  #$FF,  PACR   ;   Port A bit I/O submode
        MOVE.B  #$FF,  PBCR   ;   Port B bit I/O submode
        MOVE.B  #$0F,  PADDR  ;   Configure Port A bits
                                  0-3 as outputs and
                                  bits 4-7 as inputs
        MOVE.B  #$FF,  PBDDR  ;   Configure Port B as an
                                  output port.
```

5.11.2 MOTOROLA 68000-6821 INTERFACE

The Motorola 6821 is a 40-pin peripheral interface adapter (PIA) chip. It is provided with an 8-bit bidirectional data bus (D0-D7), two register select lines (RS0, RS1), read/write line (R/$\overline{W}$), reset line ($\overline{RESET}$), an enable line (E), two 8-bit I/O ports (PA0-PA7) and (PB0-PB7), and other pins.

There are six 6821 registers. These include two 8-bit ports (ports A and B), two data direction registers, and two control registers. Selection of these registers is controlled by the RS0 and RS1 inputs together with bit 2 of the control register. Table 5.19 shows how the registers are selected.

In Table 5.19 bit 2 in each control register (CRA-2 and CRB-2) determines selection of either an I/O port or the corresponding data direction register when the proper register select signals are applied to RS0 and RS1. A 1 in bit 2 allows access of I/O ports, while a 0 selects the data direction registers.

Each I/O port bit can be configured to act as an input or output. This is accomplished by setting a 1 in the corresponding data direction register bit for those bits which are to be output and a 0 for those bits which are to be inputs.

A $\overline{RESET}$ signal sets all PIA registers to 0. This has the effect of setting PA0-PA7 and PB0-PB7 as inputs.

TABLE 5.19
6821 Register Definition

Control register bits 2

RS1	RS0	CRA-2	CRB-2	Register selected
0	0	1	X	I/O port A
0	0	0	X	Data direction register A
0	1	X	X	Control register A
1	0	X	1	I/O port B
1	0	X	0	Data direction register B
1	1	X	X	Control register B

Note: X = Don't care.

There are three built-in signals in the 68000 which provide the interface with the 6821. These are the Enable (E), Valid Memory Access ($\overline{VMA}$), and Valid Peripheral Access ($\overline{VPA}$).

The Enable signal (E) is an output from the 68000. It corresponds to the E signal of the 6821. This signal is the clock used by the 6821 to synchronize data transfer. The frequency of the E signal is one tenth of the 68000 clock frequency. Therefore, this allows one to interface the 68000 (which operates much faster than the 6821) with the 6821. The Valid Memory Address ($\overline{VMA}$) signal is output by the 68000 to indicate to the 6800 peripherals that there is a valid address on the address bus.

The Valid Peripheral Address ($\overline{VPA}$) is an input to the 68000. This signal is used to indicate that the device addressed by the 68000 is a 6800 peripheral. This tells the 68000 to synchronize data transfer with the Enable signal (E).

Let us now discuss how the 68000 instructions can be used to configure the 6821 ports. As an example, bit 7 and bits 0-6 of port A can be configured, respectively, as input and outputs using the following instruction sequence:

```
BCLR.B  #$2,  CRA      ;      ADDRESS DDRA
MOVE.B  #$7F, DDRA     ;      CONFIGURE PORT A
BSET.B  #$2,  CRA      ;      ADDRESS PORT A
```

Once the ports are configured to the designer's specification, 6821 can be used to transfer data from an input device to the 68000 or from the 68000 to an output device by using the MOVE.B instruction as follows:

```
MOVE.B (EA), Dn    Transfer 8-bit data from an input
                   port to the specified data regis-
                   ter Dn.
MOVE.B Dn, (EA)    Transfer 8-bit data from the
                   specified data register Dn to an
                   output port.
```

Figure 5.24 shows a block diagram of how two 6821s are interfaced to the 68000 in order to generate four 8-bit I/O ports. Note that the least significant bit, A0, of the 68000 address pins is internally encoded to generate two signals called Upper Data Strobe ($\overline{\text{UDS}}$) and Lower Data Strobe ($\overline{\text{LDS}}$). For byte transfers $\overline{\text{UDS}}$ is asserted if an even-numbered byte is being transferred and $\overline{\text{LDS}}$ is asserted for odd-numbered byte.

In Figure 5.24, I/O port addresses can be obtained as follows. When A23 is HIGH and $\overline{\text{AS}}$ is LOW, the OR gate output will be LOW. This OR gate output is used to provide $\overline{\text{VPA}}$. The inverted OR gate output, in turn, makes CS1 HIGH on both the chips. Note that A23 is arbitrarily chosen. A23 is chosen to be HIGH to enable CS1 so that the addresses for the ports and the reset vector are not the same. Assuming the don't care address lines A22-A3 to be zeros, the addresses for the I/O ports, control registers, and the data direction registers for the even 6821 can be obtained as follows:

Port name	A23	A22	. . .	A3	A2	A1	A0	
I/O port A/DDRA	1	0	. . .	0	0	0	0	$= 800000_{16}$
CRA	1	0	. . .	0	0	1	0	$= 800002_{16}$
I/O port B/DDRB	1	0	. . .	0	1	0	0	$= 800004_{16}$
CRB	1	0	. . .	0	1	1	0	$= 800006_{16}$

Note that in the above, A0 = 0 for even addressing. Also, from Table 5.19, for accessing DDRA, bit 2 of CRA with memory address 800002_{16} must be set to 1 and then port A can be configured with appropriate data in 800000_{16}. Note that port A and its data direction register, DDRA, have the same address, 800000_{16}. Similarly, port B and DDRB have the same address 800004_{16}. Bit 2 in CRA or CRB identifies whether address 800000_{16} or 800004_{16} is an I/O port or data direction register.

Similarly, the addresses for the ports, control registers, and the data direction register for the odd 6821 (A0 = 1) can be determined as follows: port A/DDRA (800001_{16}), CRA (800003_{16}), port B/DDRB (800005_{16}), and CRB (800007_{16}).

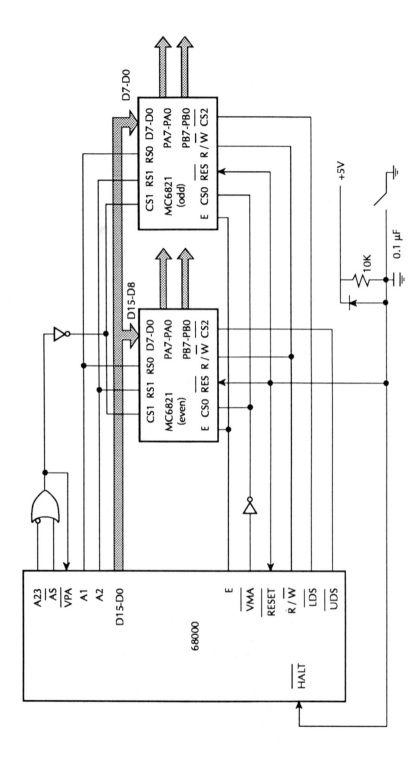

FIGURE 5.24 68000 I/O port block diagram.

5.12 68000/2716/6116/6821-BASED MICROCOMPUTER

Figure 5.25a shows the schematic of a 68000-based microcomputer with 4K EPROM, 4K Static RAM, and four 8-bit I/O ports.

Let us explain the various sections of the hardware schematic. Two 2716-1 and two 6116 chips are required to obtain the 4K EPROM and 4K RAM. The $\overline{\text{LDS}}$ and $\overline{\text{UDS}}$ pins are ORed with the memory select signal to enable the chip selects for the EPROMs and the RAMs.

Address decoding is accomplished by using a 3×8 decoder. The decoder enables the memory or I/O chips depending on the status of A12-A14 address lines and $\overline{\text{AS}}$ line of the 68000. $\overline{\text{AS}}$ is used to enable the decoder. I0 selects the EPROMs, I1 selects the RAMs, and I2 selects the I/O ports.

When addressing memory chips, $\overline{\text{DTACK}}$ input of the 68000 must be asserted for data acknowledge. The 68000 clock in the hardware schematic is 8 MHz. Therefore, each clock cycle is 125 nanoseconds. In Figure 5.25a, $\overline{\text{AS}}$ is used to enable the 3×8 decoder. The outputs of the decoder are gated to assert 68000 $\overline{\text{DTACK}}$. This means that $\overline{\text{AS}}$ is indirectly used to assert $\overline{\text{DTACK}}$. From the 68000 read timing diagram of Figure 5.16, $\overline{\text{AS}}$ goes to LOW after approximately two cycles (250 ns for 8-MHz clock) from the beginning of the bus cycle. With no wait states, the 68000 samples $\overline{\text{DTACK}}$ at the falling edge of S4 (375 ns) and, if recognized, the 68000 latches data at the falling edge of S6 (500 ns). If the $\overline{\text{DTACK}}$ is not recognized at the falling edge of S4, the 68000 inserts one cycle (125 ns in this case) wait state, samples $\overline{\text{DTACK}}$ at the end of S6, and, if recognized, latches data at the end of S8 (625 ns), and the process continues. Since the access time of 2716-1 is 350 ns, $\overline{\text{DTACK}}$ recognition by the 68000 at the falling edge of S6 (500 ns) and, hence, latching of data at the falling edge of S8 (625 ns) will satisfy the timing requirement. This means that the decoder output $\overline{\text{I0}}$ for ROM select must go Low at the end of S6. Therefore, $\overline{\text{AS}}$ must be delayed by 250 ns, i.e., two cycles (S2 through S6).

A delay circuit (Figure 5.25b) is designed using a 74LS175-D-Flip-Flop. $\overline{\text{AS}}$ activates the delay circuit. The input is then shifted right two bits to obtain a two-cycle wait state to allow sufficient time for data transfer. $\overline{\text{DTACK}}$ assertion and recognition are delayed by two cycles during data transfer with the EPROMs. A timing diagram for the $\overline{\text{DTACK}}$ delay circuit is shown in Figure 5.25c.

When ROM is not selected by the decoder, then clear pin is asserted

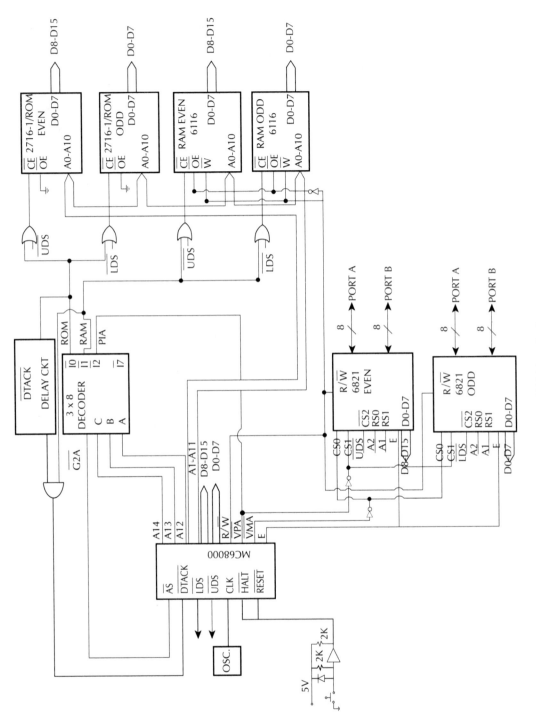

FIGURE 5.25a 68000-based microcomputer.

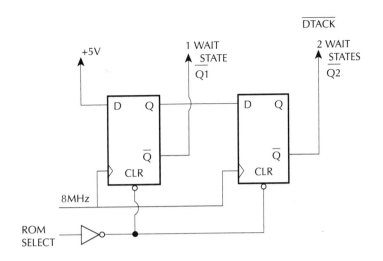

FIGURE 5.25b Delay circuit for $\overline{\text{DTACK}}$.

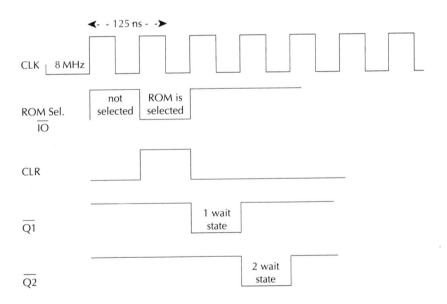

FIGURE 5.25c Timing diagram for the $\overline{\text{DTACK}}$ delay circuit.

(output of inverter). So, Q is forced LOW and $\overline{\text{Q}}$ is high. Therefore, $\overline{\text{DTACK}}$ is not asserted. When the processor is addressing the ROMs, then the output of the inverter is LOW so clear pin is not asserted. Now, the D flip-flop will accept a high at the input, and Q will output high and $\overline{\text{Q}}$ will output low. Now that $\overline{\text{Q}}$ is low, it can assert $\overline{\text{DTACK}}$. Q1 will provide one wait state and $\overline{Q2}$ will provide two wait states. Since the 2716-1 EPROM has a 350-ns access time and the microprocessor is operating at 8 MHz (125 ns clock cycle), two wait states are inserted before asserting $\overline{DTACK}$ (2*125 = 250 ns). Therefore, $\overline{Q2}$ can be connected to $\overline{DTACK}$ pin.

No wait state is required for RAMs since the access time for the RAMs is only 120 nanoseconds.

Four 8-bit I/O ports are obtained by using two 6821 chips. When the I/O ports are selected, the $\overline{VPA}$ pin is asserted instead of $\overline{DTACK}$. This will acknowledge to the 68000 that it is addressing a 6800-type peripheral. In response, the 68000 will synchronize all data transfer with the E clock.

The memory and I/O maps for the schematic are shown below:

Memory Mapping   LDS or UDS

A23—A15	A14	A13	A12	A11—A1	A0	
0—0	0	0	0	0—0	0	ROM (EVEN) = 2K
0—0	0	0	0	1—1	0	$000000, $000002, $000004 . . . ., $000FFE.
0—0	0	0	0	0—0	1	ROM (ODD) = 2K
0—0	0	0	0	1—1	1	$000001, $000003, $000005 . . . ., $000FFF
0—0	0	0	1	0—0	0	RAM (even) = 2K
0—0	0	0	1	1—1	0	$001000, $001002, . . ., $001FFE
0—0	0	0	1	0—0	1	RAM (odd) = 2K
0—0	0	0	1	1—1	1	$001001, $001003, . . ., $001FFF

Memory Mapped I/O   UDS or LDS

A23—A15	A14	A13	A12	A11—A3	RS1 A2	RS0 A1	A0	Register Selected (Address) EVEN
0—0	0	1	0	0—0	0	0	0	Port A or DDRA = $002000
0—0	0	1	0	0—0	0	1	0	CRA = $002002
0—0	0	1	0	0—0	1	0	0	Port B or DDRB = $002004
0—0	0	1	0	0—0	1	1	0	CRB = $002006

A23—A15	A14	A13	A12	A11—-A3	A2	A1	A0	ODD
					RS1	**RS0**	UDS or LDS	
0—0	0	1	0	0—0	0	0	1	Port A or DDRA = $002001
0—0	0	1	0	0—0	0	1	1	CRA = $002003
0—0	0	1	0	0—0	1	0	1	Port B or DDRB = $002005
0—0	0	1	0	0—0	1	1	1	CRB = $002007

Note that upon hardware reset, the 68000 loads the supervisor SP high and low words, respectively, from addresses $000000 and $000002 and the PC high and low words, respectively, from locations $000004 and $000006. The memory map of Figure 5.25a contains these reset vector addresses in the even and odd 2716s.

Example 5.8

Assume (assume EPROM/RAM in the system) that in the configuration of Figure 5.23, port A has three inputs and an LED connected to bits 0-3. Port B has an LED connected to bit 3. Write 68000 assembly program to

1. Turn the port A LED ON and port B LED OFF if port A has an even number of high switch inputs.
2. Turn the port A LED OFF and port B LED ON if port A has an odd number of high switch inputs.
3. Turn both LEDs off if there are no high switch inputs.

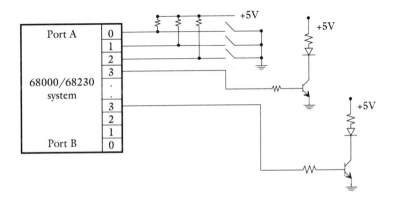

Figure for Problem 5.8.

Solution

```
PGCR    EQU  $800000
PADDR   EQU  $800004
PBDDR   EQU  $800006
PACR    EQU  $80000C
PBCR    EQU  $80000E
PADR    EQU  $800010
PBDR    EQU  $800012
        MOVE.B  #$00, PGCR    ;  Select mode 0
        MOVE.B  #$FF, PACR    ;  Port A bit I/O submode
        MOVE.B  #$FF, PBCR    ;  Port B bit I/O submode
        MOVE.B  #$08, PADDR   ;  Configure port A
        MOVE.B  #$08, PBDDR   ;  Configure port B
        MOVE.B  PADR, D1      ;  Get port A switches
        ANDI.B  #$07, D1      ;  Mask high five bits
                              ;  Are all three inputs
                              ;     low
        BEQ LOW               ;  If so, turn both LEDs
                              ;     off.
        CMPI.B  #$03, D1      ;  Are high switch inputs
                              ;     even
        BEQ EVEN              ;  If so, turn port A LED
                              ;     ON and port B LED OFF.
        CMPI.B  #$05, D1      ;  Are high switch inputs
                              ;     even
        BEQ EVEN              ;  If so, turn port A LED
                              ;     ON and port B LED OFF
        CMPI.B  #$06, D1      ;  Are high switch inputs
                              ;     even
        BEQ EVEN              ;  If so, turn port A LED
                              ;     ON and port B LED OFF.
        CMPI.B  #$07, D1      ;  Are high switch inputs
                              ;     ODD
        BEQ ODD               ;  If so, turn port A LED
                              ;     OFF and port B
                              ;     LED ON
        CMPI.B  #$04, D1      ;  Are high switch inputs
                              ;     even
        BEQ ODD               ;  If so, turn port A LED
                              ;     ON and port B LED OFF
```

```
           CMPI.B $01, D1        ; Are high switch inputs
                                     ODD
           BEQ ODD               ; If so, turn port A LED
                                     OFF and port B LED ON
           CMPI.B $02, D1        ; Are high switch inputs
                                     ODD
           BEQ ODD               ; If so, turn port A LED
                                     OFF and port B LED ON
ODD        MOVE.B #$00, PADR     ; Turn port A LED OFF
           MOVE.B #$08, PBDR     ; Turn port B LED ON
           JMP STOP              ; Halt
EVEN       MOVE.B #$08, PADR     ; Turn port A LED ON
           MOVE.B #$00, PBDR     ; Turn port B LED OFF
           JMP STOP              ; Halt
LOW        MOVE.B #$00, PADR     ; Turn port A LED OFF
           MOVE.B #$00, PBDR     ; Turn port B LED OFF
STOP       JMP STOP              ; Halt
```

5.13 68000 INTERRUPT I/O

The 68000 services interrupts in the supervisor mode. The 68000 interrupt I/O can be divided into two types: external interrupts and internal interrupts.

5.13.1 EXTERNAL INTERRUPTS

The 68000 provides seven levels of external interrupts, 1 through 7. The external hardware provides an interrupt level using the pins $\overline{IPL0}$, $\overline{IPL1}$, $\overline{IPL2}$. Like other processors, the 68000 checks for and accepts interrupts only between instructions. It compares the value of inverted $\overline{IPL0}$-$\overline{IPL2}$ with the current interrupt mask contained in the bits 10, 9, and 8 of the status register.

If the value of the inverted $\overline{IPL0}$-$\overline{IPL2}$ is greater than the value of the current interrupt mask, then the processor acknowledges the interrupt and initiates interrupt processing. Otherwise, the 68000 continues with the current interrupt. Interrupt request level zero ($\overline{IPL0}$-$\overline{IPL2}$ all HIGH) indicates that no interrupt service is requested. An inverted $\overline{IPL2}$, $\overline{IPL1}$, $\overline{IPL0}$ of 7 is always acknowledged and has the highest priority. Therefore, interrupt level 7 is "nonmaskable". Note that the interrupt level is indicated by the interrupt mask bits (inverted $\overline{IPL2}$, $\overline{IPL1}$, $\overline{IPL0}$).

To ensure that an interrupt will be recognized, the following interrupt rules should be considered:

1. The incoming interrupt request level must be at a higher priority level than the mask level set in the interrupt mask bits (except for level 7, which is always recognized).
2. The $\overline{IPL2}$-$\overline{IPL0}$ pins must be held at the interrupt request level until the 68000 acknowledges the interrupt by initiating an interrupt acknowledge ($\overline{IACK}$) bus cycle.

Interrupt level 7 is edge-triggered. On the other hand, the interrupt levels 1 to 6 are level sensitive. But as soon as one of them is acknowledged, the processor updates its interrupt mask to the same level.

The 68000 does not have any EI (Enable Interrupt) or DI (Disable Interrupt) instructions. Instead, the level indicated by I2 I1 I0 in the SR disables all interrupts below or equal to this value and enables all interrupts above this. For example, in the supervisor mode, I2, I1, and I0 can be modified by using instructions such as AND with SR. If I2, I1, and I0 are modified to contain 100_2, then interrupt levels 1 to 4 are disabled and levels 5 to 7 are enabled. Note that I2 I1 I0 = 111 disables all interrupts.

Upon hardware reset, the 68000 operates in supervisor mode and sets I2 I1 I0 to 111_2 and disables the interrupt levels 1 through 6. Note that if I2 I1 I0 is modified to 110_2, the 68000 also disables levels 1 through 6 and level 7 is, of course, always enabled.

Once the 68000 has decided to acknowledge an interrupt request, it pushes PC and SR onto the stack, enters supervisor state by setting S-bit to 1, clears TF to inhibit tracing, and updates the priority mask bits and also the address lines A3-A1 with the interrupt level. The 68000 then asserts $\overline{AS}$ to inform the external devices that A3-A1 has the interrupt level. The processor sets FC2 FC1 FC0 to 111 to run an $\overline{IACK}$ cycle for 8-bit vector number acquisition. The 68000 multiplies the 8-bit vector by 4 to determine pointer to locations containing the starting address of the service routine. The 68000 then branches to the service routine. The last instruction of the service routine should be RTE which pops PC and SR back from the stack. In order to explain how the 68000 interrupt priorities work, assume that I2 I1 I0 in SR has the value 011_2. This means that levels 1, 2, and 3 are disabled and levels 4, 5, 6, and 7 are enabled. Now, if the 68000 is interrupted with level 5, the 68000 pushes PC and SR, updates I2 I1 I0 in SR with 101_2, and loads PC with the starting address of the service routine.

Now, while in the service routine of level 5, if the 68000 is interrupted by level 6 interrupt, the 68000 pushes PC and SR onto the stack. The 68000 then completes execution of the level 6 interrupt. The RTE instruction at the end of the level 6 service routine pops old PC and old SR and returns control to the level 5 interrupt service routine at the right place and continues with the level 5 service routine.

External logic can respond to the interrupt acknowledge in one of the following ways: by requesting automatic vectoring or by placing a vector number on the data bus (nonautovector), or by indicating that no device is responding (Spurious Interrupt). If the hardware asserts $\overline{\text{VPA}}$ to terminate the $\overline{\text{IACK}}$ bus cycle, the 68000 directs itself automatically to the proper interrupt vector corresponding to the current interrupt level. No external hardware is required for providing interrupt address vector. This is known as autovectoring. The vectors for the seven autovector levels are given below:

		I2	I1	I0
Level 1 ← Interrupt vector $19 for		0	0	1
Level 2 ← Interrupt vector $1A for		0	1	0
Level 3 ← Interrupt vector $1B for		0	1	1
Level 4 ← Interrupt vector $1C for		1	0	0
Level 5 ← Interrupt vector $1D for		1	0	1
Level 6 ← Interrupt vector $1E for		1	1	0
Level 7 ← Interrupt vector $1F for		1	1	1

During autovectoring, the 68000 asserts $\overline{\text{VMA}}$ after assertion of $\overline{\text{VPA}}$ and then completes a normal 68000 read cycle as shown in Figure 5.26.

The interrupting device uses external hardware to place a vector number on data lines D0-D7, and then performs a $\overline{\text{DTACK}}$ handshake to terminate the $\overline{\text{IACK}}$ bus cycle. The vector numbers allowed are $40 to $FF, but Motorola has not implemented a protection on the first 64 entries so that user-interrupt vectors may overlap at the discretion of the system designer. This is known as nonautovectoring. The 68000 multiplies this vector by 4 and determines the pointers to interrupt address vector.

During $\overline{\text{IACK}}$ cycle, the 68000 always checks the $\overline{\text{VPA}}$ line for LOW, and if $\overline{\text{VPA}}$ is asserted, the 68000 obtains the interrupt vector address using autovectoring. If $\overline{\text{VPA}}$ is not asserted, the 68000 checks $\overline{\text{DTACK}}$ for LOW. If $\overline{\text{DTACK}}$ is asserted, the 68000 obtains the interrupt address vector using nonautovectoring.

Another way to terminate an interrupt acknowledge bus cycle is with

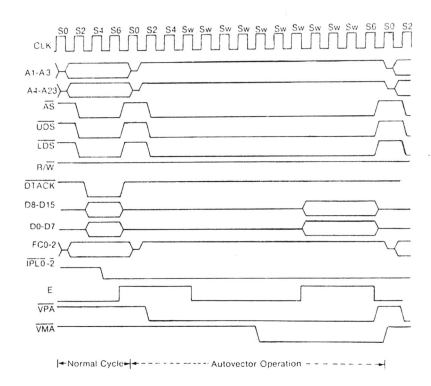

FIGURE 5.26 Autovector operation timing diagram.

the $\overline{\text{BERR}}$ (Bus Error) signal. Even though the interrupt control pins are synchronized to enhance noise immunity, it is possible that external system interrupt circuitry may initiate an $\overline{\text{IACK}}$ bus cycle as a result of noise. Since no device is requesting interrupt service, neither $\overline{\text{DTACK}}$ nor $\overline{\text{VPA}}$ will be asserted to signal the end of the nonexisting $\overline{\text{IACK}}$ bus cycle. When there is no response to an $\overline{\text{IACK}}$ bus cycle after a specified period of time (monitored by the user by an external timer), the $\overline{\text{BERR}}$ can be asserted by an external timer. This indicates to the processor that it has recognized a spurious interrupt. The 68000 provides 18H as the vector to fetch for the starting address of this exception handling routine.

The 68000 determines the interrupt address vector for each of the above cases as follows. After obtaining the 8-bit vector n, the 68000 reads the long word located at memory 4*n. This long word is the address of the service routine. Therefore, the address is found using indirect addressing. Note that the spurious interrupt and bus error interrupt due to troubled instruction (when no $\overline{\text{DTACK}}$ is received by the 68000) have two different vectors. Spurious interrupt occurs when the $\overline{\text{BUS ERROR}}$ pin is asserted during interrupt processing.

Figure 5.27a shows a flowchart for the interrupt acknowledge sequence, a timing diagram is given in Figure 4.27b, and the interrupt processing sequence is shown in Figure 5.28. In Figure 5.27b, during $\overline{IACK}$ cycle, FC2 FC1 FC0 = 111. A1-A3 has the interrupt level. The vector number is provided on the D0-D7 pins by external hardware. Note that during nonautovectoring, if $\overline{VPA}$ goes to LOW, the 68000 ignores it.

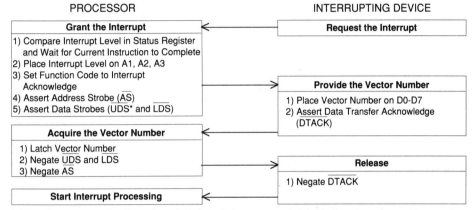

* Although a vector number is one byte, both data strobes are asserted due to the microcode used for exception processing. The processor does not recognize anything on data lines D8 through D15 at this time.

FIGURE 5.27a Vector acquisition flow chart (nonautovectoring).

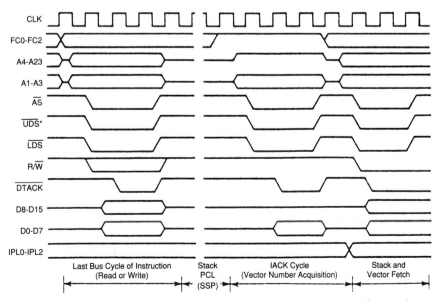

* Although a vector number is one byte, both data strobes are asserted due to the microcode used for exception processing. The processor does not recognize anything on data lines D8 through D15 at this time.

FIGURE 5.27b Interrupt acknowledge cycle timing diagram (nonautovectoring).

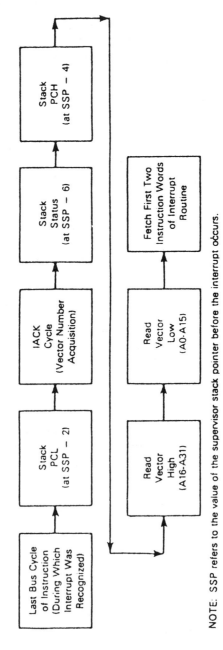

FIGURE 5.28 Interrupt processing sequence (nonautovectoring).

NOTE: SSP refers to the value of the supervisor stack pointer before the interrupt occurs.

5.13.2 INTERNAL INTERRUPTS

The internal interrupt is a software interrupt. This interrupt is generated when the 68000 executes a software interrupt instruction called TRAP or by some undesirable events such as division by zero or execution of an illegal instruction.

5.13.3 68000 EXCEPTION MAP

Figure 5.29 shows an interrupt map of the 68000. Vector addresses $00 through $2C include vector addresses for reset, bus error, trace, divide by 0, etc., and addresses $30 through $4C are unassigned. The $\overline{\text{RESET}}$ vector requires four words (addresses 0, 2, 4, and 6) and other vectors require only two words. As an example of how the 68000 determines the interrupt address vector, consider autovector 1. After $\overline{\text{VPA}}$ is asserted, if I2 I1 I0 = 001, the 68000 automatically obtains the 8-bit vector 25_{10} (19_{16}) and multiplies 19_{16} by 4 to obtain the 24-bit address 000064_{16}. The 68000 then loads the 16-bit contents of location 000064_{16} and the next location 000066_{16} into PC. For example, if the user wants to write the service routine for autovector 1 at address 271452_{16}, then $XX27_{16}$ and 1452_{16}, must, respectively, be stored at 000064_{16} and 000066_{16}. Note that XX in $XX27_{16}$ are two don't care nibbles.

After hardware reset, the 68000 loads the supervisor SP high and low words, respectively, from addresses 000000_{16} and 000002_{16}, and the PC high and low words, respectively, from 000004_{16} and 000006_{16}. Typical assembler directive, Define Constant (DC) can be used to load PC and SSP. For example, the following instruction sequence loads SSP with $004100 and PC with $001000:

```
ORG        $000000
DC.L       $00004100
DC.L       $00001000
```

5.13.4 68000 INTERRUPT ADDRESS VECTOR

Suppose that the user decides to write a service routine starting at address $123456 using autovector 1. Since the autovector 1 uses addresses $000064 and $000066, the numbers $0012 and $3456 must be stored in locations $000064 and $000066, respectively. The DC.L assembler directive can be used to load $123456 into location $000064 as follows:

```
ORG        $000064
DC.L       $00123456
```

Vector Number(s)	Address			Assignment
	Dec	Hex	Space	
0	0	000	SP	Reset: Initial SSP
–	4	004	SP	Reset: Initial PC
2	8	008	SD	Bus Error
3	12	00C	SD	Address Error
4	16	010	SD	Illegal Instruction
5	20	014	SD	Zero Divide
6	24	018	SD	CHK Instruction
7	28	01C	SD	TRAPV Instruction
8	32	020	SD	Privilege Violation
9	36	024	SD	Trace
10	40	028	SD	Line 1010 Emulator
11	44	02C	SD	Line 1111 Emulator
12*	48	030	SD	(Unassigned, Reserved)
13*	52	034	SD	(Unassigned, Reserved)
14*	56	038	SD	(Unassigned, Reserved)
15	60	03C	SD	Uninitialized Interrupt Vector
16-23*	64	04C	SD	(Unassigned, Reserved)
	95	05F		–
24	96	060	SD	Spurious Interrupt
25	100	064	SD	Level 1 Interrupt Autovector
26	104	068	SD	Level 2 Interrupt Autovector
27	108	06C	SD	Level 3 Interrupt Autovector
28	112	070	SD	Level 4 Interrupt Autovector
29	116	074	SD	Level 5 Interrupt Autovector
30	120	078	SD	Level 6 Interrupt Autovector
31	124	07C	SD	Level 7 Interrupt Autovector
32-47	128	080	SD	TRAP Instruction Vectors
	191	0BF		–
48-63*	192	0C0	SD	(Unassigned, Reserved)
	255	0FF		–
64-255	256	100	SD	User Interrupt Vectors
	1023	3FF		–

*Vector numbers 12, 13, 14, 16 through 23, and 48 through 63 are reserved for future enhancements by Motorola. No user peripheral devices should be assigned these numbers.

FIGURE 5.29 68000 exception map. 'SP' means supervisor program space; 'SD' means supervisor data space.

5.13.5 AN EXAMPLE OF AUTOVECTOR AND NONAUTOVECTOR INTERRUPTS

As an example to illustrate the concept of autovector and nonautovector interrupts, consider Figure 5.30. In this figure, I/O device 1 uses nonautovector and I/O device 2 uses autovector interrupts. The system is capable of handling interrupts from eight devices, since an 8-to-3 priority encoder such as the 74LS148 is used. Suppose that I/O device 2 drives the $\overline{I/O2}$ LOW in order to activate line 3 of this encoder. This, in turn, interrupts the processor. When the 68000 decides to acknowledge the interrupt, it drives FC0-FC2 HIGH. The interrupt level is reflected on A1-

A3 when $\overline{\text{AS}}$ is activated by the 68000. $\overline{\text{IACK3}}$ and $\overline{\text{I/O2}}$ signals are used to generate $\overline{\text{VPA}}$. Once the $\overline{\text{VPA}}$ is asserted, the 68000 obtains the interrupt vector address using autovectoring.

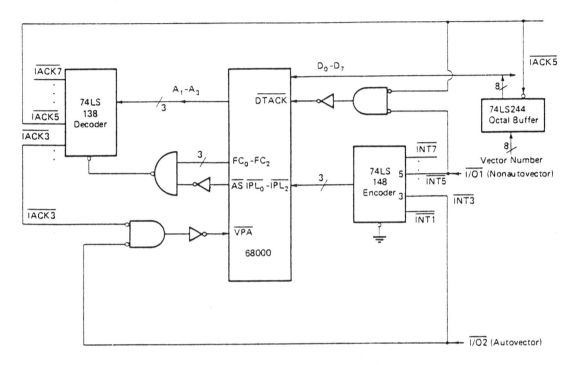

FIGURE 5.30 Autovector and nonautovector interrupts.

In case of $\overline{\text{I/O1}}$, line 5 of the priority encoder is activated to initiate the interrupt. By using appropriate logic, $\overline{\text{DTACK}}$ is asserted using $\overline{\text{IACK5}}$ and $\overline{\text{I/O1}}$. The vector number is placed on D0-D7 by enabling an octal buffer such as the 74LS244 using $\overline{\text{IACK5}}$. The 68000 inputs this vector number and multiplies it by 4 to obtain the interrupt address vector.

5.13.6 INTERFACING OF A TYPICAL A/D CONVERTER TO THE 68000 USING AUTOVECTOR AND NONAUTOVECTOR INTERRUPTS

Figure 5.31 shows interfacing of a typical A/D converter to the 68000-based microcomputer using the autovector interrupt.

In the figure, the A/D converter can be started by sending a START pulse. The $\overline{\text{DV}}$ signal can be connected to line 4 (for example) of the encoder. Note that line 4 is 100_2 for $\overline{\text{IPL2}}$, $\overline{\text{IPL1}}$, $\overline{\text{IPL0}}$, which is level 3 (inverted 100_2) interrupt. The $\overline{\text{DV}}$ can be used to assert $\overline{\text{VPA}}$ so that after

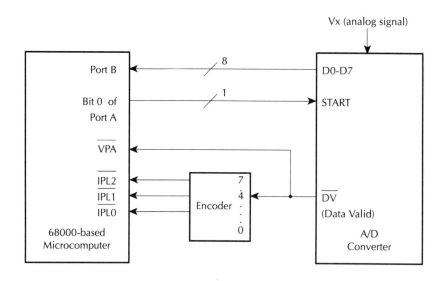

FIGURE 5.31 Interfacing of a typical 8-bit A/D converter to 68000-based microcomputer using autovector interrupt.

acknowledgment of the interrupt, the 68000 will service the interrupt as level 3 autovector interrupt. Note that the encoder in Figure 5.31 is used for illustrative purposes. This encoder is not required for a single device as the A/D converter in the above example.

Figure 5.32 shows interfacing of a typical A/D converter to the 68000-based microcomputer using the nonautovector interrupt.

In the figure, the 68000 starts the A/D converter as before. Also, the $\overline{DV}$ signal is used to interrupt the microcomputer using line 5 ($\overline{IPL2}$ $\overline{IPL1}$ $\overline{IPL0}$ = 101 which is level 2 interrupt) of the encoder. The $\overline{DV}$ can be used to assert $\overline{DTACK}$ so that after acknowledgment of the interrupt, FC2, FC1, FC0 becomes 111_2 which can be ANDed and inverted to enable an octal buffer such as the 74LS244 in order to transfer an 8-bit vector from input of the buffer to the D0-D7 lines of the 68000. The 68000 can then multiply this vector by 4 to determine the interrupt address vector. As before, the encoder in Figure 5.32 is not required for the single A/D converter.

5.14 68000 DMA

Three DMA control lines are provided with the 68000. These are $\overline{BR}$ (Bus Request), $\overline{BG}$ (Bus Grant), and $\overline{BGACK}$ (Bus Grant Acknowledge).

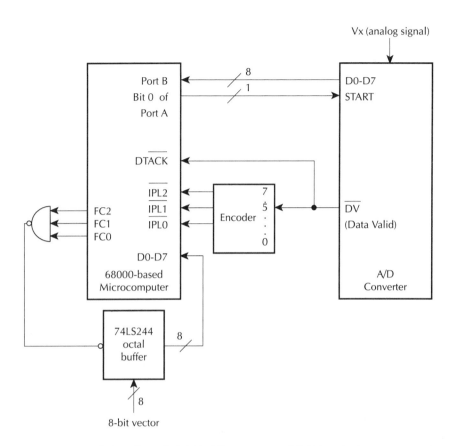

FIGURE 5.32 Interfacing of a typical 8-bit A/D converter to 68000-based microcomputer using nonautovector interrupt.

The $\overline{BR}$ line is an input to the 68000. The external device activates this line to tell the 68000 to release the system bus.

At least one clock period after receiving the $\overline{BR}$, the 68000 will enable its $\overline{BG}$ output line to acknowledge the DMA request. However, the 68000 will not relinquish the bus until it has completed the current instruction cycle. The external device must check $\overline{AS}$ (Address Strobe) line to determine the completion of instruction cycle by the 68000. When $\overline{AS}$ becomes HIGH, the 68000 will tristate its address and data lines and will give up the bus to the external device.

After taking over the bus, the external device must enable $\overline{BGACK}$ line. The $\overline{BGACK}$ line tells the 68000 and other devices connected to the bus that the bus is being used. The 68000 stays in a tristate condition until $\overline{BGACK}$ becomes HIGH.

5.15 68000 EXCEPTION HANDLING

A 16-bit microcomputer is usually capable of handling unusual or exceptional conditions. These conditions include situations such as execution of illegal instruction or division by zero. In this section, exception handling capabilities of a typical microprocessor such as the MC68000 are described.

The 68000 exceptions can be divided into three groups, namely, groups 0, 1, and 2. Group 0 has the highest priority and group 2 has the lowest priority. Within the first two groups, there are additional priority levels. A list of 68000 exceptions along with individual priorities is shown below:

Group 0   Reset (highest level in this group), Address Error (next level), and Bus Error (lowest level)

Group 1   Trace (highest level), Interrupt (next level), Illegal op code (next level), and Privilege Violation (lowest level)

Group 2   TRAP, TRAPV, CHK, and ZERO DIVIDE (no individual priorities assigned in group 2)

Exceptions from group 0 always override an active exception from group 1 or group 2. Group 0 exception processing begins at the completion of the current bus cycle (two clock cycles). Note that the number of cycles required for a READ or WRITE operation is called a bus cycle. This means that during an instruction fetch if there is a group 0 interrupt, the 68000 will complete the instruction fetch and then service the interrupt.

Group 1 exception processing begins at the completion of the current instruction.

Group 2 exceptions are initiated through execution of an instruction. Therefore, there are no individual priority levels within group 2. Exception processing occurs when a group 2 interrupt is encountered, provided there are no group 0 or group 1 interrupts.

When an exception occurs, the 68000 saves the contents of the program counter and status register onto the stack and then executes a new program whose address is provided by the exception vectors. Once this program is executed, the 68000 returns to the main program using the stored values of program counter and status register.

Exceptions can be of two types: internal or external.

The internal exceptions are generated by situations such as division by zero, execution of illegal or unimplemented instructions, and address error. As mentioned before, internal interrupts are called traps.

The external exceptions are generated by bus error, reset, or interrupts. The basic concepts associated with interrupts, relating them to the 68000, have already been described. In this section we will discuss the other exceptions.

In response to an exceptional condition, the processor executes a user-written program. In some microcomputers, one common program is provided for all exceptions. The beginning section of the program determines the cause of the exception and then branches to the appropriate routine. The 68000 utilizes a more general approach. Each exception can be handled by a separate program.

As mentioned before, the 68000 has two modes of operation: user state and supervisor state. The operating system runs in supervisor mode and all other programs are executed in user mode. The supervisor state is, therefore, privileged. Several privileged instructions such as MOVE to SR can only be executed in supervisor mode. Any attempt to execute them in user mode causes a trap.

We will now discuss how the 68000 handles exceptions which are caused by external reset, instructions causing traps, bus and address errors, tracing, execution of privileged instructions in user mode, and execution of illegal/unimplemented instructions.

The reset exception is generated internally. In response to this exception, the 68000 automatically loads the initial starting address into the processor.

The 68000 has a TRAP instruction which always causes an exception. The operand for this instruction varies from 0 to 15. This means that there are 16 TRAP instructions. Each TRAP instruction is normally used to call subroutines in an operating system. Note that this automatically places the 68000 in supervisor state. TRAPs can also be used for inserting breakpoints in a program. Two other 68000 instructions cause traps if a particular condition is true. These are TRAPV and CHK. TRAPV generates an exception if the overflow flag is set. The TRAPV instruction can be inserted after every arithmetic operation in a program for causing a trap whenever there is the possibility of an overflow. A routine can be written at the vector address for the TRAPV to indicate to the user that an overflow has occurred. The CHK instruction is designed to ensure that access to an array in memory is within the range specified by the user. If there is a violation of this range, the 68000 generates an exception.

A bus error occurs when the 68000 tries to access an address which does not belong to the device connected to the bus. This error can be detected by asserting the $\overline{\text{BERR}}$ pin on the 68000 chip by an external timer when no $\overline{\text{DTACK}}$ is received from the device after a certain period of time.

In response to this, the 68000 executes a user-written routine located at an address obtained from the exception vectors. An address error, on the other hand, occurs when the 68000 tries to READ or WRITE a word (16-bit) or long word (32-bit) in an odd address. The address error has a different exception vector from the bus error.

The trace exception in the 68000 can be generated by setting the trace bit in the status register, in response to the trace exception after execution of every instruction. The user can write a routine at the exception vectors for the trace instruction to display registers and memory. The trace exception provides the 68000 with the single-stepping debugging feature.

As mentioned before, the 68000 has some privileged instructions which must be executed in supervisor mode. An attempt to execute these instructions causes privilege violations. Finally, the 68000 causes an exception when it tries to execute an illegal or unimplemented instruction.

5.16 MULTIPROCESSING WITH 68000 USING THE TAS INSTRUCTION AND $\overline{AS}$ (ADDRESS STROBE) SIGNAL

Earlier, the 68000 TAS instruction was discussed. The TAS instruction supports the software aspects of interfacing two or more 68000s via shared RAM. When TAS is executed, an indivisible read-modify-write cycle is performed. The timing diagram for this specialized cycle is shown in Figure 5.33. During both the read and the write portions of the cycle, the $\overline{AS}$ remains LOW, and the cycle starts as the normal read cycle.

However, in the normal read the $\overline{AS}$ going inactive indicates the end of the read. During execution of the TAS, the $\overline{AS}$ stays LOW throughout the cycle, and therefore $\overline{AS}$ can be used in the design as a bus locking circuit.

Due to bus locking, only one processor at a time can perform a TAS operation in a multiprocessor system. The TAS instruction supports semaphore operations (globally shared resources) by checking a resource for availability and reserving or locking it for use by a single processor. The TAS instruction can, therefore, be used to allocate memory space reservations.

The TAS instruction execution flow for allocating memory is shown in Figure 5.34a and b. The shared RAM of Figure 5.34b is divided into M sections. The first byte of each section will be pointed to by (EA) of TAS

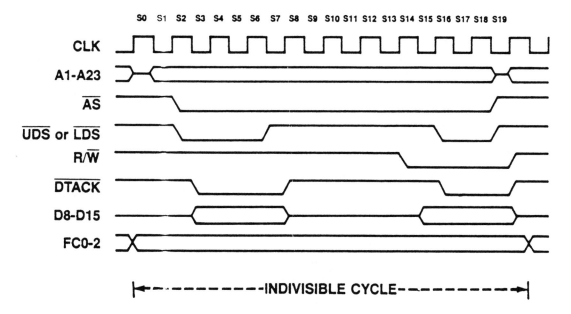

FIGURE 5.33 MC68000 read-modify-write cycle for TAS.

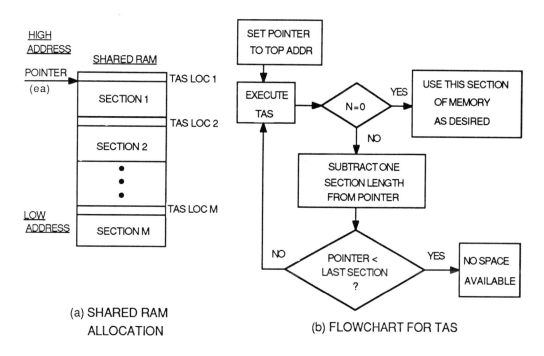

(a) SHARED RAM ALLOCATION

(b) FLOWCHART FOR TAS

FIGURE 5.34 Memory allocation using TAS.

(EA) instruction. In the flowcharts, (ea) first points to the first byte of section 1. The instruction TAS (ea) is then executed.

The TAS instruction checks the most significant bit (N bit) in (EA). N = 0 indicates that the section 1 is free; N = 1 means section 1 is busy. If N = 0, then section 1 will be allocated for use. On the other hand, if N = 1, section 1 is busy; a program will be written to subtract one section length from (EA) to check the next section for availability. Also, (EA) must be checked with the value TASLOCM. If (EA) < TASLOCM, then no space is available for allocation. However, (EA) > TASLOCM, TAS is executed and the availability of that section is determined.

In a multiprocessor environment, the TAS instruction provides software support for interfacing two or more 68000 via shared RAM. The $\overline{AS}$ signal can be used to provide the bus locking mechanism.

Figures 5.35a and 5.35b show an MC68000 multiprocessor system with shared RAM using the TAS instruction.

In Figure 5.35a, the system is comprised of two 68000 minimum systems: a shared memory subsystem and buffer control logic and an arbiter.

5.16.1 68000 MINIMUM SUBSYSTEM

The subsystem utilizes minimum 68000 configuration with ROM and RAM.

5.16.2 SHARED MEMORY AND BUFFER CONTROL LOGIC

The system takes arbiter outputs Q, $\overline{Q}$ and subdivides bus transreceivers on-line and off-line as dictated by the arbiter. Note that 74LS244 and 74LS245 are, respectively, unidirectional and bidirectional buffers. This logic, after some delay, also asserts $\overline{DTACK}$ to the microprocessors after buffers have been switched on-line, and data are valid. This is accomplished by digital delay lines. This is necessary because a processor will "throw away" its bus cycle while waiting for access to shared memory. Also, when the arbiter terminates a bus cycle, the R/$\overline{W}$ line is actively pulled HIGH several time constants before the tristated bus changes. This insures that spurious writes will not occur at random locations due to the tristate condition. This circuit is accomplished as shown on the opposite page.

5.16.3 ARBITER

In the system of Figure 5.35a, $\overline{DTACK}$ must be given to a processor whenever a processor is accessing local memory or when it is the only processor accessing shared RAM. When both processors request shared RAM, then only one processor should receive it. In this system, the

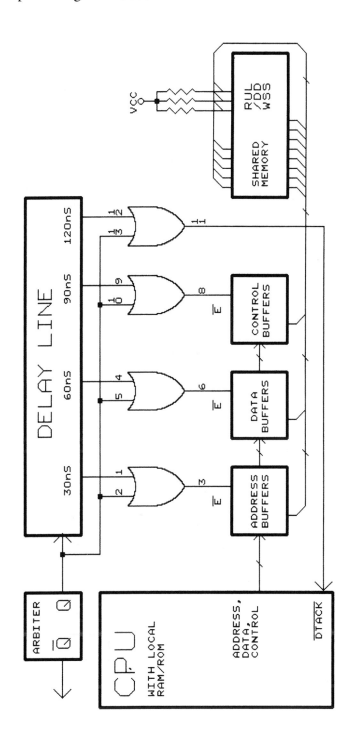

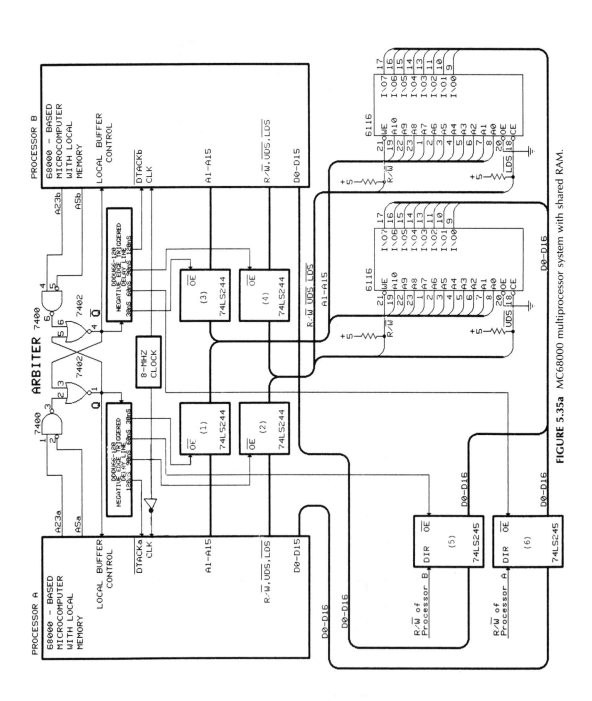

FIGURE 5.35a MC68000 multiprocessor system with shared RAM.

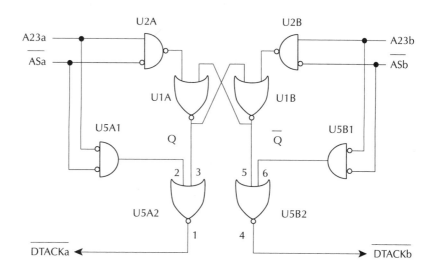

FIGURE 5.35b Details of the arbiter.

processors are given equal priority to access the shared RAM. The bus arbiter performs all the control functions.

Figure 5.35b shows the details of the bus arbiter. Shared RAM will be accessed when address line A23 (A23A or A23B) is HIGH. For each processor, when A23 is LOW and when $\overline{AS}$ is asserted, shared RAM $\overline{DTACK}$ will be given immediately (gates U5A1 and U5A2 for processor A; gates U5B1 and U5B2 for processor B).

A crucial criterion for the shared RAM system is that when a processor is given access to the shared bus, it must be allowed to complete the bus cycle without being interrupted. Thus, when a bus cycle is initiated by $\overline{AS}$ being asserted, the end of the cycle must be detected by $\overline{AS}$ being negated.

In addition to detecting the completion of the bus cycle, another processor must be inhibited from changing the state of the arbiter. This is accomplished by NOR gates U1A and U1B which act as the bus arbiter. These gates act as follows: when both processors are not accessing shared memory, both inputs are HIGH and the arbiter assumes some state. The inverter at the processor A CLK input ensures that only one processor has access to the bus if both processors access it at the same time. The arbiter will remain in a locked condition until $\overline{AS}$ is negated. When this occurs and if the second processor requests access, then the arbiter will change state. If it does not request access then the arbiter will remain idle until either processor requests shared RAM access. After completion of a bus cycle, the bus master negates $\overline{AS}$ and the bus arbiter flips state. Finally, the new output of the arbiter is propagated to the delay lines and the bus control may be offered to the next processor. After some delay time, $\overline{\text{DTACK}}$ is given if the other processor is requesting shared RAM.

In Figure 5.35a the buffers 74LS244 (1) or 74LS244 (3), respectively, transfer A0-A15 lines of processor A or B upon enabling of the $\overline{\text{OE}}$ by the bus arbiter. Since 74LS244 is an 8-bit unidirectional buffer, two 74LS244s are required for 16-bit transfer. The buffers 74LS244 (2) and 74LS244 (4) are used to transfer R/$\overline{\text{W}}$, $\overline{\text{UDS}}$, $\overline{\text{LDS}}$ lines of processor A or B to the shared memory upon enabling of $\overline{\text{OE}}$ by $\overline{\text{DTACKA}}$ or $\overline{\text{DTACKB}}$. The buffers 74LS245 (5) and 74LS245 (6) are used for bidirectional transfer of D0-D15 (from processor to RAM and vice versa).

For read or write operation consider Figure 5.35a. Assume that processor A has access to the shared RAM. This means that $\overline{\text{DTACKA}}$ is LOW. During read cycle, processor A R/$\overline{\text{W}}$ = 1 will make DIR (direction) input of the 74LS245 (5) HIGH. This will transfer data from the shared RAM to processor A via 74LS245 (5). On the other hand, during write cycle, R/$\overline{\text{W}}$ will make DIR (direction) input of 74LS245 (5) LOW. This will transfer data from processor A to shared RAM via 74LS245 (5). Note that since 74LS245 is an 8-bit bidirectional buffer, two 74LS245s are required for 16-bit transfer.

Similarly, when processor B has access to the shared RAM, buffer 75LS245 (6) is used to transfer data between the shared RAM and processor B.

5.16.4 DIGITAL DELAY LINES

The digital delay lines can delay the propagation of a digital signal by a known amount. Furthermore, by the use of taps, the digital signal can be "picked off" at various delay times. This can be very useful in "pre-event" signal switching. Examine the following theoretical case, where we wish to route several signals down some path that is several levels deep, and a control line falls LOW when we are to actually accomplish the task:

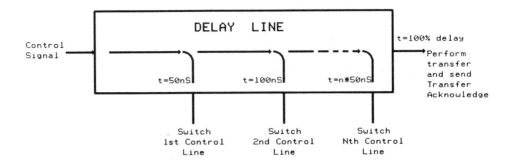

The systems designer has an advantage to using delay lines over standard TTL buffers, since the specified delay time is guaranteed to be ±2% or ±5 ns of the specified delay time, whereas a TTL gate delay time can vary by as much as 500%. This makes it difficult, if not impossible, to perform switching within a prescribed minimum and maximum timed window.

Delay lines predominately follow two pinout conventions. They are packaged as 5-tapped and 10-tapped lines. Their maximum delay times are specified in their port numbers. For example, Engineering Components Company produces the TTLDM-150 which supplies delay times of 30 ns (20%), 60 ns (40%), 90 ns (60%), 120 ns (80%), and 150 ns (100%). Pinouts are as follows:

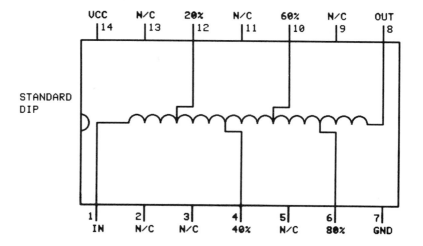

There are several major manufacturers of digital delay lines. Listed below are some major manufacturers of delay lines.

Data Delay Devices
385 Lakeview Ave.
Clifton, NJ 07011
Stock number of 120-ns device: DDU-66U-120

Engineering Components Company
3580 Sacramento Drive
San Luis Obisbo, CA 93401
Stock number of 120-ns device: TTLDM-120

Kappa Networks Inc.
13455 Ventura Blvd #220
Sherman Oaks, CA 91423
Stock number of 120-ns device: DT14CB121

5.17 68000 NANOMEMORY

The 68000 Control Unit is designed using nanomemory. This method provides significant savings in memory when a group of microoperations occur several times in a microprogram. Consider the microprogram of Figure 5.36. The microprogram in this figure contains A microinstructions B bits wide.

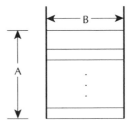

FIGURE 5.36 A microrogram of size A × B.

The size of the control memory to store this microprogram is AB bits. Assume that the microprogram has n (n < A) unique microinstructions. These n microinstructions can be held in a separate memory called the nanomemory of size nB bits. Each of these n instructions occurs once in the nanomemory. Each microinstruction in the original microprogram is replaced with the address that specifies the location of the nanomemory in which the original B-bit-wide microinstructions are held. Since the nanomemory has n addresses, only the upper integer of $\log_2 n$ bits is required to specify a nanomemory address. This is illustrated in Figure 5.37.

The operation of microprocessor employing a nanomemory can be explained as follows. The microprocessor's control unit reads an address from the microprogram. The contents of this address in the nanomemory is the desired control word. The bits in the control word are used by the control unit to accomplish the desired operation. Note that a control unit

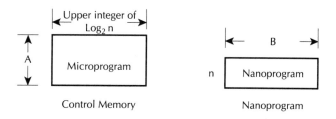

FIGURE 5.37 Nanomemory.

employing nanomemory (two-level memory) is slower than the one using a conventional control memory (single memory). This is because the nanomemory requires two memory reads (one for the control memory and the other for the nanomemory). For a single conventional control memory, only one memory fetch is necessary. This reduction in control unit speed is offset by the cost of the memory when the same microinstructions occur many times in the microprogram.

Consider a 7×4-bit microprogram stored in the single control memory of Figure 5.38. This simplified example is chosen to illustrate the nanomemory concept even though this is not a practical example.

000	0100
001	0000
010	0100
011	0100
100	0000
101	1010
110	1010

FIGURE 5.38 7×4 bit single control memory.

In this program, 3 out of 7 microinstructions are unique. Therefore, the size of the microcontrol store is 7×2 bits and the size of the nanomemory is 3×4 bits. This is shown in Figure 5.39.

Memory requirements for the single control memory = 7×4 = 28 bits. Memory requirements for nanomemory = $(7 \times 2 + 3 \times 4)$ bits = 26 bits. Therefore, saving using nanomemory = 28 − 26 = 2 bits. For a simple

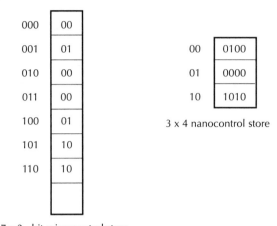

FIGURE 5.39 Two-level store (nanomemory).

example like this, 2 bits are saved. The 68000 control unit nanomemory includes a 640×9-bit microcontrol store and a 280×70 nanocontrol store as shown in Figure 5.40.

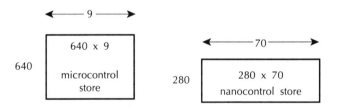

FIGURE 5.40 68000 nanomemory.

In Figure 5.40, out of 640 microinstructions, 280 are unique. If the 68000 were implemented using a single control memory, memory requirements would have been 640×70 bits. Therefore, memory savings

$$= 640 \times 70 - (640 \times 9 + 280 \times 70) \text{ bits}$$
$$= 44,800 - 25,360$$
$$= 19,440 \text{ bits}$$

This is a tremendous memory saving for the 68000 control unit.

5.18 BASIC DIFFERENCES BETWEEN THE 68000, 68008, 68010, AND 68012

The 68008 has the same register set as the 68000. The 68010 and 68012, on the other hand, include all 68000 registers plus a 32-bit vector base register (VBR) and two 3-bit alternate function code registers, SFC (source function code) and DFC (destination function code).

The 68008, like the 68000, provides an exception vector table starting at a fixed address 0. The 68010 and 68012 compute the address of the exception table by multiplying the 8-bit vector number by 4 and then adding it to VBR. This provides the user with the flexibility to provide exception vector address anywhere in memory.

The 68000 family of processors provides three function code output lines FC2, FC1, and FC0. These pins indicate to any peripherals the type of access currently in progress by the processors. The SFC and DFC registers on the 68010 and 68012 permit a system-level program to provide its own function code outputs for the source or destination during the execution of the MOVES instruction (to be discussed in Chapter 6).

The 68000, 68008, 68010, and 68012 include the same instruction set. The processors use a two-word instruction fetch. The processors begin by fetching the instruction word. As decoding starts, the processors fetch the following word from memory so that when they start executing the instruction, two words are already available. This speeds up instruction execution. However, if the processors encounter a branch instruction, the word following the instruction is discarded.

The 68010 and 68012 provide an enhancement over the two-word pipelining scheme just mentioned. In some cases, the processors can execute the looped instruction without refetching the instruction from memory. In the special case where the second word of the two prefetched words branches back to that single word instruction, the processors need not do any instruction fetches from memory while inside the loop. The pins and signals associated with the 68000, 68008, 68010, and 68012 are shown in Figure 5.41.

The 68008 has an 8-bit-wide data bus and this is the only processor in the family which has the least significant address line A0. The 68008 is also the only processor in the family which includes the single data strobe $\overline{DS}$ signal. The 68008 places a LOW on $\overline{DS}$ to indicate that its data bus is in

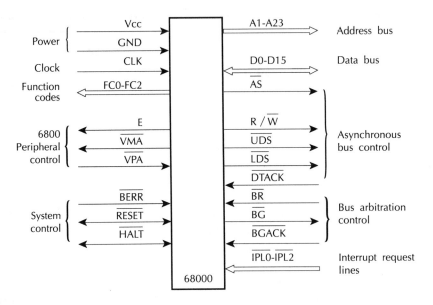

FIGURE 5.41a 68000 functional groups of signals.

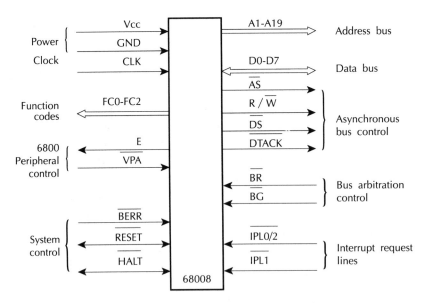

FIGURE 5.41b 68008 functional groups of signals.

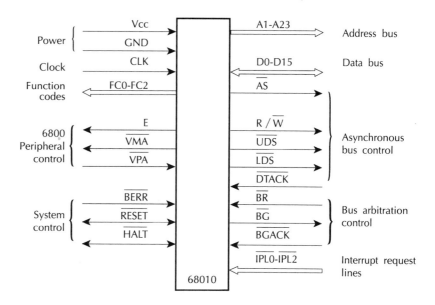

FIGURE 5.41c 68010 functional groups of signals.

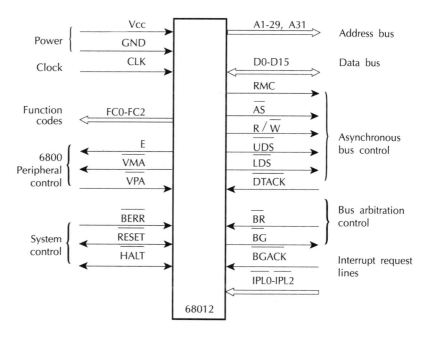

FIGURE 5.41d 68012 functional groups of signals.

use. The 68000/68010 has A1-A23 as the address lines, while the 68012 has A1-A29 and A31 with A0 on these processors encoded from $\overline{\text{UDS}}$ and $\overline{\text{LDS}}$ in the same way as the 68000.

$\overline{\text{AS}}$, R/$\overline{\text{W}}$, $\overline{\text{DTACK}}$, $\overline{\text{HALT}}$, $\overline{\text{RESET}}$, and CLK pins on the 68008, 68010, and 68012 have similar functions as the 68000.

The function code outputs (FC2, FC1, and FC0) on the 68008, 68010, and 68012, like those on the 68000, are valid when $\overline{\text{AS}}$ is low and identify the type of bus activity (user vs. supervisor) with the same encodings as the 68000, except for the 68010 and 68012 when FC2, FC1, and FC0 are all high. For the 68010 and 68012, the machine cycle with FC2 FC1 FC0 = 111 is called the CPU space cycle. In this cycle, the processors 68010 and 68012 can perform certain functions such as breakpoints. Note that in the 68000, the function code outputs FC2 FC1 FC0 = 111 indicate the interrupt acknowledge cycle. $\overline{\text{BERR}}$ input signal provides slightly different results on the virtual memory processors 68010 and 68012. In these processors, the total addressing space of the task may be greater than the physical memory space. The operating system may choose to store certain programs on disk while executing other programs. Since the processors can only execute programs in physical memory, the operating system must be able to read the programs from disk into physical memory when they need to be executed. Therefore, to implement virtual memory effectively, the processors must be able to recognize the absence of required memory, read the data from disk, and continue execution of the program. External logic should recognize the nonexistence of the required memory and assert $\overline{\text{BERR}}$. The 68010 and 68012 save a detailed stack frame in initiating bus error exception. As part of the exception routine, the 68010 and 68012 may analyze the stacked information and determine if the error was caused because of a request for data stored on disk. If so, it can read data from disk into memory.

The bus arbitration signals $\overline{\text{BR}}$, $\overline{\text{BG}}$, and $\overline{\text{BGACK}}$ are available on the 68000, 68010, and 68012. The 68008 implements fewer handshaking signals and does not include the $\overline{\text{BGACK}}$ signal.

Also, the 68008 does not implement all the 6800-type signals. For example, the 68008 does not implement the $\overline{\text{VMA}}$ signal.

The 68000 read and write timing diagrams are similar to those of 68010 and 68012. The 68008 read and write timing diagrams are a bit different from those of the other processors, since the 68008 has $\overline{\text{DS}}$ (data strobe) pin (instead of $\overline{\text{UDS}}$ and $\overline{\text{LDS}}$ pins with the 68000/68010/68012), 8 data pins D0-D7, and 20 address pins A0-A19. The details of 68008 timing can be found in Motorola manuals.

The read/modify/write cycles of all the 68000 family of processors are identical except that the 68012 provides an additional pin called the $\overline{RMC}$ (read/modify/write cycle) pin. The pin is asserted by the 68012 throughout the entire read/modify/write cycle. The $\overline{RMC}$ pin can be used by memory management schemes that require advanced indication of read/modify/write cycle. The 68020 and 68030 include the $\overline{RMC}$ pin.

External interrupts on all processors (except for the 68008) are handled via the $\overline{IPL2}$, $\overline{IPL1}$, and $\overline{IPL0}$ pin in the same way. The 68008 combines $\overline{IPL0}$ and $\overline{IPL2}$ into one signal $(\overline{IPL0}/2)$ and provides four interrupt levels.

QUESTIONS AND PROBLEMS

5.1   Assume that $[D0] = 25774411_{16}$. What will be the contents of D0 after execution of each of the following instructions:
  i)   **CLR.B D0**
  ii) **CLR D0**
  iii) **CLR.L D0**

5.2   Determine the contents of registers and the locations affected by each of the following instructions:
  i) **MOVE.L -(A2), (A3)+**
  Assume the following data prior to execution of the MOVE:
           [A2] = $300504, [A3]   = $510718,
        [$300500] = $01, [$300501] = $F1,
        [$300502] = $72, [$300503] = $A1,
        [$510718] = $53, [$510719] = $20,
        [$51071A] = $31, [51071B] = $27

  ii) **MOVEA.W D1, A4**
  Assume the following data prior to execution of the MOVEA:
               [D1] = $37158470
               [A4] = $F1218234

  iii) **MOVEA.L A2, A3**
  Assume the following data prior to execution of the MOVEA:
               [A2] = $1234F144
               [A3] = $20718714

5.3   Identify the following 68000 instructions as privileged or nonprivileged:

      i) **MOVE SR, (A2)**
     ii) **MOVE CCR, (A0)**
   iii) **LEA.L (A2), A5**
   iv) **MOVE.L A2, USP**

5.4   What are the contents of register D1 after execution of the following two instructions? Assume [D1] = $34788480 prior to the execution of the instructions:

```
EXT.L  D1
MOVEQ.L  #$2F,  D1
```

5.5   Find the contents of D1 after execution of the following DIVS instructions:

```
DIVS  (A1),  D1
```

Assume [A1] = $205014, [$205014] = $FF, [$205015] = $FE, [D1] = $00000005 prior to execution of the instruction. Identify the quotient and remainder of the result in D1. Comment on the sign of the remainder.

5.6   Write a 68000 assembly program to divide an 8-bit signed number in low byte of D1 by an 8-bit signed number in low byte of D2. Store quotient and remainder in D1.

5.7   Write a 68000 assembly language program to add two 128-bit numbers. Assume that the first number is stored in consecutive memory locations starting at $605014. The second number is stored in consecutive memory locations starting at $708020. Store the result in memory locations beginning at $708020.

5.8   Write a 68000 assembly program to add two top-two 32 bits of the stack. Store the 32-bit result onto the stack. Assume user mode.

5.9   Write a 68000 assembly program to multiply an 8-bit signed number in low byte of D1 by a 16-bit signed number in high word of D5 store the result in D3.

5.10 Write a 68000 assembly program to add twenty 32-bit numbers stored in consecutive memory locations starting at address $502040. Store the 32-bit result onto the stack. Assume that for each 32-bit number, the lowest address stores the highest byte of the number.

5.11 Write 68000 assembly language to find the minimum value of a string of ten signed 16-bit numbers using indexed addressing.

5.12 Write a 68000 assembly program to compare two strings of twenty ASCII characters. The first string is stored starting at $003000 followed by the string. The second string is stored starting at $004000. The ASCII character in location $003000 of string 1 will be compared with the ASCII character in location $004000 of string 2, [$003001] to be compared with [$003002], and so on. Each time there is a match, store $EEEE onto the stack; otherwise store $0000.

5.13 Write a 68000 assembly program to divide a 27-bit unsigned number in high 27 bits of D0 by 16_{10}. Do not use any divide instruction. Neglect remainder. Store quotient in low 27-bit of D0.

5.14 Write a subroutine in 68000 assembly language to compute

$$Z = \frac{\sum_{i=1}^{100} (Xi - Yi)}{100}$$

Assume that Xi's and Yi's are signed 16-bit and stored in consecutive locations starting at $020054 and $305116, respectively. Assume A0 and A1 point to Xi's and Yi's, respectively, and SP is already initialized.

5.15 Write a subroutine in 68000 assembly language to subtract two unsigned eight-digit BCD numbers. The BCD number 1 is stored at location starting from $300000 thru $300007, with the least significant digit at $300007 and the most significant digit at $300000. Similarly, the BCD number 2 is stored at location starting from $400000 through $400007, with the least significant digit at $400007 and the most significant digit at $400000. The BCD number 2 is to be subtracted from BCD number 1. Store result in D1.

5.16   Write a subroutine in 68000 assembly to convert a 3-digit unsigned BCD number to binary. The most significant digit is stored in memory location starting at $003000, the next digit is stored at $003001, and so on. Store the binary result in D3.

Use the value of the 3-digit BCD number in V = D2 × 10² + D1 × 10¹ + D0 = (D2 × 10 + D1) × 10 + D0).

5.17   Using LINK and UNLK instructions, write recursive subroutine (A subroutine calling itself) in 68000 assembly language to find the factorial of an 8-bit number n by using n! = n(n − 1) (n − 2) . . . 1. Store the result in D0.

5.18   Determine the status of $\overline{\text{LDS}}$, $\overline{\text{UDS}}$, $\overline{\text{AS}}$, FC2-FC0, and address lines immediately after execution of the following instruction sequence (before the 68000 tristates these lines to fetch the next instruction):

```
MOVE #$2000, SR
MOVE.B D2, $030001
 —
 —
```

Assume the 68000 is in supervisor mode prior to execution of the above instructions.

5.19   Write a 68000 assembly program to output the contents of memory locations $003000 and $003001 to two seven-segment displays connected to two 8-bit ports A and B.

5.20   Assume that in the configuration of Figure 5.23, port A and port B each has three switches and an LED connected to bits 0 through 3. Write 68000 assembly program to

  i)   Turn the port A LED ON and port B LED OFF if port A has an even and port B has an odd number of high switch inputs.

  ii)   Turn the port A LED OFF and port B LED ON if port A has an odd and port B has an even number of high switch inputs.

  iii) Turn both LEDs ON if both ports A and B have even number of high switch inputs.

  iv)   Turn both LEDs OFF if both ports A and B have odd number of high switch inputs.

5.21 Interface a 68000 to 2716s, 6116s, and a 68230 to provide 4K EPROM, 4K RAM, and two 8-bit I/O ports. Draw a neat schematic and determine memory and I/O maps. Assume 16.67 MHz internal clock for the 68000.

5.22 If the $\overline{\text{IPL2}}$ $\overline{\text{IPL1}}$ $\overline{\text{IPL0}}$ pins are interrupted by an external device with the code 001_2 when the interrupt mask value I2I1I0 is 3_{10}, will the interrupt be serviced immediately or ignored by the 68000?

5.23 Discuss briefly the various 68000 exceptions.

5.24 Write a service routine for reset that will initialize all data and address registers to zero, supervisor SP to $3F0728, user SP to $1F0524, and then jump to $002000.

5.25 Assume the following stack and register values before occurrence of an interrupt:

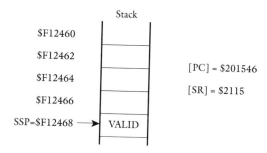

If an external device requests an interrupt by asserting the $\overline{\text{IPL2}}$ $\overline{\text{IPL1}}$ $\overline{\text{IPL0}}$ pins with the value 000, determine the contents of SSP and SR during interrupt and after execution of RTE at the end of the service routine of the interrupt. Draw the memory layouts showing where SSP points to and the stack contents during and after interrupt. Assume that the stack is not used by the service routine.

5.26 Suppose that two pumps (P1,P2) and two LEDs (L1,L2) are to be connected to a 68000-based microcomputer. Each pump has a 'pump running' output to indicate the ON/OFF status. The microcomputer starts the pumps via bits 2 and 3 of 8-bit port A and tries to turn the pumps ON. Two LEDs L1 (for P1) and L2 (for P2) are connected to bits 0 and 1 of 8-bit port B to indicate the pump statuses. If P1 runs, turn L1 ON.

On the other hand, if P2 runs, turn L2 ON. If both pumps run, turn both LEDs ON; otherwise, turn one LED (L1 or L2 depending on the pump) or both LEDs OFF if one or both pumps do not run. Assume that the pump can be turned ON by HIGH and turned OFF by LOW.

i)   Using programmed I/O, draw a block diagram and write a 68000 assembly program to accomplish the above.

ii)   Using interrupt I/O, draw a block diagram. Write the main program and service routine in 68000 assembly language to accomplish the above. The main program will perform all initializations and then start the pumps.

5.27   Compare the basic features of the 68000 with those of 68008, 68010, and 68012.

5.28   Write a 68000 assembly language program to add a 32-bit number stored in D0 (bits 0 through 15 containing the high-order 16 bits of the number and bits 16 through 31 containing the low-order 16 bits) with another 32-bit number stored in D1 (bits 0 through 15 containing the low-order 16 bits of the number and bits 16 through 31 containing the high-order 16 bits). Store the result in D0.

5.29   Write a subroutine in 68000 assembly language using the TAS instruction to find, reserve, and lock a memory segment for the main program. The memory is divided into four segments (0, 1, 2, 3) of 8 bytes each. The first byte of each segment includes a flagbyte to be used by the TAS instruction. In the subroutine, a maximum of four 8-byte memory segments must be checked for a free segment. Once a free segment is found, the TAS instruction is used to set the flagbyte. The starting address of the free segment must be stored in A5 and D5 and must be cleared to zero to indicate a free segment. If no free block is found, a nonzero value must be stored in D5.

5.30   Write a 68000 assembly language program to delete item 0 from the following linked list:

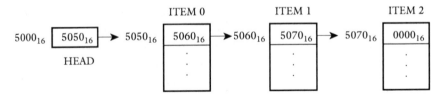

Chapter 6

MOTOROLA MC68020

This chapter describes in detail the hardware, software, and interfacing features associated with the MC68020.

Topics include MC68020 architecture, addressing modes, instruction set, I/O, coprocessors, and system design.

6.1 INTRODUCTION

The MC 68020 is a 32-bit microprocessor. The MC68020 is designed to execute all user object code written for previous members of the MC 68000 family.

The MC68020 is manufactured using HCMOS (combining HMOS and CMOS on the same device). The MC68020 consumes a maximum of 1.75 watts. It contains 200,000 transistors on a $^3/_8$" piece of silicon. The chip is packaged in a square $(1.345" \times 1.345")$ pin grid array (PGA) and contains 169 pins (114 pins used) arranged in a 13×13 matrix.

The processor speed of the MC68020 can be 12.5 MHz, 16.67 MHz, 20 MHz, 25 MHz, or 33 MHz. The chip must be operated from a minimum frequency of 8 MHz. Like the MC68000, it does not have any on-chip clock generation circuitry. The MC68020 contains 18 addressing modes and 101 instructions. All addressing modes and instructions of the MC68000 are included in the MC68020. The MC68020 supports coprocessors such as the MC68881/MC68882 floating-point and MC68851 memory management unit (MMU) coprocessors.

The features of MC68020 are compared with those of MC68000 in the following:

Characteristic	68000	68020
Technology	HMOS	HCMOS
Size	3-$\frac{1}{8}$" × $\frac{7}{8}$"	1.345" × 1.345" (square size)
Number of pins	64, 68	169 (13 × 13 matrix; pins come out at the bottom of the chip; 114 pins currently used)
Control unit	Nanomemory (two-level control memory)	Nanomemory (two-level control memory)
Clock	6 MHz, 8 MHz, 10 MHz, 12.5 MHz, and 16.67 MHz (no minimum requirements)	12.5 MHz, 16.67 MHz, 20 MHz, 25MHz, or 33 MHz (must be 8 MHz minimum)
ALU	One 16-bit ALU	Three 32-bit ALUs
Address bus size	24 bits with A0 encoded from $\overline{UDS}$ and $\overline{LDS}$	32 bits; no encoding of A0 required
Data bus size	Uses D0-D7 for odd addresses and D8-D15 for even addresses during byte transfers; for word and long word use D0-D15	8, 16, and 32 bits (byte, word, long word transfers occur, respectively, via D24-D31 lines, D16-D31 lines, and D0- D31 lines)
Instruction and data access	All word and long word accesses must be at even addresses for both instructions and data; for byte, instruction must be at even addresses, and and data can be at either odd or even addresses	Instructions must be accessed at even addresses; data accesses can be at any address for byte, word, and long word
Instruction cache	None	128-entry 16-bit word cache; at the start of an instruction fetch, the 68020 always outputs LOW on the $\overline{ECS}$ (external cycle start) pin and accesses the cache; if the instruction is found in the cache, the 68020 inhibits outputting LOW on the $\overline{AS}$ pin; otherwise the 68020 sends LOW on the $\overline{AS}$ pin and reads the instruction from the main memory
Directly addressable memory	16 megabytes	4 gigabytes (4, 294, 964, 296 bytes)

Characteristic	68000	68020
Registers	8 32-bit data registers 7 32-bit address registers 2 32-bit SPs 1 32-bit PC (24 bits used) 1 16-bit SR	8 32-bit data registers 7 32-bit address registers 3 32-bit SPs 1 32-bit PC (all bits used) 1 16-bit SR 1 32-bit VBR (vector base register) 2 3-bit function code registers (SFC and DFC) 1 32-bit CAAR (cache address register) 1 32-bit CACR (cache control register)
Addressing modes	14	18
Instruction set	56 instructions	101 instructions
Stack pointers	USP, SSP	USP, MSP (master SP), ISP (interrupt SP)
Status register	T, S, T0, I1, I2, X, N, Z, V, C	T0, T1, S, M, I0, I1, I2, X, N, Z, V, C

For the 68020 status register:

T1	T0	
0	0	No tracing
0	1	Trace on jumps
1	0	Trace on instruction execution
1	1	Undefined

S	M	
0	X	USP
1	0	ISP
1	1	MSP

Characteristic	68000	68020
Coprocessor interface	Emulated in software; that is, by writing subroutines, coprocessor functions such as floating-point arithmetic can be obtained	Can directly be interfaced to coprocessor chips and coprocessor functions, such as floating-point arithmetic can be obtained via 68020 instructions
FC2, FC0, FC1 pins	FC2, FC0, FC1 = 111 means interrupt acknowledge	FC2, FC0, FC1 = 111 means CPU space cycle and then by decoding A16-A19, one can obtain breakpoints, coprocessor functions, and interrupt acknowledge

Some of the 68020 characteristics tabulated above will now be explained:

- The three independent ALUs are provided for data manipulation and address calculations.
- A 32-bit barrel shift register (occupies 7% of silicon) is included in the 68020 for very fast shift operations regardless of the shift count.
- The 68020 has three SPs. In the supervisor mode (when S = 1), two SPs can be accessed. These are MSP (when M = 1) and ISP (when M = 0). The ISP can be used to simplify and speed up task switching for operating systems.
- The vector base register (VBR) is used in interrupt vector computation. For example, in the 68000 the interrupt address vector is obtained by multiplying an 8-bit vector by 4. In the 68020, on the other hand, the interrupt address vector is obtained by using VBR+4*8-bit vector.
- The SFC (source function code) and DFC (destination function code) registers are 3 bits wide. These registers allow the supervisor to move data between address spaces. In supervisor mode, 3-bit addresses can be written into SFC or DFC using instructions such as MOVEC A1, SFC. The upper 29 bits of SFC are assumed to be zero. The MOVES.W(A0), D0 can then be used to move a word from a location within the address space specified by SFC and (A0) to D0. The 68020 outputs [SFC] to the FC2, FC1, and FC0 pins. By decoding these pins via external decoder, the desired source memory location addressed by (A0) can be moved to D0. Now, if this data in D0 is to be moved to another space, then the following instructions will accomplish this:

```
MOVEC  A3,  DFC
MOVES.W  D0,  (A5)
```

Note that there is no MOVES mem, mem instruction. SFC and DFC allow one to move data from one space to another. Since in the above, MOVES.W D0, (A5) outputs [DFC] to FC2, FC1, and FC0 pins which can be used to enable the chip containing the memory location addressed by (A5). [D0] is then moved to this location. The new addressing modes in the 68020 include scaled indexing, 32-bit displacements, and memory indirection. In order to illustrate the concept of scaling, consider moving the contents of memory location 50_{10} to A1. Using the 68000, the following instruction sequence will accomplish this:

```
MOVEA.W #10, A0          ; Lead starting
                           address of a table to A0
MOVE.W #10, D0           ; Load index value to D0
ASL #2, D0              ; Scale index
MOVEA.L 0(A0, D0.W), A1 ; Access data
```

The scaled indexing can be used with the 68020 to perform the same as follows:

```
MOVEA.W #10, A0                ; Load starting
                                 address of a
                                 table to D0
MOVE.W #10, D0                 ; Load index value
                                 to D0
MOVE.L (0, A0, D0.W*4), A1     ; Access data
```

Note that [D0] in the above is scaled by 4. Scaling 1, 2, 4, or 8 can be obtained.

- The new 68020 instructions include bit field instructions to better support compilers and certain hardware applications such as graphics, 32-bit multiply and divide instructions, pack and unpack instructions for BCD, and coprocessor instructions. Bit field instructions can be used to input A/D converters and eliminate wasting main memory space when the A/D converter is not 32-bits.
- FC2, FC1, FC0 = 111 means CPU space cycle. The 68020 makes CPU space access for breakpoints, coprocessor operations, or interrupt acknowledge cycles. The CPU space classification is generated by the 68020 based upon execution of breakpoint instructions, coprocessor instructions, or during interrupt acknowledge cycle. The 68020 then decodes A19-A16 to determine the type of CPU space. For example, FC2, FC1, FC0 = 111 and A19, A18, A17, A16 = 0010 mean coprocessor instruction.
- For performing floating-point operations, the 68000 user must write subroutines using the 68000 instruction set. The floating-point capability in the 68020 can be obtained by connecting the floating-point coprocessor chip such as the Motorola 68881. The MC68020 currently has two coprocessor chips. These are the 68881 (floating-point) and 68851 (memory management). The MC68020 can have up to eight coprocessor chips. When a coprocessor is connected to the 68020, the coprocessor instructions are added to the 68020 instruction set automatically, and this is transparent to the user. For example, when the 68881 floating-point coprocessor is added to the 68020,

instructions such as FADD (floating-point ADD) are available to the user. The programmer can then execute the instruction:

FADD FD0, FD1

Note that registers FD0 and FD1 are in the 68881. When the 68020 encounters the FADD instruction, it writes a command in the command register in the 68881, indicating that the 68881 has to perform this operation. The 68881 then responds to this by writing in the 68881 response register. Note that all coprocessor registers are memory-mapped. The 68020 thus can read the response register and obtain the result of the floating-point ADD from the appropriate location.

6.2 PERIPHERAL SUPPORT AND APPLICATIONS

The MC68020 is supported by an array of peripheral devices that use standard microcomputer functions. These functions include MMUs, synchronous and asynchronous data communication, local area network (LAN) interface, local/global bus interface and arbitration, general-purpose I/O (serial and parallel), floppy and hard disk controller, and direct-memory access (DMA) devices.

The MC68020 derives its power from its variety of features. However, the degree to which each feature boosts performance depends on the specific application. For example, suppose that the MC68020 is being used as a communications processor. The instruction cache — which helps most in executing branches and loops — would be of limited benefit. A signal processor's job of coordinating the flow of communications suggests a linear program flow with few loops. On the other hand, new MC68020 features like scaled index, extended addressing modes, and bit-field manipulations are well-suited for communication processing.

The MC68020's bit-field instructions are valuable tools in graphics applications. The cyclical nature of a typical graphics processing algorithm would benefit from the chip's instruction cache. Robotics and numeric control applications would also make good use of the cache memory. Operating systems control is supported by privileged instructions (user/supervisor split), memory management, the interrupt and trap structure, and other specific MC68020 instructions. Multiprocessing benefits from on-chip bus arbitration logic for shared bus and memory systems.

A popular application of the MC68020 microprocessor has been as a general processor in UNIX-based supermicrocomputers and engineering computer-aided engineering design, and manufacturing (CAE/CAD/CAM) workstations that use multiuser real-time software to produce complex graphics. Additional possible applications include: next-generation personal computers that can emulate mainframe operation, large-scale small business computing systems that feature UNIX business packages, and fault-tolerant multiprocessor/multitasking systems.

6.3 FUNCTIONAL BLOCK DESCRIPTION

Figure 6.1 shows a block diagram of the MC68020. The processor can be divided into two main sections — the bus controller and the micromachine. These blocks operate independently so that the two blocks can operate concurrently, yet synchronize instruction execution and bus operation.

The bus controller loads instructions from the 68020 data bus into the instruction cache. The instruction pipe in the micromachine section inputs these instructions. The instruction decoder, sequencer, microrom/nanorom, and the control section in the micromachine perform the instruction decode and generate the control signals.

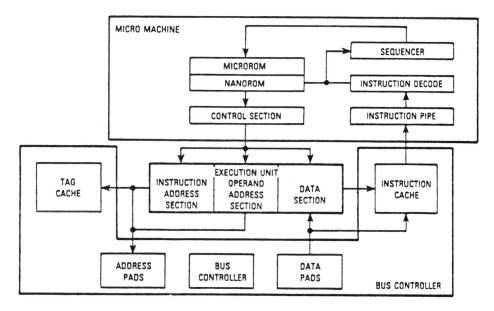

FIGURE 6.1 MC68020 block diagram.

6.4 PROGRAMMER'S MODEL

The MC68020 programmer's model is based on sequential, nonconcurrent instruction execution. This implies that each instruction is completely executed before the next instruction is executed. Although instructions might operate concurrently in actual hardware, they do not operate concurrently in the programmer's model.

Figure 6.2 shows the MC68020 programming models. The user model has sixteen 32-bit general-purpose registers (D0-D7 and A0-A7), a 32-bit program counter (PC), and a condition code register (CCR) contained within the supervisor status register (SR). The supervisor model has two 32-bit supervisor stack pointers (1SP and MSP), a 16-bit status register (SR), a 32-bit vector base register (VBR), two 3-bit alternate function code registers (SFC and DFC), and two 32-bit cache handling (address and control) registers (CAAR and CACR). General-purpose registers D0-D7 are used as data registers for operation on all data types. General-purpose registers A0-A6, user stack pointer (USP) A7, interrupt stack pointer (1SP) A7′, and master stack pointer (MSP) A7″ are address registers that may be used as software stack pointers or base address registers.

The status register (Figure 6.3) consists of a user byte (condition code register CCR) and a system byte. The system byte contains control bits to indicate that the processor is in the trace mode (T1, T0), supervisor/user state (S), and master/interrupt state (M). The user byte consists of the following condition codes: carry (C), overflow (V), zero (Z), negative (N), and extend (X).

Table 6.1 shows the conditional tests available to the MC68020.

The bits in 68020 user byte are set to reset in the same way as 68000 user byte. The bits I2, I1, I0, and S have the same meaning as 68000. In the 68020, two trace bits (T1, T0) are included as opposed to one trace bit (t) in the 68000. These two bits allow the 68000 to trace on both normal instruction execution and jumps. The 68020 M-bit is not included in the 68000 status register.

The vector base register (VBR) is used to locate the exception processing vector table in memory. The VBR supports multiple vector tables so each process can properly manage independent exceptions.

The MC68020 distinguishes address spaces as supervisor/user and program/data. To support full access privileges in the supervisor mode, the alternate function code registers (SFC and DFC) allow the supervisor to

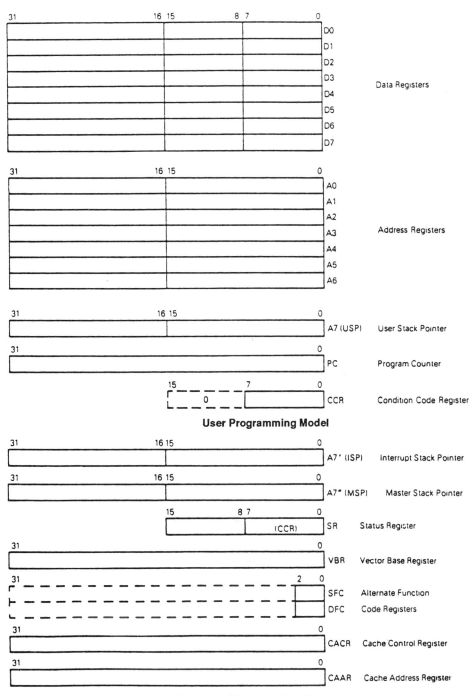

FIGURE 6.2 MC68020 programming model.

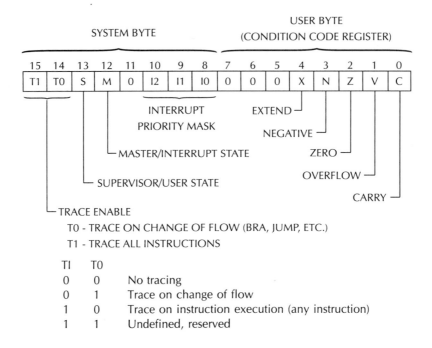

FIGURE 6.3 MC68020 status register.

access any address space by preloading the SFC/DFC registers appropriately.

The cache registers (CACR and CAAR) allow software manipulation of the instruction cache. The CACR provides control and status accesses to the instruction cache, while the CAAR holds the address for those cache control functions that require an address.

6.5 DATA TYPES, ORGANIZATION, AND CPU SPACE CYCLE

The MC68000 family supports data types of bits, byte integers (8 bits), word integers (16 bits), long word integers (32 bits), and binary coded decimal (BCD) digits. In addition to these, four new data types are supported by the MC68020: variable-width bit field, packed BCD digits, quad words (64 bits), and variable-length operands.

Data stored in memory are organized on a byte-addressable basis, where the lower addresses correspond to higher-order bytes. The MC68020

TABLE 6.1
MC68020 Conditional Tests

Mnemonic	Condition	Test
T[a]	True	1
F[a]	False	0
HI	High	$\bar{C} . \bar{Z}$
LS	Low or same	$C + Z$
CC(HS)	Carry clear	$\bar{C}$
CS(LO)	Carry set	C
NE	Not equal	$\bar{Z}$
EQ	Equal	Z
VC	Overflow clear	$\bar{V}$
VS	Overflow set	V
PL	Plus	$\bar{N}$
MI	Minus	N
GE	Greater or equal	$N . V + \bar{N} . \bar{V}$
LT	Less than	$N . \bar{V} + \bar{N} . V$
GT	Greater than	$N . V . \bar{Z} + \bar{N} . \bar{V} . Z$
LE	Less or equal	$Z + N . \bar{V} + \bar{N} . V$

Note: . = Boolean AND, + = Boolean OR, and $\bar{N}$ = Boolean NOT N.

[a] Not available for the Bcc instruction.

does not require data to be aligned on even byte boundaries, but data that are not aligned are transferred less efficiently. Instruction words must be aligned on even byte boundaries. Figure 6.4 shows how data are organized in memory.

Table 6.2 shows decoding of the function code pins. The function code pins define the user/supervisor program and data spaces in the same way as the MC68000, except that FC2 FC1 FC0 = 111 for MC68020 defines a new cycle called the CPU space cycle. Note that for MC68000, FC2, FC1, FC0 = 111 provides the interrupt acknowledge cycle. CPU space is not intended for general instruction execution, but is reserved for processor functions. The CPU space has been subdivided into 16 types of access. The type of CPU access is indicated by address bits (A19-A16) in combination with the CPU space function code (FC2 FC1 FC0 = 111).

Table 6.3 defines the four different types of CPU accesses. The definition of regions in the CPU space makes it possible to acknowledge break

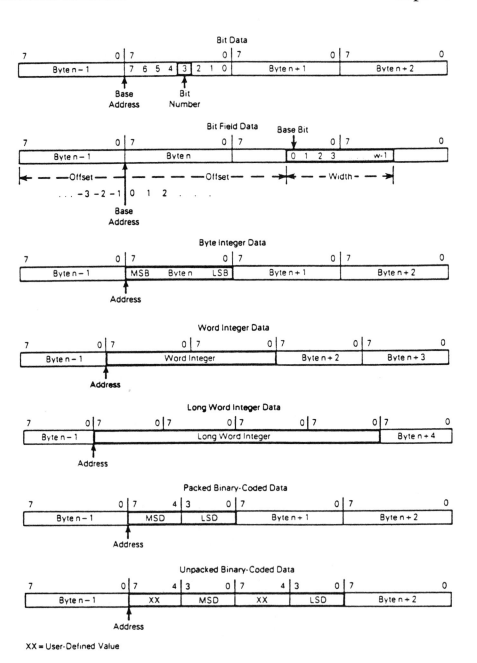

FIGURE 6.4 Memory data organization.

points and interrupts and to communicate with coprocessors and other special devices (such as the MMU) without dictating memory organization for user- and supervisor-related activity.

TABLE 6.2
Processing State Address Space

Function code			
FC2	**FC1**	**FC0**	**Address space**
0	0	0	(Undefined, reserved)[a]
0	0	1	User data space
0	1	0	User program space
0	1	1	(Undefined, reserved)[a]
1	0	0	(Undefined, reserved)[a]
1	0	1	Supervisor data space
1	1	0	Supervisor program space
1	1	1	CPU space

[a] Address space 3 is reserved for user definition, while 0 and
4 are reserved for future use by Motorola.

TABLE 6.3
CPU Space Address Access Encodings

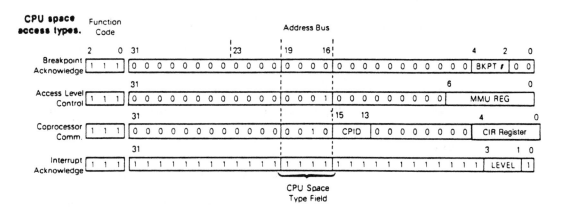

The MC68020 has three stack pointers: the user stack pointer (USP) register A7, the interrupt stack pointer (ISP) register A7′, and the master stack pointer (MSP) register A7″. During normal operation most codes will be executed in user space and programs will use A7 stack for temporary storage and parameter passing between software routines (modules). (ISP) register is only used when an exception occurs, such as an external interrupt when control is passed to supervisor mode and the relevant exception process is performed. The (MSP) holds process-related information for the various tasks and allows for the separation of task-related and non-task-related exception stacking.

When the master stack is enabled through bit (M) in the SR, all noninterrupting exceptions, such as divide by zero, software traps, and privilege violation, are placed in the user's process control block on the master stack.

6.6 MC68020 ADDRESSING MODES

Figure 6.5 lists the MC68020's 18 addressing modes. Table 6.4 compares the addressing modes of the MC68000 with those of the MC68020. All index Xn in the table can be scaled 1, 2, 4, or 8.

Since MC68000 addressing modes are covered in detail with examples, the MC68020 modes which are not available in the MC68000 will be covered in the following discussion.

6.6.1 ADDRESS REGISTER INDIRECT (ARI) WITH INDEX (SCALED) AND 8-BIT DISPLACEMENT

```
Assembler syntax:  (d8, An, Xn. size * SCALE)
EA = (An) + (Xn.size * scale value) + d8
Xn can be W or L.
```

If index register (An or Dn) is 16 bits, then it is sign-extended to 32 bits and then multiplied by 1, 2, 4, or 8 prior to being used in EA calculation. d8 is also sign-extended to 32 bits prior to EA calculation. An example is

```
MOVE.W (0, A2, D2. W*2), D1
```

Suppose that $[A2] = \$5000\ 0000$, $[D2.W] = \$1000$, and $[\$5000\ 2000] = \$1571$; then after execution of the MOVE, $[D1]_{Low\ 16\text{-}bit} = \$1571$, since EA = $\$5000\ 0000 + \$1000 * 2 + 0 = \$5000\ 2000$.

6.6.2 ARI WITH INDEX (BASE DISPLACEMENT, bd: VALUE 0 OR 16 BITS OR 32 BITS)

```
Assembler syntax:  (bd, An, Xn.size*SCALE)
EA = (An) + (Xn.size * SCALE) + bd
```

Addressing Modes	Syntax
Register Direct Data Register Direct Address Register Direct	Dn An
Register Indirect Address Register Indirect Address Register Indirect with Post Increment Address Register Indirect with Predecrement Address Register Indirect with Displacement	(An) (An)+ -(An) (d16, An)
Register Indirect with Index Address Register Indirect with Index (8-Bit Displacement) Address Register Indirect with Index (Base Displacement)	(d8, An, Xn) (bd, An, Xn)
Memory Indirect Memore Indirect Post-Indexed Memory Indirect Pre-Indexed	([bd, An], Xn, od) ([bd, An, Xn], od)
Program Counter Indirect with Displacement	(d16, PC)
Program Counter Indirect with Index PC Indirect with Index (8-Bit Displacement) PC Indirect with Index (Base Displacement)	(d8, PC, Xn) (bd, PC, Xn)
Program Counter Memory Indirect PC Memory Indirect Post-Indexed PC Memory Indirect Pre-Indexed	([bd, PC,], Xn, od) ([bd, PC, Xn], od)
Absolute Absolute Short Absolute Long	xxx.W xxx.L
Immediate	#(data)

NOTES:

Dn = Data Register, D0-D7

An = Address Register, A0-A7

d8, d16 = A twos-complement, or sign-extended displacement; added as part of the effective address calculation; size is 8 (d8) or 16 (d16) bits; when omitted, assemblers use a value of zero.

Xn = Address or data register used as an index register; form is Xn.SIZE*SCALE, where SIZE is .W or .L (indicates index register size) and SCALE is 1, 2, 4, or 8 (index register is multiplied by SCALE); use of SIZE and/or SCALE is optional.

bd = A twos-complement base displacement; when present, size can be 16 or 32 bits.

od = Outer displacement, added as part of effective address calculation after any memory indirection; use is optional with a size of 16 or 32 bits.

PC = Program Counter

(data) = Immediate value of 8, 16, or 32 bits.

( ) = Effective Address.

[ ] = Use as indirect address to long word address.

FIGURE 6.5 MC68020 addressing modes.

TABLE 6.4
Addressing Modes, MC68000 Vs. MC68020

Addressing modes available		68000	68020
Data Register Direct	Dn	Yes	Yes
Address Register Direct	An	Yes	Yes
Address Register Indirect (ARI)	(An)	Yes	Yes
ARI with Postincrement	(An)+	Yes	Yes
ARI with Predecrement	–(An)	Yes	Yes
ARI with Displacement (16-bit displ)	(d, An)	Yes	Yes
ARI with Index (8-bit displ)	(d, An, Xn)	Yes[a]	Yes
ARI with Index (Base Displ: 0, 16, 32)	(bd, An, Xn)	No	Yes
Memory Indirect (Postindexed)	([bd, An], Xn, od)	No	Yes
Memory Indirect (Preindexed)	([bd, An, Xn], od)	No	Yes
PC Indirect with Displ. (16-Bit)	(d, PC)	Yes	Yes
PC Indirect with Index (8-Bit Displ)	(d, PC, Xn)	Yes[a]	Yes
PC Indirect with Index (Base Displ)	(bd, PC, Xn)	No	Yes
PC Memory Indirect (Postindexed)	([bd, PC], Xn, od)	No	Yes
PC Memory Indirect (Preindexed)	([bd, PC, Xn], od)	No	Yes
Absolute Short	(xxx).W	Yes	Yes
Absolute Long	(xxx).L	Yes	Yes
Immediate	#<data>	Yes	Yes

[a]   68000 has no scaling capability; 68020 can scale Xn by 1, 2, 4 or 8

The figure below shows the use of ARI with index, Xn and base displacement, bd for accessing tables or arrays:

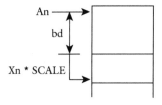

An example is **MOVE.W ($5000, A2, D1.W * 4), D5**. If [A2] = $3000 0000, [D1.W] = $0200, and [$3000 58000] = $0174, then after this **MOVE,** $[D5]_{low\ 16\ bits}$ = $0174, since EA = $5000 + $3000 0000 + $0200 * 4 = $3000 5800.

6.6.3 MEMORY INDIRECT

Memory indirect is distinguished from address register indirect by use of square brackets ([ ]) in the assembler notation.

The concept of memory indirect mode is depicted below:

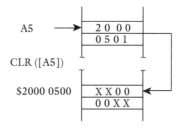

In the above, register A5 points to the effective address $2000 0501. Since CLR ([A5]) is a 16-bit clear instruction, two bytes in location $2000 0501 and $2000 0502 are cleared to zero.

Memory indirect mode can be indexed with scaling and displacements. There are two types of memory indirect with scaled index and displacements: postindexed memory indirect mode and preindexed memory indirect mode.

For postindexed memory indirect, an indirect memory address is first calculated using the base register (An) and base displacement (bd). This address is used for an indirect memory access of a long word followed by adding a scaled indexed operand and an optional outer displacement (od) to generate the effective address. bd and od can be zero, 16 bits, or 32 bits.

In postindexed memory indirect mode, indexing occurs after memory indirection.

Assembler syntax:

```
    ([bd, An], Xn.size Size * Scale, od)
EA = ([bd + An]) + Xn.size * Scale + od)
```

The concept is depicted on the following page.

An example is **MOVE.W ([$0004,A1], D1.W * 2, 2), D2.** If [A1] = $2000 0000, [$2000 0004] = $0000 3000, [D1.W] = $0002, [$0000 3006] = $1A40, then after execution of the above **MOVE,** intermediate pointer = (4 + $2000 0000) = $2000 0004, [$2000 0004], which is $0000 3000 used as a pointer. Therefore, EA = $0000 3000 + $0000 0004 + $2 = $00003006; hence, $[D2]_{\text{low 16 bits}}$ = $1A40.

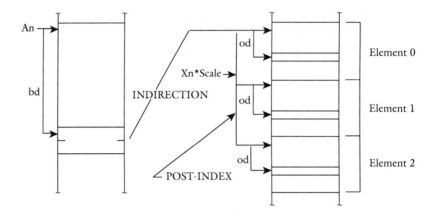

For memory indirect preindexed, the scaled index operand is added to the base register (An) and base displacement (bd). This result is then used as an indirect address into the data space. The 32-bit value at this address is fetched and an optional outer displacement (od) is added to generate the effective address. The indexing, therefore, occurs before indirection.

Assembler syntax:

```
([bd, An, Xn.size * Scale], od)
EA = (bd + An + Xn.size * Scale) + od
```

The preindexing memory indirect concept is depicted below:

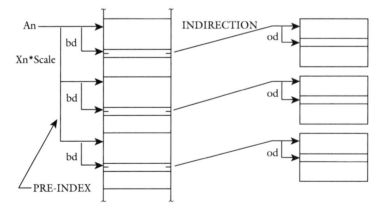

As an application of memory indirect preindexed mode, consider several I/O devices in a system. The addresses of these devices can be held in a table pointed to by An, bd, and Xn. The actual programs for the devices can be stored in memory pointed to by the respective device addresses and od.

As an example of memory indirect preindexed mode, consider **MOVE.W ([$0004, A2, D1.W * 4], 2), D5**. If [A2] = $3000 0000, [D1.W] = $0002, [$3000 000C] = $0024 1782, [$0024 1784] = $F270, then after execution of the above **MOVE**, intermediate pointer = $3000 0000 + 4 + $0002 * 4 = $3000 000C. Therefore, [$3000 000C] which is $0024 1782 is used as a pointer to memory. EA = $0024 1782 + 2 = $0024 1784. Hence, $[D5]_{\text{low 16 bits}}$ = $F270. Note that in the above, bd, Xn, and od are sign-extended to 32 bits if one (or more) of them is 16 bits wide before the calculation.

A summary of MC68020 memory indirect mode is provided below:

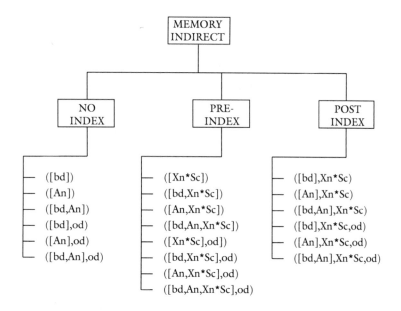

6.6.4 MEMORY INDIRECT WITH PC

In this mode, PC (program counter) is used to form the address rather than an address register. The effective address calculation is similar to address register indirect. A summary of PC indirect mode is given in the following.

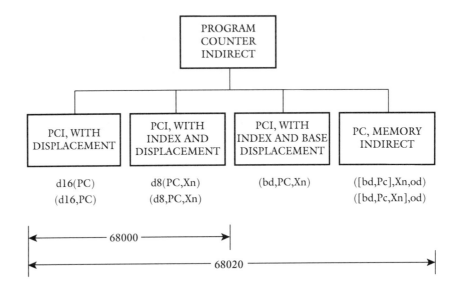

6.6.4.a PC Indirect with Index (8-Bit Displacement)

The effective address is obtained by adding the PC contents, the sign-extended displacement, and the scale indexed (sign-extended to 32 bits if it is 16 bits before calculation) register.

Assembler syntax:

$$\text{(d8, PC, Xn.size * Scale)}$$
$$\text{EA = (PC) + (Xn.size * SCALE) + D8}$$

For example, consider **MOVE.W D2, (2, PC, D1.W * 2)**. If [PC] = \$4000 0020, [D1.W] = \$0020, [D2.W] = \$20A2, then after this **MOVE,** EA = 2 + \$4000 0020 + \$0020 * 2 = \$4000 0062. Hence, [\$4000 0062] = \$20A2.

6.6.4.b PC Indirect with Index (Base Displacement)

This address of the operand is obtained by adding the PC contents, the scaled index register contents, and the base displacement.

Assembler syntax:

$$\text{(bd, PC, Xn.size * Scale)}$$
$$\text{EA = (PC) + (Xn.size * SCALE) + bd}$$

Xn and bd are sign-extended to 32 bits if either or both are 16 bits.

As an example, consider **MOVE.W (4, PC, D1.W * 2), D2.** If [PC] = $2000 0004, [D1.W] - $0020, [2000 0048] = $2560, then after this **MOVE,** [D2.W] = $2560.

6.6.4.c PC Indirect (Postindexed)

An intermediate memory pointer in program space is calculated by adding PC (used as a base register) and bd. The 32-bit content of this address is used in EA calculation. EA is obtained by adding the 32-bit contents with a scaled index register and od. Note that bd, od, or index register is sign-extended to 32 bits before using in calculation if one (or more) is 16 bits.

Assembler syntax:

```
([bd, PC], Xn.size * Scale, od)
EA = ([bd + PC] + Xn.size * Scale + od)
```

Consider another example: **MOVE.W ([2, PC], D1.W*4, 0), D1.** If [PC] = $3000 0000, [D1.W] = $0010, [$3000 0002] = $2040 0050, [$2040 0090] = $A240, then after this **MOVE,** [D1.W] = $A240.

6.6.4.d PC Indirect (Preindexed)

The scaled index register is added to the PC and bd. This sum is then used as an indirect address into the program space. The 32-bit value at this address is added to od to find EA.

Assembler syntax:

```
([bd, PC, Xn.size * Scale], od)
EA = (bd + PC + Xn.size * Scale) + od
```

od, bd, or the index register is sign-extended to 32 bits if one (or more) of them is 16 bits before the EA calculation.

As an example, consider **MOVE.W ([4, PC, D1.W * 2], 4), D5.** If [PC] = $5000 0000, [D1.W] = $0010, [$5000 0024] = $2050 7000, [$2050 7004] = $0708, then after this **MOVE,** [D5.W] = $0708.

A summary of PC modes is provided on the following page.

Example 6.1

Show the contents of registers A2, D4, A5, and the affected memory location(s), after execution of the following instruction:

MOVEA.W (0, A2, D4.L), A5

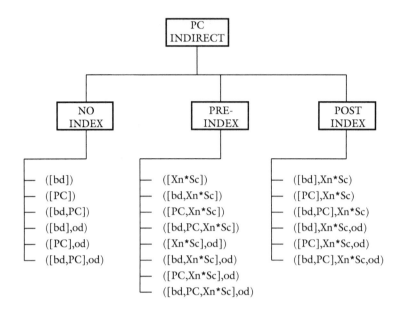

Assume prior to execution of the MOVEA instruction:

$$
\begin{array}{lcl}
\texttt{[A2]} & = & \texttt{\$0571 6660} \\
\texttt{[D4]} & = & \texttt{\$3072 8400} \\
\texttt{[A5]} & = & \texttt{\$7271 5554} \\
\texttt{[\$35E3 EA58]} & = & \texttt{\$05} \\
\texttt{[\$35E3 EA59]} & = & \texttt{\$07} \\
\texttt{[\$35E3 EA60]} & = & \texttt{\$F7} \\
\texttt{[\$35E3 EA61]} & = & \texttt{\$F1} \\
\texttt{[\$35E3 EA62]} & = & \texttt{\$40} \\
\end{array}
$$

Solution

Effective address:

$$
\begin{array}{lcl}
\texttt{D4.L} & = & \texttt{\$3072 8400} \\
\texttt{A2.L} & = & \texttt{\$0571 6660} \\
\texttt{d} & = & \texttt{\$0000 0000} \\
\hline
\texttt{EA} & = & \texttt{\$35E3 EA 60} \\
\end{array}
$$

Therefore, after execution of the MOVEA instruction:

$$
\begin{array}{lcl}
\texttt{[A2]} & = & \texttt{\$0571 6660} \\
\texttt{[D4]} & = & \texttt{\$3072 8400} \\
\texttt{[A5]} & = & \texttt{\$FFFFF7F1} \\
\end{array}
$$

Example 6.2

The following MC68000 instruction sequence:

```
MOVEA.L  6 (USP), A1
MOVE.W (A1), D5
```

is used by a subroutine to access a parameter whose address has been passed into A1 and then moves the parameter to D5.

Find the equivalent MC68020 instruction.

Solution

```
MOVE.W ([6, USP]), D5
```

Example 6.3

Find a MC68020 compare instruction with the appropriate addressing mode to replace the following MC68000 instruction sequence:

```
ASL.L     #3, D6
CMP.L     0 (A1, D6.L), D3
```

Solution

The equivalent MC 68020 instruction is

```
CMP.L (0, A1, D6.L * 8), D3
```

Example 6.4

Find the contents of register A1, D0, D5 and the affected memory locations after execution of:

```
MOVE.B (0, A1, D0.W * 2), D5
```

Assume the following data prior to execution of the MOVE instruction:

```
[A1]        =       $0000 2000
[D0]        =       $0000 0004
[D5]        =       $7124 8002
[$0000 2006] =        $51
[$0000 2007] =        $74
[$0000 2008] =        $82
[$0000 2009] =        $FO
```

Solution

Effective address:

```
= d8 + A1.L + D0.W *2
= 0 + $0000 2000 + $0000 0004 * 2
= $0000 2008
```

Therefore,

[A1]	=	$0000 2000
[D0]	=	$0000 0004
[D5]	=	$7124 8082

6.7 INSTRUCTIONS

All MC68020 instructions are at least one word, and up to 11 words long. Figure 6.6 shows the general format of an instruction. The first word in the instruction format (the operation word) determines the length of the instruction and the operation to be performed. The remaining words in the instruction are called extension words and further specify the instruction and operands. These extension words can be immediate operands, extensions to the EA mode specified in the operation word, branch displacements, bit number or bit field specifications, special register specifications, trap operands, pack/unpack constants, argument counts, or coprocessor condition codes.

15   0
Operation Word   (One Word, Specifies Operation and Modes)
Special Operand Specifiers   (If Any, One or Two Words)
Immediate Operand or Source Effective Address Extension   (If Any, One to Five Words)
Destination Effective Address Extension   (If Any, One to Five Words)

FIGURE 6.6 MC68020 instruction word general format.

The MC 68020 instruction set (Table 6.5) includes all 68000 instructions, plus some new ones. Some of the 68000 instructions are enhanced. These are listed in Table 6.6. Over 20 new instructions have been added to provide new functionality. These instructions are listed below.

BFCHG	Bit field change
BFCLR	Bit field clear
BFEXTS	Bit field signed extract
BFEXTU	Bit field unsigned extract
BFFFO	Bit field find first one set
BFINS	Bit field insert
BFSET	Bit field set
BFTST	Bit field test
CALLM	Call module
CAS	Compare and swap
CAS2	Compare and swap (two operands)
CHK2	Check register against upper and lower bounds
CMP2	Compare register against upper and lower bounds
cpBcc	Coprocessor branch on coprocessor condition
cpDBcc	Coprocessor test condition, decrement, and branch
cpGEN	Coprocessor general function
cpRESTORE	Coprocessor restore internal state
cpSAVE	Coprocessor save internal state
cpSETcc	Coprocessor set according to coprocessor condition
cpTRAPcc	Coprocessor trap on coprocessor condition
PACK	Pack BCD
RTM	Return from module
UNPK	Unpack BCD

In the following sections, the 68020 instructions listed below will be discussed in detail:

1. 68020 new privileged MOVE instructions
2. RTD instruction
3. CHK/CHK2 and CMP/CMP2 instructions
4. TRAPcc instructions
5. Bit field instructions
6. PACK and UNPK instructions
7. Multiplication and division instructions
8. 68000 enhanced instructions

TABLE 6.5
MC68020 Instruction Summary

Mnemonic	Description
ABCD	Add decimal with extend
ADD	Add
ADDA	Add address
ADDI	Add immediate
ADDQ	Add quick
ADDX	Add with extend
AND	Logical AND
ANDI	Logical AND immediate
ASL, ASR	Arithmetic shift left and right
Bcc	Branch conditionally
BCHG	Test bit and change
BCLR	Test bit and clear
BFCHG	Test bit field and change
BFCLR	Test bit field and clear
BFEXTS	Signed bit field extract
BFEXTU	Unsigned bit field extract
BFFFO	Bit field find first one
BFINS	Bit field insert
BFSET	Test bit field and set
BFTST	Test bit field
BKPT	Breakpoint
BRA	Branch
BSET	Test bit and set
BSR	Branch to subroutine
BTST	Test bit
CALLM	Call module
CAS	Compare and swap operands
CAS2	Compare and swap dual operands
CHK	Check register against bound
CHK2	Check register against upper and lower bounds
CLR	Clear
CMP	Compare
CMPA	Compare address
CMPI	Compare immediate

TABLE 6.5 (continued)
MC68020 Instruction Summary

Mnemonic	Description
CMPM	Compare memory to memory
CMP2	Compare register against upper and lower bounds
DBcc	Test condition, decrement, and branch
DIVS, DIVSL	Signed divide
DIVU,DIVUL	Unsigned divide
EOR	Logical exclusive OR
EORI	Logical exclusive OR immediate
EXG	Exchange registers
EXT, EXTB	Sign extend
ILLEGAL	Take illegal instruction trap
JMP	Jump
JSR	Jump to subroutine
LEA	Load effective address
LINK	Link and allocate
LSL, LSR	Logical shift left and right
MOVE	Move
MOVEA	Move address
MOVE CCR	Move condition code register
MOVE SR	Move status register
MOVE USP	Move user stack pointer
MOVEC	Move control register
MOVEM	Move multiple registers
MOVEP	Move peripheral
MOVEQ	Move quick
MOVES	Move alternate address space
MULS	Signed multiply
MULU	Unsigned multiply
NBCD	Negate decimal with extend
NEG	Negate

TABLE 6.5 (continued)
MC68020 Instruction Summary

Mnemonic	Description
NEGX	Negate with extend
NOP	No operation
NOT	Logical complement
OR	Logical inclusive OR
ORI	Logical inclusive OR immediate
PACK	Pack BCD
PEA	Push effective address
RESET	Reset external devices
ROL, ROR	Rotate left and right
ROXL, ROXR	Rotate with extend left and right
RTD	Return and deallocate
RTE	Return from exception
RTM	Return from module
RTR	Return and restore codes
RTS	Return from subroutine
SBCD	Subtract decimal with extend
Scc	Set conditionally
STOP	Stop
SUB	Subtract
SUBA	Subtract address
SUBI	Subtract immediate
SUBQ	Subtract quick
SUBX	Subtract with extend
SWAP	Swap register words
TAS	Test operand and set
TRAP	Trap
TRAPcc	Trap conditionally
TRAPV	Trap on overflow
TST	Test operand
UNLK	Unlink
UNPK	Unpack BCD

TABLE 6.5 (continued)
MC68020 Instruction Summary

Mnemonic	Description
	Coprocessor Instructions
cpBCC	Branch conditionally
cpDBcc	Test coprocessor condition, decrement, and branch
cpGEN	Coprocessor general instruction
cpRESTORE	Restore internal state of coprocessor
cpSAVE	Save internal state of coprocessor
cpScc	Set conditionally
cpTRAPcc	Trap conditionally

TABLE 6.6
MC68020 Instruction Enhancements

MULS, MULU, DIVS, DIVU	Operations extended to 32-bit operands
Bcc, BRA, BSR, LINK	Displacements extended to 32 bits
MOVEC	New control registers may be accessed
BKPT	Op code substitution supported

The instructions listed below are of an advanced nature and will be discussed in Chapter 7:

- BKPT instructions
- CALLM/RTM instructions
- TAS and CAS/CAS2 instructions
- Coprocessor instructions

6.7.1 NEW PRIVILEGED MOVE INSTRUCTION

The new privileged move instructions are executed by the 68000 in the supervisor mode.

The MOVE instructions are summarized in Table 6.7. The MOVEC instruction was added to allow the new supervisor registers (Rc) to be accessed. Since these registers are used for system control, they are generally referred to as control registers and include the vector base register (VBR), the source function and destination code registers (SFC, DFC), the master, interrupt, and user stack pointers (MSP, ISP, USP), and the cache control registers (CACR, CAAR). Register (Rn) can be either an address register or data register.

TABLE 6.7
MC68020 Privileged Move Instructions

Instruction	Operand size	Operation	Notation
MOVE	16	SR → destination	MOVE SR, (EA)
MOVEC	32	Rc → Rn	MOVEC.L Rc, Rn
		Rn → Rc	MOVEC.L Rn, Rc
MOVES	8, 16, 32	Rn → destination using DFC	MOVES.s Rn, (EA)
		Source using SFC → Rn	MOVES.s(EA), Rn

The operand size indicates that these MOVEC operations are always long-word. Notice only register-to-register operations are allowed.

A control register (Rc) can be copied to an address or data register (Rn), or vice versa. When copying the 3-bit, SFC, or DFC register into Rn, all 32 bits of the register are overwritten and the upper 29 bits are "0".

The MOVE to alternate space instruction (MOVES) allows the operating system to access any addressed space defined by the function codes.

It is typically used when an operating system running in the supervisor mode must pass a pointer or value to a previously defined user program or data space.

The MOVES instruction allows register-to-memory or memory-to-register operations. When a memory-to-register occurs, this instruction causes the contents of the source function code register to be placed on the external function hardware pins.

For a register-to-memory move, the processor places the destination function code register on the external function code pins.

The MOVES instruction can be used to MOVE information from one space to another. For example, in order to move the 16-bit content of a memory location addressed by A0 in supervisor data space (FC2 FC1 FC0 = 101) to a memory location addressed by A1 in user data space (FC2 FC1 FC0 = 001), the following instruction on sequence can be used:

```
MOVEQ.L #5, D0   ;  Move source space 5 to D0
MOVEQ.L #1, D1   ;  Move dest space 1 to D1
MOVEC.L D0, SFC ;  Initialize SFC
MOVEC.L D1, DFC ;  Initialize DFC
MOVES.W (A0), D2;  Move memory location addressed
                      by (A0) and SFC to D2
MOVES.W D2, (A1); Move D2 to a memory location
                      addressed by (A1) and DFC
```

In the above, the first four instructions initialize SFC to 101_2 and DFC to 001_2. Since there is no MOVES mem, mem instruction, the register D2 is used as a buffer for the memory-to-memory transfer. MOVES.W (A0), D2 transfers [SFC] to FC2 FC1 FC0 and also reads the content of a memory location addressed by SFC and (A0) to D2. The 68020 FC2 FC1 FC0 pins can be decoded to enable the appropriate memory chip containing the memory location addressed by (A0). Next, MOVES.W D2, (A1) outputs [DFC] to FC2 FC1 FC0 and then moves [D2] to a memory location addressed by (A1) contained in a memory chip which can be enabled by decoding FC2, FC1, and FC0 pins.

Example 6.5

Find the content of memory location $5000 2000 after execution by MOVE.W SR, [A6]. Assume the following data prior to execution of the MOVE instruction:

$$[A6] = \$5000\ 2000\ [SR] = \$26A1$$
$$[\$5000\ 2000] = \$02,\ [\$5000\ 2001] = \$F1$$

Also, assume supervisor mode.

Solution

SR is moved to a memory location pointed to by $5000 2000. After execution:

$$[\$5000\ 2000] = \$26$$
$$[\$5000\ 2001] = \$A1$$

Example 6.6

Find the content of DFC after execution of MOVEC.L A5, DFC. Assume the following data prior to execution of the instruction:

$$[DFC] = 100_2, \quad [A5] = \$2000\ 0105$$

Solution

After execution of the MOVEC, [DFC] = 101.

Example 6.7

Find the contents of D5 and the function code pins FC2, FC1, and FC0 after execution of MOVES.B D5, (A5). Assume the following data prior to execution of the MOVES:

$$
\begin{aligned}
&[SFC] = 101_2, \quad [DFC] = 100_2 \\
&[A5] = \$7000\ 0023 \\
&[D5] = \$718F\ 2A05 \\
&[\$7000\ 0020] = \$01, \quad [\$7000\ 0021] = \$F1 \\
&[\$7000\ 0022] = A2 \\
&[\$7000\ 0023] = \$2A
\end{aligned}
$$

Solution

After execution of the above MOVES:

$$
\begin{aligned}
&FC2\ FC1\ FC0 = 100_2 \\
&[\$7000\ 0022] = \$05
\end{aligned}
$$

6.7.2 RETURN AND DELOCATE INSTRUCTION

Return and delocate instruction RTD is useful when a subroutine has the responsibility to remove parameters off the stack that were pushed onto the stack by the calling routine. Note that the calling routine's JSR (jump to subroutine) or BSR (branch to subroutine) instructions do not automatically push parameters onto the stack prior to the call, as the CALLM instructions. Rather, the pushed parameters must be placed there using the MOVE instruction. Table 6.8 shows the format of the RTD instruction.

TABLE 6.8
RTD Instruction

Instruction	Operand size	Operation	Notation
RTD	Unsized	(SP) → PC, SP + 4 + d → SP	RTD # <displacement>

The RTD instruction operates as follows:

1. Read the long word from memory pointed to by the stack pointer.
2. Copy it into the program counter.
3. Increment the stack pointer by 4.
4. Sign-extend the 16-bit immediate data displacement to 32 bits.
5. Add it to the stack pointer.

Since parameters are pushed onto the stack to lower memory locations, only a positive displacement should be added to the SP when removing parameters from the stack. The displacement value (16 bits) is sign-extended to 32 bits.

Example 6.8
Write a 68020 instruction sequence to illustrate the use of RTD instruction by using BSR instruction and pushing three 32-bit parameters onto the stack.

Solution

```
MOVE.L PAR1, -(SP)        BSR SUBR            RTD#12
MOVE.L PAR2, -(SP)
MOVE.L PAR3, -(SP)
```

Calling routine pushes parameters on stack; this causes the stack pointer to be decremented by 12	Calling routine calls subroutine and the PC stacked; the subroutine then accesses the parameters to perform the task	Last instruction of the subroutine returns and delocates the paremeters off stack by adding (12) to the stack pointer

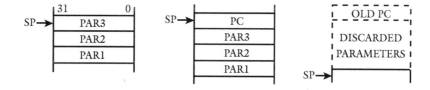

6.7.3 CHK/CHK2 AND CMP/CMP2 INSTRUCTIONS

The enhanced MC68020 check instruction (CHK) now compares a 32-bit two's complement integer value residing in a data register (Dn) against a lower bound (L.B.) value of zero and against an upper bound (U.B.) value of the programmer's choice. These bounds are located beginning at the effective address (EA) specified in the instruction format.

The CHK instruction has the following format:

$$\text{CHK.S} \quad \text{(EA.),Dn}$$

where (.S) is the operand size designator which is either word (.W) or long word (.L).

If the data register value is less than zero (Dn < 0) or if the data register is greater than the upper bound (Dn > UB), then the processor traps through exception vector 6 (offset $18) in the exception vector table. Of course, the operating system or the programmer must define a check service handler routine at this vector address. After completion of the CHK instruction, the negative (N) bit is the only condition code register (CCR) bit that is defined or affected. If the compared register (Dn) is less than zero, then the N-bit is set to one. If the data register exceeds the upper bound, then the N-bit is cleared to zero. If the CHK instruction finds that the compared register value is within bounds (i.e., 0 < Dn < UB value), then all CCR bits except X (X is unaffected) are undefined (U), and program execution resumes with the next instruction in the instruction flow. This instruction can be used for maintaining array subscripts since all subscripts can be checked against an upper bound (i.e., UB = array size minus one). If the compared subscript is within the array bounds (0 < subscript value < UB value), then the subscript is valid, and the program continues normal instruction execution. If the subscript value is out of array limits (i.e., 0 > subscript value, or the subscript value > UB value), then the processor traps through the CHK exception.

Example 6.9

Find the effects of execution of the MC68020 CHK instruction: CHK.L (A5), D3, where A5 represents a memory pointer to the array's upper bound value. Register D3 contains the subscript value to be checked against the array bounds. Assume the following data prior to execution of the CHK instruction:

$$\text{[D3]} = \$0150\ 7126, \quad \text{[A5]} = \$00710004,$$
$$\text{[\$0071 0004]} = \$0150\ 0000$$

Solution

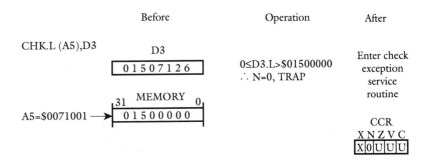

The long-word array subscript value $01507126 contained in data register D3 is compared against the long-word upper-bound value $01500000 pointed to by address register A5. Since the value $01507126 contained in D3 exceeds the upper-bound value $01500000 pointed to by A5, the N-bit is cleared. (The remaining CCR bits are either undefined or not affected.) This out-of-bound condition causes the program to trap to a check exception service routine. The operation of the CHK is summarized in Table 6.9.

TABLE 6.9
CHK Instruction Operation

Instruction	Operand size	Operation	Notation
CHK	16, 32	If Dn <0 or Dn> source then TRAP	CHK (EA), Dn

The 68020 CMP.B (EA), Dn subtracts
```
or
.W
or
.L
```
(EA) from Dn and affects the condition codes without any result.

Both the CHK2 and the CMP2 instructions have similar formats (CHK2.S (EA),Rn) and (CMP2.S (EA),Rn). They compare a value contained in a data or address register designated by (Rn) against two (2) bounds chosen by the programmer. The size of the data to be compared (.S) may be specified as either byte (.B), word (.W), or long word (.L). As shown in the figure below, the lower-bound value (LB) must be located in memory at the effective address (EA) specified in the instruction, and the upper-bound value (UB) must follow immediately at the next higher memory address [i.e., UB addr. = LB. addr + SIZE where SIZE = B (+1), W (+2), or L = (+4)].

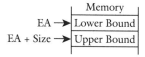

If the compared register is a data register (i.e., Rn = Dn) and the operand size (.S) is a byte or word, then only the appropriate low-order part of the data register is checked. If the compared register is an address register (i.e., Rn = An) and the operand size (.S) is a byte or word, then the bound operands are sign extended to 32 bits, and the extended operands are compared against the full 32 bits of the address register. The CHK2 and CMP2 instructions both set the CCR carry bit (C) to a one if the compared register's data are out of bounds. Likewise, the zero bit (Z) is set to a one if the data are equal to either bound or otherwise cleared to zero. In the case where an upper bound equals the lower bound, the valid range for comparison becomes a single value. The only difference between the CHK2 and CMP2 instructions is that for comparisons determined to be out of bounds, CHK2 causes exception processing utilizing the same exception vector as the CHK instructions, whereas the CMP2 instruction execution only affects the condition codes.

In both instructions, the compare is performed for either signed or unsigned bounds. The MC68020 automatically evaluates the relationship between the two bounds to determine which kind of comparison to employ. If the programmer wishes to have the bounds evaluated as signed values, the arithmetically smaller value should be the lower bound. If the bounds are to be evaluated as unsigned values, the programmer should make the logically smaller value the lower bound.

The following CHK2 and CMP2 instruction examples are identical in that they both utilize the same registers, comparison data, and bound values. The difference is how the upper and lower bounds are arranged.

Example 6.10

Determine the effects of CMP2.W (A2), D1. Assume the following data prior execution of the CMP2: [D1] = $5000 0200, [A2] = $0000 7000, [$0000 7000] = $B000, [$0000 7002] = $5000.

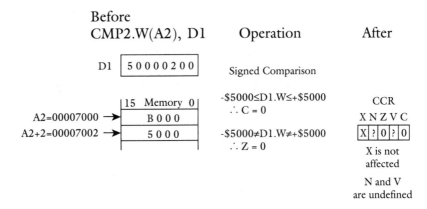

In this example, the word value $B000 contained in memory (as pointed to by address register A2) is the lower bound and the word value immediately following $5000 is the upper bound. Since the lower bound is the arithmetically smaller value, the programmer is indicating to the 68020 to interpret the bounds as signed numbers. The 2's complement value $B000 is equivalent to an actual value of −$5000. Therefore, the instruction evaluates the word contained in data register D1. ($0200) to determine if it is greater than or equal to the upper bound, +$5000, or less than or equal to the lower bound, −$5000. Since the compared value $0200 is within bounds, the carry bit (C) is cleared to zero. Also, since $0200 is not equal to either bound, the zero bit (Z) is cleared. The figure below shows the range of valid value that D1 could contain:

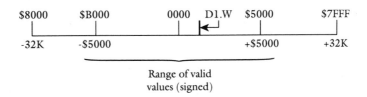

Range of valid
values (signed)

A typical application for the CHK instruction would be to read in a number of user entries and verify that each entry is valid by comparing it against the valid range bounds. In the above CMP2 example, the user-entered value would be in register D1, and register A2 would point to a range for that value. The CMP2 instruction verifies if the entry is in range by clearing the CCR carry bit if it is in bounds and setting the carry bit if it is out of bounds.

Example 6.11

Find the effects of execution of CHK2.W (A2), D1. Assume the following data prior to execution of the CHK2:

[D1] = $5000 0200, [A2] = $0000 7000, [$0000 7000] =$5000 [$0000 7002] = $B000

Solution

This time, the value $5000 is located in memory as the lower bound, and the value $B000 as the upper bound. Now, since the lower bound contains the logically smaller value, the programmer is indicating to the 68020 to interpret the bound values as unsigned number, representing only a magnitude. Therefore, the instruction evaluates the word value contained in register D1, $0200 to determine if it is greater than or equal to lower bound $5000 or less than or equal to the upper bound $B000. Since the compared value $0200 is less than $5000, the carry bit is set to indicate an out-of-bounds condition and to program traps to the CHK/CHK2 exception vector service routine. Also, since $0200 is not equal to either bound, the zero bit (Z) is cleared. The range of valid values that D1 could contain is shown below:

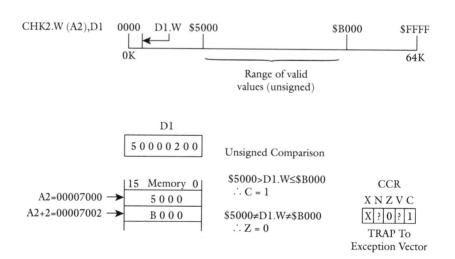

A typical application for the CHK2 instruction would be to cause a trap exception to occur if a certain subscript value is not within the bounds of some defined array. Using the CHK2 example format just given, if we define an array of 100 elements with subscripts ranging from 50_{10}-40_{10}, and if the two words located at (A2) and (A2 + 2) contain 50 and 49, respectively, and register D1 contains 100_{10}, then execution of the CHK2 instruction would cause a trap through the CHK/CHK2 exception vector. The operation of the CMP2 and the CHK2 instructions is summarized in Figure 6.7.

Instruction	Operand Size	Operation	Notation
CMP2	8, 16, 32	Compare Rn < source - lower bound or Rn > source - upper bound and set ccr	CMP2 <ea>, Rn
CHK2	8, 16, 32	If Rn < source - lower bound or Rn > source - upper bound then TRAP	CHK2 <ea>, Rn

FIGURE 6.7 Operation of CMP2 and CHK2.

6.7.4 TRAP ON CONDITION INSTRUCTIONS

The new trap on condition (Trap cc) instruction has been added to allow a conditional trap exception on any of the following conditional conditions, as shown in Table 6.10.

TABLE 6.10
Conditions for TRAPcc

CC	Carry clear	$\overline{C}$
CS	Carry set	C
EQ	Equal	Z
F	Never true	0
GE	Greater or equal	$N \cdot V + \overline{N} \cdot \overline{V}$
GT	Greater than	$N \cdot V \cdot \overline{Z} + \overline{N} \cdot \overline{V} \cdot \overline{Z}$
HI	High	$\overline{C} \cdot \overline{Z}$
LE	Less or equal	$Z + N \cdot \overline{V} + \overline{N} \cdot V$
LS	Low or same	$C + Z$
LT	Less than	$N \cdot \overline{V} + \overline{N} \cdot V$
MI	Minus	N
NE	Not equal	$\overline{Z}$
PL	Plus	N
T	Always true	1
VC	Overflow clear	$\overline{V}$
VS	Overflow set	V

These are the same conditions that are allowed for the set on condition (Scc) and the branch on condition (Bcc) instructions. The TRAPcc instruction evaluates the selected test condition based on the state of the condition code flags, and if the test is true, the MC68020 initiates exception processing by trapping through the same exceptional vector as the TRAPV instruction (vector 7, offset $1C, VBR = VBR + offset). The trap on cc instruction format is TRAPcc (or) TRAPcc (.S) # <data>, where (.S) is the operand size designator, which is either word (.W) or long word (.L).

If either a word or long word operand is specified, a 1- or 2-word immediate operand is placed following the instruction word. The immediate operand(s) consist of argument parameters that are passed to the trap handler to further define requests or services it should perform. If cc is false, the 68020 does not interpret the immediate operand(s), but instead adjusts the program counter to the beginning of the following instruction. The exception handler can access this immediate data as an offset to the stacked PC. The stacked PC is the next instruction to be executed.

A summary of the TRAPcc instruction operation is shown in Figure 6.8.

Instruction	Operand Size	Operation	Notation
TRAPcc	None	If cc then TRAP	TRAPcc
	16		TRAPcc.W #<data>
	32		TRAPcc.L #<data>

FIGURE 6.8 TRAPcc operation.

6.7.5 BIT FIELD INSTRUCTIONS

The bit field instructions allow an operation such as clear, set, one's complement, input, insert, and test one or more bits in a string of bits (bit field).

Table 6.11 lists all the bit field instructions. Note that the condition codes are affected according to the value in field before execution of the instruction. All bit field instructions affect the N and Z bits as shown for BFTST. C and V are always cleared. X is always unaffected.

For all instructions: Z = 1, if all bits in a field prior to execution of the instruction are zero; Z = 0 otherwise. N = 1 if the most significant bit of the field prior to execution of the instruction is one; N = 0 otherwise.

TABLE 6.11
Bit Field Instructions

Instruction	Operand size	Operation	Notation
BFTST	1-32	Field MSB → N, Z = 1 if all bits in field are zero; Z = 0 otherwise	BFTST (EA){offset:width}
BFCLR	1-32	0's → field	BFCLR (EA){offset:width}
BFSET	1-32	1's → field	BFSET (EA){offset:width}
BFCHG	1-32	Field' → field	BFCHG (EA){offset:width}
BFEXTS	1-32	Field → Dn; sign extended	BFEXTS (EA){offset:width}, Dn
BFEXTU	1-32	Field → Dn; zero extended	BFEXTU(EA){offset:width}, Dn
BFINS	1-32	Dn → field	BFINS Dn, (EA){offset width}
BFFFO[a]	1-32	Scan for first bit set in field	BFFFO (EA) {offset:width}, Dn

[a] The offset of the first bit set in bit field is placed in Dn; if no set bit is found, Dn contains the offset plus field width.

(EA)	address of the byte that contains bit 0 of the array
offset	#(0—31) or Dn(-2^{31} to $2^{31} - 1$)
width	#(1—32) or Dn (1—32, mod 32)

Immediate offset is from 0 to 31, while offset in Dn can be specified from -2^{31} to $2^{31} - 1$. All instructions are unsized. They are useful for memory conservation, graphics, and communications.

As an example, consider BFCLR $5002 {4:12}. Assume the following memory contents:

Bit 7 of the base address $5002 has the offset 0. Therefore, bit 3 of $5002 has offset value of 4. Bit 0 of location $5001 has offset value −1, bit 1 of $5001 has the offset value −2, and so on. The above BFCLR instruction clears 12 bits starting with bit 3 of $5002. Therefore, bits 0—3 of location $5002 and bits 0—7 of location $5003 are cleared to zero. Therefore, the above memory contents are as follows:

	7	6	5	4	3	2	1	0	
$5001	1	0	1	0	0	0	0	1	offset 4
$5002	1	0	0	1	0	0	0	0	width 12
$5003	0	0	0	0	0	0	0	0	offset 16
$5004	0	0	0	1	0	0	1	0	

The use of bit field instructions may result in memory savings. For example, assume that an input device such as a 12-bit A/D converter interfaced via a 16-bit port of a MC68020-based microcomputer. Now, suppose that one million pieces of data are to be collected from this port. Each 12 bits can be transferred to a 16-bit memory location or bit field instructions can be used.

Using 16-bit location for each 12-bit:
Memory bytes required:
= 2 * 1 million
= 2 million bytes
Using bit fields:
12 bits = 1.5 bytes
Memory requirements = 1.5 * 1 million
= 1.5 million bytes
Savings = 2 million bytes − 1.5 million bytes
= 500,000 bytes

Example 6.12
Find the effects of:

```
BFCHG     $5004         {D5 : D6}
BFEXTU    $5004         {2 : 4}, D5
BFINS     D4, (A0)      {D5 : D6}
BFFFO     $5004         {D6 : 4}, D6
```

Assume the following data prior to execution of each of the above instructions:

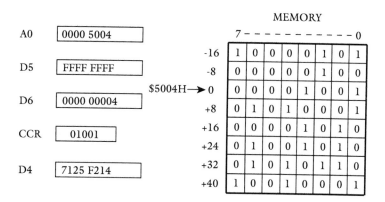

Register contents are given in hex, CCR and memory contents in binary, and offset to the left of memory in decimal.

Solutions

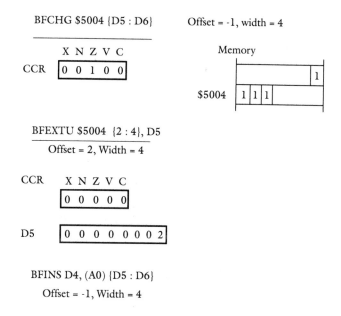

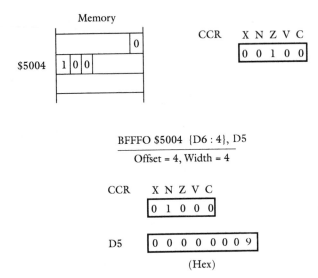

$$\text{BFFFO } \$5004 \ \{D6:4\}, \text{ D5}$$

Offset = 4, Width = 4

CCR   X N Z V C
        | 0 1 0 0 0 |

D5 | 0 0 0 0 0 0 0 9 |

(Hex)

6.7.6 PACK AND UNPACK INSTRUCTIONS

Table 6.12 lists the details of PACK and UNPK instructions. Both instructions have three operands and are unsized. They do not affect the condition codes. The PACK instruction converts two unpacked BCD digits to two packed BCD digits. The UNPK instruction reverses the process and converts two packed BCD digits to the unpacked BCD digits. Immediate data can be added to convert numbers from one code to another. That is, these instructions can be used to translate codes such as ASCII or EBCDIC to BCD and vice versa.

TABLE 6.12
Pack and Unpack Instructions

Instruction	Operand size	Operation	Notation
PACK	16 → 8	Unpacked source + # data → packed destination	PACK –(An), –(An), # <data> PACK Dn, Dn, #<data>
UNPK	8 → 16	Packed source → unpacked source unpacked source + # data → unpacked destination	UNPK –(An), –(An), # <data> UNPK Dn, Dn, # <data>

Note: Condition codes are not affected.

```
          15      12 11      8 7        4 3      0
Unpacked BCD: | 0 0 0 0 |  BCD0  | 0 0 0 0 |  BCD1 |

          7        4 3      0
Packed BCD:   |  BCD0  |  BCD1  |
```

#data - Appropriate constants can be used to translate from ASCII
or EBCDIC to BCD or from BCD to ASCII or EBCDIC.

The PACK and UNPK instructions are useful when an I/O device such as an ASCII keyboard is interfaced to a MC68020-based microcomputer. Data can be entered into the microcomputer via the keyboard in ASCII codes. The PACK instruction can be used with appropriate adjustments to convert these ASCII codes into BCD. Arithmetic operations can be performed inside the microcomputer and the result will be in PACKED BCD. The UNPK instruction can similarly be used with appropriate adjustment to convert packed BCD to ASCII codes.

Example 6.13

Find the effects of execution of the following PACK and UNPK instructions:

```
1.  PACK  D0,  D5,  # $0000
2.  PACK  - (A1),  - (A4),  # $0000
3.  UNPK  D4,  D6,  # $3030
4.  UNPK  - (A3),  - (A2),  # $3030
```

Assume the following data:

```
      31                    0
D0  | X X X X  32 37 |

      31                  0
D5  | X X X X X X  26 |

      31                  0
D4  | X X X X X X  35 |

      31                  0
D6  | X X X X X X  27 |

      31                  0
A2  | 3 0 0 5 0 0   A3 |

      31                  0
A3  | 5 0 7 1 2 4   B9 |

      31                  0
A1  | 5 0 7 1 2 4   B3 |

      31                  0
A4  | 3 0 0 5 0 0   A1 |
```

MEMORY

Address	7....0
	:
	:
$507124B1	32
$507124B2	37
$507124B3	00
$507124B4	27
$507124B5	02
$507124B6	07
$507124B7	27
$507124B8	27

Solution

1.   PACK D0, D5 # $000

                              [D0] = 32 37
                                low
                                word
                                     + 00 00
                                     ─────────
                                        32 37
                                        ↓   ↓
                                         27

Note that ASCII code for 2 is 32 and for 7 is 37. Hence the above
PACK instruction converts ASCII code to BCD.

2.   PACK - (A1), - (A4), $0000
                    [$5071 24B2] = 37   + 3237
                    [$5071 24B1] = 32   + 0000
                                              ───────
                                                3237
                                                ↙↙
                    Therefore, [3005 00A0] = 27 Packed BCD

Hence, the above instruction with the specified data converts two
ASCII digits to their equivalent PACKED BCD.

3.   UNPK D4, D6 # $3030
                        [D4] = XXXXXX 35
                                   03 05
                                + 30 30
                                ─────────
                                   33 35
                        Therefore, after this UNPK
                        [D6] = XXXX 33 35
                        [D4] = XXXXXX 35

Therefore, this instruction with the assumed data converts from
PACKED BCD 35 to ASCII 33 35.

4.   UNPK - (A3), - (A2), # $3030
                    [$5071 24B8] = 27
                                ┌──────────┐
                                │ 02   07 │
                                └──────────┘
                                  30   30
                                ────────────
                                  32   37
                    Hence,
                    [$300 500 A2] = 37
                    [$300 500 A1] = 32

This instruction with the assumed data converts two packed BCD digits to their equivalent ASCII digits.

6.7.7 MULTIPLICATION AND DIVISION INSTRUCTIONS

The MC68020 includes the following signed and unsigned multiplication instructions:

```
MULS.W (EA), Dn 16 × 16 → 32, (EA)16 * Dn16 → Dn32
  or
MULU
```

```
MULS.L (EA), Dl 32 × 32 → 32, (EA) * Dl → Dl
  or                    → Holds low 32 bits of the result
MULU                       after multiplication; upper
                           32 bits of the result are
                           discarded
```

```
MULS.L (EA), Dh:Dl 32 × 32 → 64, (EA) * Dl → Dh:Dl
  or                        → Holds 32-bit multiplicand be-
                              fore multiplication and
MULU                          low 32 bits of the product
                              after multiplication

Holds high 32 bits
 of the product af-   Holds 32-bit multiplier before
  ter multiplication    multiplication
```

(EA) in the above can be all modes except An. The condition codes N, Z, V are affected, C is always cleared to zero, and X is unaffected for both MULS and MULU. For signed multiplication, overflow (V = 1) can only occur for 32×32 multiplication producing a 32-bit result if the high-order 32 bits of 64-bit product are not the sign extension of the low-order 32 bits. In the case of unsigned multiplication, overflow (V = 1) can occur for 32×32 multiplication producing a 32-bit result if the high-order 32 bits of the 64-bit product are not zero.

Both MULS and MULU have a word form and a long-word form. For the word form (16×16) the multiplier and multiplicand are both 16 bits and the result is 32 bits. The result is saved in the destination data register. For 32 bit × 32 bit, the multiplier and multiplicand are both 32 bits and the result is either 32 bits or 64 bits. When the result is 32 bits for a 32-bit × 32-bit operation, the low-order 32 bits of the 64-bit product is provided.

The signed and unsigned division instructions of the MC68020 in-

clude the following. Source is divisor and destination is dividend. Result
(remainder and quotient) is stored in destination

```
DIVS.W (EA), Dn 32/16  ⇒  16r:16q
  or
DIVU

DIVS.L (EA), Dn 32/32  ⇒  32q (no remainder is
  or                                provided)
DIVU

DIVS.L (EA), Dr:Dq 64/32  ⇒  32r:32q
  or
DIVU

DIVSL.L (EA), Dr:Dq 32/32  ⇒  32r:32q
  or
DIVUL                       Contains the 32-bit dividend
```

Destination contains dividend and (EA) contains divisor. (EA) in the above
instructions can use all modes except An.

The condition codes for either signed or unsigned division are affected
as follows: N = 1 if the quotient is negative; N = 0 otherwise. N is undefined
if overflow or divide by zero. Z = 1 if the quotient is zero; Z = 0 otherwise.
Z is undefined for overflow or divide by zero. V = 1 for division overflow;
V = 0 otherwise. X is unaffected.

Division by zero causes a trap. If overflow is detected before completion of the instruction, V is set to one, but the operands are unaffected.

Both signed and unsigned division instructions have a word form and
three long-word forms.

For the word form, the destination operand is 32 bits and the source
operand is 16 bits. The 32-bit result in Dn contains the 16-bit quotient in
the low and the 16-bit remainder in the high word. The sign of the
remainder is the same as the sign of the dividend.

```
        For DIVS.L (EA), Dq
              or
            DIVU
```

Both destination and source operands are 32 bits. The result in Dq contains
the 32-bit quotient and the remainder is discarded.

For DIVS.L (EA), Dr:Dq

or

DIVU

The destination is 64 bits contained in any two data registers and the source is 32 bits. The 32-bit register Dr (D0-D7) contains the 32-bit remainder and the 32-bit Dq (D0-D7) contains the 32-bit quotient.

Example 6.14

Find the effects of the following multiplication and division instructions:

1. **MULU.L # $2, D5 if [D5] = $FFFFFFFF**
2. **MULS.L # $2, D5 if [D5] = $FFFFFFFF**
3. **MULU.L # $2, D5:D2**
   if [D5] = $2ABC 1800
   and [D2] = $FFFFFFFF
4. **DIVS.L # $2, D5 if [D5] = $FFFFFFFC**
5. **DIVS.L # $2, D2:D0**
   if [D2] = $FFFFFFFF
   and [D0] = $FFFFFFFC
6. **DIVSL.L # $2, D6:D1 if [D1] = $0004 1234**
   and [D1] = $FFFFFFFE

Solution

1. **MULU.L # $2, D5, [D5] = $FFFFFFFF**

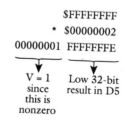

$FFFFFFFF
* $00000002
00000001 FFFFFFFE

V = 1   Low 32-bit
since   result in D5
this is
nonzero

Therefore, [D5] = $FFFFFFFE, N = 0 since the most significant bit of result is 0, Z = 0 since the result is non zero, V = 1 since the high 32 bits of the 64-bit product is not zero, C = 0 (always), and X = not affected.

2. **MULS.L # $2, D5   if [D5] = $FFFFFFFF**

$$
\begin{array}{rr}
 & \text{\$FFFFFFFF} \quad (-1) \\
* & \text{\$00000002} \quad (+2) \\
\hline
\text{\$FFFFFFFF} \quad \text{\$FFFFFFFE} & (-2)
\end{array}
$$

Result in D5

Therefore, [D5] = $FFFFFFFE, X = unaffected, C = 0, N = 1, V = 0, and Z = 0.

3. **MULU.L # $2, D5:D2   if [D5] = $2ABC 1800 and [D2] = $FFFFFFFF**

$$
\begin{array}{rr}
 & \text{\$FFFFFFFF} \\
* & \text{\$00000002} \\
\hline
\text{00000001} & \text{FFFFFFFE} \\
\text{D5} & \text{D2}
\end{array}
$$

N = 0, Z = 0, V = 1 since high 32 bits of the 64-bit product is not zero, C = 0, and X = not affected.

4. **DIVS.L # $2, D5, D5   if [D5] = $FFFFFFFC**

$$
\begin{array}{r}
-2 \\
\hline
\text{FFFF FFFE} \\
\text{00000002} \,\big|\, \text{FFFF FFFC} \\
+2 \qquad -4
\end{array}
$$

[D5] = $FFFF FFFE, X = unaffected, N = 1, Z = 0, V = 0, and C = 0 (always).

5. **DIVS.L # $2, D2:D0   if [D2] = $FFFF FFFF and [D0] = $FFFF FFFC**

$$
\begin{array}{r}
-2 \\
\hline
\text{Q = FFFF FFFE, R = 0000 0000} \\
\text{0000 0002} \,\big|\, \text{FFFF FFFF FFFF FFFC} \\
2 \qquad\qquad\qquad -4
\end{array}
$$

D2 = $0000 0000 = remainder, D0 = $FFFF FFFE = quotient, X = unaffected, Z = 0, N = 1, V = 0, and C = 0 (always).

6. **DIVSL.L # $2, D6:D1 if [D1] = $0004 1224 and [D6] = $FFFF FFFD**

$$
R = \frac{-1}{\mathrm{FFFFFFFF}}
$$

$$
Q = \frac{-1}{\mathrm{FFFFFFFF}}
$$

$$
0000\ 0002 \left| \underbrace{\mathrm{FFFFFFD}}_{-3} \right.
$$

[D6] = $FFFFFFFF = remainder, [D1] = $FFFFFFFF = quotient, X = unaffected, N = 1, Z = 0, V = 0, and C – 0 (always).

6.7.8 MC68000 ENHANCED INSTRUCTIONS

The MC68020 includes the enhanced version of the 68000 instructions listed in Table 6.13.

TABLE 6.13
Enhanced Instructions

Instruction	Operand size	Operation
BRA label	8, 16, 32	PC + d → PC
Bcc label	8, 16, 32	If cc is true, then PC + d → PC; else next instruction
BSR label	8, 16, 32	PC → – (SP); PC + d → PC
CMPI.S # data, (EA)	8, 16, 32	Destination – # data → CCR is affected
TST.S (EA)	8, 16, 32	Destination – 0 → CCR is affected
LINK.S An, – d	16, 32	An → – (SP); SP → An, SP + d → SP
EXTB.L Dn	32	Sign extend byte to long word

Note: S can be B, W, L. In addition to 8- and 16-bit signed displacements for BRA, BCC, BSR like the 68000, the 68020 also allows signed 32-bit displacements. Link is unsized in 68000. (EA) in CMPI and TST support all MC68000 modes plus PC relative. Examples are CMPI.W#$2000, (START, PC). In addition to EXT.W Dn and EXT.L Dn like the 68000, the 68020 also provides EXTB.L instruction.

Example 6.15

Write a program in MC68020 assembly language to find the first one in a bit field which is greater than 16 bits and less than or equal to 512 bits. Assume the number of bits to be checked is divisible by 16. If no ones are found, store $0000 0000 in D3. Assume A2 points to start of the array and D2 contains the number of bits in array.

Solution

```
        CLR.L D3                    ;   D3 is offset in
                                        bit field and
                                        contains the
                                        first bit
                                        number set
        DIVU #16, D2                ;   [D2] = number
                                        of searches
        SUBQ.W #1, D2              ;   Decrement D2 by
                                        1 for use in
                                        DBNE later
        MOVEQ #16, D5             ;   Load field
                                        width into D5
START   BFFFO (A2) {D3:D5}, D3   ;   Search for one
                                        in 16 bits
        DBNE D2, START            ;   Decrement branch
                                        if not equal
        BEQ STOP                   ;   If no ones
                                        found, stop
        CLR.L D3                    ;   Store 0 in D3
STOP    JMP STOP                   ;   HALT
```

Example 6.16

Write a program in MC68020 assembly language to convert 20 packed BCD digits to their ASCII equivalent and store the result to memory location $F1002004. The data bytes start at $5000.

Solution

```
        MOVEA.L # $5000, A5       ;   Load starting
                                        address of
                                        the BCD array
                                        into A5
```

```
          MOVEA.L # $F1002004, A6   ; Load starting
                                      address of the
                                      ASCII array
                                      into A6
          MOVEQ.L #20, D2           ; Load data
                                      length to D2
START     MOVE.B (A5) +, D3         ; Load BCD value
          UNPK D3, D3, # $3030      ; Convert to
                                      ASCII
          MOVE.W D3, (A6) +         ; Store ASCII
                                      data at address
                                      pointed to by
                                      A6

          DBF D2, START            ; Decrement and
                                      branch if false
STOP      JMP STOP                 ; Otherwise STOP
```

Example 6.17

Write a program in MC68020 assembly language to divide a signed 32-bit number in D0 by a signed 8-bit number in D1 by storing the division result in the following manner:

1. Store 32-bit quotient in D0 and neglect remainder.
2. Store 32-bit remainder in D1 and 32-bit quotient in D0.

Assume dividend and divisor are already in D0 and D1, respectively.

Solution

```
     1.   EXTB.L D1                ; Sign extend
                                     divisor to 32-
                                     bit
          DIVS.L D1, D0            ; 32-bit quotient
                                     in D0 and
STOP      JMP STOP                   remainder is
                                     discarded and
                                     halt
     2.   EXTB.L D1                ; Sign extend
                                     divisor to 32
                                     bits
```

```
        DIVSL.L D1, D1:D0           ; 32-bit remainder
                                      in D1 and 32-
                                      bit quotient in
                                      D0
STOP    JMP STOP                   ; Halt
```

6.8 MC68020 PINS AND SIGNALS

Figure 6.9a and 6.9b show the MC68020 functional signal groups and pin diagram. Tables 6.14a and 6.14b list these signals along with a summarized description of each, and also the pin assignments.

There are 10 VCC (+5V) and 13 ground pins to distribute the power in order to reduce the noise.

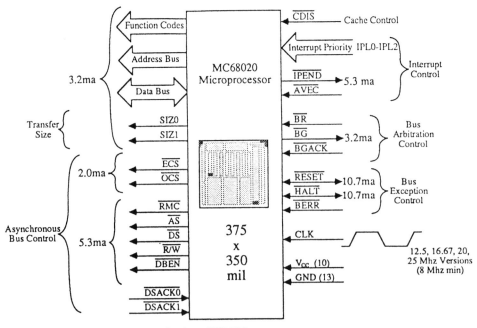

- 2 micron HCMOS process
- 200,000 transistors
- 114 lead PGA pkg
- Pd = 1.75W (max)

FIGURE 6.9a MC 68020 functional signal groups.

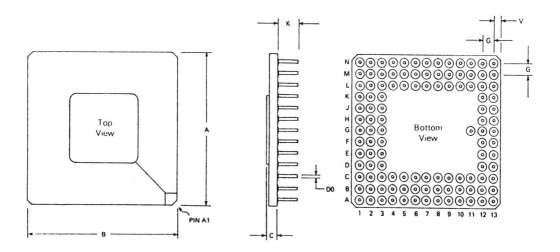

MC68020
RC Suffix Package

Mechanical
Detail

DIM	MILLIMETERS		INCHES	
	MIN	MAX	MIN	MAX
A	34.18	34.90	1.345	1.375
B	34.18	34.90	1.345	1.375
C	2.67	3.17	.100	.150
D0	.46	.51	.017	.019
G	2.54 BSC		.100 BSC	
K	4.32	4.82	.170	.190
V	1.74	2.28	.065	.095

FIGURE 6.9b MC68020 package dimensions.

TABLE 6.14a
Hardware Signal Index

Signal name	Mnemonic	Function
Address bus	A0-A31	32-bit address bus used to address any of 4,294,967,296 bytes
Data bus	D0-D31	32-bit data bus used to transfer 8, 16, 24, or 32 bits of data per bus cycle
Function codes	FC0-FC2	3-bit function code used to identify the address space of each bus cycle
Size	SIZ0/SIZ1	Indicates the number of bytes remaining to be transferred for this cycle;

TABLE 6.14a (continued)
Hardware Signal Index

Signal name	Mnemonic	Function
		these signals, together with A0 and A1, define the active sections of the data bus
Read-modify-write cycle	$\overline{\text{RMC}}$	Provides an indicator that the current bus cycle is part of an indivisible read-modify-write operation
External cycle start	$\overline{\text{ECS}}$	Provides an indication that a bus cycle is beginning
Operand cycle start	$\overline{\text{OCS}}$	Identical operation to that of ECS except that OCS is asserted only during the first bus cycle of an operand transfer
Address strobe	$\overline{\text{AS}}$	Indicates that a valid address is on the bus
Data strobe	$\overline{\text{DS}}$	Indicates that valid data is to be placed on the data bus by an external device or has been placed on the data bus by the MC68020
Read/write	$\text{R}/\overline{\text{W}}$	Defines the bus transfer as an MPU read or write
Data buffer enable	$\overline{\text{DBEN}}$	Provides an enable signal for external data buffers
Data transfer and size acknowledge	$\overline{\text{DSACK0}}/\overline{\text{DSACK1}}$	Bus response signals that indicate the requested data transfer operation are completed; in addition, these two lines indicate the size of the external

TABLE 6.14a (continued)
Hardware Signal Index

Signal name	Mnemonic	Function
		bus port on a cycle-by-cycle basis
Cache disable	$\overline{\text{CDIS}}$	Dynamically disables the on-chip cache to assist emulator support
Interrupt priority level	$\overline{\text{IPL0-IPL2}}$	Provides an encoded interrupt level to the processor
Autovector	$\overline{\text{AVEC}}$	Requests an autovector during an interrupt acknowledge cycle
Interrupt pending	$\overline{\text{IPEND}}$	Indicates than an interrupt is pending
Bus request	$\overline{\text{BR}}$	Indicates than an external device requires bus mastership
IBus grant	$\overline{\text{BG}}$	Indicates than an external device may assume bus mastership
Bus grant acknowledge	$\overline{\text{BGACK}}$	Indicates than an external device has assumed bus mastership
Reset	$\overline{\text{RESET}}$	System reset
Halt	$\overline{\text{HALT}}$	Indicates that the processor should suspend bus activity
Bus error	$\overline{\text{BERR}}$	Indicates an invalid or illegal bus operation is being attempted
Clock	CLK	Clock input to the processor
Power supply	VCC	+5 volt ± 5% power supply
Ground	GND	Ground connection

TABLE 6.14b
MC68020 Pin Assignment

Pin number	Function	Pin number	Function
A1	$\overline{\text{BGACK}}$	C9	A16
A2	A1	C10	A12
A3	A31	C11	A9
A4	A28	C12	A7
A5	A26	C13	A5
A6	A23		
A7	A22	D1	Vcc
A8	A19	D2	Vcc
A9	Vcc	D3	Vcc
A10	GND	D4-D11	—
A11	A14	D12	A4
A12	A11	D13	A3
A13	A8		
		E1	FC0
B1	GND	E2	$\overline{\text{RMC}}$
B2	$\overline{\text{BG}}$	E3	Vcc
B3	$\overline{\text{BR}}$	E12	A2
B4	A30	313	OCS
B5	A27		
B6	A24	F1	SIZ0
B7	A20	F2	FC2
B8	A18	F3	FC1
B9	GND	F12	$\overline{\text{GND}}$
B10	A15	F13	$\overline{\text{IPEND}}$
B11	A13		
B12	A10	G1	$\overline{\text{ECS}}$
B13	A6	G2	SIZ1
		G3	$\overline{\text{DBEN}}$
C1	$\overline{\text{RESET}}$	G11	Vcc
C2	CLOCK	G12	GND
C3	GND	G13	Vcc
C4	A0		
C5	A29	H1	$\overline{\text{CDIS}}$
C6	A25	H2	$\overline{\text{AVEC}}$
C7	A21	H3	$\overline{\text{DSACK0}}$
C8	A17	H12	IPL2

TABLE 6.14b (continued)
MC68020 Pin Assignment

Pin number	Function	Pin number	Function
H13	GND	M1	DS
		M2	D29
J1	$\overline{\text{DSACK1}}$	M3	D26
J2	$\overline{\text{BERR}}$	M4	D24
J3	GND	M5	D21
J12	$\overline{\text{IPL0}}$	M6	D18
J13	IPL1	M7	D16
		M8	Vcc
K1	GND	M9	D13
K2	$\overline{\text{HALT}}$	M10	D10
K3	GND	M11	D6
K12	D1	M12	D5
K13	D0	M13	D4
L1	$\overline{\text{AS}}$	N1	D31
L2	R/$\overline{\text{W}}$	N2	D28
L3	D30	N3	D25
L4	D27	N4	D22
L5	D23	N5	D20
L6	D19	N6	D17
L7	GND	N7	GND
L8	D15	N8	Vcc
L9	D11	N9	D14
L10	D7	N10	D12
L11	GND	N11	D9
L12	D3	N12	D8
L13	D2	N13	Vcc

The Vcc and GND pins are separated into three groups to provide individual power supply connections for the address bus buffers, data bus buffers, and all other output buffers and internal logic.

Group	Vcc	GND
Address bus	A9, D3	A10, B9, C3, F12
Data bus	M8, N8, N13	L7, L11, N7, K3
Logic	D1, D2, E3, G11, G13	G12, H13, J3, K1
Clock		B1

Both the 32-bit address (A0-A31) and data (D0-D31) buses are nonmultiplexed. Like the MC68000, the three function code signals FC2, FC1, and FC0 identify the processor state (supervisor or user) and the address space of the bus cycle currently being executed as follows:

FC2	FC1	FC0	Cycle type
0	0	0	(Undefined, reserved)[a]
0	0	1	User data spare
0	1	0	User program space
0	1	1	(Undefined, reserved)[a]
1	0	0	(Undefined, reserved)[a]
1	0	1	Supervisor data space
1	1	0	Supervisor program space
1	1	1	CPU space

[a] Address space 3 is reserved for user definition, while 0 and 4 are reserved for future use by Motorola.

Note that in MC68000, FC2, FC1, FC0 = 111 indicates interrupt acknowledge cycle. In the MC68020, this means CPU space cycle. In this cycle, by decoding the address lines A19-A16, the MC68020 can perform various types of functions such as coprocessor communication, breakpoint acknowledge, interrupt acknowledge, and module operations as follows:

A19	A17	A18	A16	Function performed
0	0	0	0	Breakpoint acknowledge
0	0	0	1	Module operations
0	0	1	0	Coprocessor communication
1	1	1	1	Interrupt acknowledge

Note that A19, A18, A17, A16 = 0011_2 to 1110_2 is reversed by Motorola. In the coprocessor communication CPU space cycle, the MC68020 determines the coprocessor type by decoding A15-A13 as follows:

A15	A14	A13	Coprocessor type
0	0	0	MC68851 paged memory management unit
0	0	1	MC68881 floating-point coprocessor

The MC68020 offers a feature called dynamic bus sizing which enables designers to use 8- and 16-bit memory and I/O devices without sacrificing system performance.

The key elements used to implement dynamic bus sizing are the data multiplexer, the SIZE output (SIZ0 and SIZ1 pins), and the $\overline{\text{DSACKX}}$ inputs ($\overline{\text{DSACK0}}$ and $\overline{\text{DSACK1}}$). The MC68020 uses these signals dynamically to interface to the various-sized devices (8-, 16-, or 32-bit) on a cycle-by-cycle basis. For example, if the MC68020 executes an instruction that reads a long-word operand, it will attempt to read all 32 bits during the first bus cycle. The MC68020 always assumes the memory or I/O size to be 32 bits when starting the bus cycle. Hence, it always transfers the maximum amount of data on all bus cycles. If the device responds that it is 32 bits, the processor latches all 32 bits of data and continues to the next operand. If the device responds that it is 16 bits wide, the MC68020 generates two bus cycles, obtaining 16 bits of data each time; an 8-bit transfer is handled similarly, but four bus cycles are required, obtaining 8 bits of data each time. Each device (8-, 16-, or 32-bit) assignment is fixed to particular sections of the data bus to minimize the number of bus cycles needed to transfer devices. For example, the 8-bit devices transfer data via D31-D24 pins, the 16-bit devices via D31-D16 pins, and the 32-bit devices via D31-D0 pins.

A routing and duplication multiplexor takes the four byte of 32 bits and routes them to their required positions; depending on its bus size, the positioning of bytes is determined by SIZ1, SIZ0, and address outputs A1 and A0 pins.

The MC68020 dynamic bus sizing feature for 8-, 16-, and 32-bit devices is shown in Figure 6.10. The "OPn"s define the various operand bytes with OP0 as the most significant byte. The multiplexor in the figure routes the four bytes of data (OP0-OP3) via the external data bus. For example, OP0 can be routed to D31-D24 in the normal case, or it can be routed to any other byte in order to support misaligned transfer. Note that alignment and misalignment mean that the MC68020's data transfer is with an even and odd address, respectively.

In summary, the four signals added to support dynamic bus sizing are $\overline{\text{DSACK0}}$, $\overline{\text{DSACK1}}$, SIZ0, and SIZ1. Data transfer and device size acknowledge signals ($\overline{\text{DSACK0}}$ and $\overline{\text{DSACK1}}$) are used to terminate the bus cycle and to indicate the external size of the data bus (see Table 6.15). As the MC68020 steps through memory during the data operand transfer process, the two size line outputs (SIZ0 and SIZ1) indicate how many bytes are still to be transferred during a given bus cycle (Table 6.15).

The MC68020 has no restrictions on the alignment of operands in

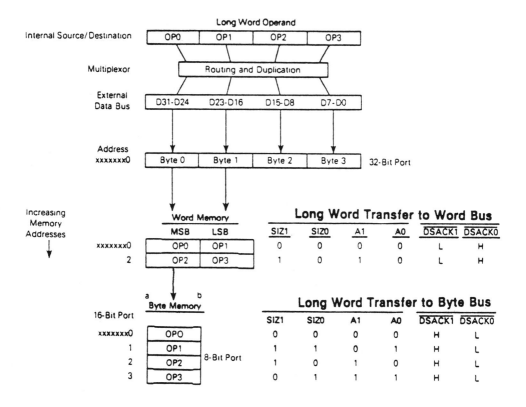

FIGURE 6.10 Dynamic bus sizing interface to port sizes.

TABLE 6.15
Dynamic Sizing Control Signals

$\overline{\text{DSACK}}$ Codes and Results

$\overline{\text{DSACK1}}$	$\overline{\text{DSACK0}}$	Result
H	H	Insert wait states in current bus cycle
H	L	Complete — data bus port size is 8 bits
L	H	Complete cycle — data bus port size is 32 bits

SIZE Output Encodings

SIZ1	SIZ0	Size
0	1	Byte

TABLE 6.15 (continued)
Dynamic Sizing Control Signals

SIZE Output Encodings

SIZ1	SIZ0	Size
1	0	Word
1	1	3 bytes
0	0	Long word

Note: To adjust the size of the physical bus interface, external circuits must issue strobe signals to gate data bus buffers. By using data strobe control, external logic can enable the proper section of the data bus.

memory — long-word operands need not be aligned on long-word address boundaries. Although the processor does not impose data alignment restrictions, some performance degradation can occur due to the multiple bus access that the processor must perform when word or long-word operands do not fall on word or long-word boundaries. The system designer can improve system performance by ensuring that all data addresses are aligned. However, instructions — and any extension words — must fall on word address boundaries. Figure 6.11 shows the aligned internal operand representation.

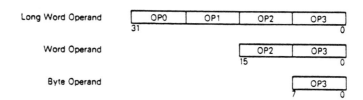

FIGURE 6.11 MC68020 internal operand representation.

The multiplexor routes and/or duplicates one or more bytes in the 32-bit data to permit any combination of aligned or misaligned transfers. The remaining number of bytes to be transferred during the second and subsequent cycles if required is defined by the SIZ0 and SIZ1 outputs. The address lines A0 and A1 define the byte position in Figure 6.10. For example, $A1A0 = 00_2$, $A1A0 = 01_2$, $A1A0 = 10_2$, and $A1A0 = 11_2$ indicate byte 0 (OP0), byte 1 (OP1), byte 2 (OP2), and byte 3 (OP3), respectively, of the 32-bit operand. A2-A31 indicate the long-word base address of that portion of the operand to be accessed.

Table 6.16 defines the data pattern along with SIZ1, SIZ0, A1, and A0 of the MC68020's internal multiplexor to the external data bus D31-D0.

TABLE 6.16
Internal to External Data Bus Multiplexor

MC68020 REGISTER

| BYTE 0 | BYTE 1 | BYTE 2 | BYTE 3 |

MULTIPLEXOR

EXTERNAL DATA PINS

Transfer size	SIZ1	SIZ0	A1	A0	D31-D24	D23-D16	D15-D8	D7-D0
Byte	0	1	X	X	BYTE 3	BYTE 3	BYTE 3	BYTE 3
Word	1	0	X	0	BYTE 2	BYTE 3	BYTE 2	BYTE 3
	1	0	X	1	BYTE 2	BYTE 2	BYTE 3	BYTE 2
3 bytes	1	1	0	0	BYTE 1	BYTE 2	BYTE 3	BYTE 0*
	1	1	0	1	BYTE 1	BYTE 1	BYTE 2	BYTE 3
	1	1	1	0	BYTE 1	BYTE 2	BYTE 1	BYTE 2
	1	1	1	1	BYTE 1	BYTE 1	BYTE 2*	BYTE 1
Long word	0	0	0	0	BYTE 0	BYTE 1	BYTE 2	BYTE 3
	0	0	0	1	BYTE 0	BYTE 0	BYTE 1	BYTE 2
	0	0	1	0	BYTE 0	BYTE 1	BYTE 0	BYTE 1
	0	0	1	1	BYTE 0	BYTE 0	BYTE 1*	BYTE 0

Note: X = don't care; * = byte ignored on read, this byte output on write.

In each cycle, the MC68020 outputs to SIZ1 SIZ0 pins to indicate to the external device the number of bytes remaining to be transferred. The $\overline{\text{DSACK1}}$ and $\overline{\text{DSACK0}}$ inputs to the MC68020 from the device terminate the bus cycle and in the subsequent cycles (if required) indicate the device size. The address pins A1 and A0 outputs to the device from the MC68020 indicate which data pins are to be used in the data transfer. For example, an 8-bit device always transfers data to MC68020 via D31-D24 pins for all combinations of A1A0 (00_2, 01_2, 10_2, 11_2). On the other hand, the 16-bit device always transfers data via D31-D16 pins. However, in the first cycle, if the address is even (A1A0 = 00_2 or 10_2), 16-bit data transfer takes place using D31-D16 pins with the data byte addressed by the odd address via D23-D16 pins. On the other hand, if the starting address is odd (A1A0 = 01_2 or 11_2) for a 16-bit device, only a byte is transferred in the first cycle via D23-D16 pins. For a 32-bit device, in the first cycle, if A1A0 = 00_2, all 32-bit data are transferred via D0-D31 pins; if A1A0 = 01_2, three bytes are transferred via D23-D0 pins; if A1A0 = 10_2, two bytes are transferred via D15-D0 pins; if A1A0 = 11_2, only one byte is transferred via D7-D0 pins.

The MC68020 always starts transferring data with the most significant byte first. As an example, consider MOVE.L D3, $50005170. Since the address is even, this is an aligned transfer from the 32-bit data register D3 to an even memory address. In the first bus cycle, the MC68020 does not know the size of the external device and hence outputs all combinations of data on D31-D0 pins, taking into consideration that the device size may be byte, word, or long word. The MC68020 outputs OP0, OP1, OP2, and OP3, respectively, on D31-D24, D23-D16, D15-D8, and D7-D8 pins. If the device is 8-bit, it will take the data OP0 from the D31-D24 pins and write to locations $50005170 in the first cycle. However, by the second cycle, the device asserts $\overline{DSACK1}$ and $\overline{DSACK0}$ as 10_2 indicating an 8-bit device; the MC68020 then transfers the remaining 24 bits via D31-D24 in three consecutive cycles. If the device is 32-bit, it obtains data bytes OP0-OP3 in one cycle. Now, let us consider a 16-bit device. During the first cycle, the MC68020 outputs A1A0 = 00_2 indicating an aligned transfer, and SIZ1 SIZ0 = 00_2 indicating 32-bit transfer. Therefore, in the first cycle, the device obtains OP0 and OP1 from D31-D24 and D23-D16, respectively. The device then asserts $\overline{DSACK1}$ and $\overline{DSACK0}$ as 01_2 to terminate the cycle and to indicate to the MC68020 that it is a 16-bit device. In the second cycle, the MC68020 outputs the A1A0 as 10_2, indicating that 16-bit data to be obtained by the device via D31-D16 pins and SIZE1 and SIZ0 as 10_2, indicating that two more bytes remain to be transferred. The MC68020 places the low two bytes (OP2 and OP3) from register D3 via the multiplexor on D31-D16 pins. The device takes these data and places them into locations $5000 5172 and $5000 5173, respectively, by activating $\overline{DSACK1}$ and $\overline{DSACK0}$ as 01_2, indicating completion of the cycle.

If [D3] = $03F1 2517 (OP0 = $03, OP1 = $F1, OP2 = $25, and OP3 = $17), then data transfer for MOVE.L D3, $5000 5170 takes place as shown in the following:

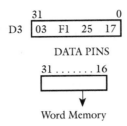

		MC68020				16-bit Memory	
		SIZ1	SIZ0	A1	A0	DSACK	DSACK0
First cycle	D31 [03] D16 [F1]	0	0	0	0	0	1
Second cycle	D31 [25] D16 [17]	1	0	1	0	0	1

Now let us consider a misaligned transfer to a 16-bit device. For example, consider MOVE.L D4, \$6017 2421. Assume [D4] = \$7126E214, that is, OP0 = \$71, OP1 = 26, OP2 = \$E2, OP3 = \$14. Now, suppose that the device is 16-bit. In the first cycle, the MC68020 outputs \$717126E2 via the multiplexor; the multiplexor places these data on D31-D0 pins considering that the device may be 8-, 16-, or 32-bit as follows:

D31 : D24	D23 : D16	D15 : D8	D7 : D0
71	71	26	E2

This is because the device accepts \$71 if it is 8-bit via D31-D24 pins, \$71 via D24-D16 pins if it is 16-bit, and 24-bit data \$7126E2 via D23-D0 pins if it is 32-bit.

For 8-bit and 32-bit devices, four and two cycles are required, respectively, to complete the long-word transfer. Now, let us consider the 16-bit device for this example in detail.

In the first cycle, the MC68020 outputs SIZ1, SIZ0 as 00_2, indicating a 32-bit transfer, and A1A0 as 01_2, indicating that a byte transfer is to take place via D23-D16 pins in the first cycle. The memory device obtains \$71 from D23-D16 and writes these data to \$60172421 and then activates $\overline{DSACK1}$ $\overline{DSACK0}$ as 01_2, indicating to the MC68020 that it is a 16-bit device. In the second cycle, the MC68020 outputs SIZ1 SIZ0 as 11_2, indicating that three more bytes remain to be transferred, and A1A0 as 10_2, indicating a 16-bit transfer is to take place via D31-D16.

The memory device activates $\overline{DSACK1}$ $\overline{DSACK0}$ as 01_2 to write \$26E2 to locations \$60172422 and \$60172423. The MC68020 then terminates the cycle.

In the third cycle, the MC68020 outputs SIZ1 SIZ0 as 01_2, indicating a byte remaining to be transferred, and A1A0 as 00_2, indicating that the remaining byte transfer is to take place via D31-D24. The MC68020 then outputs $14 to D31-D24 pins. The device activates $\overline{\text{DSACK1}}$ $\overline{\text{DSACK0}}$ as 01_2 and writes $14 to location $60172424. The MC68020 then terminates the cycle.

Note that the MC68020 outputs the 32-bit address via its A31-A0 pins and the device uses this address to write data to the selected memory location. A1 and A0 are used by the device to determine which data lines are to be used for data transfer. For example, the 16-bit device transfers data via D16-D23 for an odd memory address and it transfers data via D31-D24 for an even memory location. Therefore, SIZ1, SIZ0, A1, and A0 must be used as inputs to the address decoding logic. This is discussed later.

The data transfer for the above example takes place as follows:

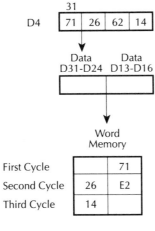

MC68020				16-Bit Memory	
SIZ1	SIZ0	A1	A0	DSACK1	DSACK0
0	0	0	1	0	1
1	1	1	0	0	1
0	1	0	0	0	1

Figure 6.12 shows a functional block diagram for MC68020 interfaces to 8-, 16-, and 32-bit memory or I/O devices.

Aligned long-word transfer to 8-, 16-, and 32-bit devices is shown in Figure 6.13.

MC68020 byte addressing is summarized in Figure 6.14.

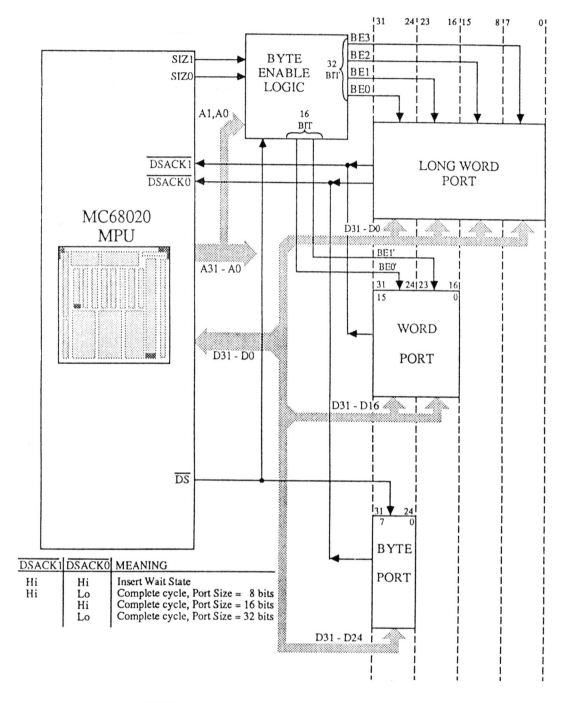

FIGURE 6.12 MC68020 dynamic bus sizing block diagram.

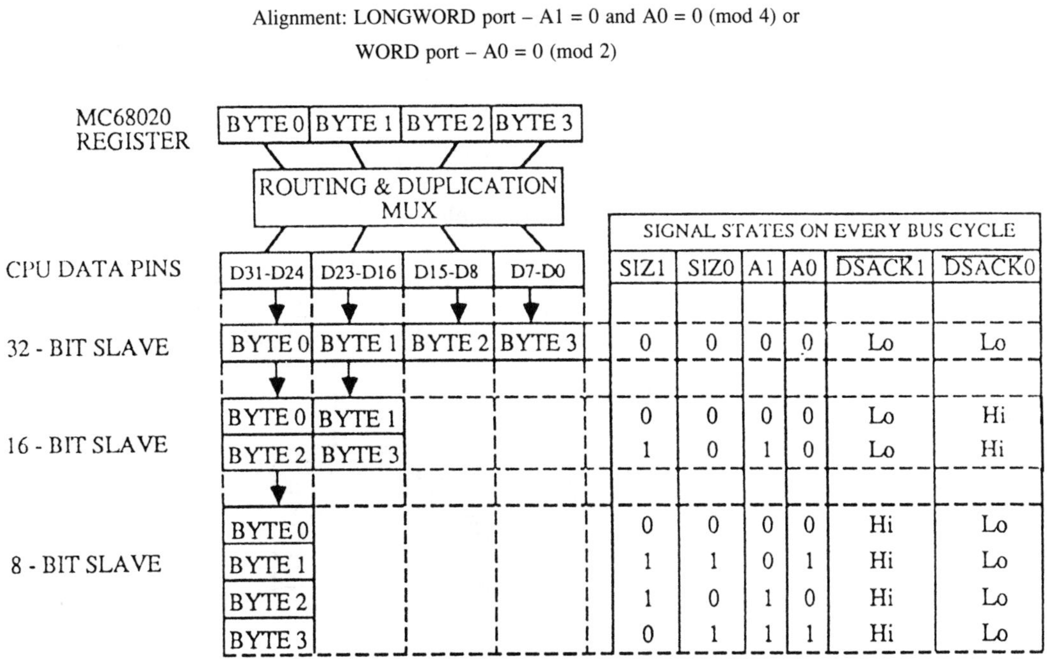

Alignment: LONGWORD port – A1 = 0 and A0 = 0 (mod 4) or
WORD port – A0 = 0 (mod 2)

MC68020 REGISTER	BYTE 0	BYTE 1	BYTE 2	BYTE 3						

ROUTING & DUPLICATION MUX

					SIGNAL STATES ON EVERY BUS CYCLE					
CPU DATA PINS	D31-D24	D23-D16	D15-D8	D7-D0	SIZ1	SIZ0	A1	A0	$\overline{DSACK1}$	$\overline{DSACK0}$
32 - BIT SLAVE	BYTE 0	BYTE 1	BYTE 2	BYTE 3	0	0	0	0	Lo	Lo
16 - BIT SLAVE	BYTE 0	BYTE 1			0	0	0	0	Lo	Hi
	BYTE 2	BYTE 3			1	0	1	0	Lo	Hi
8 - BIT SLAVE	BYTE 0				0	0	0	0	Hi	Lo
	BYTE 1				1	1	0	1	Hi	Lo
	BYTE 2				1	0	1	0	Hi	Lo
	BYTE 3				0	1	1	1	Hi	Lo

*SIZ1	*SIZ0	#BYTES
0	1	1
1	0	2
1	1	3
0	0	4

* Size pins indicate number of bytes remaining to complete the operand transfer.

FIGURE 6.13 Aligned long-word transfer.

Figure 6.15 shows misaligned long-word transfer to 8-, 16-, and 32-bit devices.

Now, let us explain the other MC68020 pins.

The $\overline{ECS}$ (external cycle start) pin is a MC68020 output pin. The MC68020 asserts this pin during the first one half clock of every bus cycle to provide the earliest indication of the start of a bus cycle. The use of $\overline{ECS}$ must be validated later with $\overline{AS}$, since the MC68020 may start an instruction fetch cycle and then abort it if the instruction is found in the cache. In the case of a cache hit, the MC68020 does not assert $\overline{AS}$, but provides A31-A0, SIZ1, SIZ0, and FC2-FC0 outputs.

The MC68020 asserts the $\overline{OCS}$ (operand cycle start) pin only during the first bus cycle of an operand transfer or instruction prefetch.

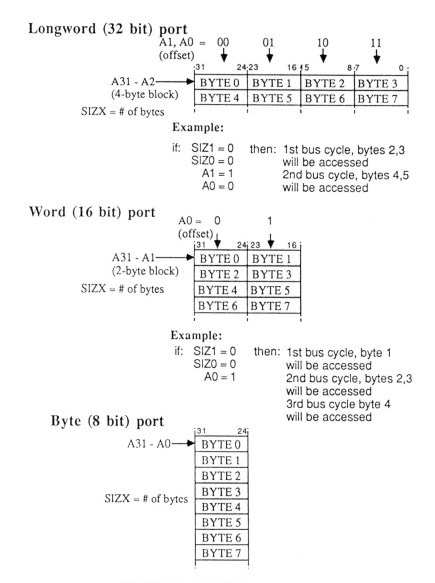

FIGURE 6.14 MC68020 byte addressing.

The MC68020 asserts the $\overline{\text{RMC}}$ (read-modify-write) pin to indicate that the current bus operation is an indivisible read-modify-write cycle. $\overline{\text{RMC}}$ should be used as a bus lock to ensure integrity of instructions which use read-modify-write operations such as TAS and CAS.

In a read cycle, the MC68020 asserts the $\overline{\text{DS}}$ (data strobe) pin to indicate that the slave device should drive the bus. During a write cycle, it indicates that the MC68020 has placed valid data on the data bus.

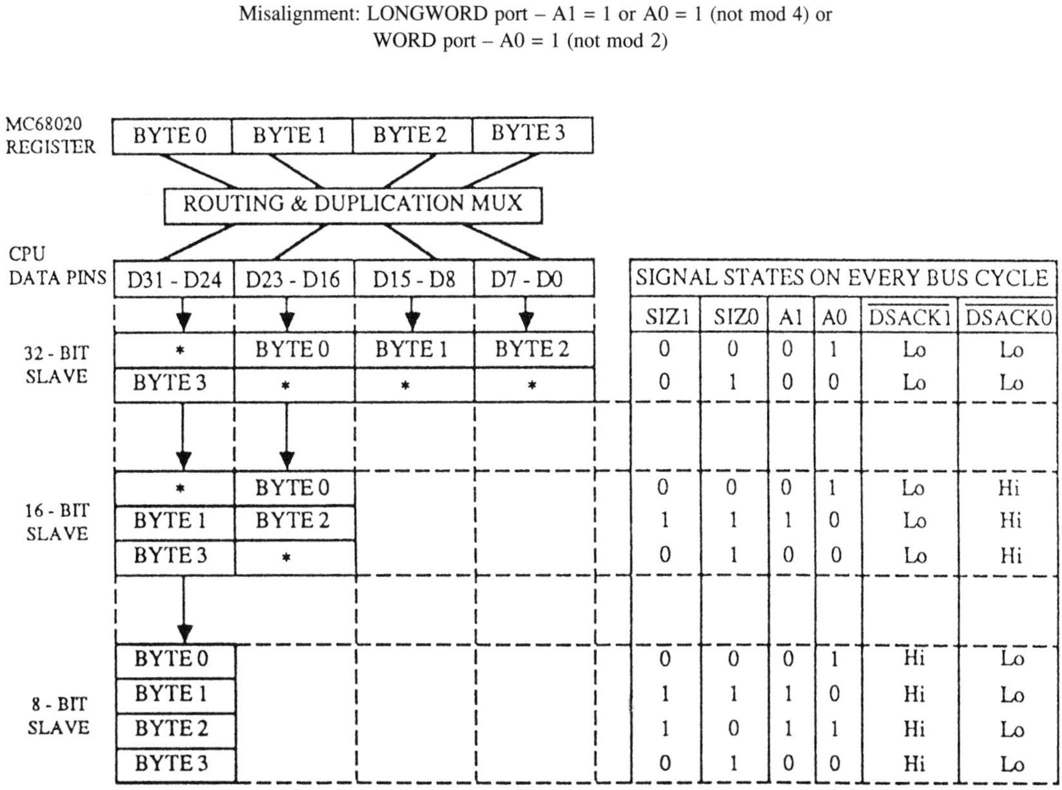

Misalignment: LONGWORD port – A1 = 1 or A0 = 1 (not mod 4) or
WORD port – A0 = 1 (not mod 2)

MC68020 REGISTER	BYTE 0	BYTE 1	BYTE 2	BYTE 3

ROUTING & DUPLICATION MUX

CPU DATA PINS	D31 - D24	D23 - D16	D15 - D8	D7 - D0	SIZ1	SIZ0	A1	A0	DSACK1	DSACK0
32 - BIT SLAVE	*	BYTE 0	BYTE 1	BYTE 2	0	0	0	1	Lo	Lo
	BYTE 3	*	*	*	0	1	0	0	Lo	Lo
16 - BIT SLAVE	*	BYTE 0			0	0	0	1	Lo	Hi
	BYTE 1	BYTE 2			1	1	1	0	Lo	Hi
	BYTE 3	*			0	1	0	0	Lo	Hi
8 - BIT SLAVE	BYTE 0				0	0	0	1	Hi	Lo
	BYTE 1				1	1	1	0	Hi	Lo
	BYTE 2				1	0	1	1	Hi	Lo
	BYTE 3				0	1	0	0	Hi	Lo

SIGNAL STATES ON EVERY BUS CYCLE

* These bytes must not be overwritten. Therefore, individual data strobes must be generated by external hardware either at the port or at the 68020.

FIGURE 6.15 Misaligned long-word transfer.

$\overline{\text{DEN}}$ (data buffer enable) is output by the MC68020 which may be used to enable external data buffers.

The $\overline{\text{CDIS}}$ (cache disable) input pin to the MC68020 dynamically disables the cache when asserted.

The interrupt pending ($\overline{\text{IPEND}}$) input pin indicates that the value of the $\overline{\text{IPL2}}\text{-}\overline{\text{IPL0}}$ pins is higher than the current I2I1I0 in SR or that a nonmaskable interrupt has been recognized.

The MC68020 $\overline{\text{AVEC}}$ input is activated by an external device to service an autovector interrupt. The $\overline{\text{AVEC}}$ has the same function as the MC68000 $\overline{\text{VPA}}$.

The functions of the other signals such as $\overline{\text{AS}}$, R/$\overline{\text{W}}$, $\overline{\text{IPL2}}\text{-}\overline{\text{IPL0}}$, $\overline{\text{BR}}$, $\overline{\text{BG}}$, and $\overline{\text{BGACK}}$ are similar to those of the MC68000.

The MC68020 system control pins are functionally similar to those of the MC68000. However, there are some minor differences. For example, for hardware reset, $\overline{RESET}$ and $\overline{HALT}$ pins need not be asserted simultaneously. Therefore, unlike the MC68000, $\overline{RESET}$ and $\overline{HALT}$ pins are not tied together in the MC68020 system.

$\overline{RESET}$ and $\overline{HALT}$ pins are bi-directional, open-drain (external pull-up resistances are required), and their functions are independent.

When $\overline{HALT}$ input is asserted by an external device, the following activities take place:

- All control signals become inactive.
- Address lines, R/$\overline{W}$ line, and function code lines remain driven with last bus cycle information.
- All bus activities stop after current bus cycle completion.

Assertion of $\overline{HALT}$ stops only external bus activities and the processor execution continues. That is, the MC68020 can continue with instruction execution internally if cache hits occur and if the external bus is not required.

The MC68020 asserts the $\overline{HALT}$ output for double bus fault. The $\overline{BERR}$ input pin, when asserted by an external device, causes the bus cycle to be aborted and strobes negated. If the $\overline{BERR}$ is asserted during operand read or write (not prefetch), exception processing occurs immediately. The $\overline{BERR}$ pin can typically be used to indicate a nonresponding device (no $\overline{DSACKX}$ received from the device), vector acquisition failure, illegal access determined by memory management unit hardware such as access fault (protected memory scheme), and page fault (virtual memory system).

Figure 6.16 shows the MC68020 reset characteristics.

The $\overline{RESET}$ signal is a bi-directional signal. The $\overline{RESET}$ pin, when asserted by an external circuit for a minimum of 520 clock periods, resets the entire system including the MC68020. Upon hardware reset, the MC68020 completes any active bus cycle in an orderly manner and then performs the following:

- Reads the 32-bit contents of address \$00000000 and loads it into ISP (contents of \$00000000 to most significant byte of ISP and so on)
- Reads the 32-bit contents of address \$00000004 into PC (contents of \$00000004 to most significant byte of PC and so on)
- Sets I2I1I0 bits of SR to 111, sets S-bit in SR to 1, and clears T1, T0, M bits in SR
- Clears VBR to \$00000000

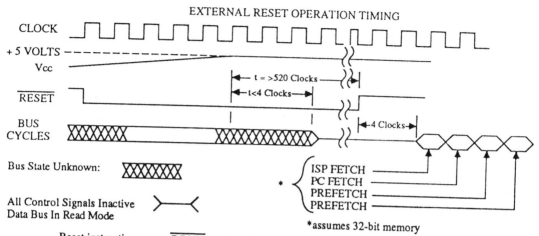

EXTERNAL RESET OPERATION TIMING

Bus State Unknown:

All Control Signals Inactive
Data Bus In Read Mode

*assumes 32-bit memory

Reset instruction asserts $\overline{\text{RESET}}$ pin for 512 clocks.

If reset instruction will not be executed,
Then $\overline{\text{RESET}}$ pin should be asserted for ≥ 10 clocks
Else RESET pin should be asserted for ≥ 520 clocks

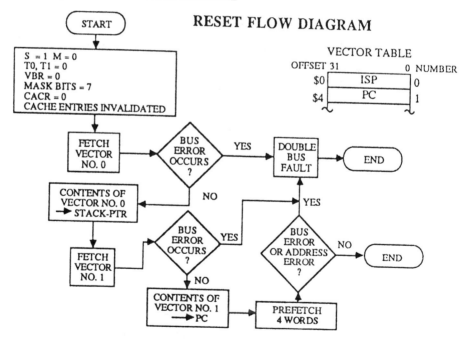

RESET FLOW DIAGRAM

FIGURE 6.16 MC68020 reset characteristics (higher level exception).

- Clears the cache enable bit in the CACR
- All other registers are unaffected by hardware reset

When the $\overline{\text{RESET}}$ instruction is executed, the MC68020 asserts the $\overline{\text{RESET}}$ pin for 512 clock cycles and the processor resets all the external devices connected to the $\overline{\text{RESET}}$ pin. Software reset does not affect any internal register.

Figure 6.17 shows a MC68020 reset circuit.

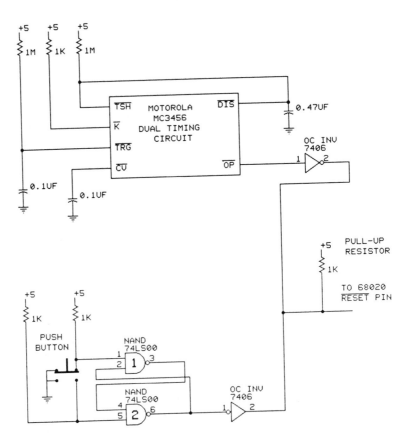

FIGURE 6.17 MC68020 reset circuit.

The Motorola MC3456 contains a dual timing circuit. The MC3456 uses an external resistor-capacitor network as its timing elements. Like the MC1455 timer used in the 68000 reset circuit, the MC3456 includes comparators and an R-S flip-flop. From the MC3456 data sheet, the RC values connected at the $\overline{\text{TRG}}$ input of the MC3456 will make output $\overline{\text{OP}}$ HIGH for T = 1.1 $R_a C_a$ seconds, where R_a = resistor connected at the $\overline{\text{TSH}}$ = 1 Mohm, and C_a = capacitor connected at $\overline{\text{DIS}}$ = 0.47 µF. This means that $\overline{\text{OP}}$ will be HIGH for 517 msec (1.1 M *0.47 µF); the $\overline{\text{OP}}$ will then go back to LOW state. Therefore, the output of the inverter (connected at $\overline{\text{OP}}$) will be LOW for 517 ms.

The push button connected to the input of the debouncing circuit, when not activated, will generate HIGH at the bottom input of AND gate #2 and LOW at the top of input of AND gate #1 (HIGH is grounded by the switch as shown in Figure 6.17).

Since a NAND gate generates a HIGH with one of the inputs as LOW, the output of NAND gate #1 will be HIGH. This means that both inputs of NAND gate #2 will be HIGH. Therefore, the output of NAND gate #2 will be LOW. This LOW level is inverted and connected to a WIRED.OR circuit along with the inverted $\overline{\text{OP}}$ of the MC3456 at the MC68020 $\overline{\text{RESET}}$ pin. The output of the debouncing circuit will be HIGH when the push button is activated. For example, activation of the push button will generate a HIGH at the top input of NAND gate #1 and a LOW at the bottom input of NAND gate #2. The AND gate #2 will generate a HIGH at its output. Therefore, the inverted output will be LOW which is presented at the WIRED.-OR circuit of the 68020 $\overline{\text{RESET}}$ pin. A LOW will be provided at the 68020 $\overline{\text{RESET}}$ pin only when both inputs are LOW, that is, when the push button is activated and inverted $\overline{\text{OP}}$ of MC3456 is LOW.

The MC3456 timer will keep this $\overline{\text{RESET}}$ pin signal LOW for 517 msec. As mentioned before, the 68020 requires the $\overline{\text{RESET}}$ pin to stay LOW for at least 520 clock cycles. For a 60-ns (16-MHz) clock, the 68020 must then be LOW for at least 31.2 µs (520 * 60 ns). Since the reset circuit of Figure 6.17 outputs a LOW for 517 msec (>31.2 µs) upon activation of the push button, the 68020 $\overline{\text{RESET}}$ pin will be asserted properly.

Example 6.18

Determine the number of bus cycles, bytes written to memory (in Hex), and signal levels of A1, A0, SIZE1, and SIZ0 pins that would occur when the instruction MOVE.L D1, (A0) with [D1] = $5012 6124 and [A0] = $2000 2053 is executed by the MC68020.

	Assume	1.	32-bit memory
		2.	16-bit memory
		3.	8-bit memory

Indicate the bus cycles in which $\overline{\text{OCS}}$ is asserted.

Solution

1.   32-bit memory; misaligned transfer since starting address is odd

	A1	A0	SIZ1	SIZ0	D31-D24	D21-D16	D15-D8	D7-D0
First bus cycle	1	1	0	0				50
Second bus cycle	0	0	1	1	12	61	24	

(MC68020 D31-D0 pins)

$\overline{OCS}$ is asserted in the first bus cycle.

2.   16-bit memory

	A1	A0	SIZ1	SIZ0	D31-D24	D23-D16
First bus cycle	1	1	0	0		50
Second bus cycle	0	0	1	1	12	61
Third bus cycle	1	0	0	1	24	

(MC68020 D31-D16 pins)

$\overline{OCS}$ is asserted in the first bus cycle.

3.   8-bit memory

	A1	A0	SIZ1	SIZ0	MC68020 D31-D24 PINS
First bus cycle	1	1	0	0	50
Second bus cycle	0	0	1	1	12
Third bus cycle	0	1	1	0	61
Fourth bus cycle	1	0	0	1	24

$\overline{OCS}$ is asserted in the first bus cycle.

Example 6.19

Determine the contents of PC, SR, MSP, ISP after MC68020 hardware reset. Assume 32-bit memory with the following data prior to the reset:

MEMORY

$00000000	$50001234
$00000004	$72152614

REGISTERS

MSP	$27140124
ISP	$61711420
PC	$35261271
SR	$0301

Solution

After hardware reset, the following are memory and register contents:

MEMORY

$00000000	$50001234
$00000004	$72152614

REGISTERS

MSP	$27140124
ISP	$50001234
PC	$72152614
SR	$2701

Note that [SR] = $2701 =

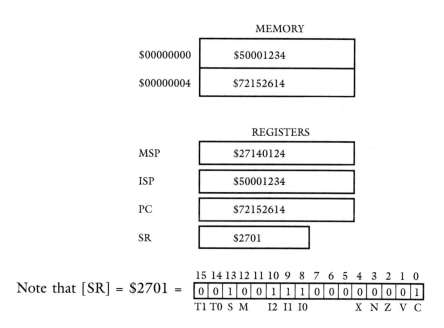

Therefore, T1T0 = 00, S = 1, M = 0, and I2I1IO = 111. Other bits are unaffected.

6.9 MC68020 TIMING DIAGRAMS

The MC68020 always activates all data lines. The MC68020 can perform either synchronous or asynchronous operation. Synchronous operation permits interfacing the devices which use the MC68020 clock to generate $\overline{\text{DSACKX}}$ and other asynchronous inputs. The asynchronous input setup and hold times must be satisfied for the assertion or negation of these inputs. The MC68020 then guarantees recognition of these signals on the current falling edge of the clock.

On the other hand, asynchronous operation provides clock frequency independence for generating $\overline{\text{DSACKX}}$ and other asynchronous inputs. This operation requires utilization of only the bus handshake signals ($\overline{\text{AS}}$, $\overline{\text{DS}}$, $\overline{\text{DSACKX}}$, $\overline{\text{BERR}}$, and $\overline{\text{HALT}}$). In asynchronous operation, $\overline{\text{AS}}$ indicates the beginning of a bus cycle and $\overline{\text{DS}}$ validates data in a write cycle. The SIZ1, SIZ0, A1, and A0 signals are decoded to generate strobe signals. These strobes indicate which data bytes are to be used in transfer. The memory or I/O devices then place data on the right portion of the data bus for a read cycle or latch data in a write cycle. The selected device finally activates the $\overline{\text{DSACKX}}$ lines according to the device size to terminate the cycle. If no $\overline{\text{DSACKX}}$ is received by the MC68020 or the access is invalid, the external device can assert $\overline{\text{BERR}}$ to abort or $\overline{\text{BERR}}$ and $\overline{\text{HALT}}$ to retry the bus cycle. There is no limit on the time from assertion of $\overline{\text{AS}}$ to the assertion of $\overline{\text{DSACKX}}$, since the MC68020 keeps inserting wait states in increments of one cycle until $\overline{\text{DSACKX}}$ is recognized by the processor.

For synchronization, the MC68020 uses a time delay to sample an external asynchronous input for high or low and then synchronizes this input to the clock.

Figure 6.18 shows an example of synchronization and recognition of asynchronous inputs.

Note that for all inputs, there is a sample window of 20 ns during which the MC68020 latches the input level. In order to guarantee the recognition of a certain level on a particular falling edge of the clock, the input level must be held stable throughout this sample window of 20 ns. If an input changes during the sample window, the level recognized by the MC68020 is unknown or illegal. One exception to this rule is the delayed assertion

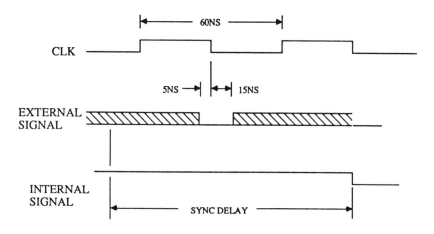

FIGURE 6.18a Synchronizing asynchronous inputs.

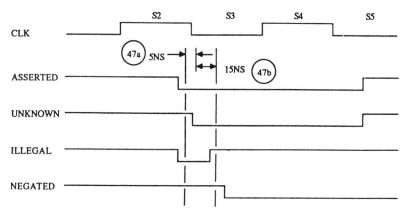

IN GENERAL, SIGNAL LEVEL MUST BE MAINTAINED FROM S2 INTO S5 OR
RESULTS WILL BE UNPREDICTABLE. AN EXCEPTION TO THIS RULE IS BUS
ERROR.

FIGURE 6.18b Asynchronous input recognition.

of $\overline{BERR}$ where the signal must be stable through the window or the
MC68020 may exhibit erratic behavior.

Note that if the $\overline{BERR}$ is asserted during an instruction prefetch, the
MC68020 delays bus error exception processing until the faulted data are
required for execution. Bus error processing will take place for faulty access
if change in program flow such as branching occurs, since the faulty data
are not required. Also, after satisfying the setup and hold times, all input
signals must meet certain protocols. For example, when $\overline{DSACKX}$ is

asserted it must remain asserted until $\overline{AS}$ is negated. Figures 6.19a and b show timing of $\overline{DSACKX}$ input recognition and the MC68020's reading of data satisfying the required protocol.

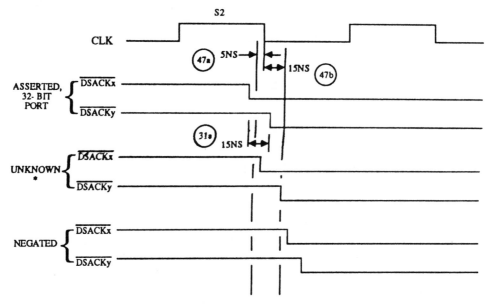

*BUT IF ASSERTED AND IF DSACKy ASSERTED WITHIN 15NS, THEN 32-BIT PORT

FIGURE 6.19a $\overline{DSACKX}$ input recognition.

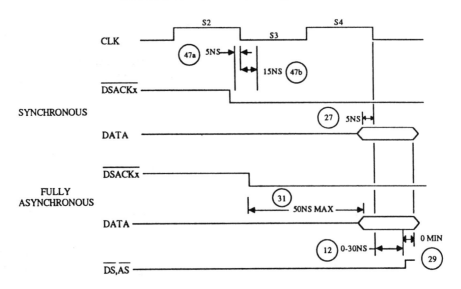

FIGURE 6.19b Protocol for reading data.

In the timing diagrams of Motorola's 68020 manuals, parameter #47 (47a and 47b) provides the asynchronous input setup time of 20 ns. All numbers circled in the timing diagrams are the timing parameters provided in Motorola manuals.

In Figure 6.19b (synchronous operation), assertion of $\overline{DSACKX}$ is recognized on the falling edge of S2; the MC68020 latches valid data on the falling edge of S4. For asynchronous operation, data are latched 50 ns (parameter 31) after assertion of $\overline{DSACKX}$. If $\overline{DSACKX}$ or $\overline{BERR}$ is not asserted by the external device during the 20 ns window of the falling edge of S2, the 68020 inserts wait states until one of these input signals is asserted. A minimum of three clock cycles is required for a read operation. $\overline{DSACKX}$ remains asserted until AS negation is satisfied in Figure 6.19a.

Figure 6.20a shows asynchronous bus cycle timing along with various parameters. Figures 6.20b, c, and d show typical MC68020 read and write timing diagrams (general form) along with their AC specifications. Note that in Figures 6.20b and c signals such as SIZ0, SIZ1, $\overline{DSACKX}$, D0-D31, A1, and A0, which precisely distinguish data transfers between 8-, 16-, and 32-bit devices, are kept in general form.

6.10 EXCEPTION PROCESSING

The MC68020 exceptions are functionally similar to those of the MC68000 with some minor variations. The MC68020 exceptions can be generated by external or internal causes. Externally generated exceptions include interrupts, bus errors, reset, and coprocessor-detected errors. Internally generated exceptions are caused by certain instructions, address errors, tracing, and breakpoints. Instructions that may cause internal exceptions as part of their instruction execution are CHK, CHK2, CALLM, RTM, RTE, DIV, and all variations of the TRAP instruction. In addition, illegal instructions, privilege violations, and coprocessor violations cause exceptions. Table 6.17 lists the priority and characteristics of all MC68020 exceptions.

MC68020 exception processing is similar in concept to the MC68000 with some minor variations. In the MC68020 exception processing occurs in four steps and varies according to the cause of the exception. The four steps are summarized below:

1. During the first step, an internal copy is made of the SR, and the SR is set for exception processing. This means that the status register enters the supervisor state and tracing is disabled.

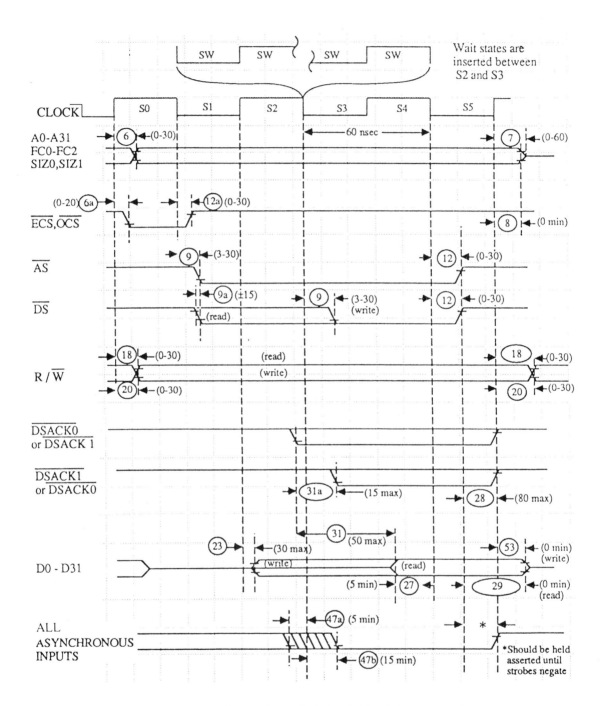

FIGURE 6.20a Asynchronous bus cycle timing. All time is in nanoseconds.

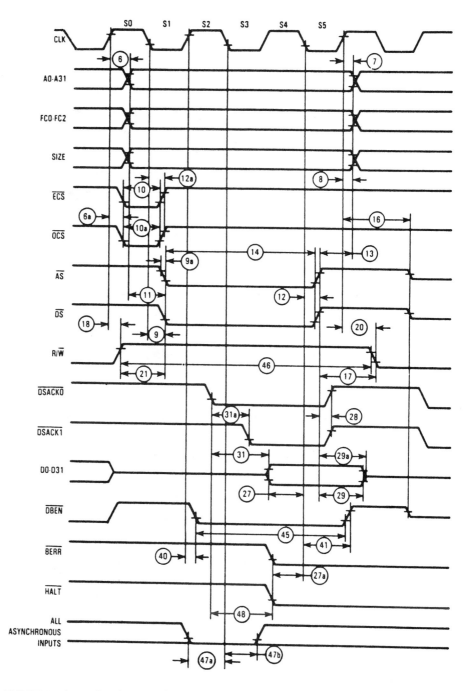

FIGURE 6.20b Read cycle timing diagram. Timing measurements are referenced to and from a low voltage of 0.8 volts and a high voltage of 2.0 volts, unless otherwise noted. The voltage swing through this range should start outside and pass through the range such that the rise or fall will be linear between 0.8 and 2.0 volts.

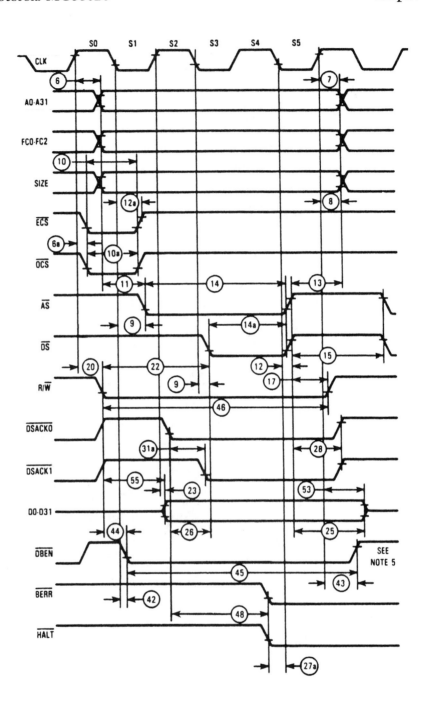

FIGURE 6.20c Write cycle timing diagram. Timing measurements are referenced to and from a low voltage of 0.8 volts and a high voltage of 2.0 volts, unless otherwise noted. The voltage swing through this range should start outside and pass through the range such that the rise or fall will be linear between 0.8 and 2.0 volts. "Note 5" refers to Figure 6.20d.

Num.	Characteristic	12.5 MHz		16.67 MHz		20 MHz		25 MHz		Unit
		Min	Max	Min	Max	Min	Max	Min	Max	
6	Clock High to Address/FC/Size/$\overline{\text{RMC}}$ Valid	0	40	0	30	0	25	0	25	ns
6A	Clock High to $\overline{\text{ECS}}$, $\overline{\text{OCS}}$ Asserted	0	30	0	20	0	15	0	15	ns
7	Clock High to Address/Data/FC/$\overline{\text{RMC}}$/Size High Impedance	0	80	0	60	0	50	0	40	ns
8	Clock High to Address/FC/Size/$\overline{\text{RMC}}$ Invalid	0	—	0	—	0	—	0	—	ns
9	Clock Low to $\overline{\text{AS}}$, $\overline{\text{DS}}$ Asserted	3	40	3	30	3	25	3	20	ns
9A[1]	$\overline{\text{AS}}$ to $\overline{\text{DS}}$ Assertion (Read) (Skew)	−20	20	−15	15	−10	10	−10	10	ns
10	$\overline{\text{ECS}}$ Width Asserted	25	—	20	—	15	—	10	—	ns
10A	$\overline{\text{OCS}}$ Width Asserted	25	—	20	—	15	—	10	—	ns
10B[7]	$\overline{\text{ECS}}$, $\overline{\text{OCS}}$ Width Negated	20	—	15	—	10	—	5	—	ns
11[6]	Address/FC/Size/$\overline{\text{RMC}}$ Valid to $\overline{\text{AS}}$ Asserted (and $\overline{\text{DS}}$ Asserted, Read)	20	—	15	—	10	—	5	—	ns
12	Clock Low to $\overline{\text{AS}}$, $\overline{\text{DS}}$ Negated	0	40	0	30	0	25	0	20	ns
12A	Clock Low to $\overline{\text{ECS}}$/$\overline{\text{OCS}}$ Negated	0	40	0	30	0	25	0	20	ns
13	$\overline{\text{AS}}$, $\overline{\text{DS}}$ Negated to Address/FC/Size/$\overline{\text{RMC}}$ Invalid	20	—	15	—	10	—	5	—	ns
14	$\overline{\text{AS}}$ (and $\overline{\text{DS}}$, Read) Width Asserted	120	—	100	—	85	—	65	—	ns
14A	$\overline{\text{DS}}$ Width Asserted, Write	50	—	40	—	38	—	30	—	ns
15	$\overline{\text{AS}}$, $\overline{\text{DS}}$ Width Negated	50	—	40	—	38	—	30	—	ns
15A[8]	$\overline{\text{DS}}$ Negated to $\overline{\text{AS}}$ Asserted	45	—	35	—	30	—	25	—	ns
16	Clock High to $\overline{\text{AS}}$/$\overline{\text{DS}}$/R/$\overline{\text{W}}$/$\overline{\text{DBEN}}$ High Impedance	—	80	—	60	—	50	—	40	ns
17[6]	$\overline{\text{AS}}$, $\overline{\text{DS}}$ Negated to R/$\overline{\text{W}}$ High	20	—	15	—	10	—	5	—	ns
18	Clock High to R/$\overline{\text{W}}$ High	0	40	0	30	0	25	0	20	ns
20	Clock High to R/$\overline{\text{W}}$ Low	0	40	0	30	0	25	0	20	ns
21[6]	R/$\overline{\text{W}}$ High to $\overline{\text{AS}}$ Asserted	20	—	15	—	10	—	5	—	ns
22[6]	R/$\overline{\text{W}}$ Low to $\overline{\text{DS}}$ Asserted (Write)	90	—	75	—	60	—	45	—	ns
23	Clock High to Data Out Valid	—	40	—	30	—	25	—	25	ns
25[6]	$\overline{\text{AS}}$, $\overline{\text{DS}}$ Negated to Data Out Invalid	20	—	15	—	10	—	5	—	ns
25A[9]	$\overline{\text{DS}}$ Negated to $\overline{\text{DBEN}}$ Negated (Write)	20	—	15	—	10	—	5	—	ns
26[6]	Data Out Valid to $\overline{\text{DS}}$ Asserted (Write)	20	—	15	—	10	—	5	—	ns
27	Data-In Valid to Clock Low (Data Setup)	10	—	5	—	5	—	5	—	ns
27A	Late $\overline{\text{BERR}}$/$\overline{\text{HALT}}$ Asserted to Clock Low Setup Time	25	—	20	—	15	—	10	—	ns
28	$\overline{\text{AS}}$, $\overline{\text{DS}}$ Negated to $\overline{\text{DSACKx}}$/$\overline{\text{BERR}}$/$\overline{\text{HALT}}$/$\overline{\text{AVEC}}$ Negated	0	110	0	80	0	65	0	50	ns
29	$\overline{\text{DS}}$ Negated to Data-In Invalid (Data-In Hold Time)	0	—	0	—	0	—	0	—	ns
29A	$\overline{\text{DS}}$ Negated to Data-In (High Impedance)	—	80	—	60	—	50	—	40	ns
31[2]	$\overline{\text{DSACKx}}$ Asserted to Data-In Valid	—	60	—	50	—	43	—	32	ns
31A[3]	$\overline{\text{DSACKx}}$ Asserted to $\overline{\text{DSACKx}}$ Valid ($\overline{\text{DSACK}}$ Asserted Skew)	—	20	—	15	—	10	—	10	ns

FIGURE 6.20d Read and write cycle specifications.

Num.	Characteristic	12.5 MHz		16.67 MHz		20 MHz		25 MHz		Unit
		Min	Max	Min	Max	Min	Max	Min	Max	
32	RESET Input Transition Time	—	1.5	—	1.5	—	1.5	—	1.5	Clks
33	Clock Low to BG Asserted	0	40	0	30	0	25	0	20	ns
34	Clock Low to BG Negated	0	40	0	30	0	25	0	20	ns
35	BR Asserted to BG Asserted (RMC Not Asserted)	1.5	3.5	1.5	3.5	1.5	3.5	1.5	3.5	Clks
37	BGACK Asserted to BG Negated	1.5	3.5	1.5	3.5	1.5	3.5	1.5	3.5	Clks
37A	BGACK Asserted to BR Negated	0	1.5	0	1.5	0	1.5	0	1.5	Clks
39	BG Width Negated	120	—	90	—	75	—	60	—	ns
39A	BG Width Asserted	120	—	90	—	75	—	60	—	ns
40	Clock High to DBEN Asserted (Read)	0	40	0	30	0	25	0	20	ns
41	Clock Low to DBEN Negated (Read)	0	40	0	30	0	25	0	20	ns
42	Clock Low to DBEN Asserted (Write)	0	40	0	30	0	25	0	20	ns
43	Clock High to DBEN Negated (Write)	0	40	0	30	0	25	0	20	ns
44[6]	R/W Low to DBEN Asserted (Write)	20	—	15	—	10	—	5	—	ns
45[5]	DBEN Width Asserted Read / Write	80 / 160	—	60 / 120	—	50 / 100	—	40 / 80	—	ns
46	R/W Width Asserted (Write or Read)	180	—	150	—	125	—	100	—	ns
47A	Asynchronous Input Setup Time	10	—	5	—	5	—	5	—	ns
47B	Asynchronous Input Hold Time	20	—	15	—	15	—	10	—	ns
48[4]	DSACKx Asserted to BERR/HALT Asserted	—	35	—	30	—	20	—	15	ns
53	Data Out Hold from Clock High	0	—	0	—	0	—	0	—	ns
55	R/W Asserted to Data Bus Impedance Change	40	—	30	—	25	—	20	—	ns
56	RESET Pulse Width (Reset Instruction)	512	—	512	—	512	—	512	—	Clks
57	BERR Negated to HALT Negated (Rerun)	0	—	0	—	0	—	0	—	ns
58[10]	BGACK Negated to Bus Driven	1	—	1	—	1	—	1	—	Clks
59[10]	BG Negated to Bus Driven	1	—	1	—	1	—	1	—	Clks

NOTES:
1. This number can be reduced to 5 nanoseconds if strobes have equal loads.
2. If the asynchronous setup time (#47) requirements are satisfied, the DSACKx low to data setup time (#31) and DSACKx low to BERR low setup time (#48) can be ignored. The data must only satisfy the data-in to clock low setup time (#27) for the following clock cycle, BERR must only satisfy the late BERR low to clock low setup time (#27A) for the following clock cycle.
3. This parameter specifies the maximum allowable skew between DSACK0 to DSACK1 asserted or DSACK1 to DSACK0 asserted, specification #47 must be met by DSACK0 or DSACK1.
4. In the absence of DSACKx, BERR is an asynchronous input using the asynchronous input setup time (#47).
5. DBEN may stay asserted on consecutive write cycles.
6. Actual value depends on the clock input waveform.
7. This is a new specification that indicates the minimum high time for ECS and OCS in the event of an internal cache hit followed immediately by a cache miss or operand cycle.
8. This is a new specification that guarantees operation with the MC68881, which specifies a minimum time for DS negated to AS asserted (specification #13A). Without this specification, incorrect interpretation of specifications #9A and #15 would indicate that the MC68020 does not meet the MC68881 requirements.
9. This is a new specificaiton that allows a system designer to guarantee data hold times on the output side of data buffers that have output enable signals generated with DBEN.
10. These are new specifications that allow system designers to guarantee that an alternate bus master has stopped driving the bus when the MC68020 regains control of the bus after an arbitration sequence.

FIGURE 6.20d (continued).

2. In the second step, the vector number of the exception vector is determined from either the exception requesting peripheral (nonautovector) or internally upon assertion of the $\overline{\text{AVEC}}$ (autovector) input. Note that in the MC68000, $\overline{\text{VPA}}$ is asserted for autovectoring. The vector base register points to the base of the 1-KB exception vector table which contains 256 exception vectors. The processor uses exception vectors as memory pointers to fetch the address of routines that handle the various exceptions. The obtained vector number is then used to generate the address of the specific exception vector. Table 6.18 lists MC68020 exception vector assignments.

3. In the third step, the processor saves PC and SR on the supervisor stack. For coprocessor exceptions, additional internal state information must be saved on the stack as well.

4. The fourth step of the execution process is the same for all exceptions. The exception vector is determined by multiplying the vector number by four and adding it to the contents of the vector base register (VBR) to determine the memory of the address of the exception vector. The PC (and 1SP for the reset exception) is loaded with the value in the exception vector. The instruction located at the address given in the exception vector is fetched and the exception handling routine is thus executed.

TABLE 6.17
Exception Priorities and Recognition Times

Exception priorities			Time of recognition
Group 0	.0	Reset	End of clock cycle
Group 1	.0	Address error	
	.1	Bus error	
Group 2	.0	BKPT #N, CALLM, CHK, CHK2, cp TRAPcc cp mid-instruction cp protocol violation, divide-by-zero, RTE, RTM, TRAP #N, TRAPV	Within an instruction cycle
Group 3	.0	Illegal instruction, unimplemented LINE F, LINE A, privilege violation, cp preinstruction	Before instruction cycle beings

TABLE 6.17 (continued)
Exception Priorities and Recognition Times

Exception priorities			Time of recognition
Group 4	.0	cp post-instruction	End of instruction cycle
	.1	Trace	
	.2	Interrupt	

Note: Halt and bus arbitration are recognized at end of bus cycle. 0.0 is highest priority; 4.2 is lowest.

TABLE 6.18
MC68020 Exception Vector Assignments

Vector number(s)	Vector offset Hex	Space	Assignment
0	000	SP	Reset: initial interrupt stack pointer
1	004	SP	Reset: initial program counter
2	008	SD	Bus error
3	00C	SD	Address error
4	010	SD	Illegal instruction
5	014	SD	Zero divide
6	018	SD	CHK, CHK2 instruction
7	01C	SD	cpTRAPcc, TRAPcc, TRAPV instructions
8	020	SD	Privilege violation
9	024	SD	Trace
10	028	SD	Line 1010 emulator
11	02C	SD	Line 1111 emulator
12	030	SD	(Unassigned, reserved)
13	034	SD	Coprocessor, protocol violation
14	038	SD	Format error
15	03C	SD	Uninitialized interrupt
16 through 23	040 05C	SD SD	(Unassigned, reserved)
24	060	SD	Spurious interrupt
25	064	SD	Level 1 interrupt auto vector

TABLE 6.18 (continued)
MC68020 Exception Vector Assignments

Vector number(s)	Vector offset Hex	Space	Assignment
26	068	SD	Level 2 interrupt auto vector
27	06C	SD	Level 3 interrupt auto vector
28	070	SD	Level 4 interrupt auto vector
29	074	SD	Level 5 interrupt auto vector
30	078	SD	Level 6 interrupt auto vector
31	07C	SD	Level 7 interrupt auto vector
32 through 47	080 0BC	SD SD	TRAP #0-15 instruction vectors
48	0CO	SD	FPCP branch or set on unordered condition
49	0C4	SD	FPCP inexact result
50	0C8	SD	FPCP divide by zero
51	0CC	SD	FPCP underflow
52	0DO	SD	FPCP operand error
53	0D4	SD	FPCP overflow
54	0D8	SD	FPCP signaling NAN
55	0DC	SD	Unassigned, reserved
56	0EO	SD	PMMU configuration
57	0E4	SD	PMMU illegal operation
58	0E8	SD	PMMU access level violation
59 through 63	0EC 0FC	SD SD	Unassigned, reserved
64 through 255	100 3FC	SD SD	User defined vectors (192)

Note: SP = supervisor program space; SD = supervisor data space.

Figure 6.21 shows an overview of exception processing.

Exception processing saves certain information on the top of the supervisor stack. This information is called the exception stack frame. The

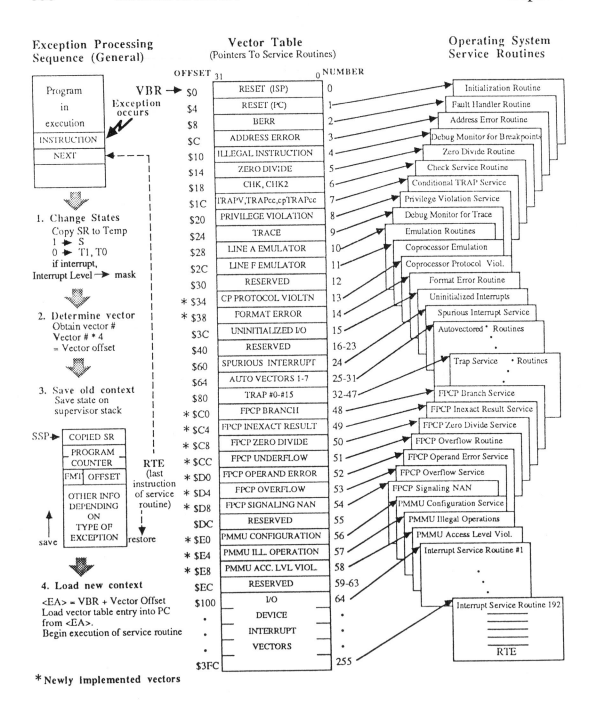

FIGURE 6.21 Exception processing overview.

exception stack frame general format is shown in Figure 6.22. The format field permits the RTE instruction to identify what information is on the stack so that it may be properly restored. Figure 6.23 shows a flowchart for the RTE instruction.

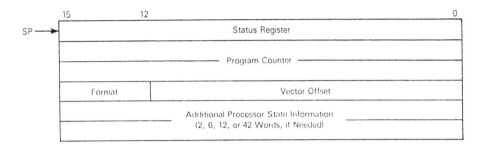

FIGURE 6.22 Exception stack frame (general form).

The MC68020 provides six different stack frames. These frames include the following:

1. Normal four-word stack frame
2. Normal six-word stack frame
3. Four-word throwaway stack frame
4. Coprocessor midinstruction exception stack frame
5. Short bus fault stack frame
6. Long bus fault stack frame

The normal four-word stack frame (FORMAT $0) is generated by interrupts, format errors (when instructions such as RTE find an invalid stack format code), TRAP#n instruction, illegal instructions, emulator traps, privilege violations, and coprocessor preinstruction exceptions.

The throwaway four-word stack frame (FORMAT $1) is generated on the interrupt stack during exception processing for an interrupt when a transition from the master to the interrupt state occurs.

The normal six-word stack frame (FORMAT $2) is generated by instruction-related exceptions such as CHK, CHK2, CPTRAPcc, TRAPcc, TRAPV, trace, and zero divide. The fifth and sixth stack words contain the instruction address that caused the exception. The other four words have the same format as the general stack format.

INSTRUCTION	OPERAND SIZE	OPERATION	NOTATION
RTE	NONE	IF S=1 THEN (SP) → SR; SP+2 → SP (SP) → PC; SP+4 → SP; RESTORE STATE FROM STACK ACCORDING TO FORMAT, ELSE TRAP	RTE

- RTE Restores a previous CPU context from one of 6 different stack frames
- Usually the last instruction of exception service routine
- Throwaway stack frame - RTE only loads SR

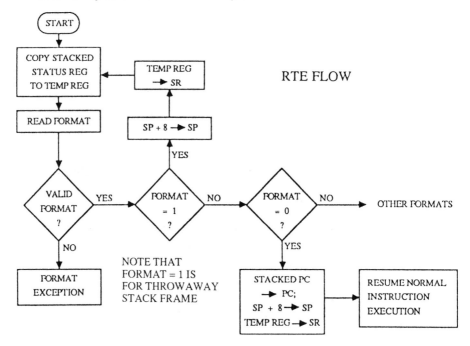

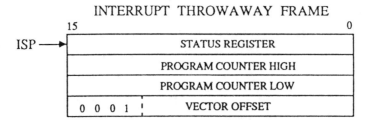

INTERRUPT THROWAWAY FRAME

FIGURE 6.23 Flowchart for RTE instruction.

The coprocessor midinstruction exception stack frame (FORMAT $9) is generated by coprocessor-related operations such as protocol violation. This frame contains ten words. The first six words are the same as the six-word stack frame; the other four words contain contents of internal registers.

The short bus cycle fault stack frame (FORMAT $A) is generated whenever a bus cycle fault is detected and the MC68020 identifies that it is at an instruction boundary and it can use this reduced version of the bus fault stack frame. This stack frame contains 16 words and words 6-16 include information such as internal registers and instruction pipes.

The long bus cycle fault stack frame (FORMAT $B) is generated whenever the MC68020 identifies bus cycle fault and finds that it is not on an instruction boundary. This stack frame contains 46 words. Words 6-46 include information such as internal registers, instruction pipes, and data input/output buffers.

The MC68020 provides the concept of two supervisor stacks pointed to by MSP and ISP. The M-bit (when S = 1) determines the active supervisor stack pointer. The MC68020 accesses MSP when S = 1, M = 0. The MSP can be used for program traps and other exceptions, while the ISP can be used for interrupts. The use of two supervisor stacks allows isolation of user processes or tasks and asynchronous supervisor I/O tasks.

$\overline{IPL2}$, $\overline{IPL1}$, $\overline{IPL0}$, $\overline{AVEC}$, and $\overline{IPEND}$ pins are used as the MC68020 hardware interrupt control signals (Figure 6.24). The MC68020 supports seven levels of prioritized interrupts encoded by using $\overline{IPL2}$, $\overline{IPL1}$, $\overline{IPL0}$ pins (Table 6.19).

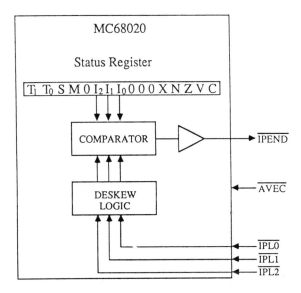

FIGURE 6.24 Interrupt control signals.

TABLE 6.19
MC68020 Interrupt Priority

Requested interrupt level	State of pins			Mask level required for recognition
	IPL2	IPL1	IPL0	
0 (no interrupt)	hi	hi	hi	N/A
1	hi	hi	lo	0
2	hi	lo	hi	1 or lower
3	hi	lo	lo	2 or lower
4	lo	hi	hi	3 or lower
5	lo	hi	lo	4 or lower
6	lo	lo	hi	5 or lower
7	lo	lo	lo	Not masked

- Interrupts allowed only above mask level.
- Level 7 may not be masked out — becomes NMI.
- Levels applied to the pins are inverted with respect to corresponding interrupt mask level.

In Figure 6.24, when an interrupting priority level 1 through 6 is requested, the MC68020 compares the interrupt level to the interrupt mask to determine whether the interrupt should be processed. Interrupt recognized as valid does not force immediate exception processing; a valid interrupt causes $\overline{\text{IPEND}}$ to be asserted, signaling to external devices that the MC68020 has an interrupt pending. Exception processing for a pending interrupt that begins at the next instruction boundary of a higher priority exception is not also currently valid. The DESKEW logic in Figure 6.24 continuously samples the $\overline{\text{IPL2}}$-$\overline{\text{IPL0}}$ pins on every falling edge of the clock, but deskews or latches an interrupt request when it remains at the same level for two consecutive falling edges of the input clock. Figure 6.25 gives an example of the MC68020 interrupt deskewing logic.

Whenever the processor reaches an instruction execution boundary, it checks for a pending interrupt. If it finds one, the MC68020 begins an exception processing and executes an interrupt acknowledge cycle (IACK) with FC2 FC1 FC0 = 111_2 and A19 A18 A17 A16 = 1111_2. The MC68020 basic hardware interrupt sequence is shown in Figure 6.26a. Figures 6.26b and c show the interrupt acknowledge flowchart and timing diagram. Before the interrupt acknowledge cycle is completed, the MC68020 must receive either $\overline{\text{AVEC}}$, $\overline{\text{DSACKX}}$, or $\overline{\text{BERR}}$; otherwise it will execute wait states until one of these input pins is activated externally.

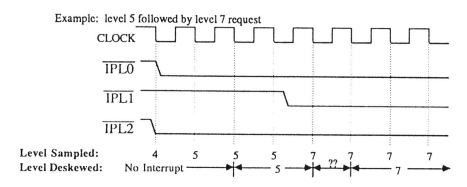

FIGURE 6.25 MC68020 interrupt deskewing logic.

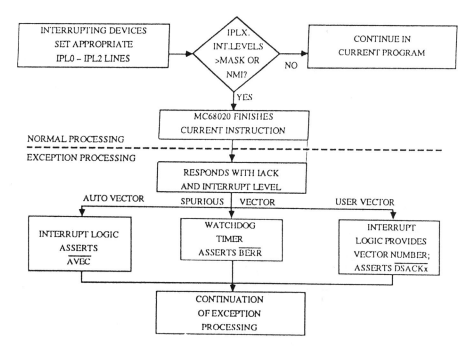

FIGURE 6.26a MC68020 basic hardware interrupt sequence.

If $\overline{\text{AVEC}}$ is asserted, the MC68020 automatically obtains the vector address internally (autovectored). If the MC68020 $\overline{\text{DSACKX}}$ pins are asserted, the MC68020 takes an 8-bit vector from the appropriate data lines (D0-D7 for 32-bit device, D16-D23 for 16-bit device, and D24-D31 for 8-bit device). This is called nonautovectored interrupts and the MC68020 obtains the interrupt vector address by adding VBR with 4 * (8-bit vector).

Figure 6.27 shows an example of autovectored and nonautovectored

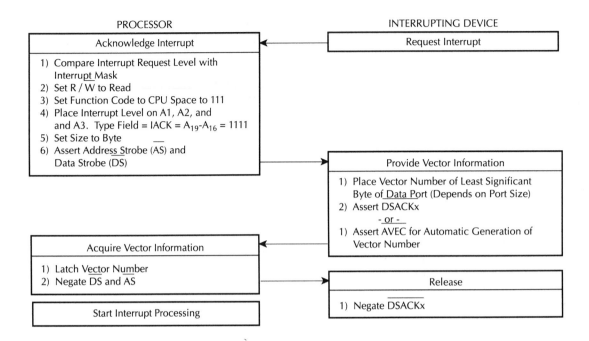

FIGURE 6.26b Interrupt acknowledge sequence flowchart.

interrupt logic. Finally, if the $\overline{\text{BERR}}$ pin is asserted, the interrupt is considered to be spurious and the MC68020 assigns the appropriate vector number for handling this.

6.11 MC68020 MEMORY AND I/O INTERFACES

In this section, simplified block diagrams illustrating interfacing of memory chips (such as 2716 and 6116) and I/O chips (68230) will be provided. Finally, an A/D converter will be interfaced to the MC68020-based microcomputer using both autovector and nonautovector interrupts. These block diagrams are self-explanatory.

Figure 6.28 shows interfacing of MC68020 to a 2716 EPROM and a 6116 RAM. Only pertinent signals are shown. Table 6.20 shows the memory selection scheme.

The delay circuit in Figure 6.28 delays $\overline{\text{DSACK0}}$ by an appropriate

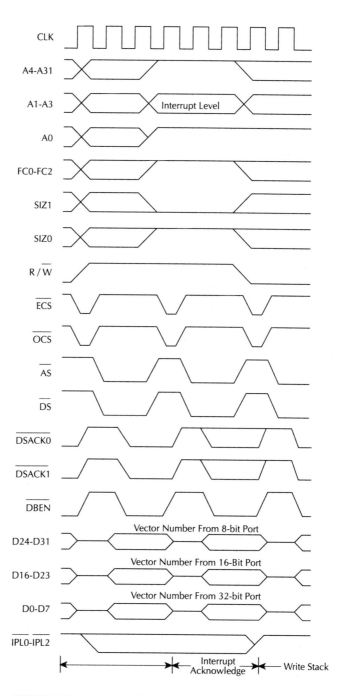

FIGURE 6.26c Interrupt acknowledge cycle timing (nonautovector).

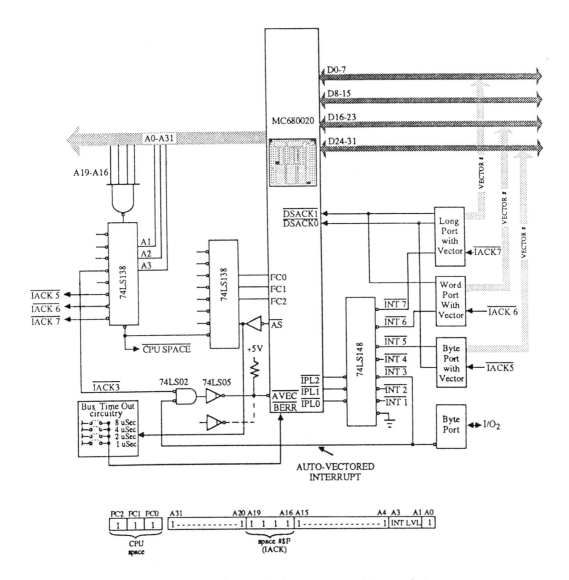

FIGURE 6.27 Autovectored and nonautovectored interrupt logic.

amount of time (determined by the access times of 2716 and 6116) so that data will be accessed when they are valid. For example, the access time of 2716 is 450 ns. The MC68020 samples $\overline{\text{DSACKX}}$ at the falling edge of S2 (two cycles; see Figure 6.20b). For an 8-bit device, $\overline{\text{DSACK1}}$ and $\overline{\text{DSACK0}}$ must have the values 1 and 0, respectively. In Figure 6.28, $\overline{\text{DSACK1}} = 1$ and $\overline{\text{DSACK0}} = 0$ after two cycles with no wait states.

If $\overline{\text{DSACK0}}$ is asserted by the external devices within two cycles and the

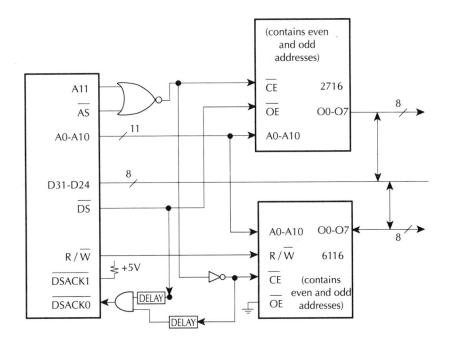

FIGURE 6.28 MC68020 interfaces to byte memory such as 2716 and 6116.

TABLE 6.20
Memory Selection Scheme

All	AS	Memory selected
0	0	6116
1	0	2716

68020 recognizes this at the falling edge of S2, then the 68020 latches date at the falling edge of S4 (three clock cycles).

For 16.67 MHz (60 ns per cycle), the 68020 latches data at 60 ns *3 = 180 ns with no wait states. If $\overline{\text{DSACKX}}$ is not recognized at the falling edge of S2, the MC68020 inserts wait states.

Since the 6116 has an access time of 120 ns, the 68020 is required to insert wait states. This can be explained as follows: the 68020 generates $\overline{\text{AS}}$ and $\overline{\text{DS}}$ LOW after 63 ns (one cycle until the falling edge of S0 plus parameter 9 in Figure 6.20b) from the start of the bus cycle. The 68020 recognizes this at the falling edge of S2. The 68020 latches invalid data at the falling edge of S4 (180 ns). Since $\overline{\text{AS}}$ is used to provide $\overline{\text{CE}}$ for the

6116, time delay between the falling edge of $\overline{AS}$ and the falling edge of S1 is approximately 70 ns (parameter 14 – parameter 12 — 100 ns – 30 ns = 70 ns), which is smaller than the 6116 access time of 120 ns. Therefore, the 6116 will not be ready with valid data unless 6116 $\overline{CE}$ (used for $\overline{DSACK0}$ recognition) is asserted at and recognized at the falling edge of S4 (70 ns) and data are latched at the falling edge of S6 (60 ns + 70 ns = 130 ns from $\overline{AS}$ going LOW).

Therefore, the 6116 $\overline{CE}$ (output of the inverter) must be delayed by, say, n50 ns (during S4 and before the falling edge of S4) so that $\overline{DSACK0}$ is asserted and recognized at the falling edge of S4 and data are latched at the falling edge of S6.

As far as the EPROM is concerned, the 2716 has an access time of 450 ns and will not work with the 16.67-MHz MC68020 unless the $\overline{DSACK0}$ in Figure 6.28 is delayed. $\overline{DS}$ is used to enable the 2716 and also to assert $\overline{DSACK0}$. $\overline{DS}$ and $\overline{AS}$ have almost identical timing characteristics (Figure 6.20b). This means that $\overline{DS}$ goes to LOW after 63 ns from the start of the bus cycle. In order to satisfy the timing requirements, time delay between the $\overline{DS}$ going LOW and data latched must be greater than 450 ns. As with the $\overline{AS}$ signal, time delay between $\overline{DS}$ LOW and the falling edge of S4 is 70 ns. $\overline{DS}$ must be delayed by about 430 ns from $\overline{DS}$ going Low ($\overline{DS}$ going LOW to the falling edge of S4 plus 6 cycles = 70 ns + 360 ns), so that $\overline{DSACK0}$ is asserted and recognized at the falling edge of S14, and then the 68020 will latch data at the falling edge of S16 (490 ns from $\overline{DS}$ going LOW). This will provide enough time for the 2716 for valid data on the data bus.

Figure 6.29a shows a simplified block diagram of the MC68020 interface to the MC68230 for I/O ports.

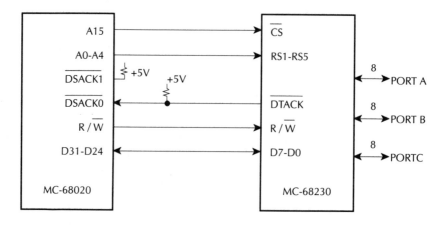

FIGURE 6.29a MC68020/68230 block diagram.

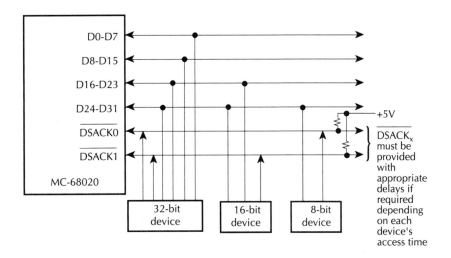

FIGURE 6.29b MC68020 interfaces to byte, word, or long-word devices.

Figure 6.29b shows a MC68020 system block diagram.

In Figure 6.29b the MC68020 always reads data from or writes data to the 8-bit device containing both odd and even addresses via D31-D24. For a 16-bit device, the MC68020 communicates via D31-D24 pins for even addresses and D23-D16 for odd addresses. Therefore, the 8-bit data lines of the even memory byte chip must be connected to D31-D24 pins; the 8-bit data lines of the odd memory byte chip must be connected to D23-D16 pins. For long-word transfer, four 2716s are required, each containing a byte, OP0 through OP3. OP0 is transferred via D31-D24, OP1 via D23-D16, OP2 via D15-D8, and OP3 via D0-D7 pins of the MC68020.

The autovector and nonautovector features of the MC68020 interrupts are illustrated in Figures 6.30a and b. Note that in Figure 6.30b $A19A18A17A16 = 1111_2$ means interrupt acknowledge. A3A2A1 has interrupt level 001 (inverted $\overline{\text{IPLs}}$).

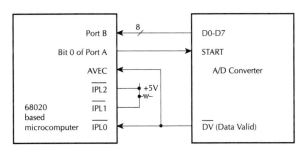

FIGURE 6.30a MC68020-A/D interface using autovector 1.

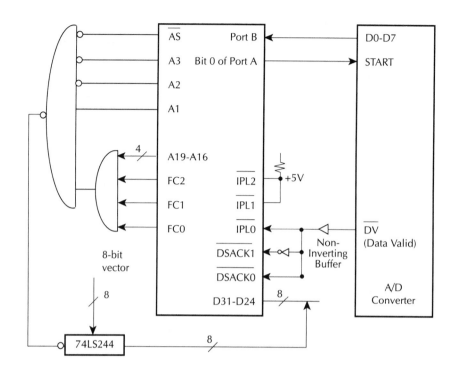

FIGURE 6.30b MC68020-A/D interface using nonautovector.

6.12 MC68020 SYSTEM DESIGN

The following MC68020 system design will use a 128-KB, 32-bit wide memory and 8-bit parallel I/O port. The memory system is partitioned into four unique address space encodings: user data, user program, supervisor data, and supervisor program. This design uses RAMs for memory accesses and EPROMs for program memory accesses. Each address has 32 KB of memory available for use. Data I/O port space is appended to both user and supervisor data spaces (see MEMORY MAP); this is done by decoding the user/supervisor data space and address line A15 signal states.

The 32-bit-wide system memory consists of 4-byte-wide memories, each connected to its associated portion of the system data bus (D24-D31, D16-D23, D8-D15, and D0-D7). To manipulate this memory configuration, 32-bit data bus control byte enable logic is incorporated to generate byte strobes (DBBEE44, DBBEE33, DBBEE22, and DBBEE11) (Table 6.21).

TABLE 6.21
Control Byte Enable State Table for 32-Bit Device

SIZ1	SIZ0	A1	A0	DBBE11	DBBE22	DBBE33	DBBE44
0	1	0	0	1	0	0	0
		0	1	0	1	0	0
		1	0	0	0	1	0
		1	1	0	0	0	1
1	0	0	0	1	1	0	0
		0	1	0	1	1	0
		1	0	0	0	1	1
		1	1	0	0	0	1
1	1	0	0	1	1	1	0
		0	1	0	0	1	1
		1	0	0	0	1	1
		1	1	0	0	0	1
0	0	0	0	1	1	1	1
		0	1	0	1	1	1
		1	0	0	0	1	1
		1	1	0	0	0	1

Hardware Design
68020 System with128K × 32-Bit Memory and 8-Bit I/O Port

MEMORY
—   —
MAP

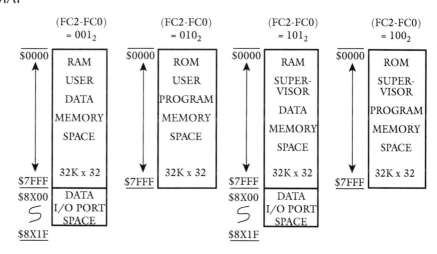

The byte strobe state table shows the necessary individual byte strobe states as dictated by the MC68020's size (SIZ1, SIZ0) and address offset (A2, A0) encodings.

Karnaugh Maps (Table 6.22) for each data strobe signal have been created to identify the logic required to implement its state table requirement. The logic created for each data strobe is then combined into a complete 32-bit control logic schematic and connected to the memory structure as shown in the system hardware schematic diagram (Figure 6.31).

The system hardware design also identifies the required interconnections between the MC68020 MPU, the 74LS138 address space decoder, the CY7C198 user/supervisor data RAMs, the NM27C256 user/supervisor program EPROMs, the 32-bit port control logic, and the MC68230 parallel I/O interface.

Since each memory is 32 KB × 8, only address lines A0-A14 are connected. The 74LS138 selects memory banks to enable, as dictated by the decoder FC2-FC0 signals. Control logic-generated data strobes (DBBE4-DBBE1) select which byte-wide portion of the data bus to activate. The 8-bit parallel I/O interface (MC68230) provides three bidirectional 8-bit ports as well as asynchronous handshake signals necessary for communication protocols.

TABLE 6.22
K Maps for Strobe Signals for 32-Bit Devices

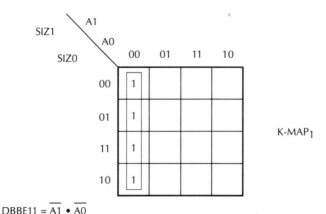

$$DBBE11 = \overline{A1} \cdot \overline{A0}$$

TABLE 6.22 (continued)
K Maps for Strobe Signals for 32-Bit Devices

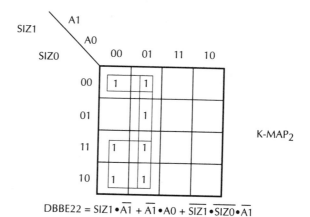

K-MAP$_2$

$$DBBE22 = SIZ1 \bullet \overline{A1} + \overline{A1} \bullet A0 + \overline{SIZ1} \bullet \overline{SIZ0} \bullet \overline{A1}$$

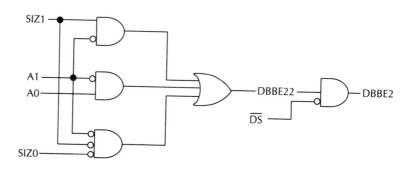

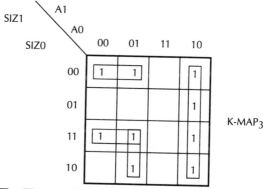

K-MAP$_3$

$$DBBE33 = \overline{A1} \bullet \overline{A0} + SIZ1 \bullet \overline{A1} \bullet A0 + SIZ1 \bullet SIZ0 \bullet \overline{A1} + \overline{SIZ1} \bullet \overline{SIZ0} \bullet \overline{A1}$$

TABLE 6.22 (continued)
K Maps for Strobe Signals for 32-Bit Devices

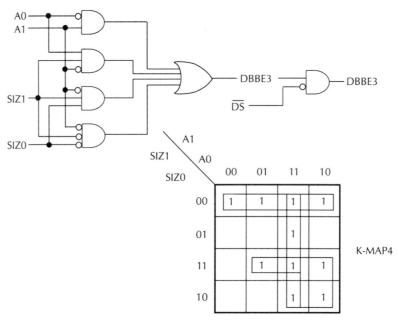

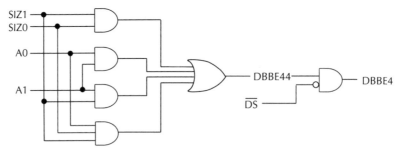

$DBBE44 = SIZ1 \bullet SIZ0 + A1 \bullet A0 + SIZ1 \bullet A1 + SIZ1 \bullet SIZ0 \bullet A0$

TABLE 6.22 (continued)
K Maps for Strobe Signals for 32-Bit Devices

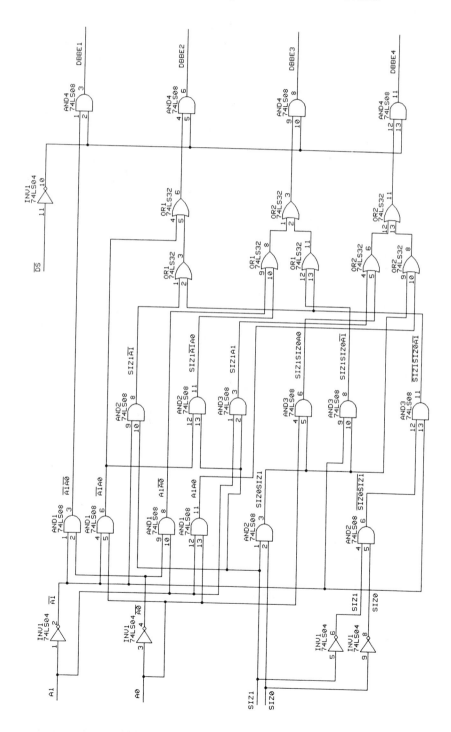

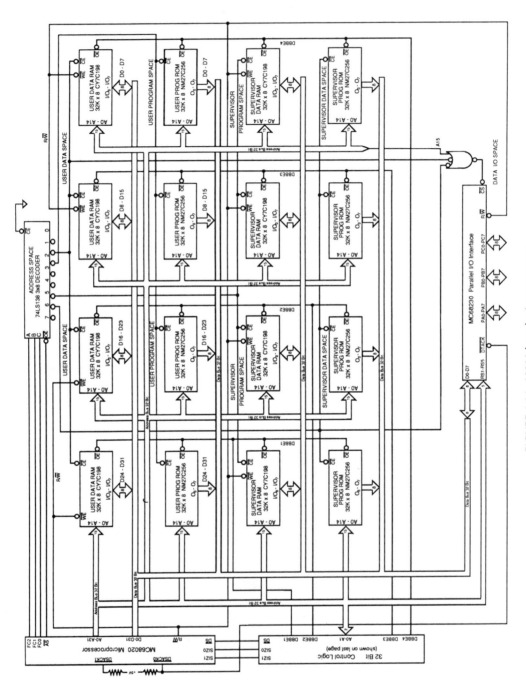

FIGURE 6.31 68020-based microcomputer.

QUESTIONS AND PROBLEMS

6.1 Find the contents of 68020 registers that are affected and the condition codes after execution of

- i) **ADD.B D2, D3**
- ii) **ADD.W D5, D6**
- iii) **ADDA.L A2, A4**

Assume the following data prior to execution of each of the above instructions:

$$
\begin{aligned}
[D2] &= \$01F462F1 \\
[D3] &= \$01001110 \\
[D5] &= \$00008210 \\
[D6] &= \$00001010 \\
[A2] &= \$71240010 \\
[A4] &= \$21040100
\end{aligned}
$$

6.2 i) How many ALUs does the 68020 have? Comment on the purpose of each.
  ii) What is the purpose of the 68020 32-bit barrel shifter?

6.3 a) Summarize the basic differences between the 68000 and 68020.
  b) Discuss the differences between 68000 and 68020 debug capabilities implemented in their status registers. Will the instructions listed below cause trace or change of flow:

- i) **MOVE SR, D5**
- ii) **TRAPEQ START**

when Z = 1?

6.4 Determine the number of bus cycles, bytes written to memory (in Hex), and signal levels of A1, A0, SIZ1, and SIZ0 pins that would occur when the following 68020 instruction

```
MOVE.W D2, (A5) with
[D2] = $20161462 and
[A5] = $10057012
```

is executed by the 68020. Assume:

    i)   16-bit memory
   ii)   8-bit memory

6.5 Show the contents of the affected 68020 registers and memory locations after execution of the instruction:

```
MOVE.W ($100, A5, D3.W *4), D1
```

Assume the following register and memory contents prior to execution of the above instruction:

```
[A5] = $0000F210
[D3] = $00001002
[D1] = $F125012A
[$00013318] = $4567
[$0001331A] = $2345
```

6.6 Show the contents of the affected 68020 registers and memory locations after execution of the instruction:

```
MOVE·B ([$102, A2, D0.W * 2],$206), D1
```

Assume the following register and memory contents prior to execution of the instructions:

```
[A2] = $0000 0100
[D0] = $0000 0020
[D1] = $0000 0300
```

	Memory
$0000 0240	1567 0200
	0300 1500

$0200 0500	1756 1020
	2050 1F21
	1072 F217

6.7 A subroutine in the supervisor mode is required to read a parameter from the stack configuration given below:

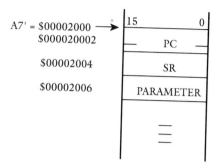

Write a 68000 instruction sequence to read the parameter into D5 and then write the equivalent 68020 instruction. Assume that the A7′ and the offset of the parameter (6) are known.

6.8 The 68000 instruction sequence below searches a table of 10_{10} 32-bit elements for a match. The address register A5 points to element 0, D3 contains the length (10_{10}) to be searched, and D2 contains the number to be matched. Find the 68020 single instruction which can replace lines 3, 4, and 5.

```
Line
1                        MOVE.B  #10, D3
2                        SUBQ.B  #1, D3
3           START        MOVE D3, D5
4                        ASL.L  #2, D5
5                        CMP.L  0(A5, D5.L), D2
6                        DBEQ D3, START
                           -
                           -
                           -
```

6.9 Find the contents of D1, D2, A4, CCR and the memory locations after execution of the following 68020 instructions:

```
i)    BFEXTS $5000 {8:16}, D4
ii)   BFINS D2, (A4) {D1:4}
iii)  BFSET $5000 {D1:10}
```

Assume the following data prior to execution of each of the above instructions:

[D1] = $0000 0004   [D4] = $0000 3000
[D2] = $1234 5678   [A4] = $0000 5000

Memory

	7							0
-16	0	1	1	0	1	1	1	1
-8	1	1	1	0	1	1	1	1
$5000 →	0	0	1	0	1	0	0	1
+8	0	1	0	1	1	1	0	0
+16	1	0	1	0	1	0	1	1

6.10   Find the 68020 condition codes after execution of CMP2.W (A2), D7. Determine the range of valid values. Indicate whether the comparison is signed or unsigned. Also, indicate the register values along with upper and lower bounds on the following:

lower bound   upper bound

Assume the following data prior to execution of CMP2:

[D7] = $F271 1020

Memory

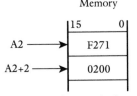

6.11 Find the 68020 condition codes and also determine if an exception occurs due to execution of

CHK2.W $5002, A1

Assume the following data prior to execution of CHK2:

$$[A1] = \$0000 \ F200$$

Memory

|15   0|

$5002 ⟶ F000

$5004 ⟶ FFFF

6.12 Fill in the missing hex values for the following 68020 instructions:

Address	Instruction	Label	Mnemonic
$0200 0200	$60 — —	START 0	BRA.B START2
.	.	.	
.	.	.	
.	.	.	
$0200 0206	$60 — —	START 1	BRA.W START0
.	— —	.	
.	.	.	
.	.	—	
$0200 020F	.	START 2	.
.			.
.			.

6.13 Identify the following 68020 instructions as valid or invalid. Comment if an instruction is valid.

    i)   **BFSET (A0) {-2:5}, D7**
    ii) **DIVS D5,D5**
    iii) **CHK.B D2, (A1)**

6.14 Determine the values of Z and C flags after execution of each of the following 68020 instructions:

    i)   **CHK2.W (A5), D3**
    ii) **CMP2.L $2001, A5**

Assume the following data prior to execution of each of the instructions:

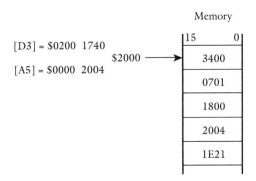

6.15 Write a 68020 assembly language program to compute

$$Y = \sum_{i=1}^{20} X_i^2 / N$$

Assume Xi's to be unsigned 32-bit numbers and the array starts at $0000 2000.

6.16 Write a 68020 assembly language program to translate 10 packed BCD digits to their ASCII equivalent. Assume that the BCD digits are stored at an address starting at $5000 and above. Store the ASCII digits starting at $6000.

6.17 What are the minimum times for a read bus cycle and a write bus cycle for a 16.67-MHz 68020?

6.18 What are the functions of 68020 VBR, CACR, and CAAR?

6.19 Determine the contents of FC2, FC1, FC0, SR, MSP, ISP, PC, A31-A0, D31-D0, SIZ1, SIZ0, and R/$\overline{W}$ pins of the 68020 upon hardware reset for the first 3 bus cycles. Assume the following memory contents prior to reset:

Memory

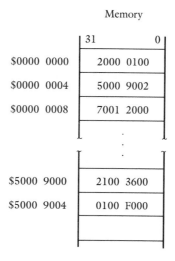

	31 0
$0000 0000	2000 0100
$0000 0004	5000 9002
$0000 0008	7001 2000
	.
	.
	.
$5000 9000	2100 3600
$5000 9004	0100 F000

6.20 For a 25-MHz 68020

    i)   Determine the length of time address has been valid during assertion of $\overline{AS}$ for a read bus cycle. Assume no wait states.

    ii)   Determine the length of time the data have been valid when $\overline{DS}$ asserts during a write bus cycle. Assume no states.

6.21   i)   What happens to the 68020 when $\overline{BERR}$ and $\overline{HALT}$ pins are asserted together?

    ii)   Identify which of the following 68020 instructions cause the $\overline{RMC}$ signal to be asserted: CAS2, TAS, CHK2, CALLM.

    iii) Which signals cause $\overline{RMC}$ to be asserted?

    iv) What happens when 68020 $\overline{IPEND}$ is asserted?

6.22   i)   Which exceptions of the 68020 are not available on the 68000?

    ii)   What is a throwaway stack frame? When is it created?

    iii) List two 68020 instructions which may cause a format error exception.

    iv) How would the 68020 get out of a double bus fault?

6.23 Draw a neat schematic to interface a 4K EPROM, 4K RAM, and 2 I/O ports. Use 2716, 6116, and 68230 to a 68020. Determine memory and I/O maps.

6.24 For a 16-bit device, use K-maps to show the following relationship for the 68020:

$$DBBE1 = \overline{A0} \cdot DS$$
$$DBBE2 = DS \, (\overline{SIZ0} + SIZ1 + A0)$$

Chapter 7

MC68020 — ADVANCED TOPICS

This chapter describes the advanced topics associated with the Motorola MC68020. Topics include the 68020 advanced instructions (such as CAS/CAS2 and CALLM/RTM instructions), cache memory, and coprocessors.

7.1 68020 ADVANCED INSTRUCTIONS

This section provides a detailed description of the 68020 advanced instructions including BKPT, CAS/CAS2, TAS, CALLM/RTM, and coprocessor instructions.

7.1.1 BREAKPOINT INSTRUCTION

A breakpoint is a debugging tool that allows the programmer to check or pass over an entire section of a program. Execution of a breakpoint usually results in exception processing. Hence, the programmer can use any of the TRAP vectors as breakpoints. Also, any of the seven interrupt levels can be used by external hardware to cause a breakpoint.

Included with the MC68020 is the breakpoint instruction (BKPT), used to support the program breakpoint function for debug monitors and real-time hardware in-circuit emulators. Real-time hardware emulators require acknowledgment of breakpoint occurrences to transfer control (i.e., trigger map switching logic) from a task to a monitor. External system hardware must be present if the breakpoint function is to be employed. The breakpoint instruction uses a special breakpoint acknowledgment bus cycle to notify external hardware that an illegal instruction (i.e., breakpoint) has been encountered. This breakpoint hardware has been included in Motorola's Paged Memory Management Unit, MC68851. The notation for the breakpoint instruction is BKPT # data. The immediate data ranges from 0 to 7 indicate eight separate breakpoint op codes, \$4848 through \$484F. These breakpoint op codes are contained in the dynamically relocatable Vector Base Register (VBR).

Upon detecting one of the breakpoint op codes, the processor informs the external hardware of its occurrence by issuing a breakpoint bus cycle to access (CPU) space #0. The breakpoint instruction format of Figure 7.1 shows how CPU space 0 is encoded during a breakpoint instruction. The three-bit breakpoint identifier on address lines A2, A3, and A4 differentiates between the eight possible breakpoints permitted.

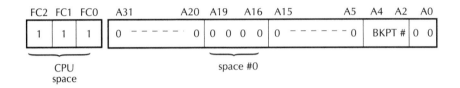

FIGURE 7.1 BKPT instruction format.

When a BKPT instruction is executed, the MC68020 reads an op word from the CPU space address corresponding to the breakpoint number. If the external hardware terminates the read cycle by asserting the $\overline{\text{DSACKX}}$ signals, then the processor replaces the breakpoint instruction in its internal pipeline with the instruction present on data bus and begins execution with that instruction. No exception processing occurs when the op code is returned along with the appropriate $\overline{\text{DSACKX}}$ signals. The data read from CPU space are the 16-bit op code that was displaced to make room in program memory for the breakpoint instruction. If the breakpoint acknowledge cycle is terminated by the $\overline{\text{BERR}}$ input control signal, then the processor performs exception processing for an illegal instruction by trapping through the illegal instruction vector contained in the vector base table. Execution of the breakpoint instruction does not affect the Condition Code Register (CCR).

The breakpoint instruction flowchart is shown in Figure 7.2.

In contrast to the TRAP or interrupt, the MC68020's BKPT instruction allows external hardware to supply a 16-bit instruction op code to be executed in place of taking the illegal instruction TRAP. This means that the processor can execute BKPT a fixed number of times, substituting the replacement op code each time through a loop until the count expires and the breakpoint halts the loop.

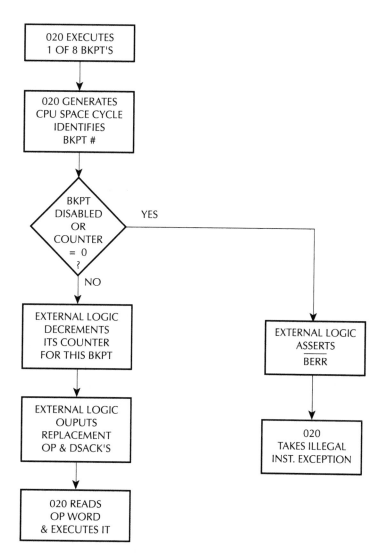

FIGURE 7.2 Breakpoint instruction flowchart.

Example 7.1
Explain the breakpoint operation shown in Figure 7.3.

Solution

In Step 1 the illegal instruction BKPT is inserted into the program flow by external hardware as requested by a user. In this example, the 16-bit op code for ADD.L D2, D3 is replaced with the 16-bit op code for BKPT #4.

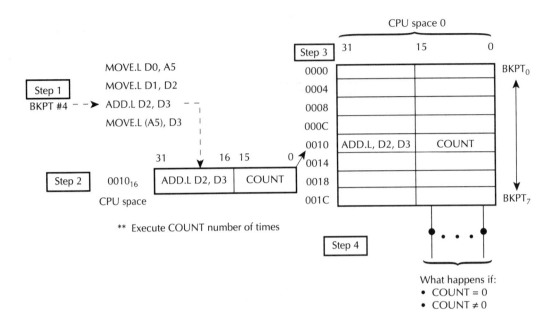

FIGURE 7.3 Executing a BKPT instruction.

In Step 2, the op code ADD.L D2, D3 is stored by the MC68020 in the CPU space long-word memory location corresponding to breakpoint number four, address $10.

Step 3 shows how long-word memory locations $00 to $1C in CPU space 0 are used to temporarily store the op codes replaced by breakpoint instructions 0 through 7. The displaced op code is stored in the upper 16 bits, and an optional count value can be loaded into the lower 16 bits through external hardware control.

In Step 4, each time BKPT #4 is executed, the MC68020 accesses CPU space 0 location $10. If the count value (bits 0-15) is not zero, the replaced op code is placed on the data bus (bits 16-31), the counter is decremented by one, and the appropriate $\overline{\text{DSACKX}}$ lines are asserted by the external hardware. The MC68020 reads this op word and executes it. If the count value is zero, the 68020 $\overline{\text{BERR}}$ pin can be asserted by external hardware to take exception.

The breakpoint function is summarized in Table 7.1. A hardware implementation to take advantage of the BKPT instruction's looping feature is shown in Figure 7.4. A debug monitor maintains a small amount of breakpoint memory. It is used to hold up to eight replacement op codes and eight counters. When a user wants a breakpoint to be encountered

TABLE 7.1
Function of the Breakpoint

Instruction	Operand size	Operation	Notation
BKPT	None	If breakpoint cycle acknowledged then execute returned op word, else trap as illegal instruction	BKPT # data

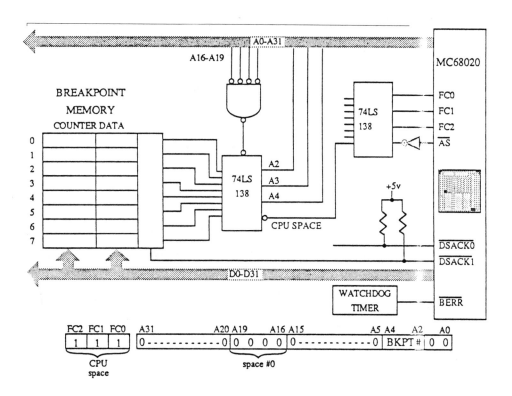

FIGURE 7.4 Breakpoint block diagram.

after say "10" passes of the op code, the debugger initiates a breakpoint counter to 10, replaces the user op code with a breakpoint instruction, saves the user op code in the breakpoint data memory, and executes the user's program. When the breakpoint op code is encountered, the MC68020 generates the breakpoint acknowledge bus cycle. The 74LS138 3-to-8 decoder shown on the right decodes the function codes as all ones (as validated by the $\overline{AS}$ signal) and asserts its bottom output indicating a CPU bus space cycle. This output enables one of the inputs of the 74LS138 shown on the left. The top enable output is enabled when address lines A 16 through A 19 are all zero, indicating a type 0 CPU space cycle. This decoder enables one of eight breakpoint counters.

If the counter $\neq 0$, then it is decremented by the external hardware and the replacement op code is returned on the data bus to the MC68020 with $\overline{DSACK1}$ asserted. In this case, we started with a count of 10, so it is decremented to 9. When the breakpoint acknowledge cycle occurs on the 11th pass, the counter = 0 and this time bus error $\overline{BERR}$ signal is asserted by the external hardware. This forces illegal instruction processing and subsequent servicing of the breakpoint. With this type of hardware, operating system support is not required until the count has been exhausted. This reduces the operating system overhead significantly. The MC68020 breakpoint instruction flow diagram is shown in Figure 7.5.

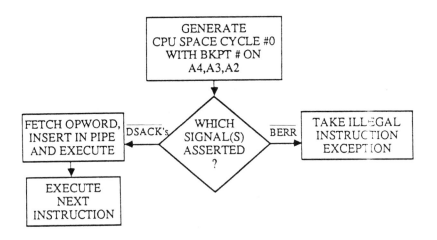

FIGURE 7.5 Breakpoint instruction flowchart.

7.1.2 CALL MODULE/RETURN FROM MODULE INSTRUCTIONS

For large programs, flowcharting does not provide an efficient software design tool. The flowcharts, however, can assist the programmer in dividing a large program into subprograms called modules (typically 20 to 50 lines). The task of dividing a large program into modules is called modular programming. Typical problems of modular programming include how to modularize a large program and then how to combine the individual modules.

One of the advantages of modular programming includes ease in writing, debugging, and testing a module rather than a large program.

One of the disadvantages of modular programming is the difficulty in modularizing a program efficiently. Some guidelines for modularizations include limiting the amount of information shared by modules and controlling the access of one module to another.

As an example of modular programming, consider that a line printer and a keyboard are to be interfaced to a microcomputer. The entire task can be divided into four sections:

- Printing module
- Data reception module
- Keyboard module
- Data transmission module

Modular programming is supported by the MC68020 call module (CALLM) and the return from module (RTM) instructions.

The CLLLM instruction creates a module stack frame on the stack (similar to an interrupt), stores the module state in that frame, and points to the address of a module descriptor (in the effective address) which contains control information for the entry into the called module.

The CALLM instruction loads the processor with the data provided by the module descriptor. Thus the CALLM instruction does not directly access the program module. Rather, it indirectly calls the routine via the module descriptor whose contents are maintained by the operating system. The module descriptor can be thought of as a gateway through which the calling program must gain access. The module being called can be thought of as a subroutine that is to act upon the arguments passed to it.

The MC68020 concept of a module is different from a subroutine in the following ways. Stack parameter passing and argument removal are handled automatically. The operating system can dynamically define the starting address of the called module, and the called module can be granted access rights that could be at a higher privilege level than those of the program calling the module. Access rights define what portions of memory can be accessed. Since all MC68020 I/O devices are memory-mapped, access to specific areas of memory are required to perform I/O functions. In the MC68020, access rights are tied to the concept of address spaces, where the function codes (FC2-FC0) define one of eight memory space access levels. The module instructions support a hierarchical resource protection mechanism which allows external hardware to implement up to 256 privileged access levels. This is accomplished through the use of an 8-bit access level number contained in each module descriptor.

When a module is called, a request can be made to change the current access level. The external hardware could be designed to interpret this access level field for level checking or level modification purposes. During execution of the module instructions, the processor can generate CPU space 1 bus cycles (i.e., FC2FC1 FC0 = 001 and A19 – A16 = 0001), called access level control cycles to which the external hardware responds. Motorola's Paged Memory Management Unit (PMMU) has this hardware built in.

The CALLM instruction syntax is

$$\texttt{CALLM \# data,   (EA)}$$

To use this instruction, an immediate data value (data 0-255) must be specified to indicate the number of bytes of argument parameters to be passed to the called module. The effective address (EA) that points to the external module descriptor must also be included. The program containing the CALLM instruction must define a RAM storage area for the module descriptor to reside in. The address of the module descriptor is known to the operating system at "run time". It is the operating system that loads the starting address of the library routine to be called into the module descriptor.

The return from module (RTM) instruction is the complement of the CALLM instruction. The RTM syntax is RTM Rn.

Register Rn (address or data) represents the module data area pointer. The RTM instruction recovers the previous module state from the stack frame and returns program execution in the calling module. The processor state (program counter, status word) comes from the previously stacked data. The operation of the module instructions is shown in Table 7.2.

TABLE 7.2
CALLM and RTM Instructions

Instruction	Operand size	Operation	Notation
CALLM	None	Save current module state on stack; load new module state from destination	CALLM data, (EA)
RTM	None	Reload saved module state in stack frame; place module data area pointer in Rn	RTM Rn

Figure 7.6 shows an overview of the CALLM and RTM operation. When the CALLM instruction executes, it creates a module call stack frame and saves the module state in that frame.

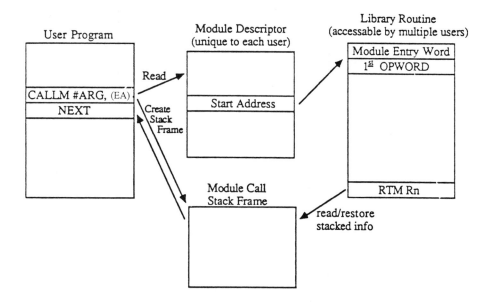

FIGURE 7.6 Overview of the CALLM and RTM operation.

It then loads the new module state from the module descriptor. The start address fetched from the module descriptor points to the module entry word of the library routine. The second word of the routine is its first op word. The last instruction of the routine is the RTM instruction.

The RTM instruction reloads the saved module state in the created stack frame, and user program execution continues with the next instruction.

During the execution of the module instructions, three components are utilized: the module descriptor, the module stack frame, and the called module. The location of the module descriptor is determined by the programmer through a descriptor declaration which ultimately must be known to the Operating System (OS). It is the operating system that maintains the contents of the module descriptor. The module descriptor format and its relation to the called module is shown in Figure 7.7.

The CALLM instruction interprets the module descriptor's information to determine: how the arguments are to be passed, the type of

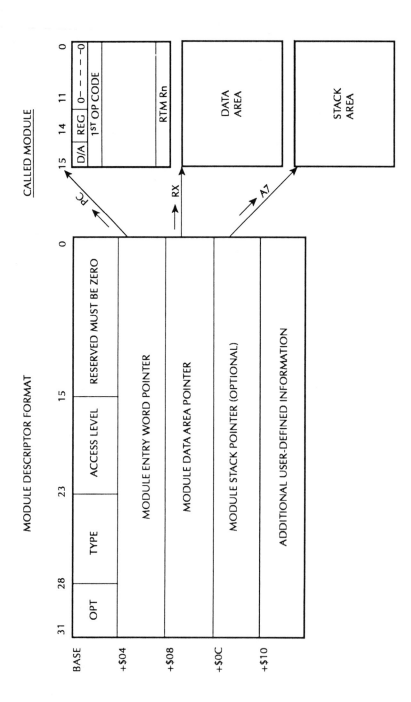

FIGURE 7.7 Module descriptor format.

descriptor, whether access level changes will be made, and the location of the called module, data area, and optional stack area. The first long word of the descriptor contains control information used during the execution of the CALLM instruction. The remaining locations contain the descriptor pointers which may be loaded into three processor registers by the CALLM instruction after first being pushed to the stack frame. The descriptor OPT field specifies how arguments are to be passed to the called module and is summarized below:

Options

000_2 The called module expects to find arguments from the calling module on the stack stack just below the module stack frame; for stack pointer changes, the MC68020 copies the arguments from old to new stack

100_2 Called module accesses arguments through an indirect pointer on the stack of the calling module; the MC68020 puts the calling module stack pointer value in the module stack frame; hence, the arguments are not copied

All other options cause a format exception. The descriptor type field specifies the type of descriptor and is summarized below:

Type	Type of descriptor
$00 (low 6 bits)	No change in module access rights or stack pointer; the called module builds its stack frame on the top of the stack used by the calling module
$01 (low 6 bits)	Possible change in module access rights, or stack pointer; the called module is allowed to have a stack area independent of the caller's stack area; if the stack changes, arguments may be copied automatically

All other types cause a format exception. The CALLM instruction flow diagrams for type 0 and type 1 formats are shown in Figure 7.8.

The descriptor's access level field (used only for type 01 descriptors) is passed to external hardware to change or monitor access control. The descriptor's module entry word pointer specifies the entry address of the called module. The first word at the entry address of the called module shown in Figure 7.9 specifies which data or address register is to be saved in the module stack frame, and subsequently loaded with the module

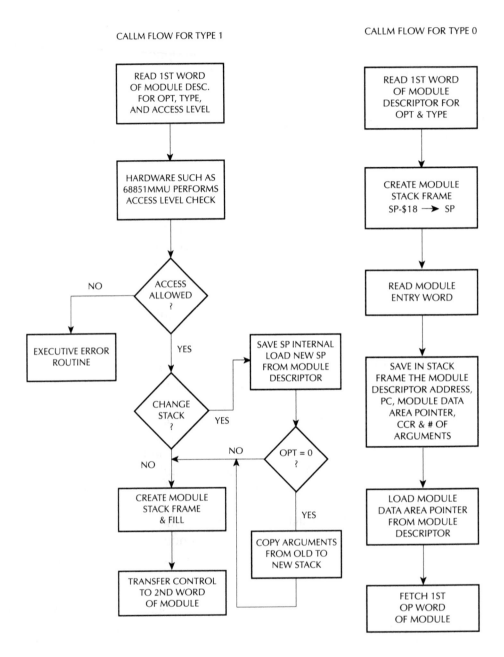

FIGURE 7.8 CALLM types 0 and 1 instruction flow diagram.

descriptor data area pointer by the CALLM instructions. D/A = 0 indicates Dn, while D/A = 1 indicates An.

15	14	13	12	11	10	9	8	7	6	5	4	3	2	1	0
D/A	REGISTER			0	0	0	0	0	0	0	0	0	0	0	0
OPERATION WORD OF FIRST INSTRUCTION															

FIGURE 7.9 Module entry word.

Thus, the CALLM instruction reads this word to determine which register is to be used as the data area pointer. The descriptor's module data area pointer field contains the address of the called module data area. The second word of the called module is the module routine's first op word. The last instruction of the called module is the RTM Rn instruction. The RTM Rn instruction loads the register specified (Rn) with the saved stack module data area pointer value and restores the program counter and optionally the stack pointer. The Rn register is usually chosen to match the register specified by the module entry word. The RTM instruction also reads the argument byte count and increments the stack pointer by the number of arguments specified in the CALLM instructions, which remove the argument from the stack.

The module stack frame is shown in Figure 7.10.

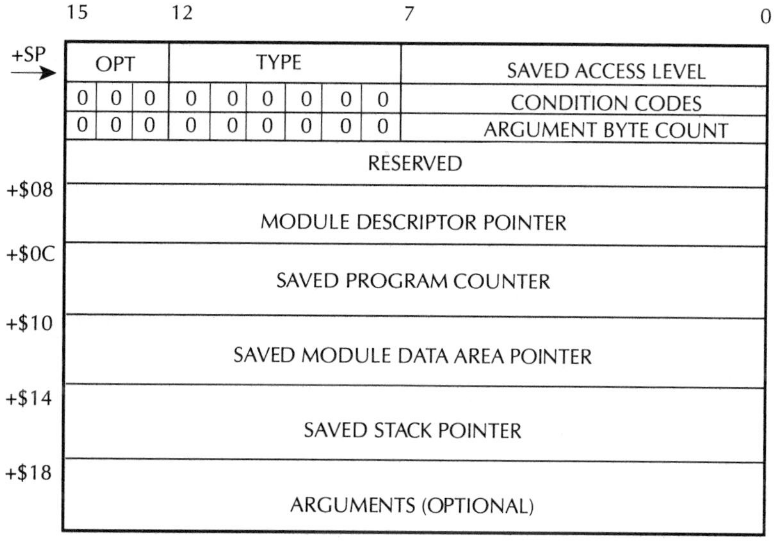

FIGURE 7.10 Module call stack frame.

This stack frame is constructed by the CALLM instruction and is removed by the RTM instruction. The first two long words contain information passed by the CALLM instruction to the RTM instruction. The contents of the Condition Code Register (CCR), as well as the OPT and type fields, are copied and saved by the CALLM instruction and removed by the RTM instruction. The access level contains control information saved from external hardware during CALLM instruction execution. The argument count field is set by the CALLM instruction and is used to remove arguments from the stack of the calling module by the RTM instruction. The module descriptor pointer contains the address of the descriptor used during the module call. The program counter is the saved address of the instruction following the CALLM instruction. The remaining locations (saved module data area pointer, saved stack pointer, optional argument) contain information to be restored on return to the calling module.

Type 01 module descriptors indicate a possible request to change access levels. While processing a type 01 descriptor, the module instructions communicate with external access control hardware (like an MMU) via accesses in CPU space. Figure 7.11 shows the MMU Access Level Control (ALC) bus registers used as an address map for CPU space accesses.

	31	23	0
$08	CAL	(UNUSED, RESERVED)	
$04	STATUS	(UNUSED, RESERVED)	
$O6	IAL	(UNUSED, RESERVED)	
$OC	DAL	(UNUSED, RESERVED)	

$40   FUNCTION CODE 0 DESCRIPTOR ADDRESS
$44   FUNCTION CODE 1 DESCRIPTOR ADDRESS (USER DATA)
$46   FUNCTION CODE 2 DESCRIPTOR ADDRESS (USER PROGRAM)
$4C   FUNCTION CODE 3 DESCRIPTOR ADDRESS
$80   FUNCTION CODE 4 DESCRIPTOR ADDRESS (SUPERVISOR DATA)
$84   FUNCTION CODE 5 DESCRIPTOR ADDRESS (SUPERVISOR PROGRAM)
$88   FUNCTION CODE 6 DESCRIPTOR ADDRESS
$8C   FUNCTION CODE 7 DESCRIPTOR ADDRESS (CPU SPACE)

FUNCTION CODES 2 - 0 1 1 1		ADDRESS BUS		
	000000000000	0001	000000000	MMU REG
	A31	A19 A16		A6 ... A0
CPU SPACE CYCLE		ACCESS LEVEL CONTROL		ADDRESS OF MMU REG

FIGURE 7.11 Access level control bus registers.

The Current Access Level Register (CAL) specifies the access level rights of the currently executing module. The increase access register (IAL) and the decrease access register (DAL) are the registers through which the MC68020 requests increased or decreased access rights, respectively.

The access status register ("STATUS") in the MMU allows the MC68020 to consult external hardware (68851 MMU) as to the legitimacy of intended access level transitions. Table 7.3 gives the valid code values of the access status register.

TABLE 7.3
Access Status Register Codes

Value	Validity	Processor action
00	Invalid	Format error
01	Valid	No change in access rights
02—03	Valid	Change access rights with no change of stack pointer
04—07	Valid	Change access rights and change stack pointer
Other	Undefined	Undefined — take format error exception

Example 7.2

Write an MC68020 instruction sequence to illustrate the use of CALLM and RTM instructions.

Solution

```
                        CALLM — RTM
CALL
PEA (EA)                SAVE 1ST PARAMETER TO STACK
PEA (EA)                SAVE 2ND PARAMETER TO STACK
CALLM #8, (A0)          8 = # OF BYTES JUST LOADED ON
                        STACK AS MODULE ARGUMENTS

MODULE ENTRY
MOVE.L $18(SP),A1       POP 2ND PARAMETER → A1 (see
                        Figure 7.7)
MOVE.L $1C(SP),A2       POP 1ST PARAMETER → A2
    .
    .
    .
RTM                     RETURN AND DEALLOCATE
                        PARAMETERS ON STACK
```

7.1.3 COMPARE, SWAP, AND CAS INSTRUCTIONS

The MC68020 compare and swap (CAS and CAS2) instructions provide support for multitasking and multiprocessing. The compare and swap instructions are used when several processors must communicate through a common block of memory, when globally shared data structures (such as counters, stack pointers, or queue pointers) must be securely updated, or when multiple bus cycles may be required. A typical application is a counting semaphore (shared incrementer). Another application of the compare and swap instructions would be to manipulate pointers for system stacks and queues that use linked lists when a new item (element) is inserted or an existing element is deleted.

When data structures are manipulated in a multiprocessor environment and a processor updates elements, the data structure can be corrupted by another processor between the time an element is obtained for update and the time the element is written back to memory. To ensure the integrity of an update operation, the CAS and CAS2 instructions check the original value of each element before it is updated, to make sure that it matches the values that were originally fetched. If the values match, elements in the data structure are updated. If not (that is, if another processor changed the value of the element since the value was fetched), the CAS and CAS2 compare registers receive the new values instead of updating them. The new values are then used to repeat the compare and swap process until the update operation is successful.

The CAS instruction uses two registers (Dc and Du) and the address (EA) of the globally shared operand variable (or pointer) to be protected. CAS operates on byte, word, and long word operands. The assembly level programming notation for the CAS instruction is

$$\texttt{CAS.S (.B or .W or .L)Dc, Du, (EA)}$$

The CAS instruction first compares the old "fetched" starting pointer in register (Dc) with the present starting pointer in the variable's original location (EA) to see if another task accessed the variable pointer and changed it while the first task was using it; if the two compared pointer values Dc and (EA) are equal (that is, pointer contents (EA) remain unchanged by interrupting tasks), then CAS passes the updated pointer value (located in Du) to the destination operand (EA) and sets the equal condition code flag in the CCR to $Z = 1$.

If the two compared values are not equal (the (EA) pointer has been changed by an interrupting task), then CAS copies the new changed pointer value contents of (EA) to register (Dc) and clears the equal condition code flag in the CCR to $Z = 0$.

A condensed version of the CAS operation is shown below:

```
CAS Dc, Du,  (EA)
     1.    (EA)  - Dc  →  cc
     2.    IF (EA)  = Dc
           THEN Du  →  <ea>
           ELSE (EA)  →  Dc
```

Next, application of the CAS for queue insertion will be discussed.

Figure 7.12a shows how to insert a new entry in a queue using the MOVE instruction.

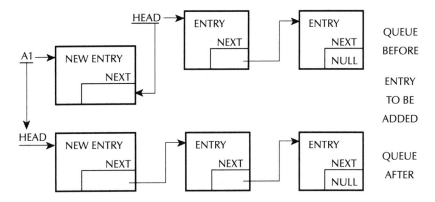

FIGURE 7.12a Inserting a new entry in queue (single user/single task).

In a single user/single task environment the above can be accomplished by the following instruction sequence:

```
MOVE.L HEAD,  (NEXT, A1)
MOVE.L A1,  HEAD
```

But in a multiuser/multitask environment, the above instruction sequence may not accomplish the task. For example, more than one user may attempt to insert a new entry in an existing queue. Suppose that after user 1 executes MOVE.L HEAD, (NEXT, A1), user 2 executes the instruction sequence

```
MOVE.L HEAD,  (NEXT, A1)
MOVE.L A1,  HEAD
```

and inserts user 2 new entry in the existing queue before user 1 gets to

MOVE.L A1, HEAD. This situation is depicted in Figures 7.12b and
7.12c. This situation can be avoided by using the CAS instruction. User 2
entry gets lost if the MOVE instruction is used for insertion. In Figure
7.12c, the HEAD (known to user 1 at the start) gets changed between the
time user 1 established the forward link and the time user 1 updated
HEAD.

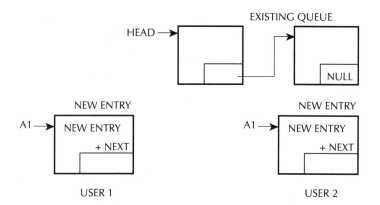

FIGURE 7.12b Two users attempting to insert a new entry into an existing queue.

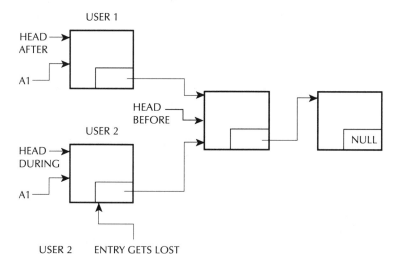

FIGURE 7.12c Insertion of entries into an existing queue in a multiuser environment using MOVE
(situation to avoid).

The following instruction sequence uses CAS to insert a new entry in
a queue in a multiuser/multitask environment:

```
        MOVE.L      HEAD, D0      Capture current HEAD
        MOVE.L      A1, D1        Need value in Du for
                                  CAS
LOOP  MOVE.L  D0, (NEXT, A1)      Establish forward link
        CAS.L   D0, D1, HEAD      If HEAD unchanged,
                                  update
        BNE     LOOP              You have new HEAD in
                                  D0, try again
```

Figures 7.12d and 7.12e illustrate the use of CAS in the above instruction sequence, respectively, in a system with no intervention and simultaneous insertion by multiusers.

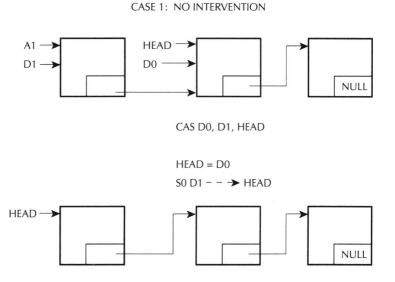

FIGURE 7.12d Inserting an element in a queue using CAS without intervention.

The CAS instruction cannot be interrupted. This ensures secure updates of variables in a multiprocessing system. Executing CAS causes the read-write-modify ($\overline{\text{RMC}}$) signal to be asserted, which locks the bus. Other bus masters in the system must wait for $\overline{\text{RMC}}$ to be deasserted before they can take control of the bus. The CAS instructions read, compare, and store operations are performed while the bus is locked. This prevents other processors from interfering with the instruction while it performs its compare and swap operation.

To illustrate the read-modify-write operation invoked during execution

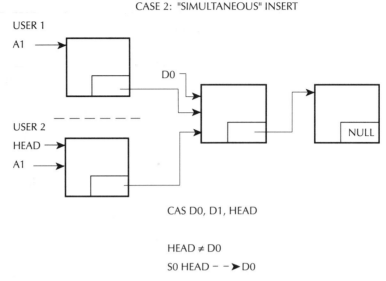

CASE 2: "SIMULTANEOUS" INSERT

CAS D0, D1, HEAD

HEAD ≠ D0

S0 HEAD − − ➤ D0

THE PROGRAM TRIES AGAIN, FROM LOOP. FIRST
INSTRUCTION NOT NECESSARY AS CAS DID IT.

FIGURE 7.12e Simultaneous insertion of elements.

of a 32-bit port CAS instruction, the following text will review the asynchronous bus signals involved and show an $\overline{\text{RMC}}$ operational flowchart with a corresponding timing diagram.

Read/Write ($R/\overline{W}$) — A high output indicates a read from an external device. A low output indicates a write to an external device.

Read-Modify-Write ($\overline{\text{RMC}}$) — Asserted indicates that the current bus cycle operation is indivisible and used a bus lock to ensure the integrity of an entire RMC sequence.

External Cycle Start ($\overline{\text{ECS}}$) — Assertion provides the earliest indication that the 68020 has accessed the cache for the instruction. In case of a cache hit, the 68020 does not assert $\overline{\text{AS}}$; otherwise the 68020 asserts AS and completes the fetch cycle.

Address Strobe ($\overline{\text{AS}}$) — Assertion indicates that the function codes (FC0-FC2), address lines (A0-A31), bus size indicators (SIZ0-SIZ1), and the read/write ($R/\overline{W}$) signal all contain valid information.

Data Strobe ($\overline{\text{DS}}$) — During a read cycle, assertion indicates the data bus is free for slave device operations during a write cycle, and the MC68020 has placed valid data on the data bus.

Data Transfer and Size Acknowledge ($\overline{\text{DSACK0}}$, $\overline{\text{DSACK1}}$) — Assertion indicates that data transfer is complete and indicates port size of the attached external device. During a read cycle, processor recognition of

$\overline{\text{DSACKX}}$ causes the data to be latched before termination of the bus cycle. During a write cycle, processor recognition of $\overline{\text{DSACKX}}$ causes the bus cycle to be terminated. The $\overline{\text{DSACKX}}$ signals are also used with the SIZE output encoding (SIZ0, SIZ1) and the addressing encoding (A0, A1) to implement the dynamic bus sizing feature.

Data Buffer Enable ($\overline{\text{DBEN}}$) — Assertion provides an enable to external data bus buffers.

The read-modify-write cycle operational flowchart for the CAS instruction along with its corresponding timing diagram is shown in Figures 7.13 and 7.14.

In a single-processor multitasking interrupt-driven system, the noninterruptible CAS update operations provide security. In a multiprocessor system, an indivisible operand bus cycle (generated by inserting $\overline{\text{RMC}}$) provides the security mechanism.

Example 7.3

Determine the effects of execution of CAS.B D3, D5, (A1). Assume the following data prior to execution of the CAS: [D3] = $2512 2551, [D5] = $7015 2652, [A1] = $5000 0004, [$5000 0004] = $5312, and [CCR] = 0000 0010₂.

Solution

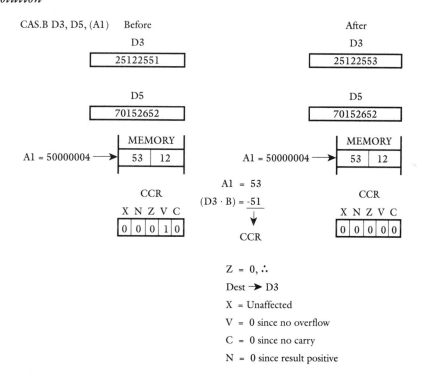

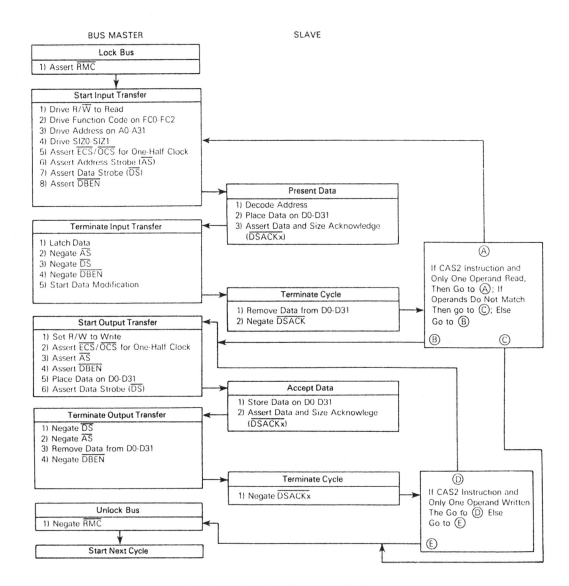

FIGURE 7.13 Read-modify-write cycle flowchart.

The CAS instruction is an extension of the test and set instruction. TAS is primarily used in a multiprocessor environment and is also performed in an indivisible noninterruptible manner. In the MC68000 system, $\overline{AS}$ stays low throughout the execution of the TAS instruction. On the other hand, in the MC68020 system, $\overline{RMC}$ is output low by the 68020 throughout the execution of the TAS instruction.

Therefore, the main difference between the 68000 and 68020 TAS implementations is that the 68000 uses $\overline{AS}$ as the bus locking control signal

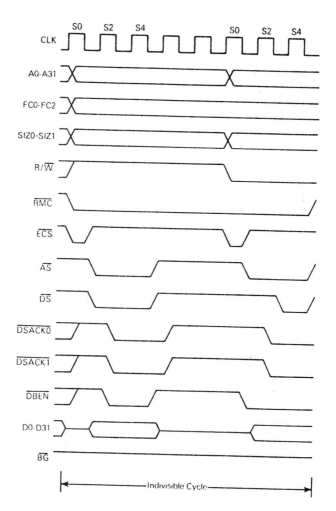

FIGURE 7.14 Read-modify-write cycle timing (32-bit port, CAS instruction).

input, while the 68020 $\overline{\text{RMC}}$ pin performs the bus locking control signal input. Other differences include the asynchronous bus control and data transfer signals used by the two MPUs.

Figure 7.15 shows a 68020 shared RAM implementation.

Shared memory bus reservation logic active outputs of the OR gates 1 and 2 indicate that the associated MPU wants exclusive use of the shared RAM. NAND gates 5 and 6 constitute an inverting latch for the outputs of NAND gates 3 and 4.

Now, if MPU-B first requests RAM, the outputs of OR gate 2 and NAND gate 4 force the MPU-A request RAM output of NAND 3 to be its "request denied" state. At the same time, the MPU-B request RAM

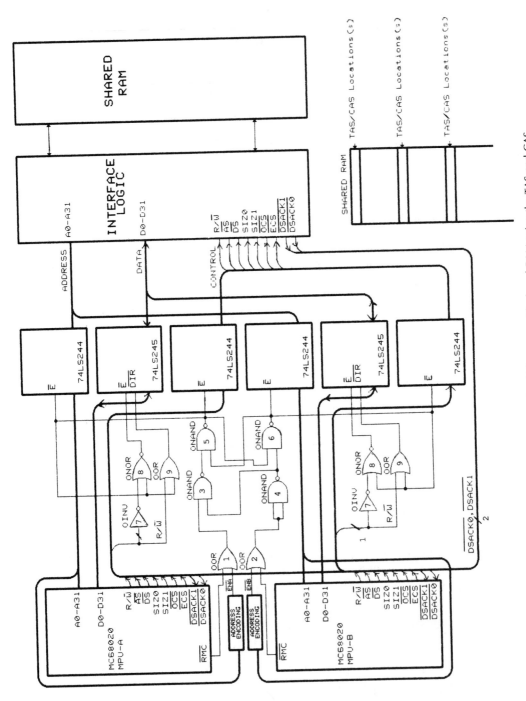

FIGURE 7.15 Multiprocessor MC68020 system with shared RAM using the TAS and CAS instructions.

output of NAND 4 is inverted and latched on the output of NAND 5. The complementary outputs of latches 5 and 6 select which MPU system bus to connect with the shared memory bus by enabling the appropriate data/ address/control bus interface logic. If MPU-A also requests use of the RAM, the outputs of NAND gates 3 and 4 both become active, but the latch does not change its previously recorded MPU-B RAM request state. Thus, the MPU-A RAM request becomes pending upon the removal of the MPU-B request. When this occurs, the changed output of NAND 4 forces the MPU-A RAM request output of NAND 3 to activate the latch into the MPU-A RAM request state. ICs 7, 8, and 9 provide bidirectional read/ write data bus control when enabled by the active RAM bus request latch output of NAND gates 5 and 6.

Example 7.4
Write a 68020 instruction sequence for counting a semaphore. That is, the instruction sequence will increment a count in a shared location.

Solution

```
        CLR.W   CNT            Clear system counter
        JSR     INIT           Initialize system
AGAIN   JSR     DOJOB          Perform some function
        MOVE.W  CNT, D0        Get a current value of
                                 the counter
LOOP    MOVE.W  D0, D1         Make a copy of it
        ADDQ.W  #1, D1         AND increment it
        CAS.W   D0, D1, CNT    If the counter value is
                                 the same, update it
        BNE     LOOP           If not, try again using
                                 new counter value in D0
        BRA     AGAIN
```

Since any system processor can update the counter, the loop guarantees that the variable is updated properly. If a processor increments a shared counter while a second processor is using the counter, the processor using the counter will continue its count sequence using the updated count value.

Instruction CAS2 is identical to CAS except that it can be used to compare and update dual operands within the same indivisible cycle. The CAS2 instruction operates on word or long word operands. The notation for the CAS2 instruction is CAS2 .W Dc1: Dc2, Du1: Du2, (Rn1):(Rn2).

or

.L

With the CAS2 instruction, both comparisons must show a match for the contents of the update registers Du1 and Du2 to be stored at the operands' destination addresses in memory pointed to by the registers Rn1 and Rn2. If either comparison fails to match, both destination operands obtained from memory are copied to the compare registers Dc1 and Dc2. The CAS2 instruction memory references to operand destination addresses must be specified using register indirect addressing with either a data or address register used as a pointer to memory.

The condensed version of CAS2 DC1: Dc2 Du1: Du2, (EA1): (EA2) operation is given below:

```
If (EA1) = Dc1 and (EA2) = Dc2, then
Du1 → (EA1) and Du2 → (EA2);
else (EA1) → Du1 and (EA2) ;→ Du2
```

Example 7.5

Determine the effects of CAS2.L D4: D5, D6: D4, (A5): (A6). Assume the following data prior execution of the CAS2:

$$[D4] = \$0000\ 7000 \qquad [A5] = \$1234\ 5000$$
$$[D5] = \$0000\ 8000 \qquad [A6] = \$5000\ 0200$$
$$[D6] = \$0000\ 9000$$

Solution

CAS2.L D4: D5, D6: D4, (A5): (A6)

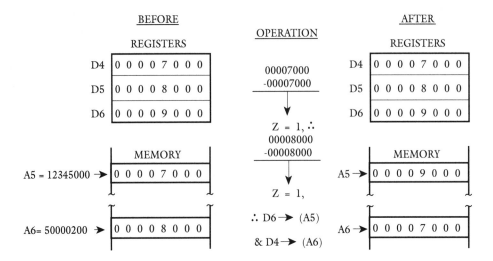

The CAS2 instruction is useful for maintaining doubly linked lists — items with both a next item pointer and a last item pointer.

Example 7.6

Write a 68020 instruction sequence to delete an element from a linked list using CAS2 instruction.

Solution

```
        LEA     HEAD, A0            ; Load address of
                                       head pointer into
                                       A0
        MOVE.L  (A0), D0           ; Move value of head
                                       pointer into D0
LOOP    TST.L   D0                 ; Check for null
                                       pointer
        BEQ     EMPTY              ; If empty, no
                                       deletion required
        LEA     (Next, D0.L), A1   ; Load address
                                       forward of link
                                       into A1
        MOVE.L  (A1), D1           ; Put value of
                                       forward link in
                                       D1
        CAS2.L  D0:D1, D1:D1,      ; If no change,
                (A0):(A1)              update head and
                                       forward pointer
        BNE     LOOP               ; D0 has new head,
                                       try again.
EMPTY   -
        -
        -
        -
        -
```

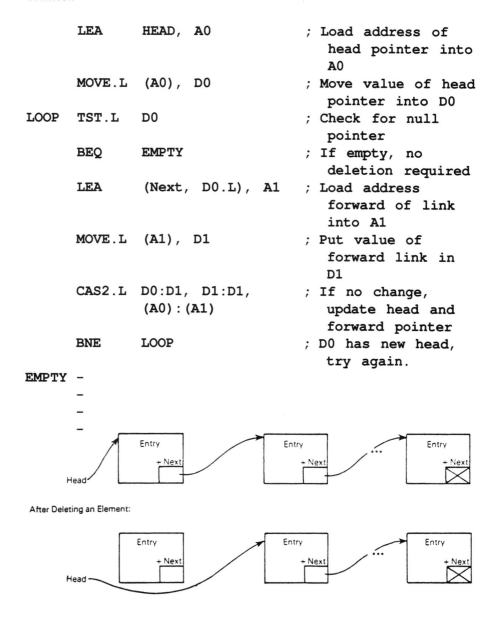

After Deleting an Element:

Table 7.4 summarizes the operation of the CAS, CAS2, and TAS instructions.

TABLE 7.4
Summary of the TAS, CAS, and CAS2 Instructions

Instruction	Operand size	Operation	Notation
TAS	8	Destination –0 → CCR 1 → bit 7 of destination	TAS (EA)
CAS	8,16,32	Destination –Dc → CCR if Z, then Du → destination; else destination → Dc	CAS.s Dc, Du, (AS)
CAS2	16,32	dest1 – Dc1 → CCR; if Z, dest2 – Dc2 → CCR; if Z, Du1 → dest 1; Du2 → dest2; else Dest 1 → DC1, dest 2 → Dc2	CAS2.s Dc1:Dc2,Du1: Du2,(Rn1):(Rn2)

Note: s = B, W, or L.

7.1.4 COPROCESSOR INSTRUCTIONS

Table 7.5 lists the MC68020 coprocessor instructions. These instructions are available on the MC68020 system when a coprocessor such as the MC68881 (floating point) or MC68851 (paged memory management unit) is interfaced to the system. Note that cp in these instructions is replaced by F for floating point (MC68881) or P for paged (MC68851), depending on the coprocessor.

The F or P provides the 3-bit cp-id in the instruction. The GEN is replaced by the specific operation. For example, FMOVE is the MOVE instruction for the floating-point coprocessor. Upon execution of the cpGEN instruction, the MC68020 passes command word to the coprocessor. The coprocessor then specifies the general data processing and movement instructions. The coprocessor finds the specific operation from the command word which follows the F-line instruction word. If the instruction requires an effective address for an operand to be fetched or stored, the third word follows the command word containing this effective address.

Note that F-line instruction word means that the high four bits of the instruction word are 1111_2. Normally, the coprocessor defines the specific instances of this instruction to provide its instruction set. The condition codes may be modified by the coprocessors. An example of a cpGEN instruction for the MC68881 is

FMOVE.L (A0) +, FP0

In this instruction F replaces cp and MOVE replaces GEN in the cpGEN format. This instruction moves 4 bytes from the MC68020-based microcomputer memory, starting with a location addressed by the contents of A0 to low 32 bits of the 80-bit register (FP0) in the MC68881; A0 is then incremented by 4.

TABLE 7.5
Coprocessor Instructions

Instruction	Operand size	Operation	Notation
cpGEN	User defined	Pass command word to coprocessor and respond to coprocessor primitives	cpGEN (parameters defined by coprocessors)
cpBcc	16,32	If cpcc true, then PC + d → PC	cpBcc (label)
cpDBcc	16	If cpcc false, then (Dn − 1 → Dn; if Dn ≠ −1, then PC + d → PC)	cpDBccDn, (label)
cpScc	8	If cpcc true, then 1's → destination, else 0's → destination	cpScc (EA)
cpTRAPcc	None $\overline{16,32}$	If cpcc true, then TRAP	cpTRAPcc cpTRAPcc # (data)
cpSAVE[a]	None	Save internal state of coprocessor	cpSAVE (EA)
cpRESTORE[a]	None	Restore internal state of coprocessor	cpRESTORE (EA)

TABLE 7.5 (continued)
Coprocessor Instructions

[a]   Privileged instructions for O.S. context switching (task switching) support.

·   MAIN and CO each do what they know how to do best
        MAIN: Tracks instruction stream
                    Takes exceptions
                    Takes branches
        CO: Does graphics manipulations
                    Calculates transcendentals, floating point
                    Does matrix manipulations
·   When MAIN obtains an F-line op word, it cooperates with a coprocessor to complete execution of the instruction

Co-Processor F-line Instruction

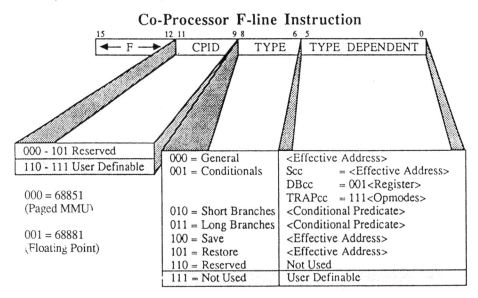

In the above for each type (bits 6-8), type dependent (bits 0-5) specifies effective address, conditional predicate, etc. For example, for general instructions (bits 8, 7, 6 = 000), type dependent (bits 0-5) specifies (ea).

The instruction F MOVE.L (A0) +, FP0 contains two words in memory as follows:

Machine Code (2 words)

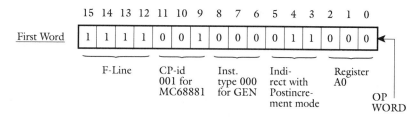

$F218

15	14	13	12	11	10	9	8	7	6	5	4	3	2	1	0

First Word:

| 1 | 1 | 1 | 1 | 0 | 0 | 1 | 0 | 0 | 0 | 0 | 1 | 1 | 0 | 0 | 0 |

F-Line | CP-id 001 for MC68881 | Inst. type 000 for GEN | Indirect with Postincrement mode | Register A0 | OP WORD

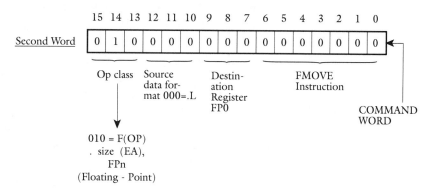

$4000

15	14	13	12	11	10	9	8	7	6	5	4	3	2	1	0

Second Word:

| 0 | 1 | 0 | 0 | 0 | 0 | 0 | 0 | 0 | 0 | 0 | 0 | 0 | 0 | 0 | 0 |

Op class | Source data format 000=.L | Destination Register FP0 | FMOVE Instruction | COMMAND WORD

010 = F(OP)
. size (EA),
FPn
(Floating - Point)

Therefore, the FMOVE.L (A0) +, FP0 contains two words in memory with the first word $F218 as the op word and the second word $4000 as the command word for the coprocessor.

The "cpBcc displacement" is the coprocessor conditional branch instruction. If the specified coprocessor condition is satisfied, program execution continues at location (PC) + displacement; otherwise the next instruction is executed. The displacement is a two's complement integer which may be either 16 or 32 bits. The coprocessor determines the specific condition from the condition field in the operation word. A typical example of this instruction is

FBEQ.L START

The cpDBcc (label) instruction works as follows. If cpcc is false, then Dn − 1 → Dn and if Dn ≠ − 1, then PC + d → PC, or if Dn = −1, then next instruction is executed. On the other hand, if cpcc is true, then the next instruction is executed.

The coprocessor determines the specific condition from the condition word which follows the operation word. A typical example of this instruction is

FDBNE.W START

The operand size is 16 bits.

The cpScc.B (EA) instruction tests a specific condition. If the condition is true, the byte specified by (EA) is set to true (all ones); otherwise that byte is set to false (all zeros). The coprocessor determines the specific condition from the condition word which follows the operation word. (EA) in the instruction can use all modes except An, immediate, (d16, PC), (d8, PC, Xn), (bd, PC, Xn), and (bd, PC, Xn, od). An example of this instruction is FSEQ.B $8000 1F20.

The cpTRAPcc or cpTRAPcc # data checks the specific condition on a coprocessor. If the selected coprocessor condition is true, the MC68020 initiates exception processing. The vector number is generated to reference the cpTRAPcc exception vector; the stacked PC is the address of the next instruction. If the selected condition is false, no operation is performed and the next instruction is executed. The coprocessor determines the specific condition from the word which follows the operation word. The user-defined optional immediate data (third word of the machine code for cpTRAPcc # data) is used by the trap handler routine. A typical example of this instruction is

FTRAPEQ

cpTRAPcc is unsized and cpTRAPcc # data has word and long word operands. cpSAVE and cpRESTORE are privileged instructions. Both instructions are unsized. cpSAVE (EA) saves the internal state of a coprocessor. (EA) can be predecrement on all alterable control addressing modes. This instruction is used by an operating system to save the context (internal state) of a coprocessor. The 68020 initiates a cpSAVE instruction by reading an internal register.

The cpRESTORE (EA) instruction restores the internal state of a coprocessor. (EA) can use postincrement or control addressing modes. This instruction is used by an operating system to restore the context of a coprocessor for both the user-visible and the user-invisible state.

7.2 MC68020 CACHE/PIPELINED ARCHITECTURE AND OPERATION

Caches have been used for years in larger machines to increase performance without greatly increasing system cost and complexity. As microprocessor clock speeds increase (the latest version of the MC68020 can run at 25 MHz), memory access time is often the limiting factor in system performance. It is possible to design a cache that is only a fraction of the size of the main memory store and yet significantly decrease the average access time to the main store.

Figure 7.16 illustrates the concept of cache memory.

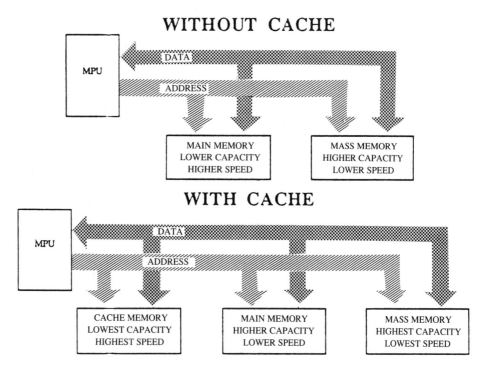

FIGURE 7.16 Cache memory concept.

This concept has been incorporated in the MC68020, which contains a 256-byte on-chip instruction cache. The cache improves performance by reducing the number of fetches required to external memory.

In a local memory, the address bits directly specify the location of the data. With a cache memory, however, the address does not specify a particular data location in the cache. Rather, the address information stored in the cache is called a tag. All cache tags are compared simultaneously to determine which cache data location is to be accessed.

The cache interface to the processor data paths within the MC68020 allows complete overlap of instruction fetches with data operand accesses. If simultaneous instruction and data operand requests are generated by MC68020 micromachine, a "hit" in the instruction cache allows concurrent fetches to take place. Also, increasing system performance is a two-clock-cycle access time for an access that "hits" the cache. This provides a 33% minimum improvement over external three-clock memory accesses. The memory access read operation flow diagram is shown in Figure 7.17.

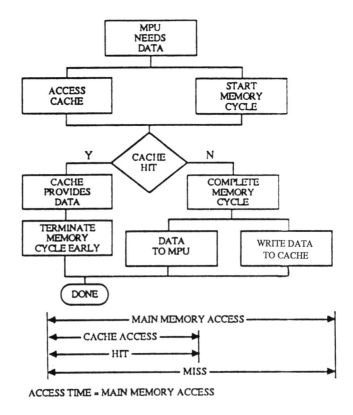

FIGURE 7.17 Memory access (read).

In systems without an instruction cache, when the processor fetches an instruction from memory, no processing can be performed until the instruction has been decoded.

When the MC68020 instruction cache is enabled and an instruction fetch can be performed from the cache, the processor spends less time waiting for information from external memory. Because the MC68020 uses the bus for a small amount of time, it increases system performance by providing more bus bandwidth for other bus masters such as an MMU, DMA devices, or coprocessors. The MC68020 processor's new three-clock bus cycles (as opposed to the four-clock cycles required by earlier MC68000 family members) also help to free the system bus for other traffic.

The MC68020 instruction cache is a 256-byte direct-mapped cache organized as 64 long word entries. Each cache entry consists of a tag field made up of the upper 24 address bits, the FC2 (user/supervisor) value, one valid bit (V), and 32 bits (two words) of instruction data. Figure 7.18 shows the MC68020 on-chip cache organization. The 68020 cache only stores instructions; data or operands are fetched directly from main memory as needed.

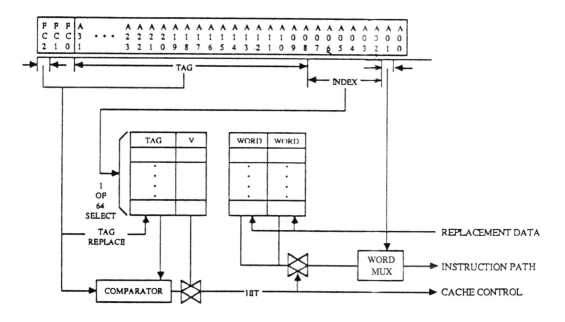

FIGURE 7.18 MC68020 on-chip cache organization.

A processor tends to execute its program from several small areas in memory. Therefore, the cache helps the processor use fewer bus cycles by storing recently executed instructions in anticipation of using them again. Further, when an instruction is supplied from a cache rather than from memory, it reaches the processor without delay and it requires zero clock cycles (parallel operation). A timing diagram showing parallel cache and external bus access is given in Figure 7.19.

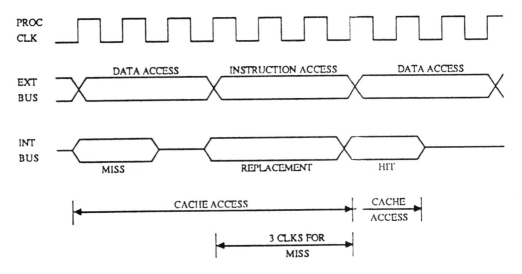

FIGURE 7.19 Parallel cache and external bus access.

When the processor fetches an instruction, it checks the cache first to determine if the word required is in the cache. First, one of 64 entries is selected by using the index field (A2-A7) of the access address as an index into the cache. Next, the 68020 compares address bits A31-A8 and function code bit FC2 with the 24-bit tag of the selected entry. If the function code and the address bit match, the 68020 sets the valid bit for the cache entry. This is called a cache hit. Finally, the 68020 uses address bit A1 to select the proper instruction word from the cache memory. If there is no match or valid bit is clear, a cache miss occurs and the instruction is fetched from external memory and put into the cache.

The MC68020 uses a 32-bit data bus and fetches instructions on long word address boundaries. Hence, each 32-bit instruction brings in two 16-bit instruction words which are then written into the on-chip cache. Subsequent prefetches will find the next 16-bit instruction word already present in the cache, and the related bus cycle is saved. Even when the cache is disabled, the subsequent prefetch will find the bus controller still holds the two instruction words and can satisfy the prefetch, again saving the related bus cycle. The bus controller provides an instruction hit rate of up to 50% even with the on-chip cache disabled.

Only the CPU uses the internal cache, so users have no direct access to the entries. However, several instructions allow the user to control the cache or dynamically disable it through the external hardware cache disable pin (CDIS). Typically, it is used by an emulator or bus state analyzer to force all bus cycles to be external cycles. The processor's two cache registers (CACR, CARR) can be programmed while in the supervisor mode by using the MOVEC instruction. Enabling, disabling, freezing, or clearing the cache is carried out by the cache control register (CACR). The CACR also allows the operating system to maintain and optimize the cache. The cache control (CACR) is shown in Figure 7.20.

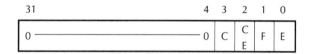

FIGURE 7.20 Cache control register format. C = clear cache, CE = clear entry, F = freeze cache, and E = enable cache.

The clear cache (C) bit of the CACR is used to invalidate all entries in the cache. This is termed as "flushing the cache". Setting the (C) bit causes all valid bits (v) in the cache to be cleared, thus invalidating all entries.

The Clear Entry (CE) of the CACR is used in conjunction with the address specified in the cache address register (CAAR). When writing to and setting the (CE) bit, the processor uses the CAAR index field to locate the selected address in the CAAR and invalidate the associated entry by clearing the valid bit.

The freeze cache (F) bit of the CACR keeps the cache enabled, but cache misses are not allowed to update the cache entries. This bit can be used by emulators to freeze the cache during emulation execution. It could be used to lock a critical region of the code in the cache after it has been executed, providing the cache is enabled and the freeze bit is cleared. The enables cache (E) bit is used for system's debug and emulation. This bit allows the designer to operate the processor with the cache disabled as long as the (E) bit remains cleared.

The cache address register (CAAR) format is shown in Figure 7.21.

The CAAR is used by the MC68020 to provide an address for the Clear Entry (CE) function as implemented in the CACR. The index portion of

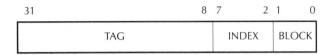

FIGURE 7.21 Cache address register format.

this register is used to specify which one of 64 entries to invalidate by clearing the associated cache entry valid bit (V).

If the cache is enabled and encounters a breakpoint instruction, it may supply the replacement op code (N) times. On the Nth execution, the breakpoint op code is fetched from the cache, and the associated loop counter is decremented to zero. At this point, an illegal instruction exception routine is evoked which clears the breakpoint entry in the cache, and the saved op code is restored in memory.

Although the micromachine of the MC68020 is highly pipelined, the predominant pipeline mechanism is a three-stage instruction pipeline. Figure 7.22 shows the MC68020 pipeline organization. The pipeline is completely internal to the processor and is used as part of the instruction fetching and decoding circuitry. Instructions from the on-chip cache, or from external memory (if the cache is disabled), go into the first stage of the pipeline and synchronously pass through the following two stages.

The pipeline output gives the 68020's control and execution unit a completely decoded instruction. The 68020 loads data and other operands into the pipeline so they are ready for immediate use. The pipeline speeds 68020 operation by making information available immediately. The benefit of the pipeline is to allow concurrent operations (parallelism) for up to three words of a single instruction or for up to three consecutive one-word instructions. Therefore, the performance benefits of a pipeline are maximized during the execution of in-line code.

7.3 MC68020 VIRTUAL MEMORY

Virtual memory is a technique that allows all user programs executing on a processor to behave as if each had the entire 4-GB addressing range of the MC68020 at its disposal, regardless of the amount of physical memory actually present in the system. Virtual memory can be supported by providing a limited amount of high-speed physical memory that can be

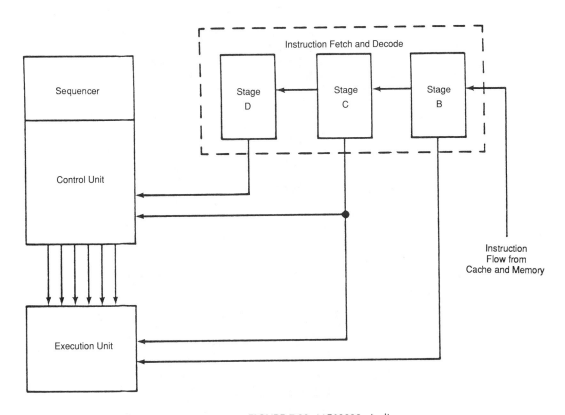

FIGURE 7.22 MC68020 pipeline.

accessed directly by the processor while maintaining an image of a much larger "virtual" memory on a secondary storage device, such as high-capacity disk drives. Figure 7.23 shows a minimal system configuration for a typical virtual memory system. Also, any given instruction must be able to be aborted and restarted. When a processor attempts to access a location in the virtual memory map that is not resident in physical memory (this is called a "page fault"), the access to that location is temporarily suspended while data are fetched from secondary storage and placed into physical memory. Page faults force a trap to the bus error exception vector.

The MC68020 processor has the abort capability via the bus error ($\overline{\text{BERR}}$) input to the processor. When $\overline{\text{BERR}}$ is asserted, exception processing causes the processor to save sufficient information to allow complete restoration of the faulted instruction. The faulted instruction will be recovered by the instruction continuation method, in which the faulted instruction is allowed to complete execution from the point of the fault. Instruction continuation is crucial for supporting virtual I/O devices in memory-

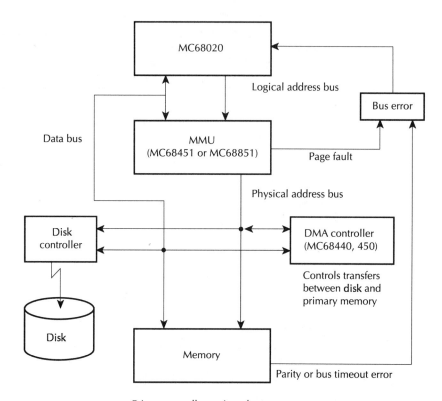

FIGURE 7.23 Typical virtual memory system, minimum configuration.

mapped I/O systems. To handle instruction continuation properly, the processor must save certain internal processor information on the stack prior to running the exception code and return this information to the processor after executing the return-from-exception (RTE) instruction. Figure 7.24 shows the BUS error processing sequence that occurs when attempting to fetch an instruction from a page not in the main memory.

7.4 MC68020 COPROCESSOR INTERFACE

The MC 68020's coprocessor interface is capable of extending the MC68020 instruction set and supporting new data types. Coprocessor support extends the instruction set by performing new instructions that the

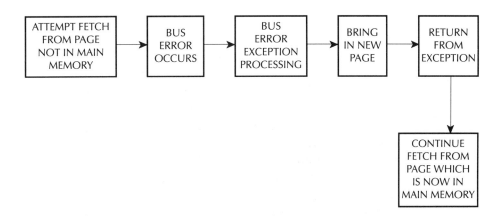

FIGURE 7.24 Bus error sequence.

main general-purpose processor cannot accommodate. The coprocessor concept allows the enhancement of general-purpose processor performance and capabilities for a particular application, without overloading the main processor architecture.

Coprocessors are DMA or non-DMA, according to the way they use the bus. A coprocessor is a Direct Memory Access (DMA) coprocessor if it can control the bus independent of the main processor. A non-DMA coprocessor cannot control the bus, so it operates as a bus slave.

The MC68020 coprocessor is not a standard peripheral hardware device. A MC68020 coprocessor communicates with the main processor through the protocol defined at the coprocessor interface. Dedicated coprocessor instructions are provided to use the coprocessor capabilities.

The interface between the main processor and a coprocessor is transparent to the user. The programmer does not have to be aware that a separate piece of hardware is executing some of the program code sequence. Hardware-implemented microcode within the MC68020 handles coprocessor interfacing so that a coprocessor can provide its capabilities to the programmer without appearing as an external hardware, but rather as a natural extension to the main processor architecture.

In contrast, standard peripheral hardware is generally accessed through the use of an interface register mapped into the memory space of the main processor. The programmer uses standard processor instructions to access the peripheral interface registers and thus use the peripheral's capabilities. Accessing coprocessors over the coprocessor interface is straightforward, because the interface uses standard MC68020 asynchronous bus structure, without any special signals.

The coprocessor does not have to be architecturally similar to the main processor, but can be designed so that it best suits its particular application. The only requirement is that it adheres to the coprocessor's interface protocol. A coprocessor can be implemented as a Very Large-Scale Integration (VLSI) device to solve some of the more common special-purpose processing needs (such as floating-point computations) or to support virtual memory/machine requirements (such as MMUs, DMA controllers, or master/slave bus arbitration devices). A board-level design particular to some limited but important application, or even a separate microcomputer system, can become a system coprocessor. The MC68020 coprocessor interface is designed to provide full support of all sequential operations necessary for nonconcurrent operation between the main processor and its associated coprocessors. The MC68020 coprocessor interface does allow concurrency in coprocessor execution, but it is the responsibility of the coprocessor designer to implement this concurrency. At the same time, the designer must maintain the MC68020 programmer's model based on sequential, nonconcurrent instruction execution.

When communicating with a coprocessor, the MC68020 executes bus cycles in CPU memory space to access a set of Coprocessor Interface Registers (CIRs). Table 7.6 shows how the separate coprocessor interface registers are located in CPU space. Within this interface register set, the various registers are allocated to specific functions required for operating the coprocessor interface. There are registers specifically for passing information such as commands, operands, and EAs. Other registers are allocated for use during a context switch operation.

TABLE 7.6
Coprocessor Interface Register

Register	Function	R/$\overline{\text{W}}$
Response	Requests action from CPU	R
Control	CPU directed control	$\overline{\text{W}}$
Save	Initiate save of internal state	R
Restore	Initiate restore of internal state	R/$\overline{\text{W}}$
Operation word	Current coprocessor instruction	$\overline{\text{W}}$
Command word	Coprocessor specific command	$\overline{\text{W}}$
Condition word	Condition to be evaluated	$\overline{\text{W}}$
Operand	32-bit operand	R/$\overline{\text{W}}$
Register select	Specifies CPU register or mask	R
Instruction address	Pointer to coprocessor instruction	R/$\overline{\text{W}}$
Operand address	Pointer to coprocessor operand	R/$\overline{\text{W}}$

Figure 7.25 shows the coprocessor interface register set map and communication protocol between the main processor and the coprocessor necessary to execute a coprocessor instruction. The MC68020 implements the CIR communication protocol automatically, so the programmer is only concerned with the coprocessor's instruction and data type extensions to the MC68020 programmer's model.

31		15	0
00	Response*		Control*
04	Save*		Restore*
08	Operation Word		Command*
OC	(Reserved)		Condition*
10	Operand*		
14	Register Select		(Reserved)
18	Instruction Address		
1C	Operand Address		

FIGURE 7.25 Coprocessor interface register set map.

Figure 7.26 shows the CIR set(s) (that is, more than one coprocessor) address map in CPU space.

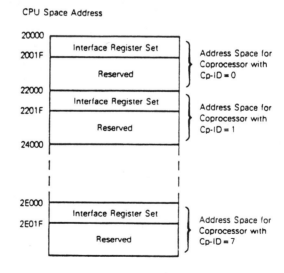

FIGURE 7.26 Coprocessor address map in CPU space.

The MC68020 indicates that it is accessing CPU memory space by encoding the function code lines high (FC0-FC2 = 111_2). Thus, the CIR set is mapped into CPU space the same way that a peripheral interface register set is generally mapped into data space. The address bus then selects the desired coprocessor chip.

Encoding the address bus during coprocessor communication is shown in Figure 7.27. By using the cp-ID field on the address bus, up to eight separate coprocessors can be interfaced concurrently to the MC68020. Figure 7.27 also shows how simply this can be done. Interfacing to these separate coprocessors is just a matter of decoding the relevant cp-ID field (address lines A13-A15) and the corresponding CPU space type field (address lines A16-A9) encoded within the coprocessor instruction, so that the MC68020 communicates with the relevant register set in CPU space.

Figure 7.28 shows a block level diagram of the MC68020 coprocessor interface signals. System designers can use multiple coprocessors of the same type (for example, several MC68881 floating-point coprocessors operating concurrently) by assigning a uniquely encoded cp-ID to each one.

Coprocessors define their own instruction set to support their specific design functions. Executing a coprocessor instruction uses an "F-line operation word" (an operation word is the first word of any instruction) to specify the type of coprocessor instruction that will be executed. Figure 7.29 shows the F-line coprocessor instruction operation word format.

The F-line operation word can be appended by extension words that provide additional instruction execution information. The F-line operation word (coprocessor instruction) contains the encoded coprocessor identification code (cp-ID) that the MC68020 uses to identify which of eight possible coprocessors to access for a given instruction. This decouples the main processor from the definition of a particular coprocessor instruction set, making the interface more general in nature. After evaluating the instruction, the coprocessor determines the service required from the main processor (if any), so that it can execute the instruction.

These service requirement requests are transmitted to the main processor in the form of an encoded "response primitive" word. The response primitive word is then evaluated and executed by the main processor. The response register of the CIR set communicates the coprocessor's service requests to the main processor. Thus, the response register contains the primitive response instruction word. Figure 7.30 shows the coprocessor response primitive format.

The MC68020's use of primitive responses minimizes coprocessor interface overhead. For example, the main processor can perform (EA) calculations and pass the result to the coprocessor or fetch a variable length operand and pass it on. By performing such complicated services for the

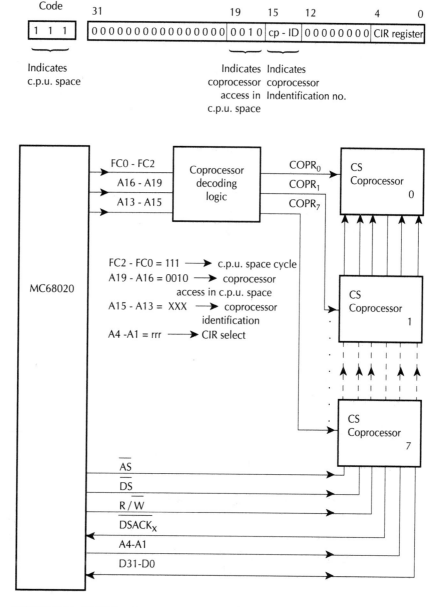

FIGURE 7.27 68020 interface to coprocessors. Coprocessor communication address bus encoding and multicoprocessor address decoding example.

coprocessor, the main processor shows the coprocessor design to be much simpler.

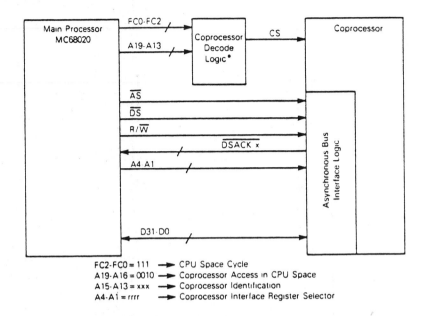

FC2-FC0 = 111 → CPU Space Cycle
A19-A16 = 0010 → Coprocessor Access in CPU Space
A15-A13 = xxx → Coprocessor Identification
A4-A1 = rrrr → Coprocessor Interface Register Selector

FIGURE 7.28 MC68020 coprocessor interface signals.

15	14	13	12	11	10	9	8	7	6	5	4	3	2	1	0
1	1	1	1	Cp-ID				Type			Type Dependent				

FIGURE 7.29 F-line coprocessor instruction operation word.

15	14	13	12	11	10	9	8	7	6	5	4	3	2	1	0
CA	PC	DR		Function				Parameter							

FIGURE 7.30 Coprocessor response primitive format.

The MC68020 supports five types of coprocessor instructions: general, branch, conditional, save state, and restore state. The general instruction (cpGEN) is used for data manipulation and movement between the coprocessor and the main processor's memory or its register. The cpGEN general instruction format is shown in Figure 7.31.

15	14	13	12	11	10	9	8	7	6	5	4	3	2	1	0
1	1	1	1	Cp-ID			0	0	0	Effective Address					
Coprocessor Command															
Optional Effective Address or Coprocessor Defined Extension Words															

FIGURE 7.31 Coprocessor general instruction format (cpGEN).

The branch instruction (cpCC) allows branching based upon a coprocessor condition. Both 16- and 32-bit displacements are supported. The conditional instructions (cpcc, cpTRAPcc, and cpDBcc) allow evaluation of one of 64 coprocessor conditions, and based upon the result, they conditionally set (cpScc), trap (cpTRAPcc), or decrement and branch (cpDBcc). For conditional instructions, the coprocessor is passed a condition for evaluation and then informs the main processor of the result.

The save and restore instructions are used to support operating system context switching. These two instruction types allow the saving and restoring of the state of a coprocessor in a virtual machine environment. During a context switch in a multitasking environment, the coprocessor state is treated as a part of the overall system state (along with the main processor's general-purpose register, PC, and SR) and must be switched out when the current task is suspended and another task takes over. The cpSAVE and cpRESTORE commands simplify this swap and reduce the amount of information that has to be saved during the context switch. Once a coprocessor instruction has been passed from the main processor to the coprocessor for evaluation, the coprocessor has a number of main processor-recognized primitives (Table 7.7) from which to implement a coprocessor instruction. Response primitives are instructions the coprocessor uses to communicate status information and processing service requests to the main processor. The main processor supports 18 basic primitives, some with several variations. Primitives can be grouped into five basic categories: processor/coprocessor synchronization, instruction stream manipulation, exception handling, general operand transfer, and register transfer.

Processor/coprocessor synchronization primitives allow the coprocessor to inform the main processor of its status. The coprocessor can perform the following functions:

- Signal that it is busy with a previous or current instruction
- Allow the main processor to process any pending interrupts while it is busy
- Request the main processor to pass the current PC value
- Direct the main processor to proceed with the next instruction, depending on whether the instruction tracing bits (T1, T0) located in the SR (see Table 7.8) are enabled
- Indicate the result of a conditional test

Instruction stream manipulation primitives allow the coprocessor to request the transfer of a coprocessor instruction to itself. The transfer instruction primitive allows the coprocessor to request the main processor to transfer up to 256 bytes from the instruction stream to the coprocessor

TABLE 7.7
MC68020 Coprocessor Primitives

Processor synchronization
    Busy with current instruction
    Proceed with next instruction, if no trace
    Service interrupts and re-query, if trace enabled
    Proceed with execution, condition true/false

Instruction manipulation
    Transfer operation word
    Transfer words from instruction stream

Exception handling
    Take privilege violation if S bit not set
    Take pre-instruction exception
    Take mid-instruction exception
    Take post-instruction exception

General operand transfer
    Evaluate and pass (EA)
    Evaluate (EA) and transfer data
    Write to previously evaluated (EA)
    Take address and transfer data
    Transfer to/from top of stack

Register transfer
    Transfer CPU register
    Transfer CPU control register
    Transfer multiple CPU registers
    Transfer multiple coprocessor registers
    Transfer CPU SR and/or ScanPC

TABLE 7.8
Instruction Tracing Control

T1	T0	Tracing function
0	0	No tracing
0	1	Trace on change of flow (BRA, JMP, etc.)
1	0	Trace on instruction execution (any instruction)
1	1	Undefined, reserved

and to update the PC appropriately. This means that coprocessor instructions can be any number of words in length.

Exception handling primitives force the main processor to check for and/or take an exception. The coprocessor can request the main processor to perform a supervisor check before executing a privileged coprocessor instruction. If the main processor is not in the supervisor state, a privilege violation exception is taken, and the main processor may be forced to save enough state information to recover from the exception later.

General operand transfer primitives are used to request the transfer of operands from or to the coprocessor. These primitives include evaluating an (EA) for the coprocessor, transferring the evaluated (EA) to the coprocessor, transfer data from/to the (EA), and transferring data to a previously evaluated (EA). Also, the coprocessor may pass an address to the main processor, as well as request an operand transfer to or from the address passed. An additional primitive allows transfer of operands to or from the top of the active system stack.

Register operand transfer primitives allow transfer of single main processor control registers, single and multiple main processor address/data registers, and multiple coprocessor registers between the main processor and the coprocessor. Additionally, the coprocessor may request a transfer to or from the main processor SR and PC.

7.4.1 MC68881 FLOATING-POINT COPROCESSOR

The MC68881 HCMOS floating-point coprocessor implements IEEE standards for binary floating-point arithmetic. When interfaced to the MC68020, the MC68881 provides a logical extension to the MC68020 interdata processing capabilities. The MC68882 is an upgrade of the MCC68881 and provides in excess of 15 times the performance of the MC68881. It is a pin and software compatible upgrade of the MC68881.

A summary of the MC68881 features is listed below:

* Eight general-purpose floating-point data registers, each supporting an 80-bit extended precision real data format (a 64-bit mantissa, plus a sign bit and a 15-bit signed exponent)
* A 67-bit arithmetic unit
* A 67-bit barrel shifter for fast shift operations
* 46 instructions with 35 arithmetic operations
* Supports trigonometric and transcendental functions
* Supports seven data types: bytes, word, long word integers; single, double, and extended precision real numbers; and packed binary coded decimal string real numbers
* 22 constants including π, e, and powers of 10

The MC68881 is a non-DMA-type coprocessor which uses a subset of the general-purpose coprocessor interface supported by the MC68020. The MC68881 programming model is shown in Figure 7.32.

The MC68881 programming model includes the following:

- Eight 80-bit floating-point registers (FP0-FP7) (These general-purpose registers are analogous to the MC68020 D0-D7 registers.)
- A 32-bit control register containing enable bits for each class of exception trap and mode bits, to set the user-selectable rounding and precision modes
- A 32-bit status register containing floating-point condition codes, quotient bits, and exception status information
- A 32-bit Floating-Point Instruction Address Register (FPIAR) containing the MC68020 memory address of the last floating-point instruction that was executed (This address is used in exception handling to locate the instruction that caused the exception.)

The MC68881 can be interfaced as a coprocessor to the MC68020. Figure 7.33 provides the MC68020/68881 block diagram.

The MC68881 is internally divided into three sections: the Bus Interface Unit (BIU), the Execution Control Unit (ECU) and the Microcode Control Unit (MCU).

The BIU communicates with the MC68020; the ECU and MCU execute all MC68881 instructions. The BIU contains the Coprocessor Interface Registers (CIRs) and the 32-bit control, status, and instruction address registers. The register select and $\overline{\text{DSACKX}}$ timing control logic are included in the BIU. The CIRS are addressed in the same way as memory by the MC68020.

The MC68020 implements the coprocessor interface protocol in hardware and microcode. When the MC68020 encounters a typical MC68881 instruction, the MC68020 writes the instruction to the memory-mapped command CIR and reads the response CIR. In this response, the BIU translates any additional action required of the MC68020 by the MC68881. Upon satisfying the coprocessor requests, the MC68020 can fetch and execute subsequent instructions.

The MC68881 supports the following data formats:

Byte Integer (B)
Word Integer (W)
Long Word Integer (L)
Single Precision Real (S)

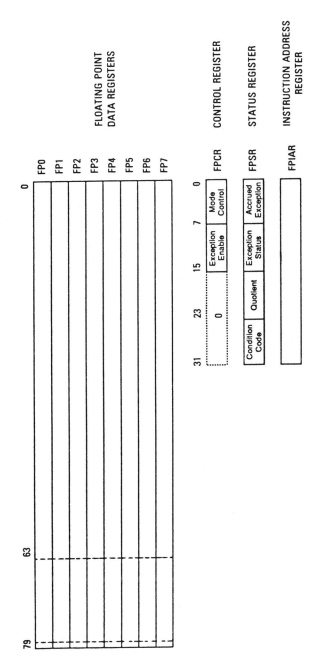

FIGURE 7.32 MC68881 programming model.

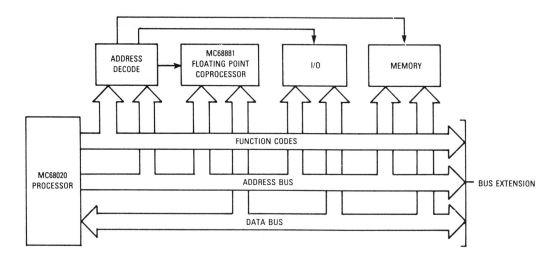

FIGURE 7.33 Typical coprocessor configuration.

Double Precision Real (D)
Extended Precision Real (X)
Packed Decimal String Real (P)

The capital letters included in parentheses denote the suffixes added to instructions in the assembly language source to specify the data format to be used

Figure 7.34 shows the MC68881 data formats. Three data types are supported: integer, floating-point, and packed decimal string real data.

These data formats are defined by IEEE standards. Integer data types do not include any fractional part of the number. The real formats contain an exponent part and a fractional (mantissa) part. The single-real and double-real formats provide sign of a fraction with 8- and 11-bit exponents and 23- and 52-bit fractional parts, respectively.

The extended real format is 96 bits wide with a 15-bit exponent, 64-bit mantissa, and a sign bit for the mantissa. The packed decimal real is 96 bits wide which provides sign for both mantissa and exponent parts. It includes a 3-digit (12 bits for BCD) base-10 exponent and a 17-digit (68 bits) base-10 mantissa. This format contains two bits to indicate infinity or not-a-number (NAN) representations. Note that NAN is a symbolic representation of a special number or situation in floating-point format. NANs include all numbers with nonzero fractions with format's maximum exponent. The infinity data types include zero fraction and maximum exponent.

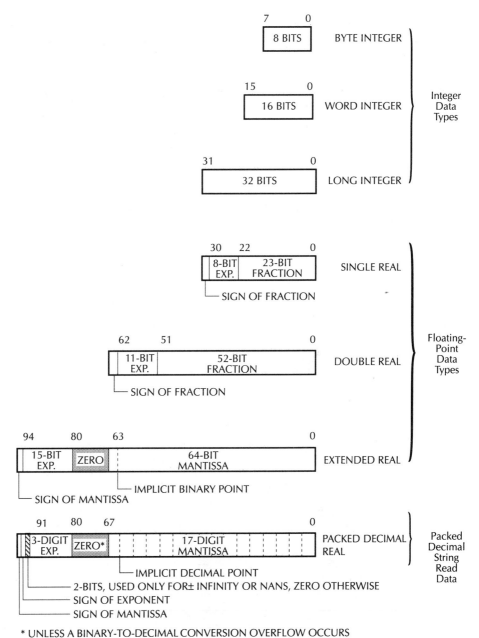

FIGURE 7.34 MC68881 data format summary.

Whenever an integer is used in a floating-point operation, the integer is automatically converted to an extended-precision floating-point number before being used. For example, the instruction FADD.W #2, FP0 converts the constant 2 to the floating-point number format in FP0, adds the two numbers, and then stores the result in FP0. This allows integer in floating-point operations and also saves user memory, since an integer representation of a number is normally smaller than the equivalent floating-point representation.

The floating-point representation contains single-precision (32 bits), double-precision (64 bits), and extended-precision numbers (96 bits) as specified by the IEEE format. The single-precision and double-precision data types should be used in most calculations involving real numbers. The exponent is biased and the mantissa is in sign and magnitude form. Single and double precision require normalized numbers. Note that a normalized number has the most significant bit of the mantissa positioned such that the one lies to the left of the radix point. Therefore, only the fractional part of the mantissa is stored in memory, which means that the most significant bit is implied and equal to one.

Extended-precision numbers are 96 bits wide but only 80 bits are used, and the unused 16 bits are for future expansion. Extended-precision numbers are for use as temporary variables, intermediate variables, or in situations where extra precision is required.

For example, a compiler might select extended-precision arithmetic for determining the value of the right side of an equation with mixed sized data, and then convert the answer to the data type on the left side of the equation. Extended-precision data should not be stored in large arrays due to the amount of memory required by each number. As with other data types, the packed BCD strings are automatically converted to extended-precision real values when they are input to the MC68881. This permits packed BCD number to be used as input to any operation such as FADD.P # − 2.012E + 18, FP1.

The MC68881 does not include any addressing modes. If the 68881 requests the 68020 to transfer an operand via the coprocessor interface, the 68020 provides the addressing mode calculations requested in the instruction.

Floating-point data registers FP0-FP7 always contain extended-precision values. Also, all data used in an operation are converted to extended precision by the MC68881 before the operation is performed. The MC68881 provides all results in extended precision. The MC68881 instructions can be grouped into six types:

1. MOVE instructions between the MC68881 and memory on the MC68020
2. MOVE multiple registers

3. Monadic operations
4. Dyadic operations
5. Branch, set, or trap conditionally
6. Miscellaneous

7.4.1.a MOVEs

All MOVE instructions from memory or from a MC68020 data register to the MC68881 convert data from the source format to the internal extended precision.

Also, all MOVE instructions from the MC68881 to memory or a MC68020 data register convert from the internal extended-precision format to the destination data.

Typical examples of MOVE instructions include:

```
F  MOVE  .  (fmt)  (EA),   FPn
F  MOVE  .  (fmt)  FPn,    (EA)
F  MOVE  .  (fmt)  FPn,    FPn
```

7.4.1.b MOVE Multiple Registers

Any floating-point register FP0 through FP7 can be moved to or from memory with one instruction. These registers are always moved as 96-bit extended data with no conversion. Typical examples of FMOVEM include:

```
FMOVEM  (EA),  FP1-FP4/FP6
FMOVEM  FP0/FP1/FP5,  (EA)
```

Any combination of FP0-FP7 can be moved, (EA) can be control modes, predecrement, or postincrement mode. For control or postincrement mode, the order of transfer is from FP7-FP0. For predecrement mode, the order of transfer is from FP0-FP7. Any combination of FPCR, FPSR, and FPIAR can also be moved by FMOVEM instruction. These registers are always moved in the order FPCR, FPSR, and FPIAR.

7.4.1.c Monadic

Monadic instructions have a single input operand. This operand may be in a floating-point data register, memory, or in a MC68020 data register. The result is always stored in a floating-point data register. Typical examples include:

```
FTAN  .  (fmt)   (EA),  FPn
                or
FTAN  .  X  FPm,  FPn
                or
FTAN  .  X   FPn
```

The FTAN instruction converts the source operand to extended precision (if necessary), computes the tangent of that number, and then stores the result in the destination floating-point data register.

Table 7.9a flowcharts the monadic function. Tables 7.9b and c list all MC68881 monadic instructions.

TABLE 7.9a
Monadic Functions

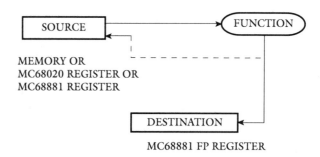

TABLE 7.9b
MC68881 — Monadic Instructions

Transcendental functions

FACOS	ARC COSINE
FASIN	ARC SINE
FATAN	ARC TANGENT
FATANH	HYPERBOLIC ARC TANGENT
FCOS	COSINE
FCOSH	HYPERBOLIC COSINE
FETOX	E TO THE X POWER
FETOXM1	E TO THE (X – 1) power
FLOG10	LOG TO THE BASE 10
FLOG2	LOG TO THE BASE 2
FLOGN	LOG BASE e OF X
FLOGNP1	LOG BASE e OF (X + 1)
FSIN	SINE
FSINCOS	SIMULTANEOUS SIN/COS
FSINH	HYPERBOLIC SINE
FTAN	TANGENT
FTANH	HYPERBOLIC TANGENT
FTENTOX	TEN TO THE X POWER
FTWOTOX	TWO TO THE X POWER

TABLE 7.9c
MC68881 — Monadic Instructions

Nontranscendental functions

FABS	ABSOLUTE VALUE
FINT	INTEGER PART
FNEG	NEGATE
FSQRT	SQUARE ROOT
FNOP	NO OPERATION (SYNCHRONIZE)
FGETEXP	GET EXPONENT
FGETMAN	GET MANTISSA
FTST	TEST

7.4.1.d Dyadic Instructions

Dyadic instructions have two input operands. The first input operand comes from a floating-point data register, memory of a MC68020 data register. The second input operand comes from a floating-point data register. The second input is also the destination floating-point data register. Typical examples include:

```
FCMP.L  (fmt) (EA), FPn
           or
FCMP.X  FPm, FPn
```

Tables 7.10a flowcharts the dyadic function and Table 7.10b lists dyadic instructions.

TABLE 7.10a
MC68881 Dyadic Functions

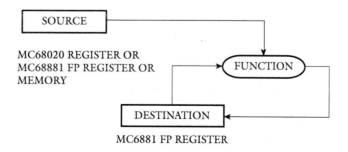

TABLE 7.10b
MC 68881 Dyadic Instructions

FADD	ADD
FCMP	COMPARE
FDIV	DIVIDE
FMOD	MOD
FMUL	MULTIPLY
FREM	IEEE REMAINDER
FSCALE	SCALE EXPONENT
FSUB	SUBTRACT

7.4.1.e BRANCH, Set, or Trap-On Condition

These instructions are similar to those of the MC68020 except that move conditions exist due to the special values in IEEE floating-point arithmetic. When the MC68020 encounters a floating-point conditional instruction, it passes the instruction to the MC68881 for performing the necessary condition checkup. The MC68881 then checks the condition and tells the MC68020 whether the condition is true or false. The MC68020 then takes the appropriate action.

The MC68881 conditional instructions are

```
FBcc.W       displ     Branch
  or .L

FDBcc.W      displ     Decrement and branch
  or .L

FScc.W       displ     Set byte according to condition
  or .L

FTRAPcc.W    displ     Trap-on condition
  or .L
```

All the above instructions can have 16- or 32-bit displacement.

cc is one of the 32 floating-point conditional test specifiers as shown in Table 7.11.

7.4.1.f Miscellaneous Instructions

These instructions include moves to and from the status, control, and instruction address registers. The virtual memory instructions FSAVE and FRESTORE that save and restore the internal state of the MC68881 also fall into this category. These instructions include:

TABLE 7.11
Floating-Point Conditional Test Specifiers

Mnemonic	Definition
F	False
EQ	Equal
OGT	Ordered greater than
OGE	Ordered greater than or equal
OLT	Ordered less than
OLE	Ordered less than or equal
OGL	Ordered greater or less than
OR	Ordered
UN	Unordered
UEQ	Unordered or equal
UGT	Unordered or greater than
UGE	Unordered or greater or equal
ULT	Unordered or less than
ULE	Unordered or less or equal
NE	Not equal
T	True

Note: The preceding conditional tests do not set the BSUN bit in the status register exception byte under any circumstances.

SF	Signaling false
SEQ	Signaling equal
GT	Greater than
GE	Greater than or equal
LT	Less than
LE	Less than or equal
GL	Greater or less than
GLE	Greater less or equal
NGLE	Not (greater, less, or equal)
NGL	Not (greater or less)
NLE	Not (less or equal)
NLT	Not (less than)
NGE	Not (greater or equal)
NGT	Not (greater than)
SNE	Signaling not equal
ST	Signaling true

Note: The preceding conditional tests set the BSUN bit in the status register exception byte if the NAN condition code bit is set when a conditional instruction is executed.

```
FMOVE      (EA),  FPcr
FMOVE      FPcr,  (EA)
FRESTORE   (EA)
```

FPcr means floating-point control register. The MC68881 does not perform addressing mode calculations. The MC68020 carries out this calculation specified in the instruction.

Typical addressing modes include immediate, postincrement, predecrement, direct, and the indexed/indirect modes of the MC68020. Some addressing modes are restricted for some instructions. For example, PC relative mode is not permitted for a destination operand.

The MC68881 can execute an instruction concurrently or nonconcurrently with the MC68020 depending on the instruction being executed. Figure 7.35 shows examples of concurrence and nonconcurrence.

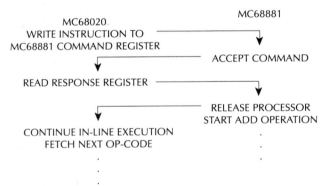

FIGURE 7.35a MC68020/MC68881 concurrence example.

Figure 7.36 shows the MC68881 pins and signals.

The 68881 is included either in a 64-pin DIP or in a 68-PGA (Pin Grid Array) package. There are 7 Vcc (+5V) and 13 grounds for power distribution to reduce noise.

The five address lines A0-A4 are used by the MC68020 to select the coprocessor interface registers mapped in the MC68020 address space. These address pins select the registers as listed in Table 7.12.

When the MC68881 is configured to operate over an 8-bit data bus for processors such as MC68808, A0 pin is used as an address signal for byte accesses of the MC68881 interface register. When the MC68881 is configured to operate over a 16-bit data bus (68000) or 32-bit data bus (68020), both A0 and SIZE pins are used, according to Table 7.13.

INSTRUCTION: FMOVE.L FP1,(AO)+

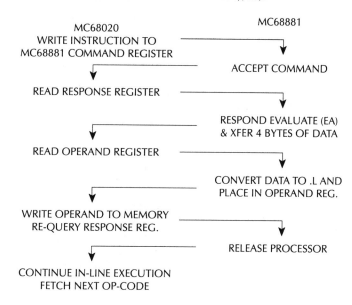

FIGURE 7.35b MC68020/MC68881 nonconcurrence example.

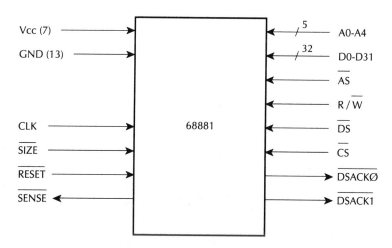

FIGURE 7.36 MC68881 I/O signals.

$\overline{\text{SIZE}}$ and A0 pins are used to configure the MC68881 for operation over 8-, 16-, or 32-bit data bus.

The address strobe $\overline{\text{AS}}$ is when LOW indicates that there is a valid address on the address bus, and both $\overline{\text{CS}}$ and R/$\overline{\text{W}}$ are valid.

TABLE 7.12
Coprocessor Interface Register Selection

A4-A0	Offset	Width	Type	Register
0000x	$00	16	Read	Response
0001x	$02	16	Write	Control
0010x	$04	16	Read	Save
0011x	$06	16	R/$\overline{\text{W}}$	Restore
0100x	$08	16	—	(reserved)
0101x	$0A	16	Write	Command
0110x	$0C	16	—	(reserved)
0111x	$0E	16	Write	Condition
100xx	$10	32	R/$\overline{\text{W}}$	Operand
1010x	$14	16	Read	Register select
1011x	$16	16	—	(reserved)
110xx	$18	32	Read	Instruction address
111xx	$1C	32	R/$\overline{\text{W}}$	Operand address

TABLE 7.13
Data Bus Configuration

A0	Size	Data bus
—	Low	8-bit
Low	High	16-bit
High	High	32-bit

A low on $\overline{\text{DS}}$ indicates that there is valid data on the data bus during a write cycle.

If the bus cycle is a MC68020 read from MC68881, the MC68881 asserts $\overline{\text{DSACK1}}$ and $\overline{\text{DSACK0}}$ to indicate that the information on the data bus is valid. If the bus cycle is a MC68020 write to the MC68881, $\overline{\text{DSACK1}}$ and $\overline{\text{DSACK0}}$ are used to acknowledge acceptance of the data by the MC68881.

The MC68881 also uses $\overline{\text{DSACK0}}$ and $\overline{\text{DSACK1}}$ to dynamically indicate the device size on a cycle-by-cycle basis.

A low on MC68881 $\overline{\text{RESET}}$ pin clears the floating-point control, status, and instruction address registers. When performing power-up reset, external circuitry should keep the $\overline{\text{RESET}}$ pin asserted for a minimum of four clock cycles after Vcc is within tolerance. After Vcc is written tolerance for more than the initial power-up time, the $\overline{\text{RESET}}$ pin must be asserted for at least two clock cycles.

The MC68881 clock input is a TTL-compatible signal that is internally buffered for generation of the internal clock signals. The clock input should be a constant frequency square wave with no stretching or shaping techniques required. The MC68881 can be operated from a 12-, 16.67-, or 20-MHz clock.

The $\overline{\text{SENSE}}$ pin may be used as an additional ground pin for more noise immunity or as an indicator to external hardware that the MC68881 is present in the system. This signal is internally connected to the GND of the die, but it is not necessary to connect it to the external ground for correct device operation. If a pullup resistor (larger than 10 K ohm) is connected to this pin location, external hardware may sense the presence of the MC68881 in a system.

Figure 7.37 shows the MC68020/MC68881 interface.

The A0 and $\overline{\text{SIZE}}$ pins are connected to Vcc for 32-bit operation. Note that A19, A18, A17, A16 = 0010_2 (indicating coprocessor function), FC2 FC1 FC0 = 111_2 (meaning CPU space cycle), and A15 A14 A13 = 001_2 (indicating 68881 floating-point coprocessor) are used to enable 68881 $\overline{\text{CS}}$. The 68020 A19 and A18 pins are not used in the chip select decode since their values are 00_2.

The $\overline{\text{BERR}}$ pin is asserted for low CS and high $\overline{\text{SENSE}}$ signals. A trap routine can be executed to perform the coprocessor operations.

The protocols involved between the MC68020 and MC68881 are shown in Figures 7.38a through 7.38f.

Let us now provide a MC68881 interface example: consider FMOVE.P (A0) +, FP0. Note that .P means "packed decimal" (12 bytes).

The above instruction moves 12 bytes from MC68020 main memory addressed by the MC68020 address register A0 to the MC68881 floating-point register, FP0. This MOVE instruction converts packed BCD numbers to extended-precision real values. The machine code equivalent of FMOVE.P (A0) +, FP0 includes two words as follows:

$F218

$4C00

The first word $F218 in Figure 7.38a specifies that the instruction is F-line, coprocessor type is MC68881, and that the instruction is general type with source operand having postincrement mode indirectly addressed by A0. The second word $4C00 in Figure 7.38a defines the op code type (FMOVE), source data format (.P), and destination register (FP0).

When the MC68020 executes the MOVE.P (A0) +, FP0 instruction,

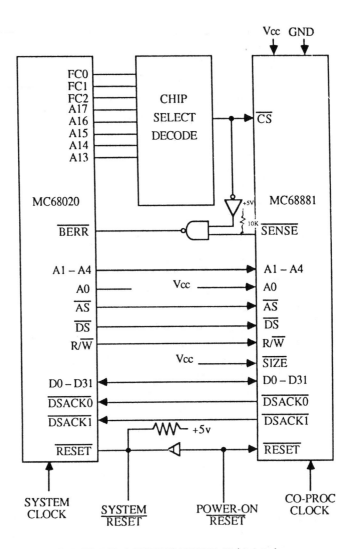

FIGURE 7.37 MC68020/MC68881 32-bit interface.

it places $0002200A on the address bus A31-A0. In this data, A19, A18, A17, A16 = 0010_2 indicates coprocessor communications and bits A15, A14, A13 = 001 specifies that the coprocessor is MC68881. Bits 31-20 and bits 5-11 are always zeros during a coprocessor access and FC2, FC1, FC0 = 111_2 indicates CPU space cycle. Figure 7.38b provides the M68020 address bus encodings for MC68881 access (see Figure 7.38b). Bits 0-4 provide $0A which is the address for the MC68881 command register. The information encoded on the FC2-FC0 lines and address lines A17-A13 (A19, A18 always zero) of the MC68020 during the MC68881 access can

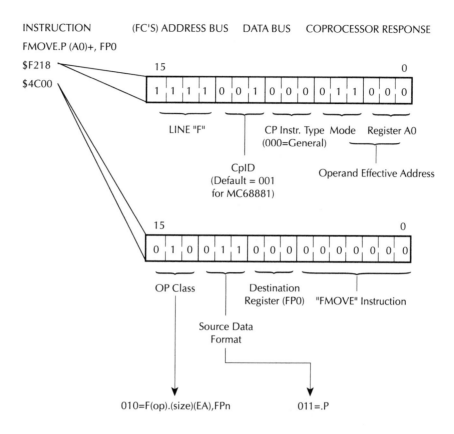

FIGURE 7.38a MC68881 interface example.

be used to generate the chip select signal ($\overline{\text{CS}}$) for the MC68881 (see Figure 7.37). The MC68020 address lines A4-A0 are used to specify that the command register (address $0A) in the command interface register set is being accessed during operand transfers between the MC68020 and the MC68881. The MC68020 also writes $4C00 [second word of the instruction FMOVE.P (A0) +, FP0] on the data bus. The MC68881 asserts $\overline{\text{DSACKX}}$, receives this datum $4C00, and places it in its command register. The MC68881 responds to the MC68020 command in the command register by writing appropriate data in the response register (address $00). The MC68881 places these data on the data bus and then asserts $\overline{\text{DSACKX}}$. The MC68020 places 111_2 on FC2FC1FC0 and $00022000 on A31-A0 (A4A3A2A1A0 = 00000_2 means response register). The MC68020 also asserts the R/$\overline{\text{W}}$ pin to read the contents of the MC68881 response register ($960C in this example) as shown in Figure 7.38c.

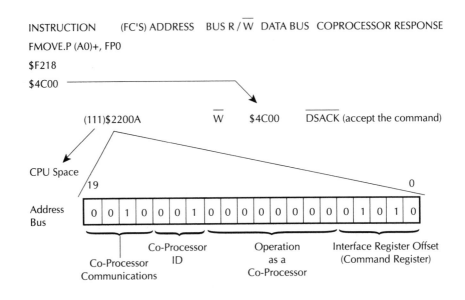

FIGURE 7.38b MC68881 interface example.

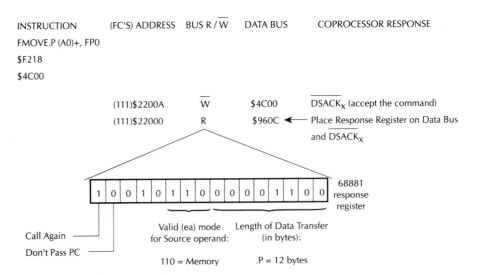

FIGURE 7.38c MC68881 interface example.

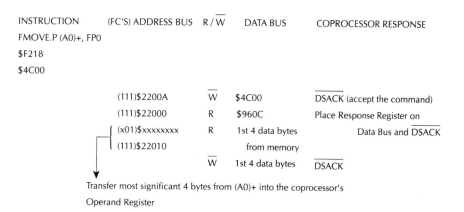

INSTRUCTION FMOVE.P (A0)+, FP0 $F218 $4C00	(FC'S) ADDRESS BUS	R/$\overline{W}$	DATA BUS	COPROCESSOR RESPONSE
	(111)$2200A	$\overline{W}$	$4C00	$\overline{DSACK}$ (accept the command)
	(111)$22000	R	$960C	Place Response Register on
	(x01)$xxxxxxxx	R	1st 4 data bytes	Data Bus and $\overline{DSACK}$
	(111)$22010		from memory	
		$\overline{W}$	1st 4 data bytes	$\overline{DSACK}$

Transfer most significant 4 bytes from (A0)+ into the coprocessor's
Operand Register

FIGURE 7.38d MC68881 interface sample.

INSTRUCTION FMOVE.P (A0)+, FP0 $F218 $4C00	(FC'S) ADDRESS BUS	R/$\overline{W}$	DATA BUS	COPROCESSOR RESPONSE
	(111)$2200A	$\overline{W}$	$4C00	$\overline{DSACK}$ (accept the command)
	(111)$22000	R	$960C	Place Response Register on
	(X01)$xxxxxxxx	R	1st 4 data bytes	Data Bus and $\overline{DSACK}$
			from memory	
	(111)$22010	$\overline{W}$	1st 4 data bytes	$\overline{DSACK}$
	(X01)$xxxxxxxx	R	memory data	
	(111)$22010	$\overline{W}$	Cp data	$\overline{DSACK}$
	(X01)$xxxxxxxx	R	memory data	
	(111)$22010	$\overline{W}$	Cp data	$\overline{DSACK}$

Transfer rest of data (8 bytes) from (A0)+ into the coprocessor's
Operand Register

FIGURE 7.38e MC68881 interface sample.

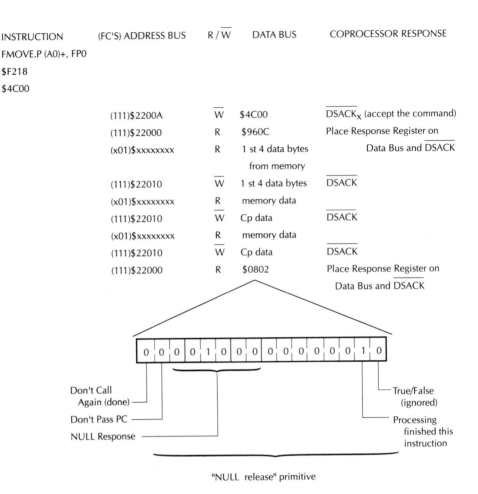

INSTRUCTION FMOVE.P (A0)+, FP0 $F218 $4C00	(FC'S) ADDRESS BUS	R/$\overline{W}$	DATA BUS	COPROCESSOR RESPONSE
	(111)$2200A	$\overline{W}$	$4C00	$\overline{DSACK_X}$ (accept the command)
	(111)$22000	R	$960C	Place Response Register on
	(x01)$xxxxxxxx	R	1 st 4 data bytes	Data Bus and $\overline{DSACK}$
			from memory	
	(111)$22010	$\overline{W}$	1 st 4 data bytes	$\overline{DSACK}$
	(x01)$xxxxxxxx	R	memory data	
	(111)$22010	$\overline{W}$	Cp data	$\overline{DSACK}$
	(x01)$xxxxxxxx	R	memory data	
	(111)$22010	$\overline{W}$	Cp data	$\overline{DSACK}$
	(111)$22000	R	$0802	Place Response Register on
				Data Bus and $\overline{DSACK}$

0 0 0 0 1 0 0 0 0 0 0 0 0 0 1 0

Don't Call
Again (done)
Don't Pass PC
NULL Response

True/False
(ignored)
Processing
finished this
instruction

"NULL release" primitive

FIGURE 7.38f MC68881 interface example.

The response primitives are encoded instructions that the coprocessor such as the MC68881 issues to the MC68020 during the execution of a coprocessor instruction. The MC68881 can communicate status information and service requests to the MC68020 through the use of the coprocessor response primitives.

The instruction FMOVE.P (A0) +, FP0 allows the MC68020 to transfer an operand from the MC68020 effective address specified in the coprocessor instruction operation word to the MC68881. This primitive is allowed with general category instructions. The format for this response primitive is given in Figure 7.39.

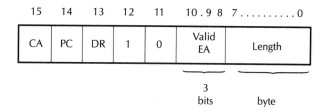

FIGURE 7.39 Evaluate effective address and transfer data primitive format.

The MC68881 response register contents of $960C in Figure 7.38c can be interpreted as follows: bit 15 in the coprocessor response primitive format, denoted by CA (call or come again), is used to specify call again operation of the MC68020. Whenever the MC68020 receives a response primitive from the response register with the CA bit set to one, it will carry out the service indicated by the primitive and then come back to read the response register.

Bit 14 in the response primitive format, denoted by PC, is used to pass program counter. If the PC bit is set to one, the MC68020 will immediately pass the current PC contents to the coprocessor instruction address interface register.

As the first operation in servicing, the primitive request bit 13 of the coprocessor response primitive format, denoted by DR, is the direction bit and is used in conjunction with operand transfers between the MC68020 and the coprocessor. If DR = 0, the direction of transfer is from the main processor to the coprocessor (MC68020 write). If DR = 1, the direction of transfer is from the coprocessor to the MC68020 (MC68020 read). If the operation does not involve operand transfer, the bit value is part of the particular primitive encoding.

In Figure 7.38c, CA = 1 for call again, PC = 0 for don't pass, and PC and DR = 0 for transfer from the MC68020 to the MC68881 as required in the FMOVE instruction. Bits 12 and 11 are always zero; bits 10, 9, and 8 contain 110 indicating value (EA) mode for the source; length byte = 12, indicating 12 bytes (.P) or 96 bits to be transferred.

Upon receipt of this primitive, the MC68020 calculates the effective address and then transfers the number of bytes (12 bytes in this case) specified in the response primitive.

As shown in Figure 7.38d, the MC68020 outputs $\chi 01$ to FC2FC1FC0 and the address \$XXXXXXXX on A31-A0 pins along with R/$\overline{W}$ = 1. The memory device places the first four bytes from memory on D31-D0 lines. In the last step of Figure 7.38d, the MC68020 outputs 111 on FC2FC1FC0 to be in CPU space and then outputs $00022010 on A31-A0 lines along with R/$\overline{W}$ line LOW to access the MC68881 operand register (low 5 bits of the address lines A0-A4 specify the coprocessor interface register and A4-A0 = $10 indicates MC68881 operand register). The MC68881 asserts $\overline{DSACKX}$, takes the first 4 bytes of the total 8 bytes, and then stores it in the operand register. Note that the MC68881 operand register is a 32-bit read/write register and is used by the MC68020 to transfer data to and from the MC68881.

In Figure 7.38e the MC68020 transfers the remaining 8 bytes of data from (A0) + into the MC68881 operand register. Since the 12-byte data transfer is complete, the MC68881 places the null primitive in its response register. The format for the null primitive is given in Figure 7.40.

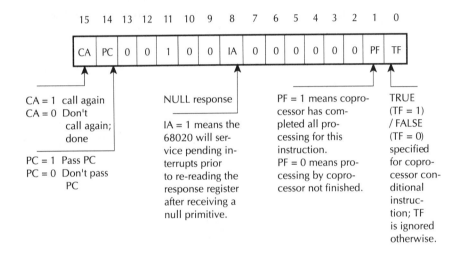

FIGURE 7.40   MC68881 null primitive format.

In Figure 7.40 CA = 0 indicates done, PC = 0 means don't pass, and PC and PF = 1 indicates the MC68881 has finished this instruction. The MC68020 places 111_2 on FC2FC1FC0 and $00022000 on A31-A0 to select the MC68881 response register, along with R/$\overline{W}$ HIGH.

After asserting $\overline{DSACKX}$, the MC68881 places the response register contents $0802 on data bus. The MC68020 reads these data and determines that the coprocessor has completed all processing associated with this instruction.

Example 7.7

For the following figure, write MC68020 assembly program using floating-point coprocessor instructions; determine X and θ.

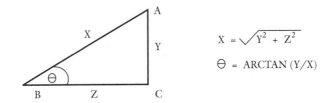

$$X = \sqrt{Y^2 + Z^2}$$

$$\theta = ARCTAN\,(Y/X)$$

Assume X, Y, and Z are 32 bits wide.

Solution

```
        MOVE.L      Y, FP2      ;     MOVE  Y  TO  FP2
        MOVE.L      Z, FP3      ;     MOVE  Z  TO  FP3
        FMOVE.L     FP2, FP0    ;     MOVE  Y  TO  FP0
        FMOVE.L     FP3, FP1    ;     MOVE  Z  TO  FP1
        FMUL.L      FP0, FP0    ;     Y²
        FMUL.L      FP1, FP1    ;     Z²
        FADD.L      FP0, FP1    ;     Z² + Y²
                                           _____
        FSQRT.L     FP1         ;     X = √Y² + Z²
        FDIV.L      FP3,FP2     ;     θ is
        FATAN       FP2         ;     ARCTAN (Y/Z)
STOP    JMP         STOP
```

7.4.2 MC68851 MMU

The MC68851 coprocessor is a demand Paged Memory Management Unit (PMMU) designed to support the MC68020-based virtual memory system. The 68851 is included in a 132-PGA package and can be operated at a frequency of either 12.5 or 16.67 MHz.

The main functions of the 68551 are to provide logical-to-physical address translation, protection mechanism, and to support the 68020 breakpoint operations.

The 68851 translates a logical address comprised of a 32-bit address and a 4-bit function code. The 68851 has four function code pins, FC0-FC3, issued by the 68020 into a corresponding 32-bit physical address in main memory. The 68851 initiates address translation by searching for the page descriptor corresponding to the logical-to-physical mapping in the on-chip 64-entry full-associative Address Translation Cache (ATC). This cache stores recently used page descriptors. If the descriptor is not found in the ATC, then the 68851 aborts the logical bus cycle, signals the 68020 to retry the operation, and requests mastership of the logical bus. Upon receiving indication that the logical bus is free, the 68851 takes over the logical bus and executes bus cycles to search the translation tables in physical (main) memory pointed to by the relevant root pointer to locate the required translation descriptor that defines the page accessed by this logical address.

After obtaining the needed translation descriptor, the 68851 returns control of the logical bus to the 68020 to retry the previous bus cycle which can now be verified for access right and properly translated by the 68851.

The 68851 automatically searches the translation tables in case of descriptor misses in the ATC using hardware without any assistance from the operating system. The 68851 translation tables have a tree structure, as depicted in Figure 7.41.

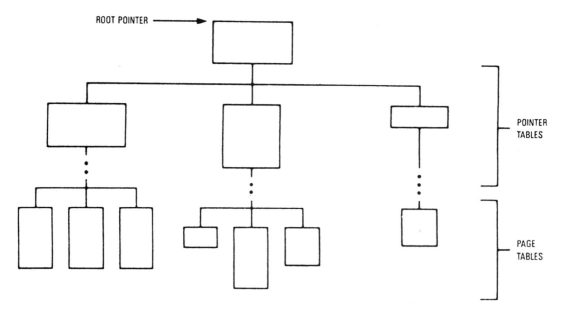

FIGURE 7.41 MC68851 translation table tree structure.

As shown in the figure, the root of a translation table is pointed to by one of the three 64-bit root pointer registers: CPU root pointer, supervisor root pointer, or DMA root pointer.

The CPU root pointer points at the translation table tree for the currently executing task; the supervisor root pointer points to the operating systems translation table; and the DMA root pointer points to a DMA controller's (if present in the system) translation table.

All addresses contained in the translation tables are physical addresses. In Figure 7.41, table entries at the higher levels of the tree (pointer tables) contain pointers to other tables. Entries at the leaf level (page tables) contain page descriptors. The pointer table lookup normally uses the function codes as the index, but they may be suppressed. The 68851 includes the 4-bit bidirectional function code pins, FC0-FC3, which indicate the address space of the current bus cycle. The 4-bit function code consists of the three function code outputs (FC0-FC2) of the 68020 and a fourth bit that indicates that a DMA access is in progress. When the 68851 is bus master, it drives the function code pins as outputs with a constant value of FC3-FC0 = $5, indicating the supervisor data space.

The 68851 hierarchical protection mechanism monitors and enforces the protection/privilege mechanism. These may be up to 8 levels with privilege hierarchy, and the upper 3 bits of the incoming logical address define these levels, with level 0 as the highest privilege in the hierarchy and level 7 as the lowest level. Privilege levels of 0, 2, or 4 can also be implemented with the 68851, in which case the access level encoding is included in the upper zero, one, or two logical address lines, respectively. The 68851 access level mechanism, when enabled, compares the access level of the memory logical address with the current access level as defined in the Current Access Level (CAL) register. The current access level defines the highest privilege level that a task may assume at that time.

If the privilege level provided by the bus cycle is more privileged than allowed, then the 68851 terminates this access as a fault.

In the 68851 protection mechanism, the privilege level of a task is defined by its access level. Smaller values for access levels specify higher privilege levels. In order to access program and/or data requiring a higher privilege level than the level of the current task, the 68851 provides CALLM (call module) and RTM (return from module) instructions. These instructions allow a program to call a module operating at the same or higher privilege level and to return from that module after completing the module function.

The 68851 provides a breakpoint acknowledge facility to support the 68020. When the 68020 executes a breakpoint instruction, it executes a breakpoint acknowledge cycle and reads a predefined address in the CPU space cycle. The 68851 decodes this address and responds by either providing a replacement op code for the breakpoint op code and asserting $\overline{\text{DSACKx}}$ inputs or by asserting 68020 $\overline{\text{BERR}}$ input to execute illegal instruction exception processing. The 68851 can be programmed to provide (1) the replacement op code n times ($1 \leq n \leq 255$) in a loop and then assert $\overline{BERR}$ or (2) assert $\overline{BERR}$ on every breakpoint.

The 68851 instructions provide extension to the 68020 instruction set via the coprocessor interface. These instructions provide:

1.   Loading and storing of MMU registers
2.   MMU control functions
3.   Access rights and conditionals checking

For example, the PMOVE instruction moves data to or from the 68851 registers using all 68020 addressing modes. PVALID compares the access level bits of an incoming logical address with those of the Valid-Access Level (VAL) register and traps if the address bits are less. PTEST searches the ATC and translation tables for an entry corresponding to a specific address and function code. The results of the test are placed in the 68851 status register which can be tested by various conditional branch and set instructions.

Optionally, the PTEST instruction can obtain the address of the page descriptor. A companion instruction, PLOAD, takes a logical address and function code, searches the translation table, and loads the ATC with an entry to translate the logical address.

PLOAD can be used to load the ATC before starting the memory transfer. This can speed up a DMA operation. PFLUSH and its variations clear the ATC of either all entries, entries with a specified function code, or those limited to a particular function code and logical address.

PSAVE saves the contents of any register that reflects the current task's state and the internal state of the 68851 dealing with coprocessor and module call operations. PRESTORE restores the information saved by PSAVE. PSAVE and PRESTORE permit the context of the 68851 to be switched.

The PBcc, PDBcc, PScc, and PTRAPcc instructions have the same meaning as those of the 68020 except that the conditions are based on the 68851 condition codes.

Figure 7.42 shows a 68020-based microcomputer system which interfaces 68881 and 68851 chips to the 68020. The 68851 MMU is placed between the logical and physical address buses. The 68851 allows interfacing memory, disk controller, and serial I/O devices to the 68020.

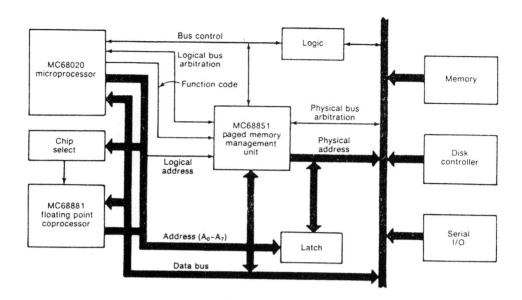

FIGURE 7.42 A 68020-based microcomputer with coprocessors.

QUESTIONS AND PROBLEMS

7.1 What is the purpose of affected 68020 CALLM and RTM instructions?

7.2 Determine the contents of 68020 register, memory locations, and condition code register after execution of CAS.B D2, D4, (A0). Assume the following data prior to execution of the instruction:

$$[D2] = \$60003002$$

$$[D4] = \$80001000$$

$$[A5] = \$30001004 = \$5004$$

$$\begin{array}{c} \text{X N Z V C} \\ \text{CCR} = \boxed{1\,|\,1\,|\,0\,|\,0\,|\,0} \end{array}$$

7.3   Determine the contents of 68020 registers and memory locations after execution of CAS2·W D5:D6, D0:D0, (A5):(A6). Assume the following data prior to execution of CAS2:

$$
\begin{aligned}
\texttt{[D0]} &= \texttt{\$0000 0000} \\
\texttt{[D5]} &= \texttt{\$AAAA AAAA} \\
\texttt{[D6]} &= \texttt{\$0000 3AAB} \\
\texttt{[D1]} &= \texttt{\$0000 0001}
\end{aligned}
$$

Memory

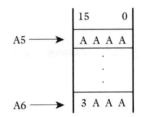

7.4   i)   Name two exception vectors for the MC68851 and the MC68881.

ii)   What is the size of the 68020 on-chip cache?

iii)   What is the 68020 cache access time?

7.5   What are the values of SIZ1, SIZ0, FC2, FC1, FC0, R/$\overline{\text{W}}$, and A31-A0 pins after execution of the 68020 BKPT #3 instruction?

7.6   Determine the values of FC2, FC1, FC0, and A31-A0 pins for a 68020 CPU space cycle with a floating-point coprocessor command register being accessed.

7.7   Assume a 68020/68881 system. Write a program in 68020 assembly language to find

$$\sqrt{X^2 + Y^2}$$

Assume X and Y are 32-bit integers.

7.8   Determine the values of 68020 operation word, command register, function code, R/$\overline{\text{W}}$, and that address bus when the 68881 asserts $\overline{\text{DSACKX}}$ to accept the command after execution of the following instruction:

FADD.L D2, FD2

Use the following data:

FADD	0100010_2
op class	010_2
.L	000_2
operand mode	000_2

7.9 i) Write a 68020 instruction sequence using CAS2 to insert an element in a double-linked list.

ii) Write a 68020 instruction sequence using CAS2 to delete the last entry in a linked list. Note that a double-linked list needs two controlled locations which point to the last element inserted in the list and the next element to be removed. If the list is empty, both pointers are NULL (0). Therefore, a double-linked list maintains a forward link and a reverse link.

7.10 i) What are the main functions of the 68851 MMU?

ii) Summarize the address translation and protection mechanism of the 68851.

iii) How does the 68851 support the 68020 breakpoint function?

Chapter 8

MOTOROLA MC68030 AND MC88100

This chapter provides an overview of the hardware, software, and interfacing features associated with the MC68030 and MC88100.

The MC68030 is a 32-bit virtual memory microprocessor based on the MC68020, while the MC88100 is a 32-bit RISC (Reduced Instruction Set Computer) microprocessor.

8.1 MOTOROLA MC68030

The MC68030 is a virtual memory microprocessor based on an MC68020 core with additional features. The MC68030 is designed by using HCMOS technology and can be operated at 16.67-, 20-, and 33-MHz clocks.

The MC68030 contains all features of the MC68020, plus some additional features. The basic differences between the MC68020 and MC68030 are listed below:

Characteristics	MC68020	MC68030
On-chip cache	256-byte instruction cache	256-byte instruction cache and 256-byte data cache
On-chip Memory Management Unit (MMU)	None	Paged data memory managment (demand page of the MC68851)
Instruction set	101	105 (four new instructions are for the chip MMU)

743

Like the MC68020, the MC68030 also supports 7 data types and 18 addressing modes. The MC68030 I/O is identical to the MC68020. The MC68020 enhancements such as instruction cache and MMU, along with the basic MC68030 features, are described in the following section.

8.1.1 MC68030 BLOCK DIAGRAM

Figure 8.1 shows the MC68030 block diagram and includes the major sections of the processor.

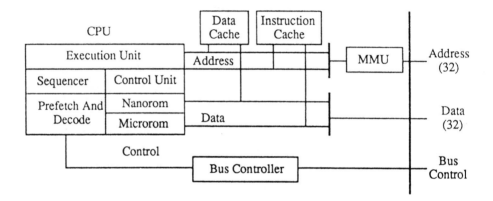

FIGURE 8.1 MC68030 block diagram.

The bus controller includes all the logic for performing bus control functions and also contains the multiplexor for dynamic bus sizing. It controls data transfer between the MC68030 and memory or I/O devices at the physical address.

The control section contains the execution unit and associated logic. Program Logic Arrays (PLAs) are utilized for instruction decode and sequencing.

The instruction and data cache units operate independently. They obtain information from the bus controller for future use. Each cache has its own address and data buses and thus permits simultaneous access. Both the caches are organized as 64 long word entries (256 bytes) with a block size of four long words. The data cache uses a write-through policy with no write allocation on cache misses.

The memory management unit maps address for page sizes from 256 bytes to 32K bytes. Mapping information stored in descriptors resides in translation tables in memory that are automatically searched by the MC68030 on demand. Most recently used descriptors are maintained in a 22-entry fully associative cache called the Address Translation Cache (ATC) in the MMU, permitting address translation and other MC68020 functions to occur simultaneously. The MMU utilizes the ATC to translate the logic address generated by the MC68030 into a physical address.

8.1.2 MC68030 PROGRAMMING MODEL

Figure 8.2 shows the MC68030 programming model.

The additional registers implemented in the 68030 beyond those of the 68020 are for supporting the MMU features. All common registers in the 68030 are the same as the 68020, except the cache control register which has additional control bits for the data cache and other new cache functions.

The 68030 additional registers are

- 32-bit translation control register (TC)
- 64-bit CPU root pointer (CRP)
- 64-bit supervisor root pointer (SRP)
- 32-bit transparent translation registers TT0 and TT1
- 16-bit MMU status register, MMUSR

The TC includes several fields that control address translation. These fields enable and disable address translation, enable and disable the use of SRP for the supervisor address space, and select or ignore the function codes in translating addresses. Other TC fields specify memory page sizes, the number of address bits used in translation, and the translation table structure.

The CRP holds a pointer to the root of the translation tree for the currently executing 68030 task. This tree includes the mapping information for the task's address space.

The SRP holds a pointer to the root of the translation tree for the supervisor's address space when the 68030 is configured to provide a separate address space for the supervisor programs.

Registers TT0 and TT1 can each specify separate memory blocks as directly addressable without address translation. Logic addresses in these areas are the same as physical addresses for memory access. Therefore, registers TT0 and TT1 provide fast movement of larger blocks of data in memory or I/O space, since delays associated with the translation scheme are not encountered. This feature is useful in graphics and real-time applications.

The MMUSR register includes memory management status information resulting from a search of the address translation cache or the translation tree for a particular logical address.

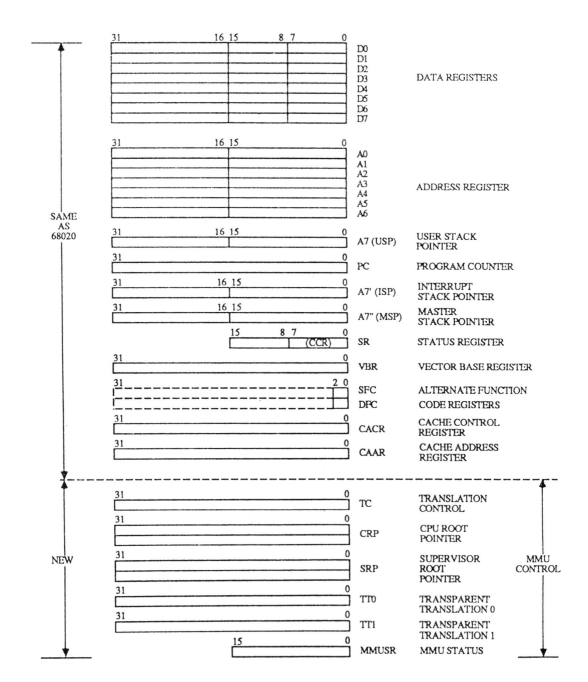

FIGURE 8.2 MC68030 programming model.

8.1.3 MC68030 DATA TYPES, ADDRESSING MODES, AND INSTRUCTIONS

Like the MC68020, seven basic data types are supported on the MC68030:

- Bits
- Bit fields
- BCD digits
- Byte integers (8 bits)
- Word integers (16 bits)
- Long word integers (32 bits)
- Quad word integers (64 bits)

The 18 addressing modes of the MC68020 are also supported by the MC68030.

The MC68030 includes all MC68020 instructions, plus a subset of the MC68851 (PMMU) instructions. These instructions (Table 8.1) include PMOVE, PTEST, PLOAD, and PFLUSH, and they are compatible with the corresponding instructions in the MC68851 PMMU. The MC68020 requires the MC68851 coprocessor interface to execute these instructions. These instructions are executed by the MC68030 just like all other instructions.

All the MMU instructions are privileged and do not affect the condition codes. These new instructions are explained in the following sections.

TABLE 8.1
MC68030 New Instructions

Instruction	Operand syntax	Operand size	Operation
PFLUSH	(FC),#mask [(EA)]	None	Invalidate ATC entries at effective address
PLOAD	(FC),(EA),{R/W}	None	Create ATC entry for effective address
PMOVE	Rn,(EA)	16, 32	Register n → destination
	(EA),Rn	16, 32	Source → register n
PTEST	(FC), (EA),#level, {R/W}An	None	Information about logical address → PMMU status

8.1.3.a PMOVE Rn, (EA) or (EA), Rn

Rn can be any MMU register. (EA) uses control alterable addressing mode. The operand size depends on the MMU registers used as follows:

```
CRP, SRP        Quad word (64-bit)
TC, TT          Long word (32-bit)
MMUSR           Word (16-bit)
```

The PMOVE instruction moves data to and from the MMU registers. This instruction is normally used to initialize the MMU registers and to read the contents of the MMUSR for determining a fault.

As an example, consider PMOVE (A5), SRP. This instruction moves a 64-bit word pointed to by A5 to the supervisor root pointer.

8.1.3.b PTEST

The PTEST has four forms:

```
PTESTR (function code), (EA), #level
PTESTR (function code), (EA), #level,An
PTESTW (function code), (EA), #level
PTESTW (function code), (EA), #level,An
```

The PTEST instruction interrogates the MMU about a logical address and is normally used to determine the cause of a fault. The PTEST instruction executes a table search for the ATC or the translation tables to a specified level for the translation descriptor corresponding to the (EA) and indicates the results of the search in the MMU status register.

The PTESTR or PTESTW means that search is to be done as if the bus cycle is a read or a write. The details of the operand are given below:

- The function code is specified in one of the following ways
  - Immediate (three bits in the command word)
  - Data register (three least-significant bits of the data register specified in the instruction)
  - Source function code register
  - Destination function code register
- The (EA) operand provides the address to be tested.
- The level operand defines the maximum depth of table or number of descriptors to be searched. Level 0 means searching ATC only while levels 1 to 7 indicate searching the translation tables only.

Execution of the PTEST instruction continues to the registry level until invalid descriptor, limit violation, or bus error assertion occurs.

When the address register, An, is specified for a translation table search, the physical address of the last table entry (last descriptor) fetched is loaded into the address register.

The MMUSR includes the results of the search. Table 8.2 shows the values in the fields of the MMUSR for an ATC search.

As an example of PTEST, consider

```
PTESTR SFC, (A3), #4, A5
```

The function code for the page is in the Source Function Code register, SFC. The content of A3 is the logical address and the search is to be extended to 4 levels. Search is to be done as if for a read bus cycle and the physical address of the last entry checked is to go to A5.

The PTEST instruction is unsized and the condition codes are unaffected, but the MMUSR contents are changed.

8.1.3.c PLOAD

The PLOAD instruction loads an entry into the ATC. This is normally used in demand paging systems to load the descriptors into the ATC before returning to execute the instruction that caused the page fault.

The two forms for the instruction are

```
PLOADR (function code), (EA)
PLOADW (function code), (EA)
```

The function code is specified in one of the following ways:

- Immediate
- Data register
- Source function code register
- Destination function code register

(EA) can be control alterable addressing modes only. The PLOAD instruction searches the ATC for (EA) and also searches the translation table for the descriptor with respect to (EA). It is used to load a descriptor from the translation tables to the address translation cache.

The condition codes and MMUSR contents are unaffected.

As an example, consider PLOADR SFC, (A5). The function code for

TABLE 8.2
MMUSR Fields for an ATC Search

MMUSR bit	PTEST, Level 0	PTEST, Level 1-7
Bus error (B)	This bit is set if the bus error bit is set in the ATC entry for the specified logical address	This bit is set if a bus error is encountered during the table search for the PTEST instruction
Limit (L)	This bit is cleared	This bit is set if an index exceeds a limit during the table search
Supervisor violation (S)	This bit is cleared	This bit is set if the S bit of a long (S) format table descriptor or long format page descriptor encountered during the search is set, and the FC2 bit of the function code specified by the PTEST instruction is not equal to one, the S bit is undefined if the I bit is set
Write protected (W)	The bit is set if the WP bit of the ATC entry is set; it is undefined if the I bit is set	This bit is set if a descriptor or page descriptor is encountered with the WP bit set during the table search, the W bit is undefined if the I bit is set
Invalid (I)	This bit indicates an invalid translation; the I bit is set if the translation for the specified logical address is not resident in the ATC, or if the B bit of the corresponding ATC entry is set	This bit indicates an invalid translation, the I bit is set if the DT field of a table or a page descriptor encountered during the search is set to invalid, or if either the B or L bits of the MMUSR are set during the table search
Modified (M)	This bit is set if the ATC entry corresponding to the specified address has the modified bit set; it is undefined if the I bit is set	This bit is set if the page descriptor for the specified address has the modified bit set; it is undefined if I bit is set
Transparent (T)	This bit is set if a match occurred in either (or both) of the transparent translation registers (TT0 or TT1)	This bit is set to zero
Number of levels (N)	This 3-bit field is cleared to zero	This 3-bit field contains the actual number of tables accessed during the search

the desired page is in SFC. The logical address for which the descriptor is desired is in A5 and the descriptor is to be loaded as for a read bus cycle.

8.1.3.d PFLUSH

The PFLUSH instruction invalidates cache entries. The forms of PFLUSH are

```
PFLUSHA
PFLUSH (function code), mask
PFLUSH (function code), mask, (EA)
```

The operands can be specified as follows:

- (Function code) can be immediate (3 bits), data register (least significant 3 bits), SFC, or DFC.
- mask when set to one uses corresponding bit in function code for matching.
- (EA) can be any one of the control alterable addressing modes.

The instruction is unsized and condition codes and MMUSR contents are unaffected.

The PFLUSHA instruction invalidates all ATC entries. When (function code) and mask are specified in the PFLUSH instruction, the instruction invalidates all entries for the specified function code or codes. When the PFLUSH instruction also specifies (EA), the instruction invalidates the page descriptor for that effective address entry in each specified function code.

The mask operand includes three bits corresponding to the function code bits. Each bit in the mask that is set to one means that the corresponding bit by the function code operand applies to the operation. Each bit in the mask with zero value means that a bit of function code operand and the function code that is ignored. As an example, consider PFLUSH #1,4. The mask operand of 100_2 causes the instruction to consider only the most significant bit of the function code operand. Since the function code is 001_2, function codes 000, 001, 010, and 011 are selected.

8.1.4 MC68030 CACHE

The 68030 cache is placed between the processor and the rest of the memory system. The effective memory access time

$$t_{acc} = h * t_{cache} + (1 - h) * t_{ext}$$

where t_{acc} = effective system access time, t_{cache} = cache access time, t_{ext} =

access time of the rest of the system, and h = hit ratio or % of time data, is found in the cache.

The instruction cache in the 68030 is a 256-byte direct-mapped cache with 16 blocks. Each block contains four long words. Each long word can be accessed independently and thus 64 entries are possible with A1 selecting a correct word during an access. Figure 8.3 shows the 68030 instruction cache.

The index or a line is addressed by address lines A4 through A7 and each entry is selected by A2 and A3. The tag includes address lines A8 through A31 along with FC2.

A0 is not used since instructions must be at even addresses (A0 is always zero).

An entry means that a line hit has occurred and the valid bit (four valid bits, one for each long word) for the selected entry is set. If an entry miss occurs, the cache entry can be updated with the instructions read from memory. If the cache is disabled, no cache hits or updates will take place, and if the cache is enabled but frozen, hits can occur without updates.

CACR can be used to clear cache entries and enable or disable the caches. The system hardware can disable the on-chip caches at any time by asserting the $\overline{CDIS}$ input pin.

Figure 8.4 shows the organization of the 68030 data cache. The data cache is organized in the same way as the instruction cache except that all three function code bits are used to determine a line hit. The data cache can be updated for both read and write. If the data cache is disabled, no hits or updates will occur. However, when the data cache is enabled but frozen, hits can occur and updates for write but not read can take place. The data cache can be updated for both read and write if enabled but not frozen.

The data cache utilizes a write-through policy with no write allocation of data writes. This means that if a cache hit takes place on a write cycle, both the data cache and the external device are updated with the new data. If a write cycle genrates a miss in the data cache, only the external device is updated and no data cache entry is replaced or allocated for that address.

Let us now consider some examples of the 68030 cache. Consider Figure 8.5 showing an instruction cache entry hit. The figure shows the CLR.W(A1) instruction with op code 4251_{16} at PC = $11CCA29E_{16}$ to be accessed in user space (FC2 = 0). The most significant column above the tag field is the FC2 bit which is 1 for supervisor space and 0 for user space. The 68030 outputs 0 on FC2 and $11CCA29E_{16}$ on its address pins. Assume that the instruction cache is enabled. Since A3-A0 is 1110_2, the address bits A3-A2 are 11_2. This means LW3 in cache is accessed. A31-A8

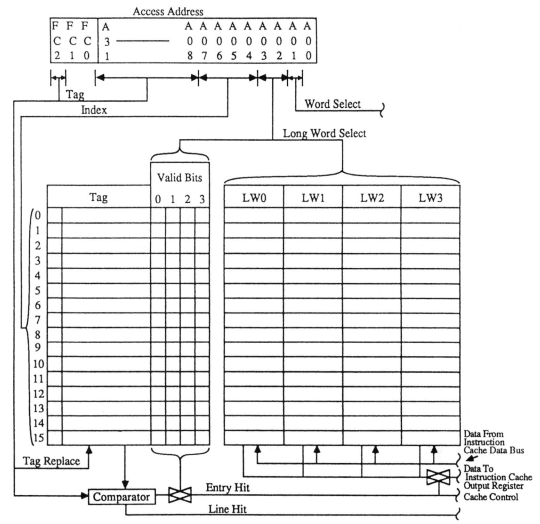

- Cache size = 64 longwords
- Line size = 4 longwords
- Set size = 1 (direct mapped)
- For an entry hit to occur
  - The access address tag field (A8-A31 and FC2) must match the tag field selected by the index field (A4-A7)
  - The selected longword entry (A2-A3) must be valid
  - The cache must be enabled in the Cache Control Register

FIGURE 8.3 MC68030 instruction cache.

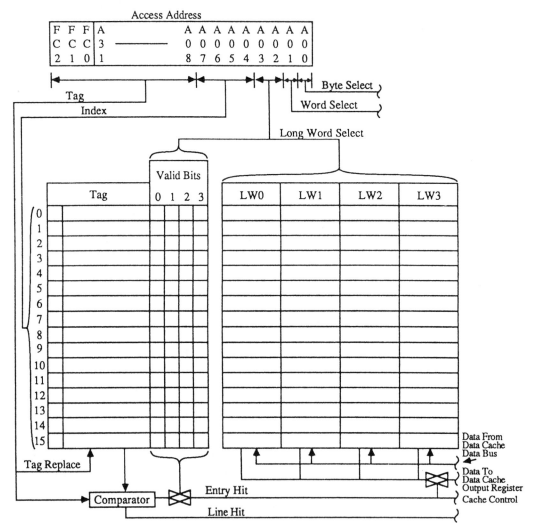

FIGURE 8.4 MC68030 data cache.

- Cache size = 64 longwords
- Line size = 4 longwords
- Set size = 1 (direct mapped)
- For an entry hit to occur
  - The access address tag field (A8-A31, FC0-FC2) must match the tag field selected by the index field (A4-A7)
  - The selected longword entry (A2-A3) must be valid
  - The cache must be enabled in the Cache Control Register

is $11CCA2_{16}$ which is used as the tag field with A7 through A4 (9_{10}) as the index field. A line hit occurs since the tag at index 9 in the cache matches

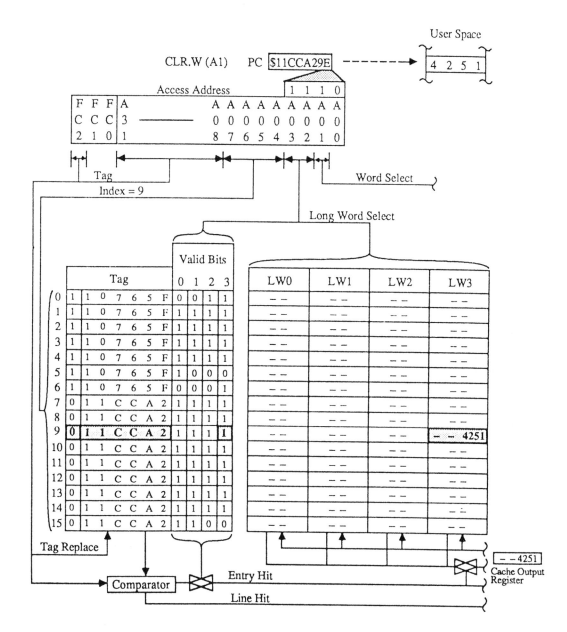

FIGURE 8.5 Instruction cache hit entry example.

A31 through A8 and FC2 = 0. Therefore, the valid bit 3 is set to one. The op code 4251_{16} is thus read into the cache output register.

Figure 8.6 illustrates instruction cache miss. In this case, the op code 4251_{16} for CLR.W(A1) stored at the PC value of $276F1A64_{16}$ in supervisor

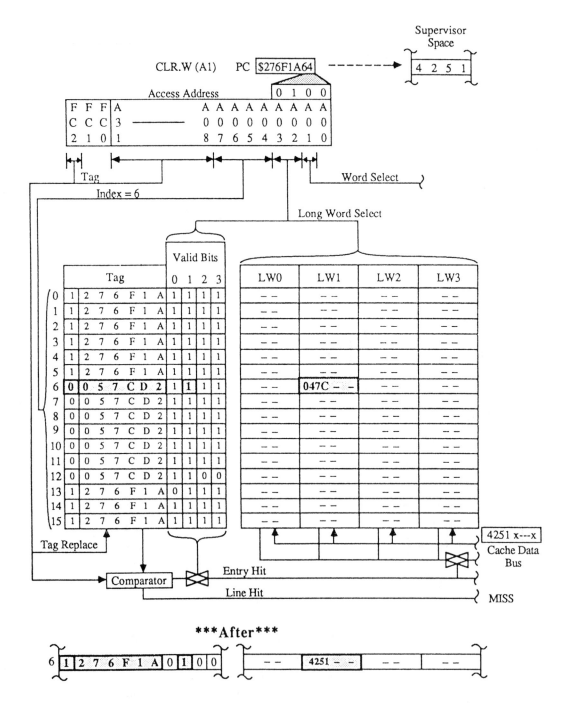

FIGURE 8.6 Instruction cache miss.

space (FC2 = 1) is to be accessed. The 68030 outputs one on the FC2 pin and $276F1A64_{16}$ on the A31-A0 pins. A miss occurs since the tag in line $6(057CD2_{16})$ does not match the address bits A31-A8 ($276F1A_{16}$) and FC2 = 1 does not match the function code bit (0), the most significant bit above the tag field. Assume the cache is enabled and not frozen. The 68030 reads 4251_{16} into LW1 from external memory and updates the FC2 field and tag field with 1 and $276F1A_{16}$, respectively. The valid bits are updated as 0100_2. Figure 8.7 shows an example of data cache hit. The 68030 executes MOVE.W(A1), D0 to read data $C28F_{16}$ at address $75B4A176_{16}$ pointed to by A1 in user data space FC2FC1FC0 = 001. Note that the most significant column shows the value on the function code pins. Since A3A2 = 01, LW1 is accessed with tag value of $75B4A1_{16}$ and index value of 7. Assume that the cache is enabled. Since the tag value in the cache matches A31-A8 and the function code values (FC2 FC1 FC0 = 001) match the function code field value of 1 in the cache, a cache hit occurs. The valid bit 1 is set to one and datum $C28F_{16}$ is placed in the cache output register. Figure 8.8 shows an example of data cache miss. The 68030 executes the instruction MOVE.W(A1), D0 to read the contents of $01F376B8_{16}$ pointed to by A1 into D0 in the supervisor data space (FC2 FC1 FC0 = 101_2). Since A3A2 = 10_2, LW2 in the cache is accessed. Assume the cache is enabled but not frozen. Since the function code pins in cache do not match the 68030 function codes, cache miss occurs. Valid bit 2 is set to one. The 68030 obtains datum 1576_{16} from external memory into low word of D0 and then updates the function code and tag fields of the cache. The 68030 then invalidates LW0, LW1, LW3 and validates LW2 by writing 0010_2 in the valid bits.

8.1.5 68030 PINS AND SIGNALS

The 68030 is housed in a 13×13 PGA package for 16.67 MHz and RC Suffix Package for 20 MHz.

Figure 8.9 shows the 68030 pin diagram. Figure 8.10 shows the 68030 functional signal groups. Table 8.3 summarizes the signal description.

8.1.6 MC68030 READ AND WRITE TIMING DIAGRAMS

The MC68030 provides three ways of data transfer between itself and the peripherals. These are

- Asynchronous transfer
  - Synchronous transfer
  - BURST mode transfer

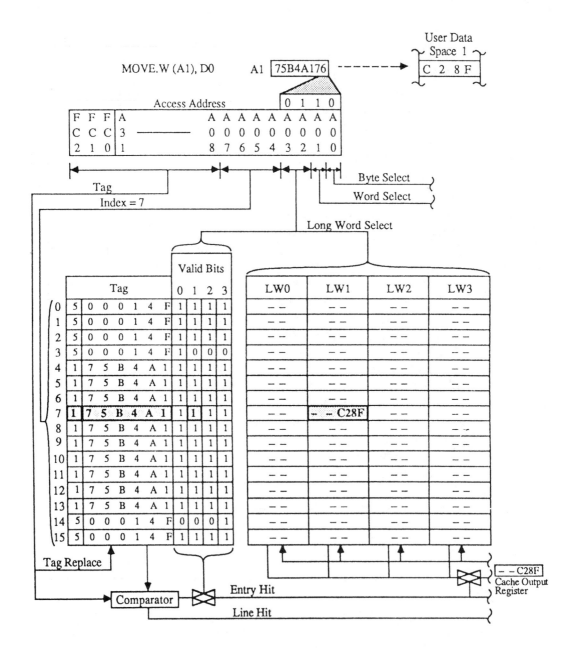

FIGURE 8.7 Data cache entry hit example.

In the asynchronous operation, the external devices connected to the system bus can operate at clock frequencies different from the MC68030 clock. Asynchronous operation requires only the handshake lines $\overline{AS}$, $\overline{DS}$,

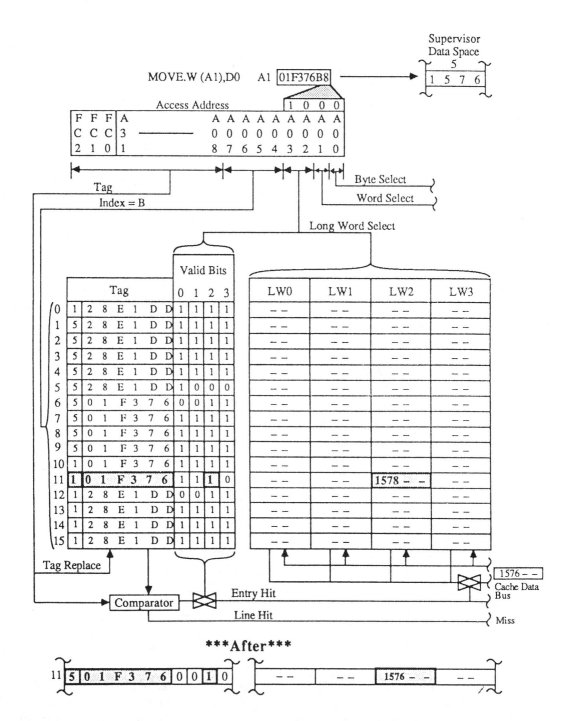

FIGURE 8.8 Data cache miss.

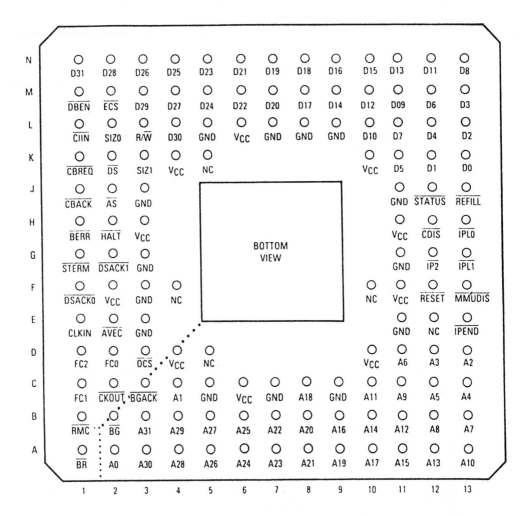

FIGURE 8.9 MC68030 pin diagram.

Group	V_{CC}	GND
Address Bus	A9, D3	A10, B9, C3, F12
Data Bus	M8, N8, N13	L7, L11, N7, K3
Logic	D1, D2, E3, G11, G13	G12, H13, J3, K1
Clock		B1

DSACKx, BERR and HALT. The asynchronous bus cycles of the MC68030
are similar to those of the MC68020. The MC68030 can transfer data in
a minimum of three clock cycles. The dynamic bus sizing using the
DSACKx signals can determine the amount of data transferred on a cycle-
by-cycle basis.

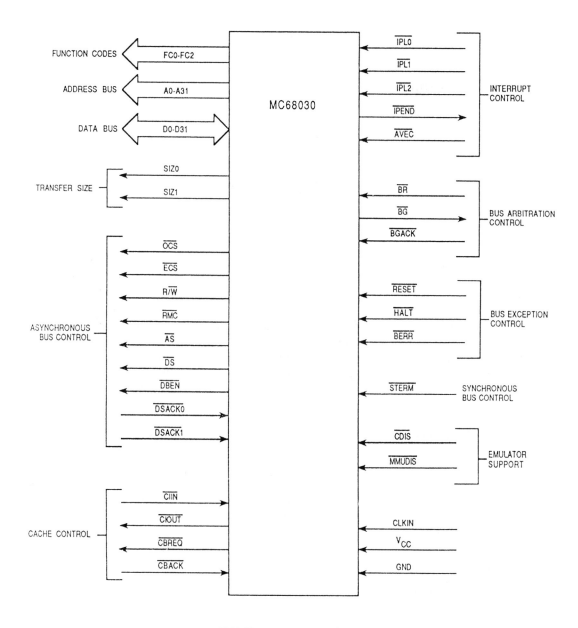

FIGURE 8.10 MC68030 functional signal groups.

Synchronous bus cycles are terminated with the $\overline{\text{STERM}}$ (synchronous termination) signal and always transfer 32-bit data in a minimum of two clock cycles. The cycles terminated with the $\overline{\text{DSACKx}}$ signals can also be classified as synchronous if the signals are interpreted relative to clock

TABLE 8.3
Signal Description

Signal name	Mnemonic	Function
Function codes	FC0-FC2	3-bit function code used to identify the address pace of each bus cycle
Address bus	A0-A31	32-bit address bus used to address any of 4,294,967,296 bytes
Data bus	D0-D31	32-bit data bus used to transfer 8, 16, 24, or 32 bits of data per bus cycle
Size	SIZ0/SIZ1	Indicates the number of bytes remaining to be transferred for this cycle; these signals, together with A0 and A1, define the active sections of the data bus
Operand cycle start	$\overline{OCS}$	Identical operation to that of $\overline{ECS}$ except that $\overline{OCS}$ is asserted only during the first bus cycle of an operand transfer
External cycle start	$\overline{ECS}$	Provides an indication that a bus cycle is beginning
Read/write	$R/\overline{W}$	Defines the bus transfer as an MPU read or write
Read-modify-write cycle	$\overline{RMC}$	Provides an indicator that the current bus cycle is part of an indivisible read-modify-write operation
Address strobe	$\overline{AS}$	Indicates that a valid address is on the bus
Data strobe	$\overline{DS}$	Indicates that valid data is to be placed on the data bus by an external device or has been placed on the data bus by the MC68020
Data buffer enable	$\overline{DBEN}$	Provides an enable signal for external data buffers
Data transfer and size acknowledge	$\overline{DSACK0}/$ $\overline{DSACK1}$	Bus response signals that indicate the requested data transfer operation is completed; in addition, these two lines indicate the size of the external bus port on a cycle-by-cycle basis and are used for asynchronous transfers
Cache inhibit in	$\overline{CIIN}$	Prevents data from being loaded into the MC68030 instruction and data caches
Cache inhibit out	$\overline{CIOUT}$	Reflects the CI bit in ATC entries; indicates that external caches should ignore these accesses
Cache burst request	$\overline{CBREQ}$	Indicates a burst request for the instruction or data cache
Cache burst acknowledge	$\overline{CBACK}$	Indicates that accessed device can operate in burst mode
Interrupt priority level	$\overline{IPL0}-\overline{IPL2}$	Provides an encoded interrupt level to the processor
Interrupt pending	$\overline{IPEND}$	Indicates that an interrupt is pending
Autovector	$\overline{AVEC}$	Requests an autovector during an interrupt acknowledge cycle

TABLE 8.3 (continued)
Signal Description

Signal name	Mnemonic	Function
Bus request	$\overline{BR}$	Indicates that an external device requires bus mastership
Bus grant	$\overline{BG}$	Indicates that an external device may assume bus mastership
Bus grant acknowledge	$\overline{BGACK}$	Indicates that an external device has assumed bus mastership
Reset	$\overline{RESET}$	System reset; same as 68020
Halt	$\overline{HALT}$	Indicates that the processor should suspend bus activity
Bus error	$\overline{BERR}$	Indicates an invalid or illegal bus operation is being attempted
Synchronous termination	$\overline{STERM}$	Bus response signal that indicates a port size of 32 bits and that data may be latched on the next falling clock edge
Cache disable	$\overline{CDIS}$	Dynamically disables the on-chip cache to assist emulator support
MMU disable	$\overline{MMUDIS}$	Dynamically disables the translation mechanism of the MMU
Clock	CLK	Clock input to the processor
Power supply	Vcc	+5 volt ± 5% power supply
Ground	GND	Ground connection

edges. The cycles that use the synchronous cycles must synchronize the responses to the MC68030 clock in order to be synchronous.

The synchronous cycles terminated with $\overline{STERM}$ are for 32-bit ports only, while the synchronous cycles terminated by $\overline{DSACKx}$ can be for 8-, 16-, or 32-bit ports. The main difference between the use of $\overline{STERM}$ and $\overline{DSACKx}$ is that $\overline{STERM}$ can be asserted and data can be transferred earlier than for a synchronous cycle terminated with $\overline{DSACKx}$. Wait cycles can be inserted by delaying the assertion of $\overline{STERM}$ if required.

BURST mode transfer can be used to fill blocks of the instruction and data caches when the MC68030 asserts $\overline{CBREQ}$ (cache burst request).

BURST mode transfer takes place in synchronous operation and requires assertion of $\overline{STERM}$ to terminate each of its cycles. BURST mode is enabled by bits in the cache control register (CACR).

As an illustration of 68030 read/time timing diagrams, 68030 longword read and write cycles for asynchronous operation will be considered.

Figure 8.11 depicts two write cycles (between two read cycles, with no idle time in-between) for a 32-bit device. The timing diagram in Figure 8.11 for read can be explained as follows:

1.   The read cycle for an instruction such as MOVE.L (A0), D1 starts in state 0 (S0). The MC68030 drives the external cycle start ($\overline{ECS}$) pin

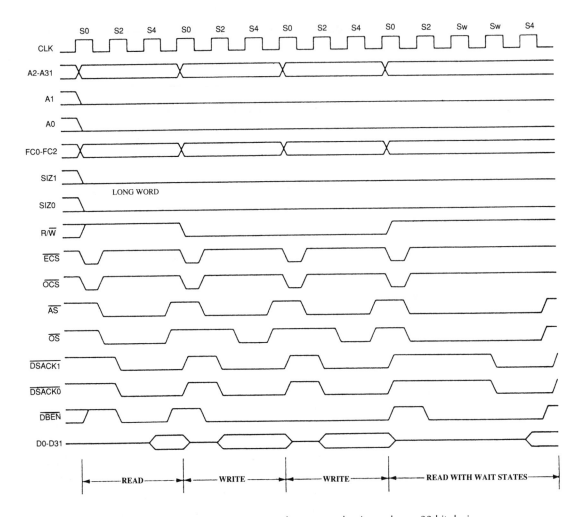

FIGURE 8.11 Asynchronous read-write cycles — 32-bit device.

LOW indicating the start of an external cycle. When the cycle is the first external cycle of a read operand, the MC68030 outputs low on the operand cycle start ($\overline{\text{OCS}}$) pin. The MC68030 then places a valid address (content of register A0 in this case) on A0-A31 pins and valid function codes on FC0-FC2 pins. The MC68030 drives R/$\overline{\text{W}}$ HIGH for read and drives data buffer enable ($\overline{\text{DBEN}}$) inactive to disable data buffers. SIZ0 and SIZ1 signals become valid, indicating the number of bytes to be transferred. Cache inhibit out ($\overline{\text{CIOUT}}$) becomes valid, indicating the state of the MMUCI bit in the address translation descriptor or in the selected TTx register.

2.   During S1, the MC68030 activates $\overline{\text{AS}}$ LOW, indicating a valid ad-

dress on A0-A31. The MC68030 then activates $\overline{DS}$ LOW and negates $\overline{ECS}$ and $\overline{OCS}$ (if asserted).

3. During S2, the MC68030 activates the $\overline{DBEN}$ pin to enable external data buffers. The selected device such as a memory chip utilizes $\overline{DS}$, SIZ0, SIZ1, R/$\overline{W}$, and $\overline{CIOUT}$ to place data on the data bus. The MC68030 outputs LOW on $\overline{CIIN}$ if appropriate. Any or all bytes on D0-D31 are selected by SIZ0, SIZ1, A0, and A1. At the same time, the selected device asserts the $\overline{DSACKx}$ signals. The MC68030 samples $\overline{DSACKx}$ at the falling edge of the S2 and if $\overline{DSACKx}$ is recognized, the MC68030 inserts no wait states.

   As long as at least one of the valid $\overline{DSACKx}$ is asserted by the end of S2 (satisfying the asynchronous setup time requirement), the MC68030 latches data on the next falling edge of the clock and ends the cycle. If $\overline{DSACKx}$ is not recognized by the MC68030 by the beginning of S3, the MC68030 inserts wait states and $\overline{DSACKx}$ must remain HIGH throughout the asynchronous input setup and holds times around the end of the S2. During MC68030's wait states, the MC68030 continually samples $\overline{DSACKx}$ on the falling edge of each of the subsequent cycles until one $\overline{DSACKx}$ is asserted.

4. With no wait states, at the end of S4, the MC68030 latches data.

5. During S5, the MC68030 negates $\overline{AS}$, $\overline{DS}$, and $\overline{DBEN}$. The MC68030 keeps the address valid during S5 to provide address hold time for memory systems R/$\overline{W}$, SIZ0, and SIZ1, and FC0-FC2 also remain valid during S5.

The timing diagram in Figure 8.11 for write can be explained as follows:

1. The MC68030 outputs LOW on both $\overline{ECS}$ and $\overline{OCS}$ and places a valid address and function codes on A0-A31 and FC2-FC0, respectively. The MC68030 also places LOW on R/$\overline{W}$ and validates SIZ0, SIZ1, and $\overline{CIOUT}$.

2. In S1, the MC68030 asserts $\overline{AS}$ and $\overline{DBEN}$ and negates $\overline{ECS}$ and $\overline{OCS}$ (if asserted).

3. During S2, the MC68030 outputs data to be written on D0-D31 and samples $\overline{DSACKx}$ at the end of S2.

4. During S3, the MC68030 outputs LOW on $\overline{DS}$, indicating that the data are stable on data bus. As long as at least one of the valid $\overline{DSACKx}$ is recognized by the end of S2, the cycle terminates after one cycle. If $\overline{DSACKx}$ is not recognized by the start of S3, the MC68030 inserts wait states. If wait states are inserted, the MC68030 continues to sample the $\overline{DSACKx}$ signals on the subsequent falling edges of the

clock, until one of the $\overline{\text{DSACKx}}$ is recognized. The selected device such as memory utilizes R/$\overline{\text{W}}$, $\overline{\text{DS}}$, SIZ0, SIZ1, and A0 and A1 to latch data from the appropriate portion of D0-D31 pins.
The MC68030 generates no new control signals during S4.

5.   During S5, the MC68030 negates $\overline{\text{AS}}$ and $\overline{\text{DS}}$. The MC68030 holds the address and data valid to provide address hold time for memory systems. The processor also keeps R/$\overline{\text{W}}$, SIZ0, SIZ1, FC0-FC2, and $\overline{\text{DBEN}}$ valid during S5.

8.1.7 MC68030 ON-CHIP MEMORY MANAGEMENT UNIT
8.1.7a MMU Basics

A Memory Management Unit (MMU) translates addresses from the microprocessor (logical) to physical addresses. Logical addresses are assigned to the task when it is linked, while physical addresses are assigned at the time the task is loaded into memory based on free physical addresses. The MMU keeps a task in its own address space. If a task attempts to go out of its own address space, the MMU asserts bus error. Besides protection, this feature is valuable in demand paging systems.

An operating system must know the free physical memory addresses available so that it can load the next task to these spaces. One way of accomplishing this is by dividing the memory into contiguous blocks of equal size. These are called pages on the logical side of the MMU and page frames on the physical side. The system memory will contain page descriptions which point to the page frames and status of the page frames.

The page size determines the number of address bits to be translated by the MMU and the number which addresses memory directly. The lower bits of the logical address related to the page size are not translated by the MMU and directly go to the physical address bus as shown in Figure 8.12. Note that A8-A3 bits provide the page number and A0-A7 bits define the 256-byte page size in this case.

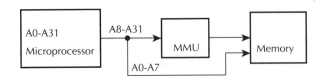

FIGURE 8.12 Logical to physical translation.

A translation table can be used to translate pages to page frames. Figure 8.13 shows an example of table translation of pages. The task control block

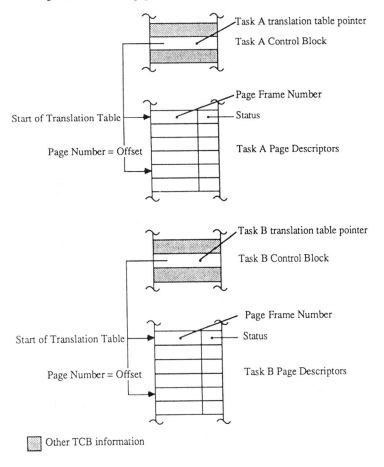

- Pages can be related to page frames with a translation table.

Task A translation table pointer

Task A Control Block

Page Frame Number

Start of Translation Table

Status

Page Number = Offset

Task A Page Descriptors

Task B translation table pointer

Task B Control Block

Page Frame Number

Start of Translation Table

Status

Page Number = Offset

Task B Page Descriptors

Other TCB information

FIGURE 8.13 Table translation of pages.

contains a pointer to the starting address of the translation table. A logical address is translated by accessing the location in the translation table determined by starting address of translation + (page number * entry size). The entry accessed contains the page frame number. Note that entry size is 4 for 32 bits (4 bytes).

Each task has a translation table. Single or multiple translation tables can be used. Figure 8.14 shows an example of a single pointer level translation. The TCB contents $00010000 contain the starting address of the translation table. The 12-bit page size ($C5E for P2) replaces the low 12 bits of the physical address directly. The logical address for P2 is translated by accessing the translation table at the location

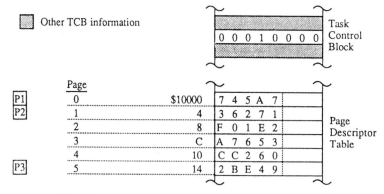

• LOGICAL ADDRESS, PAGE SIZE = 4K BYTES

• EXAMPLE

• TRANSLATION EXAMPLES

	LOGICAL	PHYSICAL
P1	$123	$745A7123
P2	$1C5E	$36271C5E
P3	$5678	$2BE49678

• If a task has only 2 pages, 0 and $FFFFF, the page descriptor table must be the same size as if the task used all pages. Size = 2^{20} x 4 bytes = 1048576 x 4 = 4194304 bytes.
• Each task has a translation table.

FIGURE 8.14 Single-pointer level translation.

```
= $10000 + (Page number * entry size)
= $10000 + ($00001 * 4)
= $100004
```

Therefore, location $100004 in the translation table is accessed and its content $36271 is obtained as the page frame number. The 12-bit page size $C5E is concatenated with the page frame number to obtain the physical address for page P2 as $36271C5E.

One of the disadvantages of the single-level translation is that for most systems, the required sizes would be too large. Therefore, multilevel translation tables are used. For example, consider the double pointer level translation table of Figure 8.15. In this case, the TCB contains a pointer

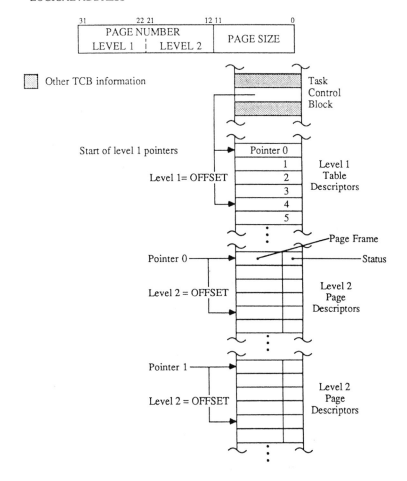

FIGURE 8.15 Double pointer level translation.

to the starting address of the level 1 translation table. Level 1 descriptors contain pointers to level 2 page descriptors.

A logical address is translated in two steps:

1. A pointer is obtained from level 1 translation table as follows: pointer from level 1 table = starting address of level 1 translation table + (level 1 * entry size of level 1 table).

2. This pointer is used to access a location in level 2 table by adding the pointer obtained from level 1 table with (level 2 * entry size of level 2 table).

The location in table 2 thus obtained contains the page frame number. Consider the logical address:

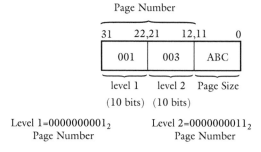

If TCB contents ($10000) point to the starting address of table 1, level 1 location

```
= $10000 + level 1 * entry size of level 1
= $10000 + 1 * 4
= $10004
```

Therefore, if the content of $10004 is $21000 pointing to the starting address of level 2 table, then the accessed location in table 2

```
= $21000 + (3₁₀ * 4)
= $2100C
```

$$= \$21000 + (3_{10} * 4)$$
$$= \$2100C$$

Assume the content of $2100C is $25719. Then $25719 is concatenated with the page size $ABC to obtain the 32-bit physical address $25719ABC. An example of the double-pointer level translation is shown at the top of the next page.

Assume a page size of 4K bytes. Let us translate the following logical addresses to physical addresses for the task shown above:

$0000072A and $00401A59

Consider the logical address $0000072A. This address has level 1 and level 2 page numbers of 0. This means that level 1 location

```
= $00780000 + 0 * 4
= $00780000
```

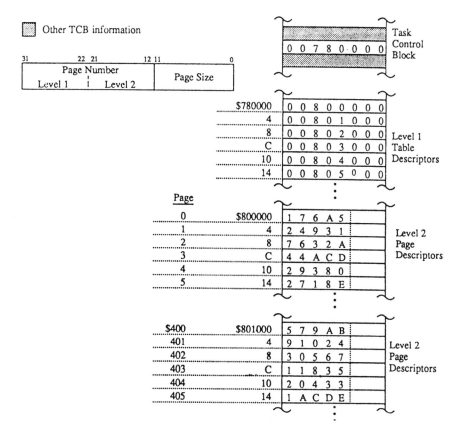

Double-pointer level translation

Therefore, [$00780000] points to the starting address of level 2 table; then the accessed location in table 2

$$= \$00800000 + 0 * 4$$
$$= \$00800000$$

The content of location $00800000 ($176A5) is concatenated with the page size $72A so that the physical address is $176A572A.

Next, consider the logical address $00401A59. The uppermost 10 bits $(0000\ 000001_2)$ define the level 1 page number as one. The next 10 bits $(0000\ 000001_2)$ define the level 2 page number as one. The page size is $A59. Level 1 location

$$= \$7800\ 0000 + (1 * 4)$$
$$= \$7800\ 0004$$

The content of location $7800 0004 ($00801000) points to the starting address of level 2 table. Level 2 location

$$= \$00800100 + 1 * 4$$
$$= \$0080\ 1004$$

The content of location $0080 1004 ($91024) is concatenated with the page size $A59 to obtain the physical address $91024 A59.

The main advantage of the multiple translation table is that it reduces the required translation table size significantly. However, multiple memory access (two in the example of two-level translation) is required to obtain a descriptor. However, address translation cache can be used to speed up memory access.

An MMU provides three basic functions:

* Translates page number to page frame number
* Restricted access, i.e., a task, is restricted to its own address space.
* Provides write protection by not allowing write access to write-protected pages

The status information is included in the low bits of the translation table entry data to provide protection information.

8.1.7.b 68030 On-chip MMU

Figure 8.16 provides a block diagram of of the MC68030 and identifies the on-chip MMU.

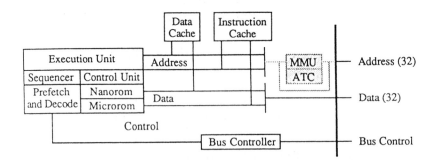

FIGURE 8.16 MC68030 on-chip MMU block diagram.

The 68030 on-chip MMU translates logical addresses to physical addresses. If the desired information is in the address translation cache, no time delay occurs due to MMU address translation. The page descriptor is obtained by the MMU by searching the translation tables if needed.

The pins used by the 68030 on-chip MMU are A31-A0, $\overline{\text{CIOUT}}$, and $\overline{\text{MMUDIS}}$.

The MMU outputs the translated physical addresses (from logical addresses) or the addresses for fetching translation data (when a table is searched) on the A31-A0 pins. The MMU asserts $\overline{\text{CIOUT}}$ pin for pages which are defined as noncacheable. The $\overline{\text{MMUDIS}}$ pin, when asserted by an external emulator, disables the MMU.

The 68030 executes a normal bus cycle when the address translation information is in the ATC. However, if the address translation information is not in the ATC, the 68030 executes additional bus cycles to obtain the desired address translation information.

The 68030 includes three main elements in its MMU: a set of registers, ATC, and table search logic.

Figure 8.17 provides the MMU registers.

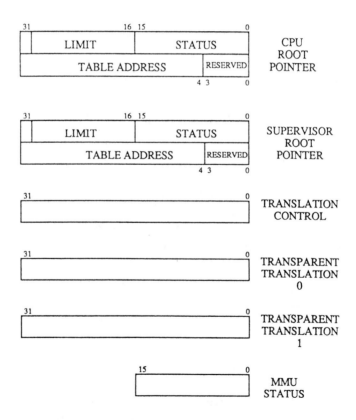

FIGURE 8.17 MC68030 MMU registers.

The CRP or SRP points to the beginning of the task translation table and supervisor table (if enabled), respectively.

The translation control register controls the MMU functions such as MMU enable.

The transparent translation registers output specified logical addresses on the A31-A0 pins.

The MMUSR provides the results of execution of the MMU instructions PMOVE (EA), MMUSR and PTEST. The MMUSR stores memory management status information resulting from a search of the address translation cache, or the translation tree, for a particular logical address.

As mentioned before, four MMU instructions — PMOVE, PTEST, PLOAD, and PFLUSH — are included in the 68030 instruction set. The MMU provides up to 5 levels of address translation tables. Address translation starts with the contents of the root pointers CRP or SRP.

Figure 8.18 provides a typical 5-level table translation scheme.

Figure 8.19 provides the ATC block diagram along with a simplified flowchart for the physical address translation.

The ATC is a content-addressable, fully associative cache with up to 22 descriptors. The ATC stores recently used descriptors so that table search is not required if future accesses are required.

There are six types of descriptors used in MMU operation. These are ATC page descriptors, table descriptors, early termination page descriptors, invalid descriptor, and indirect descriptor. Some descriptors have a long and a short form.

Figure 8.20 shows the page descriptor summary.

Each ATC entry consists of a logical address and information from a corresponding page descriptor. The 28-bit logical or tag portion of each entry consists of three fields. These are the valid bit field (bit 27), function code field (bits 26-24), and 24-bit logical address field (bits 0-23). The V-bit indicates that the entry is valid if V = 1. The function code field includes the function code bits (FC0-FC2) corresponding to the logical address in this entry. The 24-bit logical address includes the most significant logical address bits for this entry. All 24 bits are used in comparing this entry to an incoming logical address when the page size is 256 bytes. For larger page sizes, some least significant bits of this field are ignored.

Table descriptors have short (32-bit) and long (64-bit) forms. In the 32-bit short form, the table descriptor includes four status bits (bits 0-3) and a 28-bit table address. The status bit provides information such as write protection and descriptor type.

The table address contains the 28-bit physical base address of a table of descriptors. The long table descriptor includes a 28-bit table address, a

• Up to 5 level translation tables

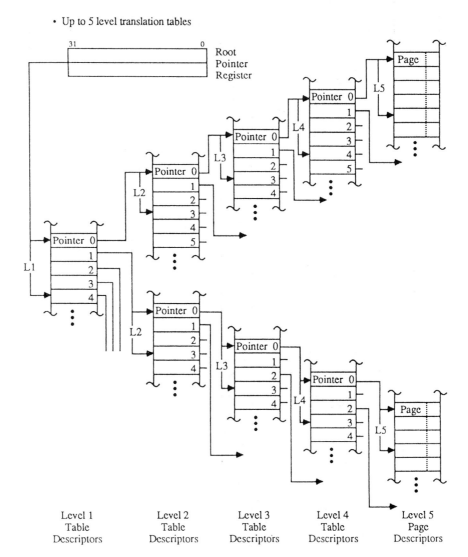

FIGURE 8.18 MC68030 MMU five-level translation scheme.

16-bit status information, and a 16-bit limit field. The status bits in the long form include additional information such as whether the table is a supervisor-only table. The limit field includes a limit to which the index portion of an address is compared to detect an out-of-bounds index.

The page descriptors also have short and long formats. The short page format is identical to the short table format except that for page tables, page table and status information related to pages are used. The long page

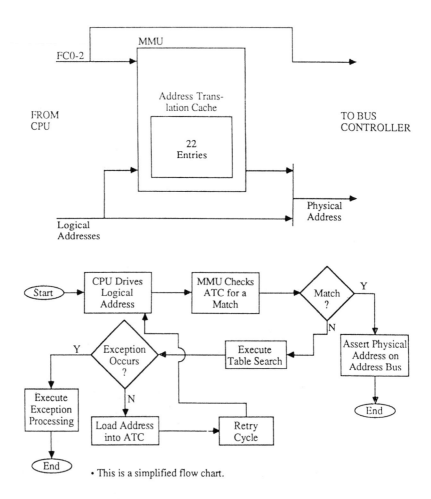

FIGURE 8.19 Address translation cache (ATCC) and flowchart for translation.

descriptor contains a 24-bit page address and 16-bit status information. The status bits provide information such as write protect, descriptor type, and identification of a modified page.

The early termination page descriptor (both short and long form) includes the page descriptor identification bits in the descriptor-type field of the status bits, but the descriptor resides in a pointer table. This means that the table in which an early termination page descriptor is located is not at the bottom level of the address translation tree. The invalid descriptors can also be short and long forms. These descriptors only contain the two descriptor-type status bits and are used with long or short page and table descriptors.

The indirect descriptors also include short and long forms. They

• Address Translation Cache Page Descriptor

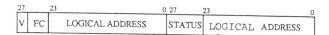

• Table Descriptors

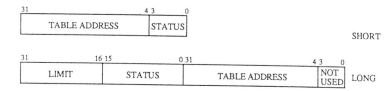

• Page Descriptors

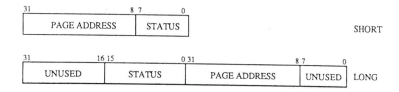

• Early Termination Page Descriptors

• Invalid Descriptors

• Indirect Descriptors

FIGURE 8.20 Page descriptor summary.

contain physical address of a page descriptor and two descriptor-type bits which identify an indirect descriptor that point to a short or long format page descriptor.

Tables 8.4 summarizes differences between 68030 on-chip MMU and 68851.

Now let us discuss the details of the 68030 MMU registers. The CRP points to the first level translation table. It is normally loaded during a context (task) switch. The ATC is automatically flushed when the CRP is loaded. Figure 8.21 shows the details of the CRP.

The limit field in the CRP limits the size of the next table. That is, it limits the size of the table index field. If the limit is exceeded during a table search, an ATC entry is created with bus error set. Two fields are assigned to the limit. These are $L/\overline{U}$ and limit. $L/\overline{U} = 1$ means a lower range limit, while $L/\overline{U} = 0$ indicates an upper range limit. If $L/\overline{U} = 0$ and limit = $7FFF or $L/\overline{U} = 1$ and limit = 0, the limit function is suppressed. The translation control register (TC) permits the user to control the translation

TABLE 8.4
68030 On-Chip MMU vs. 68851

Features of the 68851 not included on the 68030 MMU
   No access level (no CALLM or RTM instructions)
   No breakpoint registers
   No DMA root pointer
   No task aliasing
   22 entry ATC instead of 64
   No lockable content-addressable memory (CAM) entries
   No shared globally entries
   Instructions supported
      PFLUSHA, PFLUSH, PMOVE, PTEST, PLOAD
   Instructions not supported (F-line trap)
      PVALID, PFLUSHR, PFLUSHES, PBcc, PDBcc, PScc, PTRAPcc,
      PSAVE, PRESTORE
   Control alterable effective addresses only for the
      MMU instructions

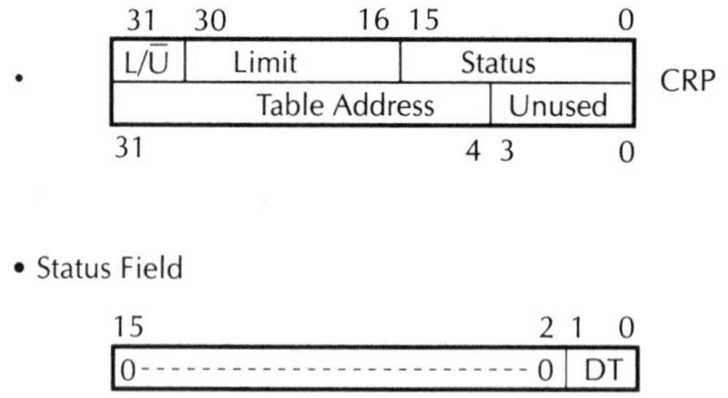

• Status Field

• DT Values

    00   Not allowed. If loaded with this value, an MMU
          Configuration Error exception occurs.

    01   Table address field is a page descriptor.

    10   Table address field points to descriptors which
          are 4 bytes long.

    11   Table address field points to descriptors which
          are 8 bytes long.

FIGURE 8.21 CRP details.

of the access. TC is also used to enable and disable the main function of the MMU. Figure 8.22 shows the details of TC.

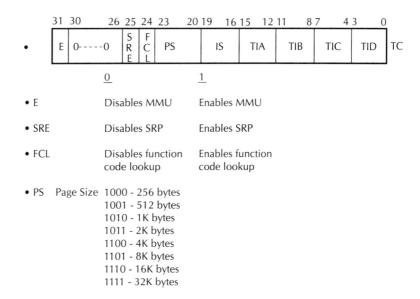

		0	1
• E		Disables MMU	Enables MMU
• SRE		Disables SRP	Enables SRP
• FCL		Disables function code lookup	Enables function code lookup

- PS   Page Size   1000 - 256 bytes
                     1001 - 512 bytes
                     1010 - 1K bytes
                     1011 - 2K bytes
                     1100 - 4K bytes
                     1101 - 8K bytes
                     1110 - 16K bytes
                     1111 - 32K bytes

- IS   Initial shift
  The number of upper address bits which are to be ignored during a table search.

- TIA, TIB, TIC, TID   Table index fields
  Specifies the number of bits of logical address to be used as an index into the table at each level

FIGURE 8.22 TC details.

The SRP is similar to the CRP except that it is used only for supervisor access. This register must be enabled in the TC before use. The format of SRP is shown in Figure 8.23.

FIGURE 8.23 SRP form.

If a task is required to access physical memory directly, such as in graphics application, TT0 or TT1 can be used to specify the physical areas of memory to be accessed.

Figure 8.24 provides formats for TT0 and TT1.

The MMUSR includes the results of execution of PTEST instruction for level = 0 or level ≠ 0.

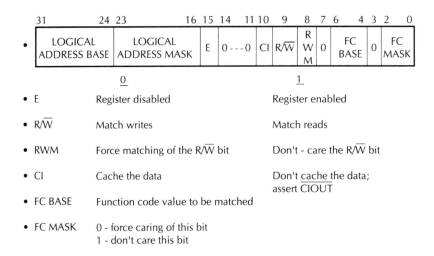

FIGURE 8.24   TT0 and TT1 details.

Figure 8.25 provides the MMUSR details.

The ATC entries include two (logical and physical) 28-bit fields. The logical field includes a valid bit, function codes, and page number. The physical field contains four control/status bits and page frame number. Figure 8.26 includes the ATC entry structure.

The translation tables supported by the 68030 contain a tree structure. The root of a translation table tree is pointed to by one or two root pointer registers.

Table entries at higher levels of the tree contain pointers to other tables, while entries at the leaf level (page tables) contain page descriptors. The technique used for table searches utilizes portions of the logical address as index for each level of the lookup. All addresses contained in the translation table entries are physical addresses.

Figure 8.27 shows the 68030 MMU translation table tree structure.

The function codes are usually used as an index in the first level of lookup in the table. However, this may be suppressed. In table searching, up to 15 of the logical address lines can be ignored. The number of levels

• The information in the MMU status register is the result of execution of the PTEST instruction.

- Level = 0   Search the ATC only
- Level ≠ 0   Search translation tables only

```
 15 14 13 12 11 10 9  8  7  6  5  4  3        0
  B  L  S  0  W  I  M  0  0  T  0  0  0   N
```

Bit	Meaning	Level = 0	Level ≠ 0
B	Bus error	Bus error is set in matching ATC entry	Bus error occurred during table walk
L	Limit bit	Always cleared	An index exceeded the limit
S	Supervisor violation	Always cleared	Supervisor bit is set in descriptor
W	Write protect	Address is write protected	Address is write protected
I	Invalid bit	No entry in ATC or B is set	No translation in table, or B or L is set
M	Modified bit	ATC entry has M bit set	Page descriptor has M bit set
T	Transparent	Address is within range of TT0 or TT1	Always cleared
N	Number of tables	0	Number of tables used in translation

FIGURE 8.25 MMUSR details.

in the table indexed by the logical address can be set from one to four and up to 15 logical address bits can be used as an index at each level. One main advantage of this tree structure is to deallocate large portions of the logical address space with a single entry at the higher levels of the tree.

The entries in the translation tables include status information with respect to the pointer for the next level of lookup or the pages themselves. These bits can be used to designate certain pages or blocks of pages as supervisor-only, write-protected, or noncacheable. The 68030 MMU exceptions include the following:

- Bus error
- F-line
- Privilege violation
- Configuration error

27 26 24 23		0	27 26 25 24 23				0
V	FC	LOGICAL ADDRESS	B	CI	WP	M	PHYSICAL ADDRESS

Bit	Meaning	0	1
V	Valid	Invalid	Valid
B	Bus error	No bus error	Error occurred when entry was formed. If this logical address occurs, a bus error exception will occur.
CI	Cache inhibit	$\overline{CIOUT}$ is negated	$\overline{CIOUT}$ is asserted disabling internal and external cache.
WP	Write protect	Page is not write protected	Page is write protected. If a write is attempted, a bus error exception occurs.
M	Modified	Page has not been modified	Page has been modified.

• FC Function Code

FIGURE 8.26 ATC entry structure.

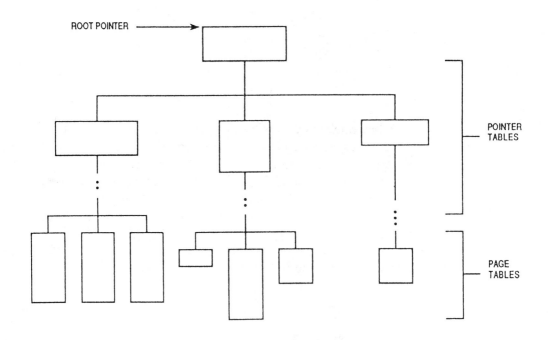

FIGURE 8.27 MC68030 MMU translation table tree structure.

All of the exceptions except configuration error exception are included in other ways besides the MMU. Table 8.5 summarizes the 68030 MMU exceptions.

TABLE 8.5
MC68030 MMU Exception Summary

	Typical cause	Possible response
Bus error		
Bit set in ATC entry due to normal tablewalk or PLOAD		
Invalid descriptor	Page not in memory	Load page to memory and rerun cycle
Limit violation or range violation	Page not in memory	Load page to memory and rerun cycle
Bus error asserted	Descriptor fetch accessed a location at which there was no device	Abort task
User attempt to write to supervisor space	Bad task	Abort task
Write to a write-protected page	Bad task	Abort task
F-line exception		
F op code with cpID = 0 was attempted and was not equal to PFLUSH, PLOAD, PMOVE, or PTEST	MC68851 instruction(s)	Rewrite instructions or write exception handler to emulate 68851 instructions
Privilege violation		
User attempt to execute PFLUSH, PLOAD, PMOVE, or PTEST	Bad task	Abort task
Configuration error		

Result of loading invalid data into CPR, SRP, and TC using
    PMOVE EA, CRP
    PMOVE EA, SRP
    PMOVE EA, TC
  Invalid data may be due to invalid descriptors
	System program error	Crash system

Example 8.1

Assume user program space. The MC68030 executes CLR.W(A1) with PC contents and instruction cache contents as follows.

Given the op code for CLR.W(A1) is 4251_{16}, [PC] = \$02513080.

Instruction Cache Contents

Function Codes = 010_2

Index			valid bits 0 1 2 3	LWO	LW1	LW2	LW3
7	2	025130	1 1 1 1	4251xxxx	—	—	—
8	2	025130	0 1 1 1	4251xxxx	—	—	—
9	2	025130	1 1 1 1	——————	—	—	—

When the instruction CLR.W(A1) is fetched by the 68030, will a cache hit or miss occur? Why?

Solution

A miss will occur since the valid bit is zero.

Example 8.2

Write an instruction sequence to freeze the data cache and disable the instruction cache.

Solution

```
MOVEC  CACR,D1      ;  Get current
                    ;  CACR
BCLR.L #0,D1        ;  Disable
                    ;  instruction
                    ;  cache
BSET.L #9,D1        ;  Freeze data cache
MOVEC  D1, CACR     ;  Write to
                    ;  CACR
```

Example 8.3

Assume a page size of 4K bytes. Determine the physical address from the logical addresses of the task shown below:

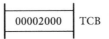

| 00002000 | TCB |

Page			
0	$002000	12345	Page
1	$002004	7AB12	Descriptor
2	$002008	1BCA7	Table

Logical addresses to be translated are $000001A5, $00002370.

Solution

From logical addresses $000001A5, the page number is upper 20 bits, i.e., page number is zero. This is because the page size is given as 4K bytes and hence the lower 12 bits ($2^{12} = 4K$) are used as the page size. Since TCB is $002000, $12345 is concatenated with the lower 12 bits ($1A5) of the logical address $000001A5 to obtain the physical address $123451A5.

Similarly, the physical address for the logical address $00002370 is $1BCA7370.

Example 8.4

Determine the contents of SRP when enabled in TC to describe a page descriptor table located at $05721050 and limited to logical address 0 – $7000.

Solution

The format for SRP is

31 30		16, 15	2, 1 0
L / $\overline{U}$	Limit	0----	DT
Table Address		Unused	
31		3	0

L/$\overline{U}$ is 0 for upper limit range. LIMIT is $7000. DT must be 01 for page descriptor. Table address is $05721050. Hence, SRP is

31			0
0	7000	0001	
05721050			

Example 8.5

What happens upon execution of the PTEST instruction with level ≠ 0 (i.e., search translation tables only)? Assume that the MMUSR contains $4005.

Solution

From Figure 8.25, level ≠ 0 means search translation tables only. Bit 14 defines the limit bit and bits 0-2 define the number of tables used in translation. [MMSUR] = $4005 indicates limit bit = 1 and number of tables used in translation is 5. Therefore, the index limit is exceeded when searching the five translation tables.

8.2 MOTOROLA MC88100 32-BIT RISC (REDUCED INSTRUCTION SET COMPUTER) MICROPROCESSOR

8.2.1 BASICS OF RISC

RISC is an acronym for Reduced Instruction Set Computer. Motorola MC88100 is a 32-bit RISC microprocessor. This type of microprocessor emphasizes simplicity and efficiency. RISC designs start with a necessary and sufficient instruction set. The purpose of using RISC architecture is to maximize speed by reducing clock cycles per instruction. Almost all computation can be obtained from a few simple operations. The goal of RISC architecture is to maximize the effective speed of a design by performing infrequent operations in software and frequent functions in hardware, thus obtaining a net performance gain.

The following summarize the typical features of a RISC microprocessor:

1. The microprocessor is designed using hardwired control with little or no microcode. Note that variable length instruction formats generally require microcode design. All RISC instructions have fixed formats, and therefore microcode design is not necessary.
2. RISC microprocessor executes most instructions in a single cycle.
3. The instruction set of RISC microprocessor typically includes only register-to-register, load, and store. All instructions involving arithmetic operations use registers, while load and store operations are utilized to access memory.
4. The instructions have simple fixed format with few addressing modes.
5. RISC microprocessor has several general-purpose registers and large cache memories.
6. RISC microprocessor processes several instructions simultaneously and thus includes pipelining.
7. Software can take advantage of more concurrency. For example, Jumps occur after execution of the instruction that follows. This

allows fetching of the next instruction during execution of the current instruction.

8.2.2 BASIC FEATURES OF THE 88100 RISC MICROPROCESSOR

MC88100 is a 32-bit microprocessor designed using HCMOS technology. The main features of the 88100 include the following:

- Hardwired control design with no microcodes
- 20 or 25 MHz internal clock frequency
- Housed in 17×17 (180 pins used) Pin Grid Array (PGA) with a maximum of $1.78'' \times 1.78''$
- Supports integers, bit field, and floating-point data types
- Includes 51 instructions which include integer arithmetic, floating-point, logical, bit-field, load/store/exchange, and branch
- Four fully parallel execution units (pipelined)
- Thirty-two 32-bit general-purpose registers
- User and supervisor modes
- 32-bit combinational multiplier
- Separate data and instruction buses that include 32-bit data bus, 32-bit instruction address bus, and 32-bit instruction bus (fixed instruction length of 32 bits)
- Directly interfaces to memory or to 88200 cache/memory management unit
- 4 gigabytes of physical memory

The 88100 performs register-to-register operation for all data manipulation instructions. Source operands are contained in source registers or are included as an immediate value inherent in the instruction. A separate destination register stores the results of an instruction. This means that source operand registers can be reused in the subsequent instructions. Register contents that can be read from or written to memory only are ld (load) and st (store) instructions. A xmem (memory exchange) instruction is included for semaphore testing and multiprocessor application.

The 88100 contains 51 instructions. All instructions are executed in one cycle. The instructions requiring more than one cycle are executed in effectively one cycle via pipelining. All instructions are decoded by hardware and no microcode is used.

The 88100 includes all data manipulation instructions as register-to-register or register plus immediate value instructions. This eliminates memory access delays in data manipulation. Only 10 memory addressing modes are provided: three modes for data memory, four modes for instruction memory, and three modes for registers.

All 88100 instructions are 32 bits wide. This fixed instruction format minimizes instruction decode time and eliminates the need for alignment. All instructions are fetched in a single memory access. The 88100 implements delayed branching to minimize pipeline delay. For pipelined architecture, branching instructions can slow down execution speed due to the time required to flush and refill the pipeline. The 88100 delayed branching feature allows fetching of the next instruction before the branch instruction is executed.

The 88100 provides two modes: supervisor and user. The supervisor mode is used by the operating system, while the application programs are executed in user mode.

The 88100 includes four execution units which operate independently and concurrently. The 88100 can perform up to five operations in parallel.

Scoreboard bits are associated with each of the general-purpose registers. When an instruction is executed or dispatched, the scoreboard bit of the destination register is set, reserving that register for that instruction. Other instructions are executed or dispatched as long as their source and destination operands have clear scoreboard bits. When an instruction completes execution, the scoreboard bit of the destination is cleared, thus freeing that register to be used by other instructions.

The 88100 memory devices can interface directly to memory. Most 88100 designs implement at least two 88200 CMMUs (one for data memory and one for instruction memory). The P-bus provides the interface to the 88200/memory system. The 88200 is an optional external chip that provides paged virtual memory support and data/instruction cache memory.

Conditional test results are provided to any specified, general-purpose register instead of a dedicated condition code register. Conditions are computed at the explicit request of the programmer using compare instructions. This eliminates contention between concurrent execution units accessing a dedicated condition code register.

8.2.3 88100/88200 INTERFACE

Figure 8.28 shows typical 88100 interfaces to several 88200s. The PBUS (processor bus) contains logical addresses, while MBUS (memory bus) contains all physical addresses. Up to 4 88200s can reside on each PBUS. Note that in the figure, the MC88000 includes the entire RISC microprocessor family, with 88100 being the first microprocessor.

Figure 8.29 shows the 88100/88200 block diagram. Each unit in the 88100 can operate independently and simultaneously. Each unit may be pipelined.

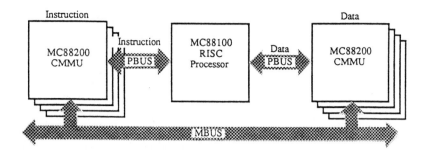

MC88100 32-Bit RISC Microprocessor

- 1.5 micron HCMOS, 180 Pins
- Highly pipelined
- Separate instruction and data buses (Harvard architecture)

MC88200 32-Bit Cache/Memory Management Unit

- 1.5 Micron HCMOS, 180 Pins
- 56 entry Page Address Translation Cache (PATC)
- 10 entry Block Address Translation Cache (BATC)
- 16Kbyte code/data cache

M88000 Processor BUS

- Synchronous, non-multiplexed, pipelined
- 33 bit logical addresses, 32 bit data path
- 1 word each clock cycle maximum transfer rate

M88000 Memory BUS

- Synchronous, multiplexed
- 32 bit physical addresses, 32 bit data path
- N words each N+1 clock cycles maximum transfer rate

FIGURE 8.28 Typical 88100 interface to 88200s. Note that MC88000 represents the 88000 family which includes 88100, 88200, and all future products.

The integer unit performs 32-bit arithmetic, logic, bit field, and address operations. All operations are performed in one clock cycle. The integer unit includes 21 control registers. The floating-point unit supports IEEE 754-1985 floating-point arithmetic, integer multiply, and divide. This unit contains 11 control registers with five-stage add pipeline and six-stage multiply pipeline. Six optional SFUs (special function units) are reserved in the architecture. The SFUs can be added to or removed from a given system with no impact on the architecture.

The data unit performs address calculation and data access and includes a three-stage pipeline.

The instruction unit fetches instruction codes and contains a three-stage pipeline.

The register file includes 32 32-bit general-purpose registers.

The sequency uses a scoreboard to control register reads/writes. It dispatches instructions and recognizes exceptions.

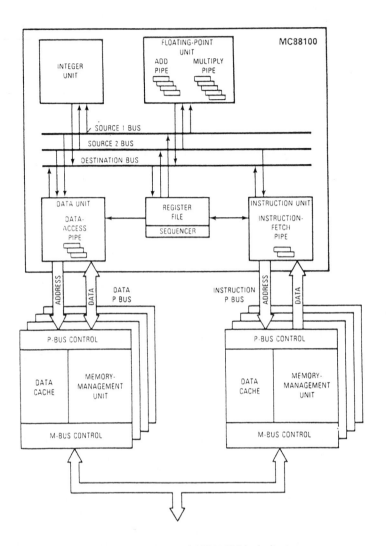

FIGURE 8.29 MC88100/MC88200 block diagram.

Figure 8.30 shows the 88200 internal block diagram.

The block address translation cache (BATC) contains 10 entries and is fully associative with software replacement.

The page address translation cache (PATC) includes 56 entries and is fully associative with hardware replacement. The SRAM (static RAM) array contains 16K bytes of static RAM and is set associative.

8.2.4 88100 REGISTERS

Figure 8.31 shows the 88100 registers. All registers are 32 bits wide. There are 32 general-purpose registers, r0-r31. These registers contain

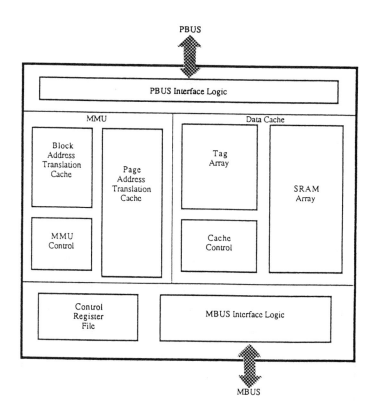

Cache Accesses in Parallel with Address Translation.

Two Level Page Address Translation Tables for Supervisor and User Programs.

FIGURE 8.30 88200 internal block diagram.

program data including instruction operand and results and provide address and bit field information. Internal registers are used by the 88100 to track instruction.

Three types of registers are included:

- 32 general-purpose registers, r0-r31, containing program data (source operand and instruction results). All of these registers except r0 (constant 0) have read/write access.
- Internal registers control instruction execution and data transfer
- Control registers in the various execution units containing status, execution control, and exception processing information

The internal registers cannot be directly accessible in software, while

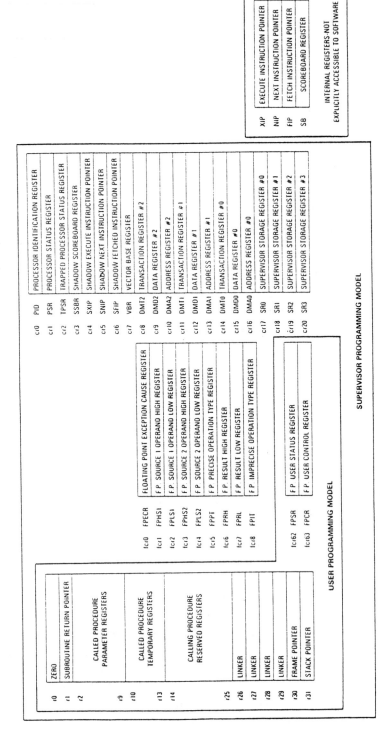

FIGURE 8.31 MC88100 register organization.

most control registers can be accessed in supervisor mode. The internal registers can only be modified and used indirectly.

The control registers include shadow registers and exception time registers, integer-unit control registers, and floating-point unit control registers.

The shadow registers are associated with several internal registers. Shadowing is utilized by the 88100 to keep track of the internal pipeline registers at each stage of the instruction execution. The shadowed registers include the three instruction pointers, the scoreboard register, the data unit pipeline registers, and the floating-point unit source operand registers. Shadowing these registers generates a copy of the instruction pipeline, the memory access pipeline, and the floating-point source operands at the end of each cycle.

Exception time registers are updated with copies of internal registers, but these registers are only written when an exception occurs. The PSR corresponds to one of the exception time registers.

There are 21 control registers (cr0 through cr20) in the integer unit. Fourteen of these registers provide exception information for integer unit or data unit exceptions. The other seven registers include status information, the base address of the exception vector table, and general-purpose storage.

The floating point includes 11 control registers (fcr0-fcr8, fcr62, and fcr63). fcr0 through fcr8 contain exception information such as the exception type, source operands and results, and the instruction in progress. These registers can only be accessed in supervisor mode. Registers fcr62 and fcr63 are not privileged. These two registers can be used to enable user-supplied exception handler software and to report exception causes in user mode.

The supervisor programmer's model contains all general-purpose and control registers. The general-purpose registers provide data and address information, while the integer unit control registers provide exception recovery and status information for the integer unit. The integer unit registers are loaded to and from general-purpose registers using ldcr (load from control register), stcr (store to control register), and xcr (exchange control register) instructions. The floating-point-unit control registers provide exception recovery, status, and control information for the floating-point unit. These registers are loaded to and from the general-purpose registers using the fldcr (load from floating-point control register), fstcvr (store to floating-point control register), and fxcr (exchange floating-point control register) instructions.

In user mode, all general-purpose registers can be accessed. Two control registers (floating-point control and status) can be accessed in the user mode.

Tables 8.6a through 8.6d summarize the 88100 general-purpose, internal, and control registers.

TABLE 8.6a
General-Purpose Register Summary

Register	Function	Convention	Access
r0	Constant zero	Hardware	Read only
r1	Subroutine return pointer	Hardware	Read/write
r2-r9	Called procedure parameter registers	Software	Read/write
r10-r13	Called procedure temporary registers	Software	Read/write
r14-r25	Called procedure reserved registers	Software	Read/write
r26-r29	Linker registers	Software	Read/write
r30	Frame pointer	Software	Read/write
r31	Stack pointer	Software	Read/write

TABLE 8.6b
Internal Register Summary

Mnemonic	Function
XIP	Pointer to currently executing instruction
NIP	Pointer to next instruction to execute
FIP	Pointer to instruction being fetched from memory
SB	Register file scoreboard

TABLE 8.6c
Integer-Unit Control Register Summary

Register	Mnemonic	Function	Shadow/ exception time	Access
cr0	PID	Processor ID field and PCE bits	—	Read only
cr1	PSR	Processor status and control bits	—	Read/write

TABLE 8.6c (continued)
Integer-Unit Control Register Summary

Register	Mnemonic	Function	Shadow/ exception time	Access
cr2	TPSR	Trapped processor status registers	Exception time	Read/write
cr3	SSBR	Shadow scoreboard register	Shadow	Read/write
cr4	SXIP	Shadow execute instruction pointer	Shadow	Read/write
cr5	SNIP	Shadow next instruction pointer	Shadow	Read/write
cr6	SFIP	Shadow fetch instruction pointer	Shadow	Read/write
cr7	VBR	Exception vector table base register	Shadow	Read/write
cr8	DMT2	Transaction information for faulted data memory transaction	Shadow	Read only
cr9	DMD2	Data for faulted data memory transaction	Shadow	Read only
cr10	DMA2	Address for faulted data memory transaction	Shadow	Read only
cr11	DMT1	Transaction information for active data memory transaction when fault occurred	Shadow	Read only
cr12	DMD1	Data for active data memory transaction when fault occurred	Shadow	Read only
cr13	DMA1	Address for active data memory transaction when fault occurred	Shadow	Read only
cr14	DMT0	Transaction information for data memory transaction being prepared when fault occurred	Shadow	Read only
cr15	DMD0	Data for data memory transaction being prepared when fault occurred	Shadow	Read only
cr16	DMA0	Address for data memory transaction being prepared when fault occurred	Shadow	Read only

TABLE 8.6d
Floating-Point Control Register Summary

Register	Mnemonic	Function	Shadow/ exception time	Access
fcr0	FPECR	Exception cause indicator	—	Read only
fcr1	FPHS1	Upper bits of floating-point source 1 operand when exception occurred	Shadow	Read only
fcr2	FPLS1	Lower bits of floating-point source 1 operand or integer source 1 operand when exception occurred	Shadow	Read only
fcr3	FPHS2	Upper bits of floating-point source 2 operand when exception occurred	Shadow	Read only
fcr4	FPLS2	Lower bits of floating-point source 2 operand or integer source 1 operand when exception occurred	Shadow	Read only
fcr5	FPPT	Information about instruction that caused a precise exception	Exception time	Read only
fcr6	FPRH	Status information and upper 21 bits of partial floating-point result when imprecise exception occurred	Exception time	Read only
fcr7	FPRL	Low-order bits of partial floating-point result when imprecise exception occurred	Exception time	Read only
fcr8	FPIT	Information about instruction that caused an imprecise exception	Exception time	Read only
fcr62	FPUSR	Flags that indicate which floating-point exception occurred	—	Read only
fcr63	FPCR	Flags that specify rounding mode and that enable user-supplied exception handlers	—	Read/write

Among the 32 general-purpose registers, r0 always contains the value 0, r1 is loaded with the subroutine return address, and r2 through r31 are general-purpose.

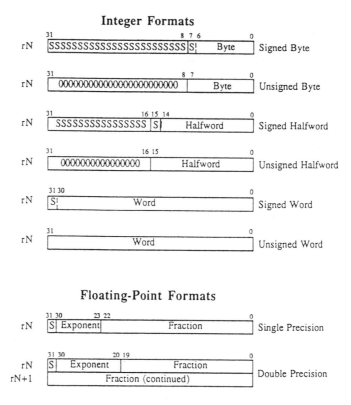

FIGURE 8.32 88100 register data formats. An "S" in the diagram above indicates a sign bit.

Figure 8.32 shows the 88000 register data formats. The 88100 supports two types of data formats, namely, integer (signed or unsigned) and floating-point real numbers. The integers can be byte, half-word (16-bit), and word (32-bit). All operations affect all 32 bits of a general-purpose register. The half-word or byte pads the sign bit; a signed byte writes the sign bit. That is, a signed byte writes the sign bit from bit 8 through bit 31. An unsigned byte, on the other hand, writes 0 from bit 8 through bit 31.

The floating-point data can be single precision and double precision. Figure 8.33 shows formats for Fer62 and Fer63.

The reserved bits in fcr62 and fcr03 are always read as zero. The FPcr defines the desired rounding mode and which exceptions are handled by user exception handles. The FPSR indicates which floating-point exceptions have occurred but were not processed by a user exception handler.

The 88100 general-purpose register convention is shown in Figure 8.34. r31 addresses the top of the stack. r30 contains the address of the current data frame in the stack.

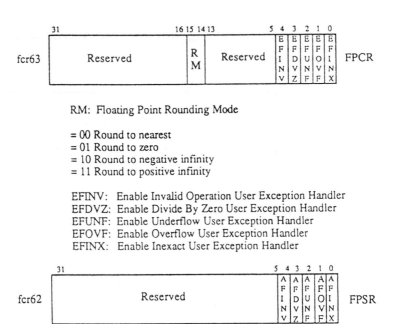

RM: Floating Point Rounding Mode

= 00 Round to nearest
= 01 Round to zero
= 10 Round to negative infinity
= 11 Round to positive infinity

EFINV: Enable Invalid Operation User Exception Handler
EFDVZ: Enable Divide By Zero User Exception Handler
EFUNF: Enable Underflow User Exception Handler
EFOVF: Enable Overflow User Exception Handler
EFINX: Enable Inexact User Exception Handler

AFINV: Accumulated Invalid Operation Flag
AFDVZ: Accumulated Divide By Zero Flag
AFUNF: Accumulated Underflow Flag
AFOVF: Accumulated Overflow Flag
AFINX: Accumulated Inexact Flag

FIGURE 8.33 88100 fcr 62 and fcr 63 formats.

Figure 8.35 shows the 88100 stack operation. The SP must always be 32-bit aligned. The stack grows from high memory to low memory addresses.

Next, consider the supervisor programmer model:

- The VBR contains the address of the exception vector table.
- The 88100 does not automatically use SR0–SR3. They are reserved for operating system use.

Figure 8.36 shows the 88100 processor status register format. In Figure 8.36, Big Endian means the most significant byte at the highest byte address. Serial instruction is to complete before the next one begins. Note that not all adds/subtracts affect C. The SFDI bit enables or disables the floating-point unit. When SFDI = 1, attempted execution of any floating-point or integer multiply/divide instructions cause floating-point precise exceptions.

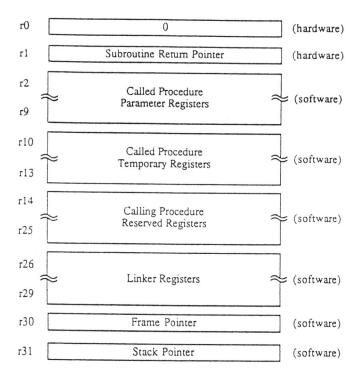

FIGURE 8.34 88100 register convention.

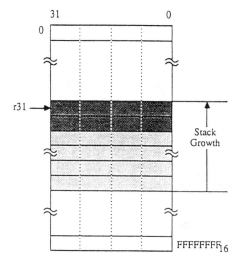

FIGURE 8.35 88100 stack operation.

31	30	29	28	27	26		10	9		4	3	2	1	0
M O D E	B O	S E R	C	D E X C	Reserved			Reserved			S F D I	M X M	I N D	S F R Z

MODE = 0 — Processor is in user mode.
        = 1 — Processor is in supervisor mode.

BO = 0 — Big Endian byte order in memory.
     = 1 — Little Endian byte order in memory.

SER = 0 — Concurrent instruction execution.
      = 1 — Serial instruction execution.

C = 0 — No carry / borrow generated.
    = 1 — Carry / borrow generated.

DEXC = 0 — Data memory exception not pending.
       = 1 — Data memory exception pending.

SFD1 = 0 — SFU1 enabled.
       = 1 — SFU1 disabled.

* MXM = 0 — Misaligned memory accesses generate exceptions.
        = 1 — Misaligned memory access truncate.
              Misaligned address to next lower aligned address.

IND = 0 — Interrupt enabled.
      = 1 — Interrupt disabled.

SFRZ = 0 — Shadow registers enabled.
       = 1 — Shadow registers frozen.

* 88100 can address each byte. For halfword, aligned addresses include all addresses in multiples of 2, for word in multiples of 4 and for doubleword in multiples of 8.

FIGURE 8.36 88100 processor status register format.

8.2.5 88100 DATA TYPES, ADDRESSING MODES, AND INSTRUCTIONS

Tables 8.7a and 8.7b list the data types and addressing modes supported by the 88100. Table 8.8 summarizes the 88100 instructions.

The 51 instructions listed in Table 8.8 of the MC88100 can be divided into 6 classes: integer arithmetic, floating-point arithmetic, logical, bit field, load/store/exchange, and flow control.

These simple instructions must be used to obtain complex operations.

TABLE 8.7a
Data Types

Data type	Represented as
Bit fields	Signed and unsigned bit fields from 1 to 32 bits
Integer	Signed and unsigned byte (8 bits)
	Signed and unsigned half-word (16 bits)
	Signed and unsigned word (32 bits)
Floating point	IEEE P754 single precision (32 bits)
	IEEE P754 double precision (64 bits)

TABLE 8.7b
Addressing Modes

Data addressing mode	Syntax
Register indirect with unsigned immediate	rD,rS1,imm16
Register indirect with index	rD,rS1,rS2
Register indirect with scaled index	rD,rS1[rS2]

Instruction addressing mode	Syntax
Register with 9-bit vector number	m5,rS1,vec9
Register with 16-bit signed displacement	m5,rS1,d16
	b5,rS1,d16
Instruction pointer relative (26-bit signed displacement)	d26
Register direct	rS2

TABLE 8.8
Instruction Set Summary

Mnemonic	Description

Integer Arithmetic Instructions

add	Add
addu	Add unsigned
cmp	Compare
div	Divide

TABLE 8.8 (continued)
Instruction Set Summary

Mnemonic	Description

Integer Arithmetic Instructions

divu	Divide unsigned
mul	Multiply
sub	Subtract
subu	Subtract unsigned

Floating-Point Arithmetic Instructions

fadd	Floating-point add
fcmp	Floating-point compare
fdiv	Floating-point divide
fldcr	Load from floating-point control register
flt	Convert integer to floating point
fmul	Floating-point multiply
fstcr	Store to floating-point control register
fsub	Floating-point subtract
fxcr	Exchange floating-point control register
int	Round floating point to integer
nint	Floating-point round to nearest integer
trnc	Truncate floating point to integer

Logical Instructions

and	AND
mask	Logical mask immediate
or	OR
xor	Exclusive OR

Bit-Field Instructions

clr	Clear bit field
ext	Extract signed bit field
extu	Extract unsigned bit field
ff0	Find first bit clear

TABLE 8.8 (continued)
Instruction Set Summary

Mnemonic	Description

Bit-Field Instructions

ff1	Find first bit set
mak	Make bit field
rot	Rotate register
set	Set bit field

Load/Store/Exchange Instructions

ld	Load register from memory
lda	Load address
ldcr	Load from control register
st	Store register to memory
stcr	Store to control register
xcr	Exchange control register
xmem	Exchange register with memory

Flow Control Instructions

bb0	Branch on bit clear
bb1	Branch on bit set
bcnd	Conditional branch
br	Unconditional branch
bsr	Branch to subroutine
jmp	Unconditional jump
jsr	Jump to subroutine
rte	Return from exception
tb0	Trap on bit clear
tb1	Trap on bit set
tbnd	Trap on bounds check
tcnd	Conditional trap

Shift and rotate operations are special cases of bit field instructions. Only ld, st, and xmem can access memory. Also, only compare instructions affect condition codes. Most MC88100 instructions can have one of the three formats:

1. Triadic register instructions (three operands). The general format is

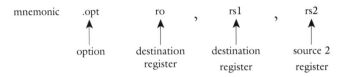

An example is add.ci r2, r7, r4. Note that Motorola's assembler expects the 88100 instructions in lower case. In the example, the mnemonic is add and the option is ci, meaning use 'carry in' in the operation. The source registers r7 and r4 remain unchanged unless one of them is used as destination. This add instruction adds [r7] and [r4] with carry and stores result in r2.

2. Triadic register instructions with 16-bit field instruction. The general format is mnemonic.opt rD, rs1, lmm16. Consider

add.Co r2, r4, 0XA125

immediate data

0X before data A125 means that A125 is in hex. This notation is used by the Motorola assembler.

3. Dyadic register instructions (two operands). The general format is mnemonic . opt rd, rs2. An example is flt.sw r5, r6 — which converts the integer source word in r6 into floating-point in r5.

Table 8.9 lists the 88100 load, store, and exchange instructions.

*   ld loads a general-purpose register from data memory. There are three operands with this instruction. Two source operands are used to calculate the address. Three forms of ld use the three addressing modes available. The (.opt) for ld specifies the size of data read from memory.

*   The st instructions are similar to ld instructions, except they are used to store source data.

*   The exchange instructions (xmem, xcr, fxcr) swap the content of a general-purpose register with data memory or with a control register.

*   Consider ld 47, r31, 0X4. The mode used here is register indirect with unsigned immediate. If $[r31] = 00005000_{16}$, the effective address is

TABLE 8.9
MC88100 LOAD, STORE, Exchange Instructions

Instructions		Exceptions
ld[.<opts>]	rD,rS1,<imm16>	
ld[.<opts>][.<space>]	rD,rS1,rS2	
ld[.<opts>][.<space>]	rD,RS1 [rS2]	
st[.<size>]	rS,rS1,<imm16>	Data access
st[.<size>][.<space>]	rS,rS1,rS2	Misaligned access
st[.<size>][.<space>]	rS,rS1 [rS2]	Privilege violation
xmem[.bu]	rS,rS1,<imm16>	
xmem[.bu][.<space>]	rS,rS1,rS2	
xmem[.bu][.<space>]	rS,rS1 [rS2]	
ldcr	rD,crCRS	
stcr	rS,crCRD	
xcr	rD,rS1,crCRS/D	Privilege violation
fldcr	rD,crFCRS	
fstcr	rS,crFCRD	
fxcr	rD,rS1,crFCRS/D	

<opts>	For	ld	<size>	For	st
.b	—	Signed byte	.b	—	Byte
.bu	—	Unsigned byte	.h	—	Halfword
.h	—	Signed halfword	none	—	Word
.hu	—	Unsigned halfword	.d	—	Doubleword
none	—	Word			
.d	—	Doubleword			

<space>	For	ld,st,xmem
.usr	—	Access user space regardless of mode bit in PSR
none	—	Access space indicated by PSR MODE bit

- rs ≡ Source register.
- crCRS ≡ Source control register.

TABLE 8.9 (continued)
MC88100 LOAD, STORE, Exchange Instructions

- crCRD ≡ Destination control register.
- crCRS/D ≡ Source/destination control register.
- crFCRS ≡ Source floating-point control register.
- crFCRD ≡ Destination floating-point control register.
- crFCRS/D ≡ Source/destination floating-point control register.
- Memory accesses for **xmem** are indivisible.

computed by adding rsl (r31) with unsigned 16-bit immediate data. Therefore, the 88100 loads the register 47 with 32-bit data from a memory location addressed by 00005004_{16}; r31 is the SP. Therefore, the access occurs within the stack. Since the immediate data are unsigned, the accessed address cannot be less than r31. This means that the stack grows toward the lower address.

- Consider st.b rs, rsl, rs2. This instruction has register indirect with index mode.

The access address is rsl + rs2 where rsl is the base register and rs2 is the index register. For example, consider st.b rl, r0, r5. If [r5] = 00010200_{16}; then since r0 is always 0, the low 8-bit content of rl is stored at address 00010200_{16}. The 88100 ignores any carry generated during address calculation. Note that in the above r0 is the base address and r5 is the index register.

Finally, consider st.hu rs, rsl [rs2]. The mode is register indirect with index. The access address is rsl + rs2* (operand size). The scaling is specified by surrounding the index register rs2 by square brackets. Operand size is 1 for byte, 2 for halfword, 4 for word, and 8 for double word.

As an example, consider st. r5, r31 [rl]. If [rl] = 00000003_{16}, [r31] = 00005000_{16}, then the effective address is

$$00005000 + \underline{4} * 00000003 = 0000500C_{16}$$

scaled by 4 for word since the instruction without any option specified means 32-bit word.

Therefore, the above store instruction stores the 32-bit contents of r5 into a memory location addressed by $0000500C_{16}$.

Table 8.10 shows the integer arithmetic instructions.

- Consider add [.<opt>] r0, rsl, rs2. Three options can be used with this instruction as follows:

TABLE 8.10
MC88100 Integer Arithmetic Instructions

Instructions		Exceptions
add[.<opt>]	rD,rS1,rS2 ⎫	Integer overflow
add	rD,rS1,<imm16> ⎬	
addu[.<opt>]	rD,rS1,rS2 ⎫	None
addu	rD,rS1,<imm16> ⎬	
sub[.<opt>]	rD,rS1,rS2 ⎫	Integer overflow
sub	rD,rS1,<imm16> ⎬	
subu[.<opt>]	rD,rS1,rS2 ⎫	None
subu	rD,rS1,<imm16> ⎬	
mul	rD,rS1,rS2 ⎫	None
mul	rD,rS1,<imm16> ⎬	
div	rD,rS1,rS2 ⎫	
div	rD,rS1,<imm16> ⎬	Integer divide
divu	rD,rS1,rS2	
divu	rD,rS1,<imm16> ⎭	
lda [.<size>]	rD,rS1,<imm16> ⎫	
lda [.<size>]	rD,rS1,rS2 ⎬	None
lda [.<size>]	rD,rS1,[rS2] ⎭	

<opt> FOR add/addu/sub/subu

none	No carry
.ci	Use carry in
.co	Propagate carry out
.cio	Use carry in and propagate carry out

<size> FOR lda

.b	Scale rS2 by 1
.h	Scale rS2 by 2
none	Scale rS2 by 4
.d	Scale rS2 by 8

- **mul** yields correct signed and unsigned results.
- Division by zero signals the integer divide exception.
- An integer divide exception occurs when either source operand is negative for **div**.
- Unscaled **lda** is functionally equivalent to **addu**.

- add.Ci rD, rs1, rs2 adds the 32-bit contents of rs1 with rs2 and the C-bit in processor status register and stores the 32-bit result in rD without providing any carry-out, and thus the C-bit in PSR is unchanged.
- add.Co rD, rs1, rs2 adds the 32-bit contents of rs1 with rs2 without any carry-in and stores the result in rD and reflects carry-out in the C-bit of PSR.
- add.Cio rD, rs1, rs2 adds the 32-bit contents of rs1 with rs2 and C-bit from PSR and stores the result in rD and reflects any carry-out to the C-bit in PSR.

- Consider add.Cio r2, r1, r5. If C-bit in PSR is 0, $[r1] = 8000 \ F102_{16}$, $[r5] = F1101100_{16}$, then after this add $[r2] = 71110202_{16}$ and C-bit in PSR is set to one.
- If no option is specified in an instruction such as add or addu, the carry-in is not included in addition and also no carry-out from the addition is provided. For example, consider addu r1, r5, 0XF112. The 16-bit immediate data $F112_{16}$ is converted to unsigned 32-bit number $0000\text{-}F112_{16}$ and is added with the 32-bit contents of r5. The 32-bit result is stored in r1. The carry-out is not provided. add instruction performs signed arithmetic. If the result cannot be accommodated in a 32-bit integer, an integer overflow exception occurs. The immediate 16-bit data in add instruction are sign-extended to 32 bits before addition.
- The sub instructions are similar to those of add instructions. The content of rs2 is subtracted from the content of rs1 with C-bit in PSR as borrow if .Ci is used for ·<opt>.
- mul instructions multiply a 32-bit number (signed or unsigned) in rs2 by a 32-bit number (signed or unsigned) in rs1 and store the low 32-bit result in rD and discard the upper 32 bits of the result.
- div instructions perform signed division while divu carries out unsigned division. divu (unsigned division) instructions divide the 32-bit content of rs1 by the 32-bit content of rs2 or 16-bit immediate value. The 32-bit quotient is stored in rD and the remainder is discarded. If the divisor is zero, an integer divide exception is taken and rD is unaffected. div (signed division) operates similarly to divu except that integer divide exception is taken if either dividend (rs1) or division (rs2) has a negative value. The exception handler must convert the negative value to positive, perform the signed integer divide, and convert the sign of the result.

- lda is the load address instruction. lda calculates the access address using one of three indirect addressing modes. lda loads rD with the access address. Unscaled lda is functionally equivalent to addu with the same operands.

Table 8.11 lists the 88100 floating-point arithmetic instructions.

TABLE 8.11
MC88100 Floating-Point Arithmetic Instructions

Instructions		Exceptions
fadd.\<sizes\>	rD,rS1,rS2	Floating point reserved operand
fsub.\<sizes\>	rD,rS1,rS2	Floating point overflow
		Floating point underflow
fmul.\<sizes\>	rD,rS1,rS2	Floating point inexact
fdiv.\<sizes\>	rD,rS1,rS2	Floating point divide by zero
trnc.\<sizes\>	rD,rS2	
nint.\<sizes\>	rD,rS2	Floating point integer conversion overflow
int.\<sizes\>	rD,rS2	Floating point reserved operand
flt.\<sizes\>	rD,rS2	Floating point inexact

\<sizes\> FOR fadd/fsub/fmul/fdiv

sss, ssd, sds, sdd, dss, dsd, dds, ddd

\<sizes\> FOR trnc/nint/int

ss, sd

\<sizes\> FOR flt

ss, ds

- The MC88100 permits a mixture of single and double precision source and destination operands.
- **trnc** performs "round to zero" rounding.
- **nint** performs "round to nearest" rounding.
- **int** performs rounding specified by the RM field of the FPCR.

- fadd adds the contents of rs1 with rs2 and stores the result in rD.
- fsub subtracts the contents of rs2 from rs1 and stores the result in rD.
- fmul multiplies the contents of rs1 by rs2 and stores the result in rD.
- fdiv divides the contents of rs1 by rs2 and stores the quotient in rD.
- The 88100 utilizes hardware to perform these IEEE floating-point computations.
- The 88100 allows single and double precision operands. <sizes> specify the operand sizes of rD, rs1, and rs2 as single or double precision. For example, .ssd means that rD and rs1 are single precision, while rs2 is double precision.
- trnc, nint, int, and flt provide conversions between integer and floating-point values. These instructions have two operands with one operand having floating point value and the other having integer value. trnc, nint, and int convert a floating-point format to equivalent format. The difference between them is the type of rounding performed. trnc rounds toward zero, and nint rounds to the nearest method. int rounds specified by the RM field in FPCR.
- Two exceptions are provided for floating-point instructions. Integer conversion overflow exception occurs when the operand value cannot be expressed as a high word. Reserved operand exception occurs by certain floating-point values.
- flt converts a signed 32-bit number into a floating-point format. The integer operand size is always specified by <sizes> indicating signed word size. A 'd' for double or 's' for single defines the floating-point operand's precision.

Table 8.12 lists the MC88100 logical instructions.

If option .u is omitted, the specified, logical operation is performed between the 16-bit immediate data <imm16> and the low-order 16 bits of rs1.

- The mask always affects all 32 bits of rD. The mask logically ANDS the 16-bit immediate value with the low 16 bits or highest 16 bits of rs1 and clears the other 16 bits to zero. If .u option is omitted, the AND is performed with low-order 16 bits of rs1 and if .u is included, the AND is performed with the high-order 16 bits of rs1.
- When both operands are registers (rs1 and rs2) for AND, OR, and XOR, the 32-bit logical operation is performed. When .c option is used, the MC88100 ones complement the contents of rs2 before performing the operation. The MC88100 only performs a 16-bit operation when the second source operand is 16-bit immediate. .u

TABLE 8.12
MC88100 Logical Instructions

Instructions		Exceptions
and [.c]	rD,rS1,rS2	
and [.u]	rD,rS1,<imm16>	
mask [.u]	rD,rS1,<imm16>	
or [.c]	rD,rS1,rS2	None
or [.u]	rD,rS1,<imm16>	
xor [.c]	rD,rS1,rS2	
xor [.u]	rD,rS1,<imm16>	

- Option .c ones complement the contents of rs2 before performing the operation.
- Option .u performs the specified logical operation between 16-bit immediate data <imm16> and high 16 bits of rs1.

option when present in AND, OR, and XOR performs the logical operation between the high 16-bit value of rs1 and the 16-bit immediate data and then stores the result in high 16 bits of rD. The low 16 bits of rs1 is copied into low the 16 bits of rD. If .u option is not present, only the low 16 bits of rs1 are used in the operation.

Table 8.13 lists the 88100 bit field instructions.

- W5 is five bit width and <05> is five bit offset.
- The number of bits in a bit field is called width. The size of width can be from 1 to 32. The least significant bit in bit field is called the offset. When the sum of width and offset is greater than 32, the bit field may be imagined to extend beyond the most significant bit of the register.

Isolated bit field ends in the least significant bit of a register with an implicit offset of zero. Bit field may contain signed and unsigned values. For unsigned isolated bit field, the high-order bits in a register are all zero and for signed isolated bit field, they are 2's complement sign bit. In either case, the entire register contains the word value equivalent to the isolated bit field value. The 88100 includes instructions to isolate embedded bit field for arithmetic manipulation. The 88100 instruction moves isolated bit field back into embedded bit field. This is illustrated in the following:

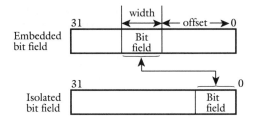

Two bit field formats are used. These are literal width with offset and register width with offset. The literal width with offset uses immediate width and offset values. An example is set r5, r1, 3 <7>. The destination register is r5; the source bit field is 3 bits wide with an offset of 7 in r1. With Motorola assembler, the offset must be included in angle brackets <>.

The register width with offset uses three operands. An example is clr r1, r3, r4. The source bit field is in r3 with offset and width determined from r4. The MC88100 obtains the offset from bits 0-4 of r4 and the width from bits 5-9 of r4. The upper 22 bits of r4 are don't cares. Both formats use an offset of 0 to 31 and width of 1 to 32 with 32 encoded as 0. The destination register (r1 in this case) stores the final result. The content of the source register (r3) does not change after the operation.

- ext (signed) and extu (unsigned) instructions extract the register value from rs1 and convert to an isolated bit field in rD. For a bit field width of 32 (encoded as 0), ext and extu perform shift right operation. The content of rs1 is shifted to the right by the number of bits specified in offset and stores the result in rD. extu performs logical shift, while ext performs arithmetic shift.
- mak creates an imbedded bit field in rD with an offset specified by an immediate value or by the content of rs2. The MC88100 stores the least significant bits of rs1 in the imbedded bit field. The bits outside the imbedded bit field in rD are cleared to zero. The mak is the inverse operation of ext and extu.
- The shift left operation may be performed by a bit field width of 32. The offset specifies the number of positions to be shifted.
- rot reads rs1 and rotates it to the right by the number of bits specified in $<0_5>$ or in bits 0-4 of rs2. The result is stored in rD.
- ff1 finds the most significant set bit in rs2 and stores the bit number in rD.
- If all bits are cleared, the 88100 loads 32 into rD. ff0 operates similarly but finds the most significant clear bit.

Table 8.14 summarizes the 88100 Integer Compare instructions.

TABLE 8.13
MC88100 Bit Field Instructions

	Instructions	**Exceptions**
clr	rD,rS1,w5 <05>	
clr	rD,rS1,rS2	
set	rD,rS1,w5 <05>	
set	rD,rS1,rS2	
ext	rD,rS1,w5 <05>	
ext	rD,rS1,rS2	
extu	rD,rS1,w5 <05>	
extu	rD,rS1,rS2	None
mak	rD,rS1,w5 <05>	
mak	rD,rS1,rS2	
rot	rD,rS1, <05>	
rot	rD,rS1,rS2	
ff1	rD,rS2	
ff0	rD,rS2	

- ext and extu affect all 32 bits of rD.
- ext and extu perform shift right operations when the width equals 32.
- mak clears rD before inserting the bit field.
- mak performs shift left operations when the width equals 32.
- **rot** rotates the bit field to the right.

- cmp provides integer data comparison. The 88100 compares the rs1 contents with either unsigned 16-bit immediate number or the content of rs2. The 16-bit immediate data are converted to a 32-bit value with zeros in high 16 bits before comparison. The result of comparison is stored in rD.

Table 8.15 shows the 88100 floating-point compare instructions. Table 8.16 lists the 88100 conditional branch instructions.

TABLE 8.14
MC88100 Integer Compare

Instructions	Exceptions
cmp rD,rS1,<imm16>	
cmp rD,rS1,rS2	} None
cmp	

cmp Predicate Bit String

	31 30 29 28 27 26 25 24 23 22 21 20 19 18 17 16 15 14 13 12 11 10 9 8 7 6 5 4 3 2 1 0
r_D	0 0 0 0 0 0 0 0 0 0 0 0 0 0 0 0 0 0 0 0 0 0	hs	lo	ls	hi	ge	lt	le	gt	ne	eq	0 0

Predicate Bits	Bit Set If And Only If:	
eq	rS1 == rS2	
ne	rS1 ≠ rS2	
gt	rS1 > rS2	
le	rS1 <= rS2	Signed Evaluation
lt	rS1 < rS2	
ge	rS1 >= rS2	
hi	rS1 > rS2	
ls	rS1 <= rS2	Unsigned Evaluation
lo	rS1 < rS2	
hs	rS1 >= rS2	

- bcnd tests the content of rs1 for = 0, ≠ 0, >0, <0, ≥0, and ≤0 and branches with 16-bit signed displacement if the condition is true. The 16-bit signed displacement is sign-extended to 32 bits, shifted twice to the left, and adds to address of bcnd to branch with a displacement of (2^{-18}) to $(2^{18} - 4)$ bytes. .n indicates 'execute next'. If .n is present and the condition is true, the bcnd executes the next instruction before taking the branch. The 'execute next' allows the 88100 to branch without flushing the execution pipeline and thus provides faster execution.

- tcnd also tests the content of rs1 for the condition but traps if the condition is true. The 88100 includes 512 vectors in the vector table. <vec9> specifies a 9-bit vector number from 0 to 511. .bb1 (branch on bit set) tests the content of rs1 for a set bit. If it is set, the 88100 takes a branch. <b5> specifies a bit number from 0 to 31. bb1 usually

TABLE 8.15
MC88100 Floating-Point Compare

Instructions	Exceptions

fcmp.sss rD,rS1,rS2 ⎞
fcmp.ssd rD,rS1,rS2 ⎟ Floating point reserved operand
fcmp.sds rD,rS1,rS2 ⎟
fcmp.sdd rD,rS1,rS2 ⎠

fcmp Predicate Bit String

31 30 29 28 27 26 25 24 23 22 21 20 19 18 17 16 15 14 13 12 11 10 9 8 7 6 5 4 3 2 1 0

rD | 0 0 0 0 0 0 0 0 0 0 0 0 0 0 0 0 0 0 0 0 0 | ob in ib ou ge lt le gt ne eq cp nc

Predicate Bits	Bit Set If And Only If:
nc	operands are not comparable
cp	operands are comparable
eq	rS1 == rS2
ne	rS1 ≠ rS2
gt	rS1 > rS2
le	rS1 <= rS2
lt	rS1 < rS2
ge	rS1 >= rS2
ou	(rS1 > rS2 OR rS1 < 0) AND rS2 > 0
ib	rS1 <= rS2 AND rS1 >= 0 and rS2 > 0
in	rS1 < rS2 AND rS1 > 0 AND rS2 > 0
ob	(rS1 >= rS2 OR rS1 <= 0) AND rS2 > 0

follows cmp and fcmp instructions. tbb1 is similar to bb1 except a trap is taken if the bit is set. bb0 (branch on bit clear) is similar to bb1 except a branch is taken if the specified bit is 0. tb0 is similar to tb1 except a trap is taken if the specified bit is 0.

- tbnd (trap on bound check) generates bound check violation. rs1 contains out of bounds; 0 is the implicit lower bound. The upper bound is either unsigned 16 bits or contained in rs2. The value of the upper bound is treated as an unsigned number. If the array limit is less than 0 or greater than the upper value, an exception is taken.

TABLE 8.16
MC88100 Conditional Flow Control Instructions

Instructions		Exceptions
bcnd [.n]	<cond>,rS1,<d16>	None
tcnd	<cond>,rS1,<vec9>	} Trap vec9 Privilege violation
bb1 [.n]	<b5>,rS1,<d16>	} None
bb0 [.n]	<b5>,rS1,<d16>	
tb1	<b5>,rS1,<vec9>	} Trap vec9 Privilege violation
tb0	<b5>,rS1,<vec9>	
tbnd	rS1,rS2	} Bounds check violation
tbnd	rS1,<imm16>	

An instruction using the .n option must not be followed by another flow control instruction. (Error undetected by the MC88100.)

<cond> for bcnd/tcnd

eq0
ne0
gt0
lt0
ge0
le0

- <d16> ≡ signed 16-bit displacement.
- <vec9> ≡ 9-bit vector number (0-511).
- <b5> ≡ 5-bit bit number (0-31).
- The .n option indicates "execute next". The next instruction executes whether or not the branch takes effect.
- tbnd traps if the value in rS1 is greater than the value in rS2 or <imm16>, or if rS1 is negative.

Table 8.17 lists the unconditional jump instructions.

TABLE 8.17
MC88100 Unconditional Flow Control Instructions

Instructions		Exceptions
br [.n]	\<d26\>	
bsr [.n]	\<d26\>	None
jmp [.n]	rS2	
jsr [.n]	rS2	
rte		Privilege violation

- \<d26\> ≡ signed 26-bit displacement.
- **.n** ≡ "execute next".
- **bsr** and **jsr** save the return address in r1.
- "**jmp r1**" performs return from subroutine.
- The last instruction of typical exception handlers is **rte**.

- br always unconditionally branches with signed 26-bit displacement with a range of (2^{-28}) to $(2^{+28} - 4)$ bytes.
- bsr is an unconditional subroutine call and saves the return address in r1. When [.n] is specified, the return address is the address of bsr plus 8.
- jmp branches to the address specified by rs2 content. The 88100 rounds the least 2 bits of rs2 to 00 before branching for alignment. However, the contents of rs2 are unchanged by the instruction. jsr is similar to jmp except it is a subroutine jump to an address specified by rs2 content and also saves the return address in r1.
- The 88100 does not provide any return from subroutine instruction. jump r1 fetches the next instruction from the return address saved by bsr or jsr.
- rte provides an orderly termination of an exception handler. It uses the shadow registers to restore the state that existed before the prior exception. rte can only clear the mode bit in PSR and ensures that the instruction is executed in user mode.

Example 8.6
Show the contents of registers and memory after the 88100 executes the following instructions:

i)   st.h r2, r3, r5
ii) xmem r2, r2[r3]

Assume the following data:

Memory

$[r2] = 00000004_{16}$

2000	FF	25	71	02
2004	00	01	02	03
2008	A2	71	36	25

$[r3] = 00002000_{16}$

$[r5] = 00000002_{16}$

8000	01	02	A2	71
8004	B1	11	26	05

Solution

i) $[r3] + [r5] = 2002_{16}$. Consider st.h r2, r3, r5 where .h stands for half-word (16 bits). The low 16 bits of r2 is stored in 2002_{16} and 2003_{16}. Therefore

2000	EF	25	00	04

ii)   xmem r2, r2[r3]. This is a 32-bit word operation. Hence, the scale factor is 4. The effective address

```
= [r2] + 4 * [r3]
= 0000 0004₁₆ + 4 * 00002000₁₆
= 0000 8004₁₆
```

Therefore, after the xmem, $[r2] = B111\ 2605_{16}$ and $[00008004] = 0000\ 0004_{16}$.

Example 8.7

Write an instruction to logically shift right by 3 bits the value of r2 into r5.

Solution

Since r2 is 32 bits wide, extu performs logical right shift and the width 32 is encoded as 0. extu r5, r2, 0<3>.

Example 8.8

Write an MC88100 instruction sequence to logically AND the 32-bit content of r7 with $F2710562_{16}$ and store the result in r5.

Solution
and logically ANDs 16-bit operands.

```
and r5, r7, 0x0562      ;  and logically ANDs 0562₁₆
                        ;  with low 16 bits of
                        ;  r7 and stores result in
                        ;  low 16 bits of r5.
and.u r5, r7, 0xF271    ;  and.u logically ANDs
                        ;  F271₁₆ with high 16 bits
                        ;  of r7 and stores result
                        ;  in high 16 bits of r5
```

Example 8.9
Find an MC88100 instruction to load register r5 with the constant value 9.

Solution
add r5, r0, 9.

Example 8.10
Find an MC88100 instruction to branch to the instruction with label START if the value in r5 is equal to zero.

Solution
bcnd eq0, r5, START.

8.2.6 88100 PINS AND SIGNALS
Figure 8.37 shows the 88100 pin diagram. Figure 8.38 shows these pins by functional group. Table 8.18 provides a brief description of the functions of these pins.

8.2.7 88100 EXCEPTION PROCESSING
The 88100 includes the following exceptions:

- Reset the hardware interrupts which are activated externally via the respective input pins
- Externally activated errors such as a memory access fault
- Internally generated errors such as divide by zero
- Trap instructions

Exceptions are processed by the 88100 after completion of the current instructions. When an exception is acknowledged, the 88100 freezes the

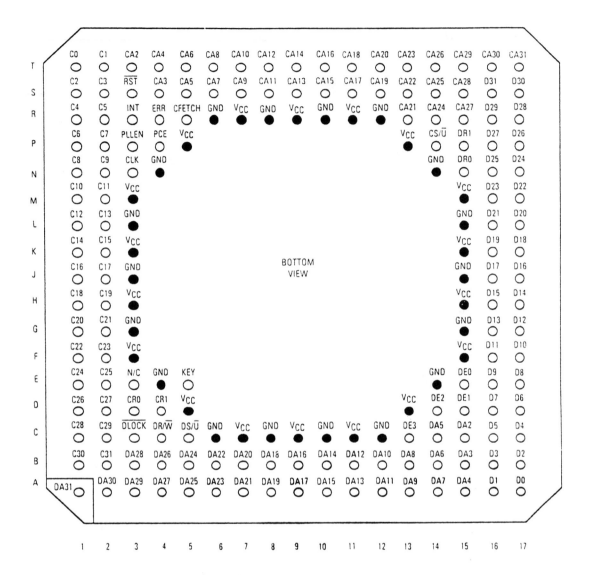

Note: The "KEY" pin is an alignment key with no internal connection.

PIN GROUP	V_CC	GND
Internal Logic	C11, K3, M3 M15, P5	C3, C12, J3 N4, N14
External Signals and Buses	C7, C9, D5, D13 F3, F15, H3, H15 P13, R7, R9, R11	C6, C8, C10, E4 E14, G3, G15, J15 L15, R6, R8 R10, R12

FIGURE 8.37 88100 pins and signals.

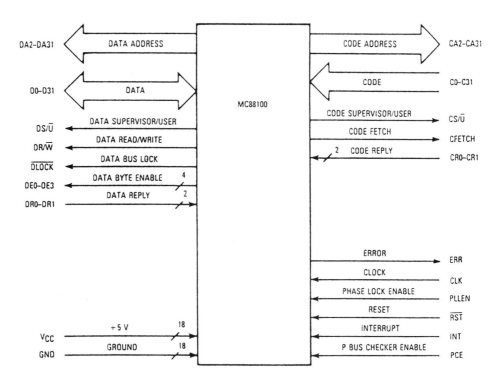

FIGURE 8.38 MC88100 signal functional diagram.

TABLE 8.18
Signal Index

Signal name	Mnemonic	Function
Data address bus	DA2-DA31	Provides the 30-bit word address to the data memory space; an entire data word (32 bits) is always addressed; individual bytes or half words are selected using the data byte strobe signals
Data bus	D0-D31	32-bit bidirectional data bus interfacing the MC88100 to the data memory space
Data supervisor/ user	DS/$\overline{\text{U}}$	This signal selects between the supervisor select data address space and the user data address space; DS/$\overline{\text{U}}$ is determined by the value of the MODE bit in the processor status register, or by the **.usr** option of the **ld** and **st** instructions
Data read/write	DR/$\overline{\text{W}}$	Indicates whether the memory transaction is a read (DT0 = 1) or a write (DT0 = 0)

TABLE 8.18 (continued)
Signal Index

Signal name	Mnemonic	Function
Data bus lock	$\overline{\text{DLOCK}}$	The memory lock pin is used by the **xmem** instruction in conjunction with the CMMU; when asserted, the CMMU maintains control of the memory bus during the two **xmem** accesses; data are guaranteed to be unaccessed between the read and write accesses of the **xmem** instruction
Data byte enable	DBE0-DBE3	Used during memory accesses, these signals indicate which bytes are accessed at the addressed location; DEB0-DEB3 are always valid during memory write cycles; a memory read is always 4 bytes wide, and the processor uses the enables to extract the valid data; that is, during an **ld** instruction, the memory system should drive all 32 data signals, regardless of whether 1, 2, or 4 bytes enables are asserted; when DEB0-DEB3 are negated, the transaction is a null; otherwise, the transaction is a valid load or store operation
Data reply	DR0-DR1	Indicates the status of the data memory transaction
Code address bus	CA2-CA31	Provides the 30-bit word address to the instruction memory space; all instructions are 32 bits wide and are aligned on 4-byte boundaries; therefore, the lower two bits of the address space are not required and are implied to be zero
Code bus	C0-C31	This read-only, 32-bit data bus interfaces the MC88100 to the instruction memory space; instructions are always 32 bits wide
Code supervisor/ user select	$\text{CS}/\overline{\text{U}}$	Selects between the user and supervisor instruction memory spaces; when asserted, selects supervisor memory and when negated, user memory; this signal is determined by the value of the MODE bit in the processor status register

TABLE 8.18 (continued)
Signal Index

Signal name	Mnemonic	Function
Code fetch	CFETCH	When asserted, signals that an instruction fetch is in progress; when negated, the transaction is a null transaction (code P bus idle)
Code reply	CR0-CR1	Signals the status of the instruction memory transaction
Error	ERR	Asserted when a bus comparator error occurs, ERR indicates that the desired signal level was not driven on the output pin; ERR is used in systems implementing a master/checker configuration of MC88100s
Clock	CLK	Internal clock normally phase locked to minimize skew between the external and internal signals; since CLK is applied to peripherals (such as CMMU devices), exact timing of internal signals is required to properly synchronize the device to the P bus
Phase lock enable	PLLEN	Asserted during reset to select phase locking, PLLEN controls the internal phase lock circuit that synchronizes the internal clocks to CLK
Reset	$\overline{\text{RST}}$	Used to perform an orderly restart of the processor; when asserted, the instruction pipeline is cleared and certain internal registers are cleared or initialized; when negated, the reset vector is fetched from memory, with execution beginning in supervisor mode
Interrupt	INT	Indicates that an interrupt request is in progress; when asserted, the processor saves the execution context and begins execution at the interrupt exception vector; software is responsible for handling all recognized interrupts (those between instructions when no higher priority exception occurs)

TABLE 8.18 (continued)
Signal Index

Signal name	Mnemonic	Function
P bus checker enable	PCE	Used in systems incorporating two or more MC88100s redundantly; when negated, the processor operates normally and when asserted, the processor monitors (but does not drive) all of its outputs except ERR as inputs
Power supply	Vcc	+ 5-volt power supply
Ground	GND	Ground connections

contents of shadow and exception time control registers, disables interrupts and all SFUs, and enters supervisor mode.

Figure 8.39 shows the 88100 general excepton (other than reset) flowchart. Note the following in the flowchart:

- The instruction pipeline shadow registers and register scoreboard are frozen by setting the SFRZ bit in PSR to one.
- The floating-point unit is disabled by setting the SFD1 bit in PSR to one.
- Interrupts are disabled by setting the IND bit to PSR to one.
- The MODE bit in PSR is set to one by the 88100 to operate in the supervisor mode.

For another exception, state information cannot be saved if shadow registers are frozen. Hence, for nested exceptions, an excepton handler must be able to save shadow registers to memory and clear SFRZ in PSR to zero.

Figures 8.40 and 8.41, respectively, show the 88100 reset flowchart and timing diagrams. When the 88100 RST pin is asserted, all outputs go into high impedance state except ERR which indicates no error. Upon hardware reset, the 88100 initializes PSR with appropriate data ($800003FF_{16}$ for supervisor mode operation, SFU1 disabled, interrupt masked, and shadow registers frozen), VBR with zero value, and fetches two 32-bit instructions from the reset vector 0. Warm reset in timing diagrams indicates push button reset.

PLLEN is the phase lock enable which controls phase locking the internal clock of the 88100 to the external clock.

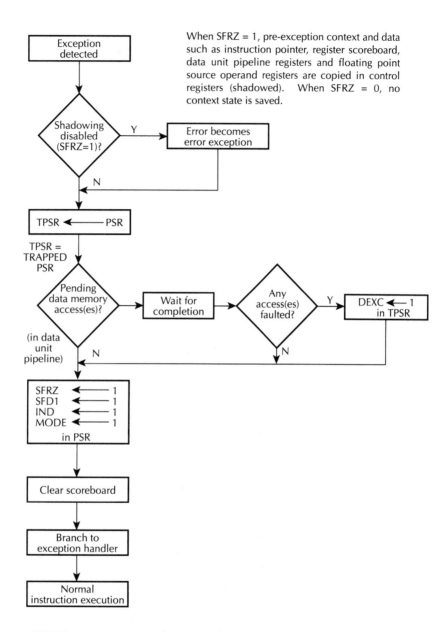

FIGURE 8.39 88100 general exception flowchart for all exceptions other than reset.

Let us discuss the timing diagrams of Figures 8.41a to d. Since the 88100 P-buses operate synchronously without asynchronous strobe signals, all devices must synchronize to the 88100 internal clock signal. The 88100 devices synchronize by phase-locking to the internal clock. During

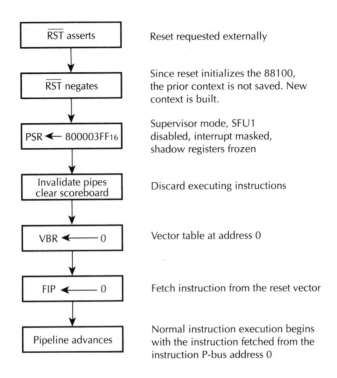

FIGURE 8.40 88100 reset exception flowchart.

reset, the assertion of phase lock enable (PLLEN) signal determines the type of phase locking performed. Figure 8.41a describes power-up reset with phase locking enabled. After power stabilizes, $\overline{RST}$ asserts and PLLEN negates together for more than 8 clock cycles. PLLEN asserts while $\overline{RST}$ remains asserted for at least 64 clock cycles. During this time, the 88100 internal clock synchronizes to the external clock input using the phase locking technique. After $\overline{RST}$ negates, the 88100 enters the exception state.

Figure 8.41b shows power-up reset with phase locking disabled. Operating the 88100 without phase locked clock is useful for debugging since this allows the 88100 to operate at clock frequencies lower than possible with phase locking enabled. After power stabilizes, $\overline{RST}$ asserts and PLLEN negates for more than 8 clock cycles. PLLEN remains negated after $\overline{RST}$ negates. The 88100 then enters the exception state.

Figure 8.41c shows a timing diagram for a warm reset after power-up reset without any change in phase locking. PLLEN remains either asserted or negated throughout the duration of the reset. $\overline{RST}$ asserts for more than 8 clock cycles. After $\overline{RST}$ negates, the 88100 enters exception.

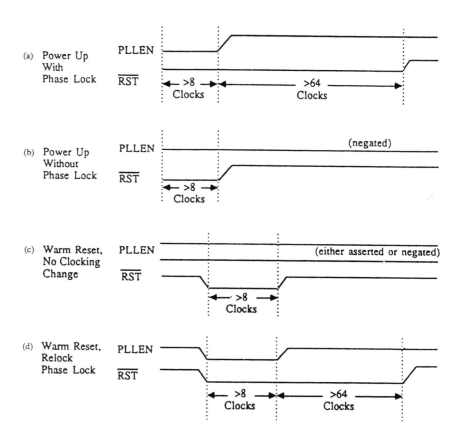

FIGURE 8.41 88100 reset exception timing diagrams.

Figure 8.41d shows the timing diagram for a warm reset with the clock relocked. $\overline{\text{RST}}$ asserts and PLLEN negates for more than 8 clock cycles. PLLEN asserts while $\overline{\text{RST}}$ remains asserted for at least 64 clock cycles. During this time, the 88100 internal clock resynchronizes to the external clock input. After $\overline{\text{RST}}$ negates, the 88100 goes into exception.

The 88100 can be interrupted when the INT pin is asserted HIGH. The 88100 completes the current instruction, then performs the following before branching to the service routine:

- Internally synchronizes INT for one clock cycle
- Fetches instruction of vector
- Propagates instruction through code pipeline

The 88100 code access faults are handled by asserting CR0 and CR1 input pins HIGH. A high on CR0 and CR1 pins indicates a fault.

Table 8.19 lists the 88100 program error exceptions.

TABLE 8.19
88100 Program Error Exceptions

Misaligned access faults
    Data memory addresses misaligned for **ld, st, xmem**
    Disabled when MXM = 1 in the PSR
    Destination register bit set in scoreboard
    Unimplemented opcode
    Unimplemented integer unit instruction execution
    Privilege violation
    User level attempted access to control registers
    User level use of **.usr** option
    User level traps to vectors 0-127
    Bounds check violation
    tbnd instruction operand failure
    Integer divide
    Zero divisor for **div, divu**
    Negative operands for **div**
    Integer overflow
    2's complement overflow for signed integer arithmetic
    Traps

Table 8.20 lists the 88100 floating-point unit exceptions.

TABLE 8.20
88100 Floating-Point Unit Exceptions

Floating-point precise exceptions
    Floating-point unit disabled
    Floating-point integer conversion overflow
    Floating-point unimplemented op code
    Floating-point privilege violation
    Floating-point reserved operand
    Floating-point divide by zero
Floating-point imprecise exceptions
    Floating-point underflow
    Floating-point overflow
    Floating-point inexact

VBR contains the address of the 88100 vector table. The vector table contains 512 vectors. Each vector corresponds to an exception. Each vector address contains the first two instructions of its exception routine. The instruction stored in the first vector is usually a branch instruction such as ' br.n START' (delayed branch) where START is the starting address of the exception routine. The second vector is normally used to save the current SP, and therefore the instruction such as stcr r31, cr17 is stored at the second vector. The first instruction of the exception routine should load the new SP to be used in the exception routine by using an instruction such as ldcr r31, cr18. The last instruction of the exception handling routine should be rte which restores the preexception state.

Table 8.21 shows the 88100 exception vector table.

TABLE 8.21
88100 VBR, Vector Table

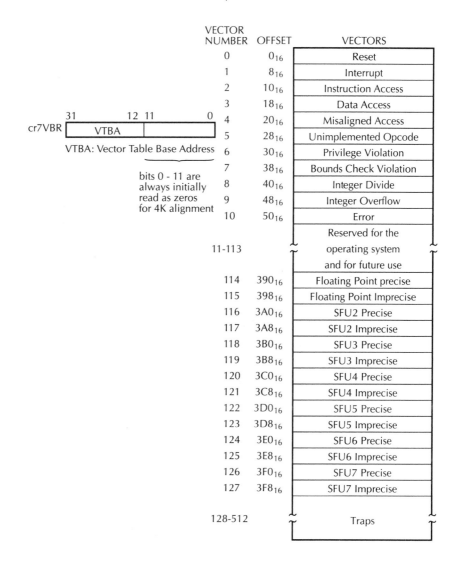

VECTOR NUMBER	OFFSET	VECTORS
0	0_{16}	Reset
1	8_{16}	Interrupt
2	10_{16}	Instruction Access
3	18_{16}	Data Access
4	20_{16}	Misaligned Access
5	28_{16}	Unimplemented Opcode
6	30_{16}	Privilege Violation
7	38_{16}	Bounds Check Violation
8	40_{16}	Integer Divide
9	48_{16}	Integer Overflow
10	50_{16}	Error
11-113		Reserved for the operating system and for future use
114	390_{16}	Floating Point precise
115	398_{16}	Floating Point Imprecise
116	$3A0_{16}$	SFU2 Precise
117	$3A8_{16}$	SFU2 Imprecise
118	$3B0_{16}$	SFU3 Precise
119	$3B8_{16}$	SFU3 Imprecise
120	$3C0_{16}$	SFU4 Precise
121	$3C8_{16}$	SFU4 Imprecise
122	$3D0_{16}$	SFU5 Precise
123	$3D8_{16}$	SFU5 Imprecise
124	$3E0_{16}$	SFU6 Precise
125	$3E8_{16}$	SFU6 Imprecise
126	$3F0_{16}$	SFU7 Precise
127	$3F8_{16}$	SFU7 Imprecise
128-512		Traps

cr7VBR

31	12	11	0
VTBA			

VTBA: Vector Table Base Address

bits 0 - 11 are always initially read as zeros for 4K alignment

The 88100 determines the starting address of the service routine by reading two consecutive 32-bit words pointed to by VBR. The VBR contents are automatically computed by the 88100 by adding VBR to (8 * vector number). For each exception type, there is a predefined vector number. The 88100 multiplies this vector number by 8 to find the offset. This offset is added to the initial VBR contents to find the VBR contents for the particular exception.

QUESTIONS AND PROBLEMS

8.1   i) Identify the 68030 registers that are not included in the 68020.
    ii) Name a 68030 register which is included in the 68020 but formatted in a different way from the 68020. Why is it structured differently?

8.2 What are the functions of 68030 $\overline{REFILL}$, $\overline{STATUS}$, and $\overline{STERM}$ pins?

8.3   i) What is the difference between 68030 $\overline{DSACK}$ and $\overline{STERM}$?
    ii) What are the minimum bus access times in clock cycles for 68030 synchronous and asynchronous operations?

8.4 What conditions must be satisfied before a cache hit occurs for either instruction or data cache in the 68030?

8.5 Assume user data space. The 68030 executes the instruction CLR.W (A1) with [A1] = $20507002 and [$20507002] = $1234 with the following information in data cache:

		Tag	Valid bits 0 1 2 3	LW0	LW1	LW2	LW3
0	1	205070	1 1 1 1	12345124	00121234	70001111	01112222
1	1	205070	0 1 1 1	77777777	12121212	FF0011EE	AAAA1111
2	1	5F1236	1 0 1 0	72101234	25252020	FEEEEEEE	00110011
3	1	021472	0 0 0 1	11223344	BBBBAAAA	71171625	00200000

Will a cache hit occur? Why or why not?

8.6 What are the functions of 68030 $\overline{\text{CBREQ}}$ and CBACK?

8.7 Write a 68030 instruction sequence to clear the entry for instruction cache for address $00005040.

8.8 For a page size of 4K bytes, translate the 68030 logical address $00000240 to physical address. Assume the following data:

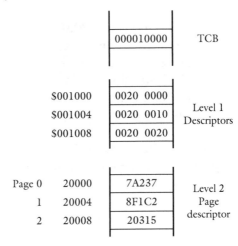

8.9 Identify the inputs and outputs that affect the 68030 MMU.

8.10 i) How many levels of translation tables does the 68030 MMU provide?

ii) What is the maximum number of page descriptor entries in the ATC?

8.11 Assume the following data contents of the 68030 CRP:

```
31                        0
0 0 1 0 0      0 0 0 3
   2 A 6 7     1 1 2  4
31              4, 3   0
```

i)   Is this a page or table descriptor?
ii) What is the address of the next table?
iii) What is the allowed range of logical addresses for the next table?

8.12 Determine the contents of the 68030 TC which will enable MMU, SRP, disable function code look-up, and will permit 2 levels of equal size look-up with a page size of 1K byte for a 30-bit address.

8.13 Show the contents of the 68030 TT0 for translating addresses $20000000—$21FFFFFF in supervisor data space. These addresses should be read-only and cacheable.

8.14 Find the following 68030 MMU instructions:
   i)   The instruction for accessing MMU register
   ii) The instruction for placing descriptors to ATC
   iii) The instruction for invalidating one or more entries in the cache
   iv) The instruction for testing a descriptor either in the memory or in the cache

8.15 Write a 68030 instruction sequence for initializing TC, CRP, and SRP registers from memory pointed to by A2. Can you initialize all MMU registers by this instruction? If not, list the register or registers.

8.16 Compare 68030 on-chip MMU features with those of the 68851 MMU.

8.17 What is meant by configuration error exception in the 68030?

8.18 In the 68030 MMU (demand paging system), what happens when a task attempts to access a page not in memory? What action should be taken by the demand paging operating system?

8.19 Summarize the basic features of RISC microprocessors. Identify how some of these features are implemented in the 88100.

8.20 Describe briefly the functional blocks included in the 88200. What does the 88200 provide to a 88100 system?

8.21 What is the maximum number of the 88200 that can be present in one 88100 processing mode?

8.22 How many pipelines are in the 88100?

8.23 What operations are controlled by the 88100 register scoreboard?

8.24 What is the size of the 88200 data cache?

8.25 Since there is no return from subroutine instruction, how does the 88100 return from subroutine?

8.26 What 88100 floating-point control registers can be accessed by the user mode programs?

8.27 Identify the stack pointer register in the 88100.

8.28 Show the contents of registers and memory locations after the 88100 executes the following instructions:
　　　i)　st.h r1, r2, r0
　　　ii)　ld.h r1, r2, 0X0A
　　　　　　Assume　[r1] = 0000 0020$_{16}$
　　　　　　　　　　[r2] = 0000 0300$_{16}$

	Memory			
0300	10	57	1F	2A
0304	A1	06	04	02
0308	27	13	20	18
030C	CC	BB	AA	FF

All numbers are in hexadecimal.

8.29 Find the contents of r5 after execution of the following 88100 instructions:
　　　i)　mask.u r5, r2, 0XFFFF
　　　ii)　mask r5, r2, r6
　　　　　　Assume　[r5] = AAAA 0100$_{16}$
　　　　　　　　　　[r2] = 0020 05FF$_{16}$
　　　　　　　　　　[r6] = 7777 7777$_{16}$

　　　prior to execution of each of the above instructions.

8.30 Write an 88100 instruction sequence to logically shift the content of r2 into r1 to the right by 8 bits.

8.31 What is the effect of the 88100 tbl r0, r1, 200 instruction?

8.32 What are the functions of 88100 CS/$\overline{U}$, BE0-BE3, C0, and C2 pins?

8.33 What 88100 registers are affected by hardware reset?

8.34 Discuss briefly the 88100 exceptions.

Chapter 9

PERIPHERAL INTERFACING

This chapter describes interfacing characteristics of a microcomputer with typical peripheral devices such as hexadecimal keyboard and display, DMA controller, printer, CRT (Cathode Ray tube) terminal, floppy disk, and coprocessor.

9.1 BASICS OF KEYBOARD AND DISPLAY INTERFACE TO A MICROPROCESSOR

A common method of entering programs into a microcomputer is via a keyboard. A popular way of displaying results by the microcomputer is by using seven segment displays. The main functions to be performed for interfacing a keyboard are

1. Sense a key actuation.
2. Debounce the key.
3. Decode the key.

Let us now elaborate on the keyboard interfacing concepts. A keyboard is arranged in rows and columns. Figure 9.1 shows a 2 × 2 keyboard interfaced to a typical microcomputer. In Figure 9.1, the columns are normally at a HIGH level. A key actuation is sensed by sending a LOW to each row one at a time via PA0 and PA1 of port A. The two columns can then be input via PB2 and PB3 of port B to see whether any of the normally HIGH columns are pulled LOW by a key actuation. If they are, the rows

835

can be checked individually to determine the row in which the key is down. The row and column code in which the key is pressed can thus be found.

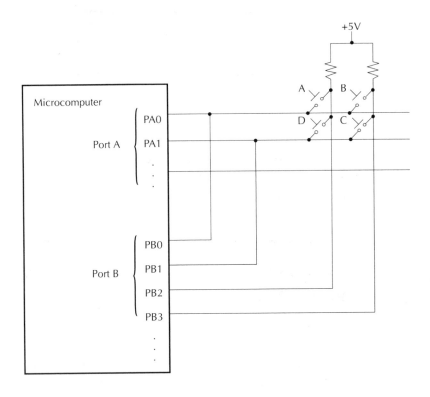

FIGURE 9.1 A 2 × 2 keyboard interfaced to a microcomputer.

The next step is to debounce the key. Key bounce occurs when a key is pressed or released — it bounces for a short time before making the contact. When this bounce occurs, it may appear to the microcomputer that the same key has been actuated several times instead of just once. This problem can be eliminated by reading the keyboard after 20 ms and then verifying to see if it is still down. If it is, then the key actuation is valid.

The next step is to translate the row and column code into a more popular code such as hexadecimal or ASCII. This can easily be accomplished by a program.

There are certain characteristics associated with keyboard actuations which must be considered while interfacing a microcomputer. Typically, these are two-key lockout and N-key rollover. The two-key lockout takes into account only one key pressed. An additional key pressed and released does not generate any codes. The system is simple to implement and most often used. However, it might slow down the typing since each key must be fully released before the next one is pressed down. On the other hand, the N-key rollover will ignore all keys pressed until only one remains down.

Now let us elaborate on the interfacing characteristics of typical displays. The following functions are to be typically performed for displays:

1. Output the appropriate display code.
2. Output the code via right entry or left entry into the displays if there is more than one display.

The above functions can easily be realized by a microcomputer program. If there is more than one key, they are typically arranged in rows. A row of four displays is shown in Figure 9.2. Note that in Figure 9.2, one has the option of outputting the display code via right entry or left entry. If it is entered via left entry, then the code for the most significant digit of the four-digit display should be output first, then the next digit code, and so on. Note that the first digit will be shifted three times, the next digit twice, the next digit once, and the last digit (least significant digit in this case) does not need to be shifted. The shifting operations are so fast that visually all four digits will appear on the display simultaneously. If the displays are entered via right entry, then the least significant digit must be output first and the rest of the sequence is similar to the left entry.

FIGURE 9.2 A row of four displays.

Two techniques are typically used to interface a hexadecimal display to the microcomputer. These are nonmultiplexed and multiplexed. In nonmultiplexed methods, each hexadecimal display digit is interfaced to the microcomputer via an I/O port. Figure 9.3 illustrates this method.

BCD to seven-segment conversion is done in software. The microcomputer can be programmed to output to the two display digits in sequence. However, the microcomputer executes the display instruction sequence so fast that the displays appear to human eyes at the same time.

Figure 9.4 illustrates the multiplexing method of interfacing the two hexadecimal displays to the microcomputer.

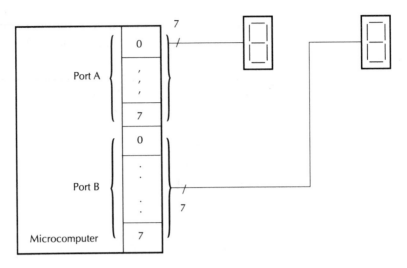

FIGURE 9.3 Nonmultiplexed hexadecimal displays.

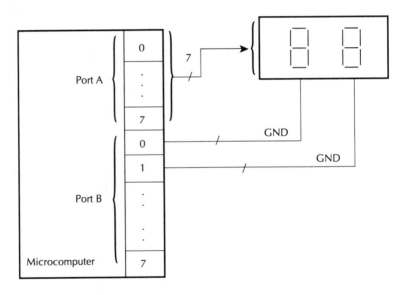

FIGURE 9.4 Multiplexed displays.

In the multiplexing scheme, seven-segment code is sent to all displays simultaneously. However, the segment to be illuminated is grounded.

The keyboard and display interfacing concepts described here can be realized by either software or hardware. In order to relieve the microprocessor of these functions, microprocessor manufacturers have developed a number of keyboard/display controller chips such as the Intel 8279. These chips are typically initialized by the microprocessor. The keyboard/display functions are then performed by the chip independent of the microprocessor.

The amount of keyboard/display functions performed by the controller chip varies from one manufacturer to another. However, these functions are usually shared between the controller chip and the microprocessor.

9.1.1 HEXADECIMAL KEYBOARD/DISPLAY INTERFACE TO THE 8085

In order to illustrate the hexadecimal keyboard/display interfacing concepts, the 8085/8156/2716-based microcomputer of Figure 2.32 will be utilized. The I/O map of the microcomputer is provided in the following:

CSR	08H
Port A	09H
Port B	0AH
Port C	0BH

The 2716 and 8156 memory maps are provided in the following:

2716 Memory Map
0000H through 07FFH
8156 Memory Map
0800H through 08FFH

Figure 9.5 shows the microcomputer's interface to a hexadecimal keyboard and two seven-segment hexadecimal displays.

The keyboard contains a 4 × 4 matrix keypad. There are eight 10K resistors which connect all columns and rows of the keypad to 5 volts such that all bits of port A will be HIGH when no key is activated.

The display includes two hexadecimal displays (TIL311). The TIL311s have on-chip decoders.

A look-up table will be used to store row and column codes for each hexadecimal digit in the 2716 EPROM.

In the software, port A is first read and checked to determine whether the previous key has been released. This will eliminate any problem when someone holds the key for a long time. When the key is released, it is debounced by calling a subroutine providing a 20-ms delay. The 8156 RAM will be used as the stack. The program will then input the rows and columns of the keyboard via port A and check for key closure. If the key

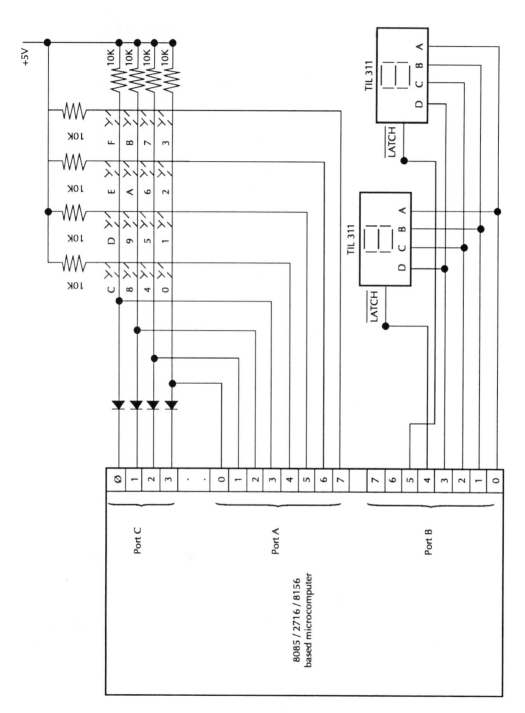

FIGURE 9.5 An 8085/2716/8156-based microcomputer's interface to hexadecimal keyboard and display.

closure is sensed, it is debounced again by waiting 20 ms, and the binary code corresponding to the key pressed is determined by using the look-up table. Rows and columns are connected to input port A. Port C is configured as an output port. The rows are also connected to port C. The rows are grounded by sending zeros to all rows via port C and key closure is sensed by inputting the column data via port A.

In order to display the keyin data, all displays are cleared first. The least significant display is the first keyin data and is stored at memory location 0800H. When the second key is pressed, the first data is displayed in the left display and the second data is displayed on the right display. The second display is also stored in location 0800H. When the third key is pressed, the left-most display is discarded. The second key from location 0800H is displayed in the left display and the third key is displayed on the right display. The third key is also stored in location 0800H and the process continues.

The assembly language program listing is given in Figure 9.6.

The data in TABLE of Figure 9.6 are obtained by inspecting the keys of Figure 9.5. For example, the code for the E key is $1011\ 0111_2$. This is because when a LOW is sent on the top row and the E key is pressed, the top row and the column connected to bit 6 of port A (normally HIGH column is grounded by activating the E key) becomes zero. This makes port A data $B7_{16}$. Similarly, the codes for the other keys in TABLE can be determined.

1	CSR	EQU08H		
2	PORTA	EQU09H		
3	PORTB	EQU0AH		
4	PORTC	EQU0BH		
5	START	MVI A, 0EH,	;	Configure Port A as
6		OUT CSR	;	input, Ports B & C as outputs
7		LXI SP, 08A0H	;	Initialize SP
8		MVI A, 0F0H	;	Set up display
9		OUT PORTB	;	To be zeros
10		NOP	;	Delay latch
11		MVI A, 00H	;	Enable both latch lines
12		OUT PORTB	;	To display zeros
13		STA 0800H	;	Store displayed data in
			;	location 0800H

FIGURE 9.6 Assembly language program for hex keyboard and displays.

14	REPEAT	XRA A	;	Clear A
15		OUT PORTC	;	Send zeros to rows
16	KEY OPEN	IN PORTA	;	Input Port A
17		CPI 0F0H	;	Compare with F0H
18		JNZ KEY OPEN	;	All keys are open
			;	If Z = 1; otherwise
			;	Wait for previous
			;	key to open
19		CALL DEBOUNCE	;	Delay 20ms
20	KEY CLOSE	IN PORTA	;	Input PortA
21	NEXT ROW	CPI 0F0H	;	Compare with F0H
22		JZ KEY CLOSE	;	Check for
			;	key closure
23		CALL DEBOUNCE	;	Delay 20ms
24		MVI A, 0FFH	;	Set 'A' to all ones
25		ORA A	;	Clear carry
26		RAL	;	Rotate zero to first row
27		MOV, B, A	;	Save row mask in B
28		OUT PORTC	;	Output to all rows
29		IN PORTA	;	Input row and column
30		MOV C, A	;	Save row and column code
31		ANI 0F0H	;	Mask row code
32		CPI 0F0H	;	Check column for HIGH
33		JNZ DECODE	;	If Z = 0, decode key
34		STC	;	If Z = 1, key not found
35		MOV A, B	;	Move one to next
36		JMP NEXT ROW	;	row
37	DECODE	LXI H, TABLE	;	Load starting address
			;	of lookup table
38		MVI B, 0FH	;	Initialize character counter
39		MOV A, C	;	Get row and column code
40	NEXT	CMP M	;	Compare row and column code
			;	with lookup table
41		JZ DONE	;	If key found, go to DONE
42		INX H	;	If not, increment HL
43		DCR B	;	Decrement character counter

FIGURE 9.6 continued.

44		JNZ NEXT	;	If Z = 0, go to NEXT for
			;	compaing with the
			;	next table code
45	DONE	MOV A, B	;	Get character
46		ORI 0F0H	;	Disable both
47		OUT PORTB	;	Latches
48		NOP	;	Delay for set-up time for
			;	data out
49		ANI 1FH	;	Enable right latch
50		OUT PORTB	;	Display key
51		NOP	;	Delay again
52		ORI 0F0H	;	Disable again
53		OUT PORTB	;	Latches
54		LDA 0800H	;	Get data
55			;	From 0800H
56		ORI 0F0H	;	Disable both LATCH
57		OUT PORTB	;	
58		ANI 0F2H	;	Enable left LATCH
59		OUT PORTB	;	Via Port B
60		MOV A, B	;	Store data in
61		STA 0800H	;	Location 0800H
62		JMP REPEAT	;	Go to another key
63	DEBOUNCE	LXI D, 09C2H	;	Delay 20 ms
64	LOOP	DCX D	;	Debounce
65		MOV A, D	;	The
66		ORA E	;	Key
67		JNZ LOOP	;	Jump if Z = 0
68		RET	;	Return
	TABLE	DB 77H	;	Code for P
		DB 0B7H	;	Code for E
		DB 0D7H	;	Code for D
		DB 0E7H	;	Code for C
		DB 7BH	;	Code for B
		DB 0BBH	;	Code for A
		DB 0DBH	;	Code for 9

FIGURE 9.6 continued.

DB 0EBH	;	Code for 8
DB 7DH	;	Code for 7
DB 0BDH	;	Code for 6
DB 0DDH	;	Code for 5
DB 0EDH	;	Code for 4
DB 7EH	;	Code for 3
DB 0BEH	;	Code for 2
DB 0DEH	;	Code for 1
DB 0EEH	;	Code for 0

FIGURE 9.6 continued.

In order to explain the program logic of Figure 9.6, let us display $E2_{16}$ in the two-digit display of Figure 9.5. The above display will take place in the following order: the E key will have to be pressed first and will be displayed on the right display. The E key code will then be saved in location 0800H until the second key '2' is pressed. When the key '2' is activated, the contents of 0800_{16} (E) will be sent to the left display and '2' will be sent to right display, and '2' is saved in 0800_{16} until the next key is pressed.

In Figure 9.6, lines 1—13 initialize ports, SP, output zeros to the two displays, and store zero in location 0800_{16}. Note that initially zeros are output to displays. Lines 14—23 detect whether the previous key is released. If it is, then the key is debounced for 20 msec. This will eliminate any problems if someone holds a key for a long time. The program then detects a key closure. If a key is pressed, it is debounced for 20 ms; otherwise the program stays in the KEYCLOSE loop.

Lines 24—32 determine exactly which key is pressed. This is done by moving all ones into the accumulator in Line 24. The CARRY is cleared and a zero is moved from this carry to a particular bit position in the accumulator. These data are used to output zero to each row in sequence. The rows and columns are read via Port A. If a key is pressed in a particular row, the column connected to that row via the depressed key will also be zero. For example, if the E key is pressed, Code $B7_{16}$ for E will appear at Port A. Since the E key is pressed in this example, the program branches from line 33 to line 37 and decodes the key. The program then branches to the label DONE; otherwise the program loops through NEXTROW until the key is found. Once the E key is found, appropriate data for the key and ones to the two $\overline{\text{LATCH}}$ lines are sent via Port B (lines 46 and 47). Instructions in lines 49 and 50 enable the right $\overline{\text{LATCH}}$ line and display E (in this case) in the right-most display.

LDA 0800H in line 54 loads 00H (stored in 0800H in line 13) into the accumulator. Lines 52 through 59 enable left $\overline{\text{LATCH}}$ line and display zero in the left display. Lines 60 and 61 store the data displayed on the right display in location 0800H.

JMP REPEAT in Line 62 branches to Line 14 from where the program is executed again, for detecting the next key pressed. The next key (if pressed), is displayed on the right display and E is moved from location 0800H to the left display and then the code for right key displayed is stored in 0800H. The process then continues.

9.1.2 INTEL 8279 KEYBOARD/DISPLAY CONTROLLER CHIP

9.1.2.a Introduction

This section is intended to aid in the use of the Intel 8279 Programmable Keyboard/Display Controller. All modes of this device will be explained in detail with examples. The 8279 description is split into three main parts: the interface to the 8085 microprocessor, interface to keyboard and display hardware, and software interface.

A block diagram is shown in Figure 9.7. As can be seen, this chip has many features which would normally require extensive external logic to perform these same functions. The chip automatically controls the display refreshing and multiplexing. It contains the debounce circuitry needed for any normal key switch. It also contains an 8×3-bit RAM which can be configured as a First-In-First-Out (FIFO) buffer or it can represent the actual condition of all the switches at any given time.

The chip is fully programmable, and many different modes can be programmed using the same external logic.

9.1.2.b Interfacing to the 8085

The 8279 was initially designed for the 8080 microprocessor, but it can work with the 8085 or 8086. As mentioned before, the main difference between the 8085 and the 8080 is the fact that the 8085 multiplexes the lower byte of address and the data on the same eight pins. Since the 8279 requires A0, the least significant bit of the address bus, we will either have to decode A0 from the multiplexed lines or use a trick of the 8085.

If the 8279 is to be I/O mapped, that is, to appear as a group of input/output ports, we can use the upper byte of the address bus to provide A0. The 8085, like the 8080, duplicates the lower byte of the address bus onto the upper byte of the address bus during I/O operations. Thus, A8 becomes A0. This is shown in Figure 9.8.

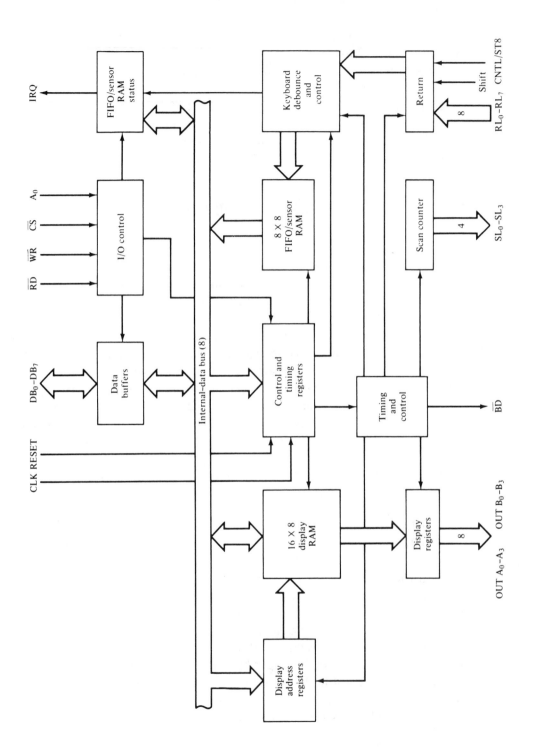

FIGURE 9.7 8279 block diagram.

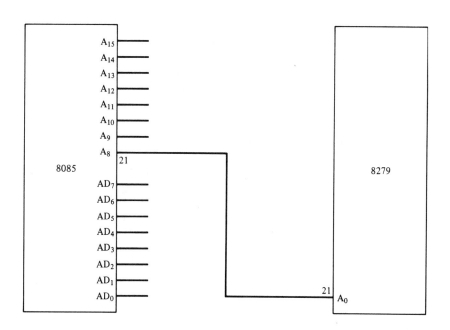

FIGURE 9.8 8085/8279 interface when the 8279 is to be I/O mapped.

If the 8279 is to be memory mapped, that is, to appear as a group of memory locations, we will have to demultiplex the address/data lines to provide the entire 16-bit address bus. This can be done by enabling an octal latch such as the Intel 8282 or a TTL 74LS373 using the 8085 ALE (Address Latch Enable). With ALE, the octal latch can store the lower byte of the address bus, thereby providing the entire 16-bit address bus for decoding. This is shown in Figure 9.9.

The 8279 has an 8-bit data bus which supplies control information and the exchange of data. This must be connected to the 8085's address/data bus.

The 8279 has two signals which control the direction of data flow on the data bus. These signals are $\overline{RD}$ and $\overline{WR}$. When $\overline{RD}$ is true, the 8085 is reading data from the 8279. When WR is true, the 8085 is writing data to the 8279. To simplify the chip select circuitry, these signals should only be active during either an I/O cycle or memory cycle, depending on the mapping selected for the 8279. The 8085 does not generate these two signals directly, but they can be generated easily.

The 8085 provides three signals which define the operation in progress. They are $\overline{WR}$, $\overline{RD}$, and IO/$\overline{M}$. The RD and $\overline{WR}$ signals specify the direction of data flow, while the IO/$\overline{M}$ signal specifies the operation in

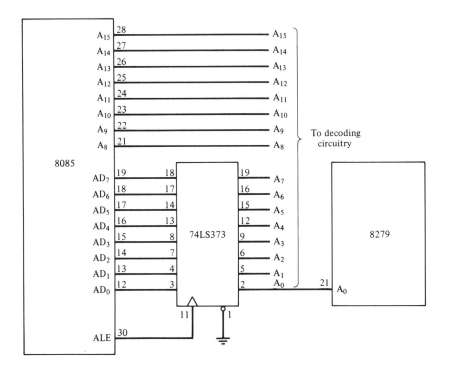

FIGURE 9.9 8085/8279 interface when the 8279 is to be memory mapped.

progress. The table below shows the decoding of these three signals and the resulting bus operation.

$\overline{\text{WR}}$	$\overline{\text{RD}}$	IO/$\overline{\text{M}}$	Operation
0	1	1	I/O write
1	0	1	I/O read
0	1	0	Memory read
1	0	0	Memory write

By using a simple 3 to 8 decoder, such as a 74LS138, we can decode these signals into $\overline{\text{IOWR}}$, $\overline{\text{IORD}}$, $\overline{\text{MEMR}}$, and $\overline{\text{MEMW}}$. Figure 9.10 shows this implementation.

The $\overline{\text{CS}}$ pin enables the 8279 for a data transfer as specified by its $\overline{\text{RD}}$, $\overline{\text{WR}}$, and A0 pins. This line goes true whenever the correct address is present on the address bus. The degree to which the address bus must be decoded depends upon how complex the system is. If the system has many

I/O devices, a more complete decoding of the address is needed to protect against bus conflicts. But in a simple system with few devices, no real decoding is needed. Each device can occupy many I/O locations.

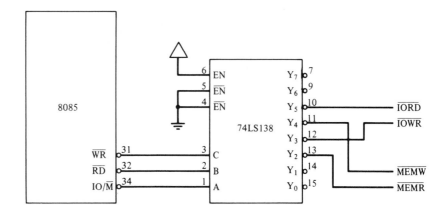

FIGURE 9.10 Decoding 8085 WR, RD, and IO/$\overline{\text{M}}$ lines.

The reset pin on the 8279 serves to reset the device during power on or reset events. This pin can be connected to the 8085 reset out pin.

The CLK pin provides the clock for the internal timing of the 8279. This clock must be greater than 200 kHz for the internal timers to provide the correct delays. This can be connected to the 8085's CLK out pin or other frequency source.

The 8279's IRQ pin signals the 8085 that the 8279 has data available and needs to be read. In an interrupt-driven system, the IRQ signal can be connected to the 8085's RST5.5, RST6.5, or RST7.5 pins to interrupt the 8085 when data are available. This will cause the 8085 to execute an interrupt service routine to read the 8279. In noninterrupt-driven systems this line is not used; the 8085 can determine if the 8279 needs service by reading the status register of the 8279.

A complete interface of the 8279 to an 8085 can be seen in Figure 9.11. This implementation is I/O mapped, interrupt driven, and uses simple decoding of the address bus.

9.1.2.c Interfacing to Keyboard Display Hardware

The 8279 interfaces typical microprocessors such as 8085 and 8086 to a keyboard and a display device. Since these two sections are separate, we first discuss the display interface.

The display interface is relatively simple. The 8279 provides the buffers, the multiplexing logic, and the refreshing needed to drive the display. This greatly simplifies the necessary hardware. In fact, if you only need a four-character display, you only need to add the display driver necessary for the particular display you are using.

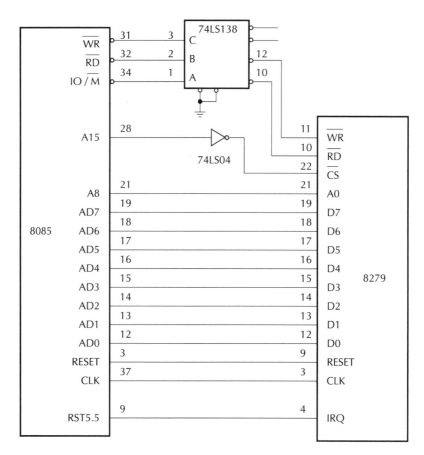

FIGURE 9.11 A complete 8085/8279 interface.

The 8279 provides refreshing of multiplexed displays. Seven-segment codes for the digits to be displayed are sent to the FIFO RAM in the 8279. The 8279 then automatically outputs the code for one digit and displays it. After some time delay (about one millisecond) the 8279 outputs code for the next digit and displays it. The process is repeated until all digits are displayed. The 8279 then goes back to the first digit.

The 8279 has two buffers: A buffer and B buffer. These buffers can be used together to form two 4 bit × 16 word displays, or they can be used together to form an 8 bit × 16 word display. Writing data into or reading data from the buffer is controlled by the mode selected, and will be discussed in the next section on software interfacing.

The 8279 provides data from the internal buffer on the out A and out B pins. Each of these ports is 4 bits wide. These data are synchronized with the scan lines, SL0 through SL3, to provide multiplexing. These scan lines are either encoded or decoded. In the decoded mode, only one scan line is active at one time. Thus, only four characters are displayed. In the encoded mode, the scan lines form a binary sequence counting from 0 to either 8 or 16, depending on the options selected. In this mode, an external decoder, such as a 4- to 16-line decoder, would have to be used. In the decoded mode, the scan lines are active low, while in the encoded mode they are active high.

There is one additional signal provided by the 8279 for the display interface. This is BD or Blank Display. This active low line goes true when the display should be blanked, either by command or between successive words. Note that the display is blanked to prevent ghosting of displays from one digit to the next when the display is switched to the next one.

If you use the two outputs together to form an 8 bit × 16 word display, you can directly drive a multiplexed LED display. Seven of the bits control the seven segments, and the eighth bit can control the decimal points. With this setup, you can display limited alphanumerics, or even special graphics. (A display much like the simple handheld games could be fashioned in this way.) For this application, you would only need to add anode and cathode drivers to buffer the signals from the 8279 and decoder chip. A sample of this display is shown in Figure 9.12.

The purpose of the keyboard section of the 8279 is to scan a keyboard, detect a key closure, and store the code for the pressed key in the internal FIFO RAM where it can be read by the microprocessor.

The keyboard interface is organized as either an 8 × 8 matrix or a 4 × 8 matrix of SPST switches. The keyboard uses the same four scan lines that the display uses (SL0-3).

The keyboard can operate in two different modes: decoded (4 × 8) or encoded (8 × 8). The scan lines behave exactly as described for the display interface. In the decoded mode, the scan lines directly do the scanning, while in the encoded mode, the scan lines must be externally decoded. Note that in the encoded mode only the first 3 bits or eight lines should be used for the keyboard. The keyboard section and the display section must be in the same scan mode, meaning that if the keyboard scan is encoded, the display scan must be encoded.

Two additional keys are provided for by the 8279. These are for the

SHIFT and CONTROL keys. These keys do not trigger the 8279 themselves, but are recorded in the FIFO along with a key in the matrix when
that key is pressed. This gives you an effective 256 codes which can be
generated by the 8279. A simple circuit for 64 keys, SHIFT, CONTROL,
and a 16-character display is shown in Figure 9.13.

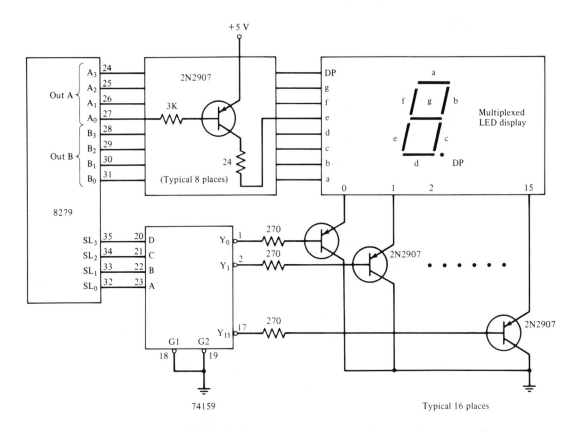

FIGURE 9.12 8279 display interface using OUT A and OUT B together.

In the scanned sensor mode, the FIFO buffer is converted into an 8 ×
8-bit map. Each bit in the map represents the state of the switch at the same
location in the keyboard matrix. If the switch is closed, then the RAM
location corresponding to that switch will be a logical zero. No key
debouncing is performed by the 8279, and the SHIFT or CONTROL
status is not recorded. In this mode, the 8279 signals any change in the
matrix by raising IRQ. A bit is also set in the status register.

In the scanned sensor mode, the sensors do not have to be switches,
but can be anything that produces a 1 or a 0 in response to the scan lines.

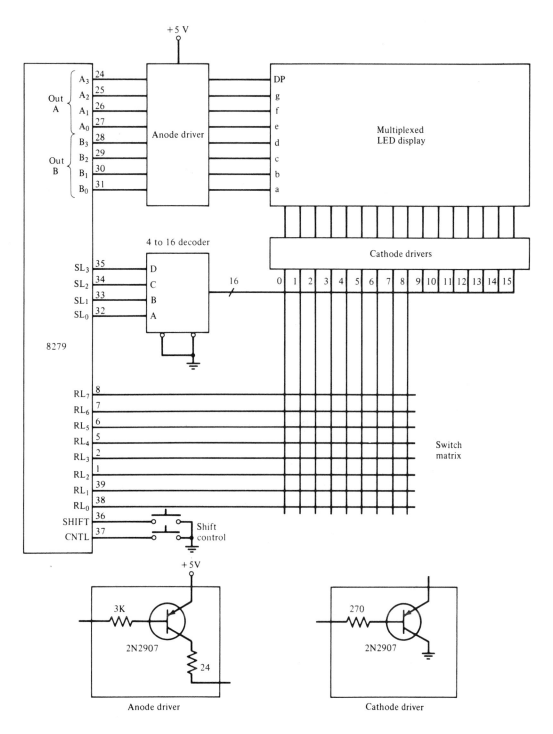

FIGURE 9.13 8279 interface to a keyboard and display.

A third mode is available for entering data into the FIFO of the 8279. This is the strobed input mode. In this mode the data present on the Return Lines (RL_{0-7}) are loaded into the FIFO by the rising edge of the CNTL/STB pulse. In this mode the scan lines do not mean anything to the keyboard section; they only control the display hardware.

9.1.2.d Software Interface

For the 8279 to work properly, it must be sent commands programming it for the specific hardware configuration. These commands are sent to the command port of the 8279 (A0 = high). The data are read from or sent to the data port of the 8279 (A0 = low). Status information is read from the command port.

The keyboard/display mode set command defines the mode the 8279 will operate in. This command is diagrammed below:

MSB   LSB

Keyboard/display mode set | 0 | 0 | 0 | D | D | K | K | K |

DD

0 0	8 8-bit character display — left entry
0 1	16 8-bit character display — left entry
1 0	8 8-bit character display — right entry
1 1	16 8-bit character display — right entry

KKK

0 0 0	Encoded scan keyboard — two-key lockout
0 0 1	Decoded scan keyboard — two-key lockout
0 1 0	Encoded scan keyboard — N-key rollover
0 1 1	Decoded scan keyboard — N-key rollover
1 0 0	Encoded scan sensor matrix
1 0 1	Decoded scan sensor matrix
1 1 0	Strobed input, encoded display scan
1 1 1	Strobed input, decoded display scan

The DD field sets the display length and the entry mode. The length of the display can be 8 or 16 words long, and we can enter data from the left or the right.

In left-entry mode, characters are entered from the left as on a typewriter. When in the autoincrementing mode, each new character will appear to the right of the old character. If you are using a 16-word display, the seventeenth character will replace the first character entered.

In right-entry mode, the characters are entered at the right side of the display and scrolled to the left with each new character, much like on a calculator. In this mode, the seventeenth character causes the first character entered to scroll off the display.

The KKK field sets the keyboard and scan mode. The scan modes have been discussed in the hardware section, along with the scanned sensor and strobed input modes.

The keyboard mode is either two-key lockout or N-key rollover. These modes determine how the 8279 deals with the problem of rollover, that is, when two or more keys are depressed at once. In two-key lockout the 8279 recognizes the first key pressed, and additional keys pressed are ignored until the first key is released. In N-key rollover, keys pressed simultaneously are entered into the FIFO in the order that the 8279 finds them. In this mode, a special error mode can be set. This error mode will consider a simultaneous key depression as an error. A bit is set in the status register, any further writing into the FIFO is inhibited, and an interrupt is requested. This error mode is set by the end interrupt/error mode set command, described later.

The 8279 has programmable counters to divide the CLK signal to 100 kHz for the internal timing. The value is set by the use of the program clock command. The P field contains the divisor necessary to give a 100-kHz internal clock. This value is in the range 2 to 31. For a 2-MHz CLK signal, the divisor would be 20_{10} or 14_{16}.

	MSB							LSB
Program clock	0	0	1	P	P	P	P	P

When the microprocessor sends a read FIFO/sensor RAM command, the 8279 responds to each successive read from the FIFO. This command is shown below:

	MSB							LSB	
Read FIFO/sensor RAM	0	1	0	AI	X	A	A	A	X = don't care

In the scanned sensor mode, AAA selects one of the eight rows of the RAM to read. AI is the autoincrement bit. If this is true, the RAM address will automatically increment after the read. If the AI bit is set, reading the RAM will *not* clear the interrupt. The AAA and AI fields are ignored during any other mode.

The read display RAM command enables the microprocessor to read the data from the display buffer. This command is diagrammed below:

	MSB							LSB
Read display RAM	0	1	1	AI	A	A	A	A

The AAAA field sets the address for this read, and the AI field controls the autoincrement mode. Since the same counter is used for reading and writing to the display RAM, this command also sets the next address and increment mode for both reading and writing.

The write display RAM command sets up the 8279 for a write to the display buffer. The addressing and autoincrement modes are identical to the Read Display RAM command, described before.

	MSB							LSB
Write display RAM	1	0	0	AI	A	A	A	A

This command does not affect the source of subsequent data reads; the CPU will read from whichever data source (FIFO/sensor RAM or display RAM) was last selected. If the source was the display RAM, the write display RAM command will change the address of the next read location.

The display inhibit/blanking command is used to inhibit writing to the display RAM or in blanking the display. This command makes using two 4-bit ports easier in that the inhibit and blanking functions can be performed on each of the two ports independently.

	MSB							LSB	
Display inhibit/blanking	1	0	1	X	IW A	IW B	BL A	BL B	X = don't care

The IW bits are used to inhibit writing to the A port or B port. If we are using BCD decoding for the two 4-bit displays, we can inhibit writing to one display while writing to the other. Port B is the lower nibble of the data written to the display, with port A being the upper nibble.

The BL bits blank the display of the selected port. The code that is sent to the display during blanking is specified by the clear command described later. When using the display as a single 8-bit display, both BL bits must be set to blank the display.

The clear command determines the codes sent to the display when it is blanked, and can also clear the display RAM and reset the device. This command, shown below,

	MSB							LSB
Clear	1	1	0	EN	CD	CD	CF	CA

consists of one field and three enable bits. The CD field determines the blanking code for the displays.

CD	**CD**	**Blanking code**
0	X	All zeros (X = don't care)
1	0	Hex 20 (ASCII space)
1	1	All ones

- The EN bit enables clearing of the display when true. During display clear, the display RAM may not be written into. This state is recorded in the status register, and remains true until the display is finished clearing.
- The CF bit, if true, clears the FIFO status, the interrupt line is reset, and the sensor RAM pointer is reset to 0.
- The CA bit, when set, has the combined effect to the EN and CF bits; in addition, it resynchronizes the internal timing chain.

The end interrupt/error mode set command lowers the interrupt request line and enables further writing into RAM. This command also sets the special error mode for the N-key rollover mode described earlier.

	MSB							LSB	
End interrupt/error mode set	1	1	1	E	X	X	X	X	X = don't care

When the E bit is set and the keyboard mode is set to N-key rollover, the special error mode is set.

Now that we have discussed all the commands, we will now look at the data formats of the various registers contained within the 8279. The FIFO status word contains information as to the state of the 8279. This word is diagrammed below:

	MSB							LSB
FIFO status word	D_U	S/E	O	U	F	N	N	N

The NNN field indicates the number of characters contained in the FIFO during keyboard or strobed input modes. This field has no meaning during the scanned sensor mode.

- The F bit indicates the FIFO is full and needs to be read before another character is entered. This bit has no meaning during the scanned sensor mode.
- The U bit indicates an underrun error has occurred. That is, the CPU has read an empty FIFO. This bit has no meaning during the scanned sensor mode.
- The 0 bit indicates a FIFO overrun has occurred. That is, a character was entered into a full FIFO. This bit has no meaning during the scanned sensor mode.
- The S/E bit has two functions, determined by the mode the 8279 is operating in. During the scanned sensor mode, this bit is set to show that at least one sensor closure indication is contained in the sensor RAM. In the N-key rollover mode, if the special error mode has been set, this bit indicates a simultaneous multiple closure error has occurred.
- The D_U bit indicates the display is unavailable because a clear display or clear all command has not completed.

The data format for the FIFO during keyboard mode is shown below:

	MSB							LSB
Keyboard data	C	S	SC	SC	SC	RL	RL	RL

This byte represents the position of the switch matrix, along with the control and shift lines.

- The RL and SC fields represent the position in the matrix of the depressed switch. The SC field is the scan line that was active when the key closure was detected, and the RL field is the return line that sampled the closed keyswitch.
- The S and C bits are the noninverted shift and control lines, respectively.
- In strobed input mode or scanned sensor mode, the FIFO contains the data present on the return lines when strobed in, with RL_0 being the least significant bit.

9.1.3 AN 8085-BASED MICROCOMPUTER USING THE 8279 FOR KEYBOARD/DISPLAY INTERFACE

In order to illustrate the application of the 8279, an example is given in the following to design an 8085-based microcomputer.

The 8085 microcomputer design uses two 8155 RAM and I/O, a 2716 EPROM, a 6116 RAM, 8279 keyboard controllers, a multiplexed 16-key keypad, six T1311 displays, and other support chips. The EPROM provides the system with 2048 bytes of ROM. 2560 bytes of RAM are available to the system through one 6116 and two 8155 chips. Memory-mapped I/O is used in this design. Two I/O ports are used by the system for displays, leaving four ports for the user. All interrupts are tied to ground.

The monitor routine consists of four control functions to change the address field, change the data field, enter data to a memory location specified by the address field, and send the microprocessor to an address specified by the address field. The address field is automatically incremented with each data entry and the new address and data are updated on the displays. User programs may call on monitor subroutines to display information or implement a delay. The four monitor functions are accessed by using a shift key along with the hex keypad. User programs can do a graceful halt by returning control to the monitor routine which then resumes polling of the keyboard controller.

A block diagram (Figure 9.14) illustrates the main components of the system. Figure 9.15 shows a detailed hardware schematic of the microcomputer.

9.1.3.a Statement of the Problem

The objective of this project is to build an experimenter's microcomputer that will illustrate the application of the 8279. A 74LS138 with its eight select lines provides for future expansion. (Currently only five lines are being used. Also with A14 of the 8085 unused, the addition of another LS138 selected by A14 could provide another eight select lines.) A memory-

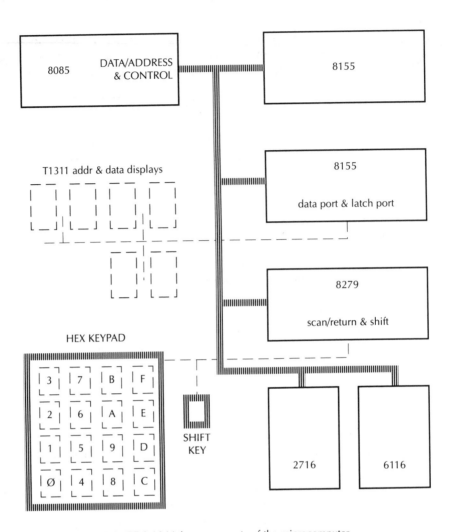

FIGURE 9.14 Main components of the microcomputer.

mapped I/O scheme is arbitrarily chosen. The 8279 keyboard controller was chosen because the shift and control/strobe lines triple the functions of a 16-key entry pad. T1311 displays are used because of on-chip decodes. Since these displays are not compatible with the output display ports of the 8279, they are driven by 8155 I/O ports.

9.1.3.b Hardware Description

9.1.3.b.i Power-On Reset

When power is applied to the 8085 it is reset by the power-on reset circuitry. A manual reset is included so that the program counter can be set

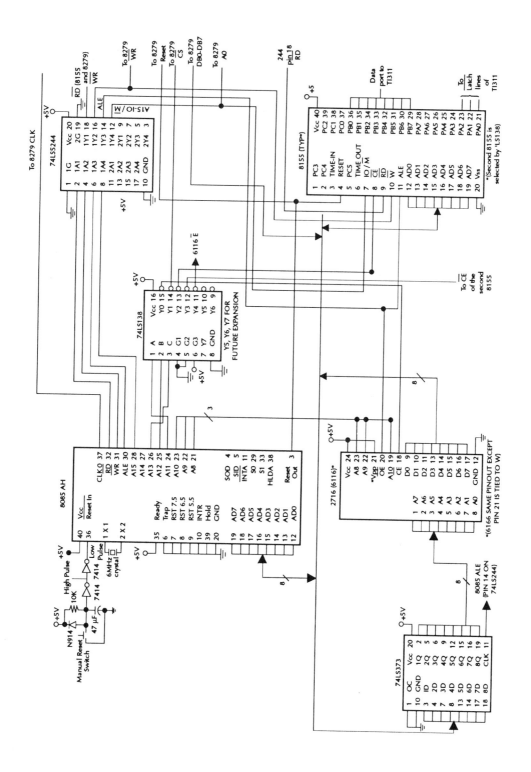

FIGURE 9.15 Detailed hardware schematic.

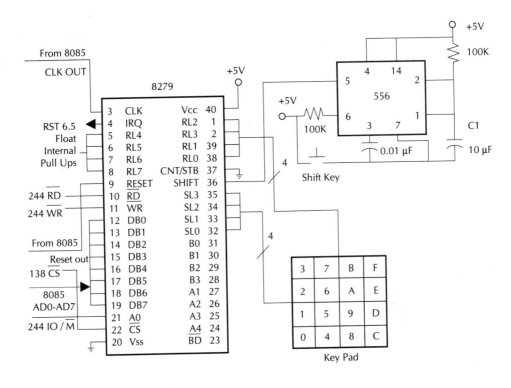

TIL311 ADDRESS AND DATA HEX DISPLAYS

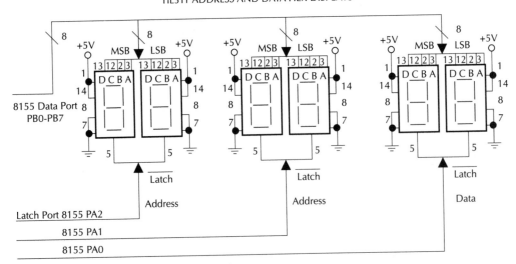

Latch
ADDR MSB 0011 F3H
ADDR LSB 0101 F5H
DATA   0110 F6H

FIGURE 9.15 continued.

to zero without turning power off. Schmitt-triggered inverters were included for increased reliability. Thus, the circuit functions so that in the case of a power transient, the diode discharges the capacitor quickly, assuring the generation of a reset pulse with the reappearance of power.

9.1.3.b.ii 8085AH Microprocessor

The 8085AH is an enhanced 8085A microprocessor implemented in N-channel, depletion load, silicon gate technology (HMOS). At 3 MHz, Icc (power supply current) is 135 mA, 20% lower than the 8085A. The instruction cycle is 1.3 μs.

A15, along with $\overline{RD}$, $\overline{WR}$, and ALE, is propagated through an LS244 line driver. A15 serves as $IO/\overline{M}$ for memory mapping and it is also tied to A0 of the 8279. Configuration commands to the 8279 and status information require a high A0; data transfer a low A0.

A11, A12, A13 are decoded through an LS138 to enable the various chips. The resulting memory addresses are contained in the table below.

9.1.3.b.iii Memory Map

2716	0000H – 07FFH	ROM MONITOR ROUTINE
8279	8800H, $\overline{RD}$	FIFO STATUS (LDA 8800H)
	8800H, $\overline{WR}$,	COMMAND (SIA 8800H);
	A = 2 × H	CMD = PROGRAM CLOCK
	A = 4 × H	CMD = READ FIFO ETC.
	0800H	DATA READ OR WRITE
8155 – 1	1000H – 10FFH	SYSTEM RAM, STACK, FLAGS, DATA
	9000H	CSR
	9001H	PORT A
	9002H	PORT B
	9003H	PORT C
	9004,5H	TIMER
8155 – 2	1800H – 18FFH	RAM
	9800H	CSR
	9801H	PORT A: DATA TO TI311 DISPLAYS
	9802H	PORT B: LATCH DISPLAYS ETC.
6116	2000H – 27FFH	MAIN USER RAM

9.1.3.b.iv Keyboard and Shift

The method to generate suitable keycodes is a mixture of hardware and software. When the 8279 is configured for a decoded scan, the four scan lines have active low outputs so that a low is placed on each line in turn at a rate determined by the programming of the 8279 clock. The return lines of the 8279 have internal pull-ups which remain high until a switch closure pulls them low. For a 16-key keypad, then, scan lines are putting a low on each row in rapid succession (5.1-ms scan cycle). Each column of the keypad is connected to a Return line. If a switch is closed this will pull a particular Return line low and this data will be recorded in the 8279 FIFO/SENSOR RAM. The status of this RAM is also recorded in an 8279 STATUS register which may be polled to determine if data are available.

Eight bits of data in the FIFO RAM are available in the scanned keyboard mode. The two most significant bits (MSBs) correspond to the status of the control and shift pins, respectively. These are high until pulled low. The next three bits correspond to the (scan) row of a key closure and the three least significant bits (LSBs) to the (return) column of the key closure. In this case, these bits will vary from 000 to 011. The monitor routine checks on the status of the shift pin and then determines which key was depressed. The 8279 automatically debounces the key depression with a 10-ms debounce (for a clock programmed to 100 kHz).

A shift key is implemented using a 556 timer chip to output a two-second pulse. Thus, simultaneous depression of the shift key with a keypad key is not required to obtain a shifted key response. The keypad key only needs to be depressed within the allotted two seconds of depressing the shift key.

9.1.3.b.v 8279 Keyboard Controller

On reset the monitor routine configures the 8279 as a decoded scan with a clock scale of 100 kHz. These parameters can be reconfigured experimentally by a user program and control can then be returned to the monitor routine to examine the results. Since the keyboard only uses four return lines, there are four more return lines that are available to the user. A user program can reconfigure the 8279 into Sensor Matrix mode and any logic that can be triggered by the scan lines can enter data to the return line inputs. Thus, the 8279 can function as another user port.

The 8279 can be polled or an interrupt output can signal the 8085 that data are available. The monitor routine polls the 8279. Depressing a key for more than 20 ms results in another entry into the FIFO 8 × 8 RAM. Since the RAM only has room for 8 entries an overrun error (entry of another character into a full FIFO) can easily occur. The monitor routine takes care of this by polling the FIFO and clearing it if there is an overrun. If a key is continuously depressed over a number of debounce cycles, data appear to scroll across the display, but at a much slower rate than every 10 ms. In fact, there has been an overrun, but it has been cleared by the monitor routine which will not poll for new data for display for a period of 1.5 sec. For the membrane-type keypad that this system uses, this delay should be extended even more to stop the inadvertent double keying of data.

A typical code sequence to program the 8279 involves two basic steps. First a command must be sent to inform the 8279 what type of data transfer is desired, such as read/write to a RAM and programming of the clock. The command code is stored in the accumulator and then an STA instruction is executed which will select the 8279 with A0 high. The actual data transfer then requires a second instruction which selects the 8279 with A0 low.

9.1.3.b.vi TIL311 Displays

The TIL311 displays with their latch, decoder, and drivers are not directly compatible with the outputs of the display ports of the 8279. The timing waveform of the 8279 (Figure 9.16) shows that the 80 μs before and 70 μs after the transition of a scan line signal, the outputs of the display ports are a blanking code consisting of all zeros or all ones or 20H. This, rather than the data in the display RAM, is what ends up as latched when using the scan lines to latch the TIL311 displays. A solution to this might be to tie the TIL311 latch pins low and use the 8279 $\overline{BD}$ signal, inverted, to blank the TIL311 displays for the 150 μs when a blanking code is being output from the 8279 display ports. For this system, data to the displays and a latch signal is sent via 8155 I/O ports.

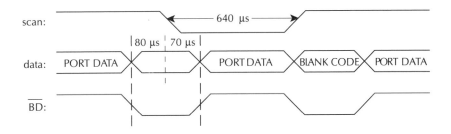

FIGURE 9.16 8279 timing diagram (blank display).

9.1.3.b.vii RAM, EPROM, and I/O

The decoding scheme for selecting and addressing RAM and I/O has already been described and a table for the locations of the ports provided. The 2716 and 6116 have their addresses latched by an LS373. Since these two chips are basically pin compatible (with pin 21 switched from high to W for the 6116), user programs can be stored in a 2716 and the 2716 used in place of the 6116.

9.1.3.c Software Description

When the system is first turned on the monitor routine loads address 2000H to the address display field. The data displayed in the data display field are unpredictable. The user may now start loading data. Data will be entered from the right and the LSB of the data display will become the MSB. Once the correct data are entered a shift-F will modify the data at the memory location indicated by the address display. The address display will be incremented and the data associated with that location will be displayed in the data field. A shift-C at any point allows the user to modify the address field. Once the correct address is displayed, a shift-D will allow modification of the data field. Or if the user desires to load the program counter with the address displayed, a shift-E accomplishes this function. The four functions may be summarized as:

Shift-C:	modify the address field
Shift-D:	load the program counter with the address field
Shift-E:	modify the data field
Shift-F:	enter data to memory; update address and data fields

9.1.3.c.i Monitor Routines: Summary

Figure 9.17 shows the flowcharts of the monitor routine. An 8085 assembly language program for the monitor is given in Figure 9.18.

1. **Start:** This routine initializes the stack pointer, configures the 8279 and 8155, sets the flag for data entry, and loads the address display field with 2000H. It then goes to the polling routine.
2. **Poll:** The 8279 FIFO status is polled. If the status indicates an error condition, the FIFO is reset. If the status indicates no data entered, then the monitor goes to the repolling routine. If data are available, then the FIFO is read.
3. **ResetFifo:** This routine resets the FIFO and then goes to the re-polling routine. After processing the keyboard input most routines return to this point. User programs can return control to the monitor

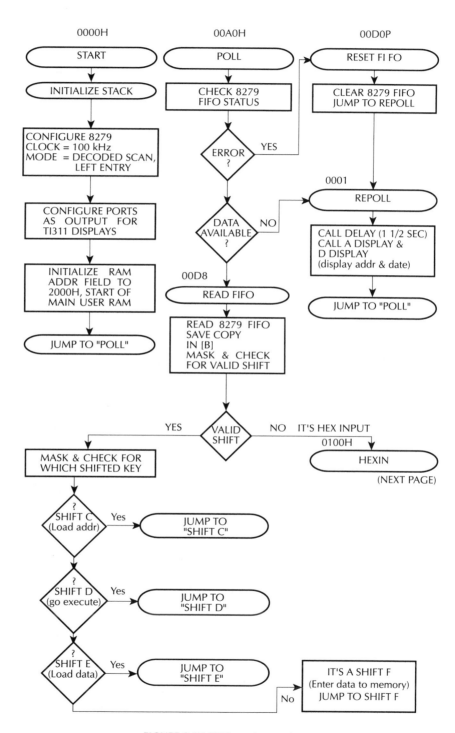

FIGURE 9.17 8085 monitor routines.

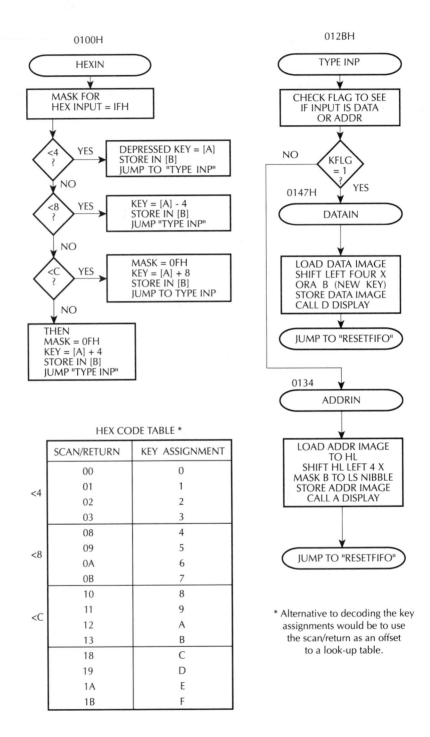

FIGURE 9.17 continued.

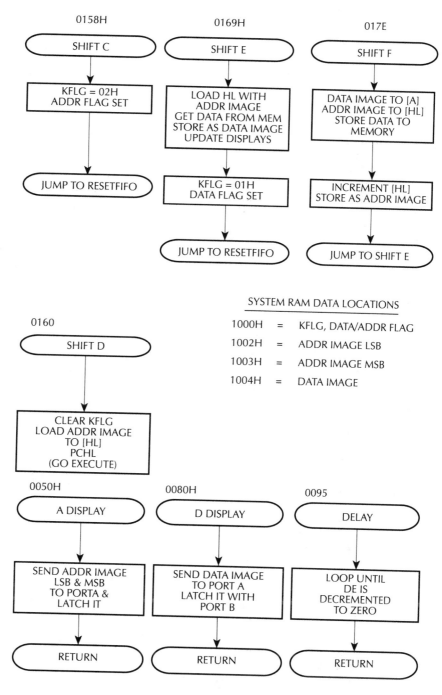

FIGURE 9.17 continued.

FILE: CLYDE:IRE   HEWLETT-PACKARD: 8085 Assembler

LOCATION OBJECT CODE LINE		SOURCE LINE		
	1	"8085"		
	2	ORG	0H	
<9801>	3 LATCH	EQU	9801H	;PORTA TO LATCH TI311
<9802>	4 PORTB	EQU	9802H	;DATA TO TI311
<1002>	5 ALSB	EQU	1002H	;ADDRESS IMAGE
<1003>	6 AMSB	EQU	1003H	;ADDRESS IMAGE
<1004>	7 DATA	EQU	1004H	;DATA IMAGE
<1000>	8 KFLG	EQU	1000H	;SHIFTKEY FLAG
0000 00	9	NOP		
0001 3110FF	10 START	LXI	SP,10FFH	
0004 3E3E	11	MVI	A,3EH	;CLOCK SCALE COMMAND
0006 328800	12	STA	8800H	;WRITE COMMAND TO 8279
0009 3E01	13	MVI	A,01H	;DECODED SCAN LEFT ENTRY
000B 328800	14	STA	8800H	;WRITE COMMAND
000E 3E03	15	MVI	A,03H	;CONFIGURE PORTS A AND B
0010 329800	16	STA	9800H	;03 TO CSR
0013 3E00	17	MVI	A,0H	;ZERO OUT FLAG
0015 321000	18	STA	KFLG	
0018 321002	19	STA	ALSB	;INITIALIZE ADDR IMAGE
001B 3E20	20	MVI	A,20H	;TO 2000H
001D 321003	21	STA	AMSB	
0020 C300A0	22	JMP	POLL	;TO POLL 8279
	23	ORG	50H	
0050 3A1002	24 ADISPLAY	LDA	ALSB	;GET ADDR OUT TO PORT
0053 329802	25	STA	PORTB	
0056 3EF5	26	MVI	A,0F5H	;LATCH LSB
0058 329801	27	STA	LATCH	
005B 3EFF	28	MVI	A,0FFH	;LATCH IT
005D 329801	29	STA	LATCH	
0060 3A1003	30	LDA	AMSB	
0063 329802	31	STA	PORTB	
0066 3EF2	32	MVI	A,0F3H	;LATCH MSB
0068 329801	33	STA	LATCH	

FIGURE 9.18 Monitor program.

```
LOCATION OBJECT
        CODE LINE                                    SOURCE LINE


006B  3EFF        34                    MVI A, 0FFH
006D  329801      35                    STA LATCH         ;LATCH IT
0070  C9          36                    RET
                  37                    ORG 80H
0080  3A1004      38  DDISPLAY          LDA DATA          ;DATA IMAGE
0083  329802      39                    STA PORTB
0086  3EF6        40                    MVI A, 0F6H
0088  329801      41                    STA LATCH         ;LATCH NEW DATA
008B  3EFF        42                    MVI A, 0FFH
008D  329801      43                    STA LATCH         ;LATCH IT
0090  C9          44                    RET
                  45                    ORG 95H
0095  1B          46  DELAY             DCX D
0096  7A          47                    MOV A, D
0097  B3          48                    ORA E
0098  C20095      49                    JNZ DELAY
009B  C9          50                    RET
                  51                    ORG 0A0H
00A0  3A8800      52  POLL              LDA 8800H         ;FIFO STATUS
00A3  47          53                    MOV B, A
00A4  17          54                    RAL
00A5  17          55                    RAL               ;SENSOR CLOSURE
                                                           ERROR
00A6  DA00D0      56                    JC RESETFIFO
00A9  17          57                    RAL               ;ERR OVERRUN BIT
00AA  DA00D0      58                    JC RESETFIFO
00AD  17          59                    RAL               ;ERR  UNDERRUN
                                                           BIT
00AE  DA00D0      60                    JC  RESETFIFO
00B1  17          61                    RAL               ;FULL FIFO
00B2  DA00D8      62                    JC READFIFO
00B5  17          63                    RAL               ;DATA AVAIL
00B6  DA00D8      64                    JC READFIFO
00B9  17          65                    RAL               ;DATA AVAIL
00BA  DA00D8      66                    JC READFIFO
00BD  17          67                    RAL               ;DATA AVAIL
00BE  DA00D8      68                    JC READFIFO       ;OTHERWISE EMPTY
00C1  110F00      69  REPOLL            LXI D, 0F00H      ;FOR DELAY
00C4  CD0095      70                    CALL DELAY
00C7  CD0050      71                    CALL ADISPLAY
00CA  CD0080      72                    CALL DDISPLAY
00CD  C300A0      73                    JMP  POLL
```

FIGURE 9.18 continued.

```
         LOCATION OBJECT
              CODE LINE                                SOURCE LINE

    00D0   3EC1      74  RESETFIFO  MVI A,0C1H      ;COMMAND  RESETS
                                                     FIFO
    00D2 328800      75             STA 8800H       ;WRITE COMMAND
    00D5 C300C1      76             JMP REPOLL
    00D8 3E40        77  READFIFO   MVI A,40H       ;COMMAND TO READ
                                                     FIFO
    00DA 328800      78             STA 8800H       ;WRITE COMMAND
    00DD 3A0800      79             LDA 0800H       ;READ FIFO
    00E0 47          80             MOV B,A         ;FIFO DATA IN B
    00E1 3E50        81             MVI A,50H       ;MASK TO CHECK
                                                     FOR VALID SHIFT
    00E3 4F          82             MDV C,A
    00E4 A0          83             ANA B           ;MASK THE FIFO
                                                     DATA
    00E5 B9          84             CMP C
    00E6 FA0100      85             JM HEXIN        ;VALID SHIFT NOT
                                                     FOUND
    00E9 3E0F        86             MVI A,0FH       ;NOW MASK FOR
                                                     WHICH SHIFTED
                                                     KEY
    00EB A0          87             ANA B
    00EC FE08        88             CPI 08H         ;08 MEANS A C
    00EE CA0158      89             JZ SHIFTC       ;SETS THE LOAD
                                                     ADDRESS FLAG
    00F1 FE09        90             CPI 09H         ;A SHIFT D
    00F3 CA0160      91             JZ SHIFTD       ;THE GO EXECUTE
                                                     KEY
    00F6 FE0A        92             CPI 0AH         ;A SHIFT  E
    00F8 CA0169      93             JZ SHIFTE       ;LOADING DATA
                                                     THENY
    00FB FE0B        94             CPI 0BH         ;A SHIFTF
    00FD  CA017E     95             JZ  SHIFTF      ;ENTER DATA  TO
                                                     MEMORY
    0100 3E1F        96  HEXIN      MVI A,1FH       ;MASK FOR HEX
                                                     INPUT
    0102 A0          97             ANA B
    0103 FE04        98             CPI 04H
    0105 D2010C      99             JNC FOUR        ;NOT LESS THAN
                                                     FOUR
    0108 47         100             MOV B,A         ;KEY IS THE
                                                     MASKED FIFO
    0109 C3012B     101             JMP TYPEINP     ;IS THIS DATA OR
                                                     ADDRESS
```

FIGURE 9.18 continued.

```
LOCATION OBJECT
         CODE LINE                                        SOURCE LINE

010C FE0C      102 FOUR       CPI 0CH              ;FOUR TO SEVEN?
010E D20117    103            JNC EIGHT            ;NO  LARGER
0111 D604      104            SUI 04               ;KEY IS MASK LESS
                                                    FOUR
0113 47        105            MOV B,A
0114 C3012B    106            JMP TYPEINP          ;IS THIS DATA OR
                                                    ADDRESS
0117 FE14      107 EIGHT      CPI 14H
0119 D20125    108            JNC HEXC             ;STILL LARGER
011C 3E0F      109            MVI A,0FH            ;MASK FOR LSB
011E A0        110            ANA B
011F C608      111            ADI 08H              ;THIS IS KEY
                                                    PRESSED
0121 47        112            MOV B,A
0122 C3012B    113            JMP TYPEINP          ;DATA OR ADDRESS
0125 3E0F      114 HEXC       MVI A,0FH            ;MASK FOR FIFO
                                                    LSB
0127 A0        115            ANA B
0128 C604      116            ADI 04H              ;THIS IS KEY
                                                    PRESSED
012A 47        117            MOV B,A
012B 211000    118 TYPEINP    LXI H,KFLG           ;GET DATA OR ADDR
                                                    FLAG
012E 7E        119            MOV A,M
012F FE01      120            CPI 01H              ;1 MEANS DATA
0131 CA0147    121            JZ DATAIN
0134 2A1002    122 ADDRIN     LHLD ALSB            ;GET MSBLSB DATA
0137 29        123            DAD H
0138 29        124            DAD H
0139 29        125            DAD H
013A 29        126            DAD H                ;SHIFT ADDR LEFT
                                                    FOUR
013B 78        127            MOV A,B              ;HEX KEY PRESSED
013C B5        128            ORA L                ;MASK IN LS
                                                    NIBBLE
013D 6F        129            MOV L,A
013E 221002    130            SHLD ALSB            ;STORE ADDR IMAGE
                                                    BACK
0141 CD0050    131            CALL ADISPLAY
0144 C300D0    132            JMP RESETFIFO
0147 3A1004    133 DATAIN     LDA DATA
014A 87        134            ADD A
014B 87        135            ADD A
```

FIGURE 9.18 continued.

```
        LOCATION OBJECT
              CODE LINE                               SOURCE LINE

        014C 87         136              ADD A
        014D 87         137              ADD A               ;SHIFT DATA LEFT
                                                               FOUR BITS
        014E B0         138              ORA B
        014F 321004     139              STA DATA            ;STORE DATA IMAGE
                                                               BACK
        0152 CD0080     140              CALL DDISPLAY
        0155 C300D0     141              JMP RESETFIFO
        0158 3E02       142 SHIFTC       MVI A,02H
        015A 321000     143              STA KFLG            ;ADDR FLAG SET
        015D C300D0     144              JMP RESETFIFO
        0160 3E00       145 SHIFTD       MVI A,0H
        0162 321000     146              STA KFLG            ;ZERO OUT FLAGS
        0165 2A1002     147              LHLD ALSB
        0168 E9         148              PCHL                ;GO EXECUTE
        0169 2A1002     149 SHIFTE       LHLD ALSB
        016C 7E         150              MOV A,M             ;GET REAL DATA
                                                               FROM MEMORY
        016D 321004     151              STA DATA            ;STORE IMAGE OF
                                                               DATA
        0170 CD0080     152              CALL DDISPLAY
        0173 CD0050     153              CALL ADISPLAY
        0176 3E01       154              MVI A,01H
        0178 321000     155              STA KFLG            ;SET DATA FLAG
        017B C300D0     156              JMP RESETFIFO
        017E 3A1004     157 SHIFTF       LDA DATA
        0181 2A1002     158              LHLD ALSB
        0184 77         159              MOV M,A             ;STORE DATA TO
                                                               MEM LOCATION
        0185 23         160              INX H
        0186 221002     161              SHLD ALSB           ;NEXT ADDRESS
        0189 C30169     162              JMP  SHIFTE
        Errors = 0
```

LINE#	SYMBOL	TYPE	REFERENCES
122	ADDRIN	A	
24	ADISPLAY	A	71,131,153
5	ALSB	A	19, 24, 122, 130, 147, 149, 158, 161
6	AMSB	A	21,30
7	DATA	A	38,133,139,151,157
133	DATAIN	A	121
38	DDISPLAY	A	72,140,152

FIGURE 9.18 continued.

LINE#	SYMBOL	TYPE	REFERENCES
46	DELAY	A	49,70
107	EIGHT	A	103
102	FOUR	A	99
114	HEXC	A	108
96	HEXIN	A	85
8	KFLG	A	18,118,143,146,155
3	LATCH	A	27,29,33,35,41,43
52	POLL	A	22,73
4	PORTB	A	25,31,39
77	READFIFO	A	62,64,66,68
69	REPOLL	A	76
74	RESETFIFO	A	56, 58, 60, 132, 141, 144, 156
142	SHIFTC	A	89
145	SHIFTD	A	91
149	SHIFTE	A	93,162
157	SHIFTF	A	95
10	START	A	
118	TYPEINP	A	101,106,113

FIGURE 9.18 continued.

by sending the PC to this point. Results of a user program can be stored in the address and data image locations and then the user program can jump to this point. The results will be displayed and the keyboard will be ready to accept new input.

4. **Repoll:** In this routine, a 1.5-second delay is implemented. After the delay the subroutines to display the address image and data image are called. From here, the monitor goes back to poll, that is, to check the status of the 8279.

5. **ReadFifo:** This routine analyzes the data in the FIFO, first determining whether a shift function is being invoked or if the input is hex key data. If no shift is found then a determination is made as to which key was pressed. Then based on the flag indicating whether the entry was to the data field or address field, a left shift is done and the field updated. From here the routine goes to ResetFifo. If, instead, a shift is detected, then ReadFifo determines which shifted key was depressed and then goes to the corresponding routine. Invalid shifted keys are treated as a normal hex key input. The functions of the shifted keys have already been described.

6. **ADisplay:** Calling this subroutine causes the data stored in locations 1002H and 1003H, the address image fields, to be displayed. DDis-

play similarly sends the contents of 1004H to the TI311 data displays.

7. **Delay:** This subroutine may be called to implement a delay proportional to the magnitude of the contents of the DE registers.

9.1.3.c.ii A Sample Program

The following program adds to 8-bit numbers in locations 2000 and 2001 and may be keyed in as follows:

```
1)  power-on;  2000 is displayed in addr field
2)  data;      any hex key pressed modifies data
                 field
3)  Shift-F;   2001 is displayed in addr field &
                 [2001] in data
4)  data;      next 8-bit number to add
5)  Shift-F;   this is entered and now 2002 in addr
                 field
6)             continue to enter in program.
```

```
    LDA  2000H
    MOV  B,A
    LDA  2001H
    ADD  B
    STA  1004H;   1004H is data image location
    CD   0080H;   Call DDisplay
    C3   00D0H;   Jmp to ResetFifo of monitor
                    routine
```

```
7)  Shift-F;   after entering last data with a
                 Shift-F load the starting address
                 of the program ie 2002H
8)  Shift-C;   keys pressed after this modify
                 address display
9)  2002;      enter starting address
10) Shift-D;   this executes the program
```

The results of the addition should be displayed in the data field. At this point the address field still shows 2002. Press Shift-C and load 2000. Now Shift-E. The first 8-bit data now are displayed in the data field. Pressing any key will modify it so that a new number may be added with the data in 2001. Loading 2002 to the address field and Shift-D will execute the program again. If the program was terminated with a Halt instruction instead of returning control to the monitor, the manual reset switch would have to be depressed to reinitiate polling of the keypad.

9.2 DMA CONTROLLERS

As mentioned before, direct memory access (DMA) is a type of data transfer between the microcomputer's main memory and an external device such as disk without involving the microprocessor. The DMA controller is an LSI (Large-Scale Integration) chip in a microcomputer system which supports DMA-type data transfer. The DMA controller can send commands to the memory in the same way as the microprocessor, and, therefore, the DMA controller can be considered as a second microprocessor in the system, except that its function is to perform I/O transfers. The DMA controllers perform data transfer at a very high rate. This is because several functions for accomplishing the transfer are implemented in hardware. The DMA controller is provided with a number of I/O ports. A typical microcomputer system with a DMA controller is shown in Figure 9.19.

The DMA controller in the figure connects one or more ports directly to memory so that data can be transferred between these ports and memory without going through the microprocessor. Therefore, the microprocessor is not involved in the data transfer.

The DMA controller in the figure has two channels (Channel 0 and 1). Each channel contains an address register, a control register, and a counter for block length. The purpose of the DMA controller is to move a string of data between the memory and an external device. In order to accomplish this, the microprocessor writes the starting address of memory where transfer is to take place in the address register, and controls information such as the direction of transfer in the control register and the length of data to be transferred in the counter.

The DMA controller then completes the transfer independent of the microprocessor. However, in order to carry out the transfer, the DMA controller must not start the transfer until the microprocessor relinquishes the system bus and the external device is ready.

The interface between an I/O port and each channel has typically a number of control signals which include DMAREQ, DMACK, and I/O read/write signals. When the I/O port is ready with an available buffer to receive data or has data ready to write into memory location, it activates the

DMAREQ line of the DMA controller. In order to accomplish the transfer, the DMA controller sends the DMACK to the port, telling the port that it can receive data from memory or send data to memory.

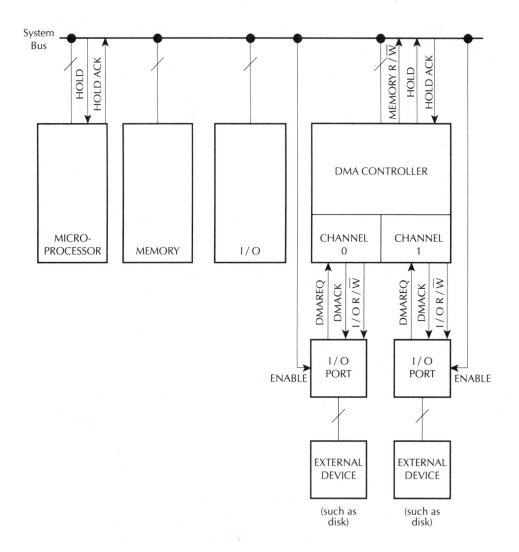

FIGURE 9.19 A microcomputer system with a DMA controller.

DMACK is similar to a chip select. This is because when the DMACK signal on the port is activated by the DMA controller, the port is selected to transfer data between the I/O device and memory. The main difference between a normal and DMA transfer is that the read or write operations have opposite meanings — that is, if the DMA controller activates the read line of the port, then data are read from a memory location to the port. However, this is a write operation to the port as far as the memory is concerned. This means that a read from a memory location is a write to the port. Similarly, a write to a memory location is equivalent to a read from the port. The figure shows two types of $R/\overline{W}$ signals. These are the usual memory $R/\overline{W}$ signal and the I/O $R/\overline{W}$ for external devices. The DMA controller activates both of these lines at the same time in opposite directions. That is, for reading data from memory and writing into a port, the DMA controller activates the memory $R/\overline{W}$ HIGH and I/O $R/\overline{W}$ LOW. The I/O ports are available with two modes of operation: non-DMA and DMA.

For non-DMA (microprocessor-controlled transfers), the ports operate in a normal mode. For DMA mode, the microprocessor first configures the port in the DMA mode and then signals the DMA controller to perform the transfer. The $R/\overline{W}$ line is complemented for providing proper direction of the data transfer during DMA transfer.

The DMA controller has a HOLD output signal and a HOLD ACK input signal. For each byte transfer, the microprocessor enables the I/O port for a DMA transfer. The port, when ready, generates the DMAREQ's signal for the DMA controller. The DMA controller then activates the HOLD input signal of microprocessor, requesting the microprocessor to relinquish the bus, and waits for a HOLD acknowledge back from the microprocessor.

After a few cycles, the microprocessor activates the HOLD acknowledge and tristates the output drivers to the system bus. The DMA controller then takes over the bus. The DMA controller:

1.   Outputs the starting address in the system bus
2.   Sends DMACK to the I/O port requesting DMA
3.   Outputs normal $R/\overline{W}$ to memory and complemented $R/\overline{W}$ to the I/O port

The I/O port and memory then complete the transfer. After the transfer, the DMA controller disables all the signals including the HOLD on the system bus and tristates all its bus drivers. The microprocessor then takes over the bus and continues with its normal operation.

For efficient operation, the DMA controller is usually provided with a burst mode in which it has control over the bus until the entire block of data is transferred.

In addition to the usual address, control, and counter registers, some

DMA controllers are also provided with data-chain registers which contain an address register, a control register, a counter, and a channel identification. These data-chain registers store the information for a specific channel for the next transfer. When the specified channel completes a DMA transfer, its registers are reloaded from the data-chain registers and the next transfer continues without any interruption from the microprocessor. In order to reload the data-chain registers for another transfer, the microprocessor can check the status register of the DMA controller to determine whether the DMA controller has already used the contents of the data-chain registers. In case it has, the microprocessor reinitializes the data-chain registers with appropriate information for the next block transfer and the process continues.

In order to illustrate the functions of a typical DMA controller just described, Motorola's MC68440 dual channel DMA controller will be considered in the following.

The MC68440 is designed for the MC68000 family microprocessors to move blocks of data between memory and peripheral using DMA.

The MC68440 includes two independent DMA channels with built-in priorities that are programmable. The MC68440 can perform two types of DMA: cycle stealing and burst. In addition, it can provide noncontinuous block transfer (continue mode) and block transfer restart operation (reload mode).

Figure 9.20 shows a typical block diagram of the MC68000/68440/68230 interface to a disk.

Data transfer between the disk and the memory takes place via port A of the MC68230, using handshaking signals H1-H4.

The A8/D0 through A23/D15 lines are multiplexed. The MC68440 multiplex control signals $\overline{\text{OWN}}$, $\overline{\text{UAS}}$ (upper address strobe), $\overline{\text{DBEN}}$ (data buffer enable), and $\overline{\text{DDIR}}$ (data direction) are used to control external demultiplexing devices such as 74LS245 bi-directional buffer and 74LS373 latch to separate address and data information on the A8/D0-A23/D15 lines. The MC68440 has 17 registers plus a general control register for each of the two channels and is selected by the lower address lines (A1-A7) in the MPU mode. A1-A7 also provides the lower 7 address outputs in the DMA mode.

A1-A7 lines can select 128 (2^7) registers; however, with A1-A7 lines, only seventeen registers with addresses are defined in the range from 00_{16} through FF_{16} and some addresses are not used. As an example, the addresses of the channel status register and the channel priority register are, respectively, 00_{16} and $2D_{16}$.

The MC68440 registers contain information about the data transfer such as:

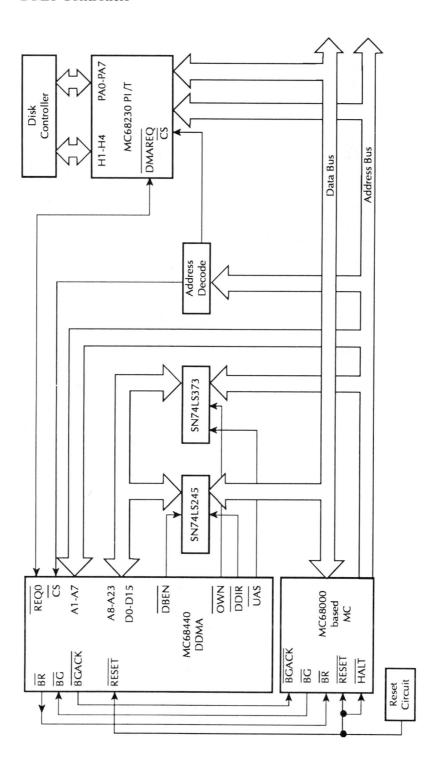

FIGURE 9.20 Typical system configuration.

1. Source and destination addresses along with function codes
2. Transfer count
3. Operand size and device port size
4. Channel priority
5. Status and error information on channel activity

The processor service request register (PSRR) of the MC68230 defines how the $\overline{\text{DMAREQ}}$ pin should be used and how the DMA transfer should take place, whether via handshaking or ports.

A data block contains a sequence of bytes or words starting at a particular address with the block length defined by the transfer count register. Figure 9.21 shows the data block format.

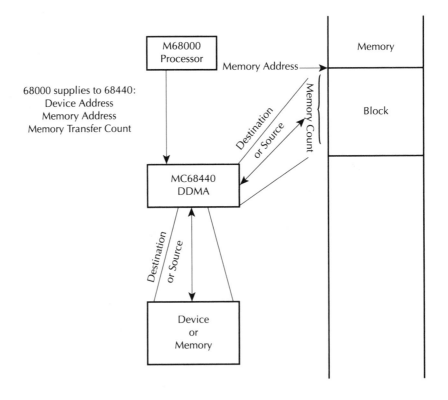

FIGURE 9.21 Data block format.

There are three phases of a DMA transfer. These are channel initialization, data transfer, and block termination. During channel initialization, the MC68000 loads the MC68440 registers with control information, address pointers, and transfer counts, and then starts the channel.

During the transfer phase, the MC68440 acknowledges data transfer requests and performs addressing and bus controls for the transfer. Finally, the block termination phase takes place when the transfer is complete. During this phase, the 68440 informs the 68000 of the completion of data transfer via a status register. During the three phases of a data transfer operation, the MC68440 will be in one of the three modes of operation. These are idle, MPU, and DMA. The MC68440 goes into the idle mode when it is reset by an external device and waits for initialization by the MC68000 or an operand transfer request from a peripheral.

The MPU mode is assumed by the MC68440 when its $\overline{CS}$ (chip select) is enabled by the MC68000. In this mode, the MC68440 internal registers can be read or written for controlling channel operation and for checking the status of a block transfer.

The MC68440 assumes the DMA mode when it takes over the bus to perform an operand transfer.

In Figure 9.20, upon reset, the MC68440 goes into idle mode. In order to initialize the MC68440 registers, the MC68000 outputs appropriate register addresses on the bus. This will enable the MC68440 $\overline{CS}$ line and places the MC68440 in the MPU mode. The MC68000 initializes the MC68440 registers in this mode. The MC68000 then executes the RESET instruction to place the MC68440 back to the idle mode.

The MC68000 now waits for a transfer request from the 68230. When the 68000 desires a DMA transfer between the disk and memory, it enables the $\overline{CS}$ line of the 68230. The 68230, when ready, activates the $\overline{DMAREQ}$ line low, which in turn drives the $\overline{REQ0}$ line of the MC68440 to low. The MC68440 then outputs low on its $\overline{BR}$ line requesting the MC68000 to relieve the bus. The MC68000, when ready, sends a low on its $\overline{BG}$ pin. This tells the MC68440 to take over the bus. The MC68440 then enters the DMA mode and sends low on its $\overline{BGACK}$ pin to inform the MC68000 of its taking over the bus. The MC68440 transfers data between the disk and memory (inside the MC68000-based microcomputer) via the MC68230. Each time a byte is transferred, the MC68440 decrements the transfer counter register and increments the address register. When the transfer is completed, the MC68440 updates a bit in the status register to indicate this. It also asserts the $\overline{DTC}$ (data transfer complete) to indicate completion of the transfer.

The MC68440 $\overline{DTC}$ pin can be connected to the MC68230 PIRQ pin. The MC68230 then outputs high on the MC68440 $\overline{REQ0}$ pin, which in turn places a HIGH on the MC68000 BR, and the MC68000 takes over the bus and goes back to normal operation.

9.3 PRINTER INTERFACE

Microprocessors are typically interfaced to two types of printers: serial and parallel.

Serial printers print one character at a time, while parallel printers print a number of characters on a single line so fast that they appear to be printed simultaneously. Depending on the character generation technique used, printers can be classified as impact or nonimpact. In impact printers, the print head strikes the printing medium, such as paper, directly, in order to print a character. In nonimpact printers, thermal or electrostatic methods are used to print a character.

Printers can also be classified based on the character formation technique used. For example, character printers use completely formed characters for character generation, while matrix printers use dots or lines to create characters.

The inexpensive serial dot matrix impact printer is very popular with microcomputers. An example of such a printer is the LRC7040 manufactured by LRC, Inc. of Riverton, Wyoming. The LRC7040 can print up to 40 columns of alphanumeric characters. The printer includes four major parts. These are the frame, the printhead, the main drive, and the paper handling components. The LRC7040 provides 8 inputs in the basic configuration. One input turns the main drive motor ON or OFF, while the other seven inputs control the print solenoids for the printhead, using TTL drivers.

The LRC7040 utilizes a 5 × 7 matrix of dots to generate characters. The columns are labeled T0 through T4 and rows are labeled S0 through S6. Each row corresponds to one of the solenoids. The entire printhead assembly is moved from left to write across the paper so that at some time the printhead is over the column T0, then it's over column T1, and so on.

A character is generated by energizing the proper solenoids at each one of the columns T0 through T4. Figure 9.22 shows how the character C is formed.

At T0, solenoids S0 through S6 are ON and at T1 through T4 solenoids S0 and S6 are active to form the character C. A number or character can be formed by the microcomputer by sending appropriate data to the printhead to generate the correct pattern of active solenoids for each of the five instants of time. The code for the character C consists of 5 bytes of data in the sequence $7F_{16}$, 41_{16}, 41_{16}, 41_{16}, 41_{16} as follows:

	S6	S5	S4	S3	S2	S1	S0	
Column T0	1	1	1	1	1	1	1	$= 7F_{16}$
Column T1	1	0	0	0	0	0	1	$= 41_{16}$
Column T2	1	0	0	0	0	0	1	$= 41_{16}$
Column T3	1	0	0	0	0	0	1	$= 41_{16}$
Column T4	1	0	0	0	0	0	1	$= 41_{16}$

Note that in the above, it is assumed that a 1 will turn a solenoid ON and a 0 will turn it OFF. Also it is assumed that S7 is zero.

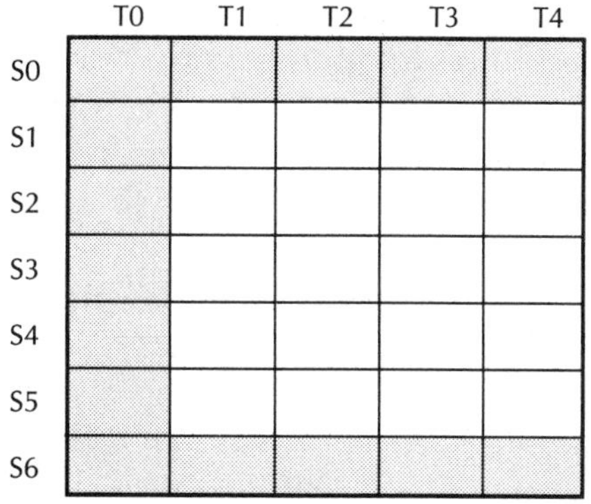

FIGURE 9.22 5 × 7 dot matrix pattern for generating the character C.

The interface signals to the printer include a pair of wires for each solenoid, a pair of wires for each motor (main drive motor and line feed motor), a pair of wires indicating the state of the HOME microswitch, and a pair of wires indicating the state of the LINEFEED microswitch.

Paper feed is accomplished by activating the line feed motor. The LINE FEED microswitch is activated by the print logic when the actual paper feed takes place. The control logic can use the trailing edge of the signal generated by the LINEFEED microswitch to turn the line feed motor OFF. The LRC7040 also has an automatic line feed version.

The HOME microswitch is activated HIGH when the printhead is at the left-hand edge of the paper. When the printhead is over the print area and moves from left to right, the HOME microswitch is deactivated to zero.

The solenoids must be driven from 40 ± 4 volts with a peak current of 3.6 A. An interface circuit is required at the microcomputer's output to provide this drive capability.

There are two ways of interfacing the printer to a microcomputer. These are

1.   Direct microcomputer control
2.   Indirect microcomputer control using a special chip called the Printer Controller

The direct microcomputer control interfaces the printer via its I/O ports and utilizes mostly software. The microcomputer performs all the functions required for printing the alphanumeric characters.

Indirect microcomputer control, on the other hand, utilizes a printer control chip such as the Intel 8295 Dot Matrix Printer Controller. The benefits of each technique depend on the specific application.

Direct microcomputer approach provides an inexpensive interface and can be appropriate when the microcomputer has a light load. The indirect microcomputer approach, on the other hand, may be useful when the microcomputer has a heavy load and cost constraint is not of concern.

9.3.1 LRC7040 PRINTER INTERFACE USING DIRECT MICROCOMPUTER CONTROL

The steps involved in starting a printing sequence by the microcomputer are provided below:

1.   The microcomputer must turn the Main Drive motor (MDM) ON by sending a HIGH output to the MDM.
2.   The microcomputer is required to detect a HIGH at the HOME microswitch. This will ensure that the printhead is at the left-hand margin of the print area.
3.   The microcomputer is then required to send five bytes of data for an alphanumeric character in sequence to energize the solenoids. Each solenoid requires a pulse of about 400 μs to generate a dot on the paper. A pause of about 900 μs is required between these pulses to provide a space between dots.

Figure 9.23 shows a block diagram interfacing the LRC7040 printer to an MC68000/6821/6116/2716-based microcomputer.

Using the hardware of Figure 9.23, an MC68000 assembly program can be written to send the start pulse for the main drive motor, detect the HOME microswitch, and then, by utilizing the timing requirements of 400 μs and 900 μs of the printer, a hexadecimal digit (0 to F) stored in a RAM location can be printed. An MC68000 assembly language program

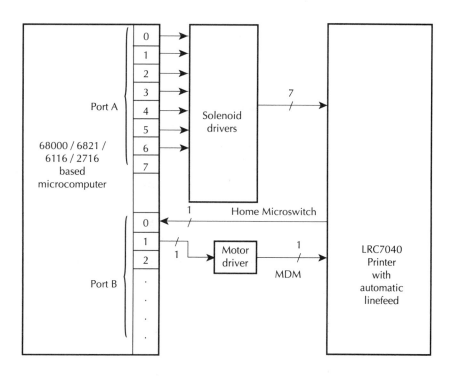

FIGURE 9.23 MC68000-based microcomputer interface to the printer.

for printing the character C is shown in Figure 9.24 assuming 68000 user mode so that USP can be initialized.

The program assumes a look-up table which stores the 5-byte code for the character C starting at $003000. Furthermore, the program assumes that the delay routines DELAY400 for 400 μs and DELAY900 for 900 μs are available. The program prints only one character C and then stops. The program is provided for illustrating the direct microcomputer control technique for printing.

9.3.2 LRC7040 PRINTER INTERFACE TO A MICROCOMPUTER USING THE 8295 PRINTER CONTROLLER CHIP

With direct microcomputer control, the microcomputer spends time in a "wait" loop for polling the status of the HOME signal from the LRC7040 printer. In order to unload the microcomputer of polling the printer status and other functions, typical LSI printer controller chips such as the Intel 8295 can be used.

The 8295 is a dot matrix printer controller. It provides an interface for

```
            ORG $500000              ;
            BCLR.B#$2, CRA           ;    Address DDRA
            MOVE.B # $7F, DDRA       ;    Configure bits 0-6
            BSET.B # $2, CRA         ;    As outputs and access Port A
            BCLR.B # $2, CRB         ;    Address DDRB
            MOVE.B # $02, DDRB       ;    Configure bit 0 and Bit 1
            BSET.B # $2, CRB         ;    of Port B as input and output
                                     ;    respectively and access Port B
            MOVEA.L # $040000, A1    ;    Initialize
            MOVE.L A1, USP           ;    USP
            MOVE.B # $02, PORT B     ;    Turn MDM on
HOME        MOVE.B PORT B, D1        ;    Input HOME switch
            ANDI.B # $01, D1         ;    Wait for HOME
            BEQ HOME                 ;    Switch to be on
            MOVEA.L # $3000, A2      ;    Move starting address
                                     ;       of character
            MOVE.B $05, D3           ;    Initialize
                                     ;    Character
                                     ;    Counter
CHARACTER   MOVE.B # $00, PORT A     ;    Generate
            MOVE. B (A2)+, PORT A    ;    Solenoid pulses
            CALL DELAY400            ;    Generate 400µs
            MOVE.B # $00, PORT A     ;    Pulses
            CALL DELAY900            ;    Delay 900µs
            SUBQ.B # $01, D3         ;    Subtract character counter
            BNE CHARACTER            ;    Loop to output all five bytes
            MOVE.B # $00, PORT B     ;    Turn MDM OFF
STOP        JMP STOP                 ;    Halt
            ORG $003000              ;
            DB $7F, $41, $41, $41, $41  ; 5-byte
            END                      ;    Code for C
```

FIGURE 9.24 Assembly language program for printing the character C.

microprocessors such as the 8085 and 8086 to dot matrix impact printers such as the LRC7040. The 8295 is packaged in a 40-pin DIP and can operate in a serial or parallel communication mode with the 8085 or 8086. In parallel mode, command and data transfers to the printer by the processor occur via polling, interrupts, or DMA using commands. The processor specifies the formats of the printing character and controls all printer functions such as linefeed and carriage return for the printer.

The 8295 includes a 40-character buffer. When the buffer is full or a carriage return is received, a line is printed automatically. The 8295 has the buffering capability of up to 40 characters and contains a 7×7 matrix character generator, which includes 64 ASCII characters. The mode selection (serial or parallel) is not software programmable and is inherent in system hardware. For example, by connecting the 8295 IRQ/$\overline{\text{SER}}$ pin to ground, the serial mode is enabled; otherwise the parallel mode is enabled. The two modes cannot be mixed in a single application. Note that IRQ/$\overline{\text{SER}}$ pin is also on 8295 interrupt request to the processor in the parallel mode.

9.3.2.a 8295 Parallel Interface

Two 8295 registers (one for input and the other for output) can be accessed by the processor in the parallel mode. The registers are selected as follows:

$\overline{\text{RD}}$	$\overline{\text{WR}}$	$\overline{\text{CS}}$	Register selected
1	0	0	Input data register
0	1	0	Output status register

Two types of data can be written in the input data register by the processor:

1. A command to be executed. The command can be 0XH or 1XH. For example, the command 08H will enable DMA mode. On the other hand, the command 11_{16} will enable normal left-to-right printing for printers whose printhead home is on the right.
2. A character data (defined in the 8295 data sheet) such as 37H for '7' or 41H for 'A' to be stored in the character buffer for printing.

The 8295 status is available in the output status register at all times. Typical status bits indicate whether the input buffer is full or DMA is enabled. For example, the IBF (Input buffer full; bit 1 of the status register) is set to one whenever data are written to the input data register. When IBF = 1, no data should be written to the 8295. The DE bit (DMA Enabled; bit 4 of the status register) is set to one whenever the 8295 is in DMA mode. Upon completion of the DMA transfer, the DE is cleared to zero.

The 8295 IRQ/SER pin is used for interrupt driven systems. This output is activated HIGH when the 8295 is ready to receive data. Using polling in parallel mode, the 8295 IRQ/SER pin can be input via the processor I/O port and data can be sent to the 8295 input data register.

Using interrupt in parallel mode, the 8295 IRQ/SER pin can be connected to the processor's interrupt pin to provide an interrupt-driven system.

Using polled or interrupt technique in parallel mode, the processor typically communicates with the 8295 by performing the following sequence of operations in the main program (polled) or service routine (interrupt):

- The processor reads the 8295 status register and checks the IBF flag for HIGH.
- If IBF = 1, the processor waits in a wait loop until IBF = 0. The processor writes data to be printed to the 8295 input data register. IBF flag is then set to one indicating no data should be written.

Data can also be transferred from the main memory to the 8295 via the DMA method using a DMA controller such as 8257.

The processor initializes the 8257 by sending a starting address and a block length. The processor also enables the 8295 DMA channel by sending it the "ENABLE DMA" command (08H) followed by two bytes specifying the block length to be transferred (low byte first). The 8295 will then activate the DMA request line of the 8257 without any further involvement by the main processor. The DMA enable (DE) flag in the status register will be HIGH until the data transfer is completed. As soon as the data transfer is completed, the DE flag is cleared to zero and IRQ/SER is set to HIGH. The 8295 then goes back to the non-DMA mode of operation.

Figure 9.25 shows a block diagram of the 8295 DMA transfer.

Typical control signals between the 8257 and the processor include HOLD, HLDA, RD, and WR. The 8295 control signals for the processor include CS, RD, WR, RESET, and IRQ/SER. CS, RD, and WR pins are used to select either 8295 input or output register. The 8295 control signals for the printer include MOT, PFM, STB, PFEED, and HOME.

The 8295 MOT output pin, when LOW, drives the motor. The MOT output is automatically in LOW on power-up. This will make the 8295 HOME input pin HIGH, indicating that the printhead of the printer is in HOME position.

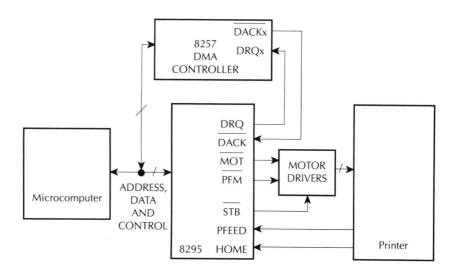

FIGURE 9.25 8295 DMA transfer.

The PFM signal, when LOW, drives the paper feed motor, and this is LOW on power-up. The PFEED is an 8295 input and indicates status of paper feed. A LOW on the PFM indicates that the paper feed mechanism is 'disabled' and a one indicates that the S1 through S7 signals, when LOW, drive the seven solenoids of the printer. Each character datum, when written into the 8295 input data register, is automatically converted to the five-byte code by the 8295 and provides the proper ON/OFF sequence for the solenoids. The STB output is used to determine duration of solenoid activation and is automatically provided by the 8295.

9.3.2.b 8295 Serial Mode

The 8295 serial mode is enabled by connecting the IRQ/SER pin to LOW. The serial mode is enabled immediately upon power-up. The serial baud rate is programmed by the D2, D1, D0 data lines. For example, D2 D1 D0 = 001 means 150 baudrate (bits/sec) and is used to set the serial transfer data rate. In this mode, RD must be tied to high and CS and WR must be tied to ground. The processor needs a UART (Universal asynchronous receiver transmitter) such as the 8251. The 8295 DACK/SIN signal (data input for serial mode) must be connected to the 8251 TXD output (8151 transmit data output bit). Also, the 8295 DRQ/CTS (clear to send in serial mode) must be connected to the 8251 CTS output. Note that a UART chip converts parallel to serial data and vice versa. The processor must wait for 8295 CTS to go LOW before sending data via TXD.

9.4 CRT (CATHODE RAY TUBE) CONTROLLER AND GRAPHICS CONTROLLER CHIPS

The CRT terminal is extensively used in microcomputer systems as an efficient man-machine interface. The users communicate with the microcomputer system via the CRT terminal. It basically consists of a typewriter keyboard and a CRT display. In order to relieve the microprocessor from performing the tedious tasks of CRT control, manufacturers have designed an LSI chip called the CRT Controller. This chip simplifies and minimizes the cost of interfacing the CRT terminal to a microcomputer.

The CRT controller supports all the functions required for interfacing a CRT terminal to a microprocessor. The microprocessor and the CRT controller usually communicate via a shared RAM. The microprocessor writes the characters to be displayed in this RAM; the CRT controller reads this memory using DMA and then generates the characters on the video display. The CRT controller provides functions such as clocking and timing, cursor placement, and scrolling. The CRT controller chip includes several registers that can be programmed to generate timing signals and video interface signals required by a terminal. The display functions are driven by clock pulses generated from a master clock. The CRT controller chip normally produces a special symbol such as a blinking signal or an underline on the CRT. This signal is commonly called the 'cursor'. It can be moved on the screen to a specific location where data need to be modified. The scrolling function implemented in the CRT controller moves currently displayed data to the top of the screen as new data are entered at the bottom.

In this section, fundamentals of CRT, character generation techniques, and graphics controllers will be discussed.

A typical CRT controller such as the Intel 8275 will then be considered to illustrate its basic functions. Finally, the graphics functions provided by Intel 82786 will be covered.

9.4.1 CRT FUNDAMENTALS

A CRT consists of an evacuated glass tube, a screen with an inner fluorescent coating, and an electron gun for producing electron beams. When the electrons generated by the gun are focused on the fluorescent inner coating of the screen, an illuminated phosphor dot is produced.

The position of the dot can be controlled by deflecting the electron beam by using an electromagnetic deflection technique. A complete display is produced by moving the beam horizontally and vertically across the entire surface of the screen and at the same time by changing its intensity.

Most modern CRT terminals generate the display by using horizontal and vertical scans. In the horizontal scan, the beam moves from the upper left-hand corner to the extreme right-hand of the line and thus travels across the screen. The beam then goes off and starts at the next lower left line for another scan. After several horizontal scans, the beam reaches the bottom of the screen to complete one vertical scan. The beam then disappears from the screen and begins another vertical scan from the top. This type of scan is also called 'raster' scan. This is because the display is produced on the screen by continuously scanning the beam across the screen for obtaining a regular pattern of closely spaced horizontal lines, or raster covering the entire screen. One of the most common examples of a raster display is the home TV set. The typical bandwidth used in these TV sets is 4.5 MHz. The raster displays used with microcomputers include a wider bandwidth from 10 MHz to 20 MHz for displaying detailed information. In most modern CRT terminals, each sweep field contains the entire picture or text to be displayed.

In order to display characters, the screen is divided by horizontal and vertical lines into a dot matrix. A matrix of 5×7 or 7×9 dots is popular for representing a character. For example, a 5×7 dot matrix can be used to represent the number '0' as shown in Figure 9.26.

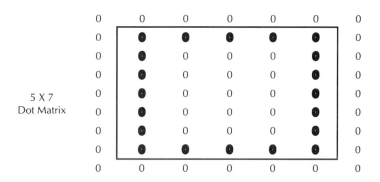

FIGURE 9.26 Generation of '0' using 5×7 dot matrix.

To provide space around the character, one top, one left, one right, and one bottom line are left blank. Each character is generated using 5×7 dot matrix. Therefore, each character requires 35 dots, which can be turned

ON or OFF depending on the dot pattern required by the character. The pattern of dots is usually stored in ROM. A ROM pattern for '0' is shown in Figure 9.27.

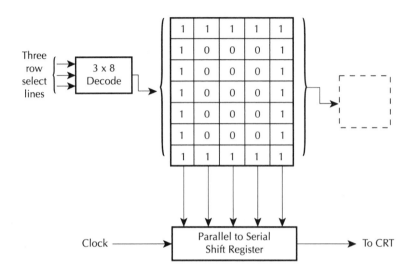

FIGURE 9.27 ROM pattern for '0'.

One character requires a 35-bit word. Each row is addressed by three bits. After reading each row data, it is transferred to a parallel to serial shift register. These data are then shifted serially by a clock to the CRT. For a standard 64-character set with each character represented by a 5×7 dot matrix, a total of 2240-bit ($64 \times 7 \times 5$) ROM is required. Each character in the 64 (2^6)-character set can be addressed using 6 address lines and three row select or seam lines (row select counter typically used) are required to identify the dot row of the character. The ROM addressing logic and parallel to serial shift register are referred to as a character generator. Also, a memory known as screen memory is required in the CRT to store the character data to be displayed. When a character is entered via the CRT keyboard, it is stored in the screen memory. The character generator compares data with the screen memory and then sends the 35-bit pattern for the matched character to the CRT.

The character generator technique described above, when combined with VLSI technology, results into graphics generation.

Graphics capability can display any figure on the CRT screen. An example of such a VLSI chip is the Intel 82786. In this chip, linked lists are used to update the display and can thus generate displays at a high speed.

Most modern graphics use the bit mapping technique rather than character generation. In order to understand bit mapping, consider a CRT screen as divided into 512 by 128 dots. Each dot is called a Pixel, or picture element, which can be illuminated by an electron beam. Each dot is a single bit in a 64K ($512 \times 128 = 65,536$) by 1 RAM and is called a bit plane. If a '1' is stored in a specific bit location, the associated Pixel is turned ON (black). On the other hand, if a '0' is stored, the corresponding Pixel is turned OFF (white). The video refresh circuitry implemented in the VLSI chip converts the ones and zeros in the bit plane to whites and blacks on the CRT screen.

Resolution is an important factor to be considered in graphics. In order to provide various colors and intensity, more than one bit is utilized in representing a Pixel. For example, Apple's 68000-based LISA microcomputer uses four bits per Pixel on a 364×720 Pixel screen. Therefore, a high speed RAM of over 1 megabit ($364 \times 720 \times 4 = 1,048,320$) is required to support such a resolution.

Therefore, graphics generation requires the bit-mapped RAM array and the LSI video interface chip. The software involves determining the information written to the bit plane array to generate the desired graphic display. Most graphics systems generate figures by combinations of straight-line segments. The software is required to generate a straight line by identifying each Pixel and write information to its corresponding bit-map position.

The concepts associated with CRT controllers and graphics described above will be illustrated by using the Intel 8275 and Intel 82786 in the following.

9.4.2 INTEL 8275 CRT CONTROLLER

The INTEL 8275 is a single chip (40-pin) CRT controller. It provides the functions required to interface CRT raster scan displays with Intel microcomputer systems using 8051, 8085, 8086, and 8088. It refreshes the display by storing (buffering) the information to be displayed from memory and controls the display position on the screen. The 8275 provides raster timing, display row buffering, visual attribute decoding, cursor timing, and light pen detection. The 8275 can be interfaced with the Intel

8257 DMA controller and character generator ROM for dot matrix decoding.

Figure 9.28 shows the 8275's interface to a microcomputer system and the 8257.

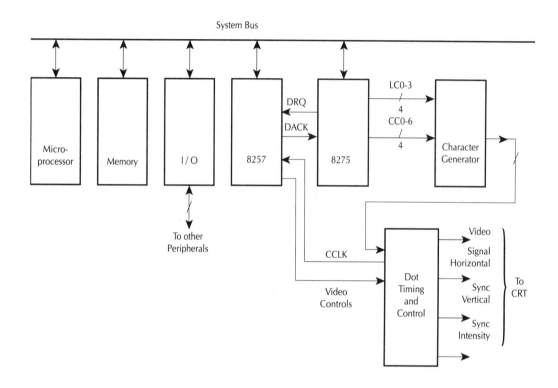

FIGURE 9.28 Microcomputer/8275/8257 interface.

The 8275 obtains display characters from memory and displays them on a row-by-row basis. There are two row buffers in the 8275. It uses one row for display, and at the same time fills the other row with the next row of characters to be displayed. The number of display characters per row and the number of character rows are software programmable.

The 8275 utilizes the 8257 DMA controller to fill the row buffer that is not being used for display. It displays character rows one line at a time.

The 8275 controller provides visual attribute codes such as graphics symbols, without the use of the character generator, and blinking, highlighting, and underlining of characters. The raster timing is controlled by the 8275. This is done by generating the horizontal retrace and vertical retrace signals on the HRTC and the VRTC pins.

The 8275 provides the light pen input and associated registers. The light pen input is used to read the registers. A command can be used to read the light pen registers. The light pen consists of a microswitch and a tiny light sensor. When the light pen is pressed against the CRT screen, the microswitch enables the light sensor. When the raster sweep reaches the light sensor, it enables the light pen output. If the output of the light pen is presented to the 8275 LPEN pin, the row and character position coordinates are stored in a pair of registers. These registers can be read by a command. A bit in the status register in the 8275 is set, indicating detection of the light pen signal. The 8275 can generate a cursor. The cursor location is determined by a cursor row register and a character position register which are added by a command to the controller.

The cursor can be programmed to appear on the display in many forms such as a blinking underline and a nonblinking underline. The 8275 does not provide scrolling function.

The 8275 outputs the line count (LC0-LC3) and character code (CC0-CC6) signals for the character generation. The LC0-LC3 signals are contents of the 8275 line counter which are used to address the character generator for the line positions on the screen. The CC0-CC6 outputs of the 8275 are the contents of the row buffers used for character selection in the character generator.

The 8275 video control signals typically include line attribute codes, highlight, and video suppression. The two line attribute codes (LA0 and LA1 pin outputs) must be decoded by the dot timing logic to produce the horizontal and vertical line combinations for the graphic displays defined by the character attribute codes. The video suppress (VSP pins) output signal is used to blank the video signal to the CRT. The highlighted (HLGT) output signal is used to intensify the display at a specific position on the screen, as defined by the attribute codes.

The dot timing and interface logic must provide the character clock (CCLK pin) input of the 8275 for proper timing.

9.4.3 INTEL 82786 GRAPHICS CONTROLLER

The Intel 82786 is a single VLSI chip providing bitmapped graphics. It is designed for microcomputer graphics applications, including personal computers, engineering workstations, terminals, and laser printers. The 82786 is designed using Intel's CHMOS III process. It is capable of both drawing and refreshing raster displays. It supports high resolution displays with a 25-MHz Pixel clock and can display up to 256 colors simultaneously. It can be interfaced to all Intel microcomputers such as 80186, 80286, and 80386. Figure 9.29 shows a block diagram of the 80186/ 80286/80386 interfaces to the 82786.

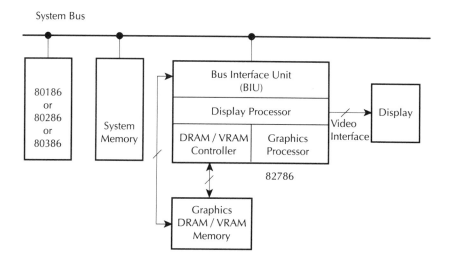

FIGURE 9.29 80186/80286/80386 interface to 82786.

The 82786 includes three basic components. These are a display processor (DP), a graphics processor (GP), and a bus interface unit (BIU), with DRAM/VRAM controller.

The display processor controls the CRT timing and provides the serial video data stream for the display. It can assemble several windows (portions of bitmaps) on the screen from different bitmaps scattered across the memory accessible to it.

The graphics processor executes commands from a graphics command block placed in memory by the 80186/80286/80386 and updates the bitmap memory for the display processor. The graphics processor has high level video display interface-like commands and can draw graphical objects and text at high speeds.

The BIU controls all communication between the 82786, 80186/ 80286/80386, and memory. The BIU contains a DRAM/VRAM controller that can perform block transfers. The display processor and graphics processor use the BIU to access the bitmaps in memory.

The system bus connects the 80186/80286/80386 and system memory to the 82786. The video interface connects the 82786 to CRT or other display. The video interface is controlled directly by the display processor. The 82786 can be programmed to generate all the CRT signals for up to 8 bits/Pixel (256 colors) displays. The other interfaces are controlled by the BIU. The BIU interfaces the graphics and display processors to the 80186/80286/80386 and system memory as well as the graphics memory via the internal DRAM/VRAM controller.

The dedicated graphics DRAM/VRAM memory provides the 82786 with fast access to memory without contention with the microprocessor and system memory.

Usually, the bitmaps to be drawn and displayed, the characters, and commands for the 82786 are all stored in this memory. The 82786 DRAM/VRAM controller interfaces directly with a number of dynamic RAMS without external logic.

Figure 9.29 shows the most common configuration. The microprocessor can access the system memory, while the 82786 accesses its dedicated graphics memory simultaneously. However, when the microprocessor accesses the graphics memory, the 82786 cannot access the system memory. Also, when the 82786 accesses the system memory, the microprocessor cannot access the graphics memory.

If DMA capability is provided, the 82786 can operate in either slave or master mode. In the slave mode, the microprocessor or DMA controller can access the 82786 internal registers or dedicated graphics memory through the 82786. In the master mode, the 82786 can access the system memory.

The microprocessor software can access both system and graphics memory in the same way. When the microprocessor accesses the 82786, the 82786 runs in slave mode.

In slave mode, the 82786 appears like an intelligent DRAM/VRAM controller to the microprocessor. The microprocessor can chip-select the 82786 and the 82786 will acknowledge when the cycle is completed by asserting a READY signal for the microprocessor.

The 82786 graphics and display processor accesses both system memory and graphics memory in the same way. When the 82786 accesses system memory, the 82786 must run in master mode.

In the master mode, the 82786 acts as a second microprocessor controlling the local bus. The 82786 activates HOLD line to take control of the system bus. When the microprocessor asserts HLDA line, the 82786 takes over the bus. When the 82786 is finished with the bus, it will disable the HOLD line and the microprocessor can remove HLDA to take over the bus.

The 82786 provides two different video interfaces when using standard

DRAMS. The 82786 reads the video data from memory and internally serializes the video data to generate the serial video data stream. When using VRAMS, the 82786 loads the VRAM shift register. Periodically, the shift register and external logic then generate the serial video data stream.

9.5 FLOPPY DISK INTERFACE

Most microcomputer systems use inexpensive removable magnetic media for storing information. There are two types of removable storage devices. These are magnetic tape and floppy disk. The floppy disk is faster than the magnetic tape, since it provides direct access to stored information, rather than serial access.

Information access on a floppy disk requires less than a second, while tape movement often requires several minutes. Because of faster speed, the floppy disk is used as an on-line mass storage device, while the magnetic tape is used as back-up storage, due to its large capacity.

Since floppy disk is very popular as an on-line secondary storage device with microcomputer systems, the structures of floppy disk and floppy disk drive will be covered in the following. Also, typical features associated with floppy disk controllers relating them to the Intel 82072 floppy disk controller will be included.

9.5.1 THE FLOPPY DISK
The floppy disk is a circular piece of thin plastic material provided with a magnetic coating and contained in a protective jacket. The floppy disk rotates at a fixed speed of approximately 360 rpm (revolutions per minute) within its jacket. Two standard sizes of the floppy disk are currently available. These are the 8 inches square and 5-1/4 inches square floppy disks. Information can either be stored on one side (single-density) or on both sides (double-density).

Information is stored on the floppy disk in concentric circles called tracks. The outermost track is defined with the lowest track number 0 and the innermost track has the highest track number.

A read/write head is moved radially across the disk by a stepper motor in increments of the distance between two tracks each time the stepper motor is stepped. In order to access a specific track (seek operation), the head is moved to track 0 and then moved to the desired track by pulsing the stepper motor an appropriate number of times. When the head is over the desired track, it is brought in contact with the floppy disk. Data are then read from or written to the disk. The head is then released from the disk in order to minimize wear on both the disk and the head. The physical beginning of a track is located by means of a small hole (physical index mark) punched through the plastic near the center of the disk. This hole is optically sensed by the disk drive on every revolution of the disk.

Each track is directed into a number of sectors. Sectors are generally 128, 256, 512, or 1024 data bytes in length. Track sectoring can be achieved in two ways: hard sectoring and soft sectoring. Hard sectoring divides each track into a maximum of 32 sectors. The start of each sector is indicated by a sector hole punched in the disk plastic. Soft sectoring, the standard for IBM, uses software to select sector sizes. In this method, each data sector is preceded by a unique sector identifier which is read or written by the disk controller.

The floppy disk often contains a write-protect notch punched at the edge of the outer jacket. This notch is sensed by the disk drive and sent to the disk controller as a write protect signal.

9.5.2 THE FLOPPY DISK DRIVE

The floppy disk drive is an electromechanical assembly that reads data from or writes data into the floppy disk. The disk drive includes all the electronics for controlling the head movement in increments toward the center of the disk (forward) or toward the edge of the disk (backward). The disk drive also connects the head to the floppy for data access and disconnects the head from floppy after data access. The drive provides certain information regarding the status of the drive and the floppy. These include status information such as drive ready (indicates that the drive door is closed and the floppy disk is inserted), track zero (indicates that the head is over track zero), and write protect (indicates that the floppy in the drive is write-protected).

9.5.3 THE FLOPPY DISK CONTROLLER

The floppy disk controller normally converts high level disk commands issued by software executed by the main microprocessor into disk drive commands. In order to accomplish this, the floppy controller performs functions such as disk drive selection, track selection, sector selection, head loading, error-checking, and data separation. The disk controller allows the main microprocessor to define a specific drive (in a system with multiple drives) to be used in a particular operation.

The disk controller positions the head from its present location to the desired track from which data are to be read from or written into.

The disk controller senses the requested sector. It also connects the head to the disk surface in order to read or write data.

Information recorded on a floppy disk is subject to both hardware and software errors. Hardware errors are due to media defects. These errors are permanent. Software errors, on the other hand, are temporary and are caused by electromagnetic noise or mechanical interference. Floppy disk controllers use a standard error checking technique known as cyclic redundancy check (CRC). As data are written to a disk, a 16-bit CRC character is computed and stored on the disk. When this datum is read, the CRC character permits the controller to detect errors. When CRC errors are detected, the controlling software retries the failed operation several times. If data cannot be reliably read or written, the system software reports the error to the operator.

The actual signal recorded on floppy disk is a combination of timing information (clock) and data. The serial read data input from the disk drive is converted by the controller into two signal streams: clock and data. The controller also assembles the serial data into 8-bit bytes before transferring them to the microcomputer main memory. Note that not all floppy disk controllers such as Intel 8272 provide the data separation feature.

New floppy disks must be written with a fixed format by the floppy controller before these disks may be used to store data. Formatting is a technique of taking raw media and adding the necessary information to allow the controller to read and write data without error. All formatting is performed by the disk controller on a track-by-track basis under the direction of the main microprocessor.

The floppy disk controller functions described above are implemented these days in a single VLSI chip such as Intel 82072. The functions provided by the 82072 will be covered in the following.

9.5.4 INTEL 82072 FLOPPY DISK CONTROLLER

The 82072 interfaces a microcomputer system based on Intel microprocessors such as 80386, 80286, and 80186 to disk drive compatible with IBM single- and double-density formats. The 82072 is designed using Intel's CHMOS III technology and is housed in a plastic 40-pin DIP or a plastic 44-leaded chip carrier package.

The 82072 includes a 16-byte FIFO to reduce the timing constraints. The point at which the 82072 generates a request for a data transfer is selectable within the 16-byte range of the FIFO.

There are three ports accessible from the microprocessor's point of view: the FIFO, the Main Status Register, and the Data Rate Select Register. Communication between the microprocessor and the 82072 is done by reading the main status register to determine if the 82072 is ready. If it is ready, a command followed by the correct parameters is sent to the 82072 through the FIFO (data port). The main status register can be read by the microprocessor at any time. The microprocessor can also write to the data rate select register at any time.

Command handling in the 82072 can be divided into three phases. These are command, execution, and result.

Upon hardware reset, the 82072 goes into the command phase and is ready to receive a command from the main microprocessor. Typical commands include recalibrate, read track, format track, read data, write data, and seek. During the command phase, the microcomputer writes a predefined set of command code bytes and parameter bytes to the 82072. These bytes of data must occur in the sequence specified by Intel. For example, the recalibrate command causes the read/write head within the floppy disk drive to retract to the track 0 position. Two bytes are provided for the recalibrate command as follows:

D7	D6	D5	D4	D3	D2	D1	D0	
0	0	0	0	0	1	1	1	First byte to the 82072
0	0	0	0	0	0	DS1	DS0	Second byte to the 82072

Note that DS1 and DS0 bits select the disk drives as follows:

DS1	DS0	Drive selected
0	0	Drive 0
0	1	Drive 1
1	0	Drive 2
1	1	Drive 3

Before writing the above data to the 82072, the microcomputer must check certain bits in the main status register. After the command phase, the 82072 automatically enters the next phase as specified by the command definition.

During the execution phases, all data transfers to or from the 82072 occur. Data are transferred in DMA or non-DMA mode as indicated in the SPECIFY command.

If DMA mode is selected, DMA transfers are initiated by the 82072 when it activates its DRQ (DMA request) pin. When ready, the DMA controller responds by activating $\overline{\text{DACK}}$ (DMA acknowledge) pin of the

82072. If the FIFO is enabled by the CONFIGURE command, the DRQ pin of the 82072 will stay active until the FIFO is filled (write) or cleared (read). If FIFO is disabled, each byte to be transferred will request a cycle.

The 82072 informs the microcomputer of the start of the result phase by activating its INT (interrupt) pin. For each of the commands, a defined set of result bytes must be read by the microcomputer before completing the result phase.

These bytes of data must be read out by the microcomputer for another command to start. Among all the Intel microprocessors, the 80186 provides the most of the required functions for interfacing to the 82072. This is because the 80186 contains on-chip DMA controller. Figure 9.30 shows a typical 80186/82072.

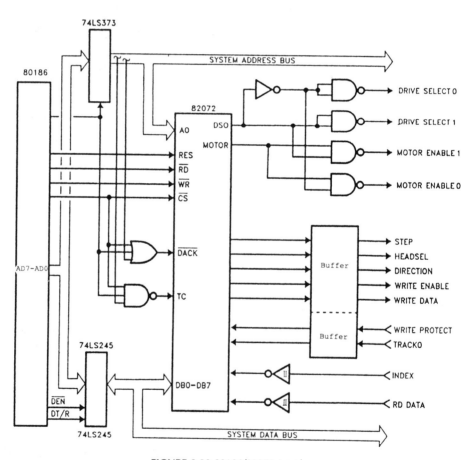

FIGURE 9.30 80186/82072 interface.

The 82072 data lines are connected to the 80186 AD0-AD7 lines via the 74LS245 buffer. The 80186 on-chip DMA controller does not provide any DMA acknowledge or terminal count signal required by the 82072. This is because the 80186 performs a read or write directly with the device requesting DMA. The DMA acknowledge signal can be obtained by using one of the 80186-generated chip select lines.

The 80186 can generate PCS0-PCS7 chip select lines for the peripheral devices. If the system does not use all the chip select lines for a specific application, one of the spare chip select lines can be used to generate the $\overline{\text{DTACK}}$ signal for the 82072.

The TC line is used to terminate the data transfer. The TC (terminal count) signal can be generated by connecting the DACK signal to one of the 80186 timers and program the timer to output a pulse after execution of a certain number of DMA cycles.

9.6 COPROCESSORS

In Chapters 1 and 7, basics of coprocessors, along with functions provided by Motorola coprocessors such as MC68851 and MC68881, are covered. In this section, a brief overview of the Intel coprocessors will be provided.

Intel offers a number of coprocessors which include numeric coprocessors such as 80872/80287/80387, DMA coprocessors such as 82258, and graphic coprocessors such as 82786. In the following, a brief overview of Intel's numeric coprocessors, which include 8087, 80287, and 80327, will be included.

9.6.1 INTEL 8087

Intel 8087 numeric data coprocessor is designed using HMOS III technology and is packaged in a 40-pin DIP. When an 8087 is present in a microcomputer system, it adds 68 numeric processing instructions and eight 80-bit registers to the microprocessor's register set. The 8087 can be interfaced to Intel microprocessors such as 8086/8088 and 80186/80188.

The 8087 supports seven data types which include 16-, 32-, and 64-bit integers, 32-, 64-, and 80-bit floating point, and 18-digit BCD operands. The 8087 is compatible with IEEE floating-point format. It includes several arithmetic, trigonometric, exponential, and logarithmic instructions.

The 8087 is treated as an exterior to the microprocessor providing additional register data types, instructions, and control at the hardware level. At the programmer level, the microprocessor and the 8087 are viewed as a single processor. For 8086/8088, the microprocessor's status (S0-S2) and queue status lines (QS0-QS1) enable the 8087 to monitor and decode instructions in synchronization. For 80186/80188 systems, the queue status signals of the 80186/80188 are synchronized to the 8087 by the 8288 bus controller. The 8087 can operate in parallel with and independent of the microprocessor. For resynchronization, the 8087's BUSY pin tells the microprocessor that the 8087 is executing an instruction and the microprocessor's WAIT instruction tests this signal to ensure that the 8087 is ready to execute subsequent instruction. The 8087 can interrupt the microprocessor when it detects an error or exception. The 8087's interrupt register line is typically connected to the microprocessor through an 8259 programmable interrupt controller for 8086/8088 systems and INT for 80186/80188 systems.

The 8087 uses the request/grant lines of the microprocessor to gain control of the system bus for data transfer.

The 8087 contains the 8086/8088 instruction set for general data manipulation and program control. The microprocessor controls overall program execution while the 8087 utilizes the coprocessor interface to recognize and perform numeric operations.

9.6.2 INTEL 80287

Intel 80287 is an enhanced 8087 that extends the 80286 microprocessor with floating-point, extended integer, and BCD data types. The 80287 adds over 50 instructions to the 80286 instruction set. The 80287 is designed using HMOS technology and is housed in a 40-pin special package called 'CERDIP'.

The 80287 supports IEEE floating-point format. The 80287 expands the 80286 data types to include 32-bit, 64-bit, and 80-bit floating point, 32-bit and 64-bit integers, and 18-digit BCD operands. It extends 80286 instruction set to trigonometric, logarithmic, exponential, and arithmetic instructions for all data types.

The 80287 executes instruction in parallel with an 80286. The 80287 has two operating modes like the 80286. Upon reset, the 80287 operates in real address mode. It can be placed in the protected virtual address mode by executing an instruction on the 80286. The 80287 cannot be placed back to the real address mode unless reset. Once in protected mode, all memory references for numeric data or status information follow the 80286 memory management and protection rules and thus the 80287 extends the 80286 protected mode.

The 80287 receives instructions and data via the data channel control signals ($\overline{\text{PEREQ}}$ — Processor Extension Data Channel Operand Transfer Request); $\overline{\text{PEACK}}$ — Processor Extension Data Channel Operand Transfer Acknowledge; $\overline{\text{BUSY}}$; NPRD — Numeric Processor $\overline{\text{RD}}$; $\overline{\text{NPWR}}$ — Numeric Processor $\overline{\text{WR}}$). When in protected mode, all information received by the 80287 is validated by the 80286 memory management and protection unit. The 80287 can operate in parallel with the 80286. When the 80287 detects an exception, it will indicate this to the 80286 by asserting the ERROR signal.

The 80286/80287 is programmed as a single processor. All memory addressing modes, physical memory, and virtual memory of the 80286 are available in the 80287.

9.6.3 INTEL 80387

Intel 80387 is a numeric coprocessor that extends the 80386 architecture with floating-point, extended integer, and BCD data types. It is compatible with IEEE floating point. The 80387 includes 32-, 64-, and 80-bit floating point, 32- and 64-bit integers, and 18-digit BCD operands. It extends the 80386 instruction set to include trigonometric, logarithmic, exponential, and arithmetic instructions of all data types. The 80387 can operate in real, protected, or virtual 8086 modes of the 80386. It is designed using CHMOS III technology and is packaged in a 68-pin PGA (Pin Grid Array).

The 80387 operates in the same manner whether the 80386 is executing in real address mode, protected mode, or virtual 86 mode. All memory access is handled by the 80386; the 80387 operates on instructions and values passed to it by the 80386. Therefore, the 80387 is independent of the 80386 mode.

The 80387 includes three functional units that can operate in parallel. The 80386 can be transferring commands and data to the 80387 bus control logic for the next instruction while the 80387 floating-point unit is performing the current numeric instruction. This parallelism improves system performance.

The 80387 adds to an 80386 system additional data types, registers, instructions, and interrupts. All communication between the 80386 and 80387 is transparent to application software. Thus, the 80387 greatly enhances the 80386 capabilities.

QUESTIONS AND PROBLEMS

9.1   Interface a hexadecimal keyboard one seven-segment display to an 8086/8255-based microcomputer.
  i)   Draw a hardware schematic of the design. Show only the pertinent signals.
  ii) Write an 8086 assembly language program to display the hex digit on the display from 0-F each time a digit is pressed on the keyboard.

9.2   Repeat Problem 9.1 using 8086/8279 configuration.

9.3   What is the purpose of A0, BD, and IRQ pins on the 8279?

9.4   What are the functions of the 8279 SL0 through SL3 lines? How would you connect an eight-digit hexadecimal display and an 8×8 keyboard via these lines? Draw a functional block diagram.

9.5   Describe the basic functions of a DMA Controller. How does it control the I/O R/W and memory R/W signals? Why is the DMA Controller faster than the microprocessor for data transfer?

9.6   Describe briefly the main features of Motorola's MC68440 DMA controller.

9.7   Draw a functional block diagram showing pertinent signals of the MC68020/68230/68440 interface.

9.8   Define the MC68440 modes of operation.

9.9   Which mode and which address lines are required by the MC68440 to decode the register addresses? Why does the MC68440 require more address lines than it requires for register address decoding?

9.10   Draw a functional block diagram of the MC68440/68008 interface.

9.11   What is the difference between the following?

i) Serial and Parallel printers
ii) Impact and Nonimpact printers
iii) Character and Matrix printers

9.12 Assume an LRC7040 printer. Draw a functional block diagram of the LRC7040 printer to an 8086-based microcomputer. Write an 8086 assembly language program to print the hexadecimal digit '0' on the printer.

9.13 Draw a functional block diagram of the 8295 printer controller interface to an 8085-based microcomputer.

9.14 How are the 8295 input data register and output status registers accessed? What are the functions of these registers?

9.15 How are the 8295 serial and parallel modes of operation selected?

9.16 In 8295 parallel mode, describe briefly how printers are interfaced via polled, interrupt, or DMA.

9.17 Summarize the basics of CRT. What is the main difference between CRT displays and graphics displays?

9.18 What are the typical functions of a CRT controller? Relate these typical functions to the Intel 8275.

9.19 Draw a functional block diagram showing an 8086-based microcomputer interface to 8275. Show only its pertinent signals.

9.20 What do you mean by bitmapping? How is it applied in graphics?

9.21 Describe briefly the functions provided by the Intel 82786 graphics controller.

9.22 Draw a functional block diagram showing 80386/82786 interface. Show only the pertinent signals.

9.23 What is the basic difference between floppy disk and magnetic tape?

9.24 Summarize the main functions provided by a floppy disk controller.

Relate these functions to those provided by the Intel 82072. Does the 82072 provide data separation? What is the purpose of the FIFO in the 82072?

9.25 Draw a functional block diagram interfacing the 80386 with the 82072.

9.26 Summarize the basic differences between the Intel 8087, the 80287, and the 80387 numeric coprocessors. Why are these three separate chips for the same coprocessor family provided by Intel?

Chapter 10

DESIGN PROBLEMS

This chapter includes a number of design problems that utilize external hardware. The systems are based on typical microprocessors such as the 8085 and 68000.

The concepts presented can be extended to other microprocessors.

10.1 DESIGN PROBLEM NO. 1

10.1.1 PROBLEM STATEMENT

An 8085-based digital voltmeter is designed which will measure a maximum of 5 V DC via an A/D converter and then display the voltage on two BCD displays. The upper display is the integer part (0 to 5 V DC) and the lower display is the fractional part (0.0 to 0.9 V DC).

10.1.2 OBJECTIVE

A digital voltmeter capable of measuring DC voltage up to and including 5 V will be built and tested. The voltmeter is to be implemented using the Intel 8085 microprocessor and an analog-to-digital converter of the designer's choice. The measured voltage is to be displayed on two seven-segment LEDs.

10.1.3 OPERATION

Figure 10.1 shows a block diagram of the digital voltmeter. It is composed of the microprocessor, 2K bytes of EPROM, 256 bytes of RAM with I/O, the A/D converter, and the display section.

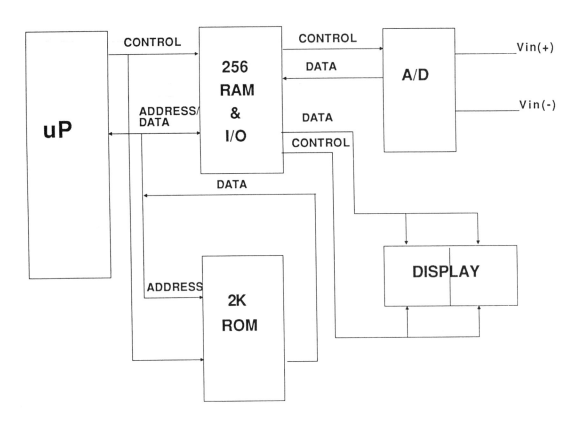

FIGURE 10.1 Voltmeter block diagram.

The Intel 8085 microprocessor provides control over all address, data, and control information involved in program execution. It also provides for manipulation of data as taken from A/D and sent to the display section.

The EPROM is a memory unit which stores the instructions necessary for system operation. The RAM and I/O section is a memory unit which provides for data as well as data transfers to and from the A/D and display. The A/D converter takes the voltage measured across Vin(+) and Vin(−) pins and converts it to an 8-bit binary message. The binary information is taken into the microprocessor via I/O and converted to its decimal equivalent. The display section takes the converted binary information from the processor so that it may be read over two seven-segment LED displays. The leftmost display provides the integer portion of the measured voltage, while the rightmost provides the fractional portion.

10.1.4 HARDWARE

Figure 10.2 shows the detailed hardware schematic. The system uses standard I/O and memory map of 0800H-08FFH. The I/O ports of the 8155 are all used. Configured as an input port, port B is connected to the output of the 0804 A/D chip. Configured as an output port, port C is connected to the TIL311 displays. Bits 0-3 are the data outputs while bits 4 and 5 are connected to the latches of the TIL311. Only three bits of port A are used, configured as an output port, to control the select, read, and write lines of the A/D chip.

Using the fully decoded memory addressing, the 74LS318, a decoder, is used to select either the RAM or the EPROM. Also, a 74LS373 is used to latch the address lines to the EPROM. The RAM does not require such a chip because the 8155 RAM has its own internal latches. The ALE line of the 8085 microprocessor controls the latches as seen in the schematic.

The EPROM contains the instructions and the algorithms for converting the binary representation of the analog voltage (applied to the A/D converter) back to decimal representation. The instructions are used to control the system operation. The algorithm uses repeated subtraction to obtain the correct voltage in decimal form. The left display is the integer part and the right display is the decimal part.

The displays, as stated before, are TIL311 hexadecimal displays. In addition, the displays have their own latches which are active low. In the 8085 microprocessor, the interrupt RST 6.5 is used to jump to the address with the algorithm to convert and display the voltage. The INTR pin of the A/D is connected directly to the RST 6.5 pin of the microprocessor. First, an active low is sent to the chip select pin, and then the write pin of the A/D converter is toggled.

Upon completion of the A/D conversion, the 8085 is interrupted. The service routine outputs an active low onto the read pin of the A/D, which latches the data. After inputting the data via the port, the read pin is toggled which then tristates the A/D output.

10.1.5 SOFTWARE

An important part of the software is to convert the A/D's 8-bit binary data into its decimal equivalent for the display. The decimal data will have two digits: one integer part and one fractional part. Two approaches can be used to accomplish this as follows.

Approach 1

Since the maximum decimal value that can be accommodated in 8 bits

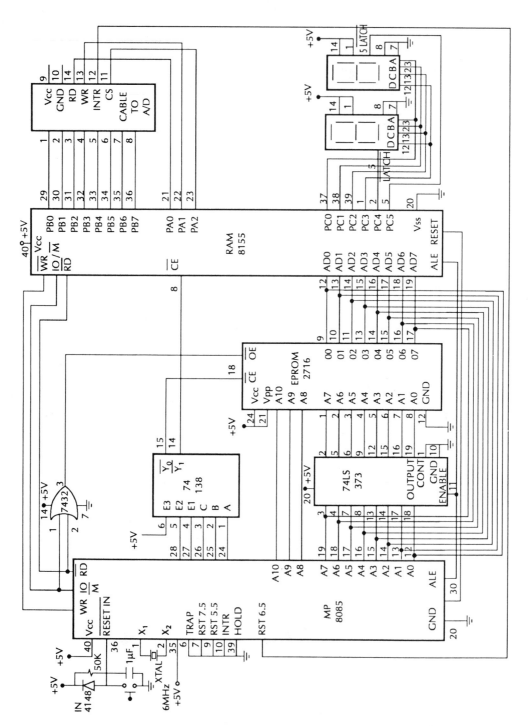

FIGURE 10.2 Digital voltmeter detailed schematic.

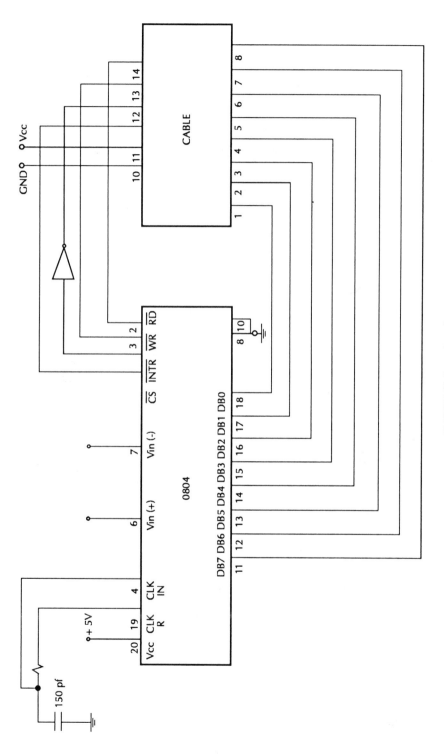

FIGURE 10.2 continued.

is 255_{10} (FF_{16}), the maximum voltage of 5 V will be equivalent to 255_{10}. This means that the display in decimal is given by:

$$
\begin{aligned}
D &= 5*(\text{Input}/255) \\
  &= \text{Input}/51 \\
  &= \text{Quotient} + (\text{Remainder}/51) \\
  &\qquad\qquad\uparrow \\
  &\text{Integer part}
\end{aligned}
$$

The fractional part in decimal is

$$
\begin{aligned}
F &= (\text{Remainder}/51)*10 \\
  &\approx \text{Remainder}/5
\end{aligned}
$$

Approach 2

In the second approach, the equivalent of 1 V ($255/5\ V = 51_{10} = 33_{16}$) is subtracted from the input data. If the input data are greater than 1 V, a counter initially cleared to zero is incremented by one. This process continues until the measured data are less than 1 V. The register keeps count of how many subtractions take place with a remainder greater than 1 V and thus contains the integer portion of the measured voltage in decimal.

The decimal portion of the fractional part is obtained in the same way except that if the input data are less than 1 V, then they are compared with the decimal equivalent ($51/10 \approx 5$) of 0.1 V. If the measured data are greater than 0.1 V, a counter initially cleared to zero is incremented by one and the process continues until the input data are less than 0.1 V. The counter contains the fractional part of the display.

Approach 2 is used as a solution to this problem. A complete listing of the 8085 assembly language program to control the digital voltmeter is given below. The program is used to begin and end the A/D conversion process as well as to manipulate the binary data into their decimal form so that they can be displayed in an easily readable format.

```
FILE: LIST1;RAT001   HEWLETT-PACKARD: 8085 Assembler

LOCATION OBJECT
  CODE LINE                   SOURCE LINE

                1  "8085"
  <09A0>        2  STACKP    EQU    09A0H
  <0009>        3  PORTA     EQU    0009H
```

FILE: LIST1;RAT001   HEWLETT-PACKARD: 8085 Assembler
(continued)

```
LOCATION OBJECT
     CODE LINE                              SOURCE LINE

   <000A>        4 PORTB    EQU    000AH
   <000B>        5 PORTC    EQU    000BH
   <0008>        6 CSR      EQU    0008H
   <0034>        7 INTR     EQU    0034H
   <0000>        8 PROG     EQU    0000H
                 9
                10           ORG    PROG
   0000 3109A0  11           LXI    SP,STACKP    ;INIT, STACK
   0003 3E0D    12 START     MVI    A,0DH        ;SET INTERRUPT
                                                  MASK
   0005 30      13           SIM                 ;SET INTERRUPT
                                                  MASK 6.5
   0006 FB      14           EI                  ;ENABLE
                                                  INTERRUPT
   0007 D308    15           OUT    CSR          ;DEFINE PORTS
                                                  A,B,C
   0009 3E30    16           MVI    A,30H        ;SET DISPLAY
                                                  ENABLES
   000B D30B    17           OUT    PORTC        ;
   000D 3EFF    18           MVI    A,0FFH       ;
   000F D309    19           OUT    PORTA        ;SET /CS,/
                                                  WR/RD HIGH
   0011 3EFE    20           MVI    A,0FEH       ;
   0013 D309    21           OUT    PORTA        ;SEND /CS LOW
   0015 3EFC    22           MVI    A,0FCH       ;
   0017 D309    23           OUT    PORTA        ;
   0019 3EFE    24           MVI    A,0FEH       ;
   001B D309    25           OUT    PORTA        ;TOGGLE /WR
   001D 76      26           HLT                 ;WAIT FOR
                                                  INTERRUPT
                27                               ;
                28                               ;
                29           ORG    INTR         ;INTERRUPT
                                                  VECTOR
                                                  ADDRESS
   0034 210900  30           LXI    H,0900H      ;INIT, MEM.
                                                  POINTER
   0037 1600    31           MVI    D,00H        ;INIT, INTEGER
                                                  COUNTER
   0039 0E33    32           MVI    C,33H        ;
   003B 3EFA    33           MVI    A,0FAH       ;SEND /RD LOW
   003D D309    34           OUT    PORTA        ;
```

```
FILE: LIST1;RAT001   HEWLETT-PACKARD: 8085 Assembler
(continued)


LOCATION OBJECT
   CODE LINE                        SOURCE LINE

  003F 00          35          NOP
  0040 DB0A         36          IN     PORTB      ;INPUT DATA
  0042 47           37          MOV    B,A        ;MOVE DATA
                                                   TEMP. TO B

  0043 3EFE         38          MVI    A,0FEH     ;
  0045 D309         39          OUT    PORTA      ;TOGGLE /RD
  0047 70           40          MOV    M,B
  0048 78           41          MOV    A,B        ;MOVE DATA TO
                                                   0900H

  0049 91           42   SUB1:  SUB    C          ;
  004A DA0052       43          JC     CONT1      ;
  004D 14           44          INR    D          ;
  004E 77           45          MOV    M,A        ;
  004F C30049       46          JMP    SUB1       ;
  0052 7A           47   CONT1: MOV    A,D        ;
  0053 D30B         48          OUT    PORTC      ;
  0055 E63F         49          ANI    3FH        ;
  0057 D30B         50          OUT    PORTC      ;
  0059 1600         51          MVI    D,00H      ;
  005B 0E05         52          MVI    C,05H      ;
  005D 7E           53          MOV    A,M        ;
  005E 91           54   SUB2:  SUB    C          ;
  005F DA0066       55          JC     CONT2      ;
  0062 14           56          INR    D          ;
  0063 C3005E       57          JMP    SUB2       ;
  0066 JA           58   CONT2: MOV    A,D        ;
  0067 F610         59          ORI    10H        ;
  0069 D30B         60          OUT    PORTC      ;
  006B E63F         61          ANI    3FH        ;
  006D D30B         62          OUT    PORTC      ;
  006F 76           63          HLT               ;

Errors = 0
```

Lines 2—8 are assembler directives which equate a recognizable label with a hex value. This is useful for values which are to be used throughout the program.

Line 10 is another assembler directive which sets the beginning of the program at address 0000H.

Line 11 initializes the stack pointer at address 09A0H. This is necessary if we are to return to a current program after an interrupt has been serviced. Although this program never returns after the interrupt has been serviced, it is a good habit to initialize the stack.

Lines 12—14 set the mask bits and enable interrupt RST6.5.

Line 15 defines port A as output, port B as input, and port C as output. Note that the data to configure the ports were already in the accumulator as per line 12.

Lines 16—17 send an active high to each display's data latch enable pin. This insures that the displays will output the correct data on the next high-to-low transition at the latch enable pins.

Lines 18—19 send an active high to the chip's select ($\overline{\text{CS}}$), write ($\overline{\text{WR}}$), and read ($\overline{\text{RD}}$) pins of the A/D converter. This insures proper start-up of the converter.

Lines 20—21 first send an active low to the converter's $\overline{\text{CS}}$ pin. Next, lines 22—25 toggle the $\overline{\text{WR}}$ pin so that conversion starts. The combination of $\overline{\text{CS}}$ and $\overline{\text{WR}}$ active low resets the A/D internally and sets it up for the start of the conversion. By sending $\overline{\text{WR}}$, an active high, the conversion starts. Figure 10.3 shows the timing diagram for the A/D.

Line 26 is a halt which is provided as a delay to wait for the interrupt request. This is necessary since it may take as long as 127 μs for the interrupt to be asserted. This is equivalent to approximately 380 clock cycles for the 8085 operating at 3 MHz.

Line 29 continues the program at the interrupt vector for interrupt RST6.5.

Line 30 loads the HL register pair with a memory address to be used later in the program.

Lines 31—32 initialize the D and C registers. D register is to hold the integer portion of the measured voltage, while C register holds a hex value equivalent to 1 V for this system.

Lines 33—34 send an active low to the $\overline{\text{RD}}$ pin of the A/D converter so that the binary information corresponding to the measured voltage may be read by the microprocessor.

Lines 36—37 take the data from the A/D converter and store them into register B.

Lines 38—39 toggle the $\overline{\text{RD}}$ pin back to active high.

Lines 40—41 move the 8-bit data into memory location 0900H and then into the accumulator.

Lines 42—46 convert the binary data into their decimal equivalent so that the integer portion may be displayed. First the equivalent of 1 V is subtracted from the input data. If the measured voltage is less than 1 V, the program jumps to line 47. If the voltage is greater than one, the program

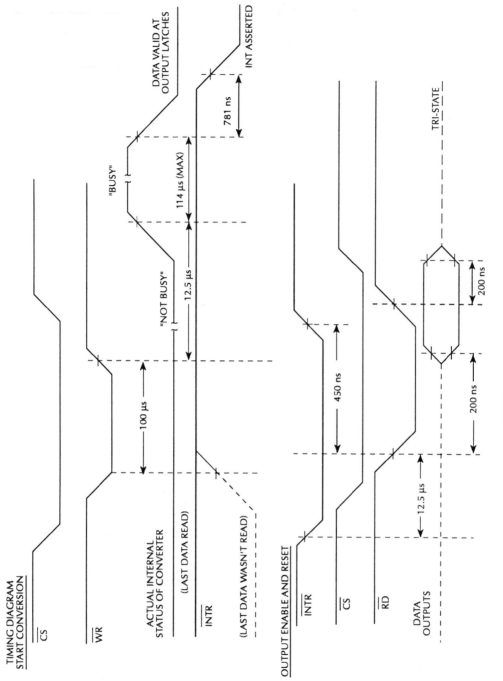

FIGURE 10.3 A/D timing diagram.

continues at line 44 where register D is incremented by one. The remainder from the subtraction is temporarily stored in memory. The program then unconditionally jumps back to line 42 so that another subtraction takes place. This loop occurs until the remainder from the subtraction is less than 1 V. Register D keeps count of how many subtractions took place with a remainder greater than 1 V and thus counts the integer number of volts measured.

Lines 47—50 send the contents of register D to the leftmost display. The AND operation unlatches the data at the display.

Lines 51—52 again initialize registers D and C, but this time register D will be counting the fractional portion of the measured voltage and register C will hold the hex equivalent of 0.1 V.

Line 53 moves the last positive remainder from memory into the accumulator.

Lines 54—57 perform the same function as lines 42—46 but with the fractional portion of the measured data.

The remaining lines output the contents of register D into the rightmost display and then halt the program.

10.2 DESIGN PROBLEM NO. 2

10.2.1 PROBLEM STATEMENT

A 68000-based system is designed to drive three seven-segment displays and monitor three key switches. The system starts by displaying 000. If the increment key is pressed, it will increment the display by one. Similarly, if the decrement key is pressed, it will decrement the display by one. The display goes from 00-FF in the hex mode and from 000-255 in the BCD mode. The system will count correctly in either mode. The change mode key will cause the display to change from hex to decimal or vice versa, depending on its present mode. Figure 10.4 depicts the block diagram.

Two solutions are provided for this problem. Solution one uses programmed I/O and no interrupts, while solution two utilizes interrupt I/O but no programmed I/O.

10.2.2 SOLUTION NO. 1

The simplest and the most straightforward system possible is built to obtain the required results. This means that there will be no RAM in the

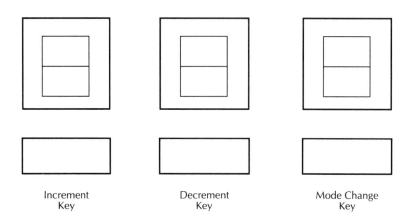

Increment   Decrement   Mode Change
Key   Key   Key

FIGURE 10.4 Block diagram for design problem no. 2.

system; therefore, no subroutine will be used in the software and only programmed I/O (no interrupt) is used.

10.2.2.a Hardware

Figure 10.5 shows the detailed hardware schematic. The circuit is divided into the following sections.

10.2.2.a.i Reset Circuit

The reset circuit for the system is basically the same as the one used for the 8085. The circuit has a 0.1-µF capacitor and 1K resistor to provide an RC time constant of 10^{-4} s for power on reset. The $\overline{\text{RESET}}$ and $\overline{\text{HALT}}$ pins of the 68000 and the $\overline{\text{RESET}}$ pin of the 6821 are tied together for complete and total reset of the system.

10.2.2.a.ii Clock Signal

An external pulse-generator is used to generate the clock signal for the system. The system is driven up to 3 MHz, the limit of the generator, without any problems.

10.2.2.a.iii Buffering

Because the 68000 is interfaced to other devices (6821 and 2716s), the outputs of the 68000 which are used to drive these chips must be buffered in order to be certain that there is enough drive current. The buffering is done by a TTL open-collector inverter buffer chip (7406). Since this chip is of the open-collector type, 1K pull-up resistor is also needed.

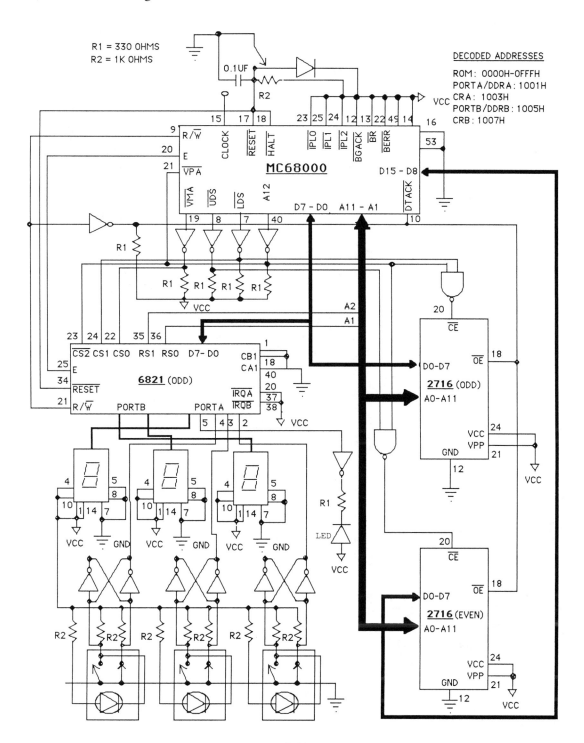

FIGURE 10.5 Detailed hardware schematic.

10.2.2.a.iv Address Mapping

The system has two 2K EPROM (2716s) and one 6800's peripheral I/O chip (6821). The 68000 address lines A1 through A11 are needed to address the EPROM. So A12 is used to select between the 2716s and the 6821 (0 for 2716s and 1 for 6821). Memory access for the EPROM is asynchronous, while the 6821 is synchronized with the E-clock. A12 is inverted, through the buffer, so the output of the inverter goes to $\overline{CS2}$ of the 6821 and also to $\overline{VPA}$ of the 68000 for synchronization. The 68000 $\overline{VMA}$ pin is also buffered and inverted and it goes to $\overline{CS0}$ of the 6821. The 6821 is chosen to be odd, so $\overline{CS1}$ is activated by inverted $\overline{LDS}$ line. Finally, address lines A1 and A2 are connected to RS0 and RS1, respectively.

The $\overline{CE}$ for the two 2716s come from two NAND gates. They are the results of the inverted A12 NANDed with the inverted $\overline{LDS}$ or the inverted $\overline{UDS}$, depending on whether the EPROM is odd or even. The $\overline{DTACK}$ pin of the 68000 and the OE pins of the 2716s are activated by the signal of $R/\overline{W}$ inverted. When the 68000 wants to read the EPROM this signal will be high, so its inverted signal will provide a low to $\overline{DTACK}$. This does not cause any problem because when the 68000 accesses the 6821, $\overline{VPA}$ is activated and so the 68000 will not look for $\overline{DTACK}$.

The configuration above causes the memory map to be as follows:

	A23...A13	A12	A11	A10	A9	A8	A7	A6	A5	A4	A3	A2	A1	HEX
4K of EPROM Memory	0 0	0	0	0	0	0	0	0	0	0	0	0	0	000000_{16}
		THROUGH												to
	0 0	0	1	1	1	1	1	1	1	1	1	1	1	$000FFF_{16}$
PA/DDRA	0 0	1	0	0	0	0	0	0	0	0	0	0	1	001001_{16}
CRA	0 0	1	0	0	0	0	0	0	0	0	0	1	1	001003_{16}
PB/DDRB	0 0	1	0	0	0	0	0	0	0	0	1	0	1	001005_{16}
CRB	0 0	1	0	0	0	0	0	0	0	0	1	1	1	001007_{16}

10.2.2.a.v I/O

There are 3 seven-segments displays in the system (TI311), an LED, and 3 switches. The 3 displays have internal latches and hex decoders. So the two least significant displays are connected directly to port B of the 6821 chip, and the most significant line is connected to the upper 4 bits of port A. The latch will enable, for the displays are tied to ground so as to enable them at all times. The LED, when ON, will indicate that the display is in the BCD mode. Each of the three switches, double-pole single throw type, with LED indicator, goes through two inverters (7404) for the hardware debounce, and the outputs of the inverters are connected to the lowest 3 bits of port A.

10.2.2.a.vi Unused-Pins Connection

For the 68000 there are 6 unused, active-low, input pins which must be disabled by connecting them to 5 V. These are $\overline{\text{IPL0}}$, $\overline{\text{IPL1}}$, $\overline{\text{IPL2}}$, $\overline{\text{BERR}}$, $\overline{\text{BR}}$, and $\overline{\text{BGACK}}$. Two of the 6821 unused pins ($\overline{\text{IRQA}}$ and $\overline{\text{IRQB}}$) are also disabled this way, while CA1 and CB1 are disabled by connecting them to ground.

10.2.2.b Microcomputer Development System

Hewlett-Packard (HP) 64000 is used to design, develop, debug and emulate the 68000-based system. Some details are given in this section.

The emulator is a very important part of the development of the software and hardware of the system. The 68000 emulator has most of the functions for emulation such as display memory or registers, modify memory or registers. But there is no single-step function. The HP 64000 emulator is divided into three modes of operations: initialization, emulation, and EPROM programming.

10.2.2.b.i Initialization
Edit

The edit function is used to create the application program in mnemonic form. The first line of the program must be "68000" to indicate that the program is to be assembled by the 68000 assembler, and that a 68000 microprocessor is to be used for emulation. Also, the special assembler mnemonic PROG should be placed before the first instruction, for linking the program later.

Assemble

When the application program has been completed and properly edited, the file is then assembled into a relocatable object code file. All errors indicated by the assembler should be corrected at this point.

In order to use the 68000 emulator special functions, a special monitor program is required. This can be copied as follows:

```
COPY Mon_68k:HP:source to MON_68k
```

Note upper and lower case. Once this monitor is copied, it must be assembled for no errors.

Linking

The two relocatable files must be linked together to create an absolute file for the emulation process. The files can be linked as follows:

```
Link <cr>
Object files? Mon_68k
Library file? <cr>
Prog, Data, Comm = 000100H, 000000H, 000000H
More files? yes
 Object file? (name of application program file)
Library file? <cr>
Prog, Data, Comm = 001100H, 000000H, 000000H
More files? no
Absolute file? (name of absolute file)
```

There are reasons why the two files were linked this way. The monitor program must be stored at 0100H through 0FFFH, and since this I/O port is mapped starting at 1001H, the application program must be stored starting at a different address, so 1100H was used. Also, address 000H through 0FFF is used for exception vectors by the 68000 microprocessor.

10.2.2.b.ii Emulation

The emulator was used as a replacement for the actual 68000 chip to test the software logic and hardware before it was actually installed into the circuit.

To start the emulation process the following soft-key parameters were entered:

```
EMULATELOAD                          (absolute file name)
Processor clock?                     external
Restrict to real time?               no
Memory block size?                   256
Significant bits?                    20
Break on write to ROM?               yes
Memory map:
0000H thru 0FFFH emulation RAM (monitor & exception
  vector)
1000H thru 10FFH user RAM (I/O PORT addresses)
1100H thru 1FFFH emulation ROM (application program)
Modify simulated I/O?                no
Reconfigure pod?                     no
Command file name?                   (name of emulation
                                       command file)
```

Note: Usually external clock requires external $\overline{\text{DTACK}}$; however, since the system only has EPROMs and for the purpose of emulation these EPROMs are not used, the external $\overline{\text{DTACK}}$ is not required.

Once the required files and memory maps are loaded, the system is ready for emulation. The monitor program must be running before the application program is executed. To run the monitor program, the following is used:

```
run from 0100H <cr>
```

Then the application program is run using:

```
run from 1100H <cr>
```

Another important part that the user should keep in mind is the processor status. There are three messages for the processor status which indicate that the emulator is not generating any bus cycles. They are

1.   Reset — Indicates that the user's hardware is asserting the Reset input. The condition can only be terminated by releasing the user's hardware.
2.   Wait — Indicates that the 68000 is waiting for a $\overline{\text{DTACK}}$ or other memory response. The condition can be terminated by asserting $\overline{\text{DTACK}}$, $\overline{\text{BERR}}$, $\overline{\text{VPA}}$ or entering "reset" from the keyboard.
3.   No memory cycle — Indicates that the 68000 has executed a STOP instruction. The condition can be terminated by asserting "break" or "reset" from the keyboard.

10.2.2.b.iii EPROM Programming

After the software and hardware have been emulated and they work properly, the final step is to program the EPROM and put the final circuit together. But before this, the program must be changed to include the addresses for the stack pointer and the initial PC. This is done by using the "ORG" and "DC" assembler directives. Then this new program is assembled and linked again. The EPROM is then programmed with the contents of this final "absolute file".

Programming EPROMs with the HP 64000 for 68000 is done by odd and even EPROMs. To program the lower 8 bits of data (odd ROM), the option bit 0 is selected, and bit 8 for the upper 8 bits (even ROM) is chosen as follows:

```
Prom_Prog                    <cr>
2716                         <cr>
Program from                 (filename: absolute:
                              bit 0 or 8)
```

Also, to check if the EPROM is clear, the command "check_sum" is used and if the result is F800H then the EPROM is clear.

10.2.2.c Software

The program consists of three major functions: initialize I/O ports and data registers, monitor and debounce key switches, and increment, decrement, or change mode. The program configures port B of the 6821 as an output port which will be used to display the two lower significant nibbles of data. Higher 4 bits of port A are configured as output to display the most significant nibble of the data. Bit 3 is also an output bit which turns ON and OFF the mode of the LEDs. The lowest 3 bits of port A are configured as inputs to detect the positions of three key switches. Register D3 is used to store the data in hex. Registers D4 and D7 are used to store the data in BCD mode with the low order byte in D4 and the high order byte in D7. Bit 3 of D0 contains a logic 1 representing BCD mode and logic 0 representing hex mode. Register D5 contains a 1 which will be used for incrementing BCD data, since ABCD doesn't have immediate mode. Register D6 contains 999 which is used for decrementing BCD.

The program monitors the three switches and stores the three input bits into register D0 if any of the keys is pressed. The processor then waits until the depressed key is released and then checks the input data one by one. The processor then branches to the increment, decrement, or mode change routine according to the depressed key. After execution, the processor will display the result on the three seven-segment displays.

Figure 10.6 shows the software flowchart.

The assembly language program is listed below:

```
FILE: LAB2:KH0A22        HEWLETT-PACKARD: 68000 Assembler

1 "68000"
2 ****************************************************************
3 *THIS PROGRAM STARTS DISPLAYING 000 AND MONITORS THREE KEY  *
4 *SWITCHES THEN INCREMENT, DECREMENT, OR CONVERT HEX TO BCD  *
5 *OR VICE VERSA, DEPENDING ON WHICH KEY IS DEPRESSED, THE    *
6 *DISPLAY GOES FROM 00-FF IN HEX MODE OR 00-255 IN BCD MODE  *
7 ****************************************************************
```

```
FILE: LAB2:KH0A22    HEWLETT-PACKARD: 68000 Assembler
(continued)


LOCATION OBJECT
   CODE LINE                              SOURCE LINE
<1001>              8 PA        EQU      001001H
<1001>              9 DDRA      EQU      001001H
<1003>             10 CRA       EQU      001003H
<1005>             11 PB        EQU      001005H
<1005>             12 DDRB      EQU      001005H
<1007>             13 CRB       EQU      001007H
                   14          ORG      00000000H
000000 FFFF FFFF   15          DC.L     0FFFFFFFFH
000004 0000 0008   16          DC.L     START
                   17 *
                   18 * CONFIGURE THE INPUT AND OUTPUT PORTS,
                   19 * DISPLAY 000 ON THE 7-SEGMENT DISPLAYS,
                   20 * AND INITIALIZE ALL THE DATA REGISTERS.
                   21 * THE HEX MODE IS STORED IN D3 AND THE
                   22 * BCD MODE IS STORED IN D7 AND D4.
000008 4238 1003   23 START     CLR.B    CRA
00000C 11FC 00FB   24           MOVE.B   #0F8H,DDRA   ;BIT 0-2 OF
                                                       PORT A AS
                                                       INPUT
000012 0BF8 0002   25           BSET.B   #02H,CRA     ;BIT 3-7 OF
                                                       PORT AS OUT-
                                                       PUT
000018 4238 1007   26           CLR.B    CRB
00001C 11FC 00FF   27           MOVE.B   #0FFH,DDRB   ;ALL 8 BITS OF
                                                       PORT B AS
                                                       OUTPUT
000022 08F8 0002   28           BSET.B   #02H,CRB
000028 4200        29           CLR.B    D0
00002A 11C0 1001   30           MOVE.B   D0,PA        ;DISPLAY 000
00002E 11C0 1005   31           MOVE.B   D0,PB
000032 4203        32           CLR.B    D3
000034 4244        33           CLR.W    D4
000036 7A01        34           MOVEQ.W  #01H,D5
000038 3C3C 0999   35           MOVE.W   #999H,D6
00003C 4207        36           CLR.B    D7
                   37 *
                   38 * DEBOUNCE THE KEY SWITCHES
                   39 *
00003E 1238 1001   40 SCAN      MOVE.B   PA,D1        ;MONITOR THE
                                                       KEYS
000042 0201 0007   41           ANDI.B   #07H,D1      ;MASK OUT THE
                                                       OUTPUT PINS
```

```
FILE: LAB2:KH0A22    HEWLETT-PACKARD: 68000 Assembler
(continued)


LOCATION OBJECT
    CODE LINE                           SOURCE LINE

000046 67F6         42          BEQ      SCAN      ;IF NO KEY IS
                                                    DEPRESSED GO TO
                                                    SCAN
000048 1438 1001 43             MOVE.B   PA,D2     ;READ THE DATA
                                                    AGAIN
00004C 0202 0007 44             ANDI.B   #07H,D2
000050 B401         45          CMP.B    D1,D2     ;CHECK TO SEE IF
                                                    THE DATA REMAIN
                                                    UNCHANGED
000052 66EA         46          BNE      SCAN      ;IF IT CHANGES GO
                                                    TO SCAN
                    47 *
                    48 * CHECK TO MAKE SURE THAT THE KEY IS
                    49 * RELEASED BEFORE THE NEXT KEY CAN BE
                    50 * ENTERED.
000054 1438 1001 51 KEYRL MOVE.B PA,D2
000058 0202 0007 52             ANDI.B   #07H,D2
00005C 66F6         53          BNE      KEYRL
                    54 * CHECK TO SEE WHICH KEY HAS BEEN EN-
                    55 * TERED. BITS 0,1, AND 2 OF D1 REPRESENT
                    56 * INCREMENT, DECREMENT, AND MODE EX-
                    57 * CHANGE RESPECTIVELY.
00005E 0801 0000 58             BTST.B   #0H,D1
000062 6600 003C 59             BNE      INCR      ;IF BIT-0 OF D1
                                                    IS 1 GOTO INCR
000066 0801 0001 60             BTST.B   #1H,D1
00006A 6700 0044 61             BEQ      MODE      ;IF BIT-1 IS 1
                                                    DECREMENT, OTHER-
                                                    WISE GOTO MODE
                    62 *
                    63 * DECREMENT BOTH HEX AND BCD AT THE SAME
                    64 * TIME.
00006E 0C03 0000 65             CMPI.B   #00H,D3
000072 67CA         66          BEQ      SCAN      ;IF THE NUMBER IS
                                                    0 NO DECREMENT,
                                                    GOTO SCAN
000074 5303         67          SUBQ.B   #1H,D3    ;DECREMENT HEX BY 1
000076 C603         68          AND.B    D3,D3     ;CLEAR THE CARRY
000078 C906         69          ABCD.B   D6,D4     ;DECREMENT BCD BY
                                                    1 BY ADDING IT
                                                    WITH 999
00007A CF06         70          ABCD.B   D6,D7
                    71 *
```

FILE: LAB2:KH0A22   HEWLETT-PACKARD: 68000 Assembler
(continued)

```
LOCATION OBJECT
     CODE LINE                          SOURCE LINE

                  72  * DISPLAY THE NUMBER IN HEX IF BIT-3 OF
                  73  * D0 IS 0, OTHERWISE DISPLAY IN BCD.
                  74  *
00007C 0800 0003  75  DISPLAY   BTST.B   #3H,D0
000080 6700 0014  76            BEQ      HEX       ;IF BIT-3 OF D0
                                                    IS 0, GOTO HEX
000084 11C4 1005  77            MOVE.B   D4,PB     ;OUTPUT THE LSB
                                                    TO PORT B
000088 E94F       78            LSL.W    #4H,D7    ;SHIFT LEFT 4
                                                    TIMES
00008A 08C7 0003  79            BSET.B   #3H,D7    ;TURN OFF THE LED
00008E 11C7 1001  80            MOVE.B   D7,PA     ;OUTPUT THE MSB
                                                    TO UPPER 4 BITS
                                                    OF PORT A
000092 E84F       81            LSR.W    #4,D7
000094 60A8       82            BRA      SCAN
000096 11C0 1001  83  HEX       MOVE.B   D0,PA     ;OUTPUT 0 TO PORT A
00009A 11C3 1005  84            MOVE.B   D3,PB     ;OUTPUT THE HEX
                                                    NUMBER TO PORT B
00009E 609E       85            BRA      SCAN
                  86  *
                  87  * INCREMENT BOTH HEX AND BCD.
                  88  *
0000A0 0C03 00FF  89  INCR      CMPI.B   #0FFH,D3
0000A4 6798       90            BEQ      SCAN      ;IF THE NUMBER IS
                                                    FF NO INCREMENT
0000A6 5203       91            ADDQ.B   #1H,D3    ;INCREMENT HEX
                                                    NUMBER BY 1
0000A8 4202       92            CLR.B    D2
0000AA C905       93            ABCD.B   D5,D4     ;INCREMENT LSB OF
                                                    BCD BY 1
0000AC CF02       94            ABCD     D2,D7     ;INCREMENT MSB OF
                                                    BCD BY 1 IF CARRY
                                                    IS 1
0000AE 60CC       95            BRA      DISPLAY
                  96  *
                  97  * EXCHANGE THE MODE THEN DISPLAY THE
                  98  * NUMBER.
0000B0 0840 0003  99  MODE      BCHG     #3H,D0    ;EXCHANGE MODE BY
                                                    CHANGING BIT-3 OF
                                                    D0
0000B4 60C6       100 BRA       DISPLAY

Errors = 0
```

LINE#	SYMBOL	TYPE	REFERENCES
***	B	U	23,24,25,26,27,28,29,30,31, 32,36,40,41,43,44,45,51, 52,58,60,65,67,68,69,70, 75,77,79,80,83,84,89,91, 92
10	CRA	A	23,25
13	CRB	A	26,28
9	DDRA	A	24
12	DDRB	A	27
75	DISPLAY	A	95,100
83	HEX	A	76
89	INCR	A	59
51	KEYRL	A	53
***	L	U	15,16
99	MODE	A	61
8	PA	A	30,40,43,51,80,83
11	PB	A	31,77,84
40	SCAN	A	42,46,66,82,85,90
23	START	A	16
***	W	U	33,34,35,78,81

10.2.3 SOLUTION NO. 2

The second solution approach uses interrupt I/O but no I/O ports.

10.2.3.a Hardware

The system includes a 3-digit and three momentary function switches (increment, decrement, and mode select). In order to minimize the complexity of the project, no I/O chips are used. Instead, a buffer and some latches as the I/O ports are used. The buffer is used to hold the status of the momentary switches and the latches are used to hold the information coming from the data bus. To further the design, three TIL311 displays are used because they contain internal data latches. Because the 68000 has 23 address lines (not including A0), the memory is linearly decoded. The even and odd memory chips are enabled by decoding pins $\overline{UDS}$, $\overline{LDS}$, and $\overline{AS}$.

To display the three-digit number, the data lines are connected to the inputs of the three TIL311 displays (D0-D3 = LSD, D4-D7 = middle digit, D8-D11 = MSD). The address strobe ($\overline{AS}$) is NANDed with the address line A14 to latch the data onto the three displays. The memory map for the displays is given in Table 10.1. Because of linear decoding, the problem of foldback exists.

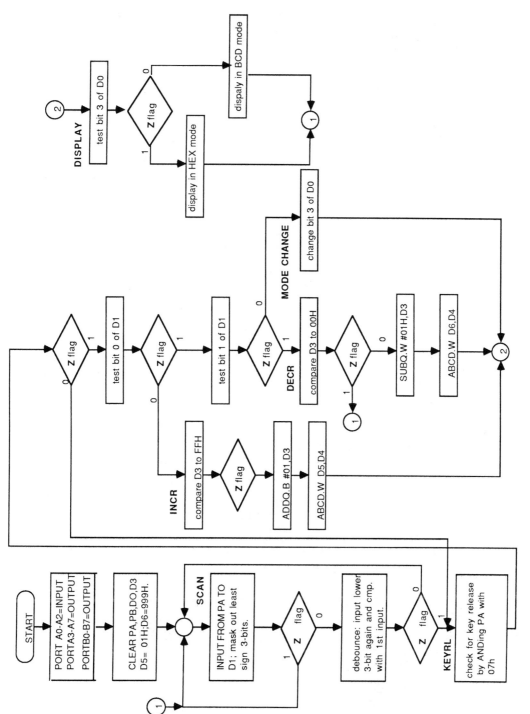

FIGURE 10.6 Software flowchart.

Two 2716s are used for the EPROM and two 6116s are used for the RAM. Both the RAM and the EPROM chips are divided into even and odd memory. The configuration enables the 68000 to access an even or an odd data bytes or a complete word in one bus cycle. The even and odd select lines are generated by ANDing the $\overline{UDS}$ and $\overline{AS}$ pins and the $\overline{LDS}$ and $\overline{AS}$ pins, respectively. To access a word, both the even and the odd enable signals are asserted. These signals are then NANDed with address lines A12 and A13 to select the EPROM and the RAM, respectively (see Figure 10.7). The odd memory chip data lines are connected to D0-D7 of the 68000. The even memory chip data lines are connected to D8-D15. Table 10.1 shows the memory map.

TABLE 10.1
Memory Map

$000000-$000FFF   EPROM
$003000-$003FFF   RAM
$005000-$005FFF   DISPLAYS
$009000-$009FFF   SWITCHES

In the system, the interrupt pins are implemented by ANDing the status of the momentary switches and connecting the output of the gate to $\overline{IPL2}$. To achieve a level 6 interrupt, $\overline{IPL1}$ and $\overline{IPL0}$ pins are connected to Vcc and ground, respectively (see Figure 10.7). To reduce the number of components, the 68000 is instructed to generate an internal autovector to service the interrupt. This is accomplished by asserting $\overline{VPA}$ and $\overline{IPL2}$ at the same time. If an interrupt occurs (switch pressed), the 68000 will compute the autovector number $1E and the vector address $78. The processor will then go to a service routine that will find the switch that was pressed.

A 4-MHz crystal oscillator is used to clock the processor. Since the 68000 is operating at 4 MHz, $\overline{AS}$ is directly connected to $\overline{DTACK}$. This gave the EPROMs (450 ns access time) about 500 ns to provide valid data. A reset circuit similar to the one used in the 8085 system is used for the 68000-based microcomputer. However, on the 68000, both the $\overline{RESET}$ and $\overline{HALT}$ pins are tied together (see Figure 10.7). Figure 10.8 shows the board layout of all the chips.

10.2.3.b Software

The first major feature of the software is the inclusion of a start-up routine. The advantage of the start-up routine is to visibly verify the system

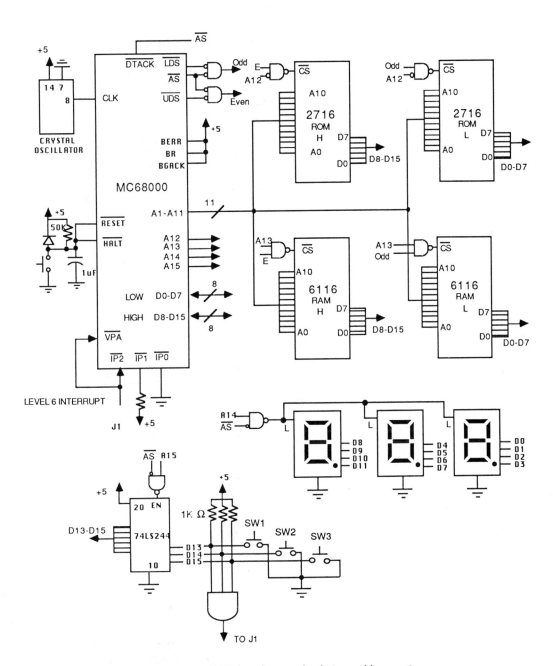

FIGURE 10.7 68000-based system for design problem no. 2.

performance. For example, if one of the displays malfunctions, the fault will not be known unless the user is able to see the display patterns. This requirement leads to the development of a start-up routine in which all

ROM CONNECTIONS

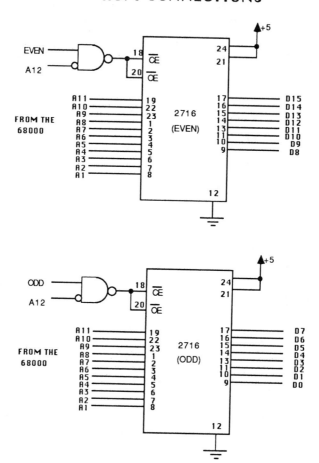

FIGURE 10.7 continued.

three displays count F down to 0 (in parallel). This routine uses a DBF loop in which the counter's value is duplicated to the two higher hex digits. The following is the actual start-up routine implemented in the program.

```
      MOVEQ   #0FH,D0      ;INITIALIZE LOOP COUNTER
                           ; TO $0000000F
LOOP  MOVE.W  D0,D1        ;COPY D0 TO D1
      ASL.W   #4,D1        ;SHIFT D1 LEFT 4 TIMES
      ADD     D0,D1        ;ADD D0 TO D1
      ASL.W   #4,D1        ;SHIFT D1 LEFT 4 TIMES
```

RAM CONNECTIONS

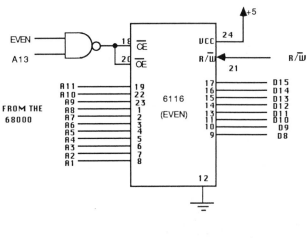

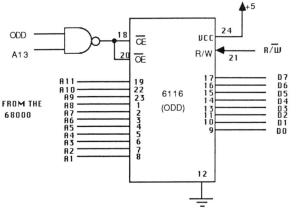

FIGURE 10.7 continued.

```
ADD.W    D0,D1           ;ADD D0 TO D1
MOVE.W   D1,DISPADDR     ;SEND RESULT TO DISPLAY
MOVE.L   #VISIBLE,D6     ;LOAD DELAY TIME
JSR      DELAY           ;CALL DELAY SUBROUTINE
DBF.W    D0,LOOP         ;DEC BRANCH IF D0 != -1,
                          NOT TO THE LOOP
CLR.L    D0              ;INITIALIZE COUNTER TO ZERO
CLR.L    D7              ;INITIALIZE MODE TO DECIMAL
MOVE.W   D0,DISPADDR     ;INITIALIZE DISPLAYS TO
                          ZERO
```

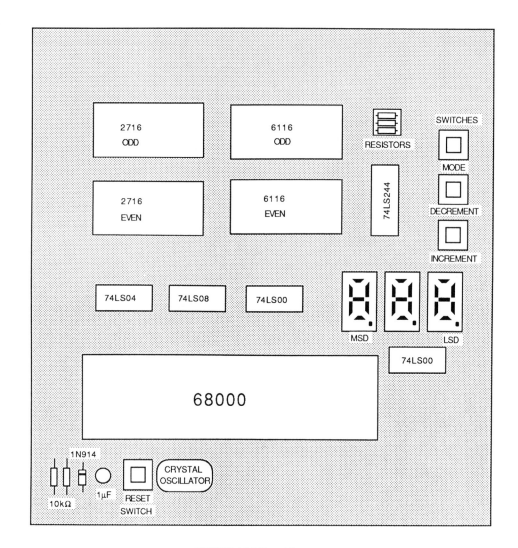

FIGURE 10.8 Board layout.

```
     MOVE.W  #INTRMASK,SR   ;SET INTR AT LEVEL 5 AND
                             SUPERVISOR MODE
WAIT BRA.B   WAIT            ;WAIT FOR INTERRUPT
```

Upon successful completion of the start-up routine, the software directs the 68000 to enter an infinite wait loop. The wait loop serves to occupy the 68000 until a level 6 interrupt signals the processor. Upon interrupt, SR is pushed and the PC is also stacked. The 68000 accesses the long word located at address $78 and jumps to that service routine. The service routine exists at location $500. In response to the interrupt, the software directs the 68000 to move in the status switches to the low word of D0. A "C"-type priority case statement executes.

The case statement has the priority of up, down, then mode. Implementation of the case statement eliminates uncertainties when multiple keys are depressed. In the following, the case statement is shown.

```
RESPONSE NOP                           ;ENTRY NO OPERATION
         MOVE.W    STATUS,D1           ;MOVE  IN  BUTTON  STATUS
                                        WORD
         BTST.W    #UPBIT,D1           ;TEST  INCREMENT  BIT
         BEQ.W     INCREASE            ;IF UPBIT=0  BRANCH  TO
                                        INCREASE
         BTST.W    #DOWNBIT,D1         ;TEST  DECREMENT  BIT
         BEQ.W     DECREASE            ;IF  DOWNBIT=0  BRANCH  TO
                                        DECREASE
         BTST.W    #MODEBIT,D1         ;TEST MODEBIT
         BEQ.B     CHMODE,D1           ;IF  MODEBIT=0  BRANCH  TO
                                        CHANGE  MODE
         BRA.B     RESPONSE            ;NO  RESPONSE,  THEN
                                        SEARCH  AGAIN
```

This segment utilizes the test bit facilities of the 68000. The algorithm first loads the status switches. The status word is then tested by the BTST instruction. The first bit test is the upbit. If the bit is found to be 0, the program will branch to an increase-update routine. If the downbit is found to be low, then the program reacts to decrement the displays. If the mode bit is found low, then the response is the base conversion of the displayed output.

The user may be tempted to indefinitely press a button or press multiple buttons. The habit is permissible. The program implements a 0.4-second wait loop at the end of any press of a key. This is a post-debounce. Without this feature, the 68000 will either count or change modes at speeds beyond recognition. The debounce routine also contains a priority. If the user constantly depresses multiple keys, the 68000 will service the input with the highest priority.

At this point, a deviation of the problem was made. The deviation was the ease of checking out the project. During checkout, when one wants to see a rollover, the increment or decrement key must be pressed 255 times. This is futile. At the end of the service routine, the software will not lock out a key entry, but rather the 68000 will immediately go to the wait state where the next interrupt may take place. To the user, it will appear that the 68000 is either autoincrementing, autodecrementing, or automatically changing modes. The post-debounce segment is displayed below.

```
VIEWER  NOP                          ;ENTRY NO OPERATION
        MOVE.1   #VISIBLE,D6         ;PLACE DELAY INTO D6
        JSR      DELAY               ;JUMP TO DELAY SUBROU-
                                        TINE
        RTE                          ;RETURN FROM EXCEPTION
DELAY   NOP                          ;ENTRY NO OPERATION
        DBF.W    D6,DELAY            ;DECREMENT FOR WAIT
        RTS                          ;RETURN FROM SUBROUTINE
```

The debounce routine implements a dummy loop that utilizes a large loop count. The routine is initialized by an immediate move long to D6. The debounce routine is called via the jump subroutine command. The delay loop contains a no-operation to increase loop time. After the NOP, the DBF.W will decrement D6 and branch if D6 is not equal to negative 1.

The software uses a hex base for counting; that is, all numbers whether decimal or hex will originate from a hex byte in data register 0 (D0). The display status exists in data register 7 (D7). If the contents of D7 are zero, this informs the program to display a decimal number on the next update. Otherwise, the program will send a hex value to the display. A typical decision-making segment (below) uses the 68000's ability to update flags on a move operation.

```
MOVE.   D7,D7        ;MOVE TO UPDATE FLAGS
BNE.B   HEX          ;IF Z=0 THEN SEND HEX TO DISPLAYS
BRA.B   DECIMAL      ;OTHERWISE, DECIMAL TO DISPLAYS
```

To convert a hex number to decimal format, the program uses the division/modulo algorithm shown in the following.

```
DECIMAL  NOP                      ;ENTRY NO OPERATION
         CLR.L    D2              ;INITIALIZE D2 TO ZERO
         CLR.L    D1              ;INITIALIZE D1 TO ZERO
         MOVE.B   D0,D1           ;COPY COUNT
         DIVU     #10,D1          ;DIVIDE D1 BY 10 MSD HEX →
                                     DECIMAL
         SWAP     D1              ;PLACE REMAINDER IN LOW
                                     WORD D1
```

```
        MOVE.W   D1,D2        ;MOVE REMAINDER TO D2
        CLR.W    D1           ;CLEAR REMAINDER
        SWAP     D1           ;REPLACE REMAINDER
        DIVU     #10,D1       ;DIVIDE D1 BY 10
        SWAP     D1           ;REMAINDER TO LOW WORD
                                D1
        ASL.W    #4,D1        ;SHIFT REMAINDER UP ONE
                                DIGIT
        ADD.W    D1,D2        ;ADD IN SECOND SIG FIG
        SWAP     D1           ;REPLACE QUOTIENT
        ASL.W    #4,D1        ;SHIFT QUOTIENT UP ONE
                                DIGIT
        ASL.W    #4,D1        ;SHIFT QUOTIENT ANOTHER
                                DIGIT
        ADD      D1,D2        ;ADD IN LSD HEX → DECI-
                                MAL
        MOVE.W   D2,DISPADDR  ;SEND DECIMAL RESULTS TO
                                DISPLAY
        BRA.W    VIEWER       ;GO TO DISPLAY BRANCH
```

The algorithm exploits the DIVU (unsigned division) facilities of the 68000. The hex byte is moved to a long word register with zero-extend (assumed by CLR.L followed by a MOVE.B operation). The number is then divided by 10. The quotient remains in the low word of the destination register (D1); the remainder lies in the high word. With the use of SWAP, the remainder and quotient words are swapped. The remainder is moved (MOVE.W D1,D2) to another register D2 (initialized to zero). At this point, the remainder is cleared in D1, and swap is used to replace the quotient in the low word of D1. The next lower significant digit is extracted. Again, DIVU uses an immediate source of 10. The remainder in D1 is swapped into the low word, shifted up four times, then added to D2. The quotient is swapped back to the low word, shifted left eight times, then added to D2. The result of this routine is (at most) a three-digit BCD number which is suitable to send to the displays.

After the update of the displays, a time delay subroutine allows execution delays from the order of microseconds to the order of seconds. The time delay subroutine is shown below.

```
DELAY   NOP                  ;ENTRY NO OPERATION
        DBF.W   D6,DELAY     ;DECREMENT FOR WAIT
        RTS                  ;RETURN FROM SUBROUTINE
```

The NOP serves to increase the delay time of the loop. The NOP takes 4 clock cycles. DBF.W (decrement and branch on false) takes 10 clocks on a branch and 14 on a skip. JSR (jump subroutine) to the delay takes 23 cycles. The time analysis is simplified when consideration is taken into the duration of the delay. A suitable delay for this project is about 0.4 s. This equates to (4-MHz clock) 1.6 million clock cycles! Because of the high number of cycles required, the "calls" and "returns" can be avoided because of their insignificance when compared to the massive number of clock delays required. A delay of about 0.4 s is used, which requires about 100,000 loops in the delay routine.

Some mention should be made of the mode features of the software. The change mode allows the user to liberally change the viewing format from hex to BCD or vice versa. The activation of this software feature simply complements D7 and then updates the displays via the previously mentioned methods. The increment facility increments D0 and updates the displays. Similarly, the decrement facility decrements D0 and updates the displays.

Expansion of the system is possible. Maybe for user entertainment, an uptone or downtone can be implemented. The tone can be generated through a variable delay routine. One of the address lines may be tied in series to a small speaker and every time the address is accessed, the speaker will "tick". Otherwise, the software, as it is, is suitable for the project. A listing of the assembly language program is provided below:

```
"68000"
;
; Microcomputer Applications
; M. Rafiquzzaman
; November 9, 1987
;
;
;  This is the software routine for Design Problem
; No. 2
;  THE BCD<>HEX COUNTER
;  Language is 68000 MACRO
;
;
           NAME      BCD<>HEX_COUNTER
AUTO6      EQU       00000074H          ;SERVICE ROUTINE ADDRESS
                                         LOCATION
TSTACK     EQU       000037FCH          ;STACK INITIALIZE
RESPONSE   EQU       00000500H          ;INTERRUPT  VECTOR
                                         ADDRESS
```

```
        DISPADDR    EQU     00005000H       ;ADDRESS OF DISPLAY
        PCINIT      EQU     00000400H       ;PC STARTUP ADDRESS
        VISIBLE     EQU     00100000H       ;DELAY TIME APPROX. 0.4
                                             SECONDS
        UPBIT       EQU     0FH             ;INCREMENT BIT LOCATION
        DOWNBIT     EQU     0EH             ;DECREMENT BIT LOCATION
        MODEBIT     EQU     0DH             ;MODE BIT LOCATION
        STATUS      EQU     00009000H       ;STATUS WORD LOCATION
        INSTRMSK    EQU     2500H           ;INTERRUPT MASK, LEVEL 7
        ;
        ; Top of the stack, program origin, and interrupt service
        ; location
        ;
                    ORG     00000000H       ;STARTUP
                    DC.L    TSTACK          ;INITIAL SUPERVISOR
                    DC.L    PCINIT          ;FIRST PROGRAM INSTR LOC
                    ORG     AUTO6           ;LOCATION OF AUTOVECTOR
                                             RESPONSE
                    DC.L    RESPONSE        ;ADDRESS OF SERVICE
                                             ROUTINE 5
                    DC.L    RESPONSE        ;ADDRESS OF SERVICE
                                             ROUTINE 6
                    DC.L    RESPONSE        ;ADDRESS OF SERVICE
                                             ROUTINE NMI
        ;
        ; Startup routine
        ;
                    ORG     PCINIT          ;BOOTUP AND TEST ROUTINE
                    NOP                     ;ENTRY NO OPERATION
                    MOVEQ   #0FH,D0         ;INITIALIZE LOOP
                                             COUNTER TO $0000000F
LOOP                MOVE.W  D0,D1           ;COPY D0 TO D1
                    ASL.W   #4,D1           ;SHIFT D1 LEFT FOUR TIMES
                    ADD.W   D0,D1           ;ADD D0 TO D1
                    ASL.W   #4,D1           ;SHIFT D1 LEFT FOUR TIMES
                    ADD.W   D0,D1           ;ADD D0 TO D1
                    MOVE.W  D1,DISPADDR     ;SEND RESULT TO DISPLAY
                    MOVE.L  #VISIBLE,D6     ;LOAD DELAY TIME
                    JSR     DELAY           ;CALL DELAY SUBROUTINE
                    DBF     D0,LOOP         ;DEC BRANCH IF D0 != -1,
                                             NOT TO LOOP
                    CLR.L   D0              ;INITIALIZE COUNTER TO
                                             ZERO
                    CLR.L   D7              ;INITIALIZE MODE TO ZERO
                    MOVE.W  D0,DISPADDR     ;INITIALIZE DISPLAYS TO
                                             ZERO
                    MOVE.W  #INTRMASK, SR   ;SET INTR AT 5 AND SUPER
                                             MODE
```

```
WAIT          BRA.B    WAIT                 ;WAIT FOR INTERRUPT
;
; INTERRUPT ROUTINE
;
              ORG      RESPONSE
RESPONSE      NOP                           ;ENTRY NO OPERATION
              MOVE.W   STATUS,D1            ;MOVE IN BUTTON STATUS
                                             WORD
              BTST.W   #UPBIT,D1            ;TEST INCREMENT BIT
              BEQ.W    INCREASE             ;IF UPBIT=0 THEN BRANCH
                                             TO INCREASE
              BTST.W   #DOWNBIT,D1          ;TEST DECREMENT BIT
              BEQ.W    DECREASE             ;IF DOWNBIT=0 BRANCH TO
                                             DECREASE
              BTST.W   #MODEBIT,D1          ;TEST MODEBIT
              BEQ.B    CHMODE,D1            ;IF MODEBIT=0 THEN
                                             BRANCH TO CHANGE MODE
              BRA.B    RESPONSE             ;NO RESPONSE, THEN
                                             SEARCH AGAIN
;
; Change mode and update displays
;
CHMODE        NOP                           ;ENTRY NO OPERATION
              EORI.B   #0FFH,D7             ;COMPLEMENT MODE MASK
              BNE.B    HEX                  ;IF EORI IS NOT ZERO
                                             THEN HEX OUT
              BRA.B    DECIMAL              ;EORI IS ZERO, THEN
                                             DECIMAL OUT
;
; Increment display count
;
INCREASE      NOP                           ;ENTRY NO OPERATION
              ADDQ.B   #1,D0                ;INCREMENT THE COUNT D0
              MOVE.B   D7,D7                ;MOVE TO UPDATE FLAGS
              BNE.B    HEX                  ;IF Z=0 THEN SEND HEX
                                             TO DISPLAYS
              BRA.B    DECIMAL              ;OTHERWISE, DECIMAL TO
                                             DISPLAYS
;
; Decrement display count
;
DECREASE      NOP                           ;ENTRY NO OPERATION
              SUBQ.B   #1,D0                ;DECREMENT COUNT
              MOVE.B   D7,D7                ;MOVE TO UPDATE FLAGS
              BNE.B    HEX                  ;IF Z=0 THEN SEND HEX
                                             TO DISPLAYS
              BRA.B    DECIMAL              ;OTHERWISE, DECIMAL
                                             DISPLAYS
```

```
        ; This routine sends hex contents of D0 to the displays
        ;
HEX         NOP                         ;ENTRY NO OPERATION
            MOVE.W  D0,DISPADDR         ;HEX DATA IS SENT TO
                                         DISPLAYS
            BRA.W   VIEWER              ;GO TO DELAY BRANCH
        ;
        ; HEX → Decimal converter
        ;
DECIMAL     NOP                         ;ENTRY NO OPERATION
            CLR.L   D2                  ;INITIALIZE D2 TO ZERO
            CLR.L   D1                  ;INITIALIZE D1 TO ZERO
            MOVE.B  D0,D1               ;COPY COUNT
            DIVU    #10,D1              ;DIVIDE D1 BY 10 MSD
                                         HEX → DECIMAL
            SWAP    D1                  ;PLACE REMAINDER IN LOW
                                         WORD D1
            MOVE.W  D1,D2               ;MOVE REMAINDER TO D2
            CLR.W   D1                  ;CLEAR REMAINDER
            SWAP    D1                  ;REPLACE REMAINDER
            DIVU    #10,D1              ;DIVIDE D1 BY 10
            SWAP    D1                  ;REMAINDER TO LOW WORD D1
            ASL.W   #4,D1               ;SHIFT REMAINDER UP ONE
                                         DIGIT
            ADD.W   D1,D2               ;ADD IN SECOND SIG FIG
            SWAP    D1                  ;REPLACE QUOTIENT
            ASL.W   #4,D1               ;SHIFT QUOTIENT UP ONE
                                         DIGIT
            ASL.W   #4,D1               ;SHIFT QUOTIENT ANOTHER
                                         DIGIT
            ADD     D1,D2               ;ADD IN LSD HEX →
                                         DECIMAL
            MOVE.W  D2,DISPADDR         ;SEND DECIMAL RESULTS
                                         TO DISPLAY
            BRA.W   VIEWER              ;GO TO DISPLAY BRANCH
        ;
        ; This sends output to displays and implements delay of 0.7
        ;   seconds
        ;
VIEWER      NOP                         ;ENTRY NO OPERATION
            MOVE.L  #VISIBLE,D6         ;PLACE ENTRY INTO D6
            JSR     DELAY               ;JUMP TO DELAY
                                         SUBROUTINE
            RTE                         ;RETURN FROM EXCEPTION
        ;
        ; Delay subroutine
        ;
DELAY       NOP                         ;ENTRY NO OPERATION
```

```
DBF.B       D6,DELAY            ;DECREMENT FOR WAIT
RTS                             ;RETURN FROM SUBROUTINE
```

The following shows 68000 Delay Analysis:

```
        MOVE.L    #VISIBLE,D6       ;MOVE IN DELAY LOOP
                                     COUNT
        JSR       DELAY             ;CALL SUBROUTINE TO
                                     DELAY LOOP
DELAY   NOP                         ;TIME DELAY INCREASE
                                     LOOP
        DBF       D6,DELAY          ;DECREMENT BRANCH FALSE
        RTS                         ;RETURN SUBROUTINE
```

Execution Time:

```
        MOVE.L    #REG          12        CLOCKS
        JSR       ADDR          10        CLOCKS
        NOP                     4         CLOCKS
        DBF       REG,ADDR      14/10     CLOCKS
        RTS                     16        CLOCKS
```

First Pass: t1 = 12 + 20 + 4 + 14 = 50 CLOCKS

Middle Pass: t(n–2) = (n – 2) (4 + 14) CLOCKS

Last Pass: tn = 4 + 10 + 16 = 30 CLOCKS

General Pass: (for n > 3)

$$\Sigma t = 50 + (n - 2)(18) + 30$$
$$= 18n + 44$$

Typical Pass: (for large n)

$$\lim_{n \to \infty} (18n + 44) = 18n \text{ for large } n$$

For 0.45-s delay with a 4-MHz clock, 1.8 million clock cycles are required (0.45 s was chosen for ease of calculations).
Therefore,

$$18n = 1,800,000$$
$$n = 100,000$$

Figure 10.9 shows the flowchart for the start-up routine.

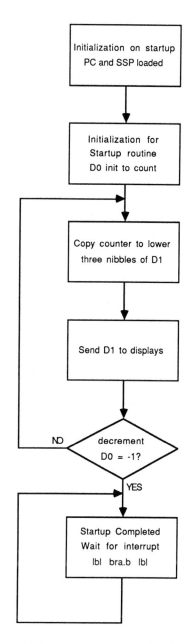

FIGURE 10.9 Start-up routine flowchart.

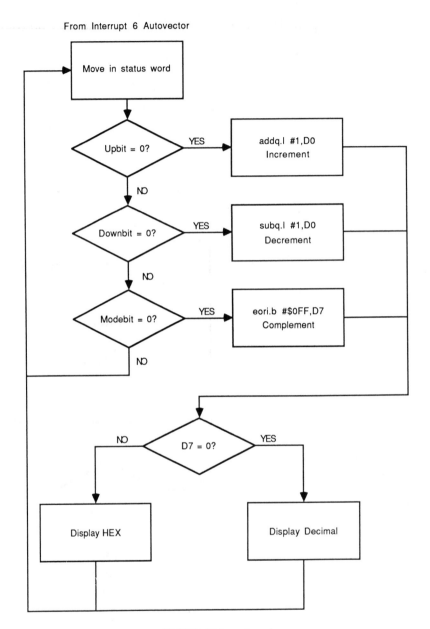

FIGURE 10.9 continued.

QUESTIONS AND PROBLEMS

Design and develop the software and hardware for the following using a particular microprocessor and its support chips with a microcomputer development system of your choice.

10.1 i)   Design and develop the hardware and software for a micropro-cessor-based system that would measure, compute, and display the Root-Mean-Square (RMS) value of a sinusoidal voltage. The system is required to:

    1. Sample a 60-Hz sinusoidal voltage 128 times.

    2. Digitize the sampled value through a microprocessor-controlled analog-to-digital converter.

    3. Input the digitized value to the microprocessor using interrupt.

    4. Compute the RMS value of the waveform using the equation RMS value = 1.11 × average value.

    5. Display the RMS value using two digits.

  ii)   Repeat Problem i) using the algorithm

$$\text{RMS value} = \sqrt{\dfrac{\Sigma X i^{2}}{N}}$$

where Xi's are the samples and N is the total number of samples.

10.2 Design a microcomputer-based capacitance meter using the following RC circuit:

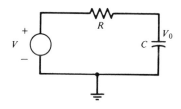 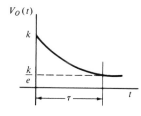

The voltage across the capacitor is $V0(t) = ke^{-t/RC}$. In one time con-stant RC, this voltage is discharged to the value k/e. For a specific value of R, the value of the capacitor C = τ/R, where τ is the time constant that can be counted by the microcomputer. Design the hardware and software for a microprocessor to charge a capacitor by using a pulse to a voltage of up to 10 V peak voltage via an amplifier. The microcomputer will then stop charging the capacitor, measure the discharge time for one time constant, and compute the capacitor value.

10.3 Design and develop the hardware and software for a microprocessor-based system to drive a four-digit seven-segment display for displaying a number from 0000H to FFFFH.

10.4 Design a microprocessor-based digital clock to display time in hours, minutes, and seconds on six-digit seven-segment displays in decimal.

10.5 Design a microcomputer-based temperature sensor. The microcomputer will measure the temperature of a thermistor. The thermistor controls the timing pulse duration of a monostable multivibrator. By using a counter to convert the timing pulse to a decimal count, the microcomputer will display the temperature in degrees Celsius.

10.6 Design a microprocessor-based system to test five different types of IC, namely, OR, NOR, AND, NAND, and XOR. The system will apply inputs to each chip and read the output. It will then compare the output with the truth table stored inside the memory. If the comparison passes, a red LED will be turned OFF. If the comparison fails, the red LED will be turned ON.

10.7 Design a microprocessor-based system that reads a thermistor via an A/D converter and then displays the temperature in degrees Celsius on three seven-segment displays.

10.8 Design a microprocessor-based system to measure the power absorbed by the 1K resistor. The system will input the voltage V across the 1K resistor and then compute the power using V^2/R.

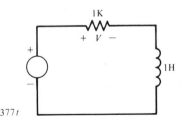

10 sin 377*t*

10.9   It is desired to design a priority vectored interrupt system using a daisy-chain structure for a microcomputer. Assume that the system includes four interrupt devices DEV0, DEV1, ..., DEV3, which, during the interrupt sequence, place the respective instructions RST0, RST1, ..., RST3 on the data bus. Also assume that DEV0, ..., DEV3 are Teledyne 8703 A/D converters (DEV3 highest, DEV0 lowest priority) or equivalent.

i) Flowchart the problem to provide service routines for inputting the A/D converters' outputs.

ii) Design and develop the hardware and software.

10.10 It is desired to drive a six-digit display through six output lines of a microcomputer system. Use eight Texas Instruments TIL311, 14-pin MSI hexadecimal displays or equivalent:

i)   Design the interface with minimum hardware.

ii)   Flowchart the software.

iii)   Convert the flowchart to the assembly language program.

iv)   Implement the hardware and software.

10.11 Design a microcomputer-based combinational lock which has a combination of five digits. The five digits are entered from a hexadecimal keyboard and they are to be entered within 10 s. If the right combination is entered within the same limit, the lock will open. If after 10 s either all five digits are not entered or a wrong combination is entered, then the display will show an error signal by displaying "E". The system will allow 5 s for the first digit to be entered the second time. If after this time the digit is not entered, the system will turn ON the alarm. If the second try fails, the alarm is also turned ON. When the alarm is ON, in order to reset the system, power has to be turned OFF.

10.12 Design a microcomputer-based stopwatch. The stopwatch will operate in the following way: the operator enters three digits (two digits for minutes and one digit for tenths of minutes) from a keyboard and then presses the GO key. The system counts down the remaining time on three seven-segment LED displays.

10.13 Design a microcomputer-based system as shown in the following diagram.The system scans a 16-key keyboard and drives three seven-segment displays. The keyboard is scanned in a 4 × 4 X-Y matrix. The system will take each key pressed and scroll them in from the right side of the displays and keep scrolling as each key is pressed. The leftmost digit is just discarded. The system continues indefinitely.

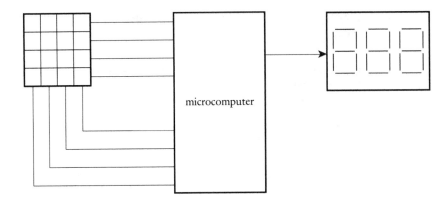

10.14 Design a microcomputer-based smart scale. The scale will measure the weight of an object in the range of 0-5 lb. The scale will use a load cell as a sensor such as the one manufactured by transducer, Inc. (Model # c462-10#-10pl strain-gage load cell). This load cell converts a weight in the range of 0-10 lb. into analog electrical voltage in the range 0-20 mV. The weight in lbs. should be displayed onto two BCD displays.

10.15 Design a microcomputer-based EPROM programmer to program 2716.

10.16 Design a microcomputer-based system to control a stepper motor.

10.17 Design a microcomputer-based sprinkler control system.

10.18 Design a phone call controller. The controller will allow the user to pass only ten random phone numbers chosen by the user. The controller will use the touch-tone frequencies to encode the user information code numbers. A device will be used to decode the touch-tone signals and convert them into a seven-bit word. A microprocessor will then interpret this word and see if it is a match with one of the ten different numbers chosen by the user. The ten numbers are inputted by the user via the * button from the touch-tone system. The controller will have a manual override via the # button from the touch-tone system.

10.19 Design a microprocessor-based appointment reminder system with a clock. The system will alert the user before the present appointment time. The user has to set the appointments into fixed slots; for example: 9 AM or 2 PM. The system will deliver a voice message such as "Your next appointment is five minutes away" five minutes before the appointment time. A real time is to be included in the system to display the current time and will show the appointment time slots. You may use the Radio Shack SP0256 narrator speech processor.

10.20 Design a microcomputer-based autoranged ohmmeter with a range of 1 ohm to 999 kohm as follows: the microcomputer generates a pulse to charge a capacitor up to 10 V peak voltage through an amplifier and then stops charging the capacitor. The microcomputer measures the discharge time of the capacitor for one time constant and then computes the value of the resistor.

10.21 Interface two microcomputers to a pair 2K × 8 dual-ported RAMs (IDT7132) without using any bus locking mechanism. Two seven-segment displays will serve as an indicator. A program will be written to verify the dual-ported RAM contents. One processor will write some known data to the dual-ported RAM and the other processor will read and verify this data against the known data.

10.22 Design a microcomputer-based low frequency (1 Hz to 10 kHz) sine waveform generator. One cycle of a sine wave will be divided into a certain amount of equal intervals. Each interval is defined as a phase increment. The precalculated sine values corresponding to the intervals are stored in ROM. The frequency of the signal will be set up by switches. When the system is started, the microprocessor will read the switches and will determine the time delay corresponding to the phase increment. The microprocessor will follow the time increments to send data to a D/A converter to convert the digital signal to an analog signal.

10.23 Design a microcomputer-based automobile alarm system. The purpose of this system is to prevent intruders from stealing a car or having enough time to steal a stereo or other valuable items in a car.

10.24 Design a microcomputer-based three-axis robot controller. The microcomputer will perform the calculations and the I/O to control movement of the arm. The microcomputer will receive destination data from an external source and perform coordinate transformations and boundary checking on the external data. It will then provide motor commands to the motor controllers to move the arm to the desired position.

10.25 Design a microcomputer-based home controller system. The system will simultaneously control six sprinkler stations, a heater, an air conditioner, and a burglar alarm. The system will contain a 12-hour clock and a temperature reader. The user will program the system through a keypad. The time and temperature will be entered to control the sprinklers, the heater, and the A/C. The alarm will be armed or disarmed by entering a 4-digit code.

10.26 Design a microcomputer-based FM modulator. The microcomputer will read an analog input, convert the signal to digital, and perform several data manipulations to generate a digital representation of the FM signal. Finally, the microcomputer will convert the FM value to an analog signal.

10.27 Design and develop a microcomputer-based system for FFT (Fast Fourier Transform) computation. The microcomputer will sample eight data points using an A/D converter and compute the time-decimation FFT. After computation of FFT, the result will be stored in system RAM where it can be used by another program for signal processing.

APPENDICES

THE HEWLETT-PACKARD (HP) 64000

A.1 System Description

The HP 64000 Microprocessor Logic Development System is a universal development system which provides all of the necessary tools to create, develop, modify, and debug software for microprocessor-based systems. In-circuit emulation provides the capability of performing an in-depth analysis of hardware and software interfacing during the integration phase of the development process.

The HP 64000 Microprocessor Logic Development System is a multi-user development system, allowing up to as many as six users to operate on the system simultaneously. All users of the system share a line printer and a common data base in the form of a 12-megabyte Winchester Technology Disc Drive or a selection of one to eight Multi-Access Controller (MAC) disk drives connected to the system via the HP Interface Bus, commonly referred to as HP-IB. Eight disk drives can provide up to 960 metabytes of HP-formatted storage space.

A.2 Development Station Description

Figure A.1 shows the front view of the HP 64000 Development Station. The keyboard (Figure A.2) is divided into four areas: (1) an ASCII-encoded typewriter-type keyboard; (2) a group of edit keys, which facilitate movement of text or cursor when in the edit mode; (3) special function keys, for system reset or pause or to access a command recall buffer; (4) the all important system "soft keys," eight unobtrusive large key pads just beneath the bezel which surrounds the display.

The soft keys provide a quick and easy means to invoke system commands, virtually eliminating the typographical errors one usually has to contend with when having to enter commands character by character. The definition of each soft key is written on the display just above the bezel. The soft key syntax changes depending on the mode of operation and the

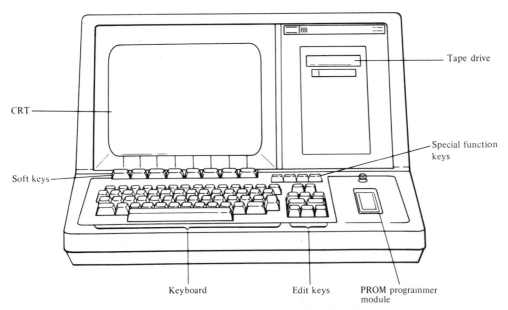

Figure A.1   Front view of the HP 64000 Development Station (Model 64100A). Front Panel: The seven major areas of the front panel are shown. Each area provides the interface necessary to operate and control the system. CRT Display: The CRT is a large-screen, raster-scan magnetic display. Screen capacity is 25 rows and 80 columns of characters. The standard 128-character (upper and lower case) ASCII set can be displayed. A blinking underline cursor is present as the prompt. Video enhancements are inverse video, blinking, and underline. Soft Keys: Just below the CRT are eight unlabeled keys. These keys are defined as the "soft keys." Each key ties to the soft key label line at the bottom of the CRT. During operation, the soft keys are labeled on the CRT screen. Source: Courtesy of Hewlett-Packard.

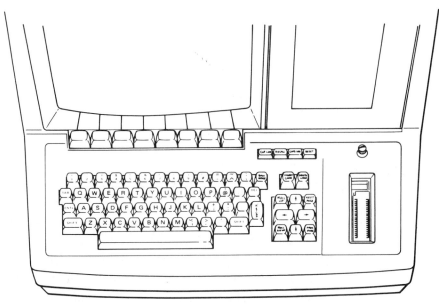

Figure A.2 Model 64100A keyboard. Source: Courtesy of Hewlett-Packard.

position of the cursor. This greatly enhances the ease of use of the system since it provides a list of alternatives available and guides the operator to use the system. In cases where the form of the input required is unknown, brackets surrounding a key word, a syntactical variable will prompt the user with the correct form of input the system expects.

The system display is a Raster Scan CRT which provides a display of 18 lines of text entry, a status line which always displays the system's status and date and time, three lines for command entry, and the soft key label line which indicates the function of each key. The display is 80 columns wide, but with the edit keys the display can be relocated to show text or data out to 240 columns. This is convenient for adding comments and really enhances the program documentation.

Other external station hardware includes RS232 ports for communication with either Data Communications Equipment (DCE) or Data Terminal Equipment (DTE). The RS232 port has a selectable baud rate up to 9,600 and uses the X-ON X-OFF convention for handshaking at baud rates 2,400 and above. There is a 20-mA current loop for TTY interfacing and two ports for triggering of external devices such as an oscilloscope during a logic trace. As system options, the front panel hosts a PROM programmer (Figure A.1) to the immediate right of the keyboard and a tape drive for file back-up. The tape drive performs a high-speed read and write and each cassette holds 250K bytes of data.

Figure A.3 shows special function keys and Table A.1 summarizes their functions.

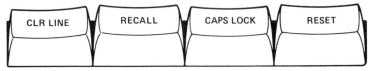

Figure A.3   Special function keys. Source: Courtesy of Hewlett-Packard.

Table A.1   Summary of Special Functions Keys

CLR LINE	Press to clear the current line containing cursor on the CRT.
RECALL	Used to recall, to the command line, previous commands from a stack. The commands are displayed one at a time for each time the RECALL key is pressed. The number of recallable commands is variable. Only valid commands are pushed into the stack. If the RECALL key is pressed and the buffer is empty the system responds with "Recall buffer is empty" message.
CAPS LOCK	Used to lock keyboard in all uppercase letters. A message is presented on the CRT indicating "CAPS LOCK on" or "CAPS LOCK off." At the next key stroke, the message is erased, but the mode remains in effect.
RESET	Pressing RESET once initiates a pause in system operation. A flashing "PAUSED" message, in inverse video, is presented on the status line. To continue operation, press any key except RESET .
	Pressing the RESET key the second time will clear the CRT and return the system to the system monitor.
SHIFT RESET	Holding the SHIFT key down and pressing RESET initiates a complete system reboot. This function should be regarded as a last resort when the system does not respond.
CNTL RESET	Holding CNTL key down and pressing RESET initiates system performance verification.

Source: Courtesy of Hewlett-Packard.

The following summarizes the HP 64000 soft keys, commands, assembler error codes, and other features.

System Monitor Soft Keys

The following provides a description of the system monitor soft keys:

userid	The userid or user identification identifies each user as being unique within the system. This facilitates file management in that once the userid command is invoked all future references to files will be to files within that userid unless explicitly stated otherwise. The HP 64000 uses six characters and must begin with an uppercase alpha character.
time	HH:MM. Allows the user to enter the correct time on the 24-hour clock displayed on the status line. This also facilitates file management since files can be referenced by time and date.
date	DD/MM/YY. (Day/Month/Year) Allows the user to enter the correct date into the system. This aids the file management system since files can be referenced by date and time.
store	This command will transfer files from the disk to the tape cartridge. The user specifies the file name and file type or all files. If all files are specified the system will store only the source files, linker command files, and emulator command files. Other file types may be stored but the file type must be specified. Other file types can readily be regenerated. This command will overwrite any previous contents of the tape cartridge.

append	Allows files to be appended to files previously stored on tape.
verify	Verify compares a file on the disk to a file resident on the tape cartridge. The user has the option of specifying a single file or all files on the tape assigned to the current userid.
restore	This command will transfer files from the tape cartridge to the disk. The user can specify file name or names and file type.
purge	This command will remove specified files from the active file list. A purged file can be recovered providing it has not been written over.
recover	Recover is used to recover files which have been purged. Files, if not written over, will be returned to the active file list.
rename	Allows the user to rename files. This is used to rename a file before recovering a previous file with the same name. This command also allows the user to transfer a file from one userid to another userid.
copy	Copy allows a disk file to be copied to, or from, the tape, display, or another file name or the RS232 port. The current display or a file may be copied to the printer.
directory	This command provides a listing of those files on the disk, the tape cartridge, and those recoverable files. The listing information consists of file name, file type, file size, last modified data, and last access date. Options: A directory can be made to include all userids, all types of files, before or after a specified date a file has been accessed or modified, and files on a specified disk unit.
library	This command is used to build libraries of relocatable files for use by the linker. These library files consist of relocatable files to be selectively loaded by the linker.
log	This creates a command file for all legal keystrokes. The log function is either toggled on or off by the "log" soft key.
(CMD_FILE)	This soft key represents a syntactical variable to be supplied by the user. This variable is a file name consisting of system commands which the development system will execute. A command file can be generated through the use of the editor or by using the log soft key.

Editor Commands

The 64000 editor commands are listed below:

revise	This mode is toggled ON and OFF and allows text to be modified. Modification may include character insertion or deletion. All appropriate command soft keys including "insert" are operational within the "revise" mode.
delete	This mode allows deletion of one line or a group of lines specified by the limit specified. The syntax "thru" includes deletion of the limit while the syntax "until" is not inclusive of the limit. The limit can be specified as a line #, string within a line, or as a start or end of text.
find	This command allows the user to search the text for the occurrence of the string. The find parameters include a (string) consisting of a single character or any combination of characters; (limit) allows the user to specify the boundaries of the search.
replace	This command allows text replacement of a string, a character, partial string with another character, string or partial string. There is an optional (limit) parameter that can specify boundaries of replacement.
(line #)	This command causes the line to become the current line of text.
end	This terminates the edit session and directs it to a specific destination. Usually this destination is a new file name. If no new file name is specified, the edit session terminates by purging the original file and replacing it with the edited file.
merge	Merge allows the user to merge an entire file or portions of it into the file being edited. Any text added to the file being edited will be added after the current line. Delimiters can be specified to determine the amount to be merged.
copy	Copy places specified text into a temporary storage buffer on disk for future use. The copy command will overwrite any text previously stored in the buffer. This is avoided by selecting the append option. The default value for (limit) is the current line only.
extract	This command removes the specified lines and places them into temporary storage space. If the append option is not selected, the extracted text will overwrite previously stored text. If (limit) is not specified, the current line will be extracted.

retrieve	This command retrieves the text from temporary storage and inserts into the program following the current line. The user has the option regarding the number of times the text is to be retrieved.
insert	This allows insertion of a combination of ASCII characters, after the current line of text. Insert is executable in the command mode, revise and insert mode.
list	This allows the user to list a file to another file or to a printer in numbered or unnumbered format. The listing will be exactly like the file text. There is also a (limit) option available.
renumber	This command renumbers the edited text starting from line one.
repeat	Repeat allows the user to duplicate the current line of text and add it immediately after the current line. The user can specify the number of times the repeat command is executed.
tabset	This command allows the user to set tabs in the desired column. The user has the choice of all 240 columns. Any character can be used to set tabs in any desired location.
range	Range restricts the columns to which find and replace commands are constrained. Columns 1 through 240 can be specified. The range function is toggled ON and OFF. When ON, the label range displays in inverse video.
autotab	This function provides an automatic tab function that is based on the first nonblank column of the previous line of text. Depressing the shift and the tab keys simultaneously allows tab back from autotab position.

Assembler Soft Key Definitions

The following provides the definitions of the 64000 assembler soft keys.

Key Label	Definition
(FILE)	This indicates the name of the source file that will be assembled.
listfile	This soft key specifies the destination of the assembler's output. The options available are listing the output to a specified file, to the display, to the printer, or to null (no generation of a list). If no list file option is specified, the assembler output listing defaults to the device previously specified by the user when the userid was declared.

options	This soft key provides the user with a selection of five options specifying the type of output listing.
list	This provides a listing of the source program excluding macro or data expansion. All no list pseudoinstructions in the source code are ignored.
nolist	Selection of this soft key provides no listing except error messages. All list pseudoinstructions in the source code are ignored.
expand	This soft key lists all source and macro generated codes. All list pseudoinstructions in the source program are ignored.
nocode	This option causes the source program to be assembled without placing it in a relocatable file.
xref	The selection of this option turns on the symbol cross-reference feature of the assembler and lists this table.

Assembler Pseudoinstructions

Pseudoinstructions are instructions used only by the assembler. They produce no executable code for the processor and normally do not take up any memory locations. They are used by the assembler to make programming easier. The following list contains those pseudo ops and their definitions supported by the HP 64000 assembler.

Op Code	Function
ASC	Stores data in memory in ASCII format.
BIN	Stores data in memory in binary format.
COMN	Assigns common block of data or code to a specific location in memory.
DATA	Assigns data to a specific location in memory.
DEC	Stores data in memory in decimal format.
END	Terminates the logical end of a program module. Operand field can be used to indicate starting address in memory for program execution.
EQU	Defines label field with operand field value. Symbol cannot be redefined.
EXPAND	Causes an output listing of all source and macro generated codes.
EXT	Indicates symbol defined in another program module.
GLB	Defines a global symbol that is used by other modules.
HEX	Stores data in memory in hexadecimal format.
LIST	Used to modify output listing of program.

MASK | Performs and/or logical operations on designated ASCII string.
NAME | Permits user to add comments for reference in the linker list.
NOLIST | Suppresses output listings (except error messages).
ORG | Sets program counter to specific memory address for absolute programming.
PROG | Assigns source statements to a specific location in memory. Assembler default condition is "PROG" storage area.
REPT | Enables user to repeat a source statement any given number of times.
SKIP | Enables user to skip to a new page to continue program listing.
SPC | Enables user to generate blank lines within program listing.
TITLE | Enables user to create a text line at the top of each page listing for the source program.

The following pseudo ops are for the 8080 and 8085 assembler.

DB | Stores data in consecutive memory locations starting with the current setting of the program counter.
DS | Reserves the number of bytes of memory as indicated by the value in the operand field.
DW | The define word pseudo stores each 16-bit value in the operand field as an address with the least significant byte stored at the current setting of the program counter. The most significant is byte stored at the next higher location.

Assembler Error Codes

The following provides a description of the 64000 assembler error codes.

Error Code | **Definition**

AS | ASCII string; the length of the ASCII string was not valid or the string was not terminated properly.
CL | Conditional label: Syntax of a conditional macro source statement requires a conditional label that is missing.
DE | Definition error: Indicated symbol must be defined prior to its being referenced. Symbol may be defined later in the program sequence.

DS   Duplicate Symbol: Indicates that the noted symbol has been previously defined in the program. This occurs when the same symbol is equated to two values (using EQU directive) or when the same symbol labels two instructions.

DZ   Division by zero: Invalid mathematical operation resulting in the assembler trying to divide by zero.

EG   External Global: Externals cannot be defined as globals.

EO   External Overflow: Program module has too may external declarations (512 externals maximum).

ES   Expanded Source: Indicates insufficient input buffer area to perform macro expansion. It could be the result of too many arguments being specified for a parameter substitution, or too many symbols being entered into the macro definition.

ET   Expression Type: The resulting type of expression is invalid. Absolute expression was expected and not found or expression contains an illegal combination of relocatable types (refer to Chapter 2 of the *Assembler Manual* for rules and conventions).

IC   Illegal Constant: Indicates that the assembler encountered a constant that is not valid.

IE   Illegal Expression: Specified expression is either incomplete or an invalid term was found within the expression.

IO   Invalid Operand: Specified operand is either incomplete or inaccurately used for this operation. This occurs when an unexpected operand is encountered or the operand is missing. If the required operand is an expression, the error indicates that the first item in the operand field is illegal.

IP   Illegal Parameter: Illegal parameters in the macro header.

IS   Illegal Symbol: Syntax expected an identifier and encountered an illegal character or token.

LR   Legal Range: Address or displacement causes the location counter to exceed the maximum memory location of the instruction's addressing capability.

MC   Macro Condition: Relational (conditional) operator in macro is invalid.

MD   Macro Definition: Macro is called before being defined in the source file. Macro definition must precede the call.

ML   Macro Label: Label not found within the macro body.

MM   Missing Mend: Indicates that a macro definition with a missing mend directive was included in the program.

MO   Missing Operator: An arithmetic operator was expected but was not found.

MP   Mismatched Parenthesis: Missing right or left parenthesis.

MS   Macro Symbol: A local symbol within a macro body was not found.

NM   Nested Macro: A macro definition is not permitted within another macro.

PC   Parameter Call: Invalid parameter in macro header.

PE   Paremeter Error: An error has been detected in the macro parameter listed in the source statement.

RC   Repeat Call: Repeat cannot precede a macro call.

RM   Repeat Macro: The repeat pseudo operation code cannot precede a macro definition.

SE   Stack Error: Indicates that a statement or expression does not conform to the required syntax.

TR   Text Replacement: Indicates that the specified text replacement string is invalid.

UC   Undefined Conditional: Conditional operation code invalid.

UO   Undefined Operation code: Operation code encountered is not defined for the microprocessor, or the assembler disallows the operation to be processed in its current context. This occurs when the operation code is misspelled or an invalid delimiter follows the label field.

UP   Undefined Parameter: The parameter found in macro body was not included in the macro header.

US   Undefined Symbol: The indicated symbol is not defined as a label or declared an external.

Linker Commands

The 64000 linker commands are defined below:

Key Label	Definition
link	Initiates the link process.
(CMDFILE)	A syntactical variable supplied by the user. This would be the name of linker command file previously established.
listfile	Allows the user to select a destination other than the system default for the linker output listing.
display	Using this command designates the display as the output destination for the linker output listing.
(FILE)	Syntactical variable supplied by the user. This would be the name of a disk file to which the output of the linker would be directed.
null	Using this command suppresses the output listing. Error messages will still be output to the default destination as previously selected by the user.

printer	This designates the printer to be the destination of the linker output listing.
options	Soft key which precedes the selection of a linker option.
edit	Available linker option to edit a previously established linker command file.
nolist	Available linker option to suppress the generation of a linker load map.

Soft Key Definitions

The 64000 emulator soft key definitions are given below:

| **Label** | **Description** |

run   This starts program execution in the emulation processor. Execution begins at the location specified by "from" and ending under the conditions specified by "until." If no limits are specified, emulation will begin at the current address until halted by a "stop run" or by a boundary specified by "until."
Syntax: run from (ADDRESS OR SYMBOL) until (AD-DRESS OR SYMBOL)

step   This function causes the emulation processor to execute one instruction at a time. Once in the step mode, each depression of the return key will cause another instruction to be executed and displayed. The user can specify the number of steps to be executed each time the return key is pressed and the address from which stepping occurs. If these parameters are not specified, the system defaults to stepping from the current program counter location, executing one instruction each time the return key is pressed.
Syntax: step # of (STATES) from (ADDRESS)

trace   This key is used to control the analysis function of the system, allowing the triggering and capturing of data of the emulation data bus.
Syntax: trace in_sequence—permits tracing on a sequence of events.
trace after—captures and displays data after the trigger qualifier word is satisfied.
trace about—captures and displays data before and after the trigger qualifier.
trace only—allows explicit definition of the information to be captured in the trace.

              trace continuous—allows continuous monitoring of trace information without reentering the trace command.

display   This command causes the system to display a variety of data types on the development station's screen. Data types can be specified as global symbols, local symbols, and last active trace specification (valid only with the analysis card), the last active run specification, the trace buffer (valid only with analysis card), contents of proper emulation microprocessor registers, absolute or relative time display (valid only with analysis card), or contents of user or emulation memory.

Syntax: display trace
Syntax: display register (REGISTER NAME)
Syntax: display memory (ADDRESS)
Syntax: display trace specification
Syntax: display run specification
Syntax: display count
Syntax: display global symbols
Syntax: display local symbols

The mode option for the trace, register, and memory display provides the user with a choice of how the data will be presented on the screen. The following modes are defined:

static	The system will display the current conditions or contents one time only. No update will be shown.
dynamic	The system will continually update the display as data are changed in the emulation system.
absolute	The system displays data in absolute numeric code (i.e., hexadecimal or octal).
mnemonic	The system presents the data in the appropriate assembly language.
offset by	The system displays program modules so that the address values are offset by a specified value.
no offset	The system displays all addresses in program modules with those values assigned by the linking loader.
packed	The system displays opcodes and operands on the same line.
block	The system displays more data on the development station by displaying multiple columns of data.
modify	This command allows the user to change the contents of the emulation memory or processor registers to correspond to data entered from the console keyboard. Syntax: modify (ADDRESS) to (VALUE)

Syntax: modify memory (ADDRESS) thru (AD-DRESS) to (VALUE)

Syntax: modify register (REGISTER NAME) to (VAL-UE)

stop This command halts the execution of either the run or trace commands. If stop-run is executed, it can be continued by a run command without skipping any of the intervening of the program code.

Syntax: stop run

Syntax: stop trace

end Selecting this soft key changes the operating mode of the station, allowing other tasks to be performed. "end" does not stop the emulation process. Emulation continues even as other functions are performed on the system.

Syntax: end_emulation

load load_memory transfers abolute object files from the system's disk into emulation or user RAM memory.

Syntax: load memory (FILE)

count The count command is used in conjunction with a trace command. The count command is used to measure the elapsed time or the number of times certain user-specified events occurred between the start and end times specified by the trace.

Syntax: count time
     count address = (ADDRESS)

copy This command allows the user to transfer data from one location of emulation or user memory to the system's disk. The content of memory from which the data are taken remains unchanged.

Syntax: copy (ADDRESS) thru (ADDRESS) to (FILE-NAME)

list_to This command allows the user to make a permanent record of the contents of the stations display by writing it to a file on the disk or to the line printer.

Syntax: list display to printer

Syntax: list display to (FILE)

restart Upon initializing the restart command, the microprocessor's program counter is reset to 0000H and the processor is reinitialized. It is important to execute the run command from the appropriate place in emulation memory.

edit_cnfg (Edit-Configuration). This command recalls the series of queries which allows mapping of memory space and fault selection. When this command is invoked the previous responses can be modified by the user.

Syntax: edit_cnfg

Following are the monitor level soft keys which will be in effect after December 1981:

```
edit compile assemble link emulate prom_prog run ---etc---
directory purge rename copy library recover log ---etc---
uerid date&time opt_test terminal (CMDFILE) --TAPE--- ---etc---
```

"--TAPE---" Soft Key

After --TAPE--- is returned the following soft keys are available.

```
store restore append verify tension directory ---etc---
```

"date&time" Soft Key

After date&time is depressed the following soft keys are available.

```
(DATE) (TIME)
```

"opt_test" Soft Key

This executes option test, which provides performance verification tests for options that are present.

Terminal Mode

"terminal Soft Key

This puts the station in an RS232 terminal mode which allows it to be a terminal to another system.

Passwords

The capability to have increased file security using passwords has been added. Following is the new syntax for userid.

"userid" Soft Key

After userid is depressed the following soft keys are available.

```
(USERID) listfile
```

After USERID is entered the following soft keys are available.

listfile password

After password is entered the following soft keys are available.

(PASSWD)

The user types in his password. This is nonprinting so he will not see on the display what he entered.

"HOST" PASCAL

"HOST" PASCAL consists of a compiler to allow users of the 64000 system to write programs that will execute on the internal host processor. In order to execute these programs the following syntax is used.

"run" Soft Key

After run is depressed the following soft key is available.

(FILE)

After a file is specified the following soft keys are available.

input output

After input is depressed the following soft keys are available.

(FILE) keyboard

After output is depressed the following soft keys are available.

(FILE) display display1 printer null

Summary of the HP 64000 Development System

Example A-1

This example shows how to create a new file and edit it. The file to be created is listed below:

```
"8085"
        ;    THIS PROGRAM STARTS AT 0 AND ADDS LOCATION 100H TO
        ;    LOCATION 101H AND STORES THE RESULT IN LOCATION 102H
             NAME    "ADD_WORKSHOP_1"
             ORG     2000H        ;    PROGRAM ORIGIN WILL BE AT
                                  ;    HEXADECIMAL 2000
START   LXI     H,100H            ;    LOAD HL PAIR WITH 100H
        MOV     A,M              ;    MOVE NUMBER IN LOCATION 100
                                 ;    INTO THE ACC.
        INX     H                ;    INCREMENT H AND L PAIR
        ADD     M                ;    ADD LOCATION 101 TO ACCUMULATOR
        INX     H                ;    INCREMENT HL PAIR
        MOV     M,A              ;    STORE ACC IN LOCATION 102H
        JMP     START
```

Procedure

Step 1: Press soft key "userid" and type in your USERID. The HP doesn't ask for the time and date after you enter your USERID. Rather, you have to press the soft key "Date&Time" to change it.

Step 2: To enter the edit mode, you have to create a new file. We'll call this new file "ADD".

               edit into ADD (RETURN)

Step 2.5: It is a good idea to set up tabs so that if you want to you may jump to the opcode, operand or comment. You do this by pressing the softkey "Tabset". The editor will then display a tab row in which you can type "T" at the current cursor position. Then when you want to move faster, the "tab" key will jump to where you set your tabs. The way we did it was:

               tabset 7 17 27 37

To save your tab sets, type the inverse softkey text "tabset" again.

Step 3: The first line of the program is the assembler directive, which lets the assembler know what microprocessor you wish to emulate.

               "8085" (RETURN)

Step 4: To enter comments, type a "*" in column 1 and then start with your comments. If you want to start it anywhere else on that line, type a ";" and enter your comment.

```
* This is a comment (The "*" is at the leftmost edge of column 1)
; This is a comment (The ";" can be at any position).
```

Note: Your comments must come after you type "*" or ";".

Step 5: Enter "Name" and a brief explanation of the file. This lets you know what a particular file does in case you have to link many files. This is optional.

```
(TAB) NAME (TAB) "ADD_WORKSHOP_I" (RETURN)
```

Step 6: Enter "ORG" to let the assembler know the starting location of your program — in this case, at 2000H.

```
(TAB) ORG (TAB) 2000H (TAB) ; COMMENTS (RETURN)
```

Step 7: Enter the label "START" at column 1 of the next line along with the first instruction. This label helps the user to remember the English word rather than what the number was, if the user wants to loop or jump to that part of the program again.

```
START (TAB) LXI (TAB) H,100H (TAB) ; COMMENTS (RETURN)
```

Step 8: If you use only a few labels in your program, it is wise to use the softkey "AUTOTAB". This softkey jumps to the next line and moves the cursor right under the first word of the previous line. This saves time. Also note that the "TAB" key can also do this if you specified the tab sets.

Step 9: Enter the rest of the program. This is the program listing called "ADD".

Step 10: To list your file to the printer, make sure the printer is on-line (the light that's adjacent to the word should be on; if not, push the "on-line" button on the printer). Then type:

```
list printer all (RETURN)
```

Step 11: To save the file, type

```
end (RETURN)
```

Note: If your file wasn't named when you entered the edit mode, then type

```
end ADD (RETURN)
```

Step 12: The file is stored onto the hard drive or disk. To see your file on it, type

```
directory (RETURN)
```

You should then see the file "ADD" with the type "SOURCE". You will also see when you last modified it and accessed it. This information is important, so that you know how updated your file is. The directory listing will only show those files under your USERID.

Step 13: To re-edit the file, type

    edit ADD (RETURN)

Notice that you don't type "edit into ADD". If you want to load your file from a disk, you have to specify the drive number. For disk drive X, type "ADD:X", where X is the disk drive number. If no drive number is specified, then the default is 0.

Step 14: To use the insert softkey, type a "NOP" after line 9 by

    9 (RETURN)
    insert (TAB) NOP (TAB) (TAB) ; NO OPERATION (RETURN)

Note: If you get an error, go to Step 15 and then back to 14. This may be because the editor was trying to find line 9, but your file has line numbers reading "NEW" instead.

Step 15: To renumber your file in order to give your editor a way to find what line to edit, type

    renumber (RETURN)

Step 16: If your file is very large and you want to search your file for a particular word like "NOP", type

    find "NOP" all (RETURN)

Note: Remember to enclose all strings with double quotes. If not, the editor will think it is a softkey command.

Step 17: To insert more text, type

    insert (RETURN)

then move the cursor up, down, or sideways and begin typing the new line.

Step 18: To revise a line, enter

    revise (RETURN)

This edits the line that the cursor is on. If that line isn't what you want, then move the cursor using the cursor keys.

Step 19: To move the display to allow for viewing all of the columns, depress the SHIFT and LEFT arrow keys simultaneously. Hitting SHIFT and

RIGHT keys will scroll the text right. To scroll the text up or down, hit the edit key ROLL UP or ROLL DOWN, respectively.

Step 20: To insert or delete character(s) when revising, hit the edit key INSERT CHAR or DELETE CHAR, respectively.

Step 21: To delete a line at the current cursor position, hit DELETE (RETURN). If you want to delete a line somewhere else, type

    extract (RETURN)

Then move the cursor to where you want to insert that line and type

    retrieve (RETURN)

Note: If you want to insert many copies of that line at the current cursor position, then type **retrieve** # (RETURN), where # is the number of copies.

Step 23: To abort the editor and not save your file, press the special function key RESET twice. Pressing it once will pause a running listing or program.

Step 24: To replace a word with another word type

    replace "word1" with "word2" all

This will replace all word1s and word2s. You can also specify where you want to stop replacing by using **thru** or **until** a certain line number.

Step 25: The "copy" command lets you copy a group of lines without erasing those lines, like "extract" does. First, place the cursor at the starting location line and then type

    copy thru line # (RETURN)

where # is the last of your lines to copy. Next, move the cursor to the place where you want it inserted, and type **retrieve**.

Step 26: The "merge" command lets you insert an entire file or copies a block of lines like the "copy" command does. To merge a file, type

    merge ADD (RETURN)

This lets you insert the file ADD at the current cursor position.

Example A-2

This example goes through the steps in assembling a file. Upon completion, it will create a "reloc" file to be later used for linking purposes.

Procedure

Step 1: Enter your userid, and optionally enter the time and date. The HP 64000 already has the current date and time, so updating isn't necessary.

        userid USERID (RETURN)

Step 2: To assemble your source file called "ADD" and make a printout of it with the cross-reference table, type

        assemble ADD listfile printer options xref (RETURN)

The printer will then output the assembled file that has both a source and object listing. It will then show the cross-reference table that lists any labels you put into that file and what lines accessed it or needed it to run.

Step 3: To show how the assembler command treats an error, we'll put one in by doing this

        edit ADD (RETURN)
        11 (RETURN)
        insert (TAB) MVI (TAB) D,FFH (RETURN)
        end (RETURN)

Step 4: Now assemble the file by typing the commands from Step 2. The assembler treated "FFH" as a symbol, not a hex value, so it generated an error. You will see the number of errors is one and that the error is an undefined symbol. On the xref table, FFH is a type U, which means it's undefined.

Step 5: To fix this error, all hex values beginning with an alpha character must be preceded with a "0". Do this by

        edit ADD (RETURN)
        12 (RETURN)
        revise (TAB) (TAB) D,0FFH (RETURN)
        end (RETURN)

Step 6: Now assemble the file again, and this time list it to the screen or display.

        assemble ADD listfile display options xref (RETURN)

To pause the display from scrolling up so fast, type RESET. To resume scrolling, type any other key.

Step 7: Your assembled file is stored on your USERID directory. To see it type

        directory (RETURN)

You will then see two more "ADD" files with the type "reloc" and "asmb_sym".

These files are useful for the assembler and linker programs. The "reloc" file is an object file containing the hex values of your program. It then must be made into an "absolute" file so it can run by itself.

Example A-3

This example goes through the steps in linking the "reloc" file to create an "absolute" file. This new file can then be run independently, emulated, or even used by the PROM programmer.

Procedure

Step 1: Initialize the linker and show the results to the display by

link listfile display (RETURN)
"Object files ?"

Step 2: This new message asks you what file(s) you want to be linked, so type

ADD (RETURN)
"Library files ?"

Step 3: There are no library routines in "ADD" so skip it by

(RETURN)
"Load addresses: PROG,DATA,COMN = 0000H,0000H,0000H"

Step 4: This command allows you to specify different memory areas for the program, data, and common modules. No memory assignment is needed because the "ADD" file already has an ORG statement, so skip it by

(RETURN)
"More files ?"

Step 5: Since there is only one file to be linked, respond by

no (RETURN)
"LIST,XREF, overlap_check,comp_db = on off on off"

Step 6: The linker is prompting the user to specify the output and declaring the default for the output listing. It then checks to see if your memory assignments overlap as well. Ignore this and type

(RETURN)
"Absolute file name ?"

Step 7: The linker wants you to enter the file name to be assigned to the absolute file.

ADD (RETURN)

Step 8: You will then see the linker examining your file

"STATUS:Linker : HP 640000S linker: Pass1"
"STATUS:Linker : HP 640000S linker: Pass2"
"STATUS:Linker : HP 640000S linker: End of link"

Note that the above display will be on a single line.

Step 9: The linker output will display the start and end location of your program, the current date and time, the assembler pseudo name "ADD_WORKSHOP_I", and extra data like XFER address and the total bytes loaded.

Step 10: To view your new files on the directory, type

directory (RETURN)

You should then see three new files with types "link_sym", "link_com", and "absolute". The absolute file is used for the emulator or the PROM programmer. The "link_com" is a command file that holds all of the data that you entered from Steps 1 to 7. This is good if you want to keep the same link configuration, but want to change or re-edit your source file(s).

If you want to save a linker listing to a file for later viewing type

link ADD listfile ADD_L (RETURN)

This will create a link listing similar to that of Step 9. Specifying "link ADD" will tell the linker to link it using its "link_com" file.

Example A-4

This example goes through the steps of emulating an absolute file without external hardware. This gives you a good idea of the importance of a development system like the HP 64000.

Procedure

Step 1: Before beginning, you must go through Examples 1 through 3. Also, the HP 64000 must have an 8085 emulator. If it is configured or has a 68000 emulator, emulation program will use only it, so be wary of this.

Step 2: To enter the emulation mode and load the absolute file do this

emulate load ADD (RETURN)
"Processor clock ?"

Step 3: This question asks if you want the source of the processor clock to be internal or external. Since there is no external hardware being used, type

internal (RETURN)
"Restrict processor to real-time runs ?"

Step 4: This question asks if you want to restrict the processor to real-time runs, which will limit the analysis functions that can be performed, such as debugging your program. An example of this would be "display registers blocked". So answer

no (RETURN)
"Stop processor on illegal opcodes ?"

Step 5: Specify "yes" so that the emulator will stop if an illegal opcode is detected.

yes (RETURN)

Step 6: The emulator will then want to specify the memory range for your emulation ram/rom and user ram/rom. Since all memory is internal (no user external hardware for this file), address 100H to 103H is used for storing the variables used in the program. Define this to be emulation RAM. To protect your program, define the memory to be emulation ROM. Thus, if something writes to your program, it will generate an error.

100H thru 103H emulation ram
2000H thru 20FFH emulation rom

Also notice that the ram and rom ranges are from 100H-3FFH and 2000H-20FFH. This may be because the emulator can only provide a range of memory area rather than a specified one.

Step 7: To keep your defined memory area, type

end (RETURN)
"Modify simulated I/O ?"

Step 8: Since we are not using any I/O ports, type

no (RETURN)
"Modify interactive measurement specification ?"

Step 8.5: This question is not in the book so type

(RETURN)
"Command file name ?"

Step 9: The emulator wants you to specify a file name to which to assign the emul_ com file configuration. Specify with

ADD (RETURN)

Once doing this, the emulator will then load your absolute file to the memory areas you specified. You should then see

"STATUS: 8085--Program loaded"

If you want to make any modifications, you have to start again, by re-editing, assembling, linking and then emulating. If you want the same emulating configuration that you specified in Steps 1 to 9, then type **emulate ADD load ADD**.

Step 11: To display your program with mnemonics, type

display memory 2000H mnemonic (RETURN)

You should then see the locations with their corresponding instructions of your program.

Step 12: To change the values that your program uses to add two numbers, you have to modify the emulation RAM by

modify memory 100H thru 102H to 02H (RETURN)
display memory 100H blocked (RETURN)

You should now see a display of your edited bytes. The memory block map will show you the address, data, and ASCII translation of each byte.

Step 13: To run your program, you can type either

run from 2000H (RETURN)

or

run from glob_sym START (RETURN)
"STATUS: 8085--Running"

Your program will keep running, so you can now modify the memory locations from Step 12 to something else, and then see the changes.

Step 14: You can also single-step the program to execute a single instruction at a time. This is a good debugging tool on the 64000.

```
break (RETURN)
"STATUS: 8085--break in background"
display registers (RETURN)
step from 2000H (RETURN)
```

or

```
step from glob_sym START (RETURN)
step (RETURN)
(RETURN)
```

Continuously pressing return will execute the "step" command again. Remember that pressing "return" will execute anything on the command prompt, no matter where the cursor is. You should then see a display of each instruction being executed with its corresponding register values. This is really good because you can trace any program, and scan the instructions, registers, flags, stack pointer, and the next IP.

Step 15: You can also set up breakpoints to stop the program when it reaches a certain argument. An example of this would be "run" from 2000H until address 2006H.

Step 16: To set up a breakpoint at address 2005H, type

```
run from 2000H until address 2005H (RETURN)
```

Step 17: Now say you want to halt the program after a memory write:

```
run from 2000H until status memory_write (RETURN)
```

Step 18: To end the emulation session, type

```
end (RETURN)
```

You can also press "RESET" twice too.

Step 19: If you want to get back to the emulation and keep the same emulator configuration, type

```
emulate ADD load ADD (RETURN)
```

If you want to change the emulator configuration type

```
modify_configuration (RETURN)
```

Note that the HP 64000 can perform in-circuit emulation with or without a large-system hardware.

Operation of the 68000 Emulator

In order to use the 68000 emulator, a monitor program must be included in the linking of the user's program. The purpose of the monitor is to provide special functions during emulation (including register display, software breakpoint setting, etc.).

The steps in the emulation process are as follows:

1. Create a program using the 64000's text edition.
    A. Make sure that "68000", including quotations, is the first line in the editor.
    B. Make the second line in the application program "PROG". (This will cause the monitor program to be successfully linked with the application.)
    C. Use "H" for Hex instead of "$" signs.
    D. Write your application program.
        Locate the program between 0FFH and 10000H-application size.
2. Assemble the program you write by typing:

    <Assemble> MON_68K

3. Make a copy of the assembly program "MON_68K" by typing:

    COPY Mon_68K:HP:source TO MON_68K

    (Note upper and lower case. Type it exactly as shown.)
4. Now assemble this program by typing:

    SOFTKEY
    <Assemble> MON_68K

5. Now, the application and monitor program must be linked together. Type:

SOFTKEY	
<LINK>	
Object File?	MYFILE
Library Files?	<CR>
Prog,Data,Comn,A5=	000XXX,0H,0H,0H where XXX=100H to 10000H
More Files?	<yes> Soft Key
Object Files?	MON_68K
Library Files?	<CR>
Prog,Data,Comn,A5=	10000H,0H,0H,0H
More Files?	<No> Soft Key
Absolute File Name=	MYFILE

A. Notes: The monitor program is position independent. Since the TARGET SYSTEM has limited address space, it is suggested that you locate your program in **THAT** address range. Furthermore, this allows the user to specify the monitor program's address in upper-address space and in emulation RAM.

B. Care should be taken so that address ranges 000H→0FFH are reserved for vectors, and that user program addresses do not conflict with the monitor program whose size is about 1000_{16} bytes. I locate the monitor at address 10000H→10FFFH.

6. Finally, the emulator is entered by answering questions with their default values (unless the user wishes otherwise).

A. For the memory map, the following should be entered:

```
0000H-0FFFH    Emulation ROM (Vectors, Interrupts, User Prog)
10000H-10FFFH  Emulation RAM (Monitor Program)
0WWWH-0VVVH    User RAM (other space for ports, tables, etc.
                 that exist in either software or the target
                 system)
```

B. Some helpful commands during emulation (<XXXX> = Soft Key):

1. <Load> MYFILE	Loads both your file and the monitor program (linked)
2. <Modify><Config>	Lets you change the emulator configuration
3. <Modify><Softwre_bkpts>	Modifies software breakpoints so that you can stop program execution anywhere

NOTE: The 68000 emulator DOES NOT allow single-stepping.

4. <BREAK>	Enter the monitor program
5. <DISPLAY><MEMORY> <MNEMONIC>	Display disassembled code
6. <MODIFY><REGISTER> <MODIFY><MEMORY>	Modify address space and registers

DO NOT put ORG statements in your program except for the interrupt vectors.

 **MOTOROLA**

Advance Information

16-BIT MICROPROCESSING UNIT

Advances in semiconductor technology have provided the capability to place on a single silicon chip a microprocessor at least an order of magnitude higher in performance and circuit complexity than has been previously available. The MC68000 is the first of a family of such VLSI microprocessors from Motorola. It combines state-of-the-art technology and advanced circuit design techniques with computer sciences to achieve an architecturally advanced 16-bit microprocessor.

The resources available to the MC68000 user consist of the following:

- 32-Bit Data and Address Registers
- 16 Megabyte Direct Addressing Range
- 56 Powerful Instruction Types
- Operations on Five Main Data Types
- Memory Mapped I/O
- 14 Addressing Modes

As shown in the programming model, the MC68000 offers seventeen 32-bit registers in addition to the 32-bit program counter and a 16-bit status register. The first eight registers (D0-D7) are used as data registers for byte (8-bit), word (16-bit), and long word (32-bit) data operations. The second set of seven registers (A0-A6) and the system stack pointer may be used as software stack pointers and base address registers. In addition, these registers may be used for word and long word address operations. All seventeen registers may be used as index registers.

MC68000L4
(4 MHz)
MC68000L6
(6 MHz)
MC68000L8
(8 MHz)
MC68000L10
(10 MHz)

HMOS
(HIGH-DENSITY, N-CHANNEL,
SILICON-GATE DEPLETION LOAD)

**16-BIT
MICROPROCESSOR**

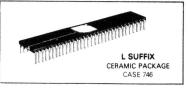

L SUFFIX
CERAMIC PACKAGE
CASE 746

64-pin dual in-line package

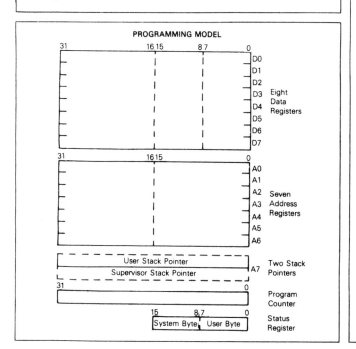

PROGRAMMING MODEL

68-Terminal Chip Carrier

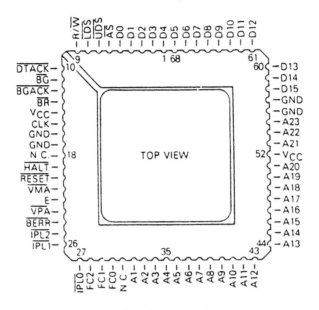

68-Pin Quad Pack

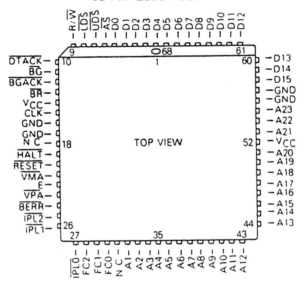

MOTOROLA

MC68230L8
MC68230L10

Advance Information

HMOS
(HIGH-DENSITY N-CHANNEL SILICON-GATE)

PARALLEL INTERFACE/TIMER

MC68230 PARALLEL INTERFACE/TIMER

The MC68230 Parallel Interface/Timer provides versatile double buffered parallel interfaces and an operating system oriented timer to MC68000 systems. The parallel interfaces operate in unidirectional or bidirectional modes, either 8 or 16 bits wide. In the unidirectional modes, an associated data direction register determines whether the port pins are inputs or outputs. In the bidirectional modes the data direction registers are ignored and the direction is determined dynamically by the state of four handshake pins. These programmable handshake pins provide an interface flexible enough for connection to a wide variety of low, medium, or high speed peripherals or other computer systems. The PI/T ports allow use of vectored or autovectored interrupts, and also provide a DMA Request pin for connection to the MC68450 Direct Memory Access Controller or a similar circuit. The PI/T timer contains a 24-bit wide counter and a 5-bit prescaler. The timer may be clocked by the system clock (PI/T CLK pin) or by an external clock (TIN pin), and a 5-bit prescaler can be used. It can generate periodic interrupts, a square wave, or a single interrupt after a programmed time period. Also it can be used for elapsed time measurement or as a device watchdog.

- MC68000 Bus Compatible
- Port Modes Include:
  Bit I/O
  Unidirectonal 8-Bit and 16-Bit
  Bidirectional 8-Bit and 16-Bit
- Selectable Handshaking Options
- 24-Bit Programmable Timer
- Software Programmable Timer Modes
- Contains Interrupt Vector Generation Logic
- Separate Port and Timer Interrupt Service Requests
- Registers are Read/Write and Directly Addressable
- Registers are Addressed for MOVEP (Move Peripheral) and DMAC Compatibility

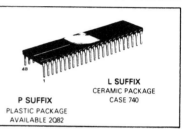

L SUFFIX
CERAMIC PACKAGE
CASE 740

P SUFFIX
PLASTIC PACKAGE
AVAILABLE 2Q82

PIN ASSIGNMENT

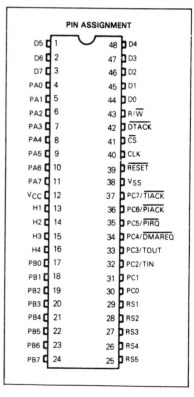

D5 □ 1	48 □ D4
D6 □ 2	47 □ D3
D7 □ 3	46 □ D2
PA0 □ 4	45 □ D1
PA1 □ 5	44 □ D0
PA2 □ 6	43 □ R/$\overline{\text{W}}$
PA3 □ 7	42 □ $\overline{\text{DTACK}}$
PA4 □ 8	41 □ $\overline{\text{CS}}$
PA5 □ 9	40 □ CLK
PA6 □ 10	39 □ $\overline{\text{RESET}}$
PA7 □ 11	38 □ V$_{SS}$
V$_{CC}$ □ 12	37 □ PC7/$\overline{\text{TIACK}}$
H1 □ 13	36 □ PC6/$\overline{\text{PIACK}}$
H2 □ 14	35 □ PC5/$\overline{\text{PIRQ}}$
H3 □ 15	34 □ PC4/$\overline{\text{DMAREQ}}$
H4 □ 16	33 □ PC3/TOUT
PB0 □ 17	32 □ PC2/TIN
PB1 □ 18	31 □ PC1
PB2 □ 19	30 □ PC0
PB3 □ 20	29 □ RS1
PB4 □ 21	28 □ RS2
PB5 □ 22	27 □ RS3
PB6 □ 23	26 □ RS4
PB7 □ 24	25 □ RS5

 **MOTOROLA**

MC6821
(1.0 MHz)
MC68A21
(1.5 MHz)
MC68B21
(2.0 MHz)

PERIPHERAL INTERFACE ADAPTER (PIA)

The MC6821 Peripheral Interface Adapter provides the universal means of interfacing peripheral equipment to the M6800 family of microprocessors. This device is capable of interfacing the MPU to peripherals through two 8-bit bidirectional peripheral data buses and four control lines. No external logic is required for interfacing to most peripheral devices.

The functional configuration of the PIA is programmed by the MPU during system initialization. Each of the peripheral data lines can be programmed to act as an input or output, and each of the four control/interrupt lines may be programmed for one of several control modes. This allows a high degree of flexibility in the overall operation of the interface.

- 8-Bit Bidirectional Data Bus for Communication with the MPU
- Two Bidirectional 8-Bit Buses for Interface to Peripherals
- Two Programmable Control Registers
- Two Programmable Data Direction Registers
- Four Individually-Controlled Interrupt Input Lines; Two Usable as Peripheral Control Outputs
- Handshake Control Logic for Input and Output Peripheral Operation
- High-Impedance Three-State and Direct Transistor Drive Peripheral Lines
- Program Controlled Interrupt and Interrupt Disable Capability
- CMOS Drive Capability on Side A Peripheral Lines
- Two TTL Drive Capability on All A and B Side Buffers
- TTL-Compatible
- Static Operation

MOS
(N-CHANNEL, SILICON-GATE, DEPLETION LOAD)

PERIPHERAL INTERFACE ADAPTER

L SUFFIX
CERAMIC PACKAGE
CASE 715

S SUFFIX
CERDIP PACKAGE
CASE 734

P SUFFIX
PLASTIC PACKAGE
CASE 711

MAXIMUM RATINGS

Characteristics	Symbol	Value	Unit
Supply Voltage	V_{CC}	-0.3 to $+7.0$	V
Input Voltage	V_{in}	-0.3 to $+7.0$	V
Operating Temperature Range MC6821, MC68A21, MC68B21 MC6821C, MC68A21C, MC68B21C	T_A	T_L to T_H 0 to 70 -40 to $+85$	°C
Storage Temperature Range	T_{stg}	-55 to $+150$	°C

THERMAL CHARACTERISTICS

Characteristic	Symbol	Value	Unit
Thermal Resistance Ceramic Plastic Cerdip	θ_{JA}	50 100 60	°C/W

This device contains circuitry to protect the inputs against damage due to high static voltages or electric fields; however, it is advised that normal precautions be taken to avoid application of any voltage higher than maximum-rated voltages to this high-impedance circuit. Reliability of operation is enhanced if unused inputs are tied to an appropriate logic voltage (i.e., either V_{SS} or V_{CC}).

PIN ASSIGNMENT

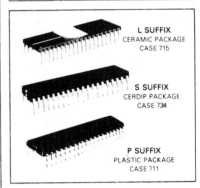

V_{SS}	1	40	CA1
PA0	2	39	CA2
PA1	3	38	$\overline{IRQA}$
PA2	4	37	$\overline{IRQB}$
PA3	5	36	RS0
PA4	6	35	RS1
PA5	7	34	$\overline{RESET}$
PA6	8	33	D0
PA7	9	32	D1
PB0	10	31	D2
PB1	11	30	D3
PB2	12	29	D4
PB3	13	28	D5
PB4	14	27	D6
PB5	15	26	D7
PB6	16	25	E
PB7	17	24	CS1
CB1	18	23	$\overline{CS2}$
CB2	19	22	CS0
V_{CC}	20	21	$R/\overline{W}$

The expanded block diagram of the MC6821 is shown in Figure B.1.

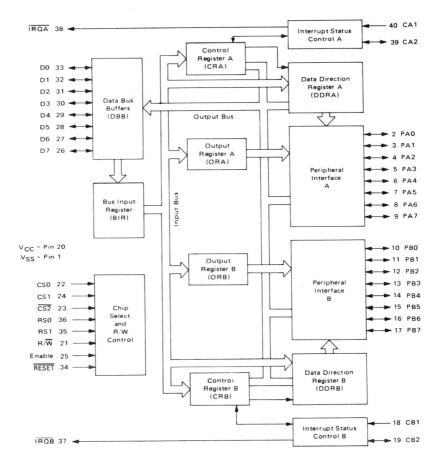

FIGURE B.1 EXPANDED BLOCK DIAGRAM

PIA INTERFACE SIGNALS FOR MPU

The PIA interfaces to the M6800 bus with an 8-bit bidirectional data bus, three chip select lines, two register select lines, two interrupt request lines, a read/write line, an enable line and a reset line. To ensure proper operation with the MC6800, MC6802, or MC6808 microprocessors, VMA should be used as an active part of the address decoding.

Bidirectional Data (D0-D7) — The bidirectional data lines (D0-D7) allow the transfer of data between the MPU and the PIA. The data bus output drivers are three-state devices that remain in the high-impedance (off) state except when the MPU performs a PIA read operation. The read/write line is in the read (high) state when the PIA is selected for a read operation.

Enable (E) — The enable pulse, E, is the only timing signal that is supplied to the PIA. Timing of all other signals is referenced to the leading and trailing edges of the E pulse.

Read/Write (R/W̄) — This signal is generated by the MPU to control the direction of data transfers on the data bus. A low state on the PIA read/write line enables the input buffers and data is transferred from the MPU to the PIA on the E signal if the device has been selected. A high on the read/write line sets up the PIA for a transfer of data to the bus. The PIA output buffers are enabled when the proper address and the enable pulse E are present.

R̄ĒS̄ĒT̄ — The active low R̄ĒS̄ĒT̄ line is used to reset all register bits in the PIA to a logical zero (low). This line can be used as a power-on reset and as a master reset during system operation.

Chip Selects (CS0, CS1, and C̄S̄2̄) — These three input signals are used to select the PIA. CS0 and CS1 must be high and C̄S̄2̄ must be low for selection of the device. Data transfers are then performed under the control of the enable and read/write signals. The chip select lines must be stable for the duration of the E pulse. The device is deselected when any of the chip selects are in the inactive state.

Register Selects (RS0 and RS1) — The two register select lines are used to select the various registers inside the PIA. These two lines are used in conjunction with internal Control Registers to select a particular register that is to be written or read.

The register and chip select lines should be stable for the duration of the E pulse while in the read or write cycle.

Interrupt Request (ĪR̄Q̄Ā and ĪR̄Q̄B̄) — The active low Interrupt Request lines (ĪR̄Q̄Ā and ĪR̄Q̄B̄) act to interrupt the MPU either directly or through interrupt priority circuitry. These lines are "open drain" (no load device on the chip). This permits all interrupt request lines to be tied together in a wire-OR configuration.

Each Interrupt Request line has two internal interrupt flag bits that can cause the Interrupt Request line to go low. Each flag bit is associated with a particular peripheral interrupt line. Also, four interrupt enable bits are provided in the PIA which may be used to inhibit a particular interrupt from a peripheral device.

Servicing an interrupt by the MPU may be accomplished by a software routine that, on a prioritized basis, sequentially reads and tests the two control registers in each PIA for interrupt flag bits that are set.

The interrupt flags are cleared (zeroed) as a result of an MPU Read Peripheral Data Operation of the corresponding data register. After being cleared, the interrupt flag bit cannot be enabled to be set until the PIA is deselected during an E pulse. The E pulse is used to condition the interrupt control lines (CA1, CA2, CB1, CB2). When these lines are used as interrupt inputs, at least one E pulse must occur from the inactive edge to the active edge of the interrupt input signal to condition the edge sense network. If the interrupt flag has been enabled and the edge sense circuit has been properly conditioned, the interrupt flag will be set on the next active transition of the interrupt input pin.

PIA PERIPHERAL INTERFACE LINES

The PIA provides two 8-bit bidirectional data buses and four interrupt/control lines for interfacing to peripheral devices.

Section A Peripheral Data (PA0-PA7) — Each of the peripheral data lines can be programmed to act as an input or output. This is accomplished by setting a "1" in the corresponding Data Direction Register bit for those lines which are to be outputs. A "0" in a bit of the Data Direction Register causes the corresponding peripheral data line to act as an input. During an MPU Read Peripheral Data Operation, the data on peripheral lines programmed to act as inputs appears directly on the corresponding MPU Data Bus lines. In the input mode, the internal pullup resistor on these lines represents a maximum of 1.5 standard TTL loads.

The data in Output Register A will appear on the data lines that are programmed to be outputs. A logical "1" written into the register will cause a "high" on the corresponding data line while a "0" results in a "low." Data in Output Register A may be read by an MPU "Read Peripheral Data A" operation when the corresponding lines are programmed as outputs. This data will be read property if the voltage on the peripheral data lines is greater than 2.0 volts for a logic "1" output and less than 0.8 volt for a logic "0" output. Loading the output lines such that the voltage on these lines does not reach full voltage causes the data transferred into the MPU on a Read operation to differ from that contained in the respective bit of Output Register A.

Section B Peripheral Data (PB0-PB7) — The peripheral data lines in the B Section of the PIA can be programmed to act as either inputs or outputs in a similar manner to PA0-PA7. They have three-state capabiity, allowing them to enter a high-impedance state when the peripheral data line is used as an input. In addition, data on the peripheral data lines

PB0-PB7 will be read properly from those lines programmed as outputs even if the voltages are below 2.0 volts for a "high" or above 0.8 V for a "low". As outputs, these lines are compatible with standard TTL and may also be used as a source of up to 1 milliampere at 1.5 volts to directly drive the base of a transistor switch.

Interrupt Input (CA1 and CB1) — Peripheral input lines CA1 and CB1 are input only lines that set the interrupt flags of the control registers. The active transition for these signals is also programmed by the two control registers.

Peripheral Control (CA2) — The peripheral control line CA2 can be programmed to act as an interrupt input or as a peripheral control output. As an output, this line is compatible with standard TTL; as an input the internal pullup resistor on this line represents 1.5 standard TTL loads. The function of this signal line is programmed with Control Register A.

Peripheral Control (CB2) — Peripheral Control line CB2 may also be programmed to act as an interrupt input or peripheral control output. As an input, this line has high input impedance and is compatible with standard TTL. As an output it is compatible with standard TTL and may also be used as a source of up to 1 milliampere at 1.5 volts to directly drive the base of a transistor switch. This line is programmed by Control Register B.

INTERNAL CONTROLS

INITIALIZATION

A $\overline{RESET}$ has the effect of zeroing all PIA registers. This will set PA0-PA7, PB0-PB7, CA2 and CB2 as inputs, and all interrupts disabled. The PIA must be configured during the restart program which follows the reset.

There are six locations within the PIA accessible to the MPU data bus: two Peripheral Registers, two Data Direction Registers, and two Control Registers. Selection of these locations is controlled by the RS0 and RS1 inputs together with bit 2 in the Control Register, as shown in Table B.1

Details of possible configurations of the Data Direction and Control Register are as follows:

TABLE B.1 INTERNAL ADDRESSING

		Control Register Bit		
RS1	RS0	CRA-2	CRB-2	Location Selected
0	0	1	X	Peripheral Register A
0	0	0	X	Data Direction Register A
0	1	X	X	Control Register A
1	0	X	1	Peripheral Register B
1	0	X	0	Data Direction Register B
1	1	X	X	Control Register B

X = Don't Care

PORT A-B HARDWARE CHARACTERISTICS

As shown in Figure B.2 the MC6821 has a pair of I/O ports whose characteristics differ greatly. The A side is designed to drive CMOS logic to normal 30% to 70% levels, and incorporates an internal pullup device that remains connected even in the input mode. Because of this, the A side requires more drive current in the input mode than Port B. In contrast, the B side uses a normal three-state NMOS buffer which cannot pullup to CMOS levels without external resistors. The B side can drive extra loads such as Darlingtons without problem. When the PIA comes out of reset, the A port represents inputs with pullup resistors, whereas the B side (input mode also) will float high or low, depending upon the load connected to it.

Notice the differences between a Port A and Port B read operation when in the output mode. When reading Port A, the actual pin is read, whereas the B side read comes from an output latch, ahead of the actual pin.

CONTROL REGISTERS (CRA and CRB)

The two Control Registers (CRA and CRB) allow the MPU to control the operation of the four peripheral control lines CA1, CA2, CB1, and CB2. In addition they allow the MPU to enable the interrupt lines and monitor the status of the interrupt flags. Bits 0 through 5 of the two registers may be written or read by the MPU when the proper chip select and register select signals are applied. Bits 6 and 7 of the two registers are read only and are modified by external interrupts occurring on control lines CA1, CA2, CB1, or CB2. The format of the control words is shown in Figure B.3

DATA DIRECTION ACCESS CONTROL BIT (CRA-2 and CRB-2)

Bit 2, in each Control Register (CRA and CRB), determines selection of either a Peripheral Output Register or the corresponding Data Direction E Register when the proper register select signals are applied to RS0 and RS1. A "1" in bit 2 allows access of the Peripheral Interface Register, while a "0" causes the Data Direction Register to be addressed.

Interrupt Flags (CRA-6, CRA-7, CRB-6, and CRB-7) — The four interrupt flag bits are set by active transitions of signals on the four Interrupt and Peripheral Control lines when those lines are programmed to be inputs. These bits cannot be set directly from the MPU Data Bus and are reset indirectly by a Read Peripheral Data Operation on the appropriate section.

Control of CA2 and CB2 Peripheral Control Lines (CRA-3, CRA-4, CRA-5, CRB-3, CRB-4, and CRB-5) — Bits 3, 4, and 5 of the two control registers are used to control the CA2 and CB2 Peripheral Control lines. These bits determine if the control lines will be an interrupt input or an output control signal. If bit CRA-5 (CRB-5) is low, CA2 (CB2) is an interrupt input line similar to CA1 (CB1). When CRA-5 (CRB-5) is high, CA2 (CB2) becomes an output signal that may be used to control peripheral data transfers. When in the output mode, CA2 and CB2 have slightly different loading characteristics.

Control of CA1 and CB1 Interrupt Input Lines (CRA-0, CRB-1, CRA-1, and CRB-1) — The two lowest-order bits of the control registers are used to control the interrupt input lines CA1 and CB1. Bits CRA-0 and CRB-0 are used to enable the MPU interrupt signals $\overline{IRQA}$ and $\overline{IRQB}$, respectively. Bits CRA-1 and CRB-1 determine the active transition of the interrupt input signals CA1 and CB1.

FIGURE B.2 PORT A AND PORT B EQUIVALENT CIRCUITS

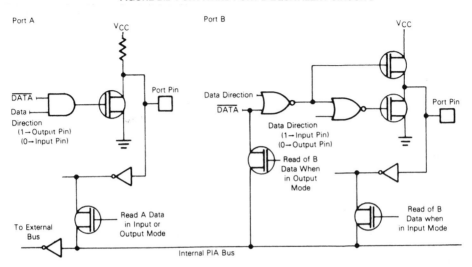

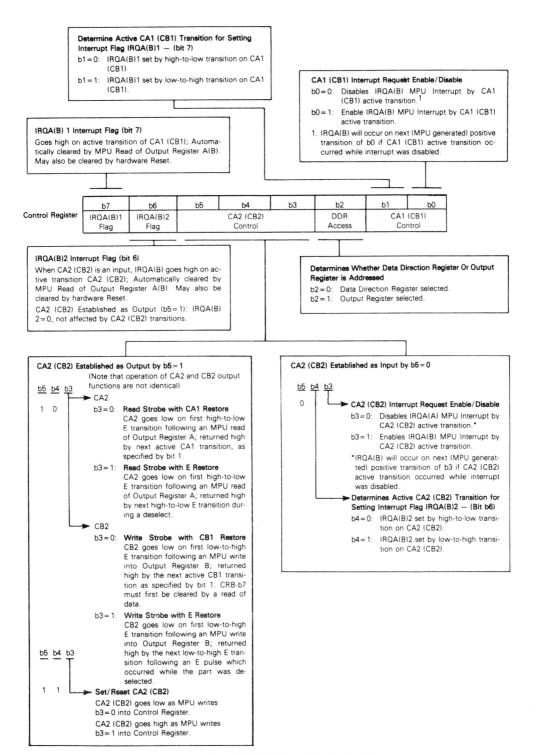

FIGURE B.3 CONTROL WORD FORMAT

MOTOROLA

MCM6116

16K BIT STATIC RANDOM ACCESS MEMORY

The MCM6116 is a 16,384-bit Static Random Access Memory organized as 2048 words by 8 bits, fabricated using Motorola's high-performance silicon-gate CMOS (HCMOS) technology. It uses a design approach which provides the simple timing features associated with fully static memories and the reduced power associated with CMOS memories. This means low standby power without the need for clocks, nor reduced data rates due to cycle times that exceed access time.

Chip Enable ($\overline{E}$) controls the power-down feature. It is not a clock but rather a chip control that affects power consumption. In less than a cycle time after Chip Enable ($\overline{E}$) goes high, the part automatically reduces its power requirements and remains in this low-power standby as long as the Chip Enable ($\overline{E}$) remains high. The automatic power-down feature causes no performance degradation.

The MCM6116 is in a 24-pin dual-in-line package with the industry standard JEDEC approved pinout and is pinout compatible with the industry standard 16K EPROM/ROM.

- Single +5 V Supply
- 2048 Words by 8-Bit Operation
- HCMOS Technology
- Fully Static: No Clock or Timing Strobe Required
- Maximum Access Time: MCM6116-12 — 120 ns
  MCM6116-15 — 150 ns
  MCM6116-20 — 200 ns
- Power Dissipation: 70 mA Maximum (Active)
  15 mA Maximum (Standby-TTL Levels)
  2 mA Maximum (Standby)
- Low Power Version Also Available — MCM61L16
- Low Voltage Data Retention (MCM61L16 Only):
  50 μA Maximum

HCMOS
(COMPLEMENTARY MOS)

2,048 × 8 BIT STATIC RANDOM ACCESS MEMORY

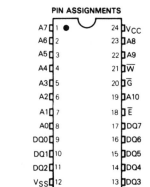

P SUFFIX
PLASTIC PACKAGE
CASE 709

PIN ASSIGNMENTS

A7	1	24	V$_{CC}$
A6	2	23	A8
A5	3	22	A9
A4	4	21	$\overline{W}$
A3	5	20	$\overline{G}$
A2	6	19	A10
A1	7	18	$\overline{E}$
A0	8	17	DQ7
DQ0	9	16	DQ6
DQ1	10	15	DQ5
DQ2	11	14	DQ4
V$_{SS}$	12	13	DQ3

PIN NAMES	
A0-A10	Address Input
DQ0-DQ7	Data Input/Output
$\overline{W}$	Write Enable
$\overline{G}$	Output Enable
$\overline{E}$	Chip Enable
V$_{CC}$	Power (+5 V)
V$_{SS}$	Ground

BLOCK DIAGRAM

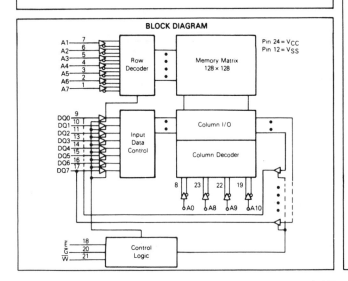

Pin 24 = V$_{CC}$
Pin 12 = V$_{SS}$

ABSOLUTE MAXIMUM RATINGS (See Note)

Rating	Value	Unit
Temperature Under Bias	− 10 to + 80	°C
Voltage on Any Pin With Respect to V_{SS}	− 1.0 to + 7.0	V
DC Output Current	20	mA
Power Dissipation	1.2	Watt
Operating Temperature Range	0 to + 70	°C
Storage Temperature Range	− 65 to + 150	°C

This device contains circuitry to protect the inputs against damage due to high static voltages or electric fields; however, it is advised that normal precautions be taken to avoid application of any voltage higher than maximum rated voltages to this high-impedance circuit.

NOTE: Permanent device damage may occur if ABSOLUTE MAXIMUM RATINGS are exceeded. Functional operation should be restricted to RECOMMENDED OPERATING CONDITIONS. Exposure to higher than recommended voltages for extended periods of time could affect device reliability.

DC OPERATING CONDITIONS AND CHARACTERISTICS
(Full operating voltage and temperature ranges unless otherwise noted.)

RECOMMENDED OPERATING CONDITIONS

Parameter	Symbol	Min	Typ	Max	Unit
Supply Voltage	V_{CC}	4.5	5.0	5.5	V
	V_{SS}	0	0	0	V
Input Voltage	V_{IH}	2.2	3.5	6.0	V
	V_{IL}	− 1.0*	−	0.8	V

*The device will withstand undershoots to the − 1.0 volt level with a maximum pulse width of 50 ns at the − 0.3 volt level. This is periodically sampled rather than 100% tested.

RECOMMENDED OPERATING CHARACTERISTICS

Parameter	Symbol	MCM6116			MCM61L16			Unit
		Min	Typ*	Max	Min	Typ*	Max	
Input Leakage Current ($V_{CC} = 5.5$ V, $V_{in} =$ GND to V_{CC})	$|I_{LI}|$	−	−	1	−	−	1	μA
Output Leakage Current ($\overline{E} = V_{IH}$ or $\overline{G} = V_{IH}$ $V_{I/O} =$ GND to V_{CC})	$|I_{LO}|$	−	−	1	−	−	1	μA
Operating Power Supply Current ($\overline{E} = V_{IL}$, $I_{I/O} = 0$ mA)	I_{CC}	−	35	70	−	35	55	mA
Average Operating Current Minimum cycle, duty = 100%	I_{CC2}	−	35	70	−	35	55	mA
Standby Power ($\overline{E} = V_{IH}$)	I_{SB}	−	5	15	−	5	12	mA
Supply Current ($\overline{E} \geq V_{CC} - 0.2$ V, $V_{in} \geq V_{CC} - 0.2$ V or $V_{in} \leq 0.2$ V)	I_{SB1}	−	20	2000	−	4	100	μA
Output Low Voltage ($I_{OL} = 2.1$ mA)	V_{OL}	−	−	0.4	−	−	0.4	V
Output High Voltage ($I_{OH} = - 1.0$ mA)**	V_{OH}	2.4	−	−	2.4	−	−	V

*$V_{CC} = 5$ V, $T_A = 25$°C
**Also, output voltages are compatible with Motorola's new high-speed CMOS logic family if the same power supply voltage is used.

CAPACITANCE (f = 1.0 MHz, $T_A = 25$°C, periodically sampled rather than 100% tested.)

Characteristic	Symbol	Typ	Max	Unit
Input Capacitance except $\overline{E}$	C_{in}	3	5	pF
Input/Output Capacitance and $\overline{E}$ Input Capacitance	$C_{I/O}$	5	7	pF

MODE SELECTION

Mode	$\overline{E}$	$\overline{G}$	$\overline{W}$	V_{CC} Current	DQ
Standby	H	X	X	I_{SB}, I_{SB1}	High Z
Read	L	L	H	I_{CC}	Q
Write Cycle (1)	L	H	L	I_{CC}	D
Write Cycle (2)	L	L	L	I_{CC}	D

AC OPERATING CONDITIONS AND CHARACTERISTICS

(Full operating voltage and temperature unless otherwise noted.)

Input Pulse Levels .... 0 Volt to 3.5 Volts   Input and Output Timing Reference Levels .... 1.5 Volts

Input Rise and Fall Times .... 10 ns   Output Load .... 1 TTL Gate and C_L = 100 pF

READ CYCLE

Parameter	Symbol	MCM6116-12 MCM61L16-12 Min	MCM6116-12 MCM61L16-12 Max	MCM6116-15 MCM61L16-15 Min	MCM6116-15 MCM61L16-15 Max	MCM6116-20 MCM61L16-20 Min	MCM6116-20 MCM61L16-20 Max	Unit
Address Valid to Address Don't Care (Cycle Time when Chip Enable is Held Active)	t_{AVAX}	120	—	150	—	200	—	ns
Chip Enable Low to Chip Enable High	t_{ELEH}	120	—	150	—	200	—	ns
Address Valid to Output Valid (Access)	t_{AVQV}	—	120	—	150	—	200	ns
Chip Enable Low to Output Valid (Access)	t_{ELQV}	—	120	—	150	—	200	ns
Address Valid to Output Invalid	t_{AVQX}	10	—	15	—	15	—	ns
Chip Enable Low to Output Invalid	t_{ELQX}	10	—	15	—	15	—	ns
Chip Enable High to Output High Z	t_{EHQZ}	0	40	0	50	0	60	ns
Output Enable to Output Valid	t_{GLQV}	—	80	—	100	—	120	ns
Output Enable to Output Invalid	t_{GLQX}	10	—	15	—	15	—	ns
Output Enable to Output High Z	t_{GLQZ}	0	40	0	50	0	60	ns
Address Invalid to Output Invalid	t_{AXQX}	10	—	15	—	15	—	ns
Address Valid to Chip Enable Low (Address Setup)	t_{AVEL}	0	—	0	—	0	—	ns
Chip Enable to Power-Up Time	t_{PU}	0	—	0	—	0	—	ns
Chip Disable to Power-Down Time	t_{PD}	—	30	—	30	—	30	ns

WRITE CYCLE

Parameter	Symbol	MCM6116-12 MCM61L16-12 Min	MCM6116-12 MCM61L16-12 Max	MCM6116-15 MCM61L16-15 Min	MCM6116-15 MCM61L16-15 Max	MCM6116-20 MCM61L16-20 Min	MCM6116-20 MCM61L16-20 Max	Unit
Chip Enable Low to Write High	t_{ELWH}	70	—	90	—	120	—	ns
Address Valid to Write High	t_{AVWH}	105	—	120	—	140	—	ns
Address Valid to Write Low (Address Setup)	t_{AVWL}	20	—	20	—	20	—	ns
Write Low to Write High (Write Pulse Width)	t_{WLWH}	70	—	90	—	120	—	ns
Write High to Address Don't Care	t_{WHAX}	5	—	10	—	10	—	ns
Data Valid to Write High	t_{DVWH}	35	—	40	—	60	—	ns
Write High to Data Don't Care (Data Hold)	t_{WHDX}	5	—	10	—	10	—	ns
Write Low to Output High Z	t_{WLQZ}	0	50	0	60	0	60	ns
Write High to Output Valid	t_{WHQV}	5	—	10	—	10	—	ns
Output Disable to Output High Z	t_{GHQZ}	0	40	0	50	0	60	ns

TIMING PARAMETER ABBREVIATIONS

```
                         t X X X X
signal name from which interval is defined ───┘ | | |
        transition direction for first signal ────┘ | |
      signal name to which interval is defined ─────┘ |
      transition direction for second signal ─────────┘
```

The transition definitions used in this data sheet are:

H = transition to high
L = transition to low
V = transition to valid
X = transition to invalid or don't care
Z = transition to off (high impedance)

TIMING LIMITS

The table of timing values shows either a minimum or a maximum limit for each parameter. Input requirements are specified from the external system point of view. Thus, address setup time is shown as a minimum since the system must supply at least that much time (even though most devices do not require it). On the other hand, responses from the memory are specified from the device point of view. Thus, the access time is shown as a maximum since the device never provides data later than that time.

APPENDIX C

intel® 8085

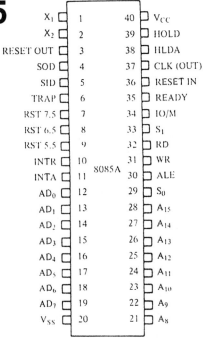

Figure C.1 8085 pinout

Figure C.1 shows 8085 pins and signals. The following table describes the function of each pin:

SYMBOL	FUNCTION
A_8-A_{15} (Output, three-state)	Address bus: The most significant 8 bits of the memory address or the 8 bits of the I/O address.
AD_{0-7} (Input/output, three-state)	Multiplexed address/data bus: Lower 8-bits of the memory address (or I/O address) appear on the bus during the first clock cycle (T state) of a machine cycle. It then becomes the data bus during the second and third clock cycles.
ALE (Output)	Address Latch Enable: It occurs during the first clock state of a machine cycle and enables the address to get latched into the on-chip latch.
S_0, S_1 and $IO/\overline{M}$ (Output)	Machine cycle status:

$IO/\overline{M}$	S_1	S_0	STATUS
0	0	1	Memory write
0	1	0	Memory read
1	0	1	I/O write

999

Symbol	Function			
	IO/$\overline{\text{M}}$	S_1	S_0	Status
	1	1	0	I/O read
	0	1	1	Op code fetch
	1	1	1	Interrupt acknowledge
	*	0	0	Halt
	*	X	X	Hold
	*	X	X	Reset

* = 3-state (high impedance)

X = unspecified

S_1 can be used as an advanced R/$\overline{\text{W}}$ status. IO/$\overline{\text{M}}$, S_0, and S_1 become valid at the beginning of a machine cycle and remain stable throughout the cycle. The falling edge of ALE may be used to latch the state of these lines.

$\overline{\text{RD}}$
(Output, three-state) READ control: A low level on $\overline{\text{RD}}$ indicates the selected memory or I/O device is to be read.

$\overline{\text{WR}}$
(Output, three-state) WRITE control: A low level on $\overline{\text{WR}}$ indicates the data on the data bus is to be written into the selected memory or I/O location.

READY
(Input) If READY is high during a read or write cycle, it indicates that the memory or peripheral is ready to send or receive data. If READY is low, the CPU will wait an integral number of clock cycles for READY to go high before completing the read or write cycle.

HOLD
(Input) HOLD indicates that another master is requesting the use of the address and data buses. The CPU, upon receiving the hold request, will relinquish the use of the bus as soon as the completion of the current bus transfer. Internal processing can continue. The processor can regain the bus only after the HOLD is removed. When the HOLD is acknowledged, the address, data, $\overline{\text{RD}}$, $\overline{\text{WR}}$, and IO/$\overline{\text{M}}$ lines are three-stated.

HLDA
(Output) HOLD ACKNOWLEDGE: Indicates that the CPU has received the HOLD request and that it will relinquish the bus in the next clock cycle. HLDA goes low after the HOLD request is removed. The CPU takes the bus one-half clock cycle after HLDA goes low.

INTR
(Input) INTERRUPT REQUEST: Is used as a general-purpose interrupt. It is sampled only during the next to the last clock cycle of an instruction and during HOLD and HALT states. If it is active, the PC will be inhibited from incrementing and an $\overline{\text{INTA}}$ will be issued. During this cycle a RESTART or CALL instruction can be inserted to jump to the interrupt service routine. The INTR is enabled and disabled by software. It is disabled by RESET and immediately after an interrupt is accepted.

$\overline{\text{INTA}}$
(Output) INTERRUPT ACKNOWLEDGE: Is used instead of (and has the same timing as) $\overline{\text{RD}}$ during the instruction cycle after an INTR is accepted. It can be used to activate the 8259 interrupt chip or some other interrupt port.

RST5.5
RST6.5
RST7.5
(Inputs) RESTART INTERRUPTS: These three inputs have the same timing as INTR except they cause an internal RESTART to be automatically inserted.

TRAP
(Input) Trap interrupt is a nonmaskable RESTART interrupt. It is recognized at the same time as INTR or RST5.5–7.5. It is unaffected by any mask or interrupt enable. It has the highest priority of any interrupt.

$\overline{\text{RESET IN}}$
(Input) Sets the program counter to zero and resets the interrupt enable and HLDA flip-flops.

RESET OUT
(Output) Indicates CPU is being reset. Can be used as a system reset.

Symbol	Function
X_1, X_2 (Input)	X_1 and X_2 are connected to a crystal, LC, or RC network to drive the internal clock generator. X_1 can also be an external clock input from a logic gate. The input frequency is divided by 2 to give the processor's internal operating frequency.
CLK (Output)	Clock output for use as a system clock. The period of CLK is twice the X_1, X_2 input period.
SID (Input)	Serial Input Data line. The data on this line is loaded into accumulator bit 7 whenever a RIM instruction is executed.
SOD (Output)	Serial Output Data line. The output SOD is set or reset as specified by the SIM instruction.
V_{cc}	$+5$ V supply.
V_{ss}	Ground reference.

8086/8086-2/8086-4
16-BIT HMOS MICROPROCESSOR

- **Direct Addressing Capability to 1 MByte of Memory**

- **Assembly Language Compatible with 8080/8085**

- **14 Word, By 16-Bit Register Set with Symmetrical Operations**

- **24 Operand Addressing Modes**

- **Bit, Byte, Word, and Block Operations**

- **8-and 16-Bit Signed and Unsigned Arithmetic in Binary or Decimal Including Multiply and Divide**

- **5 MHz Clock Rate (8 MHz for 8086-2) (4 MHz for 8086-4)**

- **MULTIBUS™ System Compatible Interface**

The Intel® 8086 is a new generation, high performance microprocessor implemented in N-channel, depletion load, silicon gate technology (HMOS), and packaged in a 40-pin CerDIP package. The processor has attributes of both 8- and 16-bit microprocessors. It addresses memory as a sequence of 8-bit bytes, but has a 16-bit wide physical path to memory for high performance.

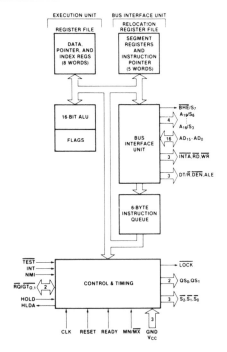

8086 CPU Functional Block Diagram

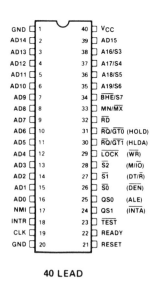

40 LEAD

8086 Pin Diagram

I8284
CLOCK GENERATOR AND DRIVER
FOR 8086, 8088, 8089 PROCESSORS

- **Generates the System Clock for the 8086, 8088 and 8089**

- **Uses a Crystal or a TTL Signal for Frequency Source**

- **Single +5V Power Supply**

- **18-Pin Package**

- **Generates System Reset Output from Schmitt Trigger Input**

- **Provides Local Ready and MULTIBUS™ Ready Synchronization**

- **Capable of Clock Synchronization with other 8284's**

- **Industrial Temperature Range −40° to +85°C**

The I8284 is a bipolar clock generator/driver designed to provide clock signals for the 8086, 8088 & 8089 and peripherals. It also contains READY logic for operation with two MULTIBUS™ systems and provides the processors required READY synchronization and timing. Reset logic with hysteresis and synchronization is also provided.

I8284 PIN CONFIGURATION

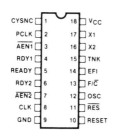

CYSNC	1		18	Vcc
PCLK	2		17	X1
AEN1	3		16	X2
RDY1	4		15	TNK
READY	5		14	EFI
RDY2	6		13	F/C̄
AEN2	7		12	OSC
CLK	8		11	RES
GND	9		10	RESET

I8284 BLOCK DIAGRAM

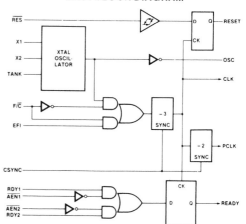

I8284 PIN NAMES

X1 X2	CONNECTIONS FOR CRYSTAL
TANK	USED WITH OVERTONE CRYSTAL
F/C̄	CLOCK SOURCE SELECT
EFI	EXTERNAL CLOCK INPUT
CSYNC	CLOCK SYNCHRONIZATION INPUT
RDY1 RDY2	READY SIGNAL FROM TWO MULTIBUS™ SYSTEMS
AEN1 AEN2	ADDRESS ENABLED QUALIFIERS FOR RDY1.2
RES	RESET INPUT
RESET	SYNCHRONIZED RESET OUTPUT
OSC	OSCILLATOR OUTPUT
CLK	MOS CLOCK FOR THE PROCESSOR
PCLK	TTL CLOCK FOR PERIPHERALS
READY	SYNCHRONIZED READY OUTPUT
Vcc	+5 VOLTS
GND	0 VOLTS

8288
BUS CONTROLLER
FOR 8086, 8088, 8089 PROCESSORS

- **Bipolar Drive Capability**

- **Provides Advanced Commands**

- **Provides Wide Flexibility in System Configurations**

- **3-State Command Output Drivers**

- **Configurable for Use with an I/O Bus**

- **Facilitates Interface to One or Two Multi-Master Busses**

The Intel® 8288 Bus Controller is a 20-pin bipolar component for use with medium-to-large 8086 processing systems. The bus controller provides command and control timing generation as well as bipolar bus drive capability while optimizing system performance.

A strapping option on the bus controller configures it for use with a multi-master system bus and separate I/O bus.

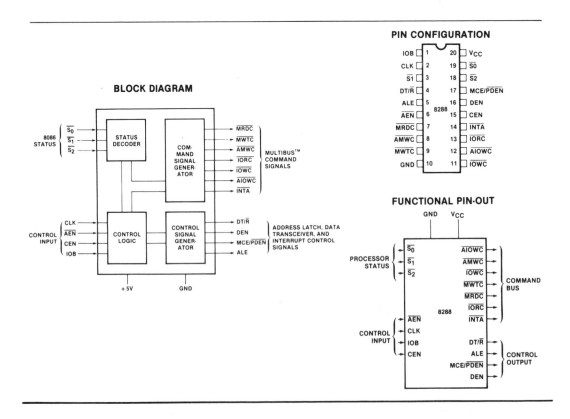

BLOCK DIAGRAM

PIN CONFIGURATION

FUNCTIONAL PIN-OUT

2142
1024 X 4 BIT STATIC RAM

	2142-2	2142-3	2142	2142L2	2142L3	2142L
Max. Access Time (ns)	200	300	450	200	300	450
Max. Power Dissipation (mw)	525	525	525	370	370	370

- **High Density 20 Pin Package**
- **Access Time Selections From 200-450ns**
- **Identical Cycle and Access Times**
- **Low Operating Power Dissipation .1mW/Bit Typical**
- **Single +5V Supply**

- **No Clock or Timing Strobe Required**
- **Completely Static Memory**
- **Directly TTL Compatible: All Inputs and Outputs**
- **Common Data Input and Output Using Three-State Outputs**

The Intel® 2142 is a 4096-bit static Random Access Memory organized as 1024 words by 4-bits using N-channel Silicon-Gate MOS technology. It uses fully DC stable (static) circuitry throughout — in both the array and the decoding — and therefore requires no clocks or refreshing to operate. Data access is particularly simple since address setup times are not required. The data is read out nondestructively and has the same polarity as the input data. Common input/output pins are provided.

The 2142 is designed for memory applications where high performance, low cost, large bit storage, and simple interfacing are important design objectives. It is directly TTL compatible in all respects: inputs, outputs, and a single +5V supply.

The 2142 is placed in a 20-pin package. Two Chip Selects ($\overline{CS}_1$ and CS_2) are provided for easy and flexible selection of individual packages when outputs are OR-tied. An Output Disable is included for direct control of the output buffers.

The 2142 is fabricated with Intel's N-channel Silicon-Gate technology — a technology providing excellent protection against contamination permitting the use of low cost plastic packaging.

PIN CONFIGURATION   **LOGIC SYMBOL**   **BLOCK DIAGRAM**

PIN CONFIGURATION:

A_6	1	20	V_{CC}
A_5	2	19	A_7
A_4	3	18	A_8
A_3	4	17	A_9
CS_2	5	16	OD
A_0	6	15	I/O_1
A_1	7	14	I/O_2
A_2	8	13	I/O_3
$\overline{CS}_1$	9	12	I/O_4
GND	10	11	$\overline{WE}$

(2142)

PIN NAMES

A_0–A_9	ADDRESS INPUTS	OD	OUTPUT DISABLE
$\overline{WE}$	WRITE ENABLE	V_{CC}	POWER (+5V)
$\overline{CS}_1$, CS_2	CHIP SELECT	GND	GROUND
I/O_1–I/O_4	DATA INPUT/OUTPUT		

Block diagram: MEMORY ARRAY 64 ROWS 64 COLUMNS, ROW SELECT, INPUT DATA CONTROL, COLUMN I/O CIRCUITS, COLUMN SELECT. ○ = PIN NUMBERS

2716
16K (2K × 8) UV ERASABLE PROM

- ■ **Fast Access Time**
  - — **350 ns Max. 2716-1**
  - — **390 ns Max. 2716-2**
  - — **450 ns Max. 2716**
  - — **650 ns Max. 2716-6**

- ■ **Single +5V Power Supply**

- ■ **Low Power Dissipation**
  - — **525 mW Max. Active Power**
  - — **132 mW Max. Standby Power**

- ■ **Pin Compatible to Intel® 2732 EPROM**

- ■ **Simple Programming Requirements**
  - — **Single Location Programming**
  - — **Programs with One 50 ms Pulse**

- ■ **Inputs and Outputs TTL Compatible during Read and Program**

- ■ **Completely Static**

The Intel® 2716 is a 16,384-bit ultraviolet erasable and electrically programmable read-only memory (EPROM). The 2716 operates from a single 5-volt power supply, has a static standby mode, and features fast single address location programming. It makes designing with EPROMs faster, easier and more economical.

The 2716, with its single 5-volt supply and with an access time up to 350 ns, is ideal for use with the newer high performance +5V microprocessors such as Intel's 8085 and 8086. The 2716 is also the first EPROM with a static standby mode which reduces the power dissipation without increasing access time. The maximum active power dissipation is 525 mW while the maximum standby power dissipation is only 132 mW, a 75% savings.

The 2716 has the simplest and fastest method yet devised for programming EPROMs — single pulse TTL level programming. No need for high voltage pulsing because all programming controls are handled by TTL signals. Program any location at any time—either individually, sequentially or at random, with the 2716's single address location programming. Total programming time for all 16,384 bits is only 100 seconds.

PIN CONFIGURATION

2716 (16K)

A_7	1	24	V_{CC}
A_6	2	23	A_8
A_5	3	22	A_9
A_4	4	21	V_{PP}
A_3	5	20	$\overline{OE}$
A_2	6	19	A_{10}
A_1	7	18	$\overline{CE}$
A_0	8	17	O_7
O_0	9	16	O_6
O_1	10	15	O_5
O_2	11	14	O_4
GND	12	13	O_3

2732† (32K)

A_7	1	24	V_{CC}
A_6	2	23	A_8
A_5	3	22	A_9
A_4	4	21	A_{11}
A_3	5	20	$\overline{OE}/V_{PP}$
A_2	6	19	A_{10}
A_1	7	18	$\overline{CE}$
A_0	8	17	O_7
O_0	9	16	O_6
O_1	10	15	O_5
O_2	11	14	O_4
GND	12	13	O_3

†Refer to 2732 data sheet for specifications

PIN NAMES

$A_0 - A_{10}$	ADDRESSES
$\overline{CE}$/PGM	CHIP ENABLE/PROGRAM
$\overline{OE}$	OUTPUT ENABLE
$O_0 - O_7$	OUTPUTS

MODE SELECTION

MODE \ PINS	$\overline{CE}$/PGM (18)	$\overline{OE}$ (20)	V_{PP} (21)	V_{CC} (24)	OUTPUTS (9-11, 13-17)
Read	V_{IL}	V_{IL}	+5	+5	D_{OUT}
Standby	V_{IH}	Don't Care	+5	+5	High Z
Program	Pulsed V_{IL} to V_{IH}	V_{IH}	+25	+5	D_{IN}
Program Verify	V_{IL}	V_{IL}	+25	+5	D_{OUT}
Program Inhibit	V_{IL}	V_{IH}	+25	+5	High Z

BLOCK DIAGRAM

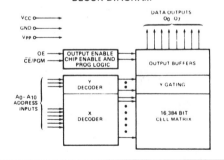

®

2732
32K (4K x 8) UV ERASABLE PROM

- **Fast Access Time:**
  - **— 450 ns Max. 2732**
  - **— 550 ns Max. 2732-6**

- **Single +5V ± 5% Power Supply**

- **Output Enable for MCS-85™ and MCS-86™ Compatibility**

- **Low Power Dissipation: 150mA Max. Active Current 30mA Max. Standby Current**

- **Pin Compatible to Intel® 2716 EPROM**

- **Completely Static**

- **Simple Programming Requirements**
  - **— Single Location Programming**
  - **— Programs with One 50ms Pulse**

- **Three-State Output for Direct Bus Interface**

The Intel® 2732 is a 32,768-bit ultraviolet erasable and electrically programmable read-only memory (EPROM). The 2732 operates from a single 5-volt power supply, has a standby mode, and features an output enable control. The total programming time for all bits is three and a half minutes. All these features make designing with the 2732 in microcomputer systems faster, easier, and more economical.

An important 2732 feature is the separate output control, Output Enable ($\overline{OE}$), from the Chip Enable control ($\overline{CE}$). The $\overline{OE}$ control eliminates bus contention in multiple bus microprocessor systems. Intel's Application Note AP-30 describes the microprocessor system implementation of the $\overline{OE}$ and $\overline{CE}$ controls on Intel's 2716 and 2732 EPROMs. AP-30 is available from Intel's Literature Department.

The 2732 has a standby mode which reduces the power dissipation without increasing access time. The maximum active current is 150mA, while the maximum standby current is only 30mA, an 80% savings. The standby mode is achieved by applying a TTL-high signal to the $\overline{CE}$ input.

PIN CONFIGURATION

```
      ┌───┬───┐
A_7  1│   24│ V_CC
A_6  2│   23│ A_8
A_5  3│   22│ A_9
A_4  4│   21│ A_11
A_3  5│   20│ OE/V_PP
A_2  6│   19│ A_10
A_1  7│   18│ CE
A_0  8│   17│ O_7
O_0  9│   16│ O_6
O_1 10│   15│ O_5
O_2 11│   14│ O_4
GND 12│   13│ O_3
      └───────┘
```

MODE SELECTION

PINS / MODE	$\overline{CE}$ (18)	$\overline{OE}$/V_PP (20)	V_CC (24)	OUTPUTS (9-11,13-17)
Read	V_{IL}	V_{IL}	+5	D_{OUT}
Standby	V_{IH}	Don't Care	+5	High Z
Program	V_{IL}	V_{PP}	+5	D_{IN}
Program Verify	V_{IL}	V_{IL}	+5	D_{OUT}
Program Inhibit	V_{IH}	V_{PP}	+5	High Z

PIN NAMES

A_0-A_{11}	ADDRESSES
$\overline{CE}$	CHIP ENABLE
$\overline{OE}$	OUTPUT ENABLE
O_0-O_7	OUTPUTS

BLOCK DIAGRAM

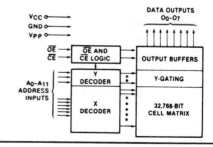

8355/8355-2
16,384-BIT ROM WITH I/O

- **2048 Words × 8 Bits**

- **Single + 5V Power Supply**

- **Directly compatible with 8085A and 8088 Microprocessors**

- **2 General Purpose 8-Bit I/O Ports**

- **Each I/O Port Line Individually Programmable as Input or Output**

- **Multiplexed Address and Data Bus**

- **Internal Address Latch**

- **40-Pin DIP**

The Intel® 8355 is a ROM and I/O chip to be used in the 8085A and 8088 microprocessor systems. The ROM portion is organized as 2048 words by 8 bits. It has a maximum acess time of 400 ns to permit use with no wait states in the 8085A CPU.

The I/O portion consists of 2 general purpose I/O ports. Each I/O port has 8 port lines and each I/O port line is individually programmable as input or output.

The 8355-2 has a 300ns access time for compatibility with the 8085A-2 and full speed 5 MHz 8088 microprocessors.

PIN CONFIGURATION

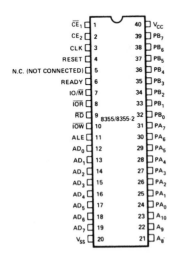

BLOCK DIAGRAM

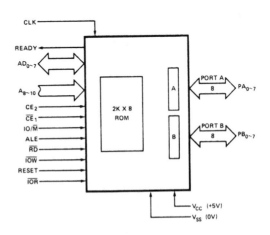

8355/8355-2

Symbol	Function
ALE (Input)	When ALE (Address Latch Enable is high, AD_{0-7}, $IO/\overline{M}$, A_{8-10}, CE, and $\overline{CE}$ enter address latched. The signals (AD, $IO/\overline{M}$, A_{8-10}, CE, $\overline{CE}$) are latched in at the trailing edge of ALE.
AD_{0-7} (Input)	Bidirectional Address/Data bus. The lower 8-bits of the ROM or I/O address are applied to the bus lines when ALE is high.
	During an I/O cycle, Port A or B are selected based on the latched value of AD_0. If $\overline{RD}$ or $\overline{IOR}$ is low when the latched chip enables are active, the output buffers present data on the bus.
A_{8-10} (Input)	These are the high order bits of the ROM address. They do not affect I/O operations.
$\overline{CE}_1$ CE_2 (Input)	Chip Enable Inputs: $\overline{CE}_1$ is active low and CE_2 is active high. The 8355 can be accessed only when BOTH Chip Enables are active at the time the ALE signal latches them up. If either Chip Enable input is not active, the AD_{0-7} and READY outputs will be in a high impedance state.
$IO/\overline{M}$ (Input)	If the latched $IO/\overline{M}$ is high when $\overline{RD}$ is low, the output data comes from an I/O port. If it is low the output data comes from the ROM.
$\overline{RD}$ (Input)	If the latched Chip Enables are active when $\overline{RD}$ goes low, the AD_{0-7} output buffers are enabled and output either the selected ROM location or I/O port. When both $\overline{RD}$ and $\overline{IOR}$ are high, the AD_{0-7} output buffers are 3-state.
$\overline{IOW}$ (Input)	If the latched Chip Enables are active, a low on $\overline{IOW}$ causes the output port pointed to by the latched value of AD_0 to be written with the data on AD_{0-7}. The state of $IO/\overline{M}$ is ignored.

Symbol	Function
CLK (Input)	The CLK is used to force the READY into its high impedance state after it has been forced low by $\overline{CE}$ low, CE high and ALE high.
READY (Output)	Ready is a 3-state output controlled by $\overline{CE}_1$, CE_2, ALE and CLK. READY is forced low when the Chip Enables are active during the time ALE is high, and remains low until the rising edge of the next CLK (see Figure 6).
PA_{0-7} (Input/ Output)	These are general purpose I/O pins. Their input/output direction is determined by the contents of Data Direction Register (DDR). Port A is selected for write operations when the Chip Enables are active and $\overline{IOW}$ is low and a 0 was previously latched from AD_0.
	Read operation is selected by either $\overline{IOR}$ low and active Chip Enables and AD_0 low, or $IO/\overline{M}$ high, $\overline{RD}$ low, active chip enables, and AD_0 low.
PB_{0-7} (Input/ Output)	This general purpose I/O port is identical to Port A except that it is selected by a 1 latched from AD_0.
RESET (Input)	An input high on RESET causes all pins in Port A and B to assume input mode.
$\overline{IOR}$ (Input)	When the Chip Enables are active, a low on $\overline{IOR}$ will output the selected I/O port onto the AD bus. $\overline{IOR}$ low performs the same function as the combination $IO/\overline{M}$ high and $\overline{RD}$ low. When $\overline{IOR}$ is not used in a system, $\overline{IOR}$ should be tied to V_{CC} ("1").
V_{CC}	+5 volt supply.
V_{SS}	Ground Reference.

8755A/8755A-2
16,384-BIT EPROM WITH I/O

- **2048 Words × 8 Bits**

- **Single +5V Power Supply (V$_{CC}$)**

- **Directly Compatible with 8085A and 8088 Microprocessors**

- **U.V. Erasable and Electrically Reprogrammable**

- **Internal Address Latch**

- **2 General Purpose 8-Bit I/O Ports**

- **Each I/O Port Line Individually Programmable as Input or Output**

- **Multiplexed Address and Data Bus**

- **40-Pin DIP**

The Intel® 8755A is an erasable and electrically reprogrammable ROM (EPROM) and I/O chip to be used in the 8085A and 8088 microprocessor systems. The EPROM portion is organized as 2048 words by 8 bits. It has a maximum access time of 450 ns to permit use with no wait states in an 8085A CPU.

The I/O portion consists of 2 general purpose I/O ports. Each I/O port has 8 port lines, and each I/O port line is individually programmable as input or output.

The 8755A-2 is a high speed selected version of the 8755A compatible with the 5 MHz 8085A-2 and the full speed 5 MHz 8088.

PIN CONFIGURATION   BLOCK DIAGRAM

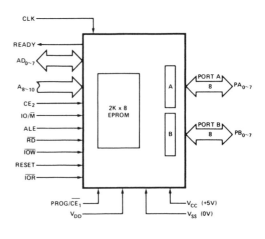

8755A FUNCTIONAL PIN DEFINITION

Symbol	Function
ALE (input)	When Address Latch Enable goes high, AD_{0-7}, IO/M, A_{8-10}, CE_2, and $\overline{CE_1}$ enter the address latches. The signals (AD, IO/M, A_{8-10}, CE) are latched in at the trailing edge of ALE.
AD_{0-7} (input/output)	Bidirectional Address/Data bus. The lower 8-bits of the PROM or I/O address are applied to the bus lines when ALE is high.
	During an I/O cycle, Port A or B are selected based on the latched value of AD_0. If $\overline{RD}$ or $\overline{IOR}$ is low when the latched Chip Enables are active, the output buffers present data on the bus.
A_{8-10} (input)	These are the high order bits of the PROM address. They do not affect I/O operations.
PROG/$\overline{CE_1}$ CE_2 (input)	Chip Enable Inputs: $\overline{CE_1}$ is active low and CE_2 is active high. The 8755A can be accessed only when *BOTH* Chip Enables are active at the time the ALE signal latches them up. If either Chip Enable input is not active, the AD_{0-7} and READY outputs will be in a high impedance state. $\overline{CE_1}$ is also used as a programming pin. (See section on programming.)
IO/$\overline{M}$ (input)	If the latched IO/$\overline{M}$ is high when $\overline{RD}$ is low, the output data comes from an I/O port. If it is low the output data comes from the PROM.
$\overline{RD}$ (input)	If the latched Chip Enables are active when $\overline{RD}$ goes low, the AD_{0-7} output buffers are enabled and output either the selected PROM location or I/O port. When both $\overline{RD}$ and $\overline{IOR}$ are high, the AD_{0-7} output buffers are 3-stated.
$\overline{IOW}$ (input)	If the latched Chip Enables are active, a low on $\overline{IOW}$ causes the output port pointed to by the latched value of AD_0 to be written with the data on AD_{0-7}. The state of IO/$\overline{M}$ is ignored.
CLK (input)	The CLK is used to force the READY into its high impedance state after it has been forced low by $\overline{CE_1}$ low, CE_2 high, and ALE high.

Symbol	Function
READY (output)	READY is a 3-state output controlled by CE_2, $\overline{CE_1}$, ALE and CLK. READY is forced low when the Chip Enables are active during the time ALE is high, and remains low until the rising edge of the next CLK. (See Figure 6.)
PA_{0-7} (input/output)	These are general purpose I/O pins. Their input/output direction is determined by the contents of Data Direction Register (DDR). Port A is selected for write operations when the Chip Enables are active and $\overline{IOW}$ is low and a 0 was previously latched from AD_0, AD_1.
	Read operation is selected by either $\overline{IOR}$ low and active Chip Enables and AD_0 and AD_1 low, *or* IO/$\overline{M}$ high, $\overline{RD}$ low, active Chip Enables, and AD_0 and AD_1 low.
PB_{0-7} (input/output)	This general purpose I/O port is identical to Port A except that it is selected by a 1 latched from AD_0 and a 0 from AD_1.
RESET (input)	In normal operation, an input high on RESET causes all pins in Ports A and B to assume input mode (clear DDR register).
$\overline{IOR}$ (input)	When the Chip Enables are active, a low on $\overline{IOR}$ will output the selected I/O port onto the AD bus. $\overline{IOR}$ low performs the same function as the combination of IO/$\overline{M}$ high and $\overline{RD}$ low. When $\overline{IOR}$ is not used in a system, $\overline{IOR}$ should be tied to V_{CC} ("1").
V_{CC}	+5 volt supply.
V_{SS}	Ground Reference.
V_{DD}	V_{DD} is a programming voltage, and must be tied to +5V when the 8755A is being read.
	For programming, a high voltage is supplied with $V_{DD} = 25V$, typical. (See section on programming.)

8155/8156/8155-2/8156-2
2048 BIT STATIC MOS RAM WITH I/O PORTS AND TIMER

- ■ **256 Word x 8 Bits**
- ■ **Single +5V Power Supply**
- ■ **Completely Static Operation**
- ■ **Internal Address Latch**
- ■ **2 Programmable 8 Bit I/O Ports**

- ■ **1 Programmable 6-Bit I/O Port**
- ■ **Programmable 14-Bit Binary Counter/ Timer**
- ■ **Compatible with 8085A and 8088 CPU**
- ■ **Multiplexed Address and Data Bus**
- ■ **40 Pin DIP**

The 8155 and 89156 are RAM and I/O chips to be used in the 8085A and 8088 microprocessor systems. The RAM portion is designed with 2048 static cells organized as 256 x 8. They have a maximum access time of 400 ns to permit use with no wait states in 8085A CPU. The 8155-2 and 8156-2 have maximum access times of 330 ns for use with the 8085A-2 and the full speed 5 MHz 8088 CPU.

The I/O portion consists of three general purpose I/O ports. One of the three ports can be programmed to be status pins, thus allowing the other two ports to operate in handshake mode.

A 14-bit programmable counter/timer is jalso included on chip to provide either a square wave or terminal count pulse for the CPU system depending on timer mode.

PIN CONFIGURATION

PC$_3$	1	40	V$_{CC}$
PC$_4$	2	39	PC$_2$
TIMER IN	3	38	PC$_1$
RESET	4	37	PC$_0$
PC$_5$	5	36	PB$_7$
$\overline{\text{TIMER OUT}}$	6	35	PB$_6$
IO/$\overline{\text{M}}$	7	34	PB$_5$
$\overline{\text{CE}}$ OR CE*	8	33	PB$_4$
$\overline{\text{RD}}$	9	32	PB$_3$
$\overline{\text{WR}}$	10	31	PB$_2$
ALE	11	30	PB$_1$
AD$_0$	12	29	PB$_0$
AD$_1$	13	28	PA$_7$
AD$_2$	14	27	PA$_6$
AD$_3$	15	26	PA$_5$
AD$_4$	16	25	PA$_4$
AD$_5$	17	24	PA$_3$
AD$_6$	18	23	PA$_2$
AD$_7$	19	22	PA$_1$
V$_{SS}$	20	21	PA$_0$

8155/8156
8155-2/8156-2

BLOCK DIAGRAM

: 8155/8155-2 = $\overline{\text{CE}}$, 8156/8156-2 = CE

8155/8156 PIN FUNCTIONS

Symbol	Function
RESET (input)	Pulse provided by the 8085A to initialize the system (connect to 8085A RESET OUT). Input high on this line resets the chip and initializes the three I/O ports to input mode. The width of RESET pulse should typically be two 8085A clock cycle times.
AD_{0-7} (input)	3-state Address/Data lines that interface with the CPU lower 8-bit Address/Data Bus. The 8-bit address is latched into the address latch inside the 8155/56 on the falling edge of ALE. The address can be either for the memory section or the I/O section depending on the $IO/\overline{M}$ input. The 8-bit data is either written into the chip or read from the chip, depending on the $\overline{WR}$ or $\overline{RD}$ input signal.
CE or $\overline{CE}$ (input)	Chip Enable: On the 8155, this pin is $\overline{CE}$ and is ACTIVE LOW. On the 8156, this pin is CE and is ACTIVE HIGH.
$\overline{RD}$ (input)	Read control: Input low on this line with the Chip Enable active enables and AD_{0-7} buffers. If $IO/\overline{M}$ pin is low, the RAM content will be read out to the AD bus. Otherwise the content of the selected I/O port or command/status registers will be read to the AD bus.
$\overline{WR}$ (input)	Write control: Input low on this line with the Chip Enable active causes the data on the Address/Data bus to be written to the RAM or I/O ports and command/status register depending on $IO/\overline{M}$.

Symbol	Function
ALE (input)	Address Latch Enable: This control signal latches both the address on the AD_{0-7} lines and the state of the Chip Enable and $IO/\overline{M}$ into the chip at the falling edge of ALE.
$IO/\overline{M}$ (input)	Selects memory if low and I/O and command/status registers if high.
$PA_{0-7}(8)$ (input/output)	These 8 pins are general purpose I/O pins. The in/out direction is selected by programming the command register.
$PB_{0-7}(8)$ (input/output)	These 8 pins are general purpose I/O pins. The in/out direction is selected by programming the command register.
$PC_{0-5}(6)$ (input/output)	These 6 pins can function as either input port, output port, or as control signals for PA and PB. Programming is done through the command register. When PC_{0-5} are used as control signals, they will provide the following: PC_0 — A INTR (Port A Interrupt) PC_1 — ABF (Port A Buffer Full) PC_2 — $\overline{A\ STB}$ (Port A Strobe) PC_3 — B INTR (Port B Interrupt) PC_4 — $\overline{B\ BF}$ (Port B Buffer Full) PC_5 — B STB (Port B Strobe)
TIMER IN (input)	Input to the counter-timer.
$\overline{\text{TIMER OUT}}$ (output)	Timer output. This output can be either a square wave or a pulse depending on the timer mode.
V_{CC}	+5 volt supply.
V_{SS}	Ground Reference.

8255A/8255A-5
PROGRAMMABLE PERIPHERAL INTERFACE

- **MCS-85™ Compatible 8255A-5**
- **24 Programmable I/O Pins**
- **Completely TTL Compatible**
- **Fully Compatible with Intel® Microprocessor Families**
- **Improved Timing Characteristics**

- **Direct Bit Set/Reset Capability Easing Control Application Interface**
- **40-Pin Dual In-Line Package**
- **Reduces System Package Count**
- **Improved DC Driving Capability**

The Intel® 8255A is a general purpose programmable I/O device designed for use with Intel® microprocessors. It has 24 I/O pins which may be individually programmed in 2 groups of 12 and used in 3 major modes of operation. In the first mode (MODE 0), each group of 12 I/O pins may be programmed in sets of 4 to be input or output. In MODE 1, the second mode, each group may be programmed to have 8 lines of input or output. Of the remaining 4 pins, 3 are used for hand-shaking and interrupt control signals. The third mode of operation (MODE 2) is a bidirectional bus mode which uses 8 lines for a bidirectional bus, and 5 lines, borrowing one from the other group, for handshaking.

PIN CONFIGURATION

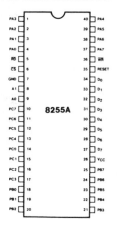

8255A BLOCK DIAGRAM

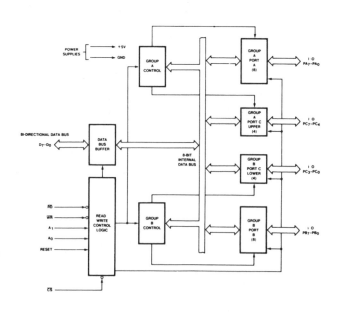

PIN NAMES

D_7-D_0	DATA BUS (BI DIRECTIONAL)
RESET	RESET INPUT
CS	CHIP SELECT
RD	READ INPUT
WR	WRITE INPUT
A0, A1	PORT ADDRESS
PA7-PA0	PORT A (BIT)
PB7-PB0	PORT B (BIT)
PC7-PC0	PORT C (BIT)
V_CC	+5 VOLTS
GND	0 VOLTS

8279/8279-5
PROGRAMMABLE KEYBOARD/DISPLAY INTERFACE

- ■ **Simultaneous Keyboard Display Operations**
- ■ **Scanned Keyboard Mode**
- ■ **Scanned Sensor Mode**
- ■ **Strobed Input Entry Mode**
- ■ **8-Character Keyboard FIFO**
- ■ **2-Key Lockout or N-Key Rollover with Contact Debounce**
- ■ **Dual 8- or 16-Numerical Display**

- ■ **Single 16-Character Display**
- ■ **Right or Left Entry 16-Byte Display RAM**
- ■ **Mode Programmable from CPU**
- ■ **Programmable Scan Timing**
- ■ **Interrupt Output on Key Entry**
- ■ **Available in EXPRESS**
  - **— Standard Temperature Range**
  - **— Extended Temperature Range**

The Intel® 8279 is a general purpose programmable keyboard and display I/O interface device designed for use with Intel® microprocessors. The keyboard portion can provide a scanned interface to a 64-contact key matrix. The keyboard portion will also interface to an array of sensors or a strobed interface keyboard, such as the hall effect and ferrite variety. Key depressions can be 2-key lockout or N-key rollover. Keyboard entries are debounced and strobed in an 8-character FIFO. If more than 8 characters are entered, overrun status is set. Key entries set the interrupt output line to the CPU.

The display portion provides a scanned display interface for LED, incandescent, and other popular display technologies. Both numeric and alphanumeric segment displays may be used as well as simple indicators. The 8279 has 16x8 display RAM which can be organized into dual 16x4. The RAM can be loaded or interrogated by the CPU. Both right entry, calculator and left entry typewriter display formats are possible. Both read and write of the display RAM can be done with auto-increment of the display RAM address.

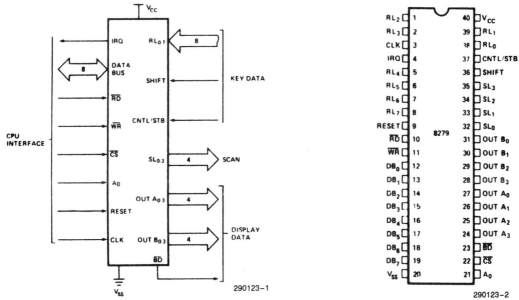

Figure 1. Logic Symbol

290123-1

September 1987
Order Number: 290123-002

Figure 2. Pin Configuration

290123-2

8279/8279-5

HARDWARE DESCRIPTION

The 8279 is packaged in a 40 pin DIP. The following is a functional description of each pin.

Table 1. Pin Description

Symbol	Pin No.	Name and Function
DB$_0$–DB$_7$	19–12	**BI-DIRECTIONAL DATA BUS:** All data and commands between the CPU and the 8279 are transmitted on these lines.
CLK	3	**CLOCK:** Clock from system used to generate internal timing.
RESET	9	**RESET:** A high signal on this pin resets the 8279. After being reset the 8279 is placed in the following mode: 1) 16 8-bit character display—left entry. 2) Encoded scan keyboard—2 key lockout. Along with this the program clock prescaler is set to 31.
CS	22	**CHIP SELECT:** A low on this pin enables the interface functions to receive or transmit.
A$_0$	21	**BUFFER ADDRESS:** A high on this line indicates the signals in or out are interpreted as a command or status. A low indicates that they are data.
$\overline{RD}$, $\overline{WR}$	10–11	**INPUT/OUTPUT READ AND WRITE:** These signals enable the data buffers to either send data to the external bus or receive it from the external bus.
IRQ	4	**INTERRUPT REQUEST:** In a keyboard mode, the interrupt line is high when there is data in the FIFO/Sensor RAM. The interrupt line goes low with each FIFO/Sensor RAM read and returns high if there is still information in the RAM. In a sensor mode, the interrupt line goes high whenever a change in a sensor is detected.
V$_{SS}$, V$_{CC}$	20, 40	**GROUND AND POWER SUPPLY PINS.**
SL$_0$–SL$_3$	32–35	**SCAN LINES:** Scan lines which are used to scan the key switch or sensor matrix and the display digits. These lines can be either encoded (1 of 16) or decoded (1 of 4).
RL$_0$–RL$_7$	38, 39, 1, 2, 5–8	**RETURN LINE:** Return line inputs which are connected to the scan lines through the keys or sensor switches. They have active internal pullups to keep them high until a switch closure pulls one low. They also serve as an 8-bit input in the Strobed Input mode.
SHIFT	36	**SHIFT:** The shift input status is stored along with the key position on key closure in the Scanned Keyboard modes. It has an active internal pullup to keep it high until a switch closure pulls it low.
CNTL/STB	37	**CONTROL/STROBED INPUT MODE:** For keyboard modes this line is used as a control input and stored like status on a key closure. The line is also the strobe line that enters the data into the FIFO in the Strobed Input mode. (Rising Edge). It has an active internal pullup to keep it high until a switch closure pulls it low.
OUT A$_0$–OUT A$_3$ OUT B$_0$–OUT B$_3$	27–24 31–28	**OUTPUTS:** These two ports are the outputs for the 16 x 4 display refresh registers. The data from these outputs is synchronized to the scan lines (SL$_0$–SL$_3$) for multiplexed digit displays. The two 4 bit ports may be blanked independently. These two ports may also be considered as one 8-bit port.
$\overline{BD}$	23	**BLANK DISPLAY:** This output is used to blank the display during digit switching or by a display blanking command.

APPENDIX D
GLOSSARY

Absolute Addressing: The specific identification number (address) permanently assigned to a storage location, device, or register by the machine designer. Used to locate information and assist in circuit fault diagnosis.

Accumulator: Used for storing the result after most ALU operations; 8 bits long for an 8-bit microprocessor.

Address: A unique identification number (or locator) of some source or destination of data. That part of an instruction which specifies the register or memory location of an operand involved in the instruction.

Addressing Mode: The manner in which a microprocessor determines the operand and destination addresses in an instruction cycle.

Address Register: A register used to store the address (label for a memory location) of data being fetched or stored, a sequence of instructions to be executed, or the location to which control will be transferred.

Address Space: The number of storage locations in a computer's memory that can be located by the addressing technique used by the CPU. The addressing range is determined by the number of bits capable of being held in the address register (that is, 2x combinations).

American Standard Code for Information Interchange (ASCII): An 8-bit code commonly used with microprocessors for representing alphanumeric codes.

Analog-to-Digital (A/D) Converter: Transforms an analog voltage into its digital equivalent.

Architecture: The organizational structure or hardware configuration of a computer system.

Arithmetic and Logic Unit (ALU): A digital circuit which performs arithmetic and logic operations on two n-bit digital words.

Assembler: A program that translates an assembly language program into a machine language program.

Assembly Language: A type of microprocessor programming language that uses a semi-English-language statement.

Asynchronous Operation: The execution of a sequence of steps such that each step is initiated upon completion of the previous step. For bus structures this implies a timing protocol that uses no clock and has no period; hence system operation proceeds at a rate governed by the time-constants of the enabled circuitry.

Asynchronous Serial Data Transmission: The transmitting device does not need to be synchronized with the receiving device.

Autodecrement Addressing Mode: The contents of the specified microprocessor register are first decremented by **K** (1 for byte, 2 for 16-bit, and 4 for 32-bit) and then the resulting value is used as the address of the operand.

Autoincrement Addressing Mode: The contents of a specified microprocessor register are used as the address of the operand first and then the register contents are automatically incremented by **K** (1 for byte, 2 for 16-bit, and 4 for 32-bit).

Bandwidth: Bandwidth of a bus or memory is a measure of communications throughput and can be represented as the product of the maximum number of transactions per second and number of data bits per transaction.

Barrel Shifter: A specially configured shift register that allows multiple shifting binary-encoded operands in one clock cycle.

Base Address: An address that is used to convert all relative addresses in a program to absolute (machine) addresses.

Base Page Addressing: This instruction uses two bytes: the first byte is the op code, and the second byte is the low-order address byte. The high-order address byte is assumed to be the base-page number.

Baud Rate: Rate of data transmission in bits per second.

Binary-Coded Decimal (BCD): The representation of 10 decimal digits, 0 through 9, by their corresponding 4-bit binary numbers.

Bit: An abbreviation for a binary digit. A unit of information equal to one binary decision or one of two possible states (one or zero, on or off, true or false) and represents the smallest piece of information in a binary notation system.

Bit-Slice Microprocessor: Divides the elements of a central processing unit (ALU, registers, and control unit) among several ICs. The registers and ALU are usually contained in a single chip. These microprocessors can be cascaded to produce microprocessors of variable word lengths such as 8, 12, 16, 32. The control unit of a bit-slice microprocessor is typically microprogrammed.

Block Transfer DMA: A peripheral device requests the DMA transfer via the DMA request line, which is connected directly or through a DMA controller chip to the microprocessor. The DMA controller chip completes the DMA transfer and transfers the control of the bus to the microprocessor.

Branch: A computer instruction that marks a decision point in the program or that point at which the path followed for the execution of instructions diverges. The branch instruction allows the computer to skip or jump out of program sequence to a designated instruction.

Breakpoint: Allows the user to execute the section of a program until one of the breakpoint conditions is met. It is then halted. The designer may then single step or examine memory and registers. Typically breakpoint conditions are program counter address or data references.

Buffer: A temporary memory storage device designed to compensate for the different data rates between a transmitting device and a receiving device (for example, between a CPU and a peripheral).

Bus: A collection of parallel unbroken electrical signal lines that interconnect or link computer modules. The typical microcomputer interface includes separate buses for address, data, control, and power functions.

Bus Arbitration: Bus operation protocols that guarantee conflict-free access to a bus. Arbitration is the process of selecting one respondent from a collection of several candidates that concurrently request service.

Bus Cycle: The period of time in which a CPU carries out all the necessary bus communications to implement a standard operation.

Byte: An 8-bit word.

Cache Memory: An ultra-high speed, directly accessible, relatively small semiconductor memory block used to store data/instructions that the computer may need in the immediate future. Increases system bandwidth by reducing the number of external memory fetches required by the processor.

Cathode Ray Tube (CRT): Evacuated glass tube with a fluorescent coating on the inner side of the screen.

Central Processing Unit (CPU): The portion of a computer containing the ALU, register section, and control unit.

Clock: Timing signals providing synchronization among the various components in a microcomputer system.

Code: A system of symbols or set of rules for the representation of data in a digital computer. Some examples include binary, BCD, and ASCII.

Compiler: A software program which translates the source code written in a high-level programming language into machine language that is understandable to the processor.

Complementary Metal Oxide Semiconductor (CMOS): Provides low power density and high noise immunity.

Concurrency: The occurrence of one or more operations at a time (see Parallel Operation).

Conditional Branching: Conditional branch instructions are used to change the order of execution of a program based on the conditions set by the status flags.

Condition Code Register: Contains information about the condition of functional units or peripheral devices. It is contained within the supervisor model's status register.

Control Register: A register which contains the address of the next instruction in the sequence of operations (that is, a program counter).

Control Store: Used to contain microcode (usually in ROM) in order to provide for microprogrammed "firmware" control functions. An integral part of a microprogrammed system controller.

Control Unit: Part of the microprocessor; its purpose is to read and decode instructions from the memory.

Controller/Sequencer: The hardware circuits which provide signals to carry out selection and retrieval of instructions from storage in sequence, interpret them, and initiate the required operation. The system functions may be implemented by hardware control, firmware control, or software control.

Coprocessor: A specialized microprocessor that performs specific functions independently from the CPU to speed up overall operations.

CPU Space: Protected memory space addressable only by the CPU itself; it is used for a processor's internal functions or vectored exception processing.

CRT Controller: Provides all logic functions for interfacing the microprocessor to a CRT.

Cycle Stealing DMA: The DMA controller transfers a byte of data between the microprocessor and a peripheral device by stealing a clock cycle of the microprocessor.

Daisy Chain Interrupt: Priorities of interrupting devices are defined by connecting them in a daisy chain.

Data: Basic elements of information represented in binary form (that is, digits consisting of bits) that can be processed or produced by a computer. Data represents any group of operands made up of numbers, letters, or symbols denoting any condition, value, or state. Current typical computer operand sizes include: a word, which contains 2 bytes or 16 bits; a long word, which contains 4 bytes or 32 bits; a quad word, which contains 8 bytes or 64 bits.

Data Counter (DC): Also known as Memory Address Register (MAR). Stores the address of data; typically, 16 bits long for 8-bit microprocessors.

Data Register: A register used to temporarily hold operational data being sent to and from a coprocessor peripheral device.

Debugger: A program that executes and debugs the object program generated by the assembler or compiler. The debugger provides a single stepping, breakpoints, and program tracing.

Decoder: A device capable of deciphering encoded signal. It interprets input instructions and initiates the appropriate control operations as a result.

Direct Address: An address that specifies the location in memory of an operand.

Direct Memory Access (DMA): A type of input/output technique in which data can be transferred between the microcomputer memory and external devices without the microprocessor's involvement.

Dynamic RAM: Stores data in capacitors and, therefore, must be refreshed; uses refresh circuitry.

EAROM (Electrically Alterable Read-Only Memory): Can be programmed without removing the memory from its sockets. This memory is also called read-mostly memory since it has much slower write times than read times.

Editor: A program that produces an error-free source program, written in assembly or high-level languages.

Effective Address: The final address used to carry out an instruction.

Emulator: A hardware device that allows a computer system to emulate (that is, mimic the procedures or protocols) of another computer system.

Encode: To apply the rules governing a specific code. For example, the selection of which hardware devices to enable during an operation can occur automatically by encoding individual device identifications into the instructions themselves. Hence, to encode is to convert data from its natural form into a machine-readable code usable to the computer.

EPROM (Erasable Programmable Read-Only Memory): Can be programmed and erased using ultraviolet light. The chip must be removed from the microcomputer system for programming.

Exception Processing: The CPU processing state associated with interrupts, trap instructions, tracing, and other exceptional conditions, whether they are initiated internally or externally.

Extended Binary-Coded Decimal Interchange Code (EBCDIC): An 8-bit code commonly used with microprocessors for representing character codes.

Firmware: Permanently stored, unalterable program instructions contained in the ROM section of a computer's memory (see Control Store).

Flag(s): An indicator, often a single bit, to indicate some condition or to mark information for processing attention. Sometimes referred to as a tag, mark, switch, or sentinel.

Flowchart: Representation of a program in a schematic form. It is convenient to flowchart a problem before writing the actual programs.

Global Bus: A computer bus system that is available to and shared by a number of processors connected together in a multiprocessor system environment.

Handshaking: Exchange of control signals between the microprocessor and an external device.

Hardware: The physical electronic circuits and electromechanical devices that make up the computer system.

HCMOS: Low-power HMOS.

Hexadecimal Number Sytem: Base-16 number system.

Hierarchical Memory: A memory organization or informational structure in which functional relationships are associated with different levels.

High-Level Language: A type of programming language that uses a more understandable human-oriented language.

HMOS: High-performance MOS reduces the channel length of the NMOS transistor and provides increased density and speed in LSI and VLSI circuits.

Immediate Address: An address that is used as an operand by the instruction itself.

Implied Address: An address not specified, but contained implicitly in the instruction.

In-Circuit Emulation: The most powerful hardware debugging technique; especially valuable when hardware and software are being debugged simultaneously.

Index: A symbol used to identify or place a particular quantity in an array (list) of similar quantities. Also, an ordered list of references to the contents of a larger body of data such as a file or record.

Indexed Addressing: Typically uses 3 bytes: the first byte for the op code and the next 2 bytes for the 16-bit address. The effective address of the instruction is determined by the sum of the 16-bit address and the contents of the index register.

Index Register: A register used to hold a value used in indexing data, such as when a value is used in indexed addressing to increment a base address contained within an instruction.

Indirect Address: An address that informs the CPU of the location of a direct address or another indirect address.

Input/Output Processor (IOP): Performs most of the I/O functions for the 16- and 32-bit microprocessors and unburdens the microprocessors of these I/O functions.

Instruction: A program statement (step) that causes the computer to carry out an operation, and specifies the values or locations of all operands.

Instruction Cycle: The sequence of operations that a microprocessor has to carry out while executing an instruction.

Instruction Register (IR): A register storing instructions; typically 8 bits long for an 8-bit microprocessor.

Instruction Set: Describes a computer's capability by listing all the instructions (available in machine code) that the computer can execute.

Interleaved DMA: Using this technique, the DMA controller takes over the system bus when the microprocessor is not using it.

Internal Interrupt: Activated internally by exceptional conditions such as overflow and division by zero.

Interpreter: A program that executes a set of machine language instructions in response to each high-level statement in order to carry out the function.

Interrupt I/O: An external device can force the microcomputer system to stop executing the current program temporarily so that it can execute another program known as the interrupt service routine.

Interrupts: A temporary break in a sequence of a program, initiated externally, causing control to pass to a routine, which performs some action while the program is stopped.

Invisible: See Transparent.

I/O (Input/Output): Describes that portion of a computer system that exchanges data between the computer system and the external world, or the data itself.

I/O Port: A module that contains control logic and data storage used to connect a computer to external peripherals.

Keyboard: Has a number of pushbutton-type switches configured in a matrix form (rows × columns).

Keybounce: When a mechanical switch opens or closes, it bounces (vibrates) for a small period of time (about 10–20 ms) before settling down.

Large-Scale Integration (LSI): An LSI chip contains more than 100 gates.

Linkage Editors: Connect the individual programs together which are assembled or compiled independently.

Linked Programming: The process of joining a subprogram with a main program or joining two separate programs together to form a single program.

Local Area Network: A collection of devices and communication channels that connect a group of computers and peripheral devices together so that they can communicate with each other.

Logic Analyzer: A hardware development aid for microprocessor-based design; gathers data on the fly and displays it.

Logical Address Space: All storage locations with a CPU's addressing range.

Loops: A programming control structure where a sequence of computer instructions are executed repeatedly (looped) until a terminating condition (result) is satisfied.

Machine Code: The binary code (composed of bit patterns) that a computer can sense, read, interpret, recognize, and manipulate.

Machine Language: A type of microprocessor programming language that uses binary or hexadecimal numbers.

Macroinstruction: Commonly known as an instruction; initiates execution of a complete microprogram.

Macroprogram: The assembly language program.

Mask: A pattern of bits used to specify (or mask) which bit parts of another bit pattern are to be operated on and which bits are to be ignored or "masked" out.

Mask ROM: Programmed by a masking operation performed on the chip during the manufacturing process; its contents cannot be changed by the user.

Maskable Interrupt: Can be enabled or disabled by executing typically the instructions EI and DI, respectively. If the microprocessor's interrupt is disabled, the microprocessor ignores the interrupt.

Memory: Any storage device which can accept, retain, and read back data. Usually refers to a computer subsystem of internal RAM- or ROM-based storage devices.

Memory Access Time: Average time taken to read a unit of information from the memory.

Memory Address Register (MAR): Also known as the Data Counter (DC). Stores the address of the data; typically 16 bits long for 8-bit microprocessors.

Memory Cycle Time: Average time lapse between two successive read operations.

Memory Map: A representation of the physical location of software within a computer's addressable main storage.

Memory-Mapped I/O: A microprocessor communications methodology (addressing scheme) where the data, address, and control buses extend throughout the system, with every connected device treated as if it were a memory location with a specific address. Manipulation of I/O data occurs in "interface registers" (as opposed to memory locations); hence there are not input (read) or output (write) instructions used in memory-mapped I/O.

Microcode: A set of "subcommands" or "pseudocommands" built into the hardware (usually stored in ROM) of a computer (that is, firmware) to handle the decoding and execution of higher-level instructions such as arithmetic operation.

Microcomputer: Consists of a microprocessor, a memory unit, and an input/output unit.

Microinstruction: Most microprocessors have an internal memory called control memory. This memory is used to store a number of codes called microinstructions. These microinstructions are combined to design the instruction set of the microprocessor.

Micro/Nano ROM: See Hierarchical Memory.

Microprocessor: The Central Processing Unit (CPU) of a microcomputer.

Microprocessor Development System: A tool for designing and debugging both hardware and software for microcomputer-based systems.

Microprocessor-Halt DMA: Data transfer is performed between the microprocessor and a peripheral device either by completely stopping the microprocessor or by a technique called cycle stealing.

Microprogramming: The microprocessor can use microprogramming to design the instruction set. Each instruction in the instruction register initiates execution of a microprogram in the control unit to perform the operation required by the instruction.

Module: (1) Any single hardware arrangement (device or component) within a computer system. (2) Any software, routine, or subroutine.

Monitor: Consists of a number of subroutines grouped together to provide "intelligence" to a microcomputer system. This intelligence gives the microcomputer system the capabilities for debugging a user program, system design, and displays.

Multiplexer: A hardware device which allows a CPU to be physically connected to a number of communication channels to receive or transmit data.

Multiprocessing: The process of executing two or more programs in parallel, handled by multiple processors all under common control. Typically each processor will be assigned specific processing tasks.

Multitasking: Operating system software that permits more than one program to run on a single CPU. Even though each program is given a small time slice in which to execute, the user has the impression that all tasks (different programs) are executing at the same time.

Multiuser: Describes a computer operating system that permits a number of users to access the system on a time-sharing basis.

Nested Subroutine: A commonly used programming technique that includes one subroutine entirely embedded within the "scope" of another subroutine.

Nibble: A 4-bit word.

NMOS: Denser and faster in comparison to PMOS. Most 8-bit microprocessors and some 16-bit microprocessors are fabricated using this technology.

Noncontiguous: Noncontiguous in nature. Refers to breaks in the linear sequential flow of any information structure.

Nonmaskable Interrupt: Occurrence of this type of interrupt cannot be ignored by the microprocessor, even though the interrupt capability of the microprocessor is disabled. Its effect cannot be disabled by instruction.

Non-Multiplexed: A non-multiplexed system indicates a direct single communication channel (that is, electrical wires) connection to the CPU.

Object Code: The binary (machine) code into which a source program is translated by a compiler, assembler, or interpreter.

Octal Number System: Base-8 number system.

One-Pass Assembler: This assembler goes through the assembly language program once and translates the assembly language program into a machine language program. This assembler has the problem of defining forward references. See Two-Pass Assembler.

Op Code (Operation Code): The instruction represented in binary form.

Operand: A datum or information item involved in an operation from which the result is obtained as a consequence of defined actions (that is, data which is operated on by an instruction). Various operand types contain information, such as source address, destination address, or immediate data.

Operating System: Consists of a number of program modules to provide resource management. Typical resources include microprocessors, disks, and printers.

Operation: (1) Means by which a result is obtained from an operand(s). (2) An action defined by a single instruction or single logical element.

Page: Some microprocessors, such as the Motorola 6800 and the MOS 6502, divide the 65,536 memory locations into 256 blocks. Each of these blocks is called a page and contains 256 addresses.

Parallel Operation: Any operation carried out simultaneously with a related operation.

Parallel Transmission: Each bit of binary data is transmitted over a separate wire.

Parity: The number of 1's in a word is odd for odd parity and even for even parity.

Peripherals: An I/O device capable of being operated under the control of a CPU through communication channels. Examples include disk drives, keyboards, CRTs, printers, modems, etc.

Personal Computer: Low-cost, affordable computer used by an individual or a small group for video games, daily schedules, and industrial applications.

Physical Address Space: Includes all internal storage.

Pipeline: A technique that allows a computer processing operation to be broken down into several steps (dictated by the number of pipeline levels or stages) so that the individual step outputs can be handled by the computer in parallel. Often used to fetch the processor's next instruction while executing the current instruction, which considerably speeds up the overall operation of the computer.

Pointer: A storage location (usually a register within a CPU) that contains the address of (or points to) a required item of data or subroutine.

Polled Interrupt: A software approach for determining the source of interrupt in a multiple interrupt system.

POP Operation: Reading from the top or bottom of the stack.

Port: An access point for a computer through which communication data may be passed to peripheral devices.

Primary Memory Store: That memory storage which is considered main, integral, or internal to the computing system. It is that storage which is physically most closely associated with the CPU and is directly controlled by it.

Primitives: A basic or fundamental unit; often refers to the lowest level of machine instruction or the lowest unit of programming language instruction.

Privileged Instructions: An instruction which is reserved for use by a computer's operating system, which will determine the range of system resources that the user is allowed to exploit.

Processor Memory: A set of microprocessor registers for holding temporary results when a computation is in progress.

Program: A self-contained sequence of computer software instructions (source code) that, when converted into machine code, directs the computer to perform specific operations for the purpose of accomplishing some processing task.

Program Counter (PC): See Control Register.

Programmed I/O: The microprocessor executes a program to perform all data transfers between the microcomputer system and external devices.

PROM (Programmable Read-Only Memory): Can be programmed by the user by using proper equipment. Once programmed, its contents cannot be altered.

Protocol: A list of data transmission conventions or procedures that encompass the timing, control, formatting, and data representations by which two devices are to communicate. Also known as hardware "handshaking", which is used to permit asynchronous communication.

Pseudo-Static RAM: Dynamic RAM with internal refresh circuitry.

PUSH Operation: Writing to the top or bottom of the stack.

Random Access Memory (RAM): A memory in which any addressable operand, disk sector, etc. can be read from and written to, and whose input-to-output access time is asynchronous in nature (that is, the access time is dictated by the time delays of the chip's internal circuitry). Internal semiconductor RAM (static or dynamic) is volatile in nature (in other words, information is lost when power is removed). External RAM examples include tape and disk formats.

Read-Only-Memory (ROM): A memory in which any addressable operand, disk sector, etc. can be read from, but not written to, after initial programming. It is an asynchronous device whose access time is dictated by its internal circuit time delays. Internal semiconductor ROM storage is non-volatile (information is not lost when power is removed).

Real-Time Software: Computer code that allows processes to be performed during the actual time that a related physical I/O action takes place.

Register: A one-word, high-speed memory device usually constructed from flip-flops (electronic switches) that are directly accessible to the processor. It can also refer to a specific location in memory that contains word(s) used during arithmetic, logic, and transfer operations.

Register Indirect: Uses a register pair which contains the address of data.

Relative Address: An address used to designate the position of a memory location in a routine or program.

Rollover: Occurs when more than one key is pushed simultaneously.

Routine: A group of instructions for carrying out a specific processing operation. Usually refers to part of a larger program. A routine and subroutine have essentially the same meaning, but a subroutine could be interpreted as a self-contained routine nested within a routine or program.

Sample and Hold Circuit: When connected to the input of an A/D converter, it keeps a rapidly varying analog signal fixed during the A/D conversion process by storing it in a capacitor.

Scaling: To adjust values to bring them into a range that is acceptable to a computer.

Secondary Memory Storage: An auxiliary data storing device that supplements the main (primary) internal memory of a computer. It is used to hold programs and data that would otherwise exceed the capacity of the main memory. Although it has a much slower access time, secondary storage is less expensive. Common devices include magnetic disk (floppy and hard), cassette tape, and videodisk.

Serial Transmission: Only one line is used to transmit the complete binary data bit by bit.

Single-Chip Microcomputer: Microcomputer (CPU, memory, and input/output) on a chip.

Single-Chip Microprocessor: Microcomputer CPU (microprocessor) on a chip.

Single Step: Allows the user to execute a program one instruction at a time and examine memory and registers.

Software: Programs in a computer.

Source Code: The high-level language code used by a programmer to write computer instructions. This code must be translated to the object (machine) code to be usable to the computer.

Stack: An area of memory reserved to hold information about the status of a computer the instant an interrupt occurs so that the computer can continue processing after the interrupt has been handled. Another common use is in handling the accessing sequence of "nested" subroutines. The stacks are the last in/first out (LIFO) devices that are manipulated by using PUSH or POP instructions.

Stack Pointer: A counter or register used to keep track of the storage and retrieval of each byte of information in the system stack.

Standard I/O: Utilizes a control pin on the microprocessor chip called the $IO/\overline{M}$ pin, in order to distinguish between input/output and memory; typically, IN and OUT instructions are used for performing input/output operations.

Static RAM: Stores data in flip-flops; does not need to be refreshed.

Status Register: A register which contains information concerning the activity within the CPU or about the condition of a functional unit or peripheral device.

Subroutine: A program carrying out a particular function and which can be called by another program known as the main program. A subroutine needs to be placed only once in memory and can be called by the main program as many times as the programmer wants.

Supervisor: Provides the procedures or instructions for coordinating the use of system resources and maintaining the flow of operations through a CPU to perform I/O operations.

Supervisor State: When internal CPU system processing operations are conducted at a higher privilege level, it is usually in the supervisor state. An operating system typically executes in the supervisor state to protect the integrity of "basic" system operations from user influences.

Synchronous Operation: Operations that occur at intervals directly related to a clock period. Also, a bus protocol in such data transactions is controlled by a master clock and is completed within a fixed clock period.

Synchronous Serial Data Transmission: Data is transmitted or received based on a clock signal.

Tracing: A dynamic diagnostic technique in which a record of internal counter events is made to permit analysis (debugging) of the program's execution.

Transparent: Processes and operations that proceed automatically in hardware while being "invisible" or transparent to the programmer.

Tristate Buffer: Has three output states: logic 0, 1, and a high-impedance state. It is typically enabled by a control signal to provide logic 0 or 1 outputs. This type of buffer can also be disabled by the control signal to place it in a high-impedance state.

2's Complement: The 2's complement of a binary number is obtained by replacing each 0 with a 1 and each 1 with a 0 and adding to the resulting number.

Two-Pass Assembler: This assembler goes through the assembly language program twice. In the first pass, the assembler defines the labels with the addresses. In the second pass, the assembler translates the assembly language program to the machine language. See One-Pass Assembler.

UART (Universal Asynchronous Receiver Transmitter): A chip that provides all the interface functions when a microprocessor transmits or receives data to or from a serial device.

User State: Typical microprocessor operations processing conducted at the user level. The user state is usually at lower privilege level than the supervisor state. This protects basic system operation resources (the operating system).

Vector Base Register (VBR): A register used during interrupts to point to predefined memory locations in CPU space which contain interrupt processing routines.

Vectored Interrupts: A device identification technique in which the highest priority device with a pending interrupt request forces program execution to branch to an interrupt routine to handle exception processing for the device.

Very Large Scale Integration (VLSI): A VLSI chip contains more than 1000 gates.

Virtual Machine: A computer whose hardware and software architecture is specifically designed to support virtual storage techniques. The virtual machine concept is widely used within multiprogramming environments.

Virtual Memory: A memory management operating system technique that allows programs or data to exceed the physical size of the main, internal, directly accessed memory. Program or data segments/pages are swapped from external disk storage as needed. The swapping is invisible (transparent) to the programmer. Therefore the programmer need not be concerned with the actual physical size of internal memory while writing the code.

Word: The bit size of a microprocessor refers to the number of bits that can be processed simultaneously by the basic arithmetic circuits of the microprocessor. A number of bits taken as a group in this manner is called a word.

BIBLIOGRAPHY

Allison, D. R., "A Design Philosophy for Microcomputer Architectures", *IEEE Trans. Computers.*

Artwick, B. A., *Microcomputer Interfacing,* Prentice-Hall, 1980.

Baer, J.-L., *Computer Systems Architecture,* Computer Science Press, 1980.

Boyce, J. C., *Microprocessor and Microcomputer Basics,* Prentice-Hall, 1979.

Burns, J., "Within the 68020," *Electronics and Wireless World,* pp 209–212, February 1985; pp 103–106, March 1985.

Chi, C. S., "Advances in Mass Storage Technology," *IEEE Computer,* Vol. 15, no. 5, pp 60–74, May 1982.

Chow, C. K., "On Optimization of Storage Hierarchies," *IBM Journal of Research and Development,* pp 194–203, May 1974.

Cohn, D. L. and Melsa, J. L., *A Step by Step Introduction to 8080 Microprocessor Systems,* Dilithium Press, 1977.

Cramer, W. and Kane, G., *68000 Microprocessor Handbook,* 2nd ed., Osborne/McGraw-Hill, 1986.

Danhor, K. J. and Smith, C. L., *Computing System Fundamentals: An Approach Based on Microcomputers,* Addison-Wesley, 1981.

Denning, P. J., "Virtual Memory," *ACM Computing Surveys,* Vol. 2, no. 3, pp 153–159, September 1970.

Electronic Industries Association, Washington, D.C., EIA Standard RS-232-C Interface, Electronic Industries Association, 1969.

Faggin, F., "How VLSI Impacts Computer Architecture," *IEEE Spectrum,* pp 28–31, May 1978.

Fisher, E. and Jensen, C. W., *Pet and the IEEE 488 Bus (BPIB),* Osborne/McGraw-Hill, 1979.

Friedman, A. D., *Logical Design of Digital Systems,* Computer Science Press, 1975.

Garland, H., *Introduction to Microprocessor System Design,* McGraw-Hill, 1979.

Gay, "68000 Family Memory Management — Part 1," *Electronic Engineering,* pp 39–48, June 1986.

Gibson, G. A. and Liu, Y., *Microprocessors for Engineers and Scientists,* Prentice-Hall, 1980.

Gill, A., *Machine and Assembly Language Programming of the PDP-11,* 2nd ed., Prentice-Hall, 1983.

Girsline, G., *16-Bit Modern Microcomputers, The Intel 8086 Family,* Prentice-Hall, 1985.

Gladstone, B. E., "Comparing Microcomputer Development System Capabilities," *Computer Design,* pp 83–90, February 1979.

Goody, R. W., *Intelligent Microcomputer,* SRA, 1982.

Goody, R., *The Versatile Microcomputer, The Motorola Family,* SRA, 1984.

Greenfield, J. D., *Practical Digital Design Using IC's,* John Wiley & Sons, 1977.

Greenfield, J. D. and Wray, WC., *Using Microprocessors and Microcomputers: The 6800 Family,* John Wiley & Sons, 1983.

Greenfield, J. D., *Practical Digital Design Using IC's,* John Wiley & Sons, 1983.

Grinich, V. H. and Jackson, H. G., *Introduction to Integrated Circuits,* McGraw-Hill, 1975.

Hall, D. V., *Microprocessors and Digital Systems,* McGraw-Hill, 1980.

Hamacher, V. C., Vranesic, Z. G., and Zaky, S. G., *Computer Organization,* McGraw-Hill, 1978.

Hamacher, V. C., Vranesic, Z. G., and Zaky, S. G., *Computer Organization,* McGraw-Hill, 1984.

Harman, T. L. and Lawson, B., *The Motorola MC68000 Microprocessor Family,* Prentice-Hall, 1984.

Hartman, B., "16-Bit 68000 Microprocessor Concepts on 32-Bit Frontier," MC 68000 Article Reprints, Motorola, pp 50–57, March 1981.

Hayes, J. P., *Computer Architecture and Organization,* McGraw-Hill, 1978.

Hayes, J. P., *Digital System Design and Microprocessors,* McGraw-Hill, 1984.

Haynes, J. L., "Circuit Design with Lotus 1-2-3," *BYTE,* Vol. 10, no. 11, pp 143–156, 1985.

Hewlett-Packard, "HP 64000," *Hewlett-Packard Journal,* 1980.

Hnatek, E. R., *A User's Handbook of Semiconductor Memories,* John Wiley & Sons, 1977.

Holt, C. A., *Electronic Circuits—Digital and Analog,* John Wiley & Sons, 1978.

Horden, I., "Microcontrollers Offer Realtime Robotics Control," *Computer Design,* pp 98–101, October 15, 1985.

Intel, *Microprocessors and Peripheral Handbook,* Vol. 1, Microprocessors, Intel Corporation, 1988.

Intel, *Microprocessors and Peripheral Handbook,* Vol. 2, Peripheral, Intel Corporation, 1988.

Intel, *80386 Programmer's Reference Manual,* Intel Corporation, 1986.

Intel, *80386 Hardware Reference Manual,* Intel Corporation, 1986.

Intel, 80386 Advance Information, Intel Corporation, 1985.

Intel, *8080 and 8085 Assembly Language Programming Manual,* Intel Corporation, 1978.

Intel, *The 8086 Family User's Family,* Intel Corporation, 1979.

Intel, *Intel Component Data Catalog,* Intel Corporation, 1979.

Intel, *MCS-85 User's Manual,* Intel Corporation, 1978.

Intel, *MCS-86 User's Manual,* Intel Corporation, 1982.

Intel, *Memory Components Handbook,* Intel Corporation, 1983.

Intel, *Microprocessor Peripheral Handbook,* Intel Corporation, 1982.

Intel, *SDK-85 User's Manual,* Intel Corporation, 1978.

Intel, "Marketing Communications," *The Semiconductor Memory Book,* John Wiley & Sons, 1978.

Isaacson, R. et al., "The Oregon Report — Personal Computing," selected reprints from *IEEE Computer,* pp 226–237.

Johnson, "A Comparison of MC68000 Family Processors," *BYTE,* pp 205–218, September 1986.

Johnson, C. D., *Process Control Instrumentation Technology,* John Wiley & Sons, 1977.

Johnson, R. C., "Microsystems Exploit Mainframe Methods," *Electronics,* 1981.

Kane, G., *CRT Controller Handbook,* Osborne/McGraw-Hill, 1980.

Kane, G., Hawkins, D., and Leventhal, L., *68000 Assembly Language Programming,* Osborne/McGraw-Hill, 1981.

King, T. and Knight, B., *Programming the MC68000,* Addison-Wesley, 1983.

Krutz, R. L., *Microprocessors and Logic Design,* John Wiley & Sons, 1980.

Krutz, R. L., *Microprocessors and Logic Design,* John Wiley & Sons, 1977.

Lesea, A. and Zaks, R., *Microprocessor Interfacing Techniques,* Sybex, 1978.

Leventhal, L. A., *8080A/8085 Assembly Language Programming,* Osborne/McGraw-Hill, 1978.

Leventhal, L. A., *Introduction to Microprocessors: Software, Hardware Programming,* Prentice-Hall, 1978.

Leventhal, L. and Walsh, C., *Microcomputer Experimentation with the Intel SDK-85,* Prentice-Hall, 1980.

Lewin, M., *Logic Design and Computer Organization,* Addison-Wesley, 1983.

Lipschutz, S., *Essential Computer Mathematics,* Schaum Outline Series, McGraw-Hill, 1982.

MacGregor, Mothersole, Meyer, "The Motorola MC68020," *IEEE MICRO,* pp 101–116, August 1984.

MacGregor, "Diverse Applications Put Spotlight on 68020's Improvements," *Electronic Design,* pp 155–164, February 7, 1985.

MacGregor, "Hardware and Software Strategies for the MC68020," *EDN,* pp 163–168, June 20, 1985.

Mano, M., *Computer System Architecture,* Prentice-Hall, 1983.

McCartney, Groepler, "The 32-Bit 68020's Power Flows Fully Through a Versatile Interface," *Electronic Design,* pp 335–343, January 10, 1985.

MITS-ALTAIR, *S-100 Bus,* MITS, Inc., Albuquerque, NM.

Morse, S., *The 8086/8088 Primer,* 2nd ed., Hayden, 1982.

Motorola, *6809 Applications Notes,* Motorola Corporation, 1978.

Motorola, *MC68000 User's Manual,* Motorola Corporation, 1979.

Motorola, *16-Bit Microprocessor — MC68000 User's Manual,* 4th ed., Prentice-Hall, 1984.

Motorola, *MC68000 16-Bit Microprocessor User's Manual,* Motorola Corporation, 1982.

Motorola, *MC68000 Supplement Material (Technical Training),* Motorola Corporation, 1982.

Motorola, *Microprocessor Data Material,* Motorola Corporation, 1981.

Motorola, *MC68020 User's Manual,* Motorola Corporation, 1985.

Motorola, "MC68020 Course Notes," MTTA20 REV 2, July 1987.

Motorola, "MC68020/68030/88100 Audio Course Notes," 1988.

Motorola, *MC88100 Data Sheets,* Motorola Corporation, 1988.

Motorola, *MC68020 User's Manual,* 2nd ed., MC68020 UM/AD Rev. 1, Prentice-Hall, 1984.

Motorola Technical Summary, *32-Bit Virtual Memory Microprocessor,* MC68020 BR243/D. Rev. 2, Motorola Corporation, 1987.

Osborne, A., *An Introduction to Microprocessors,* Vol. 1, Basic Concepts, rev. ed., Osborne/McGraw-Hill, 1980; 2nd ed., 1982.

Osborne, A. and Kane, G., *The Osborne Four- and Eight-Bit Microprocessor Handbook,* Osborne/McGraw-Hill, 1980.

Osborne, A. and Kane, G., *The Osborne 16-Bit Microprocessor Handbook,* Osborne/McGraw-Hill, 1981.

Rafiquzzaman, M., *Microprocessors and Microcomputer Development Systems — Designing Microprocessor-Based Systems,* Harper and Row, 1984.

Rafiquzzaman, M., *Microprocessors and Microcomputer Development Systems,* John Wiley & Sons, 1984.

Rafiquzzaman, M., *Microcomputer Theory and Applications with the INTEL SDK-85,* 2nd ed., John Wiley & Sons, 1987.

Rafiquzzaman, M. and Chandra, *Modern Computer Architecture,* West, 1988.

RCA, *Evaluation Kit Manual for the RCA CDP1802 COSMAC Microprocessor,* RCA Solid State Division, Somerville, NJ.

Rector, R. and Alexy, G., *The 8086 Book,* Osborne/McGraw-Hill, 1980.

Reichborn-Kjennerud, G., "Novel Methods of Integer Multiplication and Division," *BYTE,* Vol. 8, no. 6, pp 364–374, June 1983.

Ripps, Mushinsky, "32-Bit Up Speeds Code Design and Execution," *EDN,* pp 163–168, June 27, 1985.

Rockwell International, *Microelectronic Devices Data Catalog,* 1979.

Short, K. L., *Microprocessors and Programmed Logic,* Prentice-Hall, 1981.

Sloan, M. E., *Introduction to Minicomputers and Microcomputers,* Addison-Wesley, 1980.

Solomon, "Motorola's Muscular 68020," *Computers & Electronics,* pp 74–79, October 1984.

Sowell, E. F., *Programming in Assembly Language, MACRO II,* Addison-Wesley, 1984.

Starnes, T. W., "Compact Instruction Set Gives the MC68000 Power While Simplifying Its Operation," MC68000 Article Reprints, Motorola, pp 43–47, March 1981.

Strauss, E., *The Waite Group, Inside the 80286,* A Brady Book published by Prentice-Hall, 1986.

Stone, H. S., *Introduction to Computer Architecture,* SRA, 1980.

Stone, H. S., *Microcomputer Interfacing,* Addison-Wesley, 1982.

Streitmatter, G. A. and Fiore, V., *Microprocessors, Theory and Applications,* Reston Publishing, 1979.

Stritter, E. and Gunter, T., "A Microprocessor Architecture for a Changing World: The Motorola 68000," *IEEE Computers,* Vol. 12, no. 2, pp 43–52, February 1970.

Tanenbaum, A. S., *Structured Computer Organization,* Prentice-Hall, 1984.

Teledyne, *Teledyne Semiconductor Catalog,* 1977.

Texas Instruments, *The TTL Data Book,* Vol. 1, 1984.

Texas Instruments, *The TTL Data Book for Design Engineers,* 2nd ed., 1976.

Tocci, R. J. and Laskowski, L. P., *Microprocessors and Microcomputers: Hardware and Software,* Prentice-Hall, 1979.

Twaddel, "32-Bit Extension to the 68000 Family Addresses 4 GBytes, Runs at 3 MIPS," *EDN,* pp 75–77, July 12, 1984.

Wakerly, J. F., *Microcomputer Architecture and Programming,* John Wiley & Sons, 1981.

Zilog, *Z8000 Advance Specification,* Zilog, Inc., 1978.

Zoch, B., "68020 Dynamically Adjusts Its Data Transfers to Match Peripheral Ports," *Electronic Design,* pp 219–225, January 10, 1985.

Zorpette, G., "Microprocessors — The Beauty of 32-Bits," *IEEE Spectrum,* Vol. 22, no. 9, pp 65–71, September 1985.

CREDITS

The following material was reprinted by permission of the sources indicated below:

Motorola Corporation, Inc.: **Chapter 1:** Figures 1.9a and b, 1.10, 1.11; **Chapter 5:** Figures 5.1 to 5.5, 5.8 to 5.10, 5.12, 5.13b and c, 5.15, 5.16, 5.19 to 5.22, 5.26 to 5.30, 5.33, 5.34, Tables 5.1, 5.3, 5.14 to 5.19, table on page 495; **Chapter 6:** Examples 6.1 and 6.8, all figures, tables, and graphics except the tables on pages 550 to 551; **Chapter 7:** Examples 7.2, 7.4, 7.6, table on page 675, all figures, tables, and graphics except Figures 7.3, 7.15, 7.23, and 7.27; **Chapter 8:** all figures, tables, and graphics, Section 8.1.4, equation on page 751; **Chapter 9:** Figures 9.20, 9.21; **Appendix B:** data sheets.

Intel Corporation: **Chapter 2:** Figures 2.3, 2.4, 2.6 to 2.8, 2.10 to 2.13, 2.16, 2.17, 2.21, 2.23a and b, 2.26 to 2.28, Tables 2.9, 2.12, 2.13; **Chapter 3:** Figures 3.1 to 3.3, 3.5 to 3.16, 3.18, 3.21a and b, 3.22, 3.24, 3.26a and b, 3.27, Tables 3.2, 3.A-1 to 3.A-12, structure on page 251; **Chapter 4:** Figures 4.1, 4.2, 4.6 to 4.22, Tables 4.1 to 4.3, 4.5 to 4.11, table on page 382; **Chapter 9:** Figures 9.7, 9.28 to 9.30, tables on page 855; **Appendix C:** figures and data sheets.

All mnemonics in Tables 2.1 and 3.1 are courtesy of Intel Corporation.

The 80386 microprocessor referred to in text is the i386™, a trademark of Intel Corporation.

Rafiquzzaman, M., *Microcomputer Theory and Applications with the Intel SDK-85,* John Wiley & Sons, Inc., New York, New York, 1987, reprinted by permission of John Wiley & Sons, Inc.: **Chapter 2:** Tables 2.1 to 2.8, Example 2.6 solution, Example 2.11 solution, Section 2.6; **Chapter 5:** Tables 5.6 to 5.13, Examples 5.1 to 5.6; **Chapter 6:** table on pages 550 to 551.

Rafiquzzaman, M., *Microcomputer Theory and Applications with the Intel SDK-85,* John Wiley & Sons, Inc., New York, New York, 1987, reprinted by permission of Prentice Hall, Inc., Englewood Cliffs, New Jersey: **Chapter 1:** structure on page 30, Sections 1.2.4.b and c, pages 32 to 33, Section 1.2.4.e, pages 45 to 47; **Chapter 2:** Figures 2.18 to 2.20, 2.24, 2.25, 2.29a and b, 2.30, figure on page 140, Sections 2.5 and 2.9.2, pages 75 to 79, 115 to 116, 118 to 126, 130 to 133, 142 to 148, 153 to 156; **Chapter 5:** Figures 5.6, 5.7, 5.11, 5.14, 5.24, 5.31, 5.32, Tables 5.2, 5.4, 5.5, table on page 517, text on pages 405-445, 452-454, 460-465, 469-472, 478, 486-487, 506-509, 516-517, 521-527.

Rafiquzzaman, M., *Microprocessors and Microcomputer Development Systems,* copyright John Wiley & Sons, Inc., New York, New York, ©1984, reprinted by permission of John Wiley & Sons, Inc.: **Chapter 1:** Figures 1.14, 1.15, 1.21, 1.22, Sections 1.5 and 1.6; **Chapter 9:** Figures 9.1, 9.2, 9.8 to 9.13, Section 9.1.2; **Chapter 10:** Problems 10.2 to 10.13; **Appendix A; Appendix C** (excluding figures and data sheets).

Morse, S. and Albert, D., *The 80286 Architecture,* copyright John Wiley & Sons, Inc., New York, New York, ©1986, reprinted by permission of John Wiley & Sons, Inc.: **Chapter 4:** Figures 4.3 and 4.4.

Rafiquzzaman, M. and Chandra, S., *Modern Computer Architecture,* West Publishing, St. Paul, Minnesota, ©1988, reprinted by permission from West Publishing Company (all rights reserved): **Chapter 1:** Figures 1.12 and 1.13 and structures on pages 27 and 28.

Cramer, W. and Kane, G., *68000 Microprocessor Handbook,* 2nd ed., Osborne/McGraw-Hill, Berkeley, California, ©1986, reprinted by permission of Osborne/McGraw-Hill: **Chapter 5:** Figures 5.41a to d.

Osborne and Kane, G., *The Osborne Four- and Eight-Bit Microprocessor Handbook,* McGraw-Hill, ©1980, reprinted by permission of Osborne/McGraw-Hill, Berkeley, California: **Chapter 2:** Table 2.11, Figures 2.14 and 2.15.

Leventhal, *8080A/8085 Assembly Language Programming,* McGraw-Hill, ©1978, reprinted by permission of Osborne/McGraw-Hill, Berkeley, California: **Chapter 2**: Figure 2.2.

(Modified from) Leventhal and Walsh, *Microcomputer Experimentation with the Intel SDK-85,* Prentice Hall, Inc., Englewood Cliffs, New Jersey: **Chapter 2:** Table 2.10.

Practical Microprocessors — Hardware, Software and Troubleshooting, Hewlett Packard, Palo Alto, California: **Chapter 2:** Figure 2.1 and pages 73 (bottom) to 74.

The Making of a Coprocessor, *Electronics,* Groves, S., Ed., Nov. 17, 1983, reprinted with permission from Penton Publishing, Hasbrouck Heights, New Jersey, ©1983: **Chapter 1:** Section 1.2.4.h.

Burns, D. and Jones, D., Within the 68020, *Electronics and Wireless World,* Surrey, United Kingdom, ©1987: **Chapter 7:** Figures 7.3, 7.27, Example 7.1.

Gay, C., MC68000 Family Memory Management, *Electronic Engineering,* 58(714), June 1986, reprinted by permission of Electronic Engineering, London, United Kingdom, ©1986: **Chapter 7**: Figure 7.23.

CHIP INDEX

Digital Equipment Corporation chips
VAX11/750, 3
VAX11/780, 3

Hewlett-Packard (HP) Corporation
64000, 48, 52, 54, 925, 957—
986
assembler error codes, 966—968
assembler pseudoinstructions, 965—
966
assembler soft keys, 964—965
description, 957
development station, 958—960
development system, 974—984
editor commands, 963—964
emulator, 984—986
emulator soft keys, 969—972
host Pascal, 973
linker commands, 968—969
monitor soft keys, 961—962
passwords, 972—973
terminal mode, 972

Intel Corporation chips, 1, 2, 48
432, 3
2142, 167, 1005
2513, 10
2716, 117, 167, 866, 1006
2732, 1007
4004, 2
4040, 6
6116, 859, 866
8008, 2
8080, 73, 75
8085, 4, 5, 7, 9, 73—165, 170

8080 compared to, 73
8279 interface to, 845—849, 859—
877
addressing modes, 78—79
architecture, 75—77
arithmetic logic unit, 73—74
assemblers and, 61
block diagram of, 73
CALL, 60
clock frequency, 119
control logic, 75
coprocessors, 37
data sheets, 999—1001
description, 73—75
design, 156—160
design problem, 911—921
direct memory access (DMA), 77,
119, 154—155
enhanced versions, 73, see also
specific chips
flags, 75—77
input/output, 130—156
instruction decoder, 74
instruction execution, 122—129
instruction register, 74
instructions, 75, 79—112, 186
arithmetic, 96—97
logical, 98—99
instruction timing, 122—129
interrupts, 141—154
introduction of, 2
keyboard/display interface, 839—
845
logic operations, 95
memory addressing, 77—78

1045

GENERAL INDEX